W9-DAO-289

ESSENTIALS OF
Educational Psychology

Big Ideas to Guide Effective Teaching

ESSENTIALS OF
Educational Psychology

Big Ideas to Guide Effective Teaching

Third Edition

Jeanne Ellis Ormrod

University of Northern Colorado, Emerita

Boston   Columbus   Indianapolis   New York   San Francisco   Upper Saddle River
Amsterdam   Cape Town   Dubai   London   Madrid   Milan   Munich   Paris   Montreal   Toronto
Delhi   Mexico City   Sao Paulo   Sydney   Hong Kong   Seoul   Singapore   Taipei   Tokyo

Editor-in-Chief: Paul A. Smith
Development Editor: Christina Robb
Editorial Assistant: Matthew Buchholz
Vice President, Director of Marketing: Margaret Waples
Production Editor: Annette Joseph
Editorial Production Service: TexTech International
Permissions Specialist: Rebecca Savage
Manufacturing Buyer: Megan Cochran
Electronic Composition: TexTech International
Interior Design: Laurie Entringer
Photo Researcher: Annie Fuller
Cover Designer: Linda Knowles

Library of Congress Cataloging-in-Publication Data

Ormrod, Jeanne Ellis.
    Essentials of educational psychology : big ideas to guide effective teaching / Jeanne Ellis Ormrod. — 3rd ed.
       p. cm.
    ISBN-13: 978-0-13-136727-2
    ISBN-10: 0-13-136727-7
    1. Educational psychology—Textbooks.   I. Title.
    LB1051.O663 2012
    370.15—dc22

                                                                2010047894

10 9 8 7 6 5 4 3 2 1 CIN 15 14 13 12 11 10

www.pearsonhighered.com

ISBN-10: 0-13-136727-7
ISBN-13: 978-0-13-136727-2

To my children, two who have become teachers themselves and one who, in his own way, continues to teach me many things about human growth and potential

About the Author

JEANNE ELLIS ORMROD received her A.B. in psychology from Brown University and her M.S. and Ph.D. in educational psychology from The Pennsylvania State University. She earned licensure in school psychology through postdoctoral work at Temple University and the University of Colorado at Boulder and has worked as a middle school geography teacher and school psychologist. She was Professor of Educational Psychology at the University of Northern Colorado until 1998 and is currently Professor Emerita in UNC's School of Psychological Sciences. She has published numerous research articles on cognition and memory, cognitive development, and giftedness, but she is probably best known for this textbook and four others: *Educational Psychology: Developing Learners* (now in its seventh edition); *Human Learning* (now in its fifth edition); *Child Development and Education* (co-authored with Teresa McDevitt, now in its fourth edition); and *Practical Research* (co-authored with Paul Leedy, now in its ninth edition). Her most recent book—Our Minds, Our Memories: Enhancing Thinking and Learning at All Ages—introduces principles of learning and cognition to practitioners in a variety of helping professions, as well as to nonpractitioners who simply want to enhance the quality of their own lives.

After raising three children (two of whom have become teachers themselves), she now lives in New Hampshire with her husband Richard and occasionally teaches courses at the University of New Hampshire.

Brief Contents

Chapter 1 Introduction to Educational Psychology 1

Chapter 2 Learning, Cognition, and Memory 16

Chapter 3 Learning in Context 56

Chapter 4 Complex Cognitive Processes 98

Chapter 5 Cognitive Development 134

Chapter 6 Motivation and Affect 182

Chapter 7 Personal, Social, and Moral Development 236

Chapter 8 Instructional Strategies 282

Chapter 9 Strategies for Creating an Effective Classroom Environment 320

Chapter 10 Assessment Strategies 360

Appendix Interpreting Standardized Test Scores 407

Contents

PREFACE   xvii
ACKNOWLEDGMENTS   xxvii

CHAPTER 1 **Introduction to Educational Psychology   1**

Case Study: Starting High School   1

General Guiding Principles of Educational Psychology   3

An in-depth knowledge of students must drive teacher decision making.   3

The effectiveness of various classroom practices can best be determined through systematic research.   4

Research can provide quantitative information, qualitative information, or both.   6

Different kinds of research lead to different kinds of conclusions.   7

Drawing conclusions about cause–and–effect relationships requires that all other possible explanations for an outcome be eliminated.   9

Theories can help synthesize, explain, and apply research findings.   9

Developing as a Teacher   10

Keep up to date on research findings and innovative practices in education.   10

Learn as much as you can both about the subject matter you teach and about strategies for teaching it effectively.   10

Conduct your own research regarding questions and issues at your own school.   11

Learn as much as you can about the culture(s) of the community in which you are working.   11

Continually reflect on and critically examine your assumptions, inferences, and teaching practices.   11

Communicate and collaborate with colleagues.   11

Believe that you can make a difference in students' lives.   12

Strategies for Learning and Studying Effectively   12

Relate what you read to things you already know.   12

Tie abstract concepts and principles to concrete examples.   12

Elaborate on what you read, going beyond it and adding to it.   13

Periodically check yourself to make sure you remember and understand what you've read.   13

Summary   13

Practice for Your Licensure Exam: New Software   14

MyEducationLab   15

CHAPTER 2 **Learning, Cognition, and Memory   16**

Case Study: The New World   17

Learning as a Constructive Process   18

By the time they reach school age, young learners are usually actively involved in their own learning.   20

Cognitive processes influence what is learned.   20

Learners must be selective about what they focus on and learn.   21

Learners create (rather than receive) knowledge.   21

Learners use what they already know and believe to help them make sense of new experiences.   22

Thinking and Learning in the Brain   23

The various parts of the brain work closely with one another.   23

Most learning probably involves changes in neurons, astrocytes, and their interconnections.   24

Knowing how the brain functions and develops tells us only so much about learning and instruction.   24

How Human Memory Operates   25

Sensory input stays in a raw form only briefly.   26

Attention is essential for most learning and memory.   26

Working memory—where the action is in thinking and learning—has a short duration and limited capacity.   27

Long-term memory has a long duration and virtually limitless capacity.   28

Information in long-term memory is interconnected and organized to some extent.   28

Some long-term memory storage processes are more effective than others.   31

Practice makes knowledge more automatic and durable.   34

With age and experience, children acquire more effective learning strategies.   34

Prior knowledge and beliefs affect new learning, usually for the better but sometimes for the worse.   36

Why Learners May or May Not Remember What They've Learned   38

How easily something is recalled depends on how it was initially learned.   38

Remembering depends on the context.   39

How easily something is recalled and used depends on how often it has been recalled and used in the past.   40

Recall often involves reconstruction. 40

Long-term memory isn't necessarily forever. 41

Promoting Effective Cognitive Processes 41

Remembering How the Human Memory System Works 41

Grab and hold students' attention. 42

Keep the limited capacity of working memory in mind. 42

Relate new ideas to students' prior knowledge and experiences. 43

Accommodate diversity in students' background knowledge. 43

Provide experiences on which students can build. 45

Encouraging Effective Long-Term Memory Storage 45

Present questions and tasks that encourage elaboration. 45

Show how new ideas are interrelated. 45

Facilitate visual imagery. 47

Give students time to think. 47

Suggest mnemonics for hard-to-remember facts. 48

Promoting Retrieval 48

Provide many opportunities to practice important knowledge and skills. 48

Give hints that help students recall or reconstruct what they've learned. 48

Monitoring Students' Progress 50

Regularly assess students' understandings. 50

Identify and address students' misconceptions. 51

Focus assessments on meaningful learning rather than rote learning. 51

Be on the lookout for students who have unusual difficulty with certain cognitive processes. 53

Summary 54

Practice for Your Licensure Exam: Vision Unit 55

MyEducationLab 55

CHAPTER 3 Learning in Context 56

Case Study: Ben and Sylvia 57

The Immediate Environment as Context 58

Some stimuli tend to elicit certain kinds of behaviors. 58

Learners are more likely to acquire behaviors that lead to desired consequences. 59

Learners are also likely to acquire behaviors that help them avoid or escape unpleasant circumstances. 60

Learners tend to steer clear of behaviors that lead to unpleasant consequences. 62

Learners acquire many behaviors by observing other people. 63

Learners learn what behaviors are acceptable and effective by observing what happens to others. 65

By seeing what happens to themselves and others, learners form expectations about the probable outcomes of various behaviors. 65

Learned behavior and cognitive processes are sometimes situated in specific environmental contexts. 66

Social Interaction as Context 67

Learners sometimes co-construct knowledge and understandings with more experienced individuals. 67

Learners also co-construct knowledge and understandings with peers who have ability levels similar to their own. 68

Culture and Society as Context 70

The behaviors that others encourage and model are usually compatible with the culture in which they live. 71

Concepts and other cognitive tools are also the products of a culture. 72

Inconsistencies between the cultures of home and school can interfere with maximum learning and performance. 75

Many groups and institutions within a society influence children's learning and development either directly or indirectly. 77

Access to resources at home and in the community also affects learning. 78

How Learners Modify Their Own Environments 80

Learners alter their current environment both through their behaviors and through their internal traits and mental processes. 80

Learners actively seek out environments that are a good fit with their existing characteristics and behaviors. 82

Providing Supportive Contexts for Learning 83

Encouraging Productive Behaviors 83

Create conditions that elicit desired responses. 83

Make sure productive behaviors are reinforced and unproductive behaviors are not reinforced. 83

Make response–reinforcement contingencies clear. 84

As an alternative to punishment, reinforce productive behaviors that are incompatible with unproductive ones. 85

Model desired behaviors. 86

Provide a variety of role models. 86

Shape complex behaviors gradually over time. 87

Have students practice new behaviors and skills in a variety of contexts. 88

Providing Physical and Social Support for Effective Cognitive Processes 88

Provide physical and cognitive tools that can help students work and think more effectively. 88

Encourage student dialogue and collaboration. 88

Create a community of learners. 90

Taking into Account the Broader Contexts in Which Students Live 91

Learn as much as you can about students' cultural backgrounds, and come to grips with your own cultural lens. 91

Remember that membership in a particular cultural or ethnic group is not an either-or situation but, instead, a more-or-less phenomenon. 93

Incorporate the perspectives and traditions of many cultures into the curriculum. 93

Be sensitive to cultural differences in behaviors and beliefs, and accommodate them as much as possible. 94

Work hard to break down rigid stereotypes of particular cultural and ethnic groups. 94

Identify and, if possible, provide missing resources and experiences important for successful learning. 96

Summary 96

Practice for Your Licensure Exam: Adam 97

MyEducationLab 97

CHAPTER 4 **Complex Cognitive Processes** 98

Case Study: Taking Over 99

Metacognition 100

Some effective study strategies are readily apparent in learners' behaviors. 100

Even more important than observable study behaviors are the cognitive processes that underlie them. 101

Metacognitive knowledge and skills gradually improve with age. 102

Learners' views about the nature of knowledge and learning influence their approaches to learning tasks. 104

Self-Regulation 105

Self-regulating learners establish goals and standards for their own performance. 107

Self-regulating learners plan a course of action for a learning task. 107

Self-regulating learners control and monitor their cognitive processes and progress during a learning task. 108

Self-regulating learners also monitor and try to control their motivation and emotions. 108

Self-regulating learners seek assistance and support when they need it. 108

Self-regulating learners evaluate the final outcomes of their efforts. 108

Self-regulating learners self-impose consequences for their performance. 109

Learners become increasingly self-regulating over the course of childhood and adolescence. 109

Transfer 111

Transfer of knowledge and skills is most likely to occur when there is obvious similarity between the "old" and the "new." 112

Learning strategies and general beliefs and attitudes can also transfer to new situations. 112

Relevant context cues increase the probability of transfer. 113

Meaningful learning and conceptual understanding increase the probability of transfer. 113

Problem Solving and Creativity 114

The depth of learners' knowledge influences their ability to solve problems and think creatively. 115

Both convergent and divergent thinking are constrained by working memory capacity. 115

How learners encode a problem or situation influences their strategies and eventual success. 116

Problem solving and creativity often involve heuristics that facilitate—but don't guarantee—successful outcomes. 117

Effective problem solving and creativity are partly metacognitive activities. 118

Critical Thinking 119

Critical thinking requires sophisticated epistemic beliefs. 120

Critical thinking is a disposition as much as a cognitive process. 121

Promoting Complex Cognitive Processes 121

Promoting Specific Processes 121

Actively nurture students' metacognition awareness and self-reflection. 122

Explicitly teach effective learning strategies. 122

Communicate that acquiring knowledge is a dynamic, ongoing process—that one never completely "knows" something. 124

Encourage and support self-regulated learning and behavior. 125

Provide numerous and varied opportunities to apply classroom subject matter to new situations and problems. 126

Create the conditions that creative thinking and problem solving require. 128

Encourage critical thinking. 129

Promoting Complex Processes in General 129

Teach complex thinking skills within the context of academic disciplines and subject matter. 130

Pursue topics in depth rather than superficially. 130

Foster complex cognitive processes through group discussions and projects. 130

Create an overall classroom culture that values complex thinking processes. 131

Incorporate complex cognitive processes into assessment activities. 131

Summary 132

Practice for Your Licensure Exam: Interview with Emily 133

MyEducationLab 133

CHAPTER 5 **Cognitive Development** 134

Case Study: Hidden Treasure 135

General Principles of Development 136

The sequence of development is somewhat predictable. 136

Children develop at different rates. 138

Development is often marked by spurts and plateaus. 138

Development involves both quantitative and qualitative changes. 139

Heredity and environment interact in their effects on development.   139

Children's own behaviors also influence their development.   140

Developmental Processes   140

The brain continues to develop throughout childhood, adolescence, and adulthood.   140

Children have a natural tendency to organize their experiences.   142

Children are naturally inclined to make sense of and adapt to their environment.   142

Development builds on prior acquisitions.   142

Observations of the physical environment—and, ideally, frequent interactions with it—promote development.   143

Language development facilitates cognitive development.   143

Interactions with other people promote development.   143

Formal schooling promotes development.   144

Inconsistencies between existing understandings and external events promote development.   144

Challenging tasks promote development.   146

Trends in Cognitive Development   147

Children's growing working memory capacity enables them to handle increasingly complex cognitive tasks.   147

Children's growing knowledge base enhances their ability to learn new things.   147

Children's knowledge, beliefs, and thinking processes become increasingly integrated.   148

Thinking becomes increasingly logical during the elementary school years.   148

Thinking becomes increasingly abstract in the middle school and secondary school years.   150

Several logical thinking processes important for mathematical and scientific reasoning improve considerably during adolescence.   151

Children can think more logically and abstractly about tasks and topics they know well.   152

True expertise comes only after many years of study and practice.   154

To some extent, different cultures encourage different reasoning skills.   155

Intelligence   156

Intelligence can be measured only imprecisely at best.   158

To some degree, intelligence reflects speed, efficiency, and control of cognitive processing.   159

Intelligence also involves numerous specific processes and abilities.   160

Learners may be more intelligent in some domains than in others.   160

Intelligence is a product of both heredity and environment.   162

Learners may have specific cognitive styles and dispositions that predispose them to think and act in more or less intelligent ways.   162

Learners act more intelligently when they have physical, symbolic, or social support.   164

Addressing Students' Developmental Needs   164

Accommodating Developmental Differences and Diversity   164

Explore students' reasoning with problem-solving tasks and probing questions.   165

Interpret intelligence test results cautiously.   166

Look for signs of exceptional abilities and talents.   167

Consult with specialists if children show significant delays in development.   169

Fostering Cognitive Development   170

Encourage play activities.   170

Share the wisdom of previous generations.   171

Rely heavily on concrete objects and activities, especially in the early elementary grades.   171

Present abstract ideas more frequently in the middle school and high school grades, but tie them to concrete objects and events.   171

Initially introduce sophisticated reasoning processes within the context of familiar situations and group work.   172

Scaffold students' early efforts at challenging tasks and assignments.   175

Involve students in age-appropriate ways in adult activities.   176

Be optimistic that with appropriate guidance and support, all students can perform more intelligently.   177

Summary   178

Practice for Your Licensure Exam: Stones Lesson   180

MyEducationLab   181

CHAPTER 6   Motivation and Affect   182

Case Study: Passing Algebra   183

Basic Human Needs   184

Learners have a basic need for arousal.   187

Learners want to believe they are competent and have self-worth.   187

Learners want to determine the course of their lives to some degree.   188

Learners want to feel connected to other people.   189

How Motivation Affects Behavior and Cognition   190

Motivation directs behavior toward particular goals.   190

Motivation increases effort and persistence in activities.   190

Motivation affects cognitive processes.   190

Motivation determines what consequences are reinforcing and punishing.   190

Motivation often leads to improved performance.   191

Intrinsic motivation is usually more beneficial than extrinsic motivation.   191

Conditions in the learning environment influence intrinsic as well as extrinsic motivation.   192

Cognitive Factors in Motivation   192

Learners find some topics inherently interesting.   192

To engage voluntarily in activities, learners want their chances of success to be reasonably good.   195

When learners think their chances of success are slim, they may behave in ways that make success even less likely.   196

Learners are more likely to devote time to activities that have value for them.   197

Learners typically form goals related to their academic achievement; the specific nature of these goals influences learners' cognitive processes and behaviors.   199

Learners must juggle their achievement goals with their many other goals.   201

Learners identify what are, in their minds, the likely causes of their successes and failures.   202

Learners' attributions for past successes and failures affect their future performance.   204

With age, learners increasingly attribute their successes and failures to ability rather than to effort.   205

Over time, learners acquire a general attributional style.   206

Culture influences the cognitive factors underlying motivation.   208

Cognitive factors underlying sustained motivation build up over a period of time.   209

Affect and Its Effects   209

Affect and motivation are interrelated.   209

Affect is closely tied to learning and cognition.   209

Positive affect can trigger effective learning strategies.   213

Affect can also trigger certain behaviors.   213

Some anxiety is helpful, but a lot is often a hindrance.   213

Different cultures nurture different emotional responses.   216

Promoting Motivation and Positive Affect   216

Fostering Intrinsic Motivation by Addressing Students' Basic Needs   216

Conduct stimulating lessons and activities.   217

Protect and enhance students' self-efficacy and overall sense of competence and self-worth.   217

Present challenges that students can realistically accomplish.   220

Give students control over some aspects of classroom life.   221

Evaluate students' performance in a noncontrolling manner.   222

Use extrinsic reinforcers when necessary, but do so in ways that preserve students' sense of self-determination.   222

Help students meet their need for relatedness.   223

Promoting Motivation-Enhancing Cognitions   224

Relate assignments to students' personal interests, values, and goals.   224

Create conditions that foster internalization of values essential for students' long-term academic and professional success.   224

Focus students' attention more on mastery goals than on performance goals.   224

Ask students to set some personal goals for learning and performance.   225

Form and communicate optimistic expectations and attributions.   225

Minimize competition.   228

Generating Productive Affect   228

Get students emotionally involved in the subject matter.   229

Foster emotion self-regulation.   230

Keep anxiety at a low to moderate level.   230

As students make the transition to middle school or high school, make an extra effort to minimize their anxiety and address their need for relatedness.   231

Summary   233

Practice for Your Licensure Exam: Praising Students' Writing   234

MyEducationLab   235

CHAPTER 7 Personal, Social, and Moral Development   236

Case Study: The School Play   237

Personality and Sense of Self   238

Heredity and environment interact to shape personality.   238

Despite their relatively stable personality traits, children often behave somewhat differently in different contexts.   240

As children grow older, they construct increasingly multifaceted understandings of who they are as people.   240

With age, self-perceptions become more realistic, abstract, and stable.   241

As children reach puberty, they understand that they are unique individuals, but they sometimes go overboard in this respect.   242

Learners' self-perceptions influence their behaviors, and vice versa.   243

Other people's behaviors affect learners' sense of self.   243

Group memberships also affect learners' sense of self.   244

Gender plays a significant role in most learners' sense of self.   244

Despite the influence of others, learners define and socialize themselves to a considerable degree.   246

Peer Relationships   247

Peer relationships promote personal and social development in ways that adult–child relationships often cannot.   247

Peers help define "appropriate" ways of behaving.   247

Boys and girls interact with peers in distinctly different ways.   248

Social groups become increasingly important in adolescence.   248

Romantic relationships in adolescence provide valuable practice for the intimate relationships of adulthood.   250

Truly popular children have good social skills.   251

Social Cognition   252

As children get older, they become increasingly aware of other people's thoughts and emotions.   252

Children's cognitive processes in social situations influence their behaviors toward others.   254

Aggressive behavior is often the result of counterproductive cognitive processes.   254

Moral and Prosocial Development   256

At an early age, children begin applying internal standards for behavior.   256

Children increasingly distinguish between moral and conventional transgressions.   256

Children's capacity to respond emotionally to others' misfortunes and distress increases throughout the school years.   257

With age, reasoning about moral issues becomes increasingly abstract and flexible.   257

Challenges to moral reasoning promote advancement toward more sophisticated reasoning.   261

Cognition, affect, and motivation all influence moral and prosocial behavior.   261

Moral values become an important part of some learners' sense of self.   263

Promoting Personal, Social, and Moral Development   263

Fostering Personal Development   264

Accommodate students' diverse temperaments.   264

Help students get a handle on who they are as people.   264

Channel adolescents' risk-taking tendencies into safe activities.   264

Create a warm, supportive environment with clear standards for behavior and explanations of why some behaviors are unacceptable.   265

Be especially supportive of students at risk.   266

Be on the lookout for exceptional challenges that students may face at home.   267

Provide extra support and guidance for students who have disabilities that affect their personal or social functioning.   269

Be alert for signs that a student may be contemplating suicide.   270

Encouraging Effective Social Cognition and Interpersonal Skills   271

Encourage perspective taking and empathy.   271

Explicitly teach social skills to students who have trouble interacting effectively with others.   273

Provide numerous opportunities for social interaction and cooperation.   274

Talk with students about the advantages and potential dangers of Internet communications.   274

Explain what bullying is and why it cannot be tolerated.   274

Be alert for incidents of bullying and other forms of aggression, and take appropriate actions with both the victims and the perpetrators.   275

Promote understanding, communication, and interaction among diverse groups.   276

Promoting Moral Reasoning and Prosocial Behavior   277

Expose students to numerous models of moral and prosocial behavior.   277

Engage students in discussions of social and moral issues.   278

Get students actively involved in community service.   279

Summary   279

Practice for Your Licensure Exam: The Scarlet Letter   280

MyEducationLab   281

CHAPTER 8   Instructional Strategies   282

Case Study: The Oregon Trail   283

Planning Instruction   284

Identify the desired end results of instruction.   285

Ask students to identify some of their own objectives for instruction.   289

Create a class website.   289

Break complex tasks and topics into smaller pieces, identify a logical sequence for the pieces, and decide how best to teach each one.   290

Develop step-by-step lesson plans.   291

Conducting Teacher-Directed Instruction   292

Begin with what students already know and believe.   293

Promote effective cognitive processes.   293

Intermingle explanations with examples and opportunities for practice.   293

Take advantage of well-designed educational software.   295

Ask a lot of questions.   296

Extend the school day with age-appropriate homework assignments.   297

Shoot for mastery of basic knowledge and skills.   299

Conducting Learner-Directed Instruction   300

Have students discuss issues that lend themselves to multiple perspectives, explanations, or approaches.   300

Create a classroom atmosphere conducive to open debate and the constructive evaluation of ideas.   301

Conduct activities in which students must depend on one another for their learning.   302

Have students conduct their own research about new topics.   304

Have students teach one another.   307

Assign authentic real-world tasks, perhaps as group activities.   309

Use technology to enhance communication and collaboration.   310

Provide sufficient scaffolding to ensure successful accomplishment of assigned tasks.   311

General Instructional Strategies   312

Take group differences into account.   313

Take developmental levels and special educational needs into account.   313

Combine several instructional approaches into a single lesson.   316

Summary   318

Practice for Your Licensure Exam: Cooperative Learning Project   318

MyEducationLab   319

CHAPTER 9 Strategies for Creating an Effective Classroom Environment   320

Case Study: A Contagious Situation   321

Creating an Environment Conducive to Learning   322

Arrange the classroom to maximize attention and minimize disruptions.   323

Communicate acceptance, caring, and respect for every student.   323

Work hard to improve relationships that have gotten off to a bad start.   324

Create a sense of community and belongingness.   325

Create a goal-oriented, businesslike (but nonthreatening) atmosphere.   326

Establish reasonable rules and procedures.   326

Enforce rules consistently and equitably.   328

Keep students productively engaged in worthwhile tasks.   328

Plan for transitions.   329

Take individual and developmental differences into account.   330

Continually monitor what students are doing.   333

Expanding the Sense of Community Beyond the Classroom   333

Collaborate with colleagues to create an overall sense of school community.   333

Work cooperatively with other agencies that play key roles in students' lives.   334

Communicate regularly with parents and other primary caregivers.   334

Invite families to participate in the academic and social life of the school.   335

Make an extra effort with seemingly "reluctant" parents.   336

Reducing Unproductive Behaviors   337

Consider whether instructional strategies or classroom assignments might be partly to blame for off-task behaviors.   337

Consider whether cultural background might influence students' classroom behaviors.   338

Ignore misbehaviors that are temporary, minor, and unlikely to be repeated or copied.   339

Give signals and reminders about what is and is not appropriate.   340

Get students' perspectives about their behaviors.   341

Teach self-regulation strategies.   342

When administering punishment, use only those consequences that have been shown to be effective in reducing problem behaviors.   343

Confer with parents.   345

To address a chronic problem, plan and carry out a systematic intervention.   349

Determine whether certain undesirable behaviors might serve particular purposes for students.   351

Addressing Aggression and Violence at School   353

Make the creation of a nonviolent school environment a long-term effort.   354

Intervene early for students at risk.   355

Provide intensive intervention for students in trouble.   355

Take additional measures to address gang violence.   356

Summary   358

Practice for Your Licensure Exam: The Good Buddy   358

MyEducationLab   359

CHAPTER 10 Assessment Strategies   360

Case Study: Akeem   361

Using Assessment for Different Purposes   363

Guiding Instructional Decision Making   363

Diagnosing Learning and Performance Problems   364

Determining What Students Have Learned from Instruction   364

Evaluating the Quality of Instruction   364

Promoting Learning   364

Assessments influence motivation.   364

Assessments influence students' cognitive processes as they study.   365

Assessments can be learning experiences in and of themselves.   365

Assessments can provide feedback about learning progress.   366

Assessments can encourage intrinsic motivation and self-regulation if students play an active role in the assessment process.   366

Important Qualities of Good Assessment   366

A good assessment is reliable.   367

A good assessment is standardized for most students.   369

A good assessment has validity for its purpose.   369

A good assessment is practical.   373

Conducting Informal Assessments   374

Observe both verbal and nonverbal behaviors.   374

Ask yourself whether your existing beliefs and expectations might be biasing your judgments.   375

Keep a written record of your observations.   375

Don't take any single observation too seriously; instead, look for a pattern over time.   375

Designing and Giving Formal Assessments   376

Get as much information as possible within reasonable time limits.   376

When practical, use authentic tasks.   377

Use paper–pencil measures when they are consistent with instructional goals.   378

Use performance assessments when necessary to ensure validity.   379

Define tasks clearly, and give students some structure to guide their responses. 383

Carefully scrutinize items and tasks to be sure they are free from cultural bias. 383

Identify evaluation criteria in advance. 384

When giving tests, encourage students to do their best, but don't arouse a lot of anxiety. 386

Establish conditions for the assessment that enable students to maximize their performance. 386

Take reasonable steps to discourage cheating. 387

Evaluating Students' Performance on Formal Assessments 388

After students have completed an assessment, review evaluation criteria to be sure they can adequately guide scoring. 388

Be as objective as possible. 389

Make note of any significant aspects of a student's performance that a rubric doesn't address. 389

Ask students to evaluate their performance. 389

When determining overall scores, don't compare students to one another unless there is a compelling reason to do so. 390

Give detailed and constructive feedback. 390

Make allowances for risk taking and the occasional "bad day." 391

Respect students' right to privacy. 391

Summarizing Students' Achievement with Grades and Portfolios 392

Base final grades largely on achievement and hard data. 393

Use many assessments to determine final grades. 393

Share grading criteria with students, and keep students continually apprised of their progress. 393

Keep parents in the loop. 393

Accompany grades with descriptions of what the grades reflect. 394

Accompany grades with additional qualitative information about students' performance. 395

Use portfolios to show complex skills or improvements over time. 395

Assessing Students' Achievement and Abilities with Standardized Tests 397

High-Stakes Tests and Accountability 400

Using Standardized Achievement Tests Judiciously 401

When you have a choice in the test you use, choose a test that has high validity for your curriculum and students. 401

Teach to the test if—but only if—it reflects important instructional goals. 402

Make sure students are adequately prepared to take the test. 402

When administering the test, follow the directions closely and report any unusual circumstances. 403

Take students' ages and developmental levels into account when interpreting test results. 403

Make appropriate accommodations for English language learners. 403

Never use a single test score to make important decisions about students. 404

Summary 404

Practice for Your Licensure Exam: Two Science Quizzes 405

MyEducationLab 406

APPENDIX   INTERPRETING STANDARDIZED TEST SCORES 407

GLOSSARY   G-1

REFERENCES   R-1

AUTHOR INDEX   A-1

SUBJECT INDEX   S-1

Preface

New to the Third Edition

Throughout the third edition I've made many small changes to reflect research findings and new ways of thinking that have been published or presented since I wrote the second edition. I've also streamlined my prose in spots where I had previously been unnecessarily wordy, and I've reworked other spots to make my meanings more clear. More significant, however, are the following additions and modifications:

- Each chapter now begins with three to six Mega-Ideas—overarching, unifying principles that subsume the chapter's Big Ideas and can serve as advance organizers for readers. In each end-of-chapter summary, I review chapter content within the context of these Mega-Ideas.
- I've added numerous margin questions that encourage readers to reflect in certain ways on what they're reading. Some of these, marked with a **?** might be answered in a wide variety of ways; their purpose is often to encourage readers to connect what they're reading to their past experiences or current beliefs about a topic. Others, marked with a ❖ icon, have just one or only a few possible right answers; readers can develop their own answers to these questions and find my feedback in the Book-Specific Resources of MyEducationLab.
- The Developmental Trends tables in Chapters 2 through 10 now have a new "Example" column that illustrates one or more of the age-typical characteristics for each of four grade levels: K–2, 3–5, 6–8, and 9–12.
- I've added new videos to the Book-Specific Resources in MyEducationLab, with references to them in the margins at appropriate places throughout the book.

Furthermore, I've added or enhanced discussions of certain topics in every chapter, including the following:

- **Chapter 1:** Greater emphasis on the importance of evidence-based practice; expanded discussion of qualitative research; new section on "Developing as a Teacher"; discussion of action research.
- **Chapter 2:** Updated discussion of the brain, including glial cells (especially astrocytes) and recent findings regarding their probable role in thinking and learning.
- **Chapter 3:** Expanded discussion of accommodating cultural differences, including a discussion of culturally responsive teaching; new Classroom Strategies boxes on "Using Feedback to Improve Learning and Behavior" and "Addressing Students' Stereotypes and Prejudices."
- **Chapter 4:** Change from the term *epistemological beliefs* to *epistemic beliefs*, consistent with current writings in the field; importance of critical thinking when seeking information on Internet websites.
- **Chapter 5:** Ecological systems theory as an additional perspective in the Theoretical Perspectives table; discussion of the variability in width of individual children's zones of proximal development (ZPDs); addition of Cattell's fluid and crystallized intelligences

and the Cattell–Horn–Carroll theory of cognitive abilities; introduction of *intellectual disability* as a preferred term for mental retardation (consistent with current practices in special education) and introduction of a third criterion for diagnosis (early appearance of developmental delays); new discussion of inquiry learning.

- **Chapter 6:** Expanded discussions of internalized motivation, cultural diversity in motivation, and interrelationships between motivation and emotions (e.g., via *self-conscious emotions):* revision of TARGET mnemonic and table to TARGETS.
- **Chapter 7:** Expanded discussion of personality, including the Big Five personality traits and cultural differences in personality; expanded discussion of aggression and bullying (e.g., cyberbullying, effects of bullying on bystanders, whole-school antibullying programs).
- **Chapter 8:** New section on creating a class website; expanded discussions of technology in planning and instruction (e.g., the Internet as a possible source of lesson plans, teacher use of remote desktop features as a means of guiding and monitoring students' computer use, expanded discussion of simulation software programs, discussion of cross-school technology-based collaborative activities).
- **Chapter 9:** Addition of class websites as a possible medium for communicating with parents.
- **Chapter 10:** Expanded discussion of portfolios (including a new Classroom Strategies box); accommodations for English language learners.
- **Appendix:** Addition of NCE scores to the discussion of standard scores.

My Rationale for This Book

Ever since my first encounter with psychology as a college freshman many years ago, I have found psychological concepts and principles to be invaluable in helping me understand and work effectively with my fellow human beings. By the time I was a college senior, I was determined to apply psychology to an enterprise about which I care deeply: the education of children. And I've been doing so, in a variety of ways, ever since.

My undergraduate training in psychology in the late 1960s focused largely on theory and research in the behaviorist tradition. In contrast, my graduate training in educational psychology in the early 1970s had a strong information processing bent. Since then I've come to know (and love) not only behaviorism and information processing theory but also a host of other theoretical perspectives. And as a teacher and school psychologist, I've found all of these perspectives to be useful in my work with children and adolescents.

The traditional approach to teaching and writing about educational psychology is to take one theory at a time, explaining its assumptions and principles and then identifying implications for educational practice. I take this approach myself in my book *Educational Psychology: Developing Learners,* now in its seventh edition. But in recent years I've started to teach my own educational psychology courses differently, focusing more on commonalities than differences among theories. In fact, although researchers from different traditions have approached human cognition and behavior from many different angles, they sometimes arrive at more or less the same conclusions. The language they use to describe their observations is often different, to be sure, but beneath all the words are certain nuggets of truth that can be remarkably similar.

In this book I've tried to bring educational psychology to the real world of children, teachers, and classrooms. I've also tried to integrate ideas from many theoretical perspectives into what is, for me, a set of principles and concrete strategies that psychology *as a whole* can offer beginning teachers. These are, in essence, the Big Ideas I've spoken about—and increasingly heard others speak about as well—at professional meetings. After a short introduction to research and its importance (Chapter 1), I begin with the essence of the human experience: cognition (Chapter 2). From that foundation I go in five different directions—to learning in various contexts (Chapter 3), complex cognitive processes (Chapter 4), cognitive development (Chapter 5), motivation (Chapter 6), and personal and social development (Chapter 7)—but always returning to basic cognitive processes that underlie these other universal human phenomena. The last three chapters of the book build on the earlier ones to offer recommendations in instruction (Chapter 8), classroom management (Chapter 9), and assessment (Chapter 10).

Some of my colleagues may be surprised at my use of footnotes rather than APA style throughout the book. My decision was strictly a pedagogical one. Yes, students need to know that the principles and recommendations in this book are research-based. But I've found that APA style can be very distracting for someone who is reading about psychology for the first time and trying to sort out what things are and are not important to learn and remember. Novice psychologists should be concerned more with the *ideas themselves* than with the people behind the ideas, and by putting most of the people in small print at the bottom of the page, I can help novices better focus their attention on what things truly are most important to know and understand.

Features of the Book

The book's 10 chapters have a variety of features that can help my readers better understand, remember, and apply what they're reading. First, each chapter begins with three to six **Mega-Ideas**—overarching principles that guide much of the chapter's discussion, serve as advance organizers for readers, and provide an organizational scheme for the end-of-chapter summary. Then, boldfaced **Big Ideas** throughout the book highlight key principles and concrete strategies that can guide teachers in their decisions and classroom practices.

Immediately following each chapter's Mega-Ideas is a **case study** that introduces some of the ideas and issues that the chapter addresses. Throughout each chapter I periodically revisit the case to offer new insights and interpretations.

I often put readers themselves in the position of "learner" and ask them to engage in a short learning or thinking activity. These **See for Yourself** exercises are similar to ones I use in my own educational psychology classes. My students have found them to be quite helpful in making concepts and principles more "real" for them—and hence more vivid, understandable, and memorable.

SEE FOR YOURSELF   Retrieval Practice

See how quickly you can answer each of the following questions:
1. What is your name?
2. What is the capital of France?
3. In what year did Christopher Columbus first sail across the Atlantic Ocean to reach the New World?
4. What did you have for dinner three years ago today?
5. When talking about serving appetizers at a party, people sometimes use a French term instead of the word *appetizer*. What is that French term, and how is it spelled?

Using what you've just learned about attention, explain why talking on a mobile (cellular) phone while driving is illegal in many places. (Compare your response to this question with the response presented in Chapter 2 of the Book-Specific Resources in MyEducationLab.)

FIGURE 5.5 In this drawing, 8-year-old Jeff interprets the expression "Your eyes are bigger than your stomach" quite literally.

An additional feature comes in the form of **margin questions** that encourage readers to connect chapter content to their past experiences or current beliefs and in some cases also encourage readers to take concepts and principles in new directions.

If you flip through the pages of the book, you'll see many classroom artifacts—that is, **examples of work created by actual students and teachers**. I use artifacts throughout the book to help readers connect concepts, principles, and strategies to students' behavior and to classroom practices.

To a considerable degree, I talk about concepts and principles that apply to children and adolescents at all grade levels. Yet first graders often think and act very differently than sixth graders do, and sixth graders can, in turn, be quite different from eleventh graders. Chapters 2 through 10 each have one or more **Developmental Trends** tables that highlight and illustrate developmental differences that teachers are apt to see in grades K–2, 3–5, 6–8, and 9–12.

DEVELOPMENTAL TRENDS

TABLE 7.3 Moral Reasoning and Prosocial Behavior at Different Grade Levels

Grade Level	Age-Typical Characteristics	Example	Suggested Strategies
K–2	• Some awareness that behaviors causing physical or psychological harm are morally wrong • Ability to distinguish between behaviors that violate human rights and dignity versus those that violate social conventions • Guilt and shame about misbehaviors that cause obvious harm or damage • Some empathy for, as well as attempts to comfort, people in distress, especially people whom one knows well • Appreciation for the need to be fair; fairness seen as strict equality in how a desired commodity is divided • Greater concern for one's own needs than for those of others	When Jake pushes Otis off the ladder of a playground slide, several of the boys' kindergarten classmates are horrified. One child shouts, "That's wrong!" and several others rush to Otis's side to make sure he's not hurt.	• Make standards for behavior very clear. • When students misbehave, give reasons that such behaviors are unacceptable, focusing on the harm and distress they have caused for others (i.e., use *induction,* a strategy described later in the chapter). • Encourage students to comfort others in times of distress. • Model sympathetic responses; explain what you're doing and why you're doing it. • Keep in mind that some selfish behavior is typical for the age-group; when it occurs, encourage more prosocial behavior.
3–5	• Knowledge of social conventions for appropriate behavior • Growing realization that fairness doesn't necessarily mean equality—that some people (e.g., peers with disabilities) may need more of a desired commodity than others • Increasing empathy for unknown individuals who are suffering or needy • Recognition that one should strive to meet others' needs as well as one's own; growing appreciation for cooperation and compromise • Increased desire to help others as an objective in and of itself	At the suggestion of his third-grade teacher, 9-year-old Jeff acts as a "special friend" to Evan, a boy with severe physical and cognitive disabilities who joins the class two or three days a week. Evan is unable to speak, but Jeff gives him things to feel and manipulate and talks to him whenever class activities allow conversation. And the two boys regularly sit together at lunch. Jeff comments, "Doing things that make Evan happy makes me happy, too."	• Talk about how rules enable classrooms and other groups to run more smoothly. • Explain how students can often meet their own needs while helping others (e.g., when asking students to be "reading buddies" for younger children, explain that doing so will help them become better readers themselves). • Use prosocial adjectives (e.g., *kind, helpful*) when praising altruistic behaviors.

Chapters 2 through 10 also each have two or more **Classroom Strategies** boxes that offer concrete suggestions and examples of how teachers might apply a particular concept or principle. These features should provide yet another mechanism to help my readers apply educational psychology to actual classroom practices.

CLASSROOM STRATEGIES Identifying Goals and Objectives of Instruction

- Consult local, state, national, and international standards, but don't rely on them exclusively.

  In identifying instructional goals for the year, a middle school science teacher considers both the state science standards and the standards developed by the National Academy of Sciences. In addition, he identifies specific goals related to two issues directly affecting students in his inner-city school district: air pollution and poor nutrition.

- Be realistic about what can be accomplished in a given time frame; allow time to pursue important topics in depth.

  Rather than expect students to remember a lot of discrete facts in social studies, a second-grade teacher identifies several "Big Ideas" that students should master during the school year—for instance, the idea that all people have certain needs and desires that affect their behaviors and the idea that different cultural groups may strive to satisfy those needs and desires in different ways.

- Identify both short-term objectives and long-term goals.

  A fourth-grade teacher wants students to learn how to spell 10 new words each week. He also wants them to write a coherent and grammatically correct short story by the end of the school year.

- In addition to goals related to specific topics and content areas, identify goals related to students' general long-term academic success.

  A middle school teacher realizes that early adolescence is an important time for developing the learning and study strategies that students will need in high school and college. Throughout the school year, then, he continually introduces new strategies for learning and remembering classroom subject matter— effective ways that students might organize their notes, mnemonic techniques they might use to help them remember specific facts, questions they might try to answer as they read a textbook chapter, and so on.

- Include goals and objectives at varying levels of complexity and sophistication.

- A high school physics teacher wants students not only to understand basic kinds of machines (e.g., levers, wedges) but also to recognize examples of these machines in their own lives and use them to solve real-world problems.

- Consider physical, social, and affective outcomes as well as cognitive outcomes.

  A physical education teacher wants his students to know the basic rules of basketball and to dribble and pass the ball appropriately. He also wants them to acquire a love of basketball, effective ways of working cooperatively with teammates, and a general desire to stay physically fit.

- Describe goals and objectives not in terms of what the teacher will do during a lesson but in terms of what *students* should be able to do at the *end* of instruction.

  A high school Spanish teacher knows that students easily confuse the verbs *estar* and *ser* because both are translated in English as "to be." She identifies this objective for her students: "Students will correctly conjugate *estar* and *ser* in the present tense and use each one in appropriate contexts."

- When formulating short-term objectives, identify specific behaviors that will reflect accomplishment of the objectives.

  In a unit on the food pyramid, a health teacher identifies this objective for students: "Students will create menus for a breakfast, a lunch, and a dinner that, in combination, include all elements of the pyramid in appropriate proportions."

- When formulating long-term goals that involve complex topics or skills, list a few abstract outcomes and then give examples of specific behaviors that reflect each one.

  Faculty members at a junior high school identify this instructional goal for all students at their school: "Students will demonstrate effective listening skills—for example, by taking complete and accurate notes, answering teacher questions correctly, and seeking clarification when they don't understand."

Sources: Brophy, 2008; Brophy, Alleman, & Knighton, 2009; N. S. Cole, 1990; Gronlund & Brookhart, 2009; M. D. Miller, Linn, & Gronlund, 2009; Popham, 1995; Wiggins & McTighe, 2005.

In Chapter 3 I describe some of the ways in which culture influences children's learning and development. As a follow-up to that discussion, **Cultural Considerations** features describe cultural differences in specific areas—for instance, in behavior, reasoning, or motivation. These features appear in Chapters 3 through 10.

CULTURAL CONSIDERATIONS Influences of Culture and Community on Complex Cognitive Processes

Learners' experiences at home and in their general community and culture can have a significant effect on the development of complex cognitive processes. Following are several areas in which researchers have observed group differences.

Epistemic beliefs. People from various cultural groups don't completely agree on what it means to *learn* something. From the perspective of mainstream Western culture, learning is largely a mental enterprise: People learn in order to understand the world and acquire new skills and abilities. But for many people in China, learning also has moral and social dimensions: It enables an individual to become increasingly virtuous and honorable and to contribute in significant ways to the betterment of society. Furthermore, from a traditional East Asian perspective, true mastery of a topic comes only with a great deal of diligence, concentration, and perseverance—a position

that stands in stark contrast to the American students in the chapter's opening case study.[a]

Learning strategies. Consistent with a belief that learning requires diligence and perseverance, many East Asian parents and teachers encourage frequent use of rehearsal and rote memorization as learning strategies.[b] Rehearsal and memorization are also common in cultures that value committing oral histories or verbatim passages of sacred text (e.g., the Koran, the Bible) to memory.[c] In contrast, many schools in mainstream Western culture are increasingly presenting lessons and encouraging strategies that foster meaningful learning. Even so, Western schools typically insist that students learn certain things—such as multiplication tables and word spellings—by heart.[d]

Self-regulated learning. Also consistent with the importance placed on

diligence and persistence, East Asian parents and teachers are apt to encourage considerable self-discipline and stick-to-itiveness as children tackle new projects. In doing so, they foster self-regulation.[e] Self-regulation is less common when youngsters have few role models for effective study habits and self-regulation skills. Such may be the case for some (but certainly not *all!*) children and adolescents who attend schools in low-socioeconomic neighborhoods. Although these students may hope to graduate, go on to college, and eventually become successful professionals, they may have little idea about how to accomplish these things.[f] The following interview with a middle school student in inner-city Philadelphia illustrates the problem:

> **Adult:** Are you on track to meet your goals?
> **Student:** No. I need to study more.
> **Adult:** How do you know that?

Although my approach in this book is to integrate the concepts, principles, and educational strategies that diverse theoretical perspectives offer, it's also important for future teachers to have some familiarity with specific psychological theories and with a few prominent theorists who have had a significant influence on psychological thinking (e.g., Jean Piaget, Lev Vygotsky, B. F. Skinner). I occasionally mention these theories and theorists in the text discussion, but I also highlight them in **Theoretical Perspectives** tables in Chapters 2, 5, and 6.

THEORETICAL PERSPECTIVES

TABLE 5.1 General Theoretical Approaches to the Study of Child and Adolescent Development

Theoretical Perspective	General Description	Examples of Prominent Theorists	Where You Will See This Perspective in the Book
Cognitive-Developmental Theory	Cognitive-developmental theorists propose that one or more aspects of development can be characterized by a predictable sequence of stages. Each stage builds on acquisitions from any preceding stages and yet is qualitatively different from its predecessors. Most cognitive-developmentalists are *constructivists*, in that they portray children as actively trying to make sense of their world and constructing increasingly complex understandings and abilities with which to interpret and respond to experiences.	Jean Piaget Jerome Bruner Robbie Case Kurt Fischer Lawrence Kohlberg *Supplementary readings on Piaget's theory and Kohlberg's theory appear in Chapters 5 and 7, respectively, of the Book-Specific Resources in MyEducationLab.*	Piaget's ideas appear frequently in this chapter's discussions of developmental processes and trends (e.g., see the discussions of assimilation, accommodation, and equilibration, as well as Table 5.2 and some entries in Table 5.3). We will look at Kohlberg's theory in our discussion of moral development in Chapter 7.
Nativism	Some behaviors are biologically built in. A few behaviors (e.g., the reflex to suck on a nipple placed in the mouth) are evident at birth. Others (e.g., walking) emerge gradually, and usually in a predictable order, as genetic instructions propel increasing physical *maturation* of the brain and body. Nativists suggest that in addition to genetically preprogrammed behaviors, some knowledge, skills, and predispositions—or at least the basic "seeds" from which such things will grow—are also biologically built in.	Renee Baillargeon Elizabeth Spelke Noam Chomsky	The influence of nativism is most obvious in this chapter's discussions of heredity, maturation, sensitive periods, brain development, and intelligence. It will also be reflected in our discussion of *temperament* both in this chapter and in Chapter 7.

In the United States, state teacher licensing requirements in many states include passing exams such as the Praxis tests published by the Educational Testing Service (ETS). Many items on these exams involve interpreting case studies. At the end of each chapter, then, I present a **Practice for Your Licensure Exam** exercise that includes a case study along with a constructed-response question (typically requiring a one- to two-paragraph response) and a multiple-choice question based on the case. By and large, these exercises draw on content from the chapters in which they're located, but occasionally they draw on material from earlier chapters as well.

PRACTICE FOR YOUR LICENSURE EXAM

Cooperative Learning Project

One Monday morning Ms. Mihara begins the unit "Customs in Other Lands" in her fourth-grade class. She asks students to choose two or three students with whom they would like to work to study a particular country. After the students have assembled into six small groups, she assigns each group a country: Australia, Colombia, Ireland, Greece, Japan, or South Africa. She tells the students, "Today we'll go to the school library, where your group can find information on the customs of your country and check out materials you think will be useful. Every day over the next two weeks, you'll have time to work with your group. A week from Friday, each group will give an oral report to the class."

During the next few class sessions, Ms. Mihara runs into many more problems than she anticipated. She realizes that the high achievers have gotten together to form two of the groups, and many socially oriented, "popular" students have flocked to two others. The remaining two groups are comprised of whichever students were left over. Some groups get to work immediately on their task, others spend their group time joking and sharing gossip, and still others are neither academically nor socially productive.

As the unit progresses, Ms. Mihara hears more and more complaints from students about their task: "Janet and I are doing all the work; Karen and Mary Kay aren't helping at all," "Eugene thinks he can boss the rest of us around because we're studying Ireland and he's

Irish," "We're spending all this time but just can't seem to get anywhere!" And the group reports at the end of the unit differ markedly in quality: Some are carefully planned and informative, whereas others are disorganized and have little substance.

1. **Constructed-response question**

   Describe two things you might do to improve Ms. Mihara's cooperative learning activity. Base your improvements on research findings related to cooperative learning or on contemporary principles and theories of learning, development, or motivation.

2. **Multiple-choice question**

   Ms. Mihara never identifies an instructional objective for her unit "Customs in Other Lands." Which one of the following objectives reflects recommended guidelines about how instructional objectives should be formulated?

   a. "The teacher should expose students to many differences in behaviors and beliefs that exist in diverse cultures (e.g., eating habits, ceremonial practices, religious beliefs, moral values)."

   b. "The teacher should use a variety of instructional practices, including (but not limited to) lectures, direct instruction, textbook readings, and cooperative learning activities."

Observe developmental changes in metacognition as you listen to 6-year-old Brent, 10-year-old David, 12-year-old Colin, and 16-year-old Hilary reflect on their thought processes in the four "Memory and Metacognition" videos in Chapter 4 of the Book-Specific Resources in MyEducationLab.

Accompanying the book are many **video clips** in an innovative online resource called **MyEducationLab**. These videos depict numerous elementary, middle, and secondary school classrooms in action, as well as one-on-one interviews with children and adolescents.

Supplementary Materials

Many supplements to the textbook are available to enhance readers' learning and development as teachers.

PEARSON myeducationlab

THE POWER OF CLASSROOM PRACTICE

In *Preparing Teachers for a Changing World,* Linda Darling-Hammond and her colleagues point out that grounding teacher education in real classrooms—among real teachers and students and among actual examples of students' and teachers' work—is an important, and perhaps even an essential, part of training teachers for the complexities of teaching in today's classrooms. MyEducationLab is an online learning solution that provides contextualized interactive exercises, simulations, and other resources designed to help develop the knowledge and skills teachers need. All of the activities and exercises in MyEducationLab are built around essential learning outcomes for teachers and are mapped to professional teaching standards. Utilizing classroom videos, authentic student and teacher artifacts, case studies, and other resources and assessments, the scaffolded learning experiences in MyEducationLab offer preservice teachers and those who teach them a unique and valuable education tool.

For each topic covered in the course you will find most or all of the following features and resources.

CONNECTION TO NATIONAL STANDARDS

Now it is easier than ever to see how coursework is connected to national standards. Each topic on MyEducationLab lists intended learning outcomes connected to the appropriate national standards. And all of the activities and exercises in MyEducationLab are mapped to the appropriate national standards and learning outcomes as well.

ASSIGNMENTS AND ACTIVITIES

Designed to enhance student understanding of concepts covered in class and save instructors preparation and grading time, these assignable exercises show concepts in action (through videos, cases, and/or student and teacher artifacts). They help students deepen content knowledge and synthesize and apply concepts and strategies they read about in the book. (Correct answers for these assignments are available to the instructor only under the Instructor Resource tab.)

BUILDING TEACHING SKILLS AND DISPOSITIONS

These learning units help students practice and strengthen skills that are essential to effective teaching. After presenting the steps involved in a core teaching process, students are given an opportunity to practice applying this skill via videos, student and teacher artifacts, and/or case studies of authentic classrooms. Providing multiple opportunities to practice a single teaching concept, each activity encourages a deeper understanding and application of concepts, as well as the use of critical thinking skills.

IRIS CENTER RESOURCES

The IRIS Center at Vanderbilt University (http://iris.peabody.vanderbilt.edu), funded by the U.S. Department of Education's Office of Special Education Programs (OSEP), develops training enhancement materials for preservice and practicing teachers. The Center works with experts from across the country to create challenge-based interactive modules, case study units, and podcasts that provide research-validated information about working with students in inclusive settings. In your MyEducationLab course we have integrated this content where appropriate.

SIMULATIONS IN CLASSROOM MANAGEMENT

One of the most difficult challenges facing teachers today is how to balance classroom instruction with classroom management. These interactive cases focus on the classroom management issues teachers most frequently encounter on a daily basis. Each simulation presents a challenge scenario at the beginning and then offers a series of choices to solve each challenge. Along the way students receive mentor feedback on their choices and have the opportunity to make better choices if necessary. Upon exiting each simulation, students will have a clear understanding of how to address these common classroom management issues and will be better equipped to handle them in the classroom.

TEACHER TALK

This feature emphasizes the power of teaching through videos of master teachers, who each tell their own compelling stories of why they teach. These videos help teacher candidates see the bigger picture and consider why the concepts and principles they are learning are important to their career as a teacher. Each of these featured teachers has been awarded the Council of Chief State School Officers Teachers of the Year award, the oldest and most prestigious award for teachers.

STUDY PLAN AND BOOK RESOURCES SPECIFIC TO YOUR TEXT

A MyEducationLab Study Plan is a multiple-choice assessment tied to chapter Mega-Ideas, supported by study material. A well-designed Study Plan offers multiple opportunities to fully master required course content as identified by the Mega-Ideas in each chapter:

- *Mega-Ideas* identify the overarching principles for the chapter and give students targets to shoot for as they read and study.
- *Multiple-Choice Assessment*s assess mastery of the content. These assessments are mapped to Mega-Ideas, and students can take the multiple-choice quiz as many times as they want. Not only do these quizzes provide overall scores for each Mega-Idea but they also explain why responses to particular items are correct or incorrect.
- *Study Material: Review, Practice, and Enrichment* give students a deeper understanding of what they do and do not know related to chapter content. This material includes text excerpts, activities that include hints and feedback, and interactive multimedia exercises built around videos, simulations, cases, or classroom artifacts.
- *Flashcards* help students master definitions of the key terms within each chapter.

In addition to the Study Plan, there are many resources available that are specific to this book, including:

- *Focus Questions* help guide students' reading.
- *Video Examples,* referenced by margin notes in every chapter, provide concrete illustrations of the various core concepts and principles illustrated in each chapter.
- *A Practice for Your Licensure Exam Exercise* resembles the kinds of questions that appear on many teacher licensure tests. The chapter-ending exercise is also located on MyEducationLab. On MyEducationLab students can complete the exercise while receiving hints that help scaffold them toward a correct response. The students can also compare their responses to the expert feedback provided.
- *Margin Note Questions* help students connect chapter content to past experiences and/or current beliefs.
- *Supplementary Readings* provide an opportunity to explore a subject in more depth.

COURSE RESOURCES

The Course Resources section of MyEducationLab is designed to help students put together an effective lesson plan, prepare for and begin their careers, navigate their first year of teaching, and understand key educational standards, policies, and laws.

The Course Resources Tab includes the following:

- The **Lesson Plan Builder** is an effective and easy-to-use tool that students can use to create, update, and share quality lesson plans. The software also makes it easy to integrate state content standards into any lesson plan.
- The **IEP Tutorial** shows how to develop appropriate IEPs and how to conduct effective IEP conferences.
- The **Preparing a Portfolio** module provides guidelines for creating a high-quality teaching portfolio.
- **Beginning Your Career** offers tips, advice, and other valuable information on:
  - *Résumé Writing and Interviewing*: Includes expert advice on how to write impressive résumés and prepare for job interviews.
  - *Your First Year of Teaching*: Provides practical tips to set up a first classroom, manage student behavior, and more easily organize for instruction and assessment.
  - *Law and Public Policies*: Details specific directives and requirements teachers need to understand with regard to the No Child Left Behind Act and the Individuals with Disabilities Education Improvement Act of 2004.

CERTIFICATION AND LICENSURE

The Certification and Licensure section is designed to help students pass their licensure exam by giving them access to state test requirements, overviews of what tests cover, and sample test items.

The Certification and Licensure tab includes the following:

- **State Certification Test Requirements:** Here, students can click on a state and will then be taken to a list of state certification tests.
- Students can click on the **Licensure Exams** they need to take to find:
  - Basic information about each test
  - Descriptions of what is covered on each test
  - Sample test questions with explanations of correct answers
- **National Evaluation Series™** by Pearson: Here, students can see the tests in the NES, learn what is covered on each exam, and access sample test items with descriptions and rationales of correct answers. They can also purchase interactive online tutorials developed by Pearson Evaluation Systems and the Pearson Teacher Education and Development group.
- **ETS Online Praxis Tutorials:** Here students can purchase interactive online tutorials developed by ETS and by the Pearson Teacher Education and Development group. Tutorials are available for the Praxis I exams and for select Praxis II exams.

Visit www.myeducationlab.com for a demonstration of this exciting new online teaching resource.

ONLINE INSTRUCTOR'S MANUAL Available to instructors for download at www.pearsonhighered.com/educator is an *Instructor's Manual* with suggestions for learning activities, supplementary lectures, group activities, and additional media resources. These have been carefully selected to provide opportunities to support, enrich, and expand on what students read in the textbook.

ONLINE POWERPOINT® SLIDES PowerPoint slides are available to instructors for download on www.pearsonhighered.com/educator. These slides include key concept summarizations and other graphic aids to help students understand, organize, and remember core concepts and ideas.

ONLINE TEST BANK AND TESTGEN The *Test Bank* that accompanies this text contains both multiple-choice and essay questions. Some items (lower-level questions) simply ask students to identify or explain concepts and principles they have learned. But many others (higher-level questions) ask students to apply those same concepts and principles to specific classroom situations—that is, to actual student behaviors and teaching strategies. The lower-level questions assess basic knowledge of educational psychology. But ultimately it is the higher-level questions that can best assess students' ability to use principles of educational psychology in their own teaching practice. Along with the *Test Bank* is *TestGen* software that enables instructors to create and customize exams. This software is available in both Macintosh and PC/Windows versions. Both the *Test Bank* and *Test Gen* are available for instructors to download on www.pearsonhighered.com/educator.

COMPUTER SIMULATION SOFTWARE The CD *Simulations in Educational Psychology and Research,* version 2.1 (ISBN 0-13-113717-4), features five psychological/educational interactive experiments. Exercises and readings can help future teachers explore the research components and procedures connected to these experiments. Both qualitative and quantitative designs are included. Instructors should contact their local Pearson Education sales representative to order a copy of these simulations.

ARTIFACT CASE STUDIES: INTERPRETING CHILDREN'S WORK AND TEACHERS' CLASSROOM STRATEGIES I have written *Artifact Case Studies* (ISBN 0-13-114671-8) as a supplement to the textbook. It's especially useful for helping students learning to apply psychological concepts and principles related to learning, motivation, development, instruction, and assessment. The case studies, or *artifact cases,* within this text offer work samples and instructional materials that cover a broad range of topics, including literacy, mathematics, science, social studies, and art. Every artifact case includes background information and questions to consider as readers examine and interpret the artifact. Instructors should contact their local Pearson Education sales representative to order a copy of this book and its accompanying Instructor's Manual.

CASE STUDIES: APPLYING EDUCATIONAL PSYCHOLOGY With the assistance of Linda Pallock and Brian Harper, Dinah Jackson McGuire and I have coauthored *Case Studies: Applying Educational Psychology* (2nd ed., ISBN 0-13-198046-7) to give students more in-depth practice in applying educational psychology to real children, teachers, and classrooms. The 48 cases in the book address many topics in educational psychology (learning and cognition, child and adolescent development, student diversity, motivation, instruction, classroom management, and assessment) across a variety of grade levels (preschool through high school). This book, too, is accompanied by an Instructor's Manual.

Acknowledgments

Although the title page lists me as the sole author of this book, I've hardly written it alone. I am greatly indebted to the innumerable psychologists, educators, and other scholars whose insights and research findings I have pulled together in these pages. And two key individuals at Pearson Education are my former editor, Kevin Davis (who was enthusiastic about the book since its inception and devotedly guided its progress through the first two editions), and my current editor, Paul Smith (who picked up the reins for the third edition and has energized and guided me for the past two years). Others at Pearson have also helped to turn my vision into reality. Developmental editor Christie Robb has been my day-to-day counsel and sounding board for the many little things that need doing in any book revision. Project manager Annette Joseph skillfully coordinated many aspects of the production process in-house at Pearson. Also, I'm particularly grateful to Lynda Griffiths, who copyedited my manuscript with a careful yet gentle touch and handled all the nitty-gritty issues involved in changing my manuscript into the final product you see before you now.

It's important, too, to recognize the invaluable contributions of my colleagues Jayne Downey (Montana State University) and Teresa McDevitt (University of Northern Colorado), who conceptualized and produced some of the videos that I refer my readers to in MyEducationLab. And with this third edition, I'm delighted to add two people to my writing team: Brett Jones at Virginia Tech, who is authoring the Instructor's Manual and PowerPoint slides, and Zsuzsanna Szabo at Marist College, who is crafting the book-specific contents of MyEducationLab.

On the home front have been the many students and teachers whose examples, artifacts, and interviews illustrate some of the concepts, developmental trends, and classroom strategies I describe in the book: Andrew Belcher, Katie Belcher, Don Burger, Noah Davis, Shea Davis, Barbara Dee, Amaryth Gass, Anthony Gass, Ben Geraud, Darcy Geraud, Macy Gotthardt, Colin Hedges, Erin Islo, Jesse Jensen, Sheila Johnson, Shelly Lamb, Carol Lincoln, Meghan Milligan, Michele Minichiello, Susan O'Byrne, Alex Ormrod, Jeff Ormrod, Tina Ormrod, Isabelle Peters, Ann Reilly, Corey Ross, Ashton Russo, Alex Sheehan, Connor Sheehan, Matt Shump, Melinda Shump, Emma Thompson, Melissa Tillman, Grace Tober, Grant Valentine, Caroline Wilson, Hannah Wilson, and Brian Zottoli. Special gratitude goes to Ann Shump, who continues to be on the lookout for treasure troves of artifacts among her friends, neighbors, and professional colleagues.

I must also acknowledge the contributions of my professional colleagues around the country who've reviewed the first and second editions of the book and offered many invaluable insights and suggestions: Lynley H. Anderman, University of Kentucky; Heidi Andrade, State University of New York at Albany; Bonnie Armbruster, University of Illinois at Urbana-Champaign; Ty Binfet, Loyola Marymount University; Rhoda Cummings, University of Nevada at Reno; Emily de la Cruz, Portland State University; Randi A. Engle, University of California, Berkeley; Robert B. Faux, University of Pittsburgh; William M. Gray, University of Toledo; Robert L. Hohn, University of Kansas; Donna Jurich, Knox College; Julita G. Lambating, California State University at Sacramento; Frank R. Lilly, California State University at Sacramento; Jeffrey Miller, California State University at Dominguez

Hills; Marla Reese-Weber, Illinois State University; Michelle Riconscente, University of Maryland at College Park; Cecil Robinson, University of Alabama; Beverly Snyder, University of Colorado at Colorado Springs; Mark Szymanski, Pacific University; Michael P. Verdi, California State University at San Bernardino; Vickie Williams, University of Maryland, Baltimore County; Steven R. Wininger, Western Kentucky University; and John Woods, Grand Valley State University. Reviewers who helped shape this third edition were Karen A. Droms, Luzerne County Community College; Bryan Bolea, Grand Valley State University; Tenisha Tevis, American University; and Analisa L. Smith, Nova Southeastern University. I am greatly indebted to all of these individuals for their deep commitment to preparing future teachers and to getting the word out about the many things that the field of educational psychology has to offer.

Finally, of course, I must thank my husband Richard and children Tina, Alex, and Jeff, who have all shaped my life—and so also this book—in ways too numerable to mention.

ESSENTIALS OF
Educational Psychology

Big Ideas to Guide Effective Teaching

Chapter

1

Introduction to Educational Psychology

Shutterstock

CHAPTER OUTLINE

Case Study: Starting High School

General Guiding Principles of Educational Psychology

Developing as a Teacher

Strategies for Learning and Studying Effectively

Summary

Practice for Your Licensure Exam: New Software

MEGA-IDEAS TO MASTER IN THIS CHAPTER

Effective teachers use research findings and research-based theories to make decisions about instruction, classroom management, and assessment practices.

Effective teachers continually work to enhance their professional knowledge and skills.

Learners read, study, and learn more effectively when they actively try to make sense of new information.

CASE STUDY   Starting High School

Anna is an intelligent Mexican American student enrolled in Chicago's public school system. Anna has certainly had more than her share of life's challenges; for instance, her parents have divorced, and several of her friends have been victims of gang violence. Teachers and other staff members at Anna's local K–8 elementary/middle school provide considerable social and emotional support for her during such traumatic times. They also give her regular feedback and guidance to help her improve her academic skills. By eighth grade, Anna's performance on a standardized achievement test places her reading skills at a ninth-grade level—seemingly confirming that she's well equipped to tackle the high school grades.

Yet when Anna makes the transition to ninth grade at a large city high school, her academic performance quickly deteriorates, and her first-semester final grades include several Ds and an F. Anna seems overwhelmed by the new demands that high school places on her, as reflected in the following explanations she gives a researcher:

> In geography, "he said the reason why I got a lower grade is 'cause I missed one assignment and I had to do a report, and I forgot that one." In English, "I got a C . . . 'cause we were supposed to keep a journal, and I keep on forgetting it 'cause I don't have a locker. Well I do, but my locker partner she lets her cousins use it, and I lost my two books there. . . . I would forget to buy a notebook, and then I would have them on separate pieces of paper, and I would lose them." And, in biology, "the reason I failed was because I lost my folder . . . it had everything

I needed, and I had to do it again, and, by the time I had to turn in the new folder, I did, but he said it was too late . . . 'cause I didn't have the folder, and the folder has everything, all the work. . . . That's why I got an F."[1]

Although Anna's math teacher offers to find tutors for struggling students, Anna perceives most of her teachers as being uncaring, unaware of how students are progressing, and inflexible in evaluating students' achievement. Twice she goes to the school counselor's office—visits that get her in trouble for being late to her next class—but the counselor isn't available to meet with her on either occasion.

Despite her rocky start, Anna hopes to earn her high school diploma and attend college. But her first-semester performance isn't a good sign. In a study of 27,000 students in Chicago's public schools (including Anna), Roderick and Camburn found that more than 40% of first-semester ninth graders (males especially) failed at least one course, and students who achieved at low levels early in their high school career were at higher-than-average risk for dropping out before graduation.[2]

- Why does Anna's academic performance drop so dramatically in ninth grade? Drawing both from information presented in the case study and from your own experiences in middle school and high school, identify several factors that might be contributing to her academic decline.

- What things might Anna's teachers do to help her succeed in high school?

---

[1] Roderick & Camburn, 1999, p. 305.
[2] Roderick & Camburn, 1999.

Bob Daemmrich Photography

When students begin high school, they face many new challenges—classes with unfamiliar peers, more stringent course requirements, less individualized guidance and instruction, and so on—while also dealing with the unsettling physiological and social changes that come with puberty and adolescence.

A variety of factors might be contributing to the decline in Anna's school performance. For example, perhaps the subject matter and assignments in her high school classes are more challenging than those in middle school. Perhaps the high school teachers have such large classes that they have little time to give students one-on-one assistance. Given that Anna is now attending classes with many students she doesn't know, perhaps she's more focused on making friends and fitting in with her new peer group than she is on mastering school subject matter. Furthermore, Anna apparently doesn't have the organizational skills she needs to keep track of class materials and assignments.

Although students themselves certainly play a key role in their academic success, teachers can do many things to make students' success more likely. For example, they can get students genuinely interested in and excited about classroom topics. They can present information in such a way that students truly understand it, rather than simply memorize it. They can give students opportunities to practice new skills within the context of real-life situations and problems. They can teach students how to keep track of assignments and due dates, organize study materials, take good class notes, and in other ways gain self-sufficiency in academic pursuits. And they can regularly monitor students' progress and provide ongoing feedback to help students improve.

Teaching children and adolescents—whether in an elementary or secondary school classroom, in a preschool or after-school child care facility, on the playing field, or elsewhere—is one of the most rewarding activities on the planet. Yet to actually help young people *learn* what you want to teach them, you cannot be concerned only about your subject matter. You must also consider how children and adolescents typically think and learn, what abilities different age-groups are likely to have, and what conditions are likely to motivate young people to master important knowledge and skills. And you must have a large toolbox of strategies for planning and carrying out instruction, creating an environment that keeps everyone working toward important instructional goals, and regularly assessing everyone's progress and achievement.

In this book we'll explore the field of **educational psychology**, which applies concepts and theories of psychology to instructional practice and offers a wide variety of strategies that can help students of all ages succeed in the classroom. In particular, we'll look at the following:

Chapter 2: The nature of human learning, thinking, and memory. In this chapter we'll identify teaching strategies that can help students like Anna learn and remember new information and skills.

Chapter 3: Specific environmental conditions and more general social and cultural factors that foster learning and development. The chapter's discussion of one particular topic—socioeconomic status—can sensitize us to the many challenges that are apt to confront students who, like Anna, attend school in lower-income, inner-city school districts.

Chapter 4: Complex thinking processes that enable children to study and learn effectively, apply what they learn to new situations, and critically evaluate new ideas and perspectives. As we discuss self-regulation in this chapter, we'll identify strategies for helping students like Anna acquire better study habits.

Chapter 5: Trends in cognitive development that influence how students of different ages think about and learn academic subject matter. Here we'll discover how Anna, as a typical high school student, probably thinks about and understands classroom topics somewhat differently than her teachers and other adults do.

Chapter 6: Motives and emotions that turn students "on" or "off" to learning and academic achievement. As we explore various facets of human motivation and emotion, we'll identify strategies for getting students like Anna engaged in and excited about classroom topics.

educational psychology Academic discipline that (a) systematically studies the nature of learning, child development, motivation, and related topics and (b) applies its research findings to the identification and development of effective instructional practices.

Chapter 7: Aspects of personal and social development that influence school success. As we look at the development of sense of self and peer relationships, we'll find that high school students are often preoccupied with defining themselves ("Who is the *real me?*"), making and keeping friends, and finding romantic partners—preoccupations that can distract them from their academic studies.

Chapter 8: Strategies for planning and carrying out effective instruction. In this chapter we'll find that instructional methods are not one-size-fits-all—that different methods are useful in different situations and for different kinds of students.

Chapter 9: Strategies for keeping students on task and minimizing unproductive classroom behaviors. Here we'll identify strategies for establishing productive teacher–student relationships and making students feel that they are important members of the school community—conditions that can greatly enhance students' desire to stay in school.

Chapter 10: Strategies for assessing students' progress and final achievement. Our exploration of classroom assessment practices and standardized tests in this chapter will include many strategies for effectively monitoring students' learning and mastery of academic subject matter.

General Guiding Principles of Educational Psychology

As you can see from the preceding chapter descriptions, the field of educational psychology focuses on those aspects of psychology—thinking, learning, child and adolescent development, motivation, assessment of human characteristics, and so on—that have particular relevance for classroom practice. Underlying this seemingly diverse set of topics are several guiding principles that unify educational psychology as a discipline.

An in-depth knowledge of students must drive teacher decision making.

How children and adolescents think and learn, what knowledge and skills they have and have not mastered, where they are in their developmental journeys, what their interests and priorities are—all of these factors influence the effectiveness of various classroom strategies. Thus, the decisions teachers make in the classroom—decisions about what topics and skills to teach (*planning*), how to teach those topics and skills (*instruction*), how to keep students on task and supportive of one another's learning efforts (creating an effective *classroom environment*), and how best to determine what students have learned (*assessment*)—must ultimately depend on students' existing characteristics and behaviors.

Of course, teachers' classroom strategies also *change* what students know, think, and can do. Thus, the relationship between student characteristics and behaviors, on the one hand, and teacher strategies, on the other, is a two-way street. Furthermore, as you'll discover in Chapters 8 through 10, planning, instruction, the classroom environment, and assessment practices influence one another as well.

Figure 1.1 depicts how student characteristics and behaviors, planning, instruction, the classroom environment, and assessment mutually affect one another. Notice how student characteristics and behaviors are at the center of the figure, because these must drive almost everything that teachers do in the classroom. Such an approach to teaching is sometimes known as **learner-centered instruction**.[3]

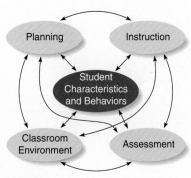

FIGURE 1.1 A learner-centered model of instruction

[3] For good general discussions of learner-centered instructional practices, see McCombs, 2005; National Research Council, 2000. You may also want to look at the American Psychological Association's (APA's) 14 *Learner-Centered Psychological Principles* on the APA website at http://www.apa.org. Type "learner-centered principles" in the search box on APA's home page.)

learner-centered instruction Approach to teaching in which instructional strategies are chosen largely on the basis of students' existing abilities, predispositions, and needs.

In many instances teachers can accommodate students' unique characteristics within the context of typical classroom practices and activities. Yet some students, known as **students with special needs**, are different enough that they require specially adapted instructional materials or practices to help them maximize their learning and development. Now, more than ever before, many of these students are in general education classrooms, a practice called **inclusion**. Regardless of the grade level or subject matter, teachers should expect to have students with a wide variety of special needs in their classrooms at one time or another. At several points in the book we'll consider students with particular kinds of special needs and identify strategies that may be especially useful in working with them.

The effectiveness of various classroom practices can best be determined through systematic research.

You yourself have been a student for many years now, and in the process you've undoubtedly learned a great deal about how children learn and develop and about how teachers can foster their learning and development. But exactly how much *do* you know? To help you find out, I've developed a short pretest, Ormrod's Own Psychological Survey (OOPS).

SEE FOR YOURSELF Ormrod's Own Psychological Survey (OOPS)

Decide whether each of the following statements is *true* or *false*.

True/False

_____ 1. The best way to learn and remember a new fact is to repeat it over and over again.

_____ 2. Most children 5 years of age and older are natural learners: They know the best way to learn something without having to be taught how to learn it.

_____ 3. When a teacher rewards one student for appropriate behavior, the behavior of other students usually suffers as a result.

_____ 4. Students are often poor judges of how much they've learned.

_____ 5. Anxiety sometimes helps students learn and perform more successfully in the classroom.

_____ 6. When teachers have children tutor their classmates in academic subject matter, the tutors gain very little from the process.

_____ 7. The ways in which teachers assess students' learning influence what and how the students actually learn.

Now let's see how well you did on the OOPS. The answers, along with an explanation for each one, are as follows:

1. The best way to learn and remember a new fact is to repeat it over and over again. FALSE—Although repeating information over and over is better than doing nothing at all, repetition is a relatively *in*effective way to learn specific pieces of information. Students learn new information more easily and remember it longer when they connect it with things they already know and when they engage in **elaboration**—that is, when they embellish on the information in some way, perhaps by drawing inferences from a historical fact, identifying new examples of a mathematical concept, or thinking of possible ways they might apply a scientific principle. Chapter 2 describes several cognitive processes that effectively help students learn and remember school subject matter.

2. Most children 5 years of age and older are natural learners: They know the best way to learn something without having to be taught how to learn it. FALSE—Many students of all ages are relatively naive about how they can best learn something, and they often use inefficient strategies when they study. For example, most elementary students and a

student with special needs Student who is different enough from peers that he or she requires specially adapted instructional materials and practices.

inclusion The practice of educating all students, including those with severe and multiple disabilities, in neighborhood schools and general education classrooms.

elaboration Cognitive process in which learners embellish on new information based on what they already know.

substantial number of high school students don't engage in elaboration as they study classroom material—that is, they don't analyze, interpret, or otherwise add their own ideas to the things they need to learn. We'll look at developmental trends in elaboration and other learning strategies in Chapter 2.

3. When a teacher rewards one student for appropriate behavior, the behavior of other students usually suffers as a result. FALSE—When teachers reward one student for behaving in a particular way, other students who have observed that student being rewarded sometimes begin to behave in a similar manner. We'll examine this phenomenon, known as *vicarious reinforcement*, in Chapter 3.

4. Students are often poor judges of how much they've learned. TRUE—Contrary to popular opinion, students are usually *not* the best judges of what they do and do not know. For example, many students think that if they've spent a long time studying a textbook chapter, they must know its contents very well. Yet if they have spent most of their study time inefficiently (perhaps by "reading" while thinking about something else altogether or by mindlessly copying definitions), they may know far less than they think they do. We'll consider this *illusion of knowing* further in Chapter 4.

5. Anxiety sometimes helps students learn and perform more successfully in the classroom. TRUE—Many people think that anxiety is always a bad thing. Yet for some classroom tasks, and especially for relatively easy tasks, a moderate level of anxiety actually *improves* students' learning and performance. We'll explore the effects of anxiety and other emotions in Chapter 6.

6. When teachers have children tutor their classmates in academic subject matter, the tutors gain very little from the process. FALSE—When students teach one another, the tutors often benefit as much as the students being tutored. For instance, in one research study,[4] when low-achieving fourth graders tutored first and second graders in basic arithmetic skills, the tutors themselves showed a substantial improvement in arithmetic. We'll look more closely at the effects of peer tutoring in Chapter 8.

7. The ways in which teachers assess students' learning influence what and how the students actually learn. TRUE—What and how students learn depend, in part, on how they expect their learning to be assessed. For example, students typically spend more time studying the things they think will be on a test than the things they think the test won't cover. And they're more likely to pull class material into an integrated, meaningful whole if they expect assessment activities to require such integration. Chapter 10 describes the effects of classroom assessment practices on students' learning.

How many of the OOPS items did you answer correctly? Did some of the false items seem convincing enough that you marked them true? Did some of the true items contradict certain beliefs you had? If either of these was the case, you're hardly alone. College students often agree with statements that seem obvious but are, in fact, partially or completely incorrect.[5] Furthermore, many students in teacher education classes reject research findings when those findings appear to contradict their personal beliefs and experiences.[6]

It's easy to be persuaded by "common sense" and assume that what seems logical must be reality. Yet common sense and logic don't always give us the real scoop about how people actually learn and develop, nor do they always give us appropriate guidance about how best to help students succeed in the classroom. Educational psychologists believe that knowledge about teaching and

When one student tutors another, the tutor often learns as much from the experience as the student being tutored.

---

[4] Inglis & Biemiller, 1997.

[5] Gage, 1991; L. S. Goldstein & Lake, 2000; Woolfolk Hoy, Davis, & Pape, 2006.

[6] Gregoire, 2003; Holt-Reynolds, 1992; T. McDevitt & Ormrod, 2008; Patrick & Pintrich, 2001.

learning should come from a more objective source of information—that is, from systematic research. Increasingly, educators and policy makers alike are calling for **evidence-based practices**—the use of instructional methods and other classroom strategies that research has consistently shown to bring about significant gains in students' development and academic achievement.[7]

When educational psychologists describe human learning, development, and motivation, and when they suggest particular instructional practices, classroom management strategies, and assessment techniques, they usually identify the particular research articles, books, conference presentations, and other sources on which they base their claims. Typically they follow **APA style,** guidelines prescribed by the American Psychological Association for identifying sources and preparing references. In APA style a source is cited by presenting the author(s) and date of publication in the body of the text. For example, let's return to the earlier paragraph that begins "How many of the OOPS items. . . ." If I had written that paragraph using APA style, it would have looked like this:[8]

> How many of the OOPS items did you answer correctly? Did some of the false items seem convincing enough that you marked them true? Did some of the true items contradict certain beliefs you had? If either of these was the case, you're hardly alone. College students often agree with statements that seem obvious but are, in fact, partially or completely incorrect (Gage, 1991; L. S. Goldstein & Lake, 2000; Woolfolk Hoy, Davis, & Pape, 2006). Furthermore, many students in teacher education classes reject research findings when those findings appear to contradict their personal beliefs and experiences (Gregoire, 2003; Holt-Reynolds, 1992; T. McDevitt & Ormrod, 2008; Patrick & Pintrich, 2001).

Notice how I've included initials for only two authors: Lisa Goldstein and Teresa McDevitt. When two or more first authors listed in the references have the same surname (as is true for the surnames Goldstein and McDevitt in this book), APA style dictates that initials be included to distinguish among those authors, making it easier for readers to find the relevant source(s) in the reference list.

Most books in the field of educational psychology use the APA style of referencing, but I've intentionally deviated from APA style in this book for pedagogical reasons. When I assign books that have citations sprinkled throughout the text, I find that some students focus too much on the names and dates and not enough on what's really important for them to learn and remember: the *ideas*. Rather than presenting my sources within the text, then, I'm presenting them in footnotes. When you find some of the book's ideas especially interesting, exciting, or surprising, I urge you to read my footnoted sources firsthand. You'll find the detailed citations for all of them in the References list at the back of the book.

Research can provide quantitative information, qualitative information, or both.

Many research studies involve **quantitative research:** They yield numbers that reflect percentages, frequencies, or averages related to certain characteristics or phenomena. For example, a quantitative study might provide information about students' performance on achievement tests, students' responses to rating-scale questionnaires, or school district records of students' attendance and dropout rates.

Other studies involve **qualitative research:** They yield nonnumeric information—perhaps in the form of verbal reports, written documents, pictures, or maps—that captures many aspects of a complex situation. For example, a qualitative study might involve lengthy interviews in which students describe their hopes for the future, a detailed case study of interpersonal relationships within a tight-knit clique of adolescent girls, or in-depth observations of several teachers who create distinctly different psychological atmospheres in their classrooms.

Ultimately, teachers gain a better understanding of students and effective classroom practices when they consider findings from *both* quantitative and qualitative research. And

evidence-based practice Instructional method or other classroom strategy that research has consistently shown to bring about significant gains in students' development and/or academic achievement.

APA style Rules and guidelines on referencing, editorial style, and manuscript format prescribed by the American Psychological Association.

quantitative research Research yielding information that is inherently numerical in nature or can easily be reduced to numbers.

qualitative research Research yielding information that cannot be easily reduced to numbers; typically involves an in-depth examination of a complex phenomenon.

---

[7] For example, see Darling-Hammond & Bransford, 2005; Waterhouse, 2006.

[8] For more information on APA style, see its *Publication Manual* (2010) or visit http://www.apastyle.org.

in fact, many studies provide both quantitative and qualitative information. For example, the study by Roderick and Camburn mentioned in the opening case study included both quantitative information (e.g., percentages of students who failed at least one course each semester) and qualitative information (e.g., students' explanations of why they were having difficulty in high school).

Different kinds of research lead to different kinds of conclusions.

Research studies typically fall into one of three general categories: descriptive, correlational, or experimental. These three categories yield different kinds of information and warrant different kinds of conclusions.

A **descriptive study** does exactly what its name implies: It *describes* a situation. Descriptive studies might give us information about the characteristics of students, teachers, or schools. They might also provide information about how frequently certain events or behaviors occur. Descriptive studies allow us to draw conclusions about the way things are—the current state of affairs. Virtually all qualitative studies are primarily descriptive in nature, and some quantitative studies fall into the descriptive category as well. The second and third columns of Table 1.1 present examples of questions we could answer with qualitative and quantitative descriptive studies.

A **correlational study** explores possible relationships among different things. For instance, it might tell us how closely two human characteristics are associated with each other, or it might give us information about the consistency with which certain human behaviors occur in conjunction with certain environmental conditions. In general, correlational studies enable us to draw conclusions about **correlation**: the extent to which two characteristics or phenomena tend to be found together or to change together. Two variables are correlated when one *increases* as the other increases (a *positive correlation*) or

descriptive study Research study that enables researchers to draw conclusions about the current state of affairs but not about correlational or cause–and–effect relationships.

correlational study Research study that explores possible relationships among variables.

correlation Extent to which two variables are associated, such that when one variable increases, the other either increases or decreases somewhat predictably.

TABLE 1.1 Examples of Questions We Might Answer with Qualitative and Quantitative Research Studies

Topic	Qualitative Research (Descriptive)	Quantitative Research		
		Descriptive Studies	Correlational Studies	Experimental Studies
Reading	What things do high-achieving students say they do "in their heads" when they read and study their textbooks?	How pervasive are gender stereotypes in books commonly used to teach reading in the elementary grades?	Are better readers also better spellers?	Which of two reading programs produces greater gains in reading comprehension?
Abstract Thinking	What misconceptions are often seen in high school students' explanations of abstract concepts?	What percentage of high school students can think abstractly about academic topics?	Are older students more capable of abstract thought than younger students?	Can abstract thinking skills be improved through specially designed educational programs?
Aggression	What distinct qualities characterize high schools in which members of violence-prone adolescent gangs interact congenially and respectfully?	What kinds of aggressive behaviors occur in schools, and with what frequencies?	Are students more likely to be aggressive at school if they often see violence at home or in their neighborhood?	Which method is most effective in reducing aggressive behavior—rewarding appropriate behavior, punishing aggressive behavior, or a combination of these two strategies?
Achievement Tests	In what ways do teachers' instructional practices change when their jobs and salaries depend on their students' scores on statewide or national achievement tests?	How well have students performed on a recent national achievement test?	Do students who get the highest scores on multiple-choice tests also get the highest scores on essays dealing with the same material?	Do different kinds of tests (e.g., multiple-choice vs. essay tests) encourage students to study in different ways and thereby affect what students actually learn?

when one *decreases* as the other increases (a *negative correlation*) in a somewhat predictable manner. The fourth column of Table 1.1 presents examples of questions we might answer with correlational studies. Notice how each of the questions asks about an association between two variables—between reading and spelling, between age and abstract thought, between student aggression and violence at home, or between multiple-choice and essay scores.

If a correlation exists between two variables, knowing the status of one variable allows us to make *predictions* about the other variable. For example, if we find that older students are more capable of abstract thought than younger students, we can predict that ninth graders will benefit more from an abstract discussion of democratic government than fourth graders. However, a correlational study cannot, in and of itself, explain *why* an association exists. In other words, *correlation does not necessarily indicate causation.* For example, Roderick and Camburn's study of the Chicago public schools had a correlational element: It revealed that early failure in high school was associated with—and so predicted—later school failure and dropping out. But it did not necessarily show that early failure was the *reason* that many students subsequently dropped out of school.

Descriptive and correlational studies describe things as they exist naturally in the environment. In contrast, an **experimental study**, or **experiment**, is a study in which the researcher somehow changes, or *manipulates,* one or more aspects of the environment (often called *independent variables*) and then measures the effects of such changes on something else. In educational research the "something else" being affected (often called the *dependent variable*) is usually some aspect of student behavior—perhaps end-of-semester grades, skill in executing a complex physical movement, persistence in tackling difficult math problems, or ability to interact appropriately with peers. In a good experiment a researcher *separates and controls variables,* testing the possible effects of one variable while holding constant all other potentially influential variables. When carefully designed and conducted, experimental studies enable us to draw conclusions about causation—about what variables cause or influence certain other variables.

Often experimental studies involve two or more groups that are treated differently. Consider these examples:

- A researcher teaches reading comprehension skills to two different groups of students using two different instructional methods. (Instructional method is the independent variable.) The researcher then tests students' reading ability (the dependent variable) and compares the average reading test scores of the two groups.
- A researcher gives three different groups of students varying amounts of practice with woodworking skills. (Amount of practice is the independent variable.) The researcher subsequently scores the quality of each student's woodworking projects (the dependent variable) and compares the average scores of the three groups.
- A researcher gives one group of students an intensive training program designed to improve their study habits. The researcher gives another group either no training at all or, better still, gives the second group training in skills unrelated to study habits. (Presence or absence of study-habits training is the independent variable.) The researcher later assesses study habits and obtains students' grade point averages (these are both dependent variables) to see if the training program had an effect.

experimental study (experiment) Research study that involves the manipulation of one variable to determine its possible influential effect on another variable.

treatment group Group of people in a research study who are given a particular experimental treatment (e.g., a particular method of instruction).

control group Group of people in a research study who are given either no treatment or a treatment that is unlikely to have an effect on the dependent variable.

Each of these examples includes one or more **treatment groups** that are the recipients of an intervention. The third example also includes a **control group** that receives either no intervention or an intervention that is unlikely to affect the dependent variable(s) in question. In many experimental studies, participants are assigned to groups *randomly*—for instance, by drawing names out of a hat. Such random assignment to groups is apt to yield groups that are, on average, roughly equivalent on other variables (ability levels, personality characteristics, motivation, etc.) that might affect the dependent variable.

The right-most column of Table 1.1 lists examples of questions that might be answered with experimental studies. Notice how each question addresses a cause–and–effect relationship—the effect of a reading program on the development of reading comprehension, the effect of educational programs on abstract thinking, the effect of rewards and punishment on aggressive behavior, or the effect of test-question format on students' learning.

Drawing conclusions about cause–and–effect relationships requires that all other possible explanations for an outcome be eliminated.

When we look at the results of a research study, we mustn't be too hasty to draw conclusions about cause–and–effect relationships. As an example, imagine that Hometown School District wants to find out which of two new reading programs, *Reading Is Great* (RIG) or *Reading and You* (RAY), leads to better reading in third grade. The district asks each of its third-grade teachers to choose one of these two reading programs and use it throughout the school year. The district then compares the end-of-year achievement test scores of students in the RIG and RAY classrooms and finds that RIG students have gotten substantially higher reading comprehension scores than RAY students. We might quickly jump to the conclusion that RIG promotes better reading comprehension than RAY—in other words, that a cause–and–effect relationship exists between instructional method and reading comprehension. But is this really so?

Not necessarily. If we look at the study more closely, we realize that the school district hasn't eliminated all other possible explanations for the difference in students' reading comprehension scores. Remember, the third-grade teachers personally *chose* the instructional program they used. Why did some teachers choose RIG and others choose RAY? Were these two groups of teachers different in some way? Had RIG teachers taken more graduate courses in reading instruction, were they more open-minded and enthusiastic about using innovative methods, or did they devote more class time to reading instruction? If the RIG and RAY teacher groups were different from each other in any of these ways—or perhaps different in some other way we might not happen to think of—then the district hasn't eliminated alternative explanations for why the RIG students have developed better reading skills than the RAY students. A better way to study the causal influence of reading program on reading comprehension would be to *randomly assign* teachers to the RIG and RAY programs, thereby making the two groups of teachers roughly equivalent in such areas as graduate-level coursework, personality, motivation, expectations for students, and class time devoted to reading instruction.

Be careful that you don't jump too quickly to conclusions about what factors are affecting students' learning, development, and behavior in particular situations. Scrutinize descriptions of research carefully, always with these questions in mind: *Have the researchers separated and controlled variables that might have an influence on the outcome? Have they ruled out other possible explanations for their results?* Only when the answers to both of these questions are undeniably *yes* should you draw a conclusion about a cause–and–effect relationship.

In this book I draw largely from descriptive and correlational studies to identify characteristics and behaviors that are typical for various age-groups and grade levels. I rely more heavily on experimental studies to identify effective teacher strategies. Keep in mind, however, that for practical or ethical reasons, many important questions about classroom instruction and children's development don't easily lend themselves to carefully controlled experimental studies. For instance, although we might reasonably hypothesize that children can better master difficult math concepts if they receive individualized instruction, most school systems can't afford such a luxury, and it would be unfair to provide tutoring for some students and deny it to a control group of other, equally needy students. And, of course, it would be highly unethical to study the effects of aggression by intentionally placing some children in a violent environment. Some important educational and developmental questions, then, can be addressed only with descriptive or correlational studies, even though such studies cannot help us pin down specific cause–and–effect relationships.

> What other possible differences between the RIG and RAY teachers might there be? (Compare your response to this question with the response presented in Chapter 1 of the Book-Specific Resources in MyEducationLab.)

Only systematic research—and ideally, experimental research—can tell us which instructional strategies truly enhance students' learning and development.

Anthony Magnacca/Merrill

Theories can help synthesize, explain, and apply research findings.

As researchers learn more and more about how things are (qualitative studies and descriptive quantitative studies), what variables are associated with one another (correlational studies), and what events cause what outcomes (experimental studies), they begin to develop **theories** that integrate and explain their findings. In their theories, researchers typically speculate about the underlying (and often unobservable) mechanisms involved in thinking, learning, development, motivation, or some other aspect of human functioning.

By giving us ideas about such mechanisms, theories can ultimately help us create learning environments that facilitate students' learning and achievement to the greatest extent possible. Let's take an example. In Chapter 2 we'll discover that a particular theory of how people learn—information processing theory—proposes that attention is an essential ingredient in the learning process. If a learner *doesn't* pay attention, information rapidly disappears from memory, essentially going "in one ear and out the other." The importance of attention in information processing theory suggests that strategies that capture and maintain students' attention—perhaps providing interesting reading materials, presenting intriguing problems, or praising good performance—are apt to enhance students' learning and achievement.

Psychological theories are rarely, if ever, set in stone. Instead, they are continually revised as additional data come to light, and in some cases one theory may be abandoned in favor of a very different one that better explains certain phenomena. Furthermore, different theories often focus on different aspects of human functioning, and psychologists have not yet been able to pull them together into a single "mega-theory" that adequately accounts for all of the diverse phenomena and experiences that comprise human existence.

The contents of upcoming chapters are based on a variety of theories related to thinking, learning, development, motivation, and behavior. Although these theories will inevitably continue to evolve over time, they can be quite useful even in their present, unfinished forms. They help us pull together thousands of research studies into concise, integrated understandings of how children typically learn and develop, and they allow us to make inferences and predictions about how students in classrooms are apt to perform and achieve in particular situations. In general, theories can help us both *explain* and *predict* human behavior, and so they will give us numerous ideas about how best to help children and adolescents achieve academic and social success at school.

• Developing as a Teacher

If you are currently enrolled in a teacher education program, you should think of your program as a good start on the road to becoming a skillful teacher.[9] But it is *only* a start. Developing true expertise in any profession, including teaching, takes many years and a great deal of experience to acquire.[10] Research indicates that several strategies can help to make you a better teacher over the long run.

Keep up to date on research findings and innovative practices in education.

Occasional university coursework and in-service training sessions are often good ways to enhance teaching effectiveness.[11] Also, effective teachers typically subscribe to one or more professional journals, and as time allows, they attend professional conferences in their region. Many Internet websites provide additional means through which teachers can gain information and ideas about effective classroom practices. Websites for the National Council of Teachers of Mathematics (www.nctm.org) and the National Council for Geographic Education (www.ncge.org) are just two of the many helpful online resources.

Learn as much as you can both about the subject matter you teach and about strategies for teaching it effectively.

When we look at effective teachers—those who are flexible in their approaches to instruction, help students develop a thorough understanding of classroom topics, convey obvious

---

theory Integrated set of concepts and principles developed to explain a particular phenomenon.

[9] Bransford, Darling-Hammond, & LePage, 2005; Brouwer & Korthagen, 2005.
[10] P. A. Alexander, 2003; Berliner, 2001; Clotfelter, Ladd, & Vigdor, 2007.

[11] Bransford, Darling-Hammond, et al., 2005; Desimone, 2009; Guskey & Sparks, 2002; Hattie, 2009.

enthusiasm for whatever they are teaching, and so on—we typically find teachers who know their subject matter extremely well.[12] Effective teachers also have many strategies for teaching particular topics and skills—strategies that are collectively known as **pedagogical content knowledge**.[13] And they can usually anticipate—and so can also address—the difficulties students will have and the kinds of errors students will make in the process of mastering a skill or body of knowledge.[14] Some teachers keep journals or other records of the strategies they develop and use in particular situations and then reuse these strategies as needed.[15]

Conduct your own research regarding questions and issues at your own school.

In their day-to-day work with students, teachers sometimes encounter problems that researchers haven't previously addressed. In **action research**, teachers conduct systematic studies of issues in their own schools, with the goal of seeking more effective strategies in working with students.[16] For instance, an action research project might involve examining the effectiveness of a new teaching technique, seeking students' opinions about a controversial school policy, or ascertaining reasons why many students rarely complete homework assignments.

Many colleges and universities now offer courses in action research. You can also find inexpensive paperback books that provide helpful guidance for novice teacher–researchers.[17]

Learn as much as you can about the culture(s) of the community in which you are working.

In Cultural Considerations boxes throughout the book, I'll describe numerous ways in which children from diverse cultural groups may think and behave differently than *you* did as a child. But a textbook can offer only a sampling of the many cultural differences you may encounter. You can become more informed about students' cultural beliefs and practices if you participate in local community activities and converse frequently with parents and other community members.[18]

Continually reflect on and critically examine your assumptions, inferences, and teaching practices.

As you'll discover in Chapter 4, one important goal of education is to nurture students' critical thinking abilities. Yet teachers must think critically as well, both about why students might be behaving in particular ways and achieving at particular levels and also about how current classroom practices might be influencing students' behavior and achievement. Effective teachers engage in **reflective teaching**: They continually examine and critique their assumptions, inferences, and instructional practices, and they regularly adjust their beliefs and strategies in light of new evidence.[19]

Communicate and collaborate with colleagues.

Good teachers rarely work in isolation. Instead, they frequently communicate with colleagues in their own school district and across the nation—perhaps with colleagues in other countries as well—and effective teachers at any single school regularly coordinate their efforts to enhance students' learning and personal well-being.[20] Thanks to both teacher lounges and the Internet, communication with professional colleagues is often quick and easy. One especially helpful website is www.tappedin.org, an online community of educators from around the world.

pedagogical content knowledge Knowledge about effective methods of teaching a specific topic or content area.

action research Research conducted by teachers and other school personnel to address issues and problems in their own schools or classrooms.

reflective teaching Regular, ongoing examination and critique of one's assumptions and instructional strategies, and revision of them as necessary to enhance students' learning and development.

---

[12] Borko & Putnam, 1996; Cochran & Jones, 1998; H. C. Hill et al., 2008; Windschitl, 2002.

[13] Cochran & Jones, 1998; Krauss et al., 2008; L. S. Shulman, 1986.

[14] Borko & Putnam, 1996; D. C. Smith & Neale, 1991.

[15] Berliner, 1988.

[16] Cochran-Smith & Lytle, 1993; G. E. Mills, 2007.

[17] For example, see Craig, 2009; Mertler, 2009; G. E.

Mills, 2007; Stringer, 2008.

[18] Castagno & Brayboy, 2008; National Research Council, 2000; Rogoff, 2003.

[19] Hammerness, Darling-Hammond, & Bransford, 2005; T. Hogan, Rabinowitz, & Craven, 2003; Larrivee, 2006.

[20] Bransford, Darling-Hammond, et al., 2005; Raudenbush, 2009.

Keep in mind that even the most masterful of teachers had to begin their teaching careers as novices, and they probably entered their first classroom with the same concerns and uncertainties that you may initially have. Most experienced teachers will be quite willing to offer you advice and support during challenging times. In fact, they'll probably be flattered that you've asked them!

Believe that you can make a difference in students' lives.

In Chapter 6 you'll discover the importance of having high self-efficacy—that is, of believing oneself capable of executing certain behaviors or reaching certain goals. Students are more likely to try to learn something if they have confidence that they can learn it. But teachers, too, must have high self-efficacy about what they can accomplish. Students who achieve at high levels are apt to be those whose teachers have confidence in what *they* can do, both individually and collectively, for their students.[21] And, in fact, high-quality instruction and teacher–student relationships can have a huge impact on students' academic success and personal well-being.[22]

• Strategies for Learning and Studying Effectively

As I've written the book, I've included many features that will, I hope, help you read about, study, and apply what researchers have learned about learning, development, motivation, and effective classroom practices. For example, I present key principles and strategies—the Big Ideas of educational psychology—as boldfaced sentences that begin new sections. I present even bigger, more general ideas—which I call Mega-Ideas—at the beginning of each chapter and then return to them in a chapter summary. In addition, the opening case studies and the figures, tables, exercises, concrete examples, and margin questions interspersed throughout the book are all designed to enhance your understanding and memory of what you're reading.

Yet ultimately, how much you learn from the book is up to you. In the next three chapters you'll learn a great deal about how human beings—including you—typically think about, learn, and remember things, and I hope you'll become a better student after reading them. But I'd like to get you off to a good start by offering four general strategies you can use as you read and study this book.

Relate what you read to things you already know.

Try to connect the ideas you read in the book with things you already know and believe. For example, relate new concepts and principles to your past experiences, your previous coursework, or your general knowledge about people and their behaviors. I'll occasionally assist you in this process by asking questions that encourage you to reflect on your prior experience, knowledge, and beliefs.

Be careful, however. As my earlier OOPS test may already have shown you, some of what you currently "know" and believe may be sort-of-but-not-quite accurate or even downright *in*accurate. As you read this book, then, think about how some ideas and research findings may actually contradict your current beliefs. In such instances I hope you'll revise your understanding of the topic at hand. That is, I hope you'll undergo *conceptual change,* a process you'll learn more about in Chapter 2.

Tie abstract concepts and principles to concrete examples.

As you'll discover in Chapter 5, children become increasingly able to think about abstract ideas as they get older, but people of *all* ages can more readily understand and remember abstract information if they tie it to concrete objects and events. Thus I will often illustrate new concepts and principles with opening case studies or brief vignettes that describe specific student and teacher behaviors in classroom settings. In addition, I will occasionally ask

---

self-efficacy Belief that one is capable of executing certain behaviors or reaching certain goals.

[21] Brophy, 2006; J. A. Langer, 2000; Skaalvik & Skaalvik, 2008; Tschannen-Moran, Woolfolk Hoy, & Hoy, 1998.

[22] Hattie, 2009; Raudenbush, 2009.

you to view certain videos in MyEducationLab, the online course that accompanies the book. I'll signal such requests with an icon like the one shown in the margin. Seeing psychological concepts and principles in action in the videos can enhance your understanding of them and help you recognize them when you see them in your own work with children and adolescents.

Sometimes it's even better to see a concept or principle in action in *oneself*. Thus I will occasionally ask you to relate a concept or principle to your own past experiences as a student. In some instances I will actually *give* you illustrative experiences in the form of See for Yourself exercises. You've completed one of these exercises—the OOPS test—already and will encounter many additional ones throughout the book.

Elaborate on what you read, going beyond it and adding to it.

Earlier I described the benefits of elaboration—embellishing on new information in some way—for learning and memory. So try to think *beyond* the things you read. Draw inferences from the ideas presented. Generate new examples of concepts. Identify your own educational applications of various principles of learning, development, and motivation.

Periodically check yourself to make sure you remember and understand what you've read.

There are times when even the most diligent students don't concentrate on what they're reading—when they're actually thinking about something else as their eyes go down the page. So stop once in a while (perhaps once every two or three pages) to make sure you've really learned and understood the things you've been reading. Try to summarize the material. Ask yourself questions about it. Make sure everything makes logical sense to you. And when you've finished reading a chapter, tackle the Practice for Your Licensure Exam exercise that appears after the chapter summary. You'll discover the nature and advantages of such *comprehension monitoring* in Chapter 4.

View Video Examples in the Book-Specific Resources section of MyEducationLab to help you tie concepts and theories of educational psychology to real children, adolescents, and classroom practices.

? How often do you elaborate while reading your textbooks? Do you learn and remember information more effectively when you elaborate on what you're reading?

Find several study aids in the Book-Specific Resources in MyEducationLab—including focus questions, self-check quizzes, and practice exercises—that can help you monitor your comprehension. Also, find additional suggestions for reading and studying in the supplementary reading "General Study Tips" in Chapter 1 of the Book-Specific Resources.

SUMMARY

Each chapter in this book includes a summary organized around the Mega-Ideas listed at the beginning of the chapter. Following are the Mega-Ideas for Chapter 1.

● ***Effective teachers use research findings and research-based theories to make decisions about instruction, classroom management, and assessment practices.*** Effective classroom practices are *learner-centered*—that is, they're chosen with students' current abilities, understandings, behaviors, and needs in mind. Effective classroom practices are also *evidence-based*—that is, they encompass strategies that research has consistently shown to bring about significant gains in students' development, academic achievement, and personal well-being. As researchers learn more and more about how things are (qualitative studies and descriptive quantitative studies), what variables are associated with one another (correlational studies), and what events cause what outcomes (experimental studies), they gradually develop and continually modify theories that integrate and explain their findings. Teachers can—and *should*—draw on research findings and well-supported theories about children's learning and development in their day-to-day and long-term instructional decision making.

● ***Effective teachers continually work to enhance their professional knowledge and skills.*** As a teacher, you must think of yourself as a life-long learner who always has new things to discover about effective educational practices, the subject matter you teach, and the out-of-school environments and cultures in which your students live. Some of these things you can learn about through books, professional journals, advanced coursework, the Internet, and consultations with colleagues, but others may require immersing yourself in the local community or conducting action research. You must also be willing to reflect on and critically analyze your current assumptions, inferences, and instructional practices—good teachers acknowledge that they can sometimes be wrong, and they adjust their beliefs and strategies accordingly. Most importantly, you must remember that, as a teacher, the many little things you do every day can have a huge impact—either positive or negative—on students' academic and personal success.

● ***Learners read, study, and learn more effectively when they actively try to make sense of new information.*** You can use what you learn about thinking and learning not only to help children and adolescents be successful in the classroom but also to help *you* learn successfully. For example, you should relate new information to what you already know, tie abstract ideas to concrete examples, embellish (elaborate) on what you're learning, and occasionally stop to test yourself on what you've read and studied.

PRACTICE FOR YOUR LICENSURE EXAM

New Software

High school math teacher Mr. Gualtieri begins his class one Monday with an important announcement: "Our school has just purchased a new instructional software program for our computer lab. This program, called 'Problem-Excel,' will give you practice in applying the concepts and procedures we'll be studying this year. I strongly encourage you to stay after school once or twice a week to get extra practice with the software whenever you're having trouble with the assignments I give you."

Mr. Gualtieri is firmly convinced that the new instructional software will help his students better understand and apply mathematics. To test his hypothesis, he keeps a record of which students report to the computer lab after school and which students do not. Later, he looks at how well the two groups of students have performed on his tests and quizzes. Much to his surprise, he discovers that, on average, the students who have stayed after school to use the computer software have gotten *lower* scores than those who haven't used the software. "How can this be?" he puzzles. "Is the computer software actually doing more harm than good?"

1. Constructed-response question

Mr. Gualtieri wonders if the computer software is hurting rather than helping his students. Assume that the software has been carefully designed by an experienced educator and that Mr. Gualtieri's tests and quizzes are good measures of how well his students have learned the material they've been studying. Then:

A. Explain why Mr. Gualtieri cannot draw a conclusion about a cause–and–effect relationship from the evidence he has. Base your response on principles of psychological and educational research.

B. Identify another plausible explanation for the results Mr. Gualtieri has obtained.

2. Multiple-choice question

Which one of the following research findings would provide the most convincing evidence that the Problem-Excel software enhances students' mathematics achievement?

a. Ten high schools in New York City purchase Problem-Excel and make it available to their students. Students at these high schools get higher mathematics achievement test scores than students at 10 other high schools that haven't purchased the software.

b. A high school purchases Problem-Excel, but only four of the eight math teachers at the school decide to have their students use it. Students of these four teachers score at higher levels on a mathematics achievement test than students of the other four teachers.

c. All tenth graders at a large high school take a mathematics achievement test in September. At some point during the next two months, they each spend 20 hours working with Problem-Excel. The students all take the same math achievement test again in December and, on average, get substantially higher scores than they did in September.

d. Students at a high school are randomly assigned to two groups. One group works with Problem-Excel, and the other group works with a software program called "Write-Away," designed to teach better writing skills. The Problem-Excel group scores higher than the Write-Away group on a subsequent mathematics achievement test.

Go to Chapter 1 of the Book-Specific Resources in MyEducationLab and click on "Practice for Your Licensure Exam" to answer these questions. Compare your responses with the feedback provided.

PEARSON
myeducationlab

Go to the Topic "Research Methods & Teacher Reflection" in the MyEducationLab (www.myeducationlab.com) for your course, where you can:

- Find learning outcomes for "Research Methods & Teacher Reflection," along with the national standards that connect to these outcomes.
- Complete Assignments and Activities that can help you more deeply understand the chapter content.
- Apply and practice your understanding of the core teaching skills identified in the chapter with the Building Teaching Skills and Dispositions learning units.
- Access video clips of CCSSO National Teachers of the Year award winners responding to the question, "Why Do I Teach?" in the Teacher Talk section.

- Check your comprehension of the content covered in the chapter by going to the Study Plan in the Book Resources for your text. Here you will be able to take a chapter quiz, receive feedback on your answers, and then access Review, Practice, and Enrichment activities to enhance your understanding of chapter content. Flashcards are also available to help you study definitions and key terms.
- Access additional Book Resources, including:
  - Focus Questions to guide your reading, a Practice for Your Licensure Exam exercise that resembles the kinds of questions appearing on many teacher licensure tests, Margin Note Questions that help you connect chapter content to your past experiences or current beliefs, and Supplementary Readings that enable you to pursue certain topics in greater depth.

Chapter

2

Learning, Cognition, and Memory

Shutterstock

CHAPTER OUTLINE

Case Study: The New World

Learning as a Constructive Process

Thinking and Learning in the Brain

How Human Memory Operates

Why Learners May or May Not Remember What They've Learned

Promoting Effective Cognitive Processes
    Remembering How the Human Memory System Works
    Encouraging Effective Long-Term Memory Storage
    Promoting Retrieval
    Monitoring Students' Progress

Summary

Practice for Your Licensure Exam: Vision Unit

MEGA-IDEAS TO MASTER IN THIS CHAPTER

Much of human learning involves a process of actively constructing—not passively absorbing—knowledge.

Knowledge about the brain is helpful, but some well-meaning educators have misinterpreted findings from brain research.

Human memory is a complex, multifaceted information processing system that is, to a considerable degree, under learners' control.

Human memory is fallible: Learners don't remember everything they learn, and sometimes they *misremember* what they've learned.

Effective teachers help students mentally process new information and skills in ways that facilitate long-term memory storage and retrieval.

CASE STUDY   The New World

Rita's fourth-grade class in Michigan recently had a unit on her state's history. Rita still knows little about U.S. history; she will study that subject as a fifth grader next year. Yet she willingly responds when an interviewer asks her if she knows why America was once called the "New World."

Rita: Because they used to live in England, the British, and they didn't know about . . . they wanted to get to China 'cause China had some things they wanted. They had some cups or whatever—no, they had furs. They had fur and stuff like that and they wanted to have a shorter way to get to China so they took it and they landed in Michigan, but it wasn't called Michigan. I think it was the British that landed in Michigan and they were there first and so they tried to claim that land, but it didn't work out for some reason so they took some furs and brought them back to Britain and they sold them, but they mostly wanted it for the furs. So then the English landed there and they claimed the land and they wanted to make it a state, and so they got it signed by the government or whoever, the big boss, then they were just starting to make it a state so the British just went up to the Upper Peninsula and they thought they could stay there for a little while. Then they had to fight a war, then the farmers, they were just volunteers, so the farmers went right back and tried to get their family put together back again.

Interviewer: Did you learn all this in state history this year?

Rita: Um hum.[1]

- Which parts of Rita's response accurately describe the history of the New World? Which parts are clearly inaccurate?

- At the time British colonists were first settling in Michigan, merchants in England were seeking a new trade route to the Far East so they could more easily secure the tea, spices, and silk available there. Why might Rita initially suggest that the British wanted to get cups from China? Why might she then say that they wanted to get furs?

[1] VanSledright & Brophy, 1992, p. 849.

Rita has certainly learned some facts about her state and its history. For example, she's aware that part of Michigan is called the Upper Peninsula, and she knows that many of the state's early European settlers were British. But she has used what she's learned to weave a tale that could give a historian heart failure. To some extent, Rita's lack of information about certain other things is limiting her ability to make sense of what she's learned about Michigan's history. Specifically, Rita doesn't know that the British and the English were the *same people*. Thinking of them as two different groups, she assumes that the arrival of the latter group drove the former group to the Upper Peninsula. Occasionally, what Rita *does* know is also a

learning Long-term change in mental representations or associations due to experience.

source of difficulty. For instance, she apparently associates China with dinnerware (including cups), and she has learned that some early European explorers sought exotic animal furs to send back to their homeland. She uses such information to draw logical but incorrect inferences about why the British were so eager to find a new route to China.

To understand how children and adolescents acquire understandings about their physical and social worlds, about academic subject matter, and about themselves as human beings, we must first understand the nature of learning. As Rita's depiction of Michigan's history clearly illustrates, learning is often a matter of creating, rather than absorbing, knowledge about the world. In other words, learning is a *constructive process*, as we shall see now.

• Learning as a Constructive Process

A good general definition of **learning** is this one: a long-term change in mental representations or associations due to experience. Let's divide this definition into its three parts. First, learning is a *long-term change* in that it isn't just a brief, transitory use of information—such as remembering a phone number only long enough to dial it—but it doesn't necessarily last forever. Second, learning involves *mental representations or associations* and so presumably has its basis in the brain. Third, learning is a change *due to experience,* rather than the result of physiological maturation, fatigue, alcohol or drugs, or onset of mental illness.

Psychologists have been studying the nature of learning for more than a century, and in the process they've taken a variety of theoretical perspectives. Table 2.1 summarizes five diverse perspectives that will contribute considerably to our understanding of what learning involves. The table also lists examples of theorists associated with each perspective. You'll find many of these theorists cited in footnotes in this and later chapters.

THEORETICAL PERSPECTIVES

TABLE 2.1 General Theoretical Approaches to the Study of Learning

Theoretical Perspective	General Description	Examples of Prominent Theorists	Where You Will See This Perspective in the Book
Behaviorism	Behaviorists argue that because thought processes cannot be directly observed and measured, it is difficult to study thinking objectively and scientifically. Instead, they focus on two things that researchers *can* observe and measure: people's behaviors (*responses*) and the environmental events (*stimuli, reinforcement*) that precede and follow those responses. Learning is viewed as a process of acquiring and modifying associations among stimuli and responses, largely through a learner's direct interactions with the environment.	B. F. Skinner Edward Thorndike Ivan Pavlov *A supplementary reading on Skinner's theory appears in Chapter 3 of the Book-Specific Resources section in MyEducationLab.*	We will examine learning from a stimulus–response perspective early in Chapter 3 (see the first four principles in the section "The Immediate Environment as Context"). We will also draw from behaviorist ideas when we address classroom management in Chapter 9 (see the discussions of cueing, punishment, applied behavior analysis, functional analysis, and positive behavioral support in the section "Reducing Unproductive Behaviors").
Social Cognitive Theory	Historically social cognitive theorists have focused largely on the ways in which people learn from observing one another. Environmental stimuli affect behavior, but cognitive processes (e.g., *awareness* of stimulus–response relationships, *expectations* about future events) also play a significant role. Oftentimes people learn through *modeling:* They watch and imitate what others do. Whether people learn and perform effectively is also a function of their *self-efficacy,* the extent to which they believe they can successfully accomplish a particular task or activity. As social cognitive theory has evolved over time, it has increasingly incorporated the concept of *self-regulation,* in which people take charge of and direct their own actions.	Albert Bandura Dale Schunk Barry Zimmerman	The social cognitive perspective will come into play in our discussions of modeling, vicarious consequences, incentives, and reciprocal causation in Chapter 3, as well as in our discussion of self-regulation in Chapter 4. Later, we will sometimes draw from social cognitive theory as we examine motivation (and especially as we focus on self-efficacy and goals) in Chapter 6.

(continued)

Theoretical Perspective	General Description	Examples of Prominent Theorists	Where You Will See This Perspective in the Book
Information Processing Theory	While not denying that the environment plays a critical role in learning, information processing theorists concern themselves with what goes on *inside* learners, focusing on the cognitive processes involved in learning, memory, and performance. From observations of how people execute various tasks and behave in various situations, these theorists draw inferences about how people may perceive, interpret, and mentally manipulate information they encounter in the environment. They speculate about what internal mechanisms underlie human cognition (e.g., *working memory* and *long-term memory*) and about how people mentally process information (e.g., through *elaboration* and *visual imagery*). Initially, some information processing theorists believed that human thinking is similar to how a computer works (hence, they borrowed terms such as *encoding, storage,* and *retrieval* from computer lingo), but in recent years many theorists have abandoned the computer analogy.	Richard Atkinson Richard Shiffrin John Anderson Alan Baddeley Elizabeth Loftus	Information processing theory is most evident in the model of human memory presented in Figure 2.5; this model provides the basis for much of the discussion of learning and memory in this chapter. Information processing theory will also help us understand the complex cognitive processes discussed in Chapter 4. It will be influential, too, in our discussions of cognitive development and intelligence in Chapter 5, cognitive factors in motivation in Chapter 6, and social cognition in Chapter 7. Furthermore, Table 8.2 in Chapter 8 draws largely from information processing theory.
Constructivism	Constructivists, like information processing theorists, concern themselves with internal aspects of learning. They propose that people create (rather than absorb) knowledge from their observations and experiences. They suggest that people combine much of what they learn into integrated bodies of knowledge and beliefs (e.g., these might take the form of *schemas* and *theories*) that may or may not be accurate, useful understandings of the world. Some constructivists focus on how individual learners create knowledge through their interactions with the environment; this approach is known as **individual constructivism**. Others emphasize that by working together, two or more people can often gain better understandings than anyone could gain alone; this approach is called **social constructivism**.	Jean Piaget Jerome Bruner John Bransford Giyoo Hatano *A supplementary reading on Piaget's theory appears in Chapter 5 of the Book-Specific Resources section in MyEducationLab.*	Constructivist ideas are intermingled with information processing theory throughout this chapter, and in fact many contemporary information processing theorists have a constructivist bent. The ideas of one of the earliest constructivists, developmental theorist Jean Piaget, are presented in Chapter 5. Constructivism will also be evident in the discussions of knowledge co-construction, epistemological beliefs, attributions, and personal and social understandings in Chapters 3, 4, 6, and 7, respectively.
Sociocultural Theory	Sociocultural theorists emphasize that the social, cultural, and historical contexts in which children grow up have profound influences on thinking, learning, and effective instructional practice. In social interactions within their communities, young learners encounter culturally appropriate ways of thinking about and interpreting objects and events. With time and practice, these ways of thinking—which are first used in a social context—are gradually *internalized* into nonspoken, mental processes that learners use on their own. Because of their varying environments, historical circumstances, and needs, children in different cultures acquire somewhat different ways of thinking, learning, and teaching.	Lev Vygotsky Barbara Rogoff Mary Gauvain Jean Lave *A supplementary reading on Vygotsky's theory appears in Chapter 5 of the Book Specific Resources section in MyEducationLab.*	We will first make use of sociocultural theory in Chapter 3, especially in the sections "Social Interaction as Context" and "Culture and Society as Context" (e.g., see the discussions of mediated learning experiences and cognitive tools). In Chapter 5, Vygotsky's theory of cognitive development will help us understand how children's social environments are essential for their cognitive development (e.g., see the discussions of internalization, self-talk, and zone of proximal development). Furthermore, the "Cultural Considerations" boxes in Chapters 3 through 10 will continually remind us how students' cultural backgrounds are likely to influence their thoughts, perceptions, and behaviors.

For the most part, diverse perspectives of learning complement rather than contradict one another, and together they can give us a rich, multifaceted picture of human learning. As we explore the nature of learning in this book, then, we'll draw useful ideas from all five perspectives. In this chapter, however, we'll be looking primarily at what goes on *inside* the learner, and so we will find the information processing and constructivist approaches most helpful.

individual constructivism Theoretical perspective that focuses on how people as individuals, construct meaning from their experiences.

social constructivism Theoretical perspective that focuses on people's collective efforts to impose meaning on the world.

Several basic principles, described in the following sections, underlie much of what information processing and constructivist theorists have learned about learning.

By the time they reach school age, young learners are usually actively involved in their own learning.

Sometimes children learn from an experience without really giving the experience much thought. For example, as infants and toddlers acquire the basic vocabulary and syntax of their first language, they seem to do so without consciously trying to acquire these things or thinking about what they're learning. Much of the learning that occurs during infancy and toddlerhood is *implicit learning,* and even older children and adults continue to learn some things about their environments in a nonintentional, "thoughtless" way.[2] But as children grow, they increasingly engage in intentional, *explicit learning:* They actively think about, interpret, and reconfigure what they see and hear in their environment. As a simple example, try the following exercise.

SEE FOR YOURSELF   Remembering Words

Study the 12 words below. Then cover up the page, and write down the words in the order they come to mind.

daisy	apple	dandelion
hammer	pear	wrench
tulip	pliers	watermelon
banana	rose	screwdriver

In what order did you remember the words? Did you recall them in their original order, or did you rearrange them somehow? If you're like most people, you grouped the words into three categories—flowers, fruit, and tools—and remembered one category at a time. In other words, you *organized* the words. As children get older, they're more likely to organize what they learn, and learners of all ages learn more effectively when they organize the subject matter at hand.

Cognitive processes influence what is learned.

The various ways in which people think about what they're seeing, hearing, studying, and learning are collectively known as **cognition**. The more specific things people do in their heads—which can have a profound effect on what they learn and can remember—are called **cognitive processes**.

An example of a cognitive process is **encoding**, in which a learner changes or adds to incoming information in some way in order to remember it more easily. For example, in the preceding "Remembering Words" exercise, chances are that you imposed a categorical structure on the words. But let's consider some alternative strategies you might have used to encode and remember the list. For instance, you might have created a story or poem that included all 12 words (e.g., "As *Daisy* and *Tulip* were walking, they ran across *Dandy* and *Rose.* They stopped in dismay when they noticed that Dandy had *pliers* on her nose . . .”). Or you might have formed a mental image of the 12 items in an elaborate, if not entirely edible, fruit salad (see Figure 2.1). All of these approaches are forms of encoding the 12-word list.

cognition Various ways of thinking about information and events.

cognitive process Particular way of mentally responding to or thinking about information or an event.

encoding Changing the format of information being stored in memory in order to remember it more easily.

---

[2] P. A. Alexander, Schallert, & Reynolds, 2009;
S. W. Kelly, Burton, Kato, & Akamatsu, 2001.

Learners must be selective about what they focus on and learn.

People are constantly bombarded with information. Consider the many stimuli you're encountering at this very moment. How many separate stimuli appear on the two open pages of your book? How many objects do you see in addition to the book? How many sounds are reaching your ears? How many objects—perhaps on your fingertips, on your toes, or around your waist—do you feel? I suspect that you've been ignoring most of these stimuli until just now; you weren't actively processing them until I asked you to do so. People can handle only so much information at any one time, and so they must be selective. Effective learners focus on what they think is important and ignore almost everything else.

FIGURE 2.1 A visual image for encoding a list of 12 words

As an analogy, consider the hundreds of items a typical adult receives in the mail each year, including all the packages, letters, bills, brochures, catalogs, credit card offers, and donation requests. Do you open, examine, and respond to every piece of mail? Probably not. If you're like me, you "process" only a few key items (e.g., packages, letters, bills, and a few miscellaneous things that catch your eye). You may inspect other items long enough to know that you don't need them. You may discard some items without even opening them.

People don't always make good choices about what to attend to, of course. Just as they might overlook a small, inconspicuous rebate check while opening a colorful "You May Already Have Won . . ." sweepstakes announcement, so, too, might they fail to catch an important idea in a classroom lesson because they're focusing on trivial details in the lesson or on a classmate's attention-getting behavior across the room. An important job for teachers, then, is to help students understand what is most important to learn and what can reasonably be cast aside as "junk mail."

Learners create (rather than receive) knowledge.

As was apparent in Rita's depiction of Michigan's history, learning isn't simply a process of absorbing information from the environment. Rather, it's a process of *making*—actively and intentionally constructing—knowledge and understandings.[3] As an example, try the following exercise.

SEE FOR YOURSELF   Rocky

Read the following passage *one time only:*

> Rocky slowly got up from the mat, planning his escape. He hesitated a moment and thought. Things were not going well. What bothered him most was being held, especially since the charge against him had been weak. He considered his present situation. The lock that held him was strong but he thought he could break it. He knew, however, that his timing would have to be perfect. Rocky was aware that it was because of his early roughness that he had been penalized so severely—much too severely from his point of view. The situation was becoming frustrating; the pressure had been grinding on him for too long. He was being ridden unmercifully. Rocky was getting angry now. He felt he was ready to make his move. He knew that his success or failure would depend on what he did in the next few seconds.[4]

Now summarize what you've just read in two or three sentences.

---

[3] For example, see Brainerd & Reyna, 2005; Neisser, 1967; Segalowitz, 2007.

[4] R. C. Anderson, Reynolds, Schallert, & Goetz, 1977, p. 372.

Were you able to make sense of the passage? What did you think it was about? A prison escape? A wrestling match? Or perhaps something else altogether? The passage includes a number of facts but leaves a lot unsaid. For instance, it tells us nothing about where Rocky was, what kind of "lock" was holding him, or why timing was important. Yet you were probably able to use the information you were given to construct an overall understanding of Rocky's situation. Most people do find meaning of one sort or another in the passage.

This active sense-making process—what theorists sometimes refer to as *constructing meaning*—is hardly limited to verbal material. For another example, try the following exercise.

SEE FOR YOURSELF   Three Faces

Look at the three pictures in Figure 2.2. What do you see in each one? Most people perceive the picture on the left as being that of a woman, even though many of her features are missing. Enough features are visible—an eye and parts of her nose, mouth, chin, and hair—that you can construct a meaningful perception from them. Do the other two pictures provide enough information to enable you to construct two more faces? Constructing a face from the figure on the right may take you a while, but it can be done.

FIGURE 2.2 Can you construct a person from each of these pictures?
Source: From "Age in the Development of Closure Ability in Children," by C. M. Mooney, 1957, *Canadian Journal of Psychology, 11,* p. 220. Copyright 1957. Canadian Psychological Association. Reprinted with permission.

Objectively speaking, the three configurations of black splotches in Figure 2.2, and especially the two rightmost ones, leave a lot to the imagination. For example, the woman in the middle is missing half of her face, and the man on the right is missing the top of his head. Yet knowing how human faces typically appear is probably enough to enable you to add the missing features (mentally) and perceive complete pictures. Curiously, once you've constructed faces from the figures, they then seem obvious. If you were to close this book now and not pick it up again for a week or more, you would probably see the faces almost immediately, even if you had had considerable difficulty perceiving them originally.

Learners use what they already know and believe to help them make sense of new experiences.

In the "Rocky" and "Three Faces" exercises you just did, you were able to make sense of situations even though a lot of information was missing. Your prior knowledge—perhaps about typical prison escapes or wrestling matches and certainly about how human facial features are arranged—allowed you to fill in many missing details. Prior knowledge and beliefs usually play a major role in the meanings people construct.

◆ Skillful readers typically skip some of the words on the page and yet accurately understand what they read. How is this possible? (Compare your response to this question with the response presented in Chapter 2 of the Book-Specific Resources in MyEducationLab.)

On many occasions different people construct different meanings from the same situation, in part because they each bring unique prior experiences and knowledge to the situation. For example, when the "Rocky" passage was used in an experiment with college students, physical education majors frequently interpreted it as a wrestling match, but music education majors (most of whom had little or no knowledge of wrestling) were more likely to think it was about a prison break.[5] Not only do learners bring different areas of expertise to a learning task, but they also bring different childhood experiences, cultural backgrounds, and assumptions about the world, and such differences are apt to have a significant impact on how they interpret new information.

The brain is, of course, the place where human beings think about, make sense of, and learn from their environment. We now look briefly at what the brain is like and how it functions.

• Thinking and Learning in the Brain

The brain is an incredibly complicated mechanism that includes several *trillion* cells. About one hundred billion of them are nerve cells—**neurons**—that are microscopic in size and interconnected in innumerable ways. Some neurons receive information from the rest of the body, others synthesize and interpret the information, and still others send messages that tell the body how to respond to its present circumstances. Curiously, neurons don't actually touch one another. Instead, they use a variety of chemical substances to send chemical messages across the tiny spaces—**synapses**—between them. Any single neuron may have synaptic connections with hundreds or even thousands of other neurons.[6]

Accompanying neurons are perhaps one to five trillion *glial cells,* which serve a variety of specialized functions. Some act as clean-up crew for unwanted garbage, others are "nutritionists" that control blood flow to neurons or "doctors" that tend to infections and injuries, and still others provide a substance known as *myelin* that enhances the efficiency of many neurons. And certain glial cells—star-shaped ones known as **astrocytes**—seem to be intimately involved in learning and memory (more about this point shortly).[7] Figure 2.3 can give you a sense of what neurons and astrocytes look like.

As you'll discover in Chapter 5, the brain changes in important ways over the course of childhood and adolescence. Yet three basic points about the brain are important to keep in mind as we explore cognition and learning in this chapter.

The various parts of the brain work closely with one another.

Groups of neurons and glial cells in different parts of the brain seem to specialize in different things. Structures in the lower and middle parts of the brain specialize in essential physiological processes (e.g., breathing, heart rate), body movements (e.g., walking, riding a bicycle), and basic perceptual skills (e.g., coordinating eye movements, diverting attention to potentially life-threatening stimuli). Complex thinking, learning, and knowledge are located primarily in the upper and outer parts of the brain collectively known as the **cortex**, which rests on the top and sides of the brain like a thick, bumpy toupee (see Figure 2.4). The portion of the cortex located near the forehead, known as the *prefrontal cortex,* is largely responsible for a wide variety of distinctly human activities, including sustained attention, reasoning, planning, decision making, coordinating complex activities, and inhibiting nonproductive thoughts and behaviors. Other parts of the cortex are important as well, being actively involved in interpreting visual and auditory information, identifying the spatial characteristics of objects and events, and keeping track of general knowledge about the world.

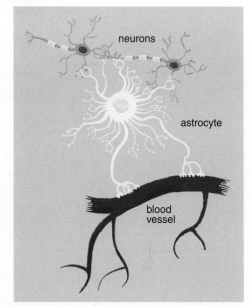

FIGURE 2.3 Two neurons, an astrocyte, and their interconnections

Prefrontal Cortex

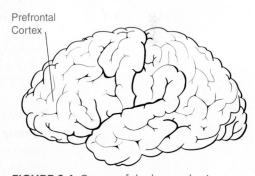

FIGURE 2.4 Cortex of the human brain

neuron Cell in the brain or another part of the nervous system that specializes in transmitting information to other cells.

synapse Tiny space across which one neuron regularly communicates with another; reflects an ongoing but modifiable connection between the two neurons.

astrocyte Star-shaped brain cell hypothesized to be involved in learning and memory; has chemically mediated connections with many other astrocytes and with neurons.

cortex Upper and outer parts of the human brain, which are largely responsible for conscious and complex cognitive processes.

[5] R. C. Anderson et al., 1977.

[6] C. S. Goodman & Tessier-Lavigne, 1997; Lichtman, 2001; Mareschal et al., 2007.

[7] Koob, 2009; Oberheim et al., 2009; Verkhratsky & Butt, 2007.

To some degree, the left and right halves of the cortex—its two *hemispheres*—have different specialties.[8] For most people, the left hemisphere takes primary responsibility for language and logical thinking, whereas the right hemisphere is more dominant in visual and spatial tasks. Yet contrary to popular belief, people rarely if ever think exclusively in one hemisphere. There is no such thing as "left-brain" or "right-brain" thinking: The two hemispheres constantly collaborate in day-to-day tasks. In fact, learning or thinking about virtually anything tends to be *distributed* across many parts of the brain. A task as seemingly simple as identifying a particular word in speech or print involves numerous areas of the cortex.[9]

Most learning probably involves changes in neurons, astrocytes, and their interconnections.

From a physiological standpoint, how and where does learning occur? Historically, many theorists and researchers have believed that the physiological basis for most learning lies in changes in the interconnections among neurons. In particular, learning may involve strengthening existing synapses or forming new ones.[10] In some instances, however, learning may actually involve *eliminating* synapses. Effective learning requires not only that people think and do certain things but also that they *not* think or do other things—in other words, that they inhibit tendencies to think or behave in particular ways.[11]

Recently some researchers have begun to speculate that astrocytes are just as important as—possibly even more important than—neurons in learning and memory. In humans, astrocytes outnumber neurons by at least 10 to 1—a ratio much larger than that for, say, mice and rats—and they have innumerable chemically mediated connections with one another and with neurons. Astrocytes appear to have some control over what neurons do and don't do and how much neurons communicate with one another.[12]

Many new astrocytes form throughout our lifetimes.[13] Some new neurons form throughout life as well, especially in the *hippocampus* (a small, seahorse-shaped structure in the middle of the brain) and possibly also in certain areas of the cortex.[14] Learning experiences seem to stimulate the formation of new brain cells, but exactly how these new cells are related to learning and memory is still unclear.[15]

As for *where* learning occurs, the answer is: many places. The prefrontal cortex is active when people must pay attention to and think about new information and events, and all of the cortex may be active to a greater or lesser extent in interpreting new input in light of previously acquired knowledge.[16] The hippocampus also seems to be a central figure in learning, in that it pulls together the information it simultaneously receives from various parts of the brain.[17]

Knowing how the brain functions and develops tells us only so much about learning and instruction.

Recent research on the human brain has given us helpful insights into the course of cognitive development (see Chapter 5) and the neurological bases of certain disabilities (e.g., dyslexia, autism spectrum disorders).[18] Yet even as researchers pin down how and where learning occurs, current knowledge of brain physiology doesn't begin to tell us everything we need to know about learning or how to foster it. For instance, brain research can't tell us much about what information and skills are most important for people to have in a particular

---

[8] Byrnes, 2001; R. Ornstein, 1997; T. Roberts & Kraft, 1987; M. S. C. Thomas & Johnson, 2008.

[9] Bressler, 2002; Huey, Krueger, & Grafman, 2006; Posner & Rothbart, 2007.

[10] Byrnes & Fox, 1998; Greenough, Black, & Wallace, 1987; Merzenich, 2001; C. A. Nelson, Thomas, & de Haan, 2006.

[11] Bruer & Greenough, 2001; Byrnes, 2001; Dempster, 1992; Haier, 2001.

[12] Koob, 2009; Oberheim et al., 2009; Verkhratsky & Butt, 2007.

[13] Koob, 2009.

[14] Gould, Beylin, Tanapat, Reeves, & Shors, 1999; C. A. Nelson et al., 2006; Sapolsky, 1999.

[15] Most newly acquired information and skills seem to need some time to "firm up" in the brain—a process called *consolidation*. An event that interferes with this consolidation (e.g., a serious brain injury) may cause a learner to forget things that happened several seconds, minutes, days, or months prior to the event; see Rasch & Born, 2008; Wixted, 2005.

[16] Byrnes, 2001; Huey et al., 2006.

[17] Bauer, 2002; Squire & Alvarez, 1998.

[18] Tager-Flusberg, 2007; Varma, McCandliss, & Schwartz, 2008.

community and culture.[19] Nor does it provide many clues about how teachers can best help their students acquire important information and skills.[20] In fact, educators who speak of "using brain research" or "brain-based learning" are, in most instances, actually talking about what psychologists have learned from studies of human *behavior* rather than from studies of brain anatomy and physiology.

By and large, if we want to understand the nature of human cognition and identify effective ways of helping children and adolescents learn more effectively, we must look primarily at what psychologists, rather than neurologists, have discovered.[21] We begin our exploration of cognitive processes by looking at what psychologists have learned about human memory.

• How Human Memory Operates

The term **memory** refers to learners' ability to mentally "save" newly acquired information and behaviors. In some cases we'll use the term to refer to the actual process of saving knowledge or skills for a period of time. In other instances we'll use it to talk about a particular "location" where knowledge is held. For instance, we will soon be talking about two components of the human memory system known as *working memory* and *long-term memory*.

The process of "putting" something into memory is called **storage**. Just as you might store groceries in a kitchen cabinet, so, too, do you store newly acquired knowledge in your memory. At some later time, you may find that you need to use what you've learned. The process of remembering previously stored information—that is, "finding" it in memory—is **retrieval**. The following exercise illustrates the retrieval process.

SEE FOR YOURSELF   Retrieval Practice

See how quickly you can answer each of the following questions:

1. What is your name?
2. What is the capital of France?
3. In what year did Christopher Columbus first sail across the Atlantic Ocean to reach the New World?
4. What did you have for dinner three years ago today?
5. When talking about serving appetizers at a party, people sometimes use a French term instead of the word *appetizer*. What is that French term, and how is it spelled?

As you probably noticed when you tried to answer these questions, retrieving some information from memory (e.g., your name) is an easy, effortless process. But other things can be retrieved only after some thought and effort. For example, it may have taken you a few seconds to recall that the capital of France is Paris and that Columbus first sailed across the Atlantic in 1492. Still other pieces of information—even though you certainly stored them in memory at one time—may be almost impossible to retrieve. Perhaps a dinner menu three years ago and the correct spelling of *hors d'oeuvre* fall into this category.

As you might guess from the preceding discussion of the brain, human memory is a very complex, multifaceted mechanism that is still somewhat of a mystery. But many psychologists have found it helpful to think of the human memory system as having three general components that hold information for different lengths of time (see Figure 2.5).[22]

---

[19] L. Bloom & Tinker, 2001; Chalmers, 1996; Gardner, 2000b.

[20] Byrnes, 2001, 2007; R. E. Mayer, 1998.

[21] For a classic article on this topic, see Bruer, 1997.

[22] For example, see R. C. Atkinson & Shiffrin, 1968; Reisberg, 1997; Willingham, 2004.

memory Ability to save something (mentally) that has been previously learned; also, the mental "location" where such information is saved.

storage Process of "putting" new information into memory.

retrieval Process of "finding" information previously stored in memory.

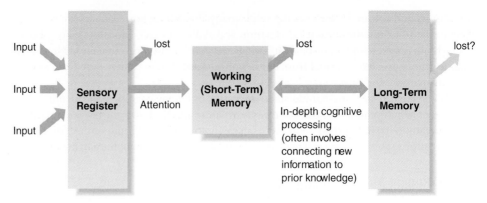

FIGURE 2.5 A model of human memory

Oversimplified as this model undoubtedly is, we can use it in combination with countless research studies to derive some general principles about how human memory operates.

Sensory input stays in a raw form only briefly.

If you have ever played with a lighted sparkler at night, then you've seen the tail of light that follows a sparkler as you wave it about. If you have ever daydreamed in class, then you may have noticed that when you tune back in to a lecture, you can still "hear" the three or four words that were spoken just *before* you started paying attention to your instructor again. The sparkler's tail and the words that linger are not "out there" in the environment. Instead, they are recorded in your sensory register.

The **sensory register** is the component of memory that holds the information you receive—*input*—in more or less its original, *un*encoded form. Much of what your body sees, hears, and otherwise senses is stored in the sensory register. In other words, the sensory register has a *large capacity:* It can hold a great deal of information at one time.

That's the good news. The bad news is that information stored in the sensory register doesn't last very long.[23] Visual information (what you see) probably lasts for less than a second. As a child, I never could spell out my entire first name (Jeanne) with a sparkler; the *J* had always faded before I got to the first *n*, no matter how quickly I wrote. Auditory information (what you hear) probably lasts slightly longer, perhaps for two or three seconds. To keep information for any time at all, then, learners need to move it to *working memory*.

Attention is essential for most learning and memory.

Information received directly from the environment, such as a sparkler's glittery light, doesn't last very long no matter what we do. But we can preserve a memory of it by encoding it in some minimal way—for instance, by interpreting a sparkler's curlicue tail as the letters *Jea*. The first step in this process is **attention**: *Whatever people pay attention to (mentally) moves into working memory.* Information in the sensory register that doesn't get a person's attention typically disappears from the memory system.[24]

Paying attention involves directing not only the appropriate sensory receptors (in the eyes, ears, fingertips, etc.) but also the *mind* toward whatever needs to be learned and remembered. Imagine yourself reading a textbook for one of your classes. Your eyes are moving down each page, but meanwhile you're thinking about something altogether different—a recent argument with a friend, a high-paying job advertised in the newspaper, or your growling stomach. What will you remember from the textbook? Absolutely nothing. Even

Observe David's realization that attention affects memory in the "Memory and Metacognition: Middle Childhood" video in Chapter 2 of the Book-Specific Resources in MyEducationLab. When David says, "My brain was turned off right now," he really means that his *attention* was turned off, or at least not focused on the interviewer's memory task.

---

sensory register Component of memory that holds incoming information in an unanalyzed form for a very brief time (perhaps one to two seconds).

attention Focusing of mental processes on particular stimuli.

[23] Cowan, 1995; Darwin, Turvey, & Crowder, 1972; Sperling, 1960.
[24] Some nonattended-to information may remain, but without the learner's conscious awareness of it, it may be extremely difficult to recall, especially over the long run; for example, see Cowan, 2007.

though your eyes were focused on the words in your book, you weren't *mentally* paying attention to the words.

Unfortunately, people can attend to only a very small amount of information at any one time. In other words, attention has a *limited capacity.*[25] For example, if you're in a room where several conversations are going on at once, you can usually attend to—and therefore can learn from—only one of the conversations. If you're sitting in front of the television with your textbook open in your lap, you can attend to the *Friends* rerun playing on the TV screen *or* to your book but not to both simultaneously. If, in class, you're pre-occupied with your instructor's ghastly taste in clothing and desperate need for a fashion makeover, you'll have a hard time paying attention to the content of the instructor's lecture.

Exactly *how* limited is the limited capacity of human attention? People can often perform two or three well-learned, automatic tasks at once. For example, you can walk and chew gum simultaneously, and you can probably drive a car and drink a cup of coffee at the same time. But when a stimulus or event is detailed and complex (as is true for both textbooks and *Friends* reruns) or when a task requires considerable thought (understanding a lecture and driving a car on an icy mountain road are examples of tasks requiring considerable concentration), then people can usually attend to only *one* thing at a time.

Let's return to a point made earlier in the chapter: Learners must be selective about what they focus on and learn. Now we see the reason why: Attention has a limited capacity, allowing only a very small amount of information stored in the sensory register to move on to working memory. The vast majority of information that the body initially receives is quickly lost from the memory system, much as we might quickly discard most of that junk mail we receive every day.

Jim Cummins/Taxi/Getty Images

Children learn effectively only when they pay attention, both physically and mentally, to the subject matter.

❖ Using what you've just learned about attention, explain why talking on a mobile (cellular) phone while driving is illegal in many places. (Compare your response to this question with the response presented in Chapter 2 of the Book-Specific Resources in MyEducationLab.)

Working memory—where the action is in thinking and learning—has a short duration and limited capacity.

Working memory is the component of memory where attended-to information stays for a short while so that we can make better sense of it. It's also where much of our thinking, or cognitive processing, occurs. It's where we try to understand new concepts presented in a lecture, draw inferences from ideas encountered in a textbook passage, or solve a problem. Basically, this is the component that does most of the mental work of the memory system—hence its name *working* memory.[26]

Information stored in working memory doesn't last very long—perhaps 5 to 20 seconds at most—unless people do something more with it.[27] Accordingly, it is sometimes called *short-term memory.* For example, imagine that you need to call a neighbor, so you look up the neighbor's number in the telephone book. Because you've paid attention to the number, it's presumably in your working memory. But you discover that you can't find your cell phone. You have no paper and pencil handy. What do you do to remember the number until you have access to a telephone?

To keep the number in your memory while you look for a phone, you might simply repeat it to yourself over and over. This process, known as **rehearsal**, keeps information in working memory for as long as you're willing to continue talking to yourself. But once you stop, the number may disappear fairly quickly.

[25] J. R. Anderson, 2005; Cowan, 2007; Reisberg, 1997.
[26] Working memory probably has several components for holding and working with different kinds of information (e.g., visual, auditory, semantic) plus a component that integrates multiple kinds of information; see Alloway, Gathercole, Kirkwood, &

Elliott, 2009; Baddeley, 2001; Cowan, Saults, & Morey, 2006; E. E. Smith, 2000.
[27] For example, see Baddeley, 2001; L. R. Peterson & Peterson, 1959.

working memory Component of memory that holds and actively thinks about and processes a limited amount of information for a short time period.

rehearsal Cognitive process in which information is repeated over and over as a possible way of learning and remembering it.

To get a better sense of the nature of working memory, put your own working memory to work for a moment in the following exercise.

SEE FOR YOURSELF A Divisive Situation

Try computing the answer to this division problem *in your head*—put the numbers in your working memory and then *don't peek* as you try to calculate the answer:

$$59 \overline{)49{,}383}$$

Did you find yourself having trouble remembering some parts of the problem while you were dealing with other parts? Did you arrive at the correct answer of 837? Most people can't solve a division problem with this many digits unless they write the problem on paper. The fact is, working memory just doesn't have enough space both to hold all that information and to perform mathematical calculations with it. Like attention, working memory has a *limited capacity*, perhaps just enough for a telephone number or very short grocery list.[28] In and of itself, it lets you hold and think about only a very small amount of material at once.

I sometimes hear students mention putting class material in "short-term memory" so that they can do well on an upcoming exam. Such a statement reflects two common misconceptions: that (1) this component of memory lasts for several days, weeks, or months; and (2) it has a fair amount of "room." Now you know otherwise: Information stored in working memory lasts only a few seconds unless it's processed further, and only a few things can be stored there at one time. Working (short-term) memory is obviously *not* the "place" to leave information you'll need for a class later today, let alone for an exam later in the week. For such memory tasks, storage in long-term memory is in order.

> ? Did you have these misconceptions about short-term memory before you read this section? If so, have you now revised your understanding?

Long-term memory has a long duration and virtually limitless capacity.

Long-term memory is where we store our general knowledge and beliefs about the world, our recollections of past experiences, and things we've learned in school. Such knowledge about *what and how things are* is known as **declarative knowledge**. Long-term memory is also where we store knowledge about how to perform various behaviors, such as how to ride a bicycle, swing a baseball bat, or write a cursive letter *J*. Such knowledge about *how to do things* is known as **procedural knowledge**. When procedural knowledge includes knowing how to respond differently under varying circumstances, it is sometimes called *conditional knowledge*.

Information stored in long-term memory lasts much longer than information stored in working memory—perhaps a day, a week, a month, a year, or a lifetime (more on the "lifetime" point later in the chapter). Even when it's there, however, people can't always find (retrieve) it when they need it. As we'll see in upcoming sections, people's ability to retrieve previously learned information from long-term memory depends on both the way in which they've initially stored it and the context in which they're trying to remember it.

Long-term memory seems to be able to hold as much information as a learner needs to store there. There is probably no such thing as someone "running out of room." In fact, for reasons we'll discover shortly, the more information already stored in long-term memory, the easier it is to learn new things.

Information in long-term memory is interconnected and organized to some extent.

To get a glimpse of how your own long-term memory is organized, try the following exercise.

long-term memory Component of memory that holds knowledge and skills for a relatively long time.

declarative knowledge Knowledge related to "what is"—that is, to the nature of how things are, were, or will be.

procedural knowledge Knowledge concerning how to do something (e.g., a skill).

---

[28] Awh, Barton, & Vogel, 2007; Baddeley, 2001; Cowan, Chen, & Rouder, 2004; G. A. Miller, 1956; Simon, 1974.

concept Mental grouping of objects or events that have something in common.

schema Tightly organized set of facts about a specific concept or phenomenon.

SEE FOR YOURSELF Horse

What's the first word that comes to mind when you see the word *horse?* And what word does that second word remind you of? And what does the third word remind you of? Beginning with the word *horse,* follow your train of thought, letting each word remind you of a new word or short phrase, for a sequence of at least eight words or phrases. Write down the sequence of things that come to mind.

You probably found yourself easily following a train of thought from the word *horse,* perhaps something like the route I followed:

horse → cowboy → lasso → rope → knot → Girl Scouts → cookies → chocolate

The last word in your sequence might be one with little or no obvious relationship to horses. Yet you can probably see a logical connection between each word or phrase and the one that follows it. Related pieces of information tend to be associated with one another in long-term memory, perhaps in a network similar to the one depicted in Figure 2.6.

FIGURE 2.6 Related ideas are often associated with one another in long-term memory. Here you see the author's train of thought from *horse* to *chocolate.*

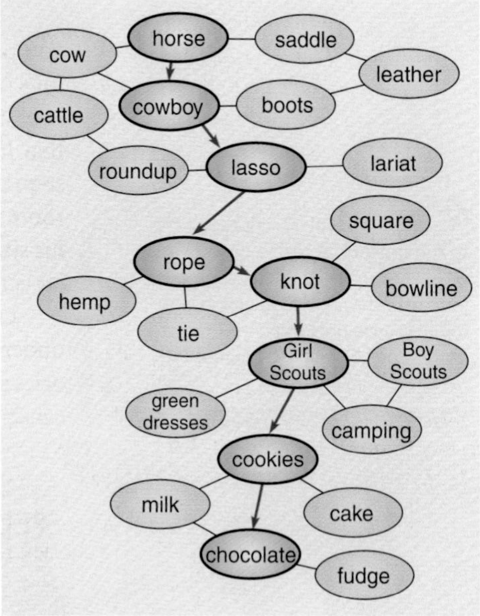

In the process of constructing knowledge, learners often create well-integrated entities that encompass particular ideas or groups of ideas. Beginning in infancy, they form **concepts** that enable them to categorize objects and events.[29] Some concepts, such as *butterfly, chair,* and *backstroke,* refer to a fairly narrow range of objects or events (e.g., see Figure 2.7). Other concepts are fairly general ones that encompass numerous more specific concepts. For example, the concept *insect* includes ants, bees, and butterflies. The concept *swimming* includes the backstroke, dog paddle, and butterfly. As you can see, some words (such as *butterfly)* can be associated with two very different, more general concepts (such as *insects* and *swimming)* and so might lead someone to follow a train of thought such as this one:

horse → cowboy → lasso → rope → knot → Girl Scouts → camping
→ outdoors → nature → insect → butterfly → swimming

Learners pull some concepts together into general understandings of what things are typically like. Some of these understandings take the form of **schemas**—tightly organized sets of facts related to particular concepts or phenomena.[30] For example, let's return to our friend the horse. You know what horses look like, of course, and you can recognize one when you see one. Hence, you have a concept for *horse.* But now think about the many things you know *about* horses. What do they eat? How do they spend their time? Where are you most likely to see them? You probably have little difficulty retrieving many facts about horses, perhaps including their fondness for oats and carrots, their love of grazing and running, and their frequent appearance in pastures and at racetracks. The various things you know about horses are closely interrelated in your long-term memory in the form of a "horse" schema.

People have schemas not only about objects but also about events. For example, read the following passage about John.

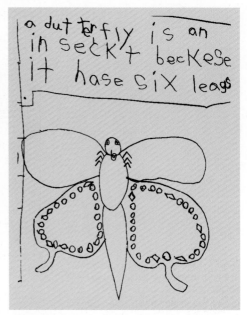

FIGURE 2.7 Eight-year-old Noah depicts organized knowledge related to the concepts *butterfly* and *insect.*

[29] Mandler, 2007; Quinn, 2002.

[30] For example, see Rumelhart & Ortony, 1977; Schraw, 2006; Willingham, 2004.

SEE FOR YOURSELF John

> Read the following passage *one time only.*
>
> John was feeling bad today so he decided to go see the family doctor. He checked in with the doctor's receptionist, and then looked through several medical magazines that were on the table by his chair. Finally the nurse came and asked him to take off his clothes. The doctor was very nice to him. He eventually prescribed some pills for John. Then John left the doctor's office and headed home.[31]

You probably had no trouble making sense of the passage because you have been to a doctor's office yourself and have a schema for how those visits usually go. You can therefore fill in a number of details that the passage doesn't tell you. For example, you probably inferred that John must have *traveled* to the doctor's office, although the story omits this essential step. Likewise, you probably concluded that John took off his clothes in the examination room, *not* in the waiting room, even though the story never makes it clear where John did his striptease. When a schema involves a predictable sequence of events related to a particular activity, such as going to see a doctor, it is sometimes called a **script**.

On a much larger scale, human beings—young children included—construct general understandings and belief systems, or **theories**, about how the world operates.[32] People's theories include many concepts and the relationships among them (e.g., frequent co-occurrence, cause–and–effect). To see what some of your own theories are like, try the next exercise.

◆ What is a typical script for a trip to the grocery store? To the movies? To a fast-food restaurant? (Compare your response to this question with the response presented in Chapter 2 of the Book-Specific Resources in MyEducationLab.)

SEE FOR YOURSELF Coffeepots and Raccoons

> Consider each of the following situations:
>
> 1. People took a coffeepot that looked like Drawing A. They removed the handle, sealed the top, took off the top knob, sealed the opening to the spout, and removed the spout. They also sliced off the base and attached a flat piece of metal. They attached a little stick, cut out a window, and filled the metal container with birdseed. When they were done, it looked like Drawing B.
>
>   After these changes, was this a coffeepot or a bird feeder?
>
> 2. Doctors took the raccoon in Drawing C and shaved away some of its fur. They dyed what was left black. Then they bleached a single stripe all white down the center of the animal's back. Then, with surgery, they put in its body a sac of supersmelly odor, just like the smell a skunk has. After they were all done, the animal looked like Drawing D.
>
>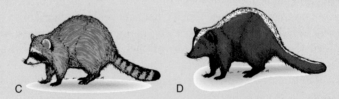
>
> After the operation, was this a skunk or a raccoon?[33]

script Schema that involves a predictable sequence of events related to a common activity.

theory Integrated set of concepts and principles developed to explain a particular phenomenon; may be constructed jointly by researchers over time (see Chapter 1) or individually by a single learner.

---

[31] G. H. Bower, Black, & Turner, 1979, p. 190.

[32] Gelman, 2003; Keil, 1989, 1994; Wellman & Gelman, 1998.

[33] Both scenarios based on Keil, 1989, p. 184.

Chances are, you concluded that the coffeepot had been transformed into a bird feeder but that the raccoon was still a raccoon despite its cosmetic makeover and stinky surgery. Now how is it possible that the coffeepot could be made into something entirely different, whereas the raccoon could not? Even young children seem to make a basic distinction between human-made objects (e.g., coffeepots, bird feeders) and biological entities (e.g., raccoons, skunks).[34] For instance, human-made objects are defined largely by the *functions* they serve (e.g., brewing coffee, feeding birds), whereas biological entities are defined primarily by their origins (e.g., the parents who brought them into being, their DNA).[35] Thus, when a coffeepot begins to hold birdseed rather than coffee, it becomes a bird feeder because its function has changed. But when a raccoon is cosmetically and surgically altered to look and smell like a skunk, it still has raccoon parents and raccoon DNA and so cannot possibly *be* a skunk.

By the time children reach school age, they have constructed basic theories about their physical, biological, and social worlds.[36] They have also constructed preliminary theories about the nature of their own and other people's thinking. For instance, they realize that people's inner thoughts are distinct from external reality, and they understand that the people in their lives have thoughts, emotions, and motives that drive much of what they do (see Chapter 7). In general, self-constructed theories help children make sense of and remember personal experiences, classroom subject matter, and other new information.[37] Yet because children's theories often evolve with little or no guidance from more knowledgeable individuals, they sometimes include erroneous beliefs about the world that can wreak havoc with new learning (more about this point shortly).

How well long-term memory is integrated and in what ways it is integrated are to some degree the result of how learners first store information in long-term memory, as we'll see in our discussion of the next principle.

Some long-term memory storage processes are more effective than others.

In the memory model presented in Figure 2.5, the arrow between working memory and long-term memory points in both directions. The process of storing new information in long-term memory often involves drawing on "old" information already stored there—that is, it involves using prior knowledge.[38] To see what I mean, try the following exercise.

SEE FOR YOURSELF   Two Letter Strings, Two Pictures

1. Study each of the following strings of letters until you can remember them perfectly:

   AIIRODFMLAWRS   FAMILIARWORDS

2. Study the two pictures in the margin until you can reproduce them accurately from memory.

Source: Figures from "Comprehension and Memory for Pictures" by G. H. Bower, M. B. Karlin, and A. Dueck, 1975, *Memory and Cognition, 3* p. 217. Reprinted by permission of Psychonomic Society, Inc.

No doubt the second letter string was easier for you to learn because you could relate it to something you already knew: the words *familiar words*. How easily were you able to

---

[34] Gelman & Kalish, 2006; Inagaki & Hatano, 2006; Keil, 1986, 1989.

[35] Greif, Kemler Nelson, Keil, & Gutierrez, 2006; Inagaki & Hatano, 2006; Keil, 1987, 1989.

[36] Geary, 2005; Torney-Purta, 1994; Wellman & Gelman, 1998.

[37] Gelman, 2003; Reiner, Slotta, Chi, & Resnick, 2000; Wellman & Gelman, 1998.

[38] For a good discussion of this point, see Kirschner, Sweller, & Clark, 2006.

rote learning Cognitive process in which learners try to remember information in a relatively uninterpreted form, with little or no effort to make sense of or attach meaning to it.

meaningful learning Cognitive process in which learners relate new information to things they already know.

learn the two pictures? Could you draw them from memory a week from now? Could you remember them more easily if they had titles such as "a very short man playing a trombone in a telephone booth" and "an early bird who caught a very strong worm"? The answer to the last question is almost certainly *yes,* because the titles help you relate the pictures to familiar shapes, such as those of trombones, telephone booths, and birds' feet.[39]

With the preceding exercise in mind, let's distinguish between two basic types of learning: rote learning and meaningful learning (e.g., see Table 2.2). People engage in **rote learning** when they try to learn and remember something without attaching much meaning to it. This would be the case, for example, if you tried to remember the letter string AIIRODFMLAWRS without trying to make some kind of "sense" of the sequence—perhaps identifying patterns in the letters or similarities to words you know. You would also be engaging in rote learning if you tried to remember the shapes in the "telephone booth" and "early bird" figures simply by trying to memorize where each line and curve is within each figure.

One common form of rote learning is *rehearsal,* repeating something over and over, perhaps by saying it aloud or perhaps by continuously thinking about it in an unaltered, verbatim fashion. We have already seen that rehearsal can help learners keep information in working memory indefinitely. Unfortunately, however, rehearsal is *not* a very effective way of storing information in *long-term* memory. If learners repeat something often enough, it might eventually "stick," but the process is slow and tedious. Furthermore, for reasons we'll identify later, people who use rehearsal and other forms of rote learning often have trouble remembering what they've learned.[40]

In contrast to rote learning, **meaningful learning** involves recognizing a relationship between new information and something previously stored in long-term memory. Seeing the words *familiar words* in the letter string FAMILIARWORDS and seeing meaningful shapes (a trombone, bird feet, etc.) in simple line drawings are two examples. Similarly, a first grader might connect subtraction facts to previously learned addition facts in the same "family" (e.g., $5 - 3 = 2$ is the reverse of $2 + 3 = 5$), and a high school student might see parallels between the "ethnic cleansing" in Kosovo in the 1990s and the Nazis' belief in white supremacy in the 1930s and 1940s. In the vast majority of cases, meaningful learning is

TABLE 2.2 Long-Term Memory Storage Processes

Process	Definition	Example	Effectiveness
Rote learning: Learning primarily through repetition and practice, with little or no attempt to make sense of what is being learned			
Rehearsal	Repeating information verbatim, either mentally or aloud	Word-for-word repetition of a formula or definition	Relatively ineffective: Storage is slow, and later retrieval is difficult
Meaningful learning: Making connections between new information and prior knowledge			
Elaboration	Embellishing on new information based on what one already knows	Generating possible reasons that historical figures made the decisions they did	Effective if associations and additions made are appropriate and productive
Organization	Making connections among various pieces of new information	Thinking about how one's lines in a play relate to the play's overall story line	Effective if organizational structure is legitimate and consists of more than just a list of separate facts
Visual imagery	Forming a mental picture of something, either by actually seeing it or by envisioning how it might look	Imagining how various characters and events in a novel might have looked	Individual differences in effectiveness; especially beneficial when used in combination with elaboration or organization

[39] G. H. Bower, Karlin, & Dueck, 1975.
[40] J. R. Anderson, 1995; Ausubel, 1968; Craik & Watkins, 1973.

more effective than rote learning for storing information in long-term memory.[41] It's especially effective when learners relate ideas to *themselves* as human beings.[42]

Meaningful learning can take a variety of forms, and in many cases it involves adding to or restructuring information in some way. For instance, in **elaboration**, learners use their prior knowledge to embellish on a new idea, thereby storing *more* information than was actually presented. For example, a student who reads that allosaurs (a species of dinosaurs) had powerful jaws and sharp teeth might correctly deduce that allosaurs were meat eaters. Similarly, if a student learns that the crew on Columbus's first trip across the Atlantic threatened to revolt and turn the ships back toward Europe, the student might speculate, "I'll bet the men were really frightened when they continued to travel west day after day without ever seeing signs of land."[43]

Another form of meaningful learning is **organization**, in which learners arrange new information in a logical structure. For example, they might group information into categories (recall the earlier "Remembering Words" exercise with the words *daisy, apple, hammer,* etc.). Alternatively, they might identify interrelationships among various pieces of information. As an illustration, students in a physics class might learn that *velocity* is the product of *acceleration* and *time* ($v = a \times t$) and that an object's *force* is determined by both the object's *mass* and its *acceleration* ($f = m \times a$). The trick is not simply to memorize the formulas (this would be rote learning) but rather to make sense of and understand the relationships that the formulas represent. In most instances, learners who learn an organized body of information remember it better—and they can use it more effectively later on—than would be the case if they tried to learn the same information as a list of separate, isolated facts.[44]

Still another effective long-term memory storage process is **visual imagery**, forming a mental picture of objects or ideas. To discover firsthand how effective visual imagery can be, try learning a bit of Mandarin Chinese in the next exercise.

> **?** In your own experiences as a student, how often have classroom assessments encouraged you to memorize information word for word rather than to learn it meaningfully?

SEE FOR YOURSELF   Five Chinese Words

Try learning these five Chinese words by forming the visual images I describe (don't worry about learning the tone marks over the words).

Chinese Word	English Meaning	Image
fáng	house	Picture a *house* with *fangs* growing on its roof and walls.
mén	door	Picture a restroom *door* with the word *MEN* painted on it.
ké	guest	Picture a person giving someone else (the *guest*) a *key* to the house.
fàn	food	Picture a plate of *food* being cooled by a *fan*.
shū	book	Picture a *shoe* with a *book* sticking out of it.

Now find something else to do for a couple of minutes. Stand up and stretch, get a glass of water, or use the restroom. But be sure to come back to your reading in just a minute or two....

Now that you're back, cover the list of Chinese words, English meanings, and visual images. Try to remember what each word means:

ké   fàn   mén   fáng   shū

---

[41] Ausubel, Novak, & Hanesian, 1978; Ghetti & Angelini, 2008; Marley, Szabo, Levin, & Glenberg, 2008; R. E. Mayer, 1996.

[42] Craik, 2006; Heatherton, Macrae, & Kelley, 2004; T. B. Rogers, Kuiper, & Kirker, 1977.

[43] Notice that I am using the term *elaboration* to describe something that *learners* do, not something that teachers do. Elaboration as a *cognitive process* occurs inside rather than outside the learner. However, teachers can certainly help students engage in elaboration, as you'll discover later in the chapter.

[44] Bjorklund, Schneider, Cassel, & Ashley, 1994; G. H. Bower, Clark, Lesgold, & Winzenz, 1969; P. A. Ornstein, Grammer, & Coffman, 2010.

elaboration Cognitive process in which learners embellish on new information based on what they already know.

organization Cognitive process in which learners find connections among various pieces of information they need to learn (e.g., by forming categories, identifying hierarchies, determining cause–and–effect relationships).

visual imagery Cognitive process in which learners form mental pictures of objects or ideas.

Did the Chinese words remind you of the visual images you stored? Did the images, in turn, help you remember the English meanings of the Chinese words? You may have remembered all five words easily, or you may have remembered only one or two. People differ in their ability to use visual imagery: Some form images quickly and easily, whereas others form them only slowly and with difficulty.[45] Especially for people in the former category, visual imagery can be a powerful means of storing information in long-term memory.[46]

The three forms of meaningful learning we've just examined—elaboration, organization, and visual imagery—are clearly *constructive* in nature: They all involve combining several pieces of information into a meaningful whole. When you elaborate on new information, you combine it with things you already know to help you make better sense of it. When you organize information, you give it a logical structure (categories, cause–and–effect relationships, etc.). And when you use visual imagery, you create mental pictures (perhaps a house with fangs or a restroom door labeled *MEN*) based on how certain objects typically look.

Practice makes knowledge more automatic and durable.

Storing something in long-term memory on one occasion is hardly the end of the learning process. When people continue to practice the information and skills they acquire—and especially when they do so in a variety of situations and contexts—they gradually become able to use what they've learned quickly, effortlessly, and automatically. In other words, people eventually achieve **automaticity** for well-practiced knowledge and skills.[47]

As noted earlier, rehearsal—repeating information over and over within the course of a few seconds or minutes—is a relatively *in*effective way of getting information into long-term memory. But when we talk about acquiring automaticity, we're talking about repetition over the long run: reviewing and practicing information and procedures at periodic intervals over the course of a few weeks, months, or years. When practice is spread out in this manner, people learn things better and remember them longer.[48]

Practice is especially important for gaining procedural knowledge. As an example, think of driving a car, a complicated skill that most of my readers can probably perform easily. Your first attempts at driving years ago may have required a great deal of mental energy and effort. But I'm guessing that you can now drive without having to pay much attention to what you're doing. Even if your car has a standard (rather than automatic) transmission, driving is, for you, an automatic activity.

Many complex procedures, such as driving a car, may begin largely as explicit, declarative knowledge—in other words, as *information* about how to execute a procedure rather than as the actual *ability* to execute it. When learners use declarative knowledge to guide them as they carry out a new procedure, their performance is slow and laborious, the activity consumes a great deal of mental effort, and learners often talk themselves through their actions. As they continue to practice the activity, however, their declarative knowledge gradually evolves into procedural knowledge. This knowledge becomes fine-tuned over time and eventually allows learners to perform an activity quickly and easily—that is, with automaticity.[49]

With age and experience, children acquire more effective learning strategies.

Sometimes learners engage in effective long-term memory storage processes (elaboration, organization, visual imagery, etc.) without intentionally trying to do so. For instance, if I tell you that *I used to live in Colorado,* you might immediately deduce that I lived in or near the Rocky Mountains, and you might even picture snow-capped mountains in your head. In this case you are automatically engaging in elaboration and visual imagery: My statement

❖ Learning something to automaticity is *not* the same thing as rote learning. In what important way are these two processes different? (Compare your response to this question with the response presented in Chapter 2 of the Book-Specific Resources in MyEducationLab.)

[45] Behrmann, 2000; J. M. Clark & Paivio, 1991; Kosslyn, 1985.

[46] Dewhurst & Conway, 1994; Johnson-Glenberg, 2000; D. B. Mitchell, 2006; Sadoski, Goetz, & Fritz, 1993; Sadoski & Paivio, 2001.

[47] J. R. Anderson, 1983; P. W. Cheng, 1985; Graham, Harris, & Fink, 2000; R. W. Proctor & Dutta, 1995; Semb & Ellis, 1994.

[48] Cepeda, Vul, Rohrer, Wixted, & Pashler, 2008; Dempster, 1991; R. W. Proctor & Dutta, 1995; Rohrer & Pashler, 2007.

[49] J. R. Anderson, 1983, 1987; Beilock & Carr, 2003.

automaticity Ability to respond quickly and efficiently while mentally processing or physically performing a task.

made no mention of the Rockies, so you supplied this information from your own long-term memory.

At other times learners deliberately use certain cognitive processes in their efforts to learn and remember information. For example, in the "Remembering Words" exercise near the beginning of the chapter, you may have quickly noticed the categorical nature of the 12 words in the list and intentionally used the categories *flowers, fruit,* and *tools* to organize them. Similarly, in the "Five Chinese Words" exercise, you intentionally formed visual images in accordance with my instructions. When learners *intentionally* engage in certain cognitive processes to help them learn and remember something, they are using a **learning strategy**.

A general inclination to relate new information to prior knowledge—meaningful learning—probably occurs in one form or another at virtually all age levels.[50] More specific and intentional learning strategies (e.g., rehearsal, organization, visual imagery) are fairly limited in the early elementary years but increase in both frequency and effectiveness over the course of childhood and adolescence. The frequency of elaboration—especially as a process that learners *intentionally* use to help them remember something—picks up a bit later, often not until adolescence, and is more common in high-achieving students. Table 2.3 summarizes developmental trends in learning strategies across the grade levels.

learning strategy Intentional use of one or more cognitive processes for a particular learning task.

 Observe how organization improves with age in the early childhood, early adolescence, and late adolescence "Memory and Metacognition" videos in Chapter 2 of the Book-Specific Resources in MyEducationLab.

DEVELOPMENTAL TRENDS

TABLE 2.3   Typical Learning Strategies at Different Grade Levels

Grade Level	Age-Typical Characteristics	Example	Suggested Strategies
K–2	• Organization of physical objects as a way to remember them • Appearance of rehearsal to remember verbal material; used infrequently and relatively ineffectively • Emerging ability to use visual imagery to enhance memory, especially if an adult suggests this strategy • Few if any intentional efforts to learn and remember verbal material; learning and memory are a byproduct of other things children do (creating things, talking about events, listening to stories, etc.)	At the end of the school day, a first-grade teacher reminds students that they need to bring three things to school tomorrow: an object that begins with the letter *W* (for a phonics lesson), a signed permission slip for a field trip to a local historic site, and a warm jacket to wear on the field trip. Six-year-old Cassie briefly mumbles "jacket" to herself a couple of times and naively assumes she'll remember all three items without any further mental effort.	• Get students actively involved in topics, perhaps through hands-on activities, engaging reading materials, or fantasy play. • Relate new topics to students' prior experiences. • Model rehearsal as a strategy for remembering things over the short run. • Provide pictures that illustrate verbal material. • Give students concrete mechanisms for remembering to bring necessary items to school (see upcoming discussions of *retrieval cues*).
3–5	• Spontaneous, intentional, and increasingly effective use of rehearsal to remember things for a short time period • Increasing use of organization as an intentional learning strategy for verbal information • Increasing effectiveness in use of visual imagery as a learning strategy	As 10-year-old Jonathan studies for an upcoming quiz on clouds, he looks at the photos of four different kinds of clouds in his science book and says each one's name aloud. Then he repeats the four cloud types several times: "Cumulus, cumulonimbus, cirrus, stratus. Cumulus, cumulonimbus, cirrus, stratus. Cumulus, cumulonimbus, cirrus, stratus."	• Emphasize the importance of making sense of, rather than memorizing, information. • Encourage students to organize what they're learning; suggest possible organizational structures for topics. • Provide a variety of visual aids to facilitate visual imagery, and suggest that students create their own drawings or visual images of things they need to remember.

(continued)

---

[50] Flavell, Miller, & Miller, 2002; Pressley & Hilden, 2006; Siegler & Alibali, 2005.

TABLE 2.3 Continued

Grade Level	Age-Typical Characteristics	Example	Suggested Strategies
 6–8	• Predominance of rehearsal as a learning strategy • Greater abstractness and flexibility in categories used to organize information • Emergence of elaboration as an intentional learning strategy	Two middle school students, Raj and Owen, are studying for a quiz on various kinds of rocks. "Let's group them somehow," Raj says. Owen suggests grouping them by color (gray, white, reddish, etc.). But after further discussion, the boys agree that sorting them into *sedimentary, igneous,* and *metamorphic* would be a more strategic approach.	• Suggest questions that students might ask themselves as they study; emphasize questions that promote elaboration (e.g., "Why would ___ do that?" "How is ___ different from ___?"). • Assess true understanding rather than rote memorization in assignments and quizzes.
 9–12	• Continuing reliance on rehearsal as an intentional learning strategy, especially by low-achieving students • Increasing use of elaboration and organization to learn new material, especially by high-achieving students	In her high school world history class, Kate focuses her studying efforts on memorizing names, dates, and places. Meanwhile, Kate's classmate Janika likes to speculate about the personalities and motives of such historical characters as Alexander the Great, Napoleon Bonaparte, and Adolf Hitler.	• Ask thought-provoking questions that engage students' interest and help students see the relevance of topics for their own lives. • Have students work in mixed-ability cooperative groups, in which high-achieving students can model effective learning strategies for low-achieving students.

Sources: Bjorklund & Coyle, 1995; Bjorklund & Jacobs, 1985; Bjorklund et al., 1994; Cowan et al., 2006; DeLoache & Todd, 1988; Gaskins & Pressley, 2007; Gathercole & Hitch, 1993; Kosslyn, Margolis, Barrett, Goldknopf, & Daly, 1990; Kunzinger, 1985; Lehmann & Hasselhorn, 2007; Lucariello et al., 1992; Marley et al., 2008; L. S. Newman, 1990; P. A. Ornstein, Grammer, & Coffman, 2010; Plumert, 1994; Pressley, 1982; Pressley & Hilden, 2006; Schneider & Pressley, 1989.

FIGURE 2.8 Learners benefit from their prior knowledge only when they make appropriate connections. Here Calvin is trying to learn new information meaningfully, but his efforts are in vain because he's unfamiliar with the word *feudal*.
Source: CALVIN AND HOBBES © 1990 Watterson. Distributed by UNIVERSAL UCLICK. Reprinted with permission. All rights reserved.

Prior knowledge and beliefs affect new learning, usually for the better but sometimes for the worse.

What learners already know provides a **knowledge base** on which new learning—especially *meaningful* learning—can build. For example, when you read the passage about John's visit to the doctor's office earlier in the chapter, you could make sense of the passage only if you yourself have visited a doctor many times and so know how such visits typically go. Generally speaking, people who already know something about a topic learn new information about the topic more effectively than people who have little relevant background.[51]

Recall how in the case study at the beginning of the chapter, Rita misinterpreted what she learned about Michigan's history in part because she didn't know that two words in her history lessons, *British* and *English*, were essentially synonyms. When learners have little relevant knowledge on which to build, they're apt to struggle in their efforts to make sense of new information.

Occasionally, however, prior knowledge *interferes* with new learning. In some instances, it may do so because a learner makes an inappropriate connection. Figure 2.8 provides an example: Calvin thinks that a *feudal* system is a *futile* system. We see additional examples in the opening case study. Rita initially associates the word *China* with dinnerware and speculates that the Europeans wanted to import cups from the Far East. She also

---

knowledge base A person's existing knowledge about specific topics and the world in general.

[51] P. A. Alexander, Kulikowich, & Schulze, 1994; Cromley & Azevedo, 2007; Schneider, 1993; Shapiro, 2004.

recalls that furs were an important commodity during the New World's colonial period but mistakenly reports that the furs came from China.

At other times things learned at an earlier time may interfere with new learning because the previous "knowledge" is incorrect. For example, imagine a group of children who think the earth is flat. Such an idea is consistent with their early experiences, especially if they live in, say, Illinois or Kansas. You now tell them that the world is actually round. Rather than replacing the *flat* idea with a *round* one, they might pull both ideas together and conclude that the earth is shaped something like a pancake, which is flat *and* round. Alternatively, they might envision a hollow-sphere version of the earth, with people living on a flat surface within it (see Figure 2.9).[52]

Figure 2.10 presents examples of misconceptions that children and adolescents may bring with them to the classroom. Especially when such misconceptions are embedded in learners' general theories about the world, instruction intended to correct them may do little to change learners' minds.[53] Instead, thanks to the process of elaboration—a process that usually facilitates learning—learners may interpret or distort the new information to be consistent with what they already "know." As a result, they can spend a great deal of time learning the wrong thing! Consider the case of Barry, an eleventh grader whose physics class was studying the idea that an object's mass and weight do *not*, by themselves,

FIGURE 2.9 One way of imagining an earth that is both flat and round

FIGURE 2.10 Common student misconceptions

ASTRONOMY
Fact: The earth revolves around the sun.
Misconception: The sun revolves around the earth. It "rises" in the morning and "sets" in the evening, at which point it "goes" to the other side of the earth.

Fact: The earth is shaped more or less like a sphere.
Misconception: The earth is shaped like a round, flat disk *or* the earth is a hollow sphere with people living on a flat surface inside.

BIOLOGY
Fact: A living thing is something that carries on such life processes as metabolism, growth, and reproduction.
Misconception: A living thing is something that moves and/or grows. The sun, wind, clouds, and fire are living things.

Fact: A plant is a living thing that produces its own food.
Misconception: A plant takes in food from the ground. It grows in a garden and is relatively small.

PHYSICS
Fact: An object remains in uniform motion until a force acts upon it; a force is needed only to *change* speed or direction.
Misconception: Any moving object has a force acting upon it. For example, a ball thrown in the air continues to be pushed upward by the force of the throw until it begins its descent.

Fact: Light objects and heavy objects fall at the same rate unless other forces (e.g., air resistance) differentially affect the objects (e.g., feathers tend to fall slowly because they encounter significant air resistance relative to their mass).
Misconception: Heavy objects fall faster than light objects.

GEOGRAPHY
Fact: The Great Lakes contain freshwater.
Misconception: The Great Lakes contain saltwater.

Fact: Rivers run from higher elevation to lower elevation.
Misconception: Rivers run from north to south (going "down" on a map). For example, rivers can run from Canada into the United States, but not vice versa.

MATHEMATICS
Fact: Multiplication and division can lead to either larger or smaller numbers (e.g., 5 divided by ½ is 10, a number larger than 5).
Misconception: Multiplication always leads to a larger number, and division always leads to a smaller number.

Fact: The size of a fraction is a function of the proportion of the top number relative to the bottom number.
Misconception: Fractions with large numbers indicate larger amounts than fractions with small numbers (e.g., 4/35 is larger than 4/5).

Sources: W. F. Brewer, 2008; S. Carey, 1986; Hynd, 1998a; Kyle & Shymansky, 1989; Maria, 1998; J. Nussbaum, 1985; K. J. Roth & Anderson, 1988; Sneider & Pulos, 1983; Vosniadou, 1994; Vosniadou & Brewer, 1987; Vosniadou et al., 2008; geography misconceptions courtesy of R. K. Ormrod.

---

[52] W. F. Brewer, 2008; Vosniadou, Vamvakoussi, & Skopeliti, 2008.
[53] Derry, 1996; P. K. Murphy & Mason, 2006; Sinatra & Pintrich, 2003; C. L. Smith, Maclin, Grosslight, & Davis, 1997.

affect the speed at which the object falls. Students were asked to design and build egg containers that would keep eggs from breaking when dropped from a third-floor window. They were told that on the day of the egg drop, they would record the time it took for the eggs to reach the ground. Convinced that heavier objects fall faster, Barry added several nails to his egg's container. Yet when he dropped it, classmates timed its fall at 1.49 seconds, a time very similar to that for other students' lighter containers. Rather than acknowledge that light and heavy objects fall at the same rate, Barry explained the result by rationalizing that "the people weren't timing real good."[54]

This tendency to look for what one thinks is true and to ignore evidence to the contrary is known as **confirmation bias**. For instance, when students in a science lab observe results that are inconsistent with their expectations, many are apt to discredit the results, perhaps complaining that "our equipment isn't working right" or "I can never do science anyway."[55] Similarly, when students in a history class read accounts of a historical event that conflicts with prior, not-quite-accurate beliefs about the event—especially if those beliefs are widely held in their cultural group—they may stick with their initial understandings, perhaps saying, "it is not written here . . . but I think this is what happened."[56]

As you can see, then, although prior knowledge and beliefs about a topic are usually a blessing, they can sometimes be a curse.

• Why Learners May or May Not Remember What They've Learned

Retrieving information from long-term memory appears to involve following a pathway of associations. Almost literally, it's a process of going down Memory Lane. One idea reminds you of another idea—that is, one idea *activates* another—the second idea reminds you of a third idea, and so on, in a manner similar to what happened when you followed a train of thought from the word *horse* earlier in the chapter. If the pathway of associations eventually leads you to what you're trying to remember, you do indeed remember it. If the path takes you in other directions, you're out of luck.

How easily and accurately people remember what they've previously learned can be described using the following general principles.

How easily something is recalled depends on how it was initially learned.

People are more likely to remember something they've previously learned if, in the process of storing it, they connected it with something else in long-term memory. Ideally, the "new" and the "old" have a logical relationship. To illustrate this idea, let's return once again to all that mail that arrives in your mailbox. Imagine that, on average, you receive five important items—things you really want to save—every day. At six postal deliveries a week and 52 weeks a year, minus a dozen or so holidays, you save about 1,500 pieces of mail each year. If you save this much mail over the course of 15 years, you eventually have more than 22,000 important things stashed somewhere in your home.

One day you hear that stock in a clothing company (Mod Bod Jeans, Inc.) has tripled in value. You remember that your wealthy Uncle Fred sent you some Mod Bod stock certificates for your birthday several years ago, and you presumably decided they were important enough to save. But where did you put them? How long will it take you to find them among the thousands of other items you've saved?

How easily you find the certificates—in fact, whether you find them at all—depends on how you've been storing your mail as you've accumulated it. If you've been storing it in a logical, organized fashion—for instance, by putting all paid bills on a closet shelf, all mail-order catalogs under your bed, and all items from relatives in a file cabinet (in alphabetical order by last name)—you should be able to retrieve Uncle Fred's gift fairly quickly. But if

---

confirmation bias Tendency to seek information that confirms rather than discredits one's current beliefs.

[54] Hynd, 1998a, p. 34.
[55] Minstrell & Stimpson, 1996, p. 192.
[56] Porat, 2004, p. 989.

you simply tossed each day's mail randomly around the house, you'll be searching your home for a long, long time, possibly without ever finding a trace of the Mod Bod stock.

Like a home with 15 years' worth of mail, long-term memory contains a great deal of information. And like finding the Mod Bod certificates, the ease with which information is retrieved from long-term memory depends somewhat on whether the information is stored in a logical "place"—that is, whether it's connected with related ideas. Through making those important connections with existing knowledge—through meaningful learning—people know where to "look" for information when they need it. In contrast, learning something by rote is like throwing Uncle Fred's gift randomly among thousands of pieces of unorganized mail: A person may never retrieve it again.

Learners are especially likely to retrieve information when they have *many* possible pathways to it—in other words, when they have associated the information with numerous other ideas in their existing knowledge. Making multiple connections is like having cross-references in your mail storage system. You may have filed the Mod Bod certificates in the "items from relatives" file drawer, but you've also written their location on notes left in many other places—perhaps with your birth certificate (after all, you received the stock on your birthday), with your income tax receipts, and in your safe deposit box. By looking in any one of these logical places, you will discover where to find your valuable stock.

Remembering depends on the context.

When I hear certain "oldies" songs (songs by the Beatles, Supremes, Mamas and Papas, etc.), I immediately recall my college years, when those songs were played regularly at parties, in my dormitory, and on the beach. The songs send me down that Memory Lane of associations that leads me to my stored versions of the people, places, and events that were so important to me in college. You too may find that certain songs, smells, pictures, or words stir up memories of days gone by. Things in the environment that remind people of something they've learned in the past—those things that facilitate retrieval—are **retrieval cues**.

Retrieval cues clearly help learners recall what they've previously learned.[57] As an example, try the following exercise.

SEE FOR YOURSELF   The Great Lakes

1. If you were educated in North America, at one time or another you probably learned the names of the five Great Lakes. See if you can recall all of them within a 15-second period.
2. If you had trouble remembering all five lakes within that short time, here's a hint: The first letters of the Great Lakes spell the word *HOMES*. Now see if you can recall all five lakes within 15 seconds.

If you did poorly at Step 1, the word *HOMES* probably helped you at Step 2 because it gave you some ideas about where to "look" in your long-term memory. For example, if you couldn't initially remember Lake Michigan, *HOMES* told you that one of the lakes begins with the letter *M*, leading you to brainstorm *M* words until, possibly, you stumbled on "Michigan." The letters in *HOMES* acted as retrieval cues that started your search of long-term memory in the right directions.

Whether people remember something they've learned when they need it later depends on whether something in their environment sends them down a productive pathway in long-term memory. In some cases the retrieval cue might be something inherent in the task to be done. For example, if I ask you to solve the problem 13 + 24 = ?, the plus sign (+) tells

Think of an exam you've recently taken. Which student would have gotten a higher score: one who had studied course material verbatim or one who had engaged in meaningful learning?

In the United States, there is only one place where four states come together at a single point. Might a misspelling of the word canoe—"CANU"—help you identify these states? (Compare your response to this question with the response presented in Chapter 2 of the Book-Specific Resources in MyEducationLab.)

retrieval cue Stimulus that provides guidance about where to "look" for a piece of information in long-term memory.

[57] Balch, Bowman, & Mohler, 1992; Holland, Hendriks, & Aarts, 2005; Tulving & Thomson, 1973.

Frequent practice of basic skills, such as addition and subtraction, makes them more durable and automatic.

you that you need to add, and so you retrieve what you know about addition. In other cases someone might give you a hint, just as I did when I suggested that you use *HOMES* to help you remember the Great Lakes. The presence or absence of such retrieval cues plays a critical role in people's ability to apply, or *transfer,* what they've learned to new situations, as you'll discover in Chapter 4.

How easily something is recalled and used depends on how often it has been recalled and used in the past.

Practice doesn't necessarily make perfect, but as we've seen, it does make knowledge more durable and automatic. Practice also makes knowledge easier to "find" when it's needed. When we use information and skills frequently, we essentially "pave" the pathways we must travel to find them, in some cases creating superhighways.

Knowledge that has been learned to automaticity has another advantage as well. Remember, working memory has a limited capacity: The active, "thinking" part of the human memory system can handle only so much at a time. Thus, when much of its capacity must be used for recalling single facts or carrying out simple procedures, little room remains for addressing more complex aspects of a task. One key reason for learning some facts and procedures to automaticity, then, is to free up working memory capacity for complex tasks and problems that require those facts and procedures.[58] For example, fourth graders who encounter the multiplication problem

$$\begin{array}{r} 87 \\ \times\ 59 \\ \hline \end{array}$$

can solve it more easily if they can quickly retrieve such basic facts as $9 \times 8 = 72$ and $5 \times 7 = 35$. High school chemistry students can more easily interpret Na_2CO_3 (sodium carbonate) if they don't have to stop to think about what the symbols *Na, C,* and *O* represent.

Recall often involves reconstruction.

Have you ever remembered an event very differently than a friend did, even though the two of you had participated actively and equally in the event? Were you and your friend both certain of the accuracy of your own memories and therefore convinced that the other person remembered the situation incorrectly? Like storage, retrieval has a constructive side, which can explain your differing recollections.

Retrieving something from long-term memory isn't necessarily an all-or-none phenomenon. Sometimes people retrieve only certain parts of something they've previously learned. In such situations they may construct their "memory" of an event by combining the tidbits they can recall with their general knowledge and assumptions about the world.[59] The following exercise illustrates this point.

SEE FOR YOURSELF   Missing Letters

Fill in the missing letters of the following words:

1. exist-nce
2. adole---nce
3. perc--ve
4. hors d'o-----

---

[58] D. Jones & Christensen, 1999; R. W. Proctor & Dutta, 1995; L. B. Resnick, 1989; Stanovich, 2000.

[59] Brainerd & Reyna, 2005; Roediger & McDermott, 2000; Schacter, 1999.

Could you retrieve the missing letters from your long-term memory? If not, you may have found yourself making guesses using either your knowledge of how the words are pronounced or your knowledge of how words in the English language are typically spelled. For example, perhaps you used the "*i* before *e* except after *c*" rule for Word 3; if so, you correctly reconstructed *perceive*. Perhaps you also recalled the *-escence* spelling pattern in such words as *obsolescence* and *effervescence,* in which case you would have spelled *adolescence* correctly. But if you applied the common spelling pattern *-ance* to Word 1, then you misspelled *existence*. Neither pronunciation nor typical English spelling patterns would have helped you with *hors d'oeuvre,* a term borrowed from the French.

When people fill in gaps in what they've retrieved based on what seems "logical," they often make mistakes—a phenomenon known as **reconstruction error**. In the opening case study, Rita's version of what she learned in history is a prime example. Rita retrieved certain facts from her history lessons (e.g., the British wanted furs; some of them eventually settled in the Upper Peninsula) and constructed what was, to her, a reasonable scenario.

Long-term memory isn't necessarily forever.

People certainly don't need to remember everything. For example, you probably have no reason to remember the phone number of a florist you called yesterday, the plot of last week's rerun of *Friends,* or the due date of an assignment you turned in last semester. Much of the information you encounter is, like junk mail, not worth keeping for the long run.

Unfortunately, people sometimes forget important things as well as inconsequential ones. Some instances of forgetting may reflect **retrieval failure**: A person simply isn't looking in the right "place" in long-term memory.[60] Perhaps the forgetful person hasn't learned the information in a meaningful way, or perhaps the person doesn't have a good retrieval cue. But other instances of forgetting may be the result of **decay**: Knowledge stored in long-term memory may gradually weaken over time and perhaps disappear altogether, especially if it isn't used very often.[61] To some degree, then, the expression "Use it or lose it" may apply to human memory.

Regardless of whether forgetting is due to retrieval failure or to decay, human beings don't always remember the things they've learned. However, teachers can do many things to increase the odds that their students *do* remember academic subject matter, as we'll see now.

• Promoting Effective Cognitive Processes

As we've seen, learning is an active, constructive process, and what students learn is rarely a carbon copy of what a teacher or textbook has presented. A teacher's goal, then, should not—and in fact *cannot*—be that students absorb all the information they are given. Instead, a more achievable goal is that students construct appropriate and useful understandings of academic subject matter—that they make reasonable *sense* of it.

How effectively students make sense and meaning from what they're studying depends in large part on the cognitive processes in which they engage. Although students are ultimately the ones in control of their own thinking and learning, a teacher can do many things to help them think and learn more effectively. I've organized these strategies into four general categories: remembering how the human memory system works, encouraging effective long-term memory storage, promoting retrieval, and monitoring students' progress.

Remembering How the Human Memory System Works

The model of memory depicted in Figure 2.5 and discussed at length in this chapter tells us several important things about human memory. First, attention is critical for moving information into working memory. Second, working memory has a short duration (less than half a minute) and limited capacity. And third, effective long-term storage typically involves

reconstruction error Construction of a logical but incorrect "memory" by combining information retrieved from one's long-term memory with one's general knowledge and beliefs about the world.

retrieval failure Inability to locate information that currently exists in long-term memory.

decay Weakening over time of information stored in long-term memory, especially if the information is used infrequently.

[60] Einstein & McDaniel, 2005; Loftus & Loftus, 1980.
[61] Altmann & Gray, 2002; J. R. Anderson, 2005; Reisberg, 1997; Schacter, 1999.

making connections between new information and prior knowledge. These points have several implications for classroom practice.

Grab and hold students' attention.

Hear 12-year-old Claudia describe things her teachers do that capture or lose her attention in the "Motivation: Early Adolescence" video in Chapter 2 of the Book-Specific Resources in MyEducationLab.

What teachers do in the classroom can have a huge impact on the extent to which students pay attention to the subject matter at hand. For example, teachers can pique students' interest in a topic, perhaps by building on students' existing interests and concerns, presenting unusual or puzzling phenomena, or modeling their own enthusiasm for a topic. Incorporating a wide variety of instructional methods into the weekly schedule (discovery learning sessions, debates about controversial issues, cooperative problem-solving activities, etc.) also helps keep students actively attentive to and engaged in mastering new information and skills. The Classroom Strategies box "Getting and Keeping Students' Attention" offers and illustrates several additional suggestions.

Keep the limited capacity of working memory in mind.

A mistake many new teachers make is to present a great deal of information very quickly, and their students' working memories simply can't handle it all. Students have only limited "space" in their working memories, imposing an upper limit on how much they can think about and learn within a given time interval. Instruction must be paced to accommodate what students' working memories can reasonably accomplish. For example, teachers might repeat the same idea several times (perhaps rewording it each time), stop to write important points on the board, provide numerous examples and illustrations, and have students use the content in a variety of activities and assignments over a period of time.

CLASSROOM STRATEGIES Getting and Keeping Students' Attention

- **Create stimulating lessons in which students *want* to pay attention.**

  In a unit on nutrition, a high school biology teacher has students determine the nutritional value of various menu items at a popular local fast-food restaurant.

- **Get students physically involved with the subject matter.**

  A middle school history teacher schedules a day late in the school year when all of his classes "go back in time" to the American Civil War. In preparation for the event, the students spend several weeks learning about the Battle of Gettysburg, researching typical dress and meals of the era, gathering appropriate clothing and equipment, and preparing snacks and lunches. On the day of the "battle," students assume various roles: Union and Confederate soldiers, government officials, journalists, merchants, housewives, doctors and nurses, and so on.

- **Incorporate a variety of instructional methods into lessons.**

  After explaining how to calculate the areas of squares and rectangles, a fourth-grade teacher has students practice calculating area in a series of increasingly challenging word problems. She then breaks the class into three- to four-member cooperative groups, gives each group a tape measure and calculator, and asks the students to calculate the area of their irregularly shaped classroom floor. To complete the task, the students must divide the room into several smaller rectangles, compute the area of each rectangle separately, and add the "subareas" together.

- **Provide frequent breaks from quiet, sedentary activities, especially when working with students in the elementary grades.**

  To provide practice with the alphabet, a kindergarten teacher occasionally has students make letters with their bodies: one child standing with arms extended up and out to make a Y, two children bending over and joining hands to form an M, and so on.

- **In the middle school and high school grades, encourage students to take notes.**

  In a middle school science class, different cooperative groups have been specializing in and researching various endangered species. As each group gives an oral report about its species to the rest of the class, the teacher asks students in the audience to jot down questions about things they would like to know about the animal. On completion of their prepared report, members of the presenting group respond to their classmates' questions.

- **Minimize distractions when students must work quietly and independently.**

  The windows of several classrooms look out onto an area where a new parking lot is being created. Teachers in those rooms have noticed that many students are being distracted by the construction activity outside. The teachers ask the principal to arrange that the construction company work elsewhere on the day that an important statewide assessment is scheduled to be administered.

Sources: Some strategies based on Di Vesta & Gray, 1972; Kiewra, 1989; Ku, Chan, Wu, & Chen, 2008; Pellegrini & Bjorklund, 1997; Posner & Rothbart, 2007.

Even with appropriate pacing, however, the amount of new information presented in a typical classroom is much more than students can reasonably learn and remember, and students aren't always the best judges of what is most important to focus on.[62] Teachers can help students make the right choices by identifying main ideas, offering guidelines on how and what to study, and omitting unnecessary details from explanations of the topic at hand.

Relate new ideas to students' prior knowledge and experiences.

Students can more effectively learn and remember classroom subject matter if they connect it to things they already know. Yet students don't always make such connections on their own, and as a result they often resort to rote learning. Teachers can encourage more meaningful learning by explicitly showing students how new material relates to one or more of the following:

- Concepts and ideas in the same subject area (e.g., showing how multiplication is related to addition)
- Concepts and ideas in other subject areas (e.g., talking about how scientific discoveries have affected historical events)
- Students' general knowledge of the world (e.g., relating the concept of *inertia* to how passengers are affected when an automobile quickly turns a sharp corner)
- Students' personal experiences (e.g., finding similarities between the family feud in *Romeo and Juliet* and students' own group conflicts)
- Students' current activities and needs outside of the classroom (e.g., showing how persuasive writing skills might be used to write a personal essay for a college application)

Ideally, teachers should use students' existing knowledge as a starting point whenever they introduce a new topic—a strategy known as **prior knowledge activation**. For example, in a first-grade classroom, teachers might begin a unit on plants by asking students to describe what their parents do to keep flowers or vegetable gardens growing. Or, in a secondary English literature class, they might introduce Sir Walter Scott's *Ivanhoe* (in which Robin Hood is a major character) by asking students to tell the tale of Robin Hood as they know it.

Accommodate diversity in students' background knowledge.

All students come to school with certain shared understandings about the world. For example, they all know that dogs and cats typically have four legs and that objects fall down (not up) when released. But in many ways students' prior knowledge and understandings are truly their own, because each one has been exposed to a unique set of experiences, interpersonal relationships, and cultural practices and beliefs. Thus students from diverse backgrounds may come to school with somewhat different knowledge—different concepts, schemas, scripts, self-constructed theories, and so on—that they will use to make sense of any new situation.[63] To see what I mean, try the next exercise.

SEE FOR YOURSELF   The War of the Ghosts

Read the following story *one time only:*

One night two young men from Egulac went down to the river to hunt seals, and while they were there it became foggy and calm. Then they heard war-cries, and they thought, "Maybe this is a war-party." They escaped to the shore, and hid behind a log. Now canoes came up, and they heard the noise of paddles, and saw one canoe coming up to them. There were five men in the canoe, and they said:

"What do you think? We wish to take you along. We are going up the river to make war on the people."

[62] P. A. Alexander & Jetton, 1996; Broekkamp, Van Hout-Wolters, Rijlaarsdam, & van den Bergh, 2002; R. E. Reynolds & Shirey, 1988.

[63] E. Fox, 2009; Lipson, 1983; Pritchard, 1990; R. E. Reynolds, Taylor, Steffensen, Shirey, & Anderson, 1982.

prior knowledge activation Process of reminding learners of things they already know relative to a new topic.

One of the young men said: "I have no arrows."

"Arrows are in the canoe," they said.

"I will not go along. I might be killed. My relatives do not know where I have gone. But you," he said, turning to the other, "may go with them."

So one of the young men went, but the other returned home.

And the warriors went on up the river to a town on the other side of Kalama. The people came down to the water, and they began to fight, and many were killed. But presently the young man heard one of the warriors say, "Quick, let us go home: that Indian has been hit." Now he thought: "Oh, they are ghosts." He did not feel sick, but they said he had been shot.

So the canoes went back to Egulac, and the young man went ashore to his house, and made a fire. And he told everybody and said, "Behold I accompanied the ghosts, and we went to fight. Many of our fellows were killed, and many of those who attacked us were killed. They said I was hit, and I did not feel sick."

He told it all, and then he became quiet. When the sun rose he fell down. Something black came out of his mouth. His face became contorted. The people jumped up and cried. He was dead.[64]

Now cover the story, and write down as much of it as you can remember.

Compare your own rendition of the story with the original. What differences do you notice? Your version is almost certainly the shorter of the two, and you probably left out many details. But did you also find yourself distorting certain parts of the story so that it made more sense to you?

A Native American ghost story, "The War of the Ghosts," may be inconsistent with some of the schemas and scripts you've acquired from your experiences, especially if you were raised in a non–Native American culture. In an early study of long-term memory, students at England's Cambridge University were asked to read the story twice and then to recall it at various times later on. Students' recollections of the story often included additions and distortions that made the story more consistent with English culture. For example, people in England rarely go "to the river to hunt seals" because seals are saltwater animals and most rivers have freshwater. Students might therefore say that the men went to the river to *fish*. Similarly, the ghostly aspect of the story didn't fit comfortably with most students' religious beliefs and so was often modified. When one student was asked to recall the story six months after he had read it, he provided the following account:

Four men came down to the water. They were told to get into a boat and to take arms with them. They inquired, "What arms?" and were answered "Arms for battle." When they came to the battle-field they heard a great noise and shouting, and a voice said: "The black man is dead." And he was brought to the place where they were, and laid on the ground. And he foamed at the mouth.[65]

Notice how the student's version of the story leaves out many of its more puzzling aspects—puzzling, at least, from his own cultural perspective.

For another example of how cultural background can influence students' interpretations of new information, let's return to the opening case study. As Rita describes the history of the New World as she understands it, notice how she focuses on what European settlers were doing. In contrast, a Native American student might look at this time period from the perspective of those whose land was being occupied and ultimately taken away by self-serving foreigners. The latter student's

Even though these two students are working together on a science activity, their prior knowledge and beliefs may lead each one to derive a different understanding from the experience.

[64] From *Remembering: A Study in Experimental and Social Psychology* (p. 65), by F. C. Bartlett, 1932, Cambridge, England: Cambridge University Press. Copyright 1932, 1955 by Cambridge University Press. Reprinted with permission of Cambridge University Press.

[65] From *Remembering: A Study in Experimental and Social Psychology* (pp. 71–72), by F. C. Bartlett, 1932, Cambridge, England: Cambridge University Press. Copyright 1932, 1955 by Cambridge University Press. Reprinted with permission of Cambridge University Press.

description of events in Michigan might reflect a theme of *invasion* rather than settlement.[66]

All of this is not to say that some students have *less* knowledge than their peers, but rather that they have *different* knowledge. For example, some (but by no means all) students from low-income families lag behind their classmates in such basic academic skills as reading, writing, and computation.[67] Yet they're apt to bring many strengths to the classroom. They may have a wealth of knowledge about pop culture—rap music lyrics, dialogues from popular films, and so on.[68] They're often quite clever at improvising with everyday objects.[69] If they work part-time to help their families make ends meet, they may have a good understanding of the working world. If they're children of single, working parents, they may know far more than their classmates do about cooking, cleaning house, and caring for younger siblings. If financial resources have been particularly scarce, they may have a special appreciation for basic human needs and true empathy for victims of war or famine around the world. In some domains, then, students who have grown up in poverty have more knowledge and skills than their economically advantaged peers.

Provide experiences on which students can build.

In some instances, of course, students simply don't have the background knowledge they need to understand a new topic. In such cases, teachers can provide concrete experiences that provide a foundation for classroom lessons. For example, students can better understand how large the dinosaurs were if they see a life-size dinosaur skeleton at a natural history museum. Students can more easily understand the events of an important battle if they visit the battlefield. Often teachers can create foundational experiences at school, perhaps by offering opportunities to work with physical objects and living creatures (e.g., timing the fall of light versus heavy objects, caring for a class pet), providing computer software that simulates complex activities (e.g., running a lemonade stand, dissecting a frog), or conducting in-class activities similar to those in the adult world (e.g., trying a mock courtroom case, conducting a political campaign).

Encouraging Effective Long-Term Memory Storage

Having prior knowledge relevant to a classroom topic is, of course, essential for meaningful learning. But it is equally important that students actively *think about* what they're studying—that they consciously and intentionally engage in effective learning strategies such as elaboration, organization, and visual imagery. The following suggestions should promote active, effective learning.

Present questions and tasks that encourage elaboration.

The more students elaborate on new material—the more they mentally expand on what they're learning—the more effectively they're apt to understand and remember it. The Classroom Strategies box "Encouraging Elaboration of Classroom Topics" describes and illustrates several ways that teachers might help students embellish on what they've learned.

Observe a teacher ask questions that encourage elaboration in the "Civil War" video in Chapter 2 of the Book-Specific Resources in MyEducationLab.

Show how new ideas are interrelated.

Let's look again at the opening case study. Rita has acquired a few tidbits about American history, but she has apparently learned them as separate, isolated facts and doesn't pull them together until an adult asks her to explain what she's learned. Unfortunately, such learning of isolated facts, without any true understanding of how they fit together, is all too common at both the elementary and secondary grade levels.[70]

The more interrelationships students identify within the subject matter they're learning—in other words, the better they *organize* it—the more easily they can remember and apply it

---

[66] Banks, 1991.
[67] Farkas, 2008; Goldenberg, 2001; Serpell, Baker, & Sonnenschein, 2005; Siegler, 2009.
[68] Freedom Writers, 1999.
[69] Torrance, 1995.
[70] M. Carr, 2010; Hollon, Roth, & Anderson, 1991; Lesgold, 2001; M. C. Linn, 2008; Paxton, 1999.

CLASSROOM STRATEGIES Encouraging Elaboration of Classroom Topics

- **Communicate the belief that students can and should make sense of the things they study.**

  A junior high school language arts teacher tells his class that he doesn't expect students to memorize the definitions he gives them for new vocabulary words. "Always put definitions in your own words," he says, "and practice using your new words in sentences. For example, one of the new words in this week's list is *garish*. Look at the definition on the handout I gave you. In what situations might you use *garish*?"

- **Ask questions that require students to draw inferences from what they're learning.**

  Students in a high school first-aid class have learned that when people suffer from traumatic shock, many normal bodily functions are depressed because less blood is circulating through the body. The teacher asks, "Given what you've learned about traumatic shock, why do experts recommend that if we find a person in shock, we *have them lie down* and *keep them warm but not hot*?"

- **Have students apply what they've learned to new situations and problems.**

  To give her class practice in creating and interpreting bar graphs, a second-grade teacher asks children to write their favorite kind of pet on a self-stick note she has given each of them. "Let's make a graph that can tell us how many children like different kinds of pets," she says. On the board the teacher draws a horizontal line and a vertical line to make the graph's *x*-axis and *y*-axis. "Let's begin by making a column for dogs," she continues. "How many of you wrote *dog* as your

  favorite pet? Seven of you? OK, come on up here and put your sticky notes on the graph where I've written *dog*. We'll put them one above another to make a bar." After the dog lovers have attached their notes to the graph, the teacher follows the same procedure for cats, birds, fish, and so on.

- **Focus on an in-depth understanding of a few key ideas instead of covering many topics superficially.**

  In planning his geography curriculum for the coming school year, a fourth-grade teacher realizes that his students may gain little from studying facts and figures about numerous countries around the globe. Instead, he chooses six countries with very different cultures—Egypt, Italy, Japan, Peru, New Zealand, and Norway—that the class will focus on that year. Through an in-depth study of these countries, the teacher plans to help his students discover how different climates, topographies, cultures, and religions lead to different lifestyles and economies.

- **Create opportunities for small-group or whole-class discussions in which students can freely exchange their views.**

  In a unit on World War II, a high school history teacher has students meet in small groups to speculate about the problems the Japanese people must have faced after atomic bombs were dropped on Hiroshima and Nagasaki.

  Sources: Some strategies based on Brophy, Alleman, & Knighton, 2009; Croninger & Valli, 2009; Middleton & Midgley, 2002; Slavin, Hurley, & Chamberlain, 2003; N. M. Webb et al., 2008.

later on.[71] When students form many logical connections within the specific concepts and ideas of a topic, they gain a **conceptual understanding** of the topic. For example, rather than simply memorize basic mathematical computation procedures, students should learn how those procedures reflect underlying principles of mathematics. And rather than learn historical facts as a list of unrelated people, places, and dates, students should place those facts within the context of major social and religious trends, migration patterns, economic considerations, human personality characteristics, and so on.

One strategy for helping students find interrelationships within a content area is to organize instructional units around a few core ideas and themes, always relating specific ideas back to this core.[72] (For example, two core ideas in this chapter are the *constructive nature of learning and memory* and the *importance of meaningful learning*.) Another strategy is to ask students to teach what they've learned to others—a task that may encourage them to focus on main ideas and pull these ideas together in a way that makes sense.[73] But ultimately, students are most likely to gain a conceptual understanding of a topic if they explore it in depth—for instance, by considering many examples, examining cause–and–effect relationships, and discovering how specific details relate to general principles. Accordingly, many educators advocate the principle *Less is more: Less* material studied *more* thoroughly is learned *more* completely and with greater understanding.[74]

---

conceptual understanding Knowledge about a topic acquired in an integrated and meaningful fashion.

[71] L. M. Anderson, 1993; Bédard & Chi, 1992; J. J. White & Rumsey, 1994.

[72] Brophy et al., 2009; Prawat, 1993; J. J. White & Rumsey, 1994.

[73] Hatano & Inagaki, 2003; McCaslin & Good, 1996; Roscoe & Chi, 2007.

[74] Brophy et al., 2009; Marshall, 1992; Sizer, 1992, 2004.

Facilitate visual imagery.

As we've discovered, visual imagery can be a highly effective way to learn and remember information. Teachers can promote students' use of visual imagery in a variety of ways.[75] For instance, they can ask students to imagine how certain events in literature or history might have looked. They can provide visual materials (pictures, charts, videos, three-dimensional models, computer animations, etc.) that illustrate or graphically organize important ideas. And they can ask students to create their *own* pictures, diagrams, or models of things they are learning.

Often teachers better help students remember new ideas when they encourage students to encode classroom subject matter *both* verbally and visually.[76] In Figure 2.11, 9-year-old Nicholas uses both words and a picture to describe his findings from a third-grade science experiment, in which he observed what happened when he dropped small, heavy objects into a glass full of water. Nick has difficulties with written language that qualify him for special educational services. Notice how he misspells many words and writes *up* from the bottom of the page. Perhaps by writing upward rather than in the normal top-down fashion, Nick is thinking about how the water traveled up and out of the glass as blocks were dropped into it.

Give students time to think.

We've talked about the importance of having students find personal meaning in, elaborate on, organize, and visualize classroom subject matter. Such processes require thought, and thought requires time. Yet teachers don't always give students that time. For instance, when teachers ask students a question, they typically wait one second or less for a response. If students don't respond in that short time, teachers tend to speak again—sometimes by asking another student the same question, sometimes by rephrasing the question, sometimes by answering the question themselves. Teachers are equally reluctant to let much time lapse after students answer questions or make comments in class—once again, they typically allow one second or less of silence before responding to a statement or asking another question.[77] The problem here is one of insufficient **wait time**.

When teachers instead allow at least *three seconds* to elapse after their own questions and after students' comments, dramatic changes can occur in students' behaviors. More students (especially more females and minority students) participate in class, and students begin to respond to one another's comments and questions. Students are more likely to support their reasoning with evidence or logic and more likely to speculate when they don't know an answer. Furthermore, they are more motivated to learn classroom subject matter, behavior problems decrease, and learning increases. Such changes are in part due to the fact that with increased wait time, *teachers'* behaviors change as well. Teachers ask fewer simplistic questions (e.g., those requiring recall of facts) and more thought-provoking ones (e.g., those requiring elaboration). They modify the direction of discussion to accommodate students' comments and questions, and they allow their classes to pursue a topic in greater depth than they had originally anticipated. And their expectations for many students, especially previously low-achieving ones, begin to improve.[78]

Observe strategies for promoting visual imagery in the "Scarlet Letter" and "Geometry Lesson" videos in Chapter 2 of the Book-Specific Resources in MyEducationLab.

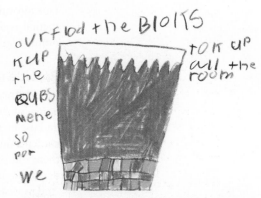

FIGURE 2.11 With both words and a picture, 9-year-old Nicholas describes his findings from a science experiment. The bottom sentence begins at the bottom and goes upward (Translation: "We poured so many cubes [that] the cup overflowed. The blocks took up all the room.")

---

[75] R. K. Atkinson et al., 1999; Carlson, Chandler, & Sweller, 2003; Edens & Potter, 2001; R. E. Mayer, 2010; Sadoski & Paivio, 2001; Van Meter, 2001; Van Meter & Garner, 2005; Verdi, Kulhavy, Stock, Rittschof, & Johnson, 1996.

[76] R. E. Mayer, 2003; Moreno, 2006; Sadoski & Paivio, 2001; Winn, 1991.

[77] Jegede & Olajide, 1995; M. B. Rowe, 1974, 1987.

[78] Castagno & Brayboy, 2008; Giaconia, 1988; Mohatt & Erickson, 1981; M. B. Rowe, 1974, 1987; Tharp, 1989; Tobin, 1987.

wait time Length of time a teacher pauses, after either asking a question or hearing a student's comment, before saying something.

Observe students' use of mnemonics in the middle childhood and late adolescence "Memory and Metacognition" videos and in the "Group Work" video in Chapter 2 of the Book-Specific Resources in MyEducationLab.

Suggest mnemonics for hard-to-remember facts.

Some things are hard to make sense of—hard to learn meaningfully. For instance, why do bones in the human body have such names as *humerus*, *fibula*, and *ulna*? Why is *fáng* the Chinese word for house? Why is Augusta the capital of Maine? For all practical purposes, there is no rhyme or reason to such facts.

When students are likely to have trouble making connections between new material and their prior knowledge, or when a body of information has an organizational structure with no obvious underlying logic (as is true for many lists), special memory tricks known as **mnemonics** can help them learn classroom material more effectively.[79] Three commonly used mnemonics are described in Figure 2.12.

Promoting Retrieval

Even when students engage in meaningful learning, they don't necessarily retrieve important information when they need it. Remember, retrieval involves following a pathway of mental associations, and students sometimes travel down the wrong path. The next two recommendations can enhance students' ability to retrieve what they've learned.

Provide many opportunities to practice important knowledge and skills.

Some information and skills are so fundamental that students must become able to retrieve and use them quickly and effortlessly—that is, with automaticity. For example, to read well, students must be able to recognize most of the words on the page without having to sound them out or look them up in the dictionary. To solve mathematical word problems, students should have such number facts as $2 + 4 = 6$ and $5 \times 9 = 45$ on the tips of their tongues. And to write well, students should be able to form letters and words without having to stop and think about how to make an uppercase *G* or spell *the*. Unless such knowledge and skills are learned to automaticity, a student may use so much working memory capacity retrieving and using them that there's little "room" to do anything more complex.[80]

Ultimately, students can learn basic information and skills to automaticity only by using and practicing them repeatedly. This is *not* to say that teachers should fill each day with endless drill-and-practice exercises involving isolated facts and procedures. Automaticity can occur just as readily when the basics are embedded in a variety of stimulating and challenging activities. Furthermore, students should practice new skills within the context of instruction and guidance that help them *improve* those skills. The Classroom Strategies box "Helping Students Acquire New Skills" provides examples of instructional strategies that can help students more effectively acquire procedural knowledge.

At the same time, teachers must be aware that automaticity has a downside.[81] In particular, students may quickly recall certain ideas or perform certain procedures when other, less automatic ideas or procedures are more useful. Students can be more flexible—and thus more likely to identify unique approaches to situations or creative solutions to problems—if they aren't automatically "locked in" to a particular response. We'll revisit this issue in our discussion of *mental set* in Chapter 4.

Observe engaging activities that encourage basic-skills practice in the "Teaching Basic Skills in Math" video in Chapter 2 of the Book-Specific Resources in MyEducationLab.

Give hints that help students recall or reconstruct what they've learned.

Sometimes forgetting is simply a matter of retrieval difficulty: Students either can't "find" knowledge that's in long-term memory or else neglect to "look" for it altogether. In such situations retrieval cues are often helpful and appropriate. For example, if a student asks how the word *liquidation* is spelled, a teacher might say, "*Liquidation* means to make something liquid. How do you spell *liquid*?" Another example comes from one of my former teacher

[79] Bulgren, Schumaker, & Deshler, 1994; M. S. Jones, Levin, Levin, & Beitzel, 2000; Pressley, Levin, & Delaney, 1982; Scruggs & Mastropieri, 1989.
[80] R. E. Mayer & Wittrock, 1996; McCutchen, 1996; Perfetti, 1983; Sweller, 1994.
[81] Killeen, 2001; E. J. Langer, 2000; LeFevre, Bisanz, & Mrkonjic, 1988.

mnemonic Memory aid or trick designed to help students learn and remember one or more specific pieces of information.

FIGURE 2.12 Common mnemonic techniques

VERBAL MEDIATION

A **verbal mediator** is a word or phrase that creates a logical connection, or "bridge," between two pieces of information. Verbal mediators can be used for such paired pieces of information as foreign language words and their English meanings, countries and their capitals, chemical elements and their symbols, and words and their spellings. Following are examples:

Information to Be Learned	Verbal Mediator
Handschuh is German for "glove."	A glove is a *shoe* for the *hand*.
Quito is the capital of Ecuador.	Mos*quito*es are at the *equator*.
Au is the symbol for gold.	'*Ay, you* stole my *gold* watch!
The word *principal* ends with the letters *pal* (not *ple*).	The *principal* is my *pal*.
The *humerus* bone is the large arm bone above the elbow.	The *humorous* bone is just above the *funny* bone.

KEYWORD METHOD

Like verbal mediation, the **keyword method** aids memory by making a connection between two things. This technique is especially helpful when there is no logical verbal mediator to fill the gap—for example, when there is no obvious sentence or phrase to relate a foreign language word to its English meaning. The keyword method involves two steps, which I will illustrate using the Spanish word *amor* and its English meaning *love:*

1. Identify a concrete object to represent each piece of information. The object may be either a commonly used symbol (e.g., a heart to symbolize *love*) or a sound-alike word (e.g., a suit of armor to represent *amor*). Such objects are *keywords.*
2. Form a mental image of the two objects together. To remember that *amor* means *love,* you might picture a knight in a suit of armor with a huge red heart painted on his chest.

You used the keyword method when you learned the meanings of *fáng, mén, ké, fàn,* and *shū* in the "Five Chinese Words" exercise earlier in the chapter. Following are additional examples:

Information to Be Learned	Visual Image
Das Pferd is German for "horse."	Picture a *horse* driving a *Ford*.
Augusta is the capital of Maine.	Picture a *gust of* wind blowing through a horse's *mane*.
Tchaikovsky composed "Swan Lake."	Picture a *swan* swimming on a *lake,* wearing a *tie* and *cough*ing.

SUPERIMPOSED MEANINGFUL STRUCTURE

A larger body of information, such as a list of items, can often be learned by superimposing a meaningful organization—a familiar shape, word, sentence, rhythm, poem, or story—on the information. Following are examples of such **superimposed meaningful structures:**

Information to Be Learned	Superimposed Meaningful Structure
The shape of Italy	A "boot"
The Great Lakes (Huron, Ontario, Michigan, Erie, Superior)	HOMES
Strings on a guitar (E A D G B E)	Edgar ate dynamite. Good-bye, Edgar.
The number of days in each month	Thirty days has September....
How to turn a screw (clockwise to tighten it; counterclockwise to loosen it)	Righty, tighty; lefty, loosey.
How to multiply in a mathematical expression of the form $(ax + b)(cx + d)$	FOIL: multiply the *first* terms within each set of parentheses, then the two *outer* terms, then the two *inner* terms, and finally the *last* terms

interns, Jesse Jensen. A student in her eighth-grade history class had been writing about the Battle of New Orleans, a decisive victory for the United States in the War of 1812. The following exchange took place:

> **Student:** Why was the Battle of New Orleans important?
> **Jesse:** Look at the map. Where is New Orleans?
> (The student locates New Orleans.)
> **Jesse:** Why is it important?
> **Student:** Oh! It's near the mouth of the Mississippi. It was important for controlling transportation up and down the river.

verbal mediator Word or phrase that forms a logical connection or "bridge" between two pieces of information.

keyword method Mnemonic technique in which an association is made between two ideas by forming a visual image of one or more concrete objects (*keywords*) that either sound similar to, or symbolically represent, those ideas.

superimposed meaningful structure Familiar shape, word, sentence, poem, or story imposed on information in order to facilitate recall.

CLASSROOM STRATEGIES Helping Students Acquire New Skills

- Help students understand the logic behind the procedures they're learning.

    As a teacher demonstrates the correct way to swing a tennis racket, he asks his students, "Why is it important to have your feet apart rather than together? Why is it important to hold your arm straight as you swing?"

- When skills are especially complex, break them into simpler tasks that students can practice one at a time.

    Knowing how overwhelming the task of driving a car can initially be, a driver education teacher begins behind-the-wheel instruction by having students practice steering and braking in an empty school parking lot. Only later, after students have mastered these skills, does she have them drive in traffic on city streets.

- Provide mnemonics that can help students remember a sequence of steps.

    A math teacher presents this equation:

$$y = \frac{3\,(x + 6)^2}{2} + 5$$

    "When x equals 4, what does y equal?" she asks. She gives students a mnemonic, *Please excuse my dear Aunt Sally*, that

they can use to help them remember how to solve problems involving such complex algebraic expressions. First, you simplify things within parentheses (this is the *P* in *Please*). Then, you simplify anything with an exponent (this is the *e* in *excuse*). Then, you do any necessary multiplication and division (these are the *m* and *d* in *my dear*). Finally, you do any remaining addition and subtraction (these are the *A* and *S* in *Aunt Sally*).

- Give students many opportunities to practice new skills, and provide the feedback they need to help them improve.

    A science teacher asks his students to write lab reports after each week's lab activity. Because many of his students have had little or no previous experience in scientific writing, he writes numerous comments when he grades the reports. Some comments describe the strengths that he sees, and others provide suggestions for making the reports more objective, precise, or clear.

Sources: P. A. Alexander & Judy, 1988; J. R. Anderson, Reder, & Simon, 1996; Beilock & Carr, 2003; R. L. Cohen, 1989; Hattie & Timperley, 2007; Hecht, Close, & Santisi, 2003; R. W. Proctor & Dutta, 1995; Shute, 2008.

In the early grades teachers typically provide many retrieval cues: They remind students about the tasks they need to do and when to do them ("I hear the fire alarm. Remember, we all walk quietly during a fire drill"; or "It's time to go home. Do you all have the field trip permission slip to take to your parents?"). But as students grow older, they must develop greater independence, relying more on themselves and less on their teachers for the things they need to remember. At all grade levels, teachers can teach students ways of providing retrieval cues for *themselves*. For example, if second-grade teachers expect children to bring signed permission slips to school the following day, they might ask the children to write a reminder on a piece of masking tape that they attach to their jackets or lunch boxes. If junior high school teachers give students a major assignment due several weeks later, they might suggest that students help themselves remember the due date by taping a note to the bedside table or typing a reminder in their cell phone calendars. In such instances teachers are fostering *self-regulation*, a topic we'll explore in Chapter 4.

Monitoring Students' Progress

As you'll learn in Chapter 10, some classroom assessments—listening to what students say in class, watching students' body language, and so on—are spontaneous, *informal* ones. Others—such as in-class quizzes and assigned projects—are more systematic, *formal* ones that require advance planning. Both informal and formal assessments are important for promoting effective cognitive processes, as the following recommendations reveal.

Regularly assess students' understandings.

Teachers must continually keep in mind that students won't necessarily construct the meanings from classroom events and lessons that teachers intend for them to construct. Rather, students will interpret classroom subject matter in their own, idiosyncratic ways. For example, a student might think that the "round" earth is shaped like a pancake or (as Barry did) believe that heavy egg containers fall faster than light ones despite evidence to the contrary.

Students may also interpret nonacademic interactions in ways that teachers don't anticipate. For example, the first day that 8-year-old Darcy attended third grade at a new school, she accidentally got egg in her hair. Her teacher, Mrs. Whaley, took her to the nurse's office to have the egg washed out. As revealed in the journal entries in Figure 2.13, Darcy initially misinterpreted Mrs. Whaley's comment as unflattering criticism. Not until five days later did she learn Mrs. Whaley's intended meaning.

It's essential, then, that teachers regularly monitor students' understandings about both academic topics and nonacademic issues. Asking questions, encouraging dialogue, listening carefully to students' ideas and explanations—all of these strategies can help teachers get a handle on the "realities" students have constructed for themselves.

Identify and address students' misconceptions.

Teachers often present new information in class with the expectation that such information will replace students' erroneous beliefs. Yet students of all ages can hold on quite stubbornly to their existing misconceptions about the world, even after considerable instruction that explicitly contradicts them.[82] In some cases students never make the connection between what they're learning and what they already believe, perhaps because they engage in rote learning as they study academic subject matter.[83] In other instances students truly try to make sense of classroom material, but—thanks to the process of elaboration—they interpret new information in light of what they already "know" about the topic, and they may reject or discredit something that doesn't fit.[84] (Recall our earlier discussion of *confirmation bias.*)

When students hold scientifically inaccurate or in other ways counterproductive beliefs about the world, teachers must work actively and vigorously to help them revise their thinking. That is, teachers must encourage **conceptual change.** The Classroom Strategies box "Promoting Conceptual Change" presents and illustrates several potentially useful techniques.

Convincing students to replace long-held and well-engrained beliefs can be quite a challenge, and ultimately it may require addressing students' *epistemic beliefs* and *motivation* as well as their long-term memory storage processes. We'll explore these two topics in Chapters 4 and 6, respectively.

Focus assessments on meaningful learning rather than rote learning.

As students get older, they increasingly encounter assignments, exams, and other formal assessments that teachers use to determine final class grades. Unfortunately, many teachers' classroom assessment practices tend to encourage students to learn school subjects in a rote rather than meaningful manner (e.g., see Figure 2.14). When students discover that assignments and exams focus on recall of unrelated facts—rather than on understanding and application of an integrated

October 22nd

I went to a new school today. My teacher's name is Mrs. Whaley. I accidentally cracked an egg on my head. Mrs. Whaley told the nurse that I was a show off and a nuisance. I got really sad and wanted to run away from school, but I didn't leave.

· · ·

October 27th

We presented our book reports today. I was the last one to present my book report. Whenever I did my book report, they laughed at me, but the teacher said they were laughing with me. I asked the teacher why she had called me a nuisance the first day. And she said, "Darcy, I didn't call you a nuisance. I was saying to Mrs. Larson that it was a nuisance to try to wash egg out of your hair." I was so happy. I decided to like Mrs. Whaley again.

FIGURE 2.13 As you can see from her journal entries, 8-year-old Darcy initially interpreted a casual remark to the school nurse in a way very different from the teacher's intended meaning. Fortunately, the teacher corrected the misunderstanding a few days later.

1) One of the coolest things about dinosaurs is that of all the millions there were, we only know about a few ___thousand___ of them.
2) The word "fossil" comes from the Latin word meaning ___dug up___.
3) What four things can fossils tell us about dinosaurs?
   1 ate   3 what they did wl young
   2 look like   4 size/weight
4) Two steps in the process of fossilization are:
   -need to die   -then are covered in layers of sediment
5) One of the processes which forms a fossil is ___pre-mineralized___ This means that minerals replace the bones of the dinosaur.
6) The evidence that dinosaurs once lived is found in discovering ___fossils___.
7) Scientists can learn about dinosaurs by observing ___where___ their fossils are buried, how ___deep___ the fossils are, and what is buried ___nearby___ the dinosaur fossils.
8) Dinosaurs lived on earth for about ___1100___ ___million___ years.
9) Dinosaurs died out about ___65___ ___million___ years ago.
10) One reason dinosaurs may have become extinct is ___a meteorite___.

FIGURE 2.14 Seventh-grade science students complete these and other fill-in-the-blank questions while they watch a video about dinosaurs. Although the questions probably help students pay attention to the video, they encourage rote rather than meaningful learning.

---

[82] Chambliss, 1994; Chinn & Brewer, 1993; Vosniadou, 2008.

[83] Chambliss, 1994; Keil & Silberstein, 1996; Strike & Posner, 1992.

[84] De Lisi & Golbeck, 1999; Gunstone & White, 1981; Hynd, 1998b; Kuhn, Amsel, & O'Loughlin, 1988.

conceptual change Significant revision of one's existing beliefs about a topic, enabling new and discrepant information to be better understood and explained.

CLASSROOM STRATEGIES Promoting Conceptual Change

- Probe for misconceptions that may lead students to interpret new information incorrectly.

    When a third-grade teacher asks, "What is gravity?" one student replies that it's "something that pulls you down." The teacher points to Australia on a globe and asks, "What do you mean by *down*? What do you think would happen if we traveled to Australia? Would gravity pull us off the earth and make us fall into space?"

- Provide information and experiences that explicitly contradict students' inaccurate beliefs.

    In a lesson about air, a first-grade teacher addresses the common misconception that air has no substance. She asks students to predict what will happen when she submerges an upside-down glass in a large bowl of water, and the children have differing opinions about whether the "empty" glass will fill with water. The teacher stuffs the glass with a crumpled paper towel, turns it upside-down, and pushes it straight down into the water. The paper towel remains dry, leading the class to a discussion of how air takes up space. (You can observe this lesson in the "Properties of Air" video in Chapter 2 of the Book-Specific Resources in MyEducationLab.)

- Ask questions that challenge students' misconceptions.

    A high school physics teacher has just begun a unit on inertia. Some students assert that when a baseball is thrown in the air, a force continues to act on the ball, pushing it upward for a short while. The teacher asks, "What force in the air could possibly be pushing that ball upward after it has left the thrower's hand?" The students offer several possibilities but acknowledge that none of them provide satisfactory explanations.

- Show students how an alternative explanation is more plausible and useful—how it makes more sense—than their original belief.

    The same physics teacher points out that the baseball continues to move upward even though no force pushes it in that direction. He brings in the concept of *inertia*: The ball needs a force only to get it *started* in a particular direction. Once the force has been exerted, other forces (gravity and air resistance) alter the ball's speed and direction.

- Give students corrective feedback about responses that reflect misunderstanding.

    Students in a fourth-grade class have just completed a small-group lab activity in which they observe the reactions of earthworms to varying conditions. Their teacher pulls the class back together and asks, "What happens if an earthworm dries out?" One student responds, "They like water, they like to splash around in it . . . if they're in the hot sun they can die because they'll dry up . . . their cells will get hard." The teacher acknowledges that the student is right about the preference for moist conditions while also gently refining the student's explanation: "Absolutely right, good. I don't think they usually like to splash around in water so much, but they like to stay where it's moist." (You can observe this lesson in the "Earthworm Investigation" video in Chapter 2 of the Book-Specific Resources in MyEducationLab.)

- Build on any kernels of truth in students' existing understandings.

    In a sixth-grade lesson about rain, the following exchange occurs between the teacher and one of her students:

    Teacher: What is rain?
    Student: It's water that falls out of a cloud when the clouds evaporate.

    Teacher: What do you mean, "clouds evaporate"?
    Student: That means water goes up in the air and then it makes clouds and then, when it gets too heavy up there, then the water comes and they call it rain.
    Teacher: Does the water stay in the sky?
    Student: Yes, and then it comes down when it rains. It gets too heavy.
    Teacher: Why does it get too heavy?
    Student: 'Cause there's too much water up there.
    Teacher: Why does it rain?
    Student: 'Cause the water gets too heavy and then it comes down.
    Teacher: Why doesn't the whole thing come down?
    Student: Well, 'cause it comes down at little times like a salt shaker when you turn it upside down. It doesn't all come down at once 'cause there's little holes and it just comes out.
    Teacher: What are the little holes in the sky?
    Student: Umm, holes in the clouds, letting the water out.

    The teacher recognizes several accurate understandings in the student's explanation: (1) clouds have water, (2) evaporation is involved in the water cycle, and (3) rain is the result of water being too heavy to remain suspended in air. She uses this knowledge as starting points for further instruction; for instance, she clarifies where in the water cycle evaporation is involved (i.e., in cloud formation) and how a cloud actually *is* water rather than a shakerlike water container.

- When pointing out misconceptions, do so in a way that maintains students' self-esteem.

    A fourth-grade teacher begins a lesson on plants by asking, "Where do plants get their food?" Various students suggest that plants get their food from dirt, water, or fertilizer. The teacher responds, "You know, many children think exactly what you think. It's a very logical way to think. But actually, plants *make* their food, using sunlight, water, and things in the soil." The teacher then introduces the process of photosynthesis.

- Engage students in discussions of the pros and cons of various explanations.

    After students express the stereotypical belief that new immigrants to the country are "lazy," a middle school social studies teacher invites several recent immigrants to visit the class and describe their efforts to adjust to their new environment. The following day, he asks students to reflect on what the guest speakers said: "Several of you have expressed the opinion that many immigrants are lazy. Do you think the people you met yesterday were lazy? Why or why not?" In the ensuing discussion the students begin to realize that most immigrants probably work very hard to adapt to and succeed in their new society and its culture.

- Ask students to apply their revised understandings to new situations and problems.

    When several students express the belief that rivers always run from north to south, a middle school geography teacher reminds them that water travels from higher elevations to lower elevations, not vice versa. She then pulls out a map of Africa. "Let's look at the Nile River," she says. "One end of the Nile is here [she points to a spot on Egypt's Mediterranean coast] and the other end is here [she points to a spot in Uganda]. In which direction must the Nile be flowing?"

Sources: C. Chan, Burtis, & Bereiter, 1997; Chinn & Samarapungavan, 2009; D. B. Clark, 2006; diSessa, 2006; Hattie & Timperley, 2007; Mason, Gava, & Boldrin, 2008; Murphy & Mason, 2006; Pine & Messer, 2000; Pintrich, Marx, & Boyle, 1993; Putnam, 1992; Slusher & Anderson, 1996; C. L. Smith, 2007; Stepans, 1991, p. 94 (salt shaker dialogue); Vosniadou, 2008; Zohar & Aharon-Kraversky, 2005.

body of knowledge—many rely on rote learning, believing that this approach will yield a higher score and that meaningful learning would be counterproductive.[85] Ultimately, teachers must communicate in every way possible—including in their classroom assessments—that it is more important to *make sense* of classroom material than to memorize it. In Chapter 10, we'll identify numerous strategies for assessing meaningful learning.

Be on the lookout for students who have unusual difficulty with certain cognitive processes.

Some students may show ongoing difficulties in processing and learning from academic (or in some cases social) situations. Students with **learning disabilities** have significant deficits in one or more specific cognitive processes. For instance, they may have trouble remembering verbal instructions, recognizing words in print (*dyslexia*), or thinking about and remembering information involving numbers (*dyscalculia*). Students with **attention-deficit hyperactivity disorder (ADHD)** may show marked deficits in attention, have trouble inhibiting inappropriate thoughts and behaviors, or both. Most experts believe that learning disabilities and ADHD have a biological basis and are often inherited.[86]

When students have been officially identified as having a learning disability or ADHD, specialists are often called on to assist them in their learning. Even so, most of these students are in general education classrooms for much or all of the school day. Strategies for working effectively with them include the following:[87]

- Identify and capitalize on the times of day when students learn best.
- Minimize distractions.
- Explicitly present the information that students need to learn; also be explicit about how various ideas are organized and interrelated.
- Use multiple modalities to present information (e.g., supplement verbal explanations with pictures or simple diagrams).
- Actively address students' areas of weakness (e.g., in reading or math).
- Teach mnemonics for specific facts.
- Help students organize and use their time effectively.
- Teach general learning and memory strategies.
- Provide a structure to guide students' learning efforts (e.g., present a partially filled-in outline for taking notes; suggest questions to answer while reading a textbook chapter; break large projects into small, manageable steps).
- Keep study sessions short; provide frequent breaks so that students can release pent-up energy.
- Regularly monitor students' recall and understanding of classroom material.

Some of these strategies should look familiar, as you've seen them at earlier points in the chapter. We'll revisit others when we discuss metacognition and self-regulation in Chapter 4. By and large, the most effective strategies for students with special educational needs are the same ones that are especially effective with *any* learner.

As you've discovered, effective instruction involves a lot more than simply telling students what they need to learn. In this chapter we've focused primarily on things that happen inside the learner when learning takes place. However, we can better understand how human beings learn when we look at *social processes* as well as internal, mental processes. We'll consider the social nature of learning as we address "Learning in Context" in Chapter 3.

❖ What kinds of assessment tasks are likely to encourage automaticity for basic knowledge and skills? (Compare your response to this question with the response presented in Chapter 2 of the Book-Specific Resources in MyEducationLab.)

---

[85] Crooks, 1988; Newstead, 2004.

[86] Barkley, 2006; Coch, Dawson, & Fischer, 2007; Shaw et al., 2007; Shaywitz, Mody, & Shaywitz, 2006.

[87] Barkley, 2006; Brigham & Scruggs, 1995; Eilam, 2001; E. S. Ellis & Friend, 1991; J. M. Fletcher, Lyon, Fuchs, & Barnes, 2007; Meltzer, 2007; Pellegrini & Bohn, 2005; Wilder & Williams, 2001.

learning disability Deficiency in one or more specific cognitive processes despite relatively normal cognitive functioning in other areas.

attention-deficit hyperactivity disorder (ADHD) Disorder marked by inattention, inability to inhibit inappropriate thoughts and behaviors, or both.

SUMMARY

As a way of summarizing the contents of the chapter, let's return to the Mega-Ideas presented at the beginning of the chapter.

● *Much of human learning involves a process of actively constructing—not passively absorbing—knowledge.* Learning is not simply a process of "soaking up" information from the environment. Rather, it is a process of *creating* meanings and interpretations from both informal experiences and formal instruction. In their attempts to make sense of the world, learners combine some (but not all) of what they observe with their existing knowledge and beliefs to create an ever-expanding and distinctly idiosyncratic understanding of the world.

● *Knowledge about the brain is helpful, but some well-meaning educators have misinterpreted findings from brain research.* At the most basic level, learning probably involves changes in neurons, astrocytes, and their interconnections in the brain. Different parts of the brain specialize in different tasks, but many parts of the brain in both hemispheres tend to work closely together in everyday tasks. Although brain research provides useful insights into cognitive development and the neurological bases of certain disabilities, teachers must ultimately look elsewhere—in particular, to psychological and educational research—for guidance about how best to help students learn.

● *Human memory is a complex, multifaceted information-processing system that is, to a considerable degree, under learners' control.* A somewhat oversimplified model of human memory—but a very helpful one nevertheless—has three distinct components. One component, the *sensory register,* holds incoming sensory information for two or three seconds at most. What a learner pays attention to moves on to *working memory,* where it is held for a somewhat longer period while the learner actively thinks about, manipulates, and interprets it. Yet working memory can hold only a small amount of information at one time, and information that is not actively being thought about tends to disappear quickly (typically in less than half a minute) unless the learner processes it sufficiently to store it in long-term memory.

Long-term memory appears to have as much capacity as human beings could ever need. In fact, the more information learners already have there, the more easily they can store new facts and ideas. Effective storage typically involves *meaningful learning*—that is, connecting new information with existing knowledge and beliefs. By making such connections, learners make better sense of their experiences, retrieve what they've learned more easily, and create an increasingly organized and integrated body of knowledge that helps them interpret new experiences. As children grow older, they gradually take charge of their own learning, and most increasingly use effective learning strategies to remember classroom subject matter. Sometimes, however, learners of all ages distort new information, such that they construct inaccurate and potentially counterproductive understandings.

● *Human memory is fallible: Learners don't remember everything they learn, and sometimes they misremember what they've learned.* Learners are more likely to remember new information over the long run if they stored it effectively to begin with—for instance, if they elaborated on, organized, or formed visual images of it—and if they've learned it to a level of automaticity. Yet retrieval is also somewhat context dependent: Learners are more likely to remember something if their environment provides retrieval cues that get them "looking" in the right "places" in long-term memory. Often retrieval involves *reconstruction:* Learners recall only part of what they've learned or experienced and then fill in the gaps in their recollections—perhaps correctly, perhaps not—based on their existing knowledge and beliefs about the world.

● *Effective teachers help students mentally process new information and skills in ways that facilitate long-term memory storage and retrieval.* Teachers must continually emphasize the importance of *understanding* classroom subject matter—making sense of it, drawing inferences from it, seeing how it all ties together, and so on—rather than simply memorizing it in a rote, "thoughtless" manner. Such an emphasis must be reflected not only in teachers' words but also in their instructional activities, assignments, and assessment practices. For instance, rather than just presenting important ideas in classroom lectures and asking students to take notes, teachers might ask thought-provoking questions that require students to evaluate, synthesize, or apply what they're learning. As an alternative to asking students to memorize procedures for adding two-digit numbers, teachers might ask them to suggest at least three different ways they might solve problems such as 15 + 45 or 29 + 68 and to justify their reasoning. Rather than assessing students' knowledge of history by asking them to recite names, places, and dates, teachers might ask them to explain why certain historical events happened and how those events altered the course of subsequent history. At the same time, teachers must also be alert to students' misconceptions about academic topics and work hard to promote *conceptual change.*

PRACTICE FOR YOUR LICENSURE EXAM

Vision Unit

Ms. Kontos is teaching a unit on human vision to her fifth-grade class. She shows her students a diagram of the various parts of the human eye: lens, cornea, retina, and so on. She then explains that people can see objects because light from the sun or another light source bounces off those objects and into the eye. To illustrate this idea, she shows them the picture to the right.

"Do you all understand how our eyes work?" she asks. Her students nod that they do.

The next day Ms. Kontos gives her students this picture:

She asks them to draw how light travels so that the child can see the tree. More than half of the students draw lines something like this:[88]

---

[88] The case presented in this exercise is based on a study by Eaton, Anderson, & Smith, 1984.

1. Constructed-response question

Obviously, most of Ms. Kontos's students have not learned what she thought she had taught them about human vision.

A. Explain why many students believe the *opposite* of what Ms. Kontos has taught them. Base your response on contemporary principles and theories of learning and cognition.

B. Describe two different ways in which you might improve on the lesson to help students gain a more accurate understanding of human vision. Base your strategies on contemporary principles and theories of learning and cognition.

2. Multiple-choice question

Many elementary school children think of human vision in the way that Ms. Kontos's fifth graders do—that is, as a process that originates in the eye and goes outward toward objects that are seen. When students revise their thinking to be more consistent with commonly accepted scientific explanations, they are said to be:

a. Acquiring a new script
b. Developing automaticity
c. Undergoing conceptual change
d. Acquiring procedural knowledge

Go to Chapter 2 of the Book-Specific Resources in MyEducationLab and click on "Practice for Your Licensure Exam" to answer these questions. Compare your responses with the feedback provided.

Chapter

3

Learning in Context

Andrew D. Brogis/The Morning Sun/AP Images

CHAPTER OUTLINE

Case Study: Ben and Sylvia

The Immediate Environment as Context

Social Interaction as Context

Culture and Society as Context

How Learners Modify Their Own Environments

Providing Supportive Contexts for Learning
  Encouraging Productive Behaviors
  Providing Physical and Social Support for Effective Cognitive
    Processes
  Taking into Account the Broader Contexts in Which Students Live

Summary

Practice for Your Licensure Exam: Adam

MEGA-IDEAS TO MASTER IN THIS CHAPTER

Learners' past and present environments influence how learners behave and think at any given time.

The general social contexts in which learners grow up—families and communities and, more broadly, cultures and societies—also influence learners' behaviors and cognitive processes.

Not only does the environment affect learners and their learning, but so, too, do learners influence their environment.

Effective teachers create a classroom environment that encourages and supports productive behaviors and ways of thinking.

Effective teachers adapt instruction to the particular social and cultural contexts in which students live.

CASE STUDY   Ben and Sylvia

For many years Frank McCourt taught English at Stuyvesant High School, a highly selective public school in New York City. One day Mr. McCourt announced that his class would be reading Charles Dickens's *A Tale of Two Cities*, a novel set partly in poverty-stricken Paris in the years leading up to the French Revolution. Several students complained loudly, arguing that they would prefer to read science fiction, such as *Dune* or *The Lord of the Rings*. Mr. McCourt admonished his students for their apparent lack of concern about the needs of individuals less fortunate than themselves: "You'll go home today to your comfortable apartments and houses, head for the refrigerator, open the door, survey contents, find nothing that will please you, ask Mom if you can send out for pizza even though you'll have dinner in an hour." The class quieted down a bit, but one student, Sylvia, remarked, "You're losing it, Mr. McCourt. Chill. Relax."

After class, a student named Ben, the son of Chinese immigrants, stayed behind. In his book *Teacher Man*, Mr. McCourt recounts Ben's comments:

> He knew what I was saying about poverty. . . . He was twelve when he came to this country four years ago. He knew no English but he studied hard and learned enough English and mathematics to pass the Stuyvesant High School entrance exam. . . . He competed against fourteen thousand kids to get into this school. His father worked six days a week, twelve hours a day, in a restaurant in Chinatown. His mother worked in a downtown sweatshop. Every night she cooked dinner for the whole family, five children, her husband, herself. Then she helped them get their clothes ready for the next day. . . . His mother made sure the children sat at the kitchen table and did their homework. . . . Ben said everyone in his family respected everyone else and they'd

never laugh at a teacher talking about the poor people of France because it could just as easily be China or even Chinatown right here in New York.

The next day, Sylvia stayed after class.

> "Mr. McCourt, about yesterday, I didn't mean to be mean. . . . I knew what you were talking about. I have to go through all kinds of stuff when I go down my street every day in Brooklyn. . . . There is nobody on my street ever gonna go to college. Whoops."
>
> "What's the matter?"
>
> "I said 'gonna.' If my mom heard me say 'gonna' she'd make me write 'going to' a hundred times. Then she'd make me say it another hundred times. So, what I'm saying is, when I walk to my house there are kids out there jeering at me. 'Oh, here she come. Here come whitey. Hey, Doc, you scrape yourself an' you find that honky skin?' They call me Doc because I wanna, want to, be a doctor."
>
> "What kind of doctor will you be?"
>
> "Pediatrician or psychiatrist. I want to get the kids before the streets get to them and tell them they're no good because I see kids in my neighborhood afraid to show how smart they are and the next thing is they're acting stupid in vacant lots and burned-out buildings. You know there's a lotta, lot of, smart kids in poor neighborhoods."

- What factors in Ben's and Sylvia's school and home environments appear to have enhanced their ability to learn in the classroom?

- What factors may have *interfered* with their ability to learn?

Note: Quotations in Case Study reprinted with permission of Scribner, a Division of Simon & Schuster, Inc., from *Teacher Man* by Frank McCourt. Copyright © 2005 by Green Peril Corp. All rights reserved.

Mr. McCourt obviously created a supportive classroom environment in which students felt comfortable voicing their opinions about classroom topics and personal matters. Furthermore, both Ben and Sylvia had parents who encouraged academic success—Ben's by making sure that he did his homework and Sylvia's by insisting that she not take "shortcuts" ("gonna," "wanna," "lotta") in her speech. Yet the two students also faced obstacles that probably made their classroom learning more challenging than was true for their classmates: Ben had immigrated to the United States and learned English only four years earlier, and some of Sylvia's neighborhood peers derided her for her high aspirations.

Learning always takes place within particular *contexts*—for instance, within a particular classroom environment, social group, culture, and society. Such contexts are the subject of this chapter. We'll begin by looking at the effects of learners' immediate surroundings. As we do so, we'll draw largely from behaviorism and social cognitive theory (recall the descriptions of these perspectives in Table 2.1 on pages 18–19 in Chapter 2). Later we'll expand our field of vision by examining more general effects that other people have in learners' lives, both through day-to-day social interactions and through the many influences of the larger culture and society. At that point, social constructivism and sociocultural theory (also described in Table 2.1) will guide much of our discussion.

• The Immediate Environment as Context

To some degree, learners' behaviors (**responses**) are influenced by the objects and events (**stimuli**, plural for **stimulus**) they are currently encountering. For instance, in the opening case study Mr. McCourt's supportive demeanor encouraged Ben and Sylvia to open up about their lives and perspectives. Several general principles sum up much of what researchers have learned about the effects that stimuli in the immediate environment have on learners' behavior and ultimately on their learning as well.

Ken Hammond/USDA/Natural Resources Conservation Service

Both physical stimuli (e.g., specimens to touch and books to read) and social stimuli (e.g., hugs from peers and explanations from teachers) can have a significant impact on children's learning.

Some stimuli tend to elicit certain kinds of behaviors.

Certain stimuli in our lives naturally lead us to behave in particular ways. A neighbor's smile might make us feel good and prompt a response such as "Hi, nice to see you." An ill-informed and highly biased newspaper editorial might make us angry and lead us to write a letter to the editor. Different pieces of music evoke different moods and behavioral states, perhaps exciting or agitating us, perhaps provoking us to tap our feet or take to the dance floor, or perhaps helping us relax and "mellow out." Stimuli that precede and evoke particular responses are known as **antecedent stimuli**.

A variety of environmental conditions have been shown to bring about particular behaviors, sometimes for the better and sometimes for the worse. For example, preschoolers are more likely to interact with their peers if they have a relatively small area in which to play and if the toys available to them (balls, puppets, toy housekeeping materials) encourage cooperation and group activity.[1] The kinds of games older children are asked to play influence their interpersonal behavior: Cooperative games promote cooperative behavior, whereas competitive games promote aggressive behavior.[2] The nature of academic assignments influences students' on-task behavior in the classroom. For instance, students are more likely to misbehave in class when think they won't be able to complete assigned tasks successfully.[3]

response   Specific behavior that an individual exhibits.

stimulus (pl. **stimuli**)   Specific object or event that influences an individual's learning or behavior.

antecedent stimulus   Stimulus that increases the likelihood that a particular response will follow.

[1] W. H. Brown, Fox, & Brady, 1987; Frost, Shin, & Jacobs, 1998; S. S. Martin, Brady, & Williams, 1991.
[2] Bay-Hinitz, Peterson, & Quilitch, 1994.

[3] Mac Iver, Reuman, & Main, 1995; Moore & Edwards, 2003; S. L. Robinson & Griesemer, 2006.

Learners are more likely to acquire behaviors that lead to desired consequences.

Learners often learn and perform new behaviors specifically because those behaviors lead to certain end results. Following are examples:

- Laura studies hard for her French vocabulary quiz. She gets an A on the quiz.
- Linda copies her answers to the French quiz from Laura's paper. She, too, gets an A.
- Julian changes the way he holds a basketball before shooting it toward the basket. He now gets more baskets than he used to.
- James throws paper clips at the girl beside him and discovers that this is one way he can get her attention.

As you can see, then, learners may acquire either productive behaviors (e.g., studying French vocabulary, shooting a basketball effectively) or nonproductive ones (e.g., cheating on a quiz, throwing paper clips at a classmate) in order to get something they want.

When we talk about the effects of desired consequences on learners' behaviors, we are talking about **operant conditioning**, a form of learning described by many behaviorists and most notably by B. F. Skinner.[4] The central principle of operant conditioning is a simple one:

> *A response that is followed by a reinforcing stimulus (a reinforcer) is more likely to occur again.*

When behaviors are consistently followed by desired consequences, they tend to increase in frequency. When behaviors don't produce results, they typically decrease and may disappear altogether.

Teachers often talk about giving students rewards for academic achievement and appropriate classroom behavior. But as you may have noticed, I haven't used the term *reward* in my description of operant conditioning, and for a very important reason. The word *reward* brings to mind things we would all agree are pleasant and desirable—perhaps praise, money, trophies, or special privileges. But some individuals increase their behavior for consequences that others wouldn't find very appealing. A **reinforcer** is *any consequence that increases the frequency of a particular behavior,* whether or not other people would find that consequence desirable. The act of following a particular response with a reinforcer is known as **reinforcement**.

Reinforcers come in all shapes and sizes, and different ones are effective for different learners. Some are **primary reinforcers**, in that they serve a basic biological need. Food, water, sources of warmth, and oxygen are all primary reinforcers. To some extent, physical affection and cuddling seem to address built-in biological needs as well, and for an adolescent addicted to an illegal substance, the next "fix" is also a primary reinforcer.[5]

In contrast, **secondary reinforcers** don't satisfy any physiological need; praise, money, good grades, and trophies are examples. Such stimuli may become reinforcing over time through their association with other reinforcers. For example, if praise is occasionally associated with a special candy treat from mother, and if money often comes with a hug from father, the praise and money eventually become reinforcing in and of themselves.

All of the examples I've mentioned so far are instances of **positive reinforcement**. Whenever a particular stimulus is *presented* after a behavior and the behavior increases as a result, positive reinforcement has occurred. Don't be misled by the word *positive,* which in this case has nothing to do with the pleasantness or general desirability of the stimulus being presented. Positive reinforcement can occur even when the presented stimulus is one that others might think is *unpleasant* or *undesirable*. Instead, *positive* simply means *adding* something to the situation. Although many students will behave in ways that earn teacher praise, others may behave to get themselves *any* form of teacher attention, even a scolding.[6] Most students will work for As, but a few may actually prefer Cs or even Fs. (As a school

Learn more about Skinner's ideas in a supplementary reading in Chapter 3 of the Book-Specific Resources in MyEducationLab.

Can you think of other examples of secondary reinforcers? (Compare your response to this question with the response presented in Chapter 3 of the Book-Specific Resources in MyEducationLab.)

operant conditioning Form of learning in which a response increases in frequency as a result of its being followed by reinforcement.

reinforcer Consequence of a response that leads to increased frequency of the response; the act of following a response with a reinforcer is known as **reinforcement**.

primary reinforcer Consequence that satisfies a biologically built-in need.

secondary reinforcer Consequence that becomes reinforcing over time through its association with another reinforcer.

positive reinforcement Phenomenon in which a response increases as a result of the presentation (rather than removal) of a stimulus.

---

[4] For example, see B. F. Skinner, 1953, 1954, 1968. Some behaviorists instead use the term *instrumental conditioning*.

[5] Harlow & Zimmerman, 1959; Lejuez, Schaal, & O'Donnell, 1998; Vollmer & Hackenberg, 2001.

[6] Flood, Wilder, Flood, & Masuda, 2002; McComas, Thompson, & Johnson, 2003.

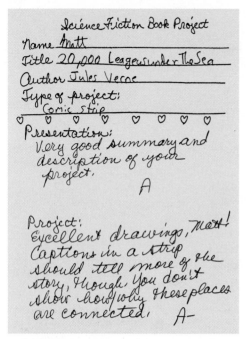

FIGURE 3.1 In commenting on Matt's book project, a middle school teacher is explicit about what Matt can do to improve but vague about what he has done well. Knowing what *specific* things made his summary and project description "very good" would help Matt repeat these things in the future.

psychologist, I once worked with a high school student who used Fs as a way to get revenge on his overbearing and overly controlling parents.) Depending on the individual, any one of these stimuli—praise, a scolding, an A, or an F—can be a positive reinforcer. Following are examples of the forms positive reinforcement might take:

- A *concrete reinforcer* is an actual object—something that can be touched (e.g., a snack, scratch-and-sniff sticker, or toy).

- A *social reinforcer* is a gesture or sign (e.g., a smile, attention, praise, or "thank you") that one person gives another, usually to communicate positive regard.

- An *activity reinforcer* is an opportunity to engage in a favorite activity. Learners will often do one thing, even something they don't like to do, if completing the task enables them to do something they enjoy.[7]

- Sometimes the simple message that an answer is correct or that a task has been done well—*positive feedback*—is reinforcement enough. Positive feedback is most effective when it tells learners in explicit terms what they're doing well and what they can do to improve their performance even further.[8] (See Figure 3.1.)

The reinforcers just listed are **extrinsic reinforcers**, those provided by the external environment (often by other people). Yet some positive reinforcers are **intrinsic reinforcers**, those supplied by learners themselves or inherent in tasks being performed. Learners engage in some activities simply because they enjoy the activities or like to feel competent and successful. When people perform certain behaviors in the absence of any observable reinforcers—when they read *The Lord of the Rings* from cover to cover in a single weekend, practice on their electric guitars into the wee hours of the morning, or do extra classwork without being asked—they are probably working for the intrinsic reinforcement that such behaviors yield.

Children's preferences for various kinds of reinforcers tend to change as they grow older. For example, concrete reinforcers (e.g., stickers, small trinkets) can be effective with young children, but teenagers are more likely to appreciate opportunities to spend time with friends. Table 3.1 presents forms of reinforcement that may be especially effective at various grade levels. An important developmental trend is evident in Table 3.1 as well: As children get older, they become better able to handle **delay of gratification**. That is, they can forego small, immediate reinforcers for the larger reinforcers that their long-term efforts may bring down the road.[9] Whereas a preschooler or kindergartner is apt to choose a small reinforcer she can have *now* over a larger and more attractive reinforcer she can't get until tomorrow, an 8-year-old may be willing to wait a day or two for the more appealing item. Some adolescents can delay gratification for several weeks or even longer.

Learners are also likely to acquire behaviors that help them avoid or escape unpleasant circumstances.

Sometimes learners behave not to get something, but instead to get *rid of* something. On such occasions negative reinforcement rather than positive reinforcement is at work. Whereas positive reinforcement involves the presentation of a stimulus, **negative reinforcement** brings about the increase of a behavior through the *removal* of a stimulus (typically an unpleasant one, at least from the perspective of the learner). The word *negative* here is not a value judgment. It simply refers to the act of *taking away* (rather than adding) a stimulus. Following are examples:

- Reuben must read *A Tale of Two Cities* for his English literature class before the end of the month. He doesn't like having this assignment hanging over his head, so he finishes it early. When he's done, he no longer has to worry about it. In other words, the annoying *worry* feeling disappears.

extrinsic reinforcer Reinforcer that comes from the outside environment, rather than from within the learner.

intrinsic reinforcer Reinforcer provided by oneself or inherent in a task being performed.

delay of gratification Ability to forego small, immediate reinforcers to obtain larger ones at a later time.

negative reinforcement Phenomenon in which a response increases as a result of the removal (rather than presentation) of a stimulus.

[7] Premack, 1959, 1963.
[8] Feltz, Chase, Moritz, & Sullivan, 1999; Hattie & Timperley, 2007; Shute, 2009.
[9] Atance, 2008; Green et al., 1994; Steinberg, Graham, et al., 2009.

DEVELOPMENTAL TRENDS

Table 3.1 Effective Reinforcers at Different Grade Levels

Grade Level	Age-Typical Characteristics	Example	Suggested Strategies

K–2
	• Preference for small, immediate rewards over larger, delayed ones
	• Examples of effective reinforcers:
	  • Concrete reinforcers (e.g., stickers, crayons, small trinkets)
	  • Teacher approval (e.g., smiles, praise)
	  • Privileges (e.g., going to lunch first)
	  • "Grown-up" responsibilities (e.g., taking absentee forms to the office)
		When a kindergarten teacher asks children to choose between a small snack before morning recess or a larger one after recess, most of them clamor for the smaller, immediate snack.	• Give immediate praise for appropriate behavior.
			• Describe enjoyable consequences that may come later as a result of students' present behaviors.
			• Use colorful stickers to indicate a job well done; choose stickers that match students' interests (e.g., use favorite cartoon characters).
			• Have students line up for recess, lunch, or dismissal based on desired behaviors (e.g., "Table 2 is the quietest and can line up first").
			• Rotate opportunities to perform classroom duties (e.g., feeding the goldfish, watering plants) among all students; make such duties contingent on appropriate behavior.

3–5
	• Increasing ability to delay gratification (i.e., to put off small reinforcers in order to gain larger ones later)
	• Examples of effective reinforcers:
	  • Concrete reinforcers (e.g., snacks, pencils, small toys)
	  • Teacher approval and positive feedback
	  • "Good citizen" certificates
	  • Free time (e.g., to draw or play games)
		Nine-year-old Li-Mei glows with pride when her teacher praises her for helping a classmate with a challenging writing assignment.	• Use concrete reinforcers only occasionally, perhaps to add novelty to a classroom activity.
			• Award a certificate to a "citizen of the week," explicitly identifying things the recipient has done especially well; be sure that every student gets at least one certificate during the school year.
			• Plan a trip to a local amusement park for students with good attendance records (especially useful for students at risk for academic failure).

6–8
	• Increasing desire to have social time with peers
	• Examples of effective reinforcers:
	  • Free time with friends
	  • Acceptance and approval from peers
	  • Teacher approval and support (becomes especially critical after the transition to middle school or junior high)
	  • Specific positive feedback about academic performance (preferably given in private)
		Students in a sixth-grade science class work diligently on an assigned lab activity, knowing that if they complete it before the end of the class session they can have a few minutes to talk with their friends.	• Make short periods of free time with peers (e.g., five minutes) contingent on accomplishing assigned tasks.
			• Spend one-on-one time with students, especially those who appear to be socially isolated.
			• Provide explicit feedback about what things students have done well (e.g., pointing out their use of colorful language in an essay or commending them for helping classmates with challenging subject matter).

9–12
	• Increasing ability to postpone immediate pleasures in order to gain desired long-term outcomes
	• Concern about getting good grades (especially for students who are applying to selective colleges)
	• Examples of effective reinforcers:
	  • Opportunities to interact with friends
	  • Specific positive feedback about academic performance
	  • Public recognition for group performance (e.g., newspaper articles about a club's public service work)
	  • Positions of responsibility (e.g., being student representative to Faculty Senate)
		When 16-year-old Deon's friends ask him to go to the movies on a Thursday evening, he declines. "I have to study for tomorrow's history test," he tells them. "If I keep my grades up, I'll have a better chance of getting a good college scholarship."	• Acknowledge students' concern about earning good grades, but focus their attention on the value of learning school subject matter for its own sake (see the discussion of achievement goals in Chapter 6).
			• Take precautions to ensure that cheating and plagiarism are *not* reinforced.
			• Publicize accomplishments of extracurricular groups and athletic teams in local news media.
			• Provide opportunities for independent decision making and responsibility, especially when students show an ability to make wise decisions.

Sources: L. H. Anderman, Patrick, Hruda, & Linnenbrink, 2002; Cizek, 2003; Fowler & Baer, 1981; L. Green, Fry, & Myerson, 1994; Hine & Fraser, 2002; Krumboltz & Krumboltz, 1972; Rimm & Masters, 1974; Rotenberg & Mayer, 1990; M. G. Sanders, 1996; Shute, 2009; Steinberg, Graham, et al., 2009.

- Rhonda is in the same literature class. Each time she sits down at home to read *A Tale of Two Cities,* she finds the novel confusing and difficult to understand. She quickly ends her study sessions by finding other things she "needs" to do instead—washing her hair, playing basketball with the neighbors, and so on. In other words, the *difficult assignment* disappears, at least for the time being.

- When students complain about having to read *A Tale of Two Cities,* Mr. McCourt rants and raves about their lack of concern for people living in poverty. They quiet down, with only one student telling him to "chill" and "relax." Through his actions, Mr. McCourt terminates a *noisy and unpleasant situation,* even if only temporarily.

In the examples just presented, notice how negative reinforcement sometimes promotes desirable behaviors (such as completing an assignment early) and at other times promotes undesirable behaviors (such as procrastination). Notice, as well, how students are not the only ones who respond to reinforcement in the classroom: Teachers are human beings too!

Negative reinforcement often comes into play when students face especially difficult academic tasks.[10] The following explanation reveals what one student with a learning disability has learned to do:

> When it comes time for reading I do everything under the sun I can to get out of it because it's my worst nightmare to read. I'll say I have to go to the bathroom or that I'm sick and I have to go to the nurse right now. My teacher doesn't know that I'll be walking around campus. She thinks I am going to the bathroom or whatever my lame excuse is. All I really want to do is get out of having to read.[11]

Occasionally, learners' attempts to avoid seemingly impossible assignments lead them to engage in blatant misbehaviors, as this statement from another student with a learning disability reveals:

> They [his teachers] used to hand us all our homework on Mondays. One day my teacher handed me a stack about an inch thick and as I was walking out of class there was a big trash can right there and I'd, in front of everybody including the teacher, just drop it in the trash can and walk out. I did this because I couldn't read what she gave me. It was kind of a point that I wanted to get the teacher to realize. That while I'm doing it, inside it kind of like hurt because I really wanted to do it but I couldn't and just so it didn't look like I was goin' soft or anything like that I'd walk over to the trash and throw it in.[12]

Learners tend to steer clear of behaviors that lead to unpleasant consequences.

Over the years I've heard many people incorrectly use the term *negative reinforcement* when they intend to impose unpleasant consequences to reduce someone's inappropriate behavior. In reality, they're talking about administering punishment, *not* negative reinforcement. Whereas negative reinforcement increases the frequency of a response, **punishment** is a consequence that *decreases* the frequency of the response it follows.

All punishing consequences fall into one of two categories. **Presentation punishment** involves presenting a new stimulus, presumably something a learner finds unpleasant and doesn't want. Scoldings and teacher scowls, *if* they lead to a reduction in the behavior they follow, are instances of presentation punishment. **Removal punishment** involves removing an existing stimulus or state of affairs, presumably one a learner finds desirable and doesn't want to lose. Loss of a privilege, a fine or penalty (involving the loss of money or previously earned points), and "grounding" (when certain pleasurable outside activities are missed) are all examples of removal punishment. Table 3.2 should help you understand how positive reinforcement, negative reinforcement, presentation punishment, and removal punishment are distinctly different concepts.

We see one clear example of punishment in the opening case study. Sylvia mentioned that her mother "makes me write 'going to' a hundred times" and then "make[s] me say it

punishment Consequence that decreases the frequency of the response it follows.

presentation punishment Punishment involving presentation of a new stimulus, presumably one a learner finds unpleasant.

removal punishment Punishment involving removal of an existing stimulus, presumably one a learner finds desirable and doesn't want to lose.

[10] McComas et al., 2003; K. A. Meyer, 1999; Van Camp et al., 2000.

[11] Zambo & Brem, 2004, p. 5.

[12] Zambo & Brem, 2004, p. 6.

TABLE 3.2 Distinguishing among Positive Reinforcement, Negative Reinforcement, and Punishment

Consequence	Effect	Examples
Positive Reinforcement	Response *increases* when a new stimulus (presumably one the learner finds desirable) is *presented.*	• A student *is praised* for writing an assignment in cursive. She begins to write other assignments in cursive as well. • A student *gets lunch money* by bullying a girl into surrendering hers. He begins bullying his classmates more frequently.
Negative Reinforcement	Response *increases* when a previously existing stimulus (presumably one the learner finds undesirable) is *removed.*	• A student *no longer has to worry* about a research paper he has completed several days before the due date. He begins to do his assignments ahead of time whenever possible. • A student *escapes the principal's wrath* by lying about her role in a recent incident of school vandalism. She begins lying to school faculty members whenever she finds herself in an uncomfortable situation.
Presentation Punishment	Response *decreases* when a new stimulus (presumably one the learner finds undesirable) is *presented.*	• A student *is scolded* for taunting other students. She taunts others less frequently after that. • A student *is ridiculed by classmates* for asking a "stupid" question during a lecture. He stops asking questions in class.
Removal Punishment	Response *decreases* when a previously existing stimulus (presumably one the learner finds desirable) is *removed.*	• A student *is removed from the softball team for a week* for showing poor sportsmanship. She rarely shows poor sportsmanship in future games. • A student *loses points on a test* for answering a question in a creative but unusual way. He takes fewer risks on future tests.

another hundred times." Such a consequence clearly influenced her behavior, because she corrected herself not only when she said "gonna" but also after saying "wanna" and "lotta." Quite possibly the neighborhood children's derisive remarks also had a punishing effect. By asking "Hey, Doc, you scrape yourself an' you find that honky skin?," Sylvia's peers were essentially accusing her of "acting white," an epithet that some African American students find aversive (more on this point in Chapter 7). The neighbors clearly didn't dissuade Sylvia from becoming a doctor, but they probably discouraged her from walking in their direction if she saw them on the street.

Certain forms of punishment, especially those that are mild in nature and cause no physical or psychological harm, can be quite effective in reducing inappropriate behaviors and, indirectly, helping children and adolescents acquire more productive ones.[13] But without proper precautions, the use of punishment in the classroom can be counterproductive. In our discussion of classroom management strategies in Chapter 9, we'll look at effective punishments and guidelines for their use.

Learners acquire many behaviors by observing other people.

Sometimes learners acquire new behaviors on their own, perhaps by "experimenting" with various responses and seeing which ones lead to reinforcement and which ones lead to punishment. But they don't always learn in this trial-and-error manner. Learners also acquire many new responses simply by observing and imitating the behaviors of other individuals (**models**).

When one person demonstrates a behavior and another person imitates it, **modeling** is occurring. Consistent with how the term is used both in everyday speech and in social cognitive theory, I will sometimes use *modeling* to describe what the model does (i.e., demonstrate a behavior) and at other times to describe what the observer does (i.e., imitate that behavior). To minimize confusion, I will often use the verb *imitate* rather than *model* when referring to what the observer does.

> **?** After studying Table 3.2, can you explain in your own words how negative reinforcement is *not* the same as punishment?

model Person who demonstrates a behavior for someone else.

modeling Demonstrating a behavior for another; also, observing and imitating another's behavior.

[13] Conyers et al., 2004; R. V. Hall et al., 1971; Landrum & Kauffman, 2006; Walters & Grusec, 1977.

Potential models are everywhere. Some are **live models**, people in learners' immediate environments. Others are **symbolic models**, real or fictional characters portrayed in books, in films, on television, and through various other media. For instance, children and adolescents can learn valuable lessons by studying the behaviors of important figures in history or by reading stories about people who accomplish great things in the face of adversity.

Learners acquire a wide variety of physical skills—for instance, complex dance steps and gymnastic skills—in part by watching other people do them first.[14] They can also gain many academic skills—for instance, solving long-division problems and writing cohesive compositions—by observing what others do.[15] Modeling of such skills can be especially effective when the model demonstrates not only how to *do* a task but also how to *think about* the task.[16] As an example, consider how a teacher might model the thinking processes involved in this long-division problem:

$$4 \overline{)276}$$

First I have to decide what number to divide 4 into. I take 276, start on the left and move toward the right until I have a number the same as or larger than 4. Is 2 larger than 4? No. Is 27 larger than 4? Yes. So my first division will be 4 into 27. Now I need to multiply 4 by a number that will give an answer the same as or slightly smaller than 27. How about 5? $5 \times 4 = 20$. No, too small. Let's try 6: $6 \times 4 = 24$. Maybe. Let's try 7: $7 \times 4 = 28$. No, too large. So 6 is correct.[17]

By observing and imitating others, learners acquire many interpersonal behaviors as well. For instance, they often learn **prosocial behaviors**—showing compassion, sharing possessions with others, and in general, putting others' needs and well-being before their own—when they see models that exhibit prosocial behavior (e.g., by watching *Sesame Street* or *Barney and Friends*). In contrast, they are more likely to be aggressive and violent when they witness aggression and violence in their personal lives or in the media.[18] What about situations in which a model advocates certain behaviors and yet does the opposite? When children hear a model say one thing and do something else, they are more likely to imitate what the model *does* than what the model *says*.[19] To be truly effective, models must practice what they preach.

Under what circumstances are learners most likely to model other people's behaviors? The next exercise should help you discover the answer.

"Don't cry, Megan. Remember, it's not whether Daddy wins the brawl in the stands that's important. It's how you played the game."

Models' actions often speak louder than their words.

Source: IN THE BLEACHERS © 2001 Steve Moore. Reprinted with permission of UNIVERSAL UCLICK. All rights reserved.

SEE FOR YOURSELF   Five People

Write down the names of five people whom you admire and whose behaviors you would like to imitate in some way. Then, beside each name, write one or more reasons *why* you admire these people.

Chances are, the five people you chose have one or more of the following characteristics:[20]

- **Competence.** Learners typically try to imitate people who do something well, not those who do it poorly.
- **Prestige and power.** Learners often imitate people who are famous or powerful, either at a national or international level (e.g., a renowned athlete, a popular rock star) or on the local scene (e.g., a head cheerleader, the captain of the high school hockey team, a gang leader).

---

live model Individual whose behavior is directly observed in one's immediate environment.

symbolic model Real or fictional character portrayed in the media that influences an observer's behavior.

prosocial behavior Behavior directed toward promoting the well-being of another person.

[14] Boyer, Miltenberger, Batsche, & Fogel, 2009; Magill, 1993; Vintere, Hemmes, Brown, & Poulson, 2004.

[15] Braaksma, Rijlaarsdam, & van den Bergh, 2002; K. R. Harris, Santangelo, & Graham, 2010; Schunk & Hanson, 1985; Schunk & Pajares, 2005; Schunk & Swartz, 1993.

[16] R. J. Sawyer, Graham, & Harris, 1992; Schunk, 1981, 1998; Schunk & Swartz, 1993; Zimmerman & Kitsantas, 1999.

[17] Schunk, 1998, p. 146.

[18] C. A. Anderson et al., 2003; Carnagey, Anderson, & Bartholow, 2007; N. E. Goldstein, Arnold, Rosenberg, Stowe, & Ortiz, 2001; Guerra, Huesmann, & Spindler, 2003; Hearold, 1986; Rushton, 1980.

[19] Bryan, 1975.

[20] Bandura, 1986; Grace, David, & Ryan, 2008; Sasso & Rude, 1987; Schunk, 1987.

- **"Gender-appropriate" behavior.** Learners are more apt to adopt behaviors they believe are appropriate for their gender (with various learners defining *gender-appropriate* somewhat differently).
- **Behavior relevant to one's own situation.** Learners are most likely to imitate behaviors they believe will help them in their own lives and circumstances.

The last of these—behavior relevant to one's own situation—leads us to the next general principle.

Learners learn what behaviors are acceptable and effective by observing what happens to others.

When I was in third grade, I entered a neighborhood Halloween costume contest dressed as "Happy Tooth," a character in several toothpaste commercials at the time. I didn't win the contest; a "witch" won first prize. So the following year I entered the same contest dressed as a witch, figuring I was a shoo-in for first place. My dressing-as-a-witch behavior increased not because I was reinforced for such behavior, but rather because I saw someone *else* being reinforced for it.

Learners sometimes experience reinforcement and punishment *vicariously*—that is, by observing the consequences of other people's behaviors. Learners who observe someone else being reinforced for a particular behavior tend to exhibit that behavior more frequently themselves—a phenomenon known as **vicarious reinforcement**. For example, by taking note of the consequences their classmates experience, students might learn that studying hard leads to good grades, that being elected to class office brings status and popularity, or that neatness counts.

Conversely, when learners see someone else get punished for a certain behavior, they are *less* likely to behave that way themselves—a phenomenon known as **vicarious punishment**. For example, when a coach benches a football player for poor sportsmanlike conduct, other players are unlikely to mimic such behavior. Unfortunately, vicarious punishment may suppress desirable behaviors as well as undesirable behaviors. For example, when a teacher belittles a student for asking a "silly question," other students may be reluctant to ask questions of their own.

By seeing what happens to themselves and others, learners form expectations about the probable outcomes of various behaviors.

So far, we've been focusing largely on what learners *do*. But the consequences of their own and others' behaviors also affect what learners *think*. In particular, learners begin to see patterns in the consequences that follow various responses, leading them to form expectations that certain responses will lead to desirable results and other responses won't. These expectations, in turn, affect what learners do and don't do in future situations.[21] To understand how this principle might play out in your own life, try the next exercise.

SEE FOR YOURSELF Dr. X

How many of the following questions can you answer about your educational psychology instructor? For lack of a better name, I'm going to call your instructor "Dr. X."

1. Is Dr. X right-handed or left-handed?
2. Is Dr. X a flashy dresser or a more conservative one?
3. What kind of shoes does Dr. X wear to class?
4. Does Dr. X wear a wedding ring?
5. Does Dr. X bring a briefcase to class each day?

vicarious reinforcement Phenomenon in which a response increases in frequency when another (observed) person is reinforced for that response.

vicarious punishment Phenomenon in which a response decreases in frequency when another (observed) person is punished for that response.

---

[21] Bandura, 1986, 2008.

If you've been going to class regularly, you probably know the answers to at least two of the questions, and possibly you can answer all five. But I'm guessing that you've never mentioned what you've learned to anyone else, because you've had no reason to believe that demonstrating your knowledge about such matters would be reinforced. When learners *do* expect reinforcement for such knowledge, it suddenly surfaces. For example, every time I teach educational psychology, I take a minute sometime during the semester to hide my feet behind the podium and then ask my students to tell me what my shoes look like. Students first look at me as if I have two heads, but after a few seconds of awkward silence, at least a half dozen of them (usually those sitting in the first two rows) begin to describe my shoes, right down to the rippled soles, scuffed leather, and beige stitching.

People learn many things that they never demonstrate because there's little likelihood that they would be reinforced for doing so. At school, for instance, children learn facts and figures, they learn ways of getting their teacher's attention, and they may even learn such tiny details as which classmate stores Twinkies in his desk and what kind of shoes the teacher wears to class. Of all the things they learn, children will be most likely to demonstrate the ones they think will bring them reinforcement. The things they think will *not* be reinforced may remain hidden forever.

When people choose to behave in a way that may bring them future reinforcement, they are working for an **incentive**. Incentives are never guaranteed—for instance, people never know for sure that they're going to get an A on a test when they study for it or that they're going to win a Halloween costume contest when they enter it. An incentive is an expected or hoped-for consequence, one that may or may not actually occur. It is apt to influence learners' behaviors only if they think that, by working hard, they can actually obtain it. For example, in a classroom of 30 children, a competition in which one prize will be awarded for the highest test score is apt to motivate just a handful of students who regularly achieve at high levels (more on this point in the discussion of *self-efficacy* in Chapter 6).

What happens when learners' expectations aren't met—for instance, when an expected reinforcement never comes? When, as a fourth grader, I entered the Halloween costume contest as a witch, I lost once again. (First prize went to a girl wearing a metal colander on her head and claiming to be *Sputnik,* the first satellite launched into space by what was then the Soviet Union.) That was the last time I entered a Halloween contest. I had expected reinforcement and felt cheated because I didn't get it. When learners think that a certain response is going to be reinforced, yet the response is *not* reinforced, they are less likely to exhibit that response in the future. In other words, the *non*occurrence of expected reinforcement is a form of punishment.[22]

Just as the nonoccurrence of reinforcement is a form of punishment, the nonoccurrence of punishment is a form of reinforcement.[23] Perhaps you can think of a time when you broke a rule, expecting to be punished, but got away with your crime. Or perhaps you can remember seeing someone else break a rule without being caught. When nothing bad happens after a forbidden behavior, people may actually feel as if they've been reinforced for the behavior.

? Can you think of a personal experience in which not receiving expected reinforcement felt like punishment?

Learned behavior and cognitive processes are sometimes situated in specific environmental contexts.

People often associate particular behaviors and ways of thinking with particular environments, and so those behaviors and ways of thinking are more frequent in such environments. In fact, sometimes people *depend* on certain aspects of their environments—perhaps certain physical objects or certain other people—to help them behave and think more effectively. This tendency for some responses and cognitive processes to be rooted in particular contexts is known as **situated learning** or **situated cognition**.[24]

Thanks (maybe I should say "*no* thanks") to situated learning and cognition, students may abandon the knowledge and skills they've learned in one class once they're in another class. For example, in one research study,[25] high school students were asked to figure out

---

incentive Hoped-for, but not guaranteed, future consequence of behavior.

situated learning and cognition Knowledge, behaviors, and thinking skills acquired and used primarily within certain contexts, with little or no use in other contexts.

[22] Bandura, 1986.

[23] Bandura, 1986.

[24] J. S. Brown, Collins, & Duguid, 1989; Greeno, Collins, & Resnick, 1996; Lave & Wenger, 1991; Light & Butterworth, 1993; Robbins & Aydede, 2009.

[25] Säljö & Wyndhamn, 1992.

how much postage they should put on an envelope of a particular weight, and they were given a table of postage rates that would enable them to determine the correct amount. When students in a social studies class were given the task, most of them used the postage table to find the answer. But when students in a math class were given the task, most of them ignored the postage table and tried to *calculate* the postage in some manner, sometimes figuring it to several decimal places. Thus the students in the social studies class were more likely to solve the problem correctly—as a former social studies teacher myself, I suspect that they were well accustomed to looking for information in tables and charts in that class. In contrast, many of the students in the math class drew on strategies they associated with that class (using formulas and performing calculations) and so overlooked the more efficient and accurate approach.

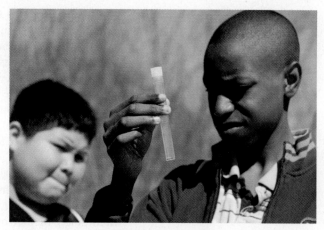

Academic learning sometimes remains "stuck" (*situated*) in the classroom environment. As often as possible, then, students should practice new skills in real-world contexts.

Fortunately, not all school learning is "stuck" in a particular classroom. People use many of the skills they've learned at school—reading, writing, arithmetic, map interpretation, and so on—in a variety of everyday situations in the outside world.[26] Nevertheless, people don't use what they've learned in the classroom as often as they might. We'll explore this issue further in our discussion of *transfer* in Chapter 4.

Social Interaction as Context

In the preceding section we discussed things that other people might do *to* or *in the presence of* a learner—providing reinforcement, modeling behavior, and so on. Yet many effective learning contexts involve active *interaction* among two or more individuals. In particular, learners may *co-construct* knowledge with others, as reflected in the following two principles.

Learners sometimes co-construct knowledge and understandings with more experienced individuals.

Adults and other more experienced individuals often help children and adolescents make sense of the world through joint discussion of a phenomenon or event they are experiencing or have recently experienced together.[27] Such an interaction, sometimes called a **mediated learning experience**, encourages a young learner to think about the phenomenon or event in particular ways: to attach labels to it, recognize concepts and principles that underlie it, draw certain inferences and conclusions from it, and so on.

As an example, consider the following exchange, in which a 5-year-old boy and his mother are talking about a prehistoric animal exhibit at a natural history museum:

Boy: Cool. Wow, look. Look giant teeth. Mom, look at his giant teeth.
Mom: He looks like a saber tooth. Do you think he eats meat or plants?
Boy: Mom, look at his giant little tooth, look at his teeth in his mouth, so big.
Mom: He looks like a saber tooth, doesn't he. Do you think he eats plants or meat?
Boy: Ouch, ouch, ouch, ouch. (referring to sharp tooth)
Mom: Do you think he eats plants or meat?
Boy: Meat.
Mom: How come?
Boy: Because he has sharp teeth. (growling noises)[28]

Even without his mother's assistance, the boy would probably learn something about the characteristics of saber-toothed tigers from his museum visit. Yet Mom helps her son make better sense of the experience than he might have done on his own—for instance, by using the label *saber tooth* and helping him connect tooth characteristics to eating preferences.

---

[26] J. R. Anderson, Reder, & Simon, 1996.
[27] Costa, 2008; Eacott, 1999; Feuerstein, Klein, & Tannenbaum, 1991; John-Steiner & Mahn, 1996.
[28] Ash, 2002, p. 378.

mediated learning experience Social interaction in which an adult helps a child interpret a phenomenon or event in particular (usually culturally appropriate) ways.

Notice how persistent Mom is in asking her son to make the tooth–food connection. She continues to ask her question about meat versus plants until the boy finally infers, correctly, that saber-toothed tigers must have been meat eaters.

As children discuss objects and events with adults and other knowledgeable individuals within the context of everyday activities, they gradually incorporate into their own thinking the ways in which the people around them talk about and interpret the world, and they begin to use many concepts, symbols, mental strategies, and problem-solving procedures that others use, model, and share.[29] In essence, they are developing a variety of **cognitive tools** that will enable them to think about and respond to situations and problems more effectively.

When children talk with parents, teachers, and other adults about past and present experiences, their memory for those experiences is better as a result.[30] Adults usually have more knowledge than children's peers do, and they tend to be more skillful teachers. Accordingly, they are often the partners of choice when children are trying to master complex new subject matter and skills.[31]

In the eyes of sociocultural theorists, mediated learning experiences and cognitive tools are not simply helpful—they are *essential* if children are to acquire the knowledge, skills, and beliefs appropriate for their culture. Accordingly, we'll return to these concepts in our discussion of cognitive development in Chapter 5.

Learners also co-construct knowledge and understandings with peers who have ability levels similar to their own.

Flip back to Figure 2.2 (the three black-and-white faces) in Chapter 2. Did you initially have trouble seeing the man on the right side of the figure? If so, perhaps you enlisted the assistance of friends or classmates to help you identify the top of the man's head, locations of the eyes and an ear, and other details. Think, too, about times when you've worked cooperatively with classmates to make sense of confusing classroom material. Quite possibly, by sharing various interpretations, your group jointly constructed a better understanding of the material than any one of you could have constructed on your own.

In addition to co-constructing meanings with more experienced individuals, learners often talk with one another to help them make better sense of their experiences—for instance, by exploring, discussing, explaining, and debating certain topics in study groups or classroom discussions. When learners work together in such a manner, they are, in essence, engaging in **distributed cognition**: They spread the learning task across many minds and can draw on multiple knowledge bases and ideas.[32] There is certainly some truth to the adage "Two heads are better than one."

As an example of distributed cognition, let's look in on Ms. Lombard's fourth-grade class, which has been studying fractions. Ms. Lombard has never taught her students how to divide a number by a fraction. Nevertheless, she gives them the following problem, which can be solved by dividing 20 by ¾:[33]

> Mom makes small apple tarts, using three-quarters of an apple for each small tart. She has 20 apples. How many small apple tarts can she make?[34]

Ms. Lombard asks the students to work in small groups to figure out how they might solve the problem. One group of four girls—Jeanette, Liz, Kerri, and Nina—has been working on the problem for some time and so far has arrived at such answers as 15, 38, and 23.

---

cognitive tool Concept, symbol, strategy, procedure, or other culturally constructed mechanism that helps people think about and respond to situations more effectively.

distributed cognition Process in which two or more learners each contribute knowledge and ideas as they work collaboratively on an issue or problem.

[29] Liben & Myers, 2007; Markus & Hamedani, 2007; K. Nelson, 1996; Vygotsky, 1962, 1978.
[30] Haden, Ornstein, Eckerman, & Didow, 2001; Hemphill & Snow, 1996; K. Nelson, 1993; Tessler & Nelson, 1994.
[31] Gauvain, 2001; Radziszewska & Rogoff, 1988.
[32] Hewitt & Scardamalia, 1998; Kuhn, 2001b; Palincsar & Herrenkohl, 1999; Salomon, 1993; Wiley & Bailey, 2006.
[33] In case your memory of how to divide by a fraction is rusty, you can approach the problem $20 \div 3/4$ by

inverting the fraction and multiplying, like so: $20 \times 4/3 = 80/3 = 26\, 2/3$. In the problem Ms. Lombard presents, Mom can make 26 tarts and have enough apple to make two-thirds of another tart. If Mom has two-thirds of the three-fourths of an apple she needs to make another whole tart, then she has half an apple left over ($2/3 \times 3/4 = 1/2$).
[34] J. Hiebert et al., 1997, p. 118.

We join the girls midway through their discussion, when they've already agreed that they can use three-fourths of each apple to make a total of 20 tarts:

Jeanette: In each apple there is a quarter left, so you've used, you've made twenty tarts already and you've got a quarter of twenty see—

Liz: So you've got twenty quarters *left*.

Jeanette: Yes, . . . and twenty quarters is equal to five apples, . . . so five apples divided by—

Liz: Six, seven, eight.

Jeanette: But three-quarters equals three.

Kerri: But she can't make only three apple tarts!

Jeanette: No, you've still got twenty.

Liz: But you've got twenty quarters, if you've got twenty quarters you might be right.

Jeanette: I'll show you.

Liz: No, I've drawn them all here.

Kerri: How many quarters have you got? Twenty?

Liz: Yes, one quarter makes five apples and out of five apples she can make five tarts which will make that twenty-five tarts and then she will have, wait, one, two, three, four, five quarters, she'll have one, two, three, four, five quarters. . . .

Nina: I've got a better . . .

Kerri: Yes?

Liz: Twenty-six quarters and a remainder of one quarter left.[35]

The discussion and occasional disagreements continue, and the girls eventually arrive at the correct answer: Mom can make 26 tarts and then will have half an apple left over.

When learners share their ideas and perspectives with one another, they can enhance their understanding of a topic in numerous ways:[36]

- They must clarify and organize their ideas well enough to explain and justify them to others.
- They tend to elaborate on what they've learned—for example, by drawing inferences, generating hypotheses, and formulating new questions.
- They are exposed to the views of others, who may have a more accurate understanding of a topic.
- They can model effective ways of thinking about and studying academic subject matter for one another.
- They may identify flaws and inconsistencies in their own thinking, thereby helping them identify gaps in their understanding.
- They may discover how people from different cultural and ethnic backgrounds may interpret the topic in different, yet perhaps equally valid, ways.
- In the process of debating controversial material, they may gain a more sophisticated view of the nature of knowledge and learning. For example, they may begin to realize that acquiring "knowledge" involves acquiring an integrated set of ideas about a topic and that such knowledge is likely to evolve gradually over time (more on this point in the discussion of *epistemic beliefs* in Chapter 4).

Such joint meaning-making doesn't necessarily have to occur in a single learning session, however. Social construction of meaning may proceed gradually over the course of several days or weeks or even longer. In fact, if we look at human beings' interpretations of their experiences on a much grander scale, the evolution of such diverse academic disciplines as mathematics, science, history, and psychology reflects co-construction of knowledge and understandings stretched out over the course of many decades or centuries.

When learners must explain their thinking to someone else, they often organize and elaborate on what they've learned. These processes help them develop a more integrated and thorough understanding of the material.

---

[35] J. Hiebert et al., 1997, p. 121.

[36] M. Carr & Biddlecomb, 1998; Chinn, 2006; Fosnot, 1996; Hatano & Inagaki, 1993, 2003; E. H. Hiebert & Raphael, 1996; K. Hogan, Nastasi, & Pressley, 2000; A. King, 1999; M. C. Linn, 2008; E. M. Nussbaum, 2008; Schwarz, Neuman, & Biezuner, 2000; Sinatra & Pintrich, 2003; N. M. Webb & Palincsar, 1996.

Shinto gods are called Kami. It is believed that these spirits are found in the basic forces of fire, wind, and water. Most influence agriculture and this of course was how the earliest people survived. They relied on what they grew to live. So the gods had to help them grow their crops or they died. It seems natural for people to worship things that will help them survive, and worshiping forces that affect what you grow was the common practice in early history. These basic forces even affect the survival of modern people. We all still need agriculture to live and forces of nature really determine whether crops grow or not.

Shintoists never developed strong doctrines, such as the belief in life after death that many other religions have. However they have developed some moral standards such as devotion, sincerity, and purity. . . .

All Shintoists have a very good and simple set of rules or practice. They want to be honorable, have feelings for others, support the government, and keep their families safe and healthy. I think these are good principles for all people, whether they practice a religion or not. . . .

FIGURE 3.2 As an assignment for his Spanish class, 14-year-old Bernie created a burlap-and-yarn eagle that was inspired by Mexican designs *(above left)*. But the true essence of a cultural group isn't found in its art, music, clothing, holiday celebrations, and other observable customs. Rather, it comprises the assumptions, beliefs, and values that underlie its members' behaviors and interpretations of the world, as revealed in excerpts from 13-year-old Melinda's essay for her language arts and social studies classes *(above right)*.

Culture and Society as Context

The term **culture** refers to the behaviors and beliefs that members of a long-standing social group tend to share and pass along to successive generations. Culture is a pervasive part of any learning environment—it permeates people's social interactions, as well as the books, toys, television shows, and other human-made objects and media that people encounter. But culture is an inside-the-head thing as well as an out-there-in-the-world thing, in that it provides an overall framework by which people determine what things are normal and abnormal, true and not true, rational and irrational, good and bad (see Figure 3.2).[37] A learner's cultural background influences the perspectives and values the learner acquires, the skills the learner masters and finds important, and the long-term goals toward which the learner strives.

A concept related to culture, but also somewhat distinct from it, is **society**: a large, enduring social group that is socially and economically organized and has collective institutions and activities. For instance, virtually any nation is a society, in that it has a government that regulates some of its activities, a set of laws that identify acceptable and unacceptable behaviors, a monetary system that allows members to exchange goods and services, and so on.

Cultures and societies aren't static entities. Instead, they continue to change over time as they incorporate new ideas, practices, and ways of thinking, and especially as they come into contact with other cultures and societies.[38] Furthermore, considerable variation exists in attitudes and behaviors within a particular culture and society, in that individual members may adopt some cultural values and societal practices but reject others.[39] For example, in the opening case study Sylvia comments on how some of her neighborhood age-mates

culture Behaviors and belief systems that members of a long-standing social group share and pass along to successive generations.

society Large, enduring social group that is socially and economically organized and has collective institutions and activities.

[37] M. Cole, 2006; Goodnow, 2010; Kağitçibaşi, 2007.
[38] Kitayama, Duffy, & Uchida, 2007; Rogoff, 2003.

[39] A. B. Cohen, 2009; Goodnow, 2010; Matute-Bianchi, 2008.

don't share her interest in academic success: "I see kids in my neighborhood afraid to show how smart they are and the next thing is they're acting stupid in vacant lots and burned-out buildings."

Sometimes the word *culture* is used to refer to behaviors and beliefs that are widely shared over a large geographic area. As an example, *mainstream Western culture* encompasses behaviors, beliefs, and values shared by many people in North American and western European societies. Among other things, members of this culture generally value self-reliance, democratic decision making, and academic achievement.[40] Other cultures are more local and self-contained. For instance, a culture might be specific to a particular island in the South Pacific. Still others may be *subcultures* that reside within, but are in some ways different from, a more widespread and dominant culture.

Although countries in North America and western Europe share a common mainstream culture, most also have many distinct cultural groups within them. For example, the United States is a nation comprised largely of immigrants and their descendents; only Native Americans lived on U.S. soil before the 1500s. People with a heritage from a particular country or region often form an **ethnic group**—a group of individuals with a common culture and the following characteristics:[41]

- Its roots either precede the creation of or are external to the country in which it currently resides. For example, it may be composed of people of the same race, national origin, or religious background.

- Its members share a sense of interdependence—a sense that their lives are intertwined.

We cannot determine people's ethnicity strictly on the basis of physical characteristics (e.g., race) or birthplace, however. For instance, although my daughter Tina was born in Colombia and has Hispanic and Native American biological ancestors, she was raised by two European American parents. Ethnically, Tina is probably more European American than anything else. In general, we can get the best sense of students' cultural backgrounds and ethnic group memberships by learning the extent to which they have participated and continue to participate in various cultural and ethnic-group activities.[42] Furthermore, some individuals participate actively in two or more cultures or ethnic groups, perhaps because their parents came from distinctly different racial or ethnic backgrounds or perhaps because they encounter new perspectives and ways of doing things as they move from one community or country to another.[43]

The culture(s) and society in which learners participate have numerous effects on their learning and development, as revealed in the following general principles.

The behaviors that others encourage and model are usually compatible with the culture in which they live.

Culture is a phenomenon that is largely unique to the human species.[44] Through its culture a human social group ensures that each new generation benefits from the wisdom that preceding generations have accumulated. For instance, with the passage of time, members of any long-standing group have learned that some interpersonal behaviors increase social harmony and thus ensure the group's survival, whereas other behaviors create discord and reduce the group's productivity. Similarly, group members have acquired numerous strategies that enhance the quality and longevity of life—preparing a healthful meal, building an energy-efficient home, transporting goods from one place to another, and so on—and they've abandoned many other, less effective, strategies. By passing along this collective knowledge about what works and what does not, a cultural group increases the chances that it will endure over the long run.

Most members of a cultural group work hard to help growing children adopt the behaviors and beliefs that the group holds dear. Beginning early in life, children learn that

---

[40] Hollins, 1996; Tamis-Lemonda & McFadden, 2010.

[41] NCSS Task Force on Ethnic Studies Curriculum Guidelines, 1992.

[42] Gutiérrez & Rogoff, 2003.

[43] A. M. Lopez, 2003; Mohan, 2009; Root, 1999.

[44] A few other species do have rudimentary cultures; for example, see M. Cole & Hatano, 2007.

ethnic group People who have common historical roots, values, beliefs, and behaviors and who share a sense of interdependence.

there are some things they can or should do and other things they definitely should *not* do, and they acquire a cultural "lens" for viewing social situations and tasks. This process of molding behavior and beliefs so that children fit in with their cultural group is called **socialization.**

Sometimes adults' socialization efforts are obvious. For instance, when an adult tells Johnny, "It's not nice to hit other children," and puts Johnny in a time-out room for his aggressive behavior, the message is crystal clear. At other times socialization is more subtle. For example, adults communicate cultural values and beliefs by encouraging and modeling certain activities ("Let's give some of our clothes and toys to the homeless shelter") and discouraging others ("Stay away from that neighborhood; there are drug dealers on every corner").

Children typically learn their earliest lessons about their culture's standards and expectations from parents and other family members, who teach them personal hygiene, table manners, rudimentary interpersonal skills (e.g., saying "please" and "thank you"), and so on. Yet once children begin school, teachers become equally important socialization agents.[45] For instance, many first-grade teachers ask their students to sit quietly rather than interrupt when an adult is speaking, middle school teachers engage students in cooperative learning activities, and high school teachers expect students to turn in homework assignments on time. In doing such things, these teachers communicate important cultural beliefs: that children should defer to and show respect for adults, that cooperation with peers can enhance learning and productivity, and that punctuality is essential for getting ahead in life.

Teachers are important socialization agents for growing children. The children in this class have learned two behaviors that are highly valued in many Western classrooms: sitting quietly and paying attention to the speaker.

To the extent that a society includes a variety of cultures and ethnic groups, different families socialize different behaviors and ways of looking at the world. Throughout the book we will examine such diversity in Cultural Considerations boxes. The first of these, "Examples of Ethnic Differences" (pp. 74–75), gives you a taste of the diversity that teachers are apt to see in school-age children. But as you read the Cultural Considerations boxes in the book, please keep in mind a point made earlier: *Considerable variation exists in the behaviors and beliefs found within a single cultural group.*[46]

Concepts and other cognitive tools are also the products of a culture.

We see obvious effects of culture in many of children's everyday activities—in the books they read, the jokes they tell, the roles they enact in pretend play, the extracurricular activities they pursue, and so on. Yet culture permeates children's thinking processes as well, for instance by providing a variety of *cognitive tools*—concepts, symbols, problem-solving strategies, and so on—that help children interpret and address the situations and problems they face. Such cognitive tools are almost invariably the products of a learner's culture.

As an example of the kinds of cognitive tools that mainstream Western culture provides, try the following exercise.

---

[45] Helton & Oakland, 1977; Hess & Holloway, 1984; Wentzel & Looney, 2007.

[46] Markus and Hamedani (2007) point out that it's easier to use a label such as "East Asians" than to say "people participating in the ideas and practices that

are pervasive in East Asian cultural contexts" (p. 11). If we're not careful, however, such simple labels can lead us to inaccurately overgeneralize about people from any geographic location or cultural background.

socialization Process of molding a child's behavior and beliefs to be appropriate for his or her cultural group.

SEE FOR YOURSELF   Building a Tree House

Imagine that you're building a tree house that has a floor four feet across, a side wall three feet high, and an opposite wall six feet high. You need to buy planks for a slanted roof that will reach from the taller wall to the shorter one. How long must the roof planks be to reach from one wall to the other? Try to solve this problem before you read further.

One way to address the problem is to measure the side walls and floor (which have known dimensions) and determine whether the drawing has been created using a particular scale. In this case the scale is one-fourth of an inch per foot. You could then apply the same scale in estimating the length of the necessary roof planks: Because the roof in the diagram is 1¼ inches long, the actual roof must be five feet long. Another approach involves geometry and algebra. If you've studied geometry, then you've probably learned the Pythagorean theorem: In any right triangle, the square of the hypotenuse (the longest side) equals the sum of the squares of the other two sides. Looking at the top part of the tree house (from the dotted line upward) as a triangle, we can find the length for the roof planks (x) this way:

$$(\text{slanted side})^2 = (\text{horizontal side})^2 + (\text{vertical side})^2$$

$$x^2 = 4^2 + (6-3)^2$$

$$x^2 = 16 + 9$$

$$x^2 = 25$$

$$x = 5$$

Regardless of which approach you took, you used several cognitive tools to solve the problem, perhaps the concepts of *measurement, inches, feet,* and *scale,* or perhaps the *Pythagorean theorem,* the concept of *variable* (x), and algebraic procedures. Mathematics provides innumerable cognitive tools that help people solve a wide variety of problems. In fact, mathematics as a discipline—even such basic elements as numbers and counting—doesn't exist in the physical, "out-there" world. Instead, it's a cultural construction.

Other academic disciplines, too, provide cognitive tools that help people think more effectively about various aspects of their lives. For instance, learners often become better

? Think about the academic discipline in which you are majoring. What cognitive tools does it provide to help you tackle new tasks and problems?

CULTURAL CONSIDERATIONS Examples of Ethnic Differences

Tremendous cultural variation exists within African American, Asian American, European American, Hispanic, and Native American groups. Thus we must be careful not to form stereotypes about *any* group. At the same time, knowledge of frequently observed differences among ethnic groups can sometimes help us better understand why learners from different backgrounds behave as they do. The following examples illustrate the kinds of cultural and ethnic diversity teachers might see in their classrooms.

Individual versus cooperative efforts. In a traditional classroom in mainstream Western culture, learning is often a solitary, individual endeavor: Students receive praise, stickers, and good grades when they personally perform at high levels. Sometimes teachers add a competitive element to personal achievement; for instance, they may grade exams "on a curve" or post "best" papers on the bulletin board. Yet many Native American, Mexican American, African, Southeast Asian, and Pacific Island cultural groups value *group* achievement over individual success. Students from such cultures are often more accustomed to working cooperatively and for the benefit of the community, rather than for themselves.[a] The Zulu word *ubuntu*,[b] reflecting the belief that people attain their "humanness"

largely through relationships with others and have a responsibility to work for the common good, epitomizes this cooperative spirit.

Eye contact. For many of us, looking someone in the eye is a way to show that we are trying to communicate or are listening intently to what another person is saying. But in many Native American, African American, Mexican American, and Puerto Rican communities, a child who looks an adult in the eye is showing disrespect. In these communities children are taught to look *down* in the presence of adults.[c]

Personal space. In some cultures, such as in some African American and Hispanic communities, people stand close together when they talk, and they may touch one another frequently.[d] In contrast, European Americans and Japanese Americans tend to keep a fair distance from one another—they maintain some **personal space**—especially if they don't know one another very well.[e]

Public versus private performance. In many classrooms learning is a very public enterprise: Individual students are often expected to answer questions or demonstrate skills in full view of their classmates, and they're encouraged to ask questions themselves when they don't understand. Such practices, which many teachers take for granted, may

confuse or even alienate the students of some ethnic groups.[f] For example, many Native American children are accustomed to practicing a skill privately at first, performing in front of a group only after they have attained a reasonable level of mastery.[g] And children in some Native American and Hawaiian communities may feel more comfortable responding to an adult's questions as a group rather than interacting with an adult one-on-one.[h]

Family relationships and expectations. In some groups—for example, in many Hispanic, Native American, and Asian communities, as well as in some rural European American communities—family bonds and relationships are especially important, and extended family members often live nearby. Children raised in these cultures are likely to feel responsibility for their family's well-being and a strong sense of loyalty to other family members. They may exhibit considerable respect for, and also go to great efforts to please, their parents.[i]

In most cultures school achievement is valued highly, and parents encourage their children to do well in school.[j] Yet certain other priorities sometimes take precedence. For instance, in some communities it's not unusual for students to leave school when their help is needed at home.[k] And in some African American and Native American families, early

musicians when they can interpret musical notation, understand what *chords* and *thirds* are, and think about particular musical pieces using such concepts. Learners can more easily understand scientific phenomena when they understand and apply concepts such as *force, gravity,* and *chemical reaction.* They can more easily find their way around their community and society when they can read street signs and interpret maps. All of these tools are social inventions that one or more cultures have created to make human endeavors easier or better in some way.

One of the most universal and basic cultural creations—language—provides many cognitive tools that shape growing children's thinking processes. For instance, preschoolers learn to categorize some people as "girls" and others as "boys," and they begin to associate

personal space Personally or culturally preferred distance between two people during social interaction.

pregnancies are cause for joy even if the mothers-to-be haven't yet completed high school.[l]

Conceptions of time.   Many people regulate their lives by the clock: Being on time to appointments, social engagements, and the dinner table is important. This emphasis on punctuality isn't characteristic of all cultures, however. For example, many Native American communities don't observe strict schedules and timelines.[m] Not surprisingly, children from these communities may often be late for school and may have trouble understanding the need to complete school tasks within a certain time frame.

Worldviews.   The cultural and ethnic differences we've identified so far reveal themselves, in one way or another, in students' behaviors. Yet recall that our definition of culture includes beliefs as well as behaviors. When people's beliefs are related to specific physical, biological, social, or mental phenomena, they are known as *theories* (see Chapter 2). In contrast, a **worldview** is a general set of beliefs and assumptions about reality— about "how things are and should be"— that influences learners' interpretations and understandings of a wide variety of phenomena.[n] Following are examples of beliefs that are apt to be components of a person's worldview:[o]

- Life and the universe came into being through random acts of nature *or* as part of a divine plan and purpose.
- Human beings are at the mercy of the forces of nature *or* must learn to live in harmony with nature *or* should strive to master the forces of nature.
- People's successes and failures in life are the result of their own actions *or* divine intervention *or* fate *or* random occurrences.
- People are most likely to enhance their well-being by relying on scientific principles and logical reasoning processes *or* by seeking guidance from authority figures.

To a considerable degree, such beliefs and assumptions are culturally transmitted, with different cultures communicating somewhat different beliefs and assumptions through adults' day-to-day interactions with children.[p]

Worldviews are often such an integral part of everyday thinking that learners take them for granted and aren't consciously aware of them. In many cases, then, worldviews reflect *implicit* rather than *explicit* learning. Nevertheless they influence learners' interpretations of current events and classroom subject matter. For instance, students might interpret a hurricane not as the unfortunate result of natural meteorological forces, but instead as divine punishment for their own or other people's wrongdoings.[q] Or they may struggle with a science curriculum that explores how human beings can manipulate and gain control over natural events, rather than how people might strive to accept and live in harmony with nature as it is.[r]

[a] X. Chen & Wang, 2010; Mejía-Arauz, Rogoff, Dexter, & Najafi, 2007; Tyler et al., 2008.
[b] In a professional trip to South Africa in 2005, I was struck by how often this word was used in daily conversation.
[c] Garrett, Bellon-Harn, Torres-Rivera, Garrett, & Roberts, 2003; Irujo, 1988; Torres-Guzmán, 1998; Tyler et al., 2008.
[d] Hale-Benson, 1986; Slonim, 1991; D. W. Sue, 1990.
[e] Irujo, 1988; Trawick-Smith, 2003.
[f] Eriks-Brophy & Crago, 1994; Garcia, 1994; Lomawaima, 1995; Tyler et al., 2008.
[g] Castagno & Brayboy, 2008; Garcia, 1994; Suina & Smolkin, 1994.
[h] K. H. Au, 1980; L. S. Miller, 1995.
[i] Banks & Banks, 1995; Fuligni, 1998; Kağitçibaşi, 2007; Timm & Borman, 1997; Tyler et al., 2008.
[j] Duran & Weffer, 1992; Goldenberg, Gallimore, Reese, & Garnier, 2001; Hossler & Stage, 1992; Okagaki, 2006.
[k] Deyhle & LeCompte, 1999; Timm & Borman, 1997.
[l] Deyhle & Margonis, 1995; Stack & Burton, 1993.
[m] Burger, 1973; Tyler et al., 2008.
[n] Koltko-Rivera, 2004.
[o] E. M. Evans, 2008; Kelemen, 2004; Koltko-Rivera, 2004; Losh, 2003; Medin, 2005.
[p] Astuti, Solomon, & Carey, 2004; Koltko-Rivera, 2004; Losh, 2003.
[q] O. Lee, 1999.
[r] Atran, Medin, & Ross, 2005; Medin, 2005.

certain behaviors with one sex or the other. Over time, the many words and concepts children acquire—for instance, *snow, yucky, birthday party, bully*—help them interpret and respond to their physical and social experiences in generally adaptive ways.

Inconsistencies between the cultures of home and school can interfere with maximum learning and performance.

For most children, expectations for behavior are different at school than they are at home. For instance, at home children may be accustomed to speaking whenever they have something to say, but at school there are times when silence is golden. Or at home children may be able to choose what they want to do and when to do it, but the school day

worldview General, culturally based set of assumptions about reality that influence understandings of a wide variety of phenomena.

Scott Cunningham/Merrill

Children may experience some culture shock when they begin school, especially if behaviors expected at school are very different from those expected at home.

typically involves a series of tasks that all children must complete at certain times. To the extent that behaviors expected at school differ from those allowed or expected at home, children may experience some confusion, or **culture shock**, when they begin school.

Culture shock is more intense for some children than for others. Most schools in North America and western Europe are based largely on mainstream Western culture, and so children with this cultural background often adjust fairly quickly to the school environment. But students who come from other cultural backgrounds, especially those with very different views about acceptable behavior, may initially find school a confusing and unsettling place. For example, recent immigrants from other parts of the world may not know what to expect from other people in their new country or what behaviors other people expect of them. Children raised in a culture where gender roles are clearly differentiated—where males and females are socialized to behave very differently—may have difficulty adjusting to a school in which similar expectations are held for both sexes.[47] Any such **cultural mismatch** between home and school cultures can interfere with students' adjustment to the school setting and ultimately with their academic achievement as well.[48]

Often children from diverse cultural backgrounds try desperately to fit in at school yet find the inconsistencies between home and school difficult to resolve. For instance, children from devout Muslim families frequently have trouble finding the time and place they need to pray during the school day, and they may have little energy for school activities during the month-long fasting period of Ramadan. And thoughtless classmates might ask Muslim girls who wear head scarves, "Are you bald? Is there something wrong with your hair?" or taunt the girls with names such as "Osama bin Laden's sister."[49]

As students gain experience with the culture of their school, they become increasingly aware of their teachers' and peers' expectations for behavior and ways of thinking. Many eventually become adept at switching their cultural vantage point as they move from home to school and back again.[50] One Mexican American student's recollection provides an example:

> At home with my parents and grandparents the only acceptable language was Spanish; actually that's all they really understood. Everything was really Mexican, but at the same time they wanted me to speak good English. . . . But at school, I felt really different because everyone was American, including me. Then I would go home in the afternoon and be Mexican again.[51]

But not all students make such an easy adjustment. Some actively resist adapting to the existing school culture, perhaps because they view it as being inconsistent with—even contradictory to—their own cultural background and identity.[52] And let's face it: Traditional classrooms don't always encourage behaviors that are in students' long-term best interests. For instance, a classroom that encourages students to compete with one another for grades—rather than fostering the cooperation that many cultural groups value—may engender an unhealthy one-upmanship that interferes with congenial peer relationships both in and outside the classroom.

The problems associated with cultural mismatch can be compounded when teachers misinterpret the behaviors of students from cultural minority groups. The following exercise provides an example.

? Can you think of ways in which your own school environment was mismatched with the culture in which you were raised?

culture shock Sense of confusion when a student encounters a culture with behavioral expectations very different from those learned previously in other contexts.

cultural mismatch Situation in which a child's home culture and the school culture hold conflicting expectations for the child's behavior.

[47] Kirschenbaum, 1989; Sirin & Ryce, 2010; Vasquez, 1988.
[48] A. S. Cole & Ibarra, 2005; García, 1995; C. D. Lee & Slaughter-Defoe, 1995; Ogbu, 1992; Phelan, Yu, & Davidson, 1994.
[49] Igoa, 1995; McBrien, 2005, p. 86; Sirin & Ryce, 2010.

[50] Y. Hong, Morris, Chiu, & Benet-Martínez, 2000; LaFromboise, Coleman, & Gerton, 1993; Phalet, Andriessen, & Lens, 2004; Phelan et al., 1994.
[51] Padilla, 1994, p. 30.
[52] Cross, Strauss, & Fhagen-Smith, 1999; Kumar, Gheen, & Kaplan, 2002; Ogbu, 2008a.

SEE FOR YOURSELF   Ruckus in the Lunchroom

In the following passage, a young adolescent named Sam is describing an incident in the school cafeteria to his friend Joe:

> I got in line behind Bubba. As usual the line was moving pretty slow and we were all getting pretty restless. For a little action Bubba turned around and said, "Hey Sam! What you doin' man? You so ugly that when the doctor delivered you he slapped your face!" Everyone laughed, but they laughed even harder when I shot back, "Oh yeah? Well, you so ugly the doctor turned around and slapped your momma!" It got even wilder when Bubba said, "Well, man, at least my daddy ain't no girl scout!" We really got into it then. After a while more people got involved—4, 5, then 6. It was a riot! People helping out anyone who seemed to be getting the worst of the deal. All of a sudden Mr. Reynolds the gym teacher came over to try to quiet things down. The next thing we knew we were all in the office. The principal made us stay after school for a week; he's so straight! On top of that, he sent word home that he wanted to talk to our folks in his office Monday afternoon. Boy! Did I get it when I got home. That's the third notice I've gotten this semester. As we were leaving the principal's office, I ran into Bubba again. We decided we'd finish where we left off, but this time we would wait until we were off the school grounds.[53]

- Exactly what happened in the school cafeteria? Were the boys fighting? Or were they simply having a good time?

The story you just read is about *playing the dozens,* a friendly exchange of insults common among male youth in some African American communities.[54] Some boys engage in such exchanges to achieve status among their peers—those hurling the most outlandish insults are the winners—whereas others do it simply for amusement. If you interpreted the cafeteria incident as a knock-down-drag-out fight, you're hardly alone, as many eighth graders in a research study did likewise.[55] But put yourself in the place of Sam, the narrator of the story. If you were punished simply for what was, in your mind, an enjoyable verbal competition, you might understandably feel angry and alienated.

Many groups and institutions within a society influence children's learning and development either directly or indirectly.

Any large society, such as a state, province, or nation, provides many "layers" of context that all affect children's learning and development in one way or another.[56] At the most basic level for most children is the *family,* which can potentially support learning in a variety of ways—for instance, by providing good nutrition, helping with homework assignments, being a "cheerleader" for academic success, and working cooperatively with teachers to address learning and behavior problems. Surrounding the family is another layer, the neighborhood and community, which can offer additional support, perhaps in the form of preschools, after-school homework assistance programs, libraries, museums, zoos, and internships in local businesses. At a still broader level, the state (or province) and country in which children reside influence learning through legislation that governs school policy, tax dollars that flow back to local schools, agencies and professional groups that offer information and training in new teaching strategies, and so on. Figure 3.3 illustrates the kinds of environmental influences that the different layers might involve.

---

[53] R. E. Reynolds, Taylor, Steffensen, Shirey, & Anderson, 1982, p. 358.
[54] DeLain, Pearson, & Anderson, 1985; R. E. Reynolds et al., 1982; you may also see the terms *joaning, sounding, signifying,* or *snapping.*

[55] R. E. Reynolds et al., 1982.
[56] Much of the discussion in this paragraph is based on Urie Bronfenbrenner's *ecological systems theory* and *bioecological model;* for instance, see Bronfenbrenner, 1989, 2005; Bronfenbrenner & Morris, 1998.

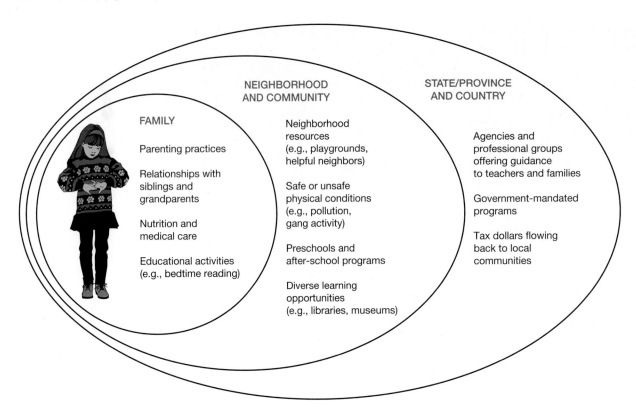

FIGURE 3.3 Examples of various layers of environmental influences

Learn more about IDEA in the supplementary reading "The Individuals with Disabilities Education Act" in Chapter 3 of the Book-Specific Resource in MyEducationLab.

In the United States the **Individuals with Disabilities Education Act (IDEA)** provides an example of how national policy can indirectly affect learning.[57] This legislation guarantees that children with disabilities have access to appropriate interventions and services designed to enhance their physical and cognitive development. It also mandates that once these children reach school age, they be educated in their neighborhood schools and with their nondisabled peers to the fullest extent possible—a practice known as *inclusion*. Early intervention clearly *is* effective in enhancing the development of children with a wide variety of special educational needs.[58] Furthermore, many children with mild disabilities achieve at higher levels if they remain in general education classrooms rather than being segregated into "special" classrooms or schools—something that often happened prior to the legislation's initial enactment in 1975. Placement in regular classes is most successful when instructional materials and practices are tailored to students' specific educational needs and academic levels.[59]

Access to resources at home and in the community also affects learning.

In virtually any society, different learners have access to different resources. For instance, some, but not all, have a quiet place to study and parents who can help them with challenging homework assignments. Some, but not all, have a home computer that provides a variety of tools (e.g., word processing programs, access to the Internet) that can enhance learning and classroom performance. Some, but not all, live near or can easily travel to public libraries, museums, and zoos.

One important factor affecting learners' access to resources is their **socioeconomic status**, often abbreviated as **SES**. This concept encompasses a number of variables, including family income, parents' education levels, and parents' occupations (e.g., whether parents

Individuals with Disabilities Education Act (IDEA) U.S. legislation granting educational rights to people with cognitive, emotional, or physical disabilities from birth until age 21; initially passed in 1975, it has been amended and reauthorized several times and is now officially known as the Individuals with Disabilities Education Improvement Act.

socioeconomic status (SES) One's general social and economic standing in society (encompasses family income, educational level, occupational status, and related factors).

---

[57] This legislation was most recently reauthorized in 2004, at which point it was renamed the Individuals with Disabilities Education Improvement Act. However, most people still refer to it by its original name.

[58] J. M. Fletcher, Lyon, Fuchs, & Barnes, 2007; Kağitçibaşi, 2007; Pelphrey & Carter, 2007.

[59] P. Hunt & Goetz, 1997; Scruggs & Mastropieri, 1994; Slavin, 1987; Soodak & McCarthy, 2006; Stainback & Stainback, 1992.

are business executives, teachers, assembly line workers, etc.). Students' socioeconomic status is correlated with their school performance: Higher-SES students tend to have higher academic achievement, and lower-SES students tend to be at greater risk for dropping out of school. As students from lower-SES families move through the grade levels, they fall further and further behind their higher-SES peers. When researchers find achievement differences among students from different ethnic groups, the differences in the students' socioeconomic status, *not* their cultural differences per se, seem to be largely to blame.[60]

Children and adolescents from low-SES families are a diverse group. Many live in inner-city neighborhoods, others live in rural areas, and some live in modest apartments or homes in wealthy suburban towns. Regardless of where they live, these learners may face one or more of the following challenges:

- **Poor nutrition and health care.** Poor nutrition in early childhood is associated with poorer attention and memory and impaired learning ability. Poor nutrition can influence school achievement both directly—for instance, by hampering early brain development—and indirectly—for instance, by leaving children listless and inattentive in class. And inadequate health care means that some conditions that interfere with school attendance and performance, such as asthma and hearing problems, go unaddressed.[61]

- **Inadequate housing and frequent moves.** Many low-SES families live in tight quarters, perhaps sharing only one or two rooms with other family members. In old, poorly maintained apartment buildings, children may be exposed to lead in the dust from deteriorating paint, and such lead can cause brain damage. In addition, if children move frequently from one rental apartment to another, they must often change schools as well. In the process they lose existing social support networks and may miss lessons on important academic skills.[62]

- **Unhealthy social environments.** On average, low-SES neighborhoods and communities have more street gangs and organized crime, higher frequencies of violence and vandalism, greater prevalence of alcoholism and drug abuse, and greater numbers of antisocial peers. Furthermore, there are fewer productive outlets for leisure time—libraries, recreation centers, sports leagues, and so on—and fewer positive adult role models. Such factors appear to be partly responsible for the lower academic achievement of students who live in poverty.[63] And, of course, the dreary physical environments that characterize many low-income inner-city neighborhoods (Sylvia spoke of "vacant lots and burned-out buildings") can be downright depressing.

- **Lower-quality schools.** Unfortunately, children who are in most need of a good education are those least likely to have access to it. Schools in low-SES neighborhoods and communities tend to receive less funding than those in higher-SES neighborhoods and, as a result, are often poorly maintained and equipped. Teacher turnover rates are high. Furthermore, some teachers at these schools have low expectations for students, offer a less-challenging curriculum,

Visits to museums, zoos, farms, and other local places of interest may be especially beneficial for children from low-income families, who often don't have the financial resources to make such visits on their own.

Shutterstock

[60] Byrnes, 2003; Farkas, 2008; N. E. Hill, Bush, & Roosa, 2003; Jimerson, Egeland, & Teo, 1999; J.-S. Lee & Bowen, 2006; McLoyd, 1998; L. S. Miller, 1995; Murdock, 2000; Sirin, 2005; Stevenson, Chen, & Uttal, 1990.

[61] Ashiabi & O'Neal, 2008; Benton, 2008; Berliner, 2005; Noble, Tottenham, & Casey, 2005; Sigman & Whaley, 1998; R. A. Thompson & Nelson, 2001.

[62] Dilworth & Moore, 2006; Gruman, Harachi, Abbott, Catalano, & Fleming, 2008; Hattie, 2009; Hernandez, Denton, & Macartney, 2008; Hubbs-Tait, Nation, Krebs, & Bellinger, 2005; Mantzicopoulos & Knutson, 2000.

[63] Aikens & Barbarin, 2008; Brooks-Gunn, Linver, & Fauth, 2005; T. D. Cook, Herman, Phillips, & Settersten, 2002; Duncan & Magnuson, 2005; Nettles, Caughy, & O'Campo, 2008; Tamis-Lemonda & McFadden, 2010.

assign less homework, and provide fewer opportunities to develop advanced thinking skills than do teachers in wealthier school districts.[64]

Children who face only one or two of these challenges often do quite well in school—Ben and Sylvia in the opening case study are two good examples—but those who face most or all of them are at high risk for academic failure.[65] Especially when poverty is an ongoing way of life rather than a temporary situation, children may feel considerable emotional stress about their life circumstances,[66] and as you'll discover in Chapter 6, students learn and perform less effectively when they're highly anxious. Not all low-SES children live in chronically stressful conditions, of course, and those whose families provide consistent support, guidance, and discipline (as was true for Ben and Sylvia) generally enjoy good mental health.[67]

• How Learners Modify Their Own Environments

In the preceding sections we've seen various ways in which people's environments affect their learning and behavior. But the reverse is true as well: Learners can have a profound influence on the environments they encounter. The following two principles describe the kinds of influences that learners can have.

Learners alter their current environment both through their behaviors and through their internal traits and mental processes.

To some degree learners change their environments through their actions. In the classroom, for example, the consequences they experience (e.g., the reinforcements and punishments) depend on whether they regularly complete assigned tasks and whether they interact with teachers and classmates in prosocial ways. But internal cognitive processes and other things that in some way "reside" inside learners come into play as well. For instance, learners are apt to focus their attention on (and so learn from) only certain aspects of their environment (see Chapter 2), and they're more likely to choose activities for which they have expectations of doing well rather than poorly. In fact, all three of these—*environment, behavior,* and *learner characteristics* (which social cognitive theorists call *person* variables)—influence one another. This interdependence among environment, behavior, and personal factors is known as **reciprocal causation**.[68] Figure 3.4 illustrates this concept, and several examples of the interplay among the three kinds of variables are presented in the "General Examples" column in Table 3.3.

As a concrete illustration of how environment, behavior, and personal factors are continually intertwined, let's consider Scene 1 in the case of a student named Lori:

Scene 1

Lori often comes late to Mr. Broderick's seventh-grade social studies class, and she's usually ill prepared for the day's activities. In class she spends more time interacting with her friends (e.g., whispering, passing notes) than getting involved in classroom activities. Lori's performance on most exams and assignments (when she turns her work in at all) is unsatisfactory.

One day in mid-October, Mr. Broderick takes Lori aside to express his concern about her lack of classroom effort. He suggests that Lori could do better if she paid more attention in class. He also offers to work with her after school twice a week to help her understand class material. Lori isn't optimistic, describing herself as "not smart enough to learn this stuff."

For a week or so after her meeting with Mr. Broderick, Lori buckles down and exerts more effort, but she never does stay after school for extra help. And before long

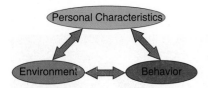

FIGURE 3.4 Environmental, behavioral, and person variables mutually influence one another.

reciprocal causation Mutual cause–and–effect relationships among environment, behavior, and personal variables as these three factors influence learning and development.

---

[64] Becker & Luthar, 2002; Eccles, Wigfield, & Schiefele, 1998; G. W. Evans, 2004; McLoyd, 1998; Skiba & Knesting, 2001.

[65] Gerard & Buehler, 2004; Grissmer, Williamson, Kirby, & Berends, 1998.

[66] Brooks-Gunn et al., 2005; G. W. Evans & Kim, 2007; Gershoff, Aber, Raver, & Lennon, 2007.

[67] N. E. Hill et al., 2003; M. O. Wright & Masten, 2006.

[68] Bandura, 1989, 2006, 2008.

TABLE 3.3 Mutual Influences (Reciprocal Causation) among Environment, Behavior, and Person

		General Examples	Examples in Lori's Case: Scene 1	Examples in Lori's Case: Scene 2
Effect of Environment	**On Behavior**	Reinforcement and punishment affect future behavior.	The teacher's decision to spend most of his time with other students leads to Lori's continuing classroom failure.	New instructional methods lead to Lori's improved academic performance.
	On Person	Feedback from others affects the learner's expectations (either positively or negatively) about future performance.	The teacher's lack of time and effort with Lori perpetuates her low self-confidence about classroom tasks.	New instructional methods capture Lori's interest and attention.
Effect of Behavior	**On Environment**	Specific behaviors affect the amount of reinforcement and punishment received.	Lori's poor classroom performance initially leads her teacher to meet privately with her and then eventually to ignore her.	Lori's improved learning strategies and academic performance lead to more frequent reinforcement.
	On Person	Current successes and failures affect expectations for future performance.	Lori's current poor classroom performance leads to her low expectations about future performance.	Lori's improved learning strategies and academic performance boost her self-confidence about future classroom performance.
Effect of Person	**On Environment**	Expectations about future performance in various domains affect the specific activities the learner chooses to engage in and therefore also affect the learning opportunities the learner encounters.	Lori's attention to classmates during instructional activities causes her peers to be more influential stimuli than her teacher.	Lori's increased attention to classroom activities enhances the effectiveness of the teacher's instruction.
	On Behavior	Attention, learning strategies, and other cognitive processes affect the learner's classroom performance.	Lori's attention to classmates rather than to instruction leads to academic failure.	Lori's greater self-confidence and increased motivation lead to more regular and effective study habits.

she's back to her old habits. Mr. Broderick eventually concludes that Lori is a lost cause and devotes most of his time and effort to helping more motivated students.

Lori's low expectations for academic achievement (a person factor) may partly explain why she spends so much time engaged in task-irrelevant activities (behaviors). The fact that she devotes her attention (another person factor) to her classmates, rather than to her teacher, affects the particular stimuli she experiences (her environment). Lori's poor study habits and resulting poor performance on assignments and exams (behaviors) adversely affect both her expectations for future academic success (person) and Mr. Broderick's treatment of her (environment). By eventually concluding that Lori is a lost cause, Mr. Broderick begins to ignore Lori (environment), contributing to her further failure (behavior) and even lower self-confidence (person). (The Scene 1 column in Table 3.3 presents examples of such interactive effects.) Clearly, Lori is showing signs of being at risk for long-term academic failure.

But now imagine that after reading several research articles about how to work with students at risk, Mr. Broderick develops greater optimism that he can break the vicious cycle of reciprocal causation for students such as Lori. Midway through the school year, he makes several changes in his teaching:

- He communicates clearly and consistently that he expects all students to succeed in his classroom.
- He incorporates students' personal experiences and interests into the study of social studies.

- He identifies specific, concrete tasks that students will accomplish each week.
- He provides guidance and structure for how students should complete each task.
- After consulting with the school's reading specialist and school psychologist, he helps students develop more effective reading and learning strategies.
- He gives a quiz every Friday so that students can see that they're making progress each week.

Let's see what happens next, as we consider Scene 2:

Scene 2

By incorporating students' personal experiences and interests into daily lessons, Mr. Broderick starts to capture Lori's interest and attention. She begins to realize that social studies has implications for her own life and so becomes more involved in classroom activities. With the more structured assignments, increased guidance about how to study, and frequent quizzes, Lori finds herself succeeding in a subject at which she has previously experienced only failure. Mr. Broderick is pleased with her performance, something he tells her frequently through his facial expressions, verbal feedback, and willingness to provide help whenever she needs it.

By the end of the school year, Lori is studying course material more effectively and completing her assignments regularly. She is eagerly looking forward to next year's social studies class, confident that she'll continue to do well.

Once again, we see the interplay among environment, behavior, and person. Mr. Broderick's new instructional methods (environment) engage Lori's attention (person), foster better study habits, and enhance academic performance (behaviors). Lori's improved classroom performance, in turn, influences Mr. Broderick's treatment of her (environment) and her own self-confidence (person). And her improved self-confidence, her greater attention to classroom activities, and her increased motivation to succeed (all person variables) affect her ability to benefit from Mr. Broderick's instruction (environment) and thus also affect her classroom success (behavior). (The Scene 2 column in Table 3.3 presents examples of the changed interactive effects.)

Learners actively seek out environments that are a good fit with their existing characteristics and behaviors.

As children get older, they can increasingly *choose* and thereby control their environments. With such choice and control, they're apt to seek out situations in which they feel comfortable—situations that match their existing abilities, interests, and needs and that allow them to engage in preferred activities. This tendency to seek out environmental conditions that are a good match with existing characteristics and behaviors—a phenomenon known as **niche-picking**—tends to increase any existing differences among learners.[69]

For example, as children move through the grade levels, they gain a wider choice of peers with whom they can spend time, and they increasingly affiliate with peers who share their interests and activities. As they reach middle school or junior high, and even more so as they reach high school, they select some of the courses they take—thus, they begin to focus on subject matter they find appealing and may steer clear of subject matter that has previously been difficult for them. As they master public transportation systems or learn how to drive, they have increasing access to environments beyond home and the immediate neighborhood. Some of these environments, such as a library, gymnasium, music studio, or (as in the case of Ben and Sylvia) good high school, can help them acquire valuable new knowledge and skills. Others, such as a gathering place for antisocial peers or an all-night dance party ("rave") where illegal drugs are readily available, can be harmful to their cognitive and social development.

Although children and adolescents influence and control their own environments to some degree, teachers, too, have considerable control over an environment that is a big part

Can you explain reciprocal causation in your own words? Can you provide an example from your own experience?

niche-picking Tendency for a learner to seek out environmental conditions that are a good match with his or her existing characteristics and behaviors.

[69] O. S. P. Davis, Haworth, & Plomin, 2009; Flynn, 2003; Halpern & LaMay, 2000; Scarr & McCartney, 1983.

of youngsters' daily lives: school. We turn now to strategies for making the school environment one that fosters young people's learning, academic achievement, and social success.

Providing Supportive Contexts for Learning

The various "layers" of the environment—from the specific stimuli learners encounter in their immediate circumstances to the general cultures and societies in which learners live—have numerous implications for classroom practice. The strategies I offer in this section fall into three general categories: encouraging productive behaviors, providing physical and social support for effective cognitive processes, and taking into account the broader contexts in which students live.

Encouraging Productive Behaviors

Applying the concepts of *antecedent stimulus, reinforcement,* and *modeling* can be quite helpful in encouraging productive behaviors, as the following recommendations reveal.

Create conditions that elicit desired responses.

Early in the chapter we noted that certain stimulus conditions—cooperative toys and games, classroom assignments appropriate for students' ability levels, and so on—tend to evoke productive behaviors. Furthermore, a general classroom climate in which students feel accepted and appreciated by teacher and classmates alike tends to bring out the best in almost everyone (more on this point in Chapter 9).

Sometimes teachers provide explicit reminders about desirable and undesirable behaviors—a strategy known as **cueing**. In some instances cueing involves a nonverbal signal, such as ringing a bell or flicking an overhead light switch to remind children to talk quietly rather than loudly. At other times it involves a verbal reminder, either direct or indirect, about what children should be doing—for example, "Remember to use your *indoor* voices as you talk" and "I see some art supplies that still need to be put away." Such statements are examples of the *retrieval cues* discussed in Chapter 2, although in this case they remind students about appropriate classroom behavior rather than about academic subject matter.

Make sure productive behaviors are reinforced and unproductive behaviors are *not* reinforced.

Teachers should be sure that desirable behaviors—reading frequently, constructing a well-researched science fair poster, working cooperatively with classmates, and so on—are regularly reinforced in some way. For reasons we'll explore in our discussion of motivation in Chapter 6, the best reinforcers are intrinsic ones, such as the pleasure one gets from reading, the pride one feels after accomplishing a challenging task, or the internal satisfaction one gains from helping others. But not all classroom tasks and activities can be intrinsically enjoyable and satisfying, and in such cases extrinsic reinforcers tailored to students' developmental levels and individual interests—stickers, special privileges, free time to engage in favorite activities, and so on—can keep students on task as they work to master important information and skills. And under certain conditions, positive feedback can be a very powerful reinforcer. The Classroom Strategies box "Using Feedback to Improve Learning and Behavior" offers several suggestions for maximizing feedback's effectiveness.

In some cases teachers can let students *choose* their reinforcers and perhaps even choose different reinforcers on different occasions.[70] One useful strategy is a **token economy**, in which students who exhibit desired behaviors receive *tokens* (e.g., poker chips or specially marked pieces of colored paper) that they can later use to "purchase" a variety of *backup reinforcers*—perhaps small treats, free time in the reading center, or a prime position in the lunch line. By and large, however, teachers should stay away from concrete

cueing Use of simple signals to indicate that a certain behavior is desired or that a certain behavior should stop.

token economy Classroom strategy in which desired behaviors are reinforced by tokens that the learner can use to "purchase" a variety of other backup reinforcers.

Observe many examples of cueing in the "Reading Group" video in Chapter 3 of the Book-Specific Resources in MyEducationLab.

Observe students' sense of pride (intrinsic reinforcement) regarding their research projects in the "Science Fair Projects" video in Chapter 3 of the Book-Specific Resources in MyEducationLab.

Today I had a soccer game to see who would go to the state finals. Unfortnly we lost. I was very dis apontated, not because we lost, but because my coach only put me in for 10 mins. I feel that the coach was ignoring me and was just focused on winning. I wish the coach would take notice of me on the side lines and not just focuse on winning.

In this journal entry, 11-year-old Amie reveals two consequences she finds reinforcing—playing soccer and gaining her coach's attention.

[70] Berg et al., 2007; Bowman, Piazza, Fisher, Hagopian, & Kogan, 1997; Fisher & Mazur, 1997.

CLASSROOM STRATEGIES Using Feedback to Improve Learning and Behavior

- **Be explicit about what students are doing well— ideally, at the time they are doing it.**

  When praising her students for appropriate classroom behavior, a second-grade teacher makes it quite clear which actions she is commending them for. For example, she says, "I like the way you're working quietly" and "You should see Ricky being so polite. Thank you, Ricky, for not disturbing the rest of the class." (This example is depicted in the "Reading Group" Video Example in Chapter 3 of the Book-Specific Resources in MyEducationLab.)

- **Give concrete guidance about how students can improve their performance.**

  A high school physical education teacher tells a student, "Your time in the 100-meter dash wasn't as fast as it could have been. It's early in the season, though, and if you work on your endurance, I know you'll improve. Also, I think you might get a faster start if you stay low when you first come out of the starting blocks."

- **Communicate optimism that students *can* improve.**

  When a student in a middle school geography class gives an oral report on Mexico, she bores her classmates with a lengthy description of her family's recent trip to Puerto Vallarta. Many students begin to communicate their displeasure through body language and occasional whispers across the aisle. At the end of class, the student is devastated that her report has been so poorly received. Her teacher takes her aside and gently says, "You included many interesting facts in your report, Julie, and your many pictures and artifacts really helped us understand Mexican culture. But you know how young teenagers are—they can have a pretty short attention span at times. I'll be assigning oral reports again next semester. Before you give yours, let's sit down and plan it so that your classmates will think, 'Wow, this is really interesting!' "

- **Don't overwhelm students with too much feedback; tell them only what they can reasonably attend to and remember at the time.**

  As a kindergarten teacher watches one of his students practice writing several alphabet letters, he helps the student hold her pencil in a way that gives her better control. He doesn't mention that she is writing her *B*s and *D*s backward; he will save this information for a later time, after she has mastered her pencil grip.

- **Minimize feedback when students already know exactly what they've done well or poorly.**

  A high school student has been getting poor grades in his math class largely as a result of insufficient effort. When he begins to buckle down and do his homework regularly, his quiz scores improve tremendously. As his teacher hands him his first quiz after his newfound diligence—a quiz on which he's earned a score of 96%—she says nothing, but she smiles and gives him a thumbs-up.

- **Teach students strategies for appropriately asking for teacher feedback.**

  A fourth-grade teacher has three students with intellectual disabilities in her class. She knows that these students may need more frequent feedback than their classmates. She teaches them three steps to take when they need her assistance: (1) They should raise their hands or walk quietly to her desk; (2) they should wait patiently until she has time to speak with them; and (3) they should make their needs known (e.g., "How am I doing?" "What do I do next?").

Sources: Bangert-Drowns, Kulik, Kulik, & Morgan, 1991; D. L. Butler & Winne, 1995; M. A. Craft, Alberg, & Heward, 1998, p. 402 (fourth-grade example); Feltz, Chase, Moritz, & Sullivan, 1999; Hattie & Timperley, 2007; K. A. Meyer, 1999; Pintrich & Schunk, 2002; Schunk & Pajares, 2005; Shute, 2008; Tunstall & Gipps, 1996.

Which form of reinforcement—continuous or intermittent—would you use to teach students to persist at difficult tasks? (Compare your response to this question with the response presented in Chapter 3 of the Book-Specific Resources in MyEducationLab.)

reinforcers such as small toys and trinkets, which can distract students' attention away from their schoolwork.

Regardless of the form reinforcement takes, *some* kind of reinforcer should follow desired behaviors. Otherwise, those behaviors might decrease and eventually disappear—a phenomenon known as **extinction**. Initially, to increase the frequency of a desired response, reinforcement should be *continuous*, occurring every time the response occurs. Once a student makes the response frequently, reinforcement can be *intermittent*—that is, given on some occasions but not others—so that the response doesn't extinguish.

Meanwhile, teachers must not inadvertently reinforce behaviors that will interfere with learners' success over the long run. For example, if a teacher repeatedly allows Carol to turn in assignments late because she says she forgot her homework, and if that teacher often lets Colin get his way by bullying classmates on the playground, the teacher is reinforcing (and hence increasing) Carol's excuse making and Colin's aggressiveness.

Make response–reinforcement contingencies clear.

Whenever teachers use reinforcement in the classroom, they should explicitly describe the cause–and–effect relationships, or **contingencies**, between responses and reinforcers. For example, kindergarten students are more likely to respond appropriately if they're told, "The quietest group will be first to get in line for lunch." Ninth graders are more likely to complete their Spanish assignments if they know that by doing so they'll be able to go on a field trip to a local Cinco de Mayo festival.

One way of explicitly communicating expectations for behavior and response–reinforcement contingencies is a **contingency contract**. To develop such a contract, the teacher meets with a student to discuss a problem behavior (e.g., talking to friends during independent seatwork or making rude comments to classmates). The teacher and student then identify and agree on desired behaviors that the student will demonstrate (e.g., completing seatwork assignments within a certain time frame; speaking with classmates in a friendly, respectful manner). The two also agree on one or more reinforcers that the student values (e.g., a certain amount of free time, or points earned toward a particular privilege or prize). Together the teacher and student write and sign a contract that describes the behaviors the student will perform and the reinforcers that will result. Contingency contracts can be a highly effective means of improving a wide variety of academic and social behaviors.[71]

Observe explicit response–reinforcement contingencies (e.g., "Thank you, Ricky, for not disturbing the rest of the class") in the "Reading Group" video in Chapter 3 of the Book-Specific Resources in MyEducationLab.

As an alternative to punishment, reinforce productive behaviors that are incompatible with unproductive ones.

As mentioned earlier, certain forms of punishment can be effective in reducing inappropriate behaviors, and in some instances punishment may be a teacher's only alternative (we'll look at the use of punishment more closely in Chapter 9). Oftentimes, however, rather than using punishment, a teacher can reduce the frequency of an unproductive behavior simply by reinforcing a *different* behavior. Ideally, the two behaviors are **incompatible behaviors**, in that they cannot be performed simultaneously. To discover examples of incompatible behaviors in your own life, try the following exercise.

SEE FOR YOURSELF   Asleep on Your Feet

Have you ever tried to sleep while standing up? Horses can do it, but most of us humans really can't. In fact, there are many pairs of responses that we can't possibly perform simultaneously. Take a minute to identify something you cannot possibly do when you perform each of these activities:

When you:	You cannot simultaneously:
Sit down	_____
Eat crackers	_____
Take a walk	_____

Obviously, there are many possible right answers in this exercise. For instance, you might have said that sitting is incompatible with standing, that eating crackers is incompatible with singing (or at least with singing *well*), and that taking a walk is incompatible with taking a nap. In each case it's physically impossible to perform both activities at exactly the same time.

To apply the concept of incompatible behaviors in the classroom, a teacher might, for example, reinforce a hyperactive student for sitting down, because sitting is incompatible with getting-out-of-seat and roaming-around-the-room behaviors. Similarly, a teacher might discourage off-task responses by reinforcing *on*-task responses or discourage verbally aggressive behavior by reinforcing socially appropriate actions. And consider how one school dealt with a chronic litterbug:

> Walt was a junior high school student who consistently left garbage (banana peels, sunflower seed shells, etc.) on the lunchroom floor, in school corridors, and on the playground. When the school faculty established an Anti-Litter Committee, it put

extinction Gradual disappearance of an acquired response; in the case of a response acquired through operant conditioning, it results from repeated lack of reinforcement for the response.

contingency Situation in which one event (e.g., reinforcement) happens only after another event (e.g., a specific response) has already occurred (one event is *contingent* on the other's occurrence).

contingency contract Written agreement between teacher and student that identifies behaviors the student will exhibit and the reinforcers that will follow.

incompatible behaviors Two or more behaviors that cannot be performed simultaneously.

---

[71] Brooke & Ruthren, 1984; D. L. Miller & Kelley, 1994; Rueger & Liberman, 1984; Welch, 1985.

Observe a special education teacher explicitly reinforce desired behaviors (including one behavior incompatible with students' previously inappropriate behaviors) in the "Incentive Systems for Academic Performance" video in Chapter 3 of the Book-Specific Resources in MyEducationLab.

Walt on the committee, and the committee eventually elected him as its chairman. Under Walt's leadership, the committee instituted a massive anti-litter campaign, complete with posters and lunchroom monitors, and Walt received considerable recognition for the campaign's success. Curiously (or perhaps not), school personnel no longer found Walt's garbage littering the school grounds.[72]

Model desired behaviors.

As we've seen, teachers teach not only by what they say but also by what they do. So it's critical that teachers model appropriate behaviors and *not* model inappropriate ones. Do they model enthusiasm and excitement about the subject matter or merely tolerance for a dreary topic the class must somehow muddle through? Do they model fairness to all students or favoritism to a small few? Do they expound on the virtues of innovation and creativity yet use the same curriculum materials year after year? Their actions often speak louder than their words.

Four conditions help students learn effectively from models:[73]

- **Attention.** Attention is critical for getting information into working memory (see Chapter 2). To learn effectively, then, students must pay attention to the model and especially to critical aspects of the modeled behavior.

- **Retention.** To learn from a model, the learner must remember what the model does—in particular, by storing it in long-term memory. Students are more likely to remember information if they encode it in more than one way, perhaps as both a visual image and a verbal message (again see Chapter 2). For instance, teachers might describe what they're doing while they demonstrate a particular skill. They might also attach descriptive labels to complex behaviors that could otherwise be difficult to remember.[74] For example, when teaching swimming, an easy way to help students remember the sequence of arm positions in the elementary backstroke is to teach them the labels *chicken, airplane,* and *soldier* (see Figure 3.5).

- **Motor reproduction.** In addition to attending and remembering, the learners must be physically able to reproduce the behavior they've observed. When students lack this ability, motor reproduction obviously can't occur; for example, kindergartners who watch a high school student throw a softball don't have the muscular coordination to mimic the throw. It's often useful to have students imitate a desired behavior immediately after they see it modeled. When they do so, their teachers can give them the feedback they need to improve their performance. Yet teachers must keep in mind a point made in the earlier Cultural Considerations box: Students from some ethnic groups may prefer to practice new behaviors in private at first and to demonstrate what they've learned only after they've achieved some degree of competence.

- **Motivation.** Finally, the learner must be motivated to demonstrate the modeled behavior. In Chapter 6 we'll identify numerous strategies for increasing students' motivation to exhibit the academic and social skills they learn in the classroom.

"Chicken" "Airplane" "Soldier"

FIGURE 3.5 Students can often more easily remember a complex behavior, such as the arm movements for the elementary backstroke, when those behaviors have verbal labels.

Provide a variety of role models.

In addition to modeling desired behaviors themselves, teachers should expose students to other models whom students are apt to perceive as competent and prestigious. For example, teachers might invite respected professionals (e.g., police officers, nurses, journalists) to demonstrate skills within particular areas of expertise. They might also have

[72] Krumboltz & Krumboltz, 1972.
[73] Bandura, 1986.

[74] Gerst, 1971; T. L. Rosenthal, Alford, & Rasp, 1972; Vintere et al., 2004.

students read about or observe positive role models in books, videos, and other media.

Furthermore, students can benefit from observing the final products of a model's efforts. Art students might gain useful strategies by studying the works of such masters as Vincent Van Gogh and Georges Seurat, and music students can acquire new strategies by listening to skillful musicians with diverse musical styles. In one seventh-grade language arts class, students found examples of figurative writing in favorite books (see Figure 3.6), and such examples served as models for their own writing efforts.

Recall that one of the characteristics of effective models listed earlier in the chapter was *behavior relevant to one's own situation.* Students are less likely to perceive a model's behaviors as relevant to their own circumstances if the model is different from them in some obvious way. For instance, students from a lower socioeconomic neighborhood or ethnic minority group won't necessarily see the actions of a middle-income European American as being useful for themselves. Similarly, students with disabilities may believe that they're incapable of accomplishing the things a nondisabled teacher demonstrates. So it's important that teachers include individuals from low-SES backgrounds and minority-group cultures, as well as individuals with disabilities, in the models they present to students. Such models can give students cause for optimism that they, too, can achieve lofty goals.[75]

"The blackness of the night came in, like snakes around the ankles."
—Caroline Cooney, *Wanted,* p. 176

"Flirtatious waves made passes at the primly pebbled beach."
—Lilian Jackson Braun, *The Cat Who Saw Stars,* p. 120

"Water boiled up white and frothy, like a milkshake."
—Lurlene McDaniel, *For Better, for Worse, Forever,* p. 60

"Solid rocket boosters suddenly belched forty-four million horsepower."
—Ben Mikaelsen, *Countdown,* p. 148

"I try to swallow the snowball in my throat."
—Laurie Halse Anderson, *Speak,* p. 72

FIGURE 3.6 Students in Barbara Dee's seventh-grade language arts class chose these models of effective figurative writing from books they were reading.

Shape complex behaviors gradually over time.

When dramatic changes are necessary, it's unreasonable to expect students to make them overnight. In such a situation, a process known as **shaping** is often effective. To shape a desired behavior, a teacher takes the following steps:

1. First reinforce any response that in some way resembles the desired behavior.
2. Then reinforce a response that more closely approximates the desired behavior (no longer reinforcing the previously reinforced response).
3. Then reinforce a response that resembles the desired behavior even more closely.
4. Continue reinforcing closer and closer approximations to the desired behavior.
5. Finally reinforce only the desired behavior.

Each response in the sequence is reinforced every time it occurs until the student exhibits it regularly. Only at that point does the teacher begin reinforcing a behavior that more closely approaches the desired behavior.

For example, imagine that a student, Bernadette, can't seem to sit still long enough to get much of anything done. Her teacher would ultimately like her to sit still for 20-minute periods. However, the teacher may first have to reinforce her for staying in her seat for just *2* minutes. As Bernadette makes progress, her teacher can gradually increase the sitting time required for reinforcement.

Shaping is often used to teach academic skills as well as appropriate classroom behaviors. For instance, kindergartners and first graders are taught to write their letters on wide-lined paper, and they're praised for well-formed letters whose bottoms rest on one line and whose tops touch a higher line. As children progress through the grade levels, the spaces between the lines become smaller, and teachers become fussier about how letters are formed. Most children begin to write consistently sized and carefully shaped letters with the benefit of only a lower line, and eventually they need no line at all. In Figure 3.7 you can see how my son Jeff's handwriting was gradually shaped from first to fourth grade. (The changing nature of the lines is an example of *scaffolding,* a concept we'll discuss in Chapter 5.)

In much the same way, teachers can (and often do) gradually shape students' ability to work independently on academic assignments. They begin by giving first graders structured

How might you use shaping to teach an 8-year-old to swing a baseball bat? How might you use it to teach an aggressive high school student to behave prosocially? (Compare your responses to these questions with the responses presented in Chapter 3 of the Book-Specific Resources in MyEducationLab.)

---

[75] Evans-Winters & Ivie, 2009; Kincheloe, 2009; Powers, Sowers, & Stevens, 1995.

shaping Process of reinforcing successively closer and closer approximations to a desired behavior.

Grade 1

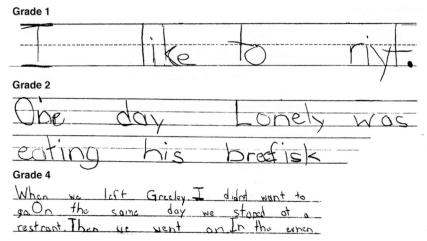

Grade 2

Grade 4

FIGURE 3.7 As Jeff moved through the elementary grades, gradual changes in his writing paper required him to write smaller and, eventually, with only a single line to guide him.

tasks that may take only 5 to 10 minutes to complete. As students move through the elementary school years, their teachers expect them to work independently for longer periods and begin to give them short assignments to do at home. By the time students reach high school, they have extended study halls and complete lengthy assignments on their own after school hours. In the college years, student assignments require a great deal of independence and self-direction.

Have students practice new behaviors and skills in a variety of contexts.

As noted earlier in the chapter, learning and cognition are sometimes *situated* in particular contexts. For instance, students may recall the Pythagorean theory *only* in a math class and neglect to use it when it might come in handy while building a tree house at home. And they may apply what they've learned about persuasive writing only in writing essays in a language arts class, rather than also using it to evaluate political campaign brochures and newspaper editorials. If teachers want students to use what they've learned in many situations both in and out of school, they should give students practice using the subject matter with a variety of stimulus materials and in many different contexts. We'll explore this idea further in our discussions of *transfer* and *authentic activities* in Chapter 4.

Providing Physical and Social Support for Effective Cognitive Processes

Environmental contexts, both past and present, affect not only students' behaviors but also their thinking processes, as reflected in the next three recommendations.

Provide physical and cognitive tools that can help students work and think more effectively.

When you think of tools, you're apt to think of physical objects: scissors, rulers, compasses, and so on. But keep in mind that many human tools—for instance, concepts, mathematical formulas, and study strategies—are entirely cognitive in nature. And still others—such as dictionaries, maps, and flowcharts—are both physical and cognitive, in that they are physical manifestations of concepts, formulas, thought processes, and other forms of human cognition. All of these tools can greatly enhance students' ability to make sense of school subject matter, solve problems, communicate with others, and, more generally, thrive and prosper.

In some cases teachers and students can work *together* to create effective tools for making better sense of classroom subject matter. For example, in the elementary grades a teacher and students might co-construct a timeline depicting forms of transportation during different time periods in history (see Figure 3.8).[76] In the secondary grades a teacher and students might collaboratively create two-dimensional charts to help them compare and contrast what they're learning about the climate, geography, and economic resources of various states or countries.

Encourage student dialogue and collaboration.

We've already identified numerous advantages to having learners talk with one another about classroom topics. And in fact, students *do* seem to make better sense of new ideas and experiences when they talk about these things with others. Accordingly, many theorists recommend that classroom dialogues be a regular feature of classroom instruction. For example, in a lesson on Nathaniel Hawthorne's *The Scarlet Letter,* high school English

Observe a high school class create a compare-and-contrast chart in the "Cause–Effect in Geography" video in Chapter 3 of the Book-Specific Resources in MyEducationLab.

---

[76] Brophy, Alleman, & Knighton, 2009.

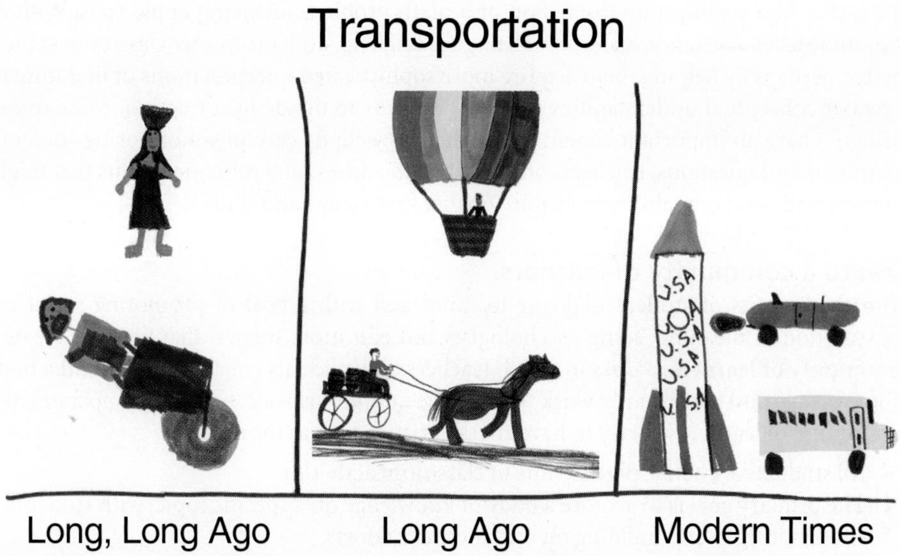

Transportation

Long, Long Ago   Long Ago   Modern Times

FIGURE 3.8 In this co-constructed timeline, a teacher provided the general framework, and two students created the drawings depicting modes of transportation during different periods in human history.

teacher Sue Southam wants students to construct an understanding of the character Arthur Dimmesdale. She reads a description of Dimmesdale in the novel and says:

> Jot down some of the important characteristics of that description. What's the diction that strikes you as being essential to understanding Dimmesdale's character? How do you see him? If you were going to draw a portrait of him, what would you make sure he had? . . . Just write some things, or draw a picture if you'd like.

Ms. Southam walks around the room, monitoring what students are doing until they appear to have finished writing. She then promotes the following discussion:

Ms. Southam: What pictures do you have in your minds of this man . . . if you were directing a film of *The Scarlet Letter*?

Mike: I don't have a person in mind, just characteristics. About five-foot-ten, short, well-groomed hair, well dressed. He looks really nervous and inexperienced. Guilty look on his face. Always nervous, shaking a lot.

Ms. Southam: He's got a guilty look on his face. His lips always trembling, always shaking.

Mike: He's very unsure about himself.

Matt: Sweating really bad. Always going like this. (He shows how Dimmesdale might be wiping his forehead.) He does . . . he has his hanky. . . .

Ms. Southam: Actually, we don't see him mopping his brow, but we do see him doing what? What's the action? Do you remember? If you go to the text, he's holding his hand over his heart, as though he's somehow suffering some pain.

Another student: Wire-framed glasses. . . . I don't know why. He's like. . . .

Mike: He's kind of like a nerd-type guy. . . . Short pants. . . .

Ms. Southam: But at the same time . . . I don't know if it was somebody in this class or somebody in another class . . . he said, "Well, she was sure *worth* it." Worth risking your immortal soul for, you know? . . . Obviously she's sinned, but so has he, right? And if she was worth it, don't we also have to see him as somehow having been worthy of her risking *her* soul for this?

By hearing such diverse ideas, students can gain an increasingly complex, multifaceted understanding of Dimmesdale that probably includes both verbal concepts (e.g., *unsure, nerd*) and visual images. (You'll see this dialogue again in Chapter 7 but at that point you'll look at it from a very different angle.)

In the lesson just presented, the teacher is actively involved in facilitating student discussion. Yet students can also co-construct understandings without teacher assistance, as we

Observe this class discussion in the "Scarlet Letter" video in Chapter 3 of the Book-Specific Resources in MyEducationLab.

saw earlier in a small-group discussion of a math problem involving apple tarts. With or without teacher assistance, classroom dialogues can help students master classroom subject matter, perhaps by helping them acquire more sophisticated interpretations of literature or a greater conceptual understanding of what it means to divide by a fraction.[77] Classroom dialogues have an important benefit for teachers as well: By carefully monitoring students' comments and questions, teachers can identify and address any misconceptions that might interfere with students' ability to acquire further knowledge and skills.[78]

Create a community of learners.

With the benefits of student dialogue in mind and with a goal of promoting social co-construction of meaning, some psychologists and educators suggest that teachers create a **community of learners**, a class in which teachers and students collaborate to build a body of knowledge and consistently work to help one another learn.[79] A class that operates as a community of learners is likely to have characteristics such as these:

- All students are active participants in classroom activities.
- The primary goal is to acquire a body of knowledge on a specific topic, with students contributing to and building on one another's efforts.
- Students draw on many resources—textbooks, magazines, the Internet, and one another—in their efforts to learn about the topic.
- Discussion and collaboration among two or more students are common occurrences and play a key role in learning.
- Diversity in students' interests and rates of progress is expected and respected.
- Students and teacher coordinate their efforts in helping one another learn; no one has exclusive responsibility for teaching others.
- Everyone is a potential resource for others; different individuals are likely to serve as resources on different occasions, depending on the topics and tasks at hand. In some cases individual students focus on particular topics and become local experts on them. Occasionally people outside the classroom share their expertise as well.
- The teacher provides some guidance and direction for classroom activities, but students also offer guidance and direction.
- Mechanisms are in place through which students can share what they've learned with others; students regularly critique one another's work.
- The process of learning is emphasized as much as, and sometimes more than, the finished product.

In one example of how a community of learners might be structured, students are divided into small groups to study different subtopics falling within a general theme. For instance, subtopics for the theme *changing populations* might be *extinct, endangered, artificial, assisted,* and *urbanized.* Each group conducts research and prepares teaching materials related to its subtopic. The class then reassembles into new groups that include at least one representative from each of the previous groups. Within these new groups students teach one another what they've learned.[80]

Another approach is to use a computer network to promote a community of learners.[81] In this electronic environment, students post their work (notes, short stories, reports, problem solutions, diagrams and flowcharts depicting scientific phenomena, etc.) as computer files that their classmates can read, react to, and possibly modify or build on. Students also interact in an ongoing computer-based chat room in which they present questions or issues to which their classmates respond. In the following online discussion, consider how three

---

community of learners Class in which teacher and students actively and collaboratively work to create a body of knowledge and help one another learn.

[77] E. H. Hiebert & Raphael, 1996; J. Hiebert et al., 1997; Lampert, Rittenhouse, & Crumbaugh, 1996; Murphy, Wilkinson, Soter, Hennessey, & Alexander, 2009; Schank & Abelson, 1995; C. L. Smith, 2007; Walshaw & Anthony, 2008.

[78] Presseisen & Beyer, 1994; Sosniak & Stodolsky, 1994.

[79] Bielaczyc & Collins, 2006; A. L. Brown & Campione, 1994; Campione, Shapiro, & Brown, 1995; A. Collins, 2006; Engle, 2006; Rogoff, Matusov, & White, 1996.

[80] A. L. Brown & Campione, 1994.

[81] Bereiter & Scardamalia, 2006; Scardamalia & Bereiter, 2006; G. Stahl, Koschmann, & Suthers, 2006; J. Zhang, Scardamalia, Reeve, & Messina, 2009.

students respond to another student's question, "How does heat affect solids?" Note that they use the headings "My theory" and "I need to understand" to structure their discussion:

JA: <u>My theory:</u> I think that heat makes solids burn or melt. I think that my prediction is right because I've seen solids melt and burn.

AR: <u>My theory:</u> I think that if a solid comes in contact with heat, it becomes hot. I also think it might change colour. Generally if any solid comes in contact with heat then it becomes hot. I think that the solid would become hot faster if it could conduct energy well. If an object didn't conduct energy well then it would heat up, but take a longer time than an object that conducts energy well. It might change colour because we think that if something is very hot it is white or red and sort of hot it is orange or yellow. There might be some truth to this.

AD: <u>My theory:</u> I think that it depends on how much heat there is. I also think that it depends on what sort of solid it is. For instance, the heat that might melt rubber might not melt metal. (This last sentence might be wrong, I'm just using it as an example.)

<u>I need to understand:</u> What makes wood burn instead of melt?

<u>My theory:</u> I think that it might have something to do with wood being organic, because I can't think of anything that is organic, and would melt.[82]

Such online discussions can be especially beneficial for students who are shy or for other reasons feel uncomfortable communicating with their classmates in a more public fashion.[83]

A classroom organized as a community of learners tends to be highly motivating for students and can promote fairly complex thinking processes for extended time periods.[84] In addition to its motivational and cognitive benefits, a community of learners can foster productive peer relationships and create a *sense of community* in the classroom—a sense that teachers and students have shared goals, are mutually respectful and supportive of one another's efforts, and believe that everyone makes an important contribution to classroom learning (more on this sense of community in Chapter 9).

A community of learners can be especially worthwhile when a classroom includes students from diverse cultural and socioeconomic backgrounds.[85] Such a community values the contributions of all students, using everyone's individual backgrounds, cultural perspectives, and unique abilities to enhance the overall performance of the class. It also provides a context in which students can form friendships across the lines of ethnicity, gender, socioeconomic status, and disability.

Yet we should note two potential weaknesses of communities of learners, as well as of group discussions in general.[86] For one thing, what students learn will inevitably be limited to the knowledge they personally acquire and share with one another. Second, students may occasionally pass their misconceptions on to classmates. Obviously, then, when teachers conduct classroom discussions or structure classrooms as communities of learners, they must carefully monitor student conversations to make sure that students ultimately acquire *accurate* understandings of the topic they're studying.

Taking into Account the Broader Contexts in Which Students Live

Students' learning and classroom achievement is influenced by what goes on *outside* as well as inside the classroom—by students' cultural groups, neighborhoods, and so on. The last set of recommendations reflects this idea.

Learn as much as you can about students' cultural backgrounds, and come to grips with your own cultural lens.

As people who grow up within a particular culture, we often interpret others' behaviors within the context of what our own culture deems to be appropriate and inappropriate, as you can see in the chapter's final exercise.

---

[82] Dialogue from Hewitt & Scardamalia, 1998, p. 85.

[83] Hewitt & Scardamalia, 1998.

[84] A. L. Brown & Campione, 1994; Engle, 2006; Engle & Conant, 2002; Rogoff, 1994; Scardamalia & Bereiter, 2006; Turkanis, 2001.

[85] Garcia, 1994; Kincheloe, 2009; Ladson-Billings, 1995b.

[86] A. L. Brown & Campione, 1994; Hynd, 1998b.

SEE FOR YOURSELF Jack

Imagine that you are a seventh-grade teacher in a Navajo school district in the American Southwest. One of your students, Jack, is a good-natured young man who enjoys school, works hard in his studies, and gets along well with his classmates. But Jack has been absent from school all week. In fact, he hasn't even been *home* all week. His family (which doesn't have a telephone) isn't sure exactly where he is but doesn't seem to be in any rush to find him.

A few days later, Jack's sister explains that her parents are now looking for Jack. "He went to see a movie with friends and never came home," she says. "If he was in trouble we would know. But now the family needs him to herd sheep tomorrow." It's spring—time for the family to plant crops and shear the sheep—and all family members need to help out.

The parents soon locate Jack but keep him home for several days to help irrigate the family's corn field. It's another week before he returns to school.[87]

With this information in mind, what might you conclude about Jack and his parents?

If you're a product of mainstream Western culture, you may have concluded that Jack and his parents don't place much value on formal education. If so, your conclusion was based on two widely held beliefs in your culture: (1) School should take priority over activities at home and elsewhere and (2) responsible parents insist that their children attend school. In reality, most Navajo children and adults fully recognize the importance of a good education. To truly understand what has transpired in Jack's family, we need to know a couple of things about Navajo culture. First, Navajos place high value on individual autonomy: People must respect others' right (even children's right) to make their own decisions.[88] From this perspective, good parenting doesn't mean demanding that children do certain things or behave in certain ways—thus, Jack's parents don't insist that he come home after the movie. Instead, Navajo parents offer suggestions and guidance that nudge children toward productive choices. If children make poor decisions despite their parents' guidance, they often learn a great deal from the consequences.

But in addition to individual autonomy, Navajos value cooperation and interdependence, believing that community members should work together for the common good. Even though Jack enjoys school, when he returns home his highest priority is helping his family. In the Navajo view, people must cooperate of their own free will; being forced to help others is not true cooperation at all. Such respect for both individual autonomy and cooperative interdependence is seen in certain other Native American cultures as well.[89]

When people act in accordance with beliefs, values, and social conventions very different from our own, it's all too easy for us to write them off as being "odd," "unmotivated," or "negligent." The assumptions and beliefs we've acquired in our own culture—perhaps including an assumption that good parents control their children's behaviors—are often integral parts of our own culturally based worldviews. As such, they're apt to be so pervasive in our lives that we tend to treat them as common sense, or even as facts, rather than as the beliefs they really are. These beliefs become a *cultural lens* through which we view events, and they may lead us to conclude—often unfairly—that other groups' practices are somehow irrational and inferior to our own.

Teachers can most effectively work with students from diverse backgrounds when they understand the fundamental assumptions and beliefs that underlie students' behavior—not only by reading about various cultures in books and journals and on Internet websites but also by participating in local community activities and conversing regularly with community members.[90] Furthermore, effective teachers are keenly aware that their own cultural

---

[87] Case described by Deyhle & LeCompte, 1999, pp. 127–128.
[88] Deyhle & LeCompte, 1999.

[89] Chisholm, 1996; Rogoff, 2003.
[90] Castagno & Brayboy, 2008; Moje & Hinchman, 2004; H. L. Smith, 1998.

beliefs are just that—*beliefs*. And they make a concerted effort *not* to pass judgment on cultural practices and beliefs very different from their own, but rather to try to understand why people of other cultural groups think and act as they do.[91]

Remember that membership in a particular cultural or ethnic group is not an either-or situation but, instead, a more-or-less phenomenon.

As noted earlier in the chapter, individuals vary considerably in how much they *participate* in various cultural and ethnic-group activities. The extent of their participation inevitably affects the strengths of their culture-specific behaviors and beliefs. For instance, some Mexican American students live in small, close-knit communities where Spanish is spoken and traditional Mexican practices and beliefs permeate everyday life, but others live in more culturally heterogeneous communities in which Mexican traditions are often cast aside. Likewise, some students who have recently emigrated from another country hold steadfastly to the customs and values of their homeland, whereas others eagerly adopt many customs and habits of their new school and community.[92]

Incorporate the perspectives and traditions of many cultures into the curriculum.

True **multicultural education** is not limited to cooking ethnic foods, celebrating Cinco de Mayo, or studying famous African Americans during Black History Month. Rather, it integrates the perspectives and experiences of numerous cultural groups throughout the curriculum and gives all students reason for pride in their cultural heritages.[93] Students from diverse backgrounds are more likely to be motivated to do well in school—and to *actually* do well there—when they perceive the school curriculum to be relevant to their own cultures.[94]

Teachers can incorporate content from diverse cultures into many aspects of the school curriculum. Following are examples:[95]

- In language arts, study the work of authors and poets from a variety of ethnic groups (e.g., study the lyrics of popular rap and hip-hop songs).
- In math, use mathematical principles to address multicultural tasks and problems (e.g., use geometry concepts to design a Navajo rug).
- In science, draw on students' experiences with the natural environment (e.g., relate biological concepts to their community's farming and hunting practices).
- In history, look at wars and other major events from diverse perspectives (e.g., the Native American perspective on the pioneers' westward migration in North America, the Spanish perspective on the Spanish–American War, the Japanese perspective on World War II).
- In both history and current events, consider such issues as discrimination and oppression.

Multicultural education involves learning about commonalities as well as differences.[96] For example, in the elementary grades students might learn that many cultural groups formally celebrate children's transition to adulthood—perhaps with *bar mitzvahs* and *bot mitzvahs* (for Jewish boys and girls), *quinceañeras* (for girls in certain Latin American cultures), or *Seijin no hi* (for 20-year-old Japanese youth). In the secondary grades students might examine issues that adolescents of all cultures face: gaining the respect of elders, forming trusting relationships with peers, and finding a meaningful place in society. One important goal of multicultural education should be to communicate that, underneath it all, people are more alike than different.

As students explore various cultures, teachers should also help them discover that diverse cultural groups have much to learn from one another. For example, students may be surprised to learn that several key practices underlying many democratic governments in Western nations—such as sending delegates to a central location to represent various

Learn what it's like for a Native American to study a strictly European American version of American history in the "Self-Concept Challenge" and "Genocide Impact" videos in Chapter 3 of the Book-Specific Resources in MyEducationLab.

[91] Banks et al., 2005; Brophy et al., 2009; Rogoff, 2003.
[92] Bornstein & Cote, 2010; S. M. Quintana et al., 2006.
[93] Banks & Banks, 1995; Hollins, 1996; Tatum, 1997.
[94] Brayboy & Searle, 2007; Moje & Hinchman, 2004; Tyler et al., 2008.
[95] Alim, 2007; J. M. Hughes, Bigler, & Levy, 2007; NCSS Task Force on Ethnic Studies Curriculum Guidelines, 1992; Nelson-Barber & Estrin, 1995; K. Schultz, Buck, & Niesz, 2000.
[96] Brophy et al., 2009; Ramsey, 1987; Ulichny, 1996.

multicultural education Instruction that integrates perspectives and experiences of numerous cultural groups throughout the curriculum.

groups, allowing only one person in a governing council to speak at a time, and keeping government and military bodies separate—were adopted from Native American governing practices (those of the Iroquois League) in the 1700s.[97]

Fostering appreciation for diverse perspectives doesn't necessarily mean portraying all cultural practices as equally acceptable, however. Rather, it means that teachers and students should try to understand another cultural group's behaviors within the context of that group's beliefs and assumptions. Teachers must certainly not embrace a culture that blatantly violates some people's basic human rights.

Be sensitive to cultural differences in behaviors and beliefs, and accommodate them as much as possible.

If students are to be successful at school and in mainstream Western culture, their teachers must gently and patiently encourage certain behaviors—being punctual, working independently, and so on—that will make such success possible. Yet many cultural differences in behavior are simply that—*differences*—and have no adverse effect on students' short- and long-term achievement. In fact, using strategies consistent with students' accustomed ways of learning and behaving—an approach known as **culturally responsive teaching**—can enhance students' academic performance and sense of well-being in the classroom. For example, if students' cultures stress the importance of cooperation with others, teachers should make frequent use of cooperative group activities.[98] And if students' home environments are high-energy ones in which several activities may take place simultaneously—as is sometimes true in African American and Hispanic families—teachers might create a similarly high-energy, multi-activity classroom environment.[99] Even the simple act of looking students in the eye—or not—can make a significant difference, as one teacher revealed in the following anecdote:

> A teacher [described a Native American] student who would never say a word, nor even answer when she greeted him. Then one day when he came in she looked in the other direction and said, "Hello, Jimmy." He answered enthusiastically, "Why hello Miss Jacobs." She found that he would always talk if she looked at a book or at the wall, but when she looked at him, he appeared frightened.[100]

Culturally responsive teaching means taking students' worldviews into account as well. For example, when discussing topics such as ecology and global climate change with Native American students, science teachers can build on a widely shared Native American conviction that people should try to live in harmony with nature rather than to control it.[101] And when discussing evolution with students whose religious beliefs include a belief in the divine creation of humankind, the goal might be to help students *understand* (rather than *accept)* scientists' explanations and lines of reasoning.[102]

Work hard to break down rigid stereotypes of particular cultural and ethnic groups.

Although teachers and students should certainly be sensitive to real differences among people from various backgrounds, it is counterproductive to hold a **stereotype**—a rigid, simplistic, and inevitably inaccurate caricature—of any particular group. Sometimes students acquire stereotypes from the prejudicial remarks and practices of friends or family members.[103] In other cases stereotypes appear in curriculum materials and classroom instruction—as happens, for instance, when American children role-play the first Thanksgiving by dressing up in paper-bag "leather" vests, painting their faces, and wearing feathers on their heads.[104] And in many instances students simply have little or no experience with a cultural group very different from their own.

When left uncorrected, students' stereotypes can lead to overtly discriminatory and malicious behaviors against others—ethnic jokes, racial taunts, social exclusion, and so

Jim Carter/Photo Researchers

In some cultures (e.g., in many Native American communities), children are taught to look down as a sign of respect to an adult who speaks to them.

culturally responsive teaching Use of instructional strategies consistent with students' culturally preferred ways of learning and behaving.

stereotype Rigid, simplistic, and erroneous view of a particular group of people.

[97] Rogoff, 2003; Weatherford, 1988.
[98] Castagno & Brayboy, 2008; Ladson-Billings, 1995a.
[99] Tyler et al., 2008.
[100] Gilliland, 1988, p. 26.
[101] Atran, Medin, & Ross, 2005.
[102] E. M. Evans, 2001; Southerland & Sinatra, 2003.
[103] Branch, 1999; Nesdale, Maass, Durkin, & Griffiths, 2005.
[104] Bigler & Liben, 2007; Brayboy & Searle, 2007.

CLASSROOM STRATEGIES Addressing Students' Stereotypes and Prejudices

- **Use curriculum materials that represent all cultures and ethnic groups as competent, legitimate participants in mainstream society, rather than as exotic curiosities who live in a separate world.**

  A history teacher peruses a history textbook to make sure that it portrays members of all ethnic groups in a nonstereotypical manner. He supplements the text with readings that highlight the important roles that members of various ethnic groups have played in history.

- **Assign literature depicting peers from diverse cultural backgrounds.**

  As part of a research project in England, several elementary school teachers read to their students a series of stories depicting close friendships between English children and refugees from other countries. Following this experimental intervention, the students express more positive attitudes toward refugee children than do control-group students who have not heard the stories.

- **Conduct class discussions about prejudice and racism that exist in the school and local community.**

  A middle school in a suburban community creates a number of mixed-race focus groups in which students regularly convene to share their views about interracial relations at the school. Although some students of European American ancestry initially feel uncomfortable talking about this topic with their minority-group peers, once the ice has been broken, greater cross-cultural understanding and communication are the long-term results.

- **Expose students to successful role models from various ethnic backgrounds.**

  A teacher invites several successful professionals from minority groups to speak with her class about their careers. When some students seem especially interested in one or more of these careers, she arranges for the students to spend time with the professionals in their workplaces.

- **Assign small-group cooperative projects in which students from diverse backgrounds must combine their unique talents to achieve a common goal.**

  A fourth-grade teacher has small cooperative groups design and conduct schoolwide surveys soliciting other students' opinions on various topics (e.g., ideas for school fundraisers, preferences for cafeteria menu items). The teacher intentionally creates groups that are heterogeneous in cultural background, knowing that the group members will draw on diverse friendship networks in seeking volunteers to take the surveys. In addition, he makes sure that every member of a group has something unique to offer in survey design or results tabulation—perhaps knowledge of word processing software, artistic talent, or math skills.

- **Emphasize that individual members of any single group are often very different from one another in their behaviors, beliefs, and values.**

  In a geography unit on major world religions, a middle school teacher regularly points out that members of any single religion often have very different customs. "For example," he says, "some Muslim women dress in much the same way that women in this country do; others wear head scarves along with regular, modern clothes; and still others dress in a burqa that covers everything except their hands and shoes. Usually the women wear a scarf or burqa to show modesty about their bodies. In fact, some Jewish women also wear head scarves as a sign of modesty, but many others don't."

Sources: Banks, 1994; Barbarin, Mercado, & Jigjidsuren, 2010; Boutte & McCormick, 1992; L. Cameron, Rutland, Brown, & Douch, 2006 (refugee stories example); Dovidio & Gaertner, 1999; Gutiérrez & Rogoff, 2003; Ladson-Billings, 1994b; O. Lee, 1999; Oskamp, 2000; Pang, 1995; J. H. Pfeifer et al., 2007; Ramsey, 1995; Schultz, Buck, & Niesz, 2000 (focus groups example); Tatum, 1997.

on—that can affect the victims' physical and mental health.[105] Teachers must work hard—sometimes *very* hard—to correct students' inaccurate and demeaning cultural and ethnic stereotypes, and they must vigorously address any acts of prejudice and discrimination witnessed in the classroom and elsewhere. The Classroom Strategies box "Addressing Students' Stereotypes and Prejudices" suggests several concrete strategies.

Multicultural understanding also comes from interacting regularly and productively with people from diverse cultural, ethnic, and racial groups. When students from diverse groups interact regularly—and especially when they come together as equals, work toward common goals, and see themselves as members of the same "team"—they are more apt to accept and, better still, *value* one another's differences.[106] In my discussion of peer relationships in Chapter 7, I suggest several strategies for promoting productive interactions and friendships among students from diverse backgrounds. By learning to appreciate multicultural differences within a single classroom, students take an important step toward appreciating the multicultural nature of the world at large.

[105] Allison, 1998; G. H. Brody et al., 2006; Killen, 2007; Pfeifer, Brown, & Juvonen, 2007; Sirin & Ryce, 2010.

[106] Dovidio & Gaertner, 1999; Oskamp, 2000; J. H. Pfeifer, Brown, & Juvonen, 2007.

Identify and, if possible, provide missing resources and experiences important for successful learning.

Some students from very poor families lack basic essentials—nutritious meals, warm clothing, adequate health care, school supplies, and so on—that will be important for their school success. Many government programs and community agencies can help to provide such essentials. School districts offer free and reduced-cost meal programs for children from low-income families. Charitable organizations often distribute warm winter jackets gathered from annual clothing drives. Many communities have low-cost health clinics. And some office supply stores and large discount chains donate notebooks, pens, and other school supplies to children who need them. Indeed, most communities provide a variety of resources for children and adolescents who have limited financial means.

In addition to connecting low-income students and families with community resources, teachers should identify any basic experiences that students may not have had. Field trips to zoos, aquariums, natural history museums, farms, the mountains, or the ocean may be in order. And, of course, teachers should identify and teach any basic skills that, for whatever reason, students haven't yet acquired. When teachers do so, they're likely to see significant improvements in students' classroom performance.[107]

Yet teachers must also remember that students who have grown up in poverty may, in some respects, have more knowledge and skills than their economically more advantaged peers (see Chapter 2). Such knowledge and skills can often provide a basis for teaching classroom subject matter. Furthermore, students who are willing to talk about the challenges they've faced can sensitize their classmates to the serious inequities that currently exist in their society. In general, research gives us cause for optimism that students from low-income backgrounds can achieve at high levels if their teachers are committed to helping them do so and give them a strong academic program that supports their learning efforts.[108]

---

[107] S. A. Griffin, Case, & Capodilupo, 1995; McLoyd, 1998; G. Phillips, McNaughton, & MacDonald, 2004; Siegler, 2009.

[108] Becker & Luthar, 2002; Goldenberg, 2001; G. Phillips et al., 2004.

SUMMARY

Our focus in this chapter has been on the many contexts that shape human beings' learning and development. The Mega-Ideas presented at the beginning of the chapter sum up much of the chapter's content, and so we return to them now.

● *Learners' past and present environments influence how learners behave and think at any given time.* Human learning takes places within many contexts that operate at a variety of levels. Learners' most local and immediate learning contexts consist of the stimuli that are present in the here–and–now—both stimuli that elicit certain behaviors and stimuli that serve as consequences of learners' behaviors. Some especially influential stimuli are the people in learners' lives who model various ways of performing and thinking about everyday tasks.

Learners acquire knowledge and skills not only from the things that environmental events and other people do *to* or *for* them but also from the things that other people do *with* them. Learners often co-construct knowledge with other people, sometimes with adults and other more experienced individuals and sometimes with peers whose ability levels equal their own. Social interaction has many benefits. For instance, it introduces learners to ways in which their culture interprets and responds to everyday experiences and problems, and it encourages learners to elaborate on prior knowledge and examine existing beliefs for possible gaps in understanding.

● *The general social contexts in which learners grow up—families and communities and, more broadly, cultures and societies—also influence learners' behaviors and cognitive processes.* Culture is a largely human phenomenon that defines appropriate and inappropriate behaviors and beliefs and enables the transmission of knowledge and skills from one generation to the next. Any culture bestows innumerable physical and cognitive tools that help learners survive and thrive in their physical and social worlds. Inconsistencies between cultures at home and at school can wreak havoc with school success, however, and teachers must bring the two contexts into alignment to the extent possible.

The society within which learners live is yet another context that can affect learning either directly or indirectly—for instance, through government policies that mandate certain instructional practices and through community institutions and agencies that offer learning opportunities and support services. Yet not everyone has equal access to the resources that a society has to offer. For instance, many students in lower socioeconomic families and neighborhoods have substandard housing, poor health care, and low-quality schools—factors that in one way or another can negatively impact students' long-term academic and social success.

● *Not only does the environment affect learners and their learning, but so, too, do learners influence their environment.* Learners' characteristics and behaviors affect the consequences they experience, the ways in which other people treat them, and the resources to which they have access. And especially as they get older and more independent, learners may actively seek out environments that are a good match with their existing characteristics and behaviors. Such niche-picking tends to increase existing differences among learners.

- *Effective teachers create a classroom environment that encourages and supports productive behaviors and ways of thinking.* Teachers can do many things to create supportive learning contexts for students. For instance, they can make sure that productive behaviors lead to desirable consequences (reinforcement) and that counterproductive ones do not. They can provide role models to illustrate effective ways of dealing with academic and social tasks. They can teach concepts, mental strategies, problem-solving procedures, and other cognitive tools that help students think about and respond to everyday situations and problems effectively. And they can conduct dialogues and cooperative activities that enable students to learn from one another.

- *Effective teachers adapt instruction to the particular social and cultural contexts in which students live.* Teachers can better promote students' learning and development when they understand and accommodate students' culture-specific behaviors and beliefs. And by providing a truly *multicultural* education—one that incorporates the perspectives and experiences of numerous cultural and ethnic groups into the curriculum—and working hard to break down inaccurate stereotypes of particular groups, teachers can better equip students for participating in a multicultural world.

PRACTICE FOR YOUR LICENSURE EXAM

Adam

Thirteen-year-old Adam seems to cause problems wherever he goes. In his sixth-grade classroom he is rude and defiant. On a typical school day, he comes to class late, slouches in his seat, rests his feet on his desk, yells obscenities at classmates and his teacher, and stubbornly refuses to participate in classroom activities. Not surprisingly, his grades are very low, just as they have been for most of his school career.

Away from his teacher's watchful eye, Adam's behavior is even worse. He shoves and pushes students in the hall, steals lunches from smaller boys in the cafeteria, and frequently initiates physical fights on the school grounds.

For obvious reasons, no one at school likes Adam very much. His classmates say he's a bully, and their parents describe him as a "bad apple," rotten to the core. Even his teacher, who tries to find the best in all of her students, has seen few redeeming qualities in Adam and is beginning to write him off as a lost cause.

Adam doesn't seem to be bothered by the hostile feelings he generates. Already he's counting the days until he can legally drop out of school.

1. Constructed-response question

Adam is the type of student whom educators often refer to as a *student at risk:* He has a high probability of failing to acquire the minimal academic skills he will need to be successful in the adult world.

   A. It is entirely possible that factors in his home and neighborhood are encouraging Adam's inappropriate behaviors. Yet factors at school may also be contributing to these behaviors. Drawing from concepts and principles of learning related to *operant conditioning,* identify two possible school-based causes for Adam's behaviors at school.

   B. Again drawing on operant conditioning concepts and principles, describe two different strategies you might use to help Adam develop more appropriate and productive behaviors.

2. Multiple-choice question

Social cognitive theorists suggest that learning environments are ultimately the result of *reciprocal causation.* Which one of the following alternatives best reflects this concept?

   a. Adam's defiant behaviors may be his way of escaping assignments he doesn't think he can complete successfully.

   b. Adam's behaviors alienate his teacher, whose subsequent actions reduce his learning opportunities and class performance.

   c. One of Adam's classmates decides that aggression is appropriate classroom behavior and acts accordingly.

   d. Many parents complain to the principal that Adam is adversely affecting the quality of their children's education.

Go to Chapter 3 of the Book-Specific Resources in MyEducationLab and click on "Practice for Your Licensure Exam" to answer these questions. Compare your responses with the feedback provided.

PEARSON myeducationlab™

Go to the Topics "Behaviorist Perspectives," "Social Cognitive Perspectives," and "Student Diversity" in the MyEducationLab (www.myeducationlab.com) for your course, where you can:

- Find learning outcomes for "Behaviorist Perspectives," "Social Cognitive Perspectives," and "Student Diversity," along with the national standards that connect to these outcomes.
- Complete Assignments and Activities that can help you more deeply understand the chapter content.
- Apply and practice your understanding of the core teaching skills identified in the chapter with the Building Teaching Skills and Dispositions learning units.
- Examine challenging situations and cases presented in the IRIS Center Resources.
- Access video clips of CCSSO National Teachers of the Year award winners responding to the question, "Why Do I Teach?" in the Teacher Talk section.

- Check your comprehension of the content covered in the chapter by going to the Study Plan in the Book Resources for your text. Here you will be able to take a chapter quiz, receive feedback on your answers, and then access Review, Practice, and Enrichment activities to enhance your understanding of chapter content. Flashcards are also available to help you study definitions and key terms.
- Access additional Book Resources, including:
  - Focus Questions to guide your reading, Video Examples of various concepts and principles presented in the chapter, a Practice for Your Licensure Exam exercise that resembles the kinds of questions appearing on many teacher licensure tests, Margin Note Questions that help you connect chapter content to your past experiences or current beliefs, and Supplementary Readings that enable you to pursue certain topics in greater depth.

Chapter

4

Complex Cognitive Processes

Shutterstock

CHAPTER OUTLINE

Case Study: Taking Over

Metacognition

Self-Regulation

Transfer

Problem Solving and Creativity

Critical Thinking

Promoting Complex Cognitive Processes
    Promoting Specific Processes
    Promoting Complex Processes in General

Summary

Practice for Your Licensure Exam: Interview with Emily

MEGA-IDEAS TO MASTER IN THIS CHAPTER

Effective learners regularly reflect on, take charge of, and strive to improve their learning efforts.

Learners often don't use the specific facts they learn at school, but they might apply the general conceptual understandings, learning strategies, and attitudes they acquire to a wide range of circumstances.

Learners are more effective problem solvers and more creative thinkers if they know the subject matter well and can think flexibly about the task at hand.

Critical thinking requires both a sophisticated understanding of the nature of knowledge and a general willingness to question the accuracy and worth of new information and ideas.

Effective teachers consistently encourage complex cognitive processes within the context of teaching academic subject matter.

CASE STUDY Taking Over

When an eighth-grade math teacher goes on maternity leave midway through the school year, substitute teacher Ms. Gaunt takes over her classes. Ms. Gaunt knows that, in accordance with Massachusetts state standards, her students should master numerous mathematical concepts and procedures, including working with exponents and irrational numbers, graphing linear equations, and applying the Pythagorean theorem. Yet many students haven't yet mastered more basic concepts and operations. Some think that any positive number less than one (e.g., a decimal such as 0.15) is a negative number. Some don't understand percentages. Some can't do long division. A few haven't even learned basic number facts.

Before long, Ms. Gaunt discovers that many students have beliefs and attitudes that also impede their learning progress. For instance, some think that a teacher's job is to present material in such a way that they "get it" immediately and will remember it forever. Thus they neither work hard to understand the material nor take notes during her explanations. And most students are concerned only with getting the right answer as quickly as possible. They depend on calculators to do their mathematical thinking for them and complain when Ms. Gaunt insists that they solve a problem with pencil and paper rather than a calculator. Students rarely check to see whether their solutions

make logical sense. For instance, in a problem such as this one:

> Louis can type 35 words a minute. He needs to type a final copy of his English composition, which is 4,200 words long. How long will it take Louis to type his paper?

a student might submit an answer of 147,000 minutes—an answer that translates into more than 100 days of around-the-clock typing—and not give the outlandishness of the solution a second thought. (It would actually take Louis two hours to type the paper.)

By mid-April, with the statewide mathematics competency exam looming on the horizon, Ms. Gaunt begins moving through lessons more rapidly so that she can cover the mandated eighth-grade math curriculum by the end of the school year. "Students can't do well on the exam if they haven't even been exposed to some of the required concepts and procedures," she reasons. "Mastery probably isn't possible at this point, but I should at least *present* what students need to know. Maybe this will help a few of them with some of the test items."[1]

- Why are the students having difficulty mastering what the state of Massachusetts considers to be an eighth-grade math curriculum? Can you identify at least three different factors that appear to be interfering with students' learning?

---

[1] I thank a friend, who must remain anonymous, for sharing this case with me.

One factor, of course, is students' lack of prerequisite knowledge and skills on which the eighth-grade curriculum depends. For instance, if students haven't learned basic number facts—let alone achieved automaticity for them—even fairly simple word problems may exceed their working memory capacity. But students' beliefs about learning and problem solving are also coming into play. In their minds, learning should come quickly and easily if the teacher does her job. They seem not to understand that understanding classroom subject matter is an active, constructive process involving considerable effort on their part and that certain strategies (e.g., taking notes) can enhance their learning. And they view mathematical problem solving as a quick, mindless enterprise that involves plugging numbers into a calculator and writing down the result, rather than a step-by-step process that requires logical reasoning and frequent self-checking.[2]

Study skills and problem solving are examples of **complex cognitive processes**, processes in which learners go far beyond the specific information they're studying, perhaps to apply it to a new situation, use it to solve a problem or create a product, or critically evaluate it. Mastering basic facts and skills is important, to be sure. But learners gain little if they cannot also *do something* with what they've learned.

In this chapter we'll look at a variety of complex cognitive processes, including self-regulation, transfer, problem solving, creativity, and critical thinking. But we'll begin with a particular set of complex processes that in one way or another influence all of the others: metacognition.

• Metacognition

The term **metacognition** literally means "thinking about thinking." It includes learners' knowledge and beliefs about their own cognitive processes, as well as their conscious attempts to engage in behaviors and thought processes that increase learning and memory. For example, metacognition includes

- Reflecting on the general nature of thinking and learning
- Knowing the limits of one's own learning and memory capabilities
- Knowing what learning tasks can realistically be accomplished within a certain time period
- Planning a reasonable approach to a learning task
- Applying effective strategies to learn and remember new material
- Reflecting on previous learning efforts—for instance, recognizing when one has or has not successfully learned something

As an illustration, you have undoubtedly learned by now that you can acquire only so much information so fast—you can't possibly absorb the contents of an entire textbook in an hour. You have also discovered that you can learn information more quickly and recall it more easily if you put it into some sort of organizational framework. And perhaps you've taken to heart one of my recommendations in Chapter 1: You periodically check yourself to make sure you remember and understand what you've read.

The more learners know about thinking and learning—the greater their metacognitive awareness—the better their learning and academic achievement will be.[3] Following are four general principles that characterize metacognition in children and adolescents.

Some effective study strategies are readily apparent in learners' behaviors.

Some study strategies are **overt strategies**—ones we can easily see in learners' behaviors. For instance, effective learners allocate specific times to study, and they find a quiet place to do their work. When they have to learn and remember a large body of information—say, for a major exam—they may spread their study sessions over several days or weeks.

Another easily observable study strategy is taking notes. In general, learners who take more notes learn and remember more. The *quality* of the notes is equally important: Good

---

complex cognitive process Cognitive process that involves going well beyond information specifically learned (e.g., by analyzing, applying, or evaluating it).

metacognition Knowledge and beliefs about one's own cognitive processes, as well as conscious attempts to engage in behaviors and thought processes that increase learning and memory.

overt strategy Learning strategy that is at least partially evident in the learner's behavior (e.g., taking notes during a lecture).

---

[2] Such beliefs about mathematics are common; see Muis, 2004.

[3] L. Baker, 1989; Hofer & Pintrich, 2002; Meltzer, 2007; D. N. Perkins, 1995.

notes reflect the main ideas of a lesson or reading assignment.[4] Figure 4.1 shows two sets of notes about King Midas taken during a seventh-grade language arts lesson on Greek mythology. Both sets were taken using a note-taking form the teacher provided. Neither set is complete, but the notes on the left should help the student recall the key characters and general plot of the King Midas story. In contrast, the notes on the right are so sketchy that the student who took them may have difficulty recalling or reconstructing the story.

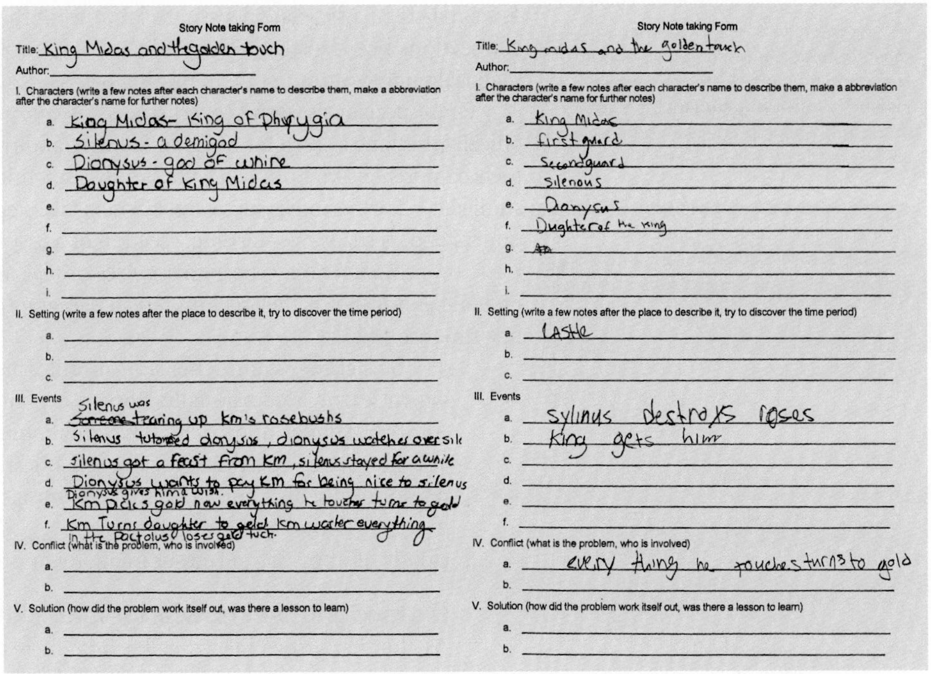

Story Note taking Form

Title: King Midas and the golden touch

Author:

I. Characters (write a few notes after each character's name to describe them, make a abbreviation after the character's name for further notes)

a. King Midas- King of Phrygia
b. Silenus - a demigod
c. Dionysus - god of whine
d. Daughter of King Midas
e.
f.
g.
h.
i.

II. Setting (write a few notes after the place to describe it, try to discover the time period)

a.
b.
c.

III. Events

a. ~~Someone~~ Silenus was tearing up km's rosebushs
b. Silenus tutored dionysus, dionysus watches over silk
c. silenus got a feast from km, silenus stayed for a while
d. Dionysus wants to pay km for being nice to silenus Dionysus gives him a wish.
e. km picks gold now everything he touches turns to gold
f. Km Turns daughter to gold km washes everything in the Pactolus loses gold tuch.

IV. Conflict (what is the problem, who is involved)

a.
b.

V. Solution (how did the problem work itself out, was there a lesson to learn)

a.
b.

Story Note taking Form

Title: King midas and the golden touch

Author:

I. Characters (write a few notes after each character's name to describe them, make a abbreviation after the character's name for further notes)

a. King Midas
b. first guard
c. Second guard
d. Silenous
e. Dionysus
f. Dughter of the king
g.
h.
i.

II. Setting (write a few notes after the place to describe it, try to discover the time period)

a. CAStle
b.
c.

III. Events

a. sylinus destroys roses
b. King gets him
c.
d.
e.
f.

IV. Conflict (what is the problem, who is involved)

a. every thing he touches turns to gold
b.

V. Solution (how did the problem work itself out, was there a lesson to learn)

a.
b.

FIGURE 4.1 Good class notes involve both quantity and quality, as seen in the notes on the left but not those on the right. Both sets were taken during a seventh-grade lesson on Greek mythology.

Still another effective overt strategy is organizing information in an explicit, concrete manner.[5] One useful way of organizing information is *outlining* the material, which may be especially helpful for low-achieving students.[6] Another approach is to create a **concept map**, a diagram that depicts the concepts of a unit and their interrelationships.[7] Figure 4.2 shows concept maps that two fifth graders constructed after watching a slide lecture on Australia. The concepts themselves are in circles, and interrelationships among them are indicated by lines with words or short phrases. As is true for class notes, both quantity and quality affect the usefulness of concept maps. The two maps in Figure 4.2 show considerable differences in depth and organization of knowledge about Australia. Furthermore, the top map has a few errors (e.g., Adelaide is *not* part of Melbourne; it's a different city altogether). If geographic knowledge about Australia is an important instructional goal, then this student clearly needs further instruction to correct such misconceptions.

Even more important than observable study behaviors are the cognitive processes that underlie them.

Such strategies as taking notes and constructing concept maps are effective, in large part, because they require effective cognitive processes, including many of those described in Chapter 2.[8] For example, to take notes, learners must *pay attention* to and *encode* information, thus facilitating effective storage in memory. To construct a concept map, learners must focus on how key concepts relate to one another and to things they already know, and so they must engage in *meaningful learning*. Both class notes and concept maps also provide a means through which learners encode information visually (i.e., forming *visual images)* as well as verbally. It is probably such **covert strategies**—mental strategies we can't directly see—that are ultimately responsible for successful learning.[9]

Oftentimes effective learners engage in study strategies that aren't evident in their observable behaviors. For instance, they may try to identify main ideas in what they're reading.[10]

[4] A. L. Brown, Campione, & Day, 1981; Kiewra, 1985; Peverly, Brobst, Graham, & Shaw, 2003.

[5] Hattie, 2009; M. A. McDaniel & Einstein, 1989; Mintzes, Wandersee, & Novak, 1997; Nesbit & Adesope, 2006.

[6] L. Baker, 1989; M. A. McDaniel & Einstein, 1989; Wade, 1992.

[7] Nesbit & Adesope, 2006; Novak, 1998; Novak & Gowin, 1984.

[8] Di Vesta & Gray, 1972; Holley & Dansereau, 1984; Katayama & Robinson, 2000; Kiewra, 1989; Rawson & Kintsch, 2005.

[9] Berthold & Renkl, 2009; Kardash & Amlund, 1991.

[10] Afflerbach & Cho, 2010; Dee-Lucas & Larkin, 1991; Dole, Duffy, Roehler, & Pearson, 1991.

concept map Diagram of concepts and their interrelationships; used to enhance learning and memory of a topic.

covert strategy Learning strategy that is strictly mental (rather than behavioral) in nature and thus cannot be observed by others.

◆◆ As you read a textbook, when is the information in working memory? in long-term memory? With your answers in mind, explain why students should monitor their comprehension both as they read and also at a later time. (Compare your response to this question with the response presented in Chapter 4 of the Book-Specific Resources in MyEducationLab.)

They may regularly relate new material to what they already know, perhaps finding logical connections between the "new" and the "old," or perhaps asking themselves whether new material might contradict their existing beliefs.[11]

One especially powerful covert strategy is **comprehension monitoring**, a process of periodically checking oneself for recall and understanding. Successful learners continually monitor their comprehension both *while* they study something and at one or more times *after* they've studied it.[12] Furthermore, successful learners take steps to correct the situation when they *don't* understand, perhaps by rereading a section of a textbook or asking a question in class. In contrast, low achievers rarely check themselves or take appropriate actions when they don't comprehend. For instance, they seldom reread paragraphs they haven't completely understood the first time around.[13]

Sometimes comprehension monitoring takes the form of *self-explanation*, in which learners occasionally stop to explain to themselves what they've learned.[14] Another, similar approach is *self-questioning*, in which learners regularly stop and ask themselves questions. Ideally, self-questions include not only simple, fact-based questions but also questions that encourage elaboration (e.g., "What might happen if _____?" "How is _____ different from _____?").[15] Yet another strategy is *summarizing* a body of information, either mentally or on paper.[16]

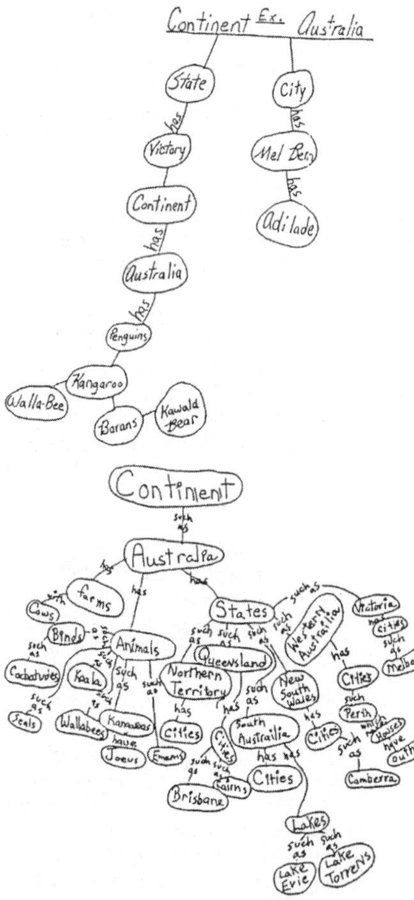

Metacognitive knowledge and skills gradually improve with age.

As children grow older, they become increasingly aware of their own thinking and learning processes and increasingly realistic about what they can learn and remember in a given time period (see Table 4.1). With this growing self-awareness come more effective study strategies.

Truly effective strategies emerge quite slowly, however, especially if young learners don't get guidance from teachers, parents, or other adults about how to study.[17] For instance, unless specifically instructed to take notes, many young adolescents take few or no notes to help them remember class material. Even when they *do* take notes, they often have trouble identifying the most important information to learn in a lesson or reading assignment. Typically, children and adolescents zero in on superficial characteristics, such as what a teacher writes on the board or what a textbook author puts in *italics* or **boldface**.[18] In the following excerpts from interviews conducted by students in my own educational psychology classes, Annie (a fifth grader) and Damon (an eighth grader) reveal their naiveté about how to identify the most important things to learn in a lesson:

Adult: When you read, how do you know what the important things are?

Annie: Most of my books have words that are written darker than all of the other words. Most of the time the "vocab" words are important. In my science books there are questions on the side of the page. You can tell that stuff is important because it is written twice.[19]

Adult: What do you think are the important things to remember when your teacher is talking?

Damon: The beginning sentences of their speech or if there's a formula or definition.[20]

Furthermore, many children and adolescents engage in little if any comprehension monitoring.[21] When they don't monitor their learning and comprehension,

FIGURE 4.2 Concept maps constructed by two fifth graders after watching a slide lecture on Australia

Source: From *Learning How to Learn* (pp. 100–101), by J. D. Novak and D. B. Gowin, 1984, Cambridge, England: Cambridge University Press. Copyright 1984 by Cambridge University Press. Reprinted with the permission of Cambridge University Press.

---

[11] Ausubel, Novak, & Hanesian, 1978; Murphy & Mason, 2006; Sinatra & Pintrich, 2003.

[12] Dunlosky & Lipko, 2007; Hacker, Bol, Horgan, & Rakow, 2000; T. O. Nelson & Dunlosky, 1991; Weaver & Kelemen, 1997.

[13] L. Baker & Brown, 1984; Hacker, 1998; Haller, Child, & Walberg, 1988; N. J. Stone, 2000.

[14] deLeeuw & Chi, 2003; Siegler & Lin, 2010; Wittwer & Renkl, 2008.

[15] De La Paz, 2005; A. King, 1992; Wong, 1985.

[16] A. King, 1992; Shanahan, 2004; Wade-Stein & Kintsch, 2004.

[17] J. E. Barnett, 2001; Pintrich & De Groot, 1990; Prawat, 1989; Rawson & Kintsch, 2005; Schneider, 2010; Schommer, 1994a.

[18] Dee-Lucas & Larkin, 1991; Dole et al., 1991; R. E. Reynolds & Shirey, 1988.

[19] Interview excerpt courtesy of a student who wishes to remain anonymous.

[20] Interview excerpt courtesy of Jenny Bressler.

[21] Dole et al., 1991; Markman, 1979; Nokes & Dole, 2004; J. W. Thomas, 1993.

comprehension monitoring Process of checking oneself to be sure one understands and remembers newly acquired information.

DEVELOPMENTAL TRENDS

TABLE 4.1 Metacognition at Different Grade Levels

Grade Level	Age-Typical Characteristics	Example	Suggested Strategies
K–2	• Awareness of thought in oneself and others, albeit in a simplistic form; limited ability to reflect on the specific nature of one's own thought processes • Considerable overestimation of what has been learned and how much can be remembered in the future • Belief that learning is a relatively passive activity • Belief that the absolute truth about any topic is "out there" somewhere, waiting to be discovered	An adult tells 6-year-old Brent that she will read him a list of 12 words; she then asks him to predict how many he'll be able to remember. Brent predicts "about 8 or 9 . . . maybe all of them," but in fact recalls only 6. Later, when the adult asks him what he did to try to remember the words, he says only "Think" and "Holded it, hold it in my brain." *(You can observe Brent's metacognitive reflection in the "Memory and Metacognition: Early Childhood" video in Chapter 4 of the Book-Specific Resources in MyEducationLab.)*	• Talk often about thinking processes (e.g., "I *wonder* if . . ." "How might you *remember* to . . . ?"). • Provide opportunities for students to "experiment" with their memories (e.g., playing "I'm going on a trip and am going to pack ___," in which each student repeats items previously mentioned and then adds another item to the list). • Introduce simple learning strategies (e.g., rehearsal of spelling words, repeated practice of motor skills).
3–5	• Increasing ability to reflect on the nature of one's own thought processes • Some overestimation of memory capabilities • Emerging realization that learning is an active, constructive process and that people may misinterpret what they observe • Continuing belief in an absolute truth "out there" somewhere	After reading several explanations of how ancient humans migrated from Asia to North America, a cooperative learning group in a combined fifth- and sixth-grade classroom includes the following points in its summary of what it has learned: "The more that we learn, the more we get confused about which is fact and which is fiction . . . We have made [our] own theories using information we found and trying to make sense of it."	• Provide simple techniques (e.g., self-test questions) that enable students to monitor their learning progress. • Examine scientific phenomena through hands-on activities and experimentation; ask students to make predictions about what will happen and to debate competing explanations for what they observe.
6–8	• Few and relatively ineffective study strategies (e.g., poor note-taking skills, little or no comprehension monitoring) • Belief that "knowledge" about a topic consists largely of a collection of discrete facts • Increasing realization that knowledge can be subjective and that conflicting perspectives may each have some validity (e.g., "people have a right to form their own opinions") • Increasing differentiation among different content domains (e.g., thinking that math involves right vs. wrong answers whereas social studies allows for diverse opinions)	The students in Ms. Gaunt's eighth-grade math class rarely take notes to help them remember new concepts and procedures, and most are more concerned about getting correct answers than about making sense of mathematical operations (see the opening case study).	• Teach and model effective strategies within the context of various subject areas. • Provide tools to assist students in their studying efforts (e.g., provide a structure for note taking, give students questions to answer as they study). • Introduce multiple perspectives about topics (e.g., asking whether Christopher Columbus was a brave scientist in search of new knowledge or, instead, an entrepreneur in search of personal wealth). • Explicitly ask students to reflect on their beliefs about the nature of various academic disciplines (e.g., "Can a math problem sometimes have two *different* right answers?").

(continued)

they don't know what they know and what they don't know, and so they may think they've mastered something when they really haven't. This **illusion of knowing** is seen in learners at all levels, even college students.[22]

Comprehension monitoring isn't just an important study strategy in its own right—it also plays a pivotal role in the development of *other* study strategies.[23] Learners will acquire and use new, more effective strategies only if they realize that their prior strategies have been *in*effective in helping them learn. If, instead, they mistakenly believe that they're

 Observe developmental changes in metacognition as you listen to 6-year-old Brent, 10-year-old David, 12-year-old Colin, and 16-year-old Hilary reflect on their thought processes in the four "Memory and Metacognition" videos in Chapter 4 of the Book-Specific Resources in MyEducationLab.

TABLE 4.1 Continued

Grade Level	Age-Typical Characteristics	Example	Suggested Strategies
 9–12	• Growing (but incomplete) knowledge of which study strategies are effective in different situations • Increasing mastery of covert learning strategies (e.g., intentional elaboration, comprehension monitoring) • Increasing recognition that knowledge involves understanding interrelationships among ideas • Increasing recognition that mastering a topic or skill takes time and practice (rather than happening quickly as a result of innate ability) • Emerging understanding that conflicting perspectives should be evaluated on the basis of evidence and logic (seen in a small minority of high school students)	When 16-year-old Hilary is asked to describe the things she does to help her remember school subject matter, she says, "When I'm trying to study for tests, I try to associate the things I'm trying to learn with familiar things . . . if I have a Spanish vocabulary test, I'll try to . . . with the Spanish words, I'll try to think of the English word that it sounds like . . . sometimes if I can't find any rule, then I just have to memorize it, just try to remember it, just go over it a lot." *(You can observe Hilary's metacognitive reflection in the "Memory and Metacognition: Late Adolescence" video in Chapter 4 of the Book-Specific Resources in MyEducationLab.)*	• Continue to teach and model effective learning strategies; ask students to describe their strategies to one another. • Develop classroom assignments and assessments that emphasize understanding, integration, and application, rather than recall of discrete facts. • Present various subject areas as dynamic entities that continue to evolve with new discoveries and theories. • Have students weigh pros and cons of various explanations and documents using objective criteria (e.g., hard evidence, logical reasoning processes).

Sources: Andre & Windschitl, 2003; Astington & Pelletier, 1996; J. E. Barnett, 2001; Buehl & Alexander, 2006; Chandler, Hallett, & Sokol, 2002; Elder, 2002; Flavell, Friedrichs, & Hoyt, 1970; Flavell, Miller, & Miller, 2002; Hatano & Inagaki, 2003; Hewitt, Brett, Scardamalia, Frecker, & Webb, 1995, p. 7 (migration example); P. M. King & Kitchener, 2002; Koob, 2009; Ku, Chan, Wu, & Chen, 2008; Kuhn, 2009; Kuhn, Garcia-Mila, Zohar, & Andersen, 1995; Kuhn & Park, 2005; Kuhn & Weinstock, 2002; Lovett & Flavell, 1990; Markman, 1977; McCrudden & Schraw, 2007; Meltzer, Pollica, & Barzillai, 2007; Muis, Bendixen, & Haerle, 2006; D. N. Perkins & Ritchhart, 2004; Schommer, 1994a, 1997; Short, Schatschneider, & Friebert, 1993; J. W. Thomas, 1993; vanSledright & Limón, 2006; Wellman, 1985, 1990; J. P. Williams, Stafford, Lauer, Hall, & Pollini, 2009.

successfully mastering school topics, they'll have little reason to abandon ineffective strategies (such as rote memorization of isolated facts) for more sophisticated ones.

Learners' views about the nature of knowledge and learning influence their approaches to learning tasks.

I once had a conversation with my son Jeff, then an eleventh grader, about the Canadian Studies program a local university had just added to its curriculum. Jeff's comments revealed a very simplistic view of what "history" is:

> **Jeff:** The Canadians don't have as much history as we [Americans] do.
> **Me:** Of course they do.
> **Jeff:** No, they don't. They haven't had as many wars.
> **Me:** History's more than wars.
> **Jeff:** Yeah, but the rest of that stuff is really boring.

Once Jeff reached college, he discovered that history is a lot more than wars and other, "really boring" stuff. In fact, he majored in history and now, as a secondary school teacher, actually *teaches* history. But it's unfortunate that he had to wait until college to discover the true nature of history as an academic discipline.

---

illusion of knowing Thinking that one knows something that one actually does *not* know.

[22] L. Baker, 1989; D. L. Butler & Winne, 1995; Dunlosky & Lipko, 2007; Hacker, 1998; Horgan, Hacker, & Huffman, 1997; N. J. Stone, 2000.

[23] Kuhn, Garcia-Mila, Zohar, & Andersen, 1995; Lodico, Ghatala, Levin, Pressley, & Bell, 1983; Loranger, 1994.

Children and adolescents have many misconceptions about academic disciplines. For instance, in the opening case study, Ms. Gaunt's students think that mathematics consists of nothing more than a collection of procedures that yield single right answers. Furthermore, most young learners have misconceptions about the general nature of learning. For instance, Ms. Gaunt's students think they should be able to learn mathematical concepts and procedures quickly and easily—with little or no effort on their part—as long as their teacher does her job.

Learners' beliefs about knowledge and learning are collectively known as **epistemic beliefs** (you may also see the term *epistemological* beliefs). Such beliefs often influence studying and learning.[24] For example, when learners believe that learning happens quickly in an all-or-none fashion (as Ms. Gaunt's students apparently do), they're apt to believe they have mastered something before they really have. Furthermore, they tend to give up quickly in the face of failure and express discouragement or dislike regarding the topic they're studying. In contrast, when learners believe that learning is a gradual process that often takes time and effort, they're likely to use a wide variety of learning strategies as they study and to persist until they've made sense of the material.[25]

As another example, some learners believe that when they read a textbook, they are passively absorbing information—often in the form of isolated facts—directly from the page to their minds. In contrast, other learners believe that learning from reading requires them to construct their own meanings by actively interpreting, organizing, and applying new information. Learners who realize that reading is a constructive, integrative process are more likely to engage in meaningful learning as they read and more likely to undergo conceptual change when they encounter ideas that contradict their existing beliefs.[26]

Epistemic beliefs tend to evolve over the course of childhood and adolescence.[27] Children in the elementary grades typically believe in the certainty of knowledge: They think that for any topic there is an absolute truth "out there" somewhere. As they reach the high school grades, some (but by no means all) of them begin to realize that knowledge is a subjective entity and that different perspectives on a topic can sometimes be equally valid. Other changes may also occur at the high school level. For example, students in twelfth grade are more likely than ninth graders to believe that knowledge consists of complex interrelationships rather than discrete facts and that learning happens slowly rather than quickly. And throughout adolescence students' epistemic beliefs become increasingly domain specific.[28] For instance, they may believe that, in math, answers are always either right or wrong (recall the students in the opening case study) but that in social studies conflicting perspectives may all have some validity. Such developmental trends are reflected in some of the entries in Table 4.1.

Yet effective study strategies and sophisticated epistemic beliefs are not the only factors affecting learning success. Self-regulation is equally important, as we shall see now.

• Self-Regulation

As you learned in Chapter 3, the environment has some influence over people's learning and behavior, but it doesn't have complete control. Learners' actions influence the environments they experience; in fact, learners often seek out certain kinds of environments (recall the discussions of *reciprocal causation* and *niche-picking*). Yet learners take control in another way as well: They make decisions about, direct, monitor, and evaluate their own learning and behavior. In other words, they engage in some degree of *self-regulated learning, self-regulated behavior,* and, more generally, **self-regulation.**[29]

Students often need help distinguishing important facts and concepts from more trivial information. Yet teachers should be careful that they don't portray academic learning as involving nothing more than *memorizing* those facts and concepts.

David Buffington/Photodisc/Getty Images

[24] Hofer & Pintrich, 1997; Purdie, Hattie, & Douglas, 1996; Schommer, 1994b, 1997.

[25] D. L. Butler & Winne, 1995; Kardash & Howell, 2000; Schommer, 1990, 1994b.

[26] Gunstone, 1994; Mason, Gava, & Boldrin, 2008; Paxton, 1999; Purdie et al., 1996; Schommer, 1994b; Schommer-Aikins, 2002; Sinatra & Pintrich, 2003; Wittrock, 1994.

[27] Astington & Pelletier, 1996; Kuhn & Park, 2005; Muis, Bendixen, & Haerle, 2006; Schommer, 1997.

[28] Buehl & Alexander, 2006; Muis et al., 2006.

[29] Good general references on this topic include Bandura, 1986, 1989; Schunk & Zimmerman, 1998; Zimmerman & Schunk, 2004.

epistemic belief Belief about the nature of knowledge or knowledge acquisition.

self-regulation Process of taking control of, monitoring, and evaluating one's own learning and behavior.

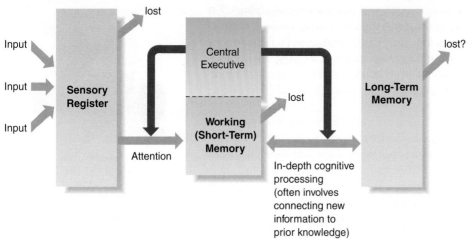

FIGURE 4.3 Adding a central executive to the model of human memory

To better understand the nature of self-regulation, let's add another component, a **central executive**, to the model of human memory presented in Chapter 2 (see Figure 4.3). In particular, this central executive (which is probably part of working memory) focuses attention and directs information processing throughout the memory system. It becomes increasingly sophisticated and effective—and perhaps most importantly, under voluntary control—as the brain continues to mature over the course of childhood and adolescence.[30]

To get a sense of how self-regulating *you* are, test yourself in the following exercise.

SEE FOR YOURSELF   Self-Reflection about Self-Regulation

In each of the following situations, choose the alternative that most accurately describes your attitudes, thoughts, and behaviors as a college student. Only *you* will see your answers, so be honest!

1. With respect to my final course grades, I am trying very hard to:
   a. Earn all As.
   b. Earn all As and Bs.
   c. Keep my overall grade point average at or above the minimally acceptable level at my college.
2. As I read or study a textbook:
   a. I often notice when my attention is wandering, and I immediately try to get my mind back on my work.
   b. I sometimes notice when my attention is wandering, but not always.
   c. I often get so lost in daydreams that I waste a lot of time.
3. Whenever I finish a study session:
   a. I write down how much time I have spent on my schoolwork.
   b. I make a mental note of how much time I have spent on my schoolwork.
   c. I don't really think much about the time I have spent.
4. When I turn in an assignment:
   a. I usually have a good idea of the grade I will get on it.
   b. I am often surprised by the grade I get.
   c. I don't think much about the quality of what I have done.
5. When I do exceptionally well on an assignment:
   a. I feel good about my performance and might reward myself in some way.
   b. I feel good about my performance but don't do anything special for myself afterward.
   c. I don't feel much differently than I had before I received a grade on the assignment.

central executive Component of the human information processing system that oversees the flow of information throughout the system.

[30] Baddeley, 2001; Demetriou, Christou, Spanoudis, & Platsidou, 2002; Fischer & Daley, 2007; Luciana, Conklin, Hooper, & Yarger, 2005; Zelazo, Müller, Frye, & Marcovitch, 2003.

Regardless of how you answered Item 1, you could probably identify a particular goal toward which you are striving. Your response to Item 2 should give you an idea of how much you monitor and try to control your thoughts when you're studying. Your responses to Items 3 and 4 tell you something about how frequently and accurately you evaluate your performance. And your response to Item 5 indicates whether you tend to reinforce yourself for desired behaviors. The following general principles illustrate these and other aspects of self-regulation.

Self-regulating learners establish goals and standards for their own performance.

Self-regulating learners know what they want to accomplish when they read or study. For instance, they may want to learn specific facts, gain a broad conceptual understanding of a topic, or simply acquire enough knowledge to do well on an upcoming test.[31] Effective learners often tie their goals for a particular activity to longer-term goals and aspirations—getting a college scholarship, exhibiting their work in a prestigious art show, becoming a veterinarian, and so on.[32] To a considerable degree, learners' goals reflect certain self-imposed general standards for performance, and these standards vary from one learner to the next. For example, one student may perceive high classroom achievement to be imperative and therefore strive for a straight-A report card, whereas another might be satisfied with mediocre performance and be quite content with Cs.

Learners' goals and standards are often modeled after those they see other people adopt.[33] For instance, at the high school I attended, many students wanted to go to the best college or university possible, and such lofty ambitions were contagious. But at a different high school, getting a job after graduation—or perhaps *instead* of graduation—might be the aspiration more commonly modeled by a student's classmates.

Self-regulating learners plan a course of action for a learning task.

Self-regulating learners determine ahead of time how best to use the time and resources they have available for a learning task.[34] They also choose different learning strategies depending on the specific goal they hope to accomplish. For example, how they read a magazine article depends on whether they're reading it for entertainment or studying for an exam.[35]

In the following interview, Shelly (a student in one of my educational psychology classes) asks her 17-year-old sister Becky about study habits. Notice how Becky chooses different study strategies for different topics. Notice, too, how she prioritizes her assignments and plans the best times for doing each one.

> **Shelly:** When you have a test, how do you study for it and when?
> **Becky:** I don't usually study; I just look over the notes. If I have to memorize something, I repeat it over and over or write it down, which is like repeating it. I sometimes use [word association], patterns, and oversimplification to remember. I will also look it over at night and then again in the morning. I derive math formulas, those I don't memorize. . . .
> **Shelly:** What types of study skills do you practice on a regular basis?
> **Becky:** Organize homework. I rewrite my assignments. I do smaller tasks first, then put the bigger ones in a pile. I do the easier ones first, then writing and studying I do last. Long-term projects I do last, or first if I want to force myself to do them. . . .
> **Shelly:** At what time of day do you learn best? [At what time do you] best study on your own?
> **Becky:** I learn better early in the day. I am in a better mood and I am not sick of school yet. . . . I study best in the morning; that's when I edit my essays from the night before.[36]

---

[31] Gaskins, Satlow, & Pressley, 2007; Muis, 2007; Nolen, 1996; Winne & Hadwin, 1998.
[32] Bandura, 2008; Bembenutty & Karabenick, 2004; R. B. Miller & Brickman, 2004; Zimmerman & Schunk, 2004.
[33] Bandura, 1986; Locke & Latham, 1990.

[34] Muis, 2007; Zimmerman, 1998; Zimmerman & Schunk, 2004.
[35] Gaskins et al., 2007; Winne, 1995a; Zimmerman, 2008.
[36] Interview excerpt courtesy of Shelly Lamb.

Jonathan Nourok/PhotoEdit

Self-regulating learners typically set one or more goals for a study session and plan a course of action that will enable them to meet their goals.

Although Becky sometimes resorts to rehearsal to learn facts verbatim, many of her strategies—review, organization (looking for patterns), elaboration (deriving formulas)—are probably quite effective. (She doesn't explain "oversimplification," but perhaps she means that she looks for key ideas or in some other way summarizes the material.) Given how well Becky takes charge of her learning, it may not surprise you to learn that at the time of the interview, she was a high-achieving high school student.

Self-regulating learners control and monitor their cognitive processes and progress during a learning task.

Self-regulating learners intentionally engage in processes that will enhance their learning. They try to focus their attention on the subject matter at hand and to clear their minds of potentially distracting thoughts.[37] They may also employ **self-instructions** that help them direct their efforts. As an example, one formerly impulsive child learned to talk himself through matching tasks in which he needed to find two identical pictures among several very similar ones:

> I have to remember to go slowly to get it right. Look carefully at this one, now look at these carefully. Is this one different? Yes, it has an extra leaf. Good, I can eliminate this one. Now, let's look at this one. I think it's this one, but let me first check the others. Good, I'm going slow and carefully. Okay, I think it's this one.[38]

Another important aspect of self-regulation is **self-monitoring**: Self-regulating learners continually check their progress toward their goals, and they change their learning strategies or modify their goals if necessary.[39] The process of *comprehension monitoring,* described earlier, is an example of such self-monitoring.

Self-regulating learners also monitor and try to control their motivation and emotions.

Self-regulating learners use a variety of strategies to keep themselves on task—perhaps embellishing on an assignment to make it more fun, reminding themselves of the importance of doing well, or promising themselves a reward after they finish.[40] For example, a middle school student named Jamaal regularly gives himself a pep talk as he works on math problems:

> I'll be, like, "Come on." I'll be thinking about different ways to solve problems and stuff like that. I'll be saying, "Come on, Jamaal, you can do this," and stuff like that . . . I don't know what it does, but it's just like extra comfort to me.[41]

Self-regulating learners also try to keep in check any emotions (anxiety, anger, etc.) that might interfere with their performance (more about such *emotion self-regulation* in Chapter 6).[42]

Self-regulating learners seek assistance and support when they need it.

Truly self-regulating learners don't necessarily try to do everything on their own. On the contrary, they recognize occasions when they need other people's help and seek it out. They're especially likely to ask for the kind of help that will enable them to work more independently in the future.[43]

Self-regulating learners evaluate the final outcomes of their efforts.

Both at home and in school, children's and adolescents' behaviors and achievements are often judged by others—their parents, teachers, classmates, and so on. But as young people become

---

self-instructions Instructions that one gives oneself while executing a complex task.

self-monitoring Observing and possibly recording one's own behavior to check progress toward a goal.

[37] Harnishfeger, 1995; Winne, 1995a; Zimmerman & Kitsantas, 2005.
[38] Meichenbaum & Goodman, 1971, p. 121.
[39] D. L. Butler & Winne, 1995; Greene & Azevedo, 2009; Schneider, 2010.
[40] Corno, 1993; Wolters, 2003.

[41] Usher, 2009, p. 295.
[42] Bronson, 2000; Winne, 1995a.
[43] R. Butler, 1998b; R. S. Newman, 2008; A. M. Ryan, Pintrich, & Midgley, 2001.

increasingly self-regulating, they also begin to judge their *own* behaviors and achievements, especially with respect to the goals and standards they've set for themselves.[44] In other words, self-regulating learners engage in **self-evaluation**. Their ability to evaluate themselves with some degree of objectivity and accuracy will ultimately be critical for their learning and achievement over the long run.[45]

Self-regulating learners self-impose consequences for their performance.

How do you feel when you accomplish a difficult task—for instance, when you earn an A in a challenging course, get elected president of an organization, or make a 3-point basket in a basketball game? How do you feel when you fail in your endeavors—for instance, when you get a D on an exam because you forgot to study, thoughtlessly hurt a friend's feelings, or miss an easy goal in a soccer game?

When you accomplish something you've set out to do—and especially when the task is complex and challenging—you might feel quite proud of yourself and give yourself a mental pat on the back. In contrast, when you fail to accomplish a task, you're probably unhappy with your performance, and you may also feel guilty, regretful, or ashamed. Likewise, as children and adolescents become increasingly self-regulating, they begin to reinforce themselves when they accomplish their goals—perhaps by engaging in a favorite activity or perhaps simply by feeling proud or telling themselves they did a good job. And they may punish themselves when they do something that does not meet their own performance standards—at a minimum, by feeling sorry, guilty, or ashamed.[46] Such self-reinforcement and self-punishment are **self-imposed contingencies**. The student poem about horseback riding presented in Figure 4.4 clearly shows both self-punishment ("Now I'm feeling guilty because I'm making the horse work harder") and self-reinforcement ("Good job! . . . Now I feel warm inside and proud").

◆ In what way are self-imposed contingencies similar to the contingencies described in Chapter 3? In what important way are they unique? (Compare your response to this question with the response presented in Chapter 4 of the Book-Specific Resources in MyEducationLab.)

Learners become increasingly self-regulating over the course of childhood and adolescence.

On average, children and adolescents become increasingly self-regulating as they grow older. As you can see in Table 4.2, a few elements of self-regulation (e.g., setting self-chosen goals, self-evaluation of behavior) are evident in the primary grades. Additional aspects (e.g., conscious attempts to focus attention, ability to complete short learning tasks at home) tend to appear in the upper elementary grades. Still others (e.g., planning, self-motivation) emerge in the middle school and high school years. One aspect of self-regulation—seeking help when needed—may actually *decline*, however, especially if students consistently struggle with their academic work but want to hide their difficulties and perceive their teachers to be aloof and nonsupportive.[47]

When children and adolescents are self-regulating, they set more ambitious academic goals for themselves, learn more effectively, and achieve at higher levels in the classroom.[48] Self-regulation becomes increasingly important in adolescence and adulthood, when many learning activities—reading, doing homework, finding information on the Internet, and so on—occur in isolation from other people and therefore require considerable self-direction.[49]

> "Sit up,
>   shoulders back,
>   drop your right shoulder."
> Now I feel guilty because I'm making the horse work harder.
> "Heels down,
>   elbows at your sides,
>   lower leg back,
>   drop your right shoulder down and back."
> Now I feel like I have no talent and like I'm hurting the horse.
> "More impulsion from the left hind leg!
>   Send him into the rein more!"
> Now I'm thinking, "This is so complicated!"
> "Good job!
>   Walk when you're ready and give him the rein.
>   Did you feel that?"
> "Yeah!"
> "Good! That was really good!
>   You've accomplished so much with him and your position."
> Now I feel warm inside and proud. All this time has paid off
>   and I realize that's why I love horseback riding so much!

FIGURE 4.4 Sixteen-year-old Melinda expresses guilt and pride—two examples of self-imposed contingencies—in this poem about horseback riding.

---

[44] D. L. Butler & Winne, 1995; Gaskins et al., 2007; Schraw & Moshman, 1995; Zimmerman & Schunk, 2004.

[45] Dunning, Heath, & Suls, 2004; Vye et al., 1998.

[46] Harter, 1999; K. R. Harris, Santangelo, & Graham, 2010; R. B. Miller & Brickman, 2004; Zimmerman & Kitsantas, 2005.

[47] Marchand & Skinner, 2007.

[48] D. L. Butler & Winne, 1995; Corno et al., 2002; Duckworth & Seligman, 2005; Zimmerman & Kitsantas, 2005.

[49] Azevedo, 2005b; Meltzer et al., 2007; Winne, 1995a.

self-evaluation Judgment of one's own performance or behavior.

self-imposed contingency Self-reinforcement or self-punishment that follows a particular behavior.

DEVELOPMENTAL TRENDS

TABLE 4.2 Self-Regulation at Different Grade Levels

Grade Level	Age-Typical Characteristics	Example	Suggested Strategies
K–2	• Some internalization of adults' standards for behavior • Emerging ability to set self-chosen goals for learning and achievement • Some use of self-instructions to guide behavior • Some self-evaluation of effectiveness and appropriateness of actions; feelings of guilt about wrongdoings • Individual differences in self-control of impulses, emotions, and attention; amount of self-control in these areas affects peer relationships and classroom performance	Most of the children in a kindergarten class can sit quietly and listen when their teacher reads a storybook. But a few of them—several boys and a couple of girls—often squirm restlessly and occasionally poke or otherwise distract their classmates.	• Discuss rationales for class rules for behavior. • Show students how some behaviors can help them reach their goals and how other behaviors interfere with goal attainment. • Organize the classroom so that students can carry out some activities on their own (e.g., have reading centers where children can listen to storybooks on tape). • When students show impulsiveness or poor emotional control, provide guidelines and consistent consequences for behavior.
3–5	• Improving ability to assess own performance and progress • Guilt and shame about unsatisfactory performance and moral transgressions • Emerging self-regulated learning strategies (e.g., conscious attempts to focus attention, ability to do short assignments independently at home) • Increasing ability to allocate study time appropriately for the learning task at hand • Difficulties with self-control for some students who have cognitive or behavioral disabilities	Every Thursday evening, 8-year-old Logan studies for the weekly spelling test his teacher will give his class the following day. Sometimes he asks his father or older brother to test him on especially difficult words.	• Have students set specific, concrete goals for their learning. • Encourage students to assess their own performance; provide criteria they can use to evaluate their work. • Ask students to engage in simple, self-regulated learning tasks (e.g., small-group learning activities, homework assignments); provide some structure to guide students' efforts. • Encourage students to use their peers as resources. • If students have continuing difficulty with self-control, teach self-instructions that can help them control their behavior.
6–8	• Increasing ability to plan future actions, due in part to increased capacity for abstract thought • Increasing mastery of some self-regulated learning strategies, especially those that involve overt behaviors (e.g., keeping a calendar of assignments and due dates) • Self-motivational strategies (e.g., minimizing distractions, devising ways to make a boring task more interesting and enjoyable, reminding oneself about the importance of doing well) • Decrease in help-seeking behaviors during times of confusion, especially if teachers appear to be aloof and nonsupportive	For fear of appearing to be "stupid" in her math class, 13-year-old Katherine rarely asks questions when she doesn't understand a new concept or procedure.	• Assign homework and other tasks that require independent learning. • Provide concrete strategies for keeping track of learning tasks and assignments (e.g., provide monthly calendars in which students can write due dates). • Provide concrete guidance about how to learn and study effectively (e.g., give students questions they should answer as they complete reading assignments at home). • Give students frequent opportunities to assess their own learning; have them compare your evaluations with their own.
9–12	• More long-range goal setting • Increasing ability to accurately self-evaluate learning and achievement • Wide variation in ability to self-regulate learning (many low-achieving high school students have few, if any, self-regulating learning strategies)	After moving from fairly small middle schools to a much larger, consolidated high school, some students diligently complete their homework assignments each night. But many others are easily enticed into more enjoyable activities with friends—hanging out at a local fast-food restaurant, instant-messaging on cell phones, and so on—and their grades decline significantly as a result.	• Relate classroom learning tasks to students' long-range personal and professional goals. • Assign complex independent learning tasks, providing the necessary structure and guidance for students who are not yet self-regulating learners. • Have high-achieving students describe their strategies for resisting attractive alternatives and keeping themselves on task when doing homework.

Sources: Blair, 2002; Bronson, 2000; Damon, 1988; Dunning et al., 2004; Eccles, Wigfield, & Schiefele, 1998; Fries, Dietz, & Schmid, 2008; M. H. Jones, Estell, & Alexander, 2008; Kochanska, Gross, Lin, & Nichols, 2002; Liew, McTigue, Barrois, & Hughes, 2008; Marchand & Skinner, 2007; J. S. Matthews, Ponitz, & Morrison, 2009; Meichenbaum & Goodman, 1971; Meltzer et al., 2007; S. D. Miller, Heafner, Massey, & Strahan, 2003; Paris & Paris, 2001; Schneider, 2010; Valiente, Lemery-Calfant, Swanson, & Reiser, 2008; Wolters & Rosenthal, 2000.

Unfortunately, not all adolescents acquire a high level of self-regulation, perhaps in part because traditional instructional practices do little to foster it.[50] The opening case study in Chapter 1, "Starting High School," provides a good example. Anna was unable to keep track of her work and assignments, and she apparently had little idea about how to keep herself on task, monitor her progress, or get help when she needed it.

To some extent, self-regulated learning probably develops from opportunities to engage in age-appropriate independent learning activities.[51] But self-regulated learning also has roots in socially regulated learning.[52] At first, other people (e.g., teachers, parents) might help children learn by setting goals for a learning activity, keeping children's attention focused on the learning task, suggesting effective strategies, monitoring progress, and so on. Over time, children assume increasing responsibility for these processes. That is, they begin to set their *own* goals, stay on task with little prodding from others, identify potentially effective strategies, and evaluate their own learning. A good bridge between other-regulated learning and self-regulated learning is **co-regulated learning**, in which an adult and one or more children share responsibility for directing various aspects of the learning process.[53] Initially, the adult (or perhaps a "virtual teacher" in the form of specially designed computer software) provides considerable structure for children's learning efforts, gradually removing it as children become more self-regulating. Co-regulated learning is an example of *scaffolding*, a concept we'll discuss in Chapter 5.

Self-regulated learning often emerges from *co-regulated learning*, in which teacher and learner share responsibility for directing various aspects of the learning process—setting goals, identifying effective strategies, evaluating progress, and so on.

Transfer

How students think about and study school subject matter has implications not only for how well they can understand and remember it but also for how effectively they can *use and apply* it on later occasions. Here we are talking about **transfer**: the extent to which knowledge and skills acquired in one situation affect a person's learning or performance in a subsequent situation. Following are examples:

- Elena speaks both English and Spanish fluently. When she begins a French course in high school, she immediately recognizes many similarities between French and Spanish. "Aha," she thinks, "what I know about Spanish will help me learn French."
- In her middle school history class, Stella discovers that she does better on exams when she takes more notes. She decides to take more notes in her geography class as well, and once again the strategy pays off.
- Ted's fifth-grade class has been working with decimals for several weeks. His teacher asks, "Which number is larger, 4.4 or 4.14?" Ted recalls something he knows about whole numbers: Numbers with three digits are larger than numbers with only two digits. "The larger number is 4.14," he mistakenly concludes.

In most cases, prior learning *helps* learning or performance in another situation. Such **positive transfer** takes place when Elena's Spanish helps her learn French and when Stella's practice with note taking in history class improves her performance in geography class. In some instances, however, existing knowledge or skills actually *hinder* later learning. Such **negative transfer** is the case for Ted, who transfers a principle related to whole numbers to a situation where it doesn't apply: comparing decimals. The opening case study in Chapter 2, "The New World" included another example of negative transfer: When thinking about *China*, Rita apparently retrieved multiple possible meanings of the word—including "dinnerware"—and erroneously concluded that Europeans wanted to import *cups* from the Far East.

? Can you think of a recent situation in which you exhibited positive transfer? A situation in which you exhibited negative transfer?

co-regulated learning Process through which an adult and child share responsibility for directing various aspects of the child's learning.

transfer Phenomenon in which something a person has learned at one time affects how the person learns or performs in a later situation.

positive transfer Phenomenon in which something learned at one time facilitates learning or performance at a later time.

negative transfer Phenomenon in which something learned at one time interferes with learning or performance at a later time.

[50] Meltzer, 2007; Paris & Ayres, 1994; Zimmerman & Risemberg, 1997.

[51] Paris & Paris, 2001; Vye et al., 1998; Zimmerman, 1998.

[52] Stright, Neitzel, Sears, & Hoke-Sinex, 2001; Vygotsky, 1962; Zimmerman, 1998.

[53] Azevedo, 2005a; McCaslin & Good, 1996; N. E. Perry, 1998; C. Quintana, Zhang, & Krajcik, 2005.

Ideally, *positive* transfer—including transfer to real-world tasks and problems—should be a major objective for classrooms at all grade levels. For instance, students should be able to use basic arithmetic skills to compute correct change and balance a checkbook, use correct grammar and spelling when completing job applications and writing newspaper editorials, and recall what they've learned in science and the social sciences while thinking about local, national, and international problems.

Four general principles can help us predict when learners are likely to transfer what they learn in one situation to a new situation.

Transfer of knowledge and skills is most likely to occur when there is obvious similarity between the "old" and the "new."

Transfer from one situation to another often occurs when the two situations overlap in content.[54] Consider Elena, the student fluent in Spanish who is now taking French. Elena should have an easy time learning to count in French because the numbers (*un, deux, trois, quatre, cinq)* are very similar to the Spanish she already knows (*uno, dos, tres, cuatro, cinco*). When transfer occurs because the original learning task and the transfer task overlap in content, we have a case of **specific transfer**.

The similarity of two situations usually promotes positive transfer from one to the other. Occasionally, however, it leads to negative transfer. As an example, try the following exercise.

SEE FOR YOURSELF A Division Problem

Quickly estimate an answer to this division problem:

$$20 \div 0.38$$

Is your answer larger or smaller than 20?

If you applied your knowledge of division by whole numbers here, you undoubtedly concluded that the answer is smaller than 20. In fact, the answer is approximately 52.63, a number *larger* than 20. Has this exercise reminded you of Ted's erroneous conclusion (that 4.14 is larger than 4.4) based on his knowledge of how whole numbers can be compared? Many students at all levels—even college students—show negative transfer of whole-number principles to situations involving decimals.[55] Working with decimals appears, on the surface, to be similar to working with whole numbers. The only difference—a very important one, as it turns out—is a tiny decimal point.

Learning strategies and general beliefs and attitudes can also transfer to new situations.

Consider Stella's strategy of taking more notes in geography because note taking has been beneficial in her history class. History and geography don't overlap much in content, but she can apply a strategy she's acquired in one class to help her in the other. Here is an instance of **general transfer**: Learning in one situation affects learning and performance in a very different situation.

We frequently see general transfer of learning and study strategies: When people acquire effective learning and study strategies within the context of one subject area, they often apply the strategies in a very different subject area.[56] In addition, the general beliefs and attitudes that learners acquire about learning and thinking—for instance, confidence in their ability to

---

specific transfer Instance of transfer in which the original learning task and the transfer task overlap in content.

general transfer Instance of transfer in which the original learning task and the transfer task are different in content.

[54] J. R. Anderson, Greeno, Reder, & Simon, 2000; Bassok, 1990; Di Vesta & Peverly, 1984.

[55] Ni & Zhou, 2005; Tirosh & Graeber, 1990.

[56] J. M. Alexander, Johnson, Scott, & Meyer, 2008; Bransford et al., 2006; Brooks & Dansereau, 1987; D. N. Perkins, 1995.

master school subject matter, recognition that learning often takes hard work, and willingness to consider multiple viewpoints on controversial issues—can have a profound impact on later learning and achievement across multiple domains and so clearly illustrate general transfer at work.[57]

When application of specific academic topics is involved, however, general transfer occurs far less often than specific transfer.[58] If transfer of these topics does occur, it typically involves *some* kind of similarity between the material involved in the two situations. Knowledge about one topic rarely transfers to a very different topic. For example, studying computer programming, though certainly a worthwhile activity in its own right, doesn't necessarily help a person with other kinds of logical thinking tasks.[59]

Relevant context cues increase the probability of transfer.

Learners can apply something they've learned to a new situation only if they *retrieve* it in the new situation.[60] Here we see one reason why specific transfer is more common than general transfer. When two situations overlap in content, the second situation is apt to provide *retrieval cues* that remind learners of relevant things they've previously learned.[61]

In Chapter 3 we examined the phenomenon of *situated cognition:* People associate particular behaviors and ways of thinking with certain contexts and tend not to use them in—that is, they don't transfer them to—other contexts. We can now explain this phenomenon quite simply. When people initially acquire knowledge and skills in a particular setting, that setting may later provide retrieval cues that help them retrieve what they've learned. Such cues may be missing in a dissimilar situation.

Meaningful learning and conceptual understanding increase the probability of transfer.

Learners are much more likely to apply new knowledge and skills when they engage in meaningful rather than rote learning.[62] Ideally, they should acquire *conceptual understanding* of a topic, such that many concepts and procedures are interrelated in a cohesive, logical whole (recall our discussion of this concept in Chapter 2). When information and skills are appropriately interconnected in memory, learners are more likely to retrieve them in relevant situations.

One critical factor affecting meaningful learning and conceptual understanding is the amount of instructional time. The more time learners spend studying a single topic, the more likely they are to transfer what they learn to a new situation, undoubtedly because they're better able to make the interconnections that meaningful, conceptual understanding involves.[63] In-depth instruction on a topic is especially effective when learners see many examples of concepts and have many opportunities to apply skills to diverse situations. In such cases learners can connect their new knowledge to a wide variety of contexts, increasing the odds that they'll retrieve it later when they need it.[64]

THE FAR SIDE® By GARY LARSON

© 1986 FarWorks, Inc. All Rights Reserved/Dist. by Creators Syndicate

Right side! One two, one two, one two, left side! One two, one two, one two, one... C'mon! Keep those cerebellums up!... One two, one two...

Brain aerobics

When transfer occurs, there is usually some similarity between the original learning situation and the transfer task. Engaging in activities simply for general mental "exercise"—for instance, memorizing poems or solving artificial logic problems—typically has little or no effect on a learner's ability to perform very dissimilar tasks.

Observe strategies for promoting conceptual understanding of addition and subtraction in the "Strategies for Learning about Operations" video in Chapter 4 of the Book-Specific Resources in MyEducationLab.

---

[57] Bransford & Schwartz, 1999; De Corte, 2003; Pugh, Bergin, & Rocks, 2003; Volet, 1999.

[58] S. M. Barnett & Ceci, 2002; W. D. Gray & Orasanu, 1987.

[59] R. E. Mayer & Wittrock, 1996; D. N. Perkins & Salomon, 1989.

[60] Cormier, 1987; Gick & Holyoak, 1987; Halpern, 1998.

[61] Gick & Holyoak, 1987; D. N. Perkins & Salomon, 1989; Sternberg & Frensch, 1993.

[62] Bereiter, 1995; Brooks & Dansereau, 1987; R. E. Mayer & Wittrock, 1996; Pugh & Bergin, 2006.

[63] Haskell, 2001; M. C. Linn, 2008; R. A. Schmidt & Bjork, 1992.

[64] Cox, 1997; M. C. Linn, 2008; D. N. Perkins & Salomon, 1987; R. A. Schmidt & Bjork, 1992.

In general, then, the *less-is-more* principle introduced in Chapter 2 applies here: Learners are more likely to transfer new knowledge and skills to new situations—including those in the outside world—when they study a few things in depth and learn them *well,* rather than studying many topics superficially.[65] The *less-is-more* principle is clearly being violated in the opening case study. Ms. Gaunt decides that she must move fairly quickly if she is to cover all of the eighth-grade math curriculum, even if it means that few students will master any particular topic or procedure. Given the upcoming statewide mathematics exam, she may have little alternative, but her students are unlikely to *use* what they're learning on future occasions.

• Problem Solving and Creativity

Both problem solving and creativity involve applying—transferring—previously learned knowledge or skills to a new situation. In **problem solving**, we use what we know to address a previously unanswered question or troubling situation. Psychologists have varying opinions about the nature of **creativity**, but in general it involves new and original behavior yielding a product appropriate for, and in some way valuable to, one's culture.[66]

To successfully tackle a problem, we typically pull together two or more pieces of information into some sort of "whole" that resolves the problem. This combining of information into a single idea or product is known as **convergent thinking**. In contrast, when we engage in creativity, we often begin with a single idea and take it in a variety of directions, at least one of which leads to something that is new, original, and culturally appropriate. This process of generating many different ideas from a single starting point is known as **divergent thinking**.

Figure 4.5 illustrates the difference between convergent and divergent thinking. To experience the difference firsthand, try the following exercise.

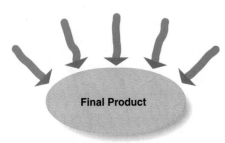

Final Product

Convergent Thinking

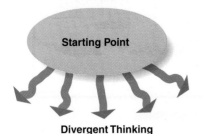

Starting Point

Divergent Thinking

FIGURE 4.5 Convergent versus divergent thinking

SEE FOR YOURSELF   Convergent and Divergent Thinking

On a sheet of paper, write your responses to each of the following:

1. You buy two apples for 25¢ each and one pear for 40¢. How much change will you get back from a dollar bill?
2. You have a rectangle with a width of 8 meters and a height of 6 meters, as shown to the right. What is the length of the diagonal line?
3. What are some possible uses of a brick? Try to think of as many different and unusual uses as you can.
4. Add improvements to the wagon to make it more fun to play with.[67]

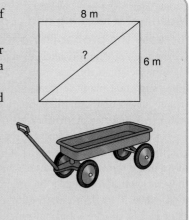

---

problem solving Using existing knowledge or skills to address an unanswered question or troubling situation.

creativity New and original behavior that yields a productive and culturally appropriate result.

convergent thinking Process of pulling several pieces of information together to draw a conclusion or solve a problem.

divergent thinking Process of mentally moving in a variety of directions from a single idea.

To answer Question 1, you must pull together at least four facts ($2 \times 25 = 50$, $50 + 40 = 90$, one dollar = 100 cents, and $100 - 90 = 10$) to arrive at the solution 10¢. To answer Question 2, you must use the Pythagorean theorem (the square of the hypotenuse equals the sum of the squares of the other two sides) plus at least four number facts ($6^2 = 36$, $8^2 = 64$, $36 + 64 = 100$,

---

[65] Brophy, 1992; M. C. Linn, 2008; Porter, 1989.

[66] Plucker, Beghetto, & Dow, 2004; Ripple, 1989; Runco, 2004; R. K. Sawyer, 2003.

[67] Problems 3 and 4 modeled after Torrance, 1970.

$\sqrt{100} = 10$) to arrive at the solution 10 meters. Both Questions 1 and 2, then, involve convergent thinking. In contrast, Questions 3 and 4 require you to think in many different ways about a single object—you must consider how a brick might be used in different contexts and how different parts of the wagon might be embellished—with some of your responses being novel and unique. (For instance, perhaps you thought a brick might make an interesting base for a small table lamp, and perhaps you fastened a hobby horse to the wagon's handle to make it look like a horse and buggy.) Questions 3 and 4, then, involve divergent thinking.

Despite the convergent–divergent dichotomy I've just described, you should think of problem solving and creativity as overlapping processes: Solving problems often involves thinking creatively, and being creative typically requires solving one or more problems. For example, consider this situation:

> As a teacher, you want to illustrate the idea that metal battleships float despite the fact that metal is denser (and so heavier) than water. You don't have any toy boats made of metal. What can you use instead to show students that a metal object with a hollow interior can float on water?

Although you ultimately need only a single solution, you must engage in divergent thinking to generate a variety of options. Many objects might serve as ship substitutes—perhaps metal pie plates, buckets, and thimbles—and some might work better than others.

Several general principles apply to both problem solving and creativity.

The depth of learners' knowledge influences their ability to solve problems and think creatively.

Successful problem solvers and creative thinkers usually have considerable knowledge and conceptual understanding of the topic in question.[68] Especially in the case of creativity, such knowledge may also involve mental associations among very different ideas and subject areas.[69]

When learners have limited knowledge about a topic and little conceptual understanding of it, they're apt to choose problem-solving strategies on the basis of superficial problem characteristics.[70] For example, when I was in elementary school, some of my classmates were having trouble with mathematical word problems. Our teacher told us that the word *left* in a problem indicates that subtraction is called for. Encoding a "left" problem as a subtraction problem works well in some instances, such as this one:

> Tim has 7 apples. He gives 3 apples to Sarah. How many apples does he have left?

But it's inappropriate in other instances, such as this one:

> At the grocery store, Tim buys some apples for $2.00. When he leaves the store, he has $1.50 left. How much money did Tim have before he bought the apples?

The latter problem requires addition, not subtraction. Obviously, words alone can be deceiving.

Both convergent and divergent thinking are constrained by working memory capacity.

You may recall from an exercise in Chapter 2 just how difficult it can be to solve a long division problem in your head. Remember, working memory has a limited capacity: It can hold only a few pieces of information and accommodate only so much cognitive processing at any one time. If a problem or task requires the learner to handle a great deal of information at once, to manipulate information in a very complex way, or to generate a wide variety of new ideas, working memory capacity may be insufficient for arriving at an accurate or creative result.[71]

[68] Amabile & Hennessey, 1992; M. Carr, 2010; Lubart & Mouchiroud, 2003; Simonton, 2000; Voss, Greene, Post, & Penner, 1983.
[69] Runco & Chand, 1995.
[70] Chi, Feltovich, & Glaser, 1981; Schoenfeld & Hermann, 1982.
[71] Hambrick & Engle, 2003; K. Lee, Ng, & Ng, 2009; H. L. Swanson, 2006; Sweller, 1994.

Learners can overcome the limits of working memory in at least two ways. One obvious approach is to create an external record of needed information—for example, by writing it down on paper. Another approach is to learn some skills to automaticity—in other words, to learn them to a point where they can be retrieved quickly and easily.[72] Yet in the case of automaticity, it's possible to have too much of a good thing, as you'll see shortly.

How learners encode a problem or situation influences their strategies and eventual success.

Any particular problem or situation might be represented in working memory—that is, *encoded*—in a variety of ways. As an example, see whether you can solve the problem in the following exercise.

SEE FOR YOURSELF Pigs and Chickens

> Old MacDonald has a barnyard full of pigs and chickens. Altogether there are 21 heads and 60 legs in the barnyard (not counting MacDonald's own head and legs). How many pigs and how many chickens are running around the barnyard?

Can you figure out the answer? If you're having difficulty, try thinking about the problem this way:

> Imagine that the pigs are standing in an upright position on only their two hind legs; their front two legs are raised over their heads. Therefore, all of the animals—pigs and chickens alike—are standing on two legs. Figure out how many legs are on the ground and how many must be in the air. From this, can you determine the number of pigs and chickens Old MacDonald has?

Some ways of encoding a problem promote more successful problem solving than others.

In case you're still having trouble solving the problem, follow this logic:

- There are 21 heads, so the total number of animals must be 21.
- If all of the pigs have their front legs in the air, there must be twice as many legs on the ground as there are number of heads. Thus, there are 42 (21 × 2) legs on the ground.
- If 42 legs are on the ground, there must be 18 (60 − 42) pigs' legs in the air.
- Each pig has 2 front legs, so there must be 9 (18 ÷ 2) pigs. Therefore, there must be 12 (21 − 9) chickens.

If you're a proficient mathematician, you may simply have used algebra to encode and solve the problem, perhaps using x for the number of pigs and y for the number of chickens and then solving for these variables in the equations $x + y = 21$ and $4x + 2y = 60$. Algebra provides many helpful procedures for solving problems involving unknown quantities. In my own experience, however, I've found that most college students rarely use algebra to solve problems outside of a math class (displaying the *situated cognition* of which I've previously spoken). And students at all grade levels often have trouble solving word problems because they don't know how to translate the problems into mathematical procedures or operations they've learned at school.[73]

Sometimes learners encode a problem or situation in a seemingly logical way that nevertheless fails to yield a workable result. As an example, take a stab at the problem in the following exercise.

---

[72] N. Frederiksen, 1984a; R. E. Mayer & Wittrock, 2006; Sweller, 1994.

[73] R. E. Mayer & Wittrock, 2006; L. B. Resnick, 1989; Reusser, 1990.

SEE FOR YOURSELF   Candle Problem

How might you stand a candle upright in front of a bulletin board attached to the wall? You don't want the candle to touch the bulletin board, because the flame might singe the board. Instead, you need to place the candle about a centimeter away from the board. How can you accomplish the task using some or all of the following materials: a small candle (birthday cake size), a metal knitting needle, matches, a box of thumbtacks, and a 12-inch plastic ruler?[74]

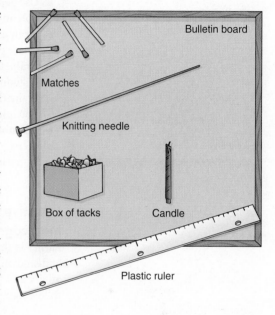

As it turns out, the ruler and knitting needle are useless in solving the problem. Piercing the candle with the knitting needle will probably break the candle, and you're unlikely to have much luck balancing the ruler on a few tacks. (I speak from experience here, as my own students have unsuccessfully tried both strategies.) The easiest solution is to fasten the thumbtack box to the bulletin board with tacks and then attach the candle to the top of the box with either a tack or some melted wax. Many people don't consider this possibility, however, because they encode the box only as a *container of tacks* and so overlook its potential use as a candle stand. When people encode a problem or situation in a way that excludes potential solutions, they're victims of a **mental set**.

Mental sets sometimes emerge when learners practice solving a particular kind of problem (e.g., doing subtraction problems in math or applying the formula $E = mc^2$ in physics) without practicing other kinds of problems at the same time.[75] In general, repetitive practice can lead learners to encode problems and situations in a particular way without really thinking about them—that is, it can lead to automaticity in encoding. Although automaticity in the basic information and skills needed for problem solving and creative thinking is often an advantage (it frees up working memory capacity), automaticity in *encoding* problems and situations may yield incorrect solutions or inappropriate products,[76] in part because it leads learners down a counterproductive path of associations in long-term memory.

Problem solving and creativity often involve heuristics that facilitate—but don't guarantee—successful outcomes.

Some problems can be successfully solved by following specific, step-by-step instructions—that is, by using an **algorithm**. We can correctly assemble the pieces of a new bookcase by following the "Directions for Assembly" that come with the package. We can calculate the hypotenuse of a right triangle by using the Pythagorean theorem. We can solve for *x* and *y* when we apply algebraic procedures to combine and manipulate the equations $x + y = 21$ and $4x + 2y = 60$. When we follow an algorithm faithfully, we invariably arrive at a correct solution.

Yet the world presents many problems for which no algorithms exist. And creativity, by its very nature,

Some problems can be solved by an algorithm, a set of step-by-step instructions that guarantees a correct solution.

mental set Inclination to encode a problem or situation in a way that excludes potential solutions.

algorithm Prescribed sequence of steps that guarantees a correct problem solution.

---

[74] Problem based on one described by Duncker, 1945.
[75] E. J. Langer, 2000; Luchins, 1942.
[76] E. J. Langer, 2000; Lubart & Mouchiroud, 2003.

requires original, nonalgorithmic approaches to situations. Furthermore, algorithms are few and far between outside the domains of mathematics and science. There are no rules we can follow to identify a substitute metal ship for a class demonstration, address ongoing ethnic and religious conflicts in the Middle East, or reduce global climate change—a problem that involves economics and political science as much as physics and meteorology.

In the absence of an algorithm, learners must instead use a **heuristic**, a general approach that may or may not yield a successful outcome. Some heuristics are specific to particular content domains. Others, such as the following, can be useful in a variety of contexts:[77]

- **Identify subgoals.** Break a large, complex task into two or more specific subtasks that can be more easily addressed.
- **Use paper and pencil.** Draw a diagram, list a problem's components, or jot down potential solutions or approaches.
- **Draw an analogy.** Identify a situation analogous to the problem situation, and derive potential solutions from the analogy.
- **Brainstorm.** Generate a wide variety of possible approaches or solutions—perhaps including some that at first glance seem outlandish or absurd—without initially evaluating any of them. After creating a lengthy list, evaluate each item for its potential relevance and usefulness.
- **"Incubate" the situation.** Let a problem remain unresolved for a few hours or days, thereby allowing mental sets to dissipate and enabling other potential approaches to be retrieved and considered.

> ? Which of these heuristics have you found to be especially helpful in solving problems?

Effective problem solving and creativity are partly metacognitive activities.

Earlier in the chapter we discovered the importance of metacognition for effective learning and studying. Metacognitive processes play an important role in problem solving and creativity as well. For instance, effective problem solvers and creative thinkers tend to do the following:[78]

- Identify one or more goals toward which to strive.
- Break a complex problem or task into two or more simpler components.
- Plan a systematic, sequential approach to addressing these components.
- Continually monitor and evaluate their progress toward their goal(s).
- Identify and address obstacles that may be impeding their progress.
- Change to new strategies if the current ones aren't working.
- Evaluate accomplishments in accordance with high standards.

Such metacognitive processes enable learners to use problem-solving and creative strategies flexibly, to apply those strategies to more complex situations, and to know when particular strategies are and are not appropriate.

In the opening case study, many of Ms. Gaunt's students rarely critique their problem solutions for logical sense—for instance, they don't recognize that typing a 4,200-word paper is unlikely to take 100 days. Essentially, the students engage in little or no self-evaluation of their problem solutions. Truly successful learners evaluate not only their own work but also the ideas and work of others. In other words, they engage in critical thinking, our next topic.

---

[77] J. E. Davidson & Sternberg, 1998, 2003; Halpern, 1997; Meltzer et al., 2007; Zimmerman & Campillo, 2003.

[78] M. Carr, 2010; Csikszentmihalyi, 1996; J. E. Davidson & Sternberg, 1998; Dominowski, 1998; Glover, Ronning, & Reynolds, 1989; Minsky, 2006; Runco & Chand, 1995.

heuristic General strategy that facilitates problem solving or creativity but does not always yield a successful outcome.

• Critical Thinking

Critical thinking involves evaluating the accuracy, credibility, and worth of information and lines of reasoning.[79] It can take a variety of forms, depending on the context. The following exercise presents four possibilities.

SEE FOR YOURSELF · Colds, Cars, Chance, and Cheer

Read and respond to each of the following situations:

1. It's autumn, and the days are becoming increasingly chilly. You see the following advertisement in the newspaper.

   > Aren't you tired of sniffles and runny noses all winter? Tired of always feeling less than your best? Get through a whole winter without colds. Take Eradicold Pills as directed.[80]

   Should you go out and buy a box of Eradicold Pills?

2. You have a beat-up old car and have invested several thousand dollars to get it in working order. You can sell the car in its present condition for $1,500, or you can invest a couple of thousand dollars more on repairs and then sell it for $3,000. What should you do?[81]

3. You have been rolling a typical six-sided die (i.e., one member of a pair of dice). You know for a fact that the die isn't heavier on one side than another, and yet in the past 30 rolls you haven't rolled a number 4 even once. What are the odds that you'll get a 4 on the next roll?

4. This research finding was presented by Dr. Edmund Emmer at an annual meeting of the American Educational Research Association:

   > Teachers who feel happy when they teach are more likely to have well-behaved students.[82]

   If you're a teacher, do such results indicate that you should try to feel happy when you enter the classroom each morning?

In each of these situations, you had to evaluate information and make some sort of judgment. In Item 1, I hope you weren't tempted to purchase Eradicold Pills, because the advertisement provided no proof that they reduce cold symptoms. It simply included the suggestion to "Take Eradicold Pills as directed" within the context of a discussion of undesirable symptoms—a common ploy in persuasive advertising.

As for Item 2, it makes more sense to sell the car now. If you sell the car for $3,000 after making $2,000 worth of repairs, you make $500 less than you would otherwise. Yet many people mistakenly believe that their past investments justify making additional ones, when in fact past investments are irrelevant to the present state of affairs.[83]

In Item 3 the chance of rolling a 4 on an evenly balanced die is—as it always is—one in six. The outcomes of previous rolls are irrelevant, because each roll is independent of the others. But when a 4 hasn't shown up even once in 30 rolls, many people believe that a 4 is long overdue and so greatly overestimate its probability.

Now what about making sure you're happy each time you enter the classroom (Item 4)? One common mistake people make in interpreting research results is to think that an association (*correlation*) between two things means that one of those things must definitely *cause* the other. As noted in Chapter 1, however, correlation doesn't necessarily indicate a

---

[79] Beyer, 1985; Heyman, 2008; J. Moon, 2008.
[80] R. J. Harris, 1977, p. 605.
[81] Modeled after Halpern, 1998.

[82] Emmer, 1994.
[83] Halpern, 1998.

critical thinking Process of evaluating the accuracy, credibility, and worth of information and lines of reasoning.

cause–and–effect relationship. Perhaps teacher happiness directly influences students' classroom behavior, but there are other possible explanations for the correlation as well. For instance, perhaps good student behavior makes teachers feel happy (rather than vice versa), or perhaps teachers who are feeling upbeat use more effective teaching techniques and keep students on task as a result of using those techniques.[84]

The four situations presented in the exercise illustrate several forms that critical thinking might take:[85]

- **Verbal reasoning:** Understanding and evaluating persuasive techniques found in oral and written language (e.g., deductive and inductive logic). You engaged in verbal reasoning when deciding whether to purchase Eradicold Pills.
- **Argument analysis:** Discriminating between reasons that do and do not support a conclusion. You engaged in argument analysis when you considered possible pros and cons of investing an additional $2,000 on car repairs.
- **Probabilistic reasoning:** Determining the likelihood and uncertainties associated with various events. You engaged in probabilistic reasoning when you determined the probability of rolling a 4 on the die.
- **Hypothesis testing:** Judging the value of data and research results in terms of the methods used to obtain them and their potential relevance to certain conclusions. When hypothesis testing includes critical thinking, it involves considering questions such as these:
  - Was an appropriate method used to measure a particular outcome?
  - Have other possible explanations or conclusions been eliminated?
  - Can the results obtained in one situation be reasonably generalized to other situations?

  You engaged in hypothesis testing when you evaluated Dr. Emmer's findings about teacher happiness.

The nature of critical thinking is, of course, different in various content domains. In writing, critical thinking may involve reading the first draft of a persuasive essay to look for errors in logical reasoning or for situations in which opinions have not been sufficiently justified. In science it may involve revising existing theories or beliefs to account for new evidence—that is, it may involve conceptual change. In history it may involve drawing inferences from historical documents, attempting to determine whether things *definitely* happened a particular way or only *maybe* happened that way.

As you might guess, critical thinking abilities emerge gradually over the course of childhood and adolescence.[86] Yet all too often, learners at all grade levels—and even many well-educated adults—take the information they see in textbooks, news reports, on the Internet, and elsewhere at face value. In other words, they engage in little or no critical thinking as they consider the accuracy, credibility, and worth of the information they encounter.[87]

The following two principles can help us understand why critical thinking tends to be the exception rather than the rule.

Critical thinking requires sophisticated epistemic beliefs.

Learners are more likely to look analytically and critically at new information if they believe that even experts' understanding of a topic continues to evolve as new evidence accumulates. They're less likely to engage in critical thinking if they believe that "knowledge" is an absolute, unchanging entity.[88] In other words, learners' *epistemic beliefs* enter into the critical thinking process.

Critical thinking takes different forms in different content domains.

[84] Emmer, 1994.

[85] Halpern, 1997, 1998, 2008.

[86] Amsterlaw, 2006; P. M. King & Kitchener, 2002; Kuhn & Franklin, 2006; D. N. Perkins & Ritchhart, 2004; Pillow, 2002.

[87] Kuhn, 2009; G. Marcus, 2008; M. J. Metzger, Flanagin, & Zwarun, 2003.

[88] Kardash & Scholes, 1996; P. M. King & Kitchener, 2002; Kuhn, 2001a; J. Moon, 2008; Schommer-Aikins, 2002.

Critical thinking is a disposition as much as a cognitive process.

By **disposition**, I mean a general inclination to approach and think about learning and problem-solving situations in a particular way—perhaps in a thoughtful, analytical, evaluative manner, on the one hand, or in a thought*less*, unquestioning way, on the other. Some learners clearly have a general disposition to think critically about the subject matter they read and study.[89] Those who do show more advanced reasoning capabilities and are more likely to undergo conceptual change when it's warranted.[90]

Researchers don't yet have a good understanding of why some learners are more predisposed to think critically than others. The larger culture and society in which learners grow up certainly have an effect, as can be seen in the Cultural Considerations box "Influences of Culture and Community on Complex Cognitive Processes." And quite possibly, teachers' actions in the classroom—for instance, whether they encourage exploration, risk taking, and critical thinking with respect to classroom topics—make a difference.[91] In the following classroom interaction, a teacher actually seems to *discourage* any disposition to think analytically and critically about classroom material:

> **Teacher:** Write this on your paper . . . it's simply memorizing this pattern. We have meters, centimeters, and millimeters. Let's say . . . write millimeters, centimeters, and meters. We want to make sure that our metric measurement is the same. If I gave you this decimal, let's say .234 m (yes, write that). In order to come up with .234 m in centimeters, the only thing that is necessary is that you move the decimal. How do we move the decimal? You move it to the right two places. (Jason, sit up please.) If I move it to the right two places, what should .234 m look like, Daniel, in centimeters? What does it look like, Ashley?
>
> **Ashley:** 23.4 cm.
>
> **Teacher:** Twenty-three point four. Simple stuff. In order to find meters, we're still moving that decimal to the right, but this time, boys and girls, we're only going to move it one place. So, if I move this decimal one place, what is my answer for millimeters?[92]

Undoubtedly, this teacher means well: She wants her students to understand how to convert from one unit of measurement to another. But notice the attitude she engenders: "Write this . . . it's simply memorizing this pattern."

Critical thinking and other complex cognitive processes will obviously enhance learners' long-term success both in higher education and in the outside world. We now look at various ways in which teachers might encourage such processes.

• Promoting Complex Cognitive Processes

If teachers focus classroom activities on the learning of isolated facts, and if they also use assessment techniques that emphasize knowledge of those facts, students will naturally begin to believe that school learning is a process of absorbing information in a rote fashion and regurgitating it at a later time. But if teachers instead focus class time and activities on *doing things with* information—applying it to new situations, using it to solve problems, critically evaluating it, and so on—then students should acquire the complex cognitive skills that will serve them well in the world beyond the classroom.

Following are numerous suggestions for encouraging students to develop and regularly use complex cognitive processes both in the classroom and in the outside world. Some focus on only one or two of the processes we've examined in this chapter, whereas others are relevant to virtually all of them.

Promoting Specific Processes

Research related to particular complex cognitive processes yields several recommendations.

---

[89] Halpern, 2008; D. N. Perkins, Tishman, Ritchhart, Donis, & Andrade, 2000; R. F. West, Toplak, & Stanovich, 2008.
[90] Southerland & Sinatra, 2003; Stanovich, 1999.

[91] Flum & Kaplan, 2006; Kuhn, 2001b, 2006; J. Moon, 2008.
[92] Dialogue from J. C. Turner, Meyer, et al., 1998, p. 741.

disposition General inclination to approach and think about learning and problem-solving tasks in a particular way.

Learners' experiences at home and in their general community and culture can have a significant effect on the development of complex cognitive processes. Following are several areas in which researchers have observed group differences.

Epistemic beliefs. People from various cultural groups don't completely agree on what it means to *learn* something. From the perspective of mainstream Western culture, learning is largely a mental enterprise: People learn in order to understand the world and acquire new skills and abilities. But for many people in China, learning also has moral and social dimensions: It enables an individual to become increasingly virtuous and honorable and to contribute in significant ways to the betterment of society. Furthermore, from a traditional East Asian perspective, true mastery of a topic comes only with a great deal of diligence, concentration, and perseverance—a position

that stands in stark contrast to the American students in the chapter's opening case study.[a]

Learning strategies. Consistent with a belief that learning requires diligence and perseverance, many East Asian parents and teachers encourage frequent use of rehearsal and rote memorization as learning strategies.[b] Rehearsal and memorization are also common in cultures that value committing oral histories or verbatim passages of sacred text (e.g., the Koran, the Bible) to memory.[c] In contrast, many schools in mainstream Western culture are increasingly presenting lessons and encouraging strategies that foster meaningful learning. Even so, Western schools typically insist that students learn certain things—such as multiplication tables and word spellings—by heart.[d]

Self-regulated learning. Also consistent with the importance placed on

diligence and persistence, East Asian parents and teachers are apt to encourage considerable self-discipline and stick-to-it-iveness as children tackle new projects. In doing so, they foster self-regulation.[e] Self-regulation is less common when youngsters have few role models for effective study habits and self-regulation skills. Such may be the case for some (but certainly not *all!*) children and adolescents who attend schools in low-socioeconomic neighborhoods. Although these students may hope to graduate, go on to college, and eventually become successful professionals, they may have little idea about how to accomplish these things.[f] The following interview with a middle school student in inner-city Philadelphia illustrates the problem:

Adult: Are you on track to meet your goals?
Student: No. I need to study more.
Adult: How do you know that?

Actively nurture students' metacognitive awareness and self-reflection.

As we've seen, children and adolescents become increasingly aware of their mental processes as they get older. Yet teachers shouldn't leave students' metacognitive development in the hands of fate. Instead, they can actively nurture students' self-reflection about mental activities. For example, a teacher might ask students to explain both what they're doing and why they're doing it while they work on a problem.[93] Alternatively, a teacher might give students questions to ask *themselves* as they work on a problem—questions such as "Are we getting closer to our goal?" and "Why is this strategy most appropriate?"[94] The right-hand column of Table 4.1 (pp. 103–104) offers additional suggestions.

Explicitly teach effective learning strategies.

Many children and adolescents know little about how they can best learn and remember information—for instance, many erroneously believe that rote learning (rehearsal, use of flash cards, etc.) is the best way to study.[95] Explicit training in study strategies—preferably integrated into ongoing instruction about academic topics—can definitely enhance students' learning and achievement and is especially important for students who have a history of academic difficulties.[96]

[93] Dominowski, 1998; Johanning, D'Agostino, Steele, & Shumow, 1999; Siegler & Lin, 2010.
[94] M. Carr, 2010; A. King, 1999, p. 101; Kramarski & Mevarech, 2003, p. 286.
[95] J. E. Barnett, 2001; Pintrich & De Groot, 1990; Prawat, 1989; Schommer, 1994a.
[96] Hattie, Biggs, & Purdie, 1996; Meltzer & Krishnan, 2007; Nokes & Dole, 2004; Pressley & Hilden, 2006.

Student: I just know by some of my grades. [mostly Cs]

Adult: Why do you think you will be more inclined to do it in high school?

Student: I don't want to get let back. I want to go to college.

Adult: What will you need to do to get better grades?

Student: Just do more and more work. I can rest when the school year is over.[9]

The student wants to get a college education, but to do so he understands only that he needs to "study more" and "do more and more work." Motivation and effort are important, to be sure, but so are planning, time management, regular self-monitoring and self-evaluation, and appropriate help-seeking—things this student seems to have little awareness of. Some learners, then, may need considerable guidance and support to acquire the learning and self-regulation strategies that will serve them well in college and the outside world.

Critical thinking. Critical thinking is another complex cognitive process that seems to depend somewhat on students' cultural backgrounds. Some cultures place high value on respecting one's elders or certain religious leaders; in doing so they may foster the epistemic belief that "truth" is a cut-and-dried entity that is best gained from authority figures.[h] In addition, a cultural emphasis on maintaining group harmony may discourage children from hashing out differences in perspectives, which critical thinking often entails.[i] Perhaps as a result of such factors, critical thinking may be less common in some groups (e.g., in some traditional Asian and Native American communities and in some fundamentalist religious groups) than in others.[j] In some situations, then, teachers must walk a fine line between teaching students to critically evaluate persuasive arguments and scientific evidence, on the one hand, and to show appropriate respect and strive for group harmony in their community and culture, on the other.

[a] Dahlin & Watkins, 2000; H. Grant & Dweck, 2001; J. Li, 2005; J. Li & Fischer, 2004.

[b] Dahlin & Watkins, 2000; D. Y. F. Ho, 1994; Purdie & Hattie, 1996.

[c] MacDonald, Uesiliana, & Hayne, 2000; Rogoff et al., 2007; Q. Wang & Ross, 2007.

[d] Q. Wang & Ross, 2007.

[e] Morelli & Rothbaum, 2007.

[f] Belfiore & Hornyak, 1998; B. L. Wilson & Corbett, 2001.

[g] B. L. Wilson & Corbett, 2001, p. 23.

[h] Delgado-Gaitan, 1994; Losh, 2003; Qian & Pan, 2002; Tyler et al., 2008.

[i] Kağitçibaşi, 2007; Kuhn & Park, 2005; J. Moon, 2008.

[j] Kuhn, Daniels, & Krishnan, 2003; Kuhn & Park, 2005; Tyler et al., 2008.

Ideally, students should learn many different learning strategies and the situations in which each one is appropriate. For instance, trying to *make sense* of new ideas—meaningful learning—is essential for learning general principles within a discipline, whereas mnemonics are often more useful in learning hard-to-remember pairs and lists. And different organizational strategies—outlines, concept maps, two-dimensional comparison tables, and so on—are more or less suitable for different situations.[97] Students should have opportunities to practice each new strategy with a variety of learning tasks over a period of time.[98] Effective strategy instruction is clearly not a one-shot deal.

When teaching learning strategies, teachers must be sure to include covert strategies—elaboration, comprehension monitoring, and so on—as well as overt ones.[99] One effective way to teach covert mental processes is to model them by thinking aloud about classroom topics.[100] For example, in a lecture on Napoleon in a world history class, a teacher might say, "Hmm . . . it seems to me that Napoleon's military tactics were similar to those of the ancient Assyrians. Let's briefly recall the things the Assyrians did." When assigning a textbook chapter for homework, a teacher might say, "Whenever I read a textbook chapter, I begin by looking at the headings and subheadings in the chapter. I then think about questions that the chapter will probably address, and I try to find the answers as I read. Let me show you how *I* might tackle the chapter I've asked you to read tonight. . . ."

[97] R. K. Atkinson et al., 1999; D. H. Robinson & Kiewra, 1995.

[98] A. L. Brown & Palincsar, 1987; A. Collins, Brown, & Newman, 1989; Gaskins & Pressley, 2007; Pressley, Harris, & Marks, 1992.

[99] Kardash & Amlund, 1991.

[100] Brophy, Alleman, & Knighton, 2009; A. L. Brown & Palincsar, 1987; Pressley, El-Dinary, Marks, Brown, & Stein, 1992.

MUSCLES

A. *Number of Muscles*

　1. There are approximately _____ muscles in the human body.

B. *How Muscles Work*

　1. Muscles work in two ways:

　　a. They _____ , or shorten.

　　b. They _____ , or lengthen.

C. *Kinds of Muscles*

　1. _____ muscles are attached to the bones by _____ .

　　a. These muscles are _____ (voluntary/involuntary).

　　b. The purpose of these muscles is to _____

　　_____ .

　2. _____ muscles line some of the body's _____ .

　　a. These muscles are _____ (voluntary/involuntary).

　　b. The purpose of these muscles is to _____

　　_____ .

　3. The _____ muscle is the only one of its kind.

　　a. This muscle is _____ (voluntary/involuntary).

　　b. The purpose of this muscle is to _____

　　_____ .

FIGURE 4.6 Example of a partially filled-in outline that can guide students' note taking

Yet students are likely to use new study strategies only if they discover for themselves that the strategies are actually helpful.[101] For instance, in my own classes I occasionally do little "experiments," presenting information that is difficult to learn and remember and giving some (but not all) students a specific strategy (e.g., a mnemonic) for learning the information. We find out how much students in the strategy and no-strategy groups can recall by writing students' "test" scores on the board. The performance of the two groups is usually so dramatically different that my students readily acknowledge the usefulness of the strategy I've taught them.

Students often need considerable guidance and support in their early efforts to use new strategies. For example, to help students identify the most important information in a lesson, a teacher might provide a list of objectives for the lesson, write key concepts and principles on the board, or ask questions that focus students' attention on central ideas.[102] To help students elaborate on what they read, teachers can provide examples of questions for students to answer (e.g., "Explain why . . ." or "What is a new example of . . . ?").[103] And to help students in their early note-taking efforts, teachers might provide a structure to fill in during a lesson. An example of such a structure for a lesson on muscles is presented in Figure 4.6. You can find another example in the two sets of notes on King Midas presented earlier in Figure 4.1.

Communicate that acquiring knowledge is a dynamic, ongoing process—that one never completely "knows" something.

Epistemic beliefs about particular academic disciplines, as well as about knowledge and learning more generally, have a significant impact on how students study, what they learn, how readily they apply classroom subject matter, and how often they critically evaluate it. Instruction in study strategies alone won't necessarily change those beliefs.[104]

One possible way to change students' epistemic beliefs is to talk specifically about the nature of knowledge and learning—for instance, to describe learning as an active, ongoing process of finding interconnections among ideas and eventually constructing one's own understanding of the world.[105] But probably a more effective approach is to provide classroom experiences that lead students to discover that knowledge must necessarily be a dynamic, rather than static, entity and to realize that successful learning sometimes occurs only through effort and persistence. For example, teachers can have students address complex issues and problems that have no clear-cut right or wrong answers.[106] They can teach

---

[101] Hattie et al., 1996; Paris & Paris, 2001; Pressley & Hilden, 2006.

[102] Ku, Chan, Wu, & Chen, 2008; McCrudden & Schraw, 2007; R. E. Reynolds & Shirey, 1988.

[103] Questions from A. King, 1992, p. 309.

[104] Schraw & Moshman, 1995.

[105] Gaskins & Pressley, 2007; Muis et al., 2006; Schommer, 1994b.

[106] Kardash & Scholes, 1996; P. M. King & Kitchener, 2002; Schommer, 1994b.

strategies for gathering data and testing competing hypotheses.[107] They can ask students to compare several explanations of a particular phenomenon or event and consider the validity and strength of evidence supporting each one.[108] And they can show students, perhaps by presenting puzzling phenomena, that their own current understandings, and in some cases even those of experts in the field, do not yet adequately explain all of human experience.[109]

Encourage and support self-regulated learning and behavior.

If students are to be productive and successful adults who work well independently, they must become increasingly self-regulating over the course of childhood and adolescence. Some students acquire self-regulation skills largely on their own, but many others need a great deal of guidance and support from teachers. For example, students with a history of academic failure acquire better study habits when they're given explicit instruction in self-regulation strategies.[110]

Consistent with the concept of *co-regulation* introduced earlier, teachers can probably best foster self-regulation skills by initially providing considerable structure and then gradually loosening the reins as students become more self-directed. The right-hand column in Table 4.2 (p. 110) offers suggestions that are apt to be appropriate at different grade levels. The Classroom Strategies box "Fostering Self-Regulation" presents several more specific ideas.

Of the many self-regulation strategies students might acquire, perhaps most important are strategies with which students can monitor and evaluate their own learning and behavior. Following are several things teachers might do to encourage self-monitoring and self-evaluation:

- Have students set specific goals and objectives for themselves, and then describe achievements in relation to them.[111]
- Provide specific criteria that students can use to judge their performance.[112]

CLASSROOM STRATEGIES Fostering Self-Regulation

- **Have students observe and record their own behavior.**

  A student with attention-deficit hyperactivity disorder frequently tips his chair back to the point where he is likely to topple over. Concerned for the student's safety, his teacher asks him to record each instance of such behavior on a sheet of graph paper. Both student and teacher notice how quickly the behavior disappears once the student has become aware of his bad habit.

- **Teach students instructions they can give themselves to remind them of what they need to do.**

  To help students remember the new dance steps they're learning, their teacher instructs them to say such things as "One, two, gallop, gallop" and "One leg, other leg, turn, and turn" while performing the steps.

- **Encourage students to evaluate their own performance.**

  A science teacher gives students a list of criteria to evaluate the lab reports they've just written. In assigning grades, she considers not only what students have written in their reports but also how accurately students have evaluated their own reports.

- **Teach students to reinforce themselves for appropriate behavior.**

  A teacher helps students develop more regular study habits by encouraging them to make a favorite activity—for example, shooting baskets, watching television, or calling a friend on the telephone—contingent on completing their homework first.

- **Give students age-appropriate opportunities to engage in learning tasks with little or no help from their teacher.**

  A middle school social studies teacher distributes various magazine articles related to current events in the Middle East, making sure that each student receives an article appropriate for his or her reading level. He asks students to read their articles over the weekend and prepare a one-paragraph summary to share with other class members. He also provides guidelines about what information students should include in their summaries.

Sources: Mace, Belfiore, & Hutchinson, 2001; Reid, Trout, & Schartz, 2005; Vintere, Hemmes, Brown, & Poulson, 2004, p. 309 (dancing self-instructions example); Zimmerman, 2004.

---

[107] Andre & Windschitl, 2003; P. M. King & Kitchener, 2002; C. L. Smith, Maclin, Houghton, & Hennessey, 2000.

[108] Andre & Windschitl, 2003; P. M. King & Kitchener, 2002; vanSledright & Limón, 2006.

[109] C. Chan, Burtis, & Bereiter, 1997; Vosniadou, 1991.

[110] Cosden, Morrison, Albanese, & Macias, 2001; Eilam, 2001; Graham & Harris, 1996; Meltzer, 2007; N. E. Perry, 1998.

[111] Eilam, 2001; Meltzer, 2007; Morgan, 1985.

[112] Meltzer, 2007; Paris & Ayres, 1994; Winne, 1995b.

Observe Keenan's self-evaluation in the "Portfolio" video in Chapter 4 of the Book-Specific Resources in MyEducationLab.

Observe the self-regulation strategies that a boy with a history of off-task behavior has acquired in the "Self-Management: Brandon's MotivAider" video in Chapter 4 of the Book-Specific Resources in MyEducationLab.

- On some occasions, delay teacher feedback so that students first have the opportunity to evaluate their own performance.[113]
- To check for long-term retention of reading material, suggest questions that students can ask themselves to assess their understanding after a significant time delay.[114]
- Ask students to keep ongoing records of their performance and to reflect on their learning in writing assignments, journals, or portfolios.[115]

One simple strategy is to provide blank forms that students can use to track their performance on classroom assessments. The daily log sheet presented in Figure 4.7 shows a form that one middle school math teacher has used. The form has its limits, however, in that it focuses students' attention only on the number of points accumulated. It provides no place for students to record the types of problems they get wrong, the kinds of errors they make, or other information that might help them improve. To help students evaluate the *quality* of their work, teachers can provide self-assessment instruments listing the criteria that students should look for. Another effective strategy is to have students compare their self-assessments with teacher assessments of their work.[116] Figure 4.8 presents a form a high school social studies teacher has used to help her students learn to evaluate their performance in a cooperative group activity.

To be successful over the long run, students must actively monitor their behavior as well as their academic performance. Yet children and adolescents aren't always aware of how frequently they do something incorrectly or ineffectively or of how *in*frequently they do something well. To help students attend to the things they do and don't do, teachers can have them observe and record their own behavior in a very concrete manner. For instance, if Raymond talks out of turn too often, his teacher can help him become aware of the problem by asking him to make a check mark on a sheet of paper every time he catches himself speaking out of turn. If Olivia has trouble staying on task during assigned activities, her teacher might give her an electronic beeper and ask her to stop, reflect on, and record her on- and off-task behaviors each time she hears a beep. Such self-focused record keeping helps students stay on task and complete assignments, and their disruptive behaviors tend to diminish.[117]

Even kindergartners and first graders can be encouraged to reflect on their performance and progress, perhaps through questions such as "What were we doing that we're proud of?" and "What can we do that we didn't do before?"[118] By regularly engaging in self-monitoring and self-evaluation of classroom assignments, students should eventually develop appropriate standards for their performance and routinely apply those standards to the things they accomplish—true hallmarks of a self-regulating learner.

Provide numerous and varied opportunities to apply classroom subject matter to new situations and problems.

As we discovered in our earlier discussion of transfer, learners will apply what they've learned only if they *retrieve* it as they encounter a new task or problem. When teachers present new material within a particular academic discipline, then, they should relate the material to other disciplines and to the outside world frequently and in a variety of ways.[119] In doing so, they help students mentally connect the concepts and procedures learned in any single classroom with

First Quarter				
Math Grade Log	Name Lea Demers			Total
				(as needed)
Assignment	Due Date	Points/Points Possible	
1 Anagram Name	8-27	5/5	5/5
2 1-1 #2-42 even	8/26	5/5	10/10
3 Your Life in Math	8/27	5/5	15/15
4 1-2 #2-52 evens	8/30	5/5	20/20
5 1-3 #7-46 even	8/31	5/5	25/25
6 1-5 #1-36	9/1	5/5	30/30
7 Quiz 1-1 to 1-3	9/2	20/25	50/55
8 4-4's Problem	9/1	6/5	56/60
9 TI Programming A	9/3	5/5	61/65
10 Quiz 1-5 to 1-6	9/10	23/25	84/90
11 1-7 #1-48	9/7	5/5	89/95

FIGURE 4.7 In this daily log sheet, 13-year-old Lea has kept track of her math assignments, their due dates, and her performance on them.

[113] D. L. Butler & Winne, 1995; Schroth, 1992.

[114] Dunning et al., 2004.

[115] Belfiore & Hornyak, 1998; Paris & Paris, 2001; N. E. Perry, 1998.

[116] McCaslin & Good, 1996; Paris & Ayres, 1994; Schraw, Potenza, & Nebelsick-Gullet, 1993.

[117] K. D. Allen, 1998; Belfiore & Hornyak, 1998; K. R. Harris, 1986; Reid, Trout, & Schartz, 2005; Webber, Scheuermann, McCall, & Coleman, 1993.

[118] N. E. Perry, VandeKamp, Mercer, & Nordby, 2002, p. 10.

[119] Bransford & Schwartz, 1999; M. C. Linn, 2008; J. R. Stone, Alfeld, & Pearson, 2008.

situations outside that classroom. For example, a teacher might show students how human digestion processes have implications for nutrition and physical well-being, how physics concepts apply to automobile engines and home construction, or how principles of economics have an impact on global climate change.

One widely recommended approach is to use **authentic activities**, activities similar to those that students are apt to encounter in real-world contexts. For example, students' writing skills may show greater improvement in both quality and quantity when students write stories, essays, and letters to real people, rather than when they complete short, artificial writing exercises.[120] Students gain a more complete understanding of how to use and interpret maps effectively when they construct their own maps than when they engage in workbook exercises involving map interpretation[121] (e.g., see Figure 4.9). Students become more proficient in math when they use their math skills for real-life tasks.[122]

Authentic activities can also be highly motivating for students.[123] As an example, consider one high school student's recollection of a ninth-grade moon-tracking activity:

> It was the first time I can remember in school doing something that wasn't in the textbook . . . like we were real scientists or something. We had to keep data sheets, measure the time and angle of the moonrise every day for a month. It drove my mom nuts because sometimes we'd be eating dinner, and I'd look at my watch and race out the door! We had to measure the river near us to see how it was affected by the moon. . . I went down to the river more than I have in my whole life, I think. Then we had to do the calculations, that was another step, and we had to chart our findings. The test was to analyze your findings and tell what they meant about the relationship of the tides and the moon. . . . I felt that I did something real, and I could see the benefit of it.[124]

Authentic activities can be developed for virtually any area of the curriculum. For example, teachers might ask students to engage in one or more of the following activities:

- Write an editorial
- Participate in a debate
- Design an electrical circuit
- Converse in a foreign language
- Make a videotape
- Perform in a concert
- Plan a personal budget
- Create a classroom website

Project description ___Travel Guide___

Evaluate with a 1 for weak, a 2 for fair, a 3 for good, a 4 for very good, and a 5 for excellent.

Student	Teacher	
4	4	1. The task was a major amount of work in keeping with a whole month of effort.
5	4	2. We used class time quite well.
4	5	3. The workload was quite evenly divided. I did a fair proportion.
4	5	4. I showed commitment to the group and to a quality project.
5	4	5. My report went into depth; it didn't just give the obvious, commonly known information.
5	5	6. The project made a point: a reader (or viewer) could figure out how all of the details fitted together to help form a conclusion.
5	5	7. The project was neat, attractive, well assembled. I was proud of the outcome.
4	5	8. We kept our work organized; we made copies; we didn't lose things or end up having to redo work that was lost.
5	4	9. The work had a lot of original thinking or other creative work.
4	4	10. The project demonstrated mastery of basic language skills—composition, planning, oral communication, writing.
45	45	Total

Comments:

46 group average

FIGURE 4.8 After a cooperative group activity with three classmates, Rochelle and her teacher used the same criteria to rate Rochelle's performance and that of her group. With the two sets of ratings side by side, Rochelle can evaluate the accuracy of her self-assessments.

Observe third graders' high level of motivation as they design and create waterwheels in the "Water Wheels" video in Chapter 4 of the Book-Specific Resources in MyEducationLab.

---

[120] E. H. Hiebert & Fisher, 1992.
[121] Gregg & Leinhardt, 1994.
[122] Cognition and Technology Group at Vanderbilt, 1993; J. R. Stone et al., 2008.
[123] M. Barnett, 2005; Marks, 2000.
[124] Wasley, Hampel, & Clark, 1997, pp. 117–118.

authentic activity Task or activity similar to one students might encounter in the outside world.

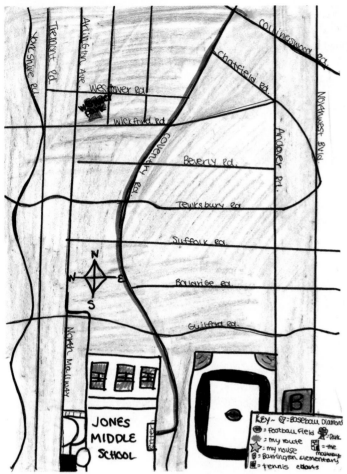

FIGURE 4.9 In an authentic mapping activity, 12-year-old Mary Lynn constructed this map of the area between her home and school.

❓ What authentic activities might you use to facilitate students' transfer of the discipline(s) you hope to teach?

In some cases authentic activities take the form of **problem-based** or **project-based learning**, in which students acquire new knowledge and skills as they work on complex problems or projects similar to those they might find in the outside world.[125] In other cases they may take the form of computer simulations (more on these in Chapter 8).

To be effective in enhancing students' learning—rather than sources of frustration and failure—most complex authentic activities require considerable teacher guidance and support.[126] Furthermore, it isn't necessarily a good idea to fill the entire school day with complex, authentic tasks. For one thing, students can sometimes achieve automaticity for basic skills more quickly when they practice them in relative isolation from other activities. For example, when learning to play the violin, students need to master their fingering before they join an orchestra, and when learning to play soccer, they need to practice dribbling and passing before they can play effectively in a game.[127] Second, some authentic tasks may be too expensive and time-consuming to warrant regular use in the classroom.[128] It's probably more important that classroom tasks encourage students to engage in learning processes that promote long-term retention and transfer of classroom subject matter—elaboration, organization, comprehension monitoring, and so on—than that tasks always be authentic.[129]

Create the conditions that creative thinking and problem solving require.

Students are more apt to think creatively when a teacher asks thought-provoking questions that require them to use previously learned information in new and unusual ways. Questions that require divergent thinking may be especially helpful.[130] Here are two examples:

- Create an alternative ending to the short story you just read that presents a different way things might have gone for the main characters in the story.
- Suppose that you were to design a new instrument to be played in a symphony orchestra for future compositions. What might that instrument be like, and why?[131]

It's important, too, to encourage students to encode situations and problems in multiple ways, so that they don't get locked into mental sets that exclude potentially effective approaches and solutions. For instance, a teacher might ask students to work in cooperative groups to identify several *different* ways of representing a single problem on paper—perhaps as a formula, a table, and a graph.[132] And certainly a teacher should mix the kinds of problems that students tackle in any single practice session, so that students must think carefully about which problem-solving procedures are appropriate for each one.[133]

If they are to think about tasks and problems creatively, students must also have the freedom and security they need to take risks, which they are unlikely to do if they're afraid of failing.[134] To encourage risk taking, teachers can allow students to engage in certain activities without evaluating their performance. They can also urge students to think of their mistakes and failures as an inevitable, but usually temporary, aspect of the creative

---

problem-based learning Classroom activity in which students acquire new knowledge and skills while working on a complex problem similar to certain real-world problems.

project-based learning Classroom activity in which students acquire new knowledge and skills while working on a complex, multifaceted project that yields a concrete end product.

[125] Gijbels, Dochy, Van den Bossche, & Segers, 2005; Hmelo-Silver, 2004, 2006; Mergendoller, Markham, Ravitz, & Larmer, 2006; Polman, 2004.

[126] Hmelo-Silver, Duncan, & China, 2007; Krajcik & Blumenfeld, 2006; Mergendoller et al., 2006.

[127] J. R. Anderson, Reder, & Simon, 1996; Bransford et al., 2006.

[128] M. M. Griffin & Griffin, 1994.

[129] J. R. Anderson et al., 1996.

[130] Feldhusen & Treffinger, 1980; D. N. Perkins, 1990; Sternberg, Grigorenko, & Zhang, 2008.

[131] Sternberg et al., 2008, p. 488.

[132] Brenner et al., 1997; J. C. Turner, Meyer, et al., 1998.

[133] E. J. Langer, 2000; Mayfield & Chase, 2002.

[134] Houtz, 1990; J. Moon, 2008; Sternberg, 2003.

process.[135] For example, when students are writing a creative short story, a teacher might give them several opportunities to get feedback before they turn in a final product.

Finally, teachers must provide the *time* that creative thinking and complex problem solving require.[136] Students need time to experiment with new materials and ideas, to think in divergent directions, and occasionally to make mistakes. For instance, when teaching a foreign language, a teacher might ask small groups of students to write and videotape a television commercial spoken entirely in that language. This is hardly a project that students can do in a day. They may need several weeks to brainstorm ideas, write and revise a script, find or develop the props they need, and rehearse their lines. Creative ideas and projects seldom emerge overnight.

Encourage critical thinking.

To become effective life-long learners, students must learn that not all sources of information can be trusted—that many of the messages they encounter in the world may be misleading or blatantly incorrect. In our current era of ever-expanding information technology, taking a critical stance toward new information is now more important than ever before. For instance, virtually anyone can post personal beliefs and opinions on the Internet—many people present these things as irrefutable "fact"—and it's all too easy to be taken in. Even many college students naively assume that virtually anything they read on the Internet is fact.[137]

Critical thinking encompasses a variety of skills, and so strategies for encouraging it are many and varied. Here are several suggestions:

- Encourage some intellectual skepticism—for instance, by urging students to question and challenge the ideas they read and hear—and communicate the epistemic belief that people's knowledge and understanding of any single topic will continue to change over time.[138]
- Model critical thinking—for instance, by thinking aloud while analyzing a persuasive argument or scientific report.[139]
- Give students many opportunities to practice critical thinking—for instance, by identifying flaws in the arguments of persuasive essays, evaluating the quality and usefulness of scientific findings, and using evidence and logic to support particular viewpoints.[140]
- Ask questions such as these to encourage critical thinking:
  - Who produced this document? What biases or predispositions did the author or authors have?
  - What persuasive technique is the author using? Is it valid, or is it designed to mislead the reader?
  - What information contradicts information in other documents?
  - What reasons support the conclusion? What reasons do *not* support the conclusion?
  - What actions might I take to improve the design of this study?[141]
- Have students debate controversial issues from several perspectives, and occasionally ask them to take a perspective quite different from their own.[142]
- Embed critical thinking skills within the context of authentic activities as a way of helping students retrieve those skills later on, both in the workplace and in other aspects of adult life.[143]

The Classroom Strategies box "Fostering Critical Thinking" presents examples of what teachers might do in language arts, social studies, and science.

Promoting Complex Processes in General

Several especially important instructional practices are apt to promote numerous complex cognitive processes simultaneously.

---

[135] Feldhusen & Treffinger, 1980; B. A. Hennessey & Amabile, 1987; Pruitt, 1989.

[136] Feldhusen & Treffinger, 1980; Pruitt, 1989; Sternberg, 2003.

[137] M. J. Metzger, Flanagin, & Zwarun, 2003; Wiley et al., 2009.

[138] Afflerbach & Cho, 2010; Kardash & Scholes, 1996; Kuhn, 2001a.

[139] J. Moon, 2008; Onosko & Newmann, 1994.

[140] Halpern, 1998; Kuhn & Pease, 2008; Kuhn & Weinstock, 2002; Monte-Sano, 2008.

[141] Questions based on Halpern, 1998, p. 454; S. A. Stahl & Shanahan, 2004, pp. 110–111.

[142] E. M. Nussbaum, 2008; Reiter, 1994.

[143] Derry et al., 1998; Halpern, 1998.

CLASSROOM STRATEGIES Fostering Critical Thinking

- **Teach elements of critical thinking.**

    In a unit on persuasion and argumentation, a junior high school language arts teacher explains that a sound argument meets three criteria: (a) The evidence presented to justify the argument is accurate and consistent; (b) the evidence is relevant to, and provides sufficient support for, the conclusion; and (c) there is little or no missing information that, if present, would lead to a contradictory conclusion. The teacher then has students practice applying these criteria to a variety of persuasive and argumentative essays.

- **Foster epistemic beliefs that encourage critical thinking.**

    Rather than teach history as a collection of facts to be memorized, a high school history teacher portrays the discipline as an attempt by informed but inevitably biased scholars to interpret and make sense of historical events. On several occasions he asks his students to read two or three different historians' accounts of the same incident and to look for evidence of personal bias in each one.

- **Embed critical thinking skills within the context of authentic activities.**

    In a unit on statistical and scientific reasoning, an eighth-grade science class studies concepts related to probability, correlation, and experimental control. Then, as part of a simulated "legislative hearing," the students work in small groups to develop arguments for or against a legislative bill concerning the marketing and use of vitamins and other dietary supplements. To find evidence to support their arguments, the students apply what they've learned about statistics and experimentation as they read and analyze journal articles and government reports about the possible benefits and drawbacks of nutritional supplements.

Sources: Derry, Levin, Osana, & Jones, 1998 (statistics example); Halpern, 1997 (criteria for sound argument); Paxton, 1999 (history example).

Teach complex thinking skills within the context of academic disciplines and subject matter.

Teachers occasionally run across packaged curricular programs designed to teach study skills, problem solving, creativity, or critical thinking. As a general rule, however, teachers should teach complex cognitive processes *not* as separate entities, but instead within the context of day-to-day academic topics. For example, they might teach critical thinking and problem-solving skills during science lessons or teach creative thinking during writing instruction.[144] And to help students become truly effective learners, teachers should teach study strategies in *every* academic discipline.[145] For example, when presenting new information in class, a teacher might (1) suggest how students can organize their notes, (2) describe mnemonics for facts and procedures that are hard to remember, and (3) ask various students to summarize the main points of a lesson. When assigning textbook pages to be read at home, a teacher might (4) suggest that students recall what they already know about a topic before they begin reading about it, (5) provide questions for students to ask themselves as they read, and (6) have students create concept maps interrelating key ideas.

Pursue topics in depth rather than superficially.

Observe a high school chemistry teacher use a variety of strategies to promote mastery of Charles's Law in the "Charles's Law" video in Chapter 4 of the Book-Specific Resources in MyEducationLab.

To apply classroom material to real-world situations and problems, use it flexibly and creatively, and think critically about it, students should not just study the material on one occasion. Instead, they must *master* it. Ultimately, students should gain a thorough, conceptual understanding of topics that can help them make better sense of their world and function more effectively in adult society. This *less-is-more* principle applies across the board: Teaching a few topics in depth is almost invariably more effective than skimming over the surface of a great many.[146]

Foster complex cognitive processes through group discussions and projects.

In Chapter 3 we noted that learners can often gain a better understanding of a topic when they discuss it with peers. A rapidly growing body of research evidence indicates that group

---

[144] Abrami et al., 2008; Beal, Arroyo, & Cohen, 2009; Desoete, Roeyers, & De Clercq, 2003; M. C. Linn, Clement, Pulos, & Sullivan, 1989; Stanley, 1980.
[145] Hattie et al., 1996; Meltzer et al., 2007; Paris & Paris, 2001; Pressley, El-Dinary, et al., 1992; Pressley, Harris, & Marks, 1992.

[146] Amabile & Hennessey, 1992; Brophy, Alleman, & Knighton, 2008; N. Frederiksen, 1984a; M. C. Linn, 2008; D. N. Perkins, 1990; Prawat, 1989; Rittle-Johnson, Siegler, & Alibali, 2001.

activities, especially when structured to some degree, can promote complex cognitive processes as well.[147] When students talk with one another, they must verbalize (and therefore become more metacognitively aware of) what and how they themselves are thinking. They also hear other (possibly better) study strategies, problem-solving techniques, and critical analyses. And by working together, they can often accomplish more difficult tasks than they would accomplish on their own.

Observe high school students engage in small-group problem solving in their history class in the "Cooperative Learning: Reconstruction" video in Chapter 4 of the Book-Specific Resources in MyEducationLab.

One effective approach is to teach students to ask one another, and then answer, thought-provoking questions about the material they're studying—for instance, "Why is it that such-and-such is true?"[148] In the following dialogue, fifth graders Katie and Janelle are working together to study class material about tide pools. Katie's job is to ask Janelle questions that encourage elaboration:

Katie: How are the upper tide zone and the lower tide zone different?

Janelle: They have different animals in them. Animals in the upper tide zone and splash zone can handle being exposed—have to be able to use the rain and sand and wind and sun—and they don't need that much water and the lower tide animals do.

Katie: And they can be softer 'cause they don't have to get hit on the rocks.

Janelle: Also predators. In the spray zone it's because there's predators like us people and all different kinds of stuff that can kill the animals and they won't survive, but the lower tide zone has not as many predators.

Katie: But wait! Why do the animals in the splash zone have to survive?[149]

Notice how the two girls are continually relating the animals' characteristics to survival in different tide zones, and eventually Katie asks why animals in the splash zone even *need* to survive—a question that clearly reflects critical thinking.

Create an overall classroom culture that values complex thinking processes.

Through both words and actions, teachers should communicate that sophisticated learning strategies, transfer, creative problem solving, and critical thinking must be commonplace in the classroom.[150] For example, teachers might:

- Have students conduct "strategy share" discussions or create "strategy books" in which class members explain their techniques for learning and remembering specific classroom topics.[151]
- Regularly encourage students to think "How might I use this information?" as they listen, read, and study.[152]
- Consistently welcome creative ideas, even those that might occasionally fly in the face of conventional ways of thinking.[153]
- Conduct extended discussions of intriguing "Why?" questions and controversial issues and ask students to defend diverse perspectives with evidence and logic.[154]

Incorporate complex cognitive processes into assessment activities.

As you'll discover in Chapter 10, it's fairly easy to construct assignments and tests that assess knowledge of basic facts and procedures. But it's ultimately more important that teachers assess what students can *do* with what they've learned. As an illustration, Figure 4.10 presents an

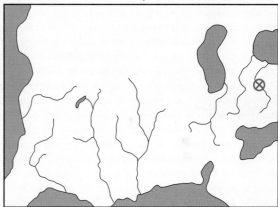

- If people living at the point marked "X" on the map began to migrate *or* expand, where would they go and what direction might they take?
- What would be the distribution of population in country "X"; that is, where would many people live, few, and so on?
- Where would large cities develop in country "X"?
- How would you judge the country's economic potential; that is, what areas might be best for development, which worst, and so on?

FIGURE 4.10 Example of an assessment activity that asks students to apply what they've learned in geography to new problems

Source: Problems and figure from B. G. Massialas and J. Zevin, *Teaching Creatively: Learning Through Discovery*, 1983, Krieger Publishing Company, Malabar, Florida, U.S.A. Reprinted with permission.

[147] Larkin, 2008; E. M. Nussbaum, 2008; A. M. O'Donnell, Hmelo-Silver, & Erkens, 2006.

[148] Kahl & Woloshyn, 1994; A. King, 1994, 1999; V. L. Martin & Pressley, 1991; Palincsar & Herrenkohl, 1999; Rosenshine, Meister, & Chapman, 1996; Woloshyn, Pressley, & Schneider, 1992; E. Wood et al., 1999.

[149] A. King, 1999, p. 97.

[150] Engle, 2006; Haskell, 2001; Muis et al., 2006; Pea, 1987; D. N. Perkins & Ritchhart, 2004.

[151] Meltzer et al., 2007.

[152] D. N. Perkins, 1992; Stein, 1989; Sternberg & Frensch, 1993.

[153] Lubart & Mouchiroud, 2003.

[154] Chinn, 2006; D. N. Perkins & Ritchhart, 2004.

assessment task that asks students to apply their knowledge of geographic principles to several new problems. By consistently incorporating application of classroom topics into assessment tasks and problems, teachers clearly communicate that academic subject matter can and should be flexibly and creatively used in many different contexts.

SUMMARY

Complex cognitive processes are processes in which learners go far beyond the information they've learned, perhaps to better understand it, apply it to a new situation, use it to solve a problem or create a product, or critically evaluate it. The Mega-Ideas presented at the beginning of the chapter can help us summarize what psychologists and educators have learned about such processes.

● **Effective learners regularly reflect on, take charge of, and strive to improve their learning efforts.** *Metacognition,* which literally means "thinking about thinking," includes knowledge and beliefs about one's own cognitive processes, along with conscious attempts to engage in behaviors and cognitive processes that maximize learning and memory. Although metacognitive awareness and effective learning strategies improve with age, even many high school students are quite naive about how they can best study and learn classroom subject matter. To some degree, learners' *epistemic beliefs* about the nature of knowledge and learning affect the study strategies they use. For example, students who realize that reading is a constructive process are more likely to engage in meaningful learning as they read and more likely to undergo conceptual change when they encounter ideas that contradict what they currently believe.

   Self-regulation—the process of directing, monitoring, and evaluating one's own performance—affects learning success as well. Self-regulation includes establishing goals and standards for performance, planning a course of action, actively controlling both external behaviors and internal thoughts and emotions, monitoring progress, evaluating final outcomes, and self-imposing consequences (either internal or external) for success and failure. *Co-regulated learning,* in which an adult and child share responsibility for directing a learning task, helps young learners gradually assume control of their own learning processes.

● **Learners often don't use the specific facts they learn at school, but they might apply the general conceptual understandings, learning strategies, and attitudes they acquire to a wide range of circumstances.** When learners apply something they've learned in one context to a new context, *transfer* is occurring. Transfer of specific facts is most common when a new situation is obviously similar to an earlier situation in which certain knowledge and skills have come into play (e.g., knowing how to count in French can help someone learn how to count in Spanish). In contrast, general study strategies, beliefs, and attitudes (e.g., knowing how to take good notes, realizing that mastering classroom topics takes hard work and persistence) often transfer from one content domain to a very

different domain. Learners are most likely to apply school subject matter to outside tasks and problems if they learn it meaningfully and have a thorough, conceptual understanding of it.

● **Learners are more effective problem solvers and more creative thinkers if they know the subject matter well and can think flexibly about the task at hand.** *Problem solving*—addressing and resolving an unanswered question or troubling situation—and *creativity*—developing an original and culturally appropriate product—involve varying degrees of convergent and divergent thinking. Learners can usually solve problems more effectively and think more creatively when they have acquired considerable knowledge about a topic, have automatized basic skills but *not* automatized particular ways of encoding problems and situations, and can metacognitively reflect on and monitor their progress.

● **Critical thinking requires both a sophisticated understanding of the nature of knowledge and a general willingness to question the accuracy and worth of new information and ideas.** *Critical thinking* involves evaluating the accuracy, credibility, and worth of information and lines of reasoning. It takes a variety of forms, such as analyzing persuasive arguments, identifying statements that do and don't support a particular conclusion, and judging the value of data collected through different research methods. When learners have sophisticated epistemic beliefs (e.g., when they realize that an understanding of a topic continues to evolve over time) and are predisposed to question and evaluate new information, they're more likely to think critically about what they read and hear.

● **Effective teachers consistently encourage complex cognitive processes within the context of teaching academic subject matter.** A variety of classroom practices can promote specific complex cognitive processes (e.g., skeletal outlines can facilitate note taking, authentic activities can encourage transfer), but several practices are applicable across the board. For example, teachers more effectively promote complex processes when they incorporate these processes into the ongoing curriculum rather than teaching separate units on, say, "study skills" or "creativity." Group discussions that enable students to critique and build on one another's ideas as they tackle challenging topics, tasks, and issues should be commonplace. And ultimately, transfer, creative problem solving, critical thinking, and other complex cognitive processes should be the expectation and norm in the classroom, not only in lessons but also in assessment activities.

PRACTICE FOR YOUR LICENSURE EXAM

Interview with Emily

In the ninth and tenth grades, Emily earns mostly Cs and Ds in her classes. When she reaches eleventh grade, however, she begins to work more diligently on her schoolwork, and by the first semester of twelfth grade, she is earning As and Bs. Ms. Tillman, a preservice teacher, interviews Emily about her study strategies:

Ms. T.: Now that you're receiving good grades, how do you study for a test?

Emily: Well, it's different for every subject. Now when I study for a math test, I do many practice problems. When I'm studying for a history or science test, I first review my notes. My favorite thing to do is make flash cards with the important facts. I then go through the flash cards many times and try to learn the facts on them.

Ms. T.: What do you mean, "learn" the facts on them?

Emily: I guess I try to memorize the facts. I'll go through the flash cards many times and say them over and over in my head until I remember them.

Ms. T.: How do you know when a fact is memorized?

Emily: I'll repeat a fact over and over in my head until I think I've memorized it. Then I'll leave and do something else, like get a snack. I know I've memorized something if I still remember it after taking my break.

Ms. T.: Do you consider yourself a good textbook reader?

Emily: Not really. Textbooks are pretty boring. I'll try to read everything in the textbook, but at times I find myself looking for boldface print. Phrases in bold print are important.

Ms. T.: What are some good methods for studying for a test?

Emily: I really like the flash card method because it helps me to memorize facts. I also like to reread the text and my notes.

---

[155] Interview courtesy of Melissa Tillman.

Another good method is outlining the text, but this method takes too long so I rarely use it.[155]

1. Constructed-response question

In the interview Emily reveals several strategies she uses to learn and remember school subject matter.

A. Identify three specific strategies that Emily uses when she studies.

B. For each of the strategies you've identified, describe the extent to which it is likely to help Emily remember and apply school subject matter over the long run. Base your explanation on contemporary principles and theories of learning, memory, metacognition, and/or self-regulation.

2. Multiple-choice question

Emily says, "My favorite thing to do is make flash cards with the important facts. I then go through the flash cards many times and try to learn the facts on them." This statement suggests that Emily views academic subject matter as being primarily a collection of discrete facts. Such a perspective is an example of:

a. A covert strategy

b. Divergent thinking

c. An illusion of knowing

d. An epistemic belief

Go to Chapter 4 of the Book-Specific Resources in MyEducationLab and click on "Practice for Your Licensure Exam" to answer these questions. Compare your responses with the feedback provided.

PEARSON
myeducationlab

Go to the Topics "Cognition and Memory" and "Social Cognitive Perspectives" in the MyEducationLab (www.myeducationlab.com) for your course, where you can:

- Find learning outcomes for "Cognition and Memory" and "Social Cognitive Perspectives," along with the national standards that connect to these outcomes.
- Complete Assignments and Activities that can help you more deeply understand the chapter content.
- Apply and practice your understanding of the core teaching skills identified in the chapter with the Building Teaching Skills and Dispositions learning units.
- Examine challenging situations and cases presented in the IRIS Center Resources.
- Access video clips of CCSSO National Teachers of the Year award winners responding to the question, "Why Do I Teach?" in the Teacher Talk section.

- Check your comprehension of the content covered in the chapter by going to the Study Plan in the Book Resources for your text. Here you will be able to take a chapter quiz, receive feedback on your answers, and then access Review, Practice, and Enrichment activities to enhance your understanding of chapter content. Flash cards are also available to help you study definitions and key terms.
- Access additional Book Resources, including:
  - Focus Questions to guide your reading, Video Examples of various concepts and principles presented in the chapter, a Practice for Your Licensure Exam exercise that resembles the kinds of questions appearing on many teacher licensure tests, and Margin Note Questions that help you connect chapter content to your past experiences or current beliefs.

Chapter

5

Cognitive Development

Bob Daemmrich Photography

CHAPTER OUTLINE

Case Study: Hidden Treasure

General Principles of Development

Developmental Processes

Trends in Cognitive Development

Intelligence

Addressing Students' Developmental Needs
    Accommodating Developmental Differences and Diversity
    Fostering Cognitive Development

Summary

Practice for Your Licensure Exam: Stones Lesson

MEGA-IDEAS TO MASTER IN THIS CHAPTER

As a result of biological and environmental factors and their continually interacting influences, children show some similar patterns but also considerable diversity in developmental pathways.

Cognitive development depends not only on brain maturation but also on stimulating physical, social, and cultural experiences and on children's natural inclinations to organize and try to make sense of those experiences.

Children continually build on existing knowledge and skills to develop more advanced thinking and reasoning abilities.

Although children in any age-group differ somewhat in intelligence, cognitive styles, and dispositions, appropriately supportive environments can significantly enhance these abilities and characteristics.

Effective teachers accommodate students' developmental differences and diversity in their curriculum planning and instructional practices.

Effective teachers also plan and conduct lessons and activities that promote students' cognitive and intellectual development.

CASE STUDY Hidden Treasure

Six-year-old Lupita has spent most of her young life in Mexico with her grandmother, a woman with limited financial means and no knowledge of English. But Lupita has recently joined her migrant-worker parents in the United States, and she is now a quiet, well-behaved student in Ms. Padilla's kindergarten class. Ms. Padilla rarely calls on Lupita because of her apparent lack of academic skills and is thinking about holding her back for a second year of kindergarten.

Yet a researcher's video camera captures a side of the child that her teacher hasn't noticed. On one occasion Lupita is quick to finish her Spanish assignment and starts to work on a puzzle during her free time. A classmate approaches, and he and Lupita begin playing with a box of toys. A teacher aide asks the boy whether he has finished his Spanish assignment, implying that he should return to complete it, but the boy doesn't understand the aide's subtle message. Lupita gently persuades the boy to go back and finish his work and then returns to her puzzle and successfully fits most of it

together. Two classmates having difficulty with their own puzzles request Lupita's assistance, and she competently and patiently shows them how to work cooperatively to assemble the puzzles.

Ms. Padilla is amazed when she views the videotape, which shows Lupita to be a competent girl with strong teaching and leadership skills. Ms. Padilla readily admits, "I had written her off . . . her and three others. They had met my expectations and I just wasn't looking for anything else." Ms. Padilla and her aides begin working closely with Lupita on academic skills and often allow her to take a leadership role in group activities. At the end of the school year, Lupita earns achievement test scores indicating exceptional competence in language skills and mathematics, and she is promoted to first grade.[1]

- Why might Ms. Padilla initially underestimate Lupita's academic potential?

- What clues in the case study suggest that Lupita is, in fact, quite bright?

[1] Case described by Carrasco, 1981.

Over the years Ms. Padilla has almost certainly had students who lacked basic knowledge and skills (color and shape names, counting, the alphabet, etc.), and many of them undoubtedly struggled with the kindergarten curriculum as a result. And in Ms. Padilla's experience, children who can answer questions and contribute to class discussions usually speak up or raise their hands, but Lupita is quiet and reserved. With such things in mind, it might be all too easy to conclude that Lupita needs a second year in kindergarten. Yet the speed with which Lupita finishes her assignment and her behavior during free time—her facility with puzzles despite little prior experience with them, her correct interpretation of an aide's subtle message, and her skill in guiding peers—suggest that she learns quickly and has considerable social know-how.

Throughout the preschool, elementary, and secondary years, children develop an ever-expanding knowledge base and a wide variety of behavioral, cognitive, and social skills for interacting effectively with their world. For instance, in previous chapters we've learned that as children get older, they acquire more effective learning and study strategies, greater metacognitive awareness, and an increasing ability to regulate their own learning. In this chapter we begin to look at child and adolescent development more closely, and we'll continue to consider developmental trends in future chapters. As we do so, we'll draw from a variety of theoretical perspectives, including two we've previously encountered in our discussions of learning and cognition: information processing theory and sociocultural theory.

Table 5.1 describes six theoretical perspectives that have been especially influential in the study of child and adolescent development. Keep in mind that, for the most part, these various perspectives aren't mutually exclusive. For example, some developmental theorists have drawn on both the cognitive-developmental and information processing perspectives in their work on cognitive development (notice how theorists Robbie Case and Kurt Fischer appear in two places in Table 5.1). Keep in mind, too, that the perspectives presented in the table are not the only ones psychologists have used in studying child development. Behaviorism, social cognitive theory, and other perspectives, although not as dominant, have made significant contributions to developmental psychology as well.

The ideas of two early developmental theorists, Jean Piaget and Lev Vygotsky, will play key roles in our discussion in the upcoming pages. Piaget, who was Swiss, developed many ingenious tasks to probe children's and adolescents' thinking and reasoning.[2] He observed that young learners often have self-constructed understandings of physical and social phenomena and that these understandings change in qualitative ways over time. Hence Piaget was a cognitive-developmental theorist. Meanwhile, Vygotsky, who was Russian, proposed mechanisms through which children's social and cultural environments influence their development, and his work provided the groundwork for sociocultural theory.[3] Some of Vygotsky's ideas—especially mediated learning, cognitive tools, and the importance of culture—appeared in Chapter 3. However, because Vygotsky was, first and foremost, concerned about children's cognitive development, we will continue to look at his ideas in this chapter.

Our initial focus in this chapter will be on general processes and trends that characterize the development of the great majority of children and adolescents. Later we'll look at the variability in cognitive abilities we're likely to see among children in any single group—variability that is sometimes referred to as *intelligence*.

 Learn more about Piaget's and Vygotsky's theories of cognitive development in supplementary readings in Chapter 5 of the Book-Specific Resources in MyEducationLab.

• General Principles of Development

Virtually any aspect of development—whether physical, cognitive, personal, or social—is characterized by several general principles.

The sequence of development is somewhat predictable.

Researchers have observed many **universals** in development—similar patterns in how children change over time despite considerable differences in their environments. Some of this universality is marked by the acquisition of **developmental milestones**—new, developmentally more advanced behaviors—in predictable sequences. For example, children usually learn to walk only after they've learned to sit up and crawl. They become capable of using fractions in mathematical problem solving only after they've mastered counting and the use of whole numbers. And they become concerned about what other people think of them only after they realize that other people *do* think about them.

---

universal (in development) Similar pattern in how children change and progress over time regardless of their specific environment.

developmental milestone Appearance of a new, developmentally more advanced behavior.

[2] For example, see Inhelder & Piaget, 1958; Piaget, 1928, 1952b, 1959, 1970, 1980.

[3] For example, see Vygotsky, 1962, 1978, 1987, 1997. Vygotsky died in 1934, but many of his works were not translated into English until considerably later.

THEORETICAL PERSPECTIVES

TABLE 5.1 General Theoretical Approaches to the Study of Child and Adolescent Development

Theoretical Perspective	General Description	Examples of Prominent Theorists	Where You Will See This Perspective in the Book
Cognitive-Developmental Theory	Cognitive-developmental theorists propose that one or more aspects of development can be characterized by a predictable sequence of stages. Each stage builds on acquisitions from any preceding stages and yet is qualitatively different from its predecessors. Most cognitive-developmentalists are *constructivists,* in that they portray children as actively trying to make sense of their world and constructing increasingly complex understandings and abilities with which to interpret and respond to experiences.	Jean Piaget Jerome Bruner Robbie Case Kurt Fischer Lawrence Kohlberg *Supplementary readings on Piaget's theory and Kohlberg's theory appear in Chapters 5 and 7, respectively, of the Book-Specific Resources in MyEducationLab.*	Piaget's ideas appear frequently in this chapter's discussions of developmental processes and trends (e.g., see the discussions of assimilation, accommodation, and equilibration, as well as Table 5.2 and some entries in Table 5.3). We will look at Kohlberg's theory in our discussion of moral development in Chapter 7.
Nativism	Some behaviors are biologically built in. A few behaviors (e.g., the reflex to suck on a nipple placed in the mouth) are evident at birth. Others (e.g., walking) emerge gradually, and usually in a predictable order, as genetic instructions propel increasing physical *maturation* of the brain and body. Nativists suggest that in addition to genetically preprogrammed behaviors, some knowledge, skills, and predispositions—or at least the basic "seeds" from which such things will grow—are also biologically built in.	Renee Baillargeon Elizabeth Spelke Noam Chomsky	The influence of nativism is most obvious in this chapter's discussions of heredity, maturation, sensitive periods, brain development, and intelligence. It will also be reflected in our discussion of *temperament* both in this chapter and in Chapter 7.
Sociocultural Theory	Sociocultural theorists emphasize the role of social interaction and children's cultural heritage in directing the course of development. Parents, teachers, and peers are especially instrumental, in that they pass along culturally prescribed ways of thinking about and responding to objects and events. As children gain practice in certain behaviors and cognitive processes within the context of social interactions, they gradually adopt and adapt these behaviors and processes as their own.	Lev Vygotsky Barbara Rogoff Jean Lave Mary Gauvain *A supplementary reading on Vygotsky's theory appears in Chapter 5 of the Book-Specific Resources in MyEducationLab.*	Vygotsky's theory and other socio-cultural perspectives come into play in this chapter whenever we discuss the influence of social interaction on cognitive development (e.g., see the discussions of internalization, zone of proximal development, cultural differences, and distributed intelligence). Sociocultural theory underlies many of the chapter's recommendations for fostering cognitive development (e.g., see the discussions of play activities, reciprocal teaching, scaffolding, and apprenticeships). It will also help us understand the effectiveness of peer mediation in Chapter 7.
Information Processing Theory	Developmental psychologists who take an information processing approach focus on how memory capabilities and specific cognitive processes change with age. For example, some examine how an expanding working memory capacity enables more complex thought. Others consider how increasingly sophisticated metacognitive knowledge and beliefs spur more advanced and effective learning strategies. Still others explore the cognitive processes involved in children's social interactions with peers.	Robert Siegler Deanna Kuhn John Flavell Robbie Case Kurt Fischer Nicki Crick Kenneth Dodge	Some trends in cognitive development described in this chapter (e.g., changes in children's working memory and knowledge bases, as well as their impacts on children's reasoning) are based on information processing research. Discussions of the cognitive processes involved in intelligence and related abilities also draw largely from information processing theory. In Chapter 7, we'll draw on this perspective once again in our discussion of social information processing.

(continued)

TABLE 5.1 Continued

Theoretical Perspective	General Description	Examples of Prominent Theorists	Where You Will See This Perspective in the Book
Ecological Systems Theory	Ecological systems theorists point out that to fully understand and explain children's development, we must consider the various environmental contexts in which children grow up—not only the immediate contexts with which children have everyday contact (e.g., home and school) but also the broader environments within which these immediate contexts exist (e.g., the community and its resources, the federal government and its laws and policies). These various layers of context interact with and affect one another in myriad ways (e.g., community employment opportunities affect a family's ability to provide nourishing food and stimulating activities for children).	Urie Bronfenbrenner	Ecological systems theory provides the basis for the discussion of the "layers" of context discussed in Chapter 3 (e.g., see Figure 3.3). It also highlights the importance of considering the cultural groups in which children grow up, as evidenced in the Cultural Considerations boxes in Chapters 3 through 10.
Psychodynamic Theory	By and large, psychodynamic theorists focus on personality development, and sometimes on abnormal development as well. They propose that a child's early experiences can have significant effects on a child's later development, even when those experiences are buried in a child's unconscious and so are unavailable for recall and self-reflection. Some theorists also propose that children go through qualitatively distinct stages in their development. One key concept in many psychodynamic theories is *identity*, one's self-constructed definition of who one is and hopes to become.	Sigmund Freud Erik Erikson *A supplementary reading on Erikson's theory appears in Chapter 7 of the Book-Specific Resources in MyEducationLab.*	Identity formation will be an important topic in our discussion of sense of self in Chapter 7. In that discussion, we'll draw on research by James Marcia (a psychologist who drew heavily from Erik Erikson's theory) to identify the various paths that adolescents might take in their search for identity.

Research often tells us the *average* age at which various developmental milestones are reached. But we must remember that individual children develop at different rates.

Children develop at different rates.

Many descriptive studies in child and adolescent development tell us the average ages at which various developmental milestones are reached. For example, the average child can hold a pencil and scribble at age 1 1/2, starts using rehearsal as a way of remembering information at age 7 or 8, and begins puberty at age 10 (for girls) or 11 1/2 (for boys).[4] But not all children reach developmental milestones at the average age—some reach them earlier, some later. Accordingly, we are apt to see considerable variability in learners' developmental accomplishments at any single grade level, and so we must never jump to conclusions about what any individual learner can and cannot do on the basis of age alone.

Development is often marked by spurts and plateaus.

Development doesn't necessarily proceed at a constant rate. Instead, periods of relatively rapid growth (*spurts*) may appear between periods of slower growth (*plateaus*). For example, toddlers may speak with a limited vocabulary and one-word "sentences" for several months, yet sometime around their

---

[4] T. M. McDevitt & Ormrod, 2010; McLane & McNamee, 1990.

second birthday their vocabulary expands rapidly and their sentences become longer and longer within just a few weeks. As another example, children gain an average of two or three inches in height per year during the early elementary school grades but may gain as much as five inches per year during their adolescent growth spurt.[5]

Development involves both quantitative and qualitative changes.

In some cases development simply means acquiring *more* of something. For example, whereas English-speaking children know about 8,000 to 14,000 words by first grade, they know about 50,000 words by sixth grade and about 80,000 words by high school.[6] Yet in many respects children tend to think and behave in qualitatively different ways at different ages. For example, as we discovered in Chapter 2, children in the elementary grades depend heavily on rehearsal when they study and try to remember classroom subject matter, with strategies such as organization and elaboration appearing later. And as we learned in Chapter 4, beliefs about the nature of knowledge often change in the high school years, gradually shifting from a view of "knowledge" as a collection of discrete facts to a realization that true mastery of a topic also includes understanding interrelationships among concepts and ideas.

Some theorists, especially those taking the cognitive-developmental approach described in Table 5.1, believe that patterns of uneven growth and qualitative change reflect distinctly different periods in children's development. In a **stage theory**, development is characterized as progressing through a predictable sequence of stages, with earlier stages providing a foundation on which later, more advanced ones build. For example, as we'll discover shortly, Piaget characterized the development of logical reasoning skills as having four distinct stages, and another prominent cognitive-developmental theorist, Lawrence Kohlberg, proposed that moral development has a stagelike nature as well (see Chapter 7).

In recent years many developmental psychologists have begun to believe that most aspects of development can be better characterized as reflecting general *trends*—for instance, a gradual transition from rehearsal to elaboration over a period of many years—rather than discrete stages.[7] Even so, developmental changes often do occur in a predictable sequence, with some acquisitions occurring before, and possibly being prerequisites for, later ones.

Heredity and environment interact in their effects on development.

As nativist theorists point out, virtually all aspects of development are affected either directly or indirectly by a child's genetic makeup. Not all inherited characteristics appear at birth, however. Heredity continues to control a child's growth through the process of **maturation**, a genetically driven progression of physical changes that occur over the course of development. For example, basic motor skills such as walking, running, and jumping emerge primarily as a result of neurological (brain) development, increased strength, and increased muscular control—changes that are largely determined by inherited biological "instructions." Children are also genetically endowed with particular ways of responding to their physical and social environments, and such **temperaments** influence their tendencies to be calm or irritable, outgoing or shy, adventuresome or cautious, cheerful or fearful.[8]

Yet the environment plays an equally critical role in most aspects of development. For example, genes require certain "supplies" and outside influences—in the forms of oxygen, nutrients, and environmental stimulation—to carry out their work. Thus, as we learned in Chapter 3, poor nutrition can hamper brain development. Although basic motor skills appear only after brain and muscle maturation make them possible, exercise and practice affect how fast children can run and how far they can jump. And although children's behaviors are partly the result of inherited temperaments, the ways in which their local environment and broader culture socialize them to behave—through reinforcement, punishment, modeling, and so on—are just as influential.

The effects of both heredity and environment are well documented, but psychologists disagree about how *much* each contributes to development—an issue known as *nature versus*

---

[5] Stang & Story, 2005.

[6] G. A. Miller & Gildea, 1987; Nippold, 1988; Owens, 1996.

[7] For example, see Flavell, 1994; Rest, Narvaez, Bebeau, & Thoma, 1999; Siegler & Lin, 2010.

[8] Kagan, Snidman, Kahn, & Towsley, 2007; Keogh, 2003; Rothbart, 2007.

stage theory Theory that depicts development as a series of relatively discrete periods (*stages*).

maturation Gradual unfolding of genetically controlled physical changes as a child develops.

temperament Genetic predisposition to respond in particular ways to one's physical and social environments.

nurture. In fact, heredity and environment typically *interact* in their effects, such that we can probably never disentangle their unique influences on development.[9] In some cases the inter-action between heredity and environment takes the form of a **sensitive period**, a biologically predetermined point in development during which a child is especially susceptible to environmental conditions. For example, the quality of nutrition has a greater impact on cognitive development in the early years, when children's brains are rapidly maturing, than in middle childhood or adolescence.[10] There may also be sensitive periods for some aspects of language development. In particular, children have an easier time mastering a language's grammatical subtleties and learning how to pronounce words flawlessly if they're immersed in the language within the first 5 to 10 years of life.[11] However, there is *no* evidence to indicate that sensitive periods exist for traditional academic subjects such as reading, writing, or mathematics.[12]

Children's own behaviors also influence their development.

Not only does heredity interact with environment, but so, too, do children's day-to-day behaviors interact with environmental factors. Furthermore, some of their behaviors are a result of inherited characteristics. Ultimately, then, we have a three-way interplay among behavior, heredity, and environment.[13] This interplay is reflected in two principles presented in Chapter 3:

- **Learners alter their current environment both through their behaviors and through their internal traits and mental processes.** For example, in the opening case study, Lupita behaves in a quiet, reserved, manner, possibly reflecting an inherited temperament to be calm and shy. Because she is so easy to overlook, Ms. Padilla gives her very little time and attention in class. Had a researcher's video camera not captured some of her strengths, Lupita might very well have spent a second year in kindergarten.
- **Learners actively seek out environments that are a good fit with their existing characteristics and behaviors.** In the opening case study, Lupita voluntarily chooses to work on a puzzle during her free time. Thus she actively seeks out an activity that will nurture an existing interest and talent.

Developmental Processes

Heredity, environment, and children's own behaviors all nudge children toward increasingly complex and sophisticated ways of thinking and behaving. The means by which they do so are reflected in the following principles.

The brain continues to develop throughout childhood, adolescence, and adulthood.

At birth the human brain has all of its basic parts, but it's hardly a finished product. Genetically driven maturational processes bring about many important changes in the brain during the first two or three decades of life. The prefrontal cortex—that part of the brain responsible for planning, decision making, and many other advanced reasoning processes—is especially slow to mature and doesn't take on a truly adultlike form until people reach their early twenties.

As we learned in Chapter 2, some new neurons and many new astrocytes form throughout life, and these new brain cells undoubtedly play a significant role in learning and development. But researchers have observed several other neurological changes that enable more efficient and effective thinking processes with age. For example, although neurons begin to form synapses with one another long before a child is born, shortly after birth the rate of synapse formation increases dramatically. Much of this early **synaptogenesis** appears to be driven primarily by genetic programming rather than by learning experiences. Thanks to synaptogenesis, children in the elementary grades have many more synapses than adults do.

> ? What kinds of extracurricular activities have you deliberately sought out? Would you say that they have strengthened abilities you already had to some degree?

---

sensitive period Genetically determined age range during which a certain aspect of a child's development is especially susceptible to environmental conditions.

synaptogenesis Universal process in early brain development in which many new synapses spontaneously form.

[9] Belsky, Bakermans-Kranenburg, & van IJzendoorn, 2007; Champagne & Mashoodh, 2009; S. W. Cole, 2009; Spencer et al., 2009.
[10] Sigman & Whaley, 1998.
[11] Bialystok, 1994; Bortfeld & Whitehurst, 2001; M. S. C. Thomas & Johnson, 2008.

[12] Bruer, 1999; Geary, 1998; Greenough, Black, & Wallace, 1987.
[13] O. S. P. Davis, Haworth, & Plomin, 2009; Mareschal et al., 2007; Plomin & Spinath, 2004; Scarr & McCartney, 1983.

As children encounter a wide variety of stimuli and experiences in their daily lives, some synapses come in quite handy and are used repeatedly. Other synapses are largely irrelevant and useless, and these gradually fade away through a process known as **synaptic pruning**. In some parts of the brain, intensive synaptic pruning occurs fairly early (e.g., in the preschool or early elementary years). In other parts, it begins later and continues until well into adolescence.[14]

Why do growing brains create a great many synapses, only to eliminate a sizable proportion of them later on? In the case of synapses, more isn't necessarily better.[15] Experts speculate that by generating more synapses than will ever be needed, human beings have the potential to adapt to a wide variety of conditions and circumstances. As children encounter certain regularities in their environment, some synapses are actually a nuisance because they're inconsistent with typical environmental events and behavior patterns. Synaptic pruning, then, may be Mother Nature's way of making the brain more efficient.

Although a high school student's brain has made great strides over the course of childhood and adolescence, it will still change in important ways in later adolescence and early adulthood.

Another developmental process that enhances the brain's efficiency over time is **myelination**: Many (but not all) neurons gradually acquire a white, fatty coating known as *myelin*. A detailed discussion of myelin is beyond the scope of this book, but we should note that its arrival means that neurons can transmit messages much faster than they could previously. A few neurons (especially those involved in basic survival skills) become myelinated before birth, but most of them don't acquire myelin until well after birth, with different areas becoming myelinated in a predictable sequence.[16]

In the cortex—and especially the prefrontal cortex—synaptic pruning continues into the middle childhood and adolescent years, and myelination continues into early adulthood.[17] And several parts of the brain, especially those that are heavily involved in thinking and learning, continue to increase in size and interconnections until late adolescence or early adulthood.[18] In addition, the beginning of puberty is marked by significant changes in hormone levels, which affect the continuing maturation of brain structures and possibly also affect the production and effectiveness of the chemical substances that enable neurons to communicate with one another.[19] Theorists have speculated that this combination of changes may affect—and possibly limit—adolescents' functioning in a variety of areas, including attention, planning, and impulse control.[20]

One widespread myth about the brain is that it does all of its "maturing" within the first few years of life and that its development can best be nurtured by bombarding it with as much stimulation as possible—reading instruction, violin lessons, art classes, and so on—before its owner ever reaches kindergarten. But as we've just seen, nothing could be further from the truth. In fact, young brains may not be capable of benefiting from some kinds of experiences, especially those that are fairly complex and multifaceted.[21] Ultimately, learning and development are, and must be, long-term endeavors.[22] People continue to form new neurons, synapses, and astrocytes—and thus continue to be able to learn quite effectively—throughout their lives. In other words, the brain retains considerable **plasticity**—a capacity to learn from and adapt itself to new circumstances—not only in childhood and adolescence but also in adulthood and old age.[23] For most topics and skills, there isn't necessarily a single "best" or "only" time to learn.

? Did you have this early-enrichment belief about the brain before you read this section? If so, have you now undergone conceptual change about the issue?

[14] Bruer, 1999; Huttenlocher & Dabholkar, 1997; M. H. Johnson & de Haan, 2001; Steinberg, 2009.

[15] Bruer & Greenough, 2001; Byrnes, 2001; Spear, 2007.

[16] Byrnes, 2001; M. Diamond & Hopson, 1998.

[17] M. H. Johnson & de Haan, 2001; Lenroot & Giedd, 2007; Merzenich, 2001; Paus et al., 1999.

[18] Giedd et al., 1999; Pribram, 1997; Sowell & Jernigan, 1998; Sowell, Thompson, Holmes, Jernigan, & Toga, 1999; E. F. Walker, 2002.

[19] Steinberg, 2009; E. F. Walker, 2002.

[20] Benes, 2007; Kuhn & Franklin, 2006; Silveri et al., 2006; Spear, 2007; Steinberg, 2009.

[21] C. A. Nelson, Thomas, & de Haan, 2006.

[22] R. D. Brown & Bjorklund, 1998.

[23] Kolb, Gibb, & Robinson, 2003; Koob, 2009; C. A. Nelson et al., 2006; Posner & Rothbart, 2007.

synaptic pruning Universal process in brain development in which many previously formed synapses wither away.

myelination Growth of a fatty coating (myelin) around neurons, enabling faster transmission of messages.

plasticity Capacity for the brain to learn and adapt to new circumstances.

Shutterstock

Children have a natural tendency to organize their experiences.

Children seem to have a genetic predisposition to detect patterns in and organize what they see and hear, and they begin to categorize aspects of their world almost from Day 1.[24] According to Piaget, the things that children learn and do are organized as schemes—groups of similar actions or thoughts that are used repeatedly in response to the environment. (Don't confuse these with the *schemas* described in Chapter 2.[25]) Initially, Piaget suggested, schemes are based largely on sensory and behavioral responses to objects. To illustrate, an infant may have a scheme for putting things in her mouth, and she may call on this scheme when dealing with a variety of objects, including her thumb, her toys, and her blanket. Over time, however, mental schemes—many of which are essentially categories or concepts—emerge as well. For example, a 7-year-old may have a scheme for identifying snakes that includes their long, thin bodies, their lack of legs, and their slithery nature. A 13-year-old may have a scheme for what constitutes *fashion*, allowing her to classify her peers as being either "totally awesome" or "real losers."

Children are naturally inclined to make sense of and adapt to their environment.

Mother Nature seems to endow children with a natural curiosity about their world. Accordingly, they actively seek out information to help them understand and make sense of it. For instance, young children continually experiment with new objects they encounter, manipulating them and observing the effects of their actions. And they may ask a seemingly endless series of questions ("Why is the sky blue?" "How does a telephone call know which house to go to?") in their efforts to understand the things they observe around them.[26]

Observe 2-year-old Maddie's curiosity about a new object in the "Cognitive Development: Early Childhood" video in Chapter 5 of the Book-Specific Resources in MyEducationLab.

Piaget proposed that underlying children's curiosity is a desire to adapt to and be successful in their environment. Such adaptation occurs through two complementary processes, assimilation and accommodation. **Assimilation** entails responding to and possibly interpreting an object or event in a way that is consistent with an existing scheme. For example, an infant may assimilate a new teddy bear into her putting-things-in-the-mouth scheme. A 7-year-old may quickly identify a new slithery object in the backyard as a snake. A 13-year-old may readily label a classmate's clothing as being either quite fashionable or "soooo yesterday."

But sometimes children cannot easily relate to a new object or event using existing schemes. In these situations one of two forms of **accommodation** occurs: Children either modify an existing scheme to account for the new object or event or else form an entirely new scheme to deal with it. For example, the infant may have to open her mouth wider than usual to accommodate a teddy bear's fat paw. The 13-year-old may have to revise her existing scheme of fashion according to changes in what's hot and what's not. The 7-year-old may find a long, thin, slithery thing that can't possibly be a snake because it has four legs. After some research, he will construct a new scheme—*salamander*—for this creature.

Assimilation and accommodation typically work hand in hand as children develop their knowledge and understanding of the world. Children interpret each new event within the context of their existing knowledge (assimilation) but at the same time may modify their knowledge as a result of the new event (accommodation). Accommodation rarely happens without assimilation. Young learners can benefit from (accommodate to) new experiences only when they can relate those experiences to their current knowledge and beliefs.

Development builds on prior acquisitions.

We've just seen how children can typically accommodate to new stimuli and events only when they can also assimilate those new stimuli and events into their existing knowledge and understandings. We encountered the same idea in our discussion of *rote* versus *meaningful learning* in Chapter 2: Children learn more effectively when they can relate new information and experiences to what they already know. This idea also underlies the notion of *stage theory* mentioned earlier: Later stages build on the accomplishments of preceding ones.

---

scheme Organized group of similar actions or thoughts that are used repeatedly in response to the environment.

assimilation Responding to and possibly interpreting a new event in a way that is consistent with an existing scheme.

accommodation Responding to a new object or event by either modifying an existing scheme or forming a new one.

[24] Behl-Chadha, 1996; Gelman, 2003; Quinn, 2007.
[25] Piaget distinguished between *schemes* and *schemas* (e.g., see Piaget, 1970, translator's footnote on p. 705), but neither concept is identical to the *schemas* about which contemporary theorists speak.

[26] Frazier, Gelman, & Wellman, 2009; Kemler Nelson, Egan, & Holt, 2004.

In general, then, children rarely start from scratch. Instead, virtually all aspects of their development involve a continual process of refining, building on, and occasionally reconfiguring previous abilities and achievements. In the opening case study, Ms. Padilla is concerned about Lupita's lack of basic academic skills. Although she mistakenly assumes that Lupita isn't capable of acquiring these skills in a single school year, she's on target in one respect: The skills will be essential for Lupita's success in first grade and beyond.

Observations of the physical environment—and, ideally, frequent interactions with it—promote development.

Piaget believed that active experimentation with the physical world is essential for cognitive growth. By exploring and manipulating physical objects—fiddling with sand and water, playing games with balls and bats, conducting science experiments, and so on—children learn the nature of such characteristics as volume and weight, discover principles related to force and gravity, acquire a better understanding of cause–and–effect relationships, and so on.

When interaction with the physical environment isn't possible, however, children must at least be able to *observe* physical phenomena. For instance, children with significant physical disabilities, who cannot actively experiment with physical objects, learn a great deal about the world simply by watching what happens around them.[27]

Language development facilitates cognitive development.

Cognitive development is, of course, essential for the development of language: Children can talk only about things that they can in some way first *think* about. But language is equally important for children's cognitive development.[28] From Piaget's perspective, it provides a set of entities (*symbols*) through which human beings can mentally represent external events and internal schemes. We often think by using specific words that our language provides. For example, when we think about household pets, our thoughts are apt to contain words such as *dog* and *cat*.

Vygotsky proposed that thought and language are separate functions for infants and young toddlers. In these early years, thinking occurs independently of language, and when language appears, it is first used primarily as a means of communication rather than as a mechanism of thought. But sometime around age 2, thought and language become intertwined: Children begin to express their thoughts when they speak, and they begin to think in words. As noted earlier, children's language skills virtually explode at this age, and their rapidly increasing vocabularies enable them to represent and think about a wide variety of objects and events.

When thought and language first merge, children often talk to themselves—a phenomenon known as **self-talk**. Vygotsky suggested that self-talk plays an important role in cognitive development. By talking to themselves, children learn to guide and direct their own behaviors through difficult tasks and complex maneuvers in much the same way that adults may have previously guided them. Self-talk eventually evolves into **inner speech**, in which children "talk" to themselves mentally rather than aloud. They continue to direct themselves verbally through tasks and activities, but others can no longer see and hear them do it.

Recent research has supported Vygotsky's views regarding the progression and role of self-talk and inner speech. The frequency of children's audible self-talk decreases during the preschool and early elementary years, but this decrease is at first accompanied by an increase in whispered mumbling and silent lip movements, presumably reflecting a transition to inner speech.[29] Furthermore, self-talk increases when children are performing more challenging tasks, at which they must exert considerable effort to be successful.[30] Even we adults occasionally talk to ourselves when we face new challenges!

Interactions with other people promote development.

Language facilitates cognitive development in a very different way as well: It enables children to exchange ideas with adults and peers. Both Piaget and Vygotsky suggested that social

What aspect of self-regulation do self-talk and inner speech remind you of? (Review the discussion of self-regulation in Chapter 4, and then compare your response to this question with the response presented in Chapter 5 of the Book-Specific Resources in MyEducationLab.)

[27] Bebko, Burke, Craven, & Sarlo, 1992; Brainerd, 2003.

[28] For contemporary discussions of language's roles in learning and cognitive development, see K. Fiedler, 2008; Ganea, Shutts, Spelke, & DeLoache, 2007; K. Nelson & Fivush, 2004; Q. Wang & Ross, 2007.

[29] Bivens & Berk, 1990; Winsler & Naglieri, 2003.

[30] Berk, 1994; Schimmoeller, 1998.

self-talk Process of talking to oneself as a way of guiding oneself through a task.

inner speech Process of talking to and guiding oneself mentally rather than aloud.

Richard Lord/Image Works

In part through sharing their thoughts with one another, children and adolescents discover that their own perspectives of the world may be different from those of others.

interaction is critical for cognitive development. In Piaget's view, exchanging ideas with others helps children realize that different individuals see things differently than they themselves do and that their own perspectives aren't necessarily completely accurate or logical ones. For example, a 9-year-old may recognize the logical inconsistencies in what she says only after someone else points them out. And through discussions with peers or adults about social and political issues, a high school student may modify some initially abstract and idealistic notions about how the world "should" be to reflect constraints that the real world imposes.

For Vygotsky, social interactions are even more important. In fact, they provide the very foundations for cognitive development. We initially encountered some of Vygotsky's ideas about social interaction in Chapter 3. For one thing, as children and adults interact, the adults often share the meanings and interpretations they attach to objects, events, and, more generally, human experience. In the process adults transform, or *mediate,* the situations that children encounter (recall the discussion of *mediated learning experiences).* Not only do adults help children interpret experiences but they also share concepts, procedures, strategies, and other *cognitive tools* that enable children to deal effectively with complex tasks and problems. To the extent that specific cultures pass along unique interpretations, beliefs, concepts, ideas, procedures, strategies, and so on, children in different cultures will acquire somewhat different knowledge, skills, and ways of thinking.

Vygotsky further proposed that social activities provide the seeds from which complex cognitive processes can grow. Essentially, children use complex processes first in interactions with other people and gradually become able to use them independently in their own thinking. Vygotsky called this phenomenon **internalization**. The progression from self-talk to inner speech just described is an example: Over time, children gradually internalize adults' directions so that they are eventually giving *themselves* directions. Yet keep in mind that children don't necessarily internalize exactly what they see and hear in a social context. Rather, internalization often involves transforming ideas and processes to make them uniquely one's own.[31]

Not all mental processes evolve as children interact with adults; some instead develop as children interact with peers. As an example, children frequently argue with one another about a variety of matters—how best to carry out an activity, what games to play, who did what to whom, and so on. Childhood arguments can help children discover that there are often several ways to view the same situation. Eventually, children internalize the "arguing" process, developing the ability to look at a situation from several different angles *on their own.*[32]

Formal schooling promotes development.

Informal conversations are one common method by which adults pass along culturally relevant ways of interpreting situations. But from the perspective of sociocultural theorists, contemporary cognitive-developmental theorists, and information processing theorists, formal education is just as important, perhaps even more so. (Recall how much progress Lupita makes once Ms. Padilla and her aides begin to work hard to help her master basic academic skills.) Through formal, preplanned lessons, teachers systematically impart the ideas, concepts, and procedures used in various academic disciplines. In this way, rather than having to reinvent the wheel (both literally and figuratively), each generation can benefit from the discoveries, understandings, and problem-solving strategies of previous generations.[33]

Inconsistencies between existing understandings and external events promote development.

Earlier we noted that children are naturally inclined to make sense of their environment. According to Piaget, when children can comfortably address new events using what they already know and believe about the world, they are in a state of **equilibrium**. But as children

internalization Process through which a learner gradually incorporates socially based activities into his or her internal cognitive processes.

equilibrium State of being able to address new events with existing schemes.

[31] Thus, Vygotsky's theory, while primarily sociocultural in nature, also has a constructivist element to it.

[32] Vygotsky, 1978.

[33] Case & Okamoto, 1996; M. Cole, 2006; Karpov & Haywood, 1998; Raudenbush, 2009; Vygotsky, 1962.

grow older and expand their horizons, they sometimes encounter situations for which their current knowledge and skills are inadequate. Such situations create **disequilibrium,** a sort of mental "discomfort" that spurs them to reexamine their current understandings. By replacing, reorganizing, or better integrating certain schemes (in other words, through accommodation), children can better understand and address previously puzzling events. The movement from equilibrium to disequilibrium and back to equilibrium again is known as **equilibration.** Piaget suggested that equilibration and children's intrinsic desire to achieve equilibrium promote the development of more complex levels of thought and knowledge.

To better understand how thinking changes with age, and to discover the circumstances under which children might revise their thinking in light of new experiences, Piaget developed a variety of tasks that would reveal children's reasoning processes and in some cases create disequilibrium. As an example of such a task, try the following exercise.

SEE FOR YOURSELF   Wooden Beads

To the right are 12 wooden beads—some brown and some white. Are there more wooden beads or more brown beads?

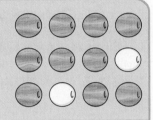

A ridiculously easy question, you might think. But in fact young children often answer incorrectly, responding that there are more *brown* beads than wooden ones. Consider the following dialogue between a 6-year-old, whom I'll call "Brian,"[34] and an adult about a set of beads similar to those I just showed you:

Adult: Are there more wooden beads or more brown beads?
Brian: More brown ones, because there are two white ones.
Adult: Are the white ones made of wood?
Brian: Yes.
Adult: And the brown ones?
Brian: Yes.
Adult: Then are there more brown ones or more wooden ones?
Brian: More brown ones.
Adult: What color would a necklace made of the wooden beads be?
Brian: Brown and white. (Here Brian shows that he understands that all the beads are wooden.)
Adult: And what color would a necklace made with the brown beads be?
Brian: Brown.
Adult: Then which would be longer, the one made with the wooden beads or the one made with the brown beads?
Brian: The one with the brown beads.
Adult: Draw the necklaces for me.
(Brian draws a series of black rings for the necklace of brown beads; he then draws a series of black rings plus two white rings for the necklace of wooden beads.)
Adult: Good. Now which will be longer, the one with the brown beads or the one with the wooden beads?
Brian: The one with the brown beads.[35]

---

[34] Piaget identified children in his studies by abbreviations. In this study he used the letters *BRI,* but I've given the child a name to allow for easier discussion.

[35] Dialogue from Piaget, 1952a, pp. 163–164.

disequilibrium State of being unable to address new events with existing schemes; typically accompanied by some mental discomfort.

equilibration Movement from equilibrium to disequilibrium and back to equilibrium, a process that promotes development of more complex thought and understandings.

class inclusion Recognition that an object simultaneously belongs to a particular category and to one of its subcategories.

zone of proximal development (ZPD) Range of tasks that a child can perform with the help and guidance of others but cannot yet perform independently.

Notice how the adult continues to probe Brian's reasoning to be sure he realizes that all of the beads are wooden but only some are brown. Even so, Brian responds that there are more brown beads than wooden ones. Piaget suggested that young children such as Brian have trouble with **class inclusion** tasks in which they must simultaneously think of an object as belonging to two categories—in this case, thinking of a bead as being both *brown* and *wooden* at the same time.

Notice, too, how the adult asks Brian to draw two necklaces, one made with the wooden beads and one made with the brown beads. The adult hopes that after Brian draws a brown-and-white necklace that is longer than an all-brown necklace, he will notice that his drawings are inconsistent with his statement that there are more brown beads. The inconsistency might lead Brian to experience disequilibrium, perhaps to the point that he will reevaluate his conclusion and realize that, logically, there *must* be more wooden beads than brown ones. In this case, however, Brian apparently is oblivious to the inconsistency, remains in equilibrium, and thus has no need to revise his thinking.

Challenging tasks promote development.

Children can typically do more difficult things in collaboration with adults or other more advanced individuals than they can do on their own.[36] For example, in the opening case study, two of Lupita's classmates can assemble puzzles only when they have Lupita's assistance. And notice how a student who cannot independently solve division problems with remainders is more successful when her teacher helps her think through the process:

Teacher: [writes $6\overline{)44}$ on the board] 44 divided by 6. What number times 6 is close to 44?
Child: 6.
Teacher: What's 6 times 6? [writes 6]
Child: 36.
Teacher: 36. Can you get one that's any closer? [erasing the 6]
Child: 8.
Teacher: What's 6 times 8?
Child: 64 . . . 48.
Teacher: 48. Too big. Can you think of something . . .
Child: 6 times 7 is 42.[37]

The range of tasks children cannot yet perform independently but *can* perform with the help and guidance of others is, in Vygotsky's terminology, the **zone of proximal development (ZPD)** (see Figure 5.1). A child's zone of proximal development includes learning and problem-solving abilities that are just beginning to emerge and develop. Naturally, children's ZPDs change over time: As some tasks are mastered, other, more complex ones appear on the horizon to take their place. Furthermore, children's ZPDs can vary considerably in "width": With assistance, some children may be able to stretch their existing abilities considerably, whereas others may be able to handle tasks that are only slightly more difficult than what they can currently do on their own.

Vygotsky proposed that children develop very little from performing tasks they can already do independently. Instead, they develop primarily by attempting tasks they can accomplish only in collaboration with a more competent individual—that is, when they attempt tasks within their zone of proximal development. But a child's ZPD also sets an upper limit on what he or she is cognitively capable of doing and learning. Impossible tasks—those that children can't complete even with considerable structure and guidance—are of no benefit whatsoever.

Observe examples of children working within their zone of proximal development in the two "Zone of Proximal Development" videos in Chapter 5 of the Book-Specific Resources in MyEducationLab.

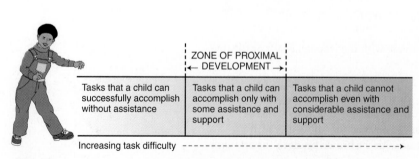

	ZONE OF PROXIMAL DEVELOPMENT	
Tasks that a child can successfully accomplish without assistance	Tasks that a child can accomplish only with some assistance and support	Tasks that a child cannot accomplish even with considerable assistance and support

Increasing task difficulty -->

FIGURE 5.1 Tasks in a child's zone of proximal development (ZPD) promote maximal cognitive growth.

[36] Fischer & Immordino-Yang, 2006; Vygotsky, 1978.
[37] Pettito, 1985, p. 251.

• Trends in Cognitive Development

In our discussions of learning and cognition in previous chapters, we've already identified several trends in cognitive development:

- With age and experience, children acquire more effective learning strategies (Chapter 2).
- Metacognitive knowledge and skills gradually improve with age (Chapter 4).
- Learners become increasingly self-regulating over the course of childhood and adolescence (Chapter 4).

We now pull from the research of information processing theorists and cognitive-developmental theorists (including both Piaget and more contemporary researchers) to identify the following additional trends.

Although easy successes may sometimes feel good, life's challenges are the things that best promote development.
CALVIN AND HOBBES © 1995 Watterson. Distributed by UCLICK. Reprinted with permission. All rights reserved.

Children's growing working memory capacity enables them to handle increasingly complex cognitive tasks.

As you should recall, working memory—the component of the human memory system where active cognitive processing occurs—has a very limited capacity. It can think about only so much, and in fact not *very* much, at once. But as children grow older, their working memory capacity seems to increase a bit, in that they can gradually handle bigger and more complex thinking and learning tasks. A good deal of this increase in capacity is probably due to the fact that children's cognitive processes become faster and more efficient and so take up less "space" in working memory. But the available physical capacity of working memory may increase somewhat as well.[38]

Children's growing knowledge base enhances their ability to learn new things.

One reason children use increasingly effective learning strategies as they grow older is that they acquire an ever-expanding body of knowledge that they can use to interpret, organize, and elaborate on new experiences.[39] As an example, consider the case of an Inuit (Eskimo) man named Tor.

SEE FOR YOURSELF   Tor of the Targa

Tor, a young man of the Targa tribe, was out hunting in the ancient hunting territory of his people. He had been away from his village for many days. The weather was bad and he had not yet managed to locate his prey. Because of the extreme temperature he knew he must soon return but it was a matter of honor among his people to track and kill the prey single-handed. Only when this was achieved could a boy be considered a man. Those who failed were made to eat and keep company with the old men and the women until they could accomplish this task.

Suddenly, in the distance, Tor could make out the outline of a possible prey. It was alone and not too much bigger than Tor, who could take him single-handed. But as he drew nearer, a hunter from a neighboring tribe came into view, also stalking the prey. The intruder was older than Tor and had around his neck evidence of his past success at the

---

[38] Ben-Yehudah & Fiez, 2007; Fry & Hale, 1996; Kail, 2007; Luna, Garver, Urban, Lazar, & Sweeney, 2004; Van Leijenhorst, Crone, & Van der Molen, 2007.

[39] J. M. Alexander, Johnson, Albano, Freygang, & Scott, 2006; Flavell, Miller, & Miller, 2002; Halford, 1989; Kail, 1990.

hunt. "Yes," thought Tor, "he is truly a man." Tor was undecided. Should he challenge the intruder or return home empty handed? To return would mean bitter defeat. The other young men of the tribe would laugh at his failure. He decided to creep up on the intruder and wait his chance.[40]

- On what kind of terrain was Tor hunting?
- What was the weather like?
- What kind of prey might Tor have been stalking?

You may have used your knowledge about Inuit people to speculate that Tor was hunting polar bears or seals on snow and ice, possibly in freezing temperatures or a bad blizzard. But notice that the story itself didn't tell you any of these things. Instead, you had to *infer* them. Like you, many older children know a fair amount about the lifestyle of Inuits and other Native Americans who live in the northernmost regions of North America. They can use that information to help them elaborate on, and so better understand and remember, this very ambiguous story about Tor.

In cases where children have more knowledge than adults, the children are often the more effective learners.[41] For example, when my son Alex and I used to read books about lizards together, Alex always remembered more than I did, because he was a self-proclaimed "lizard expert" and I myself knew very little about reptiles of any sort.

Children's knowledge, beliefs, and thinking processes become increasingly integrated.

Through such processes as knowledge construction, organization, and elaboration, children increasingly pull together what they know and believe about the world into cohesive wholes (e.g., recall the discussion of children's *theories* in Chapter 2). The knowledge base of young children is apt to consist of many separate, isolated facts. In contrast, the knowledge base of older children and adolescents typically includes many associations and interrelationships among concepts and ideas.[42]

Piaget suggested that not only children's knowledge but also their *thought processes* become increasingly integrated over time. In particular, their many "thinking" schemes gradually combine into well-coordinated systems of mental processes. These systems—which Piaget called *operations*—allow children to think in increasingly logical ways, as will be evident in the next three developmental trends.[43]

Thinking becomes increasingly logical during the elementary school years.

Piaget proposed that cognitive development proceeds through four distinct stages, which are summarized in Table 5.2. Children's thinking during the school years reflects characteristics of three of these stages—the preoperational, concrete operations, and formal operations stages—and so will be relevant to our discussion here. Yet keep in mind that children's reasoning abilities appear to emerge more gradually than Piaget's stage theory might lead us to believe. Furthermore, many contemporary theorists believe—and Piaget himself acknowledged—that the four stages better describe how children and adolescents *can* think, rather than how they always *do* think, at any particular age.[44]

In Piaget's view, reasoning in the preoperational stage (evident in most preschoolers and kindergartners) is somewhat illogical. As an example, recall 6-year-old Brian's insistence

As children grow older, they become increasingly able to draw inferences from what they see, in part because they have a larger and better integrated knowledge base to help them interpret their experiences.

Mark Richards/PhotoEdit

preoperational stage Piaget's second stage of cognitive development, in which children can think about objects beyond their immediate experience but do not yet reason in logical, adultlike ways.

conservation Realization that if nothing is added or taken away, amount stays the same regardless of alterations in shape or arrangement.

[40] A. L. Brown, Smiley, Day, Townsend, & Lawton, 1977, p. 1460.
[41] Chi, 1978; Rabinowitz & Glaser, 1985.
[42] J. M. Alexander et al., 2006; Bjorklund, 1987; Fischer & Immordino-Yang, 2006; Flavell et al., 2002.
[43] For a more recent, "neo-Piagetian" perspective on how thinking processes might become integrated,

see Kurt Fischer's discussions of *multiple, parallel strands* (e.g., Fischer & Immordino-Yang, 2006; Fischer, Knight, & Van Parys, 1993).
[44] Flavell, 1994; Halford & Andrews, 2006; Klaczynski, 2001; Morra, Gobbo, Marini, & Sheese, 2008; Tanner & Inhelder, 1960.

TABLE 5.2 Piaget's Four Stages of Cognitive Development

Stage	Proposed Age Range[a]	General Description	Examples of Abilities Acquired
Sensorimotor	Birth to age 2	Schemes are based largely on behaviors and perceptions. Especially in the early part of this stage, children cannot think about things that are not immediately in front of them, and so they focus on what they are doing and seeing at the moment.	• *Trial-and-error experimentation with physical objects:* Exploration and manipulation of objects to determine their properties • *Object permanence:* Realization that objects continue to exist even when removed from view • *Symbolic thought:* Representation of physical objects and events as mental entities (*symbols*)
Preoperational	Age 2 through age 6 or 7	Thanks in part to their rapidly developing language and the symbolic thought it enables, children can now think and talk about things beyond their immediate experience. However, they do not yet reason in logical, adultlike ways.	• *Language:* Rapid expansion of vocabulary and grammatical structures • *Intuitive thought:* Some logical thinking based on "hunches" and "intuition" rather than on conscious awareness of logical principles (especially after age 4)
Concrete Operations	Age 6 or 7 through age 11 or 12	Adultlike logic appears but is limited to reasoning about concrete, real-life situations.	• *Class inclusion:* Ability to classify objects as belonging to two or more categories simultaneously • *Conservation:* Realization that amount stays the same if nothing is added or taken away, regardless of alterations in shape or arrangement
Formal Operations	Age 11 or 12 through adulthood[b]	Logical reasoning processes are applied to abstract ideas as well as to concrete objects and situations. Many capabilities essential for advanced reasoning in science and mathematics appear.	• *Reasoning about hypothetical ideas:* Ability to draw logical deductions about situations that have no basis in physical reality • *Proportional reasoning:* Conceptual understanding of fractions, percentages, decimals, and ratios • *Separation and control of variables:* Ability to test hypotheses by manipulating one variable while holding other variables constant

[a] The age ranges presented in the table are *averages;* some children reach more advanced stages a bit earlier, others a bit later. Also, some children may be in *transition* from one stage to the next, displaying characteristics of two adjacent stages at the same time.

[b] Recent researchers have found much variability in when adolescents begin to show reasoning processes consistent with Piaget's formal operations stage. Furthermore, not all cultures value or nurture formal operational logic, perhaps because it is largely irrelevant to people's daily lives and tasks (see the Cultural Considerations box later in this chapter).

that in a set of 12 wooden beads, including 10 brown ones and 2 white ones, there are more brown beads than wooden ones. And consider the following situation:

> We show 5-year-old Nathan the three glasses depicted at the top of Figure 5.2. We ask him whether Glasses A and B contain the same amount of water, and he replies confidently that they do. We then pour the water from Glass B into Glass C and ask him whether A and C have the same amount. Nathan replies, "No, that glass [pointing to Glass A] has more because it's taller."

Nathan's response reflects lack of **conservation:** He doesn't realize that the amount of water in the two glasses must be equivalent because nothing has been added or taken away. Young children such as Nathan often confuse changes in appearance with changes in amount.

Piaget found that children as young as age 4 or 5 occasionally draw logically correct conclusions about class inclusion and conservation problems. However, he suggested that their reasoning is based on hunches and intuition rather than on any conscious awareness of underlying logical principles, and so they cannot yet explain *why* their conclusions are correct. More recently, researchers have discovered that how logically young children think depends partly on situational factors, such as how task materials are presented, how questions are worded, and whether adults provide guidance about how to think about a problem.[45]

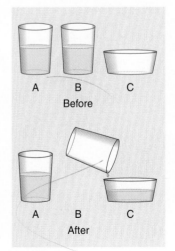

FIGURE 5.2 Conservation of liquid: Do Glasses A and C contain the same amount of water?

[45] Halford & Andrews, 2006; Morra et al., 2008; Siegler & Svetina, 2006.

Observe children's responses to tasks involving conservation of liquid and conservation of number in the "Conservation" video in Chapter 5 of the Book-Specific Resources in MyEducationLab.

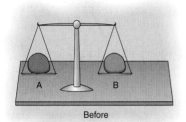

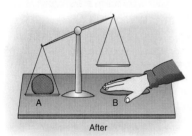

FIGURE 5.3 Conservation of weight: Ball A and Ball B initially weigh the same. When Ball B is flattened into a pancake shape, how does its weight now compare with that of Ball A?

In any event, most children have mastered simple logical thinking tasks, such as those involving class inclusion and simple forms of conservation, by age 7—an age at which, in Piaget's view, they are now in the **concrete operations stage**. As an example, consider how an 8-year-old whom we'll call "Natalie" responded to the same wooden beads problem that Brian tackled:

Adult: Are there more wooden beads or more brown beads?
Natalie: More wooden ones.
Adult: Why?
Natalie: Because the two white ones are made of wood as well.
Adult: Suppose we made two necklaces, one with all the wooden beads and one with all the brown ones. Which one would be longer?
Natalie: Well, the wooden ones and the brown ones are the same, and it would be longer with the wooden ones because there are two white ones as well.[46]

Notice how easily Natalie reaches her conclusion: Because the wooden beads include white ones as well as brown ones, there obviously must be more wooden ones.

Children continue to refine their newly acquired logical thinking capabilities throughout the elementary school years. Some simple forms of conservation, such as the conservation-of-liquid problem presented in Figure 5.2, appear at age 6 or 7. Others don't emerge until later. Consider the problem in Figure 5.3. Using a balance scale, an adult shows a child that two balls of clay have the same weight. One ball is removed from the scale and smashed into a pancake shape. Does the pancake weigh the same as the unsmashed ball, or are the weights different? Not until around age 9 do children realize that the flattened pancake must weigh the same as the round ball it was previously.[47] And some conservation-of-weight tasks are difficult even for young adolescents. For instance, although most eighth graders would acknowledge that a large block of Styrofoam has weight, they may claim that a tiny piece torn from the block has no weight at all.[48]

Thinking becomes increasingly abstract in the middle school and secondary school years.

In Piaget's theory, children in the concrete operations stage can reason only about concrete objects and events, and especially about things they can actually see. Once they acquire abilities that characterize the **formal operations stage**—perhaps at around age 11 or 12, Piaget suggested—they are capable of abstract thought and so can think about concepts and ideas that have little or no basis in everyday concrete reality. For example, in mathematics they should have an easier time understanding such concepts as *negative number*, *pi* (π), and *infinity*. In science they should be able to think about *molecules* and *atoms* and understand how it's possible for temperature to go below zero. In the poem in Figure 5.4, 11-year-old Erin uses several abstract ideas (e.g., *war darkens the day, honor is divine*) as she laments the pointlessness of war.

In Piaget's theory, formal operational thought also involves *hypothetical reasoning*, thinking logically about things that may or may not be true. In some instances, such reasoning involves things that are definitely *false*. As an example, try the following exercise.

SEE FOR YOURSELF   Beings and Basketballs

Take a moment to answer these two questions:

1. If all children are human beings,
   And if all human beings are living creatures,
   Then must all children be living creatures?

2. If all children are basketballs,
   And if all basketballs are jellybeans,
   Then must all children be jellybeans?

concrete operations stage Piaget's third stage of cognitive development, in which adultlike logic appears but is limited to concrete reality.

formal operations stage Piaget's fourth and final stage of cognitive development, in which logical reasoning processes are applied to abstract ideas as well as to concrete objects and more sophisticated scientific and mathematical reasoning processes emerge.

[46] Dialogue from Piaget, 1952a, p. 176.
[47] Morra et al., 2008; Sroufe, Cooper, DeHart, & Bronfenbrenner, 1992.
[48] C. L. Smith, Maclin, Grosslight, & Davis, 1997; Wiser & Smith, 2008.

You probably responded fairly quickly that, yes, all children must be living creatures. The second question is a bit trickier. It follows the same line of reasoning as the first but the conclusion it leads to—all children must be jellybeans—contradicts what is true in reality.

Abstract and hypothetical reasoning seem to emerge earlier and more gradually than Piaget proposed. Children in the elementary grades occasionally show an ability to reason abstractly and hypothetically about certain topics.[49] And yet once children reach puberty, they may continue to struggle with some abstract subject matter. For instance, although many can understand some abstract scientific and mathematical concepts in early adolescence, they are apt to have trouble understanding abstract concepts in history and geography until well into the high school years.[50] In fact, some adolescents never do show much evidence of formal operational thinking, especially if their culture and schooling do little to encourage it.[51]

Once learners become capable of abstract thought, they are able to look beyond the literal meanings of messages.[52] Children in the early elementary grades often take the words they hear at face value—for instance, interpreting the expression "Your eyes are bigger than your stomach" quite literally (see Figure 5.5). And they have little success determining the underlying meaning of such proverbs as "Look before you leap" or "Don't put the cart before the horse." Students' ability to interpret proverbs in a generalized, abstract fashion continues to improve even in the high school years.[53]

Another outgrowth of abstract and hypothetical thinking is the ability to envision how the world might be different from the way it actually is. In some cases adolescents envision a world much *better* than the one they live in, and they exhibit considerable concern and idealism about social and political issues. Some secondary school students devote a great deal of energy to local or global problems, such as water pollution or animal rights. However, they may offer recommendations for change that aren't practical in today's world. For example, a teenager might argue that "all you need is love" to overcome racism or suggest that a nation should eliminate its weapons and armed forces as a way of moving toward world peace. Piaget proposed that adolescent idealism reflects an inability to separate one's own logical abstractions from the perspectives of others and from practical considerations. Only through experience do adolescents eventually begin to temper their optimism with some realism about what is possible with limited resources and the foibles of human nature.

Several logical thinking processes important for mathematical and scientific reasoning improve considerably during adolescence.

In Piaget's view, several additional abilities accompany the advancement to the formal operations stage. One is *proportional reasoning,* the ability to understand and think logically about such proportions as fractions, decimals, percentages, and ratios. For example, if you can quickly and easily recognize that the following statement is true

$$\frac{2}{8} = \frac{6}{24} = 0.25 = 25\%$$

then you have mastered proportional reasoning to some degree.

Scientific reasoning skills also improve in adolescence. Two of them—*formulating and testing hypotheses* and *separating and controlling variables*—together enable learners to use a scientific method, in which several possible explanations for an observed

FIGURE 5.4 As children reach puberty, they become increasingly able to reason about abstract ideas.
(Poetry by Erin, age 11)

Observe the progression in understanding proverbs in the "Cognitive Development" videos for middle childhood and late adolescence in Chapter 5 of the Book-Specific Resources in MyEducationLab.

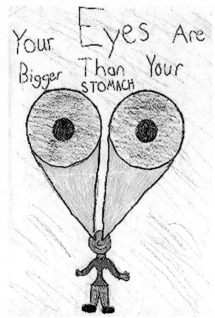

FIGURE 5.5 In this drawing, 8-year-old Jeff interprets the expression "Your eyes are bigger than your stomach" quite literally.

---

[49] Beck, Robinson, Carroll, & Apperly, 2006; S. Carey, 1985; McNeil & Uttal, 2009; Metz, 1995.
[50] Kuhn & Franklin, 2006; Lovell, 1979; Tamburrini, 1982.
[51] Flieller, 1999; Lerner, 2002; Rogoff, 2003.
[52] Owens, 1996; Winner, 1988.
[53] Owens, 1996.

phenomenon are proposed and tested in a systematic manner. As an example, consider the pendulum problem in the exercise that follows.

SEE FOR YOURSELF Pendulum Problem

In the absence of other forces, an object suspended by a rope or string—a pendulum—swings at a constant rate. (A yo-yo and a playground swing are two everyday examples.) Some pendulums swing back and forth rather slowly, others more quickly. What characteristics of a pendulum determine how fast it swings? Write down at least three hypotheses about the variable(s) that might affect a pendulum's oscillation rate.

Now gather several small, heavy objects (e.g., an eraser, a large screw or bolt, a fishing sinker) and a piece of string. Tie one of the objects to one end of the string, and set your pendulum in motion. Conduct one or more experiments to test each of your hypotheses.

What can you conclude? What variable or variables affect the rate at which a pendulum swings?

What hypotheses did you generate? Perhaps you considered the weight of the object, the length of the string, the force with which the pendulum is pushed, and the height from which the object is first released. Did you then test each hypothesis in a systematic fashion? A person capable of formal operational thinking separates and controls variables, testing one at a time while holding all others constant. (This strategy should remind you of our discussion of *experimental studies* in Chapter 1.) For example, if you were testing the hypothesis that weight makes a difference, you might have tried objects of different weights while keeping constant the length of the string, the force with which you pushed each object, and the height from which you released or pushed it. Similarly, if you hypothesized that the length of the string was a critical factor, you might have varied the length while continuing to use the same object and setting the pendulum in motion in the same manner. If you carefully separated and controlled variables, then you would have come to the correct conclusion: Only *length* affects a pendulum's oscillation rate.

Children show signs that they can think about simple proportions as early as first or second grade.[54] And by the upper elementary grades, some can separate and control variables, especially if given guidance about the importance of controlling all variables except the one they're currently testing.[55] But by and large, the mathematical and scientific reasoning abilities just described don't really take wing until puberty, and they continue to develop throughout adolescence.[56]

The progression of logical reasoning processes shown in Table 5.3 draws on both Piaget's early work and more recent research findings. It also presents examples of teaching strategies that take these processes into account.

Children can think more logically and abstractly about tasks and topics they know well.

The ability to think logically about a situation or topic depends to some degree on learners' background knowledge and educational experiences. For example, 5-year-olds are more likely to solve class inclusion problems—for instance, they're more likely to conclude that a picture of three cats and six dogs has more animals than dogs—if an adult helps them think

Observe seventh graders' difficulty separating and controlling variables in the "Designing Experiments" video in Chapter 5 of the Book-Specific Resources in MyEducationLab.

---

[54] Empson, 1999; Van Dooren, De Bock, Hessels, Janssens, & Verschaffel, 2005.
[55] Barchfeld, Sodian, Thoermer, & Bullock, 2005; Kuhn & Pease, 2008; Lorch et al., 2008.

[56] Barchfeld et al., 2005; Byrnes, 1988; Kuhn, Garcia-Mila, Zohar, & Andersen, 1995; Tourniaire & Pulos, 1985; Van Dooren et al., 2005; Zohar & Aharon-Kraversky, 2005.

DEVELOPMENTAL TRENDS

TABLE 5.3 Logical Thinking Abilities at Different Grade Levels

Grade Level	Age-Typical Characteristics	Example	Suggested Strategies
 K–2	• Emergence of class inclusion • Emergence of conservation in simple tasks • Increasing ability to explain and justify conclusions about logical reasoning tasks	Five-year-old Lucinda confidently and accurately declares that two rows of quarters each have five coins. But when an adult spreads the quarters in one row far apart, she declares that the longer row has more quarters because it's "like more far away . . . bigger." *(You can observe Lucinda's response to this conservation-of-number task in the "Conservation" video in Chapter 5 of the Book-Specific Resources in MyEducationLab.)*	• Use concrete manipulatives and experiences to illustrate new ideas. • Provide practice in classifying objects in multiple ways—for instance, by shape, size, and color. • Determine whether children have achieved conservation of number—for instance, by asking them whether a set of objects you have just rearranged has more or fewer objects than it had previously. If they haven't, ask them to explain their reasoning; also ask them to explain why someone else might think the amount *hasn't* changed.
 3–5	• Emergence of conservation in more challenging tasks (e.g., conservation of weight); full development of conservation continuing into adolescence • Ability to understand simple fractions (e.g., 1/3, 1/5, 1/8) that can be related to concrete objects and everyday events • Occasional abstract and hypothetical thinking	When students in a fourth-grade class are shown a pizza that's been cut into 12 slices, they easily identify one-half of the pizza (6 slices) and one-third of the pizza (4 slices). But when their teacher moves from concrete depictions of fractions to strictly symbolic representations, many begin to have difficulty. They are especially confused about the process of multiplying fractions, and they simply memorize—rather than make logical sense of—this mathematical operation.	• Supplement verbal explanations with concrete examples, pictures, and hands-on activities. • Introduce simple fractions by relating them to everyday objects (e.g., pizza slices, kitchen measuring cups). • Have students engage in simple scientific investigations, focusing on familiar objects and phenomena.
 6–8	• Increasing ability to reason logically about abstract, hypothetical, and contrary-to-fact situations • Some ability to test hypotheses and to separate and control variables, especially when an adult provides hints about how to proceed; conclusions sometimes affected by *confirmation bias* (see Chapter 2) • Increasing ability to understand and work with proportions • Some ability to interpret proverbs, figures of speech, and other forms of figurative language	A seventh-grade science teacher asks students to conduct experiments to determine which one or more of three variables—weight, length, and height of initial drop—affects a pendulum's oscillation rate. One group of four students consistently varies both weight and length in its experiments and ultimately concludes (erroneously) that a pendulum's weight is the deciding factor. *(You can observe this group in the "Designing Experiments" video in Chapter 5 of the Book-Specific Resources in MyEducationLab.)*	• Present abstract concepts and principles central to various academic disciplines, but make them concrete in some way (e.g., relate *gravity* to everyday experiences, show a diagram of an *atom*). • Ask students to speculate on the meanings of well-known proverbs (e.g., "Two heads are better than one," "A stitch in time saves nine"). • Assign problems that require use of simple fractions, ratios, or decimals. • Have students conduct simple experiments to answer questions about cause–and–effect; encourage them to change only one variable at a time.

(continued)

TABLE 5.3 Continued

Grade Level	Age-Typical Characteristics	Example	Suggested Strategies
 9–12	• Greater ability to think abstractly in math and science than in the social sciences • Increasing proficiency in aspects of a scientific method (e.g., formulation and testing of hypotheses, separation and control of variables); effects of confirmation bias still evident • Greater proficiency in interpreting figurative language • Idealistic (but not always realistic) views about how government, social policy, and other aspects of society should be changed	When 14-year-old Alicia is asked to explain the proverb "A rolling stone gathers no moss," she offers an interpretation that goes beyond its literal meaning: "Maybe when you go through things too fast, you don't . . . collect anything from it." *(You can observe Alicia's response in the "Cognitive Development: Late Adolescence" video in Chapter 5 of the Book-Specific Resources in MyEducationLab.)*	• Study particular topics in depth; introduce complex and abstract explanations and theories. • Ask students to speculate on the meanings of unfamiliar proverbs (e.g., "As you sow, so shall you reap," "Discretion is the better part of valor"). • Have students design some of their own experiments in science labs and science fair projects. • Encourage discussions about social, political, and ethical issues; elicit multiple perspectives on these issues.

Sources: Barchfeld et al., 2005; S. Carey, 1985; F. W. Danner & Day, 1977; M. Donaldson, 1978; Elkind, 1981; Empson, 1999; Flavell, 1963; Fujimura, 2001; Halford & Andrews, 2006; Hynd, 1998a; Inhelder & Piaget, 1958; Karplus, Pulos, & Stage, 1983; Kuhn & Dean, 2005; Kuhn & Franklin, 2006; Lorch et al., 2008; Lovell, 1979; Metz, 1995; Morra, Gobbo, Marini, & Sheese, 2008; Newcombe & Huttenlocher, 1992; Owens, 1996; Piaget, 1928, 1952b, 1959; Rosser, 1994; Siegler & Alibali, 2005; Siegler & Lin, 2010; Sroufe et al., 1992; Sund, 1976; Tamburrini, 1982; Van Dooren et al., 2005; Wiser & Smith, 2008; Zohar & Aharon-Kraversky, 2005.

Observe how fishing experience enables 10-year-old Kent to identify more variables than 14-year-old Alicia in the "Cognitive Development" videos for middle childhood and late adolescence in Chapter 5 of the Book-Specific Resources in MyEducationLab.

logically about such problems.[57] Children in the elementary grades can better understand fractions if they work with familiar concrete objects.[58] Young adolescents become increasingly able to separate and control variables if they have numerous experiences that require them to do so.[59] Junior high and high school students (and adults as well) often apply formal operational reasoning processes to topics about which they have a great deal of knowledge and yet think concretely about topics with which they're unfamiliar.[60]

As an illustration of how knowledge affects scientific reasoning processes, consider the fishing pond in Figure 5.6. In one study[61] 13-year-olds were shown a similar picture and told, "These four children go fishing every week, and one child, Herb, always catches the most fish. The other children wonder why." If you look at the picture, it's obvious that several variables might come into play here, including the child's location, kind of bait, and length of fishing rod. Adolescents who were avid fishermen more effectively separated and controlled variables for this situation than they did for the pendulum problem described earlier, whereas the reverse was true for nonfishermen.

True expertise comes only after many years of study and practice.

Some learners eventually acquire a great deal of information about a particular topic—say, lizards, World War II, auto mechanics, or photography—to the point that they are *experts*. Not only do experts know more than their peers, but their knowledge is also qualitatively different from that of others. In particular, their knowledge tends to be

---

[57] Siegler & Svetina, 2006.
[58] Empson, 1999; Fujimura, 2001.
[59] Kuhn & Pease, 2010; Lorch et al., 2008; Schauble,1990.
[60] Girotto & Light, 1993; M. C. Linn, Clement, Pulos, & Sullivan, 1989; Schliemann & Carraher, 1993.
[61] Pulos & Linn, 1981.

tightly organized, with many interrelationships among the things they know and with many abstract generalizations unifying more specific, concrete details.[62] Such qualities enable experts to retrieve the things they need more easily, to find parallels between seemingly diverse situations, and to solve problems effectively.[63]

There may be three somewhat distinct stages in the development of knowledge related to a particular topic.[64] At the first stage, *acclimation,* learners familiarize themselves with a new content domain, much as someone might do by taking an introductory course in biology, European history, or economics. At this point, learners pick up a lot of facts that they tend to store in relative isolation from one another. As a result of such fragmented learning, they are likely to hold on to many misconceptions that they may have acquired before they started studying the subject systematically.

At the second stage, *competence,* learners acquire considerably more information about the subject matter, and they also acquire some general principles that help tie the information together. People develop com-

FIGURE 5.6 What are some possible reasons that Herb is catching more fish than the others?
Based on Pulos & Linn, 1981.

petence only after studying a particular subject in depth, perhaps by taking several biology courses or reading a great many books about World War II. Because learners at the competence stage make numerous interconnections among the things they learn, they're likely to correct many of the misconceptions they've previously developed. Those misconceptions that remain, however, are apt to intrude into many learners' thoughts about the subject.

At the final stage, **expertise,** learners have truly mastered their field. They know a great deal about the subject matter, and they've pulled much of their knowledge together—including, perhaps, a few persistent misconceptions—into a tightly integrated whole. At this point, they're helping to lead the way in terms of conducting research, proposing new ways of looking at things, solving problems, and, in general, making new knowledge. Expertise comes only after many years of study and practice in a particular field.[65] As a result, few learners ever reach this stage, and we're unlikely to see it before late adolescence or adulthood.

To some extent, different cultures encourage different reasoning skills.

As noted earlier, children's developmental advancements are spurred, in part, by their desire to adapt successfully to their environment. That environment includes not only their physical surroundings but also the culture and society in which they live. Certain logical reasoning skills are more important—and so more likely to be nurtured—in some cultures than in others. The Cultural Considerations box "Cultural Differences in Reasoning Skills and Views about Intelligence" describes some of the cross-cultural differences in reasoning skills that researchers have identified.

[62] J. M. Alexander, Johnson, Leibham, & Kelley, 2008; P. A. Alexander & Judy, 1988; Bédard & Chi, 1992; R. W. Proctor & Dutta, 1995.

[63] Chi, Glaser, & Rees, 1982; De Corte, Greer, & Verschaffel, 1996; Horn, 2008; Rabinowitz & Glaser, 1985; Voss, Greene, Post, & Penner, 1983.

[64] The stages described here are based on the work of P. A. Alexander, 1997, 1998, 2004.

[65] P. A. Alexander, 1997, 1998, 2004; Ericsson, 2003; Horn, 2008.

expertise Extensive and well-integrated knowledge of a topic that comes from many years of study and practice.

CULTURAL CONSIDERATIONS Cultural Differences in Reasoning Skills and Views about Intelligence

Researchers have found that the acquisition of at least one key aspect of concrete operational thinking—conservation—and several aspects of formal operational thinking depend partly on whether a cultural group nurtures them. Furthermore, cultures differ in significant ways in their views of what it means to be an "intelligent" person.

Conservation. Imagine two balls of clay of the same size, as shown here.

You change the shape of one of these balls, perhaps flattening it into a pancake or rolling it into a sausage shape. Rather than asking a child if the two pieces of clay weigh the same (this would be the conservation-of-weight task shown in Figure 5.3), you simply ask whether the two pieces have the same amount. On average, school children in

Europe and North America master such conservation of substance with clay at around age 7. In contrast, Mexican children whose families regularly make pottery master this task a bit earlier, by age 6. Apparently, making pottery requires children to make frequent judgments about needed quantities of clay, and these judgments must be fairly accurate regardless of the specific shape of the clay.[a] Yet in other cultures, especially in some where children neither attend school nor work at activities that require keeping track of quantity, conservation may appear several years later than it does in mainstream Western societies.[b]

Formal operational reasoning skills. In some cultures, formal operational thinking skills have little relevance to people's daily lives and activities.[c] For example, let's return to the second problem in the "Beings and Basketballs" exercise presented earlier in the chapter:

If all children are basketballs,
And if all basketballs are jellybeans,
Then must all children be jellybeans?

Following rules of formal logic—that is, if we assume the first two premises to be true—the answer is *yes*. Such reasoning about hypothetical and perhaps contrary-to-fact ideas is taught and encouraged in many schools in mainstream Western societies, especially within the context of math and science instruction. But in numerous other cultures, including many modern Asian societies, logical reasoning tends to be rooted in people's everyday, concrete realities. Adults in these cultures may find little purpose in hypothetical and contrary-to-fact reasoning and so don't always nurture it in their schools or elsewhere.[d]

In some cultures, aspects of formal operational thought are inconsistent with people's worldviews.[e] For instance, whereas most people in mainstream Western culture place great value on the scientific method—forming hypotheses,

• Intelligence

What kinds of behaviors lead you to believe that someone is intelligent? Do you think of intelligence as a general ability that contributes to success in many different areas? Or is it possible for a person to be intelligent in one area yet not in another? What exactly *is* intelligence?

Psychologists haven't reached consensus on the answers to these questions. Virtually all of them agree, however, that children in any single age-group differ in how quickly they acquire new knowledge and skills, and most use the term **intelligence** to refer to this individual-differences variable. Here are several components of what many psychologists construe *intelligence* to be:[66]

- It is *adaptive*. It involves modifying and adjusting one's behaviors to accomplish new tasks successfully.
- It is related to *learning ability*. Intelligent people learn information more quickly and easily than less-intelligent people do.
- It involves the *use of prior knowledge* to analyze and understand new situations effectively.

intelligence Ability to apply prior knowledge and experiences flexibly to accomplish challenging new tasks; involves many different mental processes and may vary in nature depending on one's culture.

[66] S. M. Barnett & Ceci, 2002; Gardner, 1983; Neisser et al., 1996; Nisbett, 2009; Sternberg, 1997, 2004; Sternberg & Detterman, 1986.

collecting evidence to test them, separating and controlling variables, and so on—people in certain other cultures tend to depend on other sources of information, perhaps authority figures, holy scriptures, or general cultural folklore as a more trusted means of determining what is "truth."

Views and manifestations of intelligence. In North America and western Europe, intelligence is largely thought of as an ability that influences children's academic achievement and adults' professional success. But this view is hardly universal. Many Hispanic, African, Asian, and Native American cultures think of intelligence as involving social as well as academic skills—maintaining harmonious interpersonal relationships, working effectively with others to accomplish challenging tasks, and so on.[f] And in Buddhist and Confucian societies in the Far East (e.g., China, Taiwan), intelligence also involves acquiring strong moral values and making meaningful contributions to society.[g]

Cultural groups differ, too, in the behaviors that they believe reflect intelligence. For instance, on many traditional intelligence tests, speed is valued: Children score higher if they answer questions quickly as well as correctly. Yet people in some cultures tend to value thoroughness over speed and may even be suspicious of tasks completed very quickly.[h] As another example, many people in mainstream Western culture consider strong verbal skills to be a sign of high intelligence. In contrast, many Japanese and many Inuit people of northern Quebec interpret excessive chattiness as a sign of immaturity or low intelligence.[i] One researcher working at an Inuit school in northern Quebec asked a teacher about a boy whose language seemed unusually advanced for his age-group. The teacher replied:

Do you think he might have a learning problem? Some of these children who don't have such high intelligence have trouble stopping themselves. They don't know when to stop talking.[j]

As you'll discover as you read the rest of the chapter, intelligence tests are at best only imperfect measures of children's intellectual abilities, and so teachers must be extremely cautious in interpreting the test results for *any* child. Clearly, extra caution is warranted when children come from diverse cultural backgrounds.

[a] Price-Williams, Gordon, & Ramirez, 1969.
[b] Fahrmeier, 1978; Morra, Gobbo, Marini, & Sheese, 2008.
[c] M. Cole, 1990; J. G. Miller, 1997.
[d] Norenzayan, Choi, & Peng, 2007.
[e] Kağitçibaşi, 2007; Losh, 2003; Norenzayan et al., 2007.
[f] Greenfield et al., 2006; J. Li & Fischer, 2004; Sternberg, 2004, 2007.
[g] J. Li, 2004; Sternberg, 2003.
[h] Sternberg, 2007.
[i] Crago, 1988; Minami & McCabe, 1996; Sternberg, 2003.
[j] Crago, 1988, p. 219.

- It involves the complex interaction and coordination of *many different thinking and reasoning processes.*
- It is *culture specific.* What is "intelligent" behavior in one culture isn't necessarily intelligent behavior in another culture.

Let's consider the culture-specific aspect of intelligence for a moment. Because intelligence is adaptive, it must, of course, help learners survive and thrive in their particular culture. And because cultures can differ from one another in significant ways, intelligence must take different forms depending on the culture in which learners live (see the Cultural Considerations box).[67] But regardless of the forms intelligence might take, most psychologists think of it as being somewhat distinct from what a child has actually learned (e.g., as reflected in school achievement). At the same time, intelligent thinking and intelligent behavior *depend* on prior learning. The more young learners know about their environment and about the tasks they need to perform, the more intelligently they can behave. Intelligence, then, isn't necessarily a permanent, unchanging characteristic. As you'll soon discover, it can be modified through experience and learning.

The following general principles describe the nature of intelligence.

Intelligence often involves effectively applying prior knowledge and skills to new tasks and problems.

Bob Daemmrich Photography

---

[67] Gardner, 1983; Sternberg, 2004, 2005.

Intelligence can be measured only imprecisely at best.

Curiously, although psychologists can't pin down exactly what intelligence is, they've been trying to measure it for more than a century. In 1904 government officials in France asked Alfred Binet to develop a method of identifying students unlikely to benefit from regular school instruction and therefore in need of special educational services. To accomplish the task, Binet devised a test that measured general knowledge, vocabulary, perception, memory, and abstract thought. In doing so, he designed the earliest version of what we now call an **intelligence test**. To get a feel for what intelligence tests are like, try the following exercise.

SEE FOR YOURSELF   Mock Intelligence Test

Answer each of these questions:

1. What does the word *penitence* mean?
2. How are a goat and a beetle alike?
3. What should you do if you get separated from your family in a large department store?
4. What do people mean when they say, "A rolling stone gathers no moss"?
5. Complete the following analogy: is to as  is to:

    a. ●●   b. ●○   c. ●○   d. ▷◀

These test items are modeled after items on many modern-day intelligence tests. Think, for a moment, about the capabilities you needed to answer them successfully. Does general knowledge about the world play a role? Is knowledge of vocabulary important? Is abstract thought involved? The answer to all three questions is *yes*. Although intelligence tests have evolved considerably since Binet's time, they continue to measure many of the same abilities that Binet's original test did.

Scores on intelligence tests were originally calculated using a formula that involves division. Hence they were called "intelligence quotient scores," or **IQ scores**. Even though we still use the term *IQ*, intelligence test scores are no longer based on the old formula. Instead, they're determined by comparing a child's performance on a test with the performance of others in the same age-group. A score of 100 indicates average performance: Children with this score have performed better than half of their age-mates on the test and not as well as the other half. Scores well below 100 indicate below-average performance on the test. Scores well above 100 indicate above-average performance.

Figure 5.7 shows the percentage of individuals getting scores at different points along the scale (e.g., 12.9% get scores between 100 and 105).[68] Notice how the curve is high in the middle and low at both ends. This tells us that we have many more children obtaining scores close to 100 than we have children scoring very much higher or lower than 100. For example, if we add up the percentages in different parts of Figure 5.7, we find that approximately two-thirds of children (68%) score within 15 points of 100 (i.e., between 85 and 115). In contrast, only 2% of children score as low as 70, and only 2% score as high as 130. This symmetric and predictable distribution of scores happens by design rather than by chance: Psychologists have created a method of scoring intelligence test performance that intentionally yields such a distribution. You can learn more about the nature of IQ scores in the discussion of *standard scores* in the appendix, "Interpreting Standardized Test Scores," which appears immediately after Chapter 10.

Modern intelligence tests have been designed with Binet's original purpose in mind: to predict how well students are likely to perform in classrooms and similar situations. Studies

---

intelligence test General measure of current cognitive functioning; often used to predict academic achievement over the short run.

IQ score Score on an intelligence test; determined by comparing a person's performance with that of others in the same age-group.

[68] If you have some knowledge of descriptive statistics, it may help you to know that most intelligence tests have a mean of 100 and a standard deviation of 15.

repeatedly show that performance on intelligence tests is correlated with school achievement.[69] On average, children with higher IQ scores do better on standardized achievement tests, have higher school grades, and complete more years of education. In other words, IQ scores often *do* predict school achievement, albeit imprecisely. As a result, intelligence tests are frequently used by school psychologists and other specialists in their efforts to identify students with disabilities and other special needs who might require individualized educational programs.

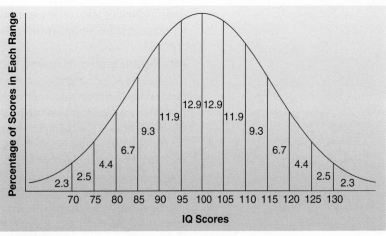

FIGURE 5.7 Percentage of IQ scores in different ranges

While recognizing the relationship between intelligence test scores and school achievement, we must also keep three points in mind about this relationship. First, intelligence doesn't necessarily *cause* achievement; it is simply correlated with it. Even though students with high IQs typically perform well in school, we cannot say conclusively that their high achievement is actually the result of their intelligence. Intelligence probably does play an important role in school achievement, but many other factors—motivation, quality of instruction, family resources, parental support, peer group expectations, and so on—are also involved. Second, the relationship between IQ scores and achievement is an imperfect one, with many exceptions to the rule. For a variety of reasons, some students with high IQ scores don't perform well in the classroom, and others achieve at higher levels than we would predict from their IQ scores alone. Third and most important, we must remember that an IQ score simply reflects a child's performance on a particular test at a particular time—it is *not* a permanent characteristic etched in stone—and that some change is to be expected over time.

? Did you have the misconception that IQ is a permanent number? If so, have you undergone conceptual change about the nature of IQ scores?

To some degree, intelligence reflects speed, efficiency, and control of cognitive processing.

Whenever we use a single IQ score as an estimate of a learner's cognitive ability, we are to some extent buying into the notion that intelligence is a single, general ability that affects performance on many different tasks. Historically, considerable evidence has supported this idea. Although different intelligence tests yield somewhat different scores, people who score high on one test tend to score high on others as well.[70] One early psychologist, Charles Spearman, called this single "intelligence" entity a *general factor,* or *g.*[71] (You may sometimes see the term *Spearman's g.*)

Recall how, in the opening case study, Lupita finishes an assignment more quickly than many of her classmates. Some contemporary information processing theorists believe that underlying *g* may be a general ability to process information quickly and efficiently.[72] Other contemporary theorists suggest that effective use of working memory—especially its central executive component (see Chapter 4)—and metacognitive abilities are also key factors in general intelligence.[73]

Several decades after Spearman's groundbreaking work, psychologist Raymond Cattell found evidence for two distinctly different components of general intelligence (*g*).[74] First, learners differ in **fluid intelligence**, their ability to acquire knowledge quickly and adapt to new situations effectively. Second, they differ in **crystallized intelligence**, the knowledge and skills they've accumulated from their experiences, schooling, and culture. Fluid intelligence is more important for new, unfamiliar tasks, especially those that require rapid

g Theoretical general factor in intelligence that influences one's ability to learn and perform in a wide variety of contexts.

fluid intelligence Ability to acquire knowledge quickly and adapt effectively to new situations.

crystallized intelligence Knowledge and skills accumulated from prior experience, schooling, and culture.

---

[69] N. Brody, 1997; Deary, Strand, Smith, & Fernandez, 2007; Gustafsson & Undheim, 1996; Sattler, 2001.

[70] McGrew, Flanagan, Zeith, & Vanderwood, 1997; Neisser et al., 1996; Spearman, 1927.

[71] Spearman, 1904, 1927.

[72] Bornstein et al., 2006; N. Brody, 1992, 2008; Haier, 2003; Vernon, 1993.

[73] Cornoldi, 2010; H. L. Swanson, 2008.

[74] Cattell, 1963, 1987; also see Nisbett, 2009.

decision making and involve nonverbal content. Crystallized intelligence is more important for familiar tasks, especially those that depend heavily on language and prior knowledge.

Intelligence also involves numerous specific processes and abilities.

Certainly intelligence isn't just a matter of doing something quickly and efficiently. Most psychologists realize that any task or activity probably involves more specific cognitive processes and abilities that are helpful in that particular task or activity but irrelevant in dissimilar ones.[75] For example, let's return to the "Mock Intelligence Test" presented in a See for Yourself exercise earlier. Defining words such as *penitence* (Item 1) requires considerable knowledge of English vocabulary plus sufficient verbal skills to explain a word's meaning with some precision. In contrast, finding analogies among geometric figures (Item 5) involves reasoning about nonverbal, visual entities.

In recent years, some theorists have built on Cattell's distinction between fluid and crystallized intelligence to suggest that intelligence may have three layers, or *strata*.[76] In this *Cattell–Horn–Carroll theory of cognitive abilities,* the top stratum is general intelligence, or *g.* Underlying it in the middle stratum are 9 or 10 more specific abilities—processing speed, general reasoning ability, general world knowledge, ability to process visual input, and so on—that encompass fluid and/or crystallized intelligence to varying degrees. And underlying *these* abilities in the bottom stratum are more than 70 very specific abilities, such as reading speed, mechanical knowledge, and number and richness of associations in memory. With its large number of specific abilities, the Cattell–Horn–Carroll theory is too complex to describe in detail here, but you should be aware that psychologists are increasingly finding it useful in predicting and understanding students' achievement in various content domains.[77]

Learners may be more intelligent in some domains than in others.

Although learners who perform well on one intelligence test also tend to perform well on others, a single high score certainly doesn't guarantee that a learner will perform well on other measures. For instance, some children score higher on tests that assess verbal abilities (e.g., knowledge of vocabulary) than on tests that assess nonverbal, spatial skills (e.g., assembling puzzles, analyzing complex geometric designs). Other children's test scores show the opposite pattern.

In response to such findings, some psychologists have suggested that children may develop two or more different "intelligences" that are somewhat independent of one another. For example, in his *triarchic* model of intelligence, psychologist Robert Sternberg suggests that people may be more or less intelligent in three different domains. *Analytical intelligence* involves making sense of, analyzing, contrasting, and evaluating the kinds of information and problems that are often seen in academic settings and on traditional intelligence tests. *Creative intelligence* involves imagination, invention, and synthesis of ideas within the context of new situations (recall the discussion of creativity in Chapter 4). *Practical intelligence* involves applying knowledge and skills effectively to manage and respond to everyday problems and social situations.[78]

Another psychologist, Howard Gardner, suggests that at least eight different, relatively independent abilities exist.[79] These *multiple intelligences* are described in Table 5.4. (Gardner suggests that there may also be a ninth, *existential* intelligence but acknowledges that he has only limited evidence for it,[80] and so I have omitted it from the table.) Gardner's multiple-intelligences perspective offers the possibility that most learners have the potential to be fairly intelligent in one way or another, perhaps showing exceptional promise in language, mathematics, music, or athletics. In the opening case study, Lupita reveals an ability that

[75] P. L. Ackerman & Lohman, 2006; Carroll, 2003; McGrew et al., 1997; Neisser et al., 1996; Spearman, 1927; Thurstone, 1938.

[76] P. L. Ackerman & Lohman, 2006; Carroll, 1993, 2003; D. P. Flanagan & Ortiz, 2001; Horn, 2008.

[77] J. J. Evans, Floyd, McGrew, & Leforgee, 2001; L. Phelps, McGrew, Knopik, & Ford, 2005; B. E. Proctor, Floyd, & Shaver, 2005.

[78] Sternberg, 1998, 2004; Sternberg et al., 2000.

[79] Gardner, 1983, 1998, 1999.

[80] Gardner, 2000a, 2003.

TABLE 5.4 Gardner's Multiple Intelligences

Type of Intelligence	Examples of Relevant Behaviors
Linguistic intelligence: Ability to use language effectively	• Making persuasive arguments • Writing poetry • Noticing subtle nuances in word meanings
Logical-mathematical intelligence: Ability to reason logically, especially in mathematics and science	• Solving mathematical problems quickly • Generating mathematical proofs • Formulating and testing hypotheses about observed phenomena[a]
Spatial intelligence: Ability to notice details of what one sees and to imagine and manipulate visual objects in one's mind	• Conjuring up mental images • Drawing a visual likeness of an object • Making fine discriminations among visually similar objects
Musical intelligence: Ability to create, comprehend, and appreciate music	• Playing a musical instrument • Composing a musical work • Identifying the underlying structure of music
Bodily-kinesthetic intelligence: Ability to use one's body skillfully	• Dancing • Playing basketball • Performing pantomime
Interpersonal intelligence: Ability to notice subtle aspects of other people's behaviors	• Reading other people's moods • Detecting other people's underlying intentions and desires • Using knowledge of others to influence their thoughts and behaviors
Intrapersonal intelligence: Awareness of one's own feelings, motives, and desires	• Discriminating among such similar emotions as sadness and regret • Identifying the motives guiding one's own behavior • Using self-knowledge to relate more effectively with others
Naturalist intelligence: Ability to recognize patterns in nature and differences among various life-forms and natural objects	• Identifying members of particular plant or animal species • Classifying natural forms (e.g., rocks, types of mountains) • Applying one's knowledge of nature in such activities as farming, landscaping, or animal training

[a] This example may remind you of Piaget's theory of cognitive development. Many of the stage-specific characteristics that Piaget described fall within the realm of logical-mathematical intelligence.

Gardner calls *interpersonal intelligence:* She correctly interprets an adult's subtle message, persuades one classmate to finish his work, and skillfully assists two others as they struggle with puzzles.

Gardner presents some evidence to support the existence of multiple intelligences. For example, he describes people who are quite skilled in one area (perhaps in composing music) and yet have seemingly average abilities in other areas. He also points out that people who suffer brain damage sometimes lose abilities that are restricted primarily to one intelligence (e.g., they may show deficits only in verbal skills). However, many psychologists don't believe that Gardner's evidence is sufficiently compelling to support the notion of eight distinctly different abilities.[81] Others disagree that abilities in specific domains, such as in music or bodily movement, are really "intelligence" per se.[82] Still others are taking a wait-and-see attitude about Gardner's theory until more research is conducted.

[81] N. Brody, 1992; Corno et al., 2002; Kail, 1998; Waterhouse, 2006.

[82] Bracken, McCallum, & Shaughnessy, 1999; Sattler, 2001.

Close attention to detail in 10-year-old Luther's drawing of a plant suggests some talent in what Gardner calls *naturalist* intelligence.

Intelligence is a product of both heredity and environment.

Children probably don't inherit a single "IQ gene" that determines their intellectual ability. However, they *do* inherit a variety of characteristics that in one way or another affect their cognitive development and intellectual abilities.[83] Thus, children who share common genes (e.g., identical twins) tend to have more similar IQ scores than children who don't.[84]

Environmental factors influence intelligence as well, sometimes for the better and sometimes for the worse. Poor nutrition in the early years of development (including the nine months before birth) leads to lower IQ scores, as does a mother's excessive use of alcohol during pregnancy.[85] Attending school has a consistently positive effect on IQ scores.[86] Moving a child from a neglectful, impoverished home environment to a more nurturing, stimulating one (e.g., through adoption) can result in IQ gains of 15 points or more.[87] Furthermore, researchers are finding that, worldwide, there has been a slow but steady increase in people's performance on intelligence tests—a trend that is probably the result of better nutrition, smaller family sizes, better schooling, increasing cognitive stimulation (through increased access to television, reading materials, etc.), and other improvements in people's environments.[88]

How *much* of a role do nature and nurture each play in the development of intelligence? This question has been a source of considerable controversy over the years, especially when IQ differences are found among various racial or ethnic groups. Increasingly, however, researchers are concluding that any *group* differences in IQ are probably due to differences in environment, and more specifically to economic circumstances that affect the quality of prenatal and postnatal nutrition, availability of stimulating books and toys, access to educational opportunities, and so on.[89] Furthermore, various groups have become increasingly *similar* in average IQ score in recent years—a trend that can be attributed only to more equitable environmental conditions.[90]

Learners may have specific cognitive styles and dispositions that predispose them to think and act in more or less intelligent ways.

Most measures of intelligence focus on specific things that a person *can* do, with little consideration of what a person is *likely* to do. For instance, intelligence tests don't evaluate the extent to which learners are willing to view a situation from multiple perspectives, examine data with a critical eye, or actively take charge of and self-regulate their own learning. Yet such inclinations are sometimes just as important as intellectual ability in determining success in academic and real-world tasks.[91]

Students with the same intelligence levels often approach classroom tasks and think about classroom topics differently. Some of these individual differences are **cognitive styles** over which students don't necessarily have much conscious control. Others are **dispositions** that students intentionally bring to bear on their efforts to master school subject matter. I urge you not to agonize over the distinction between the two concepts, because their meanings overlap considerably. Both involve not only specific cognitive tendencies but also personality characteristics. Dispositions have a motivational component as well—an I-*want*-to-do-it-this-way quality.[92]

cognitive style Characteristic way in which a learner tends to think about a task and process new information; typically comes into play automatically rather than by choice.

disposition General inclination to approach and think about learning and problem-solving tasks in a particular way; typically has a motivational component in addition to cognitive components.

[83] Kovas, Petrill, & Plomin, 2007; Kovas & Plomin, 2007; Shaw et al., 2006; Simonton, 2001.
[84] Bouchard, 1997; Kovas, Haworth, Dale, & Plomin, 2007.
[85] Benton, 2008; D'Amato, Chitooran, & Whitten, 1992; Neisser et al., 1996; Ricciuti, 1993.
[86] Ceci, 2003; Gustafsson, 2008; Nisbett, 2009.
[87] Duyme, Dumaret, & Tomkiewicz, 1999; Scarr & Weinberg, 1976; van IJzendoorn, Juffer, & Klein Poelhuis, 2005.
[88] Daley, Whaley, Sigman, Espinosa, & Neumann, 2003; Flynn, 2003, 2007; E. Hunt, 2008; Neisser, 1998b.

[89] Brooks-Gunn, Klebanov, & Duncan, 1996; Byrnes, 2003; Dickens & Flynn, 2006; McLoyd, 1998.
[90] Dickens & Flynn, 2006; Neisser et al., 1996.
[91] Duckworth & Seligman, 2005; Kuhn, 2006; Luciana, Conklin, Hooper, & Yarger, 2005; D. N. Perkins, Tishman, Ritchhart, Donis, & Andrade, 2000.
[92] Kuhn, 2001a; Messick, 1994b; D. N. Perkins & Ritchhart, 2004; Stanovich, 1999; L.-F. Zhang & Sternberg, 2006.

Over the years psychologists and educators have examined a variety of cognitive styles (some have used the term *learning styles*) and dispositions. The traits they've identified and the instruments they've developed to assess these traits don't always hold up under the scrutiny of other researchers.[93] Furthermore, matching students' self-reported "styles" to particular learning environments doesn't necessarily make a difference in academic achievement.[94] Some cognitive styles and dispositions *do* seem to influence how and what students learn, however. For instance, at least two dimensions of cognitive style appear to have an impact:

- **Analytic versus holistic processing:** Some learners tend to break new stimuli and tasks into their subordinate parts (an *analytic* approach), whereas others tend to perceive them primarily as integrated, indivisible wholes (a *holistic* approach). Overall, an analytic approach appears to be more beneficial in school learning, although research is not entirely consistent on this point. Most students become increasingly analytical as they grow older.[95]
- **Verbal versus visual learning:** Some learners seem to learn better when information is presented through words (*verbal* learners), whereas others seem to learn better when it's presented through pictures (*visual* learners). There isn't necessarily a good or not-so-good style here. Rather, learning success probably depends on which modality is used more extensively in classroom activities and instructional materials.[96]

Whereas psychologists have often been reluctant to identify some cognitive styles as being more adaptive than others, certain kinds of dispositions are clearly beneficial in the classroom. Following are several productive dispositions that researchers have identified:[97]

- **Stimulation seeking:** Eagerly interacting with one's physical and social environment
- **Need for cognition:** Regularly seeking and engaging in challenging cognitive tasks
- **Conscientiousness:** Consistently addressing assigned tasks in a careful, focused, and responsible manner
- **Critical thinking:** Consistently evaluating information or arguments in terms of their accuracy, logic, and credibility, rather than accepting them at face value (recall how, in Chapter 4, we noted that critical thinking is a disposition as well as a cognitive process)
- **Open-mindedness:** Being willing to consider alternative perspectives and multiple sources of evidence, and to suspend judgment rather than leap to immediate conclusions

> **?** Do one or more of these dispositions characterize your own thinking?

Such dispositions are often positively correlated with students' learning and achievement, and many theorists have suggested that they play a causal role in what and how much students learn. In fact, dispositions sometimes "overrule" intelligence in their influence on long-term achievement.[98] For instance, learners with a high need for cognition learn more from what they read, are more likely to base conclusions on sound evidence and logical reasoning, and are more likely to undergo conceptual change when it's warranted.[99] And learners who critically evaluate new evidence and are receptive to and open-minded about diverse perspectives show more advanced reasoning capabilities and achieve at higher levels.[100]

Researchers do not yet have a good understanding of the origins of various cognitive styles and dispositions. Perhaps inherited characteristics play a role; for instance, a student may have an energetic, inquisitive temperament or a biologically based strength in visual processing.[101] Perhaps parents or cultural groups encourage certain ways of looking at and

---

[93] Irvine & York, 1995; Krätzig & Arbuthnott, 2006; Messick, 1994b.

[94] Curry, 1990; Pashler, McDaniel, Rohrer, & Bjork, 2009.

[95] Bagley & Mallick, 1998; Irvine & York, 1995; Jonassen & Grabowski, 1993; A. Miller, 1987; Norenzayan et al., 2007; Riding & Cheema, 1991; Shipman & Shipman, 1985.

[96] R. E. Mayer & Massa, 2003; Riding & Cheema, 1991; C. W. Robinson & Sloutsky, 2004.

[97] Cacioppo, Petty, Feinstein, & Jarvis, 1996; Halpern, 2008; Hampson, 2008; Kardash & Scholes, 1996; P. M. King & Kitchener, 2002; G. Matthews, Zeidner, &

Roberts, 2006; Raine, Reynolds, & Venables, 2002; Southerland & Sinatra, 2003; Stanovich, 1999; Trautwein, Lüdtke, Schnyder, & Niggli, 2006; R. F. West, Toplak, & Stanovich, 2008.

[98] Dai & Sternberg, 2004; Kuhn & Franklin, 2006; D. N. Perkins & Ritchhart, 2004.

[99] Cacioppo et al., 1996; Dai & Wang, 2007; Murphy & Mason, 2006.

[100] G. Matthews et al., 2006; Stanovich, 1999.

[101] P. L. Harris & Leevers, 2000; Rothbart, 2007; Treffert & Wallace, 2002.

dealing with the world.[102] And quite possibly, teachers' actions in the classroom—for instance, whether they encourage exploration, risk taking, and critical thinking with respect to classroom topics—make a difference.[103]

The concept of *distributed intelligence* suggests that learners can often think more intelligently by using technology to manipulate large bodies of data, using culturally based symbolic systems to simplify complex ideas and processes, and brainstorming possible problem solutions with peers.

Learners act more intelligently when they have physical, symbolic, or social support.

Implicit in our discussion so far has been the assumption that intelligent behavior is something people engage in with little or no help from the objects or people around them. Yet people are far more likely to think and behave intelligently when they have assistance from their physical, cultural, and social environments—an idea that is sometimes referred to as **distributed intelligence**.[104] Learners can "distribute" a challenging task—that is, they can pass some of the cognitive burden onto something or someone else—in at least three ways. First, they can use physical objects, especially technology (e.g., calculators, computers), to handle and manipulate large amounts of information. Second, they can mentally encode and manipulate the situations they encounter using various symbolic systems—words, charts, diagrams, mathematical equations, and so on—and other cognitive tools their culture provides. And third, they can work with other people to explore ideas and solve problems. When learners work together on complex, challenging tasks and problems, they often think more intelligently than any one of them could think alone. In fact, they sometimes teach one another strategies and ways of thinking that can help each of them to think even *more* intelligently on future occasions.[105]

From a distributed-intelligence perspective, intelligence is not an immutable characteristic that learners "carry around" with them, nor is it something that can be easily measured and then summarized with one or more test scores. Instead, it is a highly variable, context-specific ability that increases when appropriate environmental supports are available.

• Addressing Students' Developmental Needs

In our exploration of principles of cognitive development and intelligence, we've discovered that learners of different ages, and to some extent learners of the *same* age, have different thinking and reasoning capabilities. We've also discovered that environmental factors can definitely impact learners' thinking and reasoning capabilities for the better. In this final section of the chapter, we look at (1) how to accommodate developmental differences and diversity in the classroom and (2) how to foster cognitive development in *all* children and adolescents.

Accommodating Developmental Differences and Diversity

Think, for a moment, about your own experiences in the early elementary grades. What topics did you study, and what instructional strategies did your teachers use to teach those topics? Now think about your high school years. In what ways were the subject matter and instructional methods different from those in elementary school? Certainly many differences come to mind. For instance, in the early elementary grades you probably focused on basic knowledge and skills: learning letter–sound correspondences, reading simple prose, using correct capitalization and punctuation, adding and subtracting two-digit numbers, and so on. Your teachers probably provided a lot of structure and guidance, giving you small, concrete tasks that would enable you to practice and eventually master certain information and procedures. By high school, however, you were studying complex topics—biological

---

[102] Irvine & York, 1995; Kuhn, Daniels, & Krishnan, 2003; Norenzayan et al., 2007.

[103] Flum & Kaplan, 2006; Gresalfi, 2009; Kuhn, 2001b, 2006.

[104] Barab & Plucker, 2002; T. Martin, 2009; Pea, 1993; D. N. Perkins, 1995; B. Rhodes, 2008; Salomon, 1993; Sternberg & Wagner, 1994.

[105] Applebee, Langer, Nystrand, & Gamoran, 2003; A. M. Clark et al., 2003; Salomon, 1993; Spörer & Brunstein, 2009.

distributed intelligence Thinking enhanced by physical objects and technology, concepts and symbols of one's culture, and/or social collaboration and support.

classification systems, historical events, symbolism in literature and poetry, manipulation of algebraic equations, and so on—that were abstract and multifaceted, and your teachers put much of the burden of mastering those topics on *you.*

Such differences reflect the fact that classroom instruction must be *developmentally appropriate.* That is, it must take into account the characteristics and abilities that learners of a particular age-group are likely to have. Yet as we've discovered, learners develop at different rates, and so instruction must also allow for considerable diversity in the characteristics and abilities of any single age-group. The following recommendations can help teachers in their efforts to accommodate developmental differences and student diversity in the classroom.

Explore students' reasoning with problem-solving tasks and probing questions.

In his work with children and adolescents, Piaget pioneered a technique known as the **clinical method**. In particular, he would give a child a problem and probe the child's reasoning about the problem through a series of individually tailored follow-up questions. We saw an example of the clinical method in the interview with 6-year-old Brian presented earlier. An adult asked Brian whether a set of 12 wooden beads—some brown, some white—had more wooden beads or more brown beads. When Brian responded, "More brown ones," the adult continued to press Brian (e.g., "Which would be longer, [a necklace] made with the wooden beads or . . . one made with the brown beads?") to be sure Brian truly believed there were more brown beads and possibly also to create disequilibrium.

By presenting a variety of Piagetian tasks involving either concrete or formal operational thinking skills—tasks involving class inclusion, conservation, separation and control of variables, proportional reasoning, and so on—and observing students' responses to such tasks, teachers can gain valuable insights into how their students think and reason. Typically, when teachers use the clinical method for assessment purposes, they don't give feedback about right and wrong answers. Instead, they simply ask a variety of questions to determine how a child interprets a situation. Sometimes they also ask the child to respond to alternative interpretations.[106] For example, if a child says that a tall, thin glass and a short, wider one contain the same amounts of water, a teacher might say:

> The other day a student told me that the tall glass contains more water because the water in that one is higher than it is in the short glass. What do you think about that?

Formulating follow-up questions that effectively probe a child's reasoning often comes only with considerable experience, however. In Figure 5.8, I present a procedure that a novice interviewer might use in probing students' reasoning related to *conservation of displaced volume,* a fairly advanced form of conservation that, in Piaget's theory, emerges sometime around puberty.

The clinical method isn't limited to traditional Piagetian reasoning tasks, however. On the contrary, it can be used for a wide variety of academic domains and subject matter. To illustrate, a teacher might present various kinds of maps (e.g., a road map of Arizona, a bus-route map for Chicago, a three-dimensional relief map of a mountainous area) and ask students to interpret what they see. Children in the primary grades (especially kindergartners and first graders) are apt to interpret many map symbols in a concrete fashion. For instance, they might think that roads depicted in red are *actually* red. They might also have difficulty with the scale of a map, perhaps thinking that a line can't be a road because "it's not fat enough for two cars to go on" or that a mountain depicted by a bump on a relief map isn't really a mountain because "it's not high enough."[107] Understanding the concept of *scale* of a map requires proportional reasoning—an ability that students don't fully master until adolescence—and so it's hardly surprising that young children would be confused by it.

clinical method Procedure in which an adult presents a task or problem and asks a child a series of questions about it, tailoring later questions to the child's responses to previous ones.

[106] diSessa, 2007. [107] Liben & Myers, 2007, p. 202.

FIGURE 5.8 Conservation of displaced volume: An example of how a teacher might probe a student's reasoning using Piaget's clinical method

Materials
2 glasses containing equal amounts of water
2 balls of clay equal in size and smaller in diameter than the water glasses
2 rubber bands
1 plastic knife

Procedure

1. Show the child the two glasses of water. Put one rubber band around each glass at the level of the water's surface. Ask, "Do both glasses have the same amount of water?" If the child says no, say, "Then please make them the same." Allow the child to pour water from one glass to the other until satisfied that both glasses have equal amounts. Adjust the rubber bands if necessary, or have the child adjust them.
2. Show the child the two balls of clay. Ask, "Are these balls of clay the same size?" If the child says no, say, "Then please make them the same size." Allow the child to add to or subtract from one or both of the balls until satisfied that the two are equal.
3. Being sure that the child is watching, place one ball of clay in one of the glasses of water. Say, "See how the water went up when I did that. Let's move the rubber band to the place where the surface of the water is." Move the rubber band appropriately.
4. Take the other ball of clay and other glass of water. Say, "I'm going to cut this ball of clay into several pieces." Use the plastic knife to cut the ball into four or five pieces. Ask, "How much do you think the water will rise when I drop all this clay into the glass? Move the rubber band to the level where you think the water's surface will be." Allow the child to adjust the rubber band until satisfied with its location. If the child moves the rubber band to the same level as the other rubber band, proceed with Steps 5a–7a. If the child moves it to a higher or lower level than the other rubber band, proceed with Steps 5b–6b.

If the child has predicted an equal rise in height:

5a. Say, "Tell me why you think the water will rise to that spot." Examples of possible responses are
   • "It's the same amount of clay."
   • "I don't know. I just guessed."
6a. Drop all the pieces of clay into the water. Say, "You were right. Are you surprised?" Examples of possible responses are
   • "Not surprised. Even though you cut the clay up, there's still the same amount."
   • "Surprised, because I wasn't really sure it would go there."
7a. If the child was surprised, ask, "Why do you think it rose to that level?" Listen to determine whether the child now understands the same amount of clay should, regardless of number of pieces, displace the same amount of water.

If the child has predicted an unequal rise in height:

5b. Say, "Tell me why you think the water will rise to that spot." Examples of possible responses are
   • "There's less clay."
   • "There are more pieces."
   • "I don't know. I just guessed."
6b. Drop all the pieces of clay into the water. Say, "You weren't quite right. Look, it rose the same amount of water as in the other glass. Why do you think it rose to that level?" Examples of possible responses are
   • "Even though you cut the clay up, there's still the same amount as in the other ball."
   • "It doesn't make sense, because the smaller pieces should take up less room in the glass."
   • "I don't know."

Interpretation
Children who have fully achieved conservation of displaced volume should (1) predict that the water in the second glass will rise to the same level as that in the first glass and (2) justify the prediction by saying that both the water and clay in the two glasses will be the same. Children who are on the verge of achieving conservation of displaced volume might either (3) predict the correct level without initially being able to justify it or (4) initially make an incorrect prediction. In either case, however, they should be able to explain the final result by acknowledging that, despite differences in appearance, the clay in the two glasses displaces the same amount of water. Children who can neither make a correct prediction nor explain the final result are not yet able to reason correctly about problems involving conservation of displaced volume.

Interpret intelligence test results cautiously.

As we've seen, intelligence tests are simply collections of questions and tasks that psychologists have developed and continue to revise over the years to get a handle on how well children and adolescents think, reason, and learn. These tests predict school achievement to some extent, but they are hardly magical instruments that can mysteriously determine a learner's true intelligence—if, in fact, such a thing as "true" intelligence even exists. When teachers are aware of IQ scores that have been obtained for particular students, they should keep the following points in mind:[108]

- Different kinds of intelligence tests may yield somewhat different scores.
- A student's performance on any test is inevitably affected by temporary factors present at the time the test is taken—general health, mood, motivation, time of day, distracting circumstances, and so on. Such factors are especially influential for young children, who are apt to have high energy levels, short attention spans, and little interest in sitting still for more than a few minutes. (Here we're talking about a test's *reliability,* a concept we'll consider in Chapter 10.)
- Test items typically focus on skills important in mainstream Western culture, especially in school settings. The items don't necessarily tap into skills that may be more highly valued in other contexts or cultures.
- Some students may be unfamiliar with the content or types of tasks involved in particular test items and so perform poorly on those items.
- Students with limited English proficiency (e.g., recent immigrants) are at an obvious disadvantage when an intelligence test is administered in English.
- Some students (e.g., students of color who want to avoid being perceived as conforming to "white" culture) may not be motivated to perform at their best and so may obtain scores that underestimate their capabilities.
- IQ scores have a limited "shelf life." They predict school achievement over the short run (e.g., over the next two to three years) but not necessarily over the long run, especially when the scores are obtained during the preschool or early elementary years.

Used within the context of other information, IQ scores can, in many cases, give a general idea of a student's current cognitive functioning. But as you can see from the limitations just listed, teachers should always maintain a healthy degree of skepticism about the accuracy of IQ scores, especially when students come from diverse cultural backgrounds, have acquired only limited proficiency in English, or were fairly young when the scores were obtained.

Look for signs of exceptional abilities and talents.

Earlier we discovered that a learner benefits most from tasks that he or she can accomplish only with assistance—tasks that are in the learner's *zone of proximal development.* Because different students are at different points in their cognitive development, they are apt to have different ZPDs, and almost any classroom is likely to have one or more students whose ability levels far surpass those of their peers. Although experts disagree about how such **giftedness** should be defined and identified, it is probably the result of both genetic and environmental factors.[109]

Students who are gifted tend to be among our schools' greatest underachievers. When required to progress at the same rate as their nongifted peers, they achieve at levels far short of their capabilities. Furthermore, many students with special gifts and talents become bored or frustrated when their school experiences don't provide tasks and assignments that challenge them and help them develop their unique abilities.[110]

The traditional approach to identifying giftedness is to use IQ scores, perhaps with 125 or 130 as a cutoff point.[111] Yet some students may be gifted in only one domain—say, in science or creative writing—and tests of general intelligence might not be especially helpful in identifying such students.[112] And for a variety of reasons, students from some minority-group backgrounds don't perform as well on intelligence tests as students raised in mainstream Western

Observe 9-year-old Elena's enjoyment of challenge in her school's gifted program (PEAK) in the "Motivation: Middle Childhood" video in Chapter 5 of the Book-Specific Resources in MyEducationLab.

[108] Bartholomew, 2004; Dirks, 1982; Hayslip, 1994; Heath, 1989; Neisser et al., 1996; Ogbu, 1994; D. N. Perkins, 1995; Sattler, 2001; Sternberg, 2005, 2007; Zigler & Finn-Stevenson, 1992.

[109] K. R. Carter, 1991; Keogh & MacMillan, 1996; Renzulli, 2002; Simonton, 2001; Winner, 2000b.

[110] K. R. Carter, 1991; Feldhusen, Van Winkel, & Ehle, 1996; Gallagher, 1991; Lubinski & Bleske-Rechek, 2008; Winner, 2000b.

[111] Keogh & MacMillan, 1996; J. T. Webb, Meckstroth, & Tolan, 1982.

[112] D. J. Matthews, 2009; Moran & Gardner, 2006.

giftedness Unusually high ability in one or more areas, to the point where students require special educational services to help them meet their full potential.

culture.[113] Students from some cultures may have had little experience with some of the tasks commonly used in intelligence tests, such as reasoning about self-contained logical problems or finding patterns in geometric figures (see the problems in the "Beings and Basketballs" exercise and Item 5 in the "Mock Intelligence Test" exercise on pages 150 and 158, respectively).[114] Other students, especially girls, may try to hide their talents, perhaps because they fear classmates' ridicule or perhaps because their cultures don't value high achievement in females.[115]

It is critical, then, that school personnel not rely solely on intelligence tests to identify students who may need a more challenging curriculum than their peers. The following are examples of traits teachers might look for:[116]

- More advanced vocabulary, language, and reading skills
- More general knowledge about the world
- Ability to learn more quickly, easily, and independently than peers
- More advanced and efficient cognitive processes and metacognitive skills
- Flexibility, originality, and resourcefulness in thinking and problem solving
- Ability to apply concepts and ideas to new, seemingly unrelated situations
- High standards for performance (sometimes to the point of unrealistic perfectionism)
- High motivation to accomplish challenging tasks; feelings of boredom about easy tasks
- Above-average social development and emotional adjustment (although a few extremely gifted students may have difficulties because they are so *very* different from their peers)

Researchers and expert teachers have found a variety of instructional strategies to be effective for students who are gifted. Common suggestions are presented and illustrated in the Classroom Strategies box "Working with Students Who Have Exceptional Abilities and Talents."

CLASSROOM STRATEGIES Working with Students Who Have Exceptional Abilities and Talents

- Individualize instruction in accordance with students' specific talents.

  A middle school student with exceptional reading skills and an interest in Shakespeare is assigned several Shakespearean plays. After reading each play, he discusses it with his class's teaching intern, who is an English major at a nearby university.

- Form study groups of students with similar abilities and interests.

  A music teacher forms and provides weekly instruction to a quartet of exceptionally talented music students.

- Teach complex cognitive skills within the context of specific school topics rather than separately from the regular school curriculum.

  A teacher has an advanced science study group conduct a series of experiments related to a single topic. To promote scientific reasoning and critical thinking, the teacher gives students several questions they should ask themselves as they conduct these experiments—questions that encourage them to separate and control variables, critically evaluate conclusions, and so on.

- Provide opportunities for independent study.

  A second-grade teacher finds educational software through which a mathematically gifted 8-year-old can study decimals, exponents, square roots, and other concepts that she appears to be ready to master.

- Engage students in challenging, multifaceted public service projects (i.e., *service learning;* see Chapter 8).

  Three high school students collaborate to identify and collect information about several historical buildings and monuments in their community. They then lead their classmates on a walking tour of these structures.

- Encourage students to set high goals for themselves.

  A teacher encourages a student from a lower socioeconomic background to consider going to college and helps the student explore possible sources of financial assistance for higher education.

- Seek outside resources to help students develop their exceptional talents.

  A student with an exceptional aptitude for learning foreign language studies Russian at a local university.

Sources: Ambrose, Allen, & Huntley, 1994; E. D. Fiedler, Lange, & Winebrenner, 1993; J. A. Kulik & Kulik, 1997; Lubinski & Bleske-Rechek, 2008; Lupart, 1995; S. M. Moon, Feldhusen, & Dillon, 1994; Piirto, 1999; Stanley, 1980; Terry, 2003, 2008 (walking tour example).

[113] McLoyd, 1998; Neisser, 1998a; Walton & Spencer, 2009.

[114] Nisbett, 2009; Rogoff, 2003; Sternberg, 2005.

[115] Covington, 1992; G. A. Davis & Rimm, 1998; DeLisle, 1984; Dweck, 2009.

[116] Candler-Lotven, Tallent-Runnels, Olivárez, & Hildreth, 1994; K. R. Carter & Ormrod, 1982; B. Clark, 1997; Cornell et al., 1990; Gottfried, Fleming, & Gottfried, 1994; Haywood & Lidz, 2007; Hoge & Renzulli, 1993; Janos & Robinson, 1985; Lupart, 1995; Maker & Schiever, 1989; Parker, 1997; Rabinowitz & Glaser, 1985; Steiner & Carr, 2003; Winner, 2000a, 2000b.

Consult with specialists if children show significant delays in development.

Whereas some children and adolescents show exceptionally advanced development, a few others show unusual *delays* in development. When delays appear only in a specific aspect of cognitive functioning, perhaps learners haven't had sufficient experience to develop it or perhaps a *learning disability* is present. In contrast, learners with a general **intellectual disability**—also sometimes known as *mental retardation*—show developmental delays in most aspects of their academic and social functioning.[117] More specifically, they exhibit *both* of the following characteristics:[118]

- **Significantly below-average general intelligence.** These learners have intelligence test scores that are quite low—usually no higher than 65 or 70, reflecting performance in the bottom 2% of their age-group.[119] In addition, they learn slowly and show consistently poor achievement in virtually all academic subject areas.
- **Deficits in adaptive behavior.** These learners typically behave in ways that would be expected of much younger children. Their deficits in *adaptive behavior* include limitations in practical intelligence—the ability to manage ordinary activities of daily living—and social intelligence—knowledge of appropriate conduct in social situations.

Such characteristics must be evident in childhood. Thus, a person who showed them beginning at age 16, perhaps as the result of a serious head injury, would *not* be classified as having an intellectual disability.

Intellectual disabilities are often caused by genetic conditions. For example, they are common in children with Down syndrome, a condition marked by distinctive facial features, shorter-than-average arms and legs, and poor muscle tone. Other intellectual disabilities are due to biological but noninherited causes, such as severe malnutrition or excessive alcohol consumption during the mother's pregnancy or prolonged oxygen deprivation during a difficult birth.[120] In still other situations, environmental factors, such as parental neglect or an extremely impoverished and unstimulating home environment, may be at fault.[121] Although usually a long-term condition, an intellectual disability isn't necessarily a lifelong disability, especially when its cause is environmental rather than genetic.[122]

Severe intellectual disabilities are usually identified long before children begin kindergarten or first grade. Mild cases can go undetected until school age, however. Teachers who suspect that a student has significant delays in cognitive development and adaptive behavior should definitely consult with specialists trained in identifying and working with children who have special educational needs.

Some students with mild intellectual disabilities spend part or all of the school day in general education classrooms. They are apt to have poor reading and language skills, less general knowledge about the world, poor memory for new information, difficulty with abstract ideas, and few (if any) metacognitive skills.[123] Nevertheless, they can make considerable academic progress when instruction is appropriately paced and provides a lot of guidance and support. The Classroom Strategies box "Working with Students Who Have Significant Delays in Cognitive Development" offers a few suggestions for working effectively with these students.

---

[117] Many special educators now prefer the term *intellectual disability* over the term *mental retardation* (e.g., Luckasson et al., 2002), and in 2007 the American Association on Mental Retardation changed its name to the American Association on Intellectual and Developmental Disabilities.

[118] Luckasson et al., 2002.

[119] Keogh & MacMillan, 1996; Turnbull, Turnbull, & Wehmeyer, 2007.

[120] Dorris, 1989; Keogh & MacMillan, 1996.

[121] Batshaw & Shapiro, 1997; A. A. Baumeister, 1989; D. A. Chapman, Scott, & Mason, 2002.

[122] Ormrod & McGuire, 2007; Hallahan, Kauffman, & Pullen, 2009; Landesman & Ramey, 1989.

[123] Beirne-Smith, Ittenbach, & Patton, 2002; Butterfield & Ferretti, 1987; Heward, 2009; Kail, 1990; Turnbull et al., 2007.

intellectual disability Disability characterized by significantly below-average general intelligence and deficits in adaptive behavior, both of which first appear in infancy or childhood; also known as *mental retardation*.

CLASSROOM STRATEGIES Working with Students Who Have Significant Delays in Cognitive Development

- Introduce new material at a slower pace, and provide many opportunities for practice.

  A teacher gives a student only two new addition facts a week because any more than two seems to overwhelm him. Every day the teacher has the student practice writing the new facts and review the facts learned in preceding weeks.

- Explain tasks and expected behaviors concretely and in very specific language.

  An art teacher gives a student explicit training in the steps he needs to take at the end of each painting session: (1) Rinse the paintbrush out at the sink, (2) put the brush and watercolor paints on the shelf in the back room, and (3) put the painting on the counter by the window to dry. Initially the teacher needs to remind the student of every step in the process. But with time and practice, the student eventually carries out the process independently.

- Give students explicit guidance about how to study.

  A teacher tells a student, "When you study a new spelling word, it helps if you repeat the letters out loud while you practice writing the word. Let's try it with *house,* the word you're learning this morning. Watch how I repeat the letters—H...O...U...S...E—as I write the word. Now you try doing what I just did."

- Encourage independence.

  A high school teacher teaches a student how to use her calculator to figure out what she needs to pay for lunch every day. The teacher also gives the student considerable practice in identifying the correct bills and coins to use when paying various amounts.

Sources: K. L. Fletcher & Bray, 1995; Heward, 2009; Patton, Blackbourn, & Fad, 1996; Turnbull, Turnbull, & Wehmeyer, 2007.

Fostering Cognitive Development

The findings of Vygotsky, Piaget, and contemporary developmental researchers yield numerous strategies for fostering children's and adolescents' cognitive development. The following recommendations summarize many of these strategies.

Encourage play activities.

Vygotsky suggested that play is hardly the frivolous activity it appears to be. Quite the contrary, play enables children to stretch their abilities in new ways.[124] For example, as a kindergartner, my son Jeff often played "restaurant" with his friend Scott. In a corner of our basement, the two boys created a restaurant "kitchen" with a toy sink and stove and stocked it with plastic dishes, cooking utensils, and "food" items. They created a separate dining area with child-sized tables and chairs and made menus for their customers. On one occasion they invited both sets of parents to "dine" at the restaurant, taking our orders, serving us our "meals," and eventually giving us our bills. Fortunately, they seemed quite happy with the few pennies we paid them.

In their restaurant play, the two boys took on several adult roles (restaurant manager, waiter, cook) and practiced a variety of adultlike behaviors. In real life such a scenario would, of course, be impossible: Very few 5-year-old children have the cooking, reading, writing, mathematical, or organizational skills necessary to run a restaurant. Yet the element of make-believe brought these tasks within the boys' reach.

Furthermore, as children play, their behaviors must conform to certain standards or expectations. In the preschool and early elementary school years, children often act in accordance with how a father, teacher, or waiter would behave. In the organized group games and sports that come later, children must follow a specific set of rules. By adhering to such restrictions on their behavior, children learn to plan ahead, to think before they act, and to engage in self-restraint—skills critical for successful participation in the adult world.[125]

Play, then, is hardly a waste of time. Instead, it provides a valuable training ground for the adult world, and perhaps for this reason it is seen in virtually all cultures worldwide.

---

[124] Vygotsky, 1978; also see Pellegrini, 2009.
[125] Coplan & Arbeau, 2009; A. Diamond, Barnett, Thomas, & Munro, 2007.

Share the wisdom of previous generations.

As noted in Chapter 3, the culture of any social group ensures that each generation passes the group's accumulated wisdom along to the next generation. Some aspects of a culture are transmitted through informal conversations between adults and children, but many others are passed along through formal education in various academic disciplines. Each discipline includes numerous concepts, procedures, and other cognitive tools that can help students better understand and work effectively in their physical and social worlds.

Instruction in useful cognitive tools typically begins quite early. For example, in mainstream Western culture many children learn color and shape names, counting, and the alphabet in the preschool years. For those who don't, acquiring such basic tools must be a high priority in kindergarten or first grade.[126] For example, Figure 5.9 shows an excerpt from a kindergartner's "Caterpillar Number Book," in which she practices representing the numbers 1 to 10.

Rely heavily on concrete objects and activities, especially in the early elementary grades.

As Piaget and many other researchers have discovered, children in the elementary grades often have trouble thinking and reasoning about ideas that are abstract, hypothetical, or contrary to fact. It is important, then, that elementary school teachers make classroom subject matter concrete for students. For example, in the primary grades teachers might have students use concrete manipulatives (e.g., blocks, beads, pennies) to acquire conservation of number and make sense of basic addition and subtraction facts.[127] In the middle elementary grades, paper- or computer-based illustrations can replace concrete objects to some extent, provided that mathematical concepts are still depicted in concrete terms—for instance, as pictures or diagrams.[128]

Virtually any academic discipline has its share of abstract ideas, and elementary teachers should either translate those ideas into concrete terms or else, if possible, postpone discussion of them until the upper elementary grades at the earliest. For example, in history, the very idea of historical *time*—whether it be a particular year (e.g., 1492) or a certain lengthy time span (e.g., 100 years)—is far beyond children's immediate experience. Accordingly, elementary school teachers conducting history lessons should probably minimize the extent to which they talk about specific years before the recent past.[129] Instead, especially in the primary grades, teachers might focus on important events in their nation's history—for example, having children reenact an early Thanksgiving celebration or showing photographs of covered wagons crossing the prairie—without much regard for the sequence of events over a long period. Such lessons may lead to a disjointed knowledge of history (recall Rita's understanding of Michigan's history in the opening case in Chapter 2), but they provide a concrete foundation on which more abstract and integrated history lessons can later build.

Present abstract ideas more frequently in the middle school and high school grades, but tie them to concrete objects and events.

Many of the concepts, symbols, and other useful cognitive tools that previous generations have passed along to us are fairly abstract. Yet as we've seen, abstract thinking emerges only gradually over the course of childhood and adolescence. Accordingly, abstract ideas should be introduced slowly at first, especially in the upper elementary and middle school grades, and they should be accompanied by concrete activities and illustrations as often as possible. Even in high school, actually *seeing* an abstract concept or principle in action can help students encode and remember it more effectively (recall the discussion of *visual imagery* in Chapter 2).

FIGURE 5.9 An excerpt from 5-year-old Luisa's "Caterpillar Number Book," in which she depicts each of the numbers 1 to 10 in three ways: as a numeral, segments of a caterpillar's body, and caterpillar bites in a leaf

Observe a fourth-grade teacher use manipulatives to help students understand the concept of equivalent fractions in the "Manipulative Strategies" video in Chapter 5 of the Book-Specific Resources in MyEducationLab.

Observe high school teachers making abstract ideas concrete in the "Scarlet Letter" and "Charles's Law" videos in Chapter 5 of the Book-Specific Resources in MyEducationLab.

---

[126] Siegler, 2009; Slavin, Lake, Chambers, Cheung, & Davis, 2009.

[127] Ginsburg, Cannon, Eisenband, & Pappas, 2006; T. Martin, 2009; Sherman & Bisanz, 2009.

[128] Sarama & Clements, 2009.

[129] Barton & Levstik, 1996.

At all grade levels teachers can occasionally have students engage in **discovery learning**, in which students interact with their environment to derive new concepts and principles for themselves. Teachers might also conduct **inquiry learning** activities, which typically have the goal of helping students acquire more effective *reasoning processes* either instead of or in addition to acquiring new ideas. For example, to help students learn to separate and control variables in scientific investigations, their teacher might have them design and conduct experiments related to, say, factors affecting how fast a pendulum swings or how far a ball travels after rolling down an incline.[130] Such activities can often promote more advanced reasoning skills, especially when combined with appropriate instruction and guidance.[131]

Although discovery and inquiry activities have considerable value, teachers should keep in mind two potential downsides.[132] First, students don't always have sufficient metacognitive skills to effectively direct their explorations and monitor their findings. And second, students may "discover" evidence that supports their existing misconceptions and ignore evidence that contradicts those misconceptions, reflecting *confirmation bias* (see Chapter 2). The Classroom Strategies box "Conducting Effective Discovery and Inquiry Learning Activities" offers several guidelines that can help to minimize such problems. Probably the most important of its suggestions is to *structure and guide* the activity to some extent. Occasionally students can learn from random explorations of their environment—for example, by experimenting with and thereby discovering the properties of dry sand, wet sand, and water.[133] By and large, however, students benefit more from carefully planned and structured activities that help them construct appropriate interpretations.[134] The extent to which an activity should be structured depends partly on students' reasoning and problem-solving skills. For example, some students may have trouble formulating and testing hypotheses or separating and controlling variables. Such students will gain more from their explorations if they're given specific, concrete problems and questions to address and considerable guidance about how to proceed.

Observe seventh graders erroneously conclude that weight affects a pendulum's oscillation rate (an instance of confirmation bias) in the "Designing Experiments" video in Chapter 5 of the Book-Specific Resources in MyEducationLab.

Initially introduce sophisticated reasoning processes within the context of familiar situations and group work.

Piaget proposed, and other researchers have since confirmed, that sophisticated mathematical and scientific reasoning processes—proportional reasoning, formulating and testing hypotheses, separating and controlling variables, and so on—don't fully emerge until adolescence. Such abilities are more likely to develop when they're actively nurtured rather than left to chance. Furthermore, as we discovered earlier, students are more likely to use them effectively in contexts they know well. For instance, a science teacher might initially ask students to separate and control variables related to a commonplace activity, perhaps fishing, growing sunflowers, or teaching new tricks to family pets. A social studies teacher might ask students to use proportional reasoning to compute distances on a local city map drawn to a particular scale. A physical education teacher might ask students to formulate and test various hypotheses about the most effective way to throw a softball.

The importance of group work for nurturing advanced reasoning processes can be found in Vygotsky's concept of *internalization*. Vygotsky reasoned that many complex cognitive processes have their roots in social interactions, in that children gradually internalize—and so can eventually use independently—processes that they initially use in interactions with others. We see an example of this idea in **reciprocal teaching**, an approach to teaching reading and listening comprehension strategies in which students learn to ask one another questions about textbook passages or children's literature.[135] Several students and

discovery learning Approach to instruction in which students derive their own knowledge about a topic through firsthand interaction with the environment.

inquiry learning Approach to instruction in which students seek new information through the intentional application of complex cognitive processes (e.g., scientific reasoning, critical thinking).

reciprocal teaching Approach to teaching reading and listening comprehension in which students take turns asking teacherlike questions of classmates.

[130] Lorch et al., 2008.

[131] Eysink et al., 2009; Kuhn, 2007; Kuhn & Pease, 2008; Lorch et al., 2008; Monte-Sano, 2008.

[132] Karpov, 2003; Kirschner, Sweller, & Clark, 2006; Kuhn & Pease, 2008, 2010; B. Y. White & Frederiksen, 2005.

[133] Hutt, Tyler, Hutt, & Christopherson, 1989.

[134] M. C. Brown, McNeil, & Glenberg, 2009; de Jong & van Joolingen, 1998; Hardy, Jonen, Möller, & Stern, 2006; Hickey, 1997; R. E. Mayer, 2004; B. Y. White & Frederiksen, 1998, 2005.

[135] A. L. Brown & Palincsar, 1987; Palincsar & Brown, 1984, 1989; Palincsar & Herrenkohl, 1999.

CLASSROOM STRATEGIES   Conducting Effective Discovery and Inquiry Learning Activities

- Identify a concept or principle about which students can learn something significant through interaction with their physical or social environment.

  In a unit on erosion, a sixth-grade teacher sets a 4-foot-long tray at a slight incline at the front of the classroom. The tray contains quite a bit of sand at its higher end. In a series of experiments, students pour water into the tray's higher end and look at how varying water pressures and quantities differentially affect sand movement.

- Make sure students have the necessary prior knowledge for productively interpreting their discoveries.

  A first-grade teacher asks students what they already know about air (e.g., people breathe it, wind involves its movement). After determining that they have some intuitive awareness that air has physical substance and can affect other physical substances, she and her class conduct an experiment in which a glass containing a crumpled paper towel is turned upside-down and immersed in a bowl of water. The teacher eventually removes the glass from the water and asks students to explain why the paper towel didn't get wet. (A portion of this lesson is depicted in the "Properties of Air" video in Chapter 5 of the Book-Specific Resources in MyEducationLab.)

- Show puzzling results to arouse curiosity.

  A ninth-grade science teacher shows her class two glasses of water. In one glass an egg floats at the water's surface; in the other glass an egg rests on the bottom. The students hypothesize that one egg has more air inside and is lighter as a result. But then the teacher switches the eggs into opposite glasses. The egg that the students believe to be heavier now floats, and the supposedly lighter egg sinks to the bottom. The students are quite surprised and demand to know what is going on. (Ordinarily, water is less dense than an egg, so an egg placed in it will quickly sink. But in this situation, one glass contains saltwater—a mixture denser than an egg and so capable of keeping it afloat.)

- Structure and guide a discovery session so that students proceed logically toward discoveries you want them to make.

A seventh-grade science teacher asks students to speculate about variables that might influence the rate at which a pendulum swings. His students offer three possibilities: length of the pendulum, weight of the object at the bottom, and angle at which the pendulum is initially dropped. The students work in small groups to test each of these hypotheses. When one group fails to separate and control variables, the teacher asks its members to look closely at their data: "What did you change between test one and test two? . . . Which caused the higher frequency [oscillation rate]? . . . Why can't you all come to a conclusion by looking at the numbers?" He continues to ask questions until the students realize they have simultaneously varied both length and weight in their experimentation. (This lesson is depicted in the "Designing Experiments" video in Chapter 5 of the Book-Specific Resources in MyEducation-Lab.)

- Have students record their findings.

  Students in a high school biology class collect data from a local stream and use hand-held wireless computer-networking devices to send their findings to a central class computer. Once back in the classroom, the students consolidate and graph the data and look for general patterns and trends.

- Help students relate their findings to concepts and principles in the academic discipline they're studying.

  After students in a high school social studies class have collected data on average incomes and voting patterns in different counties within their state, their teacher asks, "How can we interpret these data given what we've learned about the relative wealth of members of the two major political parties?"

Sources: Boxerman, 2009 (erosion example); M. C. Brown, McNeil, & Glenberg, 2009; Bruner, 1966; de Jong & van Joolingen, 1998; N. Frederiksen, 1984a; Hardy, Jonen, Möller, & Stern, 2006; Kirschner et al., 2006; M. C. Linn, 2008; Lorch et al., 2008; Minstrell & Stimpson, 1996; Moreno, 2006; E. L. Palmer, 1965 (egg example); Pea & Maldonado, 2006 (stream example); D. L. Schwartz & Martin, 2004; B. Y. White & Frederiksen, 1998, 2005.

their teacher meet in a group to read a piece of text, occasionally stopping to discuss and process the text aloud. Initially the teacher leads the discussion, asking questions about the text to promote four cognitive processes: summarizing, questioning, clarifying, and predicting. Gradually he or she turns the role of "teacher" over to different students, who then take charge of the discussion and ask one another the kinds of questions their teacher has modeled. Eventually students can read and discuss a text almost independently of their teacher. They work together to construct meaning and check one another for comprehension and possible misunderstandings, and they become increasingly flexible in how they apply their newly acquired strategies.

As an illustration, let's look at a reciprocal teaching session for a group of six first graders reading a passage about snowshoe rabbits. In this particular case the classroom teacher read the text in small segments (at higher grade levels, students take turns reading). After each segment, the teacher paused while students discussed and processed the segment. As you read the following dialogue, look for examples of summarizing, questioning, clarifying, and predicting (there is at least one instance of each).

The children were reading about the snowshoe rabbit, and it was the 16th day of dialogue. The teacher had just read a segment of text describing the season in which baby rabbits are born and the ways in which the mother rabbit cares for her babies. A student named Kam is the dialogue leader.

Kam: When was the babies born?

Teacher: That's a good question to ask. Call on someone to answer that question.

Kam: Robby? Milly?

Milly: Summer.

Teacher: What would happen if the babies were born in the winter? Let's think.

(Several children make a number of responses, including: "The baby would be very cold." "They would need food." "They don't have no fur when they are just born.")

Kam: I have another question. How does she get the babies safe?

Kris: She hides them.

Kam: That's right but something else. . . .

Teacher: There is something very unusual about how she hides them that surprised me. I didn't know this.

Travis: They are all in a different place.

Teacher: Why do you think she does this?

Milly: Probably because I heard another story, and when they're babies they usually eat each other or fight with each other.

Teacher: That could be! And what about when that lynx comes?

(Several children comment that that would be the end of all the babies.)

Travis: If I was the mother, I would hide mine, I would keep them all together.

Kris: If the babies are hidden and the mom wants to go and look at them, how can she remember where they are?

Teacher: Good question. Because she does have to find them again. Why? What does she bring them?

Milly: She needs to bring food. She probably leaves a twig or something.

Teacher: Do you think she puts out a twig like we mark a trail?

(Several children disagree and suggest that she uses her sense of smell. One child, recalling that the snowshoe rabbit is not all white in the winter, suggests that the mother might be able to tell her babies apart by their coloring.)

Teacher: So we agree that the mother rabbit uses her senses to find her babies after she hides them. Kam, can you summarize for us now?

Kam: The babies are born in the summer. . . .

Teacher: The mother . . .

Kam: The mother hides the babies in different places.

Teacher: And she visits them . . .

Kam: To bring them food.

Travis: She keeps them safe.

Teacher: Any predictions?

Milly: What she teaches her babies . . . like how to hop.

Kris: They know how to hop already.

Teacher: Well, let's read and see.[136]

❖ What examples of summarizing, questioning, clarifying, and predicting did you find in the dialogue? (Compare your response to this question with the response presented in Chapter 5 of the Book-Specific Resources in MyEducationLab.)

In this lesson the teacher modeled elaborative questions and connections to prior knowledge ("What would happen if the babies were born in the winter?" "Do you think she puts out a twig like we mark a trail?") and provided general guidance and occasional hints about how students should process the passage about snowshoe rabbits ("Kam, can you summarize for us now?" "And she visits them . . .". Also notice in the dialogue how students support one another in their efforts to process what they are reading. Consider this exchange as an example:

Kam: I have another question. How does she get the babies safe?

Kris: She hides them.

Kam: That's right but something else. . . .

Reciprocal teaching has been used successfully with a wide variety of students, ranging from first graders to college students, to teach effective reading and listening comprehension

---

[136] Lesson courtesy of Annemarie Palincsar, University of Michigan.

skills.[137] In an early study of reciprocal teaching,[138] six seventh-grade students with a history of poor reading comprehension participated in 20 reciprocal teaching sessions, each lasting about 30 minutes. Despite this relatively short intervention, students showed remarkable improvement in their reading comprehension skills. They became increasingly able to process reading material in an effective manner and to do so independently of their classroom teacher. Furthermore, they generalized their new reading strategies to other classes, sometimes even surpassing the achievement of their classmates.[139]

Scaffold students' early efforts at challenging tasks and assignments.

Vygotsky proposed that growing children and adolescents gain the most from challenging tasks they can accomplish only with the guidance and support of others—that is, tasks within their zone of proximal development. The guidance and support that others provide is generally known as **scaffolding**.

To better understand this concept, let's first think about how scaffolding is used in constructing a new building. The *scaffold* is an external structure that provides support for the workers (e.g., a place where they can stand) until the building itself is strong enough to support them. As the building gains stability, the scaffold becomes less necessary and is gradually removed. In much the same way, an adult guiding a child through a new task may provide an initial scaffold to support the child's early efforts. As a child becomes capable of working without such support, the adult gradually removes it; this process is known as *fading*.

Scaffolding can take a variety of forms; following are examples:[140]

- Help students develop a plan for accomplishing a new task.
- Demonstrate the proper performance of a task in a way that students can easily imitate.
- Divide a complex task into several smaller, simpler tasks.
- Provide a calculator, computer software (word processing program, spreadsheet, etc.), or other technology that makes some aspects of the task easier.
- Keep students' attention focused on the relevant aspects of the task.
- Ask questions that get students thinking about the task in productive ways.
- Keep students motivated to complete the task.
- Remind students what their goal is in performing the task (e.g., what a problem solution should look like).
- Give frequent feedback about how students are progressing.

Scaffolding can come from other students as well as from teachers. In the opening case study, Lupita scaffolds two classmates' attempts at assembling puzzles. Furthermore, when several students work together on a difficult task, they may be able to accomplish something that none of them could accomplish on their own (recall our discussions of *distributed cognition* in Chapter 3 and of *distributed intelligence* earlier in this chapter). Cross-grade tutoring is yet another possibility, and students at both the giving and receiving ends of the instruction are likely to benefit. For instance, when older children tutor younger ones in such basic subjects as writing and math, the "teachers" gradually *internalize* the suggestions they give their "students" (e.g., "Make sure every sentence has a period," "Now carry that 1 to the tens column") and so are more likely to use those suggestions themselves.[141]

Observe examples of teacher scaffolding in the "Scaffolding," "Salamander Investigation," and "Cooperative Learning: Reconstruction" videos in Chapter 5 of the Book-Specific Resources in MyEducationLab.

Jim Pickerell/Stock Connection

Through cross-grade tutoring, older students can scaffold younger students' efforts to master school subject matter.

[137] Alfassi, 2004; E. R. Hart & Speece, 1998; Johnson-Glenberg, 2000; K. D. McGee, Knight, & Boudah, 2001; Palincsar & Brown, 1989; Reinking & Leu, 2008; Rosenshine & Meister, 1994; Slater, 2004.
[138] Palincsar & Brown, 1984.
[139] A. L. Brown & Palincsar, 1987; Palincsar & Brown, 1984.

[140] A. Collins, 2006; Hmelo-Silver, 2006; Lajoie & Derry, 1993; Lodewyk & Winne, 2005; Merrill et al., 1996; Rogoff, 1990; Rosenshine & Meister, 1992; D. Wood, Bruner, & Ross, 1976.
[141] Biemiller, Shany, Inglis, & Meichenbaum, 1998.

scaffolding Support mechanism that helps a learner successfully perform a challenging task (in Vygotsky's theory, a task within the learner's zone of proximal development).

Involve students in age-appropriate ways in adult activities.

When you were a young child, did you sometimes help your mother, father, or an older sibling bake things in the kitchen? Did the cook let you pour, measure, and mix ingredients once you were old enough to do so? Did the cook also give you directions or suggestions as you performed these tasks?

Older family members often allow young children to perform household tasks (cooking, cleaning, painting, and so on) while providing guidance about how to do the tasks appropriately. Likewise, teachers should introduce students to common adult activities within a structured and supportive context. For instance, students might take active roles (cashiers, waiters, etc.) in chili dinners, multifamily garage sales, or other school fundraisers. They might assist with costume design and scenery construction for a school play. Or they might communicate with scientists or government officials through e-mail or teleconferences. When teachers get students actively involved in adult activities, they are engaging students in **guided participation** in the world of adults.[142]

In some instances adults work with children and adolescents in formal or informal **apprenticeships**, one-on-one relationships in which the adults teach the youngsters new skills, guide their initial efforts, and present increasingly difficult tasks as proficiency improves and the zone of proximal development changes.[143] Many cultures use apprenticeships as a way of gradually introducing children to particular skills and trades—perhaps playing a musical instrument, sewing, or weaving.[144]

Through an apprenticeship a student often learns not only how to perform a task but also how to *think about* a task. Such a situation is sometimes called a **cognitive apprenticeship**.[145] For instance, a student and a teacher might work together to accomplish a challenging task or solve a difficult problem (perhaps collecting data samples in biology fieldwork, solving a mathematical brainteaser, or translating a difficult passage from German to English). In the process of talking about various aspects of the task or problem, the teacher and student together analyze the situation and develop the best approach to take, and the teacher models effective ways of thinking about and mentally processing the situation.

Although apprenticeships differ widely from one context to another, they typically have many or all of these features:[146]

- **Modeling.** The teacher demonstrates the task and simultaneously thinks aloud about the process while the student observes and listens.
- **Coaching.** As the student performs the task, the teacher gives frequent suggestions, hints, and feedback.
- **Scaffolding.** The teacher provides various forms of support for the student, perhaps by simplifying the task, breaking it into smaller and more manageable components, or providing less complicated equipment.
- **Articulation.** The student explains what he or she is doing and why, allowing the teacher to examine the student's knowledge, reasoning, and problem-solving strategies.
- **Reflection.** The teacher asks the student to compare his or her performance with that of experts or perhaps with an ideal model of how the task should be done.
- **Increasing complexity and diversity of tasks.** As the student gains greater proficiency, the teacher presents more complex, challenging, and varied tasks to complete, often within real-world contexts.
- **Exploration.** The teacher encourages the student to frame questions and problems on his or her own and thereby expand and refine acquired skills.

guided participation A child's performance, with guidance and support, of an activity in the adult world.

apprenticeship Mentorship in which a novice works intensively with an expert to learn how to perform complex new skills.

cognitive apprenticeship Mentorship in which a teacher and a student work together on a challenging task and the teacher gives guidance about how to think about the task.

[142] Rogoff, 2003.
[143] A. Collins, 2006; Rogoff, 1990, 1991.
[144] D. J. Elliott, 1995; Lave & Wenger, 1991; Rogoff, 1990.

[145] J. S. Brown, Collins, & Duguid, 1989; A. Collins, 2006; John-Steiner, 1997; W. Roth & Bowen, 1995.
[146] A. Collins, 2006; A. Collins, Brown, & Newman, 1989; Hmelo-Silver, 2006.

Be optimistic that with appropriate guidance and support, all students can perform more intelligently.

Contemporary views of intelligence give us reason to be optimistic about what children and adolescents can accomplish, especially when teachers actively nurture and support their cognitive growth. If intelligence is as multifaceted as some psychologists believe, then scores from any single IQ test cannot possibly provide a complete picture of students' intelligence levels.[147] In fact, teachers are likely to see intelligent behavior in many of their students— quite possibly in *all* of them—in one way or another. One student may show promise in mathematics, another may be an exceptionally gifted writer, and a third may show talent in art or music. Furthermore, intelligent behavior draws on a variety of cognitive processes that can definitely improve over time with experience and practice.[148] And the notion of distributed intelligence suggests that intelligent behavior should be relatively commonplace when students have the right tools, symbolic systems, and social groups with which to work.

Teachers must also remember that to the extent that intelligence is dependent on culture, intelligent behavior is apt to take different forms in students from different backgrounds.[149] In mainstream Western culture children's intelligence may be reflected in their ability to deal with complex problems and abstract ideas. Among students who have been raised in predominantly African American communities, it may be reflected in oral language, such as in colorful speech, creative storytelling, or humor.[150] In Native American cultures it may be reflected in interpersonal skills or exceptional craftsmanship.[151] Teachers must be careful not to limit their conception of intelligence only to students' ability to succeed at traditional academic tasks.

It's important, too, that teachers nurture the kinds of cognitive styles and dispositions that will predispose students to think and act intelligently on a regular basis. Although

---

CLASSROOM STRATEGIES Promoting Productive Cognitive Styles and Dispositions

- When students consistently approach tasks in an impulsive, nonanalytical manner, focus their attention on accuracy rather than on speed, and teach them to talk themselves through detailed tasks.

  To help an impulsive third grader subtract two-digit numbers with regrouping ("borrowing"), his teacher instructs him to say these three phrases to himself as he solves each problem: (1) "Compare top and bottom numbers," (2) "If the top number is smaller, borrow," and (3) "Subtract."

- Present important ideas both verbally and visually, ideally with each modality offering unique insights into the subject matter.

  As a high school history teacher describes key World War II battles, he presents maps and photographs of each battlefield and describes specific strategies that one side or the other used to outfox its opponent. To get his students to think analytically about both the visual and verbal information, he asks them questions such as "What challenges did the local topography present for the troops?" and "Why did the commanders choose the strategies they did?"

- Communicate your own eagerness to learn about new topics.

  A middle school science teacher asks her students, "Have you ever wondered why so many people are concerned about global climate change? I certainly have! I've brought in some magazine articles that can help us understand why they're worried."

- Model open-mindedness about diverse viewpoints and a willingness to suspend judgment until all the facts are in. Communicate that for some issues, a single "right" answer simply isn't possible.

  In a lesson about the novel *The Scarlet Letter*, a high school English teacher encourages students to describe their diverse views of the character Arthur Dimmesdale. Students hypothesize that "He's very unsure about himself" or "He's kind of a nerd-type guy." The teacher is receptive to both possibilities but also provokes students to consider why another character, Hester Prynne, would have found him so attractive. One student suggests, "Maybe he's got a good personality," and another speculates that he has a captivating physical feature: "It's his eyes. Yeah, the eyes." (You can observe this discussion in the "Scarlet Letter" video in Chapter 5 of the Book-Specific Resources in MyEducationLab.)

---

[147] Horn, 2008; Neisser et al., 1996; Sternberg, 2005.

[148] Nisbett, 2009; Sternberg et al., 2000.

[149] Gardner, 1995; Neisser et al., 1996; Nisbett, 2009; D. N. Perkins, 1995; Sternberg, 2005.

[150] H. L. Smith, 1998; Torrance, 1989.

[151] Kirschenbaum, 1989; Maker & Schiever, 1989.

researchers haven't yet determined how best to promote productive cognitive styles and dispositions, we can reasonably assume that encouraging and modeling effective ways of thinking about classroom subject matter—for instance, paying close attention to critical details, asking students to evaluate the quality of scientific evidence, and consistently demonstrating open-mindedness about diverse perspectives—will get students off to a good start.[152] The Classroom Strategies box "Promoting Productive Cognitive Styles and Dispositions" on the preceding page presents examples of what teachers might do.

Ultimately, intelligent behavior depends *both* on students' own thought processes and on the supportive contexts in which students work.[153] Rather than asking the question, "How intelligent are my students?" teachers should instead ask themselves, "How can I help my students think as intelligently as possible? What physical and cognitive tools and what social networks can I provide?"

---

[152] Halpern, 1998; Kuhn, 2001b; Messer, 1976; D. N. Perkins & Ritchhart, 2004.

[153] B. Rhodes, 2008; Salomon, 1993; Sfard, 1998.

SUMMARY

With our discussions of cognitive development and intelligence in mind, we can now expand on the Mega-Ideas presented at the beginning of the chapter.

● *As a result of biological and environmental factors and their continually interacting influences, children show some similar patterns but also considerable diversity in developmental pathways.* Children and adolescents reach various developmental milestones in a somewhat predictable sequence, although the ages at which they reach these milestones vary considerably from one youngster to the next. The course of development is often uneven, marked by dramatic changes or qualitative shifts at some points and by slower, more gradual changes at others. Both genetic and environmental factors influence development, but because they interact in their effects and because children's own behaviors also influence the development of various characteristics, the relative contributions of heredity and environment are often impossible to determine.

● *Cognitive development depends not only on brain maturation but also on stimulating physical, social, and cultural experiences and on children's natural inclinations to organize and try to make sense of those experiences.* Although the brain changes in significant ways in the first few years of life, it continues to mature even after the teenage years. Developmental changes in the brain enable increasingly complex thought processes throughout childhood, adolescence, and early adulthood. The brain retains some plasticity throughout life, enabling people of all ages to acquire new knowledge and skills in most domains.

Young learners seem naturally inclined to learn about, organize, and adapt to their world, and they actively seek interactions both with their physical environment and with other people. Adults and other more advanced individuals foster children's cognitive development by providing labels for experiences, modeling procedures for tackling problems, and in other ways passing along culturally appropriate interpretations and behaviors. Social interaction has an additional benefit as well: Children gradually internalize the processes they initially use with others and so can eventually use those processes on their own. Ultimately, young learners benefit most from challenges, both those that call into question existing beliefs (those that create disequilibrium) and those that require use of newly emerging abilities (those that lie within learners' zones of proximal development).

● *Children continually build on existing knowledge and skills to develop more advanced thinking and reasoning abilities.* Thanks in part to growing working memory capacity and an ever-expanding and better-integrated knowledge base, young learners become increasingly capable of logical and abstract thinking over the course of childhood and adolescence. In adolescence, several abilities emerge that enhance thinking about science and math, including reasoning about contrary-to-fact situations, separating and controlling variables, and proportional reasoning. Advanced reasoning processes continue to develop during the high school years, especially if a learner's culture encourages them, but true expertise in any field comes only after many years of study and practice.

● *Although children in any age-group differ somewhat in intelligence, cognitive styles, and dispositions, appropriately supportive environments can significantly enhance these abilities and characteristics.* Virtually all children and adolescents continue to gain new cognitive abilities and skills with age, but learners in any particular age-group differ considerably in their overall ability levels. Most psychologists call this individual difference variable *intelligence*. Psychologists disagree, however, about the extent to which intelligence is a single entity that influences a wide variety of tasks, on the one hand, or a collection of distinct, semi-independent abilities, on the other. Intelligence tests provide a general idea of how a child's general cognitive ability compares to that of his or her peer group, but they are imprecise measures at best and the IQ scores they yield may change somewhat over time. Furthermore, intelligent behavior depends on environmental factors, both those that may have nurtured or impeded a child's cognitive development in the past and those that may support or hinder a child's performance at present. Intelligent behavior also depends on cognitive styles and dispositions—analytical processing, critical thinking, open-mindedness, and so on—that predispose learners to think about new ideas and events in insightful and productive ways.

- *Effective teachers accommodate students' developmental differences and diversity in their curriculum planning and instructional practices.* When considered within the context of other information, IQ scores can certainly help teachers get a general sense of students' current cognitive functioning. Equally helpful are problems and questions that reveal how students think and reason about various situations and topics. Through such information and through careful observation of students' day-to-day behaviors, teachers may discover that some students have exceptional abilities and talents begging to be nurtured and that other students have developmental delays requiring the attention of specialists and special instructional accommodations.

- *Effective teachers also plan and conduct lessons and activities that promote students' cognitive and intellectual development.* Not only must teachers ascertain where students are currently "at" in their thinking and reasoning, but they must also take active steps to help every student make advancements in cognitive abilities and skills. One important strategy is providing opportunities for pretend play, organized games and sports, and other play activities in which students practice adultlike skills and learn how to plan ahead and abide by certain rules for behavior. Another important (in fact *essential*) strategy is to pass along the collective wisdom of the culture—the many concepts, procedures, and other cognitive tools that previous generations have found to be helpful in understanding and dealing with the world. Instruction should rely heavily on concrete objects and activities in the early years but should increasingly introduce abstract ideas and encourage sophisticated reasoning processes as students move through adolescence. Teachers should structure and guide—that is, *scaffold*—students' early attempts at challenging tasks, gradually removing the scaffolding as students gain proficiency. And as ability levels improve, students should participate in meaningful ways in adult activities. In general, teachers should remember that with appropriate guidance and support, virtually all students can learn to think and act in increasingly complex, intelligent ways.

PRACTICE FOR YOUR LICENSURE EXAM

Stones Lesson

Ms. Hennessey is conducting a demonstration in her first-grade class. She shows the children a large glass tank filled with water and then also shows them two stones. One stone, a piece of granite, is fairly small (about 2 cm in diameter). The other stone, a piece of pumice (i.e., cooled volcanic lava), is much bigger (about 10 cm in diameter). Ms. Hennessey doesn't let the children touch or hold the stones, and so they have no way of knowing that the pumice, which has many small air pockets in it, is much lighter than the granite. The demonstration proceeds as follows:

Ms. H.: Would anyone like to predict what he or she thinks will happen to these stones? Yes, Brianna.

Brianna: I think the . . . both stones will sink because I know stones sink. I've seen lots of stones sink and every time I throw a rock into the water, like it always sinks, yeah, it always does.

Ms. H.: You look like you want to say something else.

Brianna: Yeah the water can't hold up rocks like it holds up boats and I know they'll sink.

Ms. H.: You sound so sure, let me try another object.

Brianna: No you gotta throw it in, you gotta test my idea first. [Ms. H. places the smaller stone in the tank; it sinks.] See, I told you I knew it would sink. [Ms. H. puts the larger, pumice stone down and picks up another object.] No you've gotta test the big one too because if the little one sunk the big one's gotta sunk (sic). [Ms. H. places the pumice stone in the tank; it floats.] No! No! That's not right! That doesn't go with my mind [Brianna grabs hold of her head], it just doesn't go with my mind.[154]

---

[154]Dialogue from M. G. Hennessey, 2003, pp. 120–121.

1. Constructed-response question

Brianna is noticeably surprised, maybe even a little upset, when she sees the pumice stone float.

A. Use one or more concepts from Jean Piaget's theory of cognitive development to explain why Brianna reacts as strongly as she does to the floating pumice.

B. Again drawing on Piaget's theory, explain why Ms. Hennessey intentionally presents a phenomenon that will surprise the children.

2. Multiple-choice question

Imagine that you perform the same demonstration with high school students rather than first graders. If you were to follow Lev Vygotsky's theory of cognitive development, which one of the following approaches would you take in helping the students understand the floating pumice?

a. Before performing the demonstration, ask students to draw a picture of the tank and two stones.

b. Drop several light objects (e.g., a feather, a piece of paper, a small sponge) into the tank before dropping either stone into it.

c. Teach the concept of *density*, and explain that an object's average density relative to water determines whether it floats or sinks.

d. Praise students who correctly predict that the larger stone will float, even if they initially give an incorrect explanation about why it will float.

Go to Chapter 5 of the Book-Specific Resources in MyEducationLab and click on "Practice for Your Licensure Exam" to answer these questions. Compare your responses with the feedback provided.

PEARSON
myeducationlab

Go to the Topic "Cognitive & Linguistic Development" in the MyEducationLab (www.myeducationlab.com) for your course, where you can:

- Find learning outcomes for "Cognitive & Linguistic Development," along with the national standards that connect to these outcomes.
- Complete Assignments and Activities that can help you more deeply understand the chapter content.
- Apply and practice your understanding of the core teaching skills identified in the chapter with the Building Teaching Skills and Dispositions learning units.
- Access video clips of CCSSO National Teachers of the Year award winners responding to the question, "Why Do I Teach?" in the Teacher Talk section.
- Check your comprehension of the content covered in the chapter by going to the Study Plan in the Book Resources for your text. Here you will be able to take a chapter quiz, receive feedback on your answers, and then access Review, Practice, and Enrichment activities to enhance your understanding of chapter content. Flashcards are also available to help you study definitions and key terms.
- Access additional Book Resources, including:
  - Focus Questions to guide your reading, Video Examples of various concepts and principles presented in the chapter, a Practice for Your Licensure Exam exercise that resembles the kinds of questions appearing on many teacher licensure tests, Margin Note Questions that help you connect chapter content to your past experiences or current beliefs, and Supplementary Readings that enable you to pursue certain topics in greater depth.

6

Motivation and Affect

Annie Pickert/Pearson

CHAPTER OUTLINE

Case Study: Passing Algebra

Basic Human Needs

How Motivation Affects Behavior and Cognition

Cognitive Factors in Motivation

Affect and Its Effects

Promoting Motivation and Positive Affect
   Fostering Intrinsic Motivation by Addressing Students'
     Basic Needs
   Promoting Motivation-Enhancing Cognitions
   Generating Productive Affect

Summary

Practice for Your Licensure Exam: Praising Students' Writing

MEGA-IDEAS TO MASTER IN THIS CHAPTER

Learners are more motivated to learn and perform at high levels when their basic psychological needs are being met.

Both intrinsic and extrinsic forms of motivation affect learners' behaviors and cognitive processes, but sometimes in different ways.

Learners' thoughts and beliefs both about themselves and about classroom subject matter can affect their motivation to learn in the classroom.

Learners' feelings and emotions—that is, their affect—influence and are influenced by both their motives and their cognitive processes.

Effective teachers create conditions that address students' basic psychological needs, help students think in ways that boost intrinsic and internalized motivation, and engender productive feelings about classroom topics.

CASE STUDY Passing Algebra

Fourteen-year-old Michael has been getting failing grades in his eighth-grade algebra class, prompting his family to ask graduate student Valerie Tucker to tutor him. In his initial tutoring session, Michael tells Ms. Tucker that he has no hope of passing algebra because he has little aptitude for math and his teacher doesn't teach the subject matter very well. In his mind, he is powerless to change either his own ability or his teacher's instructional strategies, making continuing failure inevitable.

As Ms. Tucker works with Michael over the next several weeks, she encourages him to think more about what *he* can do to master algebra and less about what his teacher may or may not be doing to help him. She points out that he did well in math in earlier years and so certainly has the ability to learn algebra if he puts his mind to it. She also teaches him a number of strategies for understanding and applying algebraic principles. Michael takes a giant step forward when he finally realizes that his own efforts play a role in his classroom success:

> Maybe I can try a little harder. . . . The teacher is still bad, but maybe some of this other stuff can work.[1]

When Michael sees gradual improvement on his algebra assignments and quizzes, he becomes increasingly aware that the specific strategies he uses are just as important as his effort:

> I learned that I need to understand information before I can hold it in my mind. . . . Now I do things in math step by step and listen to each step. I realize now that even if I don't like the teacher or don't think he is a good teacher, it is my responsibility to listen. I listen better now and ask questions more.[2]

As Michael's performance in algebra continues to improve in later weeks, he gains greater confidence that he can master algebra after all, and he comes to realize that his classroom success is ultimately up to him:

> The teacher does most of his part, but it's no use to me unless I do my part. . . . Now I try and comprehend, ask questions and figure out how he got the answer. . . . I used to just listen and not even take notes. I always told myself I would remember but I always seemed to forget. Now I take notes and I study at home every day except Friday, even if I don't have homework. Now I study so that I know that I have it. I don't just hope I'll remember.[3]

- On what factors does Michael initially blame his failure? What effects do his early beliefs appear to have on his classroom behavior and study habits?

- To what factors does Michael later attribute his success? How have his changing beliefs affected his learning strategies?

- Put yourself in Michael's shoes in this situation. How does Michael probably feel about his algebra class—and perhaps about algebra in general—when he is initially failing on his assignments and quizzes? How might he feel after he becomes more successful?

---

[1] Tucker & Anderman, 1999, p. 5.
[2] Tucker & Anderman, 1999, p. 5.
[3] Tucker & Anderman, 1999, p. 6.

Michael initially believes he's failing algebra because of two things he can't control: his own low ability and his teacher's poor instruction. As a result, he doesn't listen very attentively or take notes in class. With Ms. Tucker's guidance, however, Michael gains a better understanding of algebra and learns how to use it to solve mathematical problems. He also discovers that increased effort and better strategies (taking notes, asking questions when he doesn't understand, studying regularly, etc.) *do* affect his classroom performance. Suddenly Michael himself—not his teacher and not some genetically predetermined inability that lurks within him—is in control of the situation. As a result, his confidence skyrockets, and he works hard to master algebra.

In our discussions of learning and development in previous chapters, we've focused primarily on the question "What can children and adolescents do and learn?" As we turn to motivation in this chapter, we focus on a very different question: "How *likely* are children and adolescents to do what they're capable of doing and to learn what they're capable of learning?" Even when learners have the capabilities and prior experiences necessary to do something, their *motivation* will determine whether they actually do it. **Motivation** is an inner state that energizes, directs, and sustains behavior. It gets learners moving, points them in a particular direction, and keeps them going.

Psychologists' views about motivation have evolved considerably over the years. Within the last two or three decades, their theories have focused largely on motivation's cognitive elements—that is, on perceptions, interpretations, beliefs, and so on that affect the choices learners make and the energy and persistence with which they pursue various activities. Table 6.1 describes two early perspectives of motivation, as well as several contemporary cognitive perspectives that will guide much of our discussion in this chapter. If you look closely at the descriptions in the table, you might notice that contemporary theories overlap to some extent. For example, the concepts of *competence* (self-determination theory), *self-worth* (self-worth theory), *expectancy* (expectancy–value theory), and *self-efficacy* (social cognitive theory) all reflect two general ideas: (1) People like to believe they can perform an activity competently and (2) their self-confidence (or lack thereof) regarding that activity affects their behavior. My approach in this chapter will be to synthesize, rather than identify differences among, current theories of motivation, and in doing so I will use some terms (e.g., *self-worth, self-efficacy*) more than others.

A close partner of motivation is **affect**, the feelings, emotions, and general moods that learners bring to bear on a task. In the opening case study, Michael probably initially feels frustrated and doesn't like algebra very much. After learning effective strategies and improving his performance, however, he studies every day, "even if I don't have homework." At this point, we might suspect, Michael takes pride in his performance and perhaps even enjoys working on his algebra assignments.

In the upcoming pages we'll identify a variety of factors that influence motivation and affect—factors that we'll later translate into strategies for promoting motivation and positive affect in instructional settings. We'll begin by identifying several of human beings' most basic psychological needs.

• Basic Human Needs

Occasionally I hear educators, policy makers, or the public at large talking about "unmotivated" students. In fact, virtually all students are motivated in one way or another. For example, some students may be keenly interested in classroom subject matter and so may seek out challenging coursework, participate actively in class discussions, and earn high marks on assigned projects. Other students may be more concerned with the social side of school, interacting with classmates frequently, attending extracurricular activities almost every day, and perhaps running for a student government office. Still others may be focused on athletics, excelling in physical education classes, playing or watching sports most afternoons and weekends, and faithfully following a physical fitness regimen. And yet a few students, perhaps because of undiagnosed learning disabilities, shy temperaments, or seemingly uncoordinated bodies, may be interested primarily in *avoiding* academics, social events, or athletic activities.

Psychologists have speculated that people have a wide variety of needs. Some needs—for instance, for oxygen, food, water, and warmth—are related to physical well-being, and

motivation Inner state that energizes, directs, and sustains behavior.

affect Feelings, emotions, and moods that a learner brings to bear on a task.

THEORETICAL PERSPECTIVES

TABLE 6.1 Theoretical Approaches to the Study of Motivation

Theoretical Perspective	General Description	Examples of Prominent Theorists	Where You Will See This Perspective in the Book
EARLY PERSPECTIVES			
Behaviorism	From a behaviorist perspective, motivation is often the result of *drives,* internal states caused by a lack of something necessary for optimal functioning. Consequences of behavior (reinforcement, punishment) are effective only to the extent that they either increase or decrease a learner's drive state. In recent years some behaviorists have added a *purposeful* element to the behaviorist perspective: They suggest that learners intentionally behave in order to achieve certain end results.	Clark Hull B. F. Skinner Dorothea Lerman Jack Michael *A supplementary reading on Skinner's theory appears in Chapter 3 of the Book-Specific Resources in MyEducationLab.*	We previously examined the effects of reinforcement and punishment in Chapter 3. In this chapter we draw on behaviorist ideas primarily in our discussions of extrinsic motivation. The purposeful element of behaviorism will be useful in our discussions of functional analysis and positive behavioral support in Chapter 9.
Humanism	Historically, humanists have objected to behaviorists' depiction of people's behaviors as being largely the result of external environmental factors. In the humanist view, people have within themselves a tremendous potential for psychological growth, and they continually strive to fulfill that potential. When given a caring and supportive environment, human beings strive to understand themselves, to enhance their abilities, and to behave in ways that benefit both themselves and others. Unfortunately, early humanist ideas were grounded more in philosophy than in research findings, so many contemporary motivation theorists have largely left them by the wayside. However, one contemporary perspective, positive psychology (see the final row of this table), has some roots in the humanist perspective.	Carl Rogers Abraham Maslow *A supplementary reading on Maslow's theory appears in Chapter 6 of the Book-Specific Resources in MyEducationLab.*	Because humanists conducted little research to substantiate their ideas, we don't specifically look at them in this book. However, the humanist focus on internal, growth-producing motives has clearly influenced the contemporary cognitive perspectives we *do* consider.
CONTEMPORARY PERSPECTIVES			
Self-determination theory	Self-determination theorists propose that human beings have three basic needs: a need to be effective in dealing with the environment (*competence),* a need to control the course of their lives (*autonomy),* and a need to have close, affectionate relationships with others (*relatedness).* Learners are more effectively motivated to learn school subject matter when these three needs are met.	Edward Deci Richard Ryan Johnmarshall Reeve	Self-determination theory guides much of our discussion of basic human needs early in the chapter, and recommendations related to these needs are presented in the chapter's final section. The discussion of internalized motivation is also based on self-determination theory.
Self-worth theory	Self-worth theorists believe that protecting one's own sense of competence—that is, one's sense of *self-worth*—is a high priority for human beings. One way to maintain and possibly enhance self-worth, of course, is to be successful in daily activities. But curiously, when learners suspect that they may fail at an activity, they sometimes do things (e.g., procrastinating until the last minute) that make failure even more likely. Although such *self-handicapping* decreases the probability of success, it also enables people to justify their failure, both to themselves and to others, and so enables them to maintain their self-worth.	Martin Covington	Self-worth theory is clearly evident in the chapter's discussion of basic human needs. Also, when we look at self-handicapping midway through the chapter, we identify a variety of counterproductive behaviors through which students may try to maintain their sense of self-worth in the face of seemingly insurmountable challenges.

(continued)

TABLE 6.1 Continued

Theoretical Perspective	General Description	Examples of Prominent Theorists	Where You Will See This Perspective in the Book
Expectancy–value theory	Expectancy–value theorists propose that motivation for performing a particular task is a function of two variables. First, learners must believe they can succeed. In other words, they must have a high expectation, or *expectancy*, for their task performance. Second, learners must believe that they will gain direct or indirect benefits for performing a task. In other words, they must place *value* on the task itself or on the outcomes that are likely to result.	Jacquelynne Eccles Allan Wigfield	Expectancy–value theorists' findings related to the effects of learners' values are presented midway through the chapter. Their findings related to the effects of learners' expectancies are incorporated into the discussion of self-efficacy.
Social cognitive theory	Social cognitive theorists emphasize the importance of *self-efficacy*—the extent to which one believes oneself to be capable of successfully performing certain behaviors or reaching certain goals—in motivation. Social cognitive theorists also point out that human behavior is typically goal directed, thereby providing a foundation for *goal theory* (described separately below).	Albert Bandura Dale Schunk Barry Zimmerman Frank Pajares	As we see in this chapter, learners are more apt to initiate, exert effort in, and persist at activities for which they have high self-efficacy. To some degree high self-efficacy comes from past successes in an activity. Social factors (e.g., exposure to peer models who perform a task successfully, encouraging words from others) can also boost self-efficacy, at least for the short run.
Goal theory	Goal theorists focus on the kinds of outcomes (goals) toward which learners direct their behavior. Learners are apt to have goals in a variety of areas, including but not limited to academic performance, social relationships, careers, financial gain, and physical and psychological well-being. In recent years many goal theorists have focused on students' goals related to learning in academic settings, which they refer to as *achievement goals.*	Carol Dweck Carol Ames Paul Pintrich Edwin Locke Gary Latham Martin Ford	The goal-directed nature of human motivation is evident early in the chapter. Later we look at the effects of various kinds of goals, with a particular focus on mastery goals (reflecting a desire to gain new knowledge and skills) and performance goals (reflecting a desire to look competent in the eyes of others).
Attribution theory	Attribution theorists look at learners' beliefs about why various things happen to them—for instance, about why they do well or poorly on academic tasks. These beliefs, known as *attributions,* influence learners' optimism about future success and about the actions they might take to bring about such success. For instance, learners are more likely to work hard on classroom tasks if they believe that their ultimate success depends on something they themselves do—that is, if they attribute classroom success to internal and controllable factors.	Bernard Weiner Carol Dweck Sandra Graham	Midway through the chapter we look closely at the nature and effects of attributions. We also discover that over time, many learners acquire a general attributional style, either a realistically optimistic one (a mastery orientation) or an overly pessimistic one (learned helplessness).
Positive psychology	Positive psychology embraces early humanists' belief that people have many uniquely human qualities propelling them to engage in productive, worthwhile activities. But like other contemporary motivation theorists, it bases its views on research findings rather than philosophical speculations. As a distinct perspective of motivation, positive psychology emerged on the scene only in the late 1990s, and in its current form it is better characterized as a collection of ideas than as a full-fledged, well-integrated theory.	Martin Seligman Mihaly Csikszentmihalyi Christopher Peterson	The influence of positive psychology can best be seen in the discussions of flow (an intense form of intrinsic motivation), optimism (incorporated into sections on self-efficacy and attributions), and emotion self-regulation.

these needs undoubtedly take high priority when physical survival is in jeopardy.[4] Other needs are more closely related to *psychological* well-being—that is, to feeling comfortable and content in day-to-day activities. In the following principles, we explore several basic needs that can have a significant effect on people's motivation and psychological well-being.[5]

Learners have a basic need for arousal.

Several classic studies conducted in the 1950s and 1960s suggest that human beings have a basic need for stimulation—that is, a **need for arousal**.[6] As an example, try the following exercise.

SEE FOR YOURSELF   Doing Nothing

For the next five minutes, you're going to be a student who has nothing to do. *Remain exactly where you are,* put your book aside, and *do nothing.* Time yourself so that you spend exactly five minutes on this "task." Let's see what happens.

What kinds of responses did you make during your five-minute break? Did you fidget a bit, perhaps wiggling tired body parts or scratching newly detected itches? Did you interact in some way with something or someone else, perhaps tapping on a table or talking to another person in the room? Did you get out of your seat altogether—something I specifically asked you *not* to do? The exercise has, I hope, shown you that you tend to feel better when *something,* rather than nothing at all, is happening to you.

Some theorists have suggested that not only do people have a basic need for arousal but they also strive for a certain *optimal level* of arousal at which they feel best.[7] Too little stimulation is unpleasant, but so is too much. For example, you may enjoy watching a television game show or listening to music, but you would probably rather not have three television sets, five CD players, and a live rock band all blasting in your living room at once. Different people have different optimal levels, and they may prefer different kinds of stimulation. For instance, some children and adolescents are *sensation seekers* who thrive on physically thrilling and possibly dangerous experiences.[8] Others prefer a lot of cognitive stimulation—eagerly tackling challenging puzzles, reading about intriguing new ideas, arguing with peers about controversial issues—reflecting the *need for cognition* I mentioned in Chapter 5.[9]

The need for arousal explains some of the things students do in the classroom. For instance, it explains why many students happily pull out a favorite book and read if they finish in-class assignments before their classmates. But it also explains why students sometimes engage in off-task behaviors—for instance, passing notes or playing practical jokes—during boring lessons. Obviously, students are most likely to stay *on* task when classroom activities keep them sufficiently aroused that they have little need to look elsewhere for stimulation.

Learners want to believe they are competent and have self-worth.

In Chapter 5 we learned that children are naturally inclined to make sense of and adapt to their environment. We also learned that events inconsistent with existing knowledge and beliefs can create disequilibrium and spur children to reexamine and possibly revise their current understandings. Underlying both of these principles may be a basic **need for competence**—a need for people to believe that they can deal effectively with their environment.[10] Some evidence indicates that *protecting* this sense of competence, which is sometimes known as **self-worth**,

One early theorist, Abraham Maslow, suggested that people's various needs form a hierarchy, such that certain kinds of needs typically take precedence over others. Learn more about Maslow's hierarchy of needs in a supplementary reading in Chapter 6 of the Book-Specific Resources in MyEducationLab.

---

[4] Maslow, 1973, 1987.

[5] The second, third, and fourth principles are based loosely on Deci and Ryan's self-determination theory; for example, see Deci & Moller, 2005; Deci & Ryan, 1985, 1992; Reeve, Deci, & Ryan, 2004; R. M. Ryan & Deci, 2000.

[6] For example, see Berlyne, 1960; Heron, 1957; also see E. M. Anderman, Noar, Zimmerman, & Donohew, 2004, for a more contemporary discussion of this need.

[7] E. M. Anderman et al., 2004; Berlyne, 1960; Labouvie-Vief & González, 2004.

[8] Cleveland, Gibbons, Gerrard, Pomery, & Brody, 2005; V. F. Reyna & Farley, 2006.

[9] Cacioppo, Petty, Feinstein, & Jarvis, 1996; Raine, Reynolds, & Venables, 2002.

[10] Boggiano & Pittman, 1992; Elliot & Dweck, 2005b; Reeve et al., 2004; R. White, 1959.

need for arousal Ongoing need for either physical or cognitive stimulation.

need for competence Basic need to believe that one can deal effectively with one's overall environment.

self-worth Belief about the extent to which one is generally a good, capable individual.

DOONESBURY   **BY GARRY TRUDEAU**

Accomplishing challenging tasks can help children and adolescents maintain a sense of self-worth, but easy "successes," such as those depicted here, are unlikely to do so.

is one of people's highest priorities.[11]

Other people's judgments and approval play a key role in the development of a sense of competence and self-worth.[12] Regularly achieving success in new and challenging activities—as Michael eventually does in math in the opening case study—is another important way of maintaining, perhaps even enhancing, self-worth. But consistent success isn't always possible, especially when learners must undertake especially difficult tasks. In the face of such tasks, an alternative way to maintain self-worth is to *avoid failure,* because failure gives the impression of low ability.[13] Failure avoidance manifests itself in a variety of ways. Learners might refuse to engage in a task, minimize the task's importance, or set exceedingly low expectations for their performance.[14] They might also hold tightly to their current beliefs despite considerable evidence to the contrary.[15] The need to protect self-worth, then, may be one reason why learners are reluctant to undergo conceptual change.

Learners want to determine the course of their lives to some degree.

Some theorists suggest that human beings not only want to feel competent but also want to have a sense of autonomy and self-direction regarding the things they do and the courses their lives take. In other words, human beings may have a basic **need for self-determination**.[16] For instance, when we think "I *want* to do this" or "I would *find it valuable* to do that," we have a high sense of self-determination. In contrast, when we think "I *have to*" or "I *should,*" we're telling ourselves that someone or something else is making decisions for us. As an example of the latter situation, try the following exercise.

SEE FOR YOURSELF   Painting between the Lines

Imagine that I give you a set of watercolor paints, a paintbrush, two sheets of paper (a fairly small one glued on top of a larger one), and some paper towels. I ask you to paint a picture of your house, apartment building, or dormitory and then give you the following instructions:

> Before you begin, I want to tell you some things you will have to do. They are rules that I have about painting. You have to keep the paints clean. You can paint only on this small sheet of paper, so don't spill any paint on the big sheet. And you must wash out your brush and wipe it with a paper towel before you switch to a new color of paint, so that you don't get the colors all mixed up. In general, I want you to be a good art student and not make a mess with the paints.[17]

How much fun do you think your task would be? After reading my rules, how eager are you to begin painting?

---

need for self-determination Basic need to believe that one has some autonomy and control regarding the course of one's life.

[11] Covington, 1992; Hattie, 2008; Rhodewalt & Vohs, 2005; Sedikides & Gregg, 2008.

[12] Harter, 1999; Rudolph, Caldwell, & Conley, 2005; Weiner, 2005.

[13] Covington & Müeller, 2001; Elliot & Dweck, 2005a; Urdan & Midgley, 2001.

[14] Covington, 1992; A. J. Martin, Marsh, & Debus, 2001; Rhodewalt & Vohs, 2005.

[15] Sherman & Cohen, 2002; Sinatra & Mason, 2008.

[16] d'Ailly, 2003; deCharms, 1972; Deci & Moller, 2005; Kağitçibaşi, 2007; R. M. Ryan & Deci, 2000.

[17] Based on Koestner, Ryan, Bernieri, & Holt, 1984, p. 239.

My rules about painting are somewhat restrictive, aren't they? In fact, they're quite *controlling:* They make it clear that I am in charge of the situation and that you, as the artist, have little choice about how to go about your task. Chances are, you have little desire to paint the picture I've asked you to make.[18] Furthermore, you would probably be less creative in your painting than if I hadn't been so controlling.[19]

Even preschoolers and kindergartners seem to prefer classroom activities of their own choosing, and their perceptions of autonomy versus control are often seen in their notions of "play" or "work."[20] The following conversation among several kindergarten students and their teacher illustrates this point:

> **Mary Ann:** The boys don't like to work.
> **Teacher:** They're making a huge train setup right now.
> **Mary Ann:** That's not work. It's just playing.
> **Teacher:** When do girls play?
> **Charlotte:** In the doll corner.
> **Teacher:** How about at the painting table?
> **Mary Ann:** That's work. You could call it play sometimes, but it's really schoolwork.
> **Teacher:** When is it work and when is it play?
> **Clarice:** If you paint a real picture, it's work, but if you splatter or pour into an egg carton, then it's play.
> **Charlotte:** It's mostly work, because that's where the teacher tells you how to do stuff.[21]

Learners want to feel connected to other people.

To some extent we're all social creatures: We live, work, and play with our fellow human beings. It appears that most people of all ages have a fundamental need to feel socially connected and to secure the love and respect of others. In other words, they have a **need for relatedness**.[22]

At school the need for relatedness manifests itself in a variety of behaviors. Many children and adolescents place high priority on interacting with friends, often at the expense of getting their schoolwork done.[23] They may also be concerned about projecting a favorable public image—that is, by looking smart, popular, athletic, or cool. By looking good in the eyes of others, they not only satisfy their need for relatedness but also enhance their sense of self-worth.[24] Still another way to address the need for relatedness is to work for the betterment of others, for instance by helping peers who are struggling with classroom assignments.[25]

The need for relatedness seems to be especially high in early adolescence.[26] (For example, see 11-year-old Ben's description of his class trip to Gettysburg in Figure 6.1.) Young adolescents tend to be quite concerned about what their classmates think of them, often prefer to hang out in tight-knit groups, and are especially susceptible to peer influence (more on these points in Chapter 7).

My Trip to Gettysburg

"Honk!" sounded the bus. We had just left for one of the best times of my life. My friends, mom, teachers, and I were all going.

Last spring was my trip to Gettysburg. We had to wake up at 5:00 a.m. When we got there, I said "Hi!" to everyone in my group. We were at Gettysburg on time even though the bus was late.

When we got there, we went to the tour center and watched an informational video about Gettysburg. Now we were ready for a tour of the real battlefield the union and confederate soldiers fought on. Our guide tried to convince us that Lee was a great general. He told us the book and movie were a lie based on Longstreet's autobiography.

Then we went to the Wax Museum. It was cool! They looked so real. I liked the battlefield scene most.

We went to the Stonehenge for dinner. After that we went to the Jennie Wade house. While we where there we had a wax person talk to us. Finally we left. We watched three movies on the way home.

There were a lot of cool things I did at Gettysburg, but most of all I got closer to my friends because we spent all 18 hours together. We ate together, sat with each other on the bus, and went to every activity together. That's why I call it the best time of my life!!

FIGURE 6.1 In this personal narrative, 11-year-old Ben describes a school field trip to a Civil War battlefield. In the last paragraph he reveals what was, from his perspective, the most valuable part of the trip: the chance to be with his friends for the entire day.

---

[18] Deci, 1992; Koestner et al., 1984.

[19] Amabile & Hennessey, 1992; C. Peterson, 2006; Reeve, 2006.

[20] E. J. Langer, 1997; Paley, 1984; A. C. Schmidt, Hanley, & Layer, 2009.

[21] Dialogue from Paley, 1984, pp. 30–31.

[22] Connell & Wellborn, 1991; Kağitçibaşi, 2007; A. J. Martin & Dowson, 2009; R. M. Ryan & Deci, 2000.

[23] Dowson & McInerney, 2001; W. Doyle, 1986a; Wigfield, Eccles, Mac Iver, Reuman, & Midgley, 1991.

[24] Harter, 1999; Juvonen, 2000; Rudolph et al., 2005.

[25] Dowson & McInerney, 2001; M. E. Ford & Smith, 2007.

[26] B. B. Brown, Eicher, & Petrie, 1986; Juvonen, 2000; A. M. Ryan & Patrick, 2001.

need for relatedness Basic need to feel socially connected to others and to secure others' love and respect.

As we proceed through the chapter, we'll discover that the basic needs just described affect learners' motives, classroom behavior, and learning in a variety of ways. But first, let's look at how motivation tends to influence human behavior and cognition in general.

How Motivation Affects Behavior and Cognition

Several general principles describe how motivation is likely to affect behavior, cognition, and learning.

Motivation directs behavior toward particular goals.

Human beings seem to be purposeful by nature: They set goals for themselves and initiate courses of action they think will help them achieve those goals.[27] For school-age children and adolescents, some goals (e.g., "I want to finish reading my dinosaur book") are short-term and transitory. Others (e.g., "I want to be a paleontologist") are apt to be long-term and relatively enduring.

Motivation determines the specific goals toward which learners strive.[28] Thus it affects the choices learners make—for instance, whether to enroll in physics or studio art and whether to spend an evening playing video games with friends or, instead, completing a challenging homework assignment.

Motivation increases effort and persistence in activities.

Motivation increases the amount of effort and energy that learners expend in activities directly related to their needs and goals.[29] It determines whether they pursue a task enthusiastically and wholeheartedly, on the one hand, or apathetically and lackadaisically, on the other. Furthermore, motivated learners are more likely to continue a task until they've completed it, even if they're occasionally interrupted or frustrated in the process. In general, then, motivation increases learners' **time on task**, an important factor affecting their learning and achievement.[30]

Motivation affects cognitive processes.

Motivation affects what and how learners mentally process information.[31] For one thing, motivated learners are more likely to pay attention, and as we discovered in Chapter 2, attention is critical for getting information into working memory. Motivated learners also try to understand and elaborate on material—to learn it meaningfully—rather than simply "go through the motions" of learning in a superficial, rote manner.

We see this principle at work in the opening case study. As Michael's confidence and motivation increase, he begins to pay attention and take notes in class. He also asks questions when he doesn't understand a concept or procedure.

Motivation determines what consequences are reinforcing and punishing.

The more learners are motivated to achieve academic success, the more proud they will be of an A and the more upset they will be by an F or perhaps even a B (such feelings should remind you of the *self-imposed contingencies* discussed in Chapter 4). The more learners want to be accepted and respected by their peers, the more meaningful the approval of the "in-group" will be and the more painful the ridicule of classmates will seem.[32] To a teenage boy uninterested in athletics, making or not making the school football team is no big deal, but to a teen whose life revolves around football, making or not making the team may be a consequence of monumental importance.

---

time on task Amount of time that students are actively engaged in a learning activity.

[27] M. E. Ford & Smith, 2007; Gollwitzer & Bargh, 2005; Rovee-Collier, 1999.

[28] Locke & Latham, 2006; Maehr & Meyer, 1997; Pintrich, Marx, & Boyle, 1993; Vansteenkiste, Lens, & Deci, 2006.

[29] Csikszentmihalyi & Nakamura, 1989; Maehr, 1984; Pintrich et al., 1993.

[30] Larson, 2000; E. Skinner, Furrer, Marchand, & Kindermann, 2008; Wigfield, 1994.

[31] Blumenfeld, Kempler, & Krajcik, 2006; Hidi & Renninger, 2006; Sins, van Joolingen, Savelsbergh, & van Hout-Wolters, 2008; Voss & Schauble, 1992.

[32] Rudolph et al., 2005.

Motivation often leads to improved performance.

Because of the other effects just listed—goal-directed behavior, effort and energy, persistence, cognitive processing, and impact of consequences—motivation often leads to improved performance in the domain in question (see Figure 6.2). For instance, learners who are most motivated to learn and excel in classroom activities tend to be the highest achievers.[33] Conversely, learners who are least motivated to master academic subject matter are at high risk for dropping out before they graduate from high school.[34]

Intrinsic motivation is usually more beneficial than extrinsic motivation.

Not all forms of motivation have exactly the same effects on human learning and performance. Consider these two students in an advanced high school writing class:

- Sheryl is taking the writing class for only one reason: Earning an A or B in the class will help her earn a scholarship at State University, which she desperately wants to attend.

- Shannon has always liked to write. Doing well in class will certainly help her get a scholarship at State University, but in addition Shannon truly wants to become a better writer. She sees its usefulness for her future profession as a journalist. Besides, she's learning many new techniques for making her writing more vivid and engaging.

The first girl, Sheryl, exhibits **extrinsic motivation**: She's motivated by factors external to herself and unrelated to the task she's performing. Learners who are extrinsically motivated may want the good grades, money, or recognition that particular activities and accomplishments bring. Essentially they're motivated to perform a task as a means to an end, not as an end in and of itself. In contrast, Shannon exhibits **intrinsic motivation**: She is motivated by factors within herself or inherent in the task she is performing. Intrinsic motivation often results when learners engage in tasks that enable them to meet one or more of the basic psychological needs identified earlier.[35] Learners who are intrinsically motivated are apt to engage in an activity because it intellectually stimulates them, helps them feel competent and self-determined, or provides an enjoyable vehicle for interacting with friends.

Learners are most likely to show motivation's beneficial effects (effort and energy, persistence, etc.) when they're *intrinsically* motivated to engage in classroom activities. Intrinsically motivated learners are eager to learn classroom topics, willingly tackle assigned tasks, are more likely to process information in effective ways (e.g., by engaging in meaningful learning), and are more likely to achieve at high levels. Some learners with high levels of intrinsic motivation become so focused on and absorbed in an activity that they lose track of time and completely ignore other tasks—a phenomenon known as **flow**.[36] In contrast, extrinsically motivated learners may have to be enticed or prodded, may process information only superficially, and are often interested in performing only easy tasks and meeting minimal classroom requirements.[37]

In the early elementary grades, most students are eager and excited to learn new things at school. But sometime between grades 3 and 9, their intrinsic motivation to learn and master school subject matter declines.[38] This decline is probably the result of several factors. As learners get older, they are more frequently reminded of the importance of good grades (extrinsic motivators) for promotion, graduation, and college admission, and many begin to realize that they aren't necessarily "at the top of the heap" in comparison with their peers.[39] Furthermore, they become more cognitively able to think about and strive for long-term goals, and they begin to evaluate school subjects in terms of their relevance to such goals, rather than in terms of any intrinsic appeal.[40] And they may grow increasingly

MOTIVATION

- Goal-directed behavior
- Effort and energy
- Persistence in activities
- Cognitive processing
- Impact of consequences

ENHANCED PERFORMANCE

FIGURE 6.2 How motivation affects learning and performance

Observe numerous examples of intrinsic motivation in second graders in the "Author's Chair" video in Chapter 6 of the Book-Specific Resources in MyEducationLab.

---

[33] Gottfried, 1990; Hidi & Harackiewicz, 2000; L. H. Meyer, Weir, McClure, & Walkey, 2008.

[34] Brayboy & Searle, 2007; Hardré & Reeve, 2003; Vallerand, Fortier, & Guay, 1997.

[35] Cacioppo et al., 1996; Reeve, 2006; R. M. Ryan & Deci, 2000.

[36] Csikszentmihalyi, 1990; Csikszentmihalyi, Abuhamdeh, & Nakamura, 2005.

[37] Larson, 2000; Reeve, 2006; Schiefele, 1991; Tobias, 1994; Voss & Schauble, 1992.

[38] Corpus, McClintic-Gilberg, & Hayenga, 2009; Covington & Müeller, 2001; Lepper, Corpus, & Iyengar, 2005; Otis, Grouzet, & Pelletier, 2005.

[39] Covington & Müeller, 2001; Harter, 1992; Wigfield, Byrnes, & Eccles, 2006.

[40] Lepper et al., 2005.

extrinsic motivation Motivation resulting from factors external to the individual and unrelated to the task being performed.

intrinsic motivation Motivation resulting from personal characteristics or inherent in the task being performed.

flow Intense form of intrinsic motivation, involving complete absorption in and concentration on a challenging activity.

impatient with the overly structured, repetitive, and boring activities they often encounter at school.[41]

Extrinsic motivation isn't necessarily a bad thing, however. Oftentimes learners are motivated by both intrinsic and extrinsic factors simultaneously.[42] For example, although Shannon enjoys her writing course, she also knows that a good grade will help her get a scholarship at State U. In addition, good grades and other external rewards for high achievements may confirm for Shannon that she is, in fact, mastering school subject matter.[43] And over the course of time, extrinsic motivation may gradually move inward, as we'll discover in our discussion of *internalized motivation* later in the chapter. Thus the extrinsic–intrinsic distinction really reflects a continuum rather than an either-or situation.

In some instances extrinsic motivation, perhaps in the form of extrinsic reinforcers for academic achievement or productive behavior, may be the *only* thing that can get learners on the road to successful classroom achievement and productivity. Yet intrinsic motivation is ultimately what will sustain them over the long run. It will encourage them to make sense of and apply what they're studying and will increase the odds that they continue to read and learn about writing, science, history, and other academic subject matter long after they've left their formal education behind.

Conditions in the learning environment influence intrinsic as well as extrinsic motivation.

A common misconception is that motivation is something people "carry around" inside of them—that some people are simply motivated to do something and others are not. In fact, learners' immediate environments can have dramatic effects on their motivation to learn and achieve. Such environment-dependent motivation is known as **situated motivation**.[44] Certainly extrinsic reinforcement and punishment steer learners toward certain activities and behaviors and away from others. Yet environmental factors play a significant role in *intrinsic* motivation as well.[45] For instance, presenting an unexpected, puzzling phenomenon may pique learners' natural curiosity and interest in a topic. And providing scaffolding and guidance for challenging tasks may entice learners to tackle the tasks strictly for the pleasure and the sense of competence the tasks bring. As we examine cognitive factors in motivation in the next section, we'll identify numerous environmental factors that are apt to affect learners' intrinsic motivation.

• Cognitive Factors in Motivation

Earlier we noted that motivation affects cognitive processes: Motivated learners are likely to pay attention and engage in meaningful learning—processes that will help them understand and remember the topic at hand. But the reverse is true as well: *Cognitive processes affect motivation.* For example, in the opening case study Michael's initial beliefs about his math ability and his explanations for poor performance (low ability and poor instruction) contribute to a lackadaisical attitude: He simply *hopes* he'll remember (but usually forgets) his teacher's explanations. Later, when Michael's appraisal of the situation changes (when his self-confidence increases and he attributes success to effort and better strategies), he becomes a more engaged and proactive learner.

The following principles describe a number of cognitive factors that influence learners' motivation, sometimes for the short run and sometimes for the long haul.

Learners find some topics inherently interesting.

When we say that people have **interest** in a particular topic or activity, we mean that they find the topic or activity intriguing and engaging. Interest is typically accompanied by

---

How is *situated motivation* similar to *situated learning* and *situated cognition* (Chapter 3)? (Compare your response to this question with the response presented in Chapter 6 of the Book-Specific Resources in MyEducationLab.)

---

situated motivation Motivation that emerges at least partly from conditions in a learner's immediate environment.

interest Perception that an activity is intriguing and enticing; typically accompanied by both cognitive engagement and positive affect.

---

[41] Battistich, Solomon, Kim, Watson, & Schaps, 1995; Larson, 2000.

[42] J. Cameron, 2001; Covington, 2000; Hidi & Harackiewicz, 2000; Lepper et al., 2005.

[43] Hynd, 2003; Reeve, 2006.

[44] Boaler, 2002; Paris & Turner, 1994; Rueda & Moll, 1994; J. C. Turner & Patrick, 2008.

[45] Brophy, 2008; Deci & Moller, 2005; J. T. Guthrie et al., 2004; Kumar et al., 2002; Legault, Green-Demers, & Pelletier, 2006; Renninger, 2009.

cognitive arousal and such feelings as pleasure and excitement.[46] Interest, then, is a form of intrinsic motivation. Engaging in interesting activities is one important way in which learners satisfy their general need for arousal.

Take a minute to consider your own interests in the following exercise.

SEE FOR YOURSELF   The Doctor's Office

You have just arrived at the doctor's office for your annual checkup. The receptionist tells you that the doctor is running late and that you'll probably have to wait an hour before you can be seen. As you sit down in the waiting room, you notice six magazines on the table beside you: *Better Homes and Gardens*, *National Geographic*, *Newsweek*, *People*, *Popular Mechanics*, and *Sports Illustrated*.

1. Rate each of these magazines in terms of how *interesting* you think its articles would be to you:

	Not at All Interesting	Somewhat Interesting	Very Interesting
Better Homes and Gardens	_____	_____	_____
National Geographic	_____	_____	_____
Newsweek	_____	_____	_____
People	_____	_____	_____
Popular Mechanics	_____	_____	_____
Sports Illustrated	_____	_____	_____

2. Even though you think some of the magazines will be more interesting than others, you decide to spend 10 minutes reading each one. Estimate how much you think you might *remember* from what you read in each of the six magazines:

	Hardly Anything	A Moderate Amount	Quite a Bit
Better Homes and Gardens	_____	_____	_____
National Geographic	_____	_____	_____
Newsweek	_____	_____	_____
People	_____	_____	_____
Popular Mechanics	_____	_____	_____
Sports Illustrated	_____	_____	_____

Now compare your two sets of ratings. Chances are, the magazines you rated highest in interest to you are also the magazines from which you will learn and remember the most.

Learners who are interested in a particular topic devote more attention to it and become more cognitively engaged in it.[47] They're also apt to learn it in a more meaningful and elaborative fashion—for instance, by relating it to prior knowledge, interconnecting ideas, drawing inferences, forming visual images, generating examples, and identifying potential applications.[48] And unless they're emotionally attached to their current beliefs, interested learners are more likely to undergo conceptual change when they encounter information that contradicts their existing understandings.[49] As you might guess, then, learners who are interested in what they study show higher academic achievement and are more likely to remember the subject matter over the long run.[50]

Psychologists distinguish between two general types of interest. **Situational interest** is evoked by something in the immediate environment. Things that are new, different,

[46] Ainley, 2006; Hidi, Renninger, & Krapp, 2004; Silvia, 2008.

[47] Hidi & Renninger, 2006; E. Skinner et al., 2008.

[48] Hidi & Renninger, 2006; Pintrich & Schrauben, 1992; Schraw & Lehman, 2001; Tobias, 1994.

[49] Andre & Windschitl, 2003; Linnenbrink & Pintrich, 2003; Mason, Gava, & Boldrin, 2008.

[50] Garner, Brown, Sanders, & Menke, 1992; Hidi & Harackiewicz, 2000; Mason et al., 2008; Renninger, Hidi, & Krapp, 1992.

situational interest Interest evoked temporarily by something in the environment.

 Observe high levels of situational interest in young children in the "Snail Investigation" video in Chapter 6 of the Book-Specific Resources in MyEducationLab.

unexpected, or especially vivid often generate situational interest, as do things that involve physical activity or intense emotions.[51] Learners also tend to be intrigued by topics related to people and culture (e.g., disease, violence, holidays), nature (e.g., dinosaurs, weather, the sea), and current events (e.g., television shows, popular music, substance abuse, gangs).[52] Works of fiction (novels, short stories, movies, and so on) are more interesting and engaging when they include themes and characters with which readers can personally identify.[53] And nonfiction is more interesting when it is easy to understand and relationships among ideas are clear.[54]

Other interests lie within: Learners tend to have personal preferences about the topics they pursue and the activities in which they engage. Because such **personal interests** are relatively stable over time, we see a consistent pattern in the choices learners make (see Figure 6.3). Some personal interests probably come from learners' prior experiences with various activities and topics. For example, events and subject matter that initially invoke situational interest may provide the seeds from which a personal interest eventually grows.[55] Often interest and knowledge perpetuate each other: Personal interest in a topic fuels a quest to learn more about the topic, and the increased knowledge gained, in turn, promotes greater interest.[56]

Even in the early elementary grades, many children have specific interests—perhaps in reptiles, ballet, or outer space—that persist over time and lead to consistent patterns in the

---

Soccer, the Pride and Passion

The sharp light blinds all onlookers from the reflection off the newly polished cast iron gauntlets of the twenty-two men of steel. Helms lowered, bodies bent in preparation for the battle Royal. Weapons drawn, shields raised, minds focused, focused on their enemy, their foe, their fellow competitor. Small colored flags wave in the stands, color coded with their respective prides and passions. Noises rumble through the stadium as random as the droplets of sweat flowing down the warriors' faces; teeth gritted, fists clenched, hearts pounding, pounding in anticipation of the things to come, the ultimate challenge of wills, the will to win for your fans, for your teammates, for yourself.

Fussebol, calcio, football, soccer; hundreds of names, one sport. Soccer is the most popular and most played

game in the world, but that is not why I play the "Beautiful Game." Twenty-two players on a 120 by 90-yard battlefield scraping, fighting over one ball; that is not why I play it. Millions of players striving to be on their country's roster to play in the world's tournament that occurs only once every four years; that is not why I play it. The dream of playing in front of thousands of roaring fans and scoring the game-winning goal; that is not why I play it. For the emotion and passion of being able to walk out of my door every day to play the game I love, to give my all to the game, while taking everything I can from it, and not just progressing as a player, but a person; that is why I play it. That is why I play the "world's game." That is why I play soccer. . . .

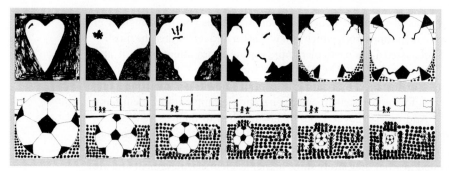

FIGURE 6.3 Many children and adolescents have personal interests that pervade much of what they do. Here we see two examples of Matt's passion for soccer during the high school years: (1) an excerpt from an essay assigned in writing class and (2) artwork created for a language arts portfolio. Matt's interest in soccer was evident many years earlier, as you'll see in excerpts from his first-grade journal in Chapter 9.

---

personal interest Long-term, relatively stable interest in a particular topic or activity.

[51] Hidi & Renninger, 2006; M. Mitchell, 1993; Renninger et al., 1992; Schank, 1979.
[52] Zahorik, 1994.
[53] Hidi & Harackiewicz, 2000; Schank, 1979; Wade, 1992.
[54] Schraw & Lehman, 2001; Wade, 1992.
[55] Hidi & Harackiewicz, 2000; Hidi & Renninger, 2006.
[56] P. A. Alexander, 1997; Hidi & McLaren, 1990; Tobias, 1994.

choices made.[57] By and large, learners form interests in activities that they can do well in and that are stereotypically appropriate for their gender and socioeconomic group.[58] Personal interests are ultimately more beneficial than situational interests. Whereas the latter may temporarily capture a learner's attention, personal interest is the force that ultimately sustains involvement in an activity over the long run.[59]

To engage voluntarily in activities, learners want their chances of success to be reasonably good.

In our earlier discussion of self-worth, we discovered that human beings have a general need to feel competent in their environment. Yet people also realize that they have both strengths and weaknesses. In other words, their beliefs about their competence are somewhat specific to different tasks and activities. The following exercise illustrates this point.

SEE FOR YOURSELF   Self-Appraisal

Take a moment to answer the following questions:

1. Do you believe you'll be able to understand and apply educational psychology by reading this book and thinking carefully about its content? Or do you believe you're going to have trouble with the material regardless of how much you read and study it?
2. Do you think you could learn to execute a reasonable swan dive from a high diving board if you were shown how to do it and given time to practice? Or do you think you're such a klutz that no amount of training and practice would help?
3. Do you think you could walk barefoot over hot coals unscathed? Or do you think the soles of your feet would burn to a crisp?

Your responses say something about your self-efficacy for the tasks about which I asked you. In general, **self-efficacy** is a learner's self-constructed judgment about his or her ability to execute certain behaviors or reach certain goals; thus, it affects the learner's expectations for future performance. For example, I hope you have high self-efficacy for learning educational psychology—a belief that with careful thought about what you're reading, you'll be able to understand and apply the ideas in this book. You may or may not have high self-efficacy about learning to execute a decent swan dive. I'm guessing that you have low self-efficacy about your ability to walk barefoot over hot coals.

Learners are more likely to initiate and persist in tasks and activities for which they have high self-efficacy.[60] High self-efficacy also leads them to engage in effective cognitive and metacognitive processes (paying attention, elaborating, effectively managing study time, etc.) that help them learn and achieve at higher levels.[61]

To a considerable degree, self-efficacy for a particular task or activity arises out of past experiences. Learners feel more confident that they can succeed at a task—that is, they have higher self-efficacy—when they've previously succeeded at that task or at similar ones.[62] In the opening case study, Michael has been getting Fs in his algebra class, and so his expectations for passing the class are initially at rock-bottom. But as he sees himself improve with

---

[57] J. M. Alexander, Johnson, Leibham, & Kelley, 2008; Nolen, 2007; Y.-M. Tsai, Kunter, Lüdtke, Trautwein, & Ryan, 2008.

[58] J. M. Alexander et al., 2008; Hidi, Renninger, & Krapp, 2004; Nolen, 2007; Wigfield, 1994.

[59] P. A. Alexander, Kulikowich, & Schulze, 1994; Hidi & Renninger, 2006; Reed, Schallert, Beth, & Woodruff, 2004.

[60] Bandura, 1997, 2000, 2006; Schunk & Pajares, 2005; Wigfield & Eccles, 2002.

[61] Bembenutty & Karabenick, 2004; Bong & Skaalvik, 2003; R. Klassen, 2002; Pajares, 2005; Shores & Shannon, 2007.

[62] J. Chen & Morris, 2008; Patrick, Anderman, & Ryan, 2002; Valentine, Cooper, Bettencourt, & DuBois, 2002; Usher & Pajares, 2008, 2009.

self-efficacy Belief that one is capable of executing certain behaviors or reaching certain goals.

effort and new strategies, he gains confidence and begins to show signs of intrinsic motivation to master algebra. He starts listening carefully and taking notes in class, and he studies "every day except Friday, even if I don't have homework."[63]

Recall how Michael's initial pessimism about his math class is based not only on his self-assessment of his math ability but also on his teacher's poor instruction. When learners form expectations about the likelihood of future success, they consider not only their own past successes but other factors as well. The quality of instruction, the perceived difficulty of a task, the amount of effort that will be needed, and the availability of resources and support will all influence their predictions.[64] Under ideal circumstances, learners identify personal strengths on which they can depend, tried-and-true strategies they can use, and environmental support systems that can help them surmount any difficulties they may encounter—a combination that gives them hope and optimism about their chances for success.[65]

Social factors, too, play a role in the development of self-efficacy. Seeing other people be successful at an activity—especially seeing successful peers—enhances learners' own self-efficacy for the activity.[66] Words of encouragement (e.g., "I bet Judy will play with you if you just ask her") and suggestions about how to improve (e.g., "I know that you can write a better essay, and here are some suggestions how") can also enhance self-efficacy, at least for the short run.[67] In addition, learners often have higher self-efficacy about accomplishing a task successfully when they work in a group rather than alone. Such **collective self-efficacy** depends not only on learners' perceptions of their own and other group members' capabilities but also on their perceptions of how effectively they can work together and coordinate their roles and responsibilities.[68]

Students often have higher self-efficacy about challenging tasks when they can work with peers rather than alone.

Bob Daemmrich Photography

Once learners have developed a high sense of self-efficacy in a particular content domain, an occasional failure is unlikely to dampen their optimism much. In fact, when these learners encounter small setbacks on the way to achieving success, they learn that sustained effort and perseverance are key ingredients of that success. In other words, they develop **resilient self-efficacy**.[69] The key word here is *occasional* failure. If, in contrast, students *consistently* fail at an activity, they gain little confidence about their chances of future success. For instance, students with learning disabilities, who may have encountered failure after failure in classroom activities, often have low self-efficacy for mastering school subject matter.[70]

Most 4- to 6-year-olds are quite confident about their ability to perform various tasks. In fact, they may overestimate what they're capable of doing.[71] As they progress through the elementary grades, however, they can better recall their past successes and failures, and they become increasingly aware that their performance doesn't always compare favorably with that of their peers.[72] Presumably as a result of these changes, they become less confident, although usually more realistic, about their chances for success in specific academic domains.[73]

When learners think their chances of success are slim, they may behave in ways that make success even *less* likely.

Even with considerable persistence, learners can't always be successful at certain tasks they're asked to perform. Repeated failures in a particular domain may lower not only their self-efficacy for the domain but also their general sense of competence and self-worth.

collective self-efficacy Shared belief of members of a group that they can be successful when they work together on a task.

resilient self-efficacy Belief that one can perform a task successfully even after experiencing setbacks.

[63] Tucker & Anderman, 1999, p. 6.
[64] Dweck & Elliott, 1983; Wigfield & Eccles, 1992, 2000, 2002; Zimmerman, Bandura, & Martinez-Pons, 1992.
[65] C. Peterson, 2006; C. R. Snyder, 1994, 2002.
[66] Dijkstra, Kuyper, van der Werf, Buunk, & van der Zee, 2008; Schunk, 1983; Schunk & Pajares, 2005; Usher, 2009; Usher & Pajares, 2009.
[67] Usher, 2009; Usher & Pajares, 2008; Zeldin & Pajares, 2000.
[68] Bandura, 1997, 2000.
[69] Bandura, 1989, 2008; Dweck, 2000.
[70] R. M. Klassen & Lynch, 2007; Lackaye & Margalit, 2006.
[71] R. Butler, 2008; Eccles, Wigfield, & Schiefele, 1998; Lockhart, Chang, & Story, 2002.
[72] R. Butler, 2008; Davis-Kean et al., 2008; Dijkstra et al., 2008.
[73] Bandura, 1986; Schunk & Zimmerman, 2006; Wigfield et al., 2006.

When learners can't avoid tasks at which they think they'll do poorly, they have alternative strategies at their disposal. Occasionally they make excuses that seemingly justify their poor performance.[74] They may also engage in **self-handicapping**—that is, doing things that actually *undermine* their chances of success. Self-handicapping takes a variety of forms, including the following:[75]

- **Reducing effort:** Putting forth an obviously insufficient amount of effort to succeed
- **Misbehaving:** Engaging in off-task behaviors in class
- **Setting unattainably high goals:** Working toward goals that even the most capable individuals couldn't achieve
- **Taking on too much:** Assuming so many responsibilities that no one could possibly accomplish them all
- **Procrastinating:** Putting off a task until success is virtually impossible
- **Cheating:** Presenting others' work as one's own
- **Using alcohol or drugs:** Taking substances that will inevitably reduce performance

It might seem paradoxical that learners who want to be successful would actually try to undermine their own success. But if they believe they're unlikely to succeed no matter what they do—and especially if failure will reflect poorly on their intelligence and ability—they increase their chances of *justifying* the failure and thereby protecting their self-worth.[76] In the following interview, a student named Christine explains why she sometimes doesn't work very hard on her assignments:

> **Interviewer:** What if you don't do so well?
>
> **Christine:** Then you've got an excuse. . . . It's just easier to cope with if you think you haven't put as much work into it.
>
> **Interviewer:** What's easier to cope with?
>
> **Christine:** From feeling like a failure because you're not good at it. It's easier to say, "I failed because I didn't put enough work into it" than "I failed because I'm not good at it."[77]

Curiously, some learners are more likely to perform at their best, and less likely to display self-handicapping behaviors, when outside, uncontrollable circumstances seemingly minimize their chances of success. In such cases failure doesn't indicate low ability and so doesn't threaten their sense of self-worth.[78]

Learners are more likely to devote time to activities that have value for them.

Another cognitive factor influencing motivation is **value:** Learners must believe there are direct or indirect benefits in performing a task. Their appraisal of the value of various tasks affects the subject matter and activities they pursue in their free time, the courses they choose in junior high and high school, and many other choices they make.[79]

Usually learners value activities that are intriguing and enjoyable—in other words, activities that are *interesting*.[80] Activities that are associated with desirable personal qualities—that is, activities viewed as *important*—also tend to be valued. For example, a boy who wants to be smart and thinks that smart people do well in school will place a premium on academic success. Still other activities have high value because they're seen as means to a desired goal; that is, they have *utility*. For example, much as my daughter Tina found mathematics confusing and frustrating, she struggled through four years of high school math classes simply because many colleges require that much math background.

Knowing how to read clocks and tell time has *utility value* in mainstream Western culture.

Ellen Senisi

---

[74] Covington, 1992; Urdan & Midgley, 2001.

[75] E. M. Anderman, Griesinger, & Westerfield, 1998; Covington, 1992; D. Y. Ford, 1996; E. E. Jones & Berglas, 1978; Hattie, 2008; Riggs, 1992; Urdan, Ryan, Anderman, & Gheen, 2002.

[76] Covington, 1992; Rhodewalt & Vohs, 2005; Sedikides & Gregg, 2008.

[77] A. J. Martin, Marsh, Williamson, & Debus, 2003, p. 621.

[78] Covington, 1992.

[79] Durik, Vida, & Eccles, 2006; Jacobs, Davis-Kean, Bleeker, Eccles, & Malanchuk, 2005; Mac Iver, Stipek, & Daniels, 1991; Wigfield & Eccles, 2002.

[80] Eccles and Wigfield have suggested four possible reasons why value might be high or low: interest, importance, utility, and cost; see Eccles, 2005, 2009; Wigfield & Eccles, 1992, 2000.

self-handicapping Behavior that undermines one's own success as a way of protecting self-worth during potentially difficult tasks.

value Belief that an activity has direct or indirect benefits.

On the other hand, learners tend *not* to value activities that require more effort than they're worth—activities that essentially *cost* too much. For example, you could probably become an expert on some little-known topic (e.g., animal-eating plants of Borneo, the nature of rats' dreams), but I'm guessing that you have more important things to which to devote your time and energy right now. Other activities may be associated with too many bad feelings. For example, if learners become frustrated often enough in their efforts to understand mathematics, they may eventually begin to steer clear of math whenever possible. And of course, anything likely to threaten a learner's sense of self-worth is a "must" to avoid.

In the early elementary years, children often pursue activities they find interesting and enjoyable, regardless of their expectations for success.[81] As they get older, however, they increasingly attach value to activities for which they have high expectations for success and to activities they think will help them meet long-term goals, and they begin to *de*value activities at which they expect to do poorly.[82]

Learners' social and cultural environments influence the things they value as well. As children grow older, they tend to adopt many of the priorities and values of the people around them. Such **internalized motivation** typically develops gradually over the course of childhood and adolescence, perhaps in the sequence depicted in Figure 6.4.[83] Initially, learners may engage in certain activities primarily because of the external consequences that result. For instance, students may do schoolwork to earn praise or to avoid being punished for poor grades. Gradually, however, they may internalize the "pressure" to perform the activities and begin to see the activities as important in their own right. Such internalization of values is most likely to take place if adults who espouse those values (parents, teachers, etc.) provide a warm, supportive, and structured environment yet also offer enough autonomy in decision making that learners have a sense of self-determination about their actions. All too often, such conditions *aren't* present when it comes to learning academic subject matter. Accordingly, the value students find in many school subjects (e.g., math, English, music, sports) declines markedly over the school years.[84]

The more learners have internalized the value of academic achievement, the more cognitively engaged they become in school subject matter and the better their overall learning is likely to be.[85] Appreciation of an activity's value also fosters self-regulated learning—a general work ethic in which learners spontaneously engage in activities that, although not always fun or immediately gratifying, are essential for reaching long-term goals.[86]

Some of my readers may think that internalized motivation is essentially the same as intrinsic motivation. Certainly both forms of motivation come from inside the learner rather than from outside factors in the immediate environment. But there's an important difference: Intrinsic motivation seems to arise spontaneously within the learner, and so it can increase or decrease somewhat unpredictably. In contrast, because internalized motivation is a product of ongoing social and cultural factors and eventually becomes an integral part of learners' sense of self—their beliefs about who they are as human beings—it remains fairly stable and dependable over time.[87]

1. External regulation: Learners are initially motivated to behave in certain ways, based primarily on the external consequences that will follow the behaviors; that is, the learners are extrinsically motivated.

2. Introjection: Learners begin to behave in ways that gain the approval of others, partly as a way of protecting and enhancing their sense of self. They feel guilty when they violate certain standards for behavior but do not fully understand the rationale behind these standards.

3. Identification: Learners now see some behaviors and activities as being personally important or valuable for them.

4. Integration: Learners integrate certain behaviors and activities into their overall system of motives and values. In essence, these behaviors become a central part of their sense of self.

FIGURE 6.4 Sequence in which internalized motivation may develop
Sources: Based on Deci & Moller, 2005; Deci & Ryan, 1995.

internalized motivation Adoption of other people's priorities and values as one's own.

[81] Wigfield, 1994.

[82] Jacobs, Lanza, Osgood, Eccles, & Wigfield, 2002; Wigfield, 1994.

[83] Deci & Moller, 2005; Deci & Ryan, 1995; R. M. Ryan & Deci, 2000.

[84] Deci & Moller, 2005; Eccles et al., 1998; Jacobs et al., 2002; La Guardia, 2009; Watt, 2004; Wigfield, Eccles, Mac Iver, Reuman, & Midgley, 1991.

[85] Assor, Vansteenkiste, & Kaplan, 2009; La Guardia, 2009; Lens, 2001; Lens, Simons, & Dewitte, 2002; R. M. Ryan & Deci, 2000.

[86] Harter, 1992; McCombs, 1996; R. M. Ryan, Connell, & Grolnick, 1992; Stipek, 1993.

[87] Otis et al., 2005; Reeve et al., 2004; Walls & Little, 2005.

Learners typically form goals related to their academic achievement; the specific nature of these goals influences learners' cognitive processes and behaviors.

As noted earlier, much of human behavior is directed toward particular goals. For school-age children and adolescents, some of these goals are apt to relate to school learning and performance. Let's consider what three different boys might be thinking during the first day of a basketball unit in Mr. Wesolowski's physical education class:

Tim: This is my chance to show all the guys what a great basketball player I am. If I stay near the basket, Travis and Tony will keep passing to me, and I'll score a lot of points. I can really impress Wesolowski and my friends.

Travis: I hope I don't screw this up. If I shoot at the basket and miss, I'll look like a real loser. Maybe I should just stay outside the 3-point line and keep passing to Tim and Tony.

Tony: I really want to become a better basketball player. I can't figure out why I don't get more of my shots into the basket. I'll ask Wesolowski to give me feedback about how I can improve my game. Maybe some of my friends will have suggestions, too.

All three boys want to play basketball well. That is, they all have *achievement goals*. But they have different reasons for wanting to play well. Tim is concerned mostly about looking good in front of his teacher and classmates and so wants to maximize opportunities to demonstrate his skill on the court. Travis, too, is concerned about the impression he'll make, but he just wants to make sure he *doesn't* look *bad*. Unlike Tim and Travis, Tony isn't thinking about how his performance will appear to others. Instead, he's interested mainly in developing his basketball skills and doesn't expect immediate success. For Tony, making mistakes is an inevitable part of learning a new skill, not a source of embarrassment or humiliation.

Tony's approach to basketball illustrates a **mastery goal**, a desire to acquire additional knowledge or master new skills.[88] Tim and Travis each have a **performance goal**, a desire to present themselves as competent in the eyes of others. More specifically, Tim has a **performance-approach goal**: He wants to look good and receive favorable judgments from others. In contrast, Travis has a **performance-avoidance goal**: He wants to avoid looking bad and receiving unfavorable judgments. Achievement goals often have an element of social comparison, in that learners are concerned about how their accomplishments compare to those of their peers.[89]

Mastery goals, performance-approach goals, and performance-avoidance goals aren't necessarily mutually exclusive. Learners may simultaneously have two kinds, or even all three.[90] For example, returning to our basketball example, we could imagine a fourth boy, Trey, who wants to improve his basketball skills *and* look good in front of his classmates *and* not come across as a klutz.

In most instances having mastery goals is the optimal situation. As Table 6.2 reveals, learners with mastery goals tend to engage in the very activities that will help them learn. They pay attention in class, process information in ways that promote effective long-term memory storage, and learn from their mistakes. Furthermore, learners with mastery goals have a healthy perspective about learning, effort, and failure. They realize that learning is a process of trying hard and continuing to persevere even in the face of temporary setbacks. Consequently, these learners are the ones who are most likely to stay on task and who benefit the most from their classroom experiences.[91]

In contrast, learners with performance goals—especially those with performance-*avoidance* goals—may stay away from the challenging tasks that would do the most to help

Which of these goals reflect intrinsic or internalized motivation? Which reflect extrinsic motivation? (Compare your response to this question with the response presented in Chapter 6 of the Book-Specific Resources in MyEducationLab.)

Observe mastery goals in the "Portfolio" and "Author's Chair" videos in Chapter 6 of the Book-Specific Resources in MyEducationLab.

mastery goal Desire to acquire new knowledge or master new skills.

performance goal Desire to demonstrate high ability and make a good impression.

performance-approach goal Desire to look good and receive favorable judgments from others.

performance-avoidance goal Desire not to look bad or receive unfavorable judgments from others.

---

[88] Some theorists distinguish between *mastery-approach* and *mastery-avoidance goals*. My focus here is on mastery-approach goals. Mastery-avoidance goals—that is, wanting to avoid the possibility of being incompetent at a task—seem to have effects similar to those of performance-avoidance goals (e.g., see Elliot, 2005; Elliot & McGregor, 2001; Witkow & Fuligni, 2007).

[89] Elliot, 2005; Midgley et al., 1998; Régner, Escribe, & Dupeyrat, 2007.

[90] Covington & Müeller, 2001; Hidi & Harackiewicz, 2000; Meece & Holt, 1993.

[91] Kumar, Gheen, & Kaplan, 2002; Shim, Ryan, & Anderson, 2008; Sins et al., 2008; Wentzel & Wigfield, 1998.

TABLE 6.2 Typical Differences between Learners with Mastery Goals and Learners with Performance Goals

Learners with Mastery Goals	Learners with Performance Goals (Especially Those with Performance-Avoidance Goals)
Are more likely to be actively engaged in classroom activities and intrinsically motivated to learn classroom subject matter	Are more likely to be extrinsically motivated (i.e., motivated by expectations of external reinforcement and punishment) and more likely to cheat to obtain good grades
Believe that competence develops over time through practice and effort; persist in the face of difficulty	Believe that competence is a stable characteristic (people either have talent or they don't); think that competent people shouldn't have to try very hard; give up quickly when facing difficulty
Exhibit more self-regulated learning and behavior	Exhibit less self-regulation
Use learning strategies that promote true comprehension and complex cognitive processes (e.g., elaboration, comprehension monitoring, transfer)	Use learning strategies that promote only rote learning (e.g., repetition, copying, word-for-word memorization); may procrastinate on assignments
Choose tasks that maximize opportunities for learning; seek out challenges	Choose tasks that maximize opportunities for demonstrating competence; avoid tasks and actions (e.g., asking for help) that make them look incompetent
Are more likely to undergo conceptual change when confronted with convincing evidence that contradicts current beliefs	Are less likely to undergo conceptual change, in part because they are less likely to notice the discrepancy between new information and existing beliefs
React to easy tasks with feelings of boredom or disappointment	React to success on easy tasks with feelings of pride or relief
Seek feedback that accurately describes their ability and helps them improve	Seek feedback that flatters them
Willingly collaborate with peers when doing so is likely to enhance learning	Collaborate with peers primarily when doing so can help them look competent or enhance social status
Evaluate their own performance in terms of the progress they make	Evaluate their own performance in terms of how they compare with others
Interpret failure as a sign that they need to exert more effort	Interpret failure as a sign of low ability and therefore predictive of future failures
View errors as a normal and useful part of the learning process; use errors to improve performance	View errors as a sign of failure and incompetence; engage in self-handicapping to provide apparent justification for errors and failures
Are satisfied with their performance if they try hard and make progress	Are satisfied with their performance only when they succeed; are apt to feel ashamed and depressed when they fail
View a teacher as a resource and guide to help them learn	View a teacher as a judge and as a rewarder or punisher
Remain relatively calm during tests and classroom assignments	Are often quite anxious about tests and other assessments
Are more likely to be enthusiastic about, and become actively involved in, school activities	Are more likely to distance themselves from the school environment

Sources: Ablard & Lipschultz, 1998; C. Ames & Archer, 1988; R. Ames, 1983; E. M. Anderman et al., 1998; E. M. Anderman & Maehr, 1994; Corpus, McClintic-Gilberg, & Hayenga, 2009; Dweck, 1986; Dweck & Elliott, 1983; Dweck, Mangels, & Good, 2004; Entwisle & Ramsden, 1983; L. S. Fuchs et al., 1997; Gabriele & Boody, 2001; Graham & Weiner, 1996; Hardré, Crowson, DeBacker, & White, 2007; Jagacinski & Nicholls, 1984, 1987; Kaplan, 1998; Kaplan & Midgley, 1999; Lau & Nie, 2008; Levy, Kaplan, & Patrick, 2000; Liem, Lau, & Nie, 2008; Linnenbrink & Pintrich, 2002, 2003; Locke & Latham, 2006; McCombs, 1988; McGregor & Elliot, 2002; Meece, 1994; Middleton & Midgley, 1997; Murphy & Alexander, 2000; R. S. Newman & Schwager, 1995; Nolen, 1996; Pekrun, Elliot, & Maier, 2006; Pugh & Bergin, 2006; Rawsthorne & Elliot, 1999; A. M. Ryan, Pintrich, & Midgley, 2001; Schiefele, 1991, 1992; Shernoff & Hoogstra, 2001; Sideridis, 2005; Sinatra & Mason, 2008; Sins et al., 2008; Skaalvik, 1997; Southerland & Sinatra, 2003; Stipek, 1993; J. C. Turner, Thorpe, & Meyer, 1998; Urdan & Midgley, 2001; Urdan, Midgley, & Anderman, 1998.

them master new skills. Furthermore, these learners tend to process information in a rote, relatively "thoughtless" manner. Performance-*approach* goals are a mixed bag. They sometimes have very positive effects, spurring learners on to achieve at high levels, especially in adolescence and especially in combination with mastery goals.[92] Yet by themselves, performance-approach goals may be less beneficial than mastery goals. To accomplish them, learners may exert only the minimal effort required, use relatively superficial learning strategies, and possibly cheat on classroom assessments.[93] Performance-approach goals appear to be most detrimental when learners are fairly young (e.g., in the elementary grades) and have low self-efficacy for classroom tasks.[94]

Most young children focus primarily on mastery goals.[95] But once they're in school, they are regularly surrounded by peers with whom they can compare their performance, and so they begin to view success as doing as well as or better than classmates. In addition, they may have trouble evaluating their progress on the complex cognitive skills they're learning (reading, writing, math, etc.) and so must rely on others (e.g., teachers) to make judgments about their competence and progress. For such reasons, performance goals become increasingly prevalent as children progress through the elementary and secondary school grades.[96] Most academically motivated high school students are primarily concerned about getting good grades, and they prefer short, easy tasks to lengthier, more challenging ones. Performance goals are also common in team sports, where the focus is often more on winning and gaining public recognition than on developing new skills and seeing improvement over time.[97]

Learners must juggle their achievement goals with their many other goals.

Children and adolescents typically have a wide variety of goals.[98] Not only might they want to do well in school but they also want to have a good time, be healthy and safe, earn money, and eventually embark on a rewarding career. Many of their goals are apt to be **social goals** that can help them meet their need for relatedness. For example, they may want to gain the approval of adults, be liked and respected by peers, belong to a supportive social group, and contribute to other people's welfare.[99] Among learners' many goals are certain **core goals** that drive much of what they do.[100] For instance, learners who attain high levels of academic achievement typically make classroom learning a high priority. Learners who achieve at lower levels are often more concerned with social relationships.[101]

Learners use several strategies to juggle their many goals.[102] Sometimes they find activities that allow them to address two or more goals simultaneously. For instance, they can address both achievement goals and social goals by forming a study group to prepare for a test. Sometimes they modify their ideas of what it means to achieve particular goals. For instance, an ambitious high school student who initially hopes to earn all As in three challenging classes may eventually decide that earning Bs in two of them is more realistic. And sometimes learners entirely abandon one goal in order to satisfy another. For instance, they may find that the multiple demands of school coerce them into focusing on performance goals (e.g., getting good grades) rather than

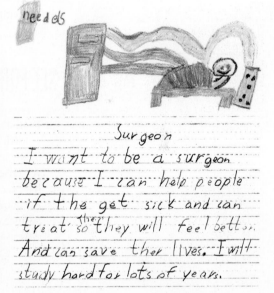

needels

Surgeon
I want to be a surgeon because I can help people if the get sick and can treat them so they will feel better. And can save ther lives. I will study hard for lots of years.

Career aspirations are often among learners' many goals. Here 7-year-old Ashton explains why he wants to be a surgeon. Notice how his career goal also has a social-goal component: "I can help people if [they] get sick."

[92] Hidi & Harackiewicz, 2000; McNeil & Alibali, 2000; Linnenbrink, 2005; Rawsthorne & Elliot, 1999; Urdan, 1997.

[93] E. M. Anderman et al., 1998; Brophy, 1987; L. H. Meyer et al., 2008; Midgley, Kaplan, & Middleton, 2001.

[94] Hidi & Harackiewicz, 2000; Kaplan, 1998; Kaplan & Midgley, 1997; Midgley et al., 2001.

[95] Bong, 2009; Dweck & Elliott, 1983.

[96] Blumenfeld, 1992; Bong, 2009; W. Doyle, 1986b; Dweck & Elliott, 1983; Elliot, 2005; Elliot & McGregor, 2000; Harter, 1992; Régner et al., 2007.

[97] G. C. Roberts, Treasure, & Kavussanu, 1997.

[98] M. E. Ford & Smith, 2007; Schutz, 1994.

[99] H. A. Davis, 2003; Dowson & McInerney, 2001; M. E. Ford & Smith, 2007; Hinkley, McInerney, & Marsh, 2001; Patrick et al., 2002; Wentzel, Filisetti, & Looney, 2007.

[100] Boekaerts, de Koning, & Vedder, 2006; Schutz, 1994.

[101] Wentzel & Wigfield, 1998; Wigfield, Eccles, & Pintrich, 1996.

[102] Covington, 2000; Dodge, Asher, & Parkhurst, 1989; McCaslin & Good, 1996; Phelan, Yu, & Davidson, 1994; Urdan & Maehr, 1995.

social goal Desire related to establishing or maintaining relationships with other people.

core goal Long-term goal that drives much of what a learner does.

studying the subject matter as thoroughly as they'd like. Brian, a junior high school student, expresses his regret about leaving mastery goals behind as he strives for performance goals:

> I sit here and I say, "Hey, I did this assignment in five minutes and I still got an A+ on it." I still have a feeling that I could do better, and it was kind of cheap that I didn't do my best and I still got this A. . . . I think probably it might lower my standards eventually, which I'm not looking forward to at all. . . . I'll always know, though, that I have it in me. It's just that I won't express it that much.[103]

Because most learners have a strong need for relatedness, their social goals often influence their classroom behavior and the priority they give to various achievement goals. If learners want to gain their teacher's attention and approval, they're apt to strive for good grades and in other ways shoot for performance goals.[104] If they seek friendly relationships with classmates or are concerned about others' welfare, they may eagerly engage in such activities as cooperative learning and peer tutoring.[105] A desire for close relationships with others may also lead them to ask peers for help, but if they want to impress peers with their high ability—a performance goal—they probably *won't* ask for help.[106] If they want to gain the approval of *low-achieving* peers, they may exert little effort in their studies and possibly even avoid classroom tasks altogether.[107]

Learners identify what are, in their minds, the likely causes of their successes and failures.

As we've seen in previous chapters, learners actively try to make sense of their experiences. Such sense-making sometimes involves identifying reasons for success or failure in particular situations. To gain insight into the kinds of explanations you yourself might identify, try the following exercise.

SEE FOR YOURSELF   Carberry and Seville

1. Professor Josiah S. Carberry has just returned the first set of exams, scored and graded, in your advanced psychoceramics class. You discover that you've gotten one of the few high test grades in the class, an A–. Why did you do so well when most of your classmates did poorly? Jot down several possible explanations for why you might have received a high grade in Carberry's class.
2. An hour later, you get the results of the first test in Professor Barbara F. Seville's socio-cosmetology class, and you learn that you *failed* it! Why did you do so poorly? Jot down several possible reasons for your F on Seville's test.

Here are some possible explanations for your A– in Carberry's class:

- You studied hard.
- You're smart.
- You have a natural talent for psychoceramics.
- You were lucky. Carberry asked the right questions; if he'd asked different questions, you might not have done so well.
- All those hours you spent brown-nosing Carberry in his office, asking questions about psychoceramics and requesting copies of articles he's written (which you never actually read), really paid off.

[103] S. Thomas & Oldfather, 1997, p. 119.
[104] Hinkley et al., 2001; Urdan & Mestas, 2006.
[105] L. H. Anderman & Anderman, 1999; Dowson & McInerney, 2001.
[106] A. M. Ryan, Hicks, & Midgley, 1997.
[107] B. B. Brown, 1990; M. E. Ford & Nichols, 1991; Schultheiss & Brunstein, 2005.

In contrast, here are some possible reasons you failed Seville's exam:

- You didn't study enough.
- You studied the wrong things.
- You've never had a knack for sociocosmetology.
- The student next to you was constantly distracting you with his wheezing and coughing.
- You were unlucky. Seville asked the wrong questions; if she'd asked different questions, you would have done better.
- It was a bad test: The questions were ambiguous and tested knowledge of trivial facts.

Learners' beliefs about what behaviors and other factors influence events in their lives are **attributions**. Learners form attributions for many events in their daily lives—why they do well or poorly on tests and assignments, why they're popular or unpopular with peers, why they're skilled athletes or total klutzes, and so on. Their attributions vary in three primary ways:[108]

- **Locus ("place"): Internal versus external.** Learners sometimes attribute the causes of events to *internal* things—to factors within themselves. Thinking that a good grade is due to your own hard work and believing that a poor grade is due to your lack of ability are examples of internal attributions. At other times learners attribute events to *external* things—to factors outside themselves. Concluding that you received a scholarship because you "lucked out" and interpreting a classmate's scowl as a sign of her bad mood (rather than as something you might have deserved because of your behavior) are examples of external attributions.
- **Stability: Stable versus unstable.** Sometimes learners believe that events are due to *stable* factors—to things that probably won't change much in the near future. For example, if you believe that you do well in science because of your innate intelligence or that you have trouble making friends because you're overweight, you're attributing events to stable, relatively long-term causes. But sometimes learners instead believe that events result from *unstable* factors—things that can change from one time to the next. Thinking that winning a tennis game was a lucky break and believing you got a bad test grade because you were exhausted when you took the test are examples of attributions involving unstable factors.
- **Controllability: Controllable versus uncontrollable.** On some occasions learners attribute events to *controllable* factors—to things they can influence and change. For example, if you think a classmate invited you to his birthday party because you often smile and say nice things to him, and if you think you probably failed a test simply because you didn't study the right things, you're attributing these events to controllable factors. On other occasions learners attribute events to *uncontrollable* factors—to things over which they have no influence. If you think that you were chosen for the lead in the school play only because you look "right" for the part or that you played a lousy game of basketball because you were sick, you're attributing these events to uncontrollable factors.

Because attributions are self-constructed, they may or may not reflect the true state of affairs. For instance, a student may blame a low test grade on a "tricky" test or an "unfair" teacher when the cause was really the student's own lack of effort or ineffective study strategies. Metacognition often enters into the picture here. In Chapter 4 we discovered that learners who don't carefully monitor their comprehension may have an *illusion of knowing*, thinking they've learned something they actually *haven't* learned. When these learners do poorly on an exam, they can't attribute their performance to internal, controllable factors because, in their minds, they studied hard and so "know" the material. Instead, they're apt to attribute the failure to such external factors as bad luck, exam difficulty, or teacher incompetence.[109]

[108] Weiner, 1986, 2000, 2005.
[109] Horgan, 1990; Rhodewalt & Vohs, 2005.

attribution Personally constructed causal explanation for a particular event, such as a success or failure.

"And remember, kids: If you play to the best of your ability and still lose the game, just blame it all on the umpire."

By blaming the umpire for a loss, children can more easily maintain a sense of self-worth. However, such external attributions are counterproductive when the true causes for success and failure are internal and within children's control.

IN THE BLEACHERS © 2002 Steve Moore. Reprinted with permission of UNIVERSAL UCLICK. All rights reserved.

In general, learners tend to attribute their successes to internal causes (e.g., high ability, hard work) and their failures to external causes (e.g., luck, other people's behaviors).[110] By patting themselves on the back for the things they do well and putting the blame elsewhere for poor performance, they can maintain their sense of self-worth.[111] Yet when learners *consistently* fail at tasks, and especially when they see their peers succeeding at those same tasks, they're apt to put the blame on a stable and seemingly uncontrollable internal factor: their own low ability.[112]

In the opening case study, Michael initially attributes his failure in algebra to two stable factors over which he has no control: low aptitude (an internal attribution) and poor instruction (an external attribution). But as his tutor helps him understand algebraic principles and procedures, and especially as he experiences success in class, he begins to attribute his performance to two unstable, internal factors he *can* control—effort and better strategies:

> I realize now that even if I don't like the teacher or don't think he is a good teacher, it is my responsibility to listen. . . . The teacher does most of his part, but it's no use to me unless I do my part. . . . Now I try and comprehend, ask questions and figure out how he got the answer.[113]

Learners' attributions for past successes and failures affect their future performance.

Let's return to those two fictional exams you considered in the earlier "Carberry and Seville" exercise—the psychoceramics exam (on which you got an A–) and the sociocosmetology exam (on which you got an F). Imagine that you'll be taking second exams in both psychoceramics and sociocosmetology in about three weeks' time. How much will you study for each exam?

The amount of time you spend studying for your upcoming exams will depend somewhat on your attributions for your earlier test grades. Let's first consider your A– on Professor Carberry's exam. If you think you did well because you studied hard, you'll probably spend a lot of time studying for the second test as well. If you think you did well because you're smart or a natural whiz at psychoceramics, you may not study quite as much. If you believe your success was a matter of luck, you may hardly study at all, but you might wear your lucky sweater when you take the next exam. And if you think the A– reflects how much Carberry likes you, you may decide that time spent flattering him is more important than time spent studying.

Now let's consider your failing grade on Professor Seville's exam. Once again, the way in which you interpret the grade will influence the ways in which you prepare for the second exam—if, in fact, you prepare at all. If you believe you didn't study enough or didn't study the right things, you may spend more time studying the next time. If you think your poor grade was due to a temporary situation—perhaps the student sitting next to you distracted you, or perhaps Seville asked the wrong questions—you may study in much the same way as you did before, hoping you'll do better the second time around. If you believe your failure was due to your low aptitude for sociocosmetology or to the fact that Seville writes lousy tests, you may study even less than you did the first time. After all, what good will it do to study when your poor test performance is beyond your control?

Learners' attributions influence a number of factors that either directly or indirectly affect their future performance:

- **Emotional reactions to success and failure.** Naturally, learners are happy when they succeed and sad when they fail. But attributions bring other emotions into the mix as well. Learners are apt to feel proud about their successes and guilty and ashamed about their failures only if they attribute these outcomes to internal causes—for instance, to things they themselves have done. Unpleasant as guilt and shame might feel, such emotions often spur learners to address their shortcomings. If, instead,

---

[110] Hattie, 2008; Rhodewalt & Vohs, 2005; Whitley & Frieze, 1985.

[111] Clifford, 1990; Paris & Byrnes, 1989.

[112] Covington, 1987; Y. Hong, Chiu, & Dweck, 1995; Schunk, 1990; Weiner, 1984.

[113] Tucker & Anderman, 1999, pp. 5–6.

learners think someone else was to blame for an undesirable outcome, they're apt to be angry—an emotion that's unlikely to lead to productive follow-up behaviors.[114]

- **Expectations for future success or failure.** When learners attribute their successes and failures to stable factors (e.g., innate ability or the lack of it), they expect their future performance to be similar to their current performance. In contrast, when they attribute their successes and failures to *un*stable factors (e.g., effort or luck), their current success rate will have little influence on their expectation for future success, and a few failures won't put much of a dent in their self-efficacy. The most optimistic learners—those with the highest expectations for future success—are the ones who attribute their successes to stable, dependable (and usually internal) factors such as innate ability and an enduring work ethic and attribute their failures to unstable factors such as lack of effort or inappropriate strategies.[115]

Learners are usually happy when they succeed at classroom tasks, but they also feel proud and satisfied if they attribute their successes to internal causes.

- **Effort and persistence.** Learners who believe their failures result from their own lack of effort (a controllable cause) are apt to try harder and persist in the face of difficulty. Learners who, instead, attribute failure to a lack of innate ability (an uncontrollable cause) give up easily and sometimes can't even perform tasks they've previously done successfully.[116]

- **Learning strategies.** Learners who expect to succeed in the classroom and believe that academic success is a result of their own doing are more likely to apply effective learning strategies—especially when they're *taught* these strategies. These learners are also more apt to be self-regulating learners and to seek help when they need it. In contrast, learners who expect failure and believe their academic performance is largely out of their hands often reject effective learning strategies in favor of rote-learning approaches.[117]

Given all of these effects, it shouldn't surprise you to learn that learners with internal, controllable attributions for classroom success (rather than external ones they can't control) are more likely to achieve at high levels and graduate from high school.[118]

Let's consider how some of the factors just listed play out in the opening case study. Michael initially attributes his failure in algebra to both his own low ability and his teacher's poor instruction, and so he probably feels a combination of shame and anger. Because the perceived causes of his failure are both stable and out of his control, he expects future failure no matter what he does and thus has little reason to exert much effort (e.g., he doesn't take notes). As Michael acquires new study strategies and gains a better understanding of algebraic concepts and procedures, he achieves greater success and realizes that his success is the direct result of his own hard work. His new internal and controllable attributions lead him to use more effective strategies and be a more self-regulating learner:

> Now I do things in math step by step and listen to each step. . . . I used to just listen and not even take notes. I always told myself I would remember but I always seemed to forget. Now I take notes and I study at home every day except Friday, even if I don't have homework. Now I study so that I know that I have it. I don't just hope I'll remember.[119]

With age, learners increasingly attribute their successes and failures to ability rather than to effort.

As children grow older, they become increasingly able to distinguish among the various possible causes of their successes and failures: effort, ability, luck, task difficulty, and so on.[120] One distinction they gradually get a better handle on is that between effort and ability. In the

[114] Hareli & Weiner, 2002; Pekrun, 2006.

[115] Dweck, 2000; Eccles, 2009; Pomerantz & Saxon, 2001; Schunk, 1990; Weiner, 2005.

[116] Blackwell, Trzesniewski, & Dweck, 2007; Dweck, 1978, 2000; Feather, 1982; Weiner, 1984.

[117] R. Ames, 1983; Dweck, Mangels, & Good, 2004; Mangels, 2004; D. J. Palmer & Goetz, 1988; Pressley, Borkowski, & Schneider, 1987; Zimmerman, 1998.

[118] L. E. Davis, Ajzen, Saunders, & Williams, 2002; Dweck et al., 2004; Pintrich, 2003.

[119] Tucker & Anderman, 1999, pp. 5–6.

[120] Dweck & Elliott, 1983; Eccles et al., 1998; Nicholls, 1990.

early elementary school grades, children think of effort and ability as positively correlated: People who try harder are more competent. Thus, they tend to attribute their successes to hard work and are usually optimistic about their chances for future success as long as they try hard. Sometime around age 9, they begin to understand that effort and ability often compensate for each other and that people with less ability may need to exert greater effort. At about the same time, many also begin to attribute their successes and failures to an inherited ability—for instance, to something they call "intelligence"—which they perceive to be fairly stable and beyond their control. If they're usually successful at school tasks, they have high self-efficacy for such tasks. If, instead, they often fail, their self-efficacy can plummet.[121]

As we discovered in Chapter 5, psychologists disagree about the extent to which intelligence is the result of heredity (and thus stable and uncontrollable) or environment (and thus able to increase with instruction and practice). Even children and adolescents have differing opinions on the matter.[122] Those with an **incremental view** believe that intelligence can and does improve with effort and practice. In contrast, those with an **entity view** believe that intelligence is a distinct ability that is built-in and relatively permanent. A student named Sarah clearly reveals an entity view in her explanation of why she has trouble in math:

> My dad is very good at math, and my brother, I, and my mom aren't good at math at all, we inherited the "not good at math gene" from my mom and I am good in English but I am not good in math.[123]

Students with an incremental view of intelligence and specific academic abilities are likely to adopt mastery goals in the classroom, to work hard at their studies, and to earn increasingly high grades. In contrast, students with an entity view (like Sarah) adopt performance goals, quickly lose interest in a topic that doesn't come easily to them, self-handicap in the face of failure, and earn lower grades over time.[124]

Over time, learners acquire a general attributional style.

Consider these two girls, who have the *same* ability:

- Jane is an enthusiastic, energetic learner. She works hard at school activities and takes obvious pleasure in doing well. She likes challenges, especially the brainteaser problems her teacher assigns as extra-credit work each day. She can't always solve the problems, but she takes failure in stride and is eager for more problems the following day.
- Julie is an anxious, fidgety student who doesn't have much confidence in her ability to accomplish school tasks successfully. In fact, she often underestimates what she can do: Even when she has succeeded, she doubts that she can do it again. She prefers filling out drill-and-practice worksheets that help her practice skills she's already mastered, rather than attempting new tasks and problems. As for those daily brainteasers Jane likes so much, Julie sometimes takes a stab at them but gives up quickly if the answer isn't obvious.

Over time, some learners, like Jane, develop an "I can do it" attitude known as a **mastery orientation**—a general sense of optimism that they can master new tasks and succeed in a variety of endeavors. Other learners, like Julie, develop an "I can't do it" attitude known as **learned helplessness**—a general sense of futility about their chances for future success. You might think of this distinction, which really reflects a continuum rather than an either-or dichotomy, as a difference between *optimists* and *pessimists*.[125]

Even when learners with a mastery orientation and those with learned helplessness have equal ability initially, those with a mastery orientation behave in ways that lead to higher achievement over the long run. In particular, they set ambitious goals, seek challenging situations, and persist in the face of failure. Learners with learned helplessness behave quite differently. Because they underestimate their ability, learners set goals they can easily

incremental view of intelligence Belief that intelligence can improve with effort and practice.

entity view of intelligence Belief that intelligence is a distinct ability that is relatively permanent and unchangeable.

mastery orientation General, fairly pervasive belief that one is capable of accomplishing challenging tasks.

learned helplessness General, fairly pervasive belief that one is incapable of accomplishing tasks and has little or no control over the environment.

[121] Dweck, 1986; Eccles [Parsons], 1983; Nicholls, 1990; Schunk, 1990.

[122] Dweck, 2000; Dweck et al., 2004; Dweck & Leggett, 1988.

[123] K. E. Ryan, Ryan, Arbuthnot, & Samuels, 2007, p. 5.

[124] Blackwell, Trzesniewski, & Dweck, 2007; Dweck & Leggett, 1988; Dweck & Molden, 2005.

[125] C. Peterson, 1990, 2006; Scheier & Carver, 1992; Seligman, 1991.

accomplish, avoid the challenges that are likely to maximize their learning and cognitive growth, and respond to failure in counterproductive ways (e.g., giving up quickly) that almost guarantee future failure.[126]

By age 5 or 6, some children begin to show a consistent tendency either to persist at a task and express confidence that they can master it, on the one hand, or to abandon a task quickly and say they don't have the ability to do it, on the other.[127] As a general rule, however, children younger than age 8 rarely exhibit extreme forms of learned helplessness, perhaps because they still believe that success is due largely to their own efforts.[128] In early adolescence, a general sense of helplessness becomes more common. Some middle schoolers believe they can't control the things that happen to them (e.g., they're apt to have an entity view of intelligence) and are at a loss for strategies about how to avert future failures.[129] In the opening case study, Michael's initial pessimism about his chances of future success in algebra suggests some degree of learned helplessness, at least about mathematics.

Table 6.3 draws from developmental trends in attributions and other cognitive factors in motivation to describe common motivational characteristics of students in the elementary, middle, and high school grades.

DEVELOPMENTAL TRENDS

TABLE 6.3 Motivation at Different Grade Levels

Grade Level	Age-Typical Characteristics	Example	Suggested Strategies
K–2	• Tendency to define teacher-chosen activities as "work" and self-chosen activities as "play" • Rapidly changing interests for many students; more stable interests for others • Pursuit of interesting and enjoyable activities regardless of expectation for success • Tendency to attribute success to hard work and practice, leading to optimism about what can be accomplished	Six-year-old Alex loves learning about lizards. He often draws lizards during his free time, and when he goes to the school library, he invariably looks for books about lizards and other reptiles. One day, with his teacher's permission, he brings his pet iguana to class and explains the things he must do to keep it healthy.	• Engage students' interest in classroom topics through hands-on, playlike activities. • Entice students into reading, writing, and other basic skills through high-interest books and subject matter (e.g., animals, superheroes, princes and princesses). • Show students how they've improved over time; point out how their effort and practice have contributed to their improvement.
 3–5	• Emergence of fairly stable personal interests • Increasing tendency to observe peers' performance as a criterion for judging one's own performance, resulting in a gradual decline in self-efficacy for overall academic performance • Increasing focus on performance goals • Increasing belief in innate ability as a significant and uncontrollable factor affecting learning and achievement	During a gymnastics unit in physical education, 9-year-old Marta watches her peers as they perform forward and backward rolls, handstands, and cartwheels. She willingly executes the rolls, but when she has trouble getting her legs up for a handstand, she quickly gives up, saying "I can't do handstands and cartwheels—not like Jessie and Sharonda can."	• Allow students to pursue personal interests in independent reading and writing tasks. • Teach students strategies for tracking their own progress over time. • Demonstrate your own fascination and enthusiasm about classroom topics; communicate that many topics are worth learning about for their own sake. • Identify strengths in every student; provide sufficient support to enable students to gain proficiency in areas of weakness.

(continued)

---

[126] Dweck, 2000; Graham, 1989; C. Peterson, 1990, 2006; Seligman, 1991.
[127] Burhans & Dweck, 1995; Ziegert, Kistner, Castro, & Robertson, 2001.
[128] Eccles et al., 1998; Lockhart, Chang, & Story, 2002; Paris & Cunningham, 1996.
[129] Dweck, 2000; Paris & Cunningham, 1996; C. Peterson, Maier, & Seligman, 1993.

TABLE 6.3 Continued

Grade Level	Age-Typical Characteristics	Example	Suggested Strategies
 6–8	• Increasing interest in activities that are stereotypically "gender-appropriate"; decrease in activities considered to be "gender-inappropriate" • Noticeable decline in perceptions of competence and intrinsic motivation for mastering academic subject matter • Increasing tendency to value activities associated with long-term goals and high expectations for success • Decline in perceived value of many content domains (e.g., English, math, music, sports) • Increasing focus on social goals (e.g., interacting with peers, making a good impression)	Thirteen-year-old Regina has always liked math. But now that she's in an advanced eighth-grade math class, she's starting to worry that her peers might think she's a "math geek." She diligently does her math homework every night and earns high grades on assignments and quizzes, but she rarely raises her hand in class to ask or answer questions. And when her friends ask her about the class, she rolls her eyes and says that she's in the class only because "Dad made me take it."	• Promote interest in classroom topics by presenting puzzling phenomena and building on students' personal interests. • Focus students' attention on their improvement; minimize opportunities for them to compare their own performance to that of classmates. • Relate classroom subject matter to students' long-term goals (e.g., through authentic activities). • Provide opportunities for social interaction as students study and learn (e.g., through role-playing activities, classroom debates, cooperative learning projects).
9–12	• Increasing integration of certain interests, values, and behaviors into one's sense of self (i.e., one's overall beliefs about who one is as a person; see Chapter 7) • Continuing decline in intrinsic motivation to master academic subject matter • Prevalence of performance goals (e.g., getting good grades) rather than mastery goals for most students • Increase in cheating as a means of accomplishing performance goals • Increasing focus on postgraduation goals (e.g., college, careers); for some students, inadequate self-regulation strategies for achieving these goals	Sixteen-year-old Randall wants to become a pediatric oncologist—"a cancer doctor for kids," he tells people, "so I can help kids with leukemia, like my sister had." He knows he needs good grades in order to get into a prestigious college, which, in turn, can help him get into medical school. Yet he has trouble saying no when his friends ask him to go to a basketball game the night before an important biology test. And when he gets home after the game, he spends an hour on Facebook instead of studying.	• Provide opportunities to pursue interests and values through out-of-class projects and extracurricular activities (e.g., community service work). • Make it possible for students to attain good grades through reasonable effort and effective strategies (e.g., minimize competitive grading practices, such as grading on a curve). • Discourage cheating (e.g., by giving individualized assignments and monitoring behavior during in-class assessments), and impose appropriate consequences when cheating occurs. • Teach self-regulation strategies that can help students reach their long-term goals (see Chapter 4).

Sources: J. M. Alexander, Johnson, Leibham, & Kelley, 2008; Blumenfeld et al., 2006; Bong, 2009; Brophy, 2008; Cizek, 2003; Corpus et al., 2009; Covington, 1992; Dijkstra, Kuyper, van der Werf, Buunk, & van der Zee, 2008; Dotterer, McHale, & Crouter, 2009; Eccles et al., 1998; Hidi et al., 2004; Jacobs, Davis-Kean, Bleeker, Eccles, & Malanchuk, 2005; Jacobs et al., 2002; Lepper, Corpus, & Iyengar, 2005; Nolen, 2007; Otis, Grouzet, & Pelletier, 2005; Paley, 1984; Patrick et al., 2002; Renninger, 2009; Schunk & Zimmerman, 2006; Shute, 2008; Watt, 2004; Wigfield, 1994; Wigfield, Byrnes, & Eccles, 2006; Wigfield et al., 1991; Wigfield & Wagner, 2005; B. L. Wilson & Corbett, 2001; Youniss & Yates, 1999.

Culture influences the cognitive factors underlying motivation.

Virtually all of the cognitive factors underlying motivation are influenced by learners' environments. Some of them—for instance, values, goals, and attributions—seem to be especially susceptible to cultural influence. The Cultural Considerations box "Cultural and Ethnic Differences in Motivation" on pages 210–211 describes numerous influences that culture is apt to have, not only on how learners prioritize various activities, form goals for themselves, and interpret consequences, but also on the specific ways in which learners satisfy their basic psychological needs.

Cognitive factors underlying sustained motivation build up over a period of time.

We've already discredited one common misconception about motivation: that it is something learners "carry around" inside of them. A second widely held misconception is that learners can turn their motivation "on" or "off" at will, much as one would flip a light switch. As should be evident from the preceding discussion, motivation—especially intrinsic motivation—is usually the result of many cognitive factors that develop gradually over time. In the opening case study, two things change for Michael during his tutoring sessions: His *self-efficacy* for mastering algebra increases, and his *attributions* for his performance begin to reflect controllable rather than uncontrollable factors. These factors don't change overnight. Instead, they evolve slowly with time, better strategies, and a regular pattern of success experiences.

• Affect and Its Effects

In reflecting earlier on the opening case, we speculated that Michael might have varying emotions—frustration, dislike, pride, enjoyment—depending on whether he was failing or succeeding in his math class. Emotions, moods, and other forms of affect permeate many aspects of learners' lives, as reflected in the following principles.

Affect and motivation are interrelated.

Without doubt, people's automatic emotional reactions to certain events—for instance, a quick, fearful retreat from a person wielding a gun or knife—increase their chances of physical survival.[130] But affect also plays a significant role in the more planful, goal-directed aspects of human motivation. As a general rule, people act in ways they think will help them feel happy and comfortable rather than sad, confused, or angry—feelings that depend, in part, on whether they're satisfying their basic needs and accomplishing their goals.[131]

Some emotions, such as pride, guilt, and shame—collectively known as **self-conscious emotions**—are closely tied to people's self-evaluations and thus affect their sense of self-worth.[132] When people evaluate their behaviors and accomplishments as being consistent with their culture's standards for appropriate and desirable behavior, they're apt to feel proud. When, in contrast, they see themselves as failing to live up to those standards—for instance, when they thoughtlessly cause harm to someone else—they're apt to feel guilty and ashamed.

Affect and motivation are interrelated in other ways as well. Learners pursuing a task they think is interesting experience considerable positive affect (e.g., pleasure, enjoyment, excitement), and such feelings can further enhance intrinsic motivation.[133] Positive affect comes with high self-efficacy as well. Furthermore, learners' reactions to the outcomes of events will depend on how they *interpret* those outcomes—in particular, whether they hold themselves, other people, environmental circumstances, or something else responsible for what has happened (recall the earlier discussion of attributions).[134]

Affect is closely tied to learning and cognition.

Affect is often an integral part of learning and cognition.[135] For example, while learning how to perform a task, learners simultaneously learn whether or not they like doing it.[136] Learners can think more creatively and solve problems more effectively when they enjoy the

Observe middle school students' pride in their accomplishments in the "Science Fair Projects" video in Chapter 6 of the Book-Specific Resources in MyEducationLab.

self-conscious emotion Affective state based on self-evaluations regarding the extent to which one's actions meet society's standards for appropriate and desirable behavior; examples are pride, guilt, and shame.

[130] Damasio, 1994; Öhman & Mineka, 2003.

[131] B. P. Ackerman, Izard, Kobak, Brown, & Smith, 2007; E. M. Anderman & Wolters, 2006; Mellers & McGraw, 2001; J. L. Tsai, 2007.

[132] M. Lewis & Sullivan, 2005; Pekrun, 2006.

[133] Hidi & Renninger, 2006; Pekrun, 2006; Pekrun, Goetz, Titz, & Perry, 2002; Schiefele, 1998.

[134] Hareli & Weiner, 2002; Harter, 1999; J. E. Turner, Husman, & Schallert, 2002.

[135] Damasio, 1994; D. K. Meyer & Turner, 2002; Minsky, 2006; Ochsner & Lieberman, 2001.

[136] Zajonc, 1980.

CULTURAL CONSIDERATIONS   Cultural and Ethnic Differences in Motivation

Virtually all children and adolescents have the basic needs we've identified in this chapter. However, the means by which they satisfy their needs, the particular goals they set for themselves, and the attributions they form for their successes and failures vary considerably depending, in part, on the behaviors and values that their culture and society model and encourage. Following are several areas in which researchers have found cultural and ethnic differences.

Achieving a sense of self-worth. In mainstream Western culture, achieving a sense of self-worth often involves *being good* at certain things and also *thinking* that one is good at these things. In such a context, learners are likely to engage in self-handicapping as a means of justifying poor performances. But not all cultures stress the importance of positive self-evaluations. For instance, many people in East Asian cultures place greater importance on how well other people view an individual as living up to society's standards for behavior. In such cultures the focus is more likely to be on correcting existing weaknesses—that is, on *self-improvement*—than on demonstrating current strengths.[a]

Achieving a sense of self-determination. Children and adolescents around the world want some autonomy and self-determination, but the amount and forms that autonomy and self-determination take may differ considerably from group to group.[b] For example, adults in some Native American groups (e.g., those living in the Navajo Nation in the southwestern United States) give children more autonomy and control over decision making, and do so at an earlier age, than do many adults in mainstream Western culture.[c] (Recall the See for Yourself exercise "Jack" on page 92 of Chapter 3.) In contrast, many Asian and African American parents give children *less* autonomy than other American adults, in some cases as a way of ensuring children's safety in potentially hostile environments.[d]

Cultural differences have also been observed in one important aspect of self-determination: opportunities to make choices. In particular, although young people around the world find choice-making opportunities highly motivating, those from Asian cultures often prefer that people they trust (e.g., parents, teachers, respected peers) make choices for them.[e] Perhaps Asian children see trusted others as people who can make *wise* choices, which will ultimately lead to higher levels of learning and competence.

Addressing the need for relatedness. Researchers have found several cultural differences in how children and adolescents address their need for relatedness. In comparison to other groups, Asian children tend to spend less time socializing with peers and place greater importance on gaining teachers' attention and approval.[f] Furthermore, whereas Asian students are likely to have friends who encourage academic achievement, some students from certain other ethnic groups (boys especially) may feel considerable peer pressure *not* to achieve at high levels, perhaps because high achievement reflects conformity to mainstream Western culture (more on this point in Chapter 7).

An additional factor in how learners address their need for relatedness is their family ties: Children and adolescents from many cultural and ethnic groups (e.g., those from many Native American, Hispanic, and Asian communities, as well as those in some rural European American communities) have especially strong loyalties to family and may have been raised to achieve for their respective communities, rather than just for themselves as individuals. Motivating statements such as "Think how proud your family will be!" and "If you go to college and get a good education, you can really help your community!" are likely to be especially effective for such learners.[g]

The need for relatedness can sometimes be at odds with the need for self-determination. In particular, achieving relatedness can involve doing what *others*

topic they're working with, and their academic successes often result in feelings of excitement, pleasure, and pride.[137] In contrast, learners may feel frustrated and anxious when they must struggle to master new material (as Michael does in the opening case study), and they may develop a dislike for the subject matter.[138] An exchange between one of my educational psychology students (Brian) and his 16-year-old sister Megan illustrates the effects of mastery and nonmastery on learners' feelings for what they are studying:

---

[137] E. M. Anderman & Wolters, 2006; Fredrickson, 2009; McLeod & Adams, 1989; Pekrun, 2006; Snow, Corno, & Jackson, 1996.

[138] C. S. Carver & Scheier, 1990; Goetz, Frenzel, Hall, & Pekrun, 2008; Stodolsky, Salk, & Glaessner, 1991.

want one to do, whereas achieving self-determination involves doing what one *personally* wants to do. Many East Asians resolve this apparent conflict by willingly agreeing to adjust personal behaviors and goals to meet social demands and maintain overall group harmony.[h]

Values and goals. Most cultural and ethnic groups place high value on getting a good education.[i] But researchers have observed differences in more specific values related to school learning. For example, many Asian cultures (e.g., in China, Japan, and Russia) emphasize learning for learning's sake: With knowledge come personal growth, better understanding of the world, and greater potential to contribute to society. Important for these cultures, too, are hard work and persistence in academic studies, even when the content isn't intrinsically enjoyable.[j] Students from European American backgrounds are less likely to be diligent when classroom topics have little intrinsic appeal, but they often find value in academic subject matter that piques their curiosity and in assignments that require creativity, independent thinking, or critical analysis.[k]

Learners from diverse cultural backgrounds may also define academic success differently and, as a result, may set different achievement goals. For example, on average, Asian American students aim for higher grades than do students from other ethnic groups, in part to win the approval of their parents and in part to bring honor to their families.[l] Even so, Asian American students—and African American students as well—tend to focus more on mastery goals (i.e., truly understanding what they are studying) than European American students do.[m] And students brought up in cultures that value group achievement over individual achievement (e.g., many Asian, Native American, Mexican American, and Pacific Islander cultures) tend to focus their mastery goals not on how much they alone can improve but instead on how much they *and their peers* can improve— or in some instances on how much their own actions can contribute to the betterment of the larger social group or society.[n]

Attributions. Learners' cultural and ethnic backgrounds influence their attributions as well. For instance, students from families with traditional Asian cultural beliefs are more likely than students from mainstream Western culture to attribute classroom success and failure to unstable factors—effort in the case of academic achievement, and temporary situational factors in the case of appropriate or inappropriate behaviors.[o] Also, some studies have found a greater tendency for African American students to develop a sense of learned helplessness about their ability to achieve academic success.[p] To some extent, racial prejudice may contribute to their learned helplessness: Students may begin to believe that because of the color of their skin, they have little chance of success no matter what they do.[q]

[a] Heine, 2007; J. Li, 2005; Sedikides & Gregg, 2008.
[b] d'Ailly, 2003; Deyhle & LeCompte, 1999; Fiske & Fiske, 2007; Rogoff, 2003.
[c] Deyhle & LeCompte, 1999.
[d] McLoyd, 1998; L. Qin, Pomerantz, & Wang, 2009; Tamis-Lemonda & McFadden, 2010.
[e] Bao & Lam, 2008; Hufton, Elliott, & Illushin, 2002; Iyengar & Lepper, 1999; Vansteenkiste, Zhou, Lens, & Soenens, 2005.
[f] Dien, 1998; Steinberg, 1996.
[g] C.-Y. Chiu & Hong, 2005; Fiske & Fiske, 2007; Kağitçibaşi, 2007; Suina & Smolkin, 1994; Timm & Borman, 1997.
[h] Heine, 2007; Iyengar & Lepper, 1999; Kağitçibaşi, 2007; J. Li & Fischer, 2004.
[i] P. J. Cook & Ludwig, 2008; Fuligni & Hardway, 2004; Phalet, Andriessen, & Lens, 2004; Spera, 2005.
[j] C.-Y. Chiu & Hong, 2005; Hufton et al., 2002; J. Li, 2006; Morelli & Rothbaum, 2007.
[k] Hess & Azuma, 1991; Kuhn & Park, 2005; Nisbett, 2009.
[l] Nisbett, 2009; Steinberg, 1996.
[m] Freeman, Gutman, & Midgley, 2002; Qian & Pan, 2002; Shim & Ryan, 2006.
[n] C.-Y. Chiu & Hong, 2005; Kağitçibaşi, 2007; J. Li, 2005, 2006.
[o] H. Grant & Dweck, 2001; Hess, Chih-Mei, & McDevitt, 1987; J. Li & Fischer, 2004; Weiner, 2004.
[p] Graham, 1989; Holliday, 1985.
[q] S. Sue & Chin, 1983; van Laar, 2000.

Brian: How do you know when you have learned something?

Megan: I know that I have learned something when I get really excited about that topic while I am talking to a person about it. When I haven't learned something I tend to say that I hate it, because I don't understand it. When I am excited and can have a discussion about something is when I know that I fully understand and have studied enough on that topic.[139]

In addition, specific facts and ideas can occasionally evoke emotional reactions, as you'll discover in the following exercise.

---

[139] Interview courtesy of Brian Zottoli.

SEE FOR YOURSELF Flying High

As you read each of the following statements, decide whether it evokes positive feelings (e.g., happiness, excitement), negative feelings (e.g., sadness, anger), or no feelings whatsoever. Check the appropriate blank in each case.

	Positive Feelings	Negative Feelings	No Feelings
1. The city of Denver opened DIA, its new international airport, in 1995.	_____	_____	_____
2. In a recent commercial airline crash, 90 passengers and 8 crew members lost their lives.	_____	_____	_____
3. A dozen people survived that crash, including a 3-month-old infant found in the rear of the plane.	_____	_____	_____
4. The area of an airplane in which food is prepared is called the *galley*.	_____	_____	_____
5. Several major airlines are offering $69 round-trip fares to a beach resort in Mexico.	_____	_____	_____
6. Those $69 fares apply only to flights leaving at 5:30 in the morning.	_____	_____	_____
7. Some flights between North America and Europe now include two full-course meals.	_____	_____	_____

You probably had little if any emotional reaction to Statements 1 (the opening of DIA) and 4 (the definition of *galley*). In contrast, you may have had pleasant feelings when you read Statements 3 (the surviving infant) and 5 (the low fares to Mexico) and unpleasant feelings when you read Statements 2 (the high number of deaths) and 6 (the dreadful departure time for those Mexico flights). Your response to Statement 7 (the two full-course meals) may have been positive, negative, or neutral, depending on your previous experiences with airline cuisine.

As learners think about, learn, or retrieve something, their very thoughts and memories may become emotionally charged—a phenomenon known as **hot cognition**. For example, learners might get excited when they read about advances in science that could lead to effective treatments for spinal cord injuries, cancer, or mental illness. They may feel sad when they read about living conditions in certain parts of the world. They will, we hope, get angry when they learn about the atrocities committed against African American slaves in the pre-Civil War days of the United States or against millions of Jewish people and members of other minority groups in Europe during World War II.

When information is emotionally charged, learners are more apt to pay attention to it, continue to think about it over a period of time, and repeatedly elaborate on it.[140] And encountering information that conflicts with what they currently know or believe can cause learners considerable mental discomfort, something that Piaget called *disequilibrium* but that many contemporary theorists call **cognitive dissonance**. Such dissonance typically leads learners to try to resolve the inconsistency in some way, perhaps by undergoing conceptual change or perhaps by finding fault with the new information (recall the discussion of *confirmation bias* in Chapter 2).[141] Later on, learners can usually retrieve material with

Observe a teacher creating cognitive dissonance in the "Properties of Air" video in Chapter 6 of the Book-Specific Resources in MyEducationLab.

hot cognition Learning or cognitive processing that is emotionally charged.

cognitive dissonance Feeling of mental discomfort caused by new information that conflicts with current knowledge or beliefs.

---

[140] G. H. Bower, 1994; Heuer & Reisberg, 1992; Schacter, 1999; Zeelenberg, Wagenmakers, & Rotteveel, 2006.

[141] Harmon-Jones, 2001; G. Marcus, 2008; Sinatra & Mason, 2008.

high emotional content more easily than they can recall relatively nonemotional informa-tion.[142] It appears that learners' affective reactions to classroom subject matter become inte-gral parts of their network of associations in long-term memory.[143]

Positive affect can trigger effective learning strategies.

How effectively learners think about and make sense of new information depends, in part, on their general mood while they're studying. In general, positive affect, such as feelings of pleasure and excitement, leads learners to attend actively to the subject matter at hand, to work hard to make sense of it, to think creatively and open-mindedly about it, and to use self-regulating learning strategies to keep themselves on task. In contrast, if learners feel generally sad or frustrated—or if they're bored with the subject matter—they're likely to process new information in more superficial, inflexible ways (e.g., by using rehearsal).[144]

Affect can also trigger certain behaviors.

Learners' emotions often lead them to behave in certain ways. For example, feeling guilty or ashamed about something they've done can lead children and adolescents to make amends for their wrongdoings (more about this point in Chapter 7). Feeling frustrated during unsuccessful attempts to reach important goals can lead them to lash out at others or with-draw from classroom activities.[145] Feeling anxious about an upcoming event can be espe-cially powerful in its influence on behavior, as the next principle reveals.

Some anxiety is helpful, but a lot is often a hindrance.

Imagine you're enrolled in Professor Josiah S. Carberry's course in advanced psychoceram-ics. Today is your day to give a half-hour presentation on the topic of psychoceramic cal-ifrications. You've read several books and numerous articles on your topic and undoubtedly know more about it than anyone else in the room. Furthermore, you've meticulously pre-pared a set of note cards to guide you during your presentation. As you sit in class waiting for your turn to speak, you should be feeling calm and confident. Instead you're a nervous wreck: Your heart is pounding wildly, your palms are sweaty, and your stomach is in a knot. When Professor Carberry calls you to the front of the room and you begin to speak, you have trouble remembering what you wanted to say, and you can barely read your note cards because your hands are shaking so much.

It's not as if you *want* to be nervous about speaking in front of your psychoceramics class. Furthermore, you can't think of a single reason why you *should* be nervous. After all, you're an expert on your topic, you're not having a bad-hair day, and your classmates aren't likely to giggle or throw rotten tomatoes if you make a mistake. So what happened to the self-assured student who stood practicing in front of the mirror last night? You're a victim of **anxiety**: You have an uncontrollable feeling of uneasiness and apprehension about an event because you're not sure what its outcome will be. This feeling is accompanied by a variety of physiological symptoms, including a rapid heartbeat, increased perspiration, and muscular tension (e.g., a "knot" or "butterflies" in the stomach).

Just as learners have an optimal level of arousal, so, too, do they have an optimal level of anxiety. A small amount of anxiety often improves performance. When it does so, it's called **facilitating anxiety**. A little anxiety spurs learners into action—for instance, they go to class, complete assignments, and study for exams (see Figure 6.5).[146] However, a great deal of anxiety usually interferes with effective performance. When it has this counterproductive effect, it's known as **debilitating anxiety**.

? Did you previously believe that *any* amount of anxiety is detrimental? If so, have you now revised your thinking about anxiety's effects?

---

[142] Barkley, 1996; E. A. Phelps & Sharot, 2008; Reisberg & Heuer, 1992. Occasionally people have trouble retrieving highly anxiety-arousing memories. This phenomenon, known as *repression,* may occasionally occur with very traumatic personal events but is unlikely to be a factor in the retrieval of academic subject matter (e.g., see G. S. Goodman et al., 2003; McNally & Geraerts, 2009).

[143] G. H. Bower & Forgas, 2001.

[144] G. H. Bower, 1994; Fredrickson, 2009; Linnenbrink & Pintrich, 2004; Pekrun, 2006; Pekrun et al., 2002; Snow et al., 1996.

[145] Berkowitz, 1989; E. Skinner et al., 2008; Wisner Fries & Pollak, 2007.

[146] Preckel, Holling, & Vock, 2006; Shipman & Shipman, 1985.

anxiety Feeling of uneasiness and apprehension concerning a situation with an uncertain outcome.

facilitating anxiety Level of anxiety (usually relatively low) that enhances performance.

debilitating anxiety Anxiety of sufficient intensity that it interferes with performance.

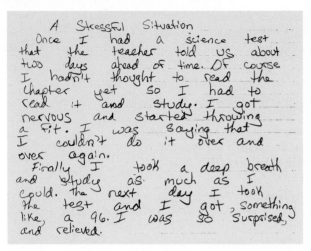

A Stressful Situation
Once I had a science test that the teacher told us about two days ahead of time. Of course I hadn't thought to read the chapter yet so I had to read it and study. I got nervous and started throwing a fit. I was saying that I couldn't do it over and over again.
  Finally I took a deep breath and study as much as I could. The next day I took the test and I got, something like, a 96. I was so surprised, and relieved.

FIGURE 6.5 This writing sample, by 14-year-old Loretta, illustrates how anxiety can sometimes improve learning and achievement.

At what point does anxiety stop facilitating and begin debilitating performance? Very easy tasks—things that learners can do almost without thinking (e.g., running)—are typically facilitated by high levels of anxiety. But more difficult tasks—those that require considerable thought and mental effort—are best performed with only a small or moderate level of anxiety.[147] A lot of anxiety in difficult situations can interfere with several processes critical for successful learning and performance:[148]

- Paying attention to what needs to be learned
- Processing information effectively (e.g., by organizing or elaborating on it)
- Retrieving and using information and skills that have previously been learned

Anxiety is especially likely to interfere with such processes when a task places heavy demands on working memory or long-term memory—for instance, when a task involves problem solving or creativity. In such situations learners may be so preoccupied about doing poorly that they can't get their minds on what they need to accomplish.[149]

In general, learners are more likely to experience debilitating anxiety when they face a **threat**, a situation in which they believe they have little or no chance of succeeding. Facilitating anxiety is more common when learners face a **challenge**, a situation in which they believe they can probably achieve success with a significant yet reasonable amount of effort.[150]

Children and adolescents are apt to have some degree of anxiety, either facilitating or debilitating, about many of the following:[151]

- **A situation in which physical safety is at risk.** For example, they will understandably feel anxious if violence is common in their school or neighborhood.
- **A situation in which self-worth is threatened.** For example, they may feel anxious when someone makes unflattering remarks about their race or gender.
- **Physical appearance.** For example, they may be concerned about being too fat or thin or about reaching puberty either earlier or later than peers.
- **A new situation.** For example, they may experience uncertainty when moving to a new school district.
- **Judgment or evaluation by others.** For example, they may worry about receiving a low grade from a teacher or about being liked and accepted by peers.
- **Frustrating subject matter.** For example, they may have considerable anxiety about mathematics if they've had difficulty with math concepts and problems in the past.
- **Excessive classroom demands.** For example, they're apt to feel anxious when teachers expect them to learn a great deal of material in a very short time.
- **Classroom tests.** For example, some students panic at the mere thought of having to take a test, and many students are exceedingly anxious about high-stakes tests that affect their chances for promotion or graduation.
- **The future.** For example, adolescents may worry about how they will make a living after they graduate from high school.

Learners' particular concerns change somewhat as they grow older. Table 6.4 describes developmental trends in anxiety, as well as in affect more generally, across childhood and adolescence.

---

threat Situation in which a learner believes there is little or no chance of success.

challenge Situation in which a learner believes that success is possible with reasonable effort.

[147] Kirkland, 1971; Landers, 2007; Zeidner & Matthews, 2005.
[148] Cassady, 2004; Eysenck, 1992; Zeidner & Matthews, 2005.
[149] Ashcraft, 2002; Beilock, 2008; Eysenck, 1992; G. Matthews, Zeidner, & Roberts, 2006; J. C. Turner, Thorpe, & Meyer, 1998.
[150] Combs, Richards, & Richards, 1976; Deci & Ryan, 1992; Zeidner & Matthews, 2005.

[151] Ashcraft, 2002; Cassady, 2004; Chabrán, 2003; Covington, 1992; DuBois, Burk-Braxton, Swenson, Tevendale, & Hardesty, 2002; Harter, 1992; Hembree, 1988; N. J. King & Ollendick, 1989; Phelan, Yu, & Davidson, 1994; I. G. Sarason, 1980; S. B. Sarason, 1972; Stipek, 1993; Stodolsky et al., 1991; Wigfield & Meece, 1988; K. M. Williams, 2001a; Zeidner & Matthews, 2005.

DEVELOPMENTAL TRENDS

TABLE 6.4 Anxiety and Other Forms of Affect at Different Grade Levels

Grade Level	Age-Typical Characteristics	Example	Suggested Strategies
 K–2	• Possible culture shock and intense anxiety upon beginning school, especially if students have had few or no preschool experiences • Possible separation anxiety when parents first leave the classroom (especially in the first few days of kindergarten) • Reduced anxiety when teachers and other adults are warm and supportive • Only limited control of overt emotional behaviors (e.g., may cry easily if distressed or act impulsively if frustrated)	Although Jeff has attended preschool since the age of 2, he's quite nervous about going to kindergarten. On his first day at the "big kids' school," he's reluctant to say good-bye to his mother. When Mom finally tells him she has to leave, he bursts into tears—a reaction that some of his classmates will taunt him about for several years.	• Ask parents about routines followed at home; when appropriate, incorporate these routines into classroom procedures. • If possible, provide an opportunity for students to meet you a few days or weeks before school begins. • Be warm, caring, and supportive with all students (but check school policies about hugs and other forms of physical affection). • Address inappropriate behaviors gently but firmly (see Chapter 9).
 3–5	• Increasing control of overt emotional behaviors • Emergence of math anxiety for some students, especially if they receive little or no assistance with math tasks • Tendency for close friends (especially girls) to talk about and dwell on negative emotional events; continues into adolescence • Possible anxiety and stress as a result of others' racist and sexist behaviors (e.g., racial slurs, unkind remarks about emerging sexual characteristics); continues into adolescence	For 9-year-old Tina, basic arithmetic procedures with whole numbers (addition, multiplication, etc.) are easy to understand. But she can make no sense of the new procedures she's learning for fractions—how to find common denominators, divide one fraction by another, and so on—and becomes increasingly frustrated when her attempts to solve fraction problems yield incorrect answers. Her aversion to math soon leads her to avoid the subject whenever possible, both in and outside of school.	• Monitor students' behaviors for subtle signs of serious anxiety or depression; talk with students privately if they seem anxious or upset, and consult with the school counselor if necessary. • Ensure that students master basic concepts and procedures before proceeding to more complex material (especially important in teaching math, a subject area in which advanced knowledge and skills build on more basic concepts and skills). • Insist on respect for all class members' characteristics, feelings, and backgrounds; don't tolerate racist or sexist actions.
 6–8	• General decline in positive, upbeat emotions; extreme mood swings, partly as a result of hormonal changes accompanying puberty • Increased anxiety and potential depression accompanying the transition to middle school or junior high school • Decrease in enjoyment of school (especially for boys) • Increasing anxiety about how one appears to others (*imaginary audience;* see Chapter 7)	At the beginning of seventh grade, 12-year-old Jeannie moves from a small, close-knit elementary school to a large junior high school. At her new school she knows only a few students in each class, and her teachers present themselves as cold, no-nonsense disciplinarians. Jeannie struggles in her efforts to make new friends and feels awkward when she must occasionally sit by herself in the cafeteria. Before long, she regularly complains of stomachaches so that she can stay home from school.	• Expect mood swings, but monitor students' behavior for signs of long-term depression. • Make a personal connection with every student; express confidence that students can succeed with effort, and offer support to facilitate success. • Design activities that capture students' interest in the subject matter; relate topics to students' personal lives and goals. • Provide opportunities for students to form friendships with classmates (e.g., cooperative group projects).

(continued)

TABLE 6.4 Continued

Grade Level	Age-Typical Characteristics	Example	Suggested Strategies
 9–12	• Continuing emotional volatility (especially in grades 9 and 10) • Increasing ability to reflect on and control extreme emotional reactions, due in part to ongoing brain maturation • Considerable anxiety about school if transition to a secondary school format has been delayed until high school • Susceptibility to serious depression in the face of significant stress • Increasing prevalence of debilitating anxiety regarding tests, especially high-stakes tests • Feelings of uncertainty about life after graduation	In a text message to a classmate, 15-year-old Jonathan reveals his crush on a popular cheerleader. The classmate thinks the message is amusing ("I can't believe that loser thinks he has a chance with the head cheerleader!") and forwards it to more than 50 members of the sophomore class. Jonathan is at a loss about how to cope with his humiliation and contemplates suicide as the only solution to the problem. *(Teachers should immediately report any suspicions of planned student suicides;* see Chapter 7.)	• Be especially supportive if students have just made the transition from an elementary school format (e.g., show personal interest in students' welfare, teach effective study skills). • Take seriously any signs that a student may be considering suicide (e.g., overt or veiled threats, such as "I won't be around much longer"; actions that indicate "putting one's affairs in order," such as giving away prized possessions). • Give frequent classroom assessments so that no single test score is a "fatal" one; help students prepare for high-stakes tests. • Present multiple options for postgraduation career paths.

Sources: Arnett, 1999; Ashcraft, 2002; Benes, 2007; Benner & Graham, 2009; Chabrán, 2003; DuBois et al., 2002; Eccles & Midgley, 1989; Elkind, 1981; Gentry, Gable, & Rizza, 2002; K. T. Hill & Sarason, 1966; Hine & Fraser, 2002; Kerns & Lieberman, 1993; Kuhl & Kraska, 1989; Lapsley, 1993; Larson & Brown, 2007; Larson, Moneta, Richards, & Wilson, 2002; D. K. Meyer & Turner, 2006; Midgley, Middleton, Gheen, & Kumar, 2002; Roderick & Camburn, 1999; A. J. Rose, 2002; Rudolph, Lambert, Clark, & Kurlakowsky, 2001; Snow et al., 1996; Spear, 2000; Wiles & Bondi, 2001.

Different cultures nurture different emotional responses.

Many human emotions—especially joy, sadness, fear, anger, disgust, and surprise—are seen even in young infants and thus are almost certainly part of our genetic heritage.[152] Nevertheless, various cultural groups have different views about what kinds of emotions and emotional reactions are appropriate, leading to differences in how they socialize growing children. The Cultural Considerations box "Cultural and Ethnic Differences in Affect" on pages 218–219 describes the kinds of cultural diversity researchers have observed. We turn our attention now to how one very important aspect of our own society and culture— *school*—can have positive influences on children's and adolescents' motivation and affect.

• Promoting Motivation and Positive Affect

As the concept of *situated motivation* reminds us, teachers' behaviors and the nature of classroom lessons and activities make a significant difference in the extent to which students are motivated to learn and achieve at school. Some instructional strategies foster intrinsic motivation by addressing students' basic needs. Others lead students to think about classroom subject matter in ways that cultivate either intrinsic or internalized motivation. Still others generate feelings and emotions—affect—that enhance students' learning and classroom performance.

Fostering Intrinsic Motivation by Addressing Students' Basic Needs

As we've discovered, students are more likely to use effective learning strategies—and thus more likely to understand and remember classroom subject matter, apply what they've learned to new situations, and undergo appropriate conceptual change—if they're intrinsically rather than extrinsically motivated. And they're more likely to be intrinsically motivated when classroom activities address one or more of their basic psychological needs. Following are several strategies that are apt to address these needs.

Conduct stimulating lessons and activities.

One essential strategy for keeping students engaged and on task in the classroom is to conduct lessons that address students' basic need for arousal. Educational psychologists have

---

[152] W. A. Collins, 2005.

identified numerous ways of provoking situational interest in classroom subject matter, and many of them work by satisfying students' need for either cognitive or physical stimulation. For instance, teachers can do the following:[153]

- Model curiosity and enthusiasm about classroom topics.
- Occasionally incorporate novelty, variety, fantasy, and mystery into lessons and procedures.
- Encourage students to identify with fictional characters or with real people in historical or contemporary events and to imagine what these people might have been thinking or feeling.
- Provide opportunities for students to respond actively to the subject matter, perhaps by manipulating and experimenting with physical objects, creating new products, discussing controversial issues, or teaching something they've learned to peers.

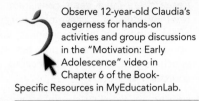

Observe 12-year-old Claudia's eagerness for hands-on activities and group discussions in the "Motivation: Early Adolescence" video in Chapter 6 of the Book-Specific Resources in MyEducationLab.

Figure 6.6 presents examples of how teachers might generate situational interest—and thereby promote intrinsic motivation—in a variety of content domains.

Protect and enhance students' self-efficacy and overall sense of competence and self-worth.

Simply telling students they're "good" or "smart" or "nice" is unlikely to boost a low sense of self-worth.[154] Furthermore, vague, abstract statements such as "You're special" have little meaning in the concrete realities of young children.[155] A more effective approach is to enhance students' self-efficacy for specific activities and tasks. As students become increasingly confident about their abilities in particular domains, they may also gain greater confidence in their general competence and worth.[156]

Observe efficacy-enhancing teacher feedback in the "Author's Chair" video in Chapter 6 of the Book-Specific Resources in MyEducationLab.

FIGURE 6.6 Examples of how teachers might generate situational interest in various content domains

Art: Have students make a mosaic from items they've found on a scavenger hunt around the school building.

Biology: Have class members debate the ethical implications of conducting medical research on animals.

Creative writing: Ask students to write newspaper-like restaurant reviews of the school cafeteria or neighborhood fast-food restaurants.

Geography: Present household objects not found locally, and ask students to guess where they might be from.

Health education: In a lesson about alcoholic beverages, have students role-play being at a party and being tempted to have a beer or wine cooler.

History: Have students read children's perspectives of historical events (e.g., Anne Frank's diary during World War II, Zlata Filipovic's diary during the Bosnian War).

Language Arts: Examine lyrics in popular hip-hop music, looking for grammatical patterns and literary themes.

Mathematics: Have students play computer games to improve their automaticity for number facts.

Music: In a unit on musical instruments, let students experiment with a variety of simple instruments.

Physical education: Incorporate steps from hip-hop, swing, or country line dancing into an aerobics workout.

Physical science: Have each student make several paper airplanes and then fly them to see which design travels farthest.

Reading: Turn a short story into a play, with each student taking a part.

Spelling: Occasionally depart from standard word lists, instead asking students to learn how to spell the names of favorite television shows or classmates' surnames.

Sources: Some ideas derived from Alim, 2007; Brophy, 1986; Lepper & Hodell, 1989; McCourt, 2005; Spaulding, 1992; Stipek, 1993; Wlodkowski, 1978.

---

[153] Ainley, 2006; Andre & Windschitl, 2003; Brophy, 2004; Brophy, Alleman, & Knighton, 2009; Chinn, 2006; Flum & Kaplan, 2006; Frenzel, Goetz, Lüdtke, Pekrun, & Sutton, 2009; Hidi & Renninger, 2006; Levstik, 1993; Patrick, Mantzicopoulos, & Samarapungavan, 2009; Zahorik, 1994.

[154] Crocker & Knight, 2005; Katz, 1993; Marsh & Craven, 1997.
[155] McMillan, Singh, & Simonetta, 1994.
[156] Bong & Skaalvik, 2003; Harter, 1999; Swann, Chang-Schneider, & McClarty, 2007.

CULTURAL CONSIDERATIONS Cultural and Ethnic Differences in Affect

Researchers have seen consistent cultural differences in several aspects of affect: emotional expressiveness, views about appropriate emotions, extent to which cognitive dissonance occurs, and sources of anxiety.

Emotional expressiveness. On average, cultural groups differ in the degree to which they show their feelings in their behaviors and facial expressions. For example, whereas Americans and Mexicans are often quite expressive, people from East Asian cultures tend to be more reserved and may be reluctant to confide in other people in times of sadness or distress.[a] Considerable variability exists in any large society, of course. For instance, in one study with Americans, people of Irish ancestry were more apt to reveal their feelings in their facial expressions than were people of Scandinavian ancestry.[b]

The emotion for which cultural differences are most prevalent is anger. Main-stream Western culture encourages children to act and speak up if someone infringes on their rights and needs, and expressing anger in a nonviolent way is considered quite acceptable. In many southeast Asian cultures, however, any expression of anger is viewed as potentially undermining adults' authority or disrupting social harmony.[c]

Views about appropriate ways to feel. Children brought up in some cultural groups, including many Buddhist groups and certain Native American and Pacific Islander communities, are encouraged not even to *feel* anger.[d] As an illustration, if a child growing up in the Tamang culture of Nepal is unfairly embarrassed or accused, he or she might respond, "Tilda bomo khaba?" ("Why be angry?"). After all, the event has already occurred and being angry about it serves no purpose.[e]

Even seemingly "positive" emotions are not always viewed favorably. Some cultures that place high priority on social harmony discourage children from feeling pride about personal accomplishments, because such an emotion focuses attention on an individual rather than on the overall group.[f] And for some cultural groups, joy and happiness can often be too much of a good thing. For instance, many Chinese and Japanese advocate striving for contentment and serenity—relatively calm emotions—rather than joy, excitement, and other intense emotions.[g]

Cognitive dissonance as a motivator. For many learners, encountering two conflicting, seemingly opposite ideas causes what Piaget called *disequilibrium* and what contemporary motivation theorists call *cognitive dissonance*—a form of mental discomfort that spurs learners to resolve the discrepancy in some way. Not all cultural groups are bothered by logical conflicts, however. When I was in China a few years ago, I was struck by

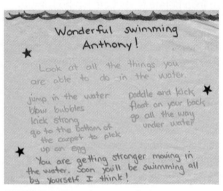

FIGURE 6.7 In this "certificate," a swimming teacher gives 5-year-old Anthony concrete feedback about skills he has mastered.

As noted earlier, learners' own past successes in an activity enhance their self-efficacy for the activity. Their previous successes are most likely to increase their self-confidence when they realize that *they themselves* have been responsible for their successes—that is, when they attribute their performance to their own effort and ability.[157] Teachers can play a role here by drawing students' attention to their successes either orally or in writing (see Figure 6.7).

But how do students acquire self-efficacy for a task they've never tried? As mentioned earlier, words of encouragement ("You can do it, I *know* you can!") can sometimes be helpful over the short run. But a more powerful approach is to show students that peers very similar to themselves have successfully mastered the task at hand.[158] For example, in one research study,[159] elementary school children having difficulty with subtraction were given 25 subtraction problems to complete. Children who had seen another student successfully complete the problems got an average of 19 correct, whereas those who saw a teacher complete the problems got only 13 correct, and those who saw no model at all solved only 8.

Ideally, learners should have a reasonably accurate sense of what they can and cannot accomplish, putting them in a good position to capitalize on their strengths,

---

[157] Dweck, 2009; Lam, Yim, & Ng, 2008; Pintrich & Schunk, 2002.

[158] Dijkstra et al., 2008; Schunk & Pajares, 2005.

[159] Schunk & Hanson, 1985.

[160] Försterling & Morgenstern, 2002; A. J. Martin, 2008; J. Wang & Lin, 2005.

how often people described something as being both one thing and also its opposite. Researchers report that many East Asians are quite tolerant and accepting of logical contradictions.[h]

Sources of anxiety.   Learners from different cultural backgrounds may have somewhat different sources of anxiety. For instance, some children and adolescents from Asian American families may feel so much family pressure to perform well in school that they regularly experience debilitating test anxiety.[i] And young people who are recent immigrants to a new country are often anxious about a variety of things: how to behave, how to interpret others' behaviors, how to make friends, and, more generally, how to make sense of the strange new culture in which they now find themselves (recall the discussion of *cultural mismatch* in Chapter 3).[j]

Anxiety may be at the root of a phenomenon known as **stereotype threat**, which can lead students from stereotypi-cally low-achieving ethnic groups to perform more poorly on classroom assessments than they would otherwise perform simply because they're aware that their group traditionally *does* do poorly.[k] When students are aware of the unflattering stereotype—and especially when they believe that the task they're performing reflects their ability in an important domain—their heart rate and other physiological correlates of anxiety go up and their performance goes down.[l] The negative effects of stereotype threat are more common when students interpret their performance on a task as an evaluation of their competence or overall self-worth.[m] Furthermore, stereotype threat is more likely to arise when students have an entity view of ability—a belief that ability is relatively fixed and permanent—rather than an incremental view.[n]

[a] Camras, Chen, Bakeman, Norris, & Cain, 2006; P. M. Cole & Tan, 2007; H. S. Kim, Sherman, & Taylor, 2008; Morelli & Rothbaum, 2007; Tyler et al., 2008.

[b] Camras et al., 2006; P. M. Cole, Tamang, & Shrestha, 2006; J. L. Tsai & Chentsova-Dutton, 2003.

[c] Mesquita & Leu, 2007; Morelli & Rothbaum, 2007; Zahn-Waxler, Friedman, Cole, Mizuta, & Hiruma, 1996.

[d] P. M. Cole, Bruschi, & Tamang, 2002; P. M. Cole et al., 2006; Solomon, 1984.

[e] P. M. Cole et al., 2002, p. 992.

[f] Eid & Diener, 2001.

[g] P. M. Cole & Tan, 2007; Kagan, 2010; Mesquita & Leu, 2007.

[h] Heine, 2007; Norenzayan, Choi, & Peng, 2007; Peng & Nisbett, 1999.

[i] Pang, 1995.

[j] P. M. Cole & Tan, 2007; Dien, 1998; Igoa, 1995.

[k] K. E. Ryan & Ryan, 2005; J. L. Smith, 2004; Steele, 1997.

[l] Aronson et al., 1999; Aronson & Steele, 2005; McKown & Weinstein, 2003; Osborne & Simmons, 2002.

[m] P. G. Davies & Spencer, 2005; Huguet & Régner, 2007; McKown & Weinstein, 2003; Walton & Spencer, 2009.

[n] Ben-Zeev et al., 2005; Dweck et al., 2004; C. Good, Aronson, & Inzlicht, 2003.

address their weaknesses, and set realistic goals.[160] Yet a tad of overconfidence can be beneficial, in that it entices learners to take on challenging activities that will help them develop new skills and abilities.[161] Within this context, it's often useful to distinguish between *self-efficacy for learning* ("I can master this if I put my mind to it") and *self-efficacy for performance* ("I already know how to do this").[162] Self-efficacy for learning (for what one can *eventually* do with effort) should be on the optimistic side, whereas self-efficacy for performance should be more in line with current ability levels.

The Classroom Strategies box "Enhancing Self-Efficacy and Self-Worth" provides several examples of how teachers can boost students' self-efficacy for specific topics and skills, as well as their more general beliefs about competence. Teachers should keep in mind, however, that academic achievement isn't necessarily the most important thing affecting students' sense of self-worth. For many children and adolescents, such factors as physical appearance, peer approval, and social success are more influential.[163] Ideally, then, teachers should help students achieve success in the nonacademic as well as academic aspects of their lives.

[161] Assor & Connell, 1992; Lockhart et al., 2002; Pajares, 2005.
[162] Lodewyk & Winne, 2005; Schunk & Pajares, 2004; Zimmerman & Kitsantas, 2005.

[163] Eccles et al., 1998; Rudolph et al., 2005.

stereotype threat Awareness of a negative stereotype about one's own group and accompanying uneasiness that low performance will confirm the stereotype; leads (often unintentionally) to a reduction in performance.

CLASSROOM STRATEGIES Enhancing Self-Efficacy and Self-Worth

- Teach basic knowledge and skills to mastery.

    A high school biology teacher makes sure all students clearly understand the basic structure of DNA before moving to mitosis and meiosis, two topics that require knowledge of DNA structure.

- Define success in terms of task accomplishment or improvement, not in terms of performance relative to others.

    A second-grade teacher and one of her students meet to discuss items in the student's end-of-year portfolio. They identify several ways in which the student's writing has improved during the past year. (This example is depicted in the "Portfolio" video in Chapter 6 of the Book-Specific Resources in MyEducationLab.)

- Assure students that they can be successful at challenging tasks, and point out that others like them have succeeded before them.

    Early in the school year, many students in beginning band express frustration about learning to play their instruments. Their teacher reminds them that students in last year's beginning band also started out with little skill but eventually mastered their instruments. A few weeks later, the beginning band class attends a concert at which the school's advanced band (last year's beginning band class) plays a medley from the Broadway musical *The Lion King*.

- Assign large, complex tasks as small-group activities.

    A middle school teacher has students work in groups of three or four to write research papers about early colonial life in North America. The teacher makes sure that the students in each group collectively have the skills in library research, writing, word processing, and art necessary to complete the task. She also makes sure that every student has unique skills to contribute to the group effort.

- Help students track their progress.

    As first graders are learning how to weave on small circular looms, one student approaches her teacher in tears, frustrated that her first few rows are full of mistakes. The teacher responds, "Look, Dorothy, this is the history, your own history, of learning to weave. You can look at this and say, 'Why, I can see how I began, here I didn't know how very well, I went over two instead of one; but I learned, and then—it is perfect all the way to the end!'" The student returns to her seat, very much comforted, and finishes her piece. She follows it with another, flawless one and proudly shows it to her teacher.

- When negative feedback is necessary, present it in a way that communicates competence and the ability to improve.

    A third-grade teacher tells a student, "I can see from the past few assignments that you're having trouble with long division. I think I know what the problem is. Here, let me show you what you need to do differently."

Sources: Bandura, 1997, 2000; R. Butler, 1998a; Covington, 1992; Deci & Ryan, 1985; Graham & Golen, 1991; Hawkins, 1997, p. 332 (weaving example); Pintrich & Schunk, 2002; Schunk, 1983; Shute, 2008; Urdan & Turner, 2005.

FIGURE 6.8 In writing about "A Book That Changed Me," 8-year-old Anthony expresses pride in reading his first book of more than 100 pages. Also notice Anthony's personal interest in sports: One book (*At the Plate*) involves baseball; the other (*On the Court*) involves basketball.

Present challenges that students can realistically accomplish.

Not only do challenges promote cognitive development (see Chapter 5) but in addition students who take on and master challenges gain a greater sense of self-efficacy and experience considerable satisfaction and pride in their accomplishments.[164] The artifact in Figure 6.8 reveals 8-year-old Anthony's pride about finishing his first 100-page book.

Challenges have another advantage as well: They heighten students' interest in the subject matter.[165] Once students are intrinsically motivated to learn about and master a topic, they often pursue further challenges of their own accord. They also exhibit considerable persistence in the face of difficulty—in part because earlier successes have led to greater self-efficacy—and they continue to remain interested even when they make frequent errors.[166] As you can see, then, challenges, self-efficacy, and intrinsic motivation mutually enhance one another, leading to a "vicious" cycle of the most desirable sort.

---

[164] Clifford, 1990; Csikszentmihalyi & Nakamura, 1989; Deci & Ryan, 1992; Shernoff, Knauth, & Makris, 2000; J. C. Turner, 1995.

[165] Deci & Ryan, 1992; S. D. Miller & Meece, 1997; N. E. Perry, Turner, & Meyer, 2006; J. C. Turner, 1995.

[166] Covington, 1992; Csikszentmihalyi et al., 2005; Deci, 1992; Harter, 1992.

When are learners most likely to take on new and potentially risky challenges? Conditions such as the following appear to be optimal:[167]

- Standards for success are realistic for each individual.
- Scaffolding is sufficient to make success possible.
- There are few, if any, penalties for errors.
- The same rewards cannot be obtained by engaging in easier tasks, *or* rewards are greater for challenging tasks than for easy ones.
- Learners attribute their success to their own ability, effort, and strategies.

Observe 15-year-old Greg's desire for challenge in the "Motivation: Late Adolescence" video in Chapter 6 of the Book-Specific Resources in MyEducationLab.

Teachers should keep in mind, however, that the school day shouldn't necessarily be one challenge after another. Such a state of affairs would be absolutely exhausting and probably quite discouraging as well. Instead, teachers should strike a balance between relatively easy tasks, which will boost students' self-confidence over the short run, and the challenging tasks so critical for longer-term self-efficacy and self-worth.[168]

Give students control over some aspects of classroom life.

When students have some sense of autonomy about events at school—in other words, when they have a sense of self-determination—they are more likely to be intrinsically motivated to engage in academic and extracurricular activities, use skills acquired at school in out-of-school settings, and stay in school until graduation.[169] Naturally, teachers can't give students total freedom about what they can and cannot do at school. Nevertheless, teachers can do several things to enhance students' sense of self-determination about school-related tasks and activities. For one thing, they can let students make decisions, either individually or as a group, about some or all of the following:[170]

- Rules and procedures to make a class run more smoothly
- Specific topics for research or writing projects
- Specific works of literature to be read
- Due dates for some assignments
- The order in which specific tasks are done during the school day
- Ways of achieving mastery of a particular skill or of demonstrating that it has been mastered (see Figure 6.9)
- Criteria by which some assignments will be evaluated
- Specific activities and procedures in extracurricular activities (school clubs, community service projects, etc.)

To the extent that students can make choices about such matters, they're more likely to be interested in what they are doing, to work diligently and persistently, and to take pride in their work.[171] Furthermore, students who are given choices—even students with serious behavior problems—are less likely to misbehave in class.[172]

In some situations students' choices can be almost limitless. For example, in a unit on expository writing,

---

Choose One!

SCIENCE FICTION BOOK PROJECTS

_____   Write a "Dear Abby" letter from one of the main characters, in which he or she asks for advice on solving his or her main problem. Then answer the letter.

_____   Draw a time line of the main events of the book.

_____   Create a comic book or a comic strip page that features a major scene from the book in each box.

_____   Make a collage of objects and printed words from newspapers and magazines that give the viewer a feeling for the mood of the book.

_____   Your book probably takes place in an unusual or exotic setting, so illustrate and write a travel brochure describing that location.

_____   Imagine yourself as a scientist who has been asked to explain the unusual events in the book. Write up a report in scientific style.

_____   With other students who have read the same book, plan a bulletin board display. Write a plot summary; character and setting descriptions; discussions of special passages. Each group member must contribute one artistic piece—for example, new book cover, bookmark, poster, banner, some of the ideas listed above. Arrange the writing and artwork under a colorful heading announcing the book.

FIGURE 6.9 By offering several options for demonstrating understanding of a science fiction book, a sixth-grade language arts teacher enhances students' sense of self-determination.

---

[167] Brophy & Alleman, 1992; Clifford, 1990; Corno & Rohrkemper, 1985; Deci & Ryan, 1985; Dweck & Elliott, 1983; Stipek, 1993.

[168] Spaulding, 1992; Stipek, 1993, 1996.

[169] Hagger, Chatzisarantis, Barkoukis, Wang, & Baranowski, 2005; Hardré & Reeve, 2003; E. J. Langer, 1997; Reeve, Bolt, & Cai, 1999; Shernoff et al., 2000; Standage, Duda, & Ntoumanis, 2003.

[170] Lane, Falk, & Wehby, 2006; Larson, 2000; Meece, 1994; Reed et al., 2004; Stipek, 1993.

[171] Deci & Ryan, 1992; Patall, Cooper, & Wynn, 2008; Reeve, 2006; J. A. Ross, 1988; J. C. Turner, 1995.

[172] Dunlap et al., 1994; Lane et al., 2006; Powell & Nelson, 1997; B. J. Vaughn & Horner, 1997.

a wide variety of student-selected research topics might be equally appropriate. In other situations teachers may need to impose certain limits on the choices students make. For example, if a teacher allows a class to set its own due dates for certain assignments, it might be with the stipulation that the schedule evenly distributes the student and teacher workload over a reasonable time period. And a teacher advisor of an extracurricular service club should help students think through the probable outcomes of various courses of action.[173]

Evaluate students' performance in a noncontrolling manner.

In most classrooms teachers have the final word in evaluating students' performance. Unfortunately, such external evaluation can undermine students' sense of self-determination and intrinsic motivation, especially if communicated in a controlling manner. Ideally, teachers should present evaluations of students' work not as "judgments" that remind students how they *should* perform but as information that can help them improve their knowledge and skills.[174] For instance, rather than saying, "You didn't follow my instructions for writing a persuasive essay" (controlling), a teacher might say, "You make some good points, but your essay could be more convincing if you also include and rebut counterarguments to your point of view" (information).

Use extrinsic reinforcers when necessary, but do so in ways that preserve students' sense of self-determination.

Although intrinsic motivation is the optimal situation, extrinsic motivation to learn is certainly better than *no* motivation to learn. Typically teachers encourage extrinsic motivation through praise, stickers, free time, good grades, and other extrinsic reinforcers. A potential problem with using extrinsic reinforcers is that they may undermine intrinsic motivation, especially if students perceive them to be limiting their choices, controlling their behavior, or in other ways undermining their sense of self-determination.[175] Extrinsic reinforcers may also communicate the message that classroom tasks are unpleasant "chores" (why else would a reinforcer be necessary?) rather than activities to be carried out and enjoyed for their own sake.[176]

Extrinsic reinforcers appear to have no adverse effects when they're unexpected (e.g., when students get special recognition for a public service project in the local community) or when they're not contingent on specific behaviors (e.g., when they're used simply to make an activity more enjoyable).[177] They can even be beneficial if used to encourage students not only to do something but also to do it *well*.[178] And if they communicate that students *have* done something well (as a high grade might) or have made considerable improvement, they can enhance students' sense of self-efficacy and competence and focus students' attention on mastering the subject matter.[179]

Sometimes students may initially find a new topic or skill boring or frustrating and therefore need external encouragement to continue.[180] So how can teachers use extrinsic reinforcers while preserving students' sense of self-determination? One strategy is to praise students in a manner that communicates information but doesn't show an intent to control behavior.[181] Consider these statements as examples:

- "Your description of the main character in your short story makes her come alive."
- "I think you've finally mastered the rolling *R* sound in Spanish."
- "This poster clearly states the hypothesis, method, results, and conclusions of your science project. Your use of a bar graph makes the differences between your treatment and control groups easy to see and interpret."

Another strategy is to teach students to reinforce *themselves* for their accomplishments, a practice that clearly keeps control in students' hands (see the discussion of *self-imposed contingencies* in Chapter 4).

Observe examples of noncontrolling, informational feedback in the "Author's Chair" video in Chapter 6 of the Book-Specific Resources in MyEducationLab.

---

[173] Larson, 2000.
[174] Deci & Moller, 2005; Reeve et al., 2004; Stipek, 1996.
[175] Deci, 1992; Lepper & Hodell, 1989; Reeve, 2006.
[176] B. A. Hennessey, 1995; Stipek, 1993.
[177] J. Cameron, 2001; Deci, Koestner, & Ryan, 2001; Reeve, 2006.

[178] J. Cameron, 2001.
[179] J. Cameron, 2001; Deci & Moller, 2005; Hynd, 2003.
[180] J. Cameron, 2001; Deci et al., 2001; Hidi & Harackiewicz, 2000.
[181] Deci, 1992; R. M. Ryan, Mims, & Koestner, 1983.

Help students meet their need for relatedness.

Warm and caring interpersonal relationships are typically among students' highest priorities.[182] Students are more likely to be academically motivated and successful—and more likely to stay in school rather than drop out—when they believe that their teachers and peers like and respect them and when they feel that they truly "belong" in the classroom community.[183]

Teachers simply cannot ignore the high need for relatedness that many students bring to the classroom. In fact, when planning daily lessons and classroom activities, teachers should include opportunities for students to interact with one another—ideally identifying ways to help students learn academic subject matter *and* address their need for relatedness simultaneously.[184] Although some instructional goals can best be accomplished when students work independently, others can be accomplished just as easily (perhaps even more easily) when students work together. Group-based activities, such as discussions, debates, role-playing, cooperative learning tasks, and competitions among two or more teams of equal ability, all provide the means through which students can satisfy their need for relatedness while simultaneously acquiring (and possibly co-constructing) new knowledge and skills.[185] Most effective are activities in which all students have something unique to contribute and so can in some way "shine" and gain the admiration of peers.

Virtually all students want good relationships with their teachers as well as their classmates. Thus teachers should show that they like their students, enjoy being with them, and are concerned about their well-being.[186] Teachers can communicate fondness for students in a variety of ways. For instance, teachers can express an interest in students' outside activities and accomplishments or provide extra assistance or a sympathetic ear when needed. Such caring messages may be especially important for students from culturally different backgrounds.[187]

The Classroom Strategies box "Addressing the Need for Relatedness" presents and illustrates several strategies for enhancing social relationships in the classroom.

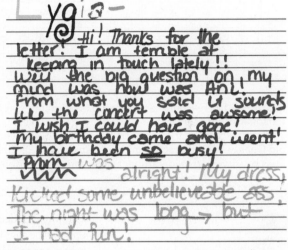

Interacting with peers—in this case, by passing a note during class—is a high priority for many students.

CLASSROOM STRATEGIES   Addressing the Need for Relatedness

- **Have students work together on some learning tasks.**

  A high school history teacher incorporates classroom debates, small-group discussions, and cooperative learning tasks into every month's activities.

- **Continually communicate the message that you like and respect your students.**

  A middle school teacher tells one of his students that he saw her dancing troupe's performance at the local shopping mall over the weekend. "I had no idea you were so talented," he says. "How many years have you been studying dance?"

- **Praise students privately when being a high achiever is not sanctioned by peers.**

  While reading a stack of short stories his students have written, a high school English teacher discovers that one of his students,

  Brigitta, has written an especially good story. Knowing that Brigitta is eager to maintain her popularity with low-achieving classmates, he writes his comments on the second page of her story, where others won't be able to see them. There he writes, "Great work, Brigitta! I think it's good enough to enter into the state writing contest. I'd like to meet with you before or after school some day this week to talk more about the contest."

- **Create a classroom culture in which respect for *everyone's* needs and well-being is paramount.**

  When a second-grade teacher overhears two boys making fun of a fellow student who stutters, she discretely pulls them aside, explains that the classmate is extremely self-conscious about his speech and is working hard to improve it, and tactfully reminds the boys that they, too, have imperfections as well as strengths.

---

[182] Dowson & McInerney, 2001; Geary, 1998; Juvonen, 2006.

[183] Furrer & Skinner, 2003; Goodenow, 1993; J. N. Hughes, Luo, Kwok, & Loyd, 2008; Hymel, Comfort, Schonert-Reichl, & McDougall, 1996; A. M. Ryan & Patrick, 2001.

[184] Wentzel & Wigfield, 1998.

[185] Blumenfeld et al., 2006; Brophy, 1987; Linnenbrink, 2005; Urdan & Maehr, 1995.

[186] Juvonen, 2006; Patrick et al., 2002; Pianta, Belsky, Vandergrift, Houts, & Morrison, 2008.

[187] Meehan, Hughes, & Cavell, 2003; Milner, 2006; Phelan, Davidson, & Cao, 1991.

Promoting Motivation-Enhancing Cognitions

Addressing specific cognitive factors that affect motivation can also have a significant impact on students' learning and classroom performance. Following are several recommendations based on such factors.

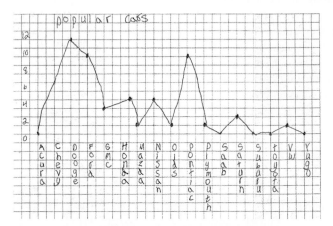

FIGURE 6.10 Teachers can capitalize on students' personal interests by allowing flexibility in the topics students explore as they work on basic skills. Twelve-year-old Connor gained practice in basic research and graphing skills by surveying fellow students about a favorite topic: cars. His findings are shown here.

Relate assignments to students' personal interests, values, and goals.

On some occasions teachers can foster intrinsic motivation by capitalizing on students' existing interests, values, and goals. For instance, teachers can have students apply new skills to authentic tasks that incorporate personal interests (see Figure 6.10). They can demonstrate how academic subject matter will help students address their present concerns and long-term career goals. And in general, teachers can convey how classroom subject matter can help students make better sense of the world around them.[188]

Create conditions that foster internalization of values essential for students' long-term academic and professional success.

No matter how much teachers try to make classroom topics and tasks interesting and engaging, some of them will have little intrinsic appeal to students. When such topics and tasks are critical for students' long-term success at school and in the outside world, students will pursue them more energetically and persistently if they truly appreciate the importance of classroom learning and achievement. The more students have internalized the value of learning and academic success, the more they will be cognitively engaged in school subject matter and the better their overall classroom performance is likely to be.[189] Internalized motivation is also an important aspect of self-regulated learning: It underlies a general work ethic in which learners spontaneously engage in activities that, although not always fun or immediately gratifying, are essential for reaching long-term goals.[190]

Many of the recommendations I've previously made—in particular, enhancing students' sense of competence, self-determination, and relatedness—are likely to help students internalize the motivation to achieve academic success. But in addition, teachers must set reasonable limits for behavior and help students understand why certain topics and skills may be critical for their long-term development and success. And teachers should refrain from asking students to engage in activities with little long-term benefit—for instance, having students memorize trivial facts for no apparent reason or requiring them to read material that's clearly beyond their comprehension levels.[191]

Focus students' attention more on mastery goals than on performance goals.

To some degree, performance goals are inevitable in today's schools and in society at large.[192] Children and adolescents often use their peers' performance as a criterion for evaluating their own performance. Universities and colleges look for high grades and test scores when screening applicants. And many aspects of the adult world (seeking employment, working in private industry, playing professional sports, etc.) are inherently competitive in nature. Ultimately, however, mastery goals are the ones most likely to lead to effective learning and performance over the long run.[193]

---

[188] P. A. Alexander et al., 1994; C. Ames, 1992; Blumenfeld et al., 2006; Brophy et al., 2009; Ferrari & Elik, 2003.

[189] Brophy, 2008; La Guardia, 2009; Otis et al., 2005; Ratelle, Guay, Vallerand, Larose, & Senécal, 2007; R. M. Ryan & Deci, 2000; Walls & Little, 2005.

[190] Harter, 1992; McCombs, 1996; R. M. Ryan et al., 1992.

[191] Brophy, 2008; Deci & Moller, 2005; Eccles, 2007; Jacobs et al., 2005; Reeve, 2009.

[192] R. Butler, 1989; Elliot & McGregor, 2000.

[193] For example, see Elliot, Shell, Henry, & Maier, 2005; Gabriele, 2007; Vansteenkiste et al., 2006.

Sometimes mastery goals come from within, especially when students have high interest in, and high self-efficacy for, learning something.[194] Yet classroom practices can also encourage mastery goals.[195] For instance, teachers can do the following:[196]

- Present subject matter that students find valuable in and of itself.
- Show how topics and skills are relevant to students' future personal and professional goals.
- Insist that students *understand,* rather than simply memorize, classroom material.
- Give specific suggestions about how students can improve.
- Encourage students to use their peers not as a reference point for their own progress, but rather as a source of ideas and help.

Focusing attention on mastery goals, especially when these goals relate to students' own lives, may especially benefit students from diverse ethnic backgrounds and students at risk for academic failure.[197]

Ask students to set some personal goals for learning and performance.

Students typically work harder toward *self-chosen* goals than toward goals that others have chosen for them, possibly because self-chosen goals help them maintain a sense of self-determination.[198] Although teachers should certainly encourage students to develop long-term goals (e.g., going to college, becoming an environmental scientist), such goals are sometimes too general and abstract to guide immediate behavior.[199] (As an example, look once again at the student interview in the Cultural Considerations box on pages 122–123 of Chapter 4.) Self-chosen goals are especially motivating when they're specific ("I want to learn how to do a cartwheel"), challenging ("Writing a limerick looks difficult, but I'm sure I can do it"), and short-term ("I'm going to learn to count to one hundred in French by the end of the month").[200] By setting and working for a series of short-term, concrete goals—sometimes called **proximal goals**—students get regular feedback about the progress they're making, develop a greater sense of self-efficacy that they can master school subject matter, and achieve at higher levels.[201]

Figure 6.11 shows a handout that one middle school teacher uses to encourage students to identify and commit to short-term goals for their learning. Such goals, accompanied by regular *achievement* of them, may be especially important for students with a history of academic failure.[202] Students' goals should, of course, be compatible with their teachers' goals for student achievement—an issue we'll address in Chapter 8.

Form and communicate optimistic expectations and attributions.

Teachers typically draw conclusions about their students relatively early in the school year, forming opinions about each one's strengths, weaknesses, and potential for academic success. In many instances teachers size up their students fairly accurately. They know which ones need help with reading skills, which ones have short attention spans, which ones have trouble working together in a cooperative group, and so on, and they can adapt their instruction and assistance accordingly.[203]

Yet even the best teachers sometimes make errors in their judgments, perhaps underestimating students who are members of ethnic minority groups or come from low socioeconomic backgrounds.[204] Furthermore, many teachers have an entity view of intelligence and

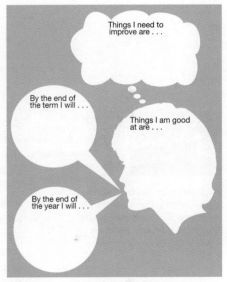

FIGURE 6.11 With this handout, a middle school information technology teacher asks students to reflect on their current strengths and identify specific goals for improvement. This handout is for girls; boys get one with shorter hair.

Source: Created by and used with permission from Jeffrey Scott Ormrod.

proximal goal Concrete goal that can be accomplished within a short time period; may be a stepping stone toward a longer-term goal.

[194] Bandura, 1997; Murphy & Alexander, 2000; Schiefele, 1992.

[195] Church, Elliot, & Gable, 2001; Midgley, 2002.

[196] C. Ames, 1992; E. M. Anderman & Maehr, 1994; Bong, 2001; Brophy, 2004, 2008; F. Danner, 2008; Graham & Weiner, 1996; Meece, 1994; Middleton & Midgley, 2002; J. C. Turner, Meyer, et al., 1998; Urdan et al., 2002.

[197] Brayboy & Searle, 2007; Garcia, 1992; S. D. Miller & Meece, 1997; Wlodkowski & Ginsberg, 1995.

[198] Reeve, 2009; Wentzel, 1999.

[199] Bandura, 1997; Husman & Freeman, 1999.

[200] Alderman, 1990; Brophy, 2004; Locke & Latham, 2006.

[201] Bandura, 1997; Locke & Latham, 2002; Page-Voth & Graham, 1999; Schunk & Pajares, 2005.

[202] E. S. Alexander, 2006.

[203] Dweck & Molden, 2005; Goldenberg, 1992.

[204] Banks & Banks, 1995; McLoyd, 1998.

so perceive students' ability levels to be relatively fixed and stable.[205] Their attributions regarding these "stable" abilities affect their expectations for students' performance, which in turn lead them to treat different students differently. When teachers have high expectations for students, they present challenging tasks, interact with students frequently, persist in their efforts to help students understand, and give a lot of positive feedback. In contrast, when teachers have low expectations for certain students, they present easy tasks, offer few opportunities for speaking in class, and give little feedback about students' responses.[206]

Teachers' beliefs about students' abilities also affect their attributions for students' successes and failures.[207] Consider the following interpretations of a student's success:

- "You did it! You're so smart!"
- "That's wonderful. Your hard work has really paid off, hasn't it?"
- "You've done very well. It's clear that you really know how to study."
- "Terrific! This is certainly your lucky day!"

And now consider these interpretations of a student's failure:

- "Hmmm, maybe this just isn't something you're good at. Perhaps we should try a different activity."
- "Why don't you practice a little more and then try again?"
- "Let's see whether we can come up with some study strategies that might work better for you."
- "Maybe you're just having a bad day."

Observe a teacher skillfully communicate internal, controllable attributions for students' writing achievement in the "Author's Chair" video in Chapter 6 of the Book-Specific Resources in MyEducationLab.

All of these comments are presumably intended to make a student feel good. But notice the different attributions they imply—in some cases to uncontrollable abilities (being smart or not "good at" something), in other cases to controllable and therefore changeable behaviors (hard work, lack of practice, effective or ineffective study strategies), and in still other cases to external, uncontrollable causes (a lucky break, a bad day).

Teachers communicate their attributions for students' performance not only through what they say but also through the emotions they convey.[208] As an example, let's return to the opening case study, in which Michael is initially doing poorly in his eighth-grade algebra class. Imagine that you're Michael's teacher. Imagine, too, that you believe Michael has low mathematical ability: He just doesn't have a "gift" for math. When you see him consistently getting Ds and Fs on assignments and quizzes, you might reasonably conclude that his poor performance is beyond his control, and so you communicate pity and sympathy. But now imagine, instead, that you believe Michael has *high* math ability: He definitely has what it takes to do well in your class. When you see his poor marks on assignments and quizzes, you naturally assume he isn't trying very hard. In your eyes, Michael has complete control over the amount of effort he exerts, and so you might express anger or annoyance when he doesn't do well. Some teachers might even punish him for his poor performance.[209]

Most children and adolescents are well aware of their teachers' differential behaviors toward different students and use such behaviors to draw inferences about their own and others' abilities.[210] When they can't figure out why they're doing well or poorly, they may eagerly seek out information to help them explain their performance.[211] If teachers repeatedly give them low-ability messages, they may begin to see themselves as their teachers see them, and their behavior may mirror their self-perceptions.[212] In some cases, then, teachers' expectations and attributions may become **self-fulfilling prophecies**: What teachers expect students to achieve becomes what students actually *do* achieve.[213] Self-fulfilling prophecies occur most frequently when students are making a significant transition in their schooling (e.g., when they enter first grade or begin junior high school), and they're more common for girls and for students from ethnic minority groups.[214]

self-fulfilling prophecy Expectation for an outcome that either directly or indirectly leads to the expected result.

[205] Oakes & Guiton, 1995; C. Reyna, 2000.
[206] Babad, 1993; Brophy, 2006; T. L. Good & Brophy, 1994; Graham, 1990; R. Rosenthal, 1994.
[207] Weiner, 2000, 2005.
[208] C. Reyna & Weiner, 2001; Weiner, 2005.
[209] C. Reyna & Weiner, 2001; Weiner, 2005.
[210] R. Butler, 1994; T. L. Good & Nichols, 2001; Weinstein, 2002.

[211] Weiner, 2000.
[212] Marachi, Friedel, & Midgley, 2001; Murdock, 1999.
[213] For a classic study of the self-fulfilling prophecy, see R. Rosenthal & Jacobson, 1968.
[214] Graham, 1990; Hinnant, O'Brien, & Ghazarian, 2009; Jussim, Eccles, & Madon, 1996; Kuklinski & Weinstein, 2001; Raudenbush, 1984.

Teachers are most likely to facilitate students' learning and motivate them to achieve at high levels when they hold optimistic expectations for students' performance (within realistic limits, of course) and when they attribute students' successes and failures to things over which either students or teachers have control (*students'* effort, *teachers'* instructional methods, etc.). The Classroom Strategies box "Forming Productive Expectations and Attributions for Student Achievement" offers several strategies that can benefit teachers and students alike. The final strategy in the box—*Remember that teachers can definitely make a difference*—is probably the most important one. Teachers must keep in mind an important point about intelligence presented in Chapter 5: Ability can and does change over time, especially when environmental conditions are conducive to such change. For this reason,

CLASSROOM STRATEGIES Forming Productive Expectations and Attributions for Student Achievement

- **Look for strengths in every student.**

  A 9-year-old boy who lives in a homeless shelter seems to have learned almost nothing about rules for punctuation and capitalization, and his spelling is more typical of a first grader than a fourth grader. Nonetheless, the stories he writes often have unusual plot twists and creative endings. His teacher suspects that his frequent moves from one school district to another have left big gaps in his knowledge of written language and so finds a parent volunteer who can work with him on his writing several times a week.

- **Consider multiple possible explanations for students' low achievement and classroom misbehaviors.**

  Several seventh-grade teachers confer regarding their experiences with a student who, at age 8, suffered a traumatic brain injury when he fell off a kitchen counter and landed on his head. His art and music teachers describe him as very disruptive in class and believe that he intentionally misbehaves in order to draw attention to himself. In contrast, his math and science teachers have found that he can easily stay on task—and can achieve at average to above-average levels—as long as they provide reasonable structure for assignments and classroom behavior. These two teachers point out that some children with brain injuries have trouble inhibiting inappropriate behaviors through no fault of their own.

- **Communicate optimism about what students can accomplish.**

  In September a high school teacher tells his class, "Next spring I'll ask you to write a 15-page research paper. That may seem like a lot now, but in the next few months we'll work on the various skills you'll need to research and write your paper. By April, 15 pages won't seem like a big deal at all!"

- **Objectively assess students' progress, and be open to evidence that contradicts your initial assessments of students' abilities.**

  A kindergarten teacher initially has low expectations for the daughter of migrant workers, a girl named Lupita who has previously had little access to books, toys, and other educational resources. When a video camera captures Lupita's strong leadership ability and her skill in assembling puzzles, the teacher realizes that Lupita has considerable potential and so works hard to help her acquire the math and literacy skills she'll need to be successful in first grade. (See the opening case study "Hidden Treasure" in Chapter 5.)

- **Attribute students' successes to a combination of high ability and such controllable factors as effort and learning strategies.**

  In a unit on basketball, a middle school physical education teacher tells students, "From what I've seen so far, you all have the capability to play a good game of basketball. And it appears that many of you have been regularly practicing after school."

- **Attribute students' failures to factors that are controllable and easily changed.**

  A high school student seeks his teacher's advice about how he might improve his performance in her class. "I know you can do better than you have been, Frank," the teacher replies. "I wonder if part of the problem might be that with your part-time job and all of your extracurricular activities, you just don't have enough time to study. Let's sit down before school tomorrow and look at what and how much you're doing to prepare for class."

- **When students fail despite obvious effort, attribute their failures to a lack of effective strategies and help them acquire such strategies.**

  A student in an advanced science class is having difficulty on the teacher's challenging weekly quizzes. The student works diligently on her science every night and attends the after-school help sessions her teacher offers on Thursdays, yet to no avail. The teacher observes that the student is trying to learn the material by rote—an ineffective strategy for answering questions that involve applying scientific principles to new situations—and so teaches her strategies that promote more meaningful learning.

- **Remember that teachers can definitely make a difference.**

  The teachers at a historically low-achieving middle school in a low-income, inner-city neighborhood meet once a month to learn about teaching strategies that are especially effective with children from low-income families. They're encouraged by the many research studies indicating that children at all socioeconomic levels can achieve at high levels when instruction takes their existing skills into account and when teachers provide reasonable guidance and support. They experiment with various strategies in their own classrooms and share especially effective ones at their group meetings.

Sources: Some ideas based on Brophy, 2006; Carrasco, 1981 (Lupita example); Curtis, 1992; Dweck, 2000, 2009; Hattie, 2009; Hawley, 2005 (brain injury example); J. A. Langer, 2000; Pressley et al., 1987; Roeser, Marachi, & Gehlbach, 2002; Skaalvik & Skaalvik, 2008; Weinstein, Madison, & Kuklinski, 1995.

teachers should take an *incremental view* of students' abilities and continually reassess and modify their expectations and attributions for student achievement as new evidence presents itself.

Minimize competition.

Competition is widespread in mainstream Western societies, not only in adult activities (e.g., in business and politics) but also in elementary and secondary schools. Schools compare students in a variety of ways. When teachers post "best work" on a bulletin board, they indirectly communicate that other papers are not as good. When teachers grade "on the curve," their grades reflect how students stack up against one another, and only those at the top of the stack are identified as being successful. When students take college aptitude tests, their test scores reflect not what they know and can do but how their performance compares with that of their peers (more on this point in the discussion of *norm-referenced scores* in Chapter 10). Participation in school sports is also competitive, especially at the high school level, in that only students with the best athletic skills can join a team, and only the *best* of the best achieve starting-player status.

Students are apt to be motivated by competition *if* they believe they have a reasonable chance of winning.[215] (For example, earlier I recommended competitions among two or more teams of equal ability as a way of helping students meet their need for relatedness.) But competition can have several negative side effects of which you should be aware:[216]

- It promotes performance goals rather than mastery goals.
- It can lead to undesirable or counterproductive behaviors, such as cheating on quizzes or preventing classmates from getting needed resources for assignments.
- For students who expect to lose, it can lead to self-handicapping.
- For the students who *actually* lose, it can lead to low self-efficacy and a poor sense of self-worth.
- Because it makes differences among students more obvious, it encourages attributions to ability rather than to effort.

For such reasons, competition ultimately leads to lower achievement for most students. When classroom success is judged on the basis of how well students perform relative to one another rather than on the basis of how much improvement they make, most students earn lower grades, show less creativity, and develop more negative attitudes toward school.[217] Competitive classroom environments may be especially disadvantageous to female students and to students from ethnic minority groups.[218]

Some motivation theorists have suggested that effective motivational strategies can be summed up in seven words: task, autonomy, recognition, grouping, evaluation, time, and social support.[219] This multifaceted "TARGETS" approach to motivation is presented in Table 6.5. If you look closely at the entries in the table, you'll notice that they address the basic needs identified early in the chapter (arousal, competence and self-worth, self-determination, and relatedness) and also take into account such cognitive factors as interests, self-efficacy, values, goals, and attributions.

Generating Productive Affect

Students learn at high levels not only when they're motivated to master classroom subject matter but also when their emotional states are conducive to productive cognitive processes and behaviors. Following are four recommendations for generating productive affect.

[215] Deci & Ryan, 1992; D. W. Johnson & Johnson, 2009a; Linnenbrink, 2005.

[216] C. Ames, 1984; Deci & Moller, 2005; Hattie, 2008; A. J. Martin et al., 2003; Nicholls, 1984; Pekrun, 2006; Stipek, 1996; Thorndike-Christ, 2008.

[217] Amabile & Hennessey, 1992; Covington, 1992; Graham & Golen, 1991; Krampen, 1987.

[218] Inglehart, Brown, & Vida, 1994; Tyler et al., 2008.

[219] L. H. Anderman & Anderman, 2009; J. L. Epstein, 1989; Maehr & Anderman, 1993.

TABLE 6.5 Seven "TARGETS" Principles of Motivation

Principle	Educational Implications	Example
Classroom **tasks** affect motivation.	• Present new topics through tasks that students find interesting, engaging, and perhaps emotionally charged. • Encourage meaningful rather than rote learning. • Relate activities to students' lives and goals. • Provide sufficient support to enable students to be successful.	Ask students to conduct a scientific investigation about an issue that concerns them.
The amount of **autonomy** students have affects motivation, especially intrinsic motivation.	• Give students some choice about what and how they learn. • Teach self-regulation strategies. • Solicit students' opinions about classroom practices and policies. • Have students take leadership roles in some activities.	Let students choose among several ways of accomplishing an instructional objective, being sure that each choice offers sufficient scaffolding to make success likely.
The amount and nature of the **recognition** students receive affect motivation.	• Acknowledge not only academic successes but also personal and social successes. • Commend students for improvement as well as for mastery. • Provide concrete reinforcers for achievement only when students are not intrinsically motivated to learn. • Show students how their own efforts and strategies are directly responsible for their successes.	Commend students for a successful community service project.
The **grouping** procedures in the classroom affect motivation.	• Provide frequent opportunities for students to interact (e.g., cooperative learning activities, peer tutoring). • Plan small-group activities in which all students can make significant contributions. • Teach the social skills that students need to interact effectively with peers.	Have students work in small groups to tackle a challenging issue or problem for which there are two or more legitimate solutions.
The forms of **evaluation** in the classroom affect motivation.	• Make evaluation criteria clear; specify them in advance. • Minimize or eliminate competition for grades (e.g., don't grade "on a curve"). • Give specific feedback about what students are doing well. • Give concrete suggestions for how students can improve.	Give students concrete criteria with which they can evaluate the quality of their own writing.
How teachers schedule **time** affects motivation.	• Give students enough time to gain mastery of important topics and skills. • Let students' interests dictate some activities. • Include variety in the school day (e.g., intersperse high-energy activities among more sedentary ones).	After explaining a new concept, engage students in a hands-on activity that lets them see the concept in action.
The amount of **social support** students believe they have in the classroom affects motivation.	• Create a general atmosphere of mutual caring, respect, and support among all class members. • Convey affection and respect for every student, along with a genuine eagerness to help every student succeed. • Create situations in which all students feel comfortable participating actively in classroom activities (including students who are excessively shy, students who have limited academic skills, students who have physical disabilities, etc.).	When working with students who seem chronically disengaged from classroom lessons, identify their specific areas of strengths and provide opportunites for them to showcase their expertise in the classroom.

Sources: L. H. Anderman & Anderman, 2009; L. H. Anderman, Andrzejewski, & Allen, in press; L. H. Anderman, Patrick, Hruda, & Linnenbrink, 2002; J. L. Epstein, 1989; Patrick et al., 1997; Maehr & Anderman, 1993.

Get students emotionally involved in the subject matter.

Academic subject matter certainly doesn't need to be dry and emotionless. On the contrary, students will often remember more if they have strong feelings about what they're studying, perhaps getting very excited about a scientific discovery or quite angry about past or present social injustices. In addition to presenting subject matter that evokes emotional reactions, teachers can promote hot cognition by revealing their own feelings about a topic. For instance, they might bring in newspaper articles and other outside materials about which they're excited, present material in an enthusiastic or impassioned fashion, and share

A teacher's enthusiasm about classroom topics can be contagious.

Observe 10-year-old Daniel, 13-year-old Crystal, and 15-year-old Greg describe their emotion self-regulation strategies in the three "Emotions" videos in Chapter 6 of the Book-Specific Resources in MyEducationLab.

the particular questions and issues about which they themselves are concerned.[220] And although teachers don't necessarily want to give the impression that schoolwork is all fun and games, they can occasionally incorporate a few gamelike features into classroom tasks and activities.[221] For example, they might assign simple crossword puzzles to introduce new spelling words or use a television game show format for a class history review (the game show strategy also addresses students' need for relatedness).

Foster emotion self-regulation.

As the Cultural Considerations box on pages 218–219 indicates, various cultural groups differ in the extent to which they encourage emotional expressiveness or restraint. Even so, all children and adolescents function better at school when they engage in **emotion self-regulation**—that is, when they keep emotional reactions to events (e.g., excitement, sadness, anger) within socially acceptable limits.[222]

Certainly teachers should refer students with severe emotional difficulties to school counselors and other specially trained professionals. But a few simple strategies can help many students cope with the everyday disappointments and frustrations of life:[223]

- Help students identify strategies for minimizing the damage.
- Encourage students to find potential benefits in an unfortunate event—for instance, to treat it as a "wake-up call" or look for the "silver lining."
- Teach students strategies that can help them prevent similar unfortunate events in the future.

Through such coping strategies, students may learn that although they can't always control everything that happens to them, they can control how they *think* about what happens, enabling them to maintain at least some sense of self-determination.[224]

Keep anxiety at a low to moderate level.

As noted earlier in the chapter, learners work most effectively and productively when they are a little bit anxious—enough to spur them into action—but not overly so. Teachers can address students' concerns about social matters (e.g., worries about peer acceptance and respect) by teaching social skills and by planning activities that foster productive peer interactions. Teachers can address students' concerns about their uncertain futures by teaching skills that will be marketable in the adult world and by providing assistance with college applications. But perhaps most importantly, teachers must take steps to ensure that students don't become overly anxious about classroom tasks and subject matter.

Because anxiety (like all emotions) is largely beyond students' immediate control, simply telling them to "Relax" or "Calm down" is unlikely to be effective. The key here is to prevent rather than "cure" debilitating anxiety. Following are several strategies that should keep students' anxiety at a facilitative level:[225]

- Communicate clear, concrete, and realistic expectations for performance.
- Match instruction to students' cognitive levels and capabilities (e.g., use concrete materials to teach mathematics to students not yet capable of abstract thought).

emotion self-regulation Process of keeping one's affective states and affect-related behaviors within productive, culturally desirable limits.

[220] Brophy, 2004; Brophy et al., 2009; Pekrun, 2006.
[221] Brophy, 2004.
[222] Labouvie-Vief & González, 2004; Wisner Fries & Pollak, 2007.
[223] J. E. Bower, Moskowitz, & Epel, 2009; N. C. Hall, Goetz, Haynes, Stupnisky, & Chipperfield, 2006; Pekrun, 2006; C. Peterson, 2006; Richards, 2004.

[224] This phenomenon is known as *secondary control;* see Rothbaum, Weisz, & Snyder, 1982.
[225] Brophy, 1986; Hattie & Timperley, 2007; Pekrun, 2006; Shute, 2008; Stipek, 1993; Zeidner, 1998.

- Provide supplementary sources of support for learning challenging topics and skills until mastery is attained (e.g., additional practice, individual tutoring, a structure for taking notes).
- Teach strategies (e.g., effective study skills) that enhance learning and performance.
- Assess students' performance independently of how well their classmates are doing, and encourage students to assess their own performance in a similar manner.
- Provide feedback about specific behaviors, rather than global evaluations of classroom performance.
- Allow students to correct errors, so that no single mistake is ever a "fatal" one.

As students make the transition to middle school or high school, make an extra effort to minimize their anxiety and address their need for relatedness.

Elementary school classrooms are often very warm, nurturing ones in which teachers get to know 20 or 30 students very well. Students in elementary classrooms also get to know *one another* quite well: They often work together on academic tasks and may even see themselves as members of a classroom "family." But somewhere around fifth to seventh grade, many students move from elementary school to a middle school or junior high school. As they do so, they simultaneously encounter several changes in the nature of their schooling:[226]

- The school is larger and has more students.
- Students have several teachers at a time, and each teacher has many students. As a result, teacher–student relationships tend to be more superficial and less personal than in elementary school, and teachers have less awareness of how well individual students are understanding and mastering classroom subject matter.
- There is more whole-class instruction, with less individualized instruction that takes into account each student's academic needs.
- Classes are less socially cohesive. Students may not know their classmates very well and may be reluctant to ask peers for assistance.
- Students have fewer opportunities to make choices about the topics they pursue and the tasks they complete. At the same time, they have more independence and responsibility regarding their learning. For example, they may have relatively unstructured assignments to be accomplished over a two- or three-week period, and they must take the initiative to seek help when they're struggling.
- Teachers place greater emphasis on demonstrating (rather than acquiring) competence. Thus mistakes are more costly for students. (This change reflects a shift from *mastery goals* to *performance goals*.)
- Standards for assigning grades are more rigorous, so students may earn lower grades than they did in elementary school. Grades are often assigned on a comparative and competitive basis, with only the highest-achieving students getting As and Bs.
- High-stakes tests (e.g., tests that affect promotion to the next grade level) become increasingly common.

Furthermore, previously formed friendships can be disrupted as students move to new (and perhaps differing) schools.[227] And, of course, students may find the physiological changes that accompany puberty and adolescence unsettling. This "multiple whammy" of changes often leads to decreased confidence, a lower sense of self-worth, less intrinsic motivation, and considerable anxiety. Focus on social relationships increases, academic achievement drops, and some students become emotionally disengaged from the school environment—a disengagement that may eventually result in dropping out of school.[228]

---

[226] H. A. Davis, 2003; Dijkstra et al., 2008; Eccles & Midgley, 1989; Hine & Fraser, 2002; Midgley et al., 2002; Wentzel & Wigfield, 1998; Wigfield et al., 2006.

[227] Pellegrini & Long, 2004; Wentzel, 1999.
[228] G. L. Cohen & Garcia, 2008; Eccles & Midgley, 1989; Gentry et al., 2002; Urdan & Maehr, 1995.

CLASSROOM STRATEGIES Easing the Transition to Middle and Secondary School

- **Provide a means through which every student can feel part of a small, close-knit group.**

  During the first week of school, a ninth-grade math teacher forms *base groups* of three or four students who provide support and assistance for one another throughout the school year. At the beginning or end of every class period, the teacher gives group members 5 minutes to help one another with questions and concerns about daily lessons and homework assignments.

- **Address students' personal and social needs as well as their academic needs.**

  Early in the school year, while his classes are working on a variety of cooperative learning activities, a middle school social studies teacher schedules individual appointments with each of his students. In these meetings he searches for interests that he and his students share and encourages the students to seek him out whenever they need help with academic or personal problems. Throughout the semester he continues to touch base with individual students (often during lunch or before or after school) to see how they're doing.

- **Teach students the skills they need to be successful independent learners.**

  After discovering that few of her students know how to take effective class notes, a high school science teacher distributes a daily "notes skeleton" that guides them through the note-taking process. The skeleton might include headings such as "Topic of the Lesson," "Definitions," "Important Ideas," and "Examples." As students' class notes improve over the course of the school year, the teacher gradually reduces the amount of structure she provides.

- **Assign grades based on mastery (not on comparisons with peers), and provide reasonable opportunities for improvement.**

  A junior high school language arts teacher requires students to submit two drafts of every essay and short story he assigns; he gives students the option of submitting additional drafts as well. He judges the compositions on several criteria, including quality of ideas, organization and cohesiveness, word usage, grammar, and spelling. He explains and illustrates each of these criteria and gives ample feedback on every draft that students turn in.

If students remain in an elementary school in early adolescence, rather than moving to a middle school or junior high environment, their attitudes and motivation are more likely to remain positive.[229] By the time they reach ninth grade, however, they almost inevitably make the transition to a secondary school format, where they will experience many of the changes that their peers in other school districts experienced a few grades earlier.[230] Students in lower-income, inner-city school districts are especially at risk for making a rough transition from an elementary to a secondary school format.[231] As an example, recall Anna's rocky start at her large city high school in the opening case study in Chapter 1.

Students who make a smooth transition to secondary school are more likely to be academically successful and, as a result, more likely to graduate from high school.[232] The Classroom Strategies box "Easing the Transition to Middle and Secondary School" offers several strategies for teachers at the middle school and high school levels.

Up to this point, we've touched only briefly on those peer relationships that can make such a difference in students' successful transitions to middle schools and high schools. As we turn to personal and social development in the next chapter, we'll look at such relationships more closely. We'll also identify factors that help or hinder young people in their efforts to establish productive relationships with their age-mates.

---

[229] Midgley et al., 2002; Rudolph, Lambert, Clark, & Kurlakowsky, 2001.
[230] Benner & Graham, 2009; Hine & Fraser, 2002; Midgley et al., 2002; Otis et al., 2005; Tomback, Williams, & Wentzel, 2005.

[231] Ogbu, 2003; Roderick & Camburn, 1999.
[232] Otis et al., 2005; Roderick & Camburn, 1999; Wigfield et al., 1996.

SUMMARY

Motivation, affect, and learning always go hand in hand, with each playing a crucial role in the development of the others. We can get a big-picture view of the interplay among motivation, affect, and learning by returning to the Mega-Ideas presented at the beginning of the chapter.

● *Learners are more motivated to learn and perform at high levels when their basic psychological needs are being met.* All human beings appear to share certain fundamental needs. In addition to basic needs for food, water, oxygen, and other substances essential for life, people seem to have a need for *arousal*—a need for some degree of physical and cognitive stimulation. They also seem to have needs for *competence, self-worth,* and *self-determination*—needs to believe that they can deal effectively with their environment; are generally good, capable individuals; and can direct the course of life events to some degree. Finally, they have a basic need for *relatedness*—a need to feel socially connected to and gain the love and respect of other people.

● *Both intrinsic and extrinsic forms of motivation affect learners' behaviors and cognitive processes, but sometimes in different ways.* In general, highly motivated learners are goal-directed, pay attention to what they need to learn, process information meaningfully, and persist in the face of failure. The best-case scenario is for learners to be intrinsically motivated to learn and master classroom subject matter; that is, their motivation arises from personal characteristics or is inherent in the task being performed. However, when learners have little or no intrinsic motivation to acquire important knowledge and skills, extrinsic reinforcers can often get them on the road to academic success.

● *Learners' thoughts and beliefs both about themselves and about classroom subject matter can affect their motivation to learn in the classroom.* Motivation is not a "switch" that learners can turn on and off at will. Rather, it depends on several cognitive factors—including interests, self-efficacy, values, goals, and attributions—that typically emerge and evolve gradually over time. Among the most important of these is self-efficacy: Learners are apt to be motivated to perform particular tasks and activities only when they're confident that they can accomplish those tasks and activities successfully. But in addition, learners' motivation in the classroom depends on the extent to which assignments are a good match with their interests, values, and goals. Finally, learners must interpret events in productive ways—for instance, by attributing both their successes and their failures to things over which they have control (e.g., effort, learning strategies).

● *Learners' feelings and emotions—that is, their affect—influence and are influenced by both their motives and their cognitive processes.* Motivation and learning are closely intertwined with affect, including both the emotions that learners bring to the learning situation and the feelings that instructional materials elicit. On average, topics that evoke strong feelings (excitement, anger, etc.) tend to be more memorable than neutral topics. However, it's possible to have too much of a good thing. For instance, situations that arouse a lot of anxiety often interfere with effective information processing and memory.

● *Effective teachers create conditions that address students' basic psychological needs, help students think in ways that boost intrinsic and internalized motivation, and engender productive feelings about classroom topics.* Some effective classroom strategies address students' basic psychological needs. For example, high-interest, stimulating activities can satisfy students' need for arousal. Age-appropriate teacher guidance and support in particular content domains can enhance students' success rates in those domains, thereby bolstering students' domain-specific self-efficacy and more general sense of competence and self-worth. Opportunities for choice making and autonomy can promote students' sense of self-determination. And through frequent small-group and whole-class activities (cooperative learning projects, class debates, etc.), students can satisfy their need for relatedness.

Other effective classroom strategies encourage students to think about themselves and academic topics in motivation-enhancing ways. For example, by demonstrating the relevance of classroom subject matter to students' personal lives, teachers can help students internalize the importance of achieving academic success. By focusing students' attention on mastery goals—that is, on truly mastering a topic rather than simply attaining high test scores and grades—teachers increase the odds that students will engage in meaningful rather than rote learning. And by portraying students' successes and failures as being within students' power to control (e.g., through reasonable effort and use of good strategies), teachers can foster an optimistic, I-can-do-it attitude toward future learning activities.

Engendering productive emotions and minimizing counterproductive ones are important as well. Ideally, teachers should promote hot cognition—that is, they should help students engage emotionally as well as cognitively with classroom topics. Furthermore, teachers can help students keep excess anxiety in check by matching instruction to students' current ability levels, communicating clear expectations for students' performance, and giving students some wiggle room to make errors without penalty. And many students are likely to need teachers' assistance in regulating intense emotional reactions to unsettling circumstances and in making the often anxiety-arousing transitions to middle school and high school.

PRACTICE FOR YOUR LICENSURE EXAM

Praising Students' Writing

Mrs. Gaskill's second graders are just beginning to learn how to write the letters of the alphabet in cursive. Every day Mrs. Gaskill introduces a new cursive letter and shows her students how to write it correctly. She also shows them some common errors in writing the letter—for instance, claiming that she's going to make the "perfect f" and then making it much too short and crossing the lines in the wrong place—and the children delight in finding her mistakes. After the class explores each letter's shape, Mrs. Gaskill asks her students to practice it, first by writing it in the air using large arm movements and then by writing it numerous times on lined paper.

Meanwhile, Mrs. Gaskill has decided to compare the effects of two kinds of praise on the children's performance. She has placed a small colored sticker on each child's desk to indicate membership in one of two groups. When children in Group 1 write a letter with good form, she gives them a happy-face token, says "Great" or "Perfect!," and either smiles or gives them a pat on the back. When children in Group 2 write a letter with good form at least once, she gives them a happy-face token and says something like "You sure are working hard," "You can write beautifully in cursive," or "You're a natural at this." When children in either group fail to meet her standards for cursive writing, she gives them whatever corrective feedback they need.

Therefore, the only way in which Mrs. Gaskill treats the two groups differently is in what she says to them when they do well, either giving them fairly cryptic feedback (for Group 1) or telling them that they are trying hard or have high ability (for Group 2). Despite such a minor difference, Mrs. Gaskill finds that the children in Group 2 say they enjoy cursive writing more, and they use it more frequently in their spelling tests and other writing tasks. Curiously, too, the children in Group 1 often seem disappointed when they receive their seemingly positive feedback. For instance, on one occasion a girl who writes beautifully but has the misfortune of being in Group 1 asks, "Am *I* a natural at this?" Although the girl consistently gets a grade of "+" for her cursive writing, she never writes in cursive voluntarily throughout the three-week period in which Mrs. Gaskill conducts her experiment.[233]

1. Constructed-response question

Mrs. Gaskill praises all of her students for their performance, yet some kinds of praise seem to be more effective than others.

A. Identify two sources of evidence to support the claim that students who receive lengthy, specific feedback (Group 2) have more intrinsic motivation to write in cursive than students who receive brief, general feedback (Group 1).

B. Explain why the praise given to Group 2 might be more motivating than the praise given to Group 1. Base your explanation on contemporary principles and theories of motivation.

2. Multiple-choice question

Which one of the following teacher behaviors in the case is an example of an *attribution*?

a. Commenting that "You sure are working hard"
b. Awarding happy-face tokens for good writing
c. Giving students a pat on the back for good work
d. Amusing the students by intentionally writing the letter *f* incorrectly

Go to Chapter 6 of the Book-Specific Resources in MyEducationLab and click on "Practice for Your Licensure Exam" to answer these questions. Compare your responses with the feedback provided.

---

[233] Study described by Gaskill, 2001.

PEARSON
myeducationlab

Go to the Topic "Motivation and Affect" in the MyEducationLab (www.myeducationlab.com) for your course, where you can:

- Find learning outcomes for "Motivation and Affect," along with the national standards that connect to these outcomes.
- Complete Assignments and Activities that can help you more deeply understand the chapter content.
- Apply and practice your understanding of the core teaching skills identified in the chapter with the Building Teaching Skills and Dispositions learning units.
- Access video clips of CCSSO National Teachers of the Year award winners responding to the question, "Why Do I Teach?" in the Teacher Talk section.
- Check your comprehension of the content covered in the chapter by going to the Study Plan in the Book Resources for your text. Here you will be able to take a chapter quiz, receive feedback on your answers, and then access Review, Practice, and Enrichment activities to enhance your understanding of chapter content. Flash cards are also available to help you study definitions and key terms.
- Access additional Book Resources, including:
  - Focus Questions to guide your reading, Video Examples of various concepts and principles presented in the chapter, a Practice for Your Licensure Exam exercise that resembles the kinds of questions appearing on many teacher licensure tests, Margin Note Questions that help you connect chapter content to your past experiences or current beliefs, and Supplementary Readings that enable you to pursue certain topics in greater depth.

Chapter

7

Personal, Social, and Moral Development

Shutterstock

CHAPTER OUTLINE

Case Study: The School Play

Personality and Sense of Self

Peer Relationships

Social Cognition

Moral and Prosocial Development

Promoting Personal, Social, and Moral Development
    Fostering Personal Development
    Encouraging Effective Social Cognition and Interpersonal Skills
    Promoting Moral Reasoning and Prosocial Behavior

Summary

Practice for Your Licensure Exam: *The Scarlet Letter*

MEGA-IDEAS TO MASTER IN THIS CHAPTER

Children's personalities and sense of self influence their behaviors to some degree.

Children and adolescents gain many benefits from productive relationships with peers.

Children's interpretations of social situations have a significant impact on their ability to interact effectively with others.

Moral reasoning and prosocial behaviors emerge early in life but continue to evolve over the course of childhood and adolescence.

Effective teachers accommodate individual differences in students' temperaments and personalities, and they help students acquire productive behaviors and a healthy sense of self.

Effective teachers create conditions that foster students' social and moral development.

CASE STUDY   The School Play

Students in Jefferson Middle School's eighth-grade class are sharply divided into two groups, the "popular" ones and the "unpopular" ones. The popular students have little time or tolerance for low-status peers, and a few of them frequently pick on a small, friendless boy named Peter. By the middle of the school year, the class's interpersonal dynamics are so bad that the faculty considers canceling the annual eighth-grade musical.

Music teacher Mr. Hughes suggests that "the show must go on" but perhaps not in the usual way. Rather than holding tryouts and selecting only a handful of students as cast members, he proposes that the school have the entire eighth-grade class participate in some way, either in the cast or in scenery construction, costume design, or lighting. "Maybe a group project will pull the class together," he explains. Other teachers are skeptical but agree to support Mr. Hughes's project.

Throughout March and April, all 92 members of the eighth-grade class and many teachers work on a production of the musical *You're a Good Man, Charlie Brown*. The sheer ambitiousness of the project and the fact that the class's efforts will be on public display on opening night instill a cohesiveness and class spirit that the faculty hasn't seen before. Peter, playing the dog Snoopy, surprises everyone with his talent, and on opening night his classmates give him rave reviews: "Did you see Peter? He was amazing." "I had no idea he was so good." "He was totally cool."[1]

- Middle school students often divide themselves into different social groups, with some groups having higher social status than others. Why might social groups be so important for young adolescents?

- What benefits might the all-class school play have? Why does it pull the class together?

[1] Case described by M. Thompson & Grace, 2001, pp. 93–94.

For many students, early adolescence can be a time of considerable anxiety. Students must grapple not only with the bodily changes of puberty but also with disruptions of previous friendships, more superficial interactions with teachers, and higher expectations for academic performance. Self-worth often plummets, at least temporarily, and students are apt to look to their peers for emotional and moral support.[2] Being in a high-status, "popular" group can be a source of comfort, but students can have high status only if some of their

[2] D. A. Cole et al., 2001; Juvonen, 2006; Levitt, Guacci-Franco, & Levitt, 1993; Seiffge-Krenke, Aunola, & Nurmi, 2009.

peers have *low* status. With the all-class school play, everything changes. Suddenly the students have a common goal, and only by working cooperatively with *all* of their classmates can *any* of them look good.[3]

School isn't just a place where children and adolescents acquire thinking skills and master academic subject matter. It's also a place where they acquire beliefs about themselves and strategies for getting along with other people. In other words, school is a place where young people grow personally and socially as well as academically.

As we consider personal, social, and moral development in this chapter, we'll draw from all six of the theoretical perspectives of child and adolescent development identified in Table 5.1 in Chapter 5 (pp. 137–138). And we'll discover that with age and experience, young learners construct increasingly sophisticated beliefs about themselves, other people, and society as a whole. Thus children's and adolescents' personal, social, and moral understandings are, like their understandings of the physical world, very much *self-constructions*.

• Personality and Sense of Self

All of us have unique qualities that make us different from the people around us. Take a minute to reflect on the qualities that make *you* unique in the following exercise.

SEE FOR YOURSELF   Describing Yourself

> On a sheet of paper, list at least 10 adjectives or phrases that describe the kind of person you think you are.

How did you describe yourself? For instance, did you say that you are smart? friendly? funny? moody? uncoordinated? open-minded? Your answers to these questions tell you something about your **sense of self**, your perceptions, beliefs, judgments, and feelings about who you are as a person. If you were able to be relatively objective, your answers also tell you something about your **personality**, your distinctive ways of behaving, thinking, and feeling.

Learners' personalities and sense of self have a significant influence on their adjustment at school and elsewhere. For example, at a typical middle school, students who are outgoing and self-assured may quickly converge to form an "in-crowd," whereas those who are shy and lack self-confidence may keep to themselves or stick close to just one or two friends. Students who have a flair for the dramatic, like Peter in the opening case study, may delight in performing for an audience, whereas those who are more reserved and reticent may prefer to stay out of the spotlight.

The following principles describe the nature, origins, and effects of a learner's personality and sense of self.

Heredity and environment interact to shape personality.

A child's **temperament** is his or her general tendency to respond to and deal with environmental stimuli and events in particular ways. Children seem to have distinct temperaments almost from birth. For instance, some are quiet and subdued, whereas others are more active and energetic. Researchers have identified many temperamental styles that emerge early in life and are relatively enduring, including general activity level, adaptability, persistence, adventurousness, shyness, inhibitedness, irritability, and distractibility. Most psychologists agree that such temperamental differences have genetic, biological origins and often persist into adolescence and adulthood.[4]

---

sense of self Perceptions, beliefs, judgments, and feelings about oneself as a person.

personality Characteristic ways in which an individual behaves, thinks, and feels.

temperament Genetic predisposition to respond in particular ways to one's physical and social environments.

---

[3] M. Thompson & Grace, 2001.
[4] Bates & Pettit, 2007; Kagan, 2010; Kagan, Snidman, Kahn, & Towsley, 2007; M. Pfeifer, Goldsmith,

Davidson, & Rickman, 2002; Rothbart, 2007; A. Thomas & Chess, 1977.

Genetic differences in temperament are only *predispositions* to behave in certain ways, however, and environmental conditions may point different children with the same predisposition in somewhat different directions.[5] One influential environmental factor is the parenting style that mothers, fathers, and other primary caregivers use in raising children. In mainstream Western culture the ideal situation seems to be **authoritative parenting**, which combines affection and respect for children with reasonable restrictions on behavior. Authoritative parents provide a loving and supportive home, communicate high standards for performance, explain why certain behaviors are unacceptable, enforce household rules consistently, involve children in decision making, and provide age-appropriate opportunities for autonomy. Children from authoritative homes tend to be self-confident, energetic, socially skillful, and compassionate. They listen respectfully to others, can follow rules by the time they reach school age, are relatively independent and self-regulating, and strive for academic achievement.[6] For the most part, such characteristics are consistent with the values espoused by mainstream Western culture.

Annie Pickert/Pearson

Children's ability to work on sedentary tasks for extended periods depends partly on biologically built-in temperaments. By nature, some children tend to be quiet and attentive, whereas others are more energetic and distractible.

Authoritative parenting isn't universally "best," however. Certain other parenting styles may be better suited to particular cultures and environments. For instance, in **authoritarian parenting**, parents expect complete and immediate compliance; they neither negotiate expectations nor provide reasons for their requests. In many African American, Asian American, and Hispanic families, high demands for obedience are made within the context of close, supportive parent–child relationships. Underlying the "control" message is a more important message: "I love you and want you to do well, but it's equally important that you act for the good of the family and community."[7] Authoritarian parenting is also more common in impoverished economic environments. When families live in low-income, inner-city neighborhoods where danger potentially lurks around every corner, parents may better serve their children by being very strict and directive about activities.[8] In any case, keep in mind that parenting styles have, at most, only a *moderate* influence on children's personalities.[9] Many children and adolescents thrive despite their caregivers' diverse parenting styles, provided that the caregivers aren't severely neglectful or abusive.[10]

A child's cultural environment also influences personality development more directly by encouraging (i.e., *socializing*) certain kinds of behaviors.[11] For example, as noted in Chapter 6, cultures vary considerably in the extent to which they encourage children to show or hide their feelings. Cultures vary, too, in the extent to which they nurture shyness, outgoingness, and assertiveness, as we'll see in a Cultural Considerations box later in the chapter.

Nature and nurture interact in numerous ways to shape children's personalities.[12] For example, children who are temperamentally energetic and adventuresome are likely to seek out a wider variety of experiences than those who are quiet and restrained (e.g., recall the discussion of *niche-picking* in Chapter 3). Children who are naturally vivacious and outgoing typically have more opportunities than shy children to learn social skills and establish rewarding interpersonal relationships. And when children have temperaments that clash with cultural norms or parental expectations, they're apt to evoke negative reactions in others and lead parents to use a more controlling, authoritarian parenting style.[13]

---

[5] Keogh, 2003; R. A. Thompson, 1998.

[6] Barber, Stolz, & Olsen, 2005; Baumrind, 1989, 1991; M. R. Gray & Steinberg, 1999; Stright, Gallagher, & Kelley, 2008; J. M. T. Walker & Hoover-Dempsey, 2006; Zhou et al., 2008.

[7] Bornstein & Lansford, 2010; X. Chen & Wang, 2010; Halgunseth, Ispa, & Rudy, 2006; McLoyd, 1998; Rothbaum & Trommsdorff, 2007.

[8] Hale-Benson, 1986; McLoyd, 1998.

[9] W. A. Collins, Maccoby, Steinberg, Hetherington, & Bornstein, 2000; Weiss & Schwarz, 1996.

[10] Belsky & Pluess, 2009; J. R. Harris, 1998; Scarr, 1992.

[11] Mendoza-Denton & Mischel, 2007; Mischel & Shoda, 1995.

[12] Bates & Pettit, 2007; N. A. Fox, Henderson, Rubin, Calkins, & Schmidt, 2001; Keogh, 2003.

[13] N. Eisenberg & Fabes, 1994; J. R. Harris, 1998; Maccoby, 2007; Scarr, 1993; Stice & Barrera, 1995.

authoritative parenting Parenting style characterized by emotional warmth, high standards for behavior, explanation and consistent enforcement of rules, inclusion of children in decision making, and reasonable opportunities for autonomy.

authoritarian parenting Parenting style characterized by rigid rules and expectations for behavior that children are asked to obey without question.

Despite their relatively stable personality traits, children often behave somewhat differently in different contexts.

As children grow older, the many interactions among their inherited temperaments and environmental circumstances lead to unique and fairly stable personality profiles. Research with both children and adults has yielded five general personality traits—known as the "Big Five" traits—that are relatively independent of one another.[14] You can remember them using the word *OCEAN*:

- *Openness:* The extent to which one is imaginative, curious about the world, and receptive to new experiences and ideas
- *Conscientiousness:* The extent to which one is careful, organized, self-disciplined, and likely to follow through on plans and commitments
- *Extraversion:* The extent to which one is socially outgoing and seeks excitement
- *Agreeableness:* The extent to which one is pleasant, kind, and cooperative in social situations
- *Neuroticism:* The extent to which one is prone to negative emotions (e.g., anxiety, anger, depression

A quick review from Chapter 2: What purpose does the word OCEAN serve here? (Compare your response to this question with the response presented in Chapter 7 of the Book-Specific Resources in MyEducationLab.)

Such traits lead to some consistency—but not *total* consistency—in children's behaviors across situations.[15] Variability is especially common when children move from one environment to a very different one. For instance, a student might be quite outgoing and sociable with his close friends but shy and withdrawn with people he doesn't know very well. And a student is more likely to be conscientious about completing schoolwork if her teacher helps her understand that academic ability improves with effort and practice (an *incremental* view of intelligence) and gives her guidance about how to organize her assignments in a "to-do" list.[16]

As children grow older, they construct increasingly multifaceted understandings of who they are as people.

Some psychologists distinguish between two aspects of people's sense of self. One aspect is *self-concept,* which includes general assessments of one's own characteristics, strengths, and weaknesses (e.g., "I'm a high-achieving student," "My nose is a bit crooked"). The other aspect is *self-esteem,* which includes judgments and feelings about one's own value and worth (e.g., "I am *proud* of my academic record," "I *hate* my crooked nose!"). We've encountered related ideas before, albeit under different names. In Chapter 6 we noted that human beings seem to have a basic need to feel competent and worthy (recall our discussion of *self-worth).* We also noted that people realize they are more likely to be successful in—that is, they have higher *self-efficacy* for—some activities than others.

So how are these four terms—self-concept, self-esteem, self-worth, and self-efficacy—different from one another? In general, *self-concept* addresses the question "*Who* am I?" The terms *self-esteem* and *self-worth* both address the question "*How good* am I as a person?" I urge you not to agonize over subtle distinctions among these three terms, because their meanings overlap considerably, and thus they're often used interchangeably.[17]

In contrast to the other three terms, *self-efficacy* addresses the question "*How well can I do* such-and-such?" In other words, it refers to people's beliefs about their competence, not in general, but in a specific domain or activity. To some extent, however, people's specific self-efficacies for various tasks and activities contribute to their more general sense of self.[18]

In their overall self-assessments, children in the early elementary grades tend to make distinctions between two general domains: how competent they are at day-to-day tasks and how well they are liked by family and friends. As they grow older, children make finer and finer distinctions. In the upper elementary grades, they realize that they may be more or less

---

[14] Caspi, 1998; G. Matthews, Zeidner, & Roberts, 2006; Saarni, Campos, Camras, & Witherington, 2006.

[15] Hampson, 2008; Mendoza-Denton & Mischel, 2007.

[16] Belfiore & Hornyak, 1998; Dweck, 2008.

[17] Byrne, 2002; Harter, 1999; McInerney, Marsh, & Craven, 2008; O'Mara, Marsh, Craven, & Debus, 2006.

[18] Bong & Skaalvik, 2003; Schunk & Pajares, 2004.

competent or "good" in various academic domains and in athletic activities, classroom behavior, acceptance by peers, and physical attractiveness. By adolescence, they also make general self-assessments about their ability to make friends, their competence at adultlike work tasks, and their romantic appeal.[19] Each of these domains may have a greater or lesser influence on learners' overall sense of self. For some, academic achievement may be the overriding factor, whereas for others physical attractiveness or popularity with peers may be more important.[20]

With age, self-perceptions become more realistic, abstract, and stable.

In the preschool and early elementary school years, children tend to think of themselves in terms of concrete, easily observable characteristics and behaviors.[21] For example, notice the many concrete characteristics in my son Alex's self-description at age 9:

> I have brown hair, brown eyes. I like wearing short-sleeved shirts. My hair is curly. I was adopted. I was born in Denver. I like all sorts of critters. The major sport I like is baseball. I do fairly well in school. I have a lizard, and I'm going to get a second one.

Like Alex, most young children have a generally positive sense of self.[22] Often they believe they're more capable than they really *are* and that they can easily overcome initial failures. Such optimism is probably due to their tendency to base self-assessments on their continuing improvement in "big boy" and "big girl" tasks. But as children have more opportunities to compare themselves with peers during the elementary school years—and also become cognitively more able to *make* such comparisons—their self-assessments become increasingly realistic.[23] Children gradually pull together their many self-observations into generalizations about the kinds of people they are (e.g., "friendly," "good at sports," "smart," "dumb"), and, for good or for bad, such generalizations lead to increasingly stable self-concepts.[24]

As children reach adolescence and gain greater capability for abstract thought, they're even more likely to think of themselves in terms of general, fairly stable traits. Consider my daughter Tina's self-description when she was in sixth grade:

> I'm cool. I'm awesome. I'm way cool. I'm 12. I'm boy crazy. I go to Brentwood Middle School. I'm popular with my fans. I play viola. My best friend is Lindsay. I have a gerbil named Taj. I'm adopted. I'm beautiful.

Although Tina listed several concrete features about herself (her school, her best friend, her gerbil), she had clearly developed a fairly abstract self-perception. Tina's focus on coolness, popularity, and beauty, rather than on intelligence or academic achievement (or, I might add, modesty), is fairly typical: Social acceptance and physical appearance are far more important to most young adolescents than academic competence.[25] In girls especially, dissatisfaction with one's physical appearance can have a significant negative impact on self-esteem and occasionally leads to bouts of depression.[26]

Older adolescents increasingly reflect on their characteristics and abilities and begin to struggle with seeming inconsistencies in their self-perceptions, perhaps wondering, "Who is the *real* me?" Eventually (perhaps around eleventh grade), they integrate their various self-perceptions into a complex, multifaceted self-concept that reconciles apparent contradictions. For instance, they may realize that diverse emotions mean they're "moody" and that their inconsistent behaviors on different occasions mean they're "flexible."[27]

Tina drew this self-portrait in second grade. For children and adolescents alike, self-perceived physical attractiveness often plays a significant role in their overall sense of self. Tina, whose genetic heritage is Hispanic and Native American, is well aware that her skin tone and hair color are darker than those of many of her classmates, some of whom she has drawn in the background.

As children get older, they increasingly include abstract qualities in their self-descriptions. In this self-description, 12-year-old Melinda identifies several abstract characteristics: musical, lovable, imaginative, noble, and animal-lover.

[19] Davis-Kean & Sandler, 2001; Harter, 1999; Marsh, Ellis, & Craven, 2002.

[20] Crocker & Knight, 2005; D. Hart, 1988; Harter, 1999.

[21] D. Hart, 1988; Harter, 1983.

[22] Harter, 1999; Lockhart, Chang, & Story, 2002; Paris & Cunningham, 1996; Robins & Trzesniewski, 2005.

[23] R. Butler, 2008; J. W. Chapman, Tunmer, & Prochnow, 2000; Davis-Kean et al., 2008; Harter, 1999.

[24] D. A. Cole et al., 2001; Harter, 1999.

[25] D. Hart, 1988; Harter, 1999.

[26] C. G. Campbell, Parker, & Kollat, 2007; Stice, 2003; E. J. Wright, 2007.

[27] Harter, 1999.

One early theorist, Erik Erikson, suggested that identity formation is a major preoccupation for adolescents. Learn more about Erikson's theory of psychosocial development in a supplementary reading in Chapter 7 of the Book-Specific Resources in MyEducationLab.

? Which of these four terms best describes your current status in your identity development?

As older adolescents pull their numerous self-perceptions together, many begin to form a general sense of **identity**: a self-constructed definition of who they are, what things they find important, and what goals they want to accomplish in life.[28] One researcher has observed four distinct patterns that characterize the status of different adolescents in the search for identity:[29]

- **Identity diffusion.** The adolescent has made no commitment to a particular career path or ideological belief system. Some haphazard experimentation with particular roles or beliefs may have taken place, but the individual hasn't yet embarked on a serious exploration of issues related to self-definition.
- **Foreclosure.** The adolescent has made a firm commitment to an occupation, a particular set of beliefs, or both. The choices have been based largely on what others (especially parents) have prescribed, without an earnest exploration of other possibilities.
- **Moratorium.** The adolescent has no strong commitment to a particular career or set of beliefs but is actively exploring and considering a variety of professions and ideologies. In essence, the individual is undergoing an identity crisis.
- **Identity achievement.** After going through a period of moratorium, the adolescent has emerged with a commitment to particular political or religious beliefs, a clear choice of occupation, or both.

For many adolescents, the ideal situation seems to be to proceed through a period of moratorium—an exploration that may continue into early adulthood—before finally settling on a clear identity.[30] Foreclosure—identity choice *without* prior exploration—rules out potentially more productive alternatives, and identity diffusion leaves young people without a clear sense of direction in life.

Even by the end of high school, however, only a small minority of teenagers in Western societies have pinned down their life-long goals and the eventual roles they'll play in the adult world.[31] In the meantime, they may sometimes take on temporary identities, aligning themselves strongly with a particular peer group, adhering rigidly to a single brand of clothing, or insisting on a certain hairstyle. Most young people need considerable time to explore various options related to careers, political beliefs, religious affiliations, and so on before they achieve a true sense of their adult identity.

As children reach puberty, they understand that they are unique individuals, but they sometimes go overboard in this respect.

Young teenagers often believe themselves to be unlike anyone else—a phenomenon known as the **personal fable**.[32] They may think their own feelings are completely unique—those around them have never experienced such emotions—and so no one else, least of all parents and teachers, can possibly know how they feel. Furthermore, some have a sense of invulnerability and immortality, believing themselves immune to the normal dangers of life. Thus they may take foolish risks, such as experimenting with drugs and alcohol, having unprotected sexual intercourse, or driving at high speeds. If admonished that they could overdose, create an unwanted pregnancy, or be in a serious automobile accident, they might think, "It won't happen to me."[33]

It's important to note, however, that adolescents are apt to take risks even when they *don't* believe themselves to be invulnerable.[34] Several other factors also predispose young people to make foolish choices. Thanks, in part, to brains that haven't yet fully matured, adolescents often have trouble planning ahead and controlling their impulses (see Chapter 5). In addition, they tend to make choices based on their emotions ("This will be a lot of fun")

---

identity Self-constructed definition of who one thinks one is and what things are important to accomplish in life.

personal fable Belief that one is completely unlike anyone else and so cannot be understood by others.

[28] Erikson, 1963, 1972; Wigfield, Eccles, & Pintrich, 1996.

[29] Marcia, 1980, 1991; also see Berzonsky & Kuk, 2000; Seaton, Scottham, & Sellers, 2006.

[30] Berzonsky, 1988; Marcia, 1988; Seaton et al., 2006.

[31] Archer, 1982; Kaplan & Flum, 2009; Marcia, 1980, 1988; Seaton et al., 2006.

[32] Elkind, 1981; Lapsley, 1993.

[33] Arnett, 1995; DeRidder, 1993; Jacobs & Klaczynski, 2002; B. Mills, Reyna, & Estrada, 2008; Nell, 2002.

[34] V. F. Reyna & Farley, 2006; Steinberg, 2007; Steinberg, Cauffman, Woolard, Graham, & Banich, 2009.

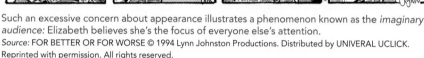

rather than on logic ("There's a high probability of a bad outcome").[35] Thus, adolescent risk taking is most common in social contexts, where having fun is typically a high priority and it's easy to get swept away by what peers are doing or suggesting.

The personal fable and risk-taking behaviors both decline in the later adolescent years, but they don't entirely disappear.[36] Hence they are—and must be—a source of concern to parents and teachers of older adolescents as well as younger ones.

Learners' self-perceptions influence their behaviors, and vice versa.

Learners tend to behave in ways that mirror their beliefs about themselves. In general, students who have positive self-perceptions are more likely to succeed academically, socially, and physically.[37] For instance, if they see themselves as good students, they're more apt to pay attention in class, follow directions, persist at difficult problems, and enroll in challenging courses. If they see themselves as friendly and socially desirable, they're more likely to seek the company of their classmates and perhaps run for student council. If they see themselves as physically competent, they'll more eagerly pursue extracurricular athletics.

If learners assess themselves fairly accurately, they're in a good position to choose age-appropriate activities and work toward realistic goals.[38] A slightly inflated self-assessment can be beneficial as well, because it may give learners the self-confidence they need to take on new challenges.[39] However, self-concepts that are *too* inflated may give some learners an unwarranted sense of superiority over classmates and lead them to bully or in other ways act aggressively toward peers.[40] And as you might guess, significant *under*estimates lead learners to avoid the many challenges that are apt to enhance their cognitive, social, and physical growth.[41]

When learners with realistically positive self-perceptions regularly experience success, their successes serve to maintain or enhance those positive self-perceptions. But an interplay between self-perceptions and behavior exists for less flattering self-perceptions as well, creating a vicious cycle: A poor sense of self leads to less productive behavior, which leads to fewer successes, which perpetuates the poor sense of self.[42]

Other people's behaviors affect learners' sense of self.

Not only do learners' past successes and failures influence their sense of self but so, too, do *other people* influence it, and in at least two ways. First, as learners get older—and especially as they reach adolescence—how they evaluate themselves depends partly on how their own performance compares to that of their peers.[43] Those who see themselves achieving at higher levels than others are apt to develop a more positive sense of self than those who consistently find themselves falling short.

Second, learners' self-perceptions are affected by how others behave *toward* them, which indirectly sends messages about strengths and weaknesses.[44] For example, adults influence children's sense of self by holding high or low expectations for academic performance and by drawing attention to the various things that children do well or poorly. Meanwhile, peers communicate information about children's social and athletic competence, perhaps by seek-

---

[35] Cleveland, Gibbons, Gerrard, Pomery, & Brody, 2005; V. F. Reyna & Farley, 2006; Steinberg, 2007.

[36] Frankenberger, 2000; Nell, 2002; V. F. Reyna & Farley, 2006.

[37] M. S. Caldwell, Rudolph, Troop-Gordon, & Kim, 2004; Marsh & Craven, 2006; Marsh, Gerlach, Trautwein, Lüdtke, & Brettschneider, 2007; Valentine, DuBois, & Cooper, 2004.

[38] R. F. Baumeister, Campbell, Krueger, & Vohs, 2003; Harter, 1999.

[39] Assor & Connell, 1992; Lockhart et al., 2002; Pajares, 2005.

[40] R. F. Baumeister et al., 2003; Menon et al., 2007; Thomaes, Bushman, Stegge, & Olthof, 2008.

[41] Assor & Connell, 1992; Marsh & O'Mara, 2008; D. Phillips & Zimmerman, 1990; Schunk & Pajares, 2004; Thomaes, Reijntjes, Orobio de Castro, & Bushman, 2009.

[42] M. S. Caldwell et al., 2004; Guay, Marsh, & Boivin, 2003; Ma & Kishor, 1997; Marsh & Craven, 2006; Thomaes et al., 2009; Valentine, Cooper, Bettencourt, & DuBois, 2002.

[43] Dijkstra, Kuyper, van der Werf, Buunk, & van der Zee, 2008; Seaton, Marsh, & Craven, 2009; Trautwein, Gerlach, & Lüdtke, 2008.

[44] Bukowski, Brendgen, & Vitaro, 2007; M. S. Caldwell et al., 2004; Dweck, 2000; M. J. Harris & Rosenthal, 1985; Harter, 1996; Rudolph, Caldwell, & Conley, 2005; Schunk & Pajares, 2005.

For Better or For Worse®   **by Lynn Johnston**

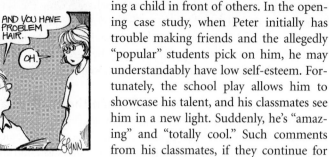

Such an excessive concern about appearance illustrates a phenomenon known as the *imaginary audience*: Elizabeth believes she's the focus of everyone else's attention.
Source: FOR BETTER OR FOR WORSE © 1994 Lynn Johnston Productions. Distributed by UNIVERAL UCLICK. Reprinted with permission. All rights reserved.

ing out a child's companionship or ridiculing a child in front of others. In the opening case study, when Peter initially has trouble making friends and the allegedly "popular" students pick on him, he may understandably have low self-esteem. Fortunately, the school play allows him to showcase his talent, and his classmates see him in a new light. Suddenly, he's "amazing" and "totally cool." Such comments from his classmates, if they continue for any length of time, should undoubtedly boost his sense of self.

In early adolescence youngsters seem to have a heightened concern about what others think of them. In fact, they may believe that in any social situation, everyone else's attention is focused squarely on them—a phenomenon known as the **imaginary audience**.[45] Because they believe themselves to be the center of attention, young teenagers (girls especially) are often preoccupied with their physical appearance and can be quite self-critical. Concerned about how others may evaluate them and wanting desperately to fit in, they can be very conforming, rigidly imitating peers' choices in dress, music, slang, and behavior.[46]

Table 7.1 summarizes developmental trends in children's and adolescents' sense of self. It also offers ideas for how teachers can enhance students' sense of self at different grade levels.

Group memberships also affect learners' sense of self.

Membership in one or more groups (e.g., being in a "popular" group, as some students in the opening case study are) can impact learners' sense of self as well.[47] If you think back to your own school years, perhaps you can recall taking pride in something your entire class accomplished, feeling good about a community service project completed through an extracurricular club, or reveling in the state championship earned by one of your school's athletic teams. In general, learners are more likely to have high self-esteem if they're members of a successful group.[48]

School groups are not the only important ones in learners' lives, however. For instance, in racially and culturally diverse communities—where different skin colors, languages, customs, and so on are obvious—children's membership in a particular racial or ethnic group may be a significant aspect of their sense of self. We'll look at the importance of this *ethnic identity* more closely in a Cultural Considerations box later in the chapter.

Gender plays a significant role in most learners' sense of self.

As young children become increasingly aware of the typical characteristics and behaviors of boys, girls, men, and women, they begin to pull their knowledge together into self-constructed understandings, or **gender schemas**, of "what males are like" and "what females are like." These gender schemas, in turn, become part of their sense of self and provide guidance for how they should behave—how to dress, what toys to play with, what interests and academic subject areas to pursue, and so on.[49]

Because gender schemas are self-constructed, their contents are apt to vary considerably from one individual to another.[50] For example, in adolescence, some girls incorporate into their "female" schema the unrealistic standards for beauty presented in popular media

---

imaginary audience Belief that one is the center of attention in any social situation.

gender schema Self-constructed, organized body of beliefs about the traits and behaviors of males or females.

[45] Elkind, 1981; Lapsley, 1993; R. M. Ryan & Kuczkowski, 1994.
[46] Hartup, 1983; Owens, 1996.
[47] Brewer & Yuki, 2007; B. B. Brown, Herman, Hamm, & Heck, 2008; Eccles, 2009; Wigfield, Byrnes, & Eccles, 2006.

[48] Harter, 1999; Phinney, 1989; Wigfield et al., 1996.
[49] Bem, 1981; Eccles, 2009; Leaper & Friedman, 2007; Ruble, Martin, & Berenbaum, 2006.
[50] Crouter, Whiteman, McHale, & Osgood, 2007; Liben & Bigler, 2002.

TABLE 7.1 Sense of Self at Different Grade Levels

Grade Level	Age-Typical Characteristics	Example	Suggested Strategies
K–2	• Self-descriptions largely limited to concrete, easily observable characteristics • Some tendency to overestimate abilities and chances of future success, especially in domains in which one has little or no prior experience	When 6-year-old Jeff is asked to describe himself, he says, "I like animals. I like making things. I do good in school. I'm happy. Blue eyes, yellow hair, light skin." He mentions nothing about his shyness, sense of humor, and ability to work and play independently—characteristics that would require considerable self-reflection and abstract thought to identify.	• Encourage students to stretch their abilities by tackling the challenging tasks they think they can accomplish. • Provide sufficient scaffolding to make success possible in various domains. • Praise students for the things they do well; be specific about the behaviors you're praising.
3–5	• Increasing awareness of, and differentiation among, particular strengths and weaknesses • Association of such emotions as pride and shame with various self-perceptions	When Kellen begins fifth grade at his neighborhood middle school, his class work rapidly deteriorates, despite individualized instruction in reading and spelling. At home he becomes increasingly irritable and soon stops doing his homework. One day his mother finds him curled in a ball under his desk, crying and saying, "I can't do this anymore!" Alarmed, she takes him to a series of specialists, who diagnose severe dyslexia. Kellen's parents eventually find a school that provides considerable structure and scaffolding for students with learning disabilities. There Kellen shows dramatic improvement in virtually every area of the curriculum, and his self-esteem skyrockets.	• Focus students' attention on their improvement over time. • Encourage pride in individual and group achievements, but be aware that students from some ethnic groups may prefer that recognition be given only for group achievements. • Provide opportunities for students to look at one another's work only when *everyone* has something to be proud of.
6–8	• Increasingly abstract conceptions of oneself • For many, a decline in self-esteem after the transition to middle or junior high school (especially for girls) • Excessive belief in one's own uniqueness (personal fable); may contribute to increase in risk-taking behaviors • Heightened concern about others' perceptions and judgments of oneself (imaginary audience)	Meghan, an eighth grader, describes a recent event in her algebra class: "I had to cough but I knew if I did everyone would stare at me and think I was stupid, hacking away. So I held my breath until I turned red and tears ran down my face and finally I coughed anyway and everyone *really* noticed then. It was horrible."	• After students make the transition to middle school or junior high, be especially supportive and optimistic about their abilities and potential for success. • Provide safe outlets for risk-taking behavior; show no tolerance for potentially dangerous behaviors on school grounds. • Be patient when students show exceptional self-consciousness; give them strategies for presenting themselves well to others.
9–12	• Search for the "real me" and an adult identity; some experimentation with a variety of possible identities • Increasing integration of diverse self-perceptions into an overall, multifaceted sense of self • Gradual increase in self-esteem • Continuing risk-taking behavior (especially for boys)	Sixteen-year-old Kayla often revises her profile on Facebook, editing her interests and favorites, the "About Me" section, and so on. And she regularly changes the photo that appears at the top of her profile. Sometimes she displays a happy Kayla, at other times a more sullen one; one photo shows her in her basketball uniform but another shows her in a skimpy party dress.	• Give students opportunities to examine and try out a variety of adultlike roles. • When discussing the potential consequences of risky behaviors, present the facts but don't make students so anxious or upset that they can't effectively learn and remember the information (e.g., avoid scare tactics). • Encourage students to explore and take pride in their cultural and ethnic heritages.

Sources: R. Butler, 2008; Davis-Kean et al., 2008; Dweck, 2000; Elkind, 1981; Greenhow, Robelia, & Hughes, 2009; Harter, 1999; Lockhart et al., 2002; Marcia, 1980, 1991; T. M. McDevitt & Ormrod, 2007 (Kellen example); Nell, 2002; Nuemi, 2008; O'Mara, Marsh, Craven, & Debus, 2006; Orenstein, 1994, p. 47 (Meghan example); Robins & Trzesniewski, 2005; Seaton, Scottham, & Sellers, 2006; Spear, 2007; Tatum, 1997; Whitesell, Mitchell, Kaufman, Spicer, & the Voices of Indian Teens Project Team, 2006.

Young adolescent girls are often preoccupied with thinness, fashion, and overall physical appearance, as this drawing by 11-year-old Marci illustrates.

(films, fashion magazines, etc.). As they compare themselves to these standards, they almost invariably come up short, their self-assessments of their physical attractiveness decline, and some fall victim to eating disorders in an effort to achieve the super-thin bodies they believe to be ideal.[51] Meanwhile, some teenage boys go out of their way to meet self-constructed "macho" standards for male behavior by putting on a tough-guy act at school and bragging (perhaps accurately, but more often not) about their many sexual conquests.[52] Fortunately, many adolescents' gender schemas become more flexible in the high school years, allowing greater freedom in behavior choices.[53]

Some researchers have found gender differences in overall self-esteem—especially in adolescence—with boys rating themselves more favorably than girls. This gender difference appears to be partly due to boys' tendency to *over*estimate their abilities and possibly also to girls' tendency to *under*estimate theirs.[54] Most adolescent boys' and girls' self-perceptions tend to be consistent with stereotypes about what males and females are "good at." Even when actual ability levels are the same—and for academic topics, ability levels *are* usually quite similar—on average boys rate themselves more highly in mathematics, whereas girls rate themselves more highly in reading and literature. On average, too, adolescent boys rate their athletic ability and physical appearance more positively than girls do.[55]

Despite the influence of others, learners define and socialize *themselves* to a considerable degree.

Young people get many messages—sometimes consistent, sometimes not—from parents, teachers, peers, and others about who they are, what they should think, and how they should behave. But rarely do they passively adopt others' ideas and opinions as their own.[56] Instead, they evaluate the information they get, choose some role models over others, weigh the pros and cons of "going along with the crowd," and gradually develop their own views about what their strengths and weaknesses are and which behaviors are and are not appropriate for themselves. Before long, much of the pressure to behave in particular ways comes from within rather than from outside (recall our discussion of self-regulation in Chapter 4). For example, when teachers actively encourage children to engage in non-gender-stereotypical activities (boys playing with dolls, girls playing with toy cars, etc.), the children may do so for a short time, but they soon revert to their earlier, more gender-typical ways.[57] This tendency for children and adolescents to conform to their own ideas about what behaviors are appropriate for themselves is known as **self-socialization**.[58]

The decisions that youngsters make about which individuals and sources of information to take seriously depend on their developmental levels and life experiences.[59] Parents are dominating forces in the lives of most children in the primary grades, and most parents continue to be influential with respect to core beliefs and values throughout their children's middle school and secondary school years. Nevertheless, growing children increasingly look to their peers for ideas about how to behave—what music to listen to, how to spend leisure time, and so on. We turn to the nature of peer relationships now.

self-socialization Tendency to integrate personal observations and others' input into self-constructed standards for behavior and to choose actions consistent with those standards.

[51] Attie, Brooks-Gunn, & Petersen, 1990; Stice, 2003; Weichold, Silbereisen, & Schmitt-Rodermund, 2003.
[52] Pollack, 2006; K. M. Williams, 2001a.
[53] Eccles, 2009; M. Rhodes & Gelman, 2008.
[54] Bornholt, Goodnow, & Cooney, 1994; D. A. Cole, Martin, Peeke, Seroczynski, & Fier, 1999; Harter, 1999; Pajares, 2005; Pajares & Valiante, 1999.
[55] D. A. Cole et al., 2001; Hattie, 2009; Herbert & Stipek, 2005; Hyde & Durik, 2005; Hyde, Lindberg,

Linn, Ellis, & Williams, 2008; Köller, Zeinz, & Trautwein, 2008; Stice, 2003; Wigfield et al., 2006.
[56] Markus & Hamedani, 2007; Nuemi, 2008.
[57] Lippa, 2002.
[58] B. B. Brown, 1990; Durkin, 1995; Leaper & Friedman, 2007; M. Lewis, 1991.
[59] Cauce, Mason, Gonzales, Hiraga, & Liu, 1994; Furman & Buhrmester, 1992; Neubauer, Mansel, Avrahami, & Nathan, 1994.

• Peer Relationships

School is very much a social place. Students interact regularly with one another, and most of them actively seek out friendly relationships with classmates. In fact, for many students, interacting with and gaining the acceptance of peers are more important than classroom learning and achievement.[60] Several principles describe the nature and effects of peer relationships in childhood and adolescence.

Peer relationships promote personal and social development in ways that adult–child relationships often cannot.

Peer relationships, especially friendships, serve several important functions in children's and adolescents' personal and social development. For one thing, they provide an arena for learning and practicing a variety of social skills, including cooperation, negotiation, emotion self-regulation, and conflict resolution.[61] In addition, peers—especially good friends—can provide companionship, safety, and emotional support: They become a group with whom to eat lunch, a safe haven from playground bullies, and shoulders to cry on in times of confusion or trouble.[62] (In the opening case study, Peter, who is initially picked on by other students, has no friends to come to his defense.) Although some children and adolescents adjust quite successfully on their own, as a general rule those who have the acceptance and support of peers have higher self-esteem, fewer emotional problems, and higher school achievement.[63]

Many adolescents (especially girls) reveal their innermost thoughts and feelings to their friends.[64] Friends often understand a teenager's perspective—the preoccupation with physical appearance, the concerns about the opposite sex, and so on—when no one else seems to. By sharing their thoughts and feelings with one another, teens may discover that they aren't as unique as they once thought. Accordingly, the personal fable I mentioned earlier gradually fades from the scene.[65]

Peers help define "appropriate" ways of behaving.

Not only do peers provide social and emotional support, but they can also be powerful socialization agents who encourage what are, at least in their own minds, appropriate ways of behaving.[66] Peers define options for leisure time, perhaps getting together in a study group or smoking cigarettes on the corner. They offer new ideas and perspectives, perhaps demonstrating how to do an "Ollie" on a skateboard or presenting arguments for becoming a vegetarian. They serve as role models and provide standards for acceptable behavior, showing what's possible, what's admirable, what's cool. They reinforce one another for acting in ways deemed appropriate for their age, gender, or ethnic group. And they sanction one another for stepping beyond acceptable bounds, perhaps through ridicule, gossip, or ostracism. Such **peer pressure** has its greatest effects during the junior high school years, and teenagers who have weak emotional bonds to their families seem to be especially vulnerable.[67]

Many peers encourage such desirable qualities as truthfulness, fairness, compassion, cooperation, and abstinence from drugs and alcohol.[68] Others, however, encourage aggression, criminal activity, and other dangerous and antisocial behaviors (recall our earlier discussion of adolescent risk taking).[69] Some peers encourage academic achievement, yet others convey the message that academic achievement is undesirable, perhaps by making

Observe 15-year-old Greg's preference for the social aspects of school (e.g., "lunch," "cliques") in the "Motivation: Late Adolescence" video in Chapter 7 of the Book-Specific Resources in MyEducationLab.

friends o ur for you when you are lonley and sad. they play with you, they are nice, they are mean, they tell stories And the things they Do. they walk you to the nurse.

In this writing sample, 7-year-old Andrew sees friends largely as companions and sources of entertainment (they're for "when you are lonely," "they play with you," "they tell stories"). Yet he also recognizes that friends can occasionally be a source of support ("they walk you to the nursce").

Observe developmental trends in the importance of friends in the three "Friendships" videos in Chapter 7 of the Book-Specific Resources in MyEducationLab. For 8-year-old Kate, having friends primarily means being nice, having companionship, and helping one another. But for 13-year-old Ryan and 17-year-old Paul, friends are also people they can trust, rely on, and confide in.

peer pressure Phenomenon whereby age-mates strongly encourage some behaviors and discourage others.

---

[60] B. B. Brown, 1993; Dowson & McInerney, 2001; W. Doyle, 1986a.

[61] Bukowski, Motzoi, & Meyer, 2009; Laursen, Bukowski, Aunola, & Nurmi, 2007; Pellegrini & Bohn, 2005.

[62] Bukowski et al., 2009; Doll, Song, & Siemers, 2004; Laursen et al., 2007; Wentzel, Barry, & Caldwell, 2004.

[63] Bukowski et al., 2009; A. J. Martin & Dowson, 2009; Wentzel, 2009.

[64] Levitt et al., 1993; A. J. Rose & Smith, 2009.

[65] Elkind, 1981.

[66] Rubin, Cheah, & Menzer, 2010; A. M. Ryan, 2000; Wentzel, 2009.

[67] Berndt, Laychak, & Park, 1990; Erwin, 1993; R. M. Ryan & Lynch, 1989; Urdan & Maehr, 1995.

[68] Berndt & Keefe, 1996; McCallum & Bracken, 1993; Wentzel & Looney, 2007.

[69] W. E. Ellis & Zarbatany, 2007; Espelage, Holt, & Henkel, 2003; Piehler & Dishion, 2007; J. Snyder et al., 2008.

fun of "brainy" students or by encouraging such behaviors as copying one another's home-work, cutting class, and skipping school.[70]

Although peer pressure certainly is a factor affecting development, its effect on chil-dren's behaviors has probably been overrated.[71] Most children and adolescents acquire a strong set of values and behavioral standards from their families, and they don't necessarily discard these values and standards in the company of peers.[72] Furthermore, they tend to choose friends who are similar to themselves in motives, styles of behavior, academic achievement, and leisure-time activities.[73] In some cases youngsters lead "double lives" that enable them to attain academic success while maintaining peer acceptance. For example, although they attend class and do their homework faithfully, they may feign disinterest in scholarly activities, disrupt class with jokes or goofy behaviors, and express surprise at receiving high grades.[74] In addition, they may act tough when they're in public, saving their softer sides for more private circumstances, as one sixth grader's explanation reveals:

> You'd still have to have your bad attitude. You have to act—it's just like a movie. You have to act. And then at home you're a regular kind of guy, you don't act mean or nothing. But when you're around your friends you have to be sharp and stuff like that, like push everybody around.[75]

Boys and girls interact with peers in distinctly different ways.

Most children and young adolescents affiliate primarily with peers of the same sex.[76] Boys' and girls' playgroups and friendships are different in key ways that affect their personal and social development. Boys tend to hang out in relatively large groups that engage in rough-and-tumble play, organized group games, and physical risk-taking activities.[77] They enjoy competition and can be fairly assertive in their efforts to achieve individual and group goals.[78] Especially as they get older, many prefer keeping some personal and emotional dis-tance between themselves and their friends—perhaps as a way of showing their "manli-ness"—and often try to hide their true emotions in social situations.[79]

Whereas boys tend to be competitive, girls are more affiliative and cooperative. Girls seem to be more attuned to others' mental states and exhibit greater sensitivity to the subtle, nonverbal messages—the body language—that others communicate.[80] They spend much of their leisure time with only a few close friends, with whom they may share their inner-most thoughts and feelings.[81] Although girls can certainly be assertive at times, they also tend to be concerned about maintaining group harmony, and so they may occasionally sub-ordinate their own wishes to those of others.[82] And they're more concerned about resolving interpersonal conflicts than boys are, as 17-year-old Paul explains:

Observe gender differences in interpersonal behaviors and conflict resolution strategies in the "Emotions: Late Adolescence" video and three "Friendships" videos in Chapter 7 of the Book-Specific Resources in MyEducationLab.

> Normally with, like, my guy friends, we just get over it. There's no working it out, you just sit . . . like, "Fine, whatever," you know? And we get over it. Girl friends, you gotta talk to them and work it out slowly. Apologize for doing whatever you did wrong. There's a whole process.

Social groups become increasingly important in adolescence.

Most children and adolescents regularly interact and enjoy being with peers besides their close friends. Over time, many form larger social groups that often get together. Initially, such groups are usually composed of a single sex, but in adolescence they often include both boys and girls.[83]

---

[70] X. Chen, Chang, Liu, & He, 2008; M. H. Jones, Estell, & Alexander, 2008; Kindermann, 2007; A. M. Ryan, 2001; Véronneau, Vitaro, Pederson, & Tremblay, 2008.

[71] Berndt & Keefe, 1996.

[72] B. B. Brown, 1990; W. A. Collins et al., 2000; Galambos, Barker, & Almeida, 2003.

[73] Card & Ramos, 2005; W. A. Collins et al., 2000; Kindermann, McCollam, & Gibson, 1996; A. M. Ryan, 2001.

[74] B. B. Brown, 1993; Covington, 1992; Hemmings, 2004; Juvonen, 2006.

[75] Juvonen & Cadigan, 2002, p. 282.

[76] Best, 2010; A. J. Rose & Smith, 2009.

[77] Best, 2010; Maccoby, 2002; Pellegrini, Kato, Blatchford, & Baines, 2002.

[78] Benenson et al., 2002; Jonkmann, Trautwein, & Lüdtke, 2009; Leaper & Friedman, 2007; Maccoby, 2002.

[79] Best, 2010; N. Eisenberg, Martin, & Fabes, 1996; Lippa, 2002; K. M. Williams, 2001a.

[80] Bosacki, 2000; Deaux, 1984.

[81] Block, 1983; N. Eisenberg et al., 1996; A. J. Rose, 2002.

[82] Benenson et al., 2002; Leaper & Friedman, 2007; Maccoby, 2002.

[83] B. B. Brown et al., 2008; N. Eisenberg et al., 1996; Furman & Collins, 2009; J. R. Harris, 1995.

Once children or adolescents gel as a group, they prefer other group members over nonmembers, and they develop feelings of loyalty to individuals within the group. In some cases they also develop feelings of hostility and rivalry toward members of other groups.[84] If you look back on your own adolescent years, you may recall that you and your friends attached names to members of different groups—not only the "popular" students mentioned in the opening case study but perhaps also "brains," "jocks," "druggies," or "nerds"— and you probably viewed some of the groups unfavorably.[85] As noted earlier, group memberships affect learners' sense of self, and associations with such unofficial groups as these are no exception. Even children in the primary grades know that social groups can vary considerably in social status.[86]

As youngsters reach puberty, larger groups become an especially prominent feature of their social worlds. Researchers have identified several distinct types of groups during the adolescent years: cliques, crowds, subcultures, and gangs. **Cliques** are moderately stable friendship groups of perhaps 3 to 10 individuals, and such groups provide the setting for most voluntary social interactions.[87] Clique boundaries tend to be fairly rigid and exclusive (some people are "in," others are "out"), and memberships in various cliques often affect social status.[88]

Crowds are considerably larger than cliques and may not have the tight-knit cohesiveness and carefully drawn boundaries of a clique. Their members tend to share common interests (e.g., "brains" study a lot, "jocks" are active in sports), attitudes about academic achievement, and (occasionally) ethnic background.[89] Sometimes a crowd takes the form of a **subculture**, a group that resists a powerful dominant culture by adopting a significantly different way of life.[90] Some subcultures are relatively benign; for example, the baggy-pants "skaters" with whom my son Alex affiliated spent much of their free time riding skateboards and addressing almost everyone (including their mothers) as "dude." Other subcultures are more worrisome, such as those that endorse racist and anti-Semitic behaviors (e.g., "skinheads") and those that practice Satanic worship and rituals. Adolescents are more likely to affiliate with troublesome subcultures when they feel alienated from the dominant culture (perhaps that of their school or that of society more generally) and want to distinguish themselves from it in some way.[91]

A **gang** is a cohesive social group characterized by initiation rites, distinctive colors and symbols, ownership of a specific "territory," and feuds with one or more rival groups. Typically, gangs are governed by strict rules for behavior, with stiff penalties for rule violations. Adolescents (and sometimes younger children as well) affiliate with gangs for a variety of reasons.[92] Some do so as a way of demonstrating loyalty to their family, friends, or neighborhood. Some seek the status and prestige that gang membership brings. Some have poor academic records and perceive the gang as an alternative arena in which they might gain recognition for their accomplishments. Many members of gangs have troubled relationships with their families or have been consistently rejected by peers, and so they turn to gangs to get the emotional support they can find nowhere else.

In the upper secondary school grades, a greater capacity for abstract thought allows many adolescents to think of other people more as unique individuals and less as members of specific categories. They gain new awareness of the characteristics they share with people from diverse backgrounds. Perhaps as a result, ties to specific peer groups tend to dissipate, hostilities between groups soften, and young people become more flexible about the peers with whom they associate.[93]

What distinct crowds existed at your high school? What labels did students give these crowds?

---

[84] Dunham, Baron, & Banaji, 2006; J. R. Harris, 1998; Nesdale, Maass, Durkin, & Griffiths, 2005.

[85] B. B. Brown et al., 2008; Eckert, 1989; J. R. Harris, 1995.

[86] Bigler, Brown, & Markell, 2001; B. B. Brown et al., 2008; Dunham et al., 2006; Nesdale et al., 2005.

[87] Crockett, Losoff, & Peterson, 1984; J. L. Epstein, 1986; Kindermann et al., 1996.

[88] Goodwin, 2006; Wigfield et al., 1996.

[89] B. B. Brown et al., 2008; Steinberg, 1996.

[90] J. S. Epstein, 1998.

[91] C. C. Clark, 1992; J. R. Harris, 1998.

[92] A. Campbell, 1984; C. C. Clark, 1992; Kodluboy, 2004; Parks, 1995; Simons, Whitbeck, Conger, & Conger, 1991.

[93] B. B. Brown, Eicher, & Petrie, 1986; Furman & Collins, 2009; Gavin & Fuhrman, 1989; Kinney, 1993; Shrum & Cheek, 1987.

clique Moderately stable friendship group of perhaps 3 to 10 members.

crowd Large, loose-knit social group that shares certain common interests and attitudes.

subculture Group that resists the ways of the dominant culture and adopts its own norms for behavior.

gang Cohesive social group characterized by initiation rites, distinctive colors and symbols, territorial orientation, and feuds with rival groups.

For many children, thoughts of romance emerge early. Here is just one of many notes 5-year-old Isabelle wrote about a classmate named Will.

Romantic relationships in adolescence provide valuable practice for the intimate relationships of adulthood.

Even in the primary grades, many children talk of having boyfriends or girlfriends, and the opposite sex is a subject of interest throughout the elementary school years. But with the onset of adolescence, the biological changes of puberty are accompanied by new, often unsettling feelings and sexual desires. Not surprisingly, then, romance is often on adolescents' minds and is a frequent topic of conversation at school.[94] From a developmental standpoint, romantic relationships have definite benefits: They can address young people's needs for companionship, affection, and security, and they provide an opportunity to experiment with new social skills and interpersonal behaviors.[95] At the same time, romance can wreak havoc with adolescents' emotions. Adolescents have more extreme mood swings than younger children or adults, and for many, this instability may be partly due to the excitement and frustrations of being romantically involved or *not* involved.[96]

Initially, "romances" often exist more in adolescents' minds than in reality.[97] Consider Sandy's recollection of her first foray into couplehood:

> In about fifth and sixth grade, all our little group that we had . . . was like, "OK," you know, "we're getting ready for junior high," you know, "it's time we all have to get a boyfriend." So I remember, it was funny, Carol, like, there were two guys who were just the heartthrobs of our class, you know . . . so, um, I guess it was Carol and Cindy really, they were, like, sort of the leaders of our group, you know, they were the, yeah, they were just the leaders, and they got Tim and Joe, each of those you know. Carol had Tim and Cindy had Joe. And then, you know, everyone else, then it kind of went down the line, everyone else found someone. I remember thinking, "Well, who am I gonna get? I don't even like anybody," you know. I remember, you know, all sitting around, we were saying, "OK, who can we find for Sandy?" you know, looking, so finally we decided, you know, we were trying to decide between Al and Dave and so finally I took Dave.[98]

For youngsters in the middle school grades, romantic thoughts may also involve crushes on people who are out of reach—perhaps favorite teachers, movie idols, or rock stars.[99]

Eventually, many adolescents begin to date, especially if their friends are also dating. Their early choices in dating partners are often based on physical attractiveness or social status, and dates may involve only limited and superficial interaction.[100] As adolescents move into the high school grades, some form more intense, affectionate, and long-term relationships with members of the opposite sex, and these relationships often (but by no means always) lead to sexual intimacy.[101] The age of first sexual intercourse has decreased steadily during the last few decades, perhaps in part because the media often communicate the message that sexual activity among unmarried partners is acceptable.[102] In the United States the average age of first sexual intercourse is now around age 16, and the majority of adolescents are sexually active by 18. However, the age varies considerably as a function of gender (boys begin earlier) and cultural background.[103]

As they reach high school (occasionally earlier), some young people find themselves attracted to their own sex either instead of or in addition to the opposite sex. Adolescence can be a particularly confusing time for gay, lesbian, and bisexual individuals. Some try to ignore or stifle what they perceive to be deviant urges, and others struggle to form an identity while feeling different and isolated from—and sometimes bullied by—peers.[104] Perhaps as a result of increasing acceptance of sexual diversity in recent years, many gay, lesbian, and bisexual adolescents are psychologically healthy and well-adjusted.[105] But others describe

[94] B. B. Brown, Feiring, & Furman, 1999.

[95] Davila, 2008; Furman & Collins, 2009; B. C. Miller & Benson, 1999.

[96] Arnett, 1999; Davila, 2008; Furman & Collins, 2009; Larson, Clore, & Wood, 1999.

[97] Gottman & Mettetal, 1986.

[98] Eckert, 1989, p. 84.

[99] B. B. Brown, 1999; B. C. Miller & Benson, 1999.

[100] Furman, Brown, & Feiring, 1999; Pellegrini, 2002.

[101] B. B. Brown, 1999; J. Connolly & Goldberg, 1999.

[102] Brooks-Gunn & Paikoff, 1993; Larson et al., 1999.

[103] Hofferth, 1990; Katchadourian, 1990; Lippa, 2002; Zimmer-Gembeck & Helfand, 2008.

[104] Filax, 2007; E. J. Meyer, 2009; Morrow, 1997; Patterson, 1995.

[105] Savin-Williams, 2008.

feelings of anger and depression, and a higher than average proportion consider suicide or drop out of school.[106]

Teenagers often have mixed feelings about their early sexual experiences, and those around them—parents, teachers, peers—are often uncertain about how to handle the topic.[107] When parents and teachers do broach the topic of sexuality, they often raise it in conjunction with *problems,* such as irresponsible behavior, substance abuse, disease, and unwanted pregnancy. And they rarely raise the issue of gay, lesbian, and bisexual orientations except within the context of acquired immune deficiency syndrome (AIDS) and other risks.[108]

Truly popular children have good social skills.

When my daughter Tina was in junior high school, she sometimes told me, "No one likes the popular kids." Her remark was, of course, self-contradictory, and I usually told her so, but in fact it was consistent with research findings. When students are asked to identify their most "popular" classmates, they identify peers who have dominant social status at school (perhaps those who belong to a prestigious social group) but in many cases are aggressive or stuck-up.[109] Truly **popular students**—those whom many classmates select as people they'd like to do things with—may or may not hold high-status positions, but they're kind and trustworthy.[110] Students who are popular in this way typically have good social skills. For instance, they know how to initiate and sustain conversations, are sensitive to the subtle social and emotional cues that others give them, and are likely to help, share, cooperate, and empathize with others.[111]

In contrast to popular students, **rejected students** are students whom classmates select as being their *least* preferred social companions. Students with few social skills—for example, those who are impulsive or aggressive, and those who continually try to draw attention to themselves—typically experience peer rejection.[112] In addition, students from racial and ethnic minority groups often find themselves the targets of derogatory remarks and other forms of racism and discrimination, as do students from low-income families.[113] Especially when peer rejection and exclusion continue over a lengthy period, rejected students are at high risk for emotional problems, low school achievement, and poor school attendance.[114]

A third group, **controversial students**, are a mixed bag, in that some peers really like them and others really *dis*like them. These students can, like rejected students, be quite aggressive, but they also have sufficiently good social skills that they are popular with at least some of their peers.[115]

Researchers have described another category as well.[116] **Neglected students** are those whom peers rarely identify as someone they would either most like or least like to do something with.[117] Neglected students tend to be quiet and keep to themselves. Some prefer to be alone, others may be very shy or may not know how to go about initiating interaction, and still others may

Having at least one good friend seems to be important for children's and adolescents' emotional well-being.

---

[106] Elia, 1994; Filax, 2007; Patterson, 1995.

[107] Alapack, 1991; Katchadourian, 1990; Zimmer-Gembeck & Helfand, 2008.

[108] Filax, 2007; M. B. Harris, 1997.

[109] Cillessen & Mayeux, 2007; Crick, Murray-Close, Marks, & Mohajeri-Nelson, 2009; W. E. Ellis & Zarbatany, 2007.

[110] Cillessen & Rose, 2005; Parkhurst & Hopmeyer, 1998.

[111] Asher & McDonald, 2009; Crick & Dodge, 1994; Mostow, Izard, Fine, & Trantacosta, 2002; Wentzel & Asher, 1995.

[112] Asher & McDonald, 2009; Pedersen, Vitaro, Barker, & Borge, 2007; Rubin et al., 2010.

[113] Banks & Banks, 1995; Graham & Hudley, 2005; McBrien, 2005; Phelan, Yu, & Davidson, 1994.

[114] Buhs, Ladd, & Herald, 2006; Ladd, 2006.

[115] Asher & McDonald, 2009; Bukowski et al., 2007; Newcomb, Bukowski, & Pattee, 1993.

[116] Altogether researchers have identified five groups of students. The fifth group, *average students,* are liked by some peers and disliked by others, but without the intensity of feelings that is true for controversial students.

[117] Asher & Renshaw, 1981.

popular student Student whom many peers like and perceive to be kind and trustworthy.

rejected student Student whom many peers identify as being an undesirable social partner.

controversial student Student whom some peers strongly like and other peers strongly dislike.

neglected student Student about whom most peers have no strong feelings, either positive or negative.

be quite content with having only one or two close friends.[118] For some students, "neglected" status is a relatively temporary situation. Others are totally friendless for extended periods, and these students are at higher-than-average risk for depression.[119]

Underlying the social skills that affect popularity are certain ways of thinking about social relationships, as we shall see now.

• Social Cognition

As children and adolescents grow older, they not only become increasingly able to understand and think logically about the physical world and academic subject matter (see Chapters 2, 4, and 5) but they also think in increasingly sophisticated ways about other people and social interactions. Such thinking about the nature of people and social events is known as **social cognition**.

At any particular age level, youngsters vary considerably in their interest in and awareness of other people's thoughts and feelings. Those who think regularly about such matters are more socially skillful, make friends more easily, and have better understandings of *themselves* as well.[120] You may occasionally see the term *emotional intelligence* in reference to such abilities.[121]

The following principles describe how social cognition influences children's and adolescents' interpersonal effectiveness.

As children get older, they become increasingly aware of other people's thoughts and emotions.

To truly understand and get along with other people, children must be able to step into others' shoes—that is, to look at the world from other viewpoints. The following situation provides an example.

SEE FOR YOURSELF Last Picked

Consider the following scenario:

Kenny and Mark are co-captains of the soccer team. They have one person left to choose for the team. Without saying anything, Mark winks at Kenny and looks at Tom, who is one of the remaining children left to be chosen for the team. Mark looks back at Kenny and smiles. Kenny nods and chooses Tom to be on their team. Tom sees Mark and Kenny winking and smiling at each other. Tom, who is usually one of the last to be picked for team sports, wonders why Kenny wants him to be on his team. . . .

- Why did Mark smile at Kenny?
- Why did Kenny nod?
- Why did Kenny choose Tom to be on the team? How do you know this?
- Do you think that Tom has any idea of why Kenny chose him to be on the team? How do you know this? . . .
- How do you think Tom feels?[122]

To answer these questions, you must look at the situation from the perspectives of the children involved. For example, if you put yourself in Tom's shoes, you might suspect that he has mixed feelings. If he enjoys soccer, he may be happy to have a chance to play, but he might also be wondering whether the other boys' nonverbal signals indicate a malicious intention to make him look foolish on the soccer field. And, of course, Tom may feel embarrassed or

[118] Gazelle & Ladd, 2003; Guay, Boivin, & Hodges, 1999; McElhaney, Antonishak, & Allen, 2008.

[119] Asher & Paquette, 2003; Gazelle & Ladd, 2003; Laursen et al., 2007.

[120] Bosacki, 2000; P. L. Harris, 2006; Izard et al., 2001.

[121] Despite the prevalence of this concept in popular media, research to date has not conclusively validated it

as a distinct ability separate from other aspects of people's intellectual and social functioning; for diverging perspectives, see J. D. Mayer, Salovey, & Caruso, 2008; Waterhouse, 2006; Zeidner, Roberts, & Matthews, 2002.

[122] Bosacki, 2000, p. 711, format adapted.

social cognition Process of thinking about how other people are likely to think, act, and react.

demoralized at consistently being one of the last children picked for a team. (Accordingly, asking some students to choose others for their teams, as might be done in a physical education class, is generally *not* recommended.) Such **perspective taking**—that is, mentally putting oneself in another's shoes—helps people to make sense of actions that might otherwise be puzzling and to choose responses that are most likely to achieve desired results and maintain positive interpersonal relationships.

Observe a discussion of perspective taking in a first-grade class in the "Promoting Perspective Taking" video in Chapter 7 of the Book-Specific Resources in MyEducationLab.

As we discovered in Chapter 4, metacognition improves with age: Children become increasingly aware of their own thought processes. In fact, as children learn more about their own thinking, they also become more adept at drawing inferences about what *other* people are thinking. More generally, children develop a **theory of mind** that encompasses increasingly complex understandings of human mental and psychological states—thoughts, beliefs, feelings, motives, and so on. Their theory of mind enables them to interpret and predict the behaviors of the important people in their lives and, as a result, to interact effectively with those individuals.[123]

Consistent with what we've learned about cognitive development, young children tend to think of other people in a fairly concrete fashion, with a focus on observable characteristics and behaviors. However, they do have some awareness of other people's inner worlds. As early as age 4 or 5, they realize that what *they* know may be different from what *other people* know.[124] They also have some ability to draw inferences about other people's mental and emotional states—for instance, to deduce that people who behave in certain ways have certain intentions or feelings.[125]

As children progress through the elementary grades, they draw more sophisticated inferences about other people's mental states. For instance, they may realize that people's actions don't always reflect their thoughts and feelings (e.g., someone who appears happy may actually feel sad).[126] Children understand, too, that people *interpret* events—rather than simply "record" events in an objective manner—and that others may therefore view a situation differently than they themselves do. In other words, children increasingly understand that thinking and learning are active, constructive processes.[127]

By early adolescence, youngsters realize that people can have mixed feelings about events and other individuals.[128] And courtesy of their expanding cognitive abilities, memory capacity, and social awareness, young adolescents become capable of **recursive thinking**.[129] That is, they can think about what other people might be thinking about them and eventually can reflect on other people's thoughts about themselves through multiple iterations (e.g., "You think that I think that you think . . ."). This is not to say that adolescents (or adults, for that matter) always use this capacity. In fact, thinking only about one's own perspective—without a realistic assessment of what others' perspectives are likely to be—is a common phenomenon in the early adolescent years (recall our earlier discussion of the *imaginary audience*).[130]

As children get older, they become increasingly able to look at situations from another person's point of view. Such perspective taking helps them interact more effectively and prosocially with one another.

Cindy Charles/PhotoEdit Inc.

In the high school years, teenagers can draw on a rich knowledge base derived from numerous social experiences and, as a result, become ever more skillful at drawing inferences about people's psychological characteristics, intentions, and needs.[131] In addition, they are more attuned to the complex dynamics that influence behavior—not only thoughts, feelings, and present circumstances but also past experiences.[132] What we see emerging in the high school years, then, is a budding psychologist: an individual who can be quite astute in deciphering and explaining the motives and actions of others.

---

[123] Flavell, 2000; Gopnik & Meltzoff, 1997; Wellman & Gelman, 1998.

[124] P. L. Harris, 2006; Wellman, Cross, & Watson, 2001; Wimmer & Perner, 1983.

[125] Astington & Pelletier, 1996; Flavell, 2000; P. L. Harris, 2006; Schult, 2002; Wellman, Phillips, & Rodriguez, 2000.

[126] Flavell, Miller, & Miller, 2002; Gnepp, 1989; Selman, 1980.

[127] Chandler & Boyes, 1982; Flavell, Green, & Flavell, 1995; Flavell et al., 2002; Wellman, 1990.

[128] Chandler, 1987; S. K. Donaldson & Westerman, 1986; Flavell & Miller, 1998; Harter & Whitesell, 1989.

[129] Flavell et al., 2002; Oppenheimer, 1986; Perner & Wimmer, 1985.

[130] Tsethlikai & Greenhoot, 2006; Tsethlikai, Guthrie-Fulbright, & Loera, 2007.

[131] N. Eisenberg, Carlo, Murphy, & Van Court, 1995; Paget, Kritt, & Bergemann, 1984.

[132] C. A. Flanagan & Tucker, 1999; Selman, 1980.

perspective taking Ability to look at a situation from someone's else viewpoint.

theory of mind Self-constructed understanding of one's own and other people's mental and psychological states (thoughts, feelings, etc.).

recursive thinking Thinking about what other people may be thinking about oneself, possibly through multiple iterations.

Children's cognitive processes in social situations influence their behaviors toward others.

Children and adolescents have a lot to think about when they consider what other people are thinking, feeling, and doing. Such **social information processing**—the mental processes involved in making sense of and responding to social events—is simply a more socially oriented version of the cognitive processes described in Chapter 2. Among other things, social information processing involves paying *attention* to certain behaviors in a social situation and trying to interpret and make sense of those behaviors through *elaboration*. For example, when children interact with peers, they might focus on certain remarks, facial expressions, and body language and try to figure out what a peer really means by, say, a thoughtless comment or sheepish grin. Children also consider one or more *goals* they hope to achieve during an interaction—perhaps preserving a friendship, on the one hand, or teaching somebody a "lesson," on the other. Then, taking into account both their interpretations and their goals, they draw on their previous knowledge and experiences to *retrieve* a number of possible responses and choose what is, in their eyes, a productive course of action.[133]

The behaviors young people attend to, the ways in which they interpret those behaviors, and the particular goals they have for their social interactions have a considerable impact on how effectively they interact with others. This point will become clear as we discuss the next principle.

Aggressive behavior is often the result of counterproductive cognitive processes.

Aggressive behavior is an action intentionally taken to hurt another person either physically or psychologically. **Physical aggression**, an action that can potentially cause bodily injury (e.g., hitting, shoving), is more common in boys. **Relational aggression**, an action that can adversely affect friendships and other interpersonal relationships (e.g., using derogatory names, ostracizing a peer), is fairly common in both boys and girls.[134] As a general rule, aggression declines over the course of childhood and adolescence, but it increases for a short time after children make the transition from elementary school to middle school or junior high.[135] For example, in the opening case study, a few of the allegedly "popular" (i.e., high-status) eighth graders regularly pick on Peter, perhaps by ridiculing him (relational aggression) and perhaps by occasionally poking or shoving him (physical aggression).

Researchers have identified two distinct groups of aggressive children.[136] Some deliberately initiate aggressive behaviors as a means of obtaining desired goals—this is **proactive aggression**. Others act aggressively primarily in response to frustration or provocation—this is **reactive aggression**. Of the two groups, children who exhibit proactive aggression are more likely to have difficulty maintaining friendships with their peers.[137] Those who direct considerable aggression toward particular individuals—whether it be physical aggression or relational aggression—are known as **bullies**. Their hapless victims often are children who are immature, anxious, friendless, and lacking in self-esteem—some also have disabilities—and so are relatively defenseless.[138] And some bullies regularly target peers whom they know or suspect to be gay, lesbian, or bisexual.[139]

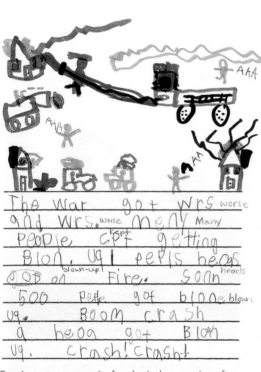

Boys' greater propensity for physical aggression often shows up in their fantasy play and fiction, as in this story by 7-year-old Grant. (His teacher has corrected some of his misspellings.)

social information processing Mental processes involved in making sense of and responding to social events.

aggressive behavior Action intentionally taken to harm another person either physically or psychologically.

physical aggression Action that can potentially cause bodily injury.

relational aggression Action that can adversely affect interpersonal relationships.

proactive aggression Deliberate aggression against another as a means of obtaining a desired goal.

reactive aggression Aggressive response to frustration or provocation.

bully Child or adolescent who frequently threatens, harasses, or causes injury to particular peers.

[133] Arsenio & Lemerise, 2004; Crick & Dodge, 1996; Dodge, 1986; Greenhoot, Tsethlikai, & Wagoner, 2006; E. R. Smith & Semin, 2007.

[134] Card, Stucky, Sawalani, & Little, 2008; Crick, Grotpeter, & Bigbee, 2002; Goodwin, 2006; Pellegrini & Archer, 2005; A. J. Rose & Smith, 2009.

[135] Pellegrini, 2002; Pellegrini & Long, 2004.

[136] Crick & Dodge, 1996; Poulin & Boivin, 1999; Vitaro, Gendreau, Tremblay, & Oligny, 1998.

[137] Hanish, Kochenderfer-Ladd, Fabes, Martin, & Denning, 2004; Poulin & Boivin, 1999.

[138] Espelage & Swearer, 2004; Hyman et al., 2004; Konishi & Hymel, 2008; R. S. Newman & Murray, 2005.

[139] Filax, 2007; E. J. Meyer, 2009.

Bullying certainly isn't limited to face-to-face interactions. For example, it might involve spreading vicious rumors that can cause considerable humiliation and emotional distress. And increasingly young people are engaging in **cyberbullying**—using modern communication technology such as cell phones and the Internet to post threats or insulting messages or to broadcast embarrassing e-mails or photographs to a wide audience of peers.[140]

Some children and adolescents are genetically more predisposed to aggression than their peers, and others may exhibit heightened aggression as a result of neurological damage.[141] Yet several cognitive factors also play a role in aggressive behavior:

- **Poor perspective-taking ability.** Many highly aggressive children have limited ability to look at situations from other people's perspectives or to empathize with their victims.[142]

- **Misinterpretation of social cues.** Children who are either physically or relationally aggressive toward peers tend to interpret others' behaviors as reflecting hostile intentions, especially when such behaviors have ambiguous meanings. This **hostile attributional bias** is especially prevalent in children who are prone to *reactive* aggression.[143]

- **Prevalence of self-serving goals.** For most young people, establishing and maintaining interpersonal relationships are a high priority. For aggressive children, however, more self-serving goals—perhaps maintaining an inflated self-image, seeking revenge, or gaining power and respect—often take precedence.[144]

- **Ineffective social problem-solving strategies.** Aggressive children often have little knowledge of how to persuade, negotiate, or compromise, and so they resort to hitting, shoving, barging into play activities, and other ineffective strategies.[145]

- **Beliefs about the appropriateness and effectiveness of aggression.** Many aggressive children believe that violence and other forms of aggression are acceptable ways of resolving conflicts and retaliating against others' misdeeds. Those who display high rates of *proactive* aggression are also apt to believe that aggressive action will yield positive results—for instance, that it will enhance their social status. Not surprisingly, aggressive children tend to associate with one another, thus confirming one another's beliefs that aggression is appropriate.[146]

Unless adults actively intervene, some aggressive children (especially those who exhibit proactive aggression) show a continuing pattern of aggression and violence as they grow older, almost guaranteeing long-term maladjustment and difficulties with peers.[147] The victims of aggression certainly suffer as well. Children who are frequent targets of bullying can become anxious, depressed, possibly even suicidal, and their classroom performance may deteriorate as a result.[148] Over time their self-esteem declines, and some begin to believe that they themselves are responsible for the harassment they endure.[149] They may fear retaliation if they alert adults to their plight and so have little optimism that things will improve.[150] One boy expressed this no-win situation as follows:

> Well I tell a teacher [when I get bullied] but that only gets me in more trouble from the bullies because they pick on me, they hit me, they call me names. Everybody except my friends in my class are bullies. They call me "stink bomb," "stinky," "dirty boy," and stuff like that.[151]

[140] Kowalski & Limber, 2007; Shariff, 2008; Valkenburg & Peter, 2009; Ybarra & Mitchell, 2007.

[141] Brendgen et al., 2008; Raine & Scerbo, 1991; D. C. Rowe, Almeida, & Jacobson, 1999.

[142] Coie & Dodge, 1998; Damon & Hart, 1988; R. F. Marcus, 1980.

[143] Bukowski et al., 2007; E. Chen, Langer, Raphaelson, & Matthews, 2004; Crick, Grotpeter, & Bigbee, 2002; Dodge et al., 2003.

[144] R. F. Baumeister, Smart, & Boden, 1996; Cillessen & Rose, 2005; Kiefer & Ryan, 2008; Menon et al., 2007; Pellegrini & Long, 2004.

[145] Neel, Jenkins, & Meadows, 1990; D. Schwartz et al., 1998; Troop-Gordon & Asher, 2005.

[146] R. P. Brown, Osterman, & Barnes, 2009; Crick et al., 2009; Dodge, Lochman, Harnish, Bates, & Pettit, 1997; Fontaine, Yang, Dodge, Bates, & Pettit, 2008; Paciello, Fida, Tramontano, Lupinetti, & Caprara, 2008; M. W. Watson, Andreas, Fischer, & Smith, 2005; Zelli, Dodge, Lochman, & Laird, 1999.

[147] Crick et al., 2009; Dodge et al., 2003; Hampson, 2008; Ladd & Troop-Gordon, 2003; Pepler, Jiang, Craig, & Connolly, 2008.

[148] Buhs et al., 2006; Hoglund, 2007; Hyman et al., 2004; D. Schwartz, Gorman, Nakamoto, & Toblin, 2005.

[149] Troop-Gordon & Ladd, 2005.

[150] Holt & Keyes, 2004; R. S. Newman & Murray, 2005.

[151] Bergamo & Evans, 2005, n.p.

cyberbullying Use of wireless technologies or the Internet to transmit hostile messages, broadcast personally embarrassing information, or in other ways cause an individual significant psychological distress.

hostile attributional bias Tendency to interpret others' behaviors as reflecting hostile or aggressive intentions.

Even children who simply observe peer-on-peer aggression can suffer considerable psychological distress, perhaps because they feel guilty that they didn't come to a victim's assistance or worry that they themselves might soon be victimized.[152]

We'll consider strategies for addressing bullying and other forms of chronic aggression near the end of the chapter. In the meantime, we turn to the development of more general beliefs about right and wrong—in other words, to moral and prosocial development.

• Moral and Prosocial Development

Some social behaviors, such as sharing, helping, and comforting, are aimed at benefiting others more than oneself. Such **prosocial behaviors**, plus such traits as honesty, fairness, and concern for other people's needs and rights, fall into the domain of **morality**.

Learners' beliefs about moral and immoral behavior—that is, their beliefs about right and wrong—affect their actions and achievement at school. For example, students are less likely to engage in theft or aggression if they respect the property and safety of their classmates. And their moral beliefs are likely to influence their cognitive and affective reactions to classroom subject matter—for instance, how they respond to descriptions of the Holocaust during World War II or to anti-Semitic dialogue in Shakespeare's *The Merchant of Venice*. By behaving and thinking morally and prosocially, students gain greater support from their teachers and classmates and thereby achieve greater academic and social success over the long run.[153]

Several principles describe the nature of moral and prosocial development over the course of childhood and adolescence.

At an early age, children begin applying internal standards for behavior.

Even preschoolers have some understanding that behaviors causing physical or psychological harm are inappropriate. By age 4, most children understand that causing harm to another person is wrong regardless of what authority figures might tell them and regardless of what consequences certain behaviors may or may not bring.[154]

Children increasingly distinguish between moral and conventional transgressions.

Virtually every culture discourages some behaviors—**moral transgressions**—because they cause damage or harm, violate human rights, or run counter to basic principles of equality, freedom, or justice. It discourages other behaviors—**conventional transgressions**—that, although not unethical, violate widely held understandings about how one should act (e.g., children shouldn't talk back to adults or burp at meals). Whereas many moral transgressions are universal across cultures, conventional transgressions are usually specific to a particular culture.[155] For instance, although burping is frowned on in mainstream Western culture, people in some cultures burp as a compliment to the cook. Occasionally, certain conventions do have moral overtones, as you can see in the Cultural Considerations box "Cultural and Ethnic Diversity in Personal, Social, and Moral Development" (pp. 258–259).

Children's awareness of social conventions increases throughout the elementary school years.[156] But especially as children reach adolescence, they don't always agree with adults about which behaviors constitute moral transgressions, which ones fall into the conventional domain, and which ones are simply a matter of personal choice. For example, many adolescents resist rules they think are infringements on their personal freedoms—rules about clothing, hair style, talking in class, and so on.[157]

prosocial behavior Behavior directed toward promoting the well-being of another person.

morality One's general standards for behaviors that preserve other people's rights and welfare.

moral transgression Action that causes harm or infringes on the needs or rights of others.

conventional transgression Action that violates a culture's general expectations regarding socially appropriate behavior.

[152] Nishina & Juvonen, 2005; Rivers, Poteat, Noret, & Ashurst, 2009.
[153] Caprara, Barbaranelli, Pastorelli, Bandura, & Zimbardo, 2000.
[154] Helwig, Zelazo, & Wilson, 2001; J. M. Kim & Turiel, 1996; Laupa & Turiel, 1995; Smetana, 1981; Tisak, 1993.

[155] Nucci, 2009; Smetana, 2006; Turiel, 2002.
[156] Helwig & Jasiobedzka, 2001; Laupa & Turiel, 1995; Nucci, 2001; Nucci & Nucci, 1982; Turiel, 1983.
[157] Nucci, 2009; Smetana, 2005.

Children's capacity to respond emotionally to others' misfortunes and distress increases throughout the school years.

Within the first two or three years of life, two emotions important for moral development emerge.[158] Children occasionally show **guilt**—a feeling of discomfort when they know they have inflicted damage or caused someone else pain or distress. They also feel **shame**—a feeling of embarrassment or humiliation when they fail to meet the standards for moral behavior that either they or others have established. Both guilt and shame, although unpleasant emotions, are good signs that children are developing a sense of right and wrong and will work hard to correct their misdeeds.[159]

Guilt and shame appear when children believe they've done something unacceptable. In contrast, **empathy**—experiencing the same feelings as someone in unfortunate circumstances—appears in the absence of wrongdoing. The ability to empathize emerges in the preschool years and continues to develop throughout childhood and adolescence (e.g., see Figure 7.1).[160] Truly prosocial children—those who help others even in the absence of their own wrongdoing—typically have a considerable capacity for perspective taking and empathy.[161] Empathy is especially likely to spur prosocial behavior when it leads to **sympathy**, whereby children not only assume another person's feelings but also have concerns for the individual's well-being.[162]

With age, reasoning about moral issues becomes increasingly abstract and flexible.

To probe people's reasoning about moral issues, researchers sometimes present **moral dilemmas**, situations in which two or more people's rights or needs may be at odds and for which there are no clear-cut right or wrong solutions. The following exercise provides an example.

SEE FOR YOURSELF   Heinz's Dilemma

Consider this situation:

> In Europe, a woman was near death from a rare form of cancer. There was one drug that the doctors thought might save her, a form of radium that a druggist in the same town had recently discovered. The druggist was charging $2,000, ten times what the drug cost him to make. The sick woman's husband, Heinz, went to everyone he knew to borrow the money, but he could only get together about half of what the drug cost. He told the druggist that his wife was dying and asked him to sell it cheaper or let him pay later. But the druggist said no. So Heinz got desperate and broke into the man's store to steal the drug for his wife.[163]

- Should Heinz have stolen the drug? What would *you* have done if you were Heinz? Which is worse, stealing something that belongs to someone else or letting another person die a preventable death? Why?

After obtaining hundreds of responses to moral dilemmas such as this one, the cognitive-developmental psychologist Lawrence Kohlberg proposed that as children grow older, they construct increasingly complex views of morality. In Kohlberg's view, the development of moral reasoning is characterized by a sequence of six stages grouped into three general

---

? How do you feel when you inadvertently inconvenience someone else? when you hurt someone else's feelings? when a friend unexpectedly loses a close family member? Do such feelings as guilt, shame, and sympathy come to mind?

hopes
goals
dreams
happiness
   broken
   destroyed
   eliminated
   exterminated
no steps forward
no evolution
no prosperity
no hope
But
maybe
perhaps
except
if we
help
together
we stand
a chance.

FIGURE 7.1 In this poem about the Holocaust, Matthew, a middle school student, expresses empathy for its victims.

guilt Feeling of discomfort about having caused someone else pain or distress.

shame Feeling of embarrassment or humiliation after failing to meet certain standards for moral behavior.

empathy Experience of sharing the same feelings as someone in unfortunate circumstances.

sympathy Feeling of sorrow for another person's distress, accompanied by concern for the person's well-being.

moral dilemma Situation in which two or more people's rights or needs may be at odds and the morally correct action is not clear-cut.

---

[158] Kochanska, Gross, Lin, & Nichols, 2002; M. Lewis & Sullivan, 2005.
[159] N. Eisenberg, 1995; Harter, 1999; Narváez & Rest, 1995.
[160] N. Eisenberg, 1982; N. Eisenberg et al., 1995; N. Eisenberg, Lennon, & Pasternack, 1986.
[161] Damon, 1988; N. Eisenberg, Zhou, & Koller, 2001; M. L. Hoffman, 1991.
[162] Batson, 1991; N. Eisenberg & Fabes, 1998; Malti, Gummerum, Keller, & Buchman, 2009; Turiel, 1998.
[163] Kohlberg, 1984, p. 186.

CULTURAL CONSIDERATIONS Cultural and Ethnic Diversity in Personal, Social, and Moral Development

Researchers have observed cultural and ethnic differences in personality, sense of self, social skills and relationships, and morality and prosocial behavior. Here we look at examples of diversity in each of these areas.

Personality. Although children's personalities are partly the result of temperamental differences, culture also plays a significant role in molding their personality characteristics.[a] For example, many Asian children are raised to be shy and reserved, whereas many in the United States are raised to be outgoing and independent.[b] Furthermore, some cultural groups explicitly nurture different characteristics in males and females. For instance, some Hispanic groups encourage boys to be strong and assertive (*machismo*) while urging girls to be demure and nurturing (*marianismo*).[c]

Sense of self. As noted earlier in the chapter, learners' group memberships affect their sense of self. In fact, in some cultures—for instance, in many Middle Eastern and Far Eastern countries, as well as in many Native American communities—children see their group membership and connections with other individuals as central parts of who they are as human beings.[d] Such cultural groups encourage children to take pride in accomplishments that contribute to the greater good of the family or larger community as well as, or perhaps *instead of*, their own accomplishments.[e]

In addition, many young people have a strong **ethnic identity**: They are both aware and proud of their ethnic group and willingly adopt some of the group's behaviors.[f] Occasionally learners' ethnic identities can lead them to reject mainstream Western values. In some ethnic minority groups, peers may accuse high-achieving students of "acting white," a label that essentially means "you're not one of us."[g] We saw an example of this phenomenon in the opening case study in Chapter 3, when Sylvia, a high-achieving African American adolescent, encountered taunts from some of her neighborhood peers:

> Oh, here she come. Here come whitey. Hey, Doc, you scrape yourself an' you find that honky skin?[h]

For the most part, however, learners with a strong and positive ethnic identity do well in school both academically and socially.[i] Also, pride in one's ethnic heritage can serve as an emotional buffer against the insults and discrimination that children and adolescents from minority groups sometimes encounter.[j] Consider this statement by Eva, an African American high school student, as an example:

> I'm proud to be black and everything. But, um, I'm aware of, you know, racist acts and racist things that are happening in the world, but I use that as no excuse, you know. I feel as though I can succeed. . . . I just know that I'm not gonna let [racism] stop me. . . . Being black is good. I'm proud to be black but you also gotta face reality. And what's going on, you know, black people are not really getting anywhere in life, but I know I will and I don't know—I just know I will.[k]

Not all young people from minority groups affiliate strongly with their cultural and ethnic groups. Some youngsters (especially those with multiple racial or cultural heritages) fluctuate in the strength of their ethnic identity depending on the context and situation.[l] In addition, older adolescents may experiment with varying forms of an ethnic identity. Some teens, for instance, may initially adopt a fairly intense, inflexible, and perhaps hostile ethnic identity before eventually settling into a more relaxed, open-minded, and productive one.[m]

Social skills and relationships. Interpersonal skills and relationships may

Learn more about Kohlberg's theory of moral development in a supplementary reading in Chapter 7 of the Book-Specific Resources in MyEducationLab.

ethnic identity Awareness of one's membership in a particular ethnic or cultural group, and willingness to adopt behaviors characteristic of the group.

preconventional morality Lack of internalized standards about right and wrong behavior; decision making based primarily on what seems best for oneself.

levels of morality: preconventional, conventional, and postconventional (see Table 7.2). A child with **preconventional morality** has not yet adopted or internalized society's conventions regarding what is right or wrong but instead focuses largely on external consequences that certain actions might bring. We see an example of preconventional reasoning in one fifth grader's response to the Heinz dilemma:

> Maybe his wife is an important person and runs a store, and the man buys stuff from her and can't get it any other place. The police would blame the owner that he didn't save the wife. He didn't save an important person, and that's just like killing with a gun or a knife. You can get the electric chair for that.[164]

---

[164] Kohlberg, 1981, pp. 265–266.

vary somewhat for students from different backgrounds. Some ethnic groups (e.g., many Asian and Native American groups and some African American communities) place particular emphasis on maintaining group harmony and resolving interpersonal conflicts peacefully, and they actively discourage physical and relational aggression. Children from these groups may be especially adept at negotiation and peace making.[n] In contrast, certain other groups encourage some forms of relational aggression. For example, teasing and ridicule are common ways of teaching children to "keep their cool" and handle criticism in some communities in northern Canada and the South Pacific.[o]

Most children and adolescents of all cultures value the company of age-mates, but the extent to which they actually spend time with their peers is partly a function of their cultural background. For instance, on average, Asian Americans spend less leisure time with friends, and are more likely to choose friends who value academic achievement, than young people from other groups.[p] Moreover, children who have recently immigrated from a non-English-speaking country may have relatively little interaction with peers because of their limited ability to communicate with other children in their neighborhoods and classrooms.[q]

Morality and prosocial behavior. Conceptions of moral and immoral behavior vary as a function of cultural background as well. Virtually all cultures espouse the importance of both individual rights and fairness (i.e., an *ethic of justice*) and compassion for others (i.e., an *ethic of caring*). However, different cultural groups tend to place greater emphasis on one than on the other.[r] For example, in the United States, helping others (or not) is often considered to be a voluntary choice, but in some societies (e.g., in many Asian and Arab countries) it is one's *duty* to help others. Such a sense of duty, which is often coupled with strong ties to family and the community, can lead to considerable prosocial behavior.[s]

Some variability is also seen in the behaviors that cultural groups view as moral transgressions versus those they see as conventional transgressions.[t] For instance, in mainstream Western culture, how one dresses is largely a matter of convention and personal choice. In some deeply religious groups, however, certain forms of dress (e.g., head coverings) are seen as moral imperatives that must be adhered to.

[a] Kagan, 2010.

[b] X. Chen, Chung, & Hsiao, 2009; Huntsinger & Jose, 2006; Rubin, Cheah, & Menzer, 2010; Tamis-Lemonda & McFadden, 2010.

[c] Goldston et al., 2008.

[d] M. B. Brewer & Yuki, 2007; Kağitçibaşi, 2007; Q. Wang, 2006; Whitesell, Mitchell, Kaufman, Spicer, & the Voices of Indian Teens Project Team, 2006.

[e] Banks & Banks, 1995; P. M. Cole & Tan, 2007.

[f] L. Allen & Aber, 2006; Y. Hong, Wan, No, & Chiu, 2007; Phinney, 1993; Sheets & Hollins, 1999.

[g] Bergin & Cooks, 2008; Cross, Strauss, & Fhagen-Smith, 1999; Ogbu, 2008a.

[h] McCourt, 2005, p. 194.

[i] Altschul, Oyserman, & Bybee, 2006; Chavous et al., 2003; Mandara, Gaylord-Harden, Richards, & Ragsdale, 2009; Nasir, McLaughlin, & Jones, 2009; Smokowski, Buchanan, & Bacalleo, 2009.

[j] L. Allen & Aber, 2006; C. H. Caldwell, Zimmerman, Bernat, Sellers, & Notaro, 2002; P. J. Cook & Ludwig, 2008; Goodnow, 2010; Pahl & Way, 2006.

[k] Way, 1998, p. 257.

[l] Hitlin, Brown, & Elder, 2006; Y. Hong, Wan, No, & Chiu, 2007; Tatum, 1997; Yip & Fuligni, 2002.

[m] Cross et al., 1999; Seaton et al., 2006.

[n] X. Chen & Wang, 2010; Gardiner & Kosmitzki, 2008; P. Guthrie, 2001; Halgunseth, Ispa, & Rudy, 2006; Rubin et al., 2010; Xu, Farver, Chang, Yu, & Zhang, 2006.

[o] Rogoff, 2003.

[p] Rubin et al., 2010; Steinberg, 1996.

[q] Ahn, 2005; A. Doyle, 1982.

[r] J. G. Miller, 2007; Shweder, Mahapatra, & Miller, 1987; Snarey, 1995; Turiel, 2002.

[s] X. Chen et al., 2009; J. G. Miller, 2007; Greenfield, 1994; Rubin et al., 2010; Triandis, 1995.

[t] Nucci, 2001.

Kohlberg's second level—**conventional morality**—is characterized by general, often unquestioning obedience either to an authority figure's dictates or to the rules and norms of society in general, even when there are no consequences for disobedience. In contrast, people at Kohlberg's third level—**postconventional morality**—view rules as useful but changeable mechanisms that ideally can maintain the general social order and protect human rights; rules are not absolute dictates that must be obeyed without question. These people live by their own abstract principles about right and wrong and may disobey rules inconsistent with these principles, as we see in one high school student's response to the Heinz dilemma:

> In that particular situation Heinz was right to do it. In the eyes of the law he would not be doing the right thing, but in the eyes of the moral law he would. If he had exhausted every other alternative I think it would be worth it to save a life.[165]

Observe examples of preconventional and conventional reasoning in the "Moral Reasoning" video in Chapter 7 of the Book-Specific Resources in MyEducationLab.

conventional morality Uncritical acceptance of society's conventions regarding right and wrong behavior.

postconventional morality Thinking in accordance with self-constructed, abstract principles regarding right and wrong behavior.

---

[165] Kohlberg, 1984, pp. 446–447.

TABLE 7.2 Kohlberg's Three Levels and Six Stages of Moral Reasoning

Level	Proposed Age Range	Stage	Nature of Moral Reasoning
Level I: Preconventional morality	Seen in preschool children, most elementary school students, some junior high school students, and a few high school students	Stage 1: Punishment-avoidance and obedience	People make decisions based on what is best for themselves, without regard for others' needs or feelings. They obey rules only if established by more powerful individuals; they may disobey if they aren't likely to get caught. "Wrong" behaviors are those that will be punished.
		Stage 2: Exchange of favors	People recognize that others also have needs. They may try to satisfy others' needs if their own needs are also met ("You scratch my back and I'll scratch yours"). They continue to define right and wrong primarily in terms of consequences to themselves.
Level II: Conventional morality	Seen in a few older elementary school students, some junior high school students, and many high school students (Stage 4 typically does not appear before high school)	Stage 3: Good boy/good girl	People make decisions based on what actions will please others, especially authority figures (e.g., teachers, popular peers). They are concerned about maintaining relationships through sharing, trust, and loyalty, and they consider other people's perspectives and intentions when making decisions.
		Stage 4: Law and order	People look to society as a whole for guidelines about right or wrong. They know rules are necessary for keeping society running smoothly and believe it is their duty to obey them. However, they perceive rules to be inflexible; they don't necessarily recognize that as society's needs change, rules should change as well.
Level III: Postconventional morality	Rarely seen before college (Stage 6 is extremely rare even in adults)	Stage 5: Social contract	People recognize that rules represent agreements among many individuals about appropriate behavior. Rules are seen as useful mechanisms that maintain the general social order and protect individual rights, rather than as absolute dictates that must be obeyed simply because they are the law. People also recognize the flexibility of rules; rules that no longer serve society's best interests can and should be changed.
		Stage 6: Universal ethical principle	Stage 6 is a hypothetical, ideal stage that few people ever reach. People in this stage adhere to a few abstract, universal principles (e.g., equality of all people, respect for human dignity, commitment to justice) that transcend specific norms and rules. They answer to a strong inner conscience and willingly disobey laws that violate their own ethical principles.

Sources: Colby & Kohlberg, 1984; Colby, Kohlberg, Gibbs, & Lieberman, 1983; Kohlberg, 1976, 1984, 1986; Reimer, Paolitto, & Hersh, 1983; Snarey, 1995.

A great deal of research on moral reasoning has followed on the heels of Kohlberg's work. Some of it supports Kohlberg's proposed sequence: Generally speaking, people seem to make advancements in the order that Kohlberg suggested.[166] Nevertheless, contemporary psychologists have identified several weaknesses in Kohlberg's theory. For one thing, Kohlberg included both moral issues (e.g., causing harm) and social conventions (e.g., having rules to help society run smoothly) in his views of morality, but as we've seen, children distinguish between these two domains, and their views about each domain may change differently over time.[167] Furthermore, Kohlberg paid little attention to one very important aspect of morality: *helping and showing compassion for* other people.[168] He also underestimated

---

[166] Boom, Brugman, & van der Heijden, 2001; Colby & Kohlberg, 1984; Snarey, 1995; Stewart & Pascual-Leone, 1992.

[167] Nucci, 2001, 2009.

[168] Gilligan, 1982, 1987; J. G. Miller, 2007.

young children, who, as we discovered earlier, acquire some internal standards of right and wrong long before they begin kindergarten or first grade. Finally, Kohlberg overlooked motives, social benefits, and other situational factors that many children (older ones especially) consider when deciding what actions are morally right and wrong.[169] For example, children and adolescents are more apt to think of lying as immoral if it causes someone else harm than if it apparently has no adverse effect—that is, if it's just a "white lie" or enables them to escape from what they believe to be unreasonable restrictions on their behavior.[170]

Many contemporary developmental psychologists believe that moral reasoning involves general *trends* rather than distinct stages. It appears that children and adolescents gradually construct several different standards that guide their moral reasoning and decision making in different situations. Such standards include the need to address one's own personal interests, consideration of other people's needs and motives, a desire to abide by society's rules and conventions, and, eventually, an appreciation for abstract ideals regarding human rights and society's overall needs.[171] With age, young people increasingly apply more advanced standards, but even a fairly primitive one—satisfying one's own needs without regard for others—may occasionally take priority.[172]

Table 7.3 describes the forms that moral reasoning and other aspects of morality are apt to take at various grade levels. As you look at the suggested strategies in the right-hand column of the table, notice how several of them are consistent with the *authoritative parenting* style described earlier in the chapter.

Challenges to moral reasoning promote advancement toward more sophisticated reasoning.

Kohlberg drew on Piaget's concept of *disequilibrium* to explain how learners progress to more advanced moral reasoning. (As you may recall from Chapter 6, some contemporary motivation theorists instead use the term *cognitive dissonance.*) In particular, growing children and adolescents occasionally encounter events and dilemmas that their existing moral beliefs can't adequately address. With time and experience, they become increasingly aware of weaknesses in their usual ways of thinking about moral dilemmas, especially if their moral judgments are challenged by people who reason at one stage above their own. For example, a Stage 3 student who agrees to let a popular cheerleader copy his homework may begin to question his decision if a Stage 4 student argues that the cheerleader would learn more by doing her own homework. By struggling with such challenges, Kohlberg suggested, children and adolescents may begin to revise their own thoughts about morality and gradually move from one stage to the next.

Although most contemporary psychologists reject Kohlberg's idea of discrete stages, researchers have confirmed his view that disequilibrium spurs moral development. For instance, classroom discussions of controversial topics and moral issues appear to promote increased perspective taking and the transition to more advanced reasoning.[173] Implicit in this finding is a very important point: Children's moral reasoning does *not* result simply from adults handing down particular moral values and preachings.[174] Instead, it emerges out of children's own, personally constructed beliefs—beliefs they often revisit and revise over time.

Cognition, affect, and motivation all influence moral and prosocial behavior.

Most children behave more morally and prosocially as they grow older, and their increasingly moral behavior is due, in part, to more advanced moral reasoning.[175] For example, children and adolescents who, from Kohlberg's perspective, reason at higher stages are less

---

[169] Helwig et al., 2001; Killen & Smetana, 2008; Nucci, 2009; Piaget, 1932/1960; Thorkildsen, 1995; Turiel, 1998.

[170] S. A. Perkins & Turiel, 2007; Turiel, Smetana, & Killen, 1991.

[171] Killen & Smetana, 2008; Krebs, 2008; Nucci, 2009; Rest, Narvaez, Bebeau, & Thoma, 1999.

[172] Rest et al., 1999; Turiel, 1998.

[173] DeVries & Zan, 1996; Power, Higgins, & Kohlberg, 1989; Schlaefli, Rest, & Thoma, 1985.

[174] Damon, 1988; Higgins, 1995; Turiel, 1998.

[175] Blasi, 1980; N. Eisenberg, 1982; N. Eisenberg, Zhou, et al., 2001; Reimer et al., 1983; Rushton, 1980.

TABLE 7.3 Moral Reasoning and Prosocial Behavior at Different Grade Levels

Grade Level	Age-Typical Characteristics	Example	Suggested Strategies
 K–2	• Some awareness that behaviors causing physical or psychological harm are morally wrong • Ability to distinguish between behaviors that violate human rights and dignity versus those that violate social conventions • Guilt and shame about misbehaviors that cause obvious harm or damage • Some empathy for, as well as attempts to comfort, people in distress, especially people whom one knows well • Appreciation for the need to be fair; fairness seen as strict equality in how a desired commodity is divided • Greater concern for one's own needs than for those of others	When Jake pushes Otis off the ladder of a playground slide, several of the boys' kindergarten classmates are horrified. One child shouts, "That's wrong!" and several others rush to Otis's side to make sure he's not hurt.	• Make standards for behavior very clear. • When students misbehave, give reasons that such behaviors are unacceptable, focusing on the harm and distress they have caused for others (i.e., use *induction*, a strategy described later in the chapter). • Encourage students to comfort others in times of distress. • Model sympathetic responses; explain what you're doing and why you're doing it. • Keep in mind that some selfish behavior is typical for the age-group; when it occurs, encourage more prosocial behavior.
 3–5	• Knowledge of social conventions for appropriate behavior • Growing realization that fairness doesn't necessarily mean equality—that some people (e.g., peers with disabilities) may need more of a desired commodity than others • Increasing empathy for unknown individuals who are suffering or needy • Recognition that one should strive to meet others' needs as well as one's own; growing appreciation for cooperation and compromise • Increased desire to help others as an objective in and of itself	At the suggestion of his third-grade teacher, 9-year-old Jeff acts as a "special friend" to Evan, a boy with severe physical and cognitive disabilities who joins the class two or three days a week. Evan is unable to speak, but Jeff gives him things to feel and manipulate and talks to him whenever class activities allow conversation. And the two boys regularly sit together at lunch. Jeff comments, "Doing things that make Evan happy makes me happy, too."	• Talk about how rules enable classrooms and other groups to run more smoothly. • Explain how students can often meet their own needs while helping others (e.g., when asking students to be "reading buddies" for younger children, explain that doing so will help them become better readers themselves). • Use prosocial adjectives (e.g., *kind, helpful*) when praising altruistic behaviors.
 6–8	• Growing awareness that some rules and conventions are arbitrary; in some cases accompanied by resistance to these rules and conventions • Interest in pleasing and helping others, but with a tendency to oversimplify what "helping" requires • Tendency to believe that people in dire circumstances (e.g., homeless people) are entirely responsible for their own fate	After the midwinter break, 13-year-old Brooke returns to school with several large nose rings and her hair styled into long, vertical spikes above her head. The school principal tells her that her appearance is inappropriate and insists that she go home to make herself more presentable. Brooke resists, claiming, "I have a right to express myself however I want!"	• Make prosocial behaviors (e.g., giving, sharing, caring for others) a high priority in the classroom. • Involve students in group projects that will benefit their school or community. • When imposing discipline for moral transgressions, accompany it with explanations about the harm that has been caused (i.e., use *induction*), especially when working with students who have deficits in empathy and moral reasoning.
 9–12	• Understanding that rules and conventions help society run more smoothly • Increasing concern about doing one's duty and abiding by the rules of society as a whole rather than simply pleasing certain authority figures • Genuine empathy for those in distress • Belief that society has an obligation to help people in need	Several high school students propose and establish a school chapter of Amnesty International, an organization dedicated to the preservation of human rights around the world. The group invites knowledgeable guest speakers from various countries and conducts several fundraisers to help combat abusive practices against women.	• Explore moral issues in social studies, science, and literature. • Encourage community service as a way of engendering feelings of commitment to helping others. Ask students to reflect on their experiences through group discussions or written essays. • Have students read autobiographies and other literature that depict heroic figures who have actively worked to help others.

Sources: N. Eisenberg, 1982; N. Eisenberg & Fabes, 1998; N. Eisenberg et al., 1986; Farver & Branstetter, 1994; C. A. Flanagan & Faison, 2001; Gibbs, 1995; Gummerum, Keller, Takezawa, & Mata, 2008; D. Hart & Fegley, 1995; Hastings, Utendale, & Sullivan, 2007; Helwig & Jasiobedzka, 2001; Helwig et al., 2001; M. L. Hoffman, 1975, 1991; Kohlberg, 1984; Krebs & Van Hesteren, 1994; Kurtines, Berman, Ittel, & Williamson, 1995; Laupa & Turiel, 1995; M. Lewis & Sullivan, 2005; Nucci, 2009; Nucci & Weber, 1995; Rushton, 1980; Smetana & Braeges, 1990; Turiel, 1983, 1998; Wainryb et al., 2005; Yates & Youniss, 1996; Yau & Smetana, 2003; Youniss & Yates, 1999; Zahn-Waxler, Radke-Yarrow, Wagner, & Chapman, 1992.

likely to cheat or insult others, more likely to help people in need, and more likely to disobey orders that would cause someone harm.[176]

Yet the correlation between moral reasoning and moral behavior isn't an especially strong one. Affective factors also enter into the picture. For instance, guilt can be an especially powerful motivator. When children feel guilty about damage or distress they've caused, they may work hard to repair the damage, soothe hurt feelings, and in other respects "make things right."[177] Guilt is limited to situations in which children themselves have caused harm, however. Truly prosocial children—those who help others even in the absence of their own wrongdoing—typically have a considerable capacity for perspective taking, empathy, and sympathy.[178]

Even when children behave prosocially, their own needs and goals often come into play as well. For instance, although children may want to do the right thing, they may also be concerned about whether others will approve of their actions and about what positive or negative consequences might result. Children are more apt to behave in accordance with their moral standards if the benefits are high (e.g., they gain others' approval or respect) and the personal costs are low (e.g., an act of altruism involves little sacrifice).[179]

Moral values become an important part of some learners' sense of self.

In adolescence some young people begin to integrate a commitment to moral values into their overall sense of identity: They think of themselves as generally moral, caring individuals who are concerned about the rights and well-being of others.[180] Their acts of altruism and compassion are not limited to their friends and acquaintances but also extend to the community at large. For example, in one study[181] researchers conducted in-depth interviews with inner-city Hispanic and African American teenagers who showed an exceptional commitment to helping others (by volunteering many hours at Special Olympics, a neighborhood political organization, a nursing home, etc.). These teens didn't necessarily display more advanced moral reasoning than their peers (as defined by Kohlberg's stages), but they were more likely to describe themselves in terms of moral traits and goals (e.g., helping others) and to mention certain ideals toward which they were striving.

As you can see, then, morality and sense of self are interrelated. In fact, the various topics we've discussed in this chapter—personality, sense of self, peer relationships, social cognition, and moral and prosocial development—are all interconnected. For example, moral beliefs influence the interpersonal behaviors that learners believe to be appropriate (social cognition). Those interpersonal behaviors influence the quality of peer relationships, which, in turn, influences learners' self-concepts and self-esteem. This ripple effect works in other directions as well. For instance, learners' sense of self is apt to influence their interpretations of other people's behaviors toward them (social cognition again) and so will also influence their responses and overall social effectiveness (e.g., recall the discussion of hostile attributional bias). And the general patterns we observe in learners' social and moral behaviors are all part of that general characteristic we call "personality."

● Promoting Personal, Social, and Moral Development

The things we've discovered about personal, social, and moral development have numerous implications for classroom practice. I've divided my recommendations into three sections, one each for the personal, social, and moral aspects of development, but keep in mind that advancements in the three domains are closely intertwined. Thus, as you'll often see in the upcoming sections, facilitating learners' development in one area is likely to enhance their development in other areas as well.

---

[176] F. H. Davidson, 1976; Kohlberg, 1975; Kohlberg & Candee, 1984; P. A. Miller, Eisenberg, Fabes, & Shell, 1996; Turiel, 2002.

[177] N. Eisenberg, 1995; Harter, 1999; Malti et al., 2009.

[178] Damon, 1988; N. Eisenberg, Zhou, et al., 2001; M. L. Hoffman, 1991; Malti et al., 2009.

[179] Arsenio & Lemerise, 2004; Batson & Thompson, 2001; N. Eisenberg, 1987; Narváez & Rest, 1995.

[180] Arnold, 2000; Blasi, 1995; Hastings, Utendale, & Sullivan, 2007; Nucci, 2001; Youniss & Yates, 1999.

[181] D. Hart & Fegley, 1995.

Fostering Personal Development

The personal characteristics students bring with them to school—their distinct temperaments and personality characteristics, their beliefs about who they are as individuals, and so on—are apt to have a significant influence on their classroom performance. The following strategies should enhance their academic and social success at school.

Accommodate students' diverse temperaments.

To some degree, students' ways of behaving in the classroom—their energy levels, their sociability, their impulse control, and so on—reflect temperamental differences that aren't entirely within their control. Many temperamental variables affect how students engage in and respond to classroom activities and so also affect students' learning and achievement.[182] Yet there is no single "best" temperament that maximizes classroom success. Instead, children are more likely to succeed at school when there is a **goodness of fit**, rather than a mismatch, between their natural inclinations and typical behaviors, on the one hand, and classroom expectations, on the other.[183] For instance, highly energetic, outgoing children often shine—but quieter students might feel anxious or intimidated—when teachers want students to participate actively in group discussions and projects. Quieter children do better—and some energetic children may be viewed as disruptive—when teachers require a lot of independent seatwork.[184] The Classroom Strategies box "Accommodating Diverse Temperaments" presents several examples of how teachers can work effectively with students' temperamental differences.

Help students get a handle on who they are as people.

A healthy sense of self includes the beliefs that one can successfully tackle certain challenging tasks (reflecting high self-efficacy) and that one is, overall, a good and capable individual (reflecting high self-worth). We identified several ways of enhancing students' sense of self-efficacy and self-worth in Chapter 6, and many additional ones are presented in the right-most column of Table 7.1 (p. 245). Undoubtedly the most important strategy is to *help students be successful,* not only at academic tasks but also in social situations.

Yet equally essential to the development of a sense of self is to gain an understanding of who one is as a person—one's strengths and weaknesses, likes and dislikes, hopes and fears, and so on. Not all students can achieve at superior levels in the classroom, nor can they all be superstars on the athletic field. Students are more likely to have a positive sense of self if they find an activity—perhaps singing, student government, or competitive jump-roping—in which they can shine.[185] And when students have long-standing difficulties in certain domains, discovering that their failures are due to a previously undiagnosed disability (e.g., dyslexia or attention-deficit hyperactivity disorder) can help repair some of the damage to self-esteem.[186] Such a discovery helps students make sense of *why* they can't perform certain tasks as well as their peers. It can also spur them and their teachers to identify effective coping strategies. In the following reflection, one student reveals how, in coming to terms with his dyslexia, he's acquired a healthy sense of self despite his disability:

> Dyslexia is your brain's wired differently and there's brick walls for some things and you just have to work either around it or break it. I'm dyslexic at reading that means I need a little bit more help. If you have dyslexia the thing you have to find is how to get over the hump, the wall. Basically you either go around it and just don't read and get along in life without it or you break down the wall.[187]

Channel adolescents' risk-taking tendencies into safe activities.

Especially at the middle school and high school levels, teachers must be aware of adolescents' propensity to engage in dangerous, high-risk behaviors. Yet scare tactics—perhaps talking about peers who've died from drug overdoses, contracted AIDS from unprotected sex, or

---

goodness of fit   Situation in which classroom conditions and expectations are compatible with students' temperaments and personality characteristics.

[182] Keogh, 2003; Rothbart, 2007; Saudino & Plomin, 2007.
[183] A. Thomas & Chess, 1977.
[184] Keogh, 2003.
[185] Harter, 1999; Jenlink, 1994.
[186] MacMaster, Donovan, & MacIntyre, 2002; Zambo, 2003.
[187] Zambo, 2003, p. 10.

CLASSROOM STRATEGIES Accommodating Diverse Temperaments

- **Minimize down time for students with high energy levels.**

  A third-grade boy seems unable to sit still for more than a couple of minutes. As a way of letting him release pent-up energy throughout the school day, his teacher gives him small chores to do between activities (e.g., erasing the board, sharpening pencils, cleaning art supplies) and shows him how to complete the chores without disturbing classmates.

- **Provide numerous opportunities for highly sociable students to interact with classmates.**

  In a unit on the colonial period in North America, a fifth-grade teacher assigns a project in which students must depict a typical colonial village in some way (e.g., by writing a research paper, drawing a map on poster board, or creating a miniature three-dimensional model). The students can choose to work on the project alone or with one or two classmates, with the stipulation that students who work with peers must undertake more complex projects than students who work alone.

- **Be especially warm and attentive with very shy students.**

  Midway through the school year, a ninth-grade science teacher gets a new student, a girl who's just moved to town from a distant state. He observes that the new girl comes to class alone each day and doesn't join in conversations with peers before or after class. One day he also sees her eating lunch by herself in the cafeteria. He sits down beside her with his own lunch and engages her in conversation about her previous school and community. The following day in class, he assigns a small-group, cooperative learning project that students will work on periodically over the next two weeks. He forms cooperative groups of three or four students each, making sure that he partners the new girl with two students who he knows will be friendly and take her under their wings.

- **When students have trouble adapting to new circumstances, give them advance notice of** unusual activities and provide extra structure and reassurance.

  A kindergarten teacher has discovered that two children in his class do well when the school day is orderly and predictable but often become anxious or upset whenever the class departs from its usual routine. To prepare the children for a field trip to the fire station on Friday, he begins talking about the trip on Monday, explaining what the class will do and see during the visit. He also recruits the father of one of the two anxiety-prone children to serve as a parent assistant that day.

- **If students seem to be overwhelmed by noisy or chaotic situations, find or create a more calm and peaceful environment for them.**

  Several middle school students find the school cafeteria loud and unsettling. Their math teacher offers her classroom as a place where they can occasionally eat instead. On some days she eats with them. At other times she sits at her desk and grades papers, but the students know she will gladly stop to talk with them if they have a question or concern.

- **Teach self-regulation strategies to students who act impulsively.**

  A high school student often shouts out comments and opinions in her history class. The student's teacher takes her aside after school one day and gently explains that her lack of restraint is interfering with her classmates' ability to participate in discussions. To sensitize the student to the extent of the problem, the teacher asks her to keep a daily tally of how many times she talks without first raising her hand. A week later the two meet again, and the teacher suggests a self-talk strategy that can help the student participate actively without dominating discussions.

Source: Some strategies based on suggestions by Keogh, 2003.

---

been killed in high-speed chases—typically have little effect on teenagers' behavior. Nor do rational explanations of probabilities—such as the likelihood of getting pregnant in a single sexual encounter—make much of a difference. When adolescents get together in recreational activities, common sense and reason seem to go out the window. Teachers, administrators, parents, and other community members must all work together to keep adolescent risk taking in check. For instance, many communities now hold all-night after-prom parties in the school building or other supervised location as a way of keeping students from drinking and driving. Another strategy is to provide outlets for *reasonable* risk taking, such as climbing walls, skateboard parks, and small-group, supervised wilderness trips.[188]

Create a warm, supportive environment with clear standards for behavior and explanations of why some behaviors are unacceptable.

An *authoritative* environment—one that combines affection and respect for children with reasonable restrictions on their behavior—seems to be important not only in parenting but also in teaching.[189] Warm teacher–student relationships can help students meet their need

---

[188] Spear, 2007; Steinberg, 2005.
[189] For example, see J. M. T. Walker & Hoover-Dempsey, 2006.

for relatedness, and positive feedback about students' strengths and successes can enhance their sense of self. At the same time, teachers must let students know in no uncertain terms what behaviors are and are not acceptable in the classroom. Behaviors that jeopardize the rights, safety, or psychological well-being of others—stealing, aggression, remarks that ridicule a particular gender or ethnic group, and so on—must be immediately addressed and discouraged.

We'll look at specific strategies both for establishing good teacher–student relationships and for responding to inappropriate behaviors in Chapter 9. But for now we should note that any disciplinary action for unacceptable behavior is most likely to foster students' long-term personal, social, and moral development when it's accompanied by **induction**—that is, by an explanation of *why* a behavior is unacceptable.[190] For example, a teacher might describe how a behavior harms another student either physically ("Having your hair pulled the way you just pulled Mai's can really be painful") or emotionally ("You hurt John's feelings when you call him names like that"). Alternatively, a teacher might explain how an action has caused someone else inconvenience ("Because you ruined Marie's jacket, her parents are making her do extra chores to earn the money for a new one"). Still another approach is to explain someone else's perspective, intention, or motive ("This science project you've just ridiculed may not be as fancy as yours, but I know that Camren spent many hours working on it and is quite proud of what he's done").

Induction is victim centered: It helps students focus on the distress of others and recognize that they themselves have been the cause. The consistent use of induction in disciplining children, especially when accompanied by *mild* punishment for misbehavior, appears to promote cooperation with rules and facilitate the development of prosocial behavior.[191]

Be especially supportive of students at risk.

Students at risk are those who have a high probability of failing to acquire the minimum academic skills necessary for success in the adult world. Many of them drop out before high school graduation, and many others graduate without basic skills in reading or math.[192] Such individuals are often ill equipped to make productive contributions to their families, communities, or society at large.

Students at risk, especially those who eventually drop out, typically have some or all of the following characteristics:

- **A history of academic failure.** On average, students who drop out have less effective reading and study skills, achieve at lower levels, and are more likely to have repeated a grade than their classmates who graduate.[193]
- **Emotional and behavioral problems.** Potential dropouts tend to have lower self-esteem than their more successful classmates. They also are more likely to exhibit serious behavioral problems (e.g., fighting, substance abuse) both in and out of school. Often their close friends are low achieving and, in some cases, antisocial, peers.[194]
- **Lack of psychological attachment to school.** Students at risk for academic failure are less likely to identify with their school or to perceive themselves to be vital members of the school community. For example, they engage in fewer extracurricular activities than their classmates and are apt to express dissatisfaction with school in general.[195]
- **Increasing disinvolvement with school.** Dropping out isn't necessarily an all-or-none event. In fact, many high school dropouts show lesser forms of "dropping out" many years before they officially leave school. Future dropouts are absent from school more frequently than their peers. They're also more likely to be occasionally

---

induction Explanation of why a certain behavior is unacceptable, often with a focus on the pain or distress that someone has caused another.

student at risk Student who has a high probability of failing to acquire the minimum academic skills necessary for success in the adult world.

[190] M. L. Hoffman, 1970, 1975; Nucci, 2009; Staub, 1995.

[191] G. H. Brody & Shaffer, 1982; M. L. Hoffman, 1975; Maccoby & Martin, 1983; Nucci, 2001; Rushton, 1980; Turiel, 2006.

[192] Boling & Evans, 2008; Laird, Kienzl, DeBell, & Chapman, 2007; Slavin, 1989.

[193] K. L. Alexander, Entwisle, & Dauber, 1995; Battin-Pearson et al., 2000; Brophy, 2002; Garnier,

Stein, & Jacobs, 1997; Hattie, 2008; Suh, Suh, & Houston, 2007.

[194] Battin-Pearson et al., 2000; Garnier et al., 1997; Jozefowicz, Arbreton, Eccles, Barber, & Colarossi, 1994; Suh et al., 2007.

[195] Christenson & Thurlow, 2004; Hymel, Comfort, Schonert-Reichl, & McDougall, 1996; Rumberger, 1995.

suspended from school or to show a long-term pattern of dropping out, returning to school, and dropping out again.[196]

A common assumption is that the reasons for dropping out lie largely within students themselves. In fact, characteristics of *schools* also play a significant role.[197] Perhaps academic subject matter is presented in such a way that students find it boring and irrelevant to their needs. Perhaps the school environment is overly controlling, on the one hand (recall our discussion of *self-determination* in Chapter 6), or violent and dangerous, on the other. Sadly, teacher behaviors can enter into the picture as well, as the following dialogue between an interviewer (Ron) and two at-risk high school students (George and Rasheed) reveals:

Many students who drop out find the school curriculum boring and irrelevant to their needs.

Ron: Why do you think someone drops out of school?

George: I think people drop out of school cuz of the pressure that school brings them. Like, sometimes the teacher might get on the back of a student so much that the student doesn't want to do the work. . . . And then that passes and he says, "I'm gonna start doing good. . . ." Then he's not doing as good as he's supposed to and when he sees his grade, he's, "you mean I'm doin' all that for nothin'? I'd rather not come to school." . . .

Rasheed: I think kids drop out of school because they gettin' too old to be in high school. And I think they got, like, they think it's time to get a responsibility and to get a job and stuff. And, like George says, sometimes the teachers, you know, tell you to drop out, knowing that you might not graduate anyway.

Ron: How does a teacher tell you to drop out?

Rasheed: No, they recommend you take the GED program sometimes. Like, some kids just say, "Why don't you just take the GED. Just get it over with." Then, job or something. [Rasheed is referring to a general equivalency diploma, obtained by taking a series of achievement tests rather than completing the requirements for high school graduation.]

Ron: You talked about a kid being too old. Why is a kid too old?

Rasheed: Cuz he got left back too many times.[198]

Teachers may begin to see indicators of "dropping out," such as low school achievement and high absenteeism, as early as elementary school. Other signs, such as low self-esteem, disruptive behavior, and lack of involvement in school activities, often appear years before students officially withdraw from school. So it's quite possible to identify at-risk students early in their school careers and take steps to prevent or remediate academic difficulties before they become insurmountable. Research indicates clearly that for students at risk, prevention, early intervention, and long-term support are more effective than later, short-term efforts.[199]

Students who are at risk for academic failure are a diverse group of individuals with a diverse set of needs, and there is probably no single strategy that can keep all of them in school until high school graduation. Nevertheless, effective teaching practices go a long way toward helping these students stay on the road to academic success and high school graduation. For instance, teachers and schools that have high success rates with students at risk tend to be those that communicate a sense of caring, concern, and high regard for students.[200] The Classroom Strategies box "Encouraging and Supporting Students at Risk" presents additional suggestions that researchers and experienced educators have found to be effective.

Be on the lookout for exceptional challenges that students may face at home.

Ideally, families provide the guidance, encouragement, emotional support, and resources that students need to succeed at school and in the outside world. Unfortunately, not all families provide nurturing environments in which to grow. Some parents have such limited

[196] Christenson & Thurlow, 2004; Finn, 1989; Raber, 1990; Suh et al., 2007.

[197] Brayboy & Searle, 2007; Hardré & Reeve, 2003; V. E. Lee & Burkam, 2003; Portes, 1996; Rumberger, 1995.

[198] Farrell, 1990, p. 91.

[199] K. L. Alexander et al., 1995; Brooks-Gunn, 2003; Christenson & Thurlow, 2004; McCall & Plemons, 2001; Paris, Morrison, & Miller, 2006; Ramey & Ramey, 1998.

[200] L. W. Anderson & Pellicer, 1998; Christenson & Thurlow, 2004; Pianta, 1999.

CLASSROOM STRATEGIES Encouraging and Supporting Students at Risk

- **Make the curriculum relevant to students' lives and needs.**

  A math class in an inner-city middle school expresses concern about the 13 liquor stores located near the school and about the shady customers and drug dealers the stores attract. The students use yardsticks and maps to calculate the distance of each store from the school, gather information about zoning restrictions and other city government regulations, identify potential violations, meet with a local newspaper editor (who publishes an editorial describing the situation), and eventually meet with state legislators and the city council. As a result of students' efforts, city police monitor the liquor stores more closely, major violations are identified (leading to the closing of two stores), and the city council makes it illegal to consume alcohol within 600 feet of the school.

- **Use students' strengths to promote a positive sense of self.**

  A low-income, inner-city elementary school forms a singing group (the Jazz Cats) for which students must try out. The group performs at a variety of community events, and the students enjoy considerable visibility for their talent. Group members exhibit increased self-esteem, improvement in other school subjects, and greater teamwork and leadership skills.

- **Provide extra support for academic success.**

  A middle school homework program meets every day after school in Room 103, where students find their homework assignments on a shelf. Students follow a particular sequence of steps to do each assignment (assembling materials, having someone check their work, etc.) and use a checklist to make sure they don't skip any steps. Initially, a supervising teacher closely monitors what they do, but with time and practice the students can complete their homework with only minimal help and guidance.

- **Communicate optimism about students' chances for long-term personal and professional success.**

  A mathematics teacher at a low-income, inner-city high school recruits students to participate in an intensive math program. The teacher and students work on evenings, Saturdays, and vacations, and many of them eventually pass the Advanced Placement calculus exam.

- **Show students that they are personally responsible for their successes.**

  A teacher says to a student, "Your essay about recent hate crimes in the community is very powerful. You've given the topic consider-

able thought, and you've clearly mastered some of the techniques of persuasive writing that we've talked about this semester. I'd like you to think seriously about submitting your essay to the local paper for its editorial page. Can we spend some time during lunch tomorrow to fine-tune the grammar and spelling?"

- **Create peer support groups that enable students to provide mutual encouragement.**

  At a school that serves a large number of minority-group students who are at risk for academic failure, faculty and students create a Minority Achievement Committee (MAC) program designed to make academic achievement a high priority. Participation in the program is selective (i.e., students must show a commitment to academic improvement) and prestigious. In regular meetings, high-achieving eleventh and twelfth graders describe, model, and encourage many effective strategies, and they help younger students who are struggling with their schoolwork.

- **Get students involved in extracurricular activities, especially those that involve making a long-term commitment to a group effort.**

  A teacher encourages a student with a strong throwing arm to go out for the school baseball team and introduces the student to the baseball coach. The coach, in turn, expresses his enthusiasm for having the student join the team and asks several current team members to help make him feel at home during team practices.

- **Involve students in school policy and management decisions.**

  At a high school that has historically had high drop-out rates, students and teachers hold regular "town meetings" to discuss issues of fairness and justice and establish rules for appropriate behavior. Meetings are democratic, with students and teachers alike having one vote apiece, and the will of the majority is binding.

Sources: Alderman, 1990; L. W. Anderson & Pellicer, 1998; Belfiore & Hornyak, 1998 (homework program example); Christenson & Thurlow, 2004; Cosden, Morrison, Albanese, & Macias, 2001; Eccles, 2007: Eilam, 2001; Feldman & Matjasko, 2005; Finn, 1989; L. S. Fuchs, Fuchs, et al., 2008; Garcia, 1994; Garibaldi, 1993; Higgins, 1995 (town meeting example); Jenlink, 1994 (Jazz Cats example); Knapp, Turnbull, & Shields, 1990; Ladson-Billings, 1994a; Lee-Pearce, Plowman, & Touchstone, 1998; McGovern, Davis, & Ogbu, 2008 (Minority Achievement Club example); Menéndez, 1988 (story of high school math teacher Jaime Escalante, portrayed in the film *Stand and Deliver*); Ramey & Ramey, 1998; M. G. Sanders, 1996; Slavin, Karweit, & Madden, 1989; Suh et al., 2007; Tate, 1995 (liquor store example); E. N. Walker, 2006; D. Wood, Larson, & Brown, 2009.

financial resources that they can't afford adequate food, housing, or medical care. Others are so overwhelmed by crises in their own lives (e.g., marital conflict, loss of employment, or a life-threatening illness) that they have little time or energy to devote to their children. Still others suffer from mental illness or have serious substance abuse problems. And in some cases parents have learned only ineffective parenting strategies from their *own* parents.[201] Such challenges increase the likelihood that children will have emotional problems (e.g., anxiety or depression) and ineffective social skills (e.g., aggression). The more challenges children face, the more vulnerable they are.[202]

---

[201] R. H. Bradley, 2010; Cummings, Schermerhorn, Davies, Goeke-Morey, & Cummings, 2006; Hemmings, 2004; Serbin & Karp, 2003; R. A. Thompson & Wyatt, 1999.

[202] Brooks-Gunn, Linver, & Fauth, 2005; P. T. Davies & Woitach, 2008; El-Sheikh et al., 2009; G. W. Evans & Kim, 2007; Maikovich, Jaffee, Odgers, & Gallop, 2008.

Through newsletters, parent–teacher conferences, and parent discussion groups, teachers can serve as valuable resources to parents about possible strategies for promoting children's personal and social development (we'll identify specific mechanisms for communicating with parents in Chapter 9). The important thing is to communicate information *without* pointing fingers or being judgmental about parenting styles. Let's revisit a point made early in the chapter: How parents treat their children is sometimes the *result,* rather than the cause, of how their children behave. If children are quick to comply with their parents' wishes, parents may have no reason to be overly strict disciplinarians. If children are hyperactive or hot tempered, parents may have to impose more restrictions on behavior and administer more severe consequences for misbehaviors. Teachers must be careful that they don't always place total credit or blame on parents for their parenting styles.

At the same time, teachers must be alert for signs of possible child maltreatment. In some cases parents and other primary caregivers neglect children: They fail to provide nutritious meals, adequate clothing, and other basic necessities of life. In other cases they abuse their children physically, sexually, or emotionally. Possible indicators of neglect or abuse are chronic hunger, lack of warm clothing in cold weather, untreated medical needs, frequent or serious physical injuries (e.g., bruises, burns, broken bones), and exceptional knowledge about sexual matters.[203]

Parental neglect and abuse can have significant adverse effects on children's personal and social development.[204] On average, children who have been routinely neglected or abused have low self-esteem, poorly developed social skills, and low school achievement. Many are angry, aggressive, and defiant. Others can be depressed, anxious, socially withdrawn, and occasionally suicidal. Teachers are both morally and legally obligated to report any cases of suspected child abuse or neglect to the proper authorities (e.g., the school principal or Child Protective Services). Two helpful resources are the National Child Abuse Hotline (1-800-4-A-CHILD, or 1-800-422-4453) and the website for Childhelp USA, www.childhelpusa.org.

Fortunately, many children and adolescents do well in school despite exceptional hardships on the home front. Some are **resilient students** who acquire characteristics and coping skills that help them rise above their adverse circumstances. As a group, resilient students have easy-going temperaments, likable personalities, positive self-concepts, and high yet realistic goals. They believe that success comes with hard work, and their bad experiences serve as constant reminders of the importance of getting a good education.[205]

Resilient students usually have one or more individuals in their lives whom they trust and can turn to in difficult times. Such individuals may be family members, neighbors, close friends, or school personnel. For example, resilient students often mention teachers who have taken a personal interest in them and been instrumental in their school success. Teachers are most likely to foster resilience in students by demonstrating true affection and respect for students, being available and willing to listen when students have concerns, holding high expectations for students' performance, and providing the encouragement and support students need to succeed both inside and outside the classroom.[206]

Provide extra support and guidance for students who have disabilities that affect their personal or social functioning.

Many students have minor social, emotional, or behavioral difficulties at one time or another, particularly during times of unusual stress or major life changes. Often these problems are temporary, especially when students have the support of caring adults and peers. Yet some students show a pattern of behavior problems that consistently interfere with their classroom performance *regardless* of others' guidance and support. Symptoms of such **emotional and behavioral disorders** typically fall into one of two broad categories.

> ? Were you an easy or difficult child to raise? How much might the parenting style in your childhood home been the result of your particular temperament?

---

[203] Crosson-Tower, 2008; Turnbull, Turnbull, & Wehmeyer, 2007.

[204] Bates & Pettit, 2007; J. Kim & Cicchetti, 2006; R. A. Thompson & Wyatt, 1999.

[205] Erath, El-Sheikh, & Cummings, 2009; S. Goldstein & Brooks, 2006; Kim-Cohen & Gold, 2009; Martinez-Torteya, Bogat, von Eye, & Levendosky, 2009; Masten & Coatsworth, 1998; Schoon, 2006; Werner & Smith, 2001.

[206] Bukowski et al., 2009; R. M. Clark, 1983; Masten & Coatsworth, 1998; McMillan & Reed, 1994; D. A. O'Donnell, Schwab-Stone, & Muyeed, 2002; Werner, 1995.

resilient student Student who succeeds in school and in life despite exceptional hardships at home.

emotional and behavioral disorders Emotional states and behavior patterns that consistently and significantly disrupt academic learning and performance.

Shutterstock

Not all students with emotional and behavioral disorders disrupt classroom activities. Students with *internalizing behaviors*—for example, students with severe depression—may be quiet and subdued.

Externalizing behaviors have direct or indirect effects on other people; examples are aggression, defiance, lying, stealing, and general lack of self-control. **Internalizing behaviors** primarily affect the student with the disorder; examples are extreme adverse emotions (e.g., severe anxiety or depression, exaggerated mood swings), withdrawal from social interaction, and eating disorders. Some emotional and behavioral disorders result from environmental factors, such as stressful living conditions, inconsistent parenting practices, child maltreatment, or family alcohol or drug abuse. But biological causes, such as inherited predispositions, chemical imbalances, and brain injuries, may also be involved.[207]

Other disabilities that adversely affect students' social functioning—and sometimes their academic learning as well—are collectively known as **autism spectrum disorders**, which are probably caused by abnormalities in the brain. Common to all of these disorders are marked impairments in social cognition (e.g., perspective taking), social skills, and social interaction. Students with autism spectrum disorders differ considerably in the severity of their condition (hence the term *spectrum*). For instance, in *Asperger syndrome*, a fairly mild form, students have normal language skills and average or above-average intelligence. In severe cases, which are often referred to simply as *autism*, children may have major delays in cognitive and linguistic development and exhibit certain bizarre behaviors—perhaps constantly rocking or waving fingers, continually repeating what someone else has said, or showing unusual fascination with certain objects (e.g., wristwatches).[208]

Professional intervention is called for whenever students are identified as having an emotional or behavior disorder or an autism spectrum disorder. Nevertheless, many students with these disabilities are in general education classrooms for much or all of the school day. Strategies for working effectively with them include the following:[209]

- Communicate a genuine interest in students' well-being.
- Explicitly teach and scaffold social cognition and effective interpersonal skills.
- Stick to a consistent and predictable weekly schedule (especially for students with autism spectrum disorders).
- Make classroom activities relevant to students' interests.
- Consistently communicate the need for appropriate classroom behavior.
- Expect gradual improvement rather than overnight success.

Be alert for signs that a student may be contemplating suicide.

Serious depression can be the result of biology (e.g., hormonal imbalances), life circumstances (e.g., a romantic breakup, chronic peer rejection or bullying, exceptional stress at home), or a combination of the two.[210] Some seriously depressed students think about taking their own lives. Warning signs include:[211]

- Sudden withdrawal from social relationships
- Increasing disregard for personal appearance
- Dramatic personality change (e.g., sudden elevation in mood)
- Preoccupation with death and morbid themes
- Overt or veiled threats (e.g., "I won't be around much longer")
- Actions that indicate "putting one's affairs in order" (e.g., giving away prized possessions)

externalizing behavior Symptom of an emotional or behavioral disorder that has a direct effect on other people.

internalizing behavior Symptom of an emotional or behavioral disorder that adversely affects the student with the disorder but has little or no direct effect on others.

autism spectrum disorders Disorders marked by impaired social cognition, social skills, and social interaction, presumably due to a brain abnormality; extreme forms often associated with significant cognitive and linguistic delays and highly unusual behaviors.

[207] Angold, Worthman, & Costello, 2003; P. T. Davies & Woitach, 2008; El-Sheikh et al., 2009; D. Glaser, 2000; H. C. Johnson & Friesen, 1993; Martinez-Torteya et al., 2009.

[208] American Psychiatric Association, 2000; Hobson, 2004; Pelphrey & Carter, 2007; Tager-Flusberg, 2007; Théoret et al., 2005.

[209] J. M. Chan & O'Reilly, 2008; Clarke et al., 1995; Dalrymple, 1995; Evertson & Weinstein, 2006; Myles &

Simpson, 2001; Wentzel, Donlan, Morrison, Russell, & Baker, 2009.

[210] Champagne & Mashoodh, 2009; Dodge, 2009; Furman & Collins, 2009; Goldston et al., 2008; Hyman et al., 2006; Leadbeater & Hoglund, 2009.

[211] Kerns & Lieberman, 1993; Wiles & Bondi, 2001.

Teachers must take any of these warning signs seriously and seek help from trained professionals, such as a school psychologist or counselor, *immediately.*

Teachers are in an excellent position to foster productive ways of thinking about social situations. They're also in a good position to help students interact effectively with others. The following recommendations are based on research related to social cognition, social skills, and peer relationships.

Encourage perspective taking and empathy.

In any classroom, day-to-day events offer many opportunities for perspective taking and empathy. One strategy is to talk frequently and explicitly about the thoughts, feelings, and needs of various members of the classroom and school community (e.g., as is done in induction).[212] Another strategy is to ask students *themselves* to consider how others might feel in a particular situation. The following report from an elementary school teacher illustrates the value of having students reflect on how their actions might affect others:

> During gym lesson five of the boys misbehaved and were dismissed from class. They acted out their anger by insulting the gym teacher and the other staff greatly by answering back, shouting and even swearing, and throwing eggs at the school buildings. . . . When the boys came to my class they were very upset. . . . I told them I was not going to blame them at this point but I wanted them to write an essay at home about what had happened. . . . [The essays] were written sincerely in the sense that they described clearly what they had done but to my surprise without any regret or tendency to see the staff members' point of view. Having read the essays I decided to discuss the event in class. . . . The children defined the problem and thought about the feelings of those involved. I spent a considerable time asking them to consider the staff members' feelings, whether they knew of somebody who worked in a place similar to the gym, which in fact they did, how that person felt, etc. Gradually, the boys' vehemence subsided. I never blamed them so that they wouldn't become defensive, because then I thought I might lose them. Instead, I tried to improve their understanding of the opinions and feelings of other people, which might differ from their own. . . . The boys improved their behavior in gym class, and this never happened again.[213]

Still another approach is to create or take advantage of opportunities in which students encounter multiple—and perhaps equally legitimate—perspectives and beliefs about a particular issue or conflict. An example is the use of **peer mediation**, in which students help one another solve interpersonal problems. More specifically, students learn how to mediate conflicts among classmates by asking opposing sides to express their differing points of view and then work together to devise a reasonable resolution.[214] In one study involving several second- through fifth-grade classrooms,[215] students were trained to help peers resolve interpersonal conflicts by asking the opposing sides to work together in taking the following steps:

Observe this process in action in the "Peer Mediation" video in Chapter 7 of the Book-Specific Resources in MyEducationLab.

1. Define the conflict (the problem).
2. Explain their own perspectives and needs.
3. Explain the other person's perspectives and needs.
4. Identify at least three possible solutions to the conflict.
5. Reach an agreement that addressed the needs of both parties.

Students took turns serving as mediator for their classmates, such that everyone had experience resolving the conflicts of others. As a result, the students more frequently resolved their *own* interpersonal conflicts in ways that addressed the needs of all involved parties, and they were less likely to ask for adult intervention than students who had not had mediation training.

In peer mediation we see an example of Vygotsky's notion that effective cognitive processes often have their roots in social interactions. In a peer mediation session, students

peer mediation Approach to conflict resolution in which a student (acting as a mediator) asks peers in conflict to express their differing viewpoints and then work together to identify a reasonable resolution.

---

[212] Ruffman, Slade, & Crowe, 2002; Woolfe, Want, & Siegal, 2002.
[213] Adalbjarnardottir & Selman, 1997, pp. 423–424.

[214] Deutsch, 1993; D. W. Johnson & Johnson, 1996, 2006.
[215] D. W. Johnson, Johnson, Dudley, Ward, & Magnuson, 1995.

model effective conflict resolution skills for one another, and they may eventually internalize the skills they use in solving others' problems to solve their *own* problems. Peer mediation is most effective when students of diverse ethnic backgrounds, socioeconomic groups, and achievement levels all serve as mediators. Furthermore, it's typically most useful for relatively small, short-term interpersonal problems (e.g., hurt feelings, conflicts over use of limited academic resources). Even the most proficient of peer mediators may be ill prepared to handle conflicts that reflect deep-seated and emotionally charged attitudes and behaviors—for instance, conflicts that involve sexual harassment or homophobia.[216]

Opportunities for perspective taking and empathy arise not only in day-to-day classroom situations but also in lessons about academic subject matter. For instance, in discussions of current events, teachers might have different students—or, using the Internet, different classrooms—take different countries' perspectives as they explore significant world problems (e.g., climate change, arms control).[217] In history lessons, teachers can ask students to imagine people's feelings or role-play events during particularly traumatic and stressful times.[218] For example, Figure 7.2 shows two writing samples created during history lessons about slavery in the pre-Civil War United States. The reaction paper on the left was written by 10-year-old Charmaine, whose fifth-grade class had been watching *Roots*, a television miniseries about a young African man (Kunta Kinte) who is captured and brought to America to be a slave. Charmaine acknowledges that she cannot fully grasp Kunta Kinte's physical pain (her own experience with pain has been limited to having a paper cut in saltwater). Even so, she talks about his "pain" and "fright" and about his

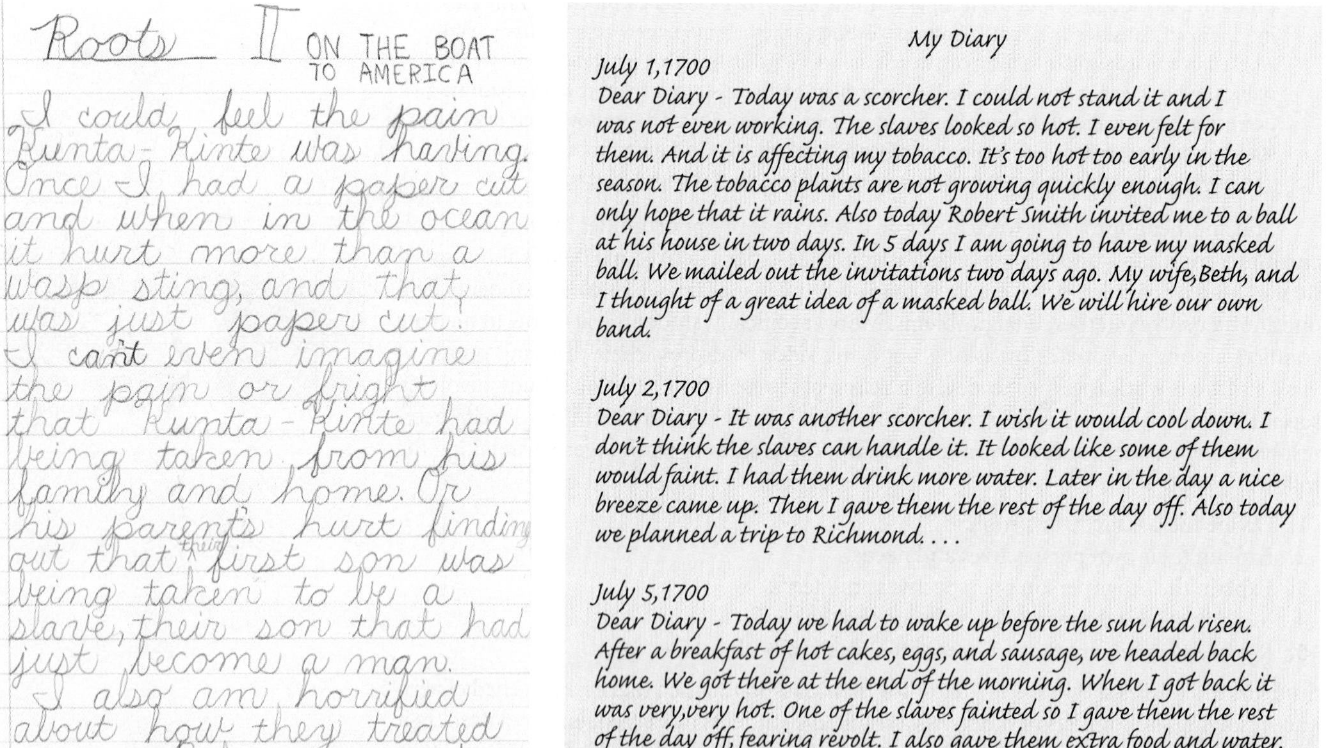

Roots II ON THE BOAT TO AMERICA

I could feel the pain Kunta-Kinte was having. Once I had a paper cut and when in the ocean it hurt more than a wasp sting, and that was just paper cut. I can't even imagine the pain or fright that Kunta-Kinte had being taken from his family and home. Or his parents hurt finding out that their first son was being taken to be a slave, their son that had just become a man. I also am horrified about how they treated women. Belly-warmers! The makes angre!

My Diary

July 1, 1700
Dear Diary - Today was a scorcher. I could not stand it and I was not even working. The slaves looked so hot. I even felt for them. And it is affecting my tobacco. It's too hot too early in the season. The tobacco plants are not growing quickly enough. I can only hope that it rains. Also today Robert Smith invited me to a ball at his house in two days. In 5 days I am going to have my masked ball. We mailed out the invitations two days ago. My wife, Beth, and I thought of a great idea of a masked ball. We will hire our own band.

July 2, 1700
Dear Diary - It was another scorcher. I wish it would cool down. I don't think the slaves can handle it. It looked like some of them would faint. I had them drink more water. Later in the day a nice breeze came up. Then I gave them the rest of the day off. Also today we planned a trip to Richmond. . . .

July 5, 1700
Dear Diary - Today we had to wake up before the sun had risen. After a breakfast of hot cakes, eggs, and sausage, we headed back home. We got there at the end of the morning. When I got back it was very, very hot. One of the slaves fainted so I gave them the rest of the day off, fearing revolt. I also gave them extra food and water. It makes me think that they are only people too. I know that this is unheard of but it really makes me think.

FIGURE 7.2 Two examples of perspective taking in history assignments

[216] Casella, 2001a; K. M. Williams, 2001b.
[217] Gehlbach et al., 2008.
[218] Brophy, Alleman, & Knighton, 2009; Brophy & VanSledright, 1997.

parents' "hurt" at losing their firstborn son, and she is incensed by some colonists' view of African women as little more than "beeby [baby] warmers." The diary entries on the right were written by 14-year-old Craig, whose ninth-grade history teacher asked his class to write journal entries that might capture the life of a southern plantation owner. Notice that Craig tries to imagine someone else (a plantation owner) taking *other people's* perspectives (those of slaves). Such two-tiered perspective taking is similar to recursive thinking but in this case involves thinking "I think that you think that someone else thinks. . . ." Notice, too, that Craig has the plantation owner engage in some minimal prosocial behavior: giving the slaves time off on hot summer days and providing extra food and water. It may not surprise you to learn that Charmaine and Craig, now young adults, are both actively involved in public service.

Explicitly teach social skills to students who have trouble interacting effectively with others.

Because of their social isolation, rejected and neglected students have few opportunities to develop the social skills that many of them desperately need.[219] When they do interact with their peers, their behaviors may be counterproductive, leaving them more isolated than ever. Consider the plight of a seventh grader named Michelle:

> Michelle is an extremely bright student whose academic accomplishments have earned much teacher praise over the years. But despite her many scholastic successes, Michelle has few friends. To draw attention to herself, she talks incessantly about her academic achievements. Her classmates interpret such bragging as a sign of undeserved arrogance and insult her frequently as a way of knocking her down a peg or two. In self-defense, Michelle begins hurling insults at her classmates as soon as she sees them—beating them to the punch, so to speak.

When students routinely offend or alienate others (as Michelle does), their peers seldom give them constructive feedback that might help them improve their behavior on future occasions, and so it may be up to teachers and other adults to give them that guidance.

Observe a special education teacher explicitly teach complimenting skills in the "Social Skills Lesson" video in Chapter 7 of the Book-Specific Resources in MyEducationLab.

Teachers and other school personnel can teach students appropriate ways of interacting with others both through explicit verbal instructions and through modeling desired behaviors. Such instruction is especially effective when students also have an opportunity to practice their newly learned social skills (perhaps through role-playing) and get concrete feedback about how well they're doing.[220]

Teaching social problem-solving skills can be helpful as well. Some students lack productive ways of solving social problems; for instance, they might rudely snatch classroom materials that a classmate has been monopolizing or barge into a playground game without asking first. One effective approach in working with such students is to teach them a series of mental steps, as follows:[221]

1. Define the problem.
2. Identify several possible solutions.
3. Predict the likely consequences of each solution.
4. Choose the best solution.
5. Identify the steps required to carry out the solution.
6. Carry out the steps.
7. Evaluate the results.

Such steps—which you may recognize as involving *social cognition*—often help students who have interpersonal problems (e.g., students who are either socially withdrawn or overly aggressive) to develop more effective social skills.[222]

---

[219] Bukowski et al., 2007; Coie & Cillessen, 1993.

[220] Bierman & Powers, 2009; S. N. Elliott & Busse, 1991; Themann & Goldstein, 2001; S. Vaughn, 1991; Watkins & Wentzel, 2008.

[221] S. N. Elliott & Busse, 1991; Meichenbaum, 1977; Shure & Aberson, 2006; Weissburg, 1985; Yell, Robinson, & Drasgow, 2001.

[222] K. R. Harris, 1982; Meichenbaum, 1977; Yell et al., 2001.

Provide numerous opportunities for social interaction and cooperation.

Schools and classrooms almost invariably involve complex social situations and thus provide ideal contexts in which children and adolescents can learn and practice new social skills. For instance, students' play activities—whether the fantasy play of preschoolers and kindergartners or the rule-based games of older children and adolescents—can promote cooperation, sharing, perspective taking, and conflict resolution skills.[223] Assignments and activities that require students to cooperate with one another to achieve a common goal (as the school play does in the opening case study) can foster leadership skills and a willingness to both help and get help from peers.[224]

Extracurricular activities provide additional opportunities for students to interact and work cooperatively with a wide range of peers.[225] Such activities can also help students find common grounds for communication, as one high school student explained:

> If you feel like you have something to do after school, it's really neat. You get to talk to people in the hall, like, "Oh, is that meeting today?" Or, "What are we doing next week?" It gives you a feeling of, I have people who are in the same club as me.[226]

Talk with students about the advantages and potential dangers of Internet communications.

With the advent of cellular telephone technology and text-messaging software, many students now communicate quite frequently—daily, sometimes almost hourly—with some of their peers.[227] And for students who have easy access to computers, the Internet provides a variety of mechanisms for interacting with peers, both those in town and those in distant places. For instance, e-mail and instant messaging ("IMing") allow quick and easy ways of asking classmates about homework assignments, making plans for social activities, and seeking friends' advice and emotional support. Networking sites (e.g., Facebook, MySpace) provide a means of sharing personal information (e.g., news, interests, photos) and potentially finding like-minded age-mates. Internet chat rooms allow group discussions about virtually any topic. Judicious use of such mechanisms can enhance students' self-esteem, connectedness with peers, and general psychological well-being.[228]

Unfortunately, wireless technologies and the Internet also provide vehicles for cyberbullying, and unscrupulous individuals (usually adults) occasionally misrepresent themselves in attempts to prey on unsuspecting children and adolescents.[229] When appropriate opportunities arise, then, teachers should talk with students about wise and socially appropriate uses of the Internet, and they must certainly monitor students' in-class use of computer technology.

In recent years wireless technologies have become increasingly important vehicles for keeping in touch with peers.

Explain what bullying is and why it cannot be tolerated.

Students often have misconceptions about bullying. For instance, they may think it involves only physical aggression, even though significant relational aggression constitutes bullying as well. An entry in one high school student's journal illustrates how bullying often involves psychological as well as physical tactics:

> One day in junior high, I was getting off the school bus from a seat in the back. . . . I heard people shouting, "Hey, Fatso!" "You big buffalo!" . . . I knew I had to face them before getting off. In order to leave the bus I had to walk through a long crowded aisle and face the obnoxious girls. As I stood up, the girls followed. They crowded together, and approached me as if they were ready to strike at me. . . . All of the [sic] sudden, the girls began to kick and sock me repeatedly. . . . They continued to hurt me as if there was nothing more important to

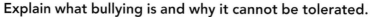

[223] Coplan & Arbeau, 2009; Creasey, Jarvis, & Berk, 1998; Gottman, 1986; Pellegrini & Bohn, 2005; Rubin, 1982.
[224] Certo, in press; Y. Li et al., 2007; N. M. Webb & Farivar, 1994.
[225] Feldman & Matjasko, 2005; Genova & Walberg, 1984; Mahoney, Cairns, & Farmer, 2003; A. J. Martin & Dowson, 2009.
[226] Certo, Cauley, & Chafin, 2002, p. 20.
[227] Greenhow, Robelia, & Hughes, 2009; Gross, 2004; Valkenburg & Peter, 2007.
[228] Ellison, Steinfield, & Lampe, 2007; Gross, 2009; Gross, Juvonen, & Gable, 2002; Valkenburg & Peter, 2009.
[229] Wolak, Finkelhor, Mitchell, & Ybarra, 2008.

them than to see me in pain. The last few kicks were the hardest; all I wanted to do was get off the bus alive. My friends were staring at me, hoping that I would do something to make the girls stop. . . . Finally, after what seemed like an eternity, I was able to release myself from their torture. I got off the bus alive. Imagining that the worst had already passed, I began to walk away from the bus and the girls stuck their heads out the window and spit on me. I could not believe it! They spit on my face! . . . While I was cleaning my face with a napkin, I could still hear the girls laughing.[230]

In some instances bullying involves *only* psychological abuse—taunts, name-calling, blatant exclusion from school social activities, and the like.[231]

Another common student misconception is that the victims of bullying somehow deserve what they get, perhaps because they display immature social and emotional behaviors or need to "toughen up" and learn to defend themselves. Thus many students condone bullying and may serve as a curious or supportive audience that encourages the perpetrators to persist.[232]

Certainly a recommendation offered earlier—*Encourage perspective taking and empathy*—can go part of the way toward discouraging bullying. But ultimately all students must be specifically educated about the nature and harmful effects of bullying. Researchers and experienced educators have found several schoolwide strategies to be helpful:[233]

- Explain that bullying doesn't necessarily involve physical aggression—that it can instead involve taunts, threats, unkind rumors, or embarrassing information communicated either face-to-face or through wireless technologies and the Internet.
- Use the mnemonic PIC to help students remember that bullying is:
  - **P**urposeful behavior ("He meant to do it")
  - **I**mbalanced ("That's not fair, he's bigger")
  - **C**ontinual ("I'm afraid to enter the classroom because she's always picking on me")
- Explicitly forbid name calling, including derogatory labels for a particular sex, ethnic group, sexual orientation, or disability.
- Explain that even seemingly mild forms of bullying can have long-term adverse effects on students' personal and emotional well-being.
- Communicate that stopping bullying is not only a school expectation but also a moral imperative—that students must safeguard other people's physical and psychological well-being as well as their own.
- Recruit well-respected students (e.g., student council members, members of school sports teams) to keep a lookout for bullying in stairways, washrooms, and other places where school faculty members might not be present.
- Teach students effective skills for discouraging bullying incidents among peers (e.g., saying "stop" and escorting the victim to a safe place).
- Prominently post a general code of conduct for student behavior throughout the school building.

As we'll discover in Chapter 9, mutual respect for one another's welfare and well-being both on and off campus is a key ingredient in the *sense of community* so important for students' school success.

Be alert for incidents of bullying and other forms of aggression, and take appropriate actions with both the victims and the perpetrators.

Teachers *must* intervene when they see some students victimize others, and they must keep alert for other possible incidents of bullying. The latter is easier said than done, because a good deal of student–to–student bullying occurs beyond the watchful eyes of school faculty members.[234] Furthermore, victims and witnesses may fear retaliation if they inform adults

---

[230] From *The Freedom Writers Diary* by The Freedom Writers with Erin Gruell, copyright © 1999 by The Tolerance Education Foundation. Used by permission of Doubleday, a division of Random House, Inc.
[231] Doll et al., 2004; Goodwin, 2006; Graham, 2006.
[232] Doll et al., 2004; Salmivalli & Peets, 2009; Shariff, 2008.

[233] D. J. Connor & Baglieri, 2009; Frey, Hirschstein, Edstrom, & Snell, 2009; Horne, Orpinas, Newman-Carlson, & Bartolomucci, 2004, pp. 298–299; E. J. Meyer, 2009; Parada, Craven, & Marsh, 2008; S. W. Ross & Horner, 2009; Willard, 2007.
[234] K. Carter & Doyle, 2006; Hyman et al., 2004.

Chapter 1
The Bully

"Mom, do I have to go to school?"
"Yes, you do Kevin."
"But what if there are bullies?"
"There will not be bullies."
"Fine, I'll go to school."
I got on the bus.
"Hey you, come here."
"No."
"I'll give you my bike if you come here!"
"No!"
"Why?"
"'Cause I have my own."
"Yeah, right. Why should I believe you?"
"I do not know."
"Because you are a liar."
"No, I am not."
"Yes, you are."
"No, I am not."
"Yes, you are."
"Fine, I am."

Most students at all grade levels encounter bullies at one time or another, as shown in this excerpt from Chapter 1 of 7-year-old Michael's story "The Biggest Bully Ever." In Chapter 2, Michael describes how he and his friends defended themselves against the bully.

about bullies' harmful behaviors.[235] It's important, then, that students have mechanisms through which they can report bullying incidents with anonymity.

Regular victims of bullies need social and emotional support from both their teachers and their classmates. Some may also need one or more sessions with a school counselor, perhaps to address feelings of vulnerability and depression or perhaps to learn social skills and help-seeking strategies that can minimize future bullying incidents.[236] One successful school program provided regular "lunch buddies" (college-student volunteers) who joined chronically bullied students in the cafeteria twice a week, indirectly conveying to peers the message that these students had many positive qualities.[237]

Aggressive students must be given appropriate consequences for their actions, of course, but they should also be helped to behave more productively. Specific strategies should be tailored to the cognitive processes and motives that underlie their aggression. Such strategies as encouraging perspective taking, helping students interpret social situations more realistically, and teaching effective social problem-solving skills are all potentially useful in reducing aggression and other disruptive behaviors.[238] For example, in one research study,[239] students with a history of bullying behavior attended a series of training sessions in which, through role-playing, discussions of personal experiences, brainstorming, and similar activities, they practiced making inferences about other people's intentions and identifying appropriate courses of action. They also learned several guidelines to remind them of how to behave in various situations—for example, thinking to themselves, "When I don't have the information to tell what he meant, I should act as if it were an accident."[240] Following the training, the students were less likely to presume hostile intent or endorse aggressive retaliation in interpersonal situations.

Yet even when an aggressive student shows dramatic improvements in behavior, classmates may continue to steer clear, perhaps thinking "Once a bully, always a bully."[241] So when teachers and other adults work to improve the behaviors of aggressive students, they must work to improve the students' reputations as well. For example, teachers might encourage active involvement in extracurricular groups or conduct cooperative learning activities in which students can exhibit their newly developed social skills. Teachers should also demonstrate through words and actions that *they* like and appreciate every student, including formerly antisocial ones. When teachers do so, their attitudes are apt to be contagious.[242]

It's important to note, however, that interventions with individual students are likely to be effective only if their school is a relatively peaceful one. At some schools violence and aggression are commonplace, and students may believe that acting aggressively is the only way to ensure that they don't become victims of *someone else's* aggression. Unfortunately, they may be right: Putting on a tough, seemingly invulnerable appearance (sometimes known as "frontin' it") can be critical for their well-being.[243] Such a situation is, of course, hardly conducive to effective learning and academic achievement. We'll look at strategies for addressing schoolwide aggression and violence in Chapter 9.

Promote understanding, communication, and interaction among diverse groups.

Even when they're in the same building with a large number of peers, students frequently congregate in small groups or cliques with whom they spend most of their time (recall the division of the popular and unpopular students in the opening case study), and a few students remain socially isolated (recall Peter's isolation before taking the role as Snoopy in the school play). Immigrant students rarely interact with long-term residents, and newcomers

[235] R. S. Newman & Murray, 2005; Salmivalli & Peets, 2009.

[236] Espelage & Swearer, 2004; Frey et al., 2009; R. S. Newman, 2008; Yeung & Leadbeater, 2007.

[237] Newgent, Cavell, Johnson, & Stegman, 2008.

[238] Crick & Dodge, 1996; Cunningham & Cunningham, 2006; Frey et al., 2009; Swearer, Grills, Haye, & Cary, 2004.

[239] Hudley & Graham, 1993.

[240] Hudley & Graham, 1993, p. 128.

[241] Bierman, Miller, & Stabb, 1987; Caprara, Dodge, Pastorelli, & Zelli, 2007; Juvonen & Weiner, 1993.

[242] Chang, 2003; Chang et al., 2004.

[243] K. M. Williams, 2001a.

to a school are often socially isolated. Many students with disabilities are neglected or rejected by their classmates.[244]

Often students divide themselves along ethnic lines when they eat lunch and interact in the school yard. In fact, ethnic segregation *increases* once students reach the middle school grades. As young adolescents from ethnic minority groups begin to look closely and introspectively at issues of racism and ethnic identity, they often find it helpful to compare experiences and perspectives with other group members.[245] Yet ethnic stereotypes and prejudices (either real or presumed) can also contribute to this self-imposed segregation.[246] And in some cases, students simply have little or no knowledge about a cultural group very different from their own.

To promote intergroup interaction, then, a necessary first step is to help students understand the customs, perspectives, and needs of their classmates from diverse backgrounds. Especially as students get older and become cognitively capable of reflecting on their own and others' thoughts and feelings, they often benefit from heart-to-heart discussions about prejudice and racism in their own community and school. Some students from mainstream Western culture may initially feel uncomfortable talking about this topic with their minority-group peers, but once the ice is broken, greater cross-cultural understanding and communication can result.[247] And students are more likely to be accepting of classmates with disabilities if they understand the nature of those disabilities, *provided that* the students and their parents give permission to share what might otherwise be confidential information.

It is equally important that schools give students many opportunities to form productive cross-group relationships. Teachers and school administrators can take a variety of proactive steps to broaden the base of students' social interactions. Several possibilities are presented in the Classroom Strategies box "Encouraging Productive Interactions among Diverse Groups," and additional strategies aimed specifically at reducing gang-related hostilities are presented in Chapter 9. When students from diverse groups interact regularly—and especially when they come together as equals, work toward a common goal, and see themselves as members of the same "team"—they are more apt to accept and possibly even *value* one another's differences.[248]

Hear Crystal's concerns about racism in the "Emotions: Early Adolescence" video in Chapter 7 of the Book-Specific Resources in MyEducationLab.

Promoting Moral Reasoning and Prosocial Behavior

Some of the recommendations in the preceding sections should promote moral and prosocial development as well as other aspects of personal and social development. For example, the use of induction—explaining *why* certain behaviors won't be tolerated—can help students acquire more prosocial tendencies toward their classmates. And by encouraging perspective taking and empathy, teachers foster advancements in moral reasoning and altruistic behavior as well as in social skills. Following are three additional recommendations.

Expose students to numerous models of moral and prosocial behavior.

Children and adolescents are more likely to exhibit moral and prosocial behavior when they see people (including their teachers!) behaving in moral rather than immoral ways. For instance, when they see adults or peers being generous and showing concern for others, they tend to do likewise.[249] When they watch television programs that illustrate perspective taking and prosocial actions (e.g., *Sesame Street, Saved by the Bell*), they're more inclined to exhibit such behaviors themselves.[250] Powerful models of moral behavior can be found in

[244] Hymel, 1986; Juvonen & Hiner, 1991; Olneck, 1995; Pérez, 1998; Schofield, 1995; Yuker, 1988.

[245] B. B. Brown et al., 2008; Schofield, 1995; Tatum, 1997.

[246] Black-Gutman & Hickson, 1996; G. L. Cohen & Garcia, 2008; Ogbu, 2008b.

[247] Schultz, Buck, & Niesz, 2000; Tatum, 1997.

[248] Dovidio & Gaertner, 1999; Oskamp, 2000; J. H. Pfeifer, Brown, & Juvonen, 2007; Ramsey, 1995.

[249] Rushton, 1980; C. C. Wilson, Piazza, & Nagle, 1990.

[250] Dubow, Huesmann, & Greenwood, 2007; Hearold, 1986; Singer & Singer, 1994.

CLASSROOM STRATEGIES Encouraging Productive Interactions among Diverse Groups

- **Set up situations in which students can form new friendships.**

  A junior high school science teacher decides how students will be paired for weekly lab activities. She changes the pairings every month and frequently pairs students from different ethnic backgrounds.

- **Minimize or eliminate barriers to social interaction.**

  Students in a third-grade class learn basic words and phrases in American Sign Language so that they can work and play with a classmate who is deaf.

- **Conduct class discussions about the negative consequences of intergroup hostilities.**

  A high school English teacher in a low-income, inner-city school district uses a lesson on Shakespeare's *Romeo and Juliet* to start a discussion about an ongoing conflict between two rival ethnic-group gangs in the community. "Don't you think this family feud is stupid?" she asks her students, referring to Shakespeare's play. When they agree, she continues, "The Capulets are like the Latino gang, and the Montagues are like the Asian gang. . . . Don't you think it's stupid that the Latino gang and the Asian gang are killing each other?" The students immediately protest, but when she presses them to justify their thinking, they gradually begin to acknowledge the pointlessness of a long-standing rivalry whose origins they can't even recall.

- **Encourage and facilitate participation in extracurricular activities, and take steps to ensure that no single group** dominates in membership or leadership in any particular activity.

  When recruiting members for the scenery committee for the eighth grade's annual school play, the committee's teacher–adviser encourages both "popular" and "unpopular" students to participate. Later he divides the workload in such a way that students who don't know one another very well must work closely and cooperatively.

- **Develop nondisabled students' understanding of students with special educational needs.**

  In a widely publicized case, Ryan White, a boy who had contracted AIDS from a blood transfusion, met considerable resistance against his return to his neighborhood school because parents and students thought he might infect others. After Ryan's family moved to a different school district, school personnel actively educated the community about the fact that AIDS doesn't spread through typical day-to-day contact. Ryan's reception at his new school was overwhelmingly positive. Later Ryan described his first day at school: "When I walked into classrooms or the cafeteria, several kids called out at once, 'Hey, Ryan! Sit with me!'"

Sources: Feldman & Matjasko, 2005; Freedom Writers, 1999, p. 33 (Shakespeare example); Genova & Walberg, 1984; Mahoney, Cairns, & Farmer, 2003; Schofield, 1995; Schultz et al., 2000; Sleeter & Grant, 1999; Tatum, 1997; R. White & Cunningham, 1991, p. 149 (Ryan White quotation).

---

literature as well—for instance, in Harper Lee's *To Kill a Mockingbird* and John Gunther's *Death Be Not Proud.*[251]

Engage students in discussions of social and moral issues.

As noted earlier, the disequilibrium (cognitive dissonance) that students experience when they wrestle with moral dilemmas can often promote more advanced moral reasoning. Social and moral dilemmas often arise within the school curriculum. Following are examples:

Observe a high school class discussing appropriate treatment of prisoners of war in the "Teaching with Current Events" video in Chapter 7 of the Book-Specific Resources in MyEducationLab.

- Is military retaliation for acts of terrorism justified even if it involves killing innocent people?
- Should laboratory rats be used to study the effects of cancer-producing agents?
- Was Hamlet justified in killing Claudius to avenge the murder of his father?

Students typically have a variety of opinions about social and moral issues, and they often get emotionally as well as cognitively involved in the subject matter (recall the discussion of *hot cognition* in Chapter 6). To facilitate productive discussions about such issues, teachers must create a trusting and nonthreatening classroom atmosphere in which students can express ideas without fear of censure or embarrassment. Teachers should also help students identify all aspects of a dilemma, including the needs and perspectives of the various individuals involved. The most fruitful discussions occur when teachers encourage students to explore their reasons for thinking as they do—that is, to clarify and reflect on the moral principles on which they're basing their judgments.[252]

---

[251] Ellenwood & Ryan, 1991; Nucci, 2001.
[252] Nucci, 2001, 2006; Reimer et al., 1983.

Get students actively involved in community service.

As we've seen, adolescents are more likely to act in moral and prosocial ways when they've integrated a commitment to moral ideals into their overall sense of identity. Regular community service—ideally beginning well before adolescence—can facilitate this aspect of identity development. Through ongoing community service activities (e.g., food and clothing drives, visits to homes for the elderly, community clean-up efforts), elementary and secondary students alike learn that they have the skills and the responsibility for helping those less fortunate than themselves and in other ways making the world a better place in which to live. In the process, they also begin to think of themselves as concerned, compassionate, and moral citizens.[253] And when high school students participate in community service projects, they gain a sense that their school activities can actually *make a difference* in other people's lives, increasing their desire to stay in school rather than drop out.[254]

Community service projects encourage students to integrate a commitment to helping others into their overall sense of identity.

Jeff Greenberg/PhotoEdit Inc.

[253] Celio, Durlak, Pachan, & Berger, 2007; Hastings et al., 2007; Kahne & Sporte, 2008; Youniss & Yates, 1999.
[254] Eccles, 2007.

SUMMARY

To summarize our discussions of personal, social, and moral development, we now return to the Mega-Ideas presented at the beginning of the chapter.

● *Children's personalities and sense of self influence their behaviors to some degree.* People's personalities are the result of complex interactions between heredity (e.g., temperament) and environment (e.g., home environments, cultural expectations for behavior). Children's and adolescents' personality characteristics lead them to behave somewhat consistently across situations, although distinctly different contexts may elicit distinctly different behaviors. For example, a child might be talkative with one or two close friends but shy and quiet in a large-group setting.

As children grow older, they construct increasingly complex and abstract understandings of who they are—understandings that affect their actions and activity choices. They derive their self-perceptions, collectively known as *sense of self*, not only from their own prior successes and failures but also from the behaviors of others, from the achievements of groups to which they belong, and, often, from their schemas about appropriate behaviors for their gender. Ultimately, children and adolescents socialize *themselves* to a considerable degree, conforming to their own, self-constructed ideas about appropriate behavior.

● *Children and adolescents gain many benefits from productive relationships with peers.* Healthy peer relationships are critical for optimal personal and social development. Peers provide a testing ground for emerging social skills, offer support and comfort in times of trouble or uncertainty, and are influential socialization agents. Furthermore, peers provide opportunities for young people to take others' perspectives, draw conclusions about others' motives and intentions, and develop workable solutions to interpersonal problems. Especially in the middle school and high school years, many older children and adolescents become part of larger social groups (perhaps cliques, crowds, or gangs) and form romantic relationships. Yet some students are consistently rejected or neglected by their peers, and these students may especially need teachers' support and guidance.

● *Children's interpretations of social situations have a significant impact on their ability to interact effectively with others.* Most children and adolescents actively try to make sense of their social world. With age, this *social cognition*—thinking about what other people might be thinking and feeling, and hypothesizing about how others might act and react in various situations—becomes increasingly complex and insightful, enabling effective interaction with adults and peers. But some young people have difficulty interpreting social cues correctly and may have few effective social skills. Such difficulties can lead to aggressive and potentially dangerous actions toward others.

Some forms of aggression involve behaviors that might cause another person physical harm. But other forms—collectively known as *relational aggression*—involve behaviors that adversely affect an individual's interpersonal relationships. For instance, through the use of a cell phone or the Internet, an individual might humiliate someone else by forwarding embarrassing e-mails or photographs to a great many peers (such technology-based aggression is known as *cyberbullying*).

● *Moral reasoning and prosocial behaviors emerge early in life but continue to evolve over the course of childhood and adolescence.* As children move through the grade levels, most acquire a clear sense of right and wrong, such that they behave in accordance with prosocial standards for behavior rather than acting solely out of self-interest. This developmental progression is the result of many things, including increasing capacities for empathy and abstract thought, an evolving appreciation for human rights and other people's welfare, and ongoing encounters with moral dilemmas and problems. Even at the high school level, however, students don't always take the moral high road, because personal needs and self-interests often enter into their moral decision making.

- **Effective teachers accommodate individual differences in students' temperaments and personalities, and they help students acquire productive behaviors and a healthy sense of self.** Although teachers should certainly accommodate students' diverse temperaments and help students identify areas of particular talent, they must also communicate clear standards for behavior and explain why some behaviors are unacceptable. All students need ongoing teacher support and guidance, but such support and guidance are especially critical for students at risk for academic failure, students who face exceptional challenges at home, and students with disabilities or emotional problems that adversely affect their psychological well-being.

- **Effective teachers create conditions that foster students' social and moral development.** Children and adolescents spend a good deal of their lives in schools and classrooms, which are therefore important contexts for social and moral development. For instance, teachers can help unpopular students acquire better social skills and more productive social information processing abilities, and they must actively discourage bullying behaviors and inappropriate Internet use. Often, too, teachers can take steps to encourage communication and interaction among students with diverse backgrounds and characteristics. And by engaging students in regular discussions about social and moral issues and getting students actively involved in community service, teachers can foster empathy and more advanced moral reasoning.

PRACTICE FOR YOUR LICENSURE EXAM

The Scarlet Letter

Ms. Southam's eleventh-grade English class has been reading Nathaniel Hawthorne's *The Scarlet Letter*. Set in seventeenth-century Boston, the novel focuses largely on two characters who have been carrying on an illicit love affair: Hester Prynne, a young woman who has not seen or heard from her husband for the past two years, and the Reverend Arthur Dimmesdale, a pious and well-respected local preacher. When Hester becomes pregnant, she is imprisoned for adultery and eventually bears a child. The class is currently discussing Chapter 3, in which the governor and town leaders, including Dimmesdale, are urging Hester to name the baby's father. (You can observe the following interaction in the "Scarlet Letter" video in Chapter 7 of the Book-Specific Resources in MyEducationLab.)

Ms. Southam: The father of the baby . . . how do you know it's Dimmesdale . . . the Reverend Arthur Dimmesdale? . . . What are the clues in the text in Chapter 3? . . . Nicole?

Nicole: He acts very withdrawn. He doesn't even want to be involved with the situation. He wants the other guy to question her, because he doesn't want to look her in the face and ask her to name *him*.

Ms. Southam: OK. Anything else? . . .

Student: The baby.

Ms. Southam: What about the baby?

Student: She starts to cry, and her eyes follow him.

Ms. Southam: That is one of my absolutely favorite little Hawthornisms.

Ms. Southam reads a paragraph about Dimmesdale and asks students to jot down their thoughts about him. She then walks around the room, monitoring what students are doing until they appear to have finished writing.

Ms. Southam: What pictures do you have in your minds of this man . . . if you were directing a film of *The Scarlet Letter*?

Mike: I don't have a person in mind, just characteristics. About five-foot-ten, short, well-groomed hair, well dressed. He looks really nervous and inexperienced. Guilty look on his face. Always nervous, shaking a lot.

Ms. Southam: He's got a guilty look on his face. His lips always trembling, always shaking.

Mike: He's very unsure about himself.

Matt: Sweating really bad. Always going like this. (He shows how Dimmesdale might be wiping his forehead.) He does . . . he has his hanky. . . .

Ms. Southam: Actually, we don't see him mopping his brow, but we do see him doing what? What's the action? Do you remember? If you go to the text, he's holding his hand over his heart, as though he's somehow suffering some pain.

Student: Wire-framed glasses. . . . I don't know why. He's like. . . .

Mike: He's kind of like a nerd-type guy. . . . Short pants. . . .

Ms. Southam: But at the same time . . . I don't know if it was somebody in this class or somebody in another class. . . . He said, "Well, she was sure *worth* it." Worth risking your immortal soul for, you know? . . . Obviously she's sinned, but so has he, right? And if she was worth it, don't we also have to see him as somehow having been worthy of her risking *her* soul for this?

Student: Maybe he's got a good personality. . . .

Ms. Southam: He apparently is, you know, a spellbinding preacher. He really can grab the crowd.

Student: It's his eyes. Yeah, the eyes.

Ms. Southam: Those brown, melancholy eyes. Yeah, those brown, melancholy eyes. Absolutely.

1. **Constructed-response question**

   In this classroom dialogue Ms. Southam and her students speculate about what the characters in the novel, especially Arthur Dimmesdale, might be thinking and feeling. In other words, they are engaging in social cognition.

   A. Identify two examples of student statements that show social cognition.

   B. For each example you identify, explain what it reveals about the speaker's social cognition.

2. **Multiple-choice question**

   Ms. Southam does several things that are apt to enhance students' perspective-taking ability. Which one of the following is the best example?

   a. She models enthusiasm for the novel ("That is one of my absolutely favorite little Hawthornisms").

b. She walks around the room as the students write down their thoughts about Dimmesdale.

c. She points out that Dimmesdale is "holding his hand over his heart, as though he's somehow suffering some pain."

d. She agrees with Mike's description of Dimmesdale as having a guilty look on his face.

Go to Chapter 7 of the Book-Specific Resources in MyEducationLab and click on "Practice for Your Licensure Exam" to answer these questions. Compare your responses with the feedback provided.

PEARSON
myeducationlab

Go to the Topic "Personal, Social & Moral Development" in the MyEducationLab (www.myeducationlab.com) for your course, where you can:

- Find learning outcomes for "Personal, Social & Moral Development," along with the national standards that connect to these outcomes.
- Complete Assignments and Activities that can help you more deeply understand the chapter content.
- Apply and practice your understanding of the core teaching skills identified in the chapter with the Building Teaching Skills and Dispositions learning units.
- Access video clips of CCSSO National Teachers of the Year award winners responding to the question, "Why Do I Teach?" in the Teacher Talk section.
- Check your comprehension of the content covered in the chapter by going to the Study Plan in the Book Resources for

your text. Here you will be able to take a chapter quiz, receive feedback on your answers, and then access Review, Practice, and Enrichment activities to enhance your understanding of chapter content. Flash cards are also available to help you study definitions and key terms.

- Access additional Book Resources, including:
  - Focus Questions to guide your reading, Video Examples of various concepts and principles presented in the chapter, a Practice for Your Licensure Exam exercise that resembles the kinds of questions appearing on many teacher licensure tests, Margin Note Questions that help you connect chapter content to your past experiences or current beliefs, and Supplementary Readings that enable you to pursue certain topics in greater depth.

Chapter 8

Instructional Strategies

Shutterstock

CHAPTER OUTLINE

Case Study: The Oregon Trail

Planning Instruction

Conducting Teacher-Directed Instruction

Conducting Learner-Directed Instruction

General Instructional Strategies

Summary

Practice for Your Licensure Exam: Cooperative
Learning Project

MEGA-IDEAS TO MASTER IN THIS CHAPTER

Effective teachers identify the knowledge and abilities they want students to acquire, and they plan instruction accordingly.

Sometimes instruction is most effective when it is teacher directed—that is, when the teacher chooses the specific topics to be studied and the general course of a lesson.

Sometimes instruction is most effective when it is learner-directed—that is, when students have some control over the issues to be addressed and the ways in which to address them.

Different instructional strategies are appropriate for different instructional goals and objectives and for different students.

CASE STUDY The Oregon Trail

Michele Minichiello's fifth-grade class is learning about the westward migration of American settlers during the middle 1800s. Today's lesson is about one well-traveled route, the Oregon Trail.[1]

"The covered wagons were about 4 feet by 10 feet," Ms. Minichiello tells her class. She has two students use masking tape to mark a 4-by-10-foot rectangle on the classroom carpet. "How much room would that give you for your family and supplies?" The students agree that people would have to be quite choosy about what they brought with them on the trip west.

"Let's brainstorm some of the things the settlers might have packed," Ms. Minichiello says. The students volunteer many possibilities—food, water, blankets, rifles, medicine, spare wagon parts—and Ms. Minichiello writes them on the dry-erase board. She asks the class to be more specific about the items on the board (e.g., What kinds of food? How much of each kind?) and then passes out reading materials that list the supplies a typical family would actually pack for the journey. As the students read and discuss the materials in small cooperative learning groups, Ms. Minichiello circulates among them to show old photographs of how the inside of a covered wagon looked when occupied by a family and its possessions.

Once the students have finished their reading, Ms. Minichiello directs their attention to their own supply list on the board and asks them to compare it to the list of typical supplies presented in the reading materials. The students notice many discrepancies:

Lacy: We need much more flour.

Janie: [Referring to an item listed in the reading materials] I don't think they should bring 100 pounds of coffee.

Curt: [Also referring to the reading materials] I don't think they need 50 pounds of lard.

Ms. M: What were some of the things that pioneers had to be prepared for?

After the class discusses possible reasons for the various items the settlers brought with them, Ms. Minichiello asks students to put themselves in the settlers' shoes.

Ms. M: If *you* were taking such a trip now—if you were moving far away from where you live now—what things would you bring with you?

Misha: Computer.

Lou: Cell phone.

Dana: Refrigerator.

Cerise: My dog.

Ms. M: Where would pioneers go now?

Curt: North or South Pole.

Tom: Space.

Ms. M: Imagine that your family isn't doing well, and so you decide to travel to a distant planet. It's very expensive to travel there. You can only take *one* item, so pick the one item you would bring. Assume there will be food and a place to sleep. Take five minutes to pick one item, and explain why you would take it.

(continued)

---

[1] I observed Michele's lesson when I was supervising her teaching internship, and she gave me permission to describe it here. The students' names are pseudonyms.

Ms. Minichiello distributes index cards on which the students can write their responses. After a few minutes she asks, "Who found that it was hard to pick just one item?" Almost all of the students raise their hands. "What I wanted you to realize is that if you had been a child back then, it would have been really hard to leave most of your things behind."

- What specific instructional strategies is Ms. Minichiello using to engage and motivate her students? What strategies is she using to help them learn and remember the content of the lesson?

To engage and motivate her students, Ms. Minichiello arouses situational interest through a physical activity (students make a "wagon" on the floor), creates cognitive dissonance (the list in the reading materials doesn't entirely match the one the class has generated), poses a challenging question ("You can only take *one* item. . . ."), and makes the lesson a very social, interactive one. Furthermore, Ms. Minichiello promotes learning and understanding by encouraging visual imagery and elaboration—for instance, by making the subject matter concrete and vivid (through the masking-tape wagon and the old photographs), having the class consider necessities and hazards that might justify items on the supply list ("What were some of the things that pioneers had to be prepared for?"), and asking students to relate the settlers' situation to a hypothetical one they themselves might face.

Much of Ms. Minichiello's lesson reflects **teacher-directed instruction**, in which the teacher calls most of the shots, choosing which topics will be addressed, directing students' activities, and so on. Even when she asks fairly open-ended questions (e.g., "If *you* were taking such a trip now . . . what things would you bring with you?") she is nudging students toward the kinds of conclusions she wants them to draw about life on the Oregon Trail. But one of her strategies—having students study reading materials in small cooperative groups—reflects **learner-directed instruction**, in which students have considerable control regarding the specific issues they address and the ways they address those issues.[2] Decisions about whether to use teacher-directed or learner-directed strategies—or to combine both kinds of strategies into a single lesson, as Ms. Minichiello does—should be based on the goals for instruction and on students' current knowledge and skill levels. And in any case the distinction I'm making is really a *continuum*—not an either-or situation—because instructional strategies can vary considerably in the degree to which teachers and students control the course of events.

In the preceding chapters, we've learned a great deal about how children and adolescents think, learn, develop, and become motivated to engage actively and productively in classroom activities. In this chapter we'll build on what we've learned to identify a variety of ways in which teachers can effectively plan and carry out instruction. As you'll soon discover, planning and carrying out instruction are closely intertwined with two other essential aspects of teaching: creating an effective classroom environment and assessing students' progress and final achievements (we'll explore these topics in depth in Chapters 9 and 10, respectively). But ultimately, student characteristics and behaviors should drive what teachers do in the classroom (see Figure 8.1). To repeat a point I made in Chapter 1, classroom practices should be *learner centered*.

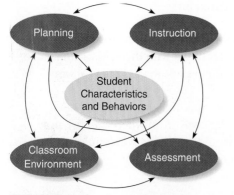

FIGURE 8.1 Planning, instruction, the classroom environment, classroom assessment practices, and student characteristics and behaviors are all interdependent and mutually influence one another.

Planning Instruction

Good teachers engage in considerable advance planning: They identify the information and skills they want students to acquire, determine an appropriate sequence in which to teach the knowledge and skills, and develop classroom lessons and activities that will maximize learning and keep students motivated and on task. Ideally, teachers also coordinate their plans with

teacher-directed instruction Approach to instruction in which the teacher is largely in control of the content and course of the lesson.

learner-directed instruction Approach to instruction in which students have considerable say in the issues addressed and the ways in which to address them.

[2] Some educators instead use the terms *teacher centered* and *learner centered* in reference to this distinction. However, as I point out in Chapter 1 and illustrate in Figure 8.1, virtually all instructional strategies should focus (center) on what and how students are learning. The essential difference here lies in who has control of the instructional activity.

one another—for example, by identifying common goals toward which everyone will strive or by developing interdisciplinary units that involve two or more classes and subject areas.

The following strategies are key elements of effective instructional planning.

Identify the desired end results of instruction.

An essential part of planning instruction is identifying the specific things students should accomplish during a lesson or unit, as well as the things they should accomplish over the course of the semester or school year. Educators use a variety of terms for such end results, including *goals, objectives, outcomes, proficiencies, targets, benchmarks,* and *standards*. In this book I'll typically use the term **instructional goals** when referring to general, long-term outcomes of instruction. I'll use the term **instructional objectives** when referring to more specific outcomes of a particular lesson or unit.

Regardless of the terminology they use, experts agree that the desired end results of instruction should influence what teachers teach, how they teach it, and how they assess students' learning and achievement.[3] In fact, as a general rule, teachers should *begin* the planning process by determining what they ultimately want students to know and be able to do. One widely recommended approach is a **backward design** in which teachers proceed through this sequence:[4]

1. Identify the desired results in terms of knowledge and skills that students should ultimately attain.
2. Determine acceptable evidence—in the form of performance on various classroom assessment tasks—to verify that students have achieved those results.
3. Plan learning experiences and instructional activities that enable students to demonstrate—through their performance on the assessment tasks—attainment of the desired results.

With such an approach, teachers essentially *begin at the end* and then choose assessment tasks and instructional strategies that are specifically related to that end. For example, if the objective for a unit on addition is *knowledge* of number facts, a teacher may want to use drill and practice (perhaps flash cards, perhaps gamelike computer software) to enhance students' automaticity for these facts and may want to use a timed test to measure students' ability to recall the facts quickly and easily. But if the objective is *application* of number facts, a teacher may instead want to focus instruction and assessment methods on word problems or on activities involving real objects and hands-on measurements.

Knowing the desired final outcomes of instruction benefits not only teachers—who can then choose appropriate content and instructional methods—but students as well. When students know what they need to accomplish, they can make more informed decisions about how to focus their efforts and allocate their study time, and they can more effectively monitor their comprehension as they read and study.[5] For example, if their teacher tells them that they should be able to apply science and math to everyday situations, they'll probably think about and study these subject areas very differently than if they need to memorize definitions and formulas.

Teachers don't pull their goals and objectives out of the blue, of course. One source of guidance comes from content area **standards** identified by national and international discipline-specific professional groups (e.g., National Council of Teachers of Mathematics, Center for Civic Education, National Association for Music Education). Such standards are typically in the form of general statements regarding the knowledge and skills that students should acquire at various grade levels, as well as the characteristics their accomplishments should reflect. Also, in the United States various state departments of education—and some local school districts as well—have established standards that identify specific goals for different grade levels in reading, writing, math, science, social studies, and sometimes also in such domains as art, music, foreign languages, and physical education.[6] As an illustration, Table 8.1 presents examples of North Carolina's standards—which state educators call *competency goals*—for English Language Arts (see the table's yellow column).

Hear a teacher describe instructional objectives for a lesson in the "Civil War" video in Chapter 8 of the Book-Specific Resources in MyEducationLab.

Find web links to content area standards developed by the 50 U.S. states and various discipline-specific professional organizations in MyEducation-Lab.

instructional goal Desired long-term outcome of instruction.

instructional objective Desired outcome of a lesson or unit.

backward design Approach to instructional planning in which a teacher first determines the desired end result (i.e., what knowledge and skills students should acquire) and then identifies appropriate assessments and instructional strategies.

standards General statements regarding the knowledge and skills that students should gain and the characteristics that their accomplishments should reflect.

---

[3] For example, see Darling-Hammond & Bransford, 2005; Kuhn, 2007.
[4] Tomlinson & McTighe, 2006; Wiggins & McTighe, 2005.

[5] Gronlund & Brookhart, 2009; McAshan, 1979.
[6] You can find many state standards online by typing "state educational standards" in a browser such as Google or Yahoo!

DEVELOPMENTAL TRENDS

TABLE 8.1 Examples of How You Might Align Classroom Goals, Objectives, and Instructional Strategies with State Standards at Different Grade Levels

Grade Level	Examples of North Carolina's Competency Goals for English Language Arts	Examples of More Specific Classroom Goals/Objectives	Examples of Relevant Instructional Strategies
Grade 1	Read and comprehend both fiction and nonfiction text appropriate for grade one using: • Prior knowledge • Summary • Questions • Graphic organizers (Competency Goal 2.03)	Use prior knowledge to draw correct inferences from a story in which the author has omitted important information.	Read high-interest stories, stopping frequently to ask questions that require students to go beyond the text itself (e.g., to speculate about what a character might be feeling).
	Respond and elaborate in answering what, when, where, and how questions. (Competency Goal 2.07)	Identify main characters, setting, and general plot line in a short story.	Have students create props for and act out a story they have recently read.
Grade 4	Interact with the text before, during, and after reading, listening, and viewing by: • Setting a purpose using prior knowledge and text information • Making predictions • Formulating questions • Locating relevant information • Making connections with previous experiences, information, and ideas (Competency Goal 2.02)	Make predictions about how a novel's plot might unfold.	As a reading group discusses Carl Hiaasen's *Hoot,* ask students to speculate about how the plot might progress and to identify clues in the text that support their predictions.
	Make inferences, draw conclusions, make generalizations, and support by referencing the text. (Competency Goal 2.05)	Identify cause–and–effect relationships in assigned readings in a history textbook.	When students are reading their history textbook, ask *why* questions that encourage cause–and–effect connections (e.g., "Why did Columbus's crew want to return home after several weeks on the open sea?").
 Grade 7	Respond to informational materials that are read, heard, and/or viewed by: • Monitoring comprehension for understanding of what is read, heard, and/or viewed • Analyzing the characteristics of informational works • Summarizing information • Determining the importance of information • Making connections to related topics/information • Drawing inferences and/or conclusions • Generating questions (Competency Goal 2.01)	Use the organizational structure of a science textbook to enhance understanding and memory of its contents.	Before students read a chapter in their science textbook, have them use its headings and subheadings to (1) create a general outline of the chapter and (2) generate questions they hope to answer as they read the chapter. Then, for homework, ask them to read and take notes on the chapter, using the outline and self-questions as guides for note taking.

(continued)

Grade Level	Examples of North Carolina's Competency Goals for English Language Arts	Examples of More Specific Classroom Goals/Objectives	Examples of Relevant Instructional Strategies
Grade 7 (continued)	Analyze the purpose of the author or creator by: • Monitoring comprehension for understanding of what is read, heard, and/or viewed • Examining any bias, apparent or hidden messages, emotional factors, and/or propaganda techniques • Exploring and evaluating the underlying assumptions of the author/creator (portion of Competency Goal 4.01)	Identify persuasive techniques used in advertisements for commercial products in magazines and online websites.	Give students an advertisement for a self-improvement product (e.g., a diet pill or exercise equipment); have them work in small cooperative learning groups to (1) identify the advertiser's motives and (2) evaluate the quality of evidence for the product's effectiveness.
Grade 11	Demonstrate the ability to read, listen to, and view a variety of increasingly complex print and non-print informational texts appropriate to grade level and course literary focus, by: • Selecting, monitoring, and modifying as necessary reading strategies appropriate to readers' purpose • Making inferences, predicting, and drawing conclusions based on text • Identifying and analyzing personal, social, historical or cultural influences, contexts, or biases (portions of Competency Goal 2.03 for English III)	Identify authors' political and cultural biases in their descriptions of current events.	Ask students to identify the unstated assumptions underlying two news magazines' depictions of the same event (e.g., an assumption that one group is good or right and another is bad or wrong).
	Develop thematic connections among works by: • Connecting themes that occur across genres or works from different time periods • Using specific references to validate connections • Examining how representative elements such as mood, tone, and style impact the development of a theme (Competency Goal 4.02 for English III)	Identify examples of racism, sexism, and classism revealed in literature from different time periods.	Conduct small-group discussions in which students compare prevailing attitudes toward women in Jane Austen's *Pride and Prejudice* and Zora Neale Hurston's *Their Eyes Were Watching God.*

Source: Competency Goals (second column) are from a website maintained by North Carolina's Department of Public Instruction and are provided with permission from the Public Schools of North Carolina. Standards are current as of October 19, 2010, from www.dpi.state.nc.us/curriculum/languagearts/scos/. Please note that North Carolina is currently revising its Standard Course of Study; thus, the Competency Goals may change within the next few years.

Existing standards for particular content domains are certainly useful in helping teachers focus instruction on important educational goals, including such complex cognitive processes as transfer, problem solving, and critical thinking. If teachers rely on content area standards exclusively, however, they're apt to neglect other, equally important goals, such as helping students acquire effective learning strategies, self-regulation techniques, and

CLASSROOM STRATEGIES Identifying Goals and Objectives of Instruction

- Consult local, state, national, and international standards, but don't rely on them exclusively.

  In identifying instructional goals for the year, a middle school science teacher considers both the state science standards and the standards developed by the National Academy of Sciences. In addition, he identifies specific goals related to two issues directly affecting students in his inner-city school district: air pollution and poor nutrition.

- Be realistic about what can be accomplished in a given time frame; allow time to pursue important topics in depth.

  Rather than expect students to remember a lot of discrete facts in social studies, a second-grade teacher identifies several "Big Ideas" that students should master during the school year—for instance, the idea that all people have certain needs and desires that affect their behaviors and the idea that different cultural groups may strive to satisfy those needs and desires in different ways.

- Identify both short-term objectives and long-term goals.

  A fourth-grade teacher wants students to learn how to spell 10 new words each week. He also wants them to write a coherent and grammatically correct short story by the end of the school year.

- In addition to goals related to specific topics and content areas, identify goals related to students' general long-term academic success.

  A middle school teacher realizes that early adolescence is an important time for developing the learning and study strategies that students will need in high school and college. Throughout the school year, then, he continually introduces new strategies for learning and remembering classroom subject matter—effective ways that students might organize their notes, mnemonic techniques they might use to help them remember specific facts, questions they might try to answer as they read a textbook chapter, and so on.

- Include goals and objectives at varying levels of complexity and sophistication.

A high school physics teacher wants students not only to understand basic kinds of machines (e.g., levers, wedges) but also to recognize examples of these machines in their own lives and use them to solve real-world problems.

- Consider physical, social, and affective outcomes as well as cognitive outcomes.

  A physical education teacher wants his students to know the basic rules of basketball and to dribble and pass the ball appropriately. He also wants them to acquire a love of basketball, effective ways of working cooperatively with teammates, and a general desire to stay physically fit.

- Describe goals and objectives not in terms of what the teacher will do during a lesson but in terms of what *students* should be able to do at the *end* of instruction.

  A high school Spanish teacher knows that students easily confuse the verbs *estar* and *ser* because both are translated in English as "to be." She identifies this objective for her students: "Students will correctly conjugate *estar* and *ser* in the present tense and use each one in appropriate contexts."

- When formulating short-term objectives, identify specific behaviors that will reflect accomplishment of the objectives.

  In a unit on the food pyramid, a health teacher identifies this objective for students: "Students will create menus for a breakfast, a lunch, and a dinner that, in combination, include all elements of the pyramid in appropriate proportions."

- When formulating long-term goals that involve complex topics or skills, list a few abstract outcomes and then give examples of specific behaviors that reflect each one.

  Faculty members at a junior high school identify this instructional goal for all students at their school: "Students will demonstrate effective listening skills—for example, by taking accurate notes, showing respect for diverse points of view, and seeking clarification when they don't understand."

Sources: Brophy, 2008; Brophy, Alleman, & Knighton, 2009; N. S. Cole, 1990; Gronlund & Brookhart, 2009; M. D. Miller, Linn, & Gronlund, 2009; Popham, 1995; Wiggins & McTighe, 2005.

social skills. In addition to considering existing local, state, national, and international standards, then, teachers should formulate some of their *own* goals and objectives. The Classroom Strategies box "Identifying Goals and Objectives of Instruction" offers suggestions for developing useful ones. Column 3 of Table 8.1 (the pink column) applies some of these suggestions in translating the examples of North Carolina's competency goals into more specific classroom goals and objectives—things that *students* should be able to do— and Column 4 (in blue) identifies relevant instructional strategies for teachers. (We'll identify assessment strategies for the same standards and goals in a separate table in Chapter 10.)

One especially important suggestion in the Classroom Strategies box is to *include goals and objectives at varying levels of complexity and sophistication.* Notice that the competency goals presented in Table 8.1 focus largely on meaningful learning and complex cognitive processes—relating new information to prior knowledge, drawing inferences, monitoring comprehension, critically evaluating ideas, and so on. Such processes must, of course, be an important part of teacher-developed goals and objectives as well. One tool that can help teachers broaden their view of what students should learn and be able to do is **Bloom's taxonomy**, a list of six general cognitive processes that vary from simple to complex:[7]

1. *Remember:* Recognizing or recalling information learned at an earlier time and stored in long-term memory
2. *Understand:* Constructing meaning from instructional materials and messages (e.g., drawing inferences, identifying new examples, summarizing)
3. *Apply:* Using knowledge in a familiar or new situation
4. *Analyze:* Breaking information into its constituent parts, and perhaps identifying interrelationships among the parts
5. *Evaluate:* Making judgments about information using certain criteria or standards
6. *Create:* Putting together knowledge, procedures, or both to form a coherent, structured, and possibly original whole

This taxonomy is hardly an exhaustive list of what students should be able to do while learning classroom subject matter—for instance, it doesn't include motor skills, attitudes, or general dispositions—but it's a helpful reminder that there's much more to school learning and academic achievement than learning and recalling facts.

Ask students to identify some of their own objectives for instruction.

With this suggestion, we're simply revisiting a suggestion I made in Chapter 6: *Ask students to set some personal goals for learning and performance.* Naturally, student-chosen goals and objectives must be compatible with any mandated standards and with their teachers' goals and objectives. However, most school curricula do allow for some flexibility in what students focus on. For example, different students might choose different gymnastic skills to master, different art media to use, or different historical events to study in depth. By allowing students to identify some of their own goals and objectives, teachers encourage the *goal setting* that is an integral aspect of self-regulation (Chapter 4) and foster the sense of *self-determination* that is so important for intrinsic motivation (Chapter 6).

Create a class website.

A long-standing practice at the secondary and college levels is to give students a printed syllabus that lists class objectives, an outline of topics, homework assignments, scheduled quizzes, and so on. But in this age of widespread access to computer technology, many teachers can now share such information—and much more—on class-specific Internet websites within their school's overall website. For example, my son Jeff (now a teacher) creates websites for each of his classes at an English-speaking school in Thailand. Figure 8.2 shows the opening screen for his sixth-grade humanities class. Notice that the course resources include two documents (a course outline and assessment criteria) that students can download. Scrolling farther down in the website, students learn about general goals for the class, get detailed information about various units and assignments, and find many more downloadable documents. Students can also interact in a class-specific chat room, and they upload their completed assignments to the website. Jeff created the site using software called Moodle (www.moodle.org); similar software is available through Sakai (www.sakaiproject.org).

FIGURE 8.2 Opening screen of a website for a sixth-grade humanities class
Source: Created by and used with permission from Jeffrey Scott Ormrod.

[7] The original taxonomy was developed in 1956 by B. S. Bloom, Englehart, Furst, Hill, and Krathwohl. The taxonomy presented here is a revision developed in 2001 by L. W. Anderson et al.

Bloom's taxonomy Taxonomy of six cognitive processes, varying in complexity, that lessons might be designed to foster.

BEHAVIORAL ANALYSIS

Playing basketball

- Dribbling
- Passing
- Shooting
- Rebounding
- etc...

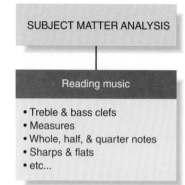

SUBJECT MATTER ANALYSIS

Reading music

- Treble & bass clefs
- Measures
- Whole, half, & quarter notes
- Sharps & flats
- etc...

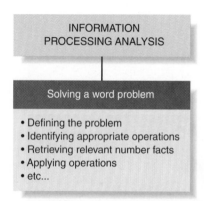

INFORMATION PROCESSING ANALYSIS

Solving a word problem

- Defining the problem
- Identifying appropriate operations
- Retrieving relevant number facts
- Applying operations
- etc...

FIGURE 8.3 Three approaches to task analysis

Break complex tasks and topics into smaller pieces, identify a logical sequence for the pieces, and decide how best to teach each one.

Instructional planning also involves determining how best to break down complex topics and skills into manageable chunks. As examples, consider these four teachers:

- Ms. Begay, a third-grade teacher, plans to teach her students how to solve arithmetic word problems. She also wants to help them learn more effectively from the things they read.
- Mr. Marzano, a middle school physical education teacher, is beginning a unit on basketball. He wants his students to develop enough proficiency in the sport to feel comfortable playing both on organized school basketball teams and in less formal games with friends and neighbors.
- Mr. Wu, a junior high school music teacher, needs to teach his new trumpet students how to play a recognizable version of "Seventy-Six Trombones" in time for the New Year's Day parade.
- Ms. Flores, a high school social studies teacher, is going to introduce the intricacies of the federal judicial system to her classes.

All four teachers want to teach complex topics or skills. Accordingly, each of them should conduct a **task analysis**, identifying the essential behavioral or cognitive aspects of mastering a particular topic or skill. The task analyses can then guide the teachers in their selections of appropriate methods and sequences in which to teach their subject matter.

Figure 8.3 illustrates three general approaches to task analysis:[8]

- **Behavioral analysis.** One way of analyzing a complex task is to identify the specific behaviors required to perform it. For example, Mr. Marzano can identify the specific physical movements involved in dribbling, passing, and shooting a basketball. Similarly, Mr. Wu can identify the behaviors that students must master to play a trumpet successfully: holding the instrument with the fingers placed appropriately on the valves, blowing correctly into the mouthpiece, and so on.
- **Subject matter analysis.** Another approach is to break down the subject matter into the specific topics, concepts, and principles it includes. For example, Ms. Flores can identify various aspects of the judicial system (concepts such as *innocent until proven guilty* and *reasonable doubt,* the roles that judges and juries play, etc.) and their interrelationships. And Mr. Wu, who needs to teach his new trumpet students how to read music as well as how to play the instrument, can identify the basic elements of written music that students must be able to interpret, such as the treble and bass clefs and whole, half, and quarter notes.
- **Information processing analysis.** A third approach is to specify the cognitive processes involved in a task. To illustrate, Ms. Begay can identify the mental processes involved in successfully solving an arithmetic word problem, such as correct classification (encoding) of the problem (e.g., determining whether it requires addition, subtraction, etc.) and rapid retrieval of basic number facts. Similarly, she can identify specific cognitive strategies useful in reading comprehension, such as finding main ideas, elaborating, and summarizing.

To get a taste of what a task analysis involves, try the following exercise.

SEE FOR YOURSELF   Peanut Butter Sandwich

Conduct a task analysis for the process of making a peanut butter sandwich:

1. Decide whether your approach should be a behavioral analysis, a subject matter analysis, or an information processing analysis.

task analysis Process of identifying the specific behaviors, knowledge, or cognitive processes necessary to master a particular topic or skill.

[8] R. E. Clark, Feldon, van Merriënboer, Yates, & Early, 2008; Jonassen, Hannum, & Tessmer, 1989.

2. Using the approach you've selected, break the sandwich-making task into a number of small, teachable steps.
3. (Optional) If you're hungry and have the necessary materials close at hand, make an actual sandwich following the steps you've identified. Did your initial analysis omit any important steps?

Chances are good that you chose a behavioral analysis, because making a peanut butter sandwich is largely a behavioral rather than mental task. For instance, you must know how to unscrew the peanut butter jar lid, get an appropriate amount of peanut butter on your knife, and spread the peanut butter gently enough that you don't tear the bread.

Conducting task analyses for complex skills and topics has at least two advantages.[9] First, by identifying a task's specific components—whether behaviors, concepts and ideas, or cognitive processes—a teacher gains a better sense of what things students need to learn and the sequence in which they can most effectively learn those things. Second, a task analysis helps a teacher choose appropriate instructional strategies. For example, if one necessary component of solving arithmetic word problems is the rapid retrieval of math facts from memory, repeated practice of these facts may be critical for developing automaticity. If another aspect of solving such problems is identifying the relevant operation to apply (addition, subtraction, etc.), then promoting a true understanding of mathematical concepts and principles (perhaps by using concrete manipulatives or authentic activities) is essential.

Sometimes a task analysis may lead a teacher to conclude that he or she can most effectively teach a complex task by teaching some or all of its components separately from one another. For instance, Mr. Wu may initially ask his beginning trumpet students to practice blowing into the mouthpiece correctly without worrying about the specific notes they produce. But on other occasions it may be more appropriate to teach the desired knowledge and behaviors entirely within the context of the overall task, in part because doing so makes the subject matter meaningful for students. For instance, Ms. Begay should almost certainly teach her students the processes involved in learning effectively from reading materials—elaborating, summarizing, and so on—primarily within the context of authentic reading tasks.

Develop step-by-step lesson plans.

Once they have identified their goals for instruction and perhaps also conducted a task analysis, effective teachers develop one or more **lesson plans** to guide them during instruction. A lesson plan typically includes the following:

- The goal(s) or objective(s) of the lesson
- Instructional materials (e.g., textbooks, handouts) and equipment required
- Instructional strategies and the sequence in which they'll be used
- Assessment method(s) planned

Any lesson plan should, of course, take into account the students who will be learning—their developmental levels, prior knowledge, cultural backgrounds, and so on.

Many beginning teachers develop fairly detailed lesson plans that describe how they're going to help students learn the subject matter in question.[10] For instance, when I began teaching middle school geography, I spent many hours each week writing down the information, examples, questions, and student activities I wanted to use during the following week. But as teachers gain experience teaching certain topics, they learn which strategies work effectively and which do not, and they use some of the effective ones frequently enough that they can retrieve them quickly and easily from long-term memory. As time goes on, planning lessons becomes far less time consuming, and much of it becomes *mental* planning rather than planning on paper.

lesson plan Predetermined guide for a lesson that identifies instructional goals or objectives, necessary materials, instructional strategies, and one or more assessment methods.

---

[9] R. E. Clark et al., 2008; Desberg & Taylor, 1986; Jonassen et al., 1989.

[10] Calderhead, 1996; Corno, 2008; Sternberg & Horvath, 1995.

In planning lessons, teachers have many resources at their disposal, including experienced teachers' lesson plans in books and on the Internet. For example, the following websites offer lesson plans and related materials concerning a wide range of topics:

- Smithsonian Institution (www.smithsonianeducation.org)
- Educator's Reference Desk (www.eduref.org)
- Discovery Education (school.discoveryeducation.com)

In taking advantage of such resources, however, teachers must always keep in mind that *lessons should be closely tied to instructional goals and objectives.*

You should probably think of a lesson plan more as a guide than as a recipe—in other words, as a general plan of attack that can and should be adjusted as events unfold.[11] For instance, during the course of a lesson, a teacher may find that students have less prior knowledge than anticipated, and so the teacher may need to back up and teach material that he or she had mistakenly assumed students had already mastered. Or, if students express considerable curiosity or have intriguing insights about a particular topic, a teacher may want to capitalize on this unique opportunity—this **teachable moment**—and spend more time exploring the topic than originally planned.

As teachers proceed through the school year, their long-range plans will also change somewhat. For instance, they may find that their initial task analyses of desired knowledge and skills were overly simplistic. Or they may discover that their expectations for students' achievement, as reflected in previously identified instructional goals, are either unrealistically high or unnecessarily low. Teachers must continually revise their plans as instruction proceeds and as classroom assessments reveal how well students are learning and achieving.

Conducting Teacher-Directed Instruction

In the opening case study, Ms. Minichiello directs the course of the lesson to a considerable degree. For example, she instructs students to mark the dimensions of a covered wagon on the floor, has them brainstorm supplies that pioneers might have needed during their journey, and asks them to consider what single item they would want to take with them to a distant planet. And through some of her questions (e.g., "What were some of the things that pioneers had to be prepared for?") she nudges students toward the kinds of conclusions she wants them to draw about life on the Oregon Trail.

A good deal of teacher-directed instruction takes the form of **expository instruction**, in which information is presented (*exposed*) in more or less the same form that students are expected to learn it.[12] Ms. Minichiello's lesson has several elements of expository instruction: She presents the dimensions of a typical covered wagon, distributes reading materials about how the settlers packed for the long trip west, and shows photographs of pioneer families and their temporary covered-wagon homes.

Some forms of expository instruction are exclusively one-way in nature, in that information goes only from teacher to learners. Examples are textbook reading assignments and educational films and videos. In each case a "teacher" (e.g., a textbook author or video narrator) presents information without any possibility of getting information from students in return. Yet other forms can be quite interactive, with an ongoing exchange of information between teacher (or perhaps a virtual "teacher," such as a computer) and students. For instance, effective classroom lectures typically include opportunities for student input, perhaps in the form of answers to teacher questions, inquiries about ambiguous points, or reactions to certain ideas. In approaches such as *direct instruction* and *computer-based instruction*—both of which we'll consider shortly—student input is a frequent and essential ingredient despite the considerable control that the teacher or computer programmer has over the content and sequence of the lesson.

---

teachable moment Situation or event (often unplanned) in which students might be especially predisposed to acquire particular knowledge or skills.

expository instruction Approach to instruction in which information is presented in essentially the same form in which students are expected to learn it.

[11] Brophy, Alleman, & Knighton, 2009; Calderhead, 1996.

[12] Some theorists use the term *expository instruction* only in reference to lectures and textbooks. I am using the term more broadly to refer to any approach that centers on the *transmission* of information from expert (e.g., classroom teacher, textbook writer, computer software designer) to student.

Strategies such as the following can enhance the effectiveness of teacher-directed instruction.

Begin with what students already know and believe.

Students are apt to engage in meaningful learning—to relate new material to things they already know—only if they have both the "new" and the "old" in working memory at the same time. Thus a strategy introduced in Chapter 2, *prior knowledge activation,* is an important first step in any teacher-directed instruction. In addition, asking students what they already know about a topic—or at least what they *think* they know about it—can uncover misconceptions that might wreak havoc with new learning and so must be vigorously addressed.

Promote effective cognitive processes.

The effectiveness of teacher-directed instruction ultimately depends on the particular cognitive processes that instruction enables and encourages.[13] To see this idea in action, try the following exercise.

SEE FOR YOURSELF   Finding Pedagogy in the Book

1. Look back at two or three of the preceding chapters. Find places where specific things I've done have helped you learn and remember the material more effectively. What strategies did I use to facilitate your cognitive processing?
2. In those same chapters, can you find places where you had difficulty processing the material presented? If so, what might I have done differently?

I'm hoping that the See for Yourself exercises have helped you relate new topics to your own knowledge and experiences. I'm hoping, too, that the case studies and the examples of students' work and teachers' strategies have made abstract ideas more concrete for you. Perhaps some of the graphics, tables, and summaries have helped you organize concepts and principles. But if you've found certain parts of the books difficult to understand or in some other way troublesome, I encourage you to let me know.[14]

Researchers have identified several factors that improve the effectiveness of teacher-directed instruction through the cognitive processes they promote. Table 8.2 describes and illustrates these factors as general principles that teachers should keep in mind whenever they need to present information in a largely one-way fashion.

Observe many principles of effective expository instruction in action in the "Civil War" and "Charles's Law" videos in Chapter 8 of the Book-Specific Resources in MyEducation-Lab. Notice how much more abstract the "Charles's Law" lesson is, consistent with older students' greater capacity for abstract thought.

Intermingle explanations with examples and opportunities for practice.

By providing numerous examples of concepts and ideas, teachers make classroom topics more concrete for students and help them relate abstract subject matter to real-world objects and events (e.g., see Figure 8.4). And by providing many opportunities to practice new knowledge and skills, teachers foster automaticity and increase the likelihood that students will transfer what they've learned to real-world tasks and problems (see Chapters 2 and 4).

An approach known as **direct instruction** makes considerable use of examples and practice opportunities to keep students actively engaged in learning and applying classroom

---

[13] R. E. Mayer, 2004, 2008; Moreno, 2006; Weinert & Helmke, 1995; Wittwer & Renkl, 2008.

[14] As I complete this book in October 2010, my e-mail addresses are jormrod@comcast.net and jormrod@alumni.brown.edu.

direct instruction Approach to instruction that uses a variety of techniques (e.g., explanations, questions, guided and independent practice) in a fairly structured manner to promote learning of basic skills.

TABLE 8.2 Enhancing Cognitive Processing in Teacher-Directed Instruction

Principle	Educational Implication	Example
An **advance organizer**—a verbal or graphic introduction that lays out the general organizational framework of upcoming material—helps students make meaningful connections among the things they learn.	Introduce a new unit by describing the major ideas and concepts to be discussed and showing how they are interrelated.	Introduce a unit on vertebrates by saying something like this: "Vertebrates all have backbones. We'll be talking about five phyla of vertebrates—mammals, birds, reptiles, amphibians, and fish—that differ from one another in several ways, including whether their members are warm blooded or cold blooded; whether they have hair, scales, or feathers; and whether they lay eggs or bear live young."
Ongoing **connections to prior knowledge** help students learn classroom material more meaningfully, provided that students' existing understandings and beliefs are accurate.	Remind students of something they already know—that is, activate their prior knowledge—and point out how a new idea is related. Also, address any erroneous beliefs students have about the topic (see the discussion of *conceptual change* in Chapter 2).	Draw an analogy between *peristalsis* (muscular contractions that push food through the digestive tract) and the process of squeezing ketchup from a packet: "You squeeze the packet near one corner and run your fingers along the length of the packet toward an opening at the other corner. When you do this, you push the ketchup through the packet, in one direction, ahead of your fingers, until it comes out of the opening."
An **organized presentation** of material helps students make appropriate interconnections among ideas.	Help students organize material in a particular way by presenting the information using that same organizational structure.	Use a concept map to depict the main concepts and ideas of a topic and their interrelationships (see the discussion of concept maps in Chapter 4).
Various **signals** built into a presentation (e.g., italicized print, interspersed questions) can draw students' attention to important points.	Stress important points—for example, by writing them on the board, asking questions about them, or simply telling students what things are most important to learn.	When assigning a textbook chapter for homework, identify several questions that students should try to answer as they read the chapter.
Visual aids help students encode material visually as well as verbally.	Illustrate new material through pictures, photographs, diagrams, maps, physical models, and demonstrations.	When describing major battles of the American Civil War, present a map showing where each battle took place; point out that some battles were fought in especially strategic locations.
Appropriate **pacing** gives students adequate time to process information.	Pace a presentation slowly enough that students can draw inferences, form visual images, and in other ways engage in effective long-term memory storage processes.	Intersperse lengthy explanations with demonstrations or hands-on activities that illustrate some of the principles you're describing.
Summaries help students review and organize material and identify main ideas.	After a lecture or reading assignment, summarize the key points of the lesson.	At the end of a unit on Emily Dickinson, summarize her work by describing the characteristics that made her poetry so unique and appealing.

Sources: Brophy et al., 2009; Bulgren, Deshler, Schumaker, & Lenz, 2000; Carney & Levin, 2002; Clement, 2008; Corkill, 1992; Dansereau, 1995; Edmonds et al., 2009; E. L. Ferguson & Hegarty, 1995; J. Hartley & Trueman, 1982; Ku, Chan, Wu, & Chen, 2008; Levin & Mayer, 1993; Lorch, Lorch, & Inman, 1993; R. E. Mayer, 2010; R. E. Mayer & Gallini, 1990; M. A. McDaniel & Einstein, 1989; Moreno, 2006; Newby, Ertmer, & Stepich, 1994, p. 4 (peristalsis example); R. E. Reynolds & Shirey, 1988; Scevak, Moore, & Kirby, 1993; M. Y. Small, Lovett, & Scher, 1993; Verdi & Kulhavy, 2002; Wade, 1992; P. T. Wilson & Anderson, 1986; Winn, 1991; Zook, 1991.

subject matter.[15] This approach involves small and carefully sequenced steps, fast pacing, and a great deal of teacher–student interaction. Each lesson typically involves most or all of the following components:[16]

1. **Review of previously learned material.** The teacher reviews relevant content from previous lessons, checks homework assignments involving that content, and reteaches any information or skills that students haven't yet mastered.

---

[15] Englemann & Carnine, 1982; R. M. Gagné, 1985; Kirschner, Sweller, & Clark, 2006; Rittle-Johnson, 2006; Rosenshine & Stevens, 1986; Tarver, 1992; Weinert & Helmke, 1995.

[16] Rosenshine & Stevens, 1986.

advance organizer Introduction to a lesson that provides an overall organizational scheme for the lesson.

2. **Statement of the objectives of the lesson.** The teacher describes one or more concepts or skills that students should master in the new lesson.
3. **Presentation of new material in small, logically sequenced steps.** The teacher presents a small amount of information or a specific skill, perhaps through a verbal explanation, modeling, and one or more examples. The teacher may also provide an advance organizer, ask questions, or in other ways scaffold students' efforts to process and remember the material.
4. **Guided student practice and assessment after each step.** Students have frequent opportunities to practice what they're learning, perhaps by answering questions, solving problems, or performing modeled procedures. The teacher gives hints during students' early responses, provides immediate feedback about their performance, makes suggestions about how to improve, and provides remedial instruction as needed. After students have completed guided practice, the teacher checks to be sure they've mastered the information or skill in question, perhaps by having them summarize what they've learned or answer a series of follow-up questions.
5. **Independent practice.** Once students have acquired some mastery (e.g., by correctly answering 80% of questions), they engage in further practice either independently or in small, cooperative groups. By doing so, they work toward achieving automaticity for the material in question.
6. **Frequent follow-up reviews.** Over the course of the school year, the teacher provides many opportunities for students to review previously learned material, perhaps through homework assignments, writing tasks, or quizzes.

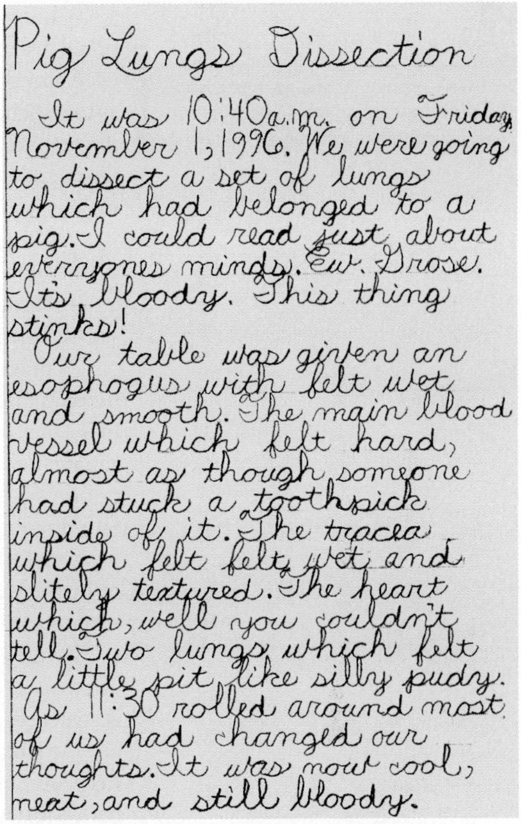
Pig Lungs Dissection
It was 10:40 a.m. on Friday November 1, 1996. We were going to dissect a set of lungs which had belonged to a pig. I could read just about everyones minds. Ew. Grose. It's bloody. This thing stinks!
Our table was given an esophogus with felt wet and smooth. The main blood vessel which felt hard, almost as though someone had stuck a toothpick inside of it. The tracea which felt felt, wet and slitely textured. The heart which, well you couldn't tell. Two lungs which felt a little pit, like silly pudy. As 11:30 rolled around most of us had changed our thoughts. It was now cool, neat, and still bloody.

FIGURE 8.4 In a unit on anatomy, 10-year-old Berlinda and her classmates gained firsthand experience with components of the respiratory and circulatory systems.

The teacher moves back and forth among these components as necessary to ensure that all students are truly mastering the subject matter.

Direct instruction is most suitable for teaching information and skills that are clear-cut and best taught in a step-by-step sequence.[17] Because of the high degree of teacher–student interaction, direct instruction is often implemented more easily with small groups than with an entire class. Under such circumstances, it can lead to substantial gains in achievement, high student interest and self-efficacy for the subject matter, and low rates of student misbehavior.[18] Using direct instruction *exclusively* may be too much of a good thing, however, especially if teachers don't vary instructional methods to maintain students' interest and engagement.[19] A teenager named Tommy shows obvious disgust about the rut one of his high school teachers has gotten into:

> [W]e just get one ditto after the next. My math teacher doesn't like the textbook, so he works up his own work sheets, and he gives us a million of them every day. If we get through all of them, we can pretty much get a good grade.[20]

Even in direct instruction, then, variety is the spice of—and an important source of motivation in—life.

Take advantage of well-designed educational software.

Many educational computer programs, collectively known as **computer-based instruction (CBI)**, incorporate principles of learning and cognition we've considered in earlier chapters. For example, effective programs often take steps to capture and hold students' attention, activate students' prior knowledge about a topic, encourage meaningful learning and effective metacognitive processes, and present diverse examples and practice exercises that promote transfer. Students tend to remain physically and cognitively engaged with such programs, in large part because they must continually respond to questions and problems.

[17] Rosenshine & Stevens, 1986.

[18] Rittle-Johnson, 2006; Rosenshine & Stevens, 1986; Tarver, 1992; Weinert & Helmke, 1995.

[19] Mac Iver, Reuman, & Main, 1995; Wasley, Hampel, & Clark, 1997.

[20] Wasley et al., 1997, p. 117.

computer-based instruction (CBI) Academic instruction provided by means of specially designed computer software.

? Judging from your own experiences in studying topics through educational software programs, what qualities lead to effective learning from CBI?

Computer-based instruction can be used either instead of or in addition to more traditional instructional methods. Some CBI programs provide drill and practice of basic knowledge and skills (e.g., math facts, typing, fundamentals of music), helping students develop automaticity in these areas. Others serve as "intelligent tutors" that skillfully guide students through complex subject matter and can anticipate and address a wide variety of misconceptions and learning difficulties. Still others teach and scaffold complex study strategies, metacognitive skills, and self-regulation.[21]

Well-designed CBI programs are often quite effective in helping students learn academic subject matter.[22] They can also be highly motivating, piquing situational interest and giving students the independence and frequent successes that can enhance their feelings of self-determination and competence.[23]

A downside of CBI is that it gives students few opportunities for social interaction and therefore does little to address their need for relatedness.[24] Yet it offers several advantages that other forms of expository instruction don't always allow. For one thing, CBI programs can include animations, video clips, and spoken messages—components that are, of course, not possible with traditional printed materials. Also, some programs can record and maintain ongoing data for every student, including such information as how far students have progressed in a program, how quickly they respond to questions, and how often they're right and wrong. With such data, teachers can monitor each student's progress and identify students who appear to be struggling with the material. And finally, a computer can be used to provide instruction when flesh-and-blood teachers aren't available. For example, CBI is often used in *distance learning,* a situation in which learners receive technology-based instruction at a location physically separate from that of their instructor.

At later points in the chapter, we'll explore additional uses of computer technology. Keep in mind, however, that using a computer is not, *in and of itself,* necessarily the key to better instruction.[25] A computer can help students achieve at higher levels only when it provides instruction that teachers can't offer as easily or effectively by other means. Little is gained when a student merely reads information on a computer screen rather than in a textbook.

Ask a lot of questions.

Virtually all effective teachers ask students a lot of questions. Some teacher questions are **lower-level questions** that call for information students have previously learned. Such questions have several benefits:[26]

- They give teachers a good idea of what prior knowledge and misconceptions students have about a topic.
- They help keep students' attention on the lesson in progress, especially when all students must respond to them in some way.
- They help teachers assess whether students are learning class material successfully or are confused about particular points. (Even very experienced teachers sometimes overestimate what students are actually learning during expository instruction.)
- They give students the opportunity to monitor their *own* comprehension—to determine whether they understand the information being presented or, instead, should ask for help or clarification.
- When students are asked questions about material they've studied earlier, they must review that material, which should promote greater recall later on.

 Observe the wide variety of teacher questions, as well as the many purposes they serve, in the videos in Chapter 8 of the Book-Specific Resources in MyEducationLab.

lower-level question Question that requires students to express what they've learned in essentially the same form they learned it.

[21] Azevedo, 2005a; Graesser, McNamara, & VanLehn, 2005; Koedinger & Corbett, 2006; Merrill et al., 1996; Moreno, Mayer, Spires, & Lester, 2001; Snir, Smith, & Raz, 2003.
[22] H. S. Kim & Kamil, 2004; Koedinger & Corbett, 2006; Slavin & Lake, 2008; Wise & Olson, 1998.
[23] Blumenfeld et al., 2006; Snir et al., 2003; Swan, Mitrani, Guerrero, Cheung, & Schoener, 1990.

[24] Winn, 2002.
[25] R. E. Clark, 1983; Moreno, 2006; Roblyer, 2003.
[26] Airasian, 1994; Brophy, 2006; Brophy et al., 2009; F. W. Connolly & Eisenberg, 1990; P. W. Fox & LeCount, 1991; Lambert, Cartledge, Heward, & Lo, 2006; Munro & Stephenson, 2009; Wixson, 1984.

Following is an example of how one eighth-grade teacher promoted review of a lesson on ancient Egypt by asking questions:

Teacher: The Egyptians believed the body had to be preserved. What did they do to preserve the body in the earliest times?

Student: They dried them and stuffed them.

Teacher: I am talking about from the earliest times. What did they do? Carey.

Carey: They buried them in the hot sands.

Teacher: Right. They buried them in the hot sands. The sand was very dry, and the body was naturally preserved for many years. It would deteriorate more slowly, at least compared with here. What did they do later on after this time?

Student: They started taking out the vital organs.

Teacher: Right. What did they call the vital organs then?

Norm: Everything but the heart and brain.

Teacher: Right, the organs in the visceral cavity. The intestines, liver, and so on, which were the easiest parts to get at. Question?

Student: How far away from the Nile River was the burial of most kings?[27]

At the end of the dialogue, a *student* asks a question—one that requests information not previously presented. The student is apparently trying to elaborate on the material, perhaps speculating that only land a fair distance from the Nile would be dry enough to preserve bodies for a lengthy period. Teachers can encourage such elaboration—and therefore also encourage new knowledge construction—by asking **higher-level questions** that require students to do something new with information they've learned.[28] For instance, a higher-level question might ask students to think of their own examples of a concept, use a new principle to solve a problem, or speculate about possible explanations for a cause–and–effect relationship.

Asking questions during a group lesson or as a follow-up to an independent reading assignment often enhances students' learning.[29] This is especially true when teachers ask higher-level questions that call for inferences, applications, justifications, or problem solving. Yet teachers must give students adequate time to respond to their questions. Just as students need time to process new information, they also need time to consider questions and retrieve knowledge relevant to possible answers. As we discovered in the discussion of *wait time* in Chapter 2, when teachers allow at least three seconds to elapse after asking a question, a greater number of students volunteer answers, and their responses tend to be more sophisticated. Furthermore, as you'll learn in a Cultural Considerations box later in the chapter, students from some ethnic backgrounds often wait for several seconds before answering a question as a way of showing courtesy and respect for the speaker.

The Classroom Strategies box "Asking Questions to Promote and Assess Learning" presents examples of how teachers might use questions to foster effective cognitive processes and enhance learning.

Extend the school day with age-appropriate homework assignments.

Students can accomplish only so much during class time, and homework provides a means through which teachers can, in essence, extend the school day. On some occasions teachers might use homework to give students extra practice with familiar information and procedures (perhaps as a way of promoting review and automaticity) or to introduce them to new yet simple material.[30] In other situations teachers might give homework assignments that ask students to apply classroom subject matter to their outside lives.[31] For example, in a

---

[27] Aulls, 1998, p. 62.

[28] Brophy, 2006; Meece, 1994; Minstrell & Stimpson, 1996.

[29] Allington & Weber, 1993; Liu, 1990; Redfield & Rousseau, 1981.

[30] Cooper, 1989.

[31] Alleman & Brophy, 1998.

higher-level question Question that requires students to do something new with something they've learned (e.g., to elaborate on or apply it).

CLASSROOM STRATEGIES Asking Questions to Promote and Assess Learning

- Direct questions to the entire class, not just to a few who seem eager to respond.

  The girls in a high school science class rarely volunteer when their teacher asks questions. Although the teacher often calls on students who raise their hands, he occasionally calls on those who do not, and he makes sure that he calls on *every* student at least once a week.

- Have all students cast votes in answering questions that have only a few possible answers.

  When beginning a lesson on dividing one fraction by another, a middle school math teacher writes this problem on the whiteboard at the front of the room:

  $$\frac{3}{4} , \frac{1}{2} = ?$$

  She asks, "Before we talk about how we solve this problem, how many of you think the answer will be less than one? How many think it will be greater than one? How many think it will be *exactly* one?" She tallies the number of hands that go up after each question and then says, "Hmmm, most of you think the answer will be less than one. Let's look at how we solve a problem like this. Then each of you will know whether you were right or wrong."

- Provide a means through which all students can write and show their answers.

- A fourth-grade teacher gives each student a laminated board on which to write their answers to questions she asks during whole-class explanations. She finds that when students can all answer her questions this way, they're more attentive and less disruptive during her lessons.

- Ask follow-up questions to probe students' reasoning.

  In a geography lesson on Canada, a sixth-grade teacher points out the St. Lawrence River on a map. "Which way does the water flow: toward the ocean or away from it?" When one student shouts out, "Away from it!" the teacher asks him, "Why do you think so?" The student's explanation reveals a common misconception: that rivers can flow only from north to south, never vice versa.

- When students initially struggle with a question, provide sufficient scaffolding to enable them to answer correctly.

  In a lesson on the food pyramid, a second-grade teacher asks students, "Which food group do you suppose orange juice comes from?" When a student responds, "Milk," the teacher replies, "Everything in the milk group comes from a cow. What does orange juice come from? . . . Orange juice comes from oranges. If it comes from oranges, which group is oranges? . . . Is it fruit or bread?" The student acknowledges that oranges are fruit and that orange juice must therefore belong to the fruit group.

Sources: Brophy et al., 2009 (food pyramid example, pp. 224–225); Lambert, Cartledge, Heward, & Lo, 2006 (laminated board example).

---

unit on lifestyle patterns, a teacher might ask second graders to compare their own homes with homes of earlier time periods (e.g., caves, log cabins) and to identify modern conveniences that make their lives easier and more comfortable.[32] On still other occasions teachers might encourage students to bring items and ideas from home (e.g., a jar of tadpoles from a local pond, descriptions of events that occurred over the weekend) and use them as the basis for in-class activities.[33] When teachers ask students to make connections between classroom material and the outside world through homework assignments, they are, of course, promoting transfer.

Doing homework appears to have a small effect on achievement in the middle school and high school grades but little if any effect at the elementary level.[34] Although homework in the elementary grades may not enhance achievement very much, it can help students develop some of the study strategies and self-regulation skills they'll need in later years.[35] Undoubtedly the *quality* of assignments—for instance, whether they encourage rote memorization or meaningful learning, whether students find them boring or engaging—makes an appreciable difference both in what and how much students learn and in what kinds of learning and self-regulation strategies they develop.[36]

When assigning homework, teachers must remember that students differ considerably in the time and resources (reference books, computers, etc.) they have at home, in the amount and quality of assistance they can get from parents and other family members, and in the extent to which they have the motivation and self-regulation strategies to keep

---

[32] Alleman & Brophy, 1998.

[33] Corno, 1996; C. Hill, 1994.

[34] Cooper, Robinson, & Patall, 2006.

[35] Cooper & Valentine, 2001; Zimmerman, 1998.

[36] Trautwein & Lüdtke, 2007; Trautwein, Lüdtke, Schnyder, & Niggli, 2006.

themselves on task.[37] Teachers can maximize the benefits of homework by following a few simple guidelines:[38]

- Use assignments primarily for instructional and diagnostic purposes; minimize the degree to which homework is used to assess learning and determine final class grades.
- Include tasks that will capture students' interest.
- Provide the information and structure students need to complete assignments with little or no assistance from others.
- Give a mixture of required and voluntary assignments. (Voluntary ones should help give students a sense of self-determination and control, enhancing their intrinsic motivation.)
- When students have poor self-regulation skills or limited resources at home, establish supervised after-school homework programs.

Teachers must remember, too, that homework is appropriate only to help students achieve important educational goals—*never* to punish students for misbehavior.

Shoot for mastery of basic knowledge and skills.

When teachers move through lessons without making sure that all students master the content of each one, they may leave more and more students behind as they go along. For example, imagine that a class of 27 students, listed in Figure 8.5, is beginning a unit on fractions. The class progresses through several lessons as follows:

Lesson 1: The class studies the basic idea that a fraction represents a part of a whole: The denominator indicates the number of pieces into which the whole has been divided, and the numerator indicates how many of those pieces are present. By the end of the lesson, 23 children understand what a fraction is. But Sarah, Laura, Jason K., and Jason M. are either partly or totally confused.

Lesson 2: The class studies the process of reducing fractions to lowest terms (e.g., $\frac{2}{4}$ can be reduced to $\frac{1}{2}$, $\frac{12}{20}$ can be reduced to $\frac{3}{5}$). By the end of the lesson, 20 children understand this process. But Alison, Reggie, and Jason S. haven't mastered the idea that they need to divide both the numerator and denominator by the same number. Sarah, Laura, and the other two Jasons still don't understand what fractions *are* and so have trouble with this lesson as well.

Lesson 3: The class studies the process of adding two fractions, for now looking only at fractions with equal denominators (e.g., $\frac{2}{5} + \frac{2}{5} = \frac{4}{5}$, $\frac{1}{20} + \frac{11}{20} = \frac{12}{20}$). By the end of the lesson, 19 children can add fractions with the same denominator. Matt, Charlie, Maria F., and Maria W. keep adding the denominators together as well as the numerators (e.g., figuring that $\frac{2}{5} + \frac{2}{5} = \frac{4}{10}$). And Sarah, Laura, Jason K., and Jason M. still don't know what fractions actually are.

Lesson 4: The class combines the processes of adding fractions and reducing fractions to lowest terms. They must first add two fractions together and then, if necessary, reduce the sum to its lowest terms (e.g., after adding $\frac{1}{20} + \frac{11}{20}$, they must reduce the sum of $\frac{12}{20}$ to $\frac{3}{5}$). Here we lose Paul, Arla, and Karen because they keep forgetting to reduce the sum to lowest terms. And of course, we've already lost Sarah, Laura, Alison, Reggie, Matt, Charlie, the two Marias, and the three Jasons on prerequisite skills. *We now have only 13 of our original 27 students understanding what they are doing—less than half the class!* (See the rightmost column of Figure 8.5.)

Mastery learning, in which students demonstrate competence in one topic before proceeding to the next, minimizes the likelihood of leaving some students

Students	Lesson 1: Concept of Fraction	Lesson 2: Reducing to Lowest Terms (Builds on Lesson 1)	Lesson 3: Adding Fractions with Same Denominators (Builds on Lesson 1)	Lesson 4: Adding Fractions & Reducing to Lowest Terms (Builds on Lessons 2 & 3)
Sarah	--→	--→	--→	--→
Laura	--→	--→	--→	--→
Jason K.	--→	--→	--→	--→
Jason M.	--→	--→	--→	--→
Alison	→	--→	--→	--→
Reggie	→	--→	--→	--→
Jason S.	→	--→	--→	--→
Matt	→	→	--→	--→
Charlie	→	→	--→	--→
Maria F.	→	→	--→	--→
Maria W.	→	→	--→	--→
Paul	→	→	→	--→
Arla	→	→	→	--→
Karen	→	→	→	--→
Kevin	→	→	→	→
Nori	→	→	→	→
Marcy	→	→	→	→
Janelle	→	→	→	→
Joyce	→	→	→	→
Ming Tang	→	→	→	→
Georgette	→	→	→	→
LaVeda	→	→	→	→
Mark	→	→	→	→
Seth	→	→	→	→
Joanne	→	→	→	→
Rita	→	→	→	→
Shauna	→	→	→	→

--→ = nonmastery of subject matter
—→ = mastery of subject matter

FIGURE 8.5 Sequential and hierarchical nature of knowledge about fractions

[37] Eilam, 2001; Fries, Dietz, & Schmid, 2008; Garbe & Guy, 2006; Hoover-Dempsey et al., 2001; Xu, 2008.
[38] Belfiore & Hornyak, 1998; Cooper, 1989; Cosden, Morrison, Albanese, & Macias, 2001; Garbe & Guy, 2006;

Patall, Cooper, & Wynn, 2008; Trautwein et al., 2006; Trautwein, Niggli, Schnyder, & Lüdtke, 2009; Xu, 2008.

mastery learning Approach to instruction in which students learn one topic thoroughly before moving to a subsequent one.

behind as a class proceeds to increasingly challenging material.[39] This approach is based on three underlying assumptions:

- Almost every student can learn a particular topic to mastery.
- Some students need more time to master a topic than others.
- Some students need more assistance than others.

As you can see, mastery learning represents a very optimistic approach to instruction. It assumes that most learners *can* learn school subject matter if given sufficient time and instruction. Furthermore, truly mastering a classroom topic increases the odds that students will be able to transfer what they've learned to new situations and problems and to think critically and creatively about it (recall the discussion of the *less-is-more* principle in Chapter 4).

A mastery learning approach to instruction looks a lot like direct instruction, in that the subject matter is broken into a series of small and logically sequenced steps, numerous opportunities for practice are provided, and learning is assessed after each step. But in addition, students move to the next step only after demonstrating mastery of the preceding one. Mastery is defined in specific, concrete terms—perhaps answering at least 90% of quiz items correctly. Students engaged in mastery learning often proceed through instructional units at their own speed, and so different students may be studying different units at any given time.

Mastery learning has several advantages over nonmastery approaches to instruction. In particular, students tend to have a better attitude toward the subject matter, learn more, and perform at higher levels on classroom assessments. The benefits are especially striking for low-ability students.[40]

Mastery learning is most appropriate when the subject matter is hierarchical in nature—that is, when certain concepts and skills provide the foundation for future learning and conceptual understanding. When instructional goals deal with such basics as word recognition, rules of grammar, arithmetic, or key scientific concepts, instruction designed to promote mastery learning may be in order. Nevertheless, the very notion of mastery may be *in*appropriate for some long-term instructional goals. For example, skills such as critical thinking, scientific reasoning, and creative writing may continue to improve throughout childhood and adolescence without ever being completely mastered.

• Conducting Learner-Directed Instruction

At one point in the opening case study, students convene in small groups to discuss reading materials about the Oregon Trail. As we discovered in Chapter 3, discussions with peers can enhance learning in numerous ways. For instance, when learners talk about and exchange ideas, they must elaborate on and organize their thoughts, may discover gaps and inconsistencies in their current understandings, and may encounter explanations that are more accurate and useful than their own. Not only can a group of learners engage in such *co-construction* of meaning but they can also *scaffold* one another's learning efforts (see Chapter 5). Clearly, then, learners have a great deal to gain from interacting frequently not only with their teachers but also with one another.

Learner-directed instruction, in which students have considerable control over what and how they learn, often—although not always—involves interaction with classmates. The following strategies can enhance the effectiveness of learner-directed lessons.

Have students discuss issues that lend themselves to multiple perspectives, explanations, or approaches.

Discussions of multifaceted and possibly controversial topics appear to have several benefits. Students are more likely to voice their opinions if they know there are multiple possible answers. They may, of their own accord, seek out new information that resolves seemingly

---

[39] For example, see B. S. Bloom, 1981; L. S. Fuchs et al., 2005; Guskey, 1985, 2010; Zimmerman & Didenedetto, 2008.

[40] Hattie, 2009; C. C. Kulik, Kulik, & Bangert-Drowns, 1990; Shuell, 1996.

contradictory data—in other words, they may be intrinsically motivated to resolve inconsistencies. They might reexamine and possibly revise their positions on issues. And they're more apt to develop a meaningful and well-integrated understanding of the subject matter they're studying.[41]

Student discussions can be fruitful in virtually any academic discipline. For example, students might discuss various interpretations of classic works of literature, addressing questions that have no easy answers.[42] In history classes, students can read and discuss various documents related to a single historical event and, as a result, come to recognize that history isn't necessarily as cut-and-dried as traditional textbooks portray it.[43] (Recall our discussion of *epistemic beliefs* in Chapter 4.) In science, discussions of various and conflicting explanations of observed phenomena can enhance scientific reasoning skills, promote conceptual change, and help students begin to understand that science isn't a collection of facts as much as it is a dynamic and continually evolving set of understandings.[44] (This point, too, has implications for students' epistemic beliefs.) And in mathematics, discussions that focus on alternative approaches to solving the same problem can promote more complete understanding, more creative problem solving, and better transfer to new situations and problems.[45]

Students gain more from a class discussion when they participate actively in it.[46] And they're often more willing to speak openly when their audience is only two or three peers rather than the class as a whole, with the difference being especially noticeable for girls and for students with disabilities.[47] On some occasions, then, teachers may want to have students discuss an issue in small groups first—thereby giving them the chance to test and possibly gain support for their ideas in a relatively private context—before bringing them together for a whole-class discussion.[48]

Observe an effective combination of small-group and whole-class discussions in a fifth-grade class in the "Debate" video in Chapter 8 of the Book-Specific Resources in MyEducationLab.

Create a classroom atmosphere conducive to open debate and the constructive evaluation of ideas.

Students are more likely to share their ideas and opinions if their teacher is supportive of multiple viewpoints and if disagreeing with classmates is socially acceptable.[49] To promote such an atmosphere, a teacher might do the following:[50]

- Communicate the message that understanding a topic at the end of a discussion is more important than having the correct answer (if there is one) at the beginning of the discussion.
- Communicate the beliefs that asking questions reflects curiosity, that differing perspectives on a controversial topic are both inevitable and healthy, and that changing one's opinion on a topic is a sign of thoughtful reflection.
- Ask students to explain their reasoning and to try to understand one another's explanations.
- Help clarify a student's line of reasoning for other group members.
- Suggest that students build on one another's ideas whenever possible.
- Encourage students to be open in their agreement or disagreement with their classmates—that is, to "agree to disagree."

[41] E. G. Cohen, 1994; E. H. Hiebert & Raphael, 1996; D. W. Johnson & Johnson, 2009b; Kuhn & Pease, 2010; Lampert, 1990; Murphy, Wilkinson, Soter, Hennessey, & Alexander, 2009; E. M. Nussbaum, 2008; Sinatra & Mason, 2008; C. L. Smith, 2007.

[42] Eeds & Wells, 1989; E. H. Hiebert & Raphael, 1996; L. M. McGee, 1992; Murphy, 2007.

[43] Leinhardt, 1994; vanSledright & Limón, 2006.

[44] Andriessen, 2006; Bell & Linn, 2002; K. Hogan, Nastasi, & Pressley, 2000; Schwarz, Neuman, & Biezuner, 2000.

[45] M. M. Chiu, 2008; Cobb et al., 1991; J. Hiebert & Wearne, 1996; Lampert, 1990; N. M. Webb et al., 2008.

[46] Lotan, 2006; A. M. O'Donnell, 1999; N. M. Webb, 1989.

[47] A.-M. Clark et al., 2003; Théberge, 1994.

[48] D. W. Johnson & Johnson, 2009b; Minstrell & Stimpson, 1996.

[49] A.-M. Clark et al., 2003; Lampert, Rittenhouse, & Crumbaugh, 1996; E. M. Nussbaum, 2008.

[50] Hadjioannou, 2007; Hatano & Inagaki, 2003; Herrenkohl & Guerra, 1998; K. Hogan et al., 2000; E. M. Nussbaum, 2008; Lampert et al., 1996; Sinatra & Mason, 2008; Staples, 2007; van Drie, van Boxtel, & van der Linden, 2006; Walshaw & Anthony, 2008.

- Depersonalize challenges to a student's line of reasoning by framing questions in a third-person voice—for example, by saying, "What if someone were to respond to your claim by saying . . . ?"
- Occasionally ask students to defend a position that directly opposes what they actually believe.
- Require students to develop compromise solutions that take into account opposing perspectives.

Not only can such strategies promote more productive classroom discussions but they also help to create a *sense of community* among students. We'll look at the benefits of creating a sense of community in Chapter 9.

When students become comfortable with disagreeing in a congenial way, they often find their interactions highly motivating, especially if they're emotionally involved in the topic under discussion (recall the concept of *hot cognition,* described in Chapter 6).[51] One fourth grader, whose class regularly engaged in small-group discussions, put it this way:

> I like it when we get to argue, because I have a big mouth sometimes, and I like to talk out in class, and I get really tired of holding my hand up in the air. Besides, we only get to talk to each other when we go outside at recess, and this gives us a chance to argue in a nice way.[52]

Furthermore, students often acquire effective social skills during classroom discussions about academic subject matter. For example, when students meet in small, self-directed groups to discuss children's literature, they may develop and model for one another such skills as expressing agreement ("I agree with Kordell because . . ."), disagreeing tactfully ("Yeah, but they could see the fox sneak in"), justifying an opinion ("I think it shouldn't be allowed, because if he got to be king, who knows what he would do to the kingdom"), and seeking everyone's participation ("Ssshhh! Be quiet! Let Zeke talk!").[53]

Conduct activities in which students must depend on one another for their learning.

In the opening case study of Chapter 7, we saw a situation in which students' success depended on their ability to work together on the annual eighth-grade class play. Cooperation with peers can enhance students' learning and achievement on smaller tasks as well. As an example, try the following exercise.

SEE FOR YOURSELF   Purple Satin

Imagine yourself as a student in each of the three classrooms described here. How would you behave in each situation?

1. Mr. Alexander tells your class, "Let's find out which students can learn the most in this week's unit on the human digestive system. The three students getting the highest scores on Friday's test will get free tickets to the Purple Satin concert." Purple Satin is a popular musical group. You'd give your eyeteeth to hear them perform, but the concert has been sold out for months.
2. Ms. Bernstein introduces her lesson this way: "I'm hoping that all of you will master the basics of human digestion this week. If you get a score of at least 90% on this Friday's test, I'll give you a free ticket to the Purple Satin concert."
3. Mr. Camacho begins the same lesson like this: "Beginning today, you'll be working in groups of three to study the human digestive system. On Friday I'll give you a test to see how much you've learned. If all three members of your group score at least 90% on the test, your group will get free tickets to the Purple Satin concert."

In which class(es) are you likely to work hard to get free tickets to Purple Satin? How might you work *differently* in the three situations?

---

[51] A.-M. Clark et al., 2003; Hadjioannou, 2007; C. L. Smith, 2007.

[52] A.-M. Clark et al., 2003, p. 194.

[53] R. C. Anderson et al., 2001, pp. 16, 25; Certo, in press.

The first class (Mr. Alexander's) is obviously a very competitive one: Only the three best students are getting tickets to the concert. Will you try to earn one of those tickets? It all depends on what you think your chances are of being a top scorer on Friday's test. If you've been doing well on tests all year, you'll undoubtedly study harder than ever during this week's unit. If, instead, you've been doing poorly in class despite your best efforts, you probably won't work for something you're unlikely to get. But in either case, will you help your fellow students learn about the digestive system? Not if you want to go to the concert yourself!

In Ms. Bernstein's class there's no competition for concert tickets. As long as you get a score of 90% or higher on the test, you'll get a ticket. But will you help your classmates understand what the pancreas does or learn the difference between the large and small intestines? Maybe . . . *if* you have the time and are feeling charitable.

Now consider Mr. Camacho's class. Whether or not you get a concert ticket depends on how well you *and two other students* score on Friday's test. Are you going to help those two students learn about salivation and digestive enzymes? And can you expect them, in turn, to help you understand where the liver fits into the whole system? Absolutely!

In **cooperative learning,**[54] students work in small groups to achieve a common goal. Unlike an individualistic classroom such as Ms. Bernstein's (where one student's success is unrelated to peers' achievement) or a competitive classroom such as Mr. Alexander's (where one student's success partly depends on the *failure* of others), students in a cooperative learning environment such as Mr. Camacho's work together to achieve joint successes. Cooperative learning yields the same advantages that emerge from class discussions, including greater comprehension and integration of the subject matter, recognition of inadequacies or misconceptions in understanding, and increased perspective taking. Furthermore, when students help one another learn, they provide scaffolding for one another's efforts and thus tend to have higher self-efficacy for accomplishing challenging tasks.[55]

Will Hart/PhotoEdit

Cooperative learning has personal and social benefits as well as academic ones. For instance, it often promotes self-efficacy, social skills, and cross-cultural friendships.

Numerous research studies indicate that cooperative learning activities, when designed and structured appropriately, are effective in many ways. Students of all ability levels show higher academic achievement, with females, members of ethnic minority groups, and students at risk for academic failure being especially likely to benefit.[56] Cooperative learning activities may also promote complex cognitive processes. Students essentially think aloud, modeling various learning and problem-solving strategies for one another and developing greater metacognitive awareness as a result.[57] Furthermore, students are more likely to believe that their classmates like them, and friendships across racial and ethnic groups and between students with and without disabilities are apt to form.[58]

Cooperative learning has several potential pitfalls, however. Some students may be more interested in meeting social and performance goals (e.g., creating a good impression, getting the right answer quickly) than they are in mastering the material, and so their willingness to assist one another or ask for help may be compromised.[59] Students who do most of the work and most of the talking are likely to learn more than other group members.[60] Students may occasionally agree to use an incorrect strategy or method that a particular group member has suggested, or they may share misconceptions about the topic they're studying.[61] And in some cases students may simply not have the skills to cooperate and help

[54] Some theorists distinguish between *cooperative* learning and *collaborative* learning, although different theorists draw the line somewhat differently. Here I'm using the term *cooperative learning* broadly to refer to any instructional method in which students work together in a somewhat structured format to achieve a shared learning goal.

[55] T. L. Good, McCaslin, & Reys, 1992; Hatano & Inagaki, 1991; A. M. O'Donnell & O'Kelly, 1994; N. M. Webb & Palincsar, 1996.

[56] Ginsburg-Block, Rohrbeck, & Fantuzzo, 2006; Lou, Abrami, & d'Apollonia, 2001; Lou et al., 1996; Nichols,

1996; Z. Qin, Johnson, & Johnson, 1995; Rohrbeck, Ginsburg-Block, Fantuzzo, & Miller, 2003; Slavin & Lake, 2008.

[57] T. L. Good et al., 1992; D. W. Johnson & Johnson, 2009a; A. King, 1999.

[58] Lou et al., 1996; Slavin, Hurley, & Chamberlain, 2003; Stevens & Slavin, 1995.

[59] Levy, Kaplan, & Patrick, 2000; M. C. Linn, Songer, & Eylon, 1996; Moje & Shepardson, 1998.

[60] Blumenfeld, 1992; Gayford, 1992; N. M. Webb, 1989.

[61] T. L. Good et al., 1992; Stacey, 1992.

cooperative learning Approach to instruction in which students work with a small group of peers to achieve a common goal and help one another learn.

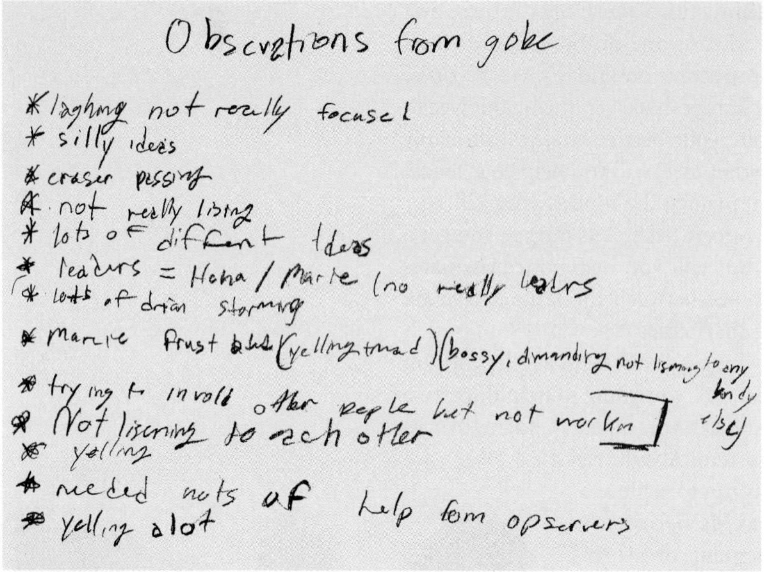
Obscvetions from gobe
*laghing not really focusel
* silly ideas
* eraser passing
* not really lising
* lots of diffrent ideas
* leaders = Hana / Marie (no really leaders
* lots of drain storming
* Marie frust (yelling mad)(bossy, dimanding not lisening to any body else)
* trying to involl other pepole but not working
* Not lisening to each other
* yelling
* needed nots of help fom opservers
* yelling alot

FIGURE 8.6 In an entry in her class journal, 12-year-old Amaryth reflects on the effectiveness of a cooperative group (she misspells *group* as "gobe").

one another learn.[62] (For example, see 12-year-old Amaryth's concerns—"not really focused," "yelling a lot," etc.—in Figure 8.6.)

As you can see, cooperative learning isn't simply a process of putting students in groups and setting them loose to work on an assignment together. Oftentimes students are more accustomed to competitive and individualistic classroom situations than they are to working cooperatively with their peers. For a cooperative learning activity to be successful, teachers must structure the activity in such a way that cooperation is not only helpful for academic success but is actually necessary for it.[63] The Classroom Strategies box "Enhancing the Effectiveness of Cooperative Learning" presents and illustrates several strategies that experts recommend for conducting effective cooperative group activities.

Have students conduct their own research about new topics.

When I've used the term *research* in previous chapters, I've been referring to planned, systematic inquiry designed to acquire new knowledge for humankind in general. Here I mean it in a much looser sense: to find new information for *oneself* rather than having it spoon-fed. In some instances such research may take the form of *discovery learning* or *inquiry learning* activities (e.g., see the Classroom Strategies box "Conducting Effective Discovery and Inquiry Learning Activities" on p. 173 of Chapter 5). But in many other cases it involves finding information already available in books, magazines, newspapers, encyclopedias, electronic databases, Internet websites, and elsewhere.

As our collective knowledge about the world grows by leaps and bounds each year, it's becoming increasingly important that students acquire **information literacy**—knowledge and skills that help them find, use, evaluate, organize, and present information about a particular topic. Information literacy includes a number of skills, all of which require teacher nurturance and guidance throughout the school years. To a large degree, these skills are *metacognitive,* in that they involve reflecting on the nature of knowledge in general as well as on specific pieces of information. One widely used approach, known as the Big6 ("big six"), involves teaching the following skills and subskills:[64]

1. Task definition
   - Defining the problem to be solved, identifying the questions to be answered
   - Identifying the information needed to solve the problem and answer the questions
2. Information-seeking strategies
   - Brainstorming all possible sources
   - Evaluating the sources and choosing the best options
3. Location and access
   - Finding the selected sources
   - Finding the needed information within those sources
4. Use of information
   - Engaging with (e.g., reading, hearing, or touching) the information
   - Extracting relevant information

information literacy Knowledge and skills that help a learner find, use, evaluate, organize, and effectively present information about a particular topic.

[62] D. M. Hogan & Tudge, 1999; N. M. Webb & Mastergeorge, 2003.
[63] D. W. Johnson & Johnson, 2009a; van Drie et al., 2006.
[64] M. B. Eisenberg & Berkowitz, 2000, 2003; Jansen, 2007, 2009; also see www.big6.com.

CLASSROOM STRATEGIES Enhancing the Effectiveness of Cooperative Learning

- Choose challenging tasks that students may have trouble accomplishing alone but *can* accomplish when several of them coordinate their efforts.

   Although they haven't yet been taught how to divide by fractions, students in a fourth-grade class are asked to solve the following problem: *Mom makes small apple tarts, using three-quarters of an apple for each small tart. She has 20 apples. How many small apple tarts can she make?* They work in small groups to solve the problem. (An example of one group's discussion appears in Chapter 3; see p. 69.)

- Form groups of students who are likely to work together productively and have unique knowledge and skills to offer.

   An elementary school teacher divides his class into cooperative groups of three or four students each to design posters depicting different African cultural groups. He makes sure that each group includes students of various ethnic backgrounds and students who will be able to contribute different skills to the task at hand. He also makes sure that students who don't work well together (e.g., close friends who get off task when they're together) are in different groups.

- Provide clear goals toward which groups should work.

   Students in a high school Spanish class work in small groups to create an episode of a soap opera (*telenovela*) spoken entirely in Spanish. Over the course of a three-week period, each cooperative group writes a short screenplay, collects the necessary props and costumes, and videotapes the episode.

- Structure tasks so that group members are dependent on one another for success.

   A high school biology teacher asks cooperative groups to prepare for an upcoming class debate on the pros and cons of mosquito control in the community. She gives each group member a unique function. One student acts as *reader* of information about the issue, another acts as *recorder* of group members' arguments, a third acts as *checker* to determine whether all group members agree with each argument, and so on.

- Provide clear guidelines about how to behave.

   A seventh-grade math teacher forms cooperative groups in which students will work on a series of math problems. Before the students begin the task, the teacher has them brainstorm ground rules for working effectively in their groups. Students volunteer such ideas as "Talk so you don't disturb the other groups," "Help someone who is having trouble," and "Be

patient." (You can observe this brainstorming session in the "Cooperative Learning" video in Chapter 8 of the Book-Specific Resources in MyEducationLab.)

- Monitor group interactions.

   A middle school social studies teacher asks cooperative groups to identify a possible plan for helping homeless people secure suitable housing. When he hears one student disparaging another because of a difference of opinion, he reminds the group that students should criticize ideas rather than people.

- Provide critical information and insights when (but only when) a group is unlikely or unable to provide such information and insights for itself.

   The same social studies teacher tells a group, "The solution you've developed assumes that most taxpayers would be willing to pay much higher taxes than they do now. Is that realistic?"

- Make students individually accountable for their achievement.

   An elementary school teacher has incorporated cooperative learning into a unit on calculating perimeters of squares, rectangles, and triangles. Later she gives all students a quiz to assess their individual mastery of perimeters.

- Reinforce group success.

   A seventh-grade math teacher awards bonus points to students whose entire group performs at or above a certain quiz score. (You can observe this strategy in the "Cooperative Learning" video in Chapter 8 of the Book-Specific Resources in MyEducationLab.)

- Ask students to evaluate their effectiveness in working as a group.

   After cooperative groups have completed their assigned tasks, a teacher asks the groups to answer questions such as these: "Did all group members actively participate?" "Did they ask questions when they didn't understand one another?" "Did they criticize ideas rather than people?"

Sources: Blumenfeld, Marx, Soloway, & Krajcik, 1996; E. G. Cohen, 1994; Crook, 1995; Deutsch, 1993; Esmonde, 2009; Finn, Pannozzo, & Achilles, 2003; Gillies & Ashman, 1998; Ginsburg-Block et al., 2006; J. Hiebert et al., 1997, p. 118 (apple tarts problem); D. W. Johnson & Johnson, 1991, 2009b; Karau & Williams, 1995; Lotan, 2006; Lou et al., 1996; A. M. O'Donnell & O'Kelly, 1994; Slavin et al., 2003; Stevens & Slavin, 1995; van Drie et al., 2006; N. M. Webb & Farivar, 1999; N. M. Webb & Palincsar, 1996.

5. Synthesis
   - Organizing information from the selected sources
   - Creating a product or performance, presenting the results
6. Evaluation
   - Judging the product or performance (in terms of its effectiveness)
   - Judging the process undertaken (in terms of its efficiency)

Learners who effectively find and use information in various media typically apply all of these skills, in some instances taking them in a sequential order and in other instances moving flexibly back and forth among them.[65] Information literacy skills are probably most

---

[65] M. B. Eisenberg, 2004.

effectively taught when teachers and school librarians collaborate to plan and teach lessons within the context of authentic learning tasks.[66]

One invaluable resource in information gathering is, of course, computer technology. For instance, most computer-based encyclopedias now take the form of **hypermedia**, collections of both visual and auditory material (printed materials, diagrams, photographs, spoken messages, videos, etc.) about a wide variety of topics. Often students begin by reading a short, introductory passage about a topic and then proceed to more specific information that addresses their specific interests and needs. For example, a student looking for information about airplanes might find a general description of airplanes with links to such topics as aerodynamics, the history of air travel, and military aircraft.

Increasingly, students are going online—to the Internet—to find needed information. Internet *search engines* such as Google (www.google.com) and Yahoo! (www.yahoo.com) allow students to find websites on almost any topic. Another good general resource is Wikipedia (www.wikipedia.org), an ever-expanding online encyclopedia to which virtually anyone can contribute about a limitless number of topics. And many government offices, public institutions, and private associations have websites that provide information, lesson plans, and links to other relevant websites. Following are just a few of the innumerable possibilities:

U.S. Geological Survey (www.usgs.gov)
U.S. Census Bureau (www.census.gov)
National Aeronautic and Space Administration (www.nasa.gov)
National Museum of Natural History (www.mnh.si.edu)
The Knowledge Loom (www.knowledgeloom.org)
Discovery Channel (school.discovery.com)

Some websites are designed specifically for elementary and secondary students. A good example is Human Anatomy Online (www.innerbody.com), which presents information about the various human anatomical systems. When first entering the website, the student chooses a particular system (e.g., skeletal, digestive, muscular, cardiovascular) and is linked to focused descriptions of that system and its various components. For instance, a student might first choose the digestive system and then, on subsequent screens, learn more about such things as teeth, the esophagus, the spleen, and the small intestine. The site also includes animated depictions of certain body parts (e.g., heart, lungs, ear) in action. Figure 8.7 illustrates this site with a screen from the ear animation.

Keep in mind, however, that students don't always have the knowledge and self-regulation skills they need to learn effectively as they explore the many resources the Internet offers.[67] Furthermore, the Internet has no good quality-control mechanism to ensure that information is accurate, especially when posted by individuals rather than by government agencies or professional organizations. (For instance, entries in Wikipedia, although generally accurate, occasionally include inaccuracies added by nonexperts.) An additional concern is that some students may venture into unproductive domains, perhaps finding research papers they can pass off as their own (thereby plagiarizing), stumbling upon sites that preach racist attitudes or offer pornographic images, or sharing personal information with people who might jeopardize their well-being.[68]

Clearly, then, students often need considerable scaffolding as they conduct online research about a topic, and their journeys into

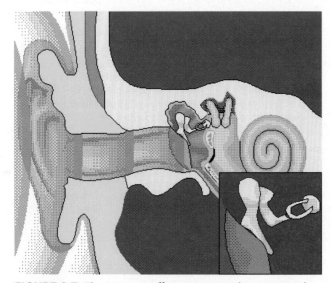

FIGURE 8.7 The Internet offers many good instructional sites. For example, at Human Anatomy Online, students can see animated depictions of such body parts as the heart, lungs, mouth and throat, and ear.
Source: Image ear5.gif from Human Anatomy Online (www.innerbody.com) provided by Pickering Brothers, LLC. All rights reserved.

---

hypermedia Collection of multimedia, computer-based instructional materials (e.g., text, pictures, sound, animations) that students can examine in a sequence of their own choosing.

[66] Afflerbach & Cho, 2010; Grover, 1996; Leu, O'Byrne, Zawilinski, McVerry, & Everett-Cacopardo, 2009.
[67] Azevedo, 2005b; K. Hartley & Bendixen, 2001; Kuiper, Volman, & Terwel, 2005.
[68] Nixon, 2005; Schofield, 2006.

cyberspace should be closely monitored. For example, elementary school librarian Carol Lincoln gives students precise, step-by-step directions on how to use Searchasaurus, a search engine available to libraries that is geared specifically for young students.[69] She tells them what icons to click on, what words to type in a search box, and so on. When students reach the website she has in mind, she provides specific questions that guide their learning (e.g., see Figure 8.8). Her approach is fairly teacher directed, but this may be necessary for students who have limited information literacy skills. As students become more proficient, they can proceed with greater independence, perhaps working in small cooperative groups to research particular topics in depth. Even in the secondary grades, however, students are likely to need considerable guidance about how to distinguish between helpful and unhelpful websites, sift through mountains of information in search of those tidbits most relevant to their own purposes, critically evaluate the quality of the information they're finding, and synthesize what they discover into a cohesive, meaningful whole.[70]

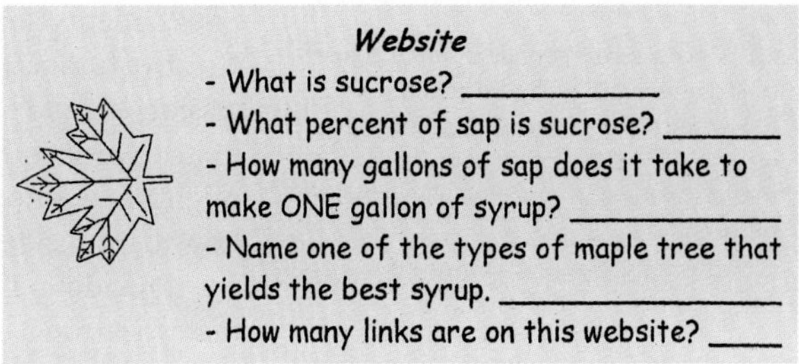

Many school computer systems now include a *remote desktop* feature that can help teachers to scaffold and monitor students' use of the Internet. With this feature, a teacher can share his or her own computer screen with students and demonstrate how to use a search engine, explore various websites, and so on. The feature also allows the teacher to view every student's computer screen from afar. If a particular student goes astray, the teacher can lock the student's screen and send an appropriate message.

Website
- What is sucrose? _____
- What percent of sap is sucrose? _____
- How many gallons of sap does it take to make ONE gallon of syrup? _____
- Name one of the types of maple tree that yields the best syrup. _____
- How many links are on this website? _____

FIGURE 8.8 Students may need some scaffolding—for instance, specific questions to answer as they look at a website about maple sugaring—to develop basic information literacy skills.

Have students teach one another.

Having some students provide instruction to other students—**peer tutoring**—is often an effective learner-directed approach to teaching fundamental knowledge and skills. For example, a teacher might have students within a single class tutor one another. Alternatively, two or more collaborating teachers might have older students teach younger ones—for instance, having fourth or fifth graders teach students in kindergarten or first grade.[71]

Peer tutoring can lead to considerable gains in academic achievement.[72] One possible reason for its effectiveness is that it provides a context in which struggling students may be more comfortable asking questions when they don't understand something. In one study[73] students asked 240 times as many questions during peer tutoring as they did during whole-class instruction!

Peer tutoring typically benefits tutors as well as those being tutored.[74] Students are more intrinsically motivated to learn something if they know they'll have to teach it to someone else, and they're apt to engage in considerable elaboration as they study and explain it.[75] Furthermore, in the process of directing and guiding other students' learning and problem solving, tutors may internalize these processes (recall our discussion of *internalization* in Chapter 5) and so become better able to direct and guide their *own* learning and problem solving. In other words, peer tutoring can foster greater self-regulation.[76] Peer tutoring has nonacademic benefits as well. Cooperation and other social skills improve, behavior problems diminish, and friendships form among students of different ethnic groups and between students with and without disabilities.[77]

[69] For more information, go to the EBSCO Information Service website at www.epnet.com/school/search.asp.

[70] Afflerbach & Cho, 2010; Egbert, 2009; Leu et al., 2009.

[71] Inglis & Biemiller, 1997; Kermani & Moallem, 1997; D. R. Robinson, Schofield, & Steers-Wentzell, 2005; J. R. Sullivan & Conoley, 2004.

[72] Ginsburg-Block et al., 2006; D. R. Robinson et al., 2005; Roscoe & Chi, 2007.

[73] Graesser & Person, 1994.

[74] Cushing & Kennedy, 1997; D. Fuchs, Fuchs, Mathes, & Simmons, 1997; Inglis & Biemiller, 1997; D. R. Robinson et al., 2005; J. R. Sullivan & Conoley, 2004.

[75] Benware & Deci, 1984; A. M. O'Donnell, 2006; Roscoe & Chi, 2007.

[76] Biemiller, Shany, Inglis, & Meichenbaum, 1998.

[77] Cushing & Kennedy, 1997; DuPaul, Ervin, Hook, & McGoey, 1998; Greenwood, Carta, & Hall, 1988; D. R. Robinson et al., 2005; J. R. Sullivan & Conoley, 2004.

peer tutoring Approach to instruction in which one student provides instruction to help another student master a classroom topic.

? Have you personally benefited from being either the tutor or the learner in a peer-tutoring session? If so, in what way(s) did you benefit? If not, how might the session have been conducted differently?

Students don't always have the knowledge and skills that will enable them to become effective tutors, however, especially in the elementary grades.[78] In most cases, then, tutoring sessions should be limited to subject matter that the tutors know well (we'll see an exception in just a moment). Training in effective tutoring skills is also helpful. For example, a teacher might show tutors how to establish a good relationship with the students they're tutoring, how to break a task into simple steps, how and when to give feedback, and so on.[79]

Providing a structure for tutoring sessions often helps students facilitate their classmates' learning, especially in situations in which all students are novices with respect to the subject matter.[80] In one approach students are given "starters" that help them form questions that encourage elaboration, critical thinking, and other effective cognitive processes as they work in pairs to study academic reading material.[81] Here are some examples of such starters:

- Describe . . . in your own words.
- What is the difference between . . . and . . . ?
- What do you think would happen to . . . if . . . happened?
- How did you figure that out?[82]

When students have guidance in formulating and asking one another good questions, highly effective tutoring sessions can result. Following is an example in which two seventh graders are following a prescribed questioning procedure as they work together to learn more about muscles, a topic that neither of them previously knew much about:

Jon: How does the muscular system work, Kyle?

Kyle: Well . . . it retracts and contracts when you move.

Jon: Can you tell me more?

Kyle: Um . . . well . . .

Jon: Um, why are muscles important, Kyle?

Kyle: They are important because if we didn't have them we couldn't move around.

Jon: But . . . how do muscles work? Explain it more.

Kyle: Um, muscles have tendons. Some muscles are called skeletal muscles. They are in the muscles that—like—in your arms—that have tendons that hold your muscles to your bones—to make them move and go back and forth. So you can walk and stuff.

Jon: Good. All right! How are the skeletal muscles and the cardiac muscles the same? . . .

Kyle: Well, they're both a muscle. And they're both pretty strong. And they hold things. I don't really think they have much in common.

Jon: Okay. Why don't you think they have much in common?

Kyle: Because the smooth muscle is—I mean the skeletal muscle is voluntary and the cardiac muscle is involuntary. Okay, I'll ask now. What do you think would happen if we didn't have smooth muscles?

Jon: We would have to be chewing harder. And so it would take a long time to digest food. We would have to think about digesting because the smooth muscles—like the intestines and stomach—are *in*voluntary. . . .

Kyle: Yeah, well—um—but, do you think it would *hurt* you if you didn't have smooth muscles?

Jon: Well, yeah—because you wouldn't have muscles to push the food along—in the stomach and intestines—you'd get plugged up! Maybe you'd hafta drink liquid—just liquid stuff. Yuk.[83]

Notice how the boys ask each other questions that encourage elaboration and metacognitive self-reflection (e.g., "Why don't you think they have much in common?" "Do you think it would hurt you if you didn't have smooth muscles?"). Through such structured

---

[78] Greenwood et al., 1988; Kermani & Moallem, 1997; D. Wood, Wood, Ainsworth, & O'Malley, 1995.

[79] Fueyo & Bushell, 1998; Inglis & Biemiller, 1997; Kermani & Moallem, 1997; D. R. Robinson et al., 2005.

[80] Fantuzzo, King, & Heller, 1992; L. S. Fuchs et al., 1996; Mathes, Torgesen, & Allor, 2001; Spörer & Brunstein, 2009.

[81] A. King, 1997, 1999.

[82] A. King, 1997, pp. 229–231.

[83] A. King, Staffieri, & Adelgais, 1998, p. 141.

interactions, students at the same grade and ability levels can provide valuable scaffolding for one another's learning efforts.[84]

Ideally, *all* students should have an opportunity to tutor others at one time or another.[85] This is often easier said than done, as a few students may consistently achieve at a lower level than most of their peers. One strategy is to ask low-achieving students to tutor younger children or same-age classmates who have cognitive or physical disabilities.[86] Another possibility is to teach the students specific tasks or procedures they can share with their higher-achieving, but in this case uninformed, classmates.[87]

Assign authentic real-world tasks, perhaps as group activities.

In Chapter 4 we noted the importance of *authentic activities*—activities similar to ones that students are apt to encounter in the outside world—as a means of promoting transfer of classroom subject matter to real-world situations. Complex tasks in the outside world must often be handled with little or no explicit guidance from others, and so growing children can best prepare for them by making many of their own decisions while completing similar tasks in the classroom. Most authentic activities, then, should be more learner directed than teacher directed.

Observe an authentic activity for high school students in the "Video Project" video in Chapter 8 of the Book-Specific Resources in MyEducationLab.

Some real-world tasks are easy to carry out within school walls. For example, students can, in a school setting, bake a cake, write a newspaper article, or calculate the amount of carpet needed for an irregularly shaped room. Other tasks can be accomplished only in the outside community. For instance, in **service learning**, students work on meaningful community service projects that are closely related to the classroom curriculum. To illustrate, children in the primary grades might regularly monitor the quantity of house pet "droppings" in an environmentally sensitive city park, and middle school students might gather information about liquor stores and possible zoning violations near school grounds (the latter example is described more fully in the Classroom Strategies box on p. 268 of Chapter 7).[88] In addition to the social, moral, and motivational benefits of community service projects (see Chapter 7), those that are closely tied to important instructional goals also appear to enhance classroom learning.[89]

Yet not all real-world tasks are possible and practical to complete either in or outside of school, and in such instances *simulations* offer a reasonable alternative. For example, students might conduct a mock trial of a historical figure (e.g., Alexander the Great, Adolf Hitler) or test the aerodynamic effectiveness of variously shaped paper airplanes. In addition, some computer programs offer simulations of such activities as dissecting a frog, building a city, or investing in the stock market. Following are three examples of software programs that require students to apply what they learn in school to complex real-world problems:

- **Gary Gadget: Building Cars.** Students assemble a car and drive to various destinations using a map; they occasionally encounter obstacles (e.g., a muddy road, a steep hill) that require making adjustments to the car.
- **Crazy Machines: The Wacky Contraptions Game.** Students use a collection of three-dimensional parts (pumps, pipes, generators, balls, etc.) to construct machines for various purposes—perhaps moving heavy objects, driving nails, or shooting cannons (see Figure 8.9).

FIGURE 8.9 In the simulation Crazy Machines: The Wacky Contraptions Game, students apply their knowledge of science to create various outcomes in a virtual world.
Source: Crazy Machines: The Wacky Contraptions Game, Courtesy of Viva Media® and FAKT Software GmbH, Crazy Machines 2™. All rights reserved.

---

[84] A. King, 1998.
[85] Greenwood, 1991; J. R. Sullivan & Conoley, 2004.
[86] Cushing & Kennedy, 1997; Inglis & Biemiller, 1997; J. R. Sullivan & Conoley, 2004.
[87] E. G. Cohen, Lockheed, & Lohman, 1976; N. M. Webb & Palincsar, 1996.
[88] Pickens, 2006; Tate, 1995.
[89] Celio, Durlak, Pachan, & Berger, 2007; Dymond, Renzaglia, & Chun, 2007.

service learning Activity that promotes learning and development through participation in a meaningful community service project.

- **Animal Hospital: Pet Vet 3D.** Students play the role of a veterinarian who must diagnose and treat a variety of sick pets and also handle the business side of a veterinary office, such as purchasing supplies and maintaining a reasonable workload.

Classroom simulations are often both motivating and challenging (thereby keeping students on task for extended periods) and can significantly enhance students' problem-solving and scientific reasoning skills.[90] In many cases the tasks involved are sufficiently complex and challenging that students must work on them in small groups rather than as individuals—a situation that many students find especially appealing.[91]

Use technology to enhance communication and collaboration.

Effective student interactions don't necessarily have to be face to face. Through such mechanisms as e-mail, Web-based chat rooms, electronic bulletin boards, and blogs, computer technology enables students to communicate with peers in their own classroom or elsewhere, exchange perspectives, and brainstorm and build on one another's ideas.[92] Technology also allows subject matter experts to be pulled occasionally into the conversation.[93]

As an example, researchers at the University of Toronto have developed software that allows students to communicate regularly using a classwide database and essentially creates a computer-based community of learners.[94] Using the database, students share their questions, ideas, notes, writing products, and graphic constructions. Their classmates (and sometimes a subject matter expert as well) respond regularly, perhaps by giving feedback, building on ideas, offering alternative perspectives, or synthesizing what has been learned. For instance, in a unit on "Prehistory of the New World," students in a combined fifth- and sixth-grade classroom worked in groups of three or four to study particular topics and then shared their findings through their computer database.[95] One group, which studied various theories about how human beings first migrated from Asia to the Americas, reported the following:

> **What We Have Learned**: We know that we have learned lots on this project, but the more that we learn the more we get confused about which is fact and which is fiction. The problem within this problem is that there isn't any real proof to say when they came or how. The theory that is most believed is the Bering Strait theory in which people from Asia walked over a land bridge. Another theory is they kayaked the distance between the two continents. We have also unfortunately found racist theories done by people who hate people unlike their own saying that the people of the New World are these people because of human sacrifices and only this race of people would do that.
>
> We have made are [our] own theories using information we found and trying to make sense of it. We have heard some people say they come from outer space but this theory is pretty much out of the question. I don't think the Native peoples or the Inuit would like to hear that theory either. How they came isn't easily answered for some of the theories but it does make since [sense] with the Bering Strait theory.[96]

Notice how the students acknowledge that several theories exist about how people first migrated to the New World (i.e., the Western Hemisphere). In other words, they've discovered that absolute truths about a topic aren't always easy to come by (recall the discussion of *epistemic beliefs* in Chapter 4). Notice, too, how the students have attempted to evaluate the credibility of various theories they've encountered in their research, reflecting considerable critical thinking.

---

[90] Cognition and Technology Group at Vanderbilt, 1996; de Jong & van Joolingen, 1998; Gehlbach et al., 2008; Kuhn & Pease, 2008; Vye et al., 1998; Zohar & Aharon-Kraversky, 2005.

[91] Lou et al., 2001.

[92] Fabos & Young, 1999; Hewitt & Scardamalia, 1996; Noss & Hoyles, 2006; G. Stahl, Koschmann, & Suthers, 2006.

[93] A. L. Brown & Campione, 1996; Winn, 2002.

[94] For example, see Hewitt & Scardamalia, 1996, 1998; Lamon, Chan, Scardamalia, Burtis, & Brett, 1993;

Scardamalia & Bereiter, 2006. An early version of this software was known as Computer Supported Intentional Learning Environment, or CSILE (pronounced like the name *Cecil*). A second generation of CSILE, called Knowledge Forum (available commercially from Learning in Motion, Inc.), allows collaboration across schools and other institutions (e.g., see www.Knowledgeforum.com).

[95] Hewitt, Brett, Scardamalia, Frecker, & Webb, 1995.

[96] Hewitt et al., 1995, p. 7.

Another option for technology-based collaborative learning is the GLOBE Program (www.globe.gov), through which student groups around the world collaborate on inquiry-based projects related to environmental and earth sciences. Students in participating schools and classrooms collect and analyze data about various environmental topics (e.g., climate change, watershed dynamics), write reports, and share their findings with students and professional scientists elsewhere. As the Internet becomes increasingly accessible to learners worldwide, then, not only do teachers have limitless sources of information on which to draw but they also have limitless mechanisms through which they and their students can communicate and collaborate with people in faraway settings about issues of common interest.

Technology-based collaborative learning appears to have several benefits. By making their findings and logical thinking processes clearly visible to one another, students can more easily reflect on and evaluate their own and others' ideas. Furthermore, students tend to focus on truly understanding classroom subject matter rather than on simply "getting things done" (i.e., they adopt mastery goals rather than performance goals), and as a result they can better remember and apply classroom subject matter.[97] Furthermore, multinational student–student collaborations are an excellent way to get young learners thinking and acting as *global* citizens as well as citizens of a particular community and country.

Provide sufficient scaffolding to ensure successful accomplishment of assigned tasks.

Regardless of the tasks that learner-directed instruction involves, students are apt to need some structure and guidance. As an example of how important structure can be, try the following exercise.

SEE FOR YOURSELF   Take Five

Grab a blank sheet of paper and a pen or pencil, and complete these two tasks:

Task A: Using single words or short phrases, list six characteristics of an effective teacher.

Task B: Explain the general effects of school attendance on children's lives.

Don't continue reading until you've spent a total of at least *five minutes* on these tasks.

Once you've completed the two tasks, answer either "Task A" or "Task B" to each of the following questions:

1. For which task did you have a better understanding of what you were being asked to do?
2. During which task did your mind more frequently wander to irrelevant topics?
3. During which task did you engage in more off-task behaviors (e.g., looking around the room, doodling, getting out of your seat)?

I'm guessing that you found the first task relatively straightforward, whereas the second wasn't at all clear-cut. Did Task B's ambiguity lead to more irrelevant thoughts and off-task behaviors for you?

Off-task behavior in the classroom occurs more frequently when activities are so loosely structured that students don't have a clear sense of what they're supposed to do. Effective teachers tend to give assignments with some degree of structure. They also give

---

[97] Bereiter & Scardamalia, 2006; Gehlbach et al., 2008; Lamon et al., 1993; Miyake, 2008; Scardamalia & Bereiter, 2006.

clear directions about how to proceed with a task and a great deal of feedback about appropriate responses, especially during the first few weeks of class.[98]

Yet teachers need to strike a happy medium here. They certainly don't want to structure classroom tasks to the point where students never make their own decisions about how to proceed or to the point where only simple tasks and thought processes are required. Ultimately, teachers want students to develop and use complex cognitive processes—for example, to think analytically, critically, and creatively—and they must have classroom assignments and activities that promote such processes.[99]

The concept of *scaffolding* is helpful in this context: Teachers can provide a great deal of structure for tasks early in the school year, gradually removing it as students become better able to structure tasks for themselves. For example, when students first engage in cooperative learning activities, a teacher might structure group meetings by breaking down each group task into several subtasks, giving clear directions about how to carry out each subtask, and assigning every group member a particular role to serve in the group. As the school year progresses and students become more adept at learning cooperatively with their classmates, their teacher can gradually become less directive about how group tasks are accomplished.

We've also seen examples of structure and scaffolding in our earlier discussions of Internet research (see the questions about maple sugaring in Figure 8.8) and peer tutoring (recall the "starter" questions). Following are additional examples:

- Students with learning disabilities use the spell-check and grammar-check functions in word processing software to help them proofread and revise their writing (e.g., see Figure 8.10).
- Before students conduct an experiment, their teacher asks them to make predictions about what will happen and to explain and defend their predictions. Later, after students have observed the experiment's outcome, the teacher asks them to explain what happened and why.[100]
- A teacher has students meet in groups of four to discuss a controversial social issue. Each group proceeds through several steps:[101]

  1. The group subdivides into two pairs.
  2. Each pair studies a particular position on the issue and presents its position to the other pair.
  3. The group has an open discussion of the issue, with each group member having an opportunity to argue persuasively for his or her own position.
  4. The group strives for consensus on a position that incorporates all the evidence presented.

The amount of structure and scaffolding teachers provide should depend on how much students need in order to be productive. For example, when monitoring small-group discussions, teachers should be more directive with a group that seems to be unfocused and floundering than with one in which students are effectively articulating, critiquing, and building on one another's ideas.[102]

• General Instructional Strategies

In planning and conducting lessons—whether they involve teacher-directed instruction, learner-directed instruction, or some combination of the two—many of the strategies we've identified in previous chapters are, of course, relevant. In my own mind, some of the most critical ones are these:

- Regularly assess students' understandings. (Chapter 2)
- Encourage and support self-regulated behavior and learning. (Chapter 4)

Observe considerable teacher scaffolding as third graders design and create water wheels in the "Water Wheels" video in Chapter 8 of the Book-Specific Resources in MyEducationLab.

When I was young it was almost impossible to read. One of my teachers told me I could learn to read if I worked hard. Learning to read was like climbing Mount Rushmore. It took a very long time but I finally got it. My Mom said she was vary proud. Reading was hard for me. It took five years for me to learn to read. Every day I would go to the learning center to learn my 400 site words. It was hard for me to learn these words but I did it. Reading is one of the most important things I have learned so far in my life.

FIGURE 8.10 Daniel, a fifth grader who struggles with reading and writing, wrote this very cohesive paragraph with the help of a word processing program. A spell-checker enabled him to spell most, but not all, of the words correctly (he meant to use the words *very* and *sight,* not *vary* and *site*).

[98] W. Doyle, 1990; Evertson & Emmer, 1982; Gettinger & Kohler, 2006; Weinert & Helmke, 1995.
[99] W. Doyle, 1986a; Weinert & Helmke, 1995.
[100] Hatano & Inagaki, 1991, 2003; B. Y. White & Frederiksen, 1998.
[101] Deutsch, 1993; D. W. Johnson & Johnson, 2009b.
[102] K. Hogan et al., 2000.

- Pursue topics in depth rather than superficially. (Chapter 4)
- Conduct stimulating lessons and activities. (Chapter 6)
- Present challenges that students can realistically accomplish. (Chapter 6)

The following three strategies also apply across the board.

Take group differences into account.

Some instructional strategies are a better fit with students' cultural backgrounds than others. Recent immigrants from some Asian countries may be more accustomed to teacher-directed instruction than to learner-directed classroom activities.[103] In contrast, students from cultures that place a high premium on interpersonal cooperation (e.g., as is true in many Hispanic and Native American communities) are apt to achieve at higher levels in classrooms with many interactive and collaborative activities.[104] Culture-specific patterns of verbal interaction may also come into play, affecting the nature and amount of students' participation in whole-class discussions and question-answer sessions (see the Cultural Considerations box "Cultural and Ethnic Differences in Verbal Interaction").

Gender differences, too, must be taken into account. Although many boys thrive on competition, girls tend to do better when instructional activities are interactive and cooperative. Girls can be intimidated by whole-class discussions, however, and are more likely to participate when discussions and activities take place in small groups.[105] Because boys sometimes take charge of small-group activities, teachers may occasionally want to form all-female groups. By doing so, they're likely to increase girls' participation and encourage them to take leadership roles.[106]

Teachers' choices of instructional strategies may be especially critical in schools in low-income neighborhoods. Students in such schools often have more than their share of drill-and-practice work in basic skills—work that is hardly conducive to fostering excitement about academic subject matter.[107] Mastering basic knowledge and skills is essential, to be sure, but teachers can often incorporate them into engaging lessons that ask students to apply what they're learning to personal interests and real-world contexts.[108] For example, in a curriculum called "Kids Voting USA," students at all grade levels have age-appropriate lessons about voting, political parties, and political issues, and they relate what they learn to local election campaigns.[109] Depending on the grade level, they might conduct their own mock elections, analyze candidates' attacks on opponents, or give speeches about particular propositions on a ballot. Students who participate in the program are more likely to attend regularly to media reports about an election, initiate discussions about the election with friends and family members, and be knowledgeable about candidates and election results. In fact, their knowledge and excitement about politics is contagious, because even their *parents* begin to pay more attention to the news, talk more frequently about politics, and gain greater knowledge about candidates and political issues.

Take developmental levels and special educational needs into account.

Instructional strategies must to some extent depend on students' ages and developmental levels. Strategies that involve teaching well-defined topics in a structured manner and giving students a lot of guidance and feedback (e.g., direct instruction, mastery learning) are often more appropriate for younger students than for older ones. Lectures (which are often somewhat abstract) and lengthy homework assignments tend to be more effective for older students.[110]

[103] Igoa, 1995.

[104] Garcia, 1994; McAlpine & Taylor, 1993; Tyler et al., 2008; N. M. Webb & Palincsar, 1996.

[105] Théberge, 1994.

[106] Fennema, 1987; MacLean, Sasse, Keating, Steward, & Miller, 1995; Slavin et al., 2003.

[107] Duke, 2000; R. Ferguson, 1998; Pianta & Hamre, 2009; Portes, 1996.

[108] Lee-Pearce, Plowman, & Touchstone, 1998; M. McDevitt & Chaffee, 1998.

[109] M. McDevitt & Chaffee, 1998; also see www .kidsvotingusa.org.

[110] Ausubel, Novak, & Hanesian, 1978; Cooper et al., 2006; Rosenshine & Stevens, 1986.

CULTURAL CONSIDERATIONS   Cultural and Ethnic Differences in Verbal Interaction

If you've grown up in mainstream Western culture, you've learned that there are certain ways of conversing with others that are socially acceptable and certain other ways that are definitely *not* acceptable. For instance, if you're having lunch with a friend, the two of you will probably try to keep a conversation going throughout the meal. And if someone else is speaking—especially if that someone else is an authority figure—you probably know not to interrupt until the speaker has finished what he or she is saying. Once the speaker *is* finished, however, you can ask a question if you need further information.

Such social conventions are by no means universal. Here we look at cultural and ethnic differences in several aspects of verbal interaction: dialect, talking versus remaining silent, asking and answering questions, and waiting versus interrupting.

Dialect.   Even if children speak English at home, they may use a form of English different from the **Standard English** typically considered acceptable at school. More specifically, they may speak in a different **dialect**, a form of English (or, more generally, a form of any language) that includes some unique pronunciations, idioms, and grammatical structures. Dialects tend to be associated either with particular geographical regions or particular ethnic and cultural groups. Perhaps the most widely studied ethnic dialect is **African American English** (you may also see the terms *Black English vernacular* and *Ebonics*). This dialect, which is actually a group of similar dialects, is used in many African American communities throughout the United States and is characterized by certain ways of speaking that are distinctly different from those of Standard English (e.g., "He got ten dollar," "Momma she mad," "He be

talkin' ").[a] At one time many researchers believed that an African American dialect represented a less complex form of speech than Standard English, and so they urged educators to teach students to speak "properly" as quickly as possible. But most researchers now realize that African American dialects are, in fact, very complex languages with their own predictable idioms and grammatical rules and that these dialects promote communication and complex thought as readily as Standard English.[b]

When a local dialect is the language preferred by residents of a community, it's often the means through which people can most effectively connect with one another in day-to-day interactions. Furthermore, many children and adolescents view their native dialect as an integral part of their ethnic identity.[c]

Nevertheless, many people in mainstream Western culture associate higher social status with people who speak Standard English, and they perceive speakers of other dialects in a lesser light.[d] In addition, children who are familiar with Standard English have an easier time learning to read than those who are not.[e] For such reasons, many experts recommend that all students in English-speaking countries develop proficiency in Standard English.[f] Ultimately, children and adolescents function most effectively when they can use both their local dialect and Standard English in appropriate contexts. For example, although teachers may wish to encourage Standard English in most written work or in formal oral presentations, they might find other dialects quite appropriate in creative writing or informal classroom discussions.[g]

Talking versus remaining silent.   In comparison to some other cultures, mainstream Western culture is a chatty one.

People often say things to one another even when they have little to communicate, making small talk as a way of maintaining interpersonal relationships and filling awkward silences.[h] In some African American communities as well, people speak frequently and often with a great deal of energy and enthusiasm.[i]

In certain other cultures, however, silence is golden. Brazilians and Peruvians often greet their guests silently, Arabs stop talking to indicate a desire for privacy, and many Native American communities value silence in general.[j] Many people from Southeast Asian countries believe that effective learning is best accomplished through attentive listening rather than through speaking.[k] And as noted in Chapter 5, some cultures (e.g., many Japanese and Canadian Inuits) interpret talking a lot as a sign of immaturity or low intelligence.[l]

Asking questions.   Different cultural and ethnic groups also have diverse views about when it's appropriate for children to speak to adults. In mainstream Western culture a common expectation is that children will speak up whenever they have comments or questions. Yet in many parts of the world, children are expected to learn primarily by close, quiet observation of adults, rather than by asking questions or otherwise interrupting what adults are doing.[m] And in some cultures—for instance, in many Mexican American and Southeast Asian communities, and in some African American communities—children learn very early that they should engage in conversation with adults only when their participation has been directly solicited.[n] In fact, children from some backgrounds—including many Puerto Ricans, Mexican Americans, and Native Americans—have been taught that speaking directly and assertively to adults is rude, perhaps even rebellious.[o]

Standard English Form of English generally considered acceptable at school, as reflected in textbooks and grammar instruction.

dialect Form of a language that has certain unique pronunciations, idioms, and grammatical structures and is characteristic of a particular region or ethnic group.

African American English Dialect of some African American communities characterized by certain pronunciations, idioms, and grammatical constructions different from those of Standard English.

Answering questions. A common interaction pattern in mainstream Western classrooms is the **IRE cycle**: A teacher *initiates* an interaction by asking a question, a student *responds* to the question, and the teacher *evaluates* the response.[p] Similar interactions are often found in parent–child interactions in middle-income European American homes. For instance, when my own children were toddlers and preschoolers, I often asked them questions such as "How old are you?" and "What does a cow say?" and praised them when they answered correctly. But children reared in other environments—for instance, in many lower-income homes, as well in some Central American, Native American, and Hawaiian communities—are unfamiliar with such question–and–answer sessions when they first come to school.[q] Furthermore, some children may be quite puzzled when a teacher asks questions to which he or she already knows the answers.[r]

The issue is not that children are unaccustomed to questions; it's only that they have little experience with certain *kinds* of questions. For example, parents in African American communities in parts of the southeastern United States are more likely to ask questions involving comparisons and analogies. Rather than asking "What's that?" they may instead ask "What's that like?"[s] In addition, children in these communities may be specifically taught *not* to answer questions from strangers about personal and home life—questions such as "What's your name?" and "Where do you live?" The complaints of parents in these communities illustrate how much of a cultural mismatch there can be between the children and their European American teachers:

- "My kid, he too scared to talk, 'cause nobody play by the rules he know. At home I can't shut him up."

- "Miss Davis, she complain 'bout Ned not answerin' back. He says she asks dumb questions she already know about."[t]

Teachers' comments about these children reflect their own lack of understanding about the culture from which the children come:

- "I would almost think some of them have a hearing problem; it is as though they don't hear me ask a question. I get blank stares to my questions. Yet when I am making statements or telling stories which interest them, they always seem to hear me."

- "The simplest questions are the ones they can't answer in the classroom; yet on the playground, they can explain a rule for a ballgame or describe a particular kind of bait with no problem."[u]

Waiting versus interrupting. After asking students a question, many teachers wait a second or less for them to respond (see Chapter 2). Not only does such a short wait time give many students insufficient time to retrieve relevant information and formulate an answer, but it's also incompatible with the interactional styles of some cultural groups. People from some cultures leave lengthy pauses before responding as a way of indicating respect, as this statement by a Northern Cheyenne illustrates:

> Even if I had a quick answer to your question, I would never answer immediately. That would be saying that your question was not worth thinking about.[v]

Students from such cultures are more likely to participate in class and answer questions when given several seconds to respond.[w] An extended wait time both allows students to show respect and gives those with limited English proficiency some mental "translation" time.

Rather than pausing as a way to show respect, children from certain other backgrounds may interrupt adults or peers who haven't finished speaking—behavior that many from mainstream Western culture might interpret as rudeness. For instance, in some African American, Hawaiian, and Jewish cultures, adults and children alike may speak spontaneously and simultaneously, perhaps to show personal involvement in a conversation or perhaps to avoid being excluded from the conversation altogether. In such settings, waiting for one's turn may mean being excluded from the conversation altogether.[x]

[a] Hulit & Howard, 2006, p. 346; Owens, 1995, p. A-8.
[b] Alim & Baugh, 2007; Fairchild & Edwards-Evans, 1990; Hulit & Howard, 2006; Spears, 2007.
[c] McAlpine, 1992; Ogbu, 2003; Tatum, 1997.
[d] DeBose, 2007; Purcell-Gates, 1995; H. L. Smith, 1998.
[e] Charity, Scarborough, & Griffin, 2004; T. A. Roberts, 2005.
[f] Casanova, 1987; M. Craft, 1984; DeBose, 2007; Ogbu, 1999.
[g] DeBose, 2007; Ogbu, 1999, 2003; Smitherman, 1994.
[h] Irujo, 1988; Trawick-Smith, 2003.
[i] Gay, 2006; Tyler et al., 2008.
[j] Basso, 1972; Menyuk & Menyuk, 1988; Trawick-Smith, 2003.
[k] J. Li, 2005; J. Li & Fischer, 2004; Volet, 1999.
[l] Crago, 1988; Minami & McCabe, 1996.
[m] Correa-Chávez, Rogoff, & Mejía Arauz, 2005; Gutiérrez & Rogoff, 2003; Kağitçibaşi, 2007.
[n] Delgado-Gaitan, 1994; C. A. Grant & Gomez, 2001; Ochs, 1982.
[o] Banks & Banks, 1995; Delgado-Gaitan, 1994.
[p] Mehan, 1979.
[q] Losey, 1995; Rogoff, 2003, 2007.
[r] Crago, Annahatak, & Ningiuruvik, 1993; Heath, 1989; Rogoff, 2003.
[s] Heath, 1980, 1989.
[t] Heath, 1980, p. 107.
[u] Heath, 1980, pp. 107–108.
[v] Gilliland, 1988, p. 27.
[w] Castagno & Brayboy, 2008; Gilliland, 1988; Mohatt & Erickson, 1981; Tharp, 1989.
[x] Farber, Mindel, & Lazerwitz, 1988; Hale-Benson, 1986; Tharp, 1989; Tyler et al., 2008.

IRE cycle Adult–child interaction marked by adult initiation (e.g., a question), child response, and adult evaluation.

Observe the effective use of a cooperative learning activity in a high school history class in the "Cooperative Learning: Reconstruction" video in Chapter 8 of the Book-Specific Resources in MyEducationLab.

The knowledge and skills that students bring to a lesson must also be a consideration.[111] Structured, teacher-directed approaches are usually most appropriate when students know little or nothing about the subject matter. But when students have mastered basic knowledge and skills, and particularly when they are self-regulating learners, they should begin directing some of their own learning, perhaps in small-group discussions, authentic activities, or independent research through hypermedia and the Internet.

Even when working with a single age-group, teachers must often modify their instructional goals and strategies for students who have exceptional cognitive abilities or disabilities. Ideally, teachers individualize instruction for *every* student—a practice known as **differentiated instruction**. For example, to ensure that all students are working within their specific *zone of proximal development* (see Chapter 5), teachers may need to identify more basic goals for some students (e.g., those with intellectual disabilities) and provide especially challenging activities for others (e.g., those who are gifted). Strictly expository instruction (e.g., a lecture or textbook chapter) can provide a quick and efficient means of presenting new ideas to students who process information quickly and abstractly, yet it may be incomprehensible and overwhelming to students with cognitive disabilities. In contrast, direct instruction and mastery learning have been shown to be effective with students who have learning difficulties (including many students with identified cognitive disabilities) yet may prevent rapid learners from progressing at a rate commensurate with their potential.[112]

Combine several instructional approaches into a single lesson.

Historically, many educators have looked for—and in some cases decided that they've found—the single "best" way to teach children and adolescents. The result has been a series of movements in which educators advocate a particular instructional approach and then, a few years later, advocate a very different approach.[113] I've often wondered why the field of education is characterized by such pendulum swings, and I've developed several hypotheses. Perhaps some people are looking for an *algorithm* for teaching—a specific procedure they can follow to guarantee high achievement. Perhaps they confuse theory with fact, thinking that the latest theoretical fad must inevitably be the one and only correct explanation of how children learn or develop, and thus conclude that the teaching implications they derive from the theory must also be correct. Or maybe they just have an overly simplistic view of what the goals of our educational system should be.

As should be clear by now, *there is no single best approach to classroom instruction.* Every instructional strategy has its merits, and each is useful in different situations. Some instructional methods are most appropriate for teaching basic skills, others are better for promoting complex cognitive processes, and so on. Table 8.3 lists several general instructional goals teachers are likely to have and suggests general instructional strategies that might be appropriate for each one. Notice that many of the strategies we've examined in this chapter appear in two or more rows in the table, reflecting the multiple purposes for which they might flexibly be used. A successful classroom—one in which students are acquiring and using school subject matter in truly meaningful ways—is undoubtedly a classroom in which a variety of approaches to instruction can be found.

---

differentiated instruction Practice of individualizing instructional methods—and possibly also individualizing specific content and instructional goals—to align with each student's existing knowledge, skills, and needs.

[111] C. M. Connor et al., 2009; Corno, 2008; Kalyuga & Sweller, 2004.

[112] Arlin, 1984; J. M. Fletcher, Lyon, Fuchs, & Barnes, 2007; Leinhardt & Pallay, 1982; Rosenshine & Stevens, 1986; Tomlinson & McTighe, 2006.

[113] K. R. Harris & Alexander, 1998; Sfard, 1998.

TABLE 8.3 Choosing an Instructional Strategy

When Your Goal Is to Help Students . . .	Consider Using . . .
Master and review basic skills.	• Direct instruction • Computer-based instruction (some programs) • Lower-level teacher questions • Mastery learning • Cooperative learning • Peer tutoring • Homework assignments (those in which students practice skills they've previously learned at school)
Gain firsthand, concrete experience with a particular topic.	• Hands-on discovery learning • Service learning activities • Computer simulations
Gain an organized, relatively abstract body of knowledge about a topic.	• Lectures • Textbooks and other assigned readings • Computer-based instruction (some programs) • Instructional websites on the Internet
Connect school subject matter to real-world contexts and problems.	• Inquiry learning • Authentic activities • Technology-based collaborative learning (either within a single classroom or in collaboration with students at other schools) • Homework assignments (those in which students are asked to relate what they're learning in class to specific issues at home or in the community)
Acquire advanced understandings about a topic and/or develop higher-level cognitive processes (e.g., problem solving, critical thinking, scientific reasoning).	• Higher-level teacher questions • Class discussions • Cooperative learning • Inquiry learning • Hypermedia and/or Internet research • Authentic activities • Computer simulations (some programs) • Technology-based collaborative learning • Peer tutoring (which requires tutors to organize and elaborate on what they've previously learned)
Acquire increased metacognitive awareness and more effective reading and self-regulation strategies.	• Computer-based instruction (some programs) • Reciprocal teaching (see Chapter 5) • Cooperative learning • Peer tutoring (which can enhance self-regulation for tutors) • Homework assignments (those appropriately scaffolded to foster planning, self-monitoring, etc.)
Acquire computer literacy skills.	• Computer-based instruction • Hypermedia and/or Internet research • Instructional websites on the Internet • Computer simulations • Technology-based collaborative learning
Acquire effective strategies for interacting and working with others.	• Class discussions • Cooperative learning • Peer tutoring • Technology-based collaborative learning

SUMMARY

Two central roles of any teacher are, of course, planning and carrying out instruction. The four Mega-Ideas presented at the beginning of the chapter can help us summarize basic principles that should guide these activities.

- *Effective teachers identify the knowledge and abilities they want students to acquire, and they plan instruction accordingly.* Good teachers engage in considerable advance planning. They identify the general instructional goals and more specific instructional objectives that they would like students to accomplish. They conduct task analyses to break complex tasks into smaller and simpler components. They develop lesson plans that spell out the activities they will use on a daily basis, and they continually evaluate and modify their plans as the school year progresses. And in recent years, many teachers have begun to create class websites on which they can communicate class-specific instructional goals and objectives, detailed information about assignments and due dates, and so on.

- *Sometimes instruction is most effective when it is teacher-directed—that is, when the teacher chooses the specific topics to be studied and the general course of a lesson.* A good deal of teacher-directed instruction is expository in nature, presenting information in essentially the same form that students are expected to learn it. In some cases (e.g., in lectures and textbook reading assignments) it's largely "one-way," with information going primarily from the teacher or some other expert (e.g., a textbook author) to students. In other cases it's more two-way, with information flowing regularly back and forth between the teacher (or perhaps a virtual "teacher," such as a computer) and students. For instance, direct instruction, computer-based instruction, and mastery learning all involve many opportunities for student practice and teacher feedback. Teacher-directed instruction is, like all instruction, most effective when

it promotes effective cognitive processes—for instance, when it captures students' attention and encourages students to elaborate on what they're learning.

- *Sometimes instruction is most effective when it is learner-directed—that is, when students have some control over the issues to be addressed and the ways in which to address them.* In class discussions, cooperative learning activities, independent learning through printed materials or technology-based media, peer tutoring, and authentic group activities, students largely control the flow of events. Learner-directed instruction is most useful when topics and tasks lend themselves to multiple perspectives and approaches, when the teacher creates an atmosphere conducive to open debate, and when students have some ability to regulate their own learning and behavior. Even so, students may need some structure and guidance to help them accomplish assigned tasks successfully.

- *Different instructional strategies are appropriate for different instructional goals and objectives and for different students.* For example, direct instruction or mastery learning is often advisable when students must learn basic skills to automaticity, whereas authentic activities are more appropriate when the goal is for students to apply those skills to real-world situations and problems. Interactive and cooperative instructional strategies may be especially effective for females, as well as for students whose cultural backgrounds have emphasized cooperation rather than competition. Abstract lectures tend to be more useful with high-achieving adolescents, whereas more concrete approaches (e.g., direct instruction) are often preferable for younger students, students who have a history of low academic achievement, and students who have little prior knowledge about the topic or skill in question. Ultimately, there is no single "best" instructional strategy.

PRACTICE FOR YOUR LICENSURE EXAM

Cooperative Learning Project

One Monday morning Ms. Mihara begins the unit "Customs in Other Lands" in her fourth-grade class. She asks students to choose two or three students with whom they would like to work to study a particular country. After the students have assembled into six small groups, she assigns each group a country: Australia, Colombia, Ireland, Greece, Japan, or South Africa. She tells the students, "Today we'll go to the school library, where your group can find information on the customs of your country and check out materials you think will be useful. Every day over the next two weeks, you'll have time to work with your group. A week from Friday, each group will give an oral report to the class."

During the next few class sessions, Ms. Mihara runs into many more problems than she anticipated. She realizes that the high achievers have gotten together to form two of the groups, and many socially oriented, "popular" students have flocked to two others. The remaining two groups are comprised of whichever students were left over. Some groups get to work immediately on their task, others spend their group time joking and sharing gossip, and still others are neither academically nor socially productive.

As the unit progresses, Ms. Mihara hears more and more complaints from students about their task: "Janet and I are doing all the work; Karen and Mary Kay aren't helping at all," "Eugene thinks he can boss the rest of us around because we're studying Ireland and he's

Irish," "We're spending all this time but just can't seem to get anywhere!" And the group reports at the end of the unit differ markedly in quality: Some are carefully planned and informative, whereas others are disorganized and have little substance.

1. **Constructed-response question**

   Describe two things you might do to improve Ms. Mihara's cooperative learning activity. Base your improvements on research findings related to cooperative learning or on contemporary principles and theories of learning, development, or motivation.

2. **Multiple-choice question**

   Ms. Mihara never identifies an instructional objective for her unit "Customs in Other Lands." Which one of the following objectives reflects recommended guidelines about how instructional objectives should be formulated?

   a. "The teacher should expose students to many differences in behaviors and beliefs that exist in diverse cultures (e.g., eating habits, ceremonial practices, religious beliefs, moral values)."

   b. "The teacher should use a variety of instructional practices, including (but not limited to) lectures, direct instruction, textbook readings, and cooperative learning activities."

c. "Students should study a variety of cultural behaviors and beliefs, including those of countries in diverse parts of the world."

d. "Students should demonstrate knowledge of diverse cultural practices—for example by describing three distinct ways in which another culture is different from their own."

Go to Chapter 8 of the Book-Specific Resources in MyEducationLab and click on "Practice for Your Licensure Exam" to answer these questions. Compare your responses with the feedback provided.

PEARSON myeducationlab

Go to the Topic "Planning and Instruction" in the MyEducationLab (www.myeducationlab.com) for your course, where you can:

- Find learning outcomes for "Planning and Instruction," along with the national standards that connect to these outcomes.
- Complete Assignments and Activities that can help you more deeply understand the chapter content.
- Apply and practice your understanding of the core teaching skills identified in the chapter with the Building Teaching Skills and Dispositions learning units.
- Examine challenging situations and cases presented in the IRIS Center Resources.
- Access video clips of CCSSO National Teachers of the Year award winners responding to the question, "Why Do I Teach?" in the Teacher Talk section.

- Check your comprehension of the content covered in the chapter by going to the Study Plan in the Book Resources for your text. Here you will be able to take a chapter quiz, receive feedback on your answers, and then access Review, Practice, and Enrichment activities to enhance your understanding of chapter content. Flashcards are also available to help you study definitions and key terms.
- Access additional Book Resources, including:
  - Focus Questions to guide your reading, Video Examples of various concepts and principles presented in the chapter, and a Practice for Your Licensure Exam exercise that resembles the kinds of questions appearing on many teacher licensure tests.

Chapter

9

Strategies for Creating an Effective Classroom Environment

Annie Pickert/Pearson

CHAPTER OUTLINE

Case Study: A Contagious Situation

Creating an Environment Conducive to Learning

Expanding the Sense of Community Beyond the Classroom

Reducing Unproductive Behaviors

Addressing Aggression and Violence at School

Summary

Practice for Your Licensure Exam: The Good Buddy

320

MEGA-IDEAS TO MASTER IN THIS CHAPTER

Effective teachers create a caring, respectful environment in which students are consistently focused on learning and on accomplishing instructional goals and objectives.

Teachers are most effective when they coordinate their efforts with colleagues, outside agencies, and parents.

Teachers must take action when students behave in ways that adversely affect their own or others' learning and achievement; interventions should be tailored to the

circumstances, with students' development and well-being being the ultimate goal.

Minimizing aggression and violence at school requires a three-tiered approach: creating a respectful and supportive school environment, intervening early for students at risk for social failure, and providing intensive interventions for chronically aggressive students.

CASE STUDY A Contagious Situation

After receiving a teaching certificate in May, Ms. Cornell has accepted a position as a fifth-grade teacher at Twin Pines Elementary School. She has spent the summer planning her classroom curriculum, identifying her instructional goals for the year, and developing numerous activities to help students achieve those goals. Today, on the first day of school, she has jumped head-long into the curriculum she planned. But three problems quickly present themselves—in the forms of Eli, Jake, and Vanessa.

These three students seem determined to disrupt the class at every possible opportunity. They move about the room without permission, intentionally annoying others as they walk to the pencil sharpener or wastebasket. They talk out of turn, sometimes being rude and disrespectful to their teacher and classmates and at other times belittling the activities Ms. Cornell has so carefully planned. They rarely complete in-class assignments, preferring instead to engage in horseplay

or practical jokes. They seem especially prone to misbehavior during downtimes in the daily schedule—for example, at the beginning and end of the school day, before and after recess and lunch, and on occasions when Ms. Cornell is preoccupied with other students.

Ms. Cornell continues to follow her daily lesson plans, ignoring her problem students and hoping they'll begin to shape up. Yet the disruptive behavior continues, with the three of them delighting in one another's antics. Furthermore, the misbehavior begins to spread to other students. By the middle of October, Ms. Cornell's classroom is out of control, and instructional objectives are rarely accomplished. The few students who still seem intent on learning are having trouble doing so.

- In what ways has Ms. Cornell planned for her classroom in advance? In what ways has she *not* planned?

As a first-year teacher, Ms. Cornell is well prepared in some respects but not at all prepared in others. She has carefully identified her instructional goals and planned relevant lessons. But she has neglected to think about how she might keep students on task or how she might adjust her lessons based on how students are progressing. And she hasn't considered how she might nip behavior problems in the bud, before they begin to interfere with instruction and students' learning. In the absence of such planning, no curriculum can be very effective—not even one grounded firmly in sound principles of learning, development, and motivation.

As we proceed through the chapter, we'll occasionally return to the opening case to identify reasons why Eli, Jake, and Vanessa are so disruptive and why their misbehaviors spread to other students. But I must make one point clear at the very beginning: The problem

A well-managed classroom is one in which students are consistently engaged in learning. It isn't necessarily one in which everyone is quiet.

in Ms. Cornell's classroom is *not* one of too much noise and activity. Effective **classroom management**—creating and maintaining a classroom environment conducive to learning and achievement—has little to do with noise or activity level. A well-managed classroom is one in which students are consistently engaged in productive learning activities and in which students' behaviors rarely interfere with their own or others' achievement of instructional goals.[1]

Creating and maintaining an environment in which students are continually engaged in productive activities can be a challenging task indeed. Teachers must tend to the unique needs of many students, must sometimes coordinate several activities occurring simultaneously, and must often make quick decisions about how to respond to unanticipated events. Furthermore, teachers must adjust their classroom management techniques to the particular instructional strategies (e.g., direct instruction, class discussions, or cooperative learning activities) in progress. So it's not surprising that many beginning teachers mention classroom management as their number one concern.[2]

A good general model of effective classroom management is *authoritative parenting,* a parenting style described in Chapter 7.[3] As you may recall, authoritative parents:

- Provide a loving and supportive environment
- Hold high expectations and standards for children's behavior
- Explain why some behaviors are acceptable and others are not
- Consistently enforce rules for behavior
- Include children in decision making
- Provide age-appropriate opportunities for independence

As we explore classroom management strategies in the following sections, we'll often see one or more of these characteristics of authoritative parenting at work. We'll begin our discussion by looking at proactive, *preventive* strategies—those designed to establish a productive learning environment right from the start. Later we'll turn to strategies for addressing the unproductive behaviors that sometimes occur even in the best-managed classrooms.

Creating an Environment Conducive to Learning

Think back on your many years as a student. Can you recall a class in which you were afraid of being ridiculed if you asked a "stupid" question? Can you recall one in which most students spent more time goofing off than getting their work done because no one had much reason to take the class seriously? Can you recall one in which you never knew what to expect because your instructor was continually changing expectations and giving last-minute assignments without warning?

When we talk about the classroom environment, to some extent we're talking about the actual physical setup—the arrangement of tables and chairs, the availability of tools and resources (painting supplies, computers, etc.), the use of bulletin boards to present information and engage students' interest, and so on. But even more important is the psychological environment, or **classroom climate**.[4] The ideal classroom is one in which students feel safe and secure, make learning a high priority, and are willing to take the risks and make the mistakes that are critical for long-term academic success. Such characteristics are especially important for students at risk for academic failure and dropping out of school.[5]

Observe the supportive classroom climates in the "Author's Chair" and "Scarlet Letter" videos in Chapter 9 of the Book-Specific Resources in MyEducationLab.

---

classroom management Establishment and maintenance of a classroom environment conducive to learning and achievement.

classroom climate Overall psychological atmosphere of the classroom.

[1] Brophy, 2006; W. Doyle, 1990; Emmer & Evertson, 1981.
[2] Evertson & Weinstein, 2006; V. Jones, 2006.
[3] For a good discussion of this point, see J. M. T. Walker & Hoover-Dempsey, 2006.

[4] Hamre & Pianta, 2005; Hardré, Crowson, DeBacker, & White, 2007; Patrick, Ryan, & Kaplan, 2007.
[5] Hamre & Pianta, 2005; V. E. Lee & Burkam, 2003.

Will Hart/PhotoEdit

The following recommendations summarize many strategies that researchers and experienced educators have identified for creating and maintaining an environment conducive to students' learning and academic achievement.

Arrange the classroom to maximize attention and minimize disruptions.

As teachers arrange classroom furniture, decide where to put instructional materials and equipment, and so on, they should consider the effects that various arrangements are likely to have on students' behavior. Here are several widely recommended strategies:[6]

- Arrange desks, tables, and chairs so that you and your students can easily interact and so that you can regularly survey the entire classroom for signs of possible confusion, frustration, or boredom.
- Establish traffic patterns that allow students to move around the classroom without disturbing one another.
- Keep intriguing materials out of sight and reach until they need to be used.
- Split up friends who easily get off task when they're together (e.g., put them on opposite sides of the room).
- Place chronically misbehaving or uninvolved students close at hand.

Hear three experienced teachers offer their suggestions in the "Arranging the Classroom" video in Chapter 9 of the Book-Specific Resources in MyEducationLab.

Communicate acceptance, caring, and respect for every student.

As you should recall from Chapter 6, human beings seem to have a fundamental need to feel socially connected with others. In the classroom this *need for relatedness* may reveal itself in a variety of ways. For instance, some students might eagerly seek their teacher's approval for something they've done well. Other students might actually misbehave to gain their teacher's attention (this may possibly be the case for Eli, Jake, and Vanessa in the opening case study). But in my own experiences as a teacher and school psychologist, I've never met a child or adolescent who, deep down, didn't want positive, productive relationships with school faculty members.

To some extent, teachers can help meet students' need for relatedness by demonstrating, through the many little things they do, that they care about and respect students as people.[7] A smile and warm greeting at the beginning of the day, a compliment about a new hairstyle, and a concerned inquiry when a student comes to school angry or upset—all of these behaviors communicate caring and respect. One high school student described caring teachers this way:

> They show it. You might see them in the hallway and they ask how you're doing, how was your last report card, is there anything you need. Or, maybe one day you're looking a little upset. They'll pull you to the side and ask you what's wrong, is there anything I can do.[8]

One effective strategy is to have students create two-way *dialogue journals* in which they regularly express their thoughts and feelings, ask questions, and request assistance. At least once a week, their teacher reads and responds to their entries. For example, Figure 9.1 shows several entries in 6-year-old Matt's journal. After each of Matt's entries is a response (indented) from his first-grade teacher. The teacher communicates caring by telling him that she often watches him playing soccer at recess and by complimenting him on his soccer skills. Through the journal the two also discover a common interest: skiing. (Matt's fourth entry is his attempt to write, "I love skiing, especially downhill skiing. Are you good at skiing?") Obviously, Matt feels comfortable enough with his teacher to engage in some one-upmanship ("I can go fastr then you"), and she is sufficiently confident about their relationship that she can tease him a bit ("I can beat a couch potato! Cinchy!") Notice that the teacher doesn't correct Matt's misspellings. Her primary purposes are to encourage him to write and to keep open the lines of communication, and negative feedback about spelling might interfere with both of these goals. Instead, she simply models correct spelling in her own entries.

How might the teacher adapt the journal assignment for students who can't yet read or write? (Compare your response to this question with the response presented in Chapter 9 of the Book-Specific Resources in MyEducationLab.)

---

[6] K. Carter & Doyle, 2006; W. Doyle, 1986a; Emmer & Evertson, 2009; Gettinger & Kohler, 2006; Sabers, Cushing, & Berliner, 1991; Woolfolk & Brooks, 1985.

[7] Allday & Pakurar, 2007; Certo, Cauley, & Chafin, 2002; D. K. Meyer & Turner, 2006.
[8] Certo et al., 2002, p. 15.

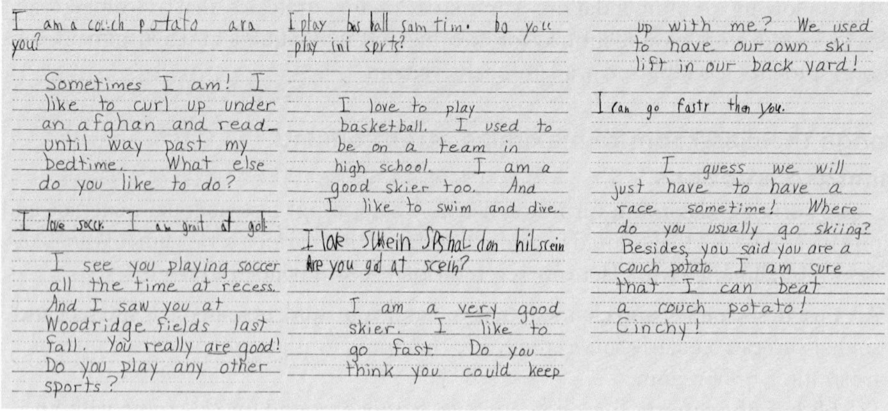

FIGURE 9.1 Six-year-old Matt and his first-grade teacher communicate regularly through a two-way dialogue journal.

Yet it isn't enough simply to be "warm and fuzzy" with students. To show genuine caring and respect for them, teachers must also do these things:[9]

- Be well prepared for class and in other ways demonstrate that they enjoy teaching and take their teaching responsibilities seriously.
- Convey high (yet realistic) expectations for student performance and provide the support students need to meet those expectations.
- Include students in decision making and in evaluations of their schoolwork.
- Acknowledge that students can occasionally have an "off" day and not hold it against them.

The quality of teacher–student relationships is one of the most influential factors affecting students' emotional well-being, motivation, and achievement at school. When students have positive, supportive relationships with teachers, they have higher self-efficacy and more intrinsic motivation to learn, engage in more self-regulated learning, are more likely to ask for help when they need it, are less apt to cheat on classroom assignments, and achieve at higher levels.[10]

Teacher affection, respect, and support are especially important for students who face exceptional hardships at home (e.g., extreme poverty, uninvolved or abusive parents, violent neighborhoods). When such students have one or more caring, trustworthy adults in their lives—and when they regularly come to a classroom that is warm, predictable, and dependable—they're more likely to have a strong sense of self-worth and to rise above their many challenges to succeed both in the classroom and in the outside world (recall the discussion of *resilient students* in Chapter 7).[11]

Work hard to improve relationships that have gotten off to a bad start.

Occasionally students come to school with an apparent chip on the shoulder, distrusting their teachers from Day 1 because of previous hurtful relationships with parents or other adults. At other times teachers get relationships with certain students off to a bad start through their own actions—perhaps because they incorrectly attribute a student's low achievement to lack of effort rather than lack of skill or perhaps because they accuse a

---

[9] L. H. Anderman, Patrick, Hruda, & Linnenbrink, 2002, p. 274; Certo et al., 2002; H. A. Davis, 2003; H. A. Davis, Schutz, & Chambless, 2001; J. M. T. Walker & Hoover-Dempsey, 2006.

[10] Hamre & Pianta, 2005; J. N. Hughes, Luo, Kwok, & Loyd, 2008; Marchand & Skinner, 2007; Marzano, 2003; Murdock, Miller, & Kohlhardt, 2004; Pianta,

Belsky, Vandergrift, Houts, & Morrison, 2008; A. M. Ryan & Patrick, 2001.

[11] Becker & Luthar, 2002; Juvonen, 2006; Masten, 2001; O'Connor & McCartney, 2007; D. A. O'Donnell, Schwab-Stone, & Muyeed, 2002; Pomeroy, 1999; Werner & Smith, 2001.

temperamentally high-energy child of being intentionally disobedient. Oftentimes students who have the poorest relationships with teachers are the ones most in need of *good* ones.[12]

Regardless of the initial causes of poor teacher–student relationships, teachers must work hard to turn them into productive ones. The first step, of course, is to *identify* poor relationships using such signs as these:[13]

- A teacher has hostile feelings (e.g., dislike, anger) toward a student.
- A teacher rarely interacts with a student.
- A teacher's messages to a student usually involve criticism or faultfinding.
- A teacher has a sense of learned helplessness about his or her ability to work effectively with a student.

Several strategies can help teachers repair these relationships. One is to think actively—perhaps in a brainstorming session with colleagues—about alternative hypotheses for why the student behaves as he or she does, being sure that the list of hypotheses offers potential solutions. Another is to meet one-on-one with the student to talk openly about the problem and possible ways to fix it (more on this point later in the chapter). Still another strategy, especially effective when working with young children, is simply to spend some time with the student in a noncontrolling, recreational context that might allow more positive feelings to emerge.[14]

Create a sense of community and belongingness.

In Chapter 3, I described a *community of learners,* a classroom in which teacher and students consistently work together to help one another learn. Ultimately, teachers should also create a general **sense of community** in the classroom—a sense that they and their students share common goals, are mutually respectful and supportive of one another's efforts, and believe that everyone makes an important contribution to classroom learning.[15] Creating a sense of community engenders feelings of **belongingness**: Students see themselves as important and valued members of the classroom.[16] In the following interview, a middle school student named Barnie describes how it feels *not* to belong at school:

Adult: Are there times when you feel you are really different from your classmates?

Barnie: Yeah, all the time. . . . Because they all answer the questions, when I raise my hand I always get it wrong. Last week I was in a group, a smart group and I am not that smart. And I mostly get all the wrong answers and they yell at me.

Adult: What do they say?

Barnie: "You're dumb! You're stupid!" . . . When I am in the gym, I cannot run as fast as everybody and they all laugh at me. . . . It feels like I am the worst student ever.[17]

Numerous strategies can create a sense of classroom community and enhance students' feelings of belongingness:[18]

- Consistently communicate the message that *all* students deserve the respect of their classmates and are important members of the classroom community.
- Emphasize such prosocial values as sharing and cooperation, and provide opportunities for students to help one another.

Scott Cunningham/Merrill

Students achieve at higher levels in the classroom when they have a *sense of community*—that is, when they have shared goals and are respectful and supportive of one another's efforts.

[12] Darch & Kame'enui, 2004; H. A. Davis, 2003; Hyman et al., 2006; Irving & Hudley, 2008; Juvonen, 2006; Keogh, 2003; Pianta, 1999; Stipek & Miles, 2008.

[13] Pianta, 1999; Sutherland & Morgan, 2003.

[14] Pianta, 1999, 2006; Silverberg, 2003; Sutton & Wheatley, 2003.

[15] Hom & Battistich, 1995; D. Kim, Solomon, & Roberts, 1995; Osterman, 2000.

[16] E. M. Anderman, 2002.

[17] Dialogue from Kumar, Gheen, & Kaplan, 2002, p. 161.

[18] D. J. Connor & Baglieri, 2009; Emmer et al., 2000; Espelage & Swearer, 2004; Hamovitch, 2007; D. Kim et al., 1995; Lickona, 1991; Nucci, 2009; Osterman, 2000; A. M. Ryan & Patrick, 2001; Sapon-Shevin, Dobbelaere, Corrigan, Goodman, & Mastin, 1998.

sense of community Shared belief that teacher and students have common goals, are mutually respectful and supportive, and all make important contributions to classroom learning.

belongingness General sense that one is an important and valued member of the classroom.

- Make frequent use of interactive and collaborative teaching strategies (class discussions, cooperative learning activities, etc.).
- Use competitive events only to create an occasional sense of playfulness in the class and only when all students have an equal chance of winning.
- Solicit students' ideas and opinions, and incorporate them into classroom discussions and activities.
- Create mechanisms through which students can help make the classroom run smoothly and efficiently (e.g., assign various "helper" roles on a rotating basis).
- Give public recognition to students' contributions toward the overall success of the classroom.
- Institute a no-exclusion policy in group activities (e.g., by insisting that any student who wants to be involved in a play activity *can* be involved).
- Encourage students to be on the lookout for classmates on the periphery of ongoing activities (perhaps students with disabilities) and to ask these classmates to join in.
- Work on social skills with students whose interpersonal behaviors may victimize or alienate others.
- Be vigilant for incidents of bullying and other forms of peer harassment, and administer appropriate consequences to the perpetrators.

When students share a sense of community, they're more likely to exhibit prosocial behavior, stay on task, express enthusiasm about classroom activities, and achieve at high levels. Furthermore, a sense of classroom community is associated with lower rates of emotional distress, disruptive classroom behavior, truancy, violence, drug use, and dropping out.[19]

Create a goal-oriented, businesslike (but nonthreatening) atmosphere.

Although caring relationships with students are essential, teachers and students alike must recognize that they're at school to get certain things accomplished. Accordingly, a relatively businesslike atmosphere should prevail in the classroom most of the time. This is not to say that classroom activities must be boring and tedious. On the contrary, they should be interesting and engaging, and they can sometimes be quite exciting. Entertainment and excitement shouldn't be thought of as goals in and of themselves, however. Rather, they're means to a more important goal: mastering academic subject matter.[20]

Despite this emphasis on business, the classroom atmosphere should never be uncomfortable or threatening. As noted in Chapter 6, students who are excessively anxious are unlikely to perform at their best. How can teachers be businesslike without being threatening? They can hold students accountable for achieving instructional objectives yet not place students under continual surveillance. They can point out mistakes without making students feel like failures. They can focus students' attention on personal progress rather than on how each one's performance compares to that of classmates. And they can admonish students for misbehavior but communicate that each new day is an opportunity for a fresh start.[21]

Establish reasonable rules and procedures.

In the opening case study, Ms. Cornell failed to provide guidelines about how students should behave—something she should have done the first week of school. A class without guidelines for appropriate behavior is apt to be chaotic and unproductive. And students must learn that certain behaviors simply won't be tolerated, especially those that cause physical or psychological harm, damage others' belongings or school property, or interfere with others' learning and performance. Setting reasonable limits on classroom behavior not only promotes a more productive learning environment but also helps prepare students to become productive members of adult society (recall the discussion of *socialization* in Chapter 3).

---

[19] Gottfredson, 2001; Hom & Battistich, 1995; Juvonen, 2006; D. Kim et al., 1995; Osterman, 2000; M. D. Resnick et al., 1997.
[20] Brophy, 2006; G. A. Davis & Thomas, 1989; Gettinger & Kohler, 2006.

[21] Dijkstra, Kuyper, van der Werf, Buunk, & van der Zee, 2008; C. R. Rogers, 1983; Spaulding, 1992.

FIGURE 9.2 Beginning the school year with a few rules

Effective teachers typically begin the school year with a few rules that will help classroom activities run smoothly. Such rules often include variations on the following:

Bring all needed materials to class. (Students should have books, homework assignments, permission slips, and any needed supplies for planned activities.)

Be in your seat and ready to work when the bell rings. (Students should be at their desks, have paper out and pencils sharpened, and be physically and mentally ready to work.)

Respect and be polite to all people. (Students should listen attentively when someone else is speaking, behave appropriately for a substitute teacher, and refrain from insults, fighting, and other disrespectful or hostile behavior.)

Respect other people's property. (Students should keep the classroom clean and neat, refrain from defacing school property, ask for permission to borrow another's possessions, and return those possessions in a timely fashion.)

Obey all school rules. (Students must obey the rules of the school building as well as the rules of the classroom.)

Sources: Based on Emmer & Evertson, 2009, pp. 22–23; Evertson & Emmer, 2009, pp. 23–24.

Effective classroom managers establish and communicate certain rules and procedures right from the start.[22] They identify acceptable and unacceptable behaviors (e.g., see Figure 9.2). They develop consistent procedures and routines for such things as completing seatwork, asking for help, and turning in assignments. And they have procedures in place for nonroutine events such as school assemblies, field trips, and fire drills. Teachers should communicate such rules and procedures clearly and explicitly and describe the consequences of noncompliance. Taking time to clarify rules and procedures seems to be especially important in the early elementary grades, when students may not be familiar with how things are typically done at school.[23]

Ideally, students should understand that rules and procedures aren't merely the result of a teacher's personal whims but are designed to help the classroom run smoothly and efficiently. And despite restrictions on their behavior, students should have some sense of *self-determination* in the classroom (see Chapter 6). One strategy is to include students in decision making about the rules and procedures by which the class will operate—a strategy that's likely to enhance their sense of ownership of and adherence to those rules and procedures.[24]

Observe two class discussions of appropriate student behaviors in the "Classroom Rules" and "Preparing for a Field Trip" videos in Chapter 9 of the Book-Specific Resources in MyEducationLab.

Another strategy for preserving students' sense of self-determination is to present rules and requirements as *information*—for instance, as conditions that can help students accomplish classroom objectives—rather than as mechanisms of *control* over students.[25] Examples of informational versus controlling messages are presented in Figure 9.3. Notice how all of the informational messages provide reasons for certain restrictions. The following scenario provides a simple illustration of how giving a reason can make all the difference in the world:

> Gerard is a student who has little tolerance for frustration. Whenever he asks Ms. Donnelly for assistance, he wants it *now.* If she can't help him immediately, he screams, "You're no good!" or "You don't care!" and shoves other students' desks as he walks angrily back to his seat.
>
> At one point during the school year, the class has a unit on interpersonal skills. One lesson in the unit addresses *timing*—the most appropriate and effective time to ask for another person's assistance with a problem.
>
> A week later, Gerard approaches Ms. Donnelly for help with a math problem. She's working with another student, but she turns briefly to Gerard and says, "Timing." She waits expectantly for Gerard's usual screaming. Instead, he responds, "Hey, Ms. D., I get it! I can ask you at another time!" He returns to his seat with a smile.[26]

Observe the teacher in the "Classroom Rules" and "Reading Groups" videos in Chapter 9 of the Book-Specific Resources in MyEducationLab. Would you characterize this teacher as "informational" or "controlling"?

Keep in mind that rules and procedures are easier to remember and therefore easier to follow if they're relatively simple and few in number.[27] Effective classroom managers tend

[22] Borko & Putnam, 1996; W. Doyle, 1990; Gettinger & Kohler, 2006.

[23] K. Carter & Doyle, 2006; Evertson & Emmer, 1982; Gettinger & Kohler, 2006.

[24] Evertson & Emmer, 2009; Nucci, 2009; M. Watson, 2008.

[25] Deci, 1992; Koestner, Ryan, Bernieri, & Holt, 1984.

[26] Based on Sullivan-DeCarlo, DeFalco, & Roberts, 1998, p. 81.

[27] G. A. Davis & Thomas, 1989; Emmer & Gerwels, 2006.

FIGURE 9.3 Presenting classroom rules and procedures as information

Students are more likely to be intrinsically motivated to follow classroom rules and procedures if teachers present them as items of information rather than as forms of control.

A teacher might say this (information):	**. . . rather than this (control):**
"You'll get your independent assignments done more quickly if you get right to work."	"Please be quiet and do your own work."
"As we practice for our fire drill, it is important to line up quickly and be quiet so that we can hear the instructions we are given and will know what to do."	"When the fire alarm sounds, line up quickly and quietly, and then wait for further instructions."
"This assignment is designed to help you develop the writing skills you will need after you graduate. It is unfair to other authors to copy their work word for word, so we will practice putting ideas into our own words and giving credit to authors whose ideas we borrow. Passing off another's writing and ideas as your own can lead to suspension in college or a lawsuit in the business world."	"Cheating and plagiarism are not acceptable in this classroom."

to stress only the most important rules and procedures at the beginning of the school year and introduce other rules and procedures later on as needed.[28] Also keep in mind that although some order and predictability are essential for student productivity, *too much* order can make a classroom a boring, routine place—one without an element of fun and spontaneity. Classrooms don't necessarily need rules and procedures for everything!

Enforce rules consistently and equitably.

Classroom rules are apt to be effective only if they're consistently enforced. For example, in the opening case study, Ms. Cornell imposes no consequences when her three troublesome students misbehave. Not only do their antics continue, but other students—realizing that "anything goes" in Ms. Cornell's classroom—follow suit. As we discovered in Chapter 3, imposing no adverse consequence for inappropriate behavior—especially when that consequence has been spelled out in advance—can actually be a form of *reinforcement* for the misbehavior.

We'll consider guidelines for administering punishment later in the chapter, but for now we should note that consistency in enforcing classroom rules should apply not only across occasions but also across *students*. Teachers almost invariably like some students more than others (e.g., they're apt to prefer high achievers), but they must keep their preferences to themselves. Students can be quite resentful of teachers who grant special favors to and overlook rule infractions of a few "pet" students.[29] And students who are unfairly accused or punished are, of course, even more resentful, as one high school student explains:

> Because like if you had a past record or whatever like in middle school if you got in trouble like at all, they would think that you're a slight trouble maker and if you got in trouble again, they would always . . . if you were anywhere that something bad happened or something against the rules or whatever, they pick you first because they think that you have a past. So they wouldn't like pick the kids that had never done anything.[30]

Thus consistency and equitable treatment for all students—or the lack thereof—is likely to have a significant effect on teacher–student relationships and overall classroom climate.[31]

Keep students productively engaged in worthwhile tasks.

As effective teachers plan lessons and classroom activities, they also plan specific ways of keeping students on task—something Ms. Cornell neglected to do in the opening case study. One strategy, of course, is to make the subject matter interesting and relevant to

? Thinking back to your years in elementary and secondary school, can you recall at least one student who was "teacher's pet"—someone who was clearly a favorite and had special privileges? Can you also recall a few students who were continually blamed for misdeeds, even when they weren't the true culprits?

---

[28] W. Doyle, 1986a.
[29] Babad, 1995; Babad, Avni-Babad, & Rosenthal, 2003; J. Baker, 1999.
[30] Certo et al., 2002, p. 25.
[31] Babad et al., 2003; J. Baker, 1999; Certo et al., 2002.

students' values and goals (see Chapter 6). Another is to incorporate variety into lessons, perhaps by using colorful audiovisual aids, conducting novel activities (e.g., small-group discussions, class debates), or occasionally moving to a different location (e.g., the computer lab or school yard).[32] But above all else, effective teachers make sure students have something to do at all times. Thanks to their basic need for arousal, human beings have a hard time doing *nothing at all* for any length of time (again see Chapter 6). Students often misbehave when they have nothing to do or are bored with what they *are* doing.[33]

Effective classroom managers make sure there is little "empty" time in which nothing is going on. Following are several strategies for keeping students productively engaged:[34]

- Have something specific for students to do each day, even on the first day of class.
- Have materials organized and equipment set up before class.
- Conduct activities that ensure *all* students' involvement and participation.
- Maintain a brisk pace throughout each lesson (but not so fast that students can't keep up).
- Ensure that students' comments are relevant and helpful but not excessively long-winded. (For example, take chronic time-monopolizers aside for a private discussion about giving classmates a chance to speak.)
- Spend only short periods of class time assisting individual students unless other students are able to work independently and productively in the meantime.
- Ensure that students who finish an assigned task quickly have something else to do (e.g., writing in a class journal or reading a book).

Plan for transitions.

In the opening case study, Eli, Jake, and Vanessa often misbehave at the beginning and end of the school day, as well as before and after recess and lunch. Misbehaviors most frequently occur during transition times—as students end one activity and begin a second, or as they move from one classroom to another. Effective classroom managers take steps to ensure that transitions proceed quickly and without a loss of momentum.[35] For example, they establish procedures for moving from one activity to the next, and they ensure that there is little between-activity slack time in which students have nothing to do. And especially in the secondary grades, when students change classes every hour or so, effective classroom managers typically have a task for students to complete as soon as they enter the classroom.

Students who are actively engaged in classroom activities rarely exhibit problem behaviors.

How might a teacher plan for the various transitions that occur throughout the school day? Here are some examples:

- An elementary school teacher has students follow the same procedure each day as lunchtime approaches: (1) Place completed assignments in a basket on the teacher's desk, (2) put away supplies, (3) get lunches from the coatroom, and (4) line up quietly by the door.
- A middle school math teacher has students copy the next homework assignment as soon as they come to class.
- As students first enter the classroom, a middle school social studies teacher always hands them a short "Do It Now" assignment. For example, on one occasion he hands out a map of U.S. states and state capitals and instructs students to identify place names that might have Native American names and those that probably have European roots—a task that soon leads to a class discussion on the origins of place names.

---

[32] Brophy, Alleman, & Knighton, 2009; G. A. Davis & Thomas, 1989; Munn, Johnstone, & Chalmers, 1990.
[33] Gettinger & Kohler, 2006; J. Hunter & Csikszentmihalyi, 2003; Shernoff, Csikszentmihalyi, Schneider, & Shernoff, 2003.
[34] G. A. Davis & Thomas, 1989; W. Doyle, 1986a; Emmer & Gerwels, 2006; Evertson & Harris, 1992; Gettinger, 1988; Munn et al., 1990.

[35] W. Doyle, 1984, 2006; Gettinger & Kohler, 2006. A phenomenon known as *behavioral momentum* is relevant here; for instance, see Ardoin, Martens, & Wolfe, 1999; Belfiore, Lee, Vargas, & Skinner, 1997; Mace et al., 1988; Nevin, Mandell, & Atak, 1983.

- Before each class period begins, a ninth-grade creative writing teacher writes a topic or question on the board (e.g., "My biggest pet peeve"). Students know that when they come to class, they should immediately begin to write on the topic or question of the day.
- A high school physical education teacher has students begin each class session with five minutes of stretching exercises.

Although very different in nature, all of these strategies share the common goal of keeping students focused on productive activities.

Keep in mind that some students may have difficulty moving from one activity to another, especially if they're deeply engaged in what they are doing. Accordingly, it's often helpful to give students advance warning that a transition is coming, describe what the subsequent activity will be, and remind them of the usual procedures for switching from one task to another.[36]

Take individual and developmental differences into account.

Earlier I mentioned the importance of consistency and equity in enforcing classroom rules. Yet when it comes to *preventing* off-task behavior, optimal strategies may differ considerably from one student to the next. For instance, during independent seatwork assignments, some students may work quite well with classmates close by, whereas others may be easily distracted unless they can work in a quiet spot, perhaps near a teacher's desk. And during small-group work, some groups may function quite effectively on their own, whereas others may need considerable guidance and supervision.

One important individual difference factor affecting classroom behavior is *temperament*—the extent to which a student is naturally inclined to be energetic, irritable, impulsive, and so on (see Chapter 7). To be truly effective classroom managers, teachers must realize that students' vastly different classroom behaviors may be due, in part, to biological predispositions that aren't entirely controllable. Such a realization will influence teachers' beliefs about why students act as they do—that is, it will influence teachers' *attributions*—and these beliefs will, in turn, affect teachers' willingness to adapt classroom strategies to foster productive classroom behavior.[37] Notice what happened to one fourth grader (now a successful college professor) when his teacher took his temperament into consideration:

> One day when I was especially restless . . . I could see Miss Rickenbrood circling to the back of the room. I wasn't aware of having done anything in particular, but I knew her eyes were on me. After a few minutes she leaned over and whispered in my ear, "Tom, would you like to go outside and run?"
>
> I was stunned. To go outside and run? On my own? When it wasn't recess? What could have possessed this woman to ignore all school rules and allow me to run? I said yes and quietly went to put on my coat. As I recall, I didn't actually run in the playground (people would be watching from inside the building), but stood outside in the doorway, in the cold, marveling at my freedom. I returned to class after about ten minutes, settled for the rest of the day.[38]

Another individual difference variable that influences classroom behavior is ability level. Students are more likely to work diligently on their classwork when they have tasks and assignments appropriate for their current knowledge and skills. They're apt to misbehave when they're asked to do things that they perceive—either accurately or not—to be too difficult for them.[39] (Such may have been the case for Eli, Jake, and Vanessa in the opening case study.) I'm *not* suggesting here that teachers assign tasks so easy that students learn nothing new in doing them (recall the concept of *zone of proximal development* described in Chapter 5). One workable strategy is to *begin* the school year with tasks that students can easily complete. Such early tasks enable students to practice required routines and procedures and also give students a sense of confidence that they can succeed at assigned activities. Once a supportive classroom climate has been established and students are comfortable with classroom procedures, teachers can gradually introduce more challenging assignments.[40]

[36] K. Carter & Doyle, 2006; Emmer & Gerwels, 2006.
[37] W. Johnson, McGue, & Iacono, 2005; Keogh, 2003; A. Miller, 2006.
[38] Newkirk, 2002, pp. 25–26.

[39] Mac Iver, Reuman, & Main, 1995; Moore & Edwards, 2003; S. L. Robinson & Griesemer, 2006.
[40] W. Doyle, 1990; Emmer & Evertson, 2009; Evertson & Emmer, 1982; N. M. Webb & Farivar, 1999.

Developmental differences, too, must dictate classroom management strategies to some degree. Many children in the early elementary grades haven't had enough experience with formal education to know all the unspoken "rules" that govern classroom interactions—for instance, that students should remain silent when a teacher or other adult is talking, that only the student who is called on should answer a question, and so on.[41] Children just beginning kindergarten or first grade may find their new school environment to be unsettling and anxiety arousing, as will many adolescents making the transition to middle school or high school (see Chapter 6). And, of course, children gain better social skills as they grow older, impacting their ability to interact effectively with their teacher and classmates (see Chapter 7). Table 9.1 presents these and other developmental differences, along with examples of how teachers might accommodate them in classroom practice.

DEVELOPMENTAL TRENDS

TABLE 9.1 Effective Classroom Management at Different Grade Levels

Grade Level	Age-Typical Characteristics	Example	Suggested Strategies
K–2	• Lack of familiarity with unspoken rules about appropriate classroom behavior • Anxiety about being in school, especially in the first few weeks and especially for students without preschool experience • Short attention span and distractibility • Little self-regulation • Desire for teacher affection and approval • Considerable individual differences in social skills	Immediately after lunch on the first day of school, a first-grade teacher gathers her students at the front of the room so that she can read them an age-appropriate storybook. Before she begins to read, she explains the importance of sitting quietly so that everyone can hear the story, and when students occasionally behave in ways that might distract others, she gently reminds them of appropriate school behaviors.	• Invite students and their parents to visit the classroom before the school year begins. • Especially during the first few weeks of school, place high priority on establishing a warm, supportive relationship with every student. • Keep assignments relatively short and focused. • Create a gathering place (e.g., a carpet) where students can sit close at hand for whole-class discussions. • Create areas where students can work independently on tasks of their choosing (e.g., a reading center where students can listen to storybooks on tape). • Be explicit about acceptable classroom behavior; correct inappropriate behavior gently but consistently.
 3–5	• Continuing desire for teacher approval, but with increasing concern about peer approval as well • Greater attentiveness to teachers who are emotionally expressive (e.g., teachers who often smile and show obvious concern in times of distress) • Increasing self-regulation skills • Gradually improving ability to reflect on one's own and others' thoughts and motives (i.e., increasing social cognition) • Increasing disengagement from school if students have consistently encountered academic and social failures	Nine-year-old Bailey is often disruptive and socially inappropriate in class—so much so that her classmates avoid her as much as possible. On several occasions her teacher takes her aside and respectfully requests more productive behavior. For example, on one occasion the teacher says, "Bailey, I'm very happy to have you in my class. I wonder if you could do me a favor. It would really help me— and I think it would help you, too—if you could raise your hand before you answer a question. That way, other kids also get a chance to answer my questions."	• Use two-way journals to communicate regularly with students about academic, social, and emotional issues. • In your words and actions, consistently show students that you care about their academic progress and emotional well-being. • Provide increasing opportunities for independent work, but with enough structure to guide students' efforts. • In times of disagreement or conflict among classmates, ask students to reflect on one another's thoughts and feelings. • Make an extra effort to establish close, supportive relationships with students who appear to be academically and socially disengaged.

(continued)

---

[41] Mehan, 1979; Myles & Simpson, 2001.

TABLE 9.1 Continued

Grade Level	Age-Typical Characteristics	Example	Suggested Strategies
 6–8	• Considerable anxiety about the transition to middle school, due in part to more distant and less supportive relationships with teachers • Decrease in intrinsic motivation to learn academic subject matter • Increase in cheating behaviors; cheating less common if students think teachers respect them and are committed to helping them learn • Heightened concern about ability to fit in and be accepted by peers • Increase in bullying behaviors	Because of a history of low achievement (due in large part to frequent moves from one relative's home to another), 14-year-old D.J. is spending a second year in seventh grade. He's extremely disruptive in class, and he often yells insulting names at his peers. On one occasion, he uses a derogatory term to describe a male classmate who behaves in stereotypically feminine ways. His teacher takes him aside and says, "I won't tolerate that word. My gay friends would find it very offensive. But listen, D.J., I know you're going through a lot at home. I really want you to be successful in my class. How can I help?" D.J. admits that he, too, has gay friends who wouldn't like the word he used. Perhaps more importantly, his teacher's obvious concern for his well-being leads to better behavior in class. Furthermore, he starts asking the teacher for help on his assignments.	• Make an effort to interact with students outside of class (e.g., attend sporting events, chaperone school dances). • Plan lessons that are engaging and relevant to students' lives and needs. • Provide sufficient academic support that students have no reason to cheat; nevertheless, be on the lookout for possible cheating. • Do not tolerate bullying and other forms of aggression; address their underlying causes (see the discussion of aggression in Chapter 7). • Reach out to students who seem socially disconnected (e.g., invite them to join you for lunch in your classroom).
 9–12	• Anxiety about the transition to high school, especially if seventh and eighth grades were part of elementary school (as in some small school districts) • Social and romantic relationships often a source of distraction • Considerable self-regulation skills in some but not all students • High incidence of cheating, in part because peers communicate that it's acceptable • Disdain for classmates who work too hard for teacher approval (i.e., "brownnosers") • Tendency for some adolescents to think that misbehavior will gain the admiration of classmates • Increase in violent behaviors, especially at schools in low-income neighborhoods	When a high school teacher sees 16-year-old Jerrod standing alone and looking apprehensive at a school dance, he approaches the boy to express empathy. "Hey, Jerrod," the teacher says, "I'm glad to see you here tonight. I remember my first school dance. Boy, did I feel awkward! I was too shy to ask a girl to dance, and I was so afraid of making a fool of myself. What do you think we might do to make these events a little less scary?" Jerrod smiles and admits that he feels much the same way that his teacher once did, and they brainstorm ideas for helping students feel more comfortable at future dances.	• Remember that even in the high school grades, students achieve at higher levels when they have close, supportive relationships with teachers. • Regularly plan activities that involve social interaction; if possible, move desks and chairs to allow students to interact more easily. • Provide guidance and support for students who have few self-regulation skills to keep them on task. • Describe what cheating is and why it's unacceptable. • Communicate approval privately rather than publicly. • Proactively address violence (see the section "Addressing Aggression and Violence at School" later in the chapter).

Sources: Some characteristics and suggestions based on Blugental, Lyon, Lin, McGrath, & Bimbela, 1999; K. Carter & Doyle, 2006; Castagno & Brayboy, 2008; Cizek, 2003; Emmer & Gerwels, 2006; Fingerhut & Christoffel, 2002; Hamre & Pianta, 2005; J. N. Hughes, Luo, Kwok, & Loyd, 2008; Ladd, Herald-Brown, & Reiser, 2008; Mehan, 1979; Murdock, Hale, & Weber, 2001; O'Connor & McCartney, 2007; Pellegrini, 2002; many other ideas derived from discussions in earlier chapters.

Continually monitor what students are doing.

Effective teachers communicate something called **withitness**: They know—and their students *know* that they know—what students are doing at all times. They regularly scan the classroom, often move from one spot to another, and make frequent eye contact with individual students. They know what misbehaviors are occurring *when* those misbehaviors occur, and they know who the perpetrators are.[42] Consider the following classroom example:

> In one second-grade classroom, an hour and a half of each morning is devoted to reading. Students spend part of this time with their teacher in small reading groups and the remainder of the time working on independent assignments tailored to their individual reading skills. As the teacher works with each reading group at the front of the classroom, she situates herself with her back to the wall so that she can simultaneously keep an eye on students working independently at their seats. She sends a quick and subtle signal—perhaps a stern expression, a finger to the lips, or a callout of a student's name—to any student who gets off task.

When teachers demonstrate such withitness, especially at the beginning of the school year, students are more likely to behave appropriately, stay on task, and achieve at high levels.[43]

Observe this classroom in action in the "Reading Group" video in Chapter 9 of the Book-Specific Resources in MyEducationLab.

• Expanding the Sense of Community Beyond the Classroom

Students' learning and development depend not only on what happens inside a particular classroom but also on what happens in other parts of the school building, in the neighborhood and community, and at home. Thus, effective teachers coordinate their efforts with other influential individuals in students' lives—with other school faculty members, with professionals at community agencies, and especially with students' parents or other primary caregivers. Ideally, teachers should think of such joint efforts as *partnerships* in which everyone is working together to promote students' long-term development and learning. Following are several recommendations.

Collaborate with colleagues to create an overall sense of school community.

Teachers are far more effective if they coordinate their efforts with other faculty members through strategies such as these:[44]

- Communicate and collaborate regularly with other classroom teachers and with specialists (e.g., special education teachers, librarians, counselors).
- Form common goals regarding what students should learn and achieve.
- Work together to identify and overcome obstacles to students' academic achievement.
- Establish a shared set of strategies for encouraging productive student behaviors.
- Make a group commitment to promote equality and multicultural sensitivity throughout the school community.

Thus, effective teachers not only create a sense of community within their individual classrooms but also create an overall **sense of school community**.[45] Students should get the same messages from every faculty member: that teachers are working together to help them become informed, successful, and productive citizens, and that students can and should help one another as well. One critical element of a sense of school community is a commitment to *respect* for people with diverse backgrounds and needs—a commitment that translates into prohibitions against malicious teasing, derogatory rumor spreading, bullying, and

---

[42] Gettinger & Kohler, 2006; T. Hogan, Rabinowitz, & Craven, 2003; Kounin, 1970.

[43] W. Doyle, 1986a; Gettinger & Kohler, 2006; Woolfolk & Brooks, 1985.

[44] Battistich, Solomon, Watson, & Schaps, 1997; Hoy, Tarter, & Woolfolk Hoy, 2006; Levine & Lezotte,

1995; T. J. Lewis, Newcomer, Trussell, & Richter, 2006; M. Watson & Battistich, 2006; Warren et al., 2006.

[45] Battistich, Solomon, Kim, Watson, & Schaps, 1995; Battistich et al., 1997; M. Watson & Battistich, 2006.

withitness Classroom management strategy in which a teacher gives the impression of knowing what all students are doing at all times.

sense of school community Shared belief that all faculty and students within a school are working together to help everyone learn and succeed.

other forms of peer harassment.[46] High school teacher Fernando Arias has described such respectfulness this way:

> In our school, our philosophy is that we treat everybody the way we'd like to be treated. . . . We have pregnant young ladies who go to our school. We have special education children. We have the regular kids, and we have the drop-out recovery program . . . we're all equal. We all have an equal chance. And we have members of every gang at our school, and we hardly have any fights, and there are close to about 300 gangs in our city. We all get along. It's one big family unit it seems like.[47]

When teachers and students share an overall sense of school community, students have more positive attitudes toward school, are more motivated to achieve at high levels, exhibit more prosocial behavior, and interact more often with peers from diverse backgrounds. Furthermore, when teachers collaborate in their efforts, they often have high *collective self-efficacy* about their ability to help students learn and achieve (recall the discussion of this concept in Chapter 6), and their high expectations for students' achievement are indeed related to students' actual performance.[48] Such a team spirit within the school faculty has an additional advantage for beginning teachers: It provides the support structure (scaffolding) they sometimes need, especially when working with students who are at risk for school failure.[49]

Work cooperatively with other agencies that play key roles in students' lives.

Students almost always have regular contact with other institutions besides their schools—possibly with community recreation centers, social services, churches, hospitals, mental health clinics, or local judicial systems. Teachers are most effective if they think of themselves as part of a larger community team that promotes growing children's long-term development. Thus, they should keep in contact with other people and institutions that play major roles in students' lives, coordinating efforts whenever possible.[50] Keep in mind, however, that school–agency cooperation regarding *individual* students—especially if it involves sharing potentially sensitive information—can typically occur only with the written permission of students' parents.

Communicate regularly with parents and other primary caregivers.

Without a doubt, productive parent–teacher relationships enhance students' learning and achievement in the classroom, and ongoing communication between school and home is critical for these relationships.[51] At a minimum, teachers must stay in regular contact with parents and other primary caregivers about students' progress. Regular communication also provides a means through which families can give *teachers* information (e.g., about current circumstances at home or about effective motivational strategies). Following are several common mechanisms for enhancing school–family communication:

- **Parent-teacher conferences.** In most school districts, formal parent–teacher conferences are scheduled one or more times a year. Teachers sometimes include students in conferences (essentially making them parent–teacher–student conferences). Inviting other family members who share caregiving responsibilities (e.g., grandparents) can also be helpful.
- **Written communication.** Written communication can take a variety of forms, including (1) homework slips explaining each night's assignments, (2) informal notes acknowledging significant accomplishments, (3) teacher-constructed checklists that describe academic progress, and (4) general newsletters describing ongoing classroom activities. Figure 9.4 shows an example of a weekly newsletter in a second-grade class.
- **Telephone conversations.** Telephone calls are useful when issues require immediate attention—for instance, when a student has won a prestigious award or, alternatively,

See a teacher and father effectively discuss how they might coordinate their efforts in the "Parent–Teacher Conference" video in Chapter 9 of the Book-Specific Resources in MyEducationLab.

---

[46] Espelage & Swearer, 2004; Langdon, 2007; S. W. Ross & Horner, 2009.

[47] Quoted in Turnbull, Pereira, & Blue-Banning, 2000, p. 67.

[48] Bandura, 2000; Goddard, Hoy, & Woolfolk Hoy, 2000; Battistich et al., 1995, 1997; Hoy et al., 2006; M. Watson & Battistich, 2006.

[49] Chester & Beaudin, 1996.

[50] J. L. Epstein, 1996.

[51] W.-B. Chen & Gregory, 2008; Gutman & McLoyd, 2000; J. Hughes & Kwok, 2007.

9/14/01

Dear Parents,

I have been lucky so far and have not had to go back for jury duty. I have two more weeks to go [in terms of possibly being summoned for duty] and hope I will continue to be in the classroom.

We have been trying to keep the routine pretty regular, despite one or two testing sessions per day. The children have been pretty focused, although it is difficult when they are unfamiliar with the format and look to us for help. I don't like telling them that they are on their own! We are done, thank goodness. I believe you will receive results in the mail.

Homework and spelling will resume next week. I could also use my regular volunteers to help get through the spelling assessments. The times you have been coming are still fine. Call or e-mail me if you need the available times for helping.

We finished our unit on germs and sanitation, although we did not get into any discussions about Anthrax. It seems that you are keeping the children protected at home from details of the scary news, as we are at school. We kept our discussions to common illnesses that they are aware of and how they can avoid them with proper sanitation.

A few classrooms are doing activities to raise money for many of the children involved in the tragedy. Sarah [the teacher intern] and I decided not to work with our children on a fundraiser because we don't want to get into anxiety-producing discussions. It is hard to help young children understand that they are safe where they are and that it is unlikely that they will be involved in such things.

Next week, we will be starting a Nutrition Unit and beginning to read some Halloween stories. We will continue working to become automatic with math facts, along with our regular routine of phonics lessons, DOL [daily oral language], reading, writing, spelling, etc.

We are running out of Kleenex and could use some donations. We would also like some boxes of baby wipes to use in cleaning hands and desks when there is not time for the entire class to wash. Someone mentioned to me that there is a homemade recipe for baby wipes out there somewhere. Is there a parent who knows and would be willing to share?

Have a great weekend.

Ann

FIGURE 9.4 Example of a teacher newsletter. This one was written on September 14, 2001, three days after the terrorist attacks on the World Trade Center and Pentagon and during a week when students were taking a districtwide standardized test.

has shown a sudden decline in performance for no apparent reason. In addition, telephone calls are a useful way of introducing oneself as a child's elementary school teacher for the coming school year.[52]

- **E-mail messages.** In the newsletter in Figure 9.4, the teacher encourages parents to contact her by e-mail, a strategy that is quite appropriate in her middle-socio-economic school district. Suggesting the use of e-mail would, of course, be inappropriate in communities where many families can't afford computers or where parents have limited knowledge of English.

- **Class websites.** As noted in Chapter 8, many teachers now create class websites on which they post instructional goals, assignments, and so on. Typically such websites are available to parents as well as students, but, as is true for e-mail messages, they're most appropriate for parents who regularly use computers and the Internet.

In their communications with students' families, teachers don't necessarily have to limit themselves to what's going on in the classroom. Many parents welcome teachers' suggestions about how best to help their children at home. For instance, parents are often grateful for suggestions about how to assist with homework or how to foster their children's development more generally. And they appreciate knowing what kinds of behaviors are and are not normal for a particular age-group.[53]

Invite families to participate in the academic and social life of the school.

In general, effective schools are *welcoming* schools that encourage not only students but also family members to participate in school activities.[54] Some parents are available on weekdays and are happy to assist with occasional field trips and class parties; a few may even be able to provide one-on-one tutoring for certain students. Most other parents are available in the evenings and can attend school open houses, school plays, band and choir performances, and fund-raising events. Some teachers have successfully used parent *coffee nights* during which they explain a new instructional strategy or *author teas* during which students read the poetry or short stories they have written.

---

[52] Striepling-Goldstein, 2004.
[53] C. Davis & Yang, 2005; J. M. T. Walker & Hoover-Dempsey, 2006.

[54] J. L. Epstein, 1996; N. E. Hill et al., 2004; G. R. López, 2001; Serpell, Baker, & Sonnenschein, 2005.

Schoolwide projects and fund-raisers, such as this pancake breakfast, provide one means of fostering productive parent–teacher relationships and getting parents actively involved in their children's schooling.

In some instances teachers or other faculty members might assemble a group of parents to discuss issues of mutual interest.[55] For example, they might use such a group as a sounding board when selecting topics to include in the classroom curriculum or thinking about assigning potentially controversial works of literature. Alternatively, teachers can use a discussion group as a mechanism through which teachers and parents alike can share ideas about how best to promote students' academic, personal, and social development on the home front.

Make an extra effort with seemingly "reluctant" parents.

Despite many opportunities, some parents remain uninvolved in their children's education; for example, they may never attend scheduled parent–teacher conferences. Rather than jumping to the conclusion that these parents are also *uninterested* in their children's education, teachers must recognize several possible reasons that parents may fail to make contact with their children's teachers. Some may have an exhausting work schedule or lack adequate child care. Others may know little English, have difficulty finding their way through the school system, or believe it's inappropriate to bother teachers with their concerns. Still others may have had such bad experiences when they themselves were students that they feel uncomfortable in a school building. And a few parents may be victims of mental illness or substance abuse, limiting their ability to support their children financially, academically, or otherwise.[56]

In some cases a personal invitation can make a difference,[57] as this parent's statement illustrates:

> The thing of it is, had someone not walked up to me and asked me specifically, I would not hold out my hand and say, "I'll do it." . . . You get parents here all the time, Black parents that are willing, but maybe a little on the shy side and wouldn't say I really want to serve on this subject. You may send me the form, I may never fill the form out. Or I'll think about it and not send it back. But you know if that principal, that teacher, my son's math teacher called and asked if I would. . . .[58]

Experienced educators have offered additional recommendations for getting seemingly reluctant parents more involved in their children's schooling:[59]

- Make an extra effort to establish parents' trust and confidence—for instance, by demonstrating that their contributions are valued and that faculty members would never try to make them appear foolish.
- Encourage parents to be assertive when they have questions or concerns.
- Invite other important family members (e.g., grandparents, aunts, uncles) to participate in school activities, especially if a student's cultural background is one that places high value on the extended family.
- Give parents suggestions about learning activities they can easily do with their children at home.
- Find out what parents do exceptionally well (e.g., carpentry, cooking), and ask them to share their talents with students.
- Provide opportunities for parents to volunteer for jobs that don't require them to leave home (e.g., to be someone whom students can call when unsure of homework assignments).

[55] J. L. Epstein, 1996; Fosnot, 1996; Rudman, 1993.
[56] Bornstein & Cote, 2010; Carbrera, Shannon, West, & Brooks-Gunn, 2006; Cazden, 2001; C. L. Green, Walker, Hoover-Dempsey, & Sandler, 2007; Hernandez, Denton, & Macartney, 2008; J.-S. Lee & Bowen, 2006; Mistry, Vandewater, Huston, & McLoyd, 2002; Pérez, 1998; Petterson & Albers, 2001.

[57] A. A. Carr, 1997; C. L. Green et al., 2007.
[58] A. A. Carr, 1997, p. 2.
[59] Castagno & Brayboy, 2008; C. Davis & Yang, 2005; J. L. Epstein, 1996; Finders & Lewis, 1994; Hidalgo, Siu, Bright, Swap, & Epstein, 1995; Howe, 1994; G. R. López, 2001; Salend & Taylor, 1993; M. G. Sanders, 1996; J. M. T. Walker & Hoover-Dempsey, 2006.

Tony Freeman/PhotoEdit

- Identify specific individuals (e.g., bilingual parents) who can translate for those who speak little or no English.
- Conduct parent–teacher conferences or parent discussions at times and locations convenient for families; make use of home visits *if* such visits are welcomed.
- Offer resources for parents at the school building (e.g., contacts with social and health services; classes in English, literacy, home repairs, arts and crafts).

Still another potentially effective strategy is to reinforce *parents* as well as students when the students do well at school. One administrator at a school serving many immigrant students put it this way:

> One of the things we do . . . is that we identify those students that had perfect attendance, those students that passed all areas of the [statewide achievement tests] and were successful. We don't honor the student, we honor the parents. We give parents a certificate. Because, we tell them, "through your efforts, and through your hard work, your child was able to accomplish this."[60]

A few parents will resist all efforts to involve them, and a subset of them may truly have little interest in helping their children do well. In such circumstances, teachers must never penalize students for their parents' actions or inactions. Teachers must also realize that *they themselves* are apt to be among the most important academic and emotional resources in these students' lives.

Reducing Unproductive Behaviors

Despite teachers' best efforts, students sometimes behave in ways that significantly disrupt classroom activities and interfere with learning. For purposes of our discussion, we'll define a **misbehavior** as any action that can potentially disrupt learning and planned classroom activities, puts one or more students' physical safety or psychological well-being in jeopardy, or violates basic moral and ethical standards. Some misbehaviors are relatively minor and have little long-term impact on students' well-being and achievement. Such behaviors as talking out of turn, writing brief notes to classmates during a lecture, and submitting homework assignments after their due date—especially if these behaviors occur infrequently—generally fall in this category. Other misbehaviors are far more serious, in that they definitely interfere with the learning or well-being of one or more students. For example, when students scream at their teachers, hit their classmates, or habitually refuse to participate in ongoing activities, then classroom learning—certainly that of the "guilty party" and sometimes that of other students as well—can be adversely affected, as can the overall classroom climate.

As is true in the opening case study, typically only a few students are responsible for the great majority of misbehaviors in any single classroom.[61] Such students are apt to be among teachers' greatest challenges, and it can be all too tempting to write them off as lost causes. Yet teachers must work vigorously to point these students in more productive directions. Without active interventions by teachers and other caring adults, students who are consistently disruptive or in other ways off task in the early grades often continue to show behavior problems in the later years as well.[62]

Teachers need to plan ahead about how they'll address students' misbehaviors. Although teachers must certainly be consistent in the consequences they impose for blatant rule infractions, different strategies for reducing counterproductive behaviors over the long run may be more or less useful under different circumstances. Following are a number of possibilities.

Consider whether instructional strategies or classroom assignments might be partly to blame for off-task behaviors.

Principles of effective classroom management go hand in hand with principles of learning and motivation. When students are learning and achieving successfully and when they clearly want to pursue the classroom's instructional goals, they're apt to be busily engaged

misbehavior Action that disrupts learning and planned classroom activities, puts students' physical safety or psychological well-being in jeopardy, or violates basic moral standards.

---

[60] G. R. López, 2001, p. 273.
[61] W. Doyle, 2006.

[62] Emmer & Gerwels, 2006; Vitaro, Brendgen, Larose, & Tremblay, 2005.

When students are frequently off task, expert teachers think about what *they themselves* might do differently to keep them engaged in classroom activities.

in productive activities for most of the school day.[63] In contrast, when they have difficulty understanding classroom subject matter or little interest in learning it, they're likely to exhibit the nonproductive or counterproductive classroom behaviors that result from frustration or boredom.

When students misbehave, beginning teachers often think about what the students are doing wrong. In contrast, experienced teachers are more likely to think about what *they themselves* could do differently to keep students on task, and they modify their plans accordingly.[64] Here are several self-questions that can help a beginning teacher start thinking like an expert:

- How can I change my instructional strategies to stimulate students' interest in a topic?
- Are instructional materials so difficult or unstructured that students are becoming frustrated? Or are they so easy or routine that students are bored?
- What are students really concerned about? For example, are they more concerned about interacting with their classmates than in gaining new knowledge and skills? How can I address students' motives and goals (e.g., their desire to affiliate with peers) while simultaneously helping them achieve classroom objectives?

Addressing such questions can help a teacher focus his or her efforts on the ultimate purpose of schooling: to help students *learn*.

Occasionally current events on the international, national, or local scene (e.g., a terrorist attack, a natural disaster, or a tragic car accident involving classmates) may take priority. When students' minds are justifiably preoccupied with something other than the topic of instruction, they'll have trouble paying attention to a preplanned lesson and are likely to learn little from it. In such circumstances, teachers may want to abandon their lesson plans altogether, at least for a short while.

Consider whether cultural background might influence students' classroom behaviors.

As teachers determine which behaviors are truly unacceptable in their classrooms, they must keep in mind that some behaviors that their own culture deems inappropriate may be quite acceptable in another culture.[65] The following exercise presents some examples.

SEE FOR YOURSELF   Identifying Misbehaviors

Read each of the three scenarios below and consider
- Whether you would classify the behavior as a *mis*behavior
- What cultural group(s) might find the behavior appropriate
- How you might deal with the behavior
  1. A student is frequently late for school, sometimes arriving more than an hour after the school bell has rung.
  2. Two students are sharing answers as they take a quiz.
  3. Several students are exchanging insults that become increasingly derogatory.

---

[63] W. Doyle, 1990; Gettinger & Kohler, 2006.
[64] Emmer & Stough, 2001; Sabers et al., 1991; H. L. Swanson, O'Connor, & Cooney, 1990.

[65] For example, see Gay, 2006.

Tardiness (Example 1) interferes with learning because the student loses valuable instructional time; thus, it might reasonably be construed as a misbehavior. However, a student who is chronically tardy may live in a community that doesn't observe strict schedules and timelines—a pattern common in some Native American groups (see the Cultural Considerations box in Chapter 3, p. 75). Furthermore, arrival time may not be entirely within the student's control. For instance, perhaps the student has household responsibilities or transportation issues that make punctuality difficult. A private conversation with the student, perhaps followed up by a conference with family members, would be the most effective way to determine the root of the problem and identify potential solutions (more about such strategies shortly).

Sharing answers during a quiz (Example 2) is a misbehavior *if* students have been specifically instructed to do their own work. Because a quiz helps a teacher determine what students have and haven't learned, inaccurate quiz scores affect the teacher's instructional planning and so indirectly affect future learning. (Sharing answers can lower the *validity* of the quiz scores; we'll discuss this concept in Chapter 10.) Although the behavior represents cheating to many people, it may reflect the cooperative spirit and emphasis on group achievement evident in the cultures of many Native American, Mexican American, and Southeast Asian students (again see the Cultural Considerations box in Chapter 3, pp. 74–75). An adverse consequence is in order *if* a teacher has previously explained what cheating is in a way that students understand and *if* the teacher has clearly described situations in which collaboration is and isn't appropriate—in other words, if students know full well that their behavior violates classroom policy. A teacher who *hasn't* laid such groundwork must soon do so in order to prevent such behavior from occurring again.

An exchange of insults (Example 3) might be psychologically harmful for the students involved and adversely affect the overall classroom climate. Alternatively, however, it might simply be an instance of *playing the dozens,* a playful verbal interaction common in some African American communities (see the "Ruckus in the Lunchroom" exercise in Chapter 3, p. 77). How a teacher handles the situation must depend on the spirit in which students seem to view the exchange. Their body language—whether they're smiling or scowling, whether they seem relaxed or tense—can reveal a great deal. If the insults truly signal escalating hostilities, an immediate intervention is in order. If, instead, the insults reflect creative verbal play, a teacher may simply need to establish reasonable boundaries (e.g., "indoor" voices should be used, racial and ethnic slurs are unacceptable).

Ignore misbehaviors that are temporary, minor, and unlikely to be repeated or copied.

On some occasions the best course of action is *no* action, at least nothing of a disciplinary nature.[66] For example, consider these situations:

> Dimitra rarely breaks classroom rules. But on one occasion, after you've just instructed students to work quietly and independently at their seats, you see her briefly whisper to the girl beside her. None of the other students seems to notice that Dimitra has disobeyed your instructions.

> Herb is careless in chemistry lab and accidentally knocks over a small container of liquid (a harmless one, fortunately). He quickly apologizes and cleans up the mess.

Will these behaviors interfere with Dimitra's or Herb's academic achievement? Are they "contagious" behaviors that will spread to other students, as the horseplay did in Ms. Cornell's class? The answer to both questions is "Probably not."

Whenever a teacher stops an instructional activity to deal with a misbehavior, even for a few seconds, the teacher runs the risk of disrupting the momentum of the activity and drawing students' attention to their misbehaving classmates. Furthermore, by drawing class attention to a particular student's behavior, the teacher may actually be reinforcing it rather than discouraging it.

---

[66] G. A. Davis & Thomas, 1989; W. Doyle, 2006.

Ignoring misbehavior is often reasonable in circumstances such as these:[67]

- When the behavior is a rare occurrence and probably won't be repeated
- When the behavior is unlikely to spread to other students
- When the behavior is the result of unusual and temporary conditions (e.g., the last day of school before a vacation, unsettling events in a student's personal life)
- When the behavior is typical for a particular age-group (e.g., when kindergartners become restless after sitting for an extended time, when sixth-grade boys and girls resist holding hands during dance instruction)
- When the behavior's natural consequence is unpleasant enough to deter a student from repeating it
- When the behavior isn't seriously affecting classroom learning

Dimitra's behavior—whispering briefly to a classmate during independent seatwork—is unlikely to spread to her classmates (they didn't see her do it) and probably isn't an instance of cheating (it occurred before she began working on the assignment). Herb's behavior—knocking over a container of liquid in chemistry lab—has, in and of itself, resulted in an unpleasant consequence: He must clean up the mess. In both situations, then, ignoring the misbehavior is probably the best thing to do.

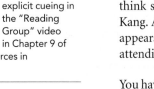

❖ Can you relate *ignoring behavior* to a specific concept in operant conditioning? Why is ignoring *not* an effective strategy in Ms. Cornell's classroom? (Compare your responses to these questions with the response presented in Chapter 9 of the Book-Specific Resources in MyEducationLab.)

Give signals and reminders about what is and is not appropriate.

In some situations off-task behaviors, although not serious in nature, *do* interfere with classroom learning and must be discouraged. Consider these situations as examples:

> As you're explaining a difficult concept, Marjorie is busily writing. At first you think she's taking notes, but then you see her pass the paper across the aisle to Kang. A few minutes later, you see Kang pass the same sheet back to Marjorie. It appears that the two students are writing personal notes when they should be attending to the lesson.

> You have separated your class into small groups for a cooperative learning exercise. One group is frequently off task and probably won't complete its task if its members don't get down to business soon.

Observe indirect and then more explicit cueing in the "Reading Group" video in Chapter 9 of the Book-Specific Resources in MyEducationLab.

Effective classroom managers handle such minor behavior problems as unobtrusively as possible. They don't stop the lesson, distract other students, or call unnecessary attention to the behavior they're trying to stop.[68] In many cases they use *cueing,* a strategy introduced in Chapter 3. That is, they let students know, through a signal of one kind or another, that they're aware of the misbehavior and want it to cease.

Cueing takes a variety of forms. For instance, a teacher might use nonverbal cues, perhaps putting a finger to the lips to signal "Shhh" or perhaps moving close to a student and standing there until the problem behavior stops. When such nonverbal signals don't work, a brief verbal cue—stating a student's name, reminding students of correct behavior, or (if necessary) specifically describing an inappropriate behavior—may be in order. Ideally, a verbal cue should focus students' attention on what *should* be done rather than on what *isn't* being done.[69] Indirect requests are often effective for older students (e.g., "I see some art supplies that still need to be put away"). More explicit ones may be necessary for young children (e.g., "Table 3 needs to clean up its art supplies before it can go to lunch").

Simple body language can often lead to more productive and on-task behavior. While this teacher is temporarily preoccupied, her hand on a student's shoulder provides a subtle reminder that he should be attending to his schoolwork.

Tom Watson/Merrill

[67] G. A. Davis & Thomas, 1989; W. Doyle, 1986a, 2006; Munn et al., 1990; Silberman & Wheelan, 1980; Wynne, 1990.

[68] K. Carter & Doyle, 2006; W. Doyle, 1990; Emmer, 1987.

[69] Emmer et al., 2000; T. L. Good & Brophy, 1994.

Get students' perspectives about their behaviors.

Sometimes brief signals are insufficient to change a student's behavior. Consider these situations:

> Alonzo is almost always a few minutes late to your third-period algebra class. When he finally arrives, he takes several additional minutes to pull his textbook and other class materials out of his backpack. You've often reminded him about the importance of coming to class on time, yet his tardiness continues.

> Trudy rarely completes class assignments. In fact, she often doesn't even *begin* them. On many previous occasions you've gently tried to get her on task, but usually without success. Today, when you look Trudy in the eye and ask her point blank to get to work, she defiantly responds, "I'm not going to do it. You can't make me!"

In such situations, talking privately with the student is the next logical step. The discussion should be *private* for several reasons.[70] First, as noted earlier, calling peers' attention to a problem behavior may actually reinforce the behavior rather than discourage it. Or, instead, the attention of classmates may cause a student to feel excessively embarrassed or humiliated—feelings that may make the student overly anxious about being in the classroom in the future. Finally, when a teacher spends too much class time dealing with a single misbehaving student, other students are apt to get off task.

Private conversations with individual students give a teacher a chance to explain why certain behaviors are unacceptable and must stop. (Recall the discussion of *induction* in Chapter 7.) They also give students a chance to explain why they behave as they do. For instance, Alonzo might explain

If cueing a misbehaving student is ineffective, a private conversation might be the best next step.

his chronic tardiness by revealing that he has diabetes and must check his blood sugar level between his second- and third-period classes. He can perform the procedure himself but would prefer to do it in the privacy of the school nurse's office at the other end of the building. Meanwhile, Trudy might reveal her long-standing frustration with subject matter and assignments she perceives as being impossible to make sense of.

Students' explanations often provide clues about how best to deal with their behavior over the long run. For example, given his diabetes, Alonzo's continued tardiness to class may be inevitable. Instead, his teacher might reassign him to a seat by the door so he can join class unobtrusively when he arrives. Trudy's frustration with her schoolwork suggests that she needs additional scaffolding to help her succeed. It also hints at a possible undiagnosed learning disability that may warrant a referral to the school psychologist or other diagnostician. In some cases conversations with students can reveal maladaptive interpretations of social situations. For instance, a chronically aggressive student may express the inaccurate belief that classmates "are always trying to pick a fight" (recall the discussion of *hostile attributional bias* in Chapter 7). In this instance a teacher might consult with the school counselor about how to help the student interpret social interactions more productively.

Yet students won't always provide explanations that lead to such straightforward solutions. For example, it may be that Alonzo is late to class simply because he wants to spend a few extra minutes hanging out with friends in the hall. Or perhaps Trudy says she doesn't want to do her assignments because she's "sick and tired" of other people telling her what to do all the time. In such circumstances it's essential that teachers not get in a power struggle—a situation in which one person wins by dominating over the other in some way.[71] Several strategies can minimize the likelihood of a power struggle:[72]

- Speak in a calm, matter-of-fact manner, describing the problem as you see it. ("You haven't turned in a single assignment in the past three weeks. You and I would both

> From a motivational standpoint, how might private discussions with students be helpful? (Compare your response to this question with the response presented in Chapter 9 of the Book-Specific Resources in MyEducationLab.)

---

[70] W. Doyle, 2006; Emmer & Gerwels, 2006; Scott & Bushell, 1974.

[71] S. C. Diamond, 1991; Emmer et al., 2000.

[72] Colvin, Ainge, & Nelson, 1997; Emmer et al., 2000; Keller & Tapasak, 2004; Lane, Falk, & Wehby, 2006.

like for you to do well in my class, but that can't happen unless we *both* work to make it happen.")

- Listen empathetically to what the student has to say, being openly accepting of the student's feelings and opinions. ("I get the impression that you don't enjoy classroom activities very much; I'd really like to hear what your concerns are.")
- Summarize what you think the student has told you, and seek clarification if necessary. ("It sounds as if you'd rather not let your classmates know how much trouble you're having with your schoolwork. Is that the problem, or is it something else?")
- Describe the effects of the problem behavior, including your personal reactions to it. ("When you come to class late each day, I worry that you're getting further and further behind. Sometimes I even feel a little hurt that you don't seem to value your time in my classroom.")
- Give the student a choice from among two or more acceptable options. ("Would you rather try to work quietly at your group's table, or would it be easier if you sat somewhere by yourself to complete your work?")
- Especially when working with an adolescent, try to identify a solution that enables the student to maintain credibility in the eyes of peers. ("I suspect you might be worrying that your friends will think less of you if you comply with my request. What might we do to address this problem?")

Ultimately, a teacher must communicate interest in the student's long-term school achievement, concern that the misbehavior is interfering with that achievement, and commitment to working cooperatively with the student to resolve the problem.

Teach self-regulation strategies.

When students express their *own* concern about their problem behaviors, teaching self-regulation strategies can be helpful. Consider the following situations as examples:

Bradley's performance on assigned tasks is usually rather poor. You know he's capable of better work, because he occasionally submits work of exceptionally high quality. The root of Bradley's problem seems to be that he's off task most of the time—perhaps sketching pictures of sports cars, mindlessly fiddling with objects he has found on the floor, or simply daydreaming. Bradley would really like to improve his academic performance but doesn't seem to know how to do it.

Georgia often speaks without permission—for instance, blurting out answers to questions, interrupting classmates who are speaking, and initiating off-task conversations at inopportune times. On several occasions you've talked with Georgia about the problem, and she always vows to exercise more self-control in the future. Her behavior improves for a day or so, but after that her mouth is off and running once again.

Bradley's off-task behavior interferes with his own learning, and Georgia's excessive chattiness interferes with the learning of her classmates. Cueing and private discussions haven't led to any improvements. But both Bradley and Georgia have something going for them: They *want* to change their behavior.

In Chapter 4 we examined a variety of strategies for promoting self-regulated learning and behavior, and some of them might be valuable for Bradley and Georgia. *Self-monitoring* is especially useful when students need a reality check about the severity of a problem. For instance, Bradley may think he's on task far more often than he really is. To help him get a sense of how frequently he's *off* task, his teacher might give him a timer set to beep every 10 minutes; each time he hears a beep, he should write down whether he's been on task. (Figure 9.5 shows the kind of recording sheet he might use.) Similarly, Georgia may not realize how frequently she prevents her classmates from speaking. To alert her to the extent of the problem, her teacher might ask her to make a check mark on a tally sheet every time she talks without permission.

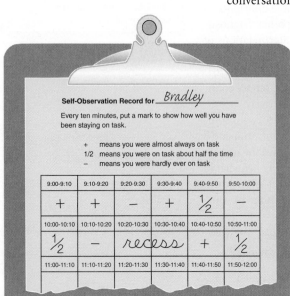

FIGURE 9.5 Example of a self-monitoring sheet for staying on task

When students genuinely want to improve their behavior, problems such as Bradley's and Georgia's can often be successfully addressed through self-monitoring alone.[73]

If self-monitoring alone doesn't do the trick, *self-instructions* might help Georgia gain some self-restraint in classroom discussions:

1. *Button* my lips (by holding them tightly together).
2. *Raise* my hand.
3. *Wait* until I'm called on.

In addition, both students might use *self-imposed contingencies* to give themselves a motivational boost. For example, Bradley might award himself a point for each 10-minute period he's been on task. Georgia might give herself five points at the beginning of each school day and then subtract a point each time she speaks out of turn. By accumulating a certain number of points, the students could earn opportunities to engage in favorite activities.

Self-regulation strategies have several advantages. They help teachers avoid power struggles with students about who's in charge. They increase students' sense of self-determination and thus also increase students' intrinsic motivation to perform well in the classroom. Furthermore, self-regulation techniques benefit students over the long run, promoting productive behaviors that are likely to continue long after students have moved on from a particular classroom or school. And when students learn how to monitor and modify their own behavior, rather than depend on adults to do it for them, their teachers become free to do other things—for instance, to teach!

When administering punishment, use only those consequences that have been shown to be effective in reducing problem behaviors.

In a well-managed classroom, reinforcement for productive behavior occurs far more often than punishment for inappropriate behavior. But consider the following situations:

> Bonnie doesn't handle frustration very well. Whenever she encounters an obstacle she can't immediately overcome, she responds by hitting, kicking, or breaking something. One day, during a class Valentine's Day party, she accidentally drops her cupcake upside-down on the floor. When she discovers that the cupcake is no longer edible, she throws her carton of milk across the room, hitting another child on the head.

> Two days before a high school football game against a cross-town rival, several members of the football team are caught spray-painting obscene words on the bleachers of the rival school's stadium.

Some misbehaviors interfere significantly with classroom learning or reflect total disregard for other people's rights and welfare. These actions require an immediate remedy, and teachers or administrators must impose consequences sufficiently unpleasant to discourage them. In other words, educators must occasionally use *punishment*. Punishment is especially useful when students appear to have little motivation to change their behavior.

As a general rule, teachers should use relatively mild forms of punishment in the classroom.[74] Severe punishment—for instance, something that lasts for several weeks or months, or something that seriously undermines students' sense of self-worth—can lead to such unwanted side effects as resentment, hostility, or truancy. Several forms of mild punishment are often effective in reducing undesirable classroom behaviors:

- **Verbal reprimands (scolding).** Although some students seem to thrive on teacher scolding because of the attention it brings, most students find verbal reprimands to be unpleasant and punishing, especially if given only infrequently. In general, reprimands are more effective when they're immediate, brief, and unemotional. They also tend to work better when given in a soft voice and in close proximity to the student, perhaps because they're less likely to draw the attention of classmates. Reprimands should be given in private whenever possible. When scolded in front of peers, some students may

---

[73] Broden, Hall, & Mitts, 1971; DuPaul & Hoff, 1998;   [74] Landrum & Kauffman, 2006.
K. R. Harris, 1986; Mace, Belfiore, & Hutchinson, 2001.

Some mild forms of punishment, such as brief time-outs, can reduce inappropriate behaviors, but teachers must monitor their effectiveness for different students.

relish the peer attention, and others (e.g., many Native American and Hispanic students) may feel totally humiliated.[75]

- **Response cost.** **Response cost** involves the loss either of a previously earned reinforcer or of an opportunity to obtain reinforcement; in either case, it's a form of *removal punishment*. Response cost is especially effective when used in combination with reinforcement of appropriate behavior.[76] For instance, when dealing with students who exhibit chronic behavior problems, teachers sometimes incorporate response cost into a point system or *token economy*, awarding points, check marks, plastic chips, or the like for good behavior (reinforcement) and taking away these things for inappropriate behavior (response cost). Students who accumulate a sufficient number of points or tokens can use them to "buy" objects, privileges, or enjoyable activities that are otherwise not available. (You may want to revisit the discussions of removal punishment and token economy in Chapter 3.)

- **Logical consequences.** A **logical consequence** is something that follows naturally or logically from a student's misbehavior; in other words, it's punishment that fits the crime. For example, if a student destroys a classmate's possession, a reasonable consequence is for the student to replace it or pay for a new one. If two close friends talk so much that they aren't completing assignments, a reasonable consequence is that they be separated.[77]

- **Time-out.** A misbehaving student given a **time-out** is placed in a dull, boring (but not scary) situation—perhaps a separate room designed especially for time-outs, a little-used office, or a remote corner of the classroom. A student in time-out has no opportunity to interact with classmates and no opportunity to obtain reinforcement. The length of the time-out is typically quite short (perhaps 2 to 10 minutes, depending on the student's age), but the student isn't released until inappropriate behavior (e.g., swearing, kicking) has stopped. Keep in mind, however, that a time-out is apt to be effective only if ongoing classroom activities are a source of pleasure and reinforcement for a student. If, instead, it allows a student to escape difficult tasks or an overwhelming amount of noise and stimulation, it might actually be reinforcing and so *increase* undesirable behavior.[78]

- **In-school suspension.** Like time-out, **in-school suspension** involves placing a student in a quiet, boring location, usually a separate room within the school building. However, it often lasts one or more school days and involves close adult supervision. Students receiving in-school suspension spend the day working on the same assignments that their nonsuspended peers do, enabling them to keep up with their schoolwork. But they have no opportunity for interaction with peers—an aspect of school that's reinforcing to most students. In-school suspension programs tend to be most effective when part of the suspension session is devoted to teaching appropriate behaviors and tutoring academic skills and when the supervising teacher acts as a supportive resource rather than punisher.[79]

Several other forms of punishment are typically *not* recommended. *Physical punishment* can, of course, lead to physical harm, and even mild forms (e.g., slapping a hand with a ruler) can lead to such undesirable behaviors as resentment of the teacher, inattention to school tasks, lying, aggression, vandalism, avoidance of school tasks, and truancy.[80] Any consequence that seriously threatens a student's sense of self-worth—*psychological punishment*— can lead to some of the same side effects as physical punishment (e.g., resentment of the teacher, inattention to school tasks, truancy from school) and may possibly inflict long-term

response cost Loss either of a previously earned reinforcer or of an opportunity to obtain reinforcement.

logical consequence Unpleasant consequence that follows naturally or logically from a student's misbehavior.

time-out Consequence for misbehavior in which a student is placed in a dull, boring situation with no opportunity for reinforcement or social interaction.

in-school suspension Consequence for misbehavior in which a student is placed in a quiet, boring room within the school building, typically to do schoolwork under close adult supervision.

[75] M. L. Fuller, 2001; Landrum & Kauffman, 2006; O'Leary, Kaufman, Kass, & Drabman, 1970; Pfiffner & O'Leary, 1993; Van Houten, Nau, MacKenzie-Keating, Sameoto, & Colavecchia, 1982.

[76] Conyers et al., 2004; Iwata & Bailey, 1974; Lentz, 1988; Rapport, Murphy, & Bailey, 1982.

[77] Dreikurs, 1998; Nucci, 2009; L. S. Wright, 1982.

[78] Alberto & Troutman, 2009; McClowry, 1998; Pfiffner, Barkley, & DuPaul, 2006; Rortvedt & Miltenberger, 1994; A. G. White & Bailey, 1990.

[79] Gootman, 1998; Huff, 1988; Pfiffner et al., 2006; J. S. Sullivan, 1989.

[80] W. Doyle, 1990; Landrum & Kauffman, 2006; Nucci, 2006.

Ellen Senisi

psychological harm.[81] *Assigning extra classwork* beyond that required for other students is inappropriate if done simply to punish a student's wrongdoing, in that it communicates the message that "schoolwork is unpleasant."[82] Finally, *out-of-school suspension* is rarely an effective means of changing a student's behavior. For one thing, suspension from school may be exactly what a student wants, in which case inappropriate behaviors are being reinforced rather than punished. Furthermore, suspension involves a loss of valuable instructional time and interferes with any psychological attachment to school, thereby reducing low-achieving students' chances for academic and social success—sometimes to the point where they have little interest in returning to school.[83]

Two additional forms of punishment get mixed reviews regarding effectiveness. In some situations *missing recess* is a logical consequence for students who fail to complete their schoolwork during regular class time because of off-task behavior. Yet research indicates that, especially at the elementary level, students can more effectively concentrate on school tasks if they have frequent breaks and opportunities to release pent-up energy.[84] And although *after-school detentions* are common practice at many schools, some students simply can't stay after school hours, perhaps because they have transportation issues, must take care of younger siblings until parents get home from work, or are justifiably afraid to walk through certain neighborhoods after dark.[85]

A frequent criticism of punishment is that it's inhumane or somehow cruel and barbaric. Indeed, certain forms of punishment, such as physical abuse or public humiliation, do constitute inhumane treatment.[86] Furthermore, physical punishment at school is illegal in many states. Teachers must be *extremely careful* in their use of punishment in the classroom. But when administered judiciously—and especially when administered within the context of a warm, supportive teacher–student relationship—some forms of mild punishment can lead to a rapid reduction in misbehavior without causing physical or psychological harm.[87] And when teachers can decrease counterproductive classroom behaviors quickly and effectively—especially when those behaviors are harmful to self or others—punishment may, in fact, be one of the most humane approaches to take.[88] The Classroom Strategies box "Using Punishment Humanely and Effectively" offers several guidelines for administering punishment in ways that will yield more productive student behavior over the long run.

Confer with parents.

Teachers may sometimes need to talk with students' parents or other primary caregivers about a serious or chronic behavior problem. Consider these situations:

> You give your students short homework assignments almost every night. Carolyn has turned in only about one-third of them. You're pretty sure she's capable of doing the work, and you know from previous parent–teacher conferences that her parents give her the time and support she needs to get her assignments done. You've spoken with Carolyn several times about the problem, but she shrugs you off as if she doesn't really care whether she does well in your class.

> Students have often found things missing from their desks or personal storage bins after Roger has been in the vicinity. A few students have told you that they've seen Roger taking things that belong to others, and many of the missing objects have later turned up in Roger's possession. When you confront him about your suspicion that he's been stealing from classmates, he adamantly denies it. He says he has no idea how Cami's gloves or Marvin's baseball trading cards ended up in his desk.

---

[81] Brendgen, Wanner, Vitaro, Bukowski, & Tremblay, 2007; G. A. Davis & Thomas, 1989; Hyman et al., 2006.
[82] Cooper, 1989; Corno, 1996.
[83] American Psychological Association Zero Tolerance Task Force, 2008; Fenning & Bohanon, 2006; Moles, 1990; Skiba & Rausch, 2006.
[84] Maxmell, Jarrett, & Dickerson, 1998; Pellegrini & Bohn, 2005; Pellegrini, Huberty, & Jones, 1995.

[85] Nichols, Ludwin, & Iadicola, 1999.
[86] For a good discussion of this point, see Hyman et al., 2004.
[87] Landrum & Kauffman, 2006; Nucci, 2001.
[88] Lerman & Vorndran, 2002.

CLASSROOM STRATEGIES Using Punishment Humanely and Effectively

- **Inform students ahead of time that certain behaviors are unacceptable, and explain how those behaviors will be punished.**

  A third-grade teacher makes one rule for recess perfectly clear: *Students must not do anything that might hurt someone else.* He gives his class several concrete examples: throwing rocks, pulling hair, pushing someone off the slide, and so on. "If you do anything that might hurt another child," he says, "you'll spend the next three recesses sitting on the bench outside the classroom door."

- **Help students understand why the punished behavior is unacceptable.**

  When several members of a high school football team are caught spray-painting obscenities on a rival school's stadium bleachers, three consequences are imposed: (1) The students will not be able to play in the upcoming game against the rival school, (2) they must visit the rival school's principal to make a formal apology and acknowledge that their actions showed poor sportsmanship and disregard for other people's property, and (3) they must repaint the affected areas of the bleachers, purchasing the paint with their own money.

- **Emphasize that it is the behavior—*not* the student—that is undesirable.**

  When a kindergartner angrily throws her carton of milk at a classmate, her teacher puts her in the "time-out corner" at the back of the room. "I like you a lot, Bonnie," the teacher tells her, "but I simply cannot have you doing something that might hurt Susan. I like her just as much as I like you, and I want both of you to feel safe in my classroom."

- **Administer punishment privately, especially when other students are not aware of the transgression.**

  As a junior high school teacher walks down the hall, she overhears a student tell two friends a "knock-knock" joke that includes an insulting racial slur, and the friends laugh uproariously. The teacher pulls the three students aside and explains that she heard the joke and found it quite offensive. "Whether you told the joke or merely laughed at it," she says, "you were all showing disrespect for certain teachers and students at this school. Not only does your disrespect undermine our overall sense of school community, but it also violates school policy. The consequence of such behavior is one day of in-school suspension. I'll notify the principal's office that you'll be reporting for in-school suspension tomorrow. Be sure to bring your textbooks and class assignments so that you won't get behind in your schoolwork."

- **Simultaneously teach and reinforce desirable alternative behaviors.**

  In small-group discussions and cooperative learning activities, a middle school student often belittles other students' ideas. Her teacher takes her aside and reprimands her but also teaches her productive strategies for disagreeing with classmates. "One strategy," he suggests, "is to say something *good* about another person's idea but then to suggest an alternative that the group might consider. For example, you might say, 'I like how carefully you've thought about the problem, Jerry. Here's a different perspective I'd like the group to think about as well. . . .'" Later, when the teacher hears the student using the strategy during a small-group project, he catches her eye and gives her a "thumbs-up" sign.

Sources: Landrum & Kauffman, 2006; Lerman & Vorndran, 2002; Moles, 1990; Nucci, 2001; Parke, 1974; D. G. Perry & Perry, 1983; Ruef, Higgins, Glaeser, & Patnode, 1998.

Conferring with parents is especially important when students' behavior problems show a pattern over time and have serious implications for students' long-term academic or social success. In some cases a simple telephone call may be sufficient. For example, Carolyn's parents may be unaware that she hasn't been doing her homework (she's been telling them she doesn't have any) and may be able to take the steps necessary to ensure that it gets done. In other instances a school conference may be more productive. For example, a teacher might want to discuss Roger's stealing habits with both Roger and his parent(s) together—something the teacher can do more effectively when everyone sits face to face in the same room.

Some ways of talking with parents are far more effective than others. Put yourself in a parent's shoes in the following exercise.

SEE FOR YOURSELF Putting Yourself in a Parent's Shoes

Imagine you're the parent of a seventh grader named Tommy. As you and Tommy are eating dinner one evening, the telephone rings. You get up and answer the phone.

You: Hello?

Ms. J.: This is Ms. Johnson, Tommy's teacher. May I talk with you for a few minutes?

> **You:** Of course. What can I do for you?
>
> **Ms. J.:** Well, I'm afraid I've been having some trouble with your son, and I thought you should know about it.
>
> **You:** Really? What's the problem?
>
> **Ms. J.:** Tommy hardly ever gets to class on time. When he does arrive, he spends most of his time talking with friends rather than paying attention to what I'm saying. It seems as if I have to speak to him three or four times every day about his behavior.
>
> **You:** How long has all this been going on?
>
> **Ms. J.:** For several weeks now. And the problem is getting worse rather than better. I'd really appreciate it if you'd talk with Tommy about the situation.
>
> **You:** Thank you for letting me know about this, Ms. Johnson.
>
> **Ms. J.:** You're most welcome. Good night.
>
> **You:** Good night, Ms. Johnson.
>
> Take a few minutes to jot down some of the things that, as a parent, you might be thinking after this telephone conversation.

You may have had a variety of thoughts in response to your conversation with Ms. Johnson. Here are some possibilities:

- Why isn't Tommy taking his schoolwork more seriously?
- Isn't Tommy doing anything *right?*
- Has Ms. Johnson tried anything besides reprimanding Tommy for his behavior? Or is she laying all of this on *my* shoulders?
- Tommy's a good kid. I should know, because I raised him. For some reason, Ms. Johnson doesn't like him and is therefore finding fault with anything he does.

Only the first of these four reactions is likely to lead to a productive response on your part.

Notice how Ms. Johnson focused strictly on the negative aspects of Tommy's classroom performance. As a result, you (as Tommy's parent) may possibly have felt anger toward your son or guilt about your ineffective parenting skills. Alternatively, if you maintained your confidence in your son's scholastic abilities and in your own ability as a parent, you may have begun to wonder about Ms. Johnson's ability to teach and motivate seventh graders. Sadly, too many teachers reach out to parents only to talk about students' weaknesses—never their strengths—as the following interview with Jamal illustrates:

> **Adult:** Has your grandpa [Jamal's primary caregiver] ever come to school?
>
> **Jamal:** Yup, when the teachers call him.
>
> **Adult:** What did they call him for?
>
> **Jamal:** The only time they call him is when I am being bad, the teacher will call him, he will come up here and have a meeting with the teacher.
>
> **Adult:** If you are being good do the teachers call?
>
> **Jamal:** No.[89]

Ideally, a teacher–parent discussion about problem behaviors is initiated within the context of an ongoing relationship characterized by mutual trust and respect and a shared concern for students' learning and well-being. For instance, a phone call to parents is most likely to yield productive results if the teacher and parents already have a good working relationship and if the teacher is confident that parents won't overreact with harsh, excessive punishment of their child. Furthermore, when communicating with parents, teachers' overall messages about students should be positive and optimistic. For instance, a teacher might describe undesirable aspects of a student's classroom performance within the context of the many things the student does *well.* (Rather than starting out by complaining about

---

[89] Dialogue from Kumar et al., 2002, p. 164.

CLASSROOM STRATEGIES Talking with Parents about Students' Misbehaviors

- **Consult with parents if a collaborative effort might bring about a behavior change.**

  At a parent–teacher–student conference, a high school math teacher expresses his concern that a student often falls asleep in class. Because the student has a computer and a cable outlet in her bedroom, her father speculates that perhaps she's surfing the Internet when she should be in bed. He looks at his daughter inquisitively, and her guilty facial expression reveals that his suspicion is justified. With the teacher's prompting, the father and the student identify an appropriate policy for home computer use—one that includes moving the computer to another room, where its use can be more closely monitored.

- **Begin with a description of a student's many strengths.**

  A teacher talks on the telephone with the father of one of her students. She describes several areas in which the student has made considerable progress and then asks for advice about strategies for helping him stay on task and be more conscientious about his work.

- **Describe the problem in terms of inappropriate behaviors, *not* in terms of undesirable personality characteristics.**

  When describing a student's poor record of turning in homework assignments, her teacher says, "Carolyn has turned in only about a third of the homework I've assigned this year. She's missed only two school days this year, so I know she's been healthy. And she's certainly capable of doing the work." At no point does the teacher suggest that Carolyn is lazy, unmotivated, or stubborn.

- **Don't place blame; instead, acknowledge that raising children is rarely easy.**

  When talking with the mother of a middle school student, a teacher mentions that the student seems to be more interested in talking with classmates than in getting her schoolwork done. The mother describes a similar problem at home: "Marnie's always been a much more social girl than I ever was. It's like pulling teeth just getting her off her phone to do her homework, and then we end up having a shouting match that

gets us nowhere!" The teacher sympathetically responds, "Students seem to become especially concerned about social matters once they reach adolescence. How about if you, Marnie, and I meet some day after school to talk about the problem? Perhaps by working together the three of us can find a way to solve it."

- **Ask for information, and express your desire to work together to address the problem.**

  When a teacher finds that a student has regularly been taking items from classmates' personal storage bins, she sets up an appointment to meet with the student and his grandmother (the student's primary caregiver). "I like Roger a lot," she says. "He has a great sense of humor, and his smile often lights up my day. I can't understand why he might want to 'borrow' items from other children without asking first. His actions have cost him several friendships. Do either of you have any ideas about how we might tackle the problem? I'd like to do whatever I can to help Roger repair his reputation in the eyes of his classmates."

- **Agree on a strategy.**

  While reviewing a student's academic progress at a parent–teacher conference, an elementary teacher says, "Mark has a tendency to fiddle with things at his desk—for example, twisting paperclips, playing with rubber bands, or making paper airplanes—when he should be getting his work done. As a result, he often doesn't complete his assignments." The student's father replies, "I've noticed the same thing when Mark works on his homework, but I bring a lot of paperwork home from the office every night and don't have time to constantly hound him to stay on task." The teacher and father talk more about the problem and agree that reinforcement for completed assignments might be helpful. Mark will earn points for high scores that will help him "buy" the new bicycle he's been asking his father for.

Sources: Christenson & Sheridan, 2001; C. Davis & Yang, 2005; Emmer & Evertson, 2009; Evertson & Emmer, 2009; A. Miller, 2006; Woolfolk Hoy, Davis, & Pape, 2006.

Tommy's behavior, Ms. Johnson might have begun by saying that Tommy is a bright and capable young man with many friends and a good sense of humor.) And teachers must be clear about their commitment to working *together* with parents to help a student succeed in the classroom. The Classroom Strategies box "Talking with Parents about Students' Misbehaviors" presents several strategies for effectively approaching parents about a challenging behavior problem.

When talking with parents, teachers must keep in mind that different cultures have different perspectives on how best to address behavior problems (see the Cultural Considerations box "Cultural Differences in Parental Discipline"). Ultimately, teachers and parents must try to find common ground on which to develop strategies for helping children and adolescents thrive at school.[90] At the same time, teachers must tactfully and sensitively help parents understand that certain consequences—for instance, severe physical and psychological punishments—are unlikely to be productive over the long run.

---

[90] T. L. Good & Nichols, 2001; Salend & Taylor, 1993.

CULTURAL CONSIDERATIONS   Cultural Differences in Parental Discipline

The vast majority of parents want what's best for their children and recognize the value of a good education for children's long-term success.[a] Yet parents from different cultural and ethnic groups sometimes have radically different ideas about what behaviors are problematic. As an example, let's return to the See for Yourself exercise titled "Jack" in Chapter 3 (p. 92). Jack, a Native American seventh grader, had been absent from school for an entire week. Not only were his parents seemingly unconcerned, but they didn't even go looking for him until they needed him at home to help with the family farm. Their attitudes and actions make sense only when we understand that they knew their son was probably safe with neighbors and believed that, as a young adolescent, Jack was essentially an adult and responsible for his own decisions.[b] In contrast, many parents from Asian cultures expect children to immediately defer to and obey adult authority figures (e.g., parents and teachers) and

think that Western teachers are much too lenient with students.[c]

Disciplinary strategies also differ from culture to culture. In mainstream Western culture, praise is widely used as a strategy for encouraging good behavior, and reprimands and denial of privileges (e.g., "grounding") are often the consequences for unacceptable behavior. But such practices are hardly universal. Children in some cultures may be unaccustomed to direct praise for appropriate behavior and personal successes, perhaps because appropriate behavior is a social obligation (and so not praiseworthy) or perhaps because adults express approval in other ways—for instance, by telling other people how skillful a child is.[d] And in certain other cultures (including some Native American and Asian groups), ostracism is a common disciplinary strategy: If a child's misbehaviors are seen as bringing shame on the family or community, the child is ignored for an extended time period.[e]

It's important to note that some cultural groups believe physical punishment

to be necessary for behavioral transgressions. When physical punishment is a common form of discipline in one's culture, children are more likely to accept *mild* physical punishment as appropriate and deserved. Even in such contexts, however, physical punishment is apt to have adverse effects on children's psychological well-being.[f] Accordingly, teachers should tactfully dissuade parents from using it, ideally by suggesting alternative consequences that can effectively reduce problem behaviors without causing harm.

[a] Gallimore & Goldenberg, 2001; Hidalgo, Siu, Bright, Swap, & Epstein, 1995; Okagaki, 2001; Spera, 2005.

[b] Deyhle & LeCompte, 1999.

[c] Dien, 1998; Hidalgo et al., 1995; Kağitçibaşi, 2007; Tamis-Lemonda & McFadden, 2010.

[d] Greenfield et al., 2006; Kitayama, Duffy, & Uchida, 2007; Rogoff, 2003.

[e] Pang, 1995; Salend & Taylor, 1993.

[f] Bornstein & Lansford, 2010; Lansford et al., 2005; Lansford, Deater-Decker, & Dodge, Bates, & Pettit, 2003.

To address a chronic problem, plan and carry out a systematic intervention.

Sometimes problem behaviors are so disruptive and persistent that they require a systematic effort to change them. Consider these situations:

> Tucker finds many reasons to roam about the room—he "has to" sharpen a pencil, "has to" get his homework out of his backpack, "has to" get a drink of water, and so on. Naturally, Tucker gets very little work done, and his classmates are continually distracted by his perpetual motion.

> Janet's verbal abusiveness is getting out of hand. She regularly insults her peers with sexually explicit language and sometimes calls you X-rated names. You've tried praising her on occasions when she's pleasant to others, and she seems to appreciate your doing so, yet her abusive remarks continue.

Imagine that both Tucker and Janet are in your class. You've already spoken with each of them about their unacceptable behavior, yet you've seen no improvement. You've suggested methods of self-regulation, but neither student seems interested in changing for the better. You've tried putting them in time-out for their actions, but Janet seems to enjoy the time away from her schoolwork, and Tucker sometimes has a valid reason for getting out of his seat. Although both students' parents are aware of and concerned about their children's classroom behaviors, their efforts at home haven't had an impact. And after all, these are largely *school* problems rather than home problems. So what do you do now?

When a serious misbehavior persists despite ongoing efforts to curtail it, a more intensive intervention is in order. Some interventions, known by such labels as **applied behavior analysis (ABA),** *behavior therapy,* or *contingency management,* focus on changing stimulus conditions and response–consequence contingencies in a student's environment.[91] These approaches are based largely on principles presented in Chapter 3:

- Some stimuli tend to elicit certain kinds of behaviors.
- Learners are more likely to acquire behaviors that lead to desired consequences.
- Learners tend to steer clear of behaviors that lead to unpleasant consequences.

With these principles in mind, effective teachers change the classroom environment to elicit more productive behaviors and establish more beneficial response–consequence contingencies. Thus they use strategies such as these:

- Identify problem behaviors and desired behaviors in explicit (and ideally measurable) terms. Often the desired behaviors identified are incompatible with problem behaviors.
- Identify reinforcers, punishments, or both that are truly effective for the student.
- Develop a specific intervention plan. The plan may involve reinforcement of desired behaviors, shaping, extinction, reinforcement of incompatible behaviors, punishment, or some combination of these.
- Modify the classroom environment to minimize conditions that might trigger inappropriate behaviors.
- Collect data on the frequency of problem behaviors and desired behaviors both before and during the intervention.
- Monitor the program's effectiveness by observing how various behaviors change over time, and modify the program if necessary.
- Take steps to promote transfer of newly acquired behaviors (e.g., by having the student practice the behaviors in a variety of realistic situations).
- Gradually phase out the intervention (e.g., through intermittent reinforcement) after the desired behaviors are acquired.

Often the strategies just listed are more effective when cognitive and motivational factors affecting students' behavior are also addressed—an approach known as *cognitive behavioral therapy.* For example, teachers might also use one or more of the following strategies:

- Teach self-regulation skills.
- Teach effective social skills.
- Encourage better perspective taking and other aspects of social cognition.
- Make changes in the curriculum, instructional methods, or both to maximize the likelihood of academic success and high self-efficacy for school tasks.

How might a teacher use some of the preceding strategies to improve Tucker's classroom behavior? One approach would be to identify one or more effective reinforcers—given Tucker's constant fidgeting, opportunities for physical activity might be reinforcing—and then gradually shape more sedentary behavior. In addition, because some out-of-seat responses are quite appropriate (e.g., getting a reference book from the bookshelf, delivering a completed assignment to the teacher's "In" basket), the teacher might give Tucker a reasonable allotment of out-of-seat "tickets" he can use during the day. Tucker can probably also benefit from instruction and scaffolding regarding general organizational skills—in particular, assembling necessary supplies (notebooks, sharpened pencils, completed homework, etc.) before lessons begin.

A systematic intervention may be helpful with Janet as well. In this case we might suspect that Janet lacks the social skills she needs to interact effectively with others. Her teacher or a school counselor might therefore need to begin by teaching her such skills through modeling, role-playing, and so on (see Chapter 7). After Janet acquires effective interpersonal skills, her teacher can begin to reinforce her for using those skills. (Praise might be an effective reinforcer, as she has responded positively to praise in the past.) Meanwhile, the teacher should also punish (perhaps with a time-out) any relapses into old, abusive behavior patterns.

---

applied behavior analysis (ABA) Systematic application of stimulus–response principles to address a chronic behavior problem.

[91] For examples of such strategies, see Alberto & Troutman, 2009; Bradshaw, Zmuda, Kellam, & Ialongo, 2009; S. N. Elliott & Busse, 1991; E. McNamara, 1987; Ormrod, 2008.

Determine whether certain undesirable behaviors might serve particular purposes for students.

Sometimes a student's misbehaviors, although maladaptive from a teacher's perspective, in one way or another help the student preserve a sense of well-being. As an example, consider 9-year-old Samantha:

> Samantha has been identified as having a mild form of autism and moderate speech disabilities. Consistent with the Individuals with Disabilities Education Act (IDEA) described in Chapter 3, she is a full-fledged member of a third-grade class. However, she frequently runs out of the classroom, damaging school property and classmates' belongings in her flight. When a teacher or other adult tries to intervene, she fights back by biting, hitting, kicking, or pulling hair. On such occasions school personnel often call her parents and ask that they come to take her home.
>
> By systematically collecting data on Samantha's classroom performance, a team of teachers and specialists discovers that her destructive and aggressive behaviors typically occur when she's given a difficult assignment or expects such an assignment. Noisy or chaotic events, departures from the routine schedule, and the absences of favorite teachers further increase the probability of inappropriate behaviors.
>
> The team hypothesizes that Samantha's undesirable behaviors serve two purposes: They (1) help her avoid overwhelming situations or unpleasant tasks and (2) enable her to gain the attention of valued adults. The team suspects, too, that Samantha feels as if she has little or no control over classroom activities and that she yearns for more social interaction with her teachers and classmates.[92]

In trying to determine why Samantha misbehaves as she does, the team is taking an approach known as **functional analysis**. That is, it identifies the specific stimulus conditions that exist both before and after Samantha makes inappropriate responses—the antecedents and consequences of particular behaviors—like so:

$$\text{Antecedent} \rightarrow \text{Behavior} \rightarrow \text{Consequence}$$

The team soon realizes that Samantha's behaviors are the result of *both* antecedent events (e.g., challenging tasks, changes in routine) and desirable consequences (e.g., getting attention, going home). In other words, Samantha's behaviors are serving certain *functions* for her: They get her attention from others (positive reinforcement) and enable her to escape things she doesn't want to do and places she doesn't want to be (such escape is negative reinforcement). Like Samantha, students with chronic behavior problems often misbehave when they're asked to do difficult or unpleasant tasks and when their misbehavior either helps them avoid those tasks or gains the attention of their teacher or peers.[93]

Once a functional analysis has been completed, an approach known as **positive behavioral support (PBS)** takes the process a step further. In particular, PBS builds on knowledge about the functions of misbehaviors to encourage more productive behaviors. Following are typical strategies:[94]

Misbehaviors often help students satisfy certain needs or achieve certain goals. In such situations a teacher may want to identify and encourage alternative behaviors that will enable students to accomplish the same ends.

- Teach behaviors that can serve the same purpose as—and can therefore replace—inappropriate behaviors.
- Modify the classroom environment to minimize conditions that might trigger inappropriate behaviors.
- Establish a predictable daily routine as a way of minimizing anxiety and making the student feel more comfortable and secure.

functional analysis Examination of inappropriate behavior and its antecedents and consequences to determine one or more purposes (functions) that the behavior might serve for the learner.

positive behavioral support (PBS) Systematic intervention that addresses chronic misbehaviors by (1) identifying the purposes those behaviors might serve for a student and (2) providing more appropriate ways for a student to achieve the same ends.

---

[92] DeVault, Krug, & Fake, 1996.

[93] K. M. Jones, Drew, & Weber, 2000; McComas, Thompson, & Johnson, 2003; McKerchar & Thompson, 2004; Mueller, Edwards, & Trahant, 2003; Van Camp et al., 2000.

[94] Crone & Horner, 2003; Koegel, Koegel, & Dunlap, 1996; Ruef, Higgins, Glaeser, & Patnode, 1998; Warren et al., 2006.

- Give the student opportunities to make choices; in this way, the student can often gain desired outcomes without having to resort to inappropriate behavior.
- Make changes in the curriculum, instruction, or both to maximize the likelihood of academic success (e.g., build on student interests, present material at a slower pace, or intersperse challenging tasks among easier and more enjoyable ones).
- Monitor the frequency of various behaviors to determine whether the intervention is working or, instead, requires modification.

For instance, after school faculty members have formed reasonable hypotheses regarding the roots of Samantha's inappropriate behaviors, they take several steps to help her acquire more productive ones:[95]

- Samantha is given a consistent and predictable daily schedule that includes frequent breaks from potentially challenging academic tasks and numerous opportunities to interact with others.
- Samantha is given "goal sheets" from which she can choose the academic tasks she'll work on, the length of time she'll work on them, and a reward she'll receive for achieving each goal.
- Samantha is taught how to ask for assistance when she needs it—a strategy she can use instead of fleeing from the classroom in the face of a challenging task.
- When Samantha feels she needs a break from academic tasks, she can ask to spend time in the "relaxation room," a quiet, private space where she can sit in a beanbag chair and listen to soothing audiotapes.
- If Samantha tries to leave the classroom, an adult immediately places her in the relaxation room, where she can calm down without a great deal of adult attention.
- Samantha is given explicit instruction in how to interact appropriately with classmates. Initially, she earns points for appropriate social behaviors and can trade them for special treats (e.g., a family trip to Dairy Queen or a video store). Eventually, her new social skills lead to natural consequences—friendly interactions with peers— that make extrinsic reinforcers unnecessary.

Samantha's teachers and parents communicate regularly to coordinate their efforts. Her problem behaviors don't disappear overnight, but they show a dramatic decline over the next several months. By the time Samantha is 12 years old and in sixth grade, her grades consistently earn her a place on the honor roll, and she has a group of friends with whom she participates in several extracurricular activities. Her teachers describe her as sociable, inquisitive, and creative. Her principal calls her a "model student."[96]

Let's return once again to Ms. Cornell's difficulties with Eli, Jake, and Vanessa in the opening case study. Here, too, a planned, systematic intervention, possibly including functional analysis and positive behavioral support, might be in order. Reinforcing appropriate behaviors (if necessary, shaping such behaviors over a period of time) and punishing inappropriate behaviors are two obvious strategies. Furthermore, Ms. Cornell should make response–consequence contingencies clear, perhaps using contingency contracts (see Chapter 3). She might also determine the purpose(s) that the students' misbehaviors serve (e.g., perhaps the three students crave attention, or perhaps they misbehave to avoid doing assignments for which they don't have adequate reading skills) and then either (1) identify more productive behaviors that can serve the same purpose(s) or (2) address academic or social problems that may be directly or indirectly contributing to the students' unproductive behaviors.

Table 9.2 summarizes the general approaches to addressing student misbehaviors described in the last few pages, and teachers are apt to use all of them at one time or another. Occasionally, however, chronic behavior problems involve not just a handful of students but an entire *school,* or at least a large subpopulation of a school's students (recall the opening case study "The School Play" in Chapter 7). Perhaps most troubling is the prevalence of aggression and violence at some schools. Teachers play a key role in—and can also be highly effective in—addressing widespread aggression and violence. In the final section of the chapter, we look at some strategies for doing so.

---

[95] DeVault et al., 1996.
[96] DeVault et al., 1996.

TABLE 9.2 Strategies for Dealing with Student Misbehavior

Strategy	Situations in Which It's Appropriate	Examples
Ignoring the behavior	• The misbehavior is unlikely to be repeated. • The misbehavior is unlikely to spread to other students. • Unusual circumstances elicit the misbehavior temporarily. • The misbehavior does not seriously interfere with learning.	• One student discreetly passes a note to another student just before the end of class. • A student accidentally drops her books, startling other students and temporarily distracting them from their work. • An entire class is hyperactive on the last afternoon before spring break.
Cueing the student	• The misbehavior is a minor infraction yet interferes with students' learning. • The behavior is likely to improve with a subtle reminder.	• A student forgets to close his notebook at the beginning of a test. • Members of a cooperative learning group are talking so loudly that they distract other groups. • Several students are exchanging jokes during an independent seatwork assignment.
Discussing the problem with the student	• Cueing has been ineffective in changing the behavior. • The reasons for the misbehavior, if made clear, might suggest possible strategies for addressing it.	• A student is frequently late to class. • A student refuses to do certain kinds of assignments. • A student shows a sudden drop in motivation for no apparent reason.
Promoting self-regulation	• The student has a strong desire to improve his or her behavior.	• A student doesn't realize how frequently she interrupts her classmates. • A student seeks help in learning to control his anger. • A student acknowledges that her inability to stay on task is adversely affecting the good grades she wants to get.
Punishment	• A behavior significantly interferes with classroom learning or reflects blatant disregard for others' rights and welfare. • The student has little or no understanding or concern that the behavior is unacceptable.	• A student punches a classmate who inadvertently brushes past him. • A student tells a joke that insults people of a particular ethnic group. • A student vandalizes other students' lockers.
Conferring with parents	• A chronic behavior problem is likely to interfere with the student's long-term academic or social success. • The source of the problem may possibly lie outside school walls. • Parents are likely to work collaboratively with school faculty members to bring about a behavior change.	• A student does well in class but rarely turns in required homework assignments. • A student falls asleep in class almost every day. • A student is caught stealing classmates' lunches.
Conducting a planned, systematic intervention (e.g., applied behavior analysis, positive behavioral support)	• The misbehavior has continued over a period of time and significantly interferes with student learning and achievement. • Other, less intensive approaches (e.g., cueing, teacher–student discussions, mild punishment) have been ineffective. • The student seems unwilling or unable to use self-regulation techniques. • The misbehavior may in some way enable a student to achieve desired outcomes.	• A student has unusual difficulty sitting still for age-appropriate time periods. • A member of the soccer team displays bursts of anger and aggression that are potentially dangerous to other players. • A student engages in disruptive behavior every time a difficult task is assigned.

Addressing Aggression and Violence at School

In recent years the news media have focused considerable attention on violent school crime, and especially on school shootings, leading many people to believe that aggression in schools is on the rise. In reality, violent aggression involving serious injury or death is relatively rare on school grounds and, in the United States at least, has been *declining* rather than increasing.[97]

---

[97] Bureau of Justice Statistics, 2005; DeVoe et al., 2003;
DeVoe, Peter, Noonan, Snyder, & Baum, 2005;
Kupchik & Bracy, 2009.

Most aggression at school involves minor physical injury, psychological harm (e.g., sexual or racial harassment), or destruction of property (e.g., vandalization of student lockers).[98]

If we consider only aggression that causes serious injury or death, then school is probably the safest place that young people can be.[99] But if we consider *all* forms of aggression (mild as well as severe), then aggression among children and adolescents occurs more frequently at school than at any other location—especially in areas where adult supervision is minimal (e.g., hallways, restrooms, parking lots).[100] The relative prevalence of aggression at school is almost certainly due to two factors. First, children and adolescents spend a great deal of time at school, more so than in any other place except home. Second, the sheer number of students attending even the smallest of schools makes some interpersonal conflict almost inevitable.

The roots of school aggression and violence are many and diverse. As we discovered in Chapter 7, a variety of cognitive factors (lack of perspective-taking, misinterpretation of social cues, poor social problem-solving skills, etc.) predispose some students to aggressive behavior. Furthermore, perhaps because of the home or neighborhood environment in which they live, some students believe that aggression is an appropriate and effective way to resolve conflicts. Developmental factors come into play as well. For instance, many young children and a few adolescents have poor impulse control. And during the unsettling transition to middle school, students who worry about fitting in may bully weaker age-mates as a way of gaining or maintaining social status.[101] The school culture is also involved. For instance, at some high schools it's acceptable practice to threaten or fight with a peer who tries to steal one's boyfriend or girlfriend.[102] Finally, aggression is a common reaction to frustration, and some students are repeatedly frustrated in their efforts to be academically and socially successful at school.[103]

Regardless of the roots of the behavior, educators must not tolerate *any* form of aggression or violence on school grounds. Students can learn and achieve at optimal levels only if they know they are both physically and psychologically safe at school. Furthermore, if they *don't* feel safe, they're at increased risk for dropping out before high school graduation.[104] To be truly effective in combating aggression and violence, teachers and other school faculty members must attack it on three levels, depicted graphically in Figure 9.6.[105] The first three of the following four recommendations reflect these three levels; the final one specifically addresses aggression that can result from hostilities among rival gangs on school grounds.

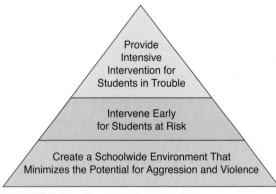

FIGURE 9.6 A three-level approach to preventing aggression and violence in schools

Note: Based on a figure in *Safeguarding Our Children: An Action Guide* (p. 3), by K. Dwyer and D. Osher, 2000, Washington, DC: U.S. Departments of Education and Justice, American Institutes for Research.

Make the creation of a nonviolent school environment a long-term effort.

One-shot "antiviolence" campaigns have little lasting effect on school aggression and violence.[106] Instead, creating a peaceful, nonviolent school environment must be a long-term effort that includes the following strategies:[107]

- Make a schoolwide commitment to supporting *all* students' academic and social success.

[98] Bender, 2001; Casella, 2001b; Pellegrini, 2002.

[99] Burstyn & Stevens, 2001; DeVoe et al., 2003, 2005; Garbarino, Bradshaw, & Vorrasi, 2002.

[100] Astor, Meyer, & Behre, 1999; Casella, 2001b; Finkelhor & Ormrod, 2000.

[101] Bronson, 2000; Espelage, Holt, & Henkel, 2003; National Center for Education Statistics, 2007; Pellegrini, 2002.

[102] K. M. Williams, 2001a, 2001b.

[103] Bender, 2001; Casella, 2001b; Miles & Stipek, 2006.

[104] Rumberger, 1995.

[105] Dwyer & Osher, 2000; Hyman et al., 2006; T. J. Lewis et al., 2006; Osher, Dwyer, & Jimerson, 2006;

H. M. Walker et al., 1996. For a more in-depth discussion of the three levels, I urge you to read *Safeguarding Our Children: An Action Guide* by K. Dwyer and D. Osher (2000). You can download a copy from a variety of Internet websites, including www.ed.gov/admins/lead/safety/actguide/index.html.

[106] Burstyn & Stevens, 2001.

[107] Burstyn & Stevens, 2001; Dwyer & Osher, 2000; Learning First Alliance, 2001; Meehan, Hughes, & Cavell, 2003; G. M. Morrison, Furlong, D'Incau, & Morrison, 2004; Osher et al., 2006; Pellegrini, 2002; S. W. Ross & Horner, 2009; Syvertsen, Flanagan, & Stout, 2009; Warren et al., 2006.

- Provide a challenging and engaging curriculum.
- Form caring, trusting faculty–student relationships.
- Insist on genuine and equal respect—among students and faculty alike—for people of diverse backgrounds, races, and ethnic groups.
- Emphasize prosocial behaviors (e.g., sharing, helping, cooperating).
- Establish schoolwide policies and practices that foster appropriate behavior (e.g., give clear guidelines for behavior, consistently apply consequences for infractions, provide instruction in effective social interaction and problem-solving skills).
- Teach specific skills that students can use to intervene during bullying incidents.
- Provide mechanisms through which students can communicate concerns about aggression and victimization openly and without fear of reprisal.
- Involve students in school decision making.
- Establish close working relationships with community agencies and families.
- Openly discuss safety issues.

Most of these strategies should look familiar, because they've surfaced at various places throughout the book. The final strategy—openly discuss safety issues—encompasses a number of more specific strategies. For example, teachers should explain what bullying is and why it's unacceptable (see Chapter 7). Faculty members might also solicit students' input on potentially unsafe areas (perhaps an infrequently used restroom or back stairwell) that require more adult supervision. And a willingness to listen to students' concerns about troublesome and potentially dangerous classmates can provide important clues about which children and adolescents are most in need of assistance and intervention.

Intervene early for students at risk.

In our discussion of students at risk in Chapter 7, we focused largely on students at risk for *academic* failure. Yet students can be at risk for *social* failure as well. For instance, they may have few or no friends, be overtly bullied or rejected by many of their peers, or in other ways find themselves excluded from the overall social life of the school.

Perhaps 10 to 15% of students will need some sort of intervention to help them interact effectively with peers, establish good working relationships with teachers, and become bona fide members of the school community.[108] Such intervention cannot be a one-size-fits-all approach but must instead be tailored to students' particular strengths and needs. For some students it might involve social skills training. In other cases it might mean getting students actively involved in school clubs or extracurricular activities. In still others it may require ongoing, systematic efforts to encourage and reinforce productive behaviors, perhaps through functional analysis and positive behavioral support. But regardless of their nature, interventions are most effective when they occur *early* in the game—before students go too far down the path of antisocial behavior—and when they're developed and implemented by a multidisciplinary team of teachers and other professionals who bring various areas of expertise to the planning table.[109]

Provide intensive intervention for students in trouble.

For a variety of reasons, minor interventions aren't always sufficient when students are predisposed to be aggressive and violent. For instance, some students have serious mental illnesses that interfere with their ability to think rationally, cope appropriately with everyday frustrations, and control impulses. Typically, schools must work closely and collaboratively with other community agencies—perhaps mental health clinics, police and probation departments, and social services—to help students at high risk for aggression and violence.[110] Teachers are a vital component of this collaborative effort, offering insights about students' strengths and weaknesses, communicating with students' families about available services, and working with specialists to develop appropriate intervention strategies.

---

[108] Dwyer & Osher, 2000; Osher et al., 2006; H. M. Walker et al., 1996.

[109] Dryfoos, 1997; Dwyer & Osher, 2000; Osher et al., 2006.

[110] Greenberg et al., 2003; Hyman et al., 2004; Rappaport, Osher, Garrison, Anderson-Ketchmark, & Dwyer, 2003.

FIGURE 9.7 Early warning signs of possible violent behavior

Experts have identified numerous warning signs that a student may possibly be contemplating violent actions against others. Any one of them alone is unlikely to signal a violent attack, but several of them *in combination* should lead a teacher to consult with school administrators and specially trained professionals about the student(s) of concern.

Social withdrawal. Over time, a student interacts less and less frequently with teachers and with all or most peers.

Excessive feelings of isolation, rejection, or persecution. A student may directly or indirectly express the belief that he or she is friendless, disliked, or unfairly picked on; such feelings may be the result of long-term physical or psychological bullying by peers.

Rapid decline in academic performance. A student shows a dramatic change in academic performance and seems unconcerned about doing well. Cognitive and physical factors (e.g., learning disabilities, ineffective study skills, brain injury) have been ruled out as causes of the decline.

Poor coping skills. A student has little ability to deal effectively with frustration, takes the smallest affront personally, and has trouble bouncing back after minor disappointments.

Lack of anger control. A student frequently responds with uncontrolled anger to even the slightest injustice and may misdirect anger at innocent bystanders.

Apparent sense of superiority, self-centeredness, and lack of empathy. A student depicts himself or herself as "smarter" or in some other way better than peers, is preoccupied with his or her own needs, and has little regard for the needs of others. Underlying such characteristics may be low self-esteem and depression.

Lengthy grudges. A student is unforgiving of others' transgressions, even after considerable time has elapsed.

Violent themes in drawings and written work. Violence predominates in a student's artwork, stories, or journal entries, and perhaps certain individuals (e.g., a parent or particular classmate) are regularly targeted in these fantasies. (Keep in mind that *occasional* violence in writing and art isn't unusual, especially for boys.)

Intolerance of individual and group differences. A student shows intense disdain and prejudice toward people of a certain race, ethnicity, gender, sexual orientation, religion, or disability.

History of violence, aggression, and other discipline problems. A student has a long record of seriously inappropriate behavior extending over several years.

Association with violent peers. A student associates regularly with a gang or other antisocial peer group.

Inappropriate role models. A student may speak with admiration about Satan, Hitler, Osama bin Laden, or some other malevolent figure.

Excessive alcohol or drug use. A student who abuses alcohol or drugs may have reduced self-control. In some cases substance abuse signals significant mental illness.

Inappropriate access to firearms. A student has easy access to guns and ammunition and may regularly practice using them.

Threats of violence. A student has openly expressed an intent to harm someone else, perhaps in explicit terms or perhaps through ambiguous references to "something spectacular" happening at school on a particular day. ***This warning sign alone requires immediate action***.

Sources: Dwyer, Osher, & Warger, 1998; O'Toole, 2000; U.S. Secret Service National Threat Assessment Center, 2000; M. W. Watson, Andreas, Fischer, & Smith, 2005.

Teachers' frequent interactions with students also put them in an ideal position to identify those children and adolescents most in need of intensive intervention to get them back on track for academic and social success. Especially after working with a particular age-group for a period of time, teachers acquire a good sense of what characteristics are and are not normal for that age level. Teachers should also be on the lookout for the early warning signs of violence presented in Figure 9.7.

Although teachers must be ever vigilant for signals that a student may be planning to cause harm to others, it is essential to keep several points in mind. First, as I mentioned earlier, extreme violence is *very rare* in schools. Unreasonable paranoia about potential school violence will prevent a teacher from working effectively with students. Second, the great majority of students who exhibit one or a few of the warning signs listed in Figure 9.7 will *not* become violent.[111] And most importantly, a teacher must *never* use the warning signs as a reason to unfairly accuse, isolate, or punish a student.[112] These signs provide a means of getting students the help they may need, not of excluding them from the education that all children and adolescents deserve.

Take additional measures to address gang violence.

A frequent source of aggression at some schools is gang-related hostilities. Although gangs are more prevalent in low-income, inner-city schools, they are sometimes found in suburban and rural schools as well.[113]

[111] U.S. Secret Service National Threat Assessment Center, 2000.
[112] Dwyer, Osher, & Warger, 1998.

[113] Howell & Lynch, 2000; Kodluboy, 2004.

The three-level approach to combating school aggression and violence just described can go a long way toward suppressing violent gang activities, but school personnel often need to take additional measures as well. Recommended strategies include the following:[114]

- Develop, communicate, and enforce clear-cut policies regarding potential threats to other students' safety.
- Identify the specific nature and scope of gang activity in the student population.
- Forbid clothing, jewelry, and behaviors that signify membership in a particular gang (e.g., bandanas, shoelaces in gang colors, certain hand signs).[115]
- Actively mediate between-gang and within-gang disputes.

A case study at one middle school[116] illustrates just how effective the last of these strategies—mediation—can sometimes be in addressing gang-related aggression. Many students belonged to one of several gangs that seemed to "rule the school." Fights among rival gangs were common, and nongang members were frequent victims of harassment. Dress codes, counseling, and suspensions of chronic troublemakers had little impact on students' behavior. In desperation, two school counselors suggested that the school implement a mediation program, beginning with three large gangs that were responsible for most of the trouble. Interpersonal problems involving two or more gangs would be brought to a mediation team, comprised of five school faculty members and three representatives from each of the three gangs. Team members had to abide by the following rules:

1. Really try to solve the problem.
2. No name-calling or put-downs.
3. No interrupting.
4. Be as honest as possible.
5. No weapons or acts of intimidation.
6. All sessions to be confidential until an agreement is reached or mediation is called off.[117]

To lay the groundwork for productive discussions, faculty members of the mediation team met separately with each of the three gangs to establish feelings of rapport and trust, explain how the mediation process would work, and gain students' cooperation with the plan.

In the first mediation session, common grievances were aired. Students agreed that they didn't like being put down or intimated, that they worried about their physical safety, and that they all wanted one another's respect. In several additional meetings during the next two weeks, the team reached agreement that a number of behaviors would be unacceptable at school: There would be no put-downs, name calling, hateful stares, threats, shoving, or gang graffiti. After the final meeting, each gang was separately called into the conference room. Its representatives on the mediation team explained the agreement, and other members of the gang were asked to sign it. Despite some skepticism, most members of all three gangs signed the agreement.

A month later, it was clear that the process had been successful. Members of rival gangs nodded pleasantly to one another or gave one another a high-five sign as they passed in the hall. Gang members no longer felt compelled to hang out in groups for safety's sake. Members of two of the gangs were seen playing soccer together one afternoon. And there had been no gang-related fights all month.

As should be apparent from our discussion in this chapter, helping growing children and adolescents develop into successful, productive adults can occasionally be quite a challenge. But in my own experience, discovering that you actually *can* make a difference in students' lives—including the lives of some who are at risk for academic or social failure—is one of the most rewarding aspects of being a teacher.

---

[114] Kodluboy, 2004.

[115] A potential problem with this strategy is that it may violate students' civil liberties. For guidance on how to walk the line between ensuring students' safety and giving them reasonable freedom of expression, see Kodluboy, 2004; Rozalski & Yell, 2004.

[116] Sanchez & Anderson, 1990.

[117] Sanchez & Anderson, 1990, p. 54.

SUMMARY

Effective classroom management involves both prevention and intervention, as reflected in the four Mega-Ideas presented at the beginning of the chapter.

• *Effective teachers create a caring, respectful environment in which students are consistently focused on learning and on accomplishing instructional goals and objectives.* Good teachers create a setting in which students are regularly engaged in planned tasks and activities and in which few student behaviors interfere with those tasks and activities. The physical arrangement of the classroom makes a difference, but more important is a psychological environment (*classroom climate*) in which students feel safe and secure, make learning a high priority, and are willing to take risks and make mistakes. Central to such a climate are (1) teacher–student relationships that communicate genuine caring and concern for every student and (2) an overall sense of community in the classroom—a sense that teachers and students have shared goals, are mutually respectful and supportive of one another's efforts, and believe that everyone makes an important contribution to classroom learning. At the same time, teachers must take charge to some extent, establishing rules and planning age-appropriate activities to ensure that students are continually working toward instructional goals and objectives.

• *Teachers are most effective when they coordinate their efforts with colleagues, outside agencies, and parents.* Effective teachers work cooperatively with other faculty members, other institutions, and families to promote students' learning, development, and achievement. It's especially important that teachers stay in regular contact with parents and other primary caregivers, sharing information in both directions about the progress that students are making and coordinating efforts at school with those at home. Teachers may need to make an extra effort to establish productive working relationships with those parents who, on the surface, seem reluctant to become involved in their children's education.

• *Teachers must take action when students behave in ways that adversely affect their own or others' learning and achievement; interventions should be tailored to the circumstances, with* *students' development and well-being being the ultimate goal.* Despite teachers' best efforts, children and adolescents sometimes engage in behaviors that disrupt classroom learning, put one or more students' physical safety or psychological well-being in jeopardy, or violate basic moral and ethical standards. Some minor misbehaviors are usually best ignored, including those that probably won't be repeated, those that are unlikely to be imitated by other students, and those that occur only temporarily and within the context of unusual circumstances. Other minor infractions can be dealt with simply and quickly by cueing students or by talking with them privately about their counterproductive behaviors. More serious and chronic behavior problems may require instruction in self-regulation strategies, punishment, consultation with parents, or intensive interventions that combine a variety of strategies in a planned, systematic manner.

• *Minimizing aggression and violence at school requires a three-tiered approach: creating a respectful and supportive school environment, intervening early for students at risk for social failure, and providing intensive interventions for chronically aggressive students.* When certain students' behaviors seriously threaten others' sense of safety and well-being, and especially when aggression and violence are prevalent throughout the school, a three-tiered approach may be necessary. First, faculty members must coordinate their efforts in creating a schoolwide environment that makes aggression and violence unlikely—for instance, by establishing trusting teacher–student relationships, fostering a sense of caring and respect among students from diverse backgrounds, and providing mechanisms through which students can communicate their concerns without fear of reprisal. Second, faculty members must intervene early for students who are at risk for academic or social failure, providing them with the cognitive and social skills they need to be successful at school. Third, school personnel must seek intensive intervention for students who are especially prone to violence, show signs of significant mental illness, or in some other way are seriously troubled. Additional measures are sometimes needed to address incidents of aggression associated with intergang hostilities.

PRACTICE FOR YOUR LICENSURE EXAM

The Good Buddy

Mr. Schulak has wanted to be a teacher for as long as he can remember. In his many volunteer activities over the years—coaching a girls' basketball team, assisting with a Boy Scout troop, teaching Sunday school—he's discovered how much he enjoys working with children. Children obviously enjoy working with him as well. Many occasionally call or stop by his home to shoot baskets, talk over old times, or just say hello. Some of them even call him by his first name.

Now that Mr. Schulak has completed his college degree and obtained his teaching certificate, he's a first-year teacher at his hometown's junior high school. He's delighted to find that he already knows many of his students, and he spends the first few days of class renewing his friendships with them. But by the end of the week, he realizes that his classes have accomplished little of an academic nature.

The following Monday Mr. Schulak vows to get down to business. He begins each of his six class sessions by describing his instructional goals for the weeks to come; he then begins his first lesson. Unfortunately, many of his students are resistant to settling down and getting to work. They move from one seat to another, talk with friends, toss wadded-up paper "basketballs" across the room, and in general do anything *except* the academic tasks Mr. Schulak has in mind. In his second week as a new teacher, Mr. Schulak has already lost control of his classroom.

1. **Constructed-response question**

   Mr. Schulak is having considerable difficulty bringing his classes to order.

   A. Identify two critical things that Mr. Schulak has *not* done to get the school year off to a good start.

   B. Describe two strategies that Mr. Schulak might now use to remedy the situation.

2. **Multiple-choice question**

   Mr. Schulak is undoubtedly aware that good teachers show that they care about and respect their students. Which one of the following statements describes the kind of teacher–student relationship that is most likely to foster students' learning and achievement?

    a. The teacher communicates optimism about a student's potential for success and offers the support necessary for that success.

    b. The teacher spends a lot of time engaging in recreational activities with students after school and on weekends.

    c. The teacher focuses almost exclusively on what students do well and ignores or downplays what students do poorly.

    d. The teacher listens empathetically to students' concerns but reminds students that he or she alone must ultimately decide what transpires in the classroom.

Go to Chapter 9 of the Book-Specific Resources in MyEducationLab and click on "Practice for Your Licensure Exam" to answer these questions. Compare your responses with the feedback provided.

PEARSON myeducationlab

Go to the Topic "Classroom Management" in the MyEducationLab (www.myeducationlab.com) for your course, where you can:

- Find learning outcomes for "Classroom Management," along with the national standards that connect to these outcomes.
- Complete Assignments and Activities that can help you more deeply understand the chapter content.
- Apply and practice your understanding of the core teaching skills identified in the chapter with the Building Teaching Skills and Dispositions learning units.
- Examine challenging situations and cases presented in the IRIS Center Resources.
- Investigate classroom management simulations on a variety of topics in the Simulations section.
- Access video clips of CCSSO National Teachers of the Year award winners responding to the question, "Why Do I Teach?" in the Teacher Talk section.

- Check your comprehension of the content covered in the chapter by going to the Study Plan in the Book Resources for your text. Here you will be able to take a chapter quiz, receive feedback on your answers, and then access Review, Practice, and Enrichment activities to enhance your understanding of chapter content. Flash cards are also available to help you study definitions and key terms.
- Access additional Book Resources, including:
  - Focus Questions to guide your reading, Video Examples of various concepts and principles presented in the chapter, a Practice for Your Licensure Exam exercise that resembles the kinds of questions appearing on many teacher licensure tests, and Margin Note Questions that help you connect chapter content to your past experiences or current beliefs.

Chapter
10

Assessment Strategies

Bob Daemmrich Photography

CHAPTER OUTLINE

Case Study: Akeem

Using Assessment for Different Purposes
  Guiding Instructional Decision Making
  Diagnosing Learning and Performance Problems
  Determining What Students Have Learned from Instruction
  Evaluating the Quality of Instruction
  Promoting Learning

Important Qualities of Good Assessment

Conducting Informal Assessments

Designing and Giving Formal Assessments

Evaluating Students' Performance on Formal Assessments

Summarizing Students' Achievement with Grades and Portfolios

Assessing Students' Achievement and Abilities with Standardized Tests
  High-Stakes Tests and Accountability
  Using Standardized Achievement Tests Judiciously

Summary

Practice for Your Licensure Exam: Two Science Quizzes

MEGA-IDEAS TO MASTER IN THIS CHAPTER

Classroom assessments serve a variety of purposes, but in one way or another they are all likely to impact students' future learning and achievement.

Ideally, classroom assessments have four RSVP characteristics—reliability, standardization, validity, and practicality—with validity being the most important.

Informal assessments of students' verbal and nonverbal behaviors can be helpful if they show a consistent pattern over time.

Formal classroom assessments must be carefully planned and conducted to ensure that their results reflect students' accomplishments of instructional goals and objectives.

Final class grades provide only minimal quantitative information about students' academic achievement; if possible, they should be supplemented with qualitative information, perhaps in student-constructed portfolios.

Large-scale standardized tests can be helpful in estimating students' general achievement levels in particular domains, but educators should never use a single test score to make important decisions about individual students.

CASE STUDY   Akeem

Midway through the school year, 9-year-old Akeem joined Susan Gordon's third-grade class. Ms. Gordon quickly discovered that there were two sides to Akeem. On some occasions he moved constantly, perhaps running and jumping on the playground or fidgeting and tapping objects in the classroom. On other occasions he was quiet, subdued, and seemingly quite sad.

Ms. Gordon soon learned, too, that Akeem had trouble with even the simplest reading, writing, and math tasks. When asked to engage in such activities, he would often respond with angry, disruptive behaviors, in some instances overturning chairs or throwing objects across the room. When given time to pursue his own interests, however, he spent much of it drawing and building things. Encouraged, Ms. Gordon gave Akeem drawing paper, wooden blocks, Legos, and other construction materials and frequently talked with him about what he was doing. In the weeks that followed, Akeem's classroom behavior improved dramatically. And before the school year was out, he had completed several complex projects, including (1) a set of airplanes and other flying vehicles, along with an illustrated book depicting the history of flight; (2) drawings and Lego constructions showing some of the city's most notable architecture; and (3) a detailed, 28-page action-figures catalog entitled "Man after Man." A typical page in this catalog appears to the right.

Although Akeem's projects enabled him to practice and strengthen his emerging literacy skills, his scores on districtwide multiple-choice achievement tests

remained low, not only that year but in the fourth and fifth grades as well. Fortunately, Akeem and Ms. Gordon compiled a portfolio that revealed his ongoing progress in reading and writing, his exceptional talents in drawing and sculpture, and his persistence and attention to

(continued)

detail in activities about which he was passionate. Several years later, in eighth grade, Akeem was still doing well in school, as Linda Darling-Hammond and her colleagues reported in their book *Authentic Assessment in Action*:

> While academics are still not easy for him, his effort and regular attendance are reflected by his record of practically all A's on his spring report card. He continues to draw and design on his own, is connected

to his strengths and to his interests. These understandings appear to serve him well as he makes plans to attend a high school oriented toward art and design. He hopes to become an architect or an engineer.[1]

- Students' abilities can be assessed in a variety of ways. What particular forms of assessment do you see in this case study? What purpose might each of these assessments have served?

[1] Case described in *Authentic Assessment in Action: Studies of Schools and Students at Work* by L. Darling-Hammond, J. Ancess, and B. Falk, pp. 217–234 (artifact appears on p. 220, excerpt appears on p. 224). Copyright 1995, Teachers College Press. Reprinted with permission.

Perhaps you identified Ms. Gordon's in-class assignments, the districtwide achievement tests, and final report card grades as assessments of Akeem's achievement. Did you also include Akeem's portfolio on your list? And did you identify Ms. Gordon's ongoing observations of Akeem's behavior as being instances of assessment? In this chapter we see that assessment can—and *should*—come in many different forms. The following definition sums up assessment's major features:

> **Assessment** is a process of observing a sample of a student's behavior and drawing inferences about the student's knowledge and abilities.

Several parts of this definition are important to note. First, assessment is an observation of students' *behavior*. It's impossible to look inside students' heads and see what knowledge and skills lurk there. Teachers can see only how students actually perform in particular situations. Second, an assessment typically involves just a *sample* of behavior. Teachers certainly can't observe and keep track of everything their students do during the school day. Finally, assessment involves drawing *inferences* from observed behaviors to make judgments about students' overall learning and achievement—a tricky business at best, and one that requires considerable thought about which behaviors can provide a reasonably accurate estimate of what students know and can do.

Some assessments reflect **informal assessment**, in that they involve spontaneous, day-to-day observations of what students say and do in the classroom. For instance, Ms. Gordon is conducting informal assessment when she notices that Akeem is most likely to engage in disruptive behaviors when he's given assignments that require reading, writing, or math. (Her detective work here should remind you of the discussion of *functional analysis* in Chapter 9.) Observing that certain topics and activities readily engage Akeem's interest and persistence also constitutes informal assessment.

Other assessments reflect **formal assessment**, in that they are planned in advance and used for a specific purpose—perhaps to determine what students have learned from an instructional unit or whether they can apply what they've learned to real-world problems. Formal assessment is *formal* in the sense that a particular time is set aside for it, students can prepare for it ahead of time, and it's intended to yield information about particular instructional objectives or content area standards. The districtwide achievement tests that Akeem took were examples of formal assessment. So, too, was the portfolio that he and his teacher created to showcase his and talents and academic progress.

Classroom assessment practices are intertwined with virtually every other aspect of classroom functioning (look once again at Figure 8.1, p. 284). Teachers' instructional goals determine—or at least *should* determine—not only the content of classroom lessons but also the nature of tests, assignments, and other measures of student learning.[2] Conversely,

assessment Process of observing a sample of a student's behavior and drawing inferences about the student's knowledge and abilities.

informal assessment Assessment that results from a teacher's spontaneous, day-to-day observations of how students behave and perform in class.

formal assessment Preplanned, systematic attempt to ascertain what students have learned.

[2] For a good discussion of this point, see Bransford, Derry, Berliner, & Hammerness, 2005.

how students perform on ongoing assessments influences teachers' future planning, instructional methods, and classroom management strategies. For example, Akeem's classroom behavior improved considerably during his third-grade year, thanks in large part to Ms. Gordon's keen observations of the things that turned him "on" and "off" and her flexibility in allowing him to pursue the "on" things.

Good classroom assessment practices also take into account students' existing characteristics and behaviors—their attention spans, vocabulary levels, reading and writing skills, and so on (reflecting the interplay of student characteristics and assessment practices depicted in Figure 8.1). Here we see a problem with the multiple-choice achievement tests that Akeem's school district used to track students' progress in basic skills. Given Akeem's occasional hyperactivity, he would have had trouble keeping his attention focused on lengthy paper–pencil tests. And his limited reading and writing skills would affect his performance not only on tests of literacy but on measures of other content domains as well.

Both informal and formal classroom assessments are *tools* that can help teachers make informed decisions about how best to help students learn and achieve and how best to sum up what students have accomplished during the school year. The usefulness of these tools depends on how well suited they are to the circumstances in which they're being used. In this final chapter of the book, we explore the various purposes for which classroom assessments might be used, and we identify characteristics and strategies that maximize their usefulness.

• Using Assessment for Different Purposes

As noted in the earlier definition, assessment involves drawing inferences, and such inferences ideally help teachers better understand their students and choose their classroom practices accordingly. On some occasions teachers engage in **formative assessment**, determining what students know and can do *before or during instruction*, perhaps to identify students' existing strengths and interests (as Ms. Gordon does), perhaps to determine what students already know and believe about a new classroom topic (e.g., see Figure 10.1), or perhaps to assess students' progress in mastering challenging subject matter.[3] At other times teachers and other school personnel engage in **summative assessment**, conducting an assessment *after instruction* to make final judgments about what students have achieved. Summative assessments are used to determine whether students have mastered the content of a lesson or unit, what final grades to assign, which students are ready for more advanced classes, and the like.

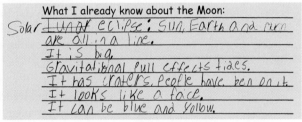

What I already know about the Moon:

Solar ~~LUNAr~~ eclipse: sun, Earth and moon are all in a line.
It is big.
Gravitational pull effects tides.
It has craters. People have been on it.
It looks like a face.
It can be blue and yellow.

FIGURE 10.1 Some assessments reflect *formative assessment,* in that they provide helpful information before or during instruction. Here 8-year-old Richard reveals his current knowledge and beliefs before a unit about the moon.

With these two basic kinds of assessment in mind, let's consider the roles that educational assessments can play in (1) guiding instructional decision making, (2) diagnosing learning and performance problems, (3) determining what students have learned at the end of instruction, (4) evaluating the quality of instruction, and, most important, (5) helping students learn *better.*

Guiding Instructional Decision Making

Both summative and formative assessments can guide instructional decision making. Any future summative assessments—annual districtwide or statewide tests of basic skills, for instance—must inevitably guide teachers somewhat as they prioritize topics and skills on which to focus. After appropriate priorities have been identified, a formative assessment can help a teacher determine a suitable point at which to begin instruction. Furthermore, conducting formative assessments throughout a lesson or unit can provide ongoing information about the appropriateness of current instructional goals and the effectiveness of

formative assessment Assessment conducted in order to facilitate instructional planning and enhance students' learning.

summative assessment Assessment conducted in order to determine students' final achievement related to a particular topic or content area.

---

[3] You may sometimes see the term *curriculum-based assessment* used in reference to ongoing, formative assessments of students' learning during instruction.

current instructional strategies. For instance, after finding that almost all students are completing assignments quickly and easily, a teacher might set instructional goals a bit higher. Alternatively, if many students struggle with material presented in class lectures, a teacher might try a different instructional approach—perhaps a more concrete, hands-on one.

Diagnosing Learning and Performance Problems

Why is Akeem having trouble learning to read? Why does Gretel misbehave every time she's given a challenging assignment? Teachers ask such questions when they suspect that certain students might learn differently from their classmates and may possibly require special educational services. Some assessment instruments are specifically designed to identify any special academic and personal needs that some students may have. Most of these instruments require explicit training in their use and so are often administered and interpreted by specialists (school psychologists, counselors, speech and language pathologists, etc.). Yet teachers' classroom assessments can provide considerable diagnostic information as well, especially when they suggest where students are going wrong and why. In other words, classroom assessments can—and ideally *should*—yield information teachers can use to help students improve.[4]

Determining What Students Have Learned from Instruction

In most instances, teachers should use formal assessments (rather than informal observations) to determine whether students have achieved instructional goals or met certain content area standards. Such information is essential when using a mastery-learning approach to instruction; it's also important for assigning final grades. School counselors and administrators, too, may use assessment results for making placement decisions, such as deciding which students are most likely to do well in advanced classes, which might need additional coursework in basic skills, and so on.

Evaluating the Quality of Instruction

Final, summative measures of student achievement are useful not only in assessing students' achievement but also in evaluating the quality of instruction. When most students perform poorly after an instructional unit, teachers should reflect not only on what students might have done differently but also on what *they themselves* might have done differently. For instance, perhaps a teacher moved too quickly through material or provided insufficient opportunities to practice critical skills. Consistently low assessment results for many or all students indicate that some modification of instruction is in order.[5]

Promoting Learning

Whenever teachers conduct formative assessments to help them develop or modify lesson plans, they're obviously using assessment to facilitate students' learning. Yet summative assessments can influence learning as well. It's likely to do so in the following ways.

Assessments influence motivation.

On average, students study class material more and learn it better when they're told they will be tested on it or in some other way held accountable for it, rather than when they're simply told to learn it.[6] Yet *how* students are assessed is as important as *whether* they're assessed. Assessments are especially effective as motivators when students are challenged to do their very best and their performance is judged on the basis of how well they've accomplished instructional goals.[7] Students' self-efficacy and attributions affect their perceptions

---

[4] Andrade & Cizek, 2010; Baek, 1994; Baxter, Elder, & Glaser, 1996; Shepard, Hammerness, Darling-Hammond, & Rust, 2005.

[5] Andrade & Cizek, 2010; Hattie, 2009; Shepard et al., 2005.

[6] Dempster, 1991; N. Frederiksen, 1984b; Halpin & Halpin, 1982.

[7] Mac Iver, Reuman, & Main, 1995; Maehr & Anderman, 1993; L. H. Meyer, Weir, McClure, & Walkey, 2008.

of the "challenge," of course. Students must believe that success on an assessment task is possible if they exert reasonable effort and use appropriate strategies.

Although regular classroom assessments can be highly motivating, they are, in and of themselves, usually *extrinsic* motivators. Thus they may direct students' attention to performance goals and undermine intrinsic motivation to learn. Assessments are especially likely to encourage performance goals when students perceive them to be an evaluation of their performance rather than a mechanism for helping them master classroom subject matter.[8]

Assessments influence students' cognitive processes as they study.

Students draw inferences about important instructional goals partly from the ways their teachers assess their learning. Thus different assessment tasks can lead them to study and learn quite differently.[9] For instance, students typically spend more time studying the things they think will be addressed on an assessment than the things they think the assessment won't cover. Furthermore, their expectations about the kinds of tasks they'll need to perform and the questions they'll need to answer influence whether they memorize isolated facts, on the one hand, or construct a meaningful, integrated body of knowledge on the other. As an example, look at the sixth-grade test about rocks shown in Figure 10.2. Part A (identifying rocks shown at the front of the room) may be assessing either basic knowledge or transfer, depending on whether the students have seen those particular rock specimens before. The rest of the test clearly focuses on memorized facts—stages of the rock cycle, definitions of terms, and so on—and might encourage students to engage in rote learning as they study for future tests. For instance, consider the last item, "Every rock has a _____." Students can answer this item correctly *only* if they have learned the material verbatim: The missing word here is "story."

Classroom assessments can also affect students' views about the nature of various academic disciplines; that is, they can influence the *epistemic beliefs* described in Chapter 4. For example, if a teacher gives quizzes that assess knowledge of specific facts (as most of the test items in Figure 10.2 do), students are apt to conclude that a discipline is just that: a collection of undisputed facts. If, instead, a teacher asks students to take a position on a controversial issue and justify that position with evidence and logic, students get a very different message: that the discipline involves an integrated set of understandings that must be supported with reasoning and are subject to change over time.

Students are more likely to study class material when they expect to be tested on it.

A. Write whether each of the rocks shown at the front of the room is a sedimentary, igneous, or metamorphic rock.
1. _____
2. _____
3. _____

B. The following are various stages of the rock cycle. Number them from 1 to 9 to indicate the order in which they occur.
____ Heat and pressure
____ Crystallization and cooling
____ Igneous rock forms
____ Magma
____ Weathering and erosion into sediments
____ Melting
____ Sedimentary rock forms
____ Pressure and cementing
____ Metamorphic rock forms

C. Write the letter for the correct definition of each rock group.
1. ____ Igneous   a. Formed when particles of eroded rock are deposited together and become cemented.
2. ____ Sedimentary   b. Produced by extreme pressures or high temperatures below the earth's surface.
3. ____ Metamorphic   c. Formed by the cooling of molten rock material from within the earth.

D. Fill in the blanks in each sentence.
1. The process of breaking down rock by the action of water, ice, plants, animals, and chemical changes is called _____ .
2. All rocks are made of _____ .
3. The hardness of rocks can be determined by a _____ .
4. Continued weathering of rock will eventually produce _____ .
5. Every rock has a _____ .

[The test continues with several additional fill-in-the-blank and short-answer items.]

FIGURE 10.2 Much of this sixth-grade geology test focuses on knowledge of specific facts and may encourage students to memorize, rather than understand, information about rocks.

Assessments can be learning experiences in and of themselves.

You can probably recall classroom assessments that actually taught you something. Perhaps an essay question asked you to compare two things you hadn't compared before and so helped you discover similarities you hadn't noticed earlier. Or perhaps a test problem asked you to apply a scientific principle to a situation you hadn't realized was related to that principle. Such tasks not only assessed what you learned; they also *helped* you learn.

---

[8] F. Danner, 2008; Grolnick & Ryan, 1987; Paris & Turner, 1994.

[9] N. Frederiksen, 1984b; Lundeberg & Fox, 1991; Shepard, 2000; Shepard et al., 2005.

In general, the very process of completing an assessment on class material helps students learn and remember the material better, especially if the assessment tasks ask students to elaborate on the material in some way.[10] But two qualifications are important to note here. First, an assessment helps students learn only the material it specifically addresses. Second, when teachers present *incorrect* information on an assessment (as they often do in true–false and multiple-choice questions), students may eventually remember that misinformation as being true rather than false. Fortunately, such misinformation doesn't appear to have a *major* impact on students' later understandings.[11]

Assessments can provide feedback about learning progress.

Regular classroom assessments can give students valuable feedback about which things they have and haven't mastered. But simply knowing one's final score on a test or assignment (e.g., knowing the percentage of items correctly answered) isn't terribly helpful. To facilitate students' learning—and ultimately to enhance their self-efficacy for mastering the subject matter—assessment results must include concrete information about where students have succeeded, where they've had difficulty, and how they might improve.[12]

Assessments can encourage intrinsic motivation and self-regulation if students play an active role in the assessment process.

As noted earlier, classroom assessments are typically extrinsic motivators that provide only an externally imposed reason for learning school subject matter. Yet students learn more effectively when they're *intrinsically* motivated, and they're more likely to be intrinsically motivated if they have some sense of autonomy and self-determination about classroom activities (see Chapter 6). Furthermore, if students are to become self-regulating learners, they must acquire skills in self-monitoring and self-evaluation (see Chapter 4). For such reasons, students should be regular and active participants in the assessment of their own learning and performance (more on this point later in the chapter). Ultimately, teachers should think of assessment as something they do *with* students rather than *to* them.[13]

The Classroom Strategies box "Using Classroom Assessments to Promote Learning and Achievement" presents several examples of how teachers might use assignments and tests to encourage effective cognitive processes, foster self-regulation skills, and enhance students' learning and motivation.

Observe 8-year-old Keenan and her teacher reflect on Keenan's writing progress in the "Portfolio" video in Chapter 10 of the Book-Specific Resources in MyEducationLab.

• Important Qualities of Good Assessment

As a student, have you ever been assessed in a way you thought was unfair? If so, *why* was it unfair? For example:

1. Did the teacher evaluate students' responses inconsistently?
2. Were some students assessed under more favorable conditions than others?
3. Was the assessment a poor measure of what you had learned?
4. Was the assessment so time consuming that eventually you no longer cared how well you performed?

In light of your experiences, what characteristics seem to be essential for a good classroom assessment instrument?

My four numbered questions reflect, respectively, four *RSVP* characteristics of good classroom assessment: reliability, standardization, validity, and practicality. The following principles reflect these characteristics.

A quick review of a concept presented in Chapter 2: What purpose might *RSVP* serve in helping you remember the four important qualities of good assessment? (Compare your response to this question with the response presented in Chapter 10 of the Book-Specific Resources in MyEducationLab.)

---

[10] Dempster, 1997; Fall, Webb, & Chudowsky, 2000; Foos & Fisher, 1988; C. I. Johnson & Mayer, 2009; Pashler, Rohrer, Cepeda, & Carpenter, 2007; Roediger & Karpicke, 2006.

[11] A. S. Brown, Schilling, & Hockensmith, 1999; N. Frederiksen, 1984b; Roediger & Karpicke, 2006; Roediger & Marsh, 2005.

[12] Baron, 1987; Hattie, 2009; Krampen, 1987; Shute, 2008.

[13] For example, see Covington, 1992; Paris & Ayres, 1994; Vye et al., 1998.

CLASSROOM STRATEGIES Using Classroom Assessments to Promote Learning and Achievement

- Give a formal or informal pretest to determine where to begin instruction.

  When beginning a new unit on cultural geography, a teacher gives a pretest designed to identify misconceptions that students might have about various cultural groups—misconceptions she can then address during instruction.

- Choose or develop an assessment instrument that reflects the actual knowledge and skills you want students to achieve.

  While planning how to assess students' achievement, a teacher initially decides to use questions from the test-item manual that accompanies the class textbook. When he looks more closely at those test items, however, he discovers that they measure only knowledge of isolated facts. Instead, he develops several assessment tasks that better reflect his primary instructional goal: Students should be able to apply what they've learned to real-world problems.

- Construct assessment instruments that reflect how you want students to think about and cognitively process information as they study.

  A teacher tells his students, "As you study for next week's vocabulary quiz, remember that the questions will ask you to put each definition in your own words and give your own example to show what a word means."

- Use an assessment task as a learning experience in and of itself.

  A high school science teacher has students collect samples of the local drinking water, test them for bacterial content, and write lab reports describing their findings. She is assessing her students' ability to use procedures she has taught them, but she also hopes they will discover the importance of protecting the community's natural resources.

- Use an assessment to give students specific feedback about what they have and have not mastered.

  As a teacher grades students' persuasive essays, he writes numerous notes in the margins to indicate places where students have analyzed a situation logically or illogically, identified a relevant or irrelevant example, proposed an appropriate or inappropriate solution, and so on.

- Provide criteria that students can use to evaluate their *own* performance.

  The teacher of a Foods and Nutrition class gives her students a checklist of qualities to look for in the pies they've baked.

A good assessment is reliable.

The **reliability** of an assessment instrument or procedure is the extent to which it yields consistent information about the knowledge, skills, or characteristics being assessed. To get a sense of what reliability involves, try the following exercise.

SEE FOR YOURSELF Fowl Play

Here is a sequence of events in the life of biology teacher Ms. Fowler:

- **Monday.** After completing a lesson on the bone structures of birds and dinosaurs, Ms. Fowler asks her students to write an essay explaining why many scientists believe that birds are descended from dinosaurs. After school she tosses the pile of essays on the back seat of her cluttered '57 Chevy.
- **Tuesday.** Ms. Fowler looks high and low for the essays both at home and in her classroom, but she can't find them anywhere.
- **Wednesday.** Because Ms. Fowler wants to use the students' essays to determine what they've learned, she asks the class to write the same essay a second time.
- **Thursday.** Ms. Fowler discovers Monday's essays on the back seat of her Chevy.
- **Friday.** Ms. Fowler grades both sets of essays. She is surprised to find little consistency between them: Students who wrote the best essays on Monday didn't necessarily do well on Wednesday, and some of Monday's poorest performers did quite well on Wednesday.

Which results should Ms. Fowler use, Monday's or Wednesday's?

reliability Extent to which an assessment instrument yields consistent information about the knowledge, skills, or characteristics being assessed.

When teachers assess learning and achievement, they must be confident that their assessment results will be essentially the same regardless of whether they give the assessment Monday or Wednesday, whether the weather is sunny or rainy, and whether they evaluate students' responses while in a good mood or a foul frame of mind. Ms. Fowler's assessment instrument has poor reliability, because the results it yields are completely different from one day to another. So which day's results should she use? I've asked you a trick question, because we have no way of knowing which set is more accurate.

Any single assessment instrument will rarely yield *exactly* the same results for the same student on two different occasions, even if the knowledge or ability being assessed remains the same. Many temporary conditions unrelated to the knowledge or ability being measured are apt to affect students' performance and almost inevitably lead to some fluctuation in assessment results. For instance, the inconsistencies in Ms. Fowler's two sets of student essays might have been due to temporary factors such as these:

- **Day-to-day changes in students**—for example, changes in health, motivation, mood, and energy level

    The 24-hour Netherlands flu was making the rounds in Ms. Fowler's classroom.

- **Variations in the physical environment**—for example, variations in room temperature, noise level, and outside distractions

    On Monday students who sat by the window in Ms. Fowler's classroom enjoyed peace and quiet, but on Wednesday they wrote their essays while noisy construction machinery tore up the pavement outside.

- **Variations in administration of the assessment**—for example, variations in instructions, timing, and the teacher's responses to students' questions

    On Monday a few students wrote the essay after school because they had attended a dress rehearsal for the school play during class time. Ms. Fowler explained the task more clearly for them than she had during class, and she gave them as much time as they needed to finish. On Wednesday a different group of students had to write the essay after school because of an across-town band concert during class time. Ms. Fowler explained the task very hurriedly and collected the essays before students had finished.

- **Characteristics of the assessment instrument**—for example, the length, clarity, and difficulty of tasks (e.g., ambiguous and very difficult tasks increase students' tendency to guess randomly)

    The essay topic, "Explain why many scientists believe that birds are descended from dinosaurs," was a vague one that students interpreted differently from one day to the next.

- **Subjectivity in scoring**—for example, judgments made on the basis of vague, imprecise criteria

    Ms. Fowler graded both sets of essays while watching *Chainsaw Murders at Central High* on television Friday night. She gave higher scores during kissing scenes, lower scores during stalking scenes.

When drawing conclusions about students' learning and achievement, teachers must be confident that the information on which they're basing their conclusions hasn't been overly distorted by temporary, irrelevant factors. Several strategies can increase the likelihood that an assessment yields reliable results:

- Include a variety of tasks, and look for consistency in students' performance on different tasks.
- Define each task clearly enough that students know exactly what they're being asked to do.
- Identify specific, concrete criteria with which to evaluate students' performance.
- Try not to let expectations for students' performance influence judgments of *actual* performance.
- Avoid assessing students' achievement when they're unlikely to give their best performance—for instance, when they're sick.
- Administer the assessment in similar ways and under similar conditions for all students.

The last of these recommendations suggests that assessment procedures be *standardized*—the second of the RSVP characteristics.

Bob Daemmrich Photography

Informal observations of student performance can yield valuable information about how students are progressing. But teachers should draw firm conclusions about students' achievement only when they know their assessment methods are *reliable*, yielding consistent results about particular students time after time.

A good assessment is standardized for most students.

The term **standardization** refers to the extent to which an assessment involves similar content and format and is administered and scored in the same way for everyone. In most situations students should all get the same instructions, perform identical or similar tasks, have the same time limits, and work under the same constraints. Furthermore, all students' responses should be scored using the same criteria. For example, unless there are extenuating circumstances, a teacher shouldn't use tougher standards for one student than for another.

Many tests constructed and published by large-scale testing companies are called *standardized tests*. This label indicates that the tests have explicit procedures for administration and scoring that are consistently applied wherever the tests are used. (We'll look at standardized tests more closely later in the chapter.) Yet standardization is important in teachers' self-constructed classroom assessments as well. Standardization increases the probability that any single assessment task will yield consistent results on different occasions—something that Ms. Fowler's essay question doesn't do.

Equity is an additional consideration. Under most circumstances, it's only fair to ask all students to be evaluated under similar conditions. We find an exception in the assessment of students with special educational needs. In the United States the Individuals with Disabilities Education Act (IDEA) mandates that schools make appropriate accommodations for students with physical, mental, social, or emotional disabilities. This mandate applies not only to instructional practices but to assessment practices as well. Specific modifications to assessment instruments and procedures must, of course, be tailored to students' particular disabilities. Following are examples:[14]

- Read paper–pencil test questions to students with limited reading skills (e.g., to students with dyslexia).
- Divide a lengthy assessment task into several shorter tasks for students with a limited attention span (e.g., for students with ADHD).
- Administer an assessment in a quiet room with few distractions (e.g., for students with learning disabilities or ADHD).
- Give more time or frequent breaks during the assessment (e.g., for students who tire easily due to a chronic illness or traumatic brain injury).
- Construct individualized assessment instruments if some students are working toward instructional goals different from those of their classmates (e.g., as may often be the case for students with intellectual disabilities).

A good assessment has validity for its purpose.

Earlier you learned about *reliability*. Let's see whether you can apply (transfer) your understanding of reliability in the following exercise.

> **?** Is this description of how standardized tests are administered consistent with your own experiences taking such tests?

SEE FOR YOURSELF FTOI

I've developed a new test called the FTOI: the Fathead Test of Intelligence. It consists of only a tape measure and a *table of norms* that shows how children and adults of various ages typically perform on the test. Administration of the FTOI is quick and easy. You simply measure a person's head circumference just above the eyebrows (firmly but not too tightly) and compare your measure against the average head circumference for the person's age-group. People with large heads (comparatively speaking) get high IQ scores. People with smaller heads get low scores.

Does the FTOI have high reliability? Answer the question before you read further.

---

[14] American Educational Research Association, American Psychological Association, & National Council on Measurement in Education, 1999; Sireci, Scarpati, & Li, 2005.

standardization Extent to which assessments involve similar content and format and are administered and scored similarly for everyone.

No matter how often you measure a person's head, you're going to get similar scores from one time to the next. Fatheads will always be fatheads, and pinheads will always be pinheads. So the answer to my question is *yes:* The FTOI has high reliability because it yields consistent results. If you answered *no,* you were probably thinking that the FTOI doesn't really measure intelligence. But that's a problem with the FTOI's *validity,* not its reliability.

The **validity** of an assessment is the extent to which it measures what it's intended to measure and allows us to draw appropriate inferences about the characteristic or ability in question. Does the FTOI measure intelligence? Are scores on a standardized, multiple-choice achievement test a good indication of whether students have mastered basic skills in reading and writing? Does students' performance at a school concert reflect what they've achieved in their instrumental music class? When assessments don't fulfill their purposes—when they're poor measures of students' knowledge and abilities—we have a validity problem.

As noted earlier, numerous irrelevant factors are apt to influence how well students perform in assessment situations. Some of these—students' health, classroom distractions, inconsistencies in scoring, and so on—are temporary conditions that lead to fluctuation in assessment results from one time to the next and thereby lower reliability. But other irrelevant factors—perhaps reading ability or chronic test anxiety—are more stable, and so their effects on assessment results may be relatively constant. For example, if Akeem has poor reading skills, he may get consistently low scores on paper–pencil, multiple-choice achievement tests regardless of how much he has actually achieved in science, math, or social studies. When assessment results continue to be affected by the same irrelevant variables, the *validity* of the assessments is in doubt.

Psychologists distinguish among different kinds of validity, which are important in different situations. In some cases we might be interested in *predictive validity.* That is, we might want to know how well scores on an assessment instrument predict performance in some future activity—for example, how well IQ scores predict students' future classroom performance. At other times we might be interested in *construct validity.* That is, we might want to know whether an assessment instrument measures a particular human trait or characteristic—for example, whether my FTOI test actually measures intelligence, or whether an alleged measure of a personality trait actually measures personality. In general, however, classroom teachers should be most concerned about **content validity**. That is, they need to be sure their assessment questions and tasks are a representative sample of the overall body of knowledge and skills—the *content domain*—they are assessing.

As an illustration, Table 10.1 revisits North Carolina's competency goals for English Language Arts (yellow column) and more specific student goals and objectives (pink column) that I presented in Chapter 8. The table's fifth (right-most) column offers examples of formal assessment strategies that might address those standards, and the instructional strategies in the fourth column provide opportunities for informal assessment. Some strategies in the table—for instance, having students write essays or create concept maps—involve **paper–pencil assessment**, whereby teachers present questions to answer, topics to address, or problems to solve, and students respond on paper. But other examples—for instance, having students respond orally to questions or act out a story—reflect **performance assessment**, in which students show what they've learned by actively *doing* something rather than simply writing about it. As we'll discover later, paper–pencil and performance assessment tasks tend to be useful in different situations.

In an assessment instrument with high content validity, questions and tasks reflect all parts of the content domain in appropriate proportions and require the particular behaviors and skills identified in instructional goals or objectives. How can a teacher make sure that a test or assignment is truly *representative* of the content domain being assessed? The most widely recommended strategy is to construct a blueprint that identifies the specific things a teacher wants to assess and the proportion of questions or tasks that should address each one. This blueprint frequently takes the form of a **table of specifications**, a two-way grid that indicates both what topics should be covered and what students should be able to *do* with each topic. Each cell of the grid indicates the relative importance of each topic–behavior combination, perhaps as a particular number or percentage of tasks or test items to be included in the overall assessment. Figure 10.3 on page 373 shows two examples, one for a paper–pencil test on addition and a second for a combined paper–pencil and performance

validity Extent to which an assessment instrument actually measures what it is intended to measure and allows appropriate inferences about the characteristic or ability in question.

content validity Extent to which an assessment includes a representative sample of tasks within the domain being assessed.

paper–pencil assessment Assessment in which students provide written responses to written items.

performance assessment Assessment in which students demonstrate their knowledge and skills in a nonwritten fashion.

table of specifications Two-way grid indicating the topics to be covered in an assessment and the things students should be able to do with those topics.

DEVELOPMENTAL TRENDS

TABLE 10.1 Examples of How You Might Align Classroom Assessments with State Standards and Classroom Goals, Objectives, and Instruction at Different Grade Levels

Grade Level	Examples of North Carolina's Competency Goals for English Language Arts	Examples of More Specific Classroom Goals/ Objectives	Examples of Relevant Instructional Strategies	Examples of Formal Assessments
 Grade 1	Read and comprehend both fiction and nonfiction text appropriate for grade one using: • Prior knowledge • Summary • Questions • Graphic organizers (Competency Goal 2.03)	Use prior knowledge to draw correct inferences from a story in which the author has omitted important information.	Read high-interest stories, stopping frequently to ask questions that require students to go beyond the text itself (e.g., to speculate about what a character might be feeling).	Ask students to read a simple story; alternatively, read them the story. Ask each student to draw inferences about certain missing details—for instance, "If [a character] was planting a garden, what time of year must it have been?" and "Why do you think [a character] was sad?"
	Respond and elaborate in answering what, when, where, and how questions. (Competency Goal 2.07)	Identify main characters, setting, and general plot line in a short story.	Have students create props for and act out a story they have recently read.	Meet with students in small groups and ask each group member to describe a story in his or her own words. To probe for understanding of specific story elements, follow up with questions such as "What happened next?" and "Why did [a character] do that?"
 Grade 4	Interact with the text before, during, and after reading, listening, and viewing by: • Setting a purpose using prior knowledge and text information • Making predictions • Formulating questions • Locating relevant information • Making connections with previous experiences, information, and ideas (Competency Goal 2.02)	Make predictions about how a novel's plot might unfold.	As a reading group discusses Carl Hiaasen's *Hoot,* ask students to speculate about how the plot might progress and to identify clues in the text that support their predictions.	After students have read the first few chapters of Natalie Babbitt's *Tuck Everlasting,* ask them to write an essay speculating on problems that the Tucks' immortality might create for them.
	Make inferences, draw conclusions, make generalizations, and support by referencing the text. (Competency Goal 2.05)	Identify cause–and–effect relationships in assigned readings in a history textbook.	When students are reading their history textbook, ask *why* questions that encourage cause–and–effect connections (e.g., "Why did Columbus's crew want to return home after several weeks on the open sea?").	Ask students to create concept maps that show cause–and–effect relationships among the actions of Native Americans and those of early European settlers during the 1600s.
 Grade 7	Respond to informational materials that are read, heard, and/or viewed by: • Monitoring comprehension for understanding of what is read, heard, and/or viewed • Analyzing the characteristics of informational works • Summarizing information • Determining the importance of information • Making connections to related topics/information • Drawing inferences and/or conclusions • Generating questions (Competency Goal 2.01)	Use the organizational structure of a science textbook to enhance understanding and memory of its contents.	Before students read a chapter in their science textbook, have them use its headings and subheadings to (1) create a general outline of the chapter and (2) generate questions they hope to answer as they read the chapter. Then, for homework, ask them to read and take notes on the chapter, using the outline and self-questions as guides for note taking.	Ask students to write a two-page summary of a chapter in their science book, using chapter headings and subheadings to organize their discussion.

(continued)

TABLE 10.1 *Continued*

Grade Level	Examples of North Carolina's Competency Goals for English Language Arts	Examples of More Specific Classroom Goals/ Objectives	Examples of Relevant Instructional Strategies	Examples of Formal Assessments
Grade 7 (continued)	Analyze the purpose of the author or creator by: • Monitoring comprehension for understanding of what is read, heard, and/or viewed • Examining any bias, apparent or hidden messages, emotional factors, and/or propaganda techniques • Exploring and evaluating the underlying assumptions of the author/creator (portion of Competency Goal 4.01)	Identify persuasive techniques used in advertisements for commercial products in magazines and online websites.	Give students an advertisement for a self-improvement product (e.g., a diet pill or exercise equipment); have them work in small cooperative learning groups to (1) identify the advertiser's motives and (2) evaluate the quality of evidence for the product's effectiveness.	Have students examine an Internet website that promotes an allegedly health-promoting product. Ask them to identify, either orally or in writing, possible flaws in the evidence and logic the website uses to convince people to purchase the product.
Grade 11	Demonstrate the ability to read, listen to, and view a variety of increasingly complex print and non-print informational texts appropriate to grade level and course literary focus, by: • Selecting, monitoring, and modifying as necessary reading strategies appropriate to readers' purpose . . . • Making inferences, predicting, and drawing conclusions based on text • Identifying and analyzing personal, social, historical or cultural influences, contexts, or biases (portions of Competency Goal 2.03 for English III)	Identify authors' political and cultural biases in their descriptions of current events.	Ask students to identify the unstated assumptions underlying two news magazines' depictions of the same event (e.g., an assumption that one group is good or right and another is bad or wrong).	Give students a magazine article describing a recent event in the national or international news. Ask them to underline five sentences that reveal the author's cultural and/or political biases and to describe those biases in a two-page essay.
	Develop thematic connections among works by: • Connecting themes that occur across genres or works from different time periods • Using specific references to validate connections • Examining how representative elements such as mood, tone, and style impact the development of a theme (Competency Goal 4.02 for English III)	Identify examples of racism, sexism, and classism revealed in literature from different time periods.	Conduct small-group discussions in which students compare prevailing attitudes toward women in Jane Austen's *Pride and Prejudice* and Zora Neale Hurston's *Their Eyes Were Watching God.*	Following the cooperative learning activity, have students write an essay in which they describe how the characters Elizabeth Bennet (*Pride and Prejudice*) and Janie Crawford (*Their Eyes Were Watching God)* ultimately dealt with certain sexist attitudes and practices of their times.

Source: Competency Goals (second column) are from a website maintained by North Carolina's Department of Public Instruction and are provided with permission from the Public Schools of North Carolina. Standards are current as of October 19, 2010, from www.dpi.state.nc.us/curriculum/languagearts/scos/. Please note that North Carolina is currently revising its Standard Course of Study; thus, the Competency Goals may change within the next few years.

assessment on simple machines. After creating a table of specifications, a teacher can develop paper–pencil items or performance tasks that reflect both the topics and the behaviors that need to be assessed and have some confidence that the assessment instrument has content validity for the domain it's intended to represent.

High content validity is *essential* whenever teachers give a test or assignment for summative assessment purposes—that is, to determine what students have ultimately learned from instruction. A teacher maximizes content validity when the tasks students are asked to perform are as similar as possible to the things students should ultimately be able to do. In other words, any assessment used in summative assessment should reflect instructional goals and objectives.

Topic	Behaviors: Computation using number line	Rapid recall of sum	Regrouping ("carrying")	Estimation	Application to word problems
Single digits	2	6			4
Multiples of 10 and 100		2			2
Two-digit numbers			2	2	3
Three-digit numbers			2	2	3

Topic	Behaviors: Make simple drawing of machine	Describe work that machine performs	Recognize examples among common objects	Solve problems by using machine
Inclined plane	5%	5%	5%	5%
Wedge	5%	5%	5%	5%
Lever	5%	5%	5%	5%
Wheel and axle	5%	5%	5%	5%
Pulley	5%	5%	5%	5%

FIGURE 10.3 Two examples of a table of specifications. The table on the left provides specifications for a 30-item paper–pencil test on addition. It assigns different weights (different numbers of items) to different topic–behavior combinations, with some combinations intentionally not being assessed at all. The table on the right provides specifications for a combination paper–pencil and performance assessment on simple machines. It assigns equal importance (the same percentage of points) to each topic–behavior combination.

A good assessment is practical.

The last of the four RSVP characteristics is **practicality**, the extent to which assessment instruments and procedures are relatively easy to use.[15] Practicality encompasses issues such as these:

- How much time will it take to develop the questions and/or tasks to be administered?
- Can the assessment be administered to many students at once, or is one-on-one administration required?
- Are expensive materials involved?
- How much time will the assessment take away from instructional activities?
- How quickly and easily can students' performance be evaluated?

There's often a trade-off between practicality and such other characteristics as validity and reliability. For example, a true–false test for a unit on tennis would be easy to construct and administer, but a performance assessment in which students actually demonstrate their tennis skills—even though it takes more time and energy—would undoubtedly be a more valid measure of how well students have mastered the game.

The four RSVP characteristics are summarized in Table 10.2. Of these, *validity is the most important.* Teachers must use assessment techniques that validly assess students' accomplishment of instructional goals and objectives. Yet it's important to note that *reliability is a necessary condition for validity.* Assessments can yield valid results only when they also yield consistent results—results that are only minimally affected by variations in administration, subjectivity in scoring, and so on. Reliability doesn't guarantee validity, however, as the earlier FTOI exercise illustrates. Standardization enhances the reliability of assessment results and so indirectly enhances validity. Practicality should be a consideration only when validity, reliability, and standardization aren't seriously jeopardized.

Now that we've examined desirable characteristics of any classroom assessment, we're in a good position to explore both informal and formal classroom assessment strategies. As we go along, we'll consider the goals and objectives for which various assessment strategies might be most appropriate and the RSVP characteristics of different approaches.

[15] Many psychologists use the term *usability*, but I think *practicality* better communicates the idea.

practicality Extent to which an assessment instrument or procedure is inexpensive and easy to use and takes only a small amount of time to administer and score.

TABLE 10.2 The RSVP Characteristics of Good Assessment

Characteristic	Definition	Questions to Consider
Reliability	The extent to which an assessment instrument or procedure yields consistent results for each student	• How much are students' scores affected by temporary conditions unrelated to the characteristic being measured? • Do different people score students' performance similarly? • Do different parts of a single assessment instrument lead to similar conclusions about a student's achievement?
Standardization	The extent to which an assessment instrument or procedure is similar for all students	• Are all students assessed on identical or similar content? • Do all students have the same types of tasks to perform? • Are instructions the same for everyone? • Do all students have similar time constraints? • Is everyone's performance evaluated using the same criteria?
Validity	The extent to which an assessment instrument or procedure measures what it is intended to measure and enables appropriate inferences to be made	• Does the assessment tap into a representative sample of the content domain being assessed *(content validity)*? • Do students' scores predict their later success in a domain *(predictive validity)*? • Does the instrument accurately measure a particular characteristic or trait *(construct validity)*?
Practicality	The extent to which an assessment instrument or procedure is easy and inexpensive to use	• How much class time does the assessment take? • How quickly and easily can students' responses be scored? • Is special training required to administer or score the assessment? • Does the assessment require specialized materials that must be purchased?

• Conducting Informal Assessments

Informal assessments—observing the many little things students say and do over the course of the school day—are helpful in several ways.[16] First and foremost, they provide continuing feedback about the effectiveness of current instructional tasks and activities. Second, they are easily adjusted at a moment's notice. For example, when students express misconceptions about a topic, a teacher's follow-up questions can probe their beliefs and reasoning processes. Third, informal assessments provide information that may either support or call into question the results obtained from more formal assessment tasks. Finally, ongoing observations of students' behaviors provide clues about social, emotional, and motivational factors affecting their classroom performance and may often be the only practical means of assessing such instructional goals as "shows courtesy" or "enjoys reading." The portfolio excerpt shown in Figure 10.4 describes 6-year-old Meghan's progress in social skills and work habits—areas that can probably be assessed only through informal observations.

Several general strategies enhance the usefulness of informal assessments.

Observe both verbal and nonverbal behaviors.

Teachers can learn a lot from what students say and do during the school day. Following are examples of informal assessment strategies:

• Ask questions during a lesson (e.g., see the Classroom Strategies box "Asking Questions to Promote and Assess Learning" on p. 298 of Chapter 8).
• Listen to what and how much students contribute to whole-class and small-group discussions; make note of the kinds of questions they ask.
• Observe how quickly and proficiently students perform various physical tasks.
• Identify the kinds of activities in which students engage voluntarily (as Ms. Gordon did in the opening case study).
• Watch for body language that might reflect students' emotional reactions to classroom tasks.

---

[16] Airasian, 1994; Stiggins, 2008.

- Look at the relative frequency of on-task and off-task behaviors; also look for patterns in *when* students are off task.
- Observe students' interactions with peers in class, at lunch, and on the playground.

By observing both verbal and nonverbal behaviors, teachers can acquire a lot of information not only about students' knowledge and misconceptions but also about students' study strategies, self-regulation skills, sense of self, interests and priorities, feelings about classroom subject matter, and attributions for success and failure.

Ask yourself whether your existing beliefs and expectations might be biasing your judgments.

Let's return to a principle presented in Chapter 2: *Prior knowledge and beliefs affect new learning.* This principle applies to teachers as well as to students. Like all human beings, teachers impose meanings on the things they see and hear, and those meanings are influenced by the things they already know or believe to be true. Teachers' existing beliefs about particular students, as well as their expectations for students' performance, inevitably affect teachers' assessments of students' behaviors.[17]

One common source of bias in teachers' informal assessments of student performance is their existing beliefs about students of different ethnic groups, genders, and socioeconomic groups. An experiment with college students[18] provides an example. Students were told that they were participating in a study on teacher evaluation methods and then shown a video of a fourth grader named Hannah. Two versions of the video gave differing impressions about Hannah's socioeconomic status. Her clothing, the kind of playground on which she played, and information about her parents' occupations indirectly conveyed to some students that she was from a high socioeconomic background and to others that she was from a low socioeconomic background. All students watched Hannah taking an oral achievement test (one on which she performed at grade level) and were asked to rate her on several characteristics. Students who had been led to believe that Hannah came from a wealthy family rated her ability well above grade level, whereas students believing that she came from a poor family evaluated her as being below grade level. The two groups of students also rated Hannah's work habits, motivation, social skills, and general maturity differently.

Keep a written record of your observations.

Let's revisit another principle presented in Chapter 2: *Long-term memory isn't necessarily forever.* Teachers' memories of students' classroom behaviors can probably never be totally accurate, dependable records of what students have actually said and done. As normal human beings, teachers are apt to remember some student behaviors but not others. When teachers must depend heavily on informal in-class observations of students' performance—and this will often be the case when working with young children who have limited reading and writing skills—they should keep ongoing, written records of what they see students do and what they hear students say.[19]

Don't take any single observation too seriously; instead, look for a pattern over time.

The greatest strength of informal assessment is its practicality. It typically involves little if any teacher time either beforehand or after the fact (except for keeping written records of

Group Participation and Work Habits

☺ **Demonstrates attentiveness as a listener through body language or facial expressions-** Meghan is still developing this skill. Sometimes it is difficult for her to listen when she is sitting near her friends.

☺ **Follows directions.**

☺ **Enters ongoing discussion on the subject.** -Sometimes needs to be encouraged to share her ideas.

☺ **Makes relevant contributions to ongoing activities.**

☺ **Completes assigned activities.** -Meghan is very responsible about her assignments.

☺ **Shows courtesy in conversations and discussions by waiting for turn to speak.**

Meghan enjoys lunch with her friends.

FIGURE 10.4 This page from 6-year-old Meghan's kindergarten portfolio shows her teacher's assessment of her work habits and social skills.

[17] Farwell & Weiner, 1996; Hattie, 2009; Ritts, Patterson, & Tubbs, 1992; Stiggins, 2008.

[18] Darley & Gross, 1983.

[19] M. D. Miller, Linn, & Gronlund, 2009; Stiggins, 2008.

Many social and emotional factors affecting students' classroom learning—for instance, how comfortable students appear to be in public speaking activities—can best be assessed through informal observations. Rather than drawing conclusions from a single event, however, teachers should look for consistent patterns over time.

observations). Furthermore, it's flexible, in that teachers can adapt their assessment procedures on the spur of the moment, altering them as circumstances change.

Despite the practicality of informal assessment, its other RSVP characteristics are often questionable. For one thing, children and adolescents can behave inconsistently from one day to the next, or even within a single day or class period. Such inconsistency calls the reliability of informal assessments into question. A teacher who asks Muhammad a question in class may happen to ask him the *only* question for which he doesn't know the answer. A teacher who sees Naomi off task during an activity may happen to look at her during the *only* time she's off task. Furthermore, informal assessments are rarely, if ever, standardized for all students. Teachers ask different questions of different students, and they're apt to observe each student's behavior in different contexts. Hence such assessments will definitely *not* yield the same kinds of information for all students.

Even when teachers see consistency in students' behavior over time, they don't always get accurate information about what students have learned. In other words, validity may be a problem. For instance, Tom may intentionally answer questions incorrectly so that he doesn't come across as a know-it-all, and Margot may be reluctant to say anything because of a chronic stuttering problem. In general, when teachers use in-class questions to assess students' learning, they must be aware that some students (especially females and students from ethnic minority groups) will be less eager to respond than others.[20]

When teachers use informal assessment to draw conclusions about what students know and can do, then, they should base their conclusions on many observations over a long period. Furthermore, they should treat any conclusions only as *hypotheses* that they must either confirm or disconfirm through other means. In the end, most teachers rely more heavily on formal assessment techniques to determine whether students have achieved instructional goals and objectives.

• Designing and Giving Formal Assessments

As we've seen, classroom assessments not only assess students' learning but also *have an impact on* students' learning. Furthermore, the conclusions teachers draw from assessment results—conclusions that affect final grades and decisions about promotion and graduation—can have a significant effect on students' future educational and career plans. Accordingly, teachers must take their formal assessments very seriously, planning and designing them carefully, administering them under optimal conditions for student performance, and scoring them reliably and equitably.

Following are a number of recommendations that should increase the RSVP characteristics of formal classroom assessments.

Get as much information as possible within reasonable time limits.

On average, longer assessment instruments have greater validity and reliability. To see why this might be so, try the next exercise.

SEE FOR YOURSELF Quick Quiz

The following multiple-choice quiz is designed to assess what you learned about motivation in Chapter 6. No peeking at the answers until you've responded to both items!

1. Which one of the following alternatives best illustrates *situated motivation*?
   a. Alexander has been interested in air travel and aerodynamics since he was a toddler, and he can often be seen sketching airplanes during his free time in class.

(continued)

---

[20] Altermatt, Jovanovic, & Perry, 1998; Rogoff, 2003; Sadker & Sadker, 1994; also see the Cultural Considerations box "Cultural and Ethnic Differences in Verbal Interaction" in Chapter 8.

> b. When Barbara gets a lower grade on an assignment than she had anticipated, she complains to her friends, "I deserved a much higher grade. Mr. Smith obviously doesn't like me very much."
>
> c. Colby is confident he'll do well on an upcoming history test because he's done well on other history tests throughout the semester.
>
> d. Although Donna has never been terribly interested in being physically fit, she eagerly learns an aerobic exercise routine that her teacher has set to some of her favorite rap music.
>
> 2. Which one of the following alternatives is the best example of *cognitive dissonance?*
>
>   a. Alicia says to herself, "I don't really like math very much, but I'm taking it because it's important for getting into a good college."
>
>   b. Bob is certain that metal always sinks, and so he is puzzled when he sees a large metal battleship floating in the harbor.
>
>   c. Carly gets so anxious during an important test that she can hardly concentrate on the test items.
>
>   d. David gets really angry when he reads about the mass murders and other atrocities that the Nazis committed during World War II.

Now score your quiz. The correct answers are *d* and *b* for Items 1 and 2, respectively. If you answered both questions correctly, you earned an A (100%) on the quiz. If you answered only one question correctly, you earned an F (50%). And, of course, two incorrect answers also mean an F.

Unfortunately, the length of my quiz is problematic. First, I assessed only two concepts (situated motivation and cognitive dissonance) out of the many concepts presented in Chapter 6. Two concepts are hardly a representative sample of what you've learned about motivation, and so the quiz has questionable validity. Second, if you interpreted one of the items differently than I intended for you to interpret it, you might have answered an item incorrectly despite having the knowledge to answer it correctly. For example, in Item 2, if you assumed that David's previous beliefs about the Nazis were positive, you might reasonably have selected *d* as an example of cognitive dissonance. With this one slip-up you would have gone from an A to an F. When a single misinterpretation moves a student from a very good grade to a very poor one—a misinterpretation that might happen on one occasion but not another—the reliability of the assessment is in doubt.

To some degree, then, longer is better when it comes to formal assessments. Ideally, a classroom assessment should include enough questions and tasks that (1) it adequately represents the content domain being assessed and (2) one or two errors due to irrelevant factors (e.g., misinterpretation of items) don't seriously impact the final result. Teachers shouldn't go overboard, however. Students become very tired—and teachers have little time left for instruction—when tests and other assessment tasks take a great deal of time to complete.

When practical, use authentic tasks.

Historically, most educational assessment instruments have focused on measuring basic knowledge and skills in relative isolation from tasks typically found in the outside world. Spelling quizzes, mathematics word problems, and physical fitness tests are examples of such traditional assessments. Yet ultimately students must be able to transfer their knowledge and skills to complex tasks outside the classroom. The notion of **authentic assessment**—assessing students' knowledge and skills in an authentic, similar-to-real-life context—is gaining increasing prominence in today's schools.[21]

In some situations an authentic assessment can involve paper and pencil. For example, a teacher might ask students to write a letter to a friend or develop a school newspaper.

---

[21] For example, see Darling-Hammond et al., 1995; DiMartino & Castaneda, 2007; Lester, Lambdin, & Preston, 1997; Paris & Paris, 2001; Valencia, Hiebert, & Afflerbach, 1994.

authentic assessment Assessment of students' knowledge and skills in a context similar to one in the outside world.

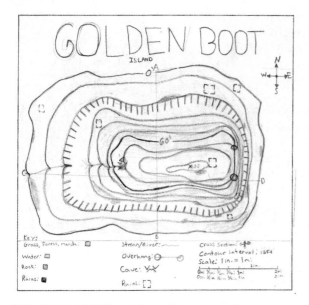

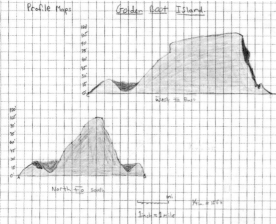

FIGURE 10.5 In his aerial and side-view drawings of "Golden Boot Island," 12-year-old Francisco demonstrates what he's learned about depicting elevation and topography.

And in the opening case study, Akeem creates an action-figures catalog and a book about the history of flight. At other times it involves performance tasks. For example, a teacher might ask students to converse in a foreign language, design and build a bookshelf, or successfully maneuver a car into a parallel parking space.[22]

Whether they be paper–pencil or performance based, assessment tasks might be authentic to varying degrees. For instance, they might ask students to apply new skills to imagined or hypothetical—rather than truly real-world—situations. As an illustration, one seventh-grade social studies teacher gave her students this semi-authentic assignment in a unit on mapping elevation and topography:

Island Map Assignment

1. Using a contour interval of 15 feet and a scale of one inch to one mile, construct a contour map of an island that:
   a. Is 6 miles from east to west and 4 miles from north to south
   b. Has a maximum elevation of 124 feet, but rises to at least 105 feet
   c. Is steepest on the east side
   d. Has a stream running into the ocean on the west shore, with its source at an elevation of 90 feet
2. Draw two profile maps of your island, one showing the island from west to east and the other showing it from north to south.

Figure 10.5 shows 12-year-old Francisco's response to this assignment.

Use paper–pencil measures when they are consistent with instructional goals.

In some situations, such as when the desired outcome is simple recall of facts, a teacher might ask students to respond to multiple-choice or short-answer questions on a paper–pencil test. In other situations—for instance, when the objective is for students to critique a literary work or to explain everyday phenomena by using principles of physics—essay tasks that require students to follow a logical line of reasoning are appropriate. *If a teacher can truly assess knowledge of a domain by having students respond in writing, then a paper–pencil assessment is a good choice.*

Paper–pencil assessment is typically easier and faster, and thus has greater practicality, than performance assessment. Usually a paper–pencil task can be administered to everyone in the classroom at the same time and under the same conditions, so it is easily standardized. To the extent that a paper–pencil assessment has a large number of items that can be objectively scored—as is true for true–false and multiple-choice tests—then it's also likely to be fairly reliable.

The RSVP characteristic of most concern in a paper–pencil assessment is its validity. When teachers ask questions that require only short, simple responses (e.g., true–false, multiple-choice, and matching questions), they can sample students' knowledge about many topics within a relatively short time period. In this sense, then, such questions can yield high content validity. Yet in some situations these types of items may not accurately reflect instructional goals. To assess students' ability to apply what they've learned to new situations, solve complex real-world problems, or engage in other complex cognitive processes, teachers may sometimes need to be satisfied with a few tasks requiring lengthy responses.[23]

---

[22] Educators are not in complete agreement in their use of the terms *performance assessment* and *authentic assessment,* and many treat the terms more or less as synonyms. I find it useful to consider separately whether an assessment involves *performance* (rather than paper and pencil) and whether it involves a complex, real-world *(authentic)* task. In the discussion here, then, I do not use the two terms interchangeably.

[23] J. R. Frederiksen & Collins, 1989; Popham, 1995; Stiggins, 2008.

Unfortunately, many paper–pencil assessment instruments—especially teacher-created tests—focus primarily on basic skills and knowledge of discrete facts.[24] (As an example, look once again at the geology test in Figure 10.2, p. 365.) But with a little ingenuity, teachers can develop a wide variety of paper–pencil assessment tasks that require conceptual understanding and complex cognitive processes. The map interpretation task presented in Figure 4.10 (Chapter 4, p. 131) and the map construction task illustrated in Figure 10.5 are two examples. The following essay task is another:

> You are to play the role of an advisor to President Nixon after his election to office in 1968. As his advisor, you are to make a recommendation about the United States' involvement in Vietnam.
>
> Your paper is to be organized around three main parts: An introduction that shows an understanding of the Vietnam War up to this point by explaining who is involved in the war and what their objectives are; also in the Introduction, you are to state a recommendation in one or two sentences to make the advice clear.
>
> The body of the paper should be written to convince the President to follow your advice by discussing: (a) the pros of the advice, including statistics, dates, examples, and general information . . . ; (b) the cons of the advice, letting the President know that the advisor is aware of how others might disagree. Anticipate one or two recommendations that others might give, and explain why they are not the best advice.
>
> The conclusion makes a final appeal for the recommendation and sells the President on the advice.[25]

Teachers can also assess complex cognitive processes with carefully constructed multiple-choice questions. In the "Quick Quiz" exercise you did earlier, you saw two multiple-choice questions that required you to transfer what you've learned about motivation to new situations. The last two items in the Classroom Strategies box "Constructing Multiple-Choice Items" are additional examples.

Use performance assessments when necessary to ensure validity.

Because paper–pencil assessment is so practical, it should generally be the method of choice *if* it can yield a valid measure of what students know and can do. But in situations where paper–pencil tasks are clearly not a good reflection of what students have learned, teachers may need to sacrifice practicality to gain the greater validity that a performance assessment provides.

A wide variety of performance tasks can be used to assess students' mastery of classroom subject matter. Here are just a few of the many possibilities:[26]

- Playing a musical instrument
- Conversing in a foreign language
- Engaging in a debate about social issues
- Fixing a malfunctioning machine
- Role-playing a job interview
- Performing a workplace routine
- Presenting research findings to a group of teachers, peers, and community members

Performance assessment lends itself especially well to the assessment of complex achievements, such as those that involve simultaneous use of multiple skills. It can also be quite helpful in assessing problem solving, creativity, and critical thinking. Furthermore, performance tasks are often more meaningful, thought provoking, and authentic for students—and so often more motivating—than paper–pencil tasks.[27]

Some performance assessments focus on tangible *products* that students create—perhaps a sculpture, scientific invention, or poster display. In situations with no tangible product, teachers must instead look at the specific *processes and behaviors* that students

? Which topics and skills in the content domain(s) you will be teaching might be validly assessed with paper–pencil assessments? Which ones would require performance assessments?

---

[24] Bransford et al., 2006; J. R. Frederiksen & Collins, 1989; Nickerson, 1989; Poole, 1994; Shepard et al., 2005.

[25] Newmann, 1997, p. 368.

[26] DiMartino & Castaneda, 2007; Gronlund & Waugh, 2009; C. Hill & Larsen, 1992; D. B. Swanson, Norman, & Linn, 1995.

[27] Darling-Hammond et al., 1995; Khattri & Sweet, 1996; Paris & Paris, 2001; D. P. Resnick & Resnick, 1996.

CLASSROOM STRATEGIES Constructing Multiple-Choice Items

- **When assessing basic knowledge, rephrase ideas presented in class or in the textbook.**

  A middle school language arts teacher uses short multiple-choice quizzes to assess students' understanding of each week's new vocabulary words. The items never include the specific definitions students have been given. For instance, for the word *manacle*, students have been given this definition: "Device used to restrain a person's hands or wrists." But the item on the quiz is this one:

  Which one of the following words or phrases is closest in meaning to the word *manacle*?

  a. Insane
  b. Handcuffs
  c. Out of control
  d. Saltwater creature that clings to hard surfaces
  (The correct answer is b.)

- **Present incorrect alternatives that are clearly wrong to students who know the material but plausible to students who haven't mastered it.**

  After a unit on the seasons, a middle school science teacher asks this question:

  What is the *main* reason that it is colder in winter than in summer?

  a. Because the earth is in the part of its orbit farthest away from the sun
  b. Because wind is more likely to come from the north than from the south
  c. Because the sun's rays hit our part of the earth at more of an angle
  d. Because the snow on the ground reflects rather than absorbs the sun's heat
  (The correct answer is c.)

- **To assess complex cognitive processes, ask students to apply what they've learned to new situations.**

  A high school physics teacher includes the following question on a quiz designed to assess what students have learned about simple machines:

  An inventor has just designed a new device for cutting paper. Without knowing anything else about his invention, we can predict that it is probably which type of machine?

  a. A lever
  b. A movable pulley
  c. An inclined plane
  d. A wedge
  (The correct answer is d.)

- **Occasionally incorporate visual materials.**

  A high school geography teacher includes maps in some of his questions. Following is an example:

  Using the map below, choose the most logical explanation for why people living in the Middle East and people living in the Far East developed distinctly different languages.

  a. People in the Far East had little contact with those who lived in the Middle East.
  b. People who lived by the ocean had very different lifestyles than people who lived in the mountains.
  c. People who lived in southern climates had very different lifestyles than people who lived in northern climates.
  d. People in the two regions were constantly fighting over desirable farmland.
  (The correct answer is a.)

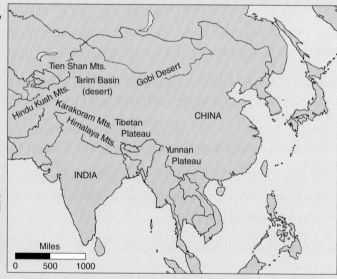

exhibit—perhaps how they give an oral presentation, execute a forward roll, or play an instrumental solo. When teachers look at processes rather than products, they may in some instances probe students' *thinking processes*. For example, a teacher who wants to determine whether students have developed some of the concrete operational or formal operational abilities that Piaget described (e.g., class inclusion, conservation, separation and control of variables) might present tasks similar to those Piaget used and ask students to explain their reasoning (see Chapter 5). And a teacher can often determine how students reason about scientific phenomena by asking them to manipulate physical objects (e.g., chemicals in a chemistry lab, electrical circuit boards in a physics class), make predictions about what will happen under varying circumstances, and then explain their results.[28] The Classroom

---

[28] De Corte, Greer, & Verschaffel, 1996; diSessa, 2007; Magnusson, Boyle, & Templin, 1994; Quellmalz & Hoskyn, 1997.

CLASSROOM STRATEGIES Developing Performance Assessments

- Have students create products that reflect what they have learned.

    A middle school science teacher asks students to make posters that summarize their projects for the school science fair. The teacher tells the students that the posters should include (1) a research question or hypothesis, (2) the method used to address the question or hypothesis, (3) results obtained, and (4) one or more conclusions.

- When the assigned task doesn't yield a tangible product, observe students' behaviors and, if appropriate, probe their thinking processes.

    After a unit on major and minor scales in an instrumental band class, a music teacher assesses students' understanding of natural minor scales by having them play three different ones on their instruments. If a student plays a scale incorrectly, the teacher asks the student to describe the structure of a minor scale (whole-step, half-step, whole-step, whole-step, half-step, whole-step, whole-step) and explain why the scale might not have sounded right.

- Consider assigning complex, lengthy tasks as group projects.

    In a unit on urban geography, a high school social studies teacher assigns this authentic assessment task as a cooperative group project:

    First, select one of the neighborhoods marked on the city map. Second, identify its current features by doing an inventory of its buildings, businesses, housing, and public facilities. Also, identify current transportation patterns and traffic flow. From the information made available, identify any special problems this neighborhood has, such as dilapidated housing, traffic congestion, or a high crime rate. Third, as a group, consider various plans for changing and improving the neighborhood.

    In evaluating students' performance, the teacher considers each group's overall accomplishments plus individual students' contributions to the group effort.

- Consider incorporating the assessment into normal instructional activities.

    To assess students' understanding of simple graphs, a first-grade teacher distributes a table that lists the 12 months of the year. She asks her students to circulate around the room, gathering each class member's signature in a box beside his or her birthday month. In this way, students create graphs showing how many class members were born in each month. The graphs indicate that some but not all students have a general understanding of graphs. In the example below, many students (e.g., Cam, Sara, Kelsey, Adrienne, Spencer) have all written their names inside a single box in the table. However, a few students (Kristen, Jesse, Kristah, and Cameron) have used two cells to write their names, perhaps because they (1) haven't mastered the idea that one person equals one box in the table or (2) can't write small enough to fit their names inside a box and don't know how to solve this problem. The graph also shows that one child (Meg, who has a March birthday) has not yet learned to write words, including her name, in the traditional left-to-right manner.

Birthday Graph

January	CAM	KRISTEN	M	
February	SARA			
March	KELSEY	EGM		
April	JESSE	P	M	TONY
May	BILLY			
June	ADRIENNE			
July	Allison	KRISTAH		
August	AJ	MAGGIE		
September	BRAB	casey	BEN B.	
October	Mrs. O'Byrne	Margaret	VICKY	
November	BEN D	Ms. Gray	CAMERON	
December	SPENCER	MAY		

Sources: Baxter, Elder, & Glaser, 1996; Boschee & Baron, 1993; DiMartino & Castaneda, 2007; Kennedy, 1992; Lester et al., 1997; Newmann, 1997 ("neighborhoods" task from p. 369); Shavelson & Baxter, 1992; Stiggins, 2008.

Strategies box "Developing Performance Assessments" offers several suggestions for using performance assessments for different age levels and content domains.

One form of performance assessment gaining popularity is **dynamic assessment**.[29] In this approach, rather than find out what students have already learned, a teacher assesses students' *ability to learn something new,* perhaps with the assistance of the teacher, a teacher aide, or a parent volunteer. Such an approach reflects Vygotsky's *zone of proximal development* and can reveal what students are likely to be able to accomplish with appropriate structure and guidance. Hence it's most appropriate for formative (rather than summative) assessment.

---

[29] For example, see Feuerstein, Feuerstein, & Gross, 1997; L. S. Fuchs, Compton, et al., 2008; Haywood & Lidz, 2007; Shepard, 2000; H. L. Swanson & Lussier, 2001; Tzuriel, 2000.

dynamic assessment Systematic examination of how readily and in what ways a student can acquire new knowledge or skills, perhaps with an adult's assistance.

TABLE 10.3 Evaluating RSVP Characteristics of Different Kinds of Assessments

Kind of Assessment	Reliability	Standardization	Validity	Practicality
Informal assessment	A single, brief assessment is not a reliable indicator of achievement. Teachers must look for consistency in a student's performance across time and in different contexts.	Informal observations are rarely, if ever, standardized. Thus teachers should not compare one student to another on the basis of informal assessments alone.	Students' public behaviors in the classroom are not always valid indicators of their achievement (e.g., some students may try to hide high achievement from peers, others may come from cultures that encourage listening more than talking).	Informal assessment is definitely practical. It is flexible and can occur sponta- neously during instruction.
Formal paper–pencil assessment	Objectively scorable items are highly reliable. Teachers can enhance the reliability of subjectively scorable items by specifying scoring criteria in concrete terms.	In most instances paper–pencil instruments are easily standardized for all students. Giving students choices (e.g., regarding topics to write about or questions to answer) may increase motivation but reduces standardization.	Using numerous questions that require short, simple responses can make an assessment a more representative sample of the content domain. But tasks requiring lengthy responses may sometimes more closely match instructional goals.	Paper–pencil assessment is usually practical. All students can be assessed at once, and no special materials are required.
Formal performance assessment	It is often difficult to score performance assessment tasks reliably. Teachers can enhance reliability by specifying scoring criteria in concrete terms.	Some performance assessment tasks are easily standardized, whereas others are not.	Performance tasks may sometimes be more consistent with instructional goals than paper–pencil tasks. A single performance task may not provide a representative sample of the content domain; several tasks may be necessary to ensure content validity.	Performance assessment is typically less practical than other approaches. It may involve special materials, and it can take a fair amount of class time, especially if students must be assessed one by one.

As previously noted, performance assessment tasks sometimes provide more valid indicators of what students have accomplished relative to instructional goals. However, students' responses to a *single* performance assessment task are frequently *not* a good indication of their overall achievement.[30] Content validity is at stake here. If time constraints allow students to perform only one or two complex tasks, those tasks may not be a representative sample of what students have learned and can do. In addition, teachers may have trouble standardizing assessment conditions for everyone and scoring students' performance consistently—problems that adversely affect reliability. And performance assessments are often less practical than more traditional paper–pencil assessments. Conducting an assessment can be quite time consuming, especially when a teacher must observe students one by one or when a task requires students to spend considerable time in the outside community.

As you can see, then, informal assessment, formal paper–pencil assessment, and formal performance assessment all have their strengths and weaknesses. Table 10.3 summarizes their RSVP characteristics and offers relevant suggestions. In the end, teachers may find that they can best assess students' achievement with a combination of paper–pencil and performance tasks and supplement their findings with informal observations of students' typical classroom behavior.[31]

[30] Crehan, 2001; R. L. Johnson, Penny, & Gordon, 2009; S. Klassen, 2006; R. L. Linn, 1994.

[31] Messick, 1994a; Stiggins, 2008; D. B. Swanson et al., 1995.

Define tasks clearly, and give students some structure to guide responses.

Contrary to what some teachers believe, there is usually little to be gained from assigning ambiguous tasks to assess students' learning and achievement. Whether or not students know how to respond to assessment tasks, they should at least understand what they're being asked to do.

As an illustration, consider this essay question in an American history class:

List the causes of the American Revolution.

What does the teacher actually want students to do? One student might take the word *list* literally and simply write "Stamp Act, Boston Massacre, Quartering Act." But another student might write several pages describing Britain's increasing restriction of navigation, the colonists' resentment of taxation without representation, and King George III's apparent lack of concern about the colonists' welfare. Responses to unstructured tasks may go in so many different directions that scoring them consistently and reliably is virtually impossible. Especially in situations where a great deal of material is potentially relevant, students need guidance about the length and completeness of desired responses and about the things they should specifically address. For example, to assess what students have learned about causes of the American Revolution, a teacher might present this task:

Identify three policies or events during the 1760s and/or 1770s that contributed to the outbreak of the American Revolution. For each of the three things you identify, explain in three to five sentences how it increased tension between England and the American colonies.

Performance assessment tasks, too, require a certain amount of structure, especially if they're used for summative (rather than formative) assessment. For instance, students should have detailed directions about what they should accomplish, what materials and equipment they can use, and how much time they have to get the job done.[32] Such structure helps to standardize the assessment and so enables a teacher to evaluate students' performance more reliably. A *lot* of structure can decrease a performance task's validity, however. Especially when giving authentic assessments, teachers want assigned tasks to be similar to those in the outside world, and real-world tasks don't always have a lot of structure. Teachers must often seek a happy medium, providing enough structure to guide students in the right direction but not so much that students make few if any decisions for themselves about how to proceed.

Carefully scrutinize items and tasks to be sure they are free from cultural bias.

An assessment instrument has **cultural bias** if any of its items either offend or unfairly penalize some students on the basis of their ethnicity, gender, or socioeconomic status.[33] There are two important points to note about this definition. First, cultural bias includes biases related to gender and socioeconomic status as well as to culture and ethnicity. Second, an assessment is biased if it either penalizes or *offends* a particular group. For example, imagine a test question that implies that boys are more competent than girls, and imagine another question that includes a picture in which members of a particular ethnic or racial group are engaging in inappropriate behavior. Such questions have cultural bias because some groups of students (girls in the first situation and members of the depicted group in the second) are likely to be offended by the questions and thus distracted from doing their best on the test.

Historically, educators have been most concerned about eliminating cultural bias in large-scale standardized tests used for assessing intelligence and overall school achievement. Yet teachers should also screen their self-constructed classroom assessment instruments for possible biases that may put some groups of students at a disadvantage. The Cultural Considerations box "Potential Sources of Cultural Bias" gives examples of things teachers should look for and think about.

cultural bias Extent to which assessment tasks either offend or unfairly penalize some students because of their ethnicity, gender, or socioeconomic status.

[32] Gronlund & Waugh, 2009; E. H. Hiebert, Valencia, & Afflerbach, 1994; Shepard et al., 2005; Stiggins, 2008.

[33] This definition is based on one suggested by Popham, 1995.

CULTURAL CONSIDERATIONS Potential Sources of Cultural Bias

Consider these two assessment tasks:

Task 1: Would you rather swim in the ocean, a lake, or a swimming pool? Write a two-page persuasive essay defending your choice.

Task 2: Mary is making a patchwork quilt from 36 separate squares of fabric, as shown here. Each square of fabric has a perimeter of 20 inches. Mary sews the squares together, using a half-inch seam allowance. She then sews the assembled set of squares to a large piece of cotton that will

serve as the flip side of the quilt, again using a half-inch seam allowance. How long is the perimeter of the finished quilt?

Task 1 would obviously be difficult for students who haven't been swimming in all three environments and would be even more difficult for students who have never swum at all. Students from low-income, inner-city families might easily fall into one of these two categories. Task 2 assumes a fair amount of knowledge about sewing (e.g., what a *seam allowance* is). This is knowledge that some students (especially girls) are more likely to have than others. Such tasks have cultural bias because some students will perform better than others

because of differences in their background experiences, *not* because of differences in what they've learned in the classroom. The "Building a Tree House" exercise in Chapter 3 (p. 73) has cultural bias as well, in that boys are more likely than girls—and children in rural areas are more likely than children in urban areas—to have had tree-house–building experience.

In considering possible sources of bias in classroom assessments, teachers must look not only at the content of their assessment tasks but also at how the tasks are being administered. For example, students who have recently immigrated and only begun to learn English—even those students with

Identify evaluation criteria in advance.

Some paper–pencil tasks, such as multiple-choice questions and many mathematics word problems, have clear-cut right and wrong answers. Some performance assessment tasks, too, are objectively scorable. A teacher can easily count the errors on a typing test or time students' performance in a 100-meter dash. But whenever a variety of student responses might be appropriate, and especially whenever students' responses might have varying degrees of quality, then teachers need to specify the criteria by which responses will be evaluated—not only for themselves but also for *students*.

Evaluating the quality as well as the quantity of what students produce is almost always in students' long-term best interest. For example, if a teacher gives full credit for completing an assignment without regard to quality, students may focus more on completing it quickly than on acquiring a conceptual understanding of what they're studying.[34] At the same time, evaluation criteria must be realistic. Overly ambitious criteria for acceptable performance are apt to discourage students from taking risks and making errors—risks and errors that are inevitable when students tackle the challenges that can best promote their cognitive development.

Teachers should typically determine the nature of good responses at the same time they develop their assessment instruments. Whenever an assessment task involves subjective evaluation of a complex performance—for instance, when it involves scoring lengthy essays, science fair posters, or art projects—teachers should list components that a good response should include or characteristics that will be considered in the evaluation. Such a list is known as a **rubric**. Some rubrics take the form of *checklists*, lists of behaviors or qualities that either are or aren't present in a student's performance. Figure 10.6 presents examples of checklists for evaluating varnishing in a high school woodworking class and

---

rubric List of components that a student's performance on an assessment task should ideally include; used to guide scoring.

[34] W. Doyle, 1983.

strong math skills—may do poorly on mathematics word problems because such problems require a good command of written English.[a] In such instances a teacher might restate the problems in simpler language and perhaps draw pictures to help students understand the problem-solving tasks. And let's return to a point made in Chapter 3: Children from some cultural groups (e.g., those from some Native American communities) prefer to practice a skill privately until they attain reasonable mastery.[b] In such cases a teacher might let students practice new skills away from the limelight and demonstrate their progress in private, one-on-one sessions.

An assessment instrument isn't necessarily biased just because one group of students gets higher scores than another group. It's biased only if the groups' scores are different when the knowledge and skills a teacher is trying to assess *aren't* different. In some cases different groups have different backgrounds that affect their classroom learning as well as their performance on assessments. For example, the fact that, on average, boys have more mathematically oriented toys and experiences than girls may give them an advantage that affects both their ability to learn certain math concepts and processes *and* their ability to

perform well on tasks assessing mastery of those concepts and processes.[c] Similarly, if students from low-income families have had few opportunities to venture beyond their immediate neighborhoods (fewer museum trips, less travel, etc.), their more limited exposure to diverse environments is likely to impact both their classroom achievement and their performance on assessments measuring that achievement.

[a] Garcia, 2005; Solano-Flores, 2008.
[b] Castagno & Brayboy, 2008; Garcia, 1994; Suina & Smolkin, 1994.
[c] Jacobs, Davis-Kean, Bleeker, Eccles, & Malanchuk, 2005; Leaper & Friedman, 2007.

work habits in a kindergarten class. Other rubrics take the form of *rating scales,* which allow teachers to rate aspects of a student's performance on one or more continua. For example, Figure 10.7 presents a 5-point rating-scale rubric that teachers at Littleton High School in Colorado have used to evaluate students' writing. Notice how the rubric addresses six distinct aspects of a writing sample that a teacher should look for: ideas and content, organization, voice, word choice, sentence fluency, and use of conventions. It also provides guidance on criteria to use in assigning high, middle, or low scores.

Teachers and students alike benefit when scoring criteria are explicit. Teachers can evaluate students' responses more consistently and reliably (and often more quickly), and their judgments are less likely to be influenced by their prior expectations for particular students' performances. Meanwhile, students have clear targets toward which to shoot as they study and practice. And, of course, a rubric helps teachers provide concrete, constructive feedback that can enable students to improve.[35]

A checklist for evaluating students' ability to apply varnish in a woodworking class

_____ Sands and prepares surface properly
_____ Applies varnish to surface with smooth strokes
_____ Works from center of surface toward the edges
_____ Brushes with the grain of the wood
_____ Uses light strokes to smooth the varnish
_____ Cleans brush with appropriate cleaner
_____ Cleans work area

A checklist for evaluating young children's work habits

_____ Follows directions
_____ Seeks help when needed
_____ Works cooperatively with others
_____ Waits turn in using materials
_____ Shares materials with others
_____ Tries new activities
_____ Completes started tasks
_____ Returns equipment to proper place
_____ Cleans work space

FIGURE 10.6 Examples of checklists
Sources: Criteria for woodworking checklist are from Gronlund, 2004, p. 113. Criteria for kindergarten checklist are from R. L. Linn and Miller, 2005, p. 274.

---

[35] Meltzer, Pollica, & Barzillai, 2007; Shepard et al., 2005.

	Ideas and Content	Organization	Voice	Word Choice	Sentence Fluency	Conventions
5	• Clear, focused topic. • Relevant and accurate supporting details.	• Clear intro and body and satisfying conclusion. • Thoughtful transitions clearly show how ideas are connected. • Sequencing is logical and effective.	• Tone furthers purpose and appeals to audience. • Appropriately individual and expressive.	• Words are specific and accurate. • Language and phrasing is natural, effective, and appropriate.	• Sentence construction produces natural flow and rhythm.	• Grammar and usage are correct and contribute to clarity and style.
3	• Broad topic. • Support is generalized or insufficient.	• Recognizable beginning, middle, and end. • Transitions often work well; sometimes connections between ideas are fuzzy. • Sequencing is functional.	• Tone is appropriate for purpose and audience. • Not fully engaged or involved.	• Words are adequate and support the meaning. • Language is general but functional.	• Sentences are constructed correctly.	• Grammar and usage mistakes do not impede meaning.
1	• Unclear topic. • Lacking or irrelevant support.	• No apparent organization. • Lack of transitions. • Sequencing is illogical.	• Not concerned with audience or fails to match purpose. • Indifferent or inappropriate.	• Improper word choice/usage makes writing difficult to understand. • Language is vague or redundant.	• Sentences are choppy, incomplete, or unnatural.	• Grammar and mistakes distract the reader or impede meaning.

FIGURE 10.7 Example of a rating-scale rubric for evaluating the quality of high school students' writing
Source: From *Breaking Ranks II: Strategies for Leading High School Reform* by the National Association of Secondary School Principals (NASSP), p. 103. Copyright 2004, National Association of Secondary School Principals, Reston, VA. Reprinted with permission.

When giving tests, encourage students to do their best, but don't arouse a lot of anxiety.

Most students get a little bit anxious about tests and other important assessments, and a small amount of anxiety can actually enhance performance (see Chapter 6). But some students become extremely anxious in test-taking situations—they have **test anxiety**—to the point that their scores significantly underestimate what they've learned.[36] Such students appear to be concerned primarily about the *evaluative* aspect of tests, worrying that someone will find them to be "stupid" or in some other way inadequate.[37] Excessive, debilitating test anxiety is especially common in students from ethnic minority groups and students with disabilities.[38]

Test anxiety interferes not only with retrieval and performance at the time of an assessment but also with encoding and storage when learners are preparing for the assessment.[39] Thus highly test-anxious students don't just *test* poorly, they also *learn* poorly. Table 10.4 distinguishes between classroom assessment practices that are likely to lead to facilitating anxiety and those that may elicit debilitating anxiety.

Establish conditions for the assessment that enable students to maximize their performance.

Administration procedures for an assessment can impact the validity of the results. For example, students are more likely to perform at their best when they complete an assessment in a comfortable environment with acceptable room temperature, adequate lighting, reasonable workspace, and minimal distractions. This comfort factor may be especially

test anxiety Excessive anxiety about a particular test or about assessment in general.

[36] Cassady & Johnson, 2002; Hembree, 1988; E. Hong, O'Neil, & Feldon, 2005.
[37] Harter, Whitesell, & Kowalski, 1992; B. N. Phillips, Pitcher, Worsham, & Miller, 1980; Wine, 1980.
[38] R. Carter, Williams, & Silverman, 2008; Putwain, 2007; Whitaker Sena, Lowe, & Lee, 2007.
[39] Cassady & Johnson, 2002; Hagtvet & Johnsen, 1992.

TABLE 10.4 Keeping Students' Anxiety at a Facilitative Level during Classroom Assessments

What to Do	What *Not* to Do
Point out the value of the assessment as a feedback mechanism to improve learning; minimize use of the word *test* in describing the assessment.	Don't stress the fact that students' competence is being evaluated.
Administer a practice assessment or pretest that gives students an idea of what the final assessment will be like.	Don't keep the nature of the assessment a secret until the day it's administered.
Encourage students to do their best but not necessarily to expect perfection; for instance, say, "We're here to learn, and you can't do that without making mistakes."	Don't tell students that failing will have dire consequences.
Provide or allow the use of memory aids (e.g., a list of formulas or a single note card containing key facts) when instructional goals don't require students to commit information to memory.	Don't insist that students commit even trivial facts to memory.
Eliminate time limits unless speed is an important part of the skill being measured.	Don't give more questions or tasks than students can possibly respond to in the allotted time.
Continually survey the room, and be available to answer students' questions.	Don't hover over students, watching them closely as they complete the assessment.
Use unannounced ("pop") quizzes only for formative assessment (e.g., to determine an appropriate starting point for instruction).	Don't give occasional pop quizzes to motivate students to study regularly and to punish those who don't.
Use the results of several assessments to make decisions (e.g., to assign grades).	Don't make important decisions on the basis of a single assessment.

Sources: Brophy, 1986, 2004 ("We're here to learn . . ." suggestion on p. 274); Cizek, 2003; Gaudry & Bradshaw, 1971; K. T. Hill, 1984; K. T. Hill & Wigfield, 1984; Popham, 1990; Sax, 1989; Sieber, Kameya, & Paulson, 1970; Spaulding, 1992; Stipek, 1993; Usher, 2009.

important for students who are easily distracted, unaccustomed to formal assessments, or unmotivated to exert much effort—for instance, it's an important consideration for students at risk.[40]

In addition, students should be able to ask questions when assigned tasks aren't clear. Despite good intentions, a teacher may present a task or question that's ambiguous or potentially misleading. (Even with more than 30 years' experience developing assignments and exams, I still have students occasionally interpreting them in ways I didn't anticipate.) To increase the likelihood that students will respond in desired ways, a teacher should encourage them to ask for clarification whenever they're uncertain about a task. Such encouragement is especially important for students from ethnic minority groups, many of whom may be reluctant to ask questions during a formal assessment situation.[41]

Take reasonable steps to discourage cheating.

The prevalence of cheating increases as students get older, and by high school the great majority of students are apt to cheat on assessments at one time or another.[42] Students cheat for a variety of reasons. Some may be more interested in doing well on an assessment than in actually learning the subject matter; for them, performance goals predominate over mastery goals. Others may believe that teachers' or parents' expectations for their performance are so high as to be unattainable and that success is out of reach unless they *do* cheat. In addition, students may perceive certain assessments (tests especially) to be poorly constructed, arbitrarily graded, or in some other way a poor reflection of what they've learned. Often, too, peers may communicate through words or actions that cheating is common and justifiable.[43]

---

[40] Popham, 1990.

[41] L. R. Cheng, 1987; C. A. Grant & Gomez, 2001; Li & Fischer, 2004.

[42] Cizek, 2003.

[43] E. M. Anderman, Griesinger, & Westerfield, 1998; Cizek, 2003; F. Danner, 2008; E. D. Evans & Craig, 1990; Murdock & Anderman, 2006; Murdock, Miller, & Kohlhardt, 2004.

When students cheat on assessments, their scores don't accurately reflect what they know and can do—hence, the scores have little or no validity. Furthermore, cheating can be habit forming if students discover that it enables them to get good grades with minimal effort.[44] The best approach is prevention—making sure students don't cheat in the first place. For instance, teachers can take the following precautions:

In the weeks or days before the assessment:

- Focus students' attention on mastery rather than performance goals.
- Make success without cheating a realistic possibility.
- Construct assessment instruments with obvious validity for important instructional goals.
- Create two or more instruments that are equivalent in form and content but have different answers (e.g., for a test, use one form in class and another for make-ups, or use different forms for different class periods).
- Explain exactly what cheating is and why it's unacceptable (e.g., explain that cheating includes plagiarism, such as copying material word for word from the Internet without giving appropriate credit).[45]
- Explain what the consequence for cheating will be.

During the assessment (especially during a test or quiz):

- Have teacher-assigned seats during any assessments that require individual (rather than group) work.
- Seat students as far away from one another as possible.
- Remain attentive to what students are doing throughout an assessment session, but without hovering over particular students.

If, despite reasonable precautions, cheating does occur, a teacher must administer the consequence he or she has previously described. This consequence should be severe enough to discourage a student from cheating again yet not so severe that the student's motivation and chances for academic success are significantly diminished over the long run. For instance, I typically require a student to redo the task, often for less credit than he or she would have earned otherwise.

Evaluating Students' Performance on Formal Assessments

As teachers evaluate students' performance on an assessment task, they must continue to be concerned about the four RSVP characteristics: reliability, standardization, validity, and practicality. Furthermore, they must keep in mind that their most important role is not to evaluate performance, but rather to help students learn. And for both pedagogical and legal reasons, they must preserve students' general sense of well-being and right to privacy. Each of the following strategies is valuable in achieving one or more of these ends.

After students have completed an assessment, review evaluation criteria to be sure they can adequately guide scoring.

Even the most experienced teachers can't anticipate the many possible directions in which students might go in responding to classroom assessment tasks. As a general rule, teachers should use the criteria they've previously told students they would use. However, they may occasionally need to adjust (or perhaps add or eliminate) one or more criteria to accommodate unexpected responses and improve their ability to score the responses consistently, fairly, and reliably. Any adjustments should be made *before* a teacher begins scoring, rather than midway through a stack of papers. For example, when grading written assessments, it's often helpful to skim a sample of students' papers first, looking for unusual responses and revising the criteria as needed.

---

[44] Cizek, 2003.
[45] One recent study found that many middle school students erroneously believe copying material verbatim from the Internet to be appropriate and acceptable (Nixon, 2005).

Be as objective as possible.

A scoring rubric can certainly help teachers apply evaluation criteria objectively and consistently for all students, thereby increasing standardization and, indirectly, reliability and validity. In addition, when assessments involve multiple tasks (e.g., several essay questions, or lab reports with several discrete sections), teachers can often score students' responses more reliably by grading everyone's response to the first task, then everyone's response to the second task, and so on. And covering students' names with small self-stick notes can help teachers keep their existing beliefs and expectations about particular students from influencing their judgments of the students' work.

Make note of any significant aspects of a student's performance that a rubric doesn't address.

Scoring rubrics are rarely perfect. Whenever teachers break down students' performance on a complex task into discrete behaviors, they can lose valuable information in the process.[46] When teachers use rubrics in scoring, then, they may occasionally want to jot down other noteworthy characteristics of students' performance. This aspect of the scoring process will be neither standardized nor reliable, of course, but it can sometimes be useful in identifying students' unique strengths and needs and can therefore be helpful in future instructional planning.

Ask students to evaluate their performance.

As noted early in the chapter, when students play an active role in assessing their own work, they develop greater proficiency in such self-regulation skills as self-monitoring and self-evaluation. Following are several strategies for helping students develop self-regulation skills by including them in the assessment process:[47]

- Provide examples of good and not-so-good products, and ask students to compare them on the basis of several criteria.
- Solicit students' ideas about evaluation criteria and rubric design.
- Have students identify their most common errors and create personalized checklists that enable them to double-check their work for these errors.
- Have students compare self-ratings with teacher ratings (e.g., note the "Self" and "Teacher" columns in the word problem rubric in Figure 10.8).
- Have students keep ongoing records of their performance and chart their progress over time.
- Have students reflect on their work in daily or weekly journal entries, where they can keep track of knowledge and skills they have and have not mastered, as well as learning strategies that have and have not been effective.
- Ask students to write practice questions similar to those they expect to see on upcoming quizzes and tests.
- Ask students to lead parent–teacher conferences.

Elements	Possible Points	Points Earned	
		Self	Teacher
1. You highlighted the question(s) to solve.	2	____	____
2. You picked an appropriate strategy.	2	____	____
3. Work is neat and organized.	2	____	____
4. Calculations are accurate.	2	____	____
5. Question(s) answered.	2	____	____
6. You have explained in words how you solved the problem.	5	____	____
Total		____	____

FIGURE 10.8 In this rubric for scoring solutions to mathematics word problems in a fourth-grade class, both teacher and student evaluate various aspects of the student's performance.

An additional strategy is having students compile portfolios of their work—a strategy we'll look at more closely later in the chapter.

---

[46] Delandshere & Petrosky, 1998.
[47] A. L. Brown & Campione, 1996; DiMartino & Castaneda, 2007; Meltzer et al., 2007; Paris & Ayres, 1994; Shepard, 2000; Stiggins, 2008; Valencia et al., 1994.

Beginner Swimmer Class
Springside Parks and Recreation Department

Students must demonstrate proficiency in each of
the following:

- ☐ Jump into chest-deep water
- ☐ Hold breath under water for 8 seconds
- ☐ Float in prone position for 10 seconds
- ☐ Glide in prone position with flutter kick
- ☐ Float on back for 10 seconds
- ☐ Glide on back with flutter kick
- ☐ Demonstrate crawl stroke and rhythmic
  breathing while standing in chest-deep water
- ☐ Show knowledge of basic water safety rules

FIGURE 10.9 In this swimming class,
students' accomplishments are reported in a
criterion-referenced fashion.

? In the opening case study, Akeem's
performance on districtwide tests
remained low even though his reading
and writing skills were improving.
Assume that the tests yielded norm-
referenced scores. With this assumption
in mind, can you explain why Akeem's
test scores did *not* increase despite
noticeable improvements in his literacy
skills? (You'll learn the answer to this
question in the upcoming section on
standardized tests.)

When determining overall scores, don't compare students to one another unless there is a compelling reason to do so.
Scores on tests and other assessments typically take one of three general forms. Most commonly used on teacher-constructed assessments is a **raw score**, which is based solely on the number or percentage of points earned or items answered correctly. For example, a student who correctly answers 15 items on a 20-item multiple-choice test might get a score of 75%. A student who gets 3 points, 8 points, and 5 points on three essay questions, respectively, might get an overall score of 16. Raw scores are easy to calculate, and they appear to be easy to understand. But in fact, we sometimes have trouble knowing what raw scores really mean. Are scores of 75% and 16 good scores or bad ones? Without knowing what kinds of tasks an assessment includes, we have no easy way of interpreting a raw score.

A **criterion-referenced score** indicates what students have achieved in relation to specific instructional objectives or standards. Some criterion-referenced scores are either–or scores indicating that a student has passed or failed a unit, mastered or not mastered a skill, or met or not met an objective. Figure 10.9 illustrates this approach in a beginning swimming class. Other criterion-referenced scores indicate various levels of competence or achievement. For instance, the rubric presented in Figure 10.7 enables teachers to assign six specific, criterion-referenced scores to students' written work, each on a scale of 1 to 5.

Both raw scores and criterion-referenced scores are determined solely by looking at an individual student's performance. In contrast, a **norm-referenced score** is determined by comparing a student's performance with the performance of others. For teacher-constructed classroom assessments, the comparison group typically consists of other students in the same class. In the case of published standardized tests, it's usually a large group of peers in a nationwide *norm group*. A norm-referenced score tells us little about what a student specifically knows and can do. Instead, it tells us whether a student's performance is typical or unusual for the age or grade level.

Norm-referenced scores—in everyday lingo, those that result from "grading on the curve"—are often used in standardized tests (more about this point later). They're far less common in teacher-constructed classroom assessments. They may occasionally be necessary when designating "first chair" in an instrumental music class or choosing the best entries for a regional science fair. Teachers may also need to resort to a norm-referenced approach when assessing complex skills (e.g., poetry writing, advanced athletic skills, or critical analysis of literature) that are difficult to describe as "mastered." Teachers should probably *not* use norm-referenced scores on a regular basis, however. Such scores create a competitive situation in which students do well only if their performance surpasses that of their classmates. Thus norm-referenced scores focus students' attention primarily on performance goals rather than mastery goals and may possibly encourage them to cheat on assessment tasks.[48] Furthermore, the competitive atmosphere that norm-referenced scores create is inconsistent with the *sense of community* described in Chapter 9.

Criterion-referenced scores communicate what teachers and students alike most need to know: whether instructional goals and objectives have been achieved. In doing so, they focus attention on mastery goals and, by showing improvement over time, can enhance students' self-efficacy for learning academic subject matter. When criterion-referenced scores are difficult to determine—perhaps because a single assessment addresses too many objectives simultaneously—raw scores are usually the second best choice, at least on teacher-constructed classroom assessment tasks.

Give detailed and constructive feedback.

As teachers score students' performance on classroom assessments, they should remember that virtually *any* assessment can promote future learning as well as determine current

raw score Assessment score based solely on the number or point value of correctly answered items.

criterion-referenced score Assessment score that specifically indicates what a student knows or can do.

norm-referenced score Assessment score that indicates how a student's performance compares with the average performance of others.

---

[48] E. M. Anderman & Anderman, 2010; E. M. Anderman et al., 1998; Mac Iver et al., 1995.

achievement levels. Accordingly, teachers should provide detailed comments that tell students what they did well, where their weaknesses lie, and how they can improve.[49]

Make allowances for risk taking and the occasional "bad day."

Students should feel comfortable enough about classroom assessments that they feel free to take risks and make mistakes. Only under these circumstances will they tackle the challenging tasks that can maximize their learning and cognitive development. Teachers encourage risk taking—and also decrease debilitating anxiety—not only when they communicate that mistakes are a normal part of learning but also when classroom assessment practices give students some leeway to be wrong without penalty.[50]

One strategy for encouraging risk taking is to *give frequent assessments.* Students who are assessed frequently are more likely to take occasional risks—and they have less test anxiety—because they know that no single assessment means "sudden death" if they earn a low score. Frequent assessment has other benefits as well. It provides ongoing information to both students and teachers about the progress students are making and about areas of weakness that need attention. It motivates students (especially those with lower ability) to study regularly, and with the pressure off to perform well on every single test and assignment, students are less likely to cheat to obtain good grades. The bottom line is that students who are assessed frequently learn and achieve at higher levels than students who are assessed infrequently.[51]

Another strategy is to *give students a chance to correct errors.* Especially when an assessment includes most or all of the content domain in question, students may learn as much—possibly even more—by correcting the errors they've made on an assessment task. For example, in an approach known as *mastery reform,* some math teachers have students correct their errors as follows:

1. **Identification of the error.** Students describe in a short paragraph exactly what they don't yet know how to do.
2. **Statement of the process.** Using words rather than mathematical symbols, students explain the steps involved in the procedure they're trying to master.
3. **Practice.** Students demonstrate their mastery of the procedure with three new problems similar to the problem(s) they previously solved incorrectly.
4. **Statement of mastery.** Students state in a sentence or two that they have now mastered the procedure.

By completing these steps, students can replace a grade on a previous assessment with the new, higher one. One high school math teacher has told me that this approach has a more general, long-term benefit as well: Many of his students eventually incorporate the four steps into their regular, internalized learning strategies.

Still another strategy is to *give retakes* when students perform poorly the first time around. As noted in the discussion of mastery learning in Chapter 8, some students need more time to master a topic than others and may therefore need to be assessed on the same material more than once. However, students who are allowed to redo the *same* test or assignment may work on the specific things the assessment covers without studying equally important but nonassessed material. (Remember, most assessment tasks can represent only small samples of the content in question.) Thus a teacher might construct two assessment instruments for the same content domain, using one as the initial assessment and the other for retakes. If this approach is too time consuming to be practical, a teacher might allow students to redo the same assessment a second time but then average the two scores earned.

Respect students' right to privacy.

How would you feel if one of your instructors did the following?

- Returned test papers in the order of students' test scores, so that those with highest scores were handed out first, and you received yours *last?*

To encourage risk taking and reduce anxiety about classroom assessments, assess students' learning frequently and provide opportunities for students to correct errors. Here a teacher uses a student's errors on a paper–pencil assessment to guide her future studying efforts.

Will Hart/PhotoEdit

[49] Bangert-Drowns, Kulik, Kulik, & Morgan, 1991; Shepard et al., 2005; Shute, 2008.
[50] Clifford, 1990; N. E. Perry & Winne, 2004; Shepard et al., 2005.
[51] Crooks, 1988; E. D. Evans & Craig, 1990; Gaynor & Millham, 1976; Glover, 1989; Roediger & Karpicke, 2006; Sax, 1989.

- Told your other instructors how poorly you had done on a test so that they could be on the lookout for other stupid things you might do?
- Looked through your school records and discovered that you scored 92 on an IQ test you took last year and furthermore that a personality test revealed some unusual sexual fantasies?

You would probably be outraged that your instructor would do any of these things. Students' performance on assessment instruments should be somewhat confidential. But exactly *how* confidential? When should people know the results of students' assessments, and who should know them?

In the United States we get legal guidance on these questions from the **Family Educational Rights and Privacy Act (FERPA),** passed by the U.S. Congress in 1974. This legislation limits normal school testing practices primarily to the assessment of achievement and scholastic aptitude, two things that are clearly within the school's domain. Furthermore, it restricts access to students' assessment results to the few individuals who really need to know them: the students who earn them, their parents, and school personnel directly involved with students' education and well-being. Assessment results can be shared with other individuals (e.g., a family doctor or psychologist in private practice) *only* if the student (if at least 18 years old) or a parent gives written permission.

This legislative mandate for confidentiality has several implications for school assessment practices:

- A teacher cannot ask students to reveal their political affiliation, sexual behavior or attitudes, illegal behaviors, potentially embarrassing psychological problems, or family income. (One exception is questions about income to determine eligibility for financial assistance.)
- A teacher cannot post test scores in ways that allow students to learn one another's scores. For example, teachers cannot post scores in alphabetical order or according to birthdays or social security numbers.
- A teacher cannot distribute papers in any way that allows students to observe one another's scores. For example, teachers cannot let students search through a stack of scored papers to find their own.

Keeping students' assessment scores confidential makes educational as well as legal sense. Students getting low scores may feel embarrassed or ashamed if classmates know their scores, and they may become more anxious about their future classroom performance than they would otherwise have been. Students with high scores may also suffer from having their scores made public. At many schools it isn't cool to be smart, and high achievers may perform at lower levels to avoid risking peer rejection. And, of course, publicizing students' assessment results focuses students' attention on performance goals—how they appear to others—rather than on mastering the subject matter.

Many educators initially interpreted FERPA as forbidding teachers to have students grade one another's test papers. In 2002, however, the U.S. Supreme Court ruled that this practice doesn't violate FERPA because the test scores obtained are not yet a part of students' permanent school records.[52] Nevertheless, having students grade one another's classroom assessments—and thereby revealing some students' exceptionally high or low performance—can have adverse effects on students' sense of psychological well-being in the classroom. For this reason, I strongly urge teachers *not* to have students swap and grade one another's papers.

Summarizing Students' Achievement with Grades and Portfolios

Teachers summarize student achievement in a variety of ways. Some preschool and early elementary teachers use checklists to indicate specific accomplishments, and others write one- to two-page summaries describing students' strengths and weaknesses. Our focus here

? Reflecting on your own experiences as a student, can you recall situations in which FERPA was violated?

Family Educational Rights and Privacy Act (FERPA) U.S. legislation passed in 1974 that gives students and parents access to school records and limits other people's access to those records.

[52] *Owasso Independent School District v. Falvo,* 534 U.S. 426; for a more detailed explanation of this ruling, see Underwood and Webb, 2006.

will be on the two most commonly used methods of summarizing achievement: grades and portfolios. Following are several recommendations for using them.

Base final grades largely on achievement and hard data.

Tempting as it might be to reward well-behaved, cooperative students with good grades and to punish chronic misbehavers with Ds or Fs, grades should ultimately reflect *how much students have learned*. Awarding good grades simply for good behavior or exceptional effort may mislead students and their parents into believing that students are making better progress than they actually are. Awarding low grades as punishment for disruptive behavior leads students to conclude (perhaps with good reason) that their teacher's grading system is arbitrary and meaningless.[53]

By and large, teachers should use hard data, such as the results of formal paper–pencil and performance assessments, when arriving at final conclusions about what students have achieved. For reasons we've previously identified, subjective teacher judgments—forming opinions based on casual observations and general impressions—tend to be unreliable and sometimes have little validity. Although teachers can generally judge the achievement of high-ability students with some accuracy, they're less accurate when they subjectively assess the achievement of low-ability students. Teachers are especially likely to underestimate the achievement of students from ethnic minority groups and those from low socioeconomic backgrounds.[54]

Use many assessments to determine final grades.

Earlier I listed several advantages of assessing students' learning and achievement frequently. Using multiple assessments to determine final grades can also help compensate for the imperfect reliability and validity of any single assessment. However, teachers probably don't want to consider *everything* students do. For instance, they may not want to include students' early efforts at new tasks, which are likely to involve considerable trial and error. And many assessments may be more appropriately used for formative purposes—to help students learn—than for summative assessment.[55]

Share grading criteria with students, and keep students continually apprised of their progress.

To give students a sense that they have some control over their grades and other summaries of achievement (recall the discussion of *internal attributions* in Chapter 6), their teachers must tell them early in the semester or school year what the grading criteria will be. In addition, by providing concrete information about how grades will be assigned, teachers avoid unpleasant surprises when students actually receive their grades. If a teacher discovers that initial grading criteria are overly stringent, he or she may need to lighten up in some way, perhaps by adjusting cutoffs or allowing retakes of critical assessments. But a teacher must never change criteria midstream in a way that unfairly penalizes some students or imposes additional, unanticipated requirements.

Keep in mind that many students—younger ones especially—have limited self-monitoring skills. Furthermore, given the undependable nature of long-term memory (see Chapter 2), students may not have an accurate recollection of their various assessment scores over a period of several weeks or months. Thus it's often helpful to provide ongoing progress reports (e.g., see Figure 10.10) or show students how to keep their own records (e.g., look once again at Figure 4.7 in Chapter 4, p. 126).

Keep parents in the loop.

Certainly parents don't need to be apprised of every score their child gets on a classroom assessment, but they have a right to know how their

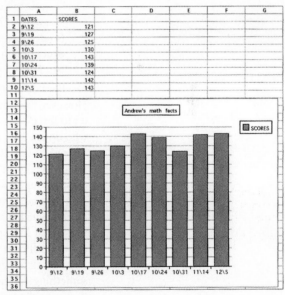

FIGURE 10.10 Computer software can often help teachers and students keep track of students' performance on classroom assessments. Here we see 10-year-old Andrew's performance on regular quizzes of math facts. Each quiz is worth 150 points.

[53] Brookhart, 2004; Cizek, 2003; Shepard et al., 2005.
[54] Brookhart, 2004; Gaines & Davis, 1990; Hoge & Coladarci, 1989; M. D. Miller et al. 2009.
[55] Andrade & Cizek, 2010; Brookhart, 2004; Frisbie & Waltman, 1992; Shepard et al., 2005.

children are progressing. In fact, in the United States, an additional provision of FERPA is that parents have the right to review any test scores and other school records. Furthermore, school personnel must present and interpret this information in a way that parents can understand.

In Chapter 9 we identified several ways of keeping the lines of communication open with parents, and some of them—parent–teacher conferences, brief notes and checklists sent home, and e-mail messages—are obviously suitable for transmitting information about students' assessment results and ongoing academic progress. For instance, the computer printout presented in Figure 10.10 can be informative to parents as well as to students.

What teachers must *not* do is use their communications with parents as punishment for what they perceive to be insufficient effort on students' part. As an example, let's look in on Ms. Ford's middle school math class. Ms. Ford has just handed back test papers with disappointing results, and the following class discussion ensues:

> **Ms. Ford:** When I corrected these papers, I was really, really shocked at some of the scores. And I think you will be too. I thought there were some that were so-so, and there were some that were devastating, in my opinion.
>
> **Student:** [Noise increasing.] Can we take them over?
>
> **Ms. Ford:** I am going to give them back to you. This is what I would like you to do: Every single math problem that you got wrong, for homework tonight and tomorrow, it is your responsibility to correct these problems and turn them in. In fact, I will say this, I want this sheet back to me by Wednesday at least. All our math problems that we got wrong I want returned to me with the correct answer.
>
> **Student:** Did anybody get 100?
>
> **Ms. Ford:** No.
>
> **Student:** Nobody got 100? [Groans]
>
> **Ms. Ford:** OK, boys and girls, shhh. I would say, on this test in particular, boys and girls, if you received a grade below 75 you definitely have to work on it. I do expect this quiz to be returned with Mom or Dad's signature on it. I want Mom and Dad to be aware of how we're doing.
>
> **Student:** No!
>
> **Student:** Do we have to show our parents? Is it a requirement to pass the class?
>
> **Ms. Ford:** If you do not return it with a signature, I will call home.[56]

Ms. Ford obviously wants parents to know that their children aren't doing well in her class. However, there are several drawbacks to her approach. First, many students may find it easier to forge an adultlike signature than to deliver bad news to their parents. Second, parents who do see their children's test papers won't have much information to help them interpret the results (are the low scores due to low effort? poor study strategies? poor instruction?). Finally, Ms. Ford focuses entirely on the problem—low achievement—without offering any concrete suggestions for *solving* it.

Ultimately, teachers must think of themselves as working in cooperation with students and parents for something that everyone wants: students' academic success. Teachers' primary goal in communicating assessment results is to share information that will foster accomplishment of that end—something Ms. Ford neglects to do. Furthermore, because virtually all of her students have done poorly on the test, Ms. Ford should consider whether something *she* has done—or not done—might account for the low scores. For instance, perhaps she allocated insufficient class time to certain concepts and skills, used ineffective strategies in teaching them, or constructed an exceptionally difficult test.

Accompany grades with descriptions of what the grades reflect.

As a general rule, final grades should reflect mastery of classroom subject matter and instructional goals. In other words, they should be criterion referenced.[57] When setting up a

---

[56] J. C. Turner, Meyer, et al., 1998, pp. 740–741.

[57] For example, see Shepard et al., 2005; Stiggins, 2008; Terwilliger, 1989. Over the past several decades, teachers have gradually moved from norm-referenced grading (i.e., grading on the curve) to criterion-referenced grading. This focus on mastery of instructional goals and objectives, rather than on comparing students with one another, partly accounts for the increasing grade point averages ("grade inflation") about which some public figures complain.

criterion-referenced grading system, teachers should determine as concretely as possible what they want each grade to communicate about students' achievement. For example, when assigning traditional letter grades, a teacher might use descriptors such as the following:

Grade	Criteria
A	The student has a firm command of both basic and advanced knowledge and skills in the content domain. He or she is well prepared for future learning tasks.
B	The student has mastered all basic knowledge and skills. Mastery at a more advanced level is evident in some, but not all, areas. In most respects, he or she is ready for future learning tasks.
C	The student has mastered basic knowledge and skills but has difficulty with more advanced aspects of the subject matter. He or she lacks a few of the prerequisites critical for future learning tasks.
D	The student has mastered some but not all of the basics in the content domain. He or she lacks many prerequisites for future learning tasks.
F	The student shows little if any mastery of instructional objectives and cannot demonstrate the most elementary knowledge and skills. He or she lacks most of the prerequisites essential for success in future learning tasks.[58]

It's especially important to specify grading criteria when different students in the same class are working toward different instructional goals. For example, in the United States the IDEA legislation stipulates that teachers and other school personnel identify appropriate instructional goals for individual children and adolescents who have special educational needs. Final evaluations of achievement, including final grades, should be based on students' accomplishment of those goals.[59]

Accompany grades with additional qualitative information about students' performance.

Even when final grades are accompanied by descriptions of what they reflect, they're at best only general indicators of the "quantity" of what students have learned. Thus, it's often helpful to accompany grades with qualitative information—for instance, information about students' particular academic strengths, work habits, attitudes, social skills, unique contributions to the classroom community, and so on. Students and parents alike often find such qualitative feedback quite informative and helpful. Comments should be fairly explicit, however. Feedback such as "a pleasure to have in class" communicates little or no new information.[60]

Use portfolios to show complex skills or improvements over time.

In the opening case study, Akeem's portfolio showed his exceptional talents in drawing and sculpture and his ongoing progress in literacy skills. In general, a **portfolio** is a collection of a student's work systematically collected over a lengthy time period. It might include writing samples, student-constructed objects (e.g., sculptures, inventions), photographs, audiotapes, video recordings, or any combination of these. For example, Figure 10.4, on page 375, presents a page from 6-year-old Meghan's portfolio that focuses on her social skills and work habits. Figure 10.11 presents another page from Meghan's portfolio, this one using photographs to show her emerging math skills. Meghan's portfolio was compiled largely by her kindergarten teacher. But once students acquire basic literacy skills, *they* are usually the primary authors of their portfolios.

Meghan makes arrangements of six in math.

Meghan displays her collection of 100.

FIGURE 10.11 In a kindergarten portfolio, Meghan and her teacher included these two digital photographs to illustrate Meghan's developing math skills.

---

[58] Based on criteria described by Frisbie & Waltman, 1992.

[59] Brookhart, 2004; Mac Iver, Stipek, & Daniels, 1991; Mastropieri & Scruggs, 2000; Venn, 2000.

[60] Brookhart, 2004, p. 183.

portfolio Collection of a student's work compiled systematically over a lengthy time period.

SELF-EVALUATION

The three pieces of writing in my portfolio that best represent who I am are: 1) "Author Ben Hoff," which is a story in the language of Ben Hoff; 2) "Quotes from <u>The Tao of Pooh</u>"; and 3) "Discrimination."

What "Author Ben Hoff" shows about me as a learner or a writer is that I am able to analyze and absorb the types and styles of an author and then transfer what I learn onto paper in a good final understandable piece of writing. This piece has good description, a good plot line, gets the point across, has a basic setting, and is understandable. I did not change too much of this piece from one draft to the next except punctuation, grammar and spelling. I did, however, add a quote from <u>The Tao of Pooh</u>.

"Quotes from <u>The Tao of Pooh</u>" shows that I am able to pull out good and significant quotes from a book, understand them, and put them into my own words. Then I can make them understandable to other people. This piece gets the point across well and is easy to understand. I really only corrected spelling and punctuation from one draft to the next.

"Discrimination" shows me that I am learning more about discrimination and how it might feel (even though I have never experienced really bad discrimination). I found I can get my ideas across through realistic writing. This piece has good description and was well written for the assignment. Besides correcting some punctuation and spelling, I changed some wording to make the story a little more clear.

For all three pieces, the mechanics of my writing tend to be fairly poor on my first draft, but that is because I am writing as thoughts come into my mind rather than focusing on details of grammar. Then my final drafts get better as I get comments and can turn my attention to details of writing.

The four most important things that I'm able to do as a writer are to: 1) get thoughts pulled into a story; 2) have that story understandable and the reader get something from it; 3) have the reader remember it was a good piece of writing; and 4) like the piece myself.

FIGURE 10.12 In this self-reflection 14-year-old Kurt explains why he has chosen certain pieces to include in his eighth-grade language arts portfolio.

The samples of student work included in a portfolio are often called *artifacts*. Most school portfolios also include student-written documentation that describes each artifact and a rationale for including it. For example, in Figure 10.12, 14-year-old Kurt describes and evaluates the writing samples he's included in a portfolio for his eighth-grade language arts class. As is true in Kurt's portfolio, many portfolios include two or more successive versions of a single item.

Portfolios take a variety of forms. Following are several types commonly used in school settings:[61]

- **Working portfolio**—Shows competencies up to the present time; is dynamic in content, with new artifacts that show increasing proficiency gradually replacing older, less skillful ones.
- **Developmental portfolio**—Includes several artifacts related to a particular set of skills; shows how a student has improved over time.
- **Course portfolio**—Includes assignments and reflections for a single course; typically also includes a summarizing reflection in which the student identifies his or her general accomplishments in the course.
- **Best-work portfolio**—Includes artifacts intended to showcase the student's particular achievements and unique talents.

These categories aren't necessarily mutually exclusive. For instance, a course portfolio might have a developmental component, showing how a student has improved in one or more skills over the school year. And a best-work portfolio may be a work-in-progress for quite some time, thereby having the dynamic nature of a working portfolio.

Some portfolios are most appropriate for formative assessment, whereas others are appropriate for summative assessment.[62] Developmental portfolios, which include products from the entire school year or perhaps an even longer period, can show whether students are making reasonable progress toward long-term instructional goals; as such, they're often best used for formative assessment. Best-work portfolios are better suited for summative assessment; for instance, they might be used to communicate students' final accomplishments to parents, school administrators, college admissions officers, or potential employers. Portfolios have several other benefits as well:[63]

 See 8-year-old Keenan use her developmental portfolio to track her progress in writing skills in the "Portfolio" video in Chapter 10 of the Book-Specific Resources in MyEducationLab.

---

[61] R. S. Johnson, Mims-Cox, & Doyle-Nichols, 2006; Spandel, 1997.
[62] R. S. Johnson et al., 2006; Spandel, 1997.
[63] Arter & Spandel, 1992; Banta, 2003; Darling-Hammond et al., 1995; DiMartino & Castaneda, 2007;

R. S. Johnson et al., 2006; Koretz, Stecher, Klein, & McCaffrey, 1994; Paulson, Paulson, & Meyer, 1991; Spandel, 1997; Vucko & Hadwin, 2004.

- They capture the multifaceted nature of students' achievement, with a particular emphasis on complex skills.
- They can demonstrate students' performance on real-world, authentic assessment tasks (e.g., science experiments, service-learning projects).
- They provide practice in self-monitoring and self-evaluation, thereby enhancing students' self-regulation skills.
- They give students a sense of accomplishment and self-efficacy about areas that have been mastered, while possibly also alerting students to areas needing improvement.
- They provide a mechanism through which teachers can easily intertwine assessment with instruction: Students often include products that their teachers have assigned primarily for instructional purposes.
- Because the focus of portfolios is usually on complex skills, teachers are more likely to *teach* those skills.

Creating a portfolio is typically a lengthy process that stretches out over several weeks or months; some best-work portfolios may evolve over several years. So that students aren't overwhelmed by such a complex undertaking, it's often helpful to break the portfolio-construction process into a series of steps, scaffolding students' efforts at each step:[64]

1. **Planning.** Decide on the purpose(s) the portfolio will serve (e.g., which instructional goals and/or content area standards it will address and whether it will be used primarily for formative or summative assessment); identify a preliminary plan of attack for creating the portfolio.
2. **Collection.** Save artifacts that demonstrate progress toward or achievement of particular goals and standards.
3. **Selection.** Review the saved artifacts, and choose those that best reflect achievement of the specified goals and standards.
4. **Reflection.** Write explanations and self-evaluations of each artifact; describe how the artifacts show current competencies and growth over time; relate achievements to previously identified goals and standards.
5. **Projection.** Identify new goals toward which to strive.
6. **Presentation.** Share the portfolio with an appropriate audience (e.g., classmates, parents, college admissions personnel).

The Classroom Strategies box "Summarizing Students' Achievements with Portfolios" offers several suggestions for scaffolding students' efforts in creating portfolios.

RSVP characteristics can be a source of concern for portfolios, however, especially if they're used to *evaluate* (rather than simply communicate) students' learning and achievement.[65] When portfolios must be scored in some way, scoring is often unreliable, with different teachers rating them differently. In addition, there's an obvious standardization problem, because their contents can vary considerably from one student to another. Validity may or may not be a problem: Some portfolios may include enough artifacts to adequately represent what students have accomplished relative to instructional goals, but others may be unrepresentative. And because portfolios are likely to take a great deal of teacher time, they're less practical than other methods of summarizing achievement. All this is *not* to say that teachers should shy away from having students create portfolios, but they should be sure the potential benefits outweigh the disadvantages. And when using portfolios as summative reflections of what students have accomplished, teachers must identify explicit criteria for evaluating them.[66]

Assessing Students' Achievement and Abilities with Standardized Tests

Final grades and portfolios are derived directly from things students do in the classroom. A different approach to summarizing what students know and can do is the **standardized test**, developed by test construction experts and published for use in many different schools

---

[64] Six steps based on R. S. Johnson et al., 2006.
[65] Arter & Spandel, 1992; Banta, 2003; R. S. Johnson et al., 2006; Koretz et al., 1994; Popham, 1995.

[66] See Darling-Hammond et al. (1995) for examples of criteria that schools have successfully used.

standardized test Test developed by test construction experts and published for use in many different schools and classrooms.

CLASSROOM STRATEGIES Summarizing Students' Achievements with Portfolios

- Identify in advance the specific purpose(s) for which a portfolio will be used.

    A third-grade teacher and her students agree to create portfolios that will show parents and other family members how much their writing skills improve over the school year. Throughout the year students save their fiction and nonfiction, and eventually they choose pieces that best demonstrate mastery of some writing skills and progress on others. The children proudly present their portfolios at parent–teacher–student conferences at the end of the year.

- Align portfolio contents with important instructional goals and/or content area standards.

    At a high school in Ohio, twelfth graders complete graduation portfolios with three components, each of which reflects one or more of the school's instructional goals for all graduates:

    - A *lifelong-learning skills section:* Includes artifacts showing one's best work in writing, math, science, and at least one other discipline or interest area, plus a personal reflection describing oneself as a learner.
    - A *democratic citizenship section:* Includes evidence of active citizenship (e.g., taking a stand on a public issue, engaging in public service) at school or in the community, plus a personal reflection on one's readiness for becoming a productive citizen in society.
    - A *career-readiness section:* Includes a résumé, a sample job or college application, recent letters of reference, and a personal reflection on one's readiness for post-graduation work or study.

- Ask students to select the contents of their portfolios; provide the scaffolding they need to make wise choices.

    A fifth-grade teacher meets one-on-one with each of his students to help them choose artifacts that best reflect their achievements for the year. To give the students an idea of the kinds of things they might include, he shows them several portfolios that students have created in previous years. He shares only those portfolios that previous students and parents have given him permission to use in this way.

- Identify specific criteria that should guide students' selections; possibly include students in the criteria identification process.

    A middle school geography teacher leads his class in a discussion of criteria that students might use to identify artifacts for a course portfolio. After reviewing the instructional goals for the course, the class agrees that each portfolio should include at least one artifact demonstrating each of the following:

    - Map interpretation skills
    - Map construction skills
    - Understanding of interrelationships between physical environments and socioeconomic practices
    - Knowledge of cultural differences within the nation
    - Recognition that all cultures have many positive qualities

- Have students include reflections on the products they include.

    At the beginning of the school year, a ninth-grade journalism teacher tells students that they will be creating portfolios that show progress in journalistic writing during the semester. She asks them to save all of their drafts—"Even simple notes and sketchy outlines," she says. Later in the semester, as students begin to compile their portfolios, she asks them to look at their various drafts of each piece and to describe how the progression from one draft to the next shows their gradual mastery of journalism skills. She occasionally assigns these reflections as homework so that students spread the portfolio construction task over a four-week period and therefore don't leave everything until the last minute.

- Give students a general organizational scheme to follow.

    When a high school requires students to complete portfolios as one of their graduation requirements, students get considerable guidance from their homeroom teachers. These teachers also provide a handout describing the elements each portfolio should include: title page, table of contents, introduction to the portfolio's contents, distinct sections for each content domain included, and final reflection summarizing the student's achievements.

- Determine whether a physical format or electronic format is more suitable for the circumstances.

    At a high school that places particular emphasis on visual and performing arts, students create electronic portfolios that showcase their talents in art, drama, dance, and/or instrumental music. They digitally photograph, videotape, or audiotape their projects and performances, and they create word processing documents that describe and evaluate each one. They then divide their electronic documents into several logical categories, each of which they put in a separate electronic folder on a flash drive, CD, or DVD.

- When using portfolios for final evaluations, develop a rubric for scoring them.

    At a high school in New York City, a key instructional goal is for students to acquire certain dispositions and thinking processes—which the school collectively calls *habits of mind*—in their academic work. One of these habits of mind is the use of credible, convincing evidence to support statements and positions. The school develops a four-point rating scale to evaluate students' work on this criterion. A score of 4 is given to work that reflects "Generalizations and ideas supported by specific relevant and accurate information, which is developed in appropriate depth." At the other end of the scale, a score of 1 is given to work that reflects "Mostly general statements; little specific evidence relating to the topic."

Sources: Banta, 2003; Darling-Hammond et al., 1995, p. 39 (New York City high school example); DiMartino & Castaneda, 2007, pp. 40–41 (Ohio high school example); R. S. Johnson et al., 2006; Paulson, Paulson, & Meyer, 1991; Popham, 1995; Spandel, 1997; Stiggins, 2008.

and classrooms. The test is *standardized* in several ways: All students are given the same instructions and time limits, respond to the same (or very similar) questions or tasks, and have their responses evaluated relative to the same criteria. A test manual describes the instructions to give students, the time limits to impose, and the specific scoring criteria to use. Often the manual also provides information about test reliability for different populations

TABLE 10.5 Commonly Used Standardized Tests

Kind of Test	Purpose	General Description	Special Considerations
Achievement tests	To assess how much students have learned from what they have specifically been taught	Test items are written to reflect the curriculum common to many schools. Test scores indicate achievement only in a very broad and (usually) norm-referenced sense: They estimate a student's general level of knowledge and skills in a particular domain relative to other students across the country.	• These tests are usually more appropriate for measuring general levels of achievement than for determining specific information and skills that students have and have not acquired.
General scholastic aptitude and intelligence tests	To assess students' general capability to learn; to predict their general academic success over the short run	Test items typically focus on what and how much students have learned and deduced from their general, everyday experiences. For example, the tests may include items that ask students to define words, draw logical deductions, recognize analogies between seemingly unrelated topics, analyze geometric figures, or solve problems.	• Test scores should not be construed as an indication of learning potential over the long run. • Individually administered tests (in which the tester works one-on-one with a particular student) are preferable when students' verbal skills are limited or when exceptional giftedness or a significant disability is suspected.
Specific aptitude and ability tests	To predict how well students are likely to perform in a specific content domain	Test items are similar to those in general scholastic aptitude tests, except that they focus on a specific domain (e.g., verbal skills, mathematical reasoning). Some aptitude tests, called *multiple aptitude batteries,* yield subscores for a variety of domains simultaneously.	• Test scores should not be construed as an indication of learning potential over the long run. • Tests tend to have only limited ability to predict students' success in a particular domain and so should be used only in combination with other information about students.
School readiness tests	To determine whether young children have the prerequisite skills to be successful in a typical kindergarten or first-grade curriculum	Test items focus on basic knowledge and skills—for instance, recognition of colors and shapes, knowledge of numbers and letters, and ability to remember and follow directions.	• Test scores should be interpreted cautiously. Young children have shorter attention spans and less motivation to perform testlike tasks than older children do, leading to lower reliability and validity of test scores. • Tests should be used primarily for instructional planning purposes, *not* for deciding whether students are ready to begin formal schooling.*

* School readiness tests have become increasingly controversial in recent years, in part because the scores they yield typically correlate only moderately with children's academic performance even a year or so later. For various perspectives on these tests, see G. J. Duncan et al., 2007; Forget-Dubois et al., 2007; La Paro & Pianta, 2000; Pellegrini, 1998; C. E. Sanders, 1997; Stipek, 2002.

and age-groups, as well as information from which teachers and school administrators can draw inferences about test validity for their own situation and purposes.

Four kinds of standardized tests that school districts use frequently—achievement tests, general scholastic aptitude tests, specific aptitude tests, and school readiness tests—are described in Table 10.5.[67] Most of these tests yield norm-referenced scores. For instance, if you look once again at the explanation of IQ scores in Chapter 5 (pp. 158–159), you'll realize that IQ scores indicate *only* how children stack up against one another and thus are norm-referenced. Common forms of norm-referenced scores used in standardized testing, including IQ scores, are described in depth in the appendix, "Interpreting Standardized Test Scores."

Consistent with our emphasis on assessing students' learning and achievement in this chapter, our focus in the upcoming pages will be on standardized *achievement* tests. Such tests are useful in at least two ways.[68] First, they enable teachers and school administrators

[67] You can find descriptions of several widely used standardized tests at the websites for CTB and McGraw-Hill (www.ctb.com) and Riverside Publishing (www.riverpub.com).

[68] Ansley, 1997.

to compare their own students' general achievement with the achievement of students elsewhere—information that may indirectly provide information about the effectiveness of the local curriculum and instructional practices. Second, standardized achievement tests provide a means of tracking students' general progress over time and raising red flags about potential trouble spots. For example, imagine that Lucas has been getting average test scores year after year but then suddenly performs well below average in eighth grade, even though the test and norm group are the same as in previous years. At this point his teacher would want to ascertain whether the low performance was a temporary fluke (e.g., was Lucas sick on the test day?) or, instead, due to other, longer-term issues that require attention.

With the preceding information in mind, let's return one final time to the opening case study. Despite Akeem's improvement in reading and writing as he moved through the grade levels, his performance on districtwide achievement tests remained low. Quite possibly those tests yielded norm-referenced scores—that is, they compared Akeem's performance to that of his age-mates around the city. He was improving, certainly, but so were most of his age-mates. Thus, his performance *relative to his peers* continued to be near the bottom of the heap. Fortunately, his elementary and middle school teachers consistently recognized and fostered his particular strengths, encouraging him to stay in school and set his sights on a rewarding career.

High-Stakes Tests and Accountability

In recent years a great deal of emphasis—entirely *too much* emphasis, in my opinion—has been placed on students' performance on standardized achievement tests. Within the past two or three decades, many politicians, business leaders, and other public figures have lamented students' low achievement test results and called for major overhauls of the public schools. Some of these reform-minded individuals equate high achievement with high scores on standardized tests and, conversely, low achievement with low test scores. Policy makers have put considerable pressure on teachers and educational administrators to get the test scores up, and some threaten serious consequences (reduced funding, restrictions on salary, etc.) for those schools and faculty members who *don't* get the scores up. Here we're talking about both **high-stakes testing**—making major decisions on the basis of single assessments—and **accountability**—a mandated obligation of teachers, administrators, and other school personnel to accept responsibility for students' performance on those assessments.

In the United States the **No Child Left Behind Act** of 2001—sometimes known simply as **NCLB**—now mandates both high-stakes testing and accountability in all public elementary and secondary schools. It also mandates that all states establish:

> challenging academic content standards in academic subjects that —
> (I) specify what children are expected to know and be able to do;
> (II) contain coherent and rigorous content; and
> (III) encourage the teaching of advanced skills[69]

School districts must annually assess students in grades 3 through 8 and at least once during grades 10 through 12 to determine whether students are making *adequate yearly progress* in meeting state-determined standards in reading, math, and science. The nature of this progress is defined by the state (and so differs from state to state), but assessment results must clearly show that all students, including those from diverse racial and socioeconomic groups, are making significant gains in knowledge and skills. (Students with significant cognitive disabilities may be given alternative assessments, but they must show improvement commensurate with their ability levels.) Schools that demonstrate progress receive rewards, such as teacher bonuses or increased funding. Schools that don't demonstrate progress are subject to sanctions and corrective actions (e.g., bad publicity, administrative restructuring, dismissal of staff members), and students have the option of attending a better public school at the school district's expense.[70] As I complete this third edition of the book in the

high-stakes testing   Practice of using students' performance on a single assessment to make major decisions about students, school personnel, or overall school quality.

accountability   Mandated obligation of teachers and other school personnel to accept responsibility for students' performance on high-stakes assessments.

No Child Left Behind Act (NCLB)   U.S. legislation passed in 2001 that mandates regular assessments of basic skills to determine whether students are making adequate yearly progress in relation to state-determined standards in reading, math, and science.

[69] P.L. 107-110, Sec. 1111.
[70] You can learn more about the No Child Left Behind Act at the U.S. Department of Education's website at www.ed.gov. You can also find a good summary in R. M. Thomas, 2005.

fall of 2010, many policy makers are talking about significant revisions to the NCLB legislation; thus, it will probably continue to be a work-in-progress for the next few years.

Sometimes individual students, too, are held accountable for their performance on statewide or schoolwide assessments. Some school districts have used students' performance on tests or other assessments as a basis for promotion to the next grade level or for awarding high school diplomas.[71] Typically, school personnel begin by identifying certain content area standards (they sometimes use the word *competencies)* that students' final achievement should reflect. They then assess students' performance levels (sometimes known as *outcomes*) at the end of instruction, and only those students whose performance meets the predetermined standards and competencies move forward. Such practice, of course, requires criterion-referenced rather than norm-referenced scores. For instance, one school district developed four possible scores for students' performance on its districtwide writing assessment, three of which reflected some degree of mastery:

In progress—Is an underdeveloped and/or unfocused message.

Essential—Is a series of related ideas. The pattern of organization and the descriptive or supporting details are adequate and appropriate.

Proficient—Meets Essential Level criteria and contains a logical progression of ideas. The pattern of organization and the transition of ideas flow. Word choice enhances the writing.

Advanced—Meets Proficient Level criteria and contains examples of one or more of the following: insight, creativity, fluency, critical thinking, or style.[72]

Such efforts to monitor schools' instructional effectiveness and students' academic progress are certainly well intentioned. Ideally, they can help schools determine whether instructional methods need revision and whether teachers need retooling, and they can help teachers identify students who are not acquiring the basic skills necessary for successful participation in the adult world. However, the current emphasis on boosting students' test scores is fraught with difficulties in implementation. For example, teachers often spend a great deal of time teaching to the tests—a serious problem if the tests reflect only a few of the many instructional goals toward which students should be striving. And recall the teacher's dilemma in the opening case study ("Taking Over") in Chapter 4. In order to "cover" all the material on the ninth-grade math competency exam, Ms. Gaunt eventually abandons her efforts to help students master basic concepts and procedures, essentially throwing the *less-is-more* principle out the window.[73]

Using Standardized Achievement Tests Judiciously

In my final set of recommendations, I offer several suggestions for using standardized and high-stakes achievement tests in ways that maximize their usefulness.

When you have a choice in the test you use, choose a test that has high validity for your curriculum and students.

Content validity is just as much a concern for standardized achievement tests as it is for teacher-constructed classroom assessments. Teachers and school administrators can best determine the content validity of a standardized achievement test by comparing a table of

---

[71] Such approaches go by a variety of names; *outcomes-based education* and *minimum competency testing* are two common ones.

[72] Criteria adapted from "District 6 Writing Assessment, Narrative and Persuasive Modes, Scoring Criteria, Intermediate Level" (Working Copy) by School District 6 (Greeley/Evans, CO), 1993; adapted by permission.

[73] For various perspectives on the problems associated with high-stakes testing and the No Child Left Behind

Act, see W. Au, 2007; Balfanz, Legters, West, & Weber, 2007; Finnigan & Gross, 2007; B. Fuller, Wright, Gesicki, & Kang, 2007; A. D. Ho, 2008; Hursh, 2007; S. Kelly & Monczunski, 2007; La Guardia, 2009; J. Lee, 2008; Mintrop & Sunderman, 2009; Nisbett, 2009; Porter & Polikoff, 2007; Solórzano, 2008; Stringfield & Yakimowski-Srebnick, 2005; R. M. Thomas, 2005; Valli & Buese, 2007; W. E. Wright, 2006.

Some standardized tests are administered one-on-one. Such tests minimize the importance of testwiseness, and they enable the examiner to observe a student's attention span, motivation, and other factors that may affect the student's performance. For these reasons, individually administered tests are typically used when identifying students who have special educational needs.

specifications for the test to their own curriculum.[74] School faculty members should also scrutinize the actual test items to see whether they address only basic knowledge and skills (as some tests do[75]) or, instead, also address conceptual understanding and complex cognitive processes. A test has high content validity for a particular school and classroom only if the topics and thinking skills emphasized in test items match local instructional goals and content area standards.

Teach to the test if—but only if—it reflects important instructional goals.

When teachers are held accountable for their students' performance on a particular test, many of them understandably devote many class hours to the knowledge and skills the test assesses, and students may focus their studying efforts accordingly.[76] The result is often that students perform at higher levels on a high-stakes test *without* improving their achievement and abilities more generally.[77] If a test truly measures the things that are most important for students to learn—including such complex cognitive processes as transfer, problem solving, and critical thinking—then focusing on those things is quite appropriate. If the test primarily assesses rote knowledge and basic skills, however, then such emphasis may undermine the improvements teachers *really* want to see in students' achievement.[78]

Make sure students are adequately prepared to take the test.

Teachers should typically prepare students ahead of time for a standardized test. For instance, teachers can do the following:[79]

- Explain the general nature of the test and the tasks it involves (e.g., if applicable, mention that students aren't expected to know all the answers and that many students won't have enough time to respond to every item).
- Encourage students to do their best, but without describing the test as a life–or–death matter.
- Give students practice with the test's format and item types (e.g., demonstrate how to answer multiple-choice questions and fill in computer-scored answer sheets).
- Encourage students to get a full night's sleep and eat a good breakfast before taking the test.

To some degree, teachers can also help students prepare for standardized achievement tests by teaching them useful test-taking strategies, such as temporarily skipping difficult items, double-checking to be sure answers are marked in the correct spots, and so on. Teachers should keep in mind, however, that having effective test-taking skills—**testwiseness**—typically makes only a small difference in students' test scores.[80] Furthermore, test-taking skills and student achievement are positively correlated: Students with many test-taking strategies tend to be higher achievers than students with few strategies. In other words, very few students get low test scores *only* because they're poor test takers.[81] In most cases teachers better serve their students by teaching them the knowledge and skills that tests are designed to assess rather than spending an inordinate amount of time teaching them how to take tests.[82]

---

testwiseness Test-taking know-how that enhances test performance.

[74] Test publishers typically construct a table of specifications and either include it in the test manual or make it available upon request. If a table is not available, school personnel can construct one by tallying the number of items that tap into various topics and thinking skills.

[75] Alleman & Brophy, 1997; Bransford et al., 2006; Mintrop & Sunderman, 2009; Porter & Polikoff, 2007.

[76] Jacob, 2003; R. L. Linn, 2000; Pianta, Belsky, Houts, & Morrison, 2007; R. M. Thomas, 2005.

[77] Amrein & Berliner, 2002a, 2002b, 2002c; Jacob, 2003; Shepard et al., 2005.

[78] Amrein & Berliner, 2002b; W. Au, 2007; Mintrop & Sunderman, 2009; R. M. Ryan, 2005; Valli & Buese, 2007.

[79] Kirkland, 1971; Popham, 1990; Sax, 1989; Shepard et al., 2005.

[80] Bangert-Drowns, Kulik, & Kulik, 1983; Hembree, 1987; A. J. Reynolds & Oberman, 1987; Scruggs & Lifson, 1985; Shepard et al., 2005.

[81] Geiger, 1997; Scruggs & Lifson, 1985.

[82] J. R. Frederiksen & Collins, 1989; Shepard et al., 2005.

When administering the test, follow the directions closely and report any unusual circumstances.

Once the testing session begins, teachers should follow the test administration procedures to the letter, distributing test booklets as directed, asking students to complete any practice items provided, keeping time faithfully, and responding to students' questions in the prescribed manner. Remember, students in the test's norm group have taken the test under certain standardized conditions, and teachers must replicate those conditions as closely as possible. Occasionally teachers will encounter events (a noisy construction project nearby, an unexpected power failure, etc.) that are beyond their control. When such events significantly alter the conditions under which students are taking the test, they jeopardize the validity of the test results and so must be reported. Teachers should also make note of any individual students who are behaving in ways unlikely to lead to maximum performance—students who appear exceptionally nervous, stare out the window for long periods, seem to be marking answers haphazardly, and so on.[83]

Take students' ages and developmental levels into account when interpreting test results.

Virtually any test score will be influenced by a variety of irrelevant factors—language and literacy skills, motivation, mood, energy level, general health, and so on—that will impact the score's reliability and validity. Such factors are especially likely to influence the test results of young children, many of whom may have limited verbal skills, short attention spans, little motivation to do their best, and low tolerance for frustration. Furthermore, young children's erratic behaviors may make it difficult to maintain standardized testing conditions.[84]

In adolescence other variables can affect the validity of scores on standardized tests. Although students may get a bit nervous about tests in the elementary grades (e.g., see Figure 10.13), test anxiety increases in the middle school and high school grades, sometimes to the point of interfering with students' concentration during a test. Furthermore, especially in high school, some students become quite cynical about the validity and usefulness of standardized paper–pencil tests.[85] If students see little point to taking a test, they may read test items superficially, if at all, and a few may complete answer sheets simply by following a certain pattern (e.g., alternating between A and B) or filling in bubbles to make pictures or designs.[86] At *any* grade level, then, teachers and educational administrators must be careful not to place too much stock in the specific scores that tests yield.

FIGURE 10.13 Eight-year-old Connie describes how overwhelming test anxiety can be.

Make appropriate accommodations for English language learners.

Without question, students' experience and facility with English affects their performance on English-based achievement tests, including high-stakes tests.[87] For instance, when children come to school after growing up in a non-English-speaking environment, it typically takes them considerable time—perhaps five to seven years—to gain sufficient proficiency in English to perform at their best in English-speaking classrooms.[88] Yet many school districts require these students to take high-stakes tests in English long before they achieve this proficiency.[89] Clearly such a policy leads to significant underestimations of English language learners' academic achievement. Ideally, educators should modify achievement tests in ways that yield greater content validity. Following are several recommended practices:[90]

- Translate a test into a student's native language.

---

[83] M. D. Miller et al., 2009.

[84] Bracken & Walker, 1997; S. M. Carver, 2006; Fleege, Charlesworth, & Burts, 1992; Messick, 1983; Stipek, 2002; Wodtke, Harper, & Schommer, 1989.

[85] Paris, Lawton, Turner, & Roth, 1991.

[86] Paris et al., 1991; W. E. Wright, 2006.

[87] Carhill, Suárez-Orozco, & Páez, 2008; Solórzano, 2008.

[88] Carhill et al., 2008; Cummins, 1984, 2008; Padilla, 2006.

[89] Solórzano, 2008; W. E. Wright, 2006.

[90] Haywood & Lidz, 2007; R. S. Johnson et al., 2006; Solórzano, 2008; W. E. Wright, 2006.

- Administer a test one on one, perhaps eliminating time limits, presenting questions orally, and allowing students to respond in their native language. (This practice reduces the second RSVP characteristic—standardization—but may be the only way to ensure the third RSVP characteristic—validity of the results.)
- Use alternative assessment methods (e.g., dynamic assessment, portfolios) to document achievement.
- Exclude students' test scores when computing averages that reflect the overall achievement of a school or a particular subgroup within the school.

Never use a single test score to make important decisions about students.

What I've seen and heard in the media leads me to think that many politicians and other policy makers overestimate how much high-stakes and other standardized achievement tests can tell us: They assume that such instruments are highly accurate, comprehensive measures of students' academic achievement. True, these tests are often developed by experts with considerable training in test construction, but no test is completely reliable, and its validity will vary considerably depending on the context in which it's being used.[91] Every test is fallible, and students do poorly on tests for a variety of reasons. Thus teachers, school administrators, parents, and others should never—and I do mean *never*—use a single assessment instrument or single test score to make important decisions about individual students. Nor should they use the results of a single test to make important decisions about large groups of students or about the teachers who teach them. It behooves everyone who has a personal or professional stake in children's education to be aware of the limitations of standardized tests and enlighten their fellow citizens accordingly.

Regardless of how students' learning and achievement are assessed, we must continually keep one point in mind: *Tests and other educational assessments are useful but imperfect tools.* Standardized tests, teacher quizzes, classroom assignments, performance tasks, portfolios—all of these can tell us something about what students know and can do and what students still need to learn and master. The usefulness of any assessment strategy depends on how well matched it is to the situation in which it will be used and how reliable and valid it is for that situation. As a general rule, we should think of any educational assessment as a tool that, in combination with the other tools at teachers' disposal, can help improve classroom instruction and maximize students' learning and achievement over the long run.

---

[91] Kane, 2008.

SUMMARY

Regular assessments of students' learning and achievement are an essential component of effective classroom instruction. The Mega-Ideas presented at the beginning of the chapter can help us summarize the key concepts and principles that must guide teachers' assessment practices.

- *Classroom assessments serve a variety of purposes, but in one way or another they are all likely to impact students' future learning and achievement.* Assessment is a process of observing a sample of a student's behavior and drawing inferences about the student's knowledge and abilities. Some classroom assessments are used for formative assessment, to guide future instruction. Others are used for summative assessment, to determine what students ultimately know and can do at the end of instruction. But regardless of

a teacher's purpose in assessing students' knowledge and skills, the nature of the teacher's assessment instruments gives students messages about what things are most important to learn and about how students should study and think about classroom subject matter. Not only is assessment closely interconnected with instruction, but in a very real sense it *is* instruction.

- *Ideally, classroom assessments have four RSVP characteristics—reliability, standardization, validity, and practicality—with validity being the most important.* Teachers should keep four characteristics in mind when identifying assessment strategies and developing assessment instruments. First, an assessment should be *reliable*, yielding consistent results regardless of the specific circumstances in which a teacher administers and scores it. Second, it should be *standardized,* in that it has similar content and is administered and evaluated in a similar manner for everyone (some students with disabilities may be exceptions). Third, it should be *valid,* being an accurate reflection of the knowledge and skills the teacher is trying to assess. Finally, it should be *practical,* staying within reasonable costs and time constraints.

● ***Informal assessments of students' verbal and nonverbal behaviors can be helpful if they show a consistent pattern over time.*** Teachers sometimes assess achievement informally, perhaps by simply observing what students do and listening to what they say in everyday classroom activities. Informal assessment is flexible and practical and requires little or no advance planning. Unfortunately, it usually doesn't provide a representative sample of what students know and can do, and teachers' judgments are often biased by their beliefs and expectations about particular students.

● ***Formal classroom assessments must be carefully planned and conducted to ensure that their results reflect students' accomplishments of instructional goals and objectives.*** When drawing firm conclusions about what students have and have not achieved—for instance, when assigning final grades—teachers should base their conclusions largely on preplanned, formal assessments. Paper–pencil assessment tasks are usually more practical, and so they are often preferable *if* they truly reflect instructional goals. Performance assessment tasks are often more appropriate for assessing complex achievements that require the integration of numerous skills, and accomplishment of some instructional objectives can be assessed *only* through direct observation of what students can do. Paper–pencil and performance assessments alike usually yield more useful information when tasks have some structure and when explicit, concrete scoring criteria are identified ahead of time.

Although teachers must be the final judges of students' performance on classroom assessments, involving students in the assessment process—for instance, soliciting students' input about evaluation criteria and asking them to rate their own performance—can encourage intrinsic motivation and foster self-regulation skills. Furthermore, classroom assessment practices should allow leeway for students to take the risks so essential for the pursuit of challenging tasks. No single failure should seriously impact a student's long-term academic success.

For both legal and educational reasons, teachers must keep students' assessment results confidential, communicating students' test scores, grades, and other information only to the students themselves, to their parents, and to school personnel directly involved in the students' education and well-being. Teachers must also remember that the ultimate purpose of *any* assessment is not to pass judgment, but rather to help students learn and achieve more effectively.

● ***Final class grades provide only minimal quantitative information about students' academic achievement; if possible, they should be supplemented with qualitative information, perhaps in student-constructed portfolios.*** Most teachers eventually need to boil down the results of classroom assessments into more general indicators of what students have learned. The most common procedure is to assign final grades that summarize what students have achieved over the course of the term or school year. In most instances final grades should reflect actual achievement and be based on hard data. The problem with grades, of course, is that they communicate very little about what a student specifically has learned and can do. Student portfolios, which can represent the multifaceted, complex nature of students' achievements, can often be an effective alternative or supplement to overall class grades.

● ***Large-scale standardized tests can be helpful in estimating students' general achievement levels in particular domains, but educators should never use a single test score to make important decisions about individual students.*** Standardized achievement tests provide a means of tracking students' general progress over time and getting a rough idea of how students at a particular school compare to their peers elsewhere. In recent years standardized achievement tests have increasingly been used to make important decisions about students and to hold school personnel accountable for students' achievement (e.g., as is reflected in the No Child Left Behind Act in the United States in 2001). Such *high-stakes testing* is here to stay, at least for the foreseeable future, and teachers must become vocal advocates for reasonable and valid approaches to assessing students' overall progress and achievement. For instance, any high-stakes tests should be closely matched to important instructional goals, and students' ages, developmental levels, and proficiency in English must be accommodated in test design, administration, and interpretation.

PRACTICE FOR YOUR LICENSURE EXAM

Two Science Quizzes

Knowing that frequent paper–pencil quizzes will encourage students to study and review class material regularly, Mr. Bloskas tells his ninth-grade science students that they'll have a quiz every Friday. As a first-year teacher, he has had little experience developing test questions, so he decides to use the questions in the test-item manual that accompanies the class textbook. The night before the first quiz, Mr. Bloskas types 30 multiple-choice and true–false items from the manual, making sure they cover the specific topics that he has addressed in class.

His students complain that the questions are "picky." As he looks carefully at his quiz, he realizes that the students are right: The quiz measures nothing more than memorization of trivial details. So when he prepares the second quiz, he casts the test-item manual aside and

writes two essay questions asking students to apply scientific principles they've studied to new, real-life situations.

The following Friday, students complain even more loudly about the second quiz: "This is too hard!" "We never studied this stuff!" "I liked the first quiz better!" Later, as Mr. Bloskas grades the essays, he's appalled to discover how poorly his students have performed.

1. **Constructed-response question**

   When identifying classroom assessment tasks, teachers must be sure that the tasks have validity, especially *content validity.*

   A. Compare the content validity of Mr. Bloskas's two quizzes.
   B. Describe a reasonable approach Mr. Bloskas might use to create quizzes that have good content validity for his classes.

2. **Multiple-choice question**

   The following alternatives present four possible explanations for the students' negative reactions to the second quiz. Drawing on contemporary theories of learning and motivation, choose the most likely explanation.

   a. Multiple-choice and true–false items are more likely than essay questions to enhance students' sense of self-determination.

   b. Learners are most likely to behave and study in ways that they expect will lead to reinforcement.

   c. Multiple-choice and true–false items are apt to foster learning goals, whereas essay questions are more likely to foster performance goals.

   d. Multiple-choice and true–false items assess information in short-term memory, whereas essay questions usually assess information in long-term memory.

   Go to Chapter 10 of the Book-Specific Resources in MyEducationLab and click on "Practice for Your Licensure Exam" to answer these questions. Compare your responses with the feedback provided.

PEARSON
myeducationlab

Go to the Topic "Assessment" in the MyEducationLab (www.myeducationlab.com) for your course, where you can:

- Find learning outcomes for "Assessment," along with the national standards that connect to these outcomes.
- Complete Assignments and Activities that can help you more deeply understand the chapter content.
- Apply and practice your understanding of the core teaching skills identified in the chapter with the Building Teaching Skills and Dispositions learning units.
- Examine challenging situations and cases presented in the IRIS Center Resources.
- Access video clips of CCSSO National Teachers of the Year award winners responding to the question, "Why Do I Teach?" in the Teacher Talk section.
- Check your comprehension of the content covered in the chapter by going to the Study Plan in the Book Resources for your text. Here you will be able to take a chapter quiz, receive feedback on your answers, and then access Review, Practice, and Enrichment activities to enhance your understanding of chapter content. Flash cards are also available to help you study definitions and key terms.
- Access additional Book Resources, including:
  - Focus Questions to guide your reading, Video Examples of various concepts and principles presented in the chapter, a Practice for Your Licensure Exam exercise that resembles the kinds of questions appearing on many teacher licensure tests, Margin Note Questions that help you connect chapter content to your past experiences or current beliefs, and Supplementary Readings that enable you to pursue certain topics in greater depth.

Appendix

Interpreting Standardized Test Scores

Students' performance on standardized tests is often reported in terms of one or more *norm-referenced* scores—in particular, as scores that show a student's performance relative to others in a nationwide *norm group*. In some cases the scores are derived by comparing a student's performance with the performance of students at a variety of grade or age levels; such comparisons yield grade- or age-equivalent scores. In other cases the scores are based on comparisons only with students of the *same* age or grade; these comparisons yield either percentile ranks or standard scores.

● Grade-Equivalent and Age-Equivalent Scores

Imagine that Shawn takes a standardized test, the Reading Achievement Test (RAT). He gets 46 of the 60 test items correct; thus, 46 is his raw score. We turn to the norms reported in the test manual and find the average raw scores for students at different grade and age levels, shown in Figure A.1. Shawn's raw score of 46 is the same as the average score of eleventh graders in the norm group, so he has a **grade-equivalent score** of 11. His score is halfway between the average score of 16-year-old and 17-year-old students, so he has an **age-equivalent score** of about 16½. Shawn is 13 years old and in eighth grade, so he has obviously done well on the RAT.

In general, grade- and age-equivalent scores are determined by matching a student's raw score to a particular grade or age level in the norm group. A student who performs as well as the average second grader on a reading test will get a grade-equivalent score of 2, regardless of the student's actual grade level. A student who gets the same raw score as the average 10-year-old on a physical fitness test will get an age-equivalent score of 10, regardless of whether that student is 5, 10, or 15 years old.

Grade- and age-equivalent scores are frequently used because they seem so simple and straightforward. But they have a serious drawback: They give us no idea of the typical *range* of performance for students at a particular grade or age level. For example, a raw score of 34 on the RAT gives us a grade-equivalent score of 8, but obviously not all eighth graders will get raw scores of exactly 34. It's possible, and in fact quite likely, that many eighth graders will get raw scores several points above or below 34, thus getting grade-equivalent scores of 9 or 7 (perhaps even 10 or higher, or 6 or lower). Yet grade-equivalent scores are often used inappropriately as a standard for performance: Parents, school personnel, government officials, and the public at large may believe that *all* students should perform at grade level on an achievement test. Given the normal variability within most classrooms, this goal is impossible to meet.

● Percentile Ranks

A different approach is to compare students only with others at the *same* age or grade level. One way of making such a peer-based comparison is to use a **percentile rank**: the percentage of people getting a raw score less than or equal to the student's raw score. (Such a score is sometimes known simply as a *percentile*.) To illustrate, let's once again consider Shawn's

Norms for Grade Levels		Norms for Age Levels	
Grade	Average Raw Score	Age	Average Raw Score
5	19	10	18
6	25	11	24
7	30	12	28
8	34	13	33
9	39	14	37
10	43	15	41
11	46	16	44
12	50	17	48

FIGURE A.1 Hypothetical norm-group data for the Reading Achievement Test (RAT)

grade-equivalent score Test score matching a particular student's performance with the average performance of students at a certain grade level.

age-equivalent score Test score matching a particular student's performance with the average performance of students of a certain age.

percentile rank (percentile) Test score indicating the percentage of peers in the norm group getting a raw score less than or equal to a particular student's raw score.

performance on the RAT. Because Shawn is in eighth grade, we would turn to the eighth-grade norms in the RAT test manual. If we discover that a raw score of 46 is at the 98th percentile for eighth graders, we know that Shawn has done as well as or better than 98% of eighth graders in the norm group. Similarly, a student getting a percentile rank of 25 has performed as well as or better than 25% of the norm group, and a student getting a score at the 60th percentile has done as well as or better than 60%. It's important to note that a percentile rank refers to a percentage of *people,* not to the percentage of correct items—a common misconception among teacher education students.[1]

Percentile ranks are relatively simple to understand and therefore used frequently in reporting test results. But they have a major weakness: They distort actual differences among students. As an illustration, consider the RAT percentile ranks of these four boys:

Student	Percentile Rank
Ernest	45
Frank	55
Giorgio	89
Wayne	99

In *actual achievement* (as measured by the RAT), Ernest and Frank are probably very similar to one another even though their percentile ranks are 10 points apart. However, a 10-point difference at the upper end of the scale probably reflects a substantial difference in achievement: Giorgio's percentile rank of 89 tells us that he knows quite a bit, but Wayne's percentile rank of 99 tells us that he knows an exceptional amount. In general, percentiles tend to *over*estimate differences in the middle range of the characteristic being measured: Scores a few points apart reflect similar achievement or ability. Meanwhile, percentiles *under*estimate differences at the upper and lower extremes: Scores only a few points apart often reflect significant differences in achievement or ability. We avoid this problem when we use standard scores.

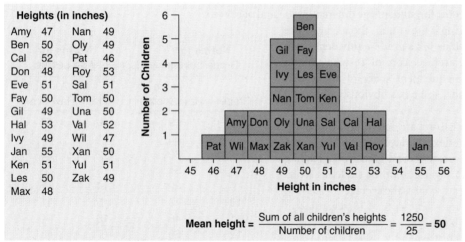

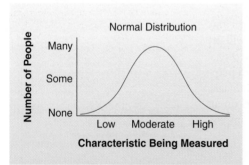

$$\text{Mean height} = \frac{\text{Sum of all children's heights}}{\text{Number of children}} = \frac{1250}{25} = 50$$

FIGURE A.2 Heights of children in Ms. Oppenheimer's third-grade class

• Standard Scores

The school nurse measures the heights of the 25 students in Ms. Oppenheimer's third-grade class, as shown on the left side of Figure A.2. The nurse then creates a graph of the children's heights, shown on the right side of Figure A.2. Notice that the graph is high in the middle and low on both ends. This shape tells us that most of Ms. Oppenheimer's students are more or less average in height, with only a few very short students (e.g., Pat, Amy, and Wil) and only a few very tall ones (e.g., Hal, Roy, and Jan).

Many psychologists believe that educational and psychological characteristics (including academic achievement and abilities) typically follow the same pattern we see for height: Most people are close to average, with fewer and fewer people being counted as we move farther from the average. This theoretical pattern of educational and psychological characteristics, known as the **normal distribution** (or **normal curve**), is shown to the left. Standard scores reflect this normal distribution: Many students get scores in the middle range, and only a few get very high or very low scores.

normal distribution (normal curve)
Theoretical pattern of educational and psychological characteristics in which most individuals score somewhere in the middle range and only a few score at either extreme.

Before we examine standard scores in detail, we need to understand two numbers used to derive them: the mean and standard deviation. The **mean (M)** is the average of a set of scores: We add all the scores together and divide by the total number of scores (or people). For example, if we add the heights of all 25 students in Ms. Oppenheimer's class and then divide by 25, we get a mean height of 50 inches (see the calculation in Figure A.2).

The **standard deviation (SD)** indicates the *variability* of a set of scores. A small number tells us that, generally speaking, the scores are close together, and a large number tells us that they're far apart. For example, third graders tend to be more similar in height than eighth graders (some eighth graders are less than five feet tall; others may be almost six feet). The standard deviation for the heights of third graders is therefore smaller than the standard deviation for the heights of eighth graders. The formula for computing a standard deviation is fairly complex; fortunately, we don't need to know it in order to understand the role that a standard deviation plays in standard scores. Furthermore, the standard deviation for any published test is typically provided in the test manual.

Learn how to calculate standard deviations in a supplementary reading in the Homework and Exercises section in Chapter 10 of the Book-Specific Resources in MyEducationLab.

The mean and standard deviation can be used to divide the normal distribution into several parts, as shown in Figure A.3. The vertical line at the middle of the curve shows the mean; for a normal distribution, it's both the midpoint and the highest point of the curve. The thinner lines to either side reflect the standard deviation: We count out 1 standard deviation higher and lower than the mean and mark those two spots with vertical lines, and then we count another standard deviation to either side and draw two more lines. When we divide a normal distribution in this way, the percentages of students getting scores in each part are always the same. Approximately two-thirds (68%) get scores within one standard deviation of the mean (34% in each direction). As we go farther away from the mean, we find fewer and fewer students, with 28% lying between one and two standard deviations away (14% on each side) and only about 4% being more than two standard deviations away (2% at each end).

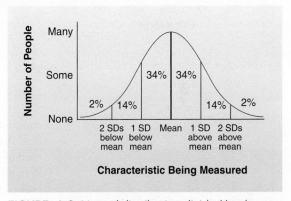

FIGURE A.3 Normal distribution divided by the mean and standard deviation

Now that we better understand the normal distribution and two statistics that describe it, let's look at standard scores. A **standard score** reflects a student's position in the normal distribution: It tells us how far the student's performance is from the mean in terms of standard deviation units. Unfortunately, not all standard scores use the same scale: Scores used for various tests have different means and standard deviations. Four commonly used standard scores, depicted graphically in Figure A.4, are the following:

- **IQ scores.** IQ scores are frequently used to report students' performance on intelligence tests. They have a *mean of 100* and, for most tests, a *standard deviation of 15*. (If you look back at Figure 5.7 in Chapter 5, p. 159, you'll see that I've broken up that curve by thirds of a standard deviation unit. The lines for 85 and 115 reflect 1 standard deviation from the mean score of 100. The lines for 70 and 130 reflect 2 SDs from the mean.)
- **ETS scores.** ETS scores are used on tests published by the Educational Testing Service, such as the SAT and the Graduate Record Examination (GRE). They have a *mean of 500* and a *standard deviation of 100*. However, no scores fall below 200 or above 800.
- **Stanines.** Stanines (short for *standard nines*) are often used to report standardized achievement test results. They have a *mean of 5* and a *standard deviation of 2*. Because they are always reported as whole numbers, each score reflects a *range* of test performance (reflected by the shaded and unshaded portions of the upper right-hand curve in Figure A.4).
- *z*-**scores.** Standard scores known as *z*-scores are often used by statisticians. They have a *mean of 0* and a *standard deviation of 1*.

Increasingly I'm seeing yet a fifth type of standard score being used to report students' achievement test results. These scores, known as **NCE scores** (short for *normal-curve-equivalent scores*) have a *mean of 50* and a *standard deviation of 21.06*. Why such an odd standard deviation? It turns out that with this particular standard deviation, an NCE score of 1 is equivalent to a percentile score of 1 and, likewise, an NCE score of 99 is equivalent

mean (M) Mathematical average of a set of scores.

standard deviation (SD) Statistic indicating the amount of variability characterizing a set of scores.

standard score Test score indicating how far a student's performance is from the mean with respect to standard deviation units.

IQ score Score on an intelligence test, determined by comparing a student's performance on the test with the performance of others in the same age-group; for most tests, it's a standard score with a mean of 100 and a standard deviation of 15.

ETS score Standard score with a mean of 500 and a standard deviation of 100.

stanine Standard score with a mean of 5 and a standard deviation of 2; always reported as a whole number.

z-score Standard score with a mean of 0 and a standard deviation of 1.

NCE score Standard score with a mean of 50 and a standard deviation of 21.06; an NCE score of 1 equals a percentile rank of 1, and an NCE score of 99 equals a percentile rank of 99.

confidence interval Range around a test score that reflects the amount of error likely to be affecting the score's accuracy.

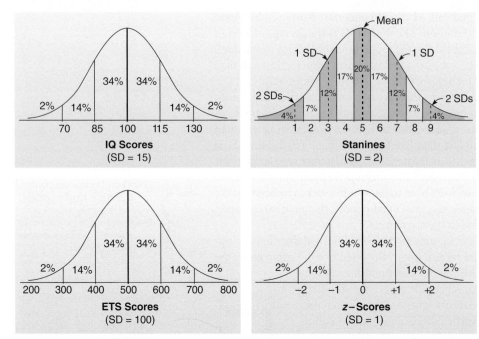

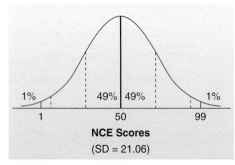

FIGURE A.4 Distributions of four types of standard scores

FIGURE A.5 Distribution of NCE (normal curve equivalent) scores

to a percentile score of 99. And, of course, an NCE score of 50 (being the mean and midpoint of the curve) is also a percentile score of 50 (see Figure A.5).

Interpreting Test Scores: An Example

Figure A.6 presents a computer print-out of 12-year-old Ingrid's scores on various subtests of a national achievement test. Ingrid's percentile ranks and stanines have been computed by comparing her raw scores with those of a national norm group. On the basis of her test scores, Ingrid appears to have achieved at average to below-average levels in spelling and math computation, an average to above-average level in math concepts, and above-average to well-above-average levels in reading comprehension, science, and social studies.

The "national percentile bands" in Figure A.6 (i.e., the rows of Xs) are **confidence intervals** that reflect the amount of error (due to imperfect reliability) that is apt to be in Ingrid's percentile scores. Ingrid's confidence intervals for spelling and math overlap, so even though she has gotten somewhat higher scores in math concepts than in spelling or math computation, the scores aren't different *enough* to say that she is better at math concepts than in the other two areas. The confidence intervals for reading comprehension, science, and social studies overlap as well, so she performed similarly in these three areas. The confidence intervals for her three highest scores *don't* overlap with those for her lowest three scores. We can say, then, that Ingrid's relative strengths are in reading comprehension, science, and social studies, and that she has achieved at lower levels in spelling and math.

Notice that the numbers for the percentile confidence intervals (the numbers on the bottom line of the computer printout) are unevenly spaced. Remember, percentile ranks tend to overestimate differences near the mean and underestimate differences at the extremes. The uneven spacing is the test publisher's way of showing this fact: It squishes the middle percentile scores close together and spreads high and low percentile scores farther apart. In this way, it tries to give students and parents an idea about where students' test scores fall in a normal distribution.

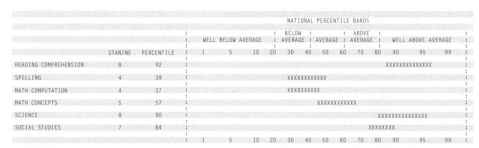

FIGURE A.6 Computer printout showing 12-year-old Ingrid's performance on a standardized achievement test

accommodation Responding to a new object or event by either modifying an existing scheme or forming a new one.

accountability Mandated obligation of teachers and other school personnel to accept responsibility for students' performance on high-stakes assessments.

action research Research conducted by teachers and other school personnel to address issues and problems in their own schools or classrooms.

advance organizer Introduction to a lesson that provides an overall organizational scheme for the lesson.

affect Feelings, emotions, and moods that a learner brings to bear on a task.

African American English Dialect of some African American communities characterized by certain pronunciations, idioms, and grammatical constructions different from those of Standard English.

age-equivalent score Test score matching a particular student's performance with the average performance of students of a certain age.

aggressive behavior Action intentionally taken to harm another person either physically or psychologically.

algorithm Prescribed sequence of steps that guarantees a correct problem solution.

antecedent stimulus Stimulus that increases the likelihood that a particular response will follow.

anxiety Feeling of uneasiness and apprehension concerning a situation with an uncertain outcome.

APA style Rules and guidelines on referencing, editorial style, and manuscript format prescribed by the American Psychological Association.

applied behavior analysis (ABA) Systematic application of stimulus–response principles to address a chronic behavior problem.

apprenticeship Mentorship in which a novice works intensively with an expert to learn how to perform complex new skills.

arousal See *need for arousal.*

assessment Process of observing a sample of a student's behavior and drawing inferences about the student's knowledge and abilities.

assimilation Responding to and possibly interpreting a new event in a way that is consistent with an existing scheme.

astrocyte Star-shaped brain cell hypothesized to be involved in learning and memory; has chemically mediated connections with many other astrocytes and with neurons.

attention Focusing of mental processes on particular stimuli.

attention-deficit hyperactivity disorder (ADHD) Disorder marked by inattention, inability to inhibit inappropriate thoughts and behaviors, or both.

attribution Personally constructed causal explanation for a particular event, such as a success or failure.

attribution theory Theoretical perspective that focuses on people's explanations (*attributions*) concerning the causes of events that befall them, as well as on the behaviors that result from such explanations.

authentic activity Task or activity similar to one students might encounter in the outside world.

authentic assessment Assessment of students' knowledge and skills in a context similar to one in the outside world.

authoritarian parenting Parenting style characterized by rigid rules and expectations for behavior that children are asked to obey without question.

authoritative parenting Parenting style characterized by emotional warmth, high standards for behavior, explanation and consistent enforcement of rules, inclusion of children in decision making, and reasonable opportunities for autonomy.

autism spectrum disorders Disorders marked by impaired social cognition, social skills, and social interaction, presumably due to a brain abnormality; extreme forms often associated with significant cognitive and linguistic delays and highly unusual behaviors.

automaticity Ability to respond quickly and efficiently while mentally processing or physically performing a task.

backward design Approach to instructional planning in which a teacher first determines the desired end result (i.e., what knowledge and skills students should acquire) and then identifies appropriate assessments and instructional strategies.

behaviorism Theoretical perspective in which learning and behavior are described and explained in terms of stimulus–response relationships, and motivation is often the result of deficit-based drives. Adherents to this perspective are called **behaviorists**.

belongingness General sense that one is an important and valued member of the classroom.

Bloom's taxonomy Taxonomy of six cognitive processes, varying in complexity, that lessons might be designed to foster.

bully Child or adolescent who frequently threatens, harasses, or causes injury to particular peers.

central executive Component of the human information processing system that oversees the flow of information throughout the system.

challenge Situation in which a learner believes that success is possible with reasonable effort.

class inclusion Recognition that an object simultaneously belongs to a particular category and to one of its subcategories.

classroom climate Overall psychological atmosphere of the classroom.

classroom management Establishment and maintenance of a classroom environment conducive to learning and achievement.

clinical method Procedure in which an adult presents a task or problem and asks a child a series of questions about it, tailoring later questions to the child's responses to previous ones.

clique Moderately stable friendship group of perhaps 3 to 10 members.

cognition Various ways of thinking about information and events.

cognitive apprenticeship Mentorship in which a teacher and a student work together on a challenging task and the teacher gives guidance about how to think about the task.

cognitive-developmental theory Theoretical perspective that focuses on qualitative, stage-like changes in children's characteristics and abilities, with a particular emphasis on how children's active, constructive thinking processes contribute to such changes.

cognitive dissonance Feeling of mental discomfort caused by new information that conflicts with current knowledge or beliefs.

cognitive process Particular way of mentally responding to or thinking about information or an event.

cognitive style Characteristic way in which a learner tends to think about a task and process new information; typically comes into play automatically rather than by choice.

cognitive tool Concept, symbol, strategy, procedure, or other culturally constructed mechanism that helps people think about and respond to situations more effectively.

collective self-efficacy Shared belief of members of a group that they can be successful when they work together on a task.

community of learners Class in which teacher and students actively and collaboratively work to create a body of knowledge and help one another learn.

competence See *need for competence.*

complex cognitive process Cognitive process that involves going well beyond information specifically learned (e.g., by analyzing, applying, or evaluating it).

comprehension monitoring Process of checking oneself to be sure one understands and remembers newly acquired information.

computer-based instruction (CBI) Academic instruction provided by means of specially designed computer software.

concept Mental grouping of objects or events that have something in common.

concept map Diagram of concepts and their interrelationships; used to enhance learning and memory of a topic.

conceptual change Significant revision of one's existing beliefs about a topic, enabling new and discrepant information to be better understood and explained.

conceptual understanding Knowledge about a topic acquired in an integrated and meaningful fashion.

concrete operations stage Piaget's third stage of cognitive development, in which adultlike logic appears but is limited to concrete reality.

confidence interval Range around a test score that reflects the amount of error likely to be affecting the score's accuracy.

confirmation bias Tendency to seek information that confirms rather than discredits one's current beliefs.

conservation Realization that if nothing is added or taken away, amount stays the same regardless of alterations in shape or arrangement.

constructivism Theoretical perspective proposing that learners construct (rather than absorb) a body of knowledge from their experiences—knowledge that may or may not be an accurate representation of external reality. Adherents to this perspective are called **constructivists**.

content validity Extent to which an assessment includes a representative sample of tasks within the domain being assessed.

contingency Situation in which one event (e.g., reinforcement) happens only after another event (e.g., a specific response) has already occurred (one event is *contingent* on the other's occurrence).

contingency contract Written agreement between teacher and student that identifies behaviors the student will exhibit and the reinforcers that will follow.

control group Group of people in a research study who are given either no treatment or a treatment that is unlikely to have an effect on the dependent variable.

controversial student Student whom some peers strongly like and other peers strongly dislike.

conventional morality Uncritical acceptance of society's conventions regarding right and wrong behavior.

conventional transgression Action that violates a culture's general expectations regarding socially appropriate behavior.

convergent thinking Process of pulling several pieces of information together to draw a conclusion or solve a problem.

cooperative learning Approach to instruction in which students work with a small group of peers to achieve a common goal and help one another learn.

core goal Long-term goal that drives much of what a learner does.

co-regulated learning Process through which an adult and child share responsibility for directing various aspects of the child's learning.

correlation Extent to which two variables are associated, such that when one variable increases, the other either increases or decreases somewhat predictably.

correlational study Research study that explores possible relationships among variables.

cortex Upper and outer parts of the human brain, which are largely responsible for conscious and complex cognitive processes.

covert strategy Learning strategy that is strictly mental (rather than behavioral) in nature and thus cannot be observed by others.

creativity New and original behavior that yields a productive and culturally appropriate result.

criterion-referenced score Assessment score that specifically indicates what a student knows or can do.

critical thinking Process of evaluating the accuracy, credibility, and worth of information and lines of reasoning.

crowd Large, loose-knit social group that shares certain common interests and attitudes.

crystallized intelligence Knowledge and skills accumulated from prior experience, schooling, and culture.

cueing Use of simple signals to indicate that a certain behavior is desired or that a certain behavior should stop.

cultural bias Extent to which assessment tasks either offend or unfairly penalize some students because of their ethnicity, gender, or socioeconomic status.

cultural mismatch Situation in which a child's home culture and the school culture hold conflicting expectations for the child's behavior.

culturally responsive teaching Use of instructional strategies consistent with students' culturally preferred ways of learning and behaving.

culture Behaviors and belief systems that members of a long-standing social group share and pass along to successive generations.

culture shock Sense of confusion when a student encounters a culture with behavioral expectations very different from those learned previously in other contexts.

cyberbullying Use of wireless technologies or the Internet to transmit hostile messages, broadcast personally embarrassing information, or in other ways cause an individual significant psychological distress.

debilitating anxiety Anxiety of sufficient intensity that it interferes with performance.

decay Weakening over time of information stored in long-term memory, especially if the information is used infrequently.

declarative knowledge Knowledge related to "what is"—that is, to the nature of how things are, were, or will be.

delay of gratification Ability to forego small, immediate reinforcers to obtain larger ones at a later time.

descriptive study Research study that enables researchers to draw conclusions about the current state of affairs but not about correlational or cause–and–effect relationships.

developmental milestone Appearance of a new, developmentally more advanced behavior.

dialect Form of a language that has certain unique pronunciations, idioms, and grammatical structures and is characteristic of a particular region or ethnic group.

differentiated instruction Practice of individualizing instructional methods—and possibly also individualizing specific content and instructional goals—to align with each student's existing knowledge, skills, and needs.

direct instruction Approach to instruction that uses a variety of techniques (e.g., explanations, questions, guided and independent practice) in a fairly structured manner to promote learning of basic skills.

discovery learning Approach to instruction in which students derive their own knowledge about a topic through firsthand interaction with the environment.

disequilibrium State of being unable to address new events with existing schemes; typically accompanied by some mental discomfort.

disposition General inclination to approach and think about learning and problem-solving tasks in a particular way; typically has a motivational component in addition to cognitive components.

distributed cognition Process in which two or more learners each contribute knowledge and ideas as they work collaboratively on an issue or problem.

distributed intelligence Thinking enhanced by physical objects and technology, concepts and symbols of one's culture, and/or social collaboration and support.

divergent thinking Process of mentally moving in a variety of directions from a single idea.

dynamic assessment Systematic examination of how readily and in what ways a student can acquire new knowledge or skills, perhaps with an adult's assistance.

ecological systems theory Theoretical perspective that takes into account the various "layers" of contexts in which children grow up, including both the immediate contexts with which children have everyday contact (e.g., home, school) and the broader environments within which these immediate contexts exist (e.g., community, federal government).

educational psychology Academic discipline that (a) systematically studies the nature of learning, child development, motivation, and related topics and (b) applies its research findings to the identification and development of effective instructional practices.

elaboration Cognitive process in which learners embellish on new information based on what they already know.

emotional and behavioral disorders Emotional states and behavior patterns that consistently and significantly disrupt academic learning and performance.

emotion self-regulation Process of keeping one's affective states and affect-related behaviors within productive, culturally desirable limits.

empathy Experience of sharing the same feelings as someone in unfortunate circumstances.

encoding Changing the format of information being stored in memory in order to remember it more easily.

entity view of intelligence Belief that intelligence is a distinct ability that is relatively permanent and unchangeable.

epistemic belief Belief about the nature of knowledge or knowledge acquisition.

equilibration Movement from equilibrium to disequilibrium and back to equilibrium, a process that promotes development of more complex thought and understandings.

equilibrium State of being able to address new events with existing schemes.

ethnic group People who have common historical roots, values, beliefs, and behaviors and who share a sense of interdependence.

ethnic identity Awareness of one's membership in a particular ethnic or cultural group, and willingness to adopt behaviors characteristic of the group.

ETS score Standard score with a mean of 500 and a standard deviation of 100.

evidence-based practice Instructional method or other classroom strategy that research has consistently shown to bring about significant gains in students' development and/or academic achievement.

expectancy–value theory Theoretical perspective proposing that human motivation is a function of two psychological variables: the extent to which one has confidence about being successful in an activity (*expectancy*) and the extent to which one believes there are direct or indirect benefits in performing the activity (*value*).

experimental study (experiment) Research study that involves the manipulation of one variable to determine its possible influential effect on another variable.

expertise Extensive and well-integrated knowledge of a topic that comes from many years of study and practice.

expository instruction Approach to instruction in which information is presented in essentially the same form in which students are expected to learn it.

externalizing behavior Symptom of an emotional or behavioral disorder that has a direct effect on other people.

extinction Gradual disappearance of an acquired response; in the case of a response acquired through operant conditioning, it results from repeated lack of reinforcement for the response.

extrinsic motivation Motivation resulting from factors external to the individual and unrelated to the task being performed.

extrinsic reinforcer Reinforcer that comes from the outside environment, rather than from within the learner.

facilitating anxiety Level of anxiety (usually relatively low) that enhances performance.

Family Educational Rights and Privacy Act (FERPA) U.S. legislation passed in 1974 that gives students and parents access to school records and limits other people's access to those records.

flow Intense form of intrinsic motivation, involving complete absorption in and concentration on a challenging activity.

fluid intelligence Ability to acquire knowledge quickly and adapt effectively to new situations.

formal assessment Preplanned, systematic attempt to ascertain what students have learned.

formal operations stage Piaget's fourth and final stage of cognitive development, in which logical reasoning processes are applied to abstract ideas as well as to concrete objects and more sophisticated scientific and mathematical reasoning processes emerge.

formative assessment Assessment conducted in order to facilitate instructional planning and enhance students' learning.

functional analysis Examination of inappropriate behavior and its antecedents and consequences to determine one or more purposes (functions) that the behavior might serve for the learner.

g Theoretical general factor in intelligence that influences one's ability to learn and perform in a wide variety of contexts.

gang Cohesive social group characterized by initiation rites, distinctive colors and symbols, territorial orientation, and feuds with rival groups.

gender schema Self-constructed, organized body of beliefs about the traits and behaviors of males or females.

general transfer Instance of transfer in which the original learning task and the transfer task are different in content.

giftedness Unusually high ability in one or more areas, to the point where students require special educational services to help them meet their full potential.

goal theory Theoretical perspective that portrays human motivation as being directed toward particular goals, which influence the specific ways in which people think and behave in various situations.

goodness of fit Situation in which classroom conditions and expectations are compatible with students' temperaments and personality characteristics.

grade-equivalent score Test score matching a particular student's performance with the average performance of students at a certain grade level.

guided participation A child's performance, with guidance and support, of an activity in the adult world.

guilt Feeling of discomfort about having caused someone else pain or distress.

heuristic General strategy that facilitates problem solving or creativity but does not always yield a successful outcome.

higher-level question Question that requires students to do something new with something they've learned (e.g., to elaborate on or apply it).

high-stakes testing Practice of using students' performance on a single assessment to make major decisions about students, school personnel, or overall school quality.

hostile attributional bias Tendency to interpret others' behaviors as reflecting hostile or aggressive intentions.

hot cognition Learning or cognitive processing that is emotionally charged.

humanism Philosophical perspective in which people are seen as having tremendous potential for psychological growth and as continually striving to fulfill that potential. Adherents to this perspective are called **humanists**.

hypermedia Collection of multimedia, computer-based instructional materials (e.g., text, pictures, sound, animations) that students can examine in a sequence of their own choosing.

identity Self-constructed definition of who one thinks one is and what things are important to accomplish in life.

illusion of knowing Thinking that one knows something that one actually does *not* know.

imaginary audience Belief that one is the center of attention in any social situation.

incentive Hoped-for, but not guaranteed, future consequence of behavior.

inclusion The practice of educating all students, including those with severe and multiple disabilities, in neighborhood schools and general education classrooms.

incompatible behaviors Two or more behaviors that cannot be performed simultaneously.

incremental view of intelligence Belief that intelligence can improve with effort and practice.

individual constructivism Theoretical perspective that focuses on how people, as individuals, construct meaning from their experiences.

Individuals with Disabilities Education Act (IDEA) U.S. legislation granting educational rights to people with cognitive, emotional, or physical disabilities from birth until age 21; initially passed in 1975, it has been amended and reauthorized several times and is now officially known as the Individuals with Disabilities Education Improvement Act.

induction Explanation of why a certain behavior is unacceptable, often with a focus on the pain or distress that someone has caused another.

informal assessment Assessment that results from a teacher's spontaneous, day-to-day observations of how students behave and perform in class.

information literacy Knowledge and skills that help a learner find, use, evaluate, organize, and effectively present information about a particular topic.

information processing theory Theoretical perspective that focuses on how learners mentally think about (process) new information and events and how such processes change with development.

inner speech Process of talking to and guiding oneself mentally rather than aloud.

inquiry learning Approach to instruction in which students seek new information through the intentional application of complex cognitive processes (e.g., scientific reasoning, critical thinking).

in-school suspension Consequence for misbehavior in which a student is placed in a quiet, boring room within the school building, typically to do schoolwork under close adult supervision.

instructional goal Desired long-term outcome of instruction.

instructional objective Desired outcome of a lesson or unit.

intellectual disability Disability characterized by significantly below-average general intelligence and deficits in adaptive behavior, both of which first appear in infancy or childhood; also known as *mental retardation.*

intelligence Ability to apply prior knowledge and experiences flexibly to accomplish challenging new tasks; involves many different mental processes and may vary in nature depending on one's culture.

intelligence test General measure of current cognitive functioning; often used to predict academic achievement over the short run.

interest Perception that an activity is intriguing and enticing; typically accompanied by both cognitive engagement and positive affect.

internalization Process through which a learner gradually incorporates socially based activities into his or her internal cognitive processes.

internalized motivation Adoption of other people's priorities and values as one's own.

internalizing behavior Symptom of an emotional or behavioral disorder that adversely affects the student with the disorder but has little or no direct effect on others.

intrinsic motivation Motivation resulting from personal characteristics or inherent in the task being performed.

intrinsic reinforcer Reinforcer provided by oneself or inherent in a task being performed.

IQ score Score on an intelligence test, determined by comparing a student's performance on the test with the performance of others in the same age-group; for most tests, it's a standard score with a mean of 100 and a standard deviation of 15.

IRE cycle Adult–child interaction marked by adult initiation (e.g., a question), child response, and adult evaluation.

keyword method Mnemonic technique in which an association is made between two ideas by forming a visual image of one or more concrete objects (*keywords*) that either sound similar to, or symbolically represent, those ideas.

knowledge base A person's existing knowledge about specific topics and the world in general.

learned helplessness General, fairly pervasive belief that one is incapable of accomplishing tasks and has little or no control over the environment.

learner-centered instruction Approach to teaching in which instructional strategies are chosen largely on the basis of students' existing abilities, predispositions, and needs.

learner-directed instruction Approach to instruction in which students have considerable say in the issues addressed and the ways in which to address them.

learning Long-term change in mental representations or associations due to experience.

learning disability Deficiency in one or more specific cognitive processes despite relatively normal cognitive functioning in other areas.

learning strategy Intentional use of one or more cognitive processes for a particular learning task.

lesson plan Predetermined guide for a lesson that identifies instructional goals or objectives, necessary materials, instructional strategies, and one or more assessment methods.

live model Individual whose behavior is directly observed in one's immediate environment.

logical consequence Unpleasant consequence that follows naturally or logically from a student's misbehavior.

long-term memory Component of memory that holds knowledge and skills for a relatively long time.

lower-level question Question that requires students to express what they've learned in essentially the same form they learned it.

mastery goal Desire to acquire new knowledge or master new skills.

mastery learning Approach to instruction in which students learn one topic thoroughly before moving to a subsequent one.

mastery orientation General, fairly pervasive belief that one is capable of accomplishing challenging tasks.

maturation Gradual unfolding of genetically controlled physical changes as a child develops.

mean (M) Mathematical average of a set of scores.

meaningful learning Cognitive process in which learners relate new information to things they already know.

mediated learning experience Social interaction in which an adult helps a child interpret a phenomenon or event in particular (usually culturally appropriate) ways.

memory Ability to save something (mentally) that has been previously learned; also, the mental "location" where such information is saved.

mental retardation See *intellectual disability.*

mental set Inclination to encode a problem or situation in a way that excludes potential solutions.

metacognition Knowledge and beliefs about one's own cognitive processes, as well as conscious attempts to engage in behaviors and thought processes that increase learning and memory.

misbehavior Action that disrupts learning and planned classroom activities, puts students' physical safety or psychological well-being in jeopardy, or violates basic moral standards.

mnemonic Memory aid or trick designed to help students learn and remember one or more specific pieces of information.

model Person who demonstrates a behavior for someone else.

modeling Demonstrating a behavior for another; also, observing and imitating another's behavior.

moral dilemma Situation in which two or more people's rights or needs may be at odds and the morally correct action is not clear-cut.

moral transgression Action that causes harm or infringes on the needs or rights of others.

morality One's general standards for behaviors that preserve other people's rights and welfare.

motivation Inner state that energizes, directs, and sustains behavior.

multicultural education Instruction that integrates perspectives and experiences of numerous cultural groups throughout the curriculum.

myelination Growth of a fatty coating (myelin) around neurons, enabling faster transmission of messages.

nativism Theoretical perspective that proposes that certain characteristics, behaviors, knowledge, and predispositions are biologically built in.

NCE score Standard score with a mean of 50 and a standard deviation of 21.06; an NCE score of 1 equals a percentile rank of 1, and an NCE score of 99 equals a percentile rank of 99.

need for arousal Ongoing need for either physical or cognitive stimulation.

need for competence Basic need to believe that one can deal effectively with one's overall environment.

need for relatedness Basic need to feel socially connected to others and to secure others' love and respect.

need for self-determination Basic need to believe that one has some autonomy and control regarding the course of one's life.

negative reinforcement Phenomenon in which a response increases as a result of the removal (rather than presentation) of a stimulus.

negative transfer Phenomenon in which something learned at one time interferes with learning or performance at a later time.

neglected student Student about whom most peers have no strong feelings, either positive or negative.

neuron Cell in the brain or another part of the nervous system that specializes in transmitting information to other cells.

niche-picking Tendency for a learner to seek out environmental conditions that are a good match with his or her existing characteristics and behaviors.

No Child Left Behind Act (NCLB) U.S. legislation passed in 2001 that mandates regular assessments of basic skills to determine whether students are making adequate yearly progress in relation to state-determined standards in reading, math, and science.

normal distribution (normal curve) Theoretical pattern of educational and psychological characteristics in which most individuals score somewhere in the middle range and only a few score at either extreme.

norm-referenced score Assessment score that indicates how a student's performance compares with the average performance of others.

operant conditioning Form of learning in which a response increases in frequency as a result of its being followed by reinforcement.

organization Cognitive process in which learners find connections among various pieces of information they need to learn (e.g., by forming categories, identifying hierarchies, determining cause–and–effect relationships).

overt strategy Learning strategy that is at least partially evident in the learner's behavior (e.g., taking notes during a lecture).

paper–pencil assessment Assessment in which students provide written responses to written items.

pedagogical content knowledge Knowledge about effective methods of teaching a specific topic or content area.

peer mediation Approach to conflict resolution in which a student (acting as a mediator) asks peers in conflict to express their differing viewpoints and then work together to identify a reasonable resolution.

peer pressure Phenomenon whereby agemates strongly encourage some behaviors and discourage others.

peer tutoring Approach to instruction in which one student provides instruction to help another student master a classroom topic.

percentile rank (percentile) Test score indicating the percentage of peers in the norm group getting a raw score less than or equal to a particular student's raw score.

performance-approach goal Desire to look good and receive favorable judgments from others.

performance assessment Assessment in which students demonstrate their knowledge and skills in a nonwritten fashion.

performance-avoidance goal Desire not to look bad or receive unfavorable judgments from others.

performance goal Desire to demonstrate high ability and make a good impression.

personal fable Belief that one is completely unlike anyone else and so cannot be understood by others.

personal interest Long-term, relatively stable interest in a particular topic or activity.

personal space Personally or culturally preferred distance between two people during social interaction.

personality Characteristic ways in which an individual behaves, thinks, and feels.

perspective taking Ability to look at a situation from someone's else viewpoint.

physical aggression Action that can potentially cause bodily injury.

plasticity Capacity for the brain to learn and adapt to new circumstances.

popular student Student whom many peers like and perceive to be kind and trustworthy.

portfolio Collection of a student's work compiled systematically over a lengthy time period.

positive behavioral support (PBS) Systematic intervention that addresses chronic misbehaviors by (1) identifying the purposes those behaviors might serve for a student and (2) providing more appropriate ways for a student to achieve the same ends.

positive psychology Theoretical perspective that portrays people as having many unique qualities that propel them to engage in productive, worthwhile activities; it shares early humanists' belief that people strive to fulfill their potential but also shares contemporary psychologists' belief that theories of motivation must be research-based.

positive reinforcement Phenomenon in which a response increases as a result of the presentation (rather than removal) of a stimulus.

positive transfer Phenomenon in which something learned at one time facilitates learning or performance at a later time.

postconventional morality Thinking in accordance with self-constructed, abstract principles regarding right and wrong behavior.

practicality Extent to which an assessment instrument or procedure is inexpensive and easy to use and takes only a small amount of time to administer and score.

preconventional morality Lack of internalized standards about right and wrong behavior; decision making based primarily on what seems best for oneself.

preoperational stage Piaget's second stage of cognitive development, in which children can think about objects beyond their immediate experience but do not yet reason in logical, adultlike ways.

presentation punishment Punishment involving presentation of a new stimulus, presumably one a learner finds unpleasant.

primary reinforcer Consequence that satisfies a biologically built-in need.

prior knowledge activation Process of reminding learners of things they already know relative to a new topic.

proactive aggression Deliberate aggression against another as a means of obtaining a desired goal.

problem-based learning Classroom activity in which students acquire new knowledge and skills while working on a complex problem similar to certain real-world problems.

problem solving Using existing knowledge or skills to address an unanswered question or troubling situation.

procedural knowledge Knowledge concerning how to do something (e.g., a skill).

project-based learning Classroom activity in which students acquire new knowledge and skills while working on a complex, multifaceted project that yields a concrete end product.

prosocial behavior Behavior directed toward promoting the well-being of another person.

proximal goal Concrete goal that can be accomplished within a short time period; may be a stepping stone toward a longer-term goal.

psychodynamic theory Theoretical perspective proposing that a person's development is greatly affected by the person's early experiences, including experiences that are unavailable for conscious recall and reflection.

punishment Consequence that decreases the frequency of the response it follows.

qualitative research Research yielding information that cannot be easily reduced to numbers; typically involves an in-depth examination of a complex phenomenon.

quantitative research Research yielding information that is inherently numerical in nature or can easily be reduced to numbers.

raw score Assessment score based solely on the number or point value of correctly answered items.

reactive aggression Aggressive response to frustration or provocation.

reciprocal causation Mutual cause-and-effect relationships among environment, behavior, and personal variables as these three factors influence learning and development.

reciprocal teaching Approach to teaching reading and listening comprehension in which students take turns asking teacherlike questions of classmates.

reconstruction error Construction of a logical but incorrect "memory" by combining information retrieved from one's long-term memory with one's general knowledge and beliefs about the world.

recursive thinking Thinking about what other people may be thinking about oneself, possibly through multiple iterations.

reflective teaching Regular, ongoing examination and critique of one's assumptions and instructional strategies, and revision of them as necessary to enhance students' learning and development.

rehearsal Cognitive process in which information is repeated over and over as a possible way of learning and remembering it.

reinforcer Consequence of a response that leads to increased frequency of the response; the act of following a response with a reinforcer is known as **reinforcement**.

rejected student Student whom many peers identify as being an undesirable social partner.

relatedness See *need for relatedness.*

relational aggression Action that can adversely affect interpersonal relationships.

reliability Extent to which an assessment instrument yields consistent information about the knowledge, skills, or characteristics being assessed.

removal punishment Punishment involving removal of an existing stimulus, presumably one a learner finds desirable and doesn't want to lose.

resilient self-efficacy Belief that one can perform a task successfully even after experiencing setbacks.

resilient student Student who succeeds in school and in life despite exceptional hardships at home.

response Specific behavior that an individual exhibits.

response cost Loss either of a previously earned reinforcer or of an opportunity to obtain reinforcement.

retrieval Process of "finding" information previously stored in memory.

retrieval cue Stimulus that provides guidance about where to "look" for a piece of information in long-term memory.

retrieval failure Inability to locate information that currently exists in long-term memory.

rote learning Cognitive process in which learners try to remember information in a relatively uninterpreted form, with little or no effort to make sense of or attach meaning to it.

rubric List of components that a student's performance on an assessment task should ideally include; used to guide scoring.

scaffolding Support mechanism that helps a learner successfully perform a challenging task (in Vygotsky's theory, a task within the learner's zone of proximal development).

schema Tightly organized set of facts about a specific concept or phenomenon.

scheme In Piaget's theory, organized group of similar actions or thoughts that are used repeatedly in response to the environment.

script Schema that involves a predictable sequence of events related to a common activity.

secondary reinforcer Consequence that becomes reinforcing over time through its association with another reinforcer.

self-conscious emotion Affective state based on self-evaluations regarding the extent to which one's actions meet society's standards for appropriate and desirable behavior; examples are pride, guilt, and shame.

self-determination theory Theoretical perspective proposing that human beings have a basic need for autonomy (*self-determination*) about the courses that their lives take; it further proposes that humans also have basic needs to feel competent and to have close, affectionate relationships with others. Also see *need for self-determination*.

self-efficacy Belief that one is capable of executing certain behaviors or reaching certain goals.

self-evaluation Judgment of one's own performance or behavior.

self-fulfilling prophecy Expectation for an outcome that either directly or indirectly leads to the expected result.

self-handicapping Behavior that undermines one's own success as a way of protecting self-worth during potentially difficult tasks.

self-imposed contingency Self-reinforcement or self-punishment that follows a particular behavior.

self-instructions Instructions that one gives oneself while executing a complex task.

self-monitoring Observing and possibly recording one's own behavior to check progress toward a goal.

self-regulation Process of taking control of, monitoring, and evaluating one's own learning and behavior.

self-socialization Tendency to integrate personal observations and others' input into self-constructed standards for behavior and to choose actions consistent with those standards.

self-talk Process of talking to oneself as a way of guiding oneself through a task.

self-worth Belief about the extent to which one is generally a good, capable individual.

self-worth theory Theoretical perspective proposing that protecting one's own sense of competence (one's sense of *self-worth*) is a high priority for human beings.

sense of community Shared belief that teacher and students have common goals, are mutually respectful and supportive, and all make important contributions to classroom learning.

sense of school community Shared belief that all faculty and students within a school are working together to help everyone learn and succeed.

sense of self Perceptions, beliefs, judgments, and feelings about oneself as a person.

sensitive period Genetically determined age range during which a certain aspect of a child's development is especially susceptible to environmental conditions.

sensorimotor stage Piaget's first stage of cognitive development, in which schemes are based largely on behaviors and perceptions.

sensory register Component of memory that holds incoming information in an unanalyzed form for a very brief time (perhaps one to two seconds).

service learning Activity that promotes learning and development through participation in a meaningful community service project.

shame Feeling of embarrassment or humiliation after failing to meet certain standards for moral behavior.

shaping Process of reinforcing successively closer and closer approximations to a desired behavior.

situated learning and cognition Knowledge, behaviors, and thinking skills acquired and used primarily within certain contexts, with little or no use in other contexts.

situated motivation Motivation that emerges at least partly from conditions in a learner's immediate environment.

situational interest Interest evoked temporarily by something in the environment.

social cognition Process of thinking about how other people are likely to think, act, and react.

social cognitive theory Theoretical perspective that focuses on how people learn by observing others and how they eventually assume control over their own behavior; previously known as *social learning theory*.

social constructivism Theoretical perspective that focuses on people's collective efforts to impose meaning on the world.

social goal Desire related to establishing or maintaining relationships with other people.

social information processing Mental processes involved in making sense of and responding to social events.

social learning theory See *social cognitive theory*.

socialization Process of molding a child's behavior and beliefs to be appropriate for his or her cultural group.

society Large, enduring social group that is socially and economically organized and has collective institutions and activities.

sociocultural theory Theoretical perspective that emphasizes the importance of society and culture for promoting learning and cognitive development.

socioeconomic status (SES) One's general social and economic standing in society (encompasses family income, educational level, occupational status, and related factors).

specific transfer Instance of transfer in which the original learning task and the transfer task overlap in content.

stage theory Theory that depicts development as a series of relatively discrete periods (*stages*).

standard deviation (SD) Statistic indicating the amount of variability characterizing a set of scores.

Standard English Form of English generally considered acceptable at school, as reflected in textbooks and grammar instruction.

standard score Test score indicating how far a student's performance is from the mean with respect to standard deviation units.

standardization Extent to which assessments involve similar content and format and are administered and scored similarly for everyone.

standardized test Test developed by test construction experts and published for use in many different schools and classrooms.

standards General statements regarding the knowledge and skills that students should gain and the characteristics that their accomplishments should reflect.

stanine Standard score with a mean of 5 and a standard deviation of 2; always reported as a whole number.

stereotype Rigid, simplistic, and erroneous view of a particular group of people.

stereotype threat Awareness of a negative stereotype about one's own group and accompanying uneasiness that low performance will confirm the stereotype; leads (often unintentionally) to a reduction in performance.

stimulus (pl. stimuli) Specific object or event that influences an individual's learning or behavior.

storage Process of "putting" new information into memory.

student at risk Student who has a high probability of failing to acquire the minimum academic skills necessary for success in the adult world.

student with special needs Student who is different enough from peers that he or she requires specially adapted instructional materials and practices.

subculture Group that resists the ways of the dominant culture and adopts its own norms for behavior.

summative assessment Assessment conducted in order to determine students' final achievement related to a particular topic or content area.

superimposed meaningful structure Familiar shape, word, sentence, poem, or story imposed on information in order to facilitate recall.

symbolic model Real or fictional character portrayed in the media that influences an observer's behavior.

sympathy Feeling of sorrow for another person's distress, accompanied by concern for the person's well-being.

synapse Tiny space across which one neuron regularly communicates with another; reflects an ongoing but modifiable connection between the two neurons.

synaptic pruning Universal process in brain development in which many previously formed synapses wither away.

synaptogenesis Universal process in early brain development in which many new synapses spontaneously form.

table of specifications Two-way grid indicating the topics to be covered in an assessment and the things students should be able to do with those topics.

task analysis Process of identifying the specific behaviors, knowledge, or cognitive processes necessary to master a particular topic or skill.

teachable moment Situation or event (often unplanned) in which students might be especially predisposed to acquire particular knowledge or skills.

teacher-directed instruction Approach to instruction in which the teacher is largely in control of the content and course of the lesson.

temperament Genetic predisposition to respond in particular ways to one's physical and social environments.

test anxiety Excessive anxiety about a particular test or about assessment in general.

testwiseness Test-taking know-how that enhances test performance.

theory Integrated set of concepts and principles developed to explain a particular phenomenon; may be constructed jointly by researchers over time (see Chapter 1) or individually by a single learner (see Chapter 2).

theory of mind Self-constructed understanding of one's own and other people's mental and psychological states (thoughts, feelings, etc.).

threat Situation in which a learner believes there is little or no chance of success.

time on task Amount of time that students are actively engaged in a learning activity.

time-out Consequence for misbehavior in which a student is placed in a dull, boring situation with no opportunity for reinforcement or social interaction.

token economy Classroom strategy in which desired behaviors are reinforced by tokens that the learner can use to "purchase" a variety of other, backup reinforcers.

transfer Phenomenon in which something a person has learned at one time affects how the person learns or performs in a later situation.

treatment group Group of people in a research study who are given a particular experimental treatment (e.g., a particular method of instruction).

universal (in development) Similar pattern in how children change and progress over time regardless of their specific environment.

validity Extent to which an assessment instrument actually measures what it is intended to measure and allows appropriate inferences about the characteristic or ability in question.

value Belief that an activity has direct or indirect benefits.

verbal mediator Word or phrase that forms a logical connection or "bridge" between two pieces of information.

vicarious punishment Phenomenon in which a response decreases in frequency when another (observed) person is punished for that response.

vicarious reinforcement Phenomenon in which a response increases in frequency when another (observed) person is reinforced for that response.

visual imagery Cognitive process in which learners form mental pictures of objects or ideas.

wait time Length of time a teacher pauses, after either asking a question or hearing a student's comment, before saying something.

withitness Classroom management strategy in which a teacher gives the impression of knowing what all students are doing at all times.

working memory Component of memory that holds and actively thinks about and processes a limited amount of information for a short time period.

worldview General, culturally based set of assumptions about reality that influence understandings of a wide variety of phenomena.

zone of proximal development (ZPD) Range of tasks that a child can perform with the help and guidance of others but cannot yet perform independently.

z-score Standard score with a mean of 0 and a standard deviation of 1.

Ablard, K. E., & Lipschultz, R. E. (1998). Self-regulated learning in high-achieving students: Relations to advanced reasoning, achievement goals, and gender. *Journal of Educational Psychology, 90,* 94–101.

Abrami, P. C., Bernard, R. M., Borokhovski, E., Wade, A., Surkes, M. A., Tamim, R., et al. (2008). Instructional interventions affecting critical thinking skills and dispositions: A stage 1 meta-analysis. *Review of Educational Research, 78,* 1102–1134.

Ackerman, B. P., Izard, C. E., Kobak, R., Brown, E. D., & Smith, C. (2007). Relation between reading problems and internalizing behavior in school for preadolescent children from economically disadvantaged families. *Child Development, 78,* 581–596.

Ackerman, P. L., & Lohman, D. F. (2006). Individual differences in cognitive functions. In P. A. Alexander & P. H. Winne (Eds.), *Handbook of educational psychology* (2nd ed., pp. 139–161). Mahwah, NJ: Erlbaum.

Adalbjarnardottir, S., & Selman, R. L. (1997). "I feel I have received a new vision": An analysis of teachers' professional development as they work with students on interpersonal issues. *Teaching and Teacher Education, 13,* 409–428.

Afflerbach, P., & Cho, B.-Y. (2010). Determining and describing reading strategies: Internet and traditional forms of reading. In H. S. Waters & W. Schneider (Eds.), *Metacognition, strategy use, and instruction* (pp. 201–225). New York: Guilford Press.

Ahn, J. (2005, April). *Young immigrant children's cultural transition and self-transformation.* Paper presented at the annual meeting of the American Educational Research Association, Montreal.

Aikens, N. L., & Barbarin, O. (2008). Socioeconomic differences in reading trajectories: The contribution of family, neighborhood, and school contexts. *Journal of Educational Psychology, 100,* 235–251.

Ainley, M. (2006). Connecting with learning: Motivation, affect, and cognition in interest processes. *Educational Psychology Review, 18,* 391–405.

Airasian, P. W. (1994). *Classroom assessment* (2nd ed.). New York: McGraw-Hill.

Alapack, R. (1991). The adolescent first kiss. *Humanistic Psychologist, 19,* 48–67.

Alberto, P. A., & Troutman, A. C. (2009). *Applied behavior analysis for teachers* (8th ed.). Upper Saddle River, NJ: Merrill/Pearson Education.

Alderman, M. K. (1990). Motivation for at-risk students. *Educational Leadership, 48*(1), 27–30.

Alexander, E. S. (2006, April). *Beyond S.M.A.R.T.? Integrating hopeful thinking into goal setting for adolescents at-risk of dropping out of high school.* Paper presented at the annual meeting of the American Educational Research Association, San Francisco.

Alexander, J. M., Johnson, K. E., Albano, J., Freygang, T., & Scott, B. (2006). Relations between intelligence and the development of metaconceptual knowledge. *Metacognition and Learning, 1,* 51–67.

Alexander, J. M., Johnson, K. E., Leibham, M. E., & Kelley, K. (2008). The development of conceptual interests in young children. *Cognitive Development, 23,* 324–334.

Alexander, J. M., Johnson, K. E., Scott, B., & Meyer, R. D. (2008). Stegosaurus and spoonbills: Mechanisms for transfer across biological domains. In M. F. Shaughnessy, M. V. E. Vennemann, & C. K. Kennedy (Eds.), *Metacognition: A recent review of research, theory, and perspectives* (pp. 63–83). Happauge, NY: Nova.

Alexander, K. L., Entwisle, D. R., & Dauber, S. L. (1995). On the success of failure. New York: Cambridge University Press.

Alexander, P. A. (1997). Mapping the multidimensional nature of domain learning: The interplay of cognitive, motivational, and strategic forces. In P. R. Pintrich & M. L. Maehr (Eds.), *Advances in motivation and achievement* (Vol. 10). Greenwich, CT: JAI Press.

Alexander, P. A. (1998). Positioning conceptual change within a model of domain literacy. In B. Guzzetti & C. Hynd (Eds.), *Perspectives on conceptual change: Multiple ways to understand knowing and learning in a complex world* (pp. 55–76). Mahwah, NJ: Erlbaum.

Alexander, P. A. (2003). The development of expertise: The journey from acclimation to proficiency. *Educational Researcher, 32*(8), 10–14.

Alexander, P. A. (2004). A model of domain learning: Reinterpreting expertise as a multidimensional, multistage process. In D. Y. Dai & R. J. Sternberg (Eds.), *Motivation, emotion, and cognition: Integrative perspectives on intellectual functioning and development* (pp. 273–298). Mahwah, NJ: Erlbaum.

Alexander, P. A., & Jetton, T. L. (1996). The role of importance and interest in the processing of text. *Educational Psychology Review, 8,* 89–121.

Alexander, P. A., & Judy, J. E. (1988). The interaction of domain-specific and strategic knowledge in academic performance. *Review of Educational Research, 58,* 375–404.

Alexander, P. A., Kulikowich, J. M., & Schulze, S. K. (1994). How subject-matter knowledge affects recall and interest. *American Educational Research Journal, 31,* 313–337.

Alexander, P. A., Schallert, D. L., & Reynolds, R. E. (2009). What is learning anyway? A topographic perspective considered. *Educational Psychologist, 44,* 176–192.

Alfassi, M. (2004). Reading to learn: Effects of combined strategy instruction on high school students. *Journal of Educational Research, 97,* 171–184.

Alim, H. S. (2007). "The Whig party don't exist in my hood": Knowledge, reality, and education in the hip hop nation. In H. S. Alim & J. Baugh (Eds.), *Talkin Black talk: Language, education, and social change* (pp. 15–29). New York: Teachers College Press.

Alim, H. S., & Baugh, J. (Eds.). (2007). *Talkin Black talk: Language, education, and social change.* New York: Teachers College Press.

Allday, R. A., & Pakurar, K. (2007). Effects of teacher greetings on student on-task behavior. *Journal of Applied Behavior Analysis, 40,* 317–320.

Alleman, J., & Brophy, J. (1997). Elementary social studies: Instruments, activities, and standards. In G. D. Phye (Ed.), *Handbook of classroom assessment: Learning, achievement, and adjustment.* San Diego, CA: Academic Press.

Alleman, J., & Brophy, J. (1998). Strategic learning opportunities during out-of-school hours. *Social Studies and the Young Learner, 10*(4), 10–13.

Allen, K. D. (1998). The use of an enhanced simplified habit-reversal procedure to reduce disruptive outbursts during athletic performance. *Journal of Applied Behavior Analysis, 31,* 489–492.

Allen, L., & Aber, J. L. (2006). The development of ethnic identity during adolescence. *Developmental Psychology, 42,* 1–10.

Allington, R. L., & Weber, R. (1993). Questioning questions in teaching and learning from texts. In B. K. Britton, A. Woodward, & M. Binkley (Eds.), *Learning from textbooks: Theory and practice.* Mahwah, NJ: Erlbaum.

Allison, K. W. (1998). Stress and oppressed social category membership. In J. Swim & C. Stangor (Eds.), *Prejudice: The target's perspective* (pp. 149–170). San Diego, CA: Academic Press.

Alloway, T. P., Gathercole, S. E., Kirkwood, H., & Elliott, J. (2009). The cognitive and behavioral characteristics of children with low working memory. *Child Development, 80,* 606–621.

Altermatt, E. R., Jovanovic, J., & Perry, M. (1998). Bias or responsivity? Sex and achievement-level effects on teachers' classroom questioning practices. *Journal of Educational Psychology, 90,* 516–527.

Altmann, E. M., & Gray, W. D. (2002). Forgetting to remember: The functional relationship of decay and interference. *Psychological Science, 13,* 27–33.

Altschul, I., Oyserman, D., & Bybee, D. (2006). Racial-ethnic identity in mid-adolescence: Content and change as predictors of academic achievement. *Child Development, 77,* 1155–1169.

Amabile, T. M., & Hennessey, B. A. (1992). The motivation for creativity in children. In A. K. Boggiano & T. S. Pittman (Eds.), *Achievement and motivation: A social-developmental perspective.* Cambridge, England: Cambridge University Press.

Ambrose, D., Allen, J., & Huntley, S. B. (1994). Mentorship of the highly creative. *Roeper Review, 17,* 131–133.

American Educational Research Association, American Psychological Association, & National

Council on Measurement in Education. (1999). *Standards for educational and psychological testing* (2nd ed.). Washington, DC: American Educational Research Association.

American Psychiatric Association. (2000). *Diagnostic and statistical manual of mental disorders* (4th ed.). Washington, DC: Author.

American Psychological Association. (2010). *Publication manual of the American Psychological Association* (6th ed.). Washington, DC: Author.

American Psychological Association Zero Tolerance Task Force. (2008). Are zero tolerance policies effective in the schools? An evidentiary review and recommendations. *American Psychologist, 63,* 852–862.

Ames, C. (1984). Competitive, cooperative, and individualistic goal structures: A cognitive-motivational analysis. In R. Ames & C. Ames (Eds.), *Research on motivation in education: Vol. 1. Student motivation.* San Diego, CA: Academic Press.

Ames, C. (1992). Classrooms: Goals, structures, and student motivation. *Journal of Educational Psychology, 84,* 261–271.

Ames, C., & Archer, J. (1988). Achievement goals in the classroom: Students' learning strategies and motivation processes. *Journal of Educational Psychology, 80,* 260–267.

Ames, R. (1983). Help-seeking and achievement orientation: Perspectives from attribution theory. In A. Nadler, J. Fisher, & B. DePaulo (Eds.), *New directions in helping* (Vol. 2). New York: Academic Press.

Amrein, A. L., & Berliner, D. C. (2002a, December). *An analysis of some unintended and negative consequences of high-stakes testing* (Report EPSL-0211-125-EPRU). Educational Policy Study Laboratory Web site: Retrieved April 28, 2003, from Arizona State University, www.asu.edu/educ/epsl/EPRU/epru_2002_Research_Writing.htm

Amrein, A. L., & Berliner, D. C. (2002b, March). High-stakes testing, uncertainty, and student learning. *Education Policy Analysis Archives, 10*(18). Retrieved April 9, 2002, from http://epaa.asu.edu/ epaa/v10n18/

Amrein, A. L., & Berliner, D. C. (2002c). The impact of high-stakes tests on student academic performance: An analysis of NAEP results in states with high-stakes tests and ACT, SAT, and AP test results in states with high school graduation exams. Retrieved April 28, 2003, from Arizona State University, Education Policy Studies Laboratory Web site: http://www.asu.edu/educ/epsl/EPRU/epru_2002_Research_Writing.htm

Amsterlaw, J. (2006). Children's beliefs about everyday reasoning. *Child Development, 77,* 443–464.

Anderman, E. M. (2002). School effects on psychological outcomes during adolescence. *Journal of Educational Psychology, 94,* 795–809.

Anderman, E. M., & Anderman, L. H. (2010). *Classroom motivation.* Upper Saddle River, NJ: Pearson.

Anderman, E. M., Griesinger, T., & Westerfield, G. (1998). Motivation and cheating during early adolescence. *Journal of Educational Psychology, 90,* 84–93.

Anderman, E. M., & Maehr, M. L. (1994). Motivation and schooling in the middle grades. *Review of Educational Research, 64,* 287–309.

Anderman, E. M., Noar, S., Zimmerman, R. S., & Donohew, L. (2004). The need for sensation as a prerequisite for motivation to engage in academic tasks. In M. L. Maehr & P. Pintrich (Eds.), *Advances in motivation and achievement: Motivating students, improving schools: The legacy of Carol Midgley* (Vol. 13). Greenwich, JAI Press.

Anderman, E. M., & Wolters, C. A. (2006). Goals, values, and affect: Influences on student motivation. In P. A. Alexander & P. H. Winne (Eds.), *Handbook of educational psychology* (2nd ed., pp. 369–389). Mahwah, NJ: Erlbaum.

Anderman, L. H., & Anderman, E. M. (1999). Social predictors of changes in students' achievement goal orientation. *Contemporary Educational Psychology, 25,* 21–37.

Anderman, L. H., & Anderman, E. M. (2009). Oriented towards mastery: Promoting positive motivational goals for students. In R. Gilman, E. S. Huebner, & M. J. Furlong (Eds.), *Handbook of positive psychology in schools* (pp. 161–173). New York: Routledge.

Anderman, L. H., Andrzejewski, C. E., & Allen, J. (in press). How do teachers support students' motivation and learning in their classrooms? *Teachers College Record, 113*(5).

Anderman, L. H., Patrick, H., Hruda, L. Z., & Linnenbrink, E. A. (2002). Observing classroom goal structures to clarify and expand goal theory. In C. Midgley (Ed.), *Goals, goal structures, and patterns of adaptive learning* (pp. 243–278). Mahwah, NJ: Erlbaum.

Anderson, C. A., Berkowitz, L., Donnerstein, E., Huesmann, L. R., Johnson, J. D., Linz, D., et al. (2003). The influence of media violence on youth. *Psychological Science in the Public Interest, 4,* 81–110.

Anderson, J. R. (1983). *The architecture of cognition.* Cambridge, MA: Harvard University Press.

Anderson, J. R. (1987). Skill acquisition: Compilation of weak-method problem solutions. *Psychological Review, 94,* 192–210.

Anderson, J. R. (1995). *Learning and memory: An integrated approach.* New York: Wiley.

Anderson, J. R. (2005). *Cognitive psychology and its implications* (6th ed.). New York: Worth.

Anderson, J. R., Greeno, J. G., Reder, L. M., & Simon, H. A. (2000). Perspectives on learning, thinking, and activity. *Educational Researcher, 29*(4), 11–13.

Anderson, J. R., Reder, L. M., & Simon, H. A. (1996). Situated learning and education. *Educational Researcher, 25*(4), 5–11.

Anderson, L. H. (1999). *Speak.* New York: Puffin Books.

Anderson, L. M. (1993). Auxiliary materials that accompany textbooks: Can they promote "higher-order" learning? In B. K. Britton, A. Woodward, & M. Binkley (Eds.), *Learning from textbooks: Theory and practice.* Mahwah, NJ: Erlbaum.

Anderson, L. W., Krathwohl, D. R., Airasian, P. W., Cruikshank, K. A., Mayer, R. E., Pintrich, P. R., et al. (Eds.). (2001). *A taxonomy for learning, teaching, and assessing: A revision of Bloom's taxonomy of educational objectives.* New York: Longman.

Anderson, L. W., & Pellicer, L. O. (1998). Toward an understanding of unusually successful programs for economically disadvantaged students. *Journal of Education for Students Placed at Risk, 3,* 237–263.

Anderson, R. C., Nguyen-Jahiel, K., McNurlen, B., Archodidou, A., Kim, S.-Y., Reznitskaya, A., et al. (2001). The snowball phenomenon: Spread of ways of talking and ways of thinking across groups of children. *Cognition and Instruction, 19,* 1–46.

Anderson, R. C., Reynolds, R. E., Schallert, D. L., & Goetz, E. T. (1977). Frameworks for comprehending discourse. *American Educational Research Journal, 14,* 367–381.

Andrade, H. L. (2010). Students as the definitive source of formative assessment: Academic self-assessment and the self-regulation of learning. In H. L. Andrade & G. G. Cizek (Eds.), *Handbook of formative assessment* (pp. 90–105). New York: Routledge.

Andre, T., & Windschitl, M. (2003). Interest, epistemological belief, and intentional conceptual change. In G. M. Sinatra & P. R. Pintrich (Eds.), *Intentional conceptual change* (pp. 173–197). Mahwah, NJ: Erlbaum.

Andriessen, J. (2006). Arguing to learn. In R. K. Sawyer (Ed.), *The Cambridge handbook of the learning sciences* (pp. 443–459). Cambridge, England: Cambridge University Press.

Angold, A., Worthman, C., & Costello, E. J. (2003). Puberty and depression. In C. Hayward (Ed.), *Gender differences at puberty* (pp. 137–164). Cambridge, England: Cambridge University Press.

Ansley, T. (1997). The role of standardized achievement tests in grades K–12. In G. D. Phye (Ed.), *Handbook of classroom assessment: Learning, achievement, and adjustment.* San Diego, CA: Academic Press.

Applebee, A. N., Langer, J. A., Nystrand, M., & Gamoran, A. (2003). Discussion-based approaches to developing understanding: Classroom instruction and student performance in middle and high school English. *American Educational Research Journal, 40,* 685–730.

Archer, S. L. (1982). The lower age boundaries of identity development. *Child Development, 53,* 1551–1556.

Ardoin, S. P., Martens, B. K., & Wolfe, L. A. (1999). Using high-probability instructional sequences with fading to increase student compliance during transitions. *Journal of Applied Behavior Analysis, 32,* 339–351.

Arlin, M. (1984). Time, equality, and mastery learning. *Review of Educational Research, 54,* 65–86.

Arnett, J. (1995). The young and the reckless: Adolescent reckless behavior. *Current Directions in Psychological Science, 4,* 67–71.

Arnett, J. (1999). Adolescent storm and stress, reconsidered. *American Psychologist, 54,* 317–326.

Arnold, M. L. (2000). Stage, sequence, and sequels: Changing conceptions of morality, post-Kohlberg. *Educational Psychology Review, 12,* 365–383.

Aronson, J., Lustina, M. J., Good, C., Keough, K., Steele, C. M., & Brown, J. (1999). When white men can't do math: Necessary and sufficient factors in stereotype threat. *Journal of Experimental Social Psychology, 35,* 29–46.

Aronson, J., & Steele, C. M. (2005). Stereotypes and the fragility of academic competence, motivation, and self-concept. In A. J. Elliot & C. S. Dweck (Eds.), *Handbook of competence and motivation* (pp. 436–456). New York: Guilford Press.

Arsenio, W. F., & Lemerise, E. A. (2004). Aggression and moral development: Integrating social information processing and moral domain models. *Child Development, 75,* 987–1002.

Arter, J. A., & Spandel, V. (1992). Using portfolios of student work in instruction and assessment. *Educational Measurement: Issues and Practice, 11*(1), 36–44.

Ash, D. (2002). Negotiations of thematic conversations about biology. In G. Leinhardt, K. Crowley, & K. Knutson (Eds.), *Learning conversations in museums* (pp. 357–400). Mahwah, NJ: Erlbaum.

Ashcraft, M. H. (2002). Math anxiety: Personal, educational, and cognitive consequences. *Current Directions in Psychological Science, 11*, 181–184.

Asher, S. R., & McDonald, K. A. (2009). The behavioral basis of acceptance, rejection, and perceived popularity. In K. H. Rubin, W. M. Bukowski, & B. Laursen (Eds.), *Handbook of peer interactions, relationships, and groups* (pp. 232–248). New York: Guilford.

Asher, S. R., & Paquette, J. A. (2003). Loneliness and peer relations in childhood. *Current Directions in Psychological Science, 12*, 75–78.

Asher, S. R., & Renshaw, P. D. (1981). Children without friends: Social knowledge and social skill training. In S. R. Asher & J. M. Gottman (Eds.), *The development of children's friendships.* New York: Cambridge University Press.

Ashiabi, G. S., & O'Neal, K. K. (2008). A framework for understanding the association between food insecurity and children's developmental outcomes. *Child Development Perspectives, 2*, 71–77.

Assor, A., & Connell, J. P. (1992). The validity of students' self-reports as measures of performance affecting self-appraisals. In D. H. Schunk & J. L. Meece (Eds.), *Student perceptions in the classroom.* Mahwah, NJ: Erlbaum.

Assor, A., Vansteenkiste, M., & Kaplan, A. (2009). Identified versus introjected approach and introjected avoidance motivations in school and in sports: The limited benefits of self-worth strivings. *Journal of Educational Psychology, 101*, 482–497.

Astington, J. W., & Pelletier, J. (1996). The language of mind: Its role in teaching and learning. In D. R. Olson & N. Torrance (Eds.), *The handbook of education and human development: New models of learning, teaching, and schooling.* Cambridge, MA: Blackwell.

Astor, R. A., Meyer, H. A., & Behre, W. J. (1999). Unowned places and times: Maps and interviews about violence in high schools. *American Educational Research Journal, 36*, 3–42.

Astuti, R., Solomon, G. E. A., & Carey, S. (2004). Constraints on conceptual development. *Monographs of the Society for Research in Child Development, 69*(3, Serial No. 277).

Atance, C. M. (2008). Future thinking in young children. *Current Directions in Psychological Science, 17*, 295–298.

Atkinson, R. C., & Shiffrin, R. M. (1968). Human memory: A proposed system and its control processes. In K. W. Spence & J. T. Spence (Eds.), *The psychology of learning and motivation: Advances in research and theory* (Vol. 2). San Diego, CA: Academic Press.

Atkinson, R. K., Levin, J. R., Kiewra, K. A., Meyers, T., Kim, S., Atkinson, L. A., et al. (1999). Matrix and mnemonic text-processing adjuncts: Comparing and combining their components. *Journal of Educational Psychology, 91*, 342–357.

Atran, S., Medin, D. L., & Ross, N. O. (2005). The cultural mind: Environmental decision making and cultural modeling within and across populations. *Psychological Review, 112*, 744–776.

Attie, I., Brooks-Gunn, J., & Petersen, A. (1990). A developmental perspective on eating disorders and eating problems. In M. Lewis &

S. M. Miller (Eds.), *Handbook of developmental psychopathology* (pp. 409–420). New York: Plenum Press.

Au, K. H. (1980). Participation structures in a reading lesson with Hawaiian children: Analysis of a culturally appropriate instructional event. *Anthropology and Education Quarterly, 11*, 91–115.

Au, W. (2007). High-stakes testing and curricular control: A qualitative metasynthesis. *Educational Researcher, 36*(5), 258–267.

Aulls, M. W. (1998). Contributions of classroom discourse to what content students learn during curriculum enactment. *Journal of Educational Psychology, 90*, 56–69.

Ausubel, D. P. (1968). *Educational psychology: A cognitive view.* New York: Holt, Rinehart & Winston.

Ausubel, D. P., Novak, J. D., & Hanesian, H. (1978). *Educational psychology: A cognitive view* (2nd ed.). New York: Holt, Rinehart & Winston.

Awh, E., Barton, B., & Vogel, E. D. (2007). Visual working memory represents a fixed number of items regardless of complexity. *Psychological Science, 18*, 622–628.

Azevedo, R. (2005a). Computer environments as metacognitive tools for enhancing learning. *Educational Psychologist, 40*, 193–197.

Azevedo, R. (2005b). Using hypermedia as a metacognitive tool for enhancing student learning? The role of self-regulated learning. *Educational Psychologist, 40*, 199–209.

Babad, E. (1993). Teachers' differential behavior. *Educational Psychology Review, 5*, 347–376.

Babad, E. (1995). The "teacher's pet phenomenon," students' perceptions of teachers' differential behavior, and students' morale. *Journal of Educational Psychology, 87*, 361–374.

Babad, E., Avni-Babad, D., & Rosenthal, R. (2003). Teachers' brief nonverbal behaviors in defined instructional situations can predict students' evaluations. *Journal of Educational Psychology, 95*, 553–562.

Baddeley, A. D. (2001). Is working memory still working? *American Psychologist, 56*, 851–864.

Baek, S. (1994). Implications of cognitive psychology for educational testing. *Educational Psychology Review, 6*, 373–389.

Bagley, C., & Mallick, K. (1998). Field independence, cultural context and academic achievement: A commentary. *British Journal of Educational Psychology, 68*, 581–587.

Baker, J. (1999). Teacher-student interaction in urban at-risk classrooms: Differential behavior, relationship quality, and student satisfaction with school. *The Elementary School Journal, 100*, 57–70.

Baker, L. (1989). Metacognition, comprehension monitoring, and the adult reader. *Educational Psychology Review, 1*, 3–38.

Baker, L., & Brown, A. L. (1984). Metacognitive skills of reading. In D. Pearson (Ed.), *Handbook of reading research.* White Plains, NY: Longman.

Balch, W., Bowman, K., & Mohler, L. (1992). Music-dependent memory in immediate and delayed word recall. *Memory and Cognition, 20*, 21–28.

Balfanz, R., Legters, N., West, T. C., & Weber, L. M. (2007). Are NCLB's measures, incentives, and improvement strategies the right ones for the nation's low-performing high schools? *American Educational Research Journal, 44*, 559–593.

Bandura, A. (1986). *Social foundations of thought and action: A social cognitive theory.* Upper Saddle River, NJ: Prentice Hall.

Bandura, A. (1989). Human agency in social cognitive theory. *American Psychologist, 44*, 1175–1184.

Bandura, A. (1997). *Self-efficacy: The exercise of control.* New York: Freeman.

Bandura, A. (2000). Exercise of human agency through collective efficacy. *Current Directions in Psychological Science, 9*, 75–78.

Bandura, A. (2006). Toward a psychology of human agency. *Perspectives on Psychological Science, 1*, 164–180.

Bandura, A. (2008). Toward an agentic theory of the self. In H. W. Marsh, R. G. Craven, & D. M. McInerney (Eds.), *Self-processes, learning, and enabling human potential* (pp. 15–49). Charlotte, NC: Information Age.

Bangert-Drowns, R. L., Kulik, J. A., & Kulik, C.-L. C. (1983). Effects of coaching programs on achievement test performance. *Review of Educational Research, 53*, 571–585.

Bangert-Drowns, R. L., Kulik, C. C., Kulik, J. A., & Morgan, M. (1991). The instructional effect of feedback in test-like events. *Review of Educational Research, 61*, 213–238.

Banks, J. A. (1991). Multicultural literacy and curriculum reform. *Educational Horizons, 69*(3), 135–140.

Banks, J. A. (1994). *An introduction to multicultural education.* Boston: Allyn & Bacon.

Banks, J. A., & Banks, C. A. M. (Eds.). (1995). *Handbook of research on multicultural education.* New York: Macmillan.

Banks, J., Cochran-Smith, M., Moll, L., Richert, A., Zeichner, K., LePage, P., Darling-Hammond, L., & Duffy, H. (with McDonald, M.) (2005). Teaching diverse learners. In L. Darling-Hammond & J. Bransford (Eds.), *Preparing teachers for a changing world: What teachers should learn and be able to do* (pp. 232–274). San Francisco: Jossey-Bass/Wiley.

Banta, T. W. (Ed.). (2003). *Portfolio assessment: Uses, cases, scoring, and impact.* San Francisco: Jossey-Bass.

Bao, X., & Lam, S. (2008). Who makes the choice? Rethinking the role of autonomy and relatedness in Chinese children's motivation. *Child Development, 79*, 269–283.

Barab, S. A., & Plucker, J. A. (2002). Smart people or smart contexts? Cognition, ability, and talent development in an age of situated approaches to knowing and learning. *Educational Psychologist, 37*, 165–182.

Barbarin, O., Mercado, M., & Jigjidsuren, D. (2010). Development for tolerance and respect for diversity in the context of immigration. In E. L. Grigorenko & R. Takanishi (Eds.), *Immigration, diversity, and education* (pp. 276–288). New York: Routledge.

Barber, B. K., Stolz, H. E., & Olsen, J. A. (2005). Parental support, psychological control, and behavioral control: Assessing relevance across time, culture, and method. *Monographs of the Society for Research in Child Development, 70*(4, Serial No. 282).

Barchfeld, P., Sodian, B., Thoermer, C., & Bullock, M. (2005, April). *The development of experiment generation abilities from primary school to late adolescence.* Poster presented at the biennial meeting of the Society for Research in Child Development, Atlanta.

Barkley, R. A. (1996). Linkages between attention and executive functions. In G. R. Lyon & N. A. Krasnegor (Eds.), *Attention, memory, and executive function.* Baltimore: Brookes.

Barkley, R. A. (2006). *Attention-deficit hyperactivity disorder: A handbook for diagnosis and treatment* (3rd ed.). New York: Guilford Press.

Barnett, J. E. (2001, April). *Study strategies and preparing for exams: A survey of middle and high school students.* Paper presented at the annual meeting of the American Educational Research Association, Seattle, WA.

Barnett, M. (2005, April). *Engaging inner city students in learning through designing remote operated vehicles.* Paper presented at the annual meeting of the American Educational Research Association, Montreal.

Barnett, S. M., & Ceci, S. J. (2002). When and where do we apply what we learn? A taxonomy of far transfer. *Psychological Bulletin, 128,* 612–637.

Baron, J. B. (1987). Evaluating thinking skills in the classroom. In J. B. Baron & R. J. Sternberg (Eds.), *Teaching thinking skills: Theory and practice.* New York: Freeman.

Bartholomew, D. J. (2004). *Measuring intelligence: Facts and fallacies.* Cambridge, England: Cambridge University Press.

Bartlett, F. C. (1932). *Remembering: A study in experimental and social psychology.* Cambridge, England: Cambridge University Press.

Barton, K. C., & Levstik, L. S. (1996). "Back when God was around and everything": Elementary children's understanding of historical time. *American Educational Research Journal, 33,* 419–454.

Basso, K. (1972). To give up on words: Silence in western Apache culture. In P. Giglioli (Ed.), *Language and social context.* New York: Penguin Books.

Bassok, M. (1990). Transfer of domain-specific problem-solving procedures. *Journal of Experimental Psychology: Learning, Memory, and Cognition, 16,* 522–533.

Bates, J. E., & Pettit, G. S. (2007). Temperament, parenting, and socialization. In J. E. Grusec & P. D. Hastings (Eds.), *Handbook of socialization: Theory and research* (pp. 153–177). New York: Guilford Press.

Batshaw, M. L., & Shapiro, B. K. (1997). Mental retardation. In M. L. Batshaw (Ed.), *Children with disabilities* (4th ed.). Baltimore: Brookes.

Batson, C. D. (1991). *The altruism question: Toward a social-psychological answer.* Hillsdale, NJ: Erlbaum.

Batson, C. D., & Thompson, E. R. (2001). Why don't moral people act morally? Motivational considerations. *Current Directions in Psychological Science, 10,* 54–57.

Battin-Pearson, S., Newcomb, M. D., Abbott, R. D., Hill, K. G., Catalano, R. F., & Hawkins, J. D. (2000). Predictors of early high school dropout: A test of five theories. *Journal of Educational Psychology, 92,* 568–582.

Battistich, V., Solomon, D., Kim, D., Watson, M., & Schaps, E. (1995). Schools as communities, poverty levels of student populations, and students' attitudes, motives, and performance: A multilevel analysis. *American Educational Research Journal, 32,* 627–658.

Battistich, V., Solomon, D., Watson, M., & Schaps, E. (1997). Caring school communities. *Educational Psychologist, 32,* 137–151.

Bauer, P. J. (2002). Long-term recall memory: Behavioral and neuro-developmental changes in the first 2 years of life. *Current Directions in Psychological Science, 11,* 137–141.

Baumeister, A. A. (1989). Mental retardation. In C. G. Lask & M. Hersen (Eds.), *Handbook of child psychiatric diagnosis.* New York: Wiley.

Baumeister, R. F., Campbell, J. D., Krueger, J. I., & Vohs, K. D. (2003). Does high self-esteem cause better performance, interpersonal success, happiness, or healthier lifestyles? *Psychological Science in the Public Interest, 4,* 1–44.

Baumeister, R. F., Smart, L., & Boden, J. M. (1996). Relation of threatened egotism to violence and aggression: The dark side of high self-esteem. *Psychological Review, 103,* 5–33.

Baumrind, D. (1989). Rearing competent children. In W. Damon (Ed.), *Child development today and tomorrow.* San Francisco: Jossey-Bass.

Baumrind, D. (1991). Parenting styles and adolescent development. In R. M. Lerner, A. C. Petersen, & J. Brooks-Gunn (Eds.), *Encyclopedia of adolescence.* New York: Garland.

Baxter, G. P., Elder, A. D., & Glaser, R. (1996). Knowledge-based cognition and performance assessment in the science classroom. *Educational Psychologist, 31,* 133–140.

Bay-Hinitz, A. K., Peterson, R. F., & Quilitch, H. R. (1994). Cooperative games: A way to modify aggressive and cooperative behaviors in young children. *Journal of Applied Behavior Analysis, 27,* 435–446.

Beal, C. R., Arroyo, I., & Cohen, P. R. (2009, April). *Experimental evaluation of an intelligent tutoring system for middle school mathematics word problem solving.* Paper presented at the annual meeting of the American Educational Research Association, San Diego, CA.

Bebko, J. M., Burke, L., Craven, J., & Sarlo, N. (1992). The importance of motor activity in sensorimotor development: A perspective from children with physical handicaps. *Human Development, 35,* 226–240.

Beck, S. R., Robinson, E. J., Carroll, D. J., & Apperly, I. A. (2006). Children's thinking about counterfactuals and future hypotheticals as possibilities. *Child Development, 77,* 413–426.

Becker, B. E., & Luthar, S. S. (2002). Social-emotional factors affecting achievement outcomes among disadvantaged students: Closing the achievement gap. *Educational Psychologist, 37,* 197–214.

Bédard, J., & Chi, M. T. H. (1992). Expertise. *Current Directions in Psychological Science, 1,* 135–139.

Behl-Chadha, G. (1996). Basic-level and superordinate-like categorical representations in early infancy. *Cognition, 60,* 105–141.

Behrmann, M. (2000). The mind's eye mapped onto the brain's matter. *Current Directions in Psychological Science, 9,* 50–54.

Beilock, S. L. (2008). Math performance in stressful situations. *Current Directions in Psychological Science, 17,* 339–343.

Beilock, S. L., & Carr, T. H. (2003). From novice to expert performance: Memory, attention, and the control of complex sensorimotor skills. In A. M. Williams, N. J. Hodges, M. A. Scott, & M. L. J. Court (Eds.), *Skill acquisition in sport: Research, theory, and practice.* New York: Routledge.

Beirne-Smith, M., Ittenbach, R. F., & Patton, J. R. (2002). *Mental retardation* (6th ed.). Upper Saddle River, NJ: Merrill/Prentice Hall.

Belfiore, P. J., & Hornyak, R. S. (1998). Operant theory and application to self-monitoring in adolescents. In D. H. Schunk & B. J. Zimmerman (Eds.), *Self-regulated learning: From teaching to self-reflective practice.* New York: Guilford Press.

Belfiore, P. J., Lee, D. L., Vargas, A. U., & Skinner, C. H. (1997). Effects of high-preference single-digit mathematics problem completion on multiple-digit mathematics problem performance. *Journal of Applied Behavior Analysis, 30,* 327–330.

Bell, P., & Linn, M. C. (2002). Beliefs about science: How does science instruction contribute? In B. K. Hofer & P. R. Pintrich (Eds.), *Personal epistemology: The psychology of beliefs about knowledge and knowing* (pp. 321–346). Mahwah, NJ: Erlbaum.

Belsky, J., Bakermans-Kranenburg, M. J., & van IJzendoorn, M. H. (2007). For better *and* for worse: Differential susceptibility to environmental influences. *Current Directions in Psychological Science, 16,* 300–304.

Belsky, J., & Pluess, M. (2009). The nature (and nurture?) of plasticity in early human development. *Perspectives on Psychological Science, 4,* 345–351.

Bem, S. L. (1981). Gender schema theory: A cognitive account of sex typing. *Psychological Review, 88,* 354–364.

Bembenutty, H., & Karabenick, S. A. (2004). Inherent association between academic delay of gratification, future time perspective, and self-regulated learning. *Educational Psychology Review, 16,* 35–57.

Bender, G. (2001). Resisting dominance? The study of a marginalized masculinity and its construction within high school walls. In J. N. Burstyn, G. Bender, R. Casella, H. W. Gordon, D. P. Guerra, K. V. Luschen, et al., *Preventing violence in schools: A challenge to American democracy* (pp. 61–77). Mahwah, NJ: Erlbaum.

Benenson, J. F., Maiese, R., Dolenszky, E., Dolensky, N., Sinclair, N., & Simpson, A. (2002). Group size regulates self-assertive versus self-deprecating responses to interpersonal competition. *Child Development, 73,* 1818–1829.

Benes, F. M. (2007). Corticolimbic circuitry and psychopathology: Development of the corticolimbic system. In D. Coch, G. Dawson, & K. W. Fischer (Eds.), *Human behavior, learning, and the developing brain: Atypical development* (pp. 331–361). New York: Guilford Press.

Benner, A. D., & Graham, S. (2009). The transition to high school as a developmental process among multiethnic urban youth. *Child Development, 80,* 356–376.

Benton, D. (2008). Nutrition and intellectual development. In P. C. Kyllonen, R. D. Roberts, & L. Stankov (Eds.), *Extending intelligence: Enhancement and new constructs* (pp. 373–394). New York: Erlbaum/Taylor & Francis.

Benware, C., & Deci, E. L. (1984). Quality of learning with an active versus passive motivational set. *American Educational Research Journal, 21,* 755–765.

Ben-Yehudah, G., & Fiez, J. A. (2007). Development of verbal working memory. In D. Coch, K. W. Fischer, & G. Dawson (Eds.), *Human behavior, learning, and the developing brain: Typical development* (pp. 301–328). New York: Guilford Press.

Ben-Zeev, T., Carrasquillo, C. M., Ching, A. M. L., Kliengklom, T. J., McDonald, K. L., Newhall, D. C., et al. (2005). "Math is hard!" (Barbie™, 1994): Responses of threat vs. challenge-mediated arousal to stereotypes alleging intellectual inferiority. In A. M. Gallagher & J. C. Kaufman (Eds.), *Gender differences in mathematics: An integrative psychological approach* (pp. 189–206). Cambridge, England: Cambridge University Press.

Bereiter, C. (1995). A dispositional view of transfer. In A. McKeough, J. Lupart, & A. Marini (Eds.), *Teaching for transfer: Fostering generalization in learning*. Mahwah, NJ: Erlbaum.

Bereiter, C., & Scardamalia, M. (2006). Education for the Knowledge Age: Design-centered models of teaching and instruction. In P. A. Alexander & P. H. Winne (Eds.), *Handbook of educational psychology* (2nd ed., pp. 695–713). Mahwah, NJ: Erlbaum.

Berg, W. K., Wacker, D. P., Cigrand, K., Merkle, S., Wade J., Henry, K., et al. (2007). Comparing functional analysis and paired-choice assessment results in classroom settings. *Journal of Applied Behavior Analysis, 40,* 545–552.

Bergamo, M., & Evans, M. A. (2005, April). *Rules of surviving peer relationships: Advice from middle school students.* Poster presented at the annual meeting of the American Educational Research Association, Montreal.

Bergin, D. A., & Cooks, H. C. (2008). High school students of color talk about accusations of "acting White." In J. U. Ogbu (Ed.), *Minority status, oppositional culture, and schooling* (pp. 145–166). New York: Routledge.

Berk, L. E. (1994). Why children talk to themselves. *Scientific American, 271,* 78–83.

Berkowitz, L. (1989). Frustration-aggression hypothesis: Examination and reformulation. *Psychological Bulletin, 106,* 59–73.

Berliner, D. C. (1988, February). *The development of expertise in pedagogy.* Paper presented at the American Association of Colleges for Teacher Education, New Orleans, LA.

Berliner, D. C. (2001). Learning about and learning from expert teachers. *International Journal of Educational Research, 35,* 463–483.

Berliner, D. C. (2005, April). *Ignoring the forest, blaming the trees: Our impoverished view of educational reform.* Paper presented at the annual meeting of the American Educational Research Association, Montreal.

Berlyne, D. E. (1960). *Conflict, arousal, and curiosity.* New York: McGraw-Hill.

Berndt, T. J., & Keefe, K. (1996). Friends' influence on school adjustment: A motivational analysis. In J. Juvonen & K. R. Wentzel (Eds.), *Social motivation: Understanding children's school adjustment* (pp. 248–278). Cambridge, England: Cambridge University Press.

Berndt, T. J., Laychak, A. E., & Park, K. (1990). Friends' influence on adolescents' academic achievement motivation: An experimental study. *Journal of Educational Psychology, 82,* 664–670.

Berthold, K., & Renkl, A. (2009). Instructional aids to support a conceptual understanding of multiple representations. *Journal of Educational Psychology, 101,* 70–87.

Berzonsky, M. D. (1988). Self-theorists, identity status, and social cognition. In D. K. Lapsley & F. C. Power (Eds.), *Self, ego, and identity: Integrative approaches* (pp. 243–261). New York: Springer-Verlag.

Berzonsky, M. D., & Kuk, L. S. (2000). Identity status, identity processing style, and the transition to university. *Journal of Adolescent Research, 15,* 81–98.

Best, D. L. (2010). Gender. In M. H. Bornstein (Ed.), *Handbook of cultural developmental science* (pp. 209–222). New York: Psychology Press.

Beyer, B. K. (1985). Critical thinking: What is it? *Social Education, 49,* 270–276.

Bialystok, E. (1994). Representation and ways of knowing: Three issues in second language acquisition. In N. C. Ellis (Ed.), *Implicit and explicit learning of languages*. London: Academic Press.

Bielaczyc, K., & Collins, A. (2006). Fostering knowledge-creating communities. In A. M. O'Donnell, C. E. Hmelo-Silver, & G. Erkens (Eds.), *Collaborative learning, reasoning, and technology* (pp. 37–60). Mahwah, NJ: Erlbaum.

Biemiller, A., Shany, M., Inglis, A., & Meichenbaum, D. (1998). Factors influencing children's acquisition and demonstration of self-regulation on academic tasks. In D. H. Schunk & B. J. Zimmerman (Eds.), *Self-regulated learning: From teaching to self-reflective practice* (pp. 203–224). New York: Guilford Press.

Bierman, K. L., Miller, C. L., & Stabb, S. D. (1987). Improving the social behavior and peer acceptance of rejected boys: Effect of social skill training with instructions and prohibitions. *Journal of Consulting and Clinical Psychology, 55,* 194–200.

Bierman, K. L., & Powers, C. J. (2009). Social skills training to improve peer relations. In K. H. Rubin, W. M. Bukowski, & B. Laursen (Eds.), *Handbook of peer interactions, relationships, and groups* (pp. 603–621). New York: Guilford Press.

Bigler, R. S., Brown, C. S., & Markell, M. (2001). When groups are not created equal: Effects of group status on the formation of intergroup attitudes in children. *Child Development, 72,* 1151–1162.

Bigler, R. S., & Liben, L. S. (2007). Developmental intergroup theory: Explaining and reducing children's social stereotyping and prejudice. *Current Directions in Psychological Science, 16,* 162–166.

Bivens, J. A., & Berk, L. E. (1990). A longitudinal study of the development of elementary school children's private speech. *Merrill-Palmer Quarterly, 36,* 443–463.

Bjorklund, D. F. (1987). How age changes in knowledge base contribute to the development of children's memory: An interpretive review. *Developmental Review, 7,* 93–130.

Bjorklund, D. F., & Coyle, T. R. (1995). Utilization deficiencies in the development of memory strategies. In F. E. Weinert & W. Schneider (Eds.), *Research on memory development: State of the art and future directions*. Mahwah, NJ: Erlbaum.

Bjorklund, D. F., & Jacobs, J. W. (1985). Associative and categorical processes in children's memory: The role of automaticity in the development of organization in free recall. *Journal of Experimental Child Psychology, 39,* 599–617.

Bjorklund, D. F., Schneider, W., Cassel, W. S., & Ashley, E. (1994). Training and extension of a memory strategy: Evidence for utilization deficiencies in high- and low-IQ children. *Child Development, 65,* 951–965.

Black-Gutman, D., & Hickson, F. (1996). The relationship between racial attitudes and social-cognitive development in children: An Australian study. *Developmental Psychology, 32,* 448–456.

Blackwell, L. S., Trzesniewski, K. H., & Dweck, C. S. (2007). Implicit theories of intelligence predict achievement across an adolescent transition: A longitudinal study and an intervention. *Child Development, 78,* 246–263.

Blair, C. (2002). School readiness: Integrating cognition and emotion in a neurobiological conceptualization of children's functioning at school entry. *American Psychologist, 57,* 111–127.

Blasi, A. (1980). Bridging moral cognition and moral action: A critical review of the literature. *Psychological Bulletin, 88,* 593–637.

Blasi, A. (1995). Moral understanding and the moral personality: The process of moral integration. In W. M. Kurtines & J. L. Gewirtz (Eds.), *Moral development: An introduction*. Boston: Allyn & Bacon.

Block, J. H. (1983). Differential premises arising from differential socialization of the sexes: Some conjectures. *Child Development, 54,* 1335–1354.

Bloom, B. S. (1981). *All our children learning*. New York: McGraw-Hill.

Bloom, B. S., Englehart, M. D., Furst, E. J., Hill, W. H., & Krathwohl, D. R. (1956). *Taxonomy of educational objectives. The classification of educational goals: Handbook I. Cognitive domain*. New York: David McKay.

Bloom, L., & Tinker, E. (2001). The intentionality model and language acquisition. *Monographs of the Society for Research in Child Development, 66*(4, Serial No. 267).

Blugental, D. B., Lyon, J. E., Lin, E. K., McGrath, E. P., & Bimbela, A. (1999). Children "tune out" to the ambiguous communication style of powerless adults. *Child Development, 70,* 214–230.

Blumenfeld, P. C. (1992). The task and the teacher: Enhancing student thoughtfulness in science. In J. Brophy (Ed.), *Advances in research on teaching: Vol. 3. Planning and managing learning tasks and activities*. Greenwich, CT: JAI Press.

Blumenfeld, P. C., Kempler, T. M., & Krajcik, J. S. (2006). Motivation and cognitive engagement in learning environments. In R. K. Sawyer (Ed.), *The Cambridge handbook of the learning sciences* (pp. 475–488). Cambridge, England: Cambridge University Press.

Blumenfeld, P. C., Marx, R. W., Soloway, E., & Krajcik, J. (1996). Learning with peers: From small group cooperation to collaborative communities. *Educational Researcher, 25*(8), 37–40.

Boaler, J. (2002). *Experiencing school mathematics: Traditional and reform approaches to teaching and their impact on student learning*. Mahwah, NJ: Erlbaum.

Boekaerts, M., de Koning, E., & Vedder, P. (2006). Goal-directed behavior and contextual factors in the classroom: An innovative approach to the study of multiple goals. *Educational Psychologist, 41,* 33–51.

Boggiano, A. K., & Pittman, T. S. (Eds.). (1992). *Achievement and motivation: A social-developmental perspective*. Cambridge, England: Cambridge University Press.

Boling, C. J., & Evans, W. H. (2008). Reading success in the secondary classroom. *Preventing School Failure, 52*(2), 59–66.

Bong, M. (2001). Between- and within-domain relations of academic motivation among middle and high school students: Self-efficacy, task-value, and achievement goals. *Journal of Educational Psychology, 93,* 23–34.

Bong, M. (2009). Age-related differences in achievement goal differentiation. *Journal of Educational Psychology, 101,* 879–896.

Bong, M., & Skaalvik, E. M. (2003). Academic self-concept and self-efficacy: How different are they really? *Educational Psychology Review, 15,* 1–40.

Boom, J., Brugman, D., & van der Heijden, P. G. M. (2001). Hierarchical structure of moral stages assessed by a sorting task. *Child Development, 72,* 535–548.

Borko, H., & Putnam, R. T. (1996). Learning to teach. In D. C. Berliner & R. C. Calfee (Eds.), *Handbook of educational psychology.* New York: Macmillan.

Bornholt, L. J., Goodnow, J. J., & Cooney, G. H. (1994). Influences of gender stereotypes on adolescents' perceptions of their own achievement. *American Educational Research Journal, 31,* 675–692.

Bornstein, M. H., & Cote, L. R. (2010). Immigration and acculturation. In M. H. Bornstein (Ed.), *Handbook of cultural developmental science* (pp. 531–552). New York: Psychology Press.

Bornstein, M. H., Hahn, C.-S., Bell, C., Haynes, O. M., Slater, A., Golding, J., et al. (2006). Stability in cognition across early childhood: A developmental cascade. *Psychological Science, 17,* 151–158.

Bornstein, M. H., & Lansford, J. E. (2010). Parenting. In M. H. Bornstein (Ed.), *Handbook of cultural developmental science* (pp. 259–277). New York: Psychology Press.

Bortfeld, H., & Whitehurst, G. J. (2001). Sensitive periods in first language acquisition. In D. B. Bailey, Jr., J. T. Bruer, F. J. Symons, & J. W. Lichtman (Eds.), *Critical thinking about critical periods* (pp. 173–192). Baltimore: Brookes.

Bosacki, S. L. (2000). Theory of mind and self-concept in preadolescents: Links with gender and language. *Journal of Educational Psychology, 92,* 709–717.

Boschee, F., & Baron, M. A. (1993). *Outcome-based education: Developing programs through strategic planning.* Lancaster, PA: Technomic.

Bouchard, T. J., Jr. (1997). IQ similarity in twins reared apart: Findings and responses to critics. In R. J. Sternberg & E. L. Grigorenko (Eds.), *Intelligence, heredity, and environment* (pp. 126–160). Cambridge, England: Cambridge University Press.

Boutte, G. S., & McCormick, C. B. (1992). Authentic multicultural activities: Avoiding pseudo-multiculturalism. *Childhood Education, 68,* 140–144.

Bower, G. H. (1994). Some relations between emotions and memory. In P. Ekman & R. J. Davidson (Eds.), *The nature of emotion: Fundamental questions.* New York: Oxford University Press.

Bower, G. H., Black, J. B., & Turner, T. J. (1979). Scripts in memory for text. *Cognitive Psychology, 11,* 177–220.

Bower, G. H., Clark, M. C., Lesgold, A. M., & Winzenz, D. (1969). Hierarchical retrieval schemes in recall of categorized word lists. *Journal of Verbal Learning and Verbal Behavior, 8,* 323–343.

Bower, G. H., & Forgas, J. P. (2001). Mood and social memory. In J. P. Forgas (Ed.), *Handbook of affect and social cognition* (pp. 95–120). Mahwah, NJ: Erlbaum.

Bower, G. H., Karlin, M. B., & Dueck, A. (1975). Comprehension and memory for pictures. *Memory and Cognition, 3,* 216–220.

Bower, J. E., Moskowitz, J. T., & Epel, E. (2009). Is benefit finding good for your health? Pathways linking positive life changes after stress and physical health outcomes. *Current Directions in Psychological Science, 18,* 337–341.

Bowman, L. G., Piazza, C. C., Fisher, W. W., Hagopian, L. P., & Kogan, J. S. (1997). Assessment of preference for varied versus constant reinforcers. *Journal of Applied Behavior Analysis, 30,* 451–458.

Boxerman, J. Z. (2009, April). *Students' understanding of erosion.* Paper presented at the annual meeting of the American Educational Research Association, San Diego, CA.

Boyer, E., Miltenberger, R. G., Batsche, C., & Fogel, V. (2009). Video modeling by experts with video feedback to enhance gymnastics skills. *Journal of Applied Behavior Analysis, 42,* 855–860.

Braaksma, M. A. H., Rijlaarsdam, G., & van den Bergh, H. (2002). Observational learning and the effects of model-observer similarity. *Journal of Educational Psychology, 94,* 405–415.

Bracken, B. A., McCallum, R. S., & Shaughnessy, M. F. (1999). An interview with Bruce A. Bracken and R. Steve McCallum, authors of the Universal Nonverbal Intelligence Test (UNIT). *North American Journal of Psychology, 1,* 277–288.

Bracken, B. A., & Walker, K. C. (1997). The utility of intelligence tests for preschool children. In D. P. Flanagan, J. L. Genshaft, & P. L. Harrison (Eds.), *Contemporary intellectual assessment: Theories, tests, and issues* (pp. 484–502). New York: Guilford Press.

Bradley, R. H. (2010). The HOME environment. In M. H. Bornstein (Ed.), *Handbook of cultural developmental science* (pp. 505–530). New York: Psychology Press.

Bradshaw, C. P., Zmuda, J. H., Kellam, S. G., & Ialongo, N. S. (2009). Longitudinal impact of two universal preventive interventions in first grade on educational outcomes in high school. *Journal of Educational Psychology, 101,* 926–937.

Brainerd, C. J. (2003). Jean Piaget, learning research, and American education. In B. J. Zimmerman & D. H. Schunk (Eds.), *Educational psychology: A century of contributions* (pp. 251–287). Mahwah, NJ: Erlbaum.

Brainerd, C. J., & Reyna, V. F. (2005). *The science of false memory.* Oxford, England: Oxford University Press.

Branch, C. (1999). Race and human development. In R. H. Sheets & E. R. Hollins (Eds.), *Racial and ethnic identity in school practices: Aspects of human development* (pp. 7–28). Mahwah, NJ: Erlbaum.

Bransford, J., Darling-Hammond, L., & LePage, P. (2005). Introduction. In L. Darling-Hammond & J. Bransford (Eds.), *Preparing teachers for a changing world: What teachers should learn and be able to do* (pp. 1–39). San Francisco: Jossey-Bass/Wiley.

Bransford, J., Derry, S., Berliner, D., & Hammerness, K. (with Beckett, K. L.). (2005). Theories of learning and their roles in teaching. In L. Darling-Hammond & J. Bransford (Eds.), *Preparing teachers for a changing world: What teachers should learn and be able to do* (pp. 40–87). San Francisco: Jossey-Bass/Wiley.

Bransford, J. D., & Schwartz, D. L. (1999). Rethinking transfer: A simple proposal with multiple implications. *Review of Research in Education* (Vol. 24, pp. 61–100). Washington, DC: American Educational Research Association.

Bransford, J., Stevens, R., Schwartz, D., Meltzoff, A., Pea, R., Reschelle, J., et al. (2006). Learning theories and education: Toward a decade of synergy. In P. A. Alexander & P. H. Winne (Eds.), *Handbook of educational psychology* (2nd ed., pp. 209–244). Mahwah, NJ: Erlbaum.

Braun, L. J. (1998). *The cat who saw stars.* New York: G. P. Putnam's Sons.

Brayboy, B. M. J., & Searle, K. A. (2007). Thanksgiving and serial killers: Representations of American Indians in schools. In S. Books (Ed.), *Invisible children in the society and its schools* (3rd ed., pp. 173–192). Mahwah, NJ: Erlbaum.

Brendgen, M., Boivin, M., Vitaro, F., Bukowski, W. M., Dionne, G., Tremblay, R. E., et al. (2008). Linkages between children's and their friends' social and physical aggression: Evidence for a gene-environment interaction? *Child Development, 79,* 13–29.

Brendgen, M., Wanner, G., Vitaro, F., Bukowski, W. M., & Tremblay, R. E. (2007). Verbal abuse by the teacher during childhood and academic, behavioral, and emotional adjustment in young adulthood. *Journal of Educational Psychology, 99,* 26–38.

Brenner, M. E., Mayer, R. E., Moseley, B., Brar, T., Durán, R., Reed, B. S., et al. (1997). Learning by understanding: The role of multiple representations in learning algebra. *American Educational Research Journal, 34,* 663–689.

Bressler, S. L. (2002). Understanding cognition through large-scale cortical networks. *Current Directions in Psychological Science, 11,* 58–61.

Brewer, M. B., & Yuki, M. (2007). Culture and social identity. In S. Kitayama & D. Cohen (Eds.), *Handbook of cultural psychology* (pp. 307–322). New York: Guilford Press.

Brewer, W. F. (2008). Naive theories of observational astronomy: Review, analysis, and theoretical implications. In S. Vosniadou (Ed.), *International handbook on conceptual change* (pp. 155–204). New York: Routledge.

Brigham, F. J., & Scruggs, T. E. (1995). Elaborative maps for enhanced learning of historical information: Uniting spatial, verbal, and imaginal information. *Journal of Special Education, 28,* 440.

Broden, M., Hall, R. V., & Mitts, B. (1971). The effect of self-recording on the classroom behavior of two eighth-grade students. *Journal of Applied Behavior Analysis, 4,* 191–199.

Brody, G. H., Chen, Y.-F., Murry, V. M., Ge, X., Simons, R. L., Gibbons, F. X., et al. (2006). Perceived discrimination and the adjustment of African American youths: A five-year longitudinal analysis with contextual moderation effects. *Child Development, 77,* 1170–1189.

Brody, G. H., & Shaffer, D. R. (1982). Contributions of parents and peers to children's moral socialization. *Developmental Review, 2,* 31–75.

Brody, N. (1992). *Intelligence* (2nd ed.). San Diego, CA: Academic Press.

Brody, N. (1997). Intelligence, schooling, and society. *American Psychologist, 52,* 1046–1050.

Brody, N. (2008). Does education influence intelligence? In P. C. Kyllonen, R. D. Roberts, & L. Stankov (Eds.), *Extending intelligence: Enhancement and new constructs* (pp. 85–92). New York: Erlbaum/Taylor & Francis.

Broekkamp, H., van Hout-Wolters, B. H. A. M., Rijlaarsdam, G., & van den Bergh, H. (2002). Importance in instructional text: Teachers' and students' perceptions of task demands. *Journal of Educational Psychology, 94,* 260–271.

Bronfenbrenner, U. (1989). Ecological systems theory. In R. Vasta (Ed.), *Annals of child development* (Vol. 6, pp. 187–251). Greenwich, CT: JAI Press.

Bronfenbrenner, U. (2005). *Making human beings human: Bioecological perspectives on human development.* Thousand Oaks, CA: Sage.

Bronfenbrenner, U., & Morris, P. A. (1998). The ecology of developmental processes. In W. Damon (Series Ed.) & R. M. Lerner (Vol. Ed.), *Handbook of child psychology: Vol. 1. Theoretical models of human development* (5th ed., pp. 993–1028). New York: Wiley.

Bronson, M. B. (2000). *Self-regulation in early childhood: Nature and nurture.* New York: Guilford Press.

Brooke, R. R., & Ruthren, A. J. (1984). The effects of contingency contracting on student performance in a PSI class. *Teaching of Psychology, 11,* 87–89.

Brookhart, S. M. (2004). *Grading.* Upper Saddle River, NJ: Merrill/Prentice Hall.

Brooks, L. W., & Dansereau, D. F. (1987). Transfer of information: An instructional perspective. In S. M. Cormier & J. D. Hagman (Eds.), *Transfer of learning: Contemporary research and applications.* San Diego, CA: Academic Press.

Brooks-Gunn, J. (2003). Do you believe in magic?: What we can expect from early childhood intervention programs. *Social Policy Report of the Society for Research in Child Development, 17*(1), 3–14.

Brooks-Gunn, J., Klebanov, P. K., & Duncan, G. J. (1996). Ethnic differences in children's intelligence test scores: Role of economic deprivation, home environment, and maternal characteristics. *Child Development, 67,* 396–408.

Brooks-Gunn, J., Linver, M. R., & Fauth, R. C. (2005). Children's competence and socioeconomic status in the family and neighborhood. In A. J. Elliot & C. S. Dweck (Eds.), *Handbook of competence and motivation* (pp. 414–435). New York: Guilford Press.

Brooks-Gunn, J., & Paikoff, R. L. (1993). "Sex is a gamble, kissing is a game": Adolescent sexuality and health promotion. In S. G. Millstein, A. C. Petersen, & E. O. Nightingale (Eds.), *Promoting the health of adolescents: New directions for the twenty-first century* (pp. 180–208). New York: Oxford University Press.

Brophy, J. E. (1986). *On motivating students* (Occasional Paper No. 101). East Lansing: Michigan State University, Institute for Research on Teaching.

Brophy, J. E. (1987). Synthesis of research on strategies for motivating students to learn. *Educational Leadership, 45*(2), 40–48.

Brophy, J. E. (1992). Probing the subtleties of subject-matter teaching. *Educational Leadership, 49*(7), 4–8.

Brophy, J. E. (2002). Social promotion. In J. Guthrie (Ed.), *Encyclopedia of education* (2nd ed., Vol. 6, pp. 2262–2265). New York: Macmillan.

Brophy, J. E. (2004). *Motivating students to learn* (2nd ed.). Mahwah, NJ: Erlbaum.

Brophy, J. E. (2006). Observational research on generic aspects of classroom teaching. In P. A. Alexander & P. H. Winne (Eds.), *Handbook of educational psychology* (2nd ed., pp. 755–780). Mahwah, NJ: Erlbaum.

Brophy, J. E. (2008). Developing students' appreciation for what is taught in school. *Educational Psychologist, 43,* 132–141.

Brophy, J. E., & Alleman, J. (1992). Planning and managing learning activities: Basic principles. In J. Brophy (Ed.), *Advances in research on teaching: Vol. 3. Planning and managing learning tasks and activities.* Greenwich, CT: JAI Press.

Brophy, J. E., Alleman, J., & Knighton, B. (2009). *Inside the social studies classroom.* New York: Routledge.

Brophy, J. E., & VanSledright, B. (1997). *Teaching and learning history in elementary schools.* New York: Teachers College Press.

Brouwer, N., & Korthagen, F. (2005). Can teacher education make a difference? *American Educational Research Journal, 42,* 153–224.

Brown, A. L., & Campione, J. C. (1994). Guided discovery in a community of learners. In K. McGilly (Ed.), *Classroom lessons: Integrating cognitive theory and classroom practice.* Cambridge, MA: MIT Press.

Brown, A. L., & Campione, J. C. (1996). Psychological theory and the design of innovative learning environments: On procedures, principles, and systems. In L. Schauble & R. Glaser (Eds.), *Innovations in learning: New environments for education.* Mahwah, NJ: Erlbaum.

Brown, A. L., Campione, J., & Day, J. (1981). Learning to learn: On training students to learn from texts. *Educational Researcher, 10*(2), 14–21.

Brown, A. L., & Palincsar, A. S. (1987). Reciprocal teaching of comprehension strategies: A natural history of one program for enhancing learning. In J. Borkowski & J. D. Day (Eds.), *Cognition in special education: Comparative approaches to retardation, learning disabilities, and giftedness.* Norwood, NJ: Ablex.

Brown, A. L., Smiley, S. S., Day, J. D., Townsend, M. A. R., & Lawton, S. C. (1977). Intrusion of a thematic idea in children's comprehension and retention of stories. *Child Development, 48,* 1454–1466.

Brown, A. S., Schilling, H. E. H., & Hockensmith, M. L. (1999). The negative suggestion effect: Pondering incorrect alternatives may be hazardous to your knowledge. *Journal of Educational Psychology, 91,* 756–764.

Brown, B. B. (1990). Peer groups. In S. Feldman & G. Elliott (Eds.), *At the threshold: The developing adolescent* (pp. 171–196). Cambridge, MA: Harvard University Press.

Brown, B. B. (1993). School culture, social politics, and the academic motivation of U.S. students. In T. M. Tomlinson (Ed.), *Motivating students to learn: Overcoming barriers to high achievement.* Berkeley, CA: McCutchan.

Brown, B. B. (1999). "You're going out with *who*?" Peer group influences on adolescent romantic relationships. In W. Furman, B. B. Brown, & C. Feiring (Eds.), *The development of romantic relationships in adolescence* (pp. 291–329). Cambridge, England: Cambridge University Press.

Brown, B. B., Eicher, S. A., & Petrie, S. (1986). The importance of peer group ("crowd") affiliation in adolescence. *Journal of Adolescence, 9,* 73–96.

Brown, B. B., Feiring, C., & Furman, W. (1999). Missing the love boat: Why researchers have shied away from adolescent romance. In W. Furman, B. B. Brown, & C. Feiring (Eds.), *The development of romantic relationships in adolescence* (pp. 1–16). Cambridge, England: Cambridge University Press.

Brown, B. B., Herman, M., Hamm, J. V., & Heck, D. J. (2008). Ethnicity and image: Correlates of crowd affiliation among ethnic minority youth. *Child Development, 79,* 529–546.

Brown, J. S., Collins, A., & Duguid, P. (1989). Situated cognition and the culture of learning. *Educational Researcher, 18*(1), 32–42.

Brown, M. C., McNeil, N. M., & Glenberg, A. M. (2009). Using concreteness in education: Real problems, potential solutions. *Child Development Perspectives, 3,* 160–164.

Brown, R. D., & Bjorklund, D. F. (1998). The biologizing of cognition, development, and education: Approach with cautious enthusiasm. *Educational Psychology Review, 10,* 355–373.

Brown, R. P., Osterman, L. L., & Barnes, C. D. (2009). School violence and the culture of honor. *Psychological Science, 20,* 1400–1405.

Brown, W. H., Fox, J. J., & Brady, M. P. (1987). Effects of spatial density on 3- and 4-year-old children's socially directed behavior during freeplay: An investigation of a setting factor. *Education and Treatment of Children, 10,* 247–258.

Bruer, J. T. (1997). Education and the brain: A bridge too far. *Educational Researcher, 26*(8), 4–16.

Bruer, J. T. (1999). *The myth of the first three years: A new understanding of early brain development and lifelong learning.* New York: Free Press.

Bruer, J. T., & Greenough, W. T. (2001). The subtle science of how experience affects the brain. In D. B. Bailey, Jr., J. T. Bruer, F. J. Symons, & J. W. Lichtman (Eds.), *Critical thinking about critical periods* (pp. 209–232). Baltimore: Brookes.

Bruner, J. S. (1966). *Toward a theory of instruction.* Cambridge, MA: Harvard University Press.

Bryan, J. H. (1975). Children's cooperation and helping behaviors. In E. M. Hetherington (Ed.), *Review of child development research* (Vol. 5). Chicago: University of Chicago Press.

Buehl, M. M., & Alexander, P. A. (2006). Examining the dual nature of epistemological beliefs. *International Journal of Educational Research, 45,* 28–42.

Buhs, E. S., Ladd, G. W., & Herald, S. L. (2006). Peer exclusion and victimization: Processes that mediate the relation between peer group rejection and children's classroom engagement and achievement. *Journal of Educational Psychology, 98,* 1–13.

Bukowski, W. M., Brendgan, M., & Vitaro, F. (2007). Peers and socialization: Effects on externalizing and internalizing problems. In J. E. Grusec & P. D. Hastings (Eds.), *Handbook of socialization: Theory and research* (pp. 355–381). New York: Guilford Press.

Bukowski, W. M., Motzoi, C., & Meyer, F. (2009). Friendship as process, function, and outcome. In K. H. Rubin, W. M. Bukowski, & B. Laursen (Eds.), *Handbook of peer interactions, relationships, and groups* (pp. 217–231). New York: Guilford.

Bulgren, J. A., Deshler, D. D., Schumaker, J. B., & Lenz, B. K. (2000). The use and effectiveness of analogical instruction in diverse secondary content classrooms. *Journal of Educational Psychology, 92,* 426–441.

Bulgren, J. A., Schumaker, J. B., & Deshler, D. D. (1994). The effects of a recall enhancement routine on the test performance of secondary students with and without learning disabilities. *Learning Disabilities Research and Practice, 9,* 2–11.

Bureau of Justice Statistics. (2005). *Sourcebook of criminal justice statistics.* Washington, DC: Author.

Burger, H. G. (1973). Cultural pluralism and the schools. In C. S. Brembeck & W. H. Hill (Eds.), *Cultural challenges to education: The influence of cultural factors in school learning.* Lexington, MA: Heath.

Burhans, K. K., & Dweck, C. S. (1995). Helplessness in early childhood: The role of contingent worth. *Child Development, 66,* 1719–1738.

Burstyn, J. N., & Stevens, R. (2001). Involving the whole school in violence prevention. In J. N. Burstyn, G. Bender, R. Casella, H. W. Gordon, D. P. Guerra, K. V. Luschen, et al., *Preventing violence in schools: A challenge to American democracy* (pp. 139–158). Mahwah, NJ: Erlbaum.

Butler, D. L., & Winne, P. H. (1995). Feedback and self-regulated learning: A theoretical synthesis. *Review of Educational Research, 65,* 245–281.

Butler, R. (1989). Mastery versus ability appraisal: A developmental study of children's observations of peers' work. *Child Development, 60,* 1350–1361.

Butler, R. (1994). Teacher communication and student interpretations: Effects of teacher responses to failing students on attributional inferences in two age groups. *British Journal of Educational Psychology, 64,* 277–294.

Butler, R. (1998a). Age trends in the use of social and temporal comparison for self-evaluation: Examination of a novel developmental hypothesis. *Child Development, 69,* 1054–1073.

Butler, R. (1998b). Determinants of help seeking: Relations between perceived reasons for classroom help-avoidance and help-seeking behaviors in an experimental context. *Journal of Educational Psychology, 90,* 630–644.

Butler, R. (2008). Evaluating competence and maintaining self-worth between early and middle childhood: Blissful ignorance or the construction of knowledge and strategies in context? In H. W. Marsh, R. G. Craven, & D. M. McInerney (Eds.), *Self-processes, learning, and enabling human potential* (pp. 193–222). Charlotte, NC: Information Age.

Butterfield, E. C., & Ferretti, R. P. (1987). Toward a theoretical integration of cognitive hypotheses about intellectual differences among children. In J. G. Borkowski & J. D. Day (Eds.), *Cognition in special children: Approaches to retardation, learning disabilities, and giftedness.* Norwood, NJ: Ablex.

Byrne, B. M. (2002). Validating the measurement and structure of self-concept: Snapshots of past, present, and future research. *American Psychologist, 57,* 897–909.

Byrnes, J. P. (1988). Formal operations: A systematic reformulation. *Developmental Review, 8,* 66–87.

Byrnes, J. P. (2001). *Minds, brains, and learning: Understanding the psychological and educational relevance of neuroscientific research.* New York: Guilford Press.

Byrnes, J. P. (2003). Factors predictive of mathematics achievement in White, Black, and Hispanic 12th graders. *Journal of Educational Psychology, 95,* 316–326.

Byrnes, J. P. (2007). Some ways in which neuroscientific research can be relevant to education. In D. Coch, K. W. Fischer, & G. Dawson (Eds.), *Human behavior, learning, and the developing brain: Typical development* (pp. 30–49). New York: Guilford Press.

Byrnes, J. P., & Fox, N. A. (1998). The educational relevance of research in cognitive neuroscience. *Educational Psychology Review, 10,* 297–342.

Cacioppo, J. T., Petty, R. E., Feinstein, J. A., & Jarvis, W. B. G. (1996). Dispositional differences in cognitive motivation: The life and times of individuals varying in need for cognition. *Psychological Bulletin, 119,* 197–253.

Calderhead, J. (1996). Teachers: Beliefs and knowledge. In D. C. Berliner & R. C. Calfee (Eds.), *Handbook of educational psychology.* New York: Macmillan.

Caldwell, C. H., Zimmerman, M. A., Bernat, D. H., Sellers, R. M., & Notaro, P. C. (2002). Racial identity, maternal support, and psychological distress among African American adolescents. *Child Development, 73,* 1322–1336.

Caldwell, M. S., Rudolph, K. D., Troop-Gordon, W., & Kim, D. (2004). Reciprocal influences among relational self-views, social disengagement, and peer stress during early adolescence. *Child Development, 75,* 1140–1154.

Cameron, J. (2001). Negative effects of reward on intrinsic motivation—A limited phenomenon: Comment on Deci, Koestner, and Ryan (2001). *Review of Educational Research, 71,* 29–42.

Cameron, L., Rutland, A., Brown, R., & Douch, R. (2006). Changing children's intergroup attitudes toward refugees: Testing different models of extended contact. *Child Development, 77,* 1208–1219.

Campbell, A. (1984). *The girls in the gang: A report from New York City.* New York: Blackwell.

Campbell, C. G., Parker, J. G., & Kollat, S. H. (2007, March). *The influence of contingent self-esteem and appearance.* Paper presented at the biennial meeting of the Society for Research in Child Development, Boston.

Campione, J. C., Shapiro, A. M., & Brown, A. L. (1995). Forms of transfer in a community of learners: Flexible learning and understanding. In A. McKeough, J. Lupart, & A. Marini (Eds.), *Teaching for transfer: Fostering generalization in learning.* Mahwah, NJ: Erlbaum.

Camras, L. A., Chen, Y., Bakeman, R., Norris, K., & Cain, T. R. (2006). Culture, ethnicity, and children's facial expressions: A study of European American, Mainland Chinese, Chinese American, and adopted Chinese girls. *Emotion, 6,* 103–114.

Candler-Lotven, A., Tallent-Runnels, M. K., Olivárez, A., & Hildreth, B. (1994, April). *A comparison of learning and study strategies of gifted, average-ability, and learning-disabled ninth-grade students.* Paper presented at the annual meeting of the American Educational Research Association, New Orleans, LA.

Capara, G. V., Barbaranelli, C., Pastorelli, C., Bandura, A., & Zimbardo, P. G. (2000). Prosocial foundations of children's academic achievement. *Psychological Science, 11,* 302–306.

Caprara, G. V., Dodge, K. A., Pastorelli, C., & Zelli, A. (2007). How marginal deviations sometimes grow into serious aggression. *Child Development Perspectives, 1,* 33–39.

Carbrera, N. J., Shannon, J. D., West, J., & Brooks-Gunn, J. (2006). Parental interactions with Latino infants: Variation by country of origin and English proficiency. *Child Development, 77,* 1190–1207.

Card, N. A., & Ramos, J. F. (2005, April). *Friends' similarity on academic characteristics: A meta-analytic review.* Paper presented at the annual meeting of the American Educational Research Association, Montreal.

Card, N. A., Stucky, B. D., Sawalani, G. M., & Little T. D. (2008). Direct and indirect aggression during childhood and adolescence: A meta-analytic review of gender differences, intercorrelations, and relations to maladjustment. *Child Development, 79,* 1185–1229.

Carey, S. (1985). *Conceptual change in childhood.* Cambridge, MA: MIT Press.

Carey, S. (1986). Cognitive science and science education. *American Psychologist, 41,* 1123–1130.

Carhill, A., Suárez-Orozco, C., & Páez, M. (2008). Explaining English language proficiency among adolescent immigrant students. *American Educational Research Journal, 45,* 1045–1079.

Carlson, R., Chandler, P., & Sweller, J. (2003). Learning and understanding science instructional material. *Journal of Educational Psychology, 95,* 629–640.

Carnagey, N. L., Anderson, C. A., & Bartholow, B. D. (2007). Media violence and social neuroscience: New questions and new opportunities. *Current Directions in Psychological Science, 16,* 178–182.

Carney, R. N., & Levin, J. R. (2002). Pictorial illustrations *still* improve students' learning from text. *Educational Psychology Review, 14,* 5–26.

Carr, A. A. (1997, March). *The participation "race": Kentucky's site based decision teams.* Paper presented at the annual meeting of the American Educational Research Association, Chicago.

Carr, M. (2010). The importance of metacognition for conceptual change and strategy use in mathematics. In H. S. Waters & W. Schneider (Eds.), *Metacognition, strategy use, and instruction* (pp. 176–197). New York: Guilford.

Carr, M., & Biddlecomb, B. (1998). Metacognition in mathematics from a constructivist perspective. In D. J. Hacker, J. Dunlosky, & A. C. Graesser (Eds.), *Metacognition in educational theory and practice* (pp. 69–91). Mahwah, NJ: Erlbaum.

Carrasco, R. L. (1981). Expanded awareness of student performance: A case study in applied ethnographic monitoring in a bilingual classroom. In H. T. Trueba, G. P. Guthrie, & K. H. Au (Eds.), *Culture and the bilingual classroom: Studies in classroom ethnography.* Rowley, MA: Newbury House.

Carroll, J. B. (1993) *Human cognitive abilities: A survey of factor-analytic studies.* New York: Cambridge University Press.

Carroll, J. B. (2003). The higher stratum structure of cognitive abilities: Current evidence supports *g* and about ten broad factors. In H. Nyborg (Ed.), *The scientific study of general intelligence.* New York: Pergamon.

Carter, K., & Doyle, W. (2006). Classroom management in early childhood and elementary classrooms. In C. M. Evertson & C. S. Weinstein (Eds.), *Handbook of classroom management: Research, practice, and contemporary issues* (pp. 373–406). Mahwah, NJ: Erlbaum.

Carter, K. R. (1991). Evaluation of gifted programs. In N. Buchanan & J. Feldhusen (Eds.), *Conducting research and evaluation in gifted education: A handbook of methods and applications.* New York: Teachers College Press.

Carter, K. R., & Ormrod, J. E. (1982). Acquisition of formal operations by intellectually gifted children. *Gifted Child Quarterly, 26,* 110–115.

Carter, R., Williams, S., & Silverman, W. K. (2008). Cognitive and emotional facets of test anxiety in African American school children. *Cognition and Emotion, 22,* 539–551.

Carver, C. S., & Scheier, M. F. (1990). Origins and functions of positive and negative affect: A control-process view. *Psychological Review, 97,* 19–35.

Carver, S. M. (2006). Assessing for deep understanding. In R. K. Sawyer (Ed.), *The Cambridge handbook of the learning sciences* (pp. 205–221). Cambridge, England: Cambridge University Press.

Casanova, U. (1987). Ethnic and cultural differences. In V. Richardson-Koehler (Ed.), *Educator's handbook: A research perspective.* White Plains, NY: Longman.

Case, R., & Okamoto, Y., in collaboration with Griffin, S., McKeough, A., Bleiker, C., Henderson, B., & Stephenson, K. M. (1996). The role of central conceptual structures in the development of children's thought. *Monographs of the Society for Research in Child Development, 61*(1, Serial No. 246).

Casella, R. (2001a). The cultural foundations of peer mediation: Beyond a behaviorist model of urban school conflict. In J. N. Burstyn, G. Bender, R. Casella, H. W. Gordon, D. P. Guerra, K. V. Luschen, et al., *Preventing violence in schools: A challenge to American democracy* (pp. 159–179). Mahwah, NJ: Erlbaum.

Casella, R. (2001b). What is violent about "school violence"? The nature of violence in a city high school. In J. N. Burstyn, G. Bender, R. Casella, H. W. Gordon, D. P. Guerra, K. V. Luschen, et al., *Preventing violence in schools: A challenge to American democracy* (pp. 15–46). Mahwah, NJ: Erlbaum.

Caspi, A. (1998). Personality development across the life course. In W. Damon (Series Ed.) & N. Eisenberg (Vol. Ed.), *Handbook of child psychology: Vol. 3. Social, emotional, and personality development* (5th ed., pp. 311–388). New York: Wiley.

Cassady, J. C. (2004). The influence of cognitive test anxiety across the learning-testing cycle. *Learning and Instruction, 14,* 569–592.

Cassady, J. C., & Johnson, R. E. (2002). Cognitive test anxiety and academic performance. *Contemporary Educational Psychology, 27,* 270–295.

Castagno, A. E., & Brayboy, B. M. J. (2008). Culturally responsive schooling for Indigenous youth: A review of the literature. *Review of Educational Research, 78,* 941–993.

Cattell, R. B. (1963). Theory of fluid and crystallized intelligence: A critical experiment. *Journal of Educational Psychology, 54,* 1–22.

Cattell, R. B. (1987). *Intelligence: Its structure, growth, and action.* Amsterdam: North-Holland.

Cauce, A. M., Mason, C., Gonzales, N., Hiraga, Y., & Liu, G. (1994). Social support during adolescence: Methodological and theoretical considerations. In F. Nestemann & K. Hurrelmann (Eds.), *Social networks and social support in childhood and adolescence.* Berlin, Germany: Aldine de Gruyter.

Cazden, C. B. (2001). *Classroom discourse: The language of teaching and learning* (2nd ed.). Portsmouth, NH: Heinemann.

Ceci, S. J. (2003). Cast in six ponds and you'll reel in something: Looking back on 25 years of research. *American Psychologist, 58,* 855–864.

Celio, C. I., Durlak, J. A., Pachan, M. K., & Berger, S. R. (2007, March). *Helping others and helping oneself: A meta-analysis of service-learning programs.* Paper presented at the biennial meeting of the Society for Research in Child Development, Boston.

Cepeda, N. J., Vul, E., Rohrer, D., Wixted, J. T., & Pashler, H. (2008). Spacing effects in learning: A temporal ridgeline of optimal retention. *Psychological Science, 19,* 1095–1102.

Certo, J. (in press). Social skills and leadership abilities among children in small group literature discussions. *Journal of Research in Childhood Education.*

Certo, J. L., Cauley, K. M., & Chafin, C. (2002, April). *Students' perspectives on their high school experience.* Paper presented at the annual meeting of the American Educational Research Association, New Orleans, LA.

Chabrán, M. (2003). Listening to talk from and about students on accountability. In M. Carnoy, R. Elmore, & L. S. Siskin (Eds.), *The new accountability: High schools and high-stakes testing* (pp. 129–145). New York: RoutledgeFalmer.

Chalmers, D. J. (1996). *The conscious mind: In search of a fundamental theory.* New York: Oxford University Press.

Chambliss, M. J. (1994). Why do readers fail to change their beliefs after reading persuasive text? In R. Garner & P. A. Alexander (Eds.), *Beliefs about text and instruction with text.* Mahwah, NJ: Erlbaum.

Champagne, F. A., & Mashoodh, R. (2009). Genes in context: Gene–environment interplay and the origins of individual differences in behavior. *Current Directions in Psychological Science, 18,* 127–131.

Chan, C., Burtis, J., & Bereiter, C. (1997). Knowledge building as a mediator of conflict in conceptual change. *Cognition and Instruction, 15,* 1–40.

Chan, J. M., & O'Reilly, M. F. (2008). A Social Stories™ intervention package for students with autism in inclusive classroom settings. *Journal of Applied Behavior Analysis, 41,* 405–409.

Chandler, M. (1987). The Othello effect: Essay on the emergence and eclipse of skeptical doubt. *Human Development, 30,* 137–159.

Chandler, M., & Boyes, M. (1982). Social-cognitive development. In B. Wolman (Ed.), *Handbook of developmental psychology.* Upper Saddle River, NJ: Prentice Hall.

Chandler, M., Hallett, D., & Sokol, B. W. (2002). Competing claims about competing knowledge claims. In B. K. Hofer & P. R. Pintrich (Eds.), *Personal epistemology: The psychology of beliefs about knowledge and knowing* (pp. 145–168). Mahwah, NJ: Erlbaum.

Chang, L. (2003). Variable effects of children's aggression, social withdrawal, and prosocial leadership as functions of teacher beliefs and behaviors. *Child Development, 74,* 535–548.

Chang, L., Liu, H., Wen, Z., Fung, K. Y., Wang, Y, & Xu, Y. (2004). Mediating teacher liking and moderating authoritative teaching on Chinese adolescents' perceptions of antisocial and prosocial behaviors. *Journal of Educational Psychology, 96,* 369–380.

Chapman, D. A., Scott, K. G., & Mason, C. A. (2002). Early risk factors for mental retardation: Role of maternal age and maternal education. *American Journal on Mental Retardation, 107,* 46–59.

Chapman, J. W., Tunmer, W. E., & Prochnow, J. E. (2000). Early reading-related skills and performance, reading self-concept, and the development of academic self-concept: A longitudinal study. *Journal of Educational Psychology, 92,* 703–708.

Charity, A. H., Scarborough, H. S., & Griffin, D. M. (2004). Familiarity with school English in African American children and its relation to early reading achievement. *Child Development, 75,* 1340–1356.

Chavous, T. M., Bernat, D. H., Schmeelk-Cone, K., Caldwell, C. H., Kohn-Wood, L., & Zimmerman, M. A. (2003). Racial identity and academic attainment among African American adolescents. *Child Development, 74,* 1076–1090.

Chen, E., Langer, D. A., Raphaelson, Y. E., & Matthews, K. A. (2004). Socioeconomic status and health in adolescents: The role of stress interpretations. *Child Development, 75,* 1039–1052.

Chen, J., & Morris, D. (2008, March). *Sources of science self-efficacy beliefs among high school students in different tracking levels.* Paper presented at the annual meeting of the American Educational Research Association, New York.

Chen, W.-B., & Gregory, A. (2008, March). *Parental involvement in schooling: What types work for low-achieving adolescents and what does this mean for schools?* Paper presented at the annual meeting of the American Educational Research Association, New York.

Chen, X., Chang, L., Liu, H., & He, Y. (2008). Effects of the peer group on the development of social functioning and academic achievement: A longitudinal study in Chinese children. *Child Development, 79,* 235–251.

Chen, X., Chung, J., & Hsiao, C. (2009). Peer interactions and relationships from a cross-cultural perspective. In K. H. Rubin, W. M. Bukowski, & B. Laursen (Eds.), *Handbook of peer interactions, relationships, and groups* (pp. 432–451). New York: Guilford.

Chen, X., & Wang, L. (2010). China. In M. H. Bornstein (Ed.), *Handbook of cultural developmental science* (pp. 429–444). New York: Psychology Press.

Cheng, L. R. (1987). *Assessing Asian language performance.* Rockville, MD: Aspen.

Cheng, P. W. (1985). Restructuring versus automaticity: Alternative accounts of skill acquisition. *Psychological Review, 92,* 414–423.

Chester, M. D., & Beaudin, B. Q. (1996). Efficacy beliefs of newly hired teachers in urban schools. *American Educational Research Journal, 33,* 233–257.

Chi, M. T. H. (1978). Knowledge structures and memory development. In R. S. Siegler (Ed.), *Children's thinking: What develops?* Mahwah, NJ: Erlbaum.

Chi, M. T. H., Feltovich, P., & Glaser, R. (1981). Categorization and representation of physics problems by experts and novices. *Cognitive Science, 5,* 121–152.

Chi, M. T. H., Glaser, R., & Rees, E. (1982). Expertise in problem solving. In R. J. Sternberg (Ed.), *Advances in the psychology of human intelligence.* Hillsdale, NJ: Erlbaum.

Chinn, C. A. (2006). Learning to argue. In A. M. O'Donnell, C. E. Hmelo-Silver, & G. Erkens (Eds.), *Collaborative learning, reasoning, and technology* (pp. 355–383). Mahwah, NJ: Erlbaum.

Chinn, C. A., & Brewer, W. F. (1993). The role of anomalous data in knowledge acquisition: A theoretical framework and implications for science instruction. *Review of Educational Research, 63,* 1–49.

Chinn, C. A., & Samarapungavan, A. (2009). Conceptual change—Multiple routes, multiple mechanisms: A commentary on Ohlsson (2009). *Educational Psychologist, 44,* 48–57.

Chisholm, J. S. (1996). Learning "respect for everything": Navajo images of development. In C. P. Hwant, M. E. Lamb, & I. E. Sigel (Eds.), *Images of childhood* (pp. 167–183). Mahwah, NJ: Erlbaum.

Chiu, C.-Y., & Hong, Y.-Y. (2005). Cultural competence: Dynamic processes. In A. J. Elliot & C. S. Dweck (Eds.), *Handbook of competence and motivation* (pp. 489–505). New York: Guilford Press.

Chiu, M. M. (2008). Effects of argumentation on group micro-creativity: Statistical discourse analyses of algebra students' collaborative problem solving. *Contemporary Educational Psychology, 33,* 382–402.

Christenson, S. L., & Sheridan, S. M. (2001). *Schools and families: Creating essential connections for learning.* New York: Guilford Press.

Christenson, S. L., & Thurlow, M. L. (2004). School dropouts: Prevention, considerations, interventions, and challenges. *Current Directions in Psychological Science, 13*, 36–39.

Church, M. A., Elliot, A. J., & Gable, S. L. (2001). Perceptions of classroom environment, achievement goals, and achievement outcomes. *Journal of Educational Psychology, 93*, 43–54.

Cillessen, A. H. N., & Mayeux, L. (2007). Variations in the association between aggression and social status: Theoretical and empirical perspectives. In P. H. Hawley, T. D. Little, & P. C. Rodkin (Eds.), *Aggression and adaptation: The bright side to bad behavior* (pp. 135–156). Mahwah, NJ: Erlbaum.

Cillessen, A. H. N., & Rose, A. J. (2005). Understanding popularity in the peer system. *Current Directions in Psychological Science, 14*, 102–105.

Cizek, G. J. (2003). *Detecting and preventing classroom cheating: Promoting integrity in assessment.* Thousand Oaks, CA: Corwin.

Clark, A.-M., Anderson, R. C., Kuo, L., Kim, I., Archodidou, A., & Nguyen-Jahiel, K. (2003). Collaborative reasoning: Expanding ways for children to talk and think in school. *Educational Psychology Review, 15*, 181–198.

Clark, B. (1997). *Growing up gifted* (5th ed.). Upper Saddle River, NJ: Merrill/Prentice Hall.

Clark, C. C. (1992). Deviant adolescent subcultures: Assessment strategies and clinical interventions. *Adolescence, 27*(106), 283–293.

Clark, D. B. (2006). Longitudinal conceptual change in students' understanding of thermal equilibrium: An examination of the process of conceptual restructuring. *Cognition and Instruction, 24*, 467–563.

Clark, J. M., & Paivio, A. (1991). Dual coding theory and education. *Educational Psychology Review, 3*, 149–210.

Clark, R. E. (1983). Reconsidering research on learning from media. *Review of Educational Research, 53*, 445–459.

Clark, R. E., Feldon, D. F., van Merriënboer, J. J. G., Yates, K. A., & Early, S. (2008). Cognitive task analysis. In J. M. Spector, M. D. Merrill, J. van Merriënboer, & M. P. Driscoll (Eds.), *Handbook of research on educational communications and technology* (3rd ed., pp. 577–593). New York: Routledge.

Clarke, S. Dunlap, G., Foster-Johnson, L., Childs, K. E., Wilson, D., White, R., & Vera, A. (1995). Improving the conduct of students with behavioral disorders by incorporating student interests into curriculuar areas. *Behavioral Disorders, 20*, 221–237.

Clement, J. (2008). The role of explanatory models in teaching for conceptual change. In S. Vosniadou (Ed.), *International handbook on conceptual change* (pp. 417–452). New York: Routledge.

Cleveland, M. J., Gibbons, F. X., Gerrard, M., Pomery, E. A., & Brody, G. H. (2005). The impact of parenting on risk cognitions and risk behavior: A study of mediation and moderation in a panel of African American adolescents. *Child Development, 76*, 900–916.

Clifford, M. M. (1990). Students need challenge, not easy success. *Educational Leadership, 48*(1), 22–26.

Clotfelter, C. T., Ladd, H. F., & Vigdor, J. (2007). Who teaches whom? Race and the distribution of novice teachers. *Economics of Education Review, 24*, 377–392.

Cobb, P., Wood, T., Yackel, E., Nicholls, J., Wheatley, G., Trigatti, B., et al. (1991). Assessment of a problem centered second-grade mathematics project. *Journal for Research in Mathematics Education, 22*, 3–29.

Coch, D., Dawson, G., & Fischer, K. W. (Eds.). (2007). *Human behavior, learning, and the developing brain: Atypical development.* New York: Guilford Press.

Cochran, K. F., & Jones, L. L. (1998). The subject matter knowledge of preservice science teachers. In B. J. Fraser & K. G. Tobin (Eds.), *International handbook of science education* (Pt. II). Dordrecht, Netherlands: Kluwer.

Cochran-Smith, M., & Lytle, S. (1993). *Inside out: Teacher research and knowledge.* New York: Teachers College Press.

Cognition and Technology Group at Vanderbilt. (1993). Anchored instruction and situated cognition revisited. *Educational Technology, 33*(3), 52–70.

Cognition and Technology Group at Vanderbilt. (1996). Looking at technology in context: A framework for understanding technology and education research. In D. C. Berliner & R. C. Calfee (Eds.), *Handbook of educational psychology* (pp. 807–840). New York: Macmillan.

Cohen, A. B. (2009). Many forms of culture. *American Psychologist, 64*, 194–204.

Cohen, E. G. (1994). Restructuring the classroom: Conditions for productive small groups. *Review of Educational Research, 64*, 1–35.

Cohen, E. G., Lockheed, M. E., & Lohman, M. R. (1976). The center for interracial cooperation: A field experiment. *Sociology of Education, 59*, 47–58.

Cohen, G. L., & Garcia, J. (2008). Identity, belonging, and achievement: A model, interventions, implications. *Current Directions in Psychological Science, 17*, 365–369.

Cohen, R. L. (1989). Memory for action events: The power of enactment. *Educational Psychology Review, 1*, 57–80.

Coie, J. D., & Cillessen, A. H. N. (1993). Peer rejection: Origins and effects on children's development. *Current Directions in Psychological Science, 2*, 89–92.

Coie, J. D., & Dodge, K. A. (1998). Aggression and antisocial behavior. In W. Damon (Series Ed.) & N. Eisenberg (Vol. Ed.), *Handbook of child psychology: Vol. 3. Social, emotional, and personality development* (5th ed., pp. 779–862). New York: Wiley.

Colby, A., & Kohlberg, L. (1984). Invariant sequence and internal consistency in moral judgment stages. In W. M. Kurtines & J. L. Gewirtz (Eds.), *Morality, moral behavior, and moral development.* New York: Wiley.

Colby, A., Kohlberg, L., Gibbs, J., & Lieberman, M. (1983). A longitudinal study of moral judgment. *Monographs of the Society for Research in Child Development, 48*(1–2, Serial No. 200).

Cole, A. S., & Ibarra, R. A. (2005). Examining gender-related differential item functioning using insights from psychometric and multicontext theory. In A. M. Gallagher & J. C. Kaufman (Eds.), *Gender differences in mathematics: An integrative psychological approach* (pp. 143–171). Cambridge, England: Cambridge University Press.

Cole, D. A., Martin, J. M., Peeke, L. A., Seroczynski, A. D., & Fier, J. (1999). Children's over- and underestimation of academic competence: A longitudinal study of gender differences, depression, and anxiety. *Child Development, 70*, 459–473.

Cole, D. A., Maxwell, S. E., Martin, J. M., Peeke, L. G., Seroczynski, A. D., Tram, et al. (2001). The development of multiple domains of child and adolescent self-concept: A cohort sequential longitudinal design. *Child Development, 72*, 1723–1746.

Cole, M. (1990). Cognitive development and formal schooling: The evidence from cross-cultural research. In L. C. Moll (Ed.), *Vygotsky and education* (pp. 89–110). New York: Cambridge University Press.

Cole, M. (2006). Culture and cognitive development in phylogenetic, historical and ontogenetic perspective. In W. Damon & R. M. Lerner (Series Eds.), D. Kuhn & R. Siegler (Vol. Eds.), *Handbook of child psychology: Vol. 2. Cognition, perception, and language* (6th ed.). New York: Wiley.

Cole, M., & Hatano, G. (2007). Cultural-historical activity theory: Integrating phylogeny, cultural history, and ontogenesis in cultural psychology. In S. Kitayama & D. Cohen (Eds.), *Handbook of cultural psychology* (pp. 109–135). New York: Guilford Press.

Cole, N. S. (1990). Conceptions of educational achievement. *Educational Researcher, 19*(3), 2–7.

Cole, P. M., Bruschi, C. J., & Tamang, B. L. (2002). Cultural differences in children's emotional reactions to difficult situations. *Child Development, 73*, 983–996.

Cole, P. M., Tamang, B. L., & Shrestha, S. (2006). Cultural variations in the socialization of young children's anger and shame. *Child Development, 77*, 1237–1251.

Cole, P. M., & Tan, P. Z. (2007). Emotion socialization from a cultural perspective. In J. E. Grusec & P. D. Hastings (Eds.), *Handbook of socialization: Theory and research* (pp. 516–542). New York: Guilford Press.

Cole, S. W. (2009). Social regulation of human gene expression. *Current Directions in Psychological Science, 18*, 133–137.

Collins, A. (2006). Cognitive apprenticeship. In R. K. Sawyer (Ed.), *The Cambridge handbook of the learning sciences* (pp. 47–60). Cambridge, England: Cambridge University Press.

Collins, A., Brown, J. S., & Newman, S. E. (1989). Cognitive apprenticeship: Teaching the crafts of reading, writing, and mathematics. In L. B. Resnick (Ed.), *Knowing, learning, and instruction: Essays in honor of Robert Glaser.* Mahwah, NJ: Erlbaum.

Collins, W. A. (2005, April). *A "new look" in social development? Re-framing and extending the canon.* Invited address at the Developmental Science Teaching Institute at the biennial meeting of the Society for Research in Child Development, Atlanta.

Collins, W. A., Maccoby, E. E., Steinberg, L., Hetherington, E. M., & Bornstein, M. H. (2000). Contemporary research on parenting: The case for nature and nurture. *American Psychologist, 55*, 218–232.

Colvin, G., Ainge, D., & Nelson, R. (1997). How to defuse defiance, threats, challenges, confrontations. *Teaching Exceptional Children, 29*(6), 47–51.

Combs, A. W., Richards, A. C., & Richards, F. (1976). *Perceptual psychology.* New York: Harper & Row.

Connell, J. P., & Wellborn, J. G. (1991). Competence, autonomy, and relatedness: A motivational analysis of self-system processes. In M. R. Gunnar & L. A. Sroufe (Eds.), *Self processes and* development: The Minnesota Symposia on Child Psychology (Vol. 23). Mahwah, NJ: Erlbaum.

Connolly, F. W., & Eisenberg, T. E. (1990). The feedback classroom: Teaching's silent friend. T.H.E. Journal, 17(5), 75–77.

Connolly, J., & Goldberg, A. (1999). Romantic relationships in adolescence: The role of friends and peers in their emergence and development. In W. Furman, B. B. Brown, & C. Feiring (Eds.), The development of romantic relationships in adolescence (pp. 266–290). Cambridge, England: Cambridge University Press.

Connor, C. M., Piasta, S. B., Fishman, B., Glasney, S., Schatschneider, C., Crowe, E., et al. (2009). Individualizing student instruction precisely: Effects of child X instruction interactions on first graders' literacy development. Child Development, 80, 77–100.

Connor, D. J., & Baglieri, S. (2009). Tipping the scales: Disabilities studies asks "How much diversity can you take?" In S. R. Steinberg (Ed.), Diversity and multiculturalism: A reader (pp. 341–361). New York: Peter Lang.

Conyers, C., Miltenberger, R., Maki, A., Barenz, R., Jurgens, M., Sailer, A., et al. (2004). A comparison of response cost and differential reinforcement of other behavior to reduce disruptive behavior in a preschool classroom. Journal of Applied Behavior Analysis, 37, 411–415.

Cook, P. J., & Ludwig, J. (2008). The burden of "acting White": Do Black adolescents disparage academic achievement? In J. U. Ogbu (Ed.), Minority status, oppositional culture, and schooling (pp. 275–297). New York: Routledge.

Cook, T. D., Herman, M. R., Phillips, M., & Settersten, R. A., Jr. (2002). Some ways in which neighborhoods, nuclear families, friendship groups, and schools jointly affect changes in early adolescent development. Child Development, 73, 1283–1309.

Cooper, H. (1989). Synthesis of research on homework. Educational Leadership, 47(3), 85–91.

Cooper, H., Robinson, J. C., & Patall, E. A. (2006). Does homework improve academic achievement? A synthesis of research, 1987–2003. Review of Educational Research, 76, 1–62.

Cooper, H., & Valentine, J. C. (2001). Using research to answer practical questions about homework. Educational Psychologist, 36, 143–153.

Coplan, R. J., & Arbeau, K. A. (2009). Peer interactions and play in early childhood. In K. H. Rubin, W. M. Bukowski, & B. Laursen (Eds.), Handbook of peer interactions, relationships, and groups (pp. 143–161). New York: Guilford Press.

Corkill, A. J. (1992). Advance organizers: Facilitators of recall. Educational Psychology Review, 4, 33–67.

Cormier, S. M. (1987). The structural processes underlying transfer of training. In S. M. Cormier & J. D. Hagman (Eds.), Transfer of learning: Contemporary research and applications. San Diego, CA: Academic Press.

Cornell, D. G., Pelton, G. M., Bassin, L. E., Landrum, M., Ramsay, S. G., Cooley, M. R., et al. (1990). Self-concept and peer status among gifted program youth. Journal of Educational Psychology, 82, 456–463.

Corno, L. (1993). The best-laid plans: Modern conceptions of volition and educational research. Educational Researcher, 22(2), 14–22.

Corno, L. (1996). Homework is a complicated thing. Educational Researcher, 25(8), 27–30.

Corno, L. (2008). On teaching adaptively. Educational Psychologist, 43, 161–173.

Corno, L., Cronbach, L. J., Kupermintz, H., Lohman, D. F., Mandinach, E. B., Porteu, A. W., et al. (2002). Remaking the concept of aptitude: Extending the legacy of Richard E. Snow. Mahwah, NJ: Erlbaum.

Corno, L., & Rohrkemper, M. M. (1985). The intrinsic motivation to learn in classrooms. In C. Ames & R. Ames (Eds.), Research on motivation in education: Vol. 2. The classroom milieu. San Diego, CA: Academic Press.

Cornoldi, C. (2010). Metacognition, intelligence, and academic performance. In H. S. Waters & W. Schneider (Eds.), Metacognition, strategy use, and instruction (pp. 257–277). New York: Guilford Press.

Corpus, J. H., McClintic-Gilbert, M. S., & Hayenga, A. O. (2009). Within-year changes in children's intrinsic and extrinsic motivational orientations: Contextual predictors and academic outcomes. Contemporary Educational Psychology, 34, 154–166.

Correa-Chávez, M., Rogoff, B., & Mejía Arauz, R. (2005). Cultural patterns in attending to two events at once. Child Development, 76, 664–678.

Cosden, M., Morrison, G., Albanese, A. L., & Macias, S. (2001). When homework is not home work: After-school programs for homework assistance. Educational Psychologist, 36, 211–221.

Costa, A. L. (2008). Mediative environments: Creating conditions for intellectual grouth. Thousand Oaks, CA: Corwin.

Covington, M. V. (1987). Achievement motivation, self-attributions, and the exceptional learner. In J. D. Day & J. G. Borkowski (Eds.), Intelligence and exceptionality. Norwood, NJ: Ablex.

Covington, M. V. (1992). Making the grade: A self-worth perspective on motivation and school reform. Cambridge, England: Cambridge University Press.

Covington, M. V. (2000). Intrinsic versus extrinsic motivation in schools: A reconciliation. Current Directions in Psychological Science, 9, 22–25.

Covington, M. V., & Müeller, K. J. (2001). Intrinsic versus extrinsic motivation: An approach/avoidance reformulation. Educational Psychology Review, 13, 157–176.

Cowan, N. (1995). Attention and memory: An integrated framework. New York: Oxford University Press.

Cowan, N. (2007). What infants can tell us about working memory development. In L. M. Oakes & P. J. Bauer (Eds.), Short- and long-term memory in infancy and early childhood: Taking the first steps toward remembering (pp. 126–150). New York: Oxford University Press.

Cowan, N., Chen, Z., & Rouder, J. N. (2004). Constant capacity in an immediate serial-recall task: A logical sequel to Miller (1956). Psychological Science, 15, 634–640.

Cowan, N., Saults, J. S., & Morey, C. C. (2006). Development of working memory for verbal-spatial associations. Journal of Memory and Language, 55, 274–289.

Cox, B. D. (1997). The rediscovery of the active learner in adaptive contexts: A developmental-historical analysis of transfer of training. Educational Psychologist, 32, 41–55.

Craft, M. (1984). Education for diversity. In M. Craft (Ed.), Educational and cultural pluralism. London: Falmer Press.

Craft, M. A., Alberg, S. R., & Heward, W. L. (1998). Teaching elementary students with developmental disabilities to recruit teacher attention in a general education classroom: Effects on teacher praise and academic productivity. Journal of Applied Behavior Analysis, 31, 399–415.

Crago, M. B. (1988). Cultural context in the communicative interaction of young Inuit children. Unpublished doctoral dissertation, McGill University, Montreal, Canada.

Crago, M. B., Annahatak, B., & Ningiuruvik, L. (1993). Changing patterns of language socialization in Inuit homes. Anthropology and Education Quarterly, 24, 205–223.

Craig, D. V. (2009). Action research essentials. San Francisco: Jossey-Bass.

Craik, F. I. M. (2006). Distinctiveness and memory: Comments and a point of view. In R. R. Hunt & J. B. Worthen (Eds.), Distinctiveness and memory (pp. 425–442). Oxford, England: Oxford University Press.

Craik, F. I. M., & Watkins, M. J. (1973). The role of rehearsal in short-term memory. Journal of Verbal Learning and Verbal Behavior, 12, 598–607.

Creasey, G. L., Jarvis, P. A., & Berk, L. E. (1998). Play and social competence. In O. N. Saracho & B. Spodek (Eds.), Multiple perspectives on play in early childhood education. Albany: State University of New York Press.

Crehan, K. D. (2001). An investigation of the validity of scores on locally developed performance measures in a school assessment program. Educational and Psychological Measurement, 61, 841–848.

Crick, N. R., & Dodge, K. A. (1994). A review and reformulation of social information-processing mechanisms in children's social adjustment. Psychological Bulletin, 115, 74–101.

Crick, N. R., & Dodge, K. A. (1996). Social information-processing mechanisms in reactive and proactive aggression. Child Development, 67, 993–1002.

Crick, N. R., Grotpeter, J. K., & Bigbee, M. A. (2002). Relationally and physically aggressive children's intent attributions and feelings of distress for relational and instrumental peer provocation. Child Development, 73, 1134–1142.

Crick, N. R., Murray-Close, D., Marks, P. E. L., & Mohajeri-Nelson, N. (2009). Aggression and peer relationships in school-age children: Relational and physical aggression in group and dyadic contexts. In K. H. Rubin, W. M. Bukowski, & B. Laursen (Eds.), Handbook of peer interactions, relationships, and groups (pp. 287–302). New York: Guilford Press.

Crocker, J., & Knight, K. M. (2005). Contingencies of self-worth. Current Directions in Psychological Science, 14, 200–203.

Crockett, L., Losoff, M., & Peterson, A. C. (1984). Perceptions of the peer group and friendship in early adolescence. Journal of Early Adolescence, 4, 155–181.

Cromley, J. G., & Azevedo, R. (2007). Testing and refining the direct and inferential mediation model of reading comprehension. Journal of Educational Psychology, 99, 311–325.

Crone, D. A., & Horner, R. H. (2003). Building positive behavior support systems in schools: Functional behavioral assessment. New York: Guilford Press.

Croninger, R. G., & Valli, L. (2009). "Where is the action?" Challenges to studying the teaching of reading in elementary classrooms. Educational Researcher, 38, 100–108.

Crook, C. (1995). On resourcing a concern for collaboration within peer interactions. Cognition and Instruction, 13, 541–547.

Crooks, T. J. (1988). The impact of classroom evaluation practices on students. *Review of Educational Research, 58,* 438–481.

Cross, W. E., Jr., Strauss, L., & Fhagen-Smith, P. (1999). African American identity development across the life span: Educational implications. In R. H. Sheets & E. R. Hollins (Eds.), *Racial and ethnic identity in school practices: Aspects of human development* (pp. 29–47). Mahwah, NJ: Erlbaum.

Crosson-Tower, C. (2008). *Understanding child abuse and neglect.* Boston: Pearson/Allyn & Bacon.

Crouter, A. C., Whiteman, S. D., McHale, S. M., & Osgood, D. W. (2007). Development of gender attitude traditionality across middle childhood and adolescence. *Child Development, 78,* 911–926.

Csikszentmihalyi, M. (1990). *Flow: The psychology of optimal experience.* New York: Harper-Perennial.

Csikszentmihalyi, M. (1996). *Creativity: Flow and the psychology of discovery and invention.* New York: HarperCollins.

Csikszentmihalyi, M., Abuhamdeh, S., & Nakamura, J. (2005). Flow. In A. J. Elliot & C. S. Dweck (Eds.), *Handbook of competence and motivation* (pp. 598–608). New York: Guilford Press.

Csikszentmihalyi, M., & Nakamura, J. (1989). The dynamics of intrinsic motivation: A study of adolescents. In C. Ames & R. Ames (Eds.), *Research on motivation in education: Vol. 3. Goals and cognitions.* San Diego, CA: Academic Press.

Cummins, J. (1984). *Bilingualism and special education: Issues in assessment and pedagogy.* Clevedon, England: Multilingual Matters.

Cummins, J. (2008). BICS and CALP: Empirical and theoretical status of the distinction. In B. Street & N. H. Hornberger (Eds.), *Encyclopedia of language and education* (2nd ed., Vol. 2, pp. 71–83). New York: Springer.

Cummings, E. M., Schermerhorn, A. C., Davies, P. T., Goeke-Morey, M. C., & Cummings, J. S. (2006). Interparental discord and child adjustment: Prospective investigations of emotional security as an explanatory mechanism. *Child Development, 77,* 132–152.

Cunningham, C. E., & Cunningham, L. J. (2006). Student-mediated conflict resolution programs. In R. A. Barkley, *Attention-deficit hyperactivity disorder: A handbook for diagnosis and treatment* (3rd ed., pp. 590–607). New York: Guilford Press.

Curry, L. (1990). A critique of the research on learning styles. *Educational Leadership, 47*(2), 50–56.

Curtis, K. A. (1992). Altering beliefs about the importance of strategy: An attributional intervention. *Journal of Applied Social Psychology, 22,* 953–972.

Cushing, L. S., & Kennedy, C. H. (1997). Academic effects of providing peer support in general education classrooms on students without disabilities. *Journal of Applied Behavior Analysis, 30,* 139–151.

Dahlin, B., & Watkins, D. (2000). The role of repetition in the processes of memorizing and understanding: A comparison of the views of Western and Chinese secondary students in Hong Kong. *British Journal of Educational Psychology, 70,* 65–84.

Dai, D. Y., & Sternberg, R. J. (2004). Beyond cognitivism: Toward an integrated understanding of intellectual functioning and development. In D. Y. Dai & R. J. Sternberg (Eds.), *Motivation, emotion, and cognition: Integrative perspectives on intellectual functioning and development* (pp. 3–38). Mahwah, NJ: Erlbaum.

Dai, D. Y., & Wang, X. (2007). The role of need for cognition and reader beliefs in text comprehension and interest development. *Contemporary Educational Psychology, 32,* 332–347.

d'Ailly, H. (2003). Children's autonomy and perceived control in learning: A model of motivation and achievement in Taiwan. *Journal of Educational Psychology, 95,* 84–96.

Daley, T. C., Whaley, S. E., Sigman, M. D., Espinosa, M. P., & Neumann, C. (2003). IQ on the rise: The Flynn effect in rural Kenyan children. *Psychological Science, 14,* 215–219.

Dalrymple, N. J. (1995). Environmental supports to develop flexibility and independence. In K. A. Quill (Ed.), *Teaching children with autism: Strategies to enhance communication and socialization.* New York: Delmar.

Damasio, A. R. (1994). *Descartes' error: Emotion, reason, and the human brain.* New York: Avon Books.

D'Amato, R. C., Chitooran, M. M., & Whitten, J. D. (1992). Neuropsychological consequences of malnutrition. In D. I. Templer, L. C. Hartlage, & W. G. Cannon (Eds.), *Preventable brain damage: Brain vulnerability and brain health.* New York: Springer.

Damon, W. (1988). *The moral child: Nurturing children's natural moral growth.* New York: Free Press.

Damon, W., & Hart, D. (1988). *Self-understanding from childhood and adolescence.* New York: Cambridge University Press.

Danner, F. (2008, March). *The effects of perceptions of classroom assessment practices and academic press on classroom mastery goals and high school students' self-reported cheating.* Paper presented at the annual meeting of the American Educational Research Association, New York.

Danner, F. W., & Day, M. C. (1977). Eliciting formal operations. *Child Development, 48,* 1600–1606.

Dansereau, D. F. (1995). Derived structural schemas and the transfer of knowledge. In A. McKeough, J. Lupart, & A. Marini (Eds.), *Teaching for transfer: Fostering generalization in learning.* Mahwah, NJ: Erlbaum.

Darch, C. B., & Kame'enui, E. J. (2004). *Instructional classroom management: A proactive approach to behavior management* (2nd ed.). Upper Saddle River, NJ: Merrill/Prentice Hall.

Darley, J. M., & Gross, P. H. (1983). A hypothesis-confirming bias in labeling effects. *Journal of Personality and Social Psychology, 44,* 20–33.

Darling-Hammond, L., Ancess, J., & Falk, B. (1995). *Authentic assessment in action: Studies of schools and students at work.* New York: Teachers College Press.

Darling-Hammond, L., & Bransford, J. (Eds.). (2005). *Preparing teachers for a changing world: What teachers should learn and be able to do.* San Francisco: Jossey-Bass/Wiley.

Darwin, C. J., Turvey, M. T., & Crowder, R. G. (1972). An auditory analogue of the Sperling partial report procedure: Evidence for brief auditory storage. *Cognitive Psychology, 3,* 255–267.

Davidson, F. H. (1976). Ability to respect persons compared to ethnic prejudice in childhood. *Journal of Personality and Social Psychology, 34,* 1256–1267.

Davidson, J. E., & Sternberg, R. J. (1998). Smart problem solving: How metacognition helps. In D. J. Hacker, J. Dunlosky, & A. C. Graesser (Eds.), *Metacognition in educational theory and practice* (pp. 47–68). Mahwah, NJ: Erlbaum.

Davidson, J. E., & Sternberg, R. J. (Eds.). (2003). *The psychology of problem solving.* Cambridge, England: Cambridge University Press.

Davies, P. G., & Spencer, S. J. (2005). The gender-gap artifact: Women's underperformance in quantitative domains through the lens of stereotype threat. In A. M. Gallagher & J. C. Kaufman (Eds.), *Gender differences in mathematics: An integrative psychological approach* (pp. 172–188). Cambridge, England: Cambridge University Press.

Davies, P. T., & Woitach, M. J. (2008). Children's emotional security in the interparental relationship. *Current Directions in Psychological Science, 17,* 269–274.

Davila, J. (2008). Depressive symptoms and adolescent romance: Theory, research, and implications. *Child Development Perspectives, 2*(1), 26–31.

Davis, C., & Yang, A. (2005). *Parents and teachers working together.* Turners Falls, MA: Northeast Foundation for Children.

Davis, G. A., & Rimm, S. B. (1998). *Education of the gifted and talented* (4th ed.). Boston: Allyn & Bacon.

Davis, G. A., & Thomas, M. A. (1989). *Effective schools and effective teachers.* Boston: Allyn & Bacon.

Davis, H. A. (2003). Conceptualizing the role and influence of student-teacher relationships on children's social and cognitive development. *Educational Psychologist, 38,* 207–234.

Davis, H. A., Schutz, P. A., & Chambless, C. B. (2001, April). *Uncovering the impact of social relationships in the classroom: Viewing relationships with teachers from different lenses.* Paper presented at the annual meeting of the American Educational Research Association, Seattle, WA.

Davis, L. E., Ajzen, I., Saunders, J., & Williams, T. (2002). The decision of African American students to complete high school: An application of the theory of planned behavior. *Journal of Educational Psychology, 94,* 810–819.

Davis, O. S. P., Haworth, C. M. A., & Plomin, R. (2009). Dramatic increase in heritability of cognitive development from early to middle childhood: An 8-year longitudinal study of 8,700 pairs of twins. *Psychological Science, 20,* 1301–1308.

Davis-Kean, P. E., Huesmann, R., Jager, J., Collins, W. A., Bates, J. E., & Lansford, J. E. (2008). Changes in the relation of self-efficacy beliefs and behaviors across development. *Child Development, 79,* 1257–1269.

Davis-Kean, P. E., & Sandler, H. M. (2001). A meta-analysis of measures of self-esteem for young children: A framework for future measures. *Child Development, 72,* 887–906.

Deary, I. J., Strand, S., Smith, P., & Fernandez, C. (2007). Intelligence and educational achievement. *Intelligence, 35,* 13–21.

Deaux, K. (1984). From individual differences to social categories: Analysis of a decade's research on gender. *American Psychologist, 39,* 105–116.

DeBose, C. E. (2007). The Ebonics phenomenon, language planning, and the hegemony of Standard English. In H. S. Alim & J. Baugh (Eds.), *Talkin Black talk: Language, education, and social change* (pp. 30–42). New York: Teachers College Press.

deCharms, R. (1972). Personal causation training in the schools. *Journal of Applied Social Psychology, 2,* 95–113.

Deci, E. L. (1992). The relation of interest to the motivation of behavior: A self-determination theory perspective. In K. A. Renninger, S. Hidi, & A. Krapp (Eds.), *The role of interest in learning and development.* Mahwah, NJ: Erlbaum.

Deci, E. L., Koestner, R., & Ryan, R. M. (2001). Extrinsic rewards and intrinsic motivation in education: Reconsidered once again. *Review of Educational Research, 71,* 1–27.

Deci, E. L., & Moller, A. C. (2005). The concept of competence: A starting place for understanding intrinsic motivation and self-determined extrinsic motivation. In A. J. Elliot & C. S. Dweck (Eds.), *Handbook of competence and motivation* (pp. 579–597). New York: Guilford Press.

Deci, E. L., & Ryan, R. M. (1985). *Intrinsic motivation and self-determination in human behavior.* New York: Plenum Press.

Deci, E. L., & Ryan, R. M. (1992). The initiation and regulation of intrinsically motivated learning and achievement. In A. K. Boggiano & T. S. Pittman (Eds.), *Achievement and motivation: A social-developmental perspective.* Cambridge, England: Cambridge University Press.

Deci, E. L., & Ryan, R. M. (1995). Human autonomy: The basis for true self-esteem. In M. H. Kernis (Ed.), *Efficacy, agency, and self-esteem.* New York: Plenum Press.

De Corte, E. (2003). Transfer as the productive use of acquired knowledge, skills, and motivations. *Current Directions in Psychological Science, 12,* 142–146.

De Corte, E., Greer, B., & Verschaffel, L. (1996). Mathematics teaching and learning. In D. C. Berliner & R. C. Calfee (Eds.), *Handbook of educational psychology.* New York: Macmillan.

Dee-Lucas, D., & Larkin, J. H. (1991). Equations in scientific proofs: Effects on comprehension. *American Educational Research Journal, 28,* 661–682.

de Jong, T., & van Joolingen, W. R. (1998). Scientific discovery learning with computer simulations of conceptual domains. *Review of Educational Research, 68,* 179–201.

DeLain, M. T., Pearson, P. D., & Anderson, R. C. (1985). Reading comprehension and creativity in black language use: You stand to gain by playing the sounding game! *American Educational Research Journal, 22,* 155–173.

Delandshere, G., & Petrosky, A. R. (1998). Assessment of complex performances: Limitations of key measurement assumptions. *Educational Researcher, 27*(2), 14–24.

De La Paz, S. (2005). Effects of historical reasoning instruction and writing strategy mastery in culturally and academically diverse middle school classrooms. *Journal of Educational Psychology, 97,* 139–156.

deLeeuw, N., & Chi, M. T. H. (2003). Self-explanation: Enriching a situation model or repairing a domain model? In G. M. Sinatra & P. R. Pintrich (Eds.), *Intentional conceptual change* (pp. 55–78). Mahwah, NJ: Erlbaum.

Delgado-Gaitan, C. (1994). Socializing young children in Mexican-American families: An intergenerational perspective. In P. M. Greenfield & R. R. Cocking (Eds.), *Cross-cultural roots of minority child development.* Mahwah, NJ: Erlbaum.

De Lisi, R., & Golbeck, S. L. (1999). Implications of Piagetian theory for peer learning. In A. M. O'Donnell & A. King (Eds.), *Cognitive perspectives on peer learning* (pp. 3–37). Mahwah, NJ: Erlbaum.

DeLisle, J. R. (1984). *Gifted children speak out.* New York: Walker.

DeLoache, J. S., & Todd, C. M. (1988). Young children's use of spatial categorization as a mnemonic strategy. *Journal of Experimental Child Psychology, 46,* 1–20.

Demetriou, A., Christou, C., Spanoudis, G., & Platsidou, M. (2002). The development of mental processing: Efficiency, working memory, and thinking. *Monographs of the Society for Research in Child Development, 67*(1, Serial No. 268).

Dempster, F. N. (1991). Synthesis of research on reviews and tests. *Educational Leadership, 48*(7), 71–76.

Dempster, F. N. (1992). The rise and fall of the inhibitory mechanism: Toward a unified theory of cognitive development and aging. *Developmental Review, 12,* 45–75.

Dempster, F. N. (1997). Using tests to promote classroom learning. In R. F. Dillon (Ed.), *Handbook on testing* (pp. 332–346). Westport, CT: Greenwood Press.

DeRidder, L. M. (1993). Teenage pregnancy: Etiology and educational interventions. *Educational Psychology Review, 5,* 87–107.

Derry, S. J. (1996). Cognitive schema theory in the constructivist debate. *Educational Psychologist, 31,* 163–174.

Derry, S. J., Levin, J. R., Osana, H. P., & Jones, M. S. (1998). Developing middle school students' statistical reasoning abilities through simulation gaming. In S. P. Lajoie (Ed.), *Reflections on statistics: Learning, teaching, and assessment in grades K–12* (pp. 175–195). Mahwah, NJ: Erlbaum.

Desberg, P., & Taylor, J. H. (1986). *Essentials of task analysis.* Lanham, MD: University Press of America.

Desimone, L. M. (2009). Improving impact studies of teachers' professional development: Toward better conceptualizations and measures. *Educational Researcher, 38,* 181–199.

Desoete, A., Roeyers, H., & De Clercq, A. (2003). Can offline metacognition enhance mathematical problem solving? *Journal of Educational Psychology, 95,* 188–200.

Deutsch, M. (1993). Educating for a peaceful world. *American Psychologist, 48,* 510–517.

DeVault, G., Krug, C., & Fake, S. (1996, September). Why does Samantha act that way: Positive behavioral support leads to successful inclusion. *Exceptional Parent,* 43–47.

DeVoe, J. F., Peter, K., Kaufman, P., Ruddy, S. A., Miller, A. K., Planty, M., et al. (2003). *Indicators of school crime and safety: 2003* (NCES 2004-004/NCJ 201257). Washington, DC: U.S. Departments of Education and Justice. Retrieved February 27, 2004, from http://nces.ed.gov/

DeVoe, J. F., Peter, K., Noonan, M., Snyder, T. D., & Baum, K. (2005). *Indicators of school crime and safety: 2005* (NCES 2006–001/NCJ 210697). Washington, DC: U.S. Departments of Education and Justice. Retrieved February 6, 2007, from http://ojp.usdoj.gov/bjs/abstract/iscs05.htm

DeVries, R., & Zan, B. (1996). A constructivist perspective on the role of the sociomoral atmosphere in promoting children's development. In C. T. Fosnot (Ed.), *Constructivism: Theory, perspectives, and practice.* New York: Teachers College Press.

Dewhurst, S. A., & Conway, M. A. (1994). Pictures, images, and recollective experience. *Journal of Experimental Psychology: Learning, Memory, and Cognition, 20,* 1088–1098.

Deyhle, D., & LeCompte, M. (1999). Cultural differences in child development: Navajo adolescents in middle schools. In R. H. Sheets & E. R. Hollins (Eds.), *Racial and ethnic identity in school practices: Aspects of human development* (pp. 123–139). Mahwah, NJ: Erlbaum.

Deyhle, D., & Margonis, F. (1995). Navajo mothers and daughters: Schools, jobs, and the family. *Anthropology and Education Quarterly, 26,* 135–167.

Diamond, A., Barnett, W. S., Thomas, J., & Munro, S. (2007). Preschool program improves cognitive control. *Science, 318,* 1387–1388.

Diamond, M., & Hopson, J. (1998). *Magic trees of the mind.* New York: Dutton.

Diamond, S. C. (1991). What to do when you can't do anything: Working with disturbed adolescents. *Clearing House, 64,* 232–234.

Dickens, W. T., & Flynn, J. R. (2006). Black Americans reduce the racial IQ gap: Evidence from standardization samples. *Psychological Science, 17,* 913–920.

Dien, T. (1998). Language and literacy in Vietnamese American communities. In B. Pérez (Ed.), *Sociocultural contexts of language and literacy.* Mahwah, NJ: Erlbaum.

Dijkstra, P., Kuyper, H., van der Werf, G., Buunk, A. P., & van der Zee, Y. G. (2008). Social comparison in the classroom: A review. *Review of Educational Research, 78,* 828–879.

Dilworth, J. E., & Moore, C. F. (2006). Mercy mercy me: Social injustice and the prevention of environmental pollutant exposures among ethnic minority and poor children. *Child Development, 77,* 247–265.

DiMartino, J., & Castaneda, A. (2007). Assessing applied skills. *Educational Leadership, 64,* 38–42.

Dirks, J. (1982). The effect of a commercial game on children's Block Design scores on the WISC-R test. *Intelligence, 6,* 109–123.

diSessa, A. A. (2006). A history of conceptual change research. In R. K. Sawyer (Ed.), *The Cambridge handbook of the learning sciences* (pp. 265–281). Cambridge, England: Cambridge University Press.

diSessa, A. A. (2007). An interactional analysis of clinical interviewing. *Cognition and Instruction, 25,* 523–565.

Di Vesta, F. J., & Gray, S. G. (1972). Listening and notetaking. *Journal of Educational Psychology, 63,* 8–14.

Di Vesta, F. J., & Peverly, S. T. (1984). The effects of encoding variability, processing activity and rule example sequences on the transfer of conceptual rules. *Journal of Educational Psychology, 76,* 108–119.

Dodge, K. A. (1986). A social information processing model of social competence in children. In M. Perlmutter (Ed.), *Minnesota Symposia on Child Psychology: Vol. 18. Cognitive perspectives in children's social and behavioral development.* Mahwah, NJ: Erlbaum.

Dodge, K. A. (2009). Mechanisms of gene–environment interaction effects in the development of conduct disorder. *Perspectives on Psychological Science, 4,* 408–414.

Dodge, K. A., Asher, S. R., & Parkhurst, J. T. (1989). Social life as a goal-coordination task. In C. Ames & R. Ames (Eds.), *Research on motivation in education: Vol. 3. Goals and cognitions.* San Diego, CA: Academic Press.

Dodge, K. A., Lansford, J. E., Burks, V. S., Bates, J. E., Pettit, G. S., Fontaine, R., et al. (2003). Peer rejection and social information-processing factors in the development of aggressive behavior problems in children. *Child Development, 74,* 374–393.

Dodge, K. A., Lochman, J. E., Harnish, J. D., Bates, J. E., & Pettit, G. S. (1997). Reactive and proactive aggression in school children and psychiatrically impaired chronically assaultive youth. *Journal of Abnormal Psychology, 106,* 37–51.

Dole, J. A., Duffy, G. G., Roehler, L. R., & Pearson, P. D. (1991). Moving from the old to the new: Research on reading comprehension instruction. *Review of Educational Research, 61,* 239–264.

Doll, B., Song, S., & Siemers, E. (2004). Classroom ecologies that support or discourage bullying. In D. L. Espelage & S. M. Swearer (Eds.), *Bullying in American schools: A social-ecological perspective on prevention and intervention* (pp. 161–183). Mahwah, NJ: Erlbaum.

Dominowski, R. L. (1998). Verbalization and problem solving. In D. J. Hacker, J. Dunlosky, & A. C. Graesser (Eds.), *Metacognition in educational theory and practice* (pp. 25–45). Mahwah, NJ: Erlbaum.

Donaldson, M. (1978). *Children's minds.* New York: Norton.

Donaldson, S. K., & Westerman, M. A. (1986). Development of children's understanding of ambivalence and causal theories of emotion. *Developmental Psychology, 22,* 655–662.

Dorris, M. (1989). *The broken cord.* New York: Harper & Row.

Dotterer, A. M., McHale, S. M., & Crouter, A. C. (2009). The development and correlates of academic interests from childhood through adolescence. *Journal of Educational Psychology, 101,* 509–519.

Dovidio, J. F., & Gaertner, S. L. (1999). Reducing prejudice: Combating intergroup biases. *Current Directions in Psychological Science, 8,* 101–105.

Dowson, M., & McInerney, D. M. (2001). Psychological parameters of students' social and work avoidance goals: A qualitative investigation. *Journal of Educational Psychology, 93,* 35–42.

Doyle, A. (1982). Friends, acquaintances, and strangers: The influence of familiarity and ethnolinguistic backgrounds on social interaction. In K. Rubin & H. Ross (Eds.), *Peer relationships and social skills in childhood.* New York: Springer-Verlag.

Doyle, W. (1983). Academic work. *Review of Educational Research, 53,* 159–199.

Doyle, W. (1984). How order is achieved in classrooms: An interim report. *Journal of Curriculum Studies, 16,* 259–277.

Doyle, W. (1986a). Classroom organization and management. In M. C. Wittrock (Ed.), *Handbook of research on teaching* (3rd ed.). New York: Macmillan.

Doyle, W. (1986b). Content representation in teachers' definitions of academic work. *Journal of Curriculum Studies, 18,* 365–379.

Doyle, W. (1990). Classroom management techniques. In O. C. Moles (Ed.), *Student discipline strategies: Research and practice.* Albany: State University of New York Press.

Doyle, W. (2006). Ecological approaches to classroom management. In C. M. Evertson & C. S. Weinstein (Eds.), *Handbook of classroom management: Research, practice, and contemporary issues* (pp. 97–125). Mahwah, NJ: Erlbaum.

Dreikurs, R. (1998). *Maintaining sanity in the classroom: Classroom management techniques* (2nd ed.). Bristol, PA: Hemisphere.

Dryfoos, J. G. (1997). The prevalence of problem behaviors: Implications for programs. In R. P. Weissberg, T. P. Gullotta, R. L. Hampton, B. A. Ryan, & G. R. Adams (Eds.), *Enhancing children's wellness* (Vol. 8, pp. 17–46). Thousand Oaks, CA: Sage.

DuBois, D. L., Burk-Braxton, C., Swenson, L. P., Tevendale, H. D., & Hardesty, J. L. (2002). Race and gender influences on adjustment in early adolescence: Investigation of an integrative model. *Child Development, 73,* 1573–1592.

Dubow, E. F., Huesmann, L. R., & Greenwood, D. (2007). Media and youth socialization: Underlying processes and moderators of effects. In J. E. Grusec & P. D. Hastings (Eds.), *Handbook of socialization: Theory and research* (pp. 404–430). New York: Guilford Press.

Duckworth, A. L., & Seligman, M. E. P. (2005). Self-discipline outdoes IQ in predicting academic performance of adolescents. *Psychological Science, 16,* 939–944.

Duke, N. K. (2000). For the rich it's richer: Print experiences and environments offered to children in very low- and very high-socioeconomic status first-grade classrooms. *American Educational Research Journal, 37,* 441–478.

Duncan, G. J., Dowsett, C. J., Claessens, A., Magnuson, K., Huston, A. C., Klevanov, P., et al. (2007). School readiness and later achievement. *Developmental Psychology, 43,* 1428–1446.

Duncan, G. J., & Magnuson, K. A. (2005). Can family socioeconomic resources account for racial and ethnic test score gaps? *The Future of Children, 15*(1), 35–54.

Duncker, K. (1945). On problem solving. *Psychological Monographs, 58* (Whole No. 270).

Dunham, Y., Baron, A. S., & Banaji, M. R. (2006). From American city to Japanese village: A cross-cultural investigation of implicit race attitudes. *Child Development, 77,* 1268–1281.

Dunlap, G., dePerczel, M., Clarke, S., Wilson, D., Wright, S., White, R., et al. (1994). Choice making to promote adaptive behavior for students with emotional and behavioral challenges. *Journal of Applied Behavior Analysis, 27,* 505–518.

Dunlosky, J., & Lipko, A. R. (2007). Metacomprehension: A brief history and how to improve its accuracy. *Current Directions in Psychological Science, 16,* 228–232.

Dunning, D., Heath, C., & Suls, J. M. (2004). Flawed self-assessment: Implications for health, education, and the workplace. *Psychological Science in the Public Interest, 5,* 69–106.

DuPaul, G. J., Ervin, R. A., Hook, C. L., & McGoey, K. E. (1998). Peer tutoring for children with attention deficit hyperactivity disorder: Effects on classroom behavior and academic performance. *Journal of Applied Behavior Analysis, 31,* 579–592.

DuPaul, G., & Hoff, K. (1998). Reducing disruptive behavior in general education classrooms: The use of self-management strategies. *School Psychology Review, 27,* 290–304.

Duran, B. J., & Weffer, R. E. (1992). Immigrants' aspirations, high school process, and academic outcomes. *American Educational Research Journal, 29,* 163–181.

Durik, A. M., Vida, M., & Eccles, J. S. (2006). Task values and ability beliefs as predictors of high school literacy choices: A developmental analysis. *Journal of Educational Psychology, 98,* 382–393.

Durkin, K. (1995). *Developmental social psychology: From infancy to old age.* Cambridge, MA: Blackwell.

Duyme, M., Dumaret, A., & Tomkiewicz, S. (1999). How can we boost IQs of "dull" children? A late adoption study. *Proceedings of the National Academy of Sciences, USA, 96,* 8790–8794.

Dweck, C. S. (1978). Achievement. In M. E. Lamb (Ed.), *Social and personality development.* New York: Holt, Rinehart & Winston.

Dweck, C. S. (1986). Motivational processes affecting learning. *American Psychologist, 41,* 1040–1048.

Dweck, C. S. (2000). *Self-theories: Their role in motivation, personality, and development.* Philadelphia: Psychology Press.

Dweck, C. S. (2008). Can personality be changed? The role of beliefs in personality and change. *Current Directions in Psychological Science, 17,* 391–394.

Dweck, C. S. (2009). Foreword. In F. D. Horowitz, R. F. Subotnik, & D. J. Matthews (Eds.), *The development of giftedness and talent across the life span* (pp. xi–xiv). Washington, DC: American Psychological Association.

Dweck, C. S., & Elliott, E. S. (1983). Achievement motivation. In E. M. Hetherington (Ed.), *Handbook of child psychology: Vol. 4. Socialization, personality, and social development* (4th ed., pp. 643–691). New York: Wiley.

Dweck, C. S., & Leggett, E. L. (1988). A social-cognitive approach to motivation and personality. *Psychological Review, 95,* 256–273.

Dweck, C. S., Mangels, J. A., & Good, C. (2004). Motivational effects on attention, cognition, and performance. In D. Y. Dai & R. J. Sternberg (Eds.), *Motivation, emotion, and cognition: Integrative perspectives on intellectual functioning and development* (pp. 41–55). Mahwah, NJ: Erlbaum.

Dweck, C. S., & Molden, D. C. (2005). Self-theories: Their impact on competence motivation and acquisition. In A. J. Elliot & C. S. Dweck (Eds.), *Handbook of competence and motivation* (pp. 122–140). New York: Guilford Press.

Dwyer, K., & Osher, D. (2000). *Safeguarding our children: An action guide.* Washington, DC: U.S. Departments of Education and Justice, American Institutes for Research. Retrieved February 26, 2004, from www.ed.gov/pubs/edpubs.html

Dwyer, K., Osher, D., & Warger, C. (1998). *Early warning, timely response: A guide to safe schools.* Washington, DC: U.S. Department of Education. Retrieved February 26, 2004, from www.ed.gov/offices/OSERS/OSEP/earlywrn.html

Dymond, S. K., Renzaglia, A., & Chun, E. (2007). Elements of effective high school service learning programs that include students with and without disabilities. *Remedial and Special Education, 28,* 227–243.

Eacott, M. J. (1999). Memory for the events of early childhood. *Current Directions in Psychological Science, 8,* 46–49.

Eaton, J. F., Anderson, C. W., & Smith, E. L. (1984). Students' misconceptions interfere with science learning: Case studies of fifth-grade students. *Elementary School Journal, 84,* 365–379.

Eccles, J. S. (2005). Subjective task value and the Eccles et al. model of achievement-related choices. In A. J. Elliot & C. S. Dweck (Eds.), *Handbook of competence and motivation* (pp. 105–121). New York: Guilford Press.

Eccles, J. S. (2007). Families, schools, and developing achievement-related motivations and engagement. In J. E. Grusec & P. D. Hastings

(Eds.), *Handbook of socialization: Theory and research* (pp. 665–691). New York: Guilford Press.

Eccles, J. (2009). Who am I and what am I going to do with my life? Personal and collective identities as motivators of action. *Educational Psychologist, 44,* 78–89.

Eccles, J. S., & Midgley, C. (1989). Stage-environment fit: Developmentally appropriate classrooms for young adolescents. In C. Ames & R. Ames (Eds.), *Research on motivation in education: Vol. 3. Goals and cognitions.* San Diego, CA: Academic Press.

Eccles, J. S., Wigfield, A., & Schiefele, U. (1998). Motivation to succeed. In W. Damon (Series Ed.) & N. Eisenberg (Vol. Ed.), *Handbook of child psychology: Vol. 3. Social, emotional, and personality development* (5th ed., pp. 1017–1095). New York: Wiley.

Eccles (Parsons), J. S. (1983). Expectancies, values, and academic behaviors. In J. T. Spence (Ed.), *Achievement and achievement motivation.* San Francisco: Freeman.

Eckert, P. (1989). *Jocks and burnouts: Social categories and identity in the high school.* New York: Teachers College Press.

Edens, K. M., & Potter, E. F. (2001). Promoting conceptual understanding through pictorial representation. *Studies in Art Education, 42,* 214–233.

Edmonds, M. S., Vaughn, S., Wexler, J., Reutebuch, C., Cable, A., Tackett, K. K., et al. (2009). A synthesis of reading interventions and effects of reading comprehension outcomes for older struggling students. *Review of Educational Research, 79,* 262–300.

Eeds, M., & Wells, D. (1989). Grand conversations: An explanation of meaning construction in literature study groups. *Research in the Teaching of English, 23,* 4–29.

Egbert, J. (2009). *Supporting learning with technology: Essentials of classroom practice.* Upper Saddle River, NJ: Pearson/Merrill Prentice Hall.

Eid, M., & Diener, E. (2001). Norms for experiencing emotions in different cultures: Inter- and intranational differences. *Journal of Personality and Social Psychology, 81,* 869–885.

Eilam, B. (2001). Primary strategies for promoting homework performance. *American Educational Research Journal, 38,* 691–725.

Einstein, G. O., & McDaniel, M. A. (2005). Prospective memory: Multiple retrieval processes. *Current Directions in Psychological Science, 14,* 286–290.

Eisenberg, M. B. (2004). *A Big6™ skills overview.* Retrieved April 23, 2004, from http://big6.com/showarticle/php?id=16

Eisenberg, M. B., & Berkowitz, R. E. (2000). *Teaching information and technology skills: The Big6 in elementary schools.* Worthington, OH: Linworth.

Eisenberg, N. (1982). The development of reasoning regarding prosocial behavior. In N. Eisenberg (Ed.), *The development of prosocial behavior.* San Diego, CA: Academic Press.

Eisenberg, N. (1987). The relation of altruism and other moral behaviors to moral cognition: Methodological and conceptual issues. In N. Eisenberg (Ed.), *Contemporary topics in developmental psychology* (pp. 165–189). New York: Wiley.

Eisenberg, N. (1995). Prosocial development: A multifaceted model. In W. M. Kurtines & J. L. Gewirtz (Eds.), *Moral development: An introduction.* Boston: Allyn & Bacon.

Eisenberg, N., Carlo, G., Murphy, B., & Van Court, N. (1995). Prosocial development in late adolescence: A longitudinal study. *Child Development, 66,* 1179–1197.

Eisenberg, N., & Fabes, R. A. (1994). Mothers' reactions to children's negative emotions: Relations to children's temperament and anger behavior. *Merrill-Palmer Quarterly, 40,* 138–156.

Eisenberg, N., & Fabes, R. A. (1998). Prosocial development. In W. Damon (Series Ed.) & N. Eisenberg (Vol. Ed.), *Handbook of child psychology: Vol. 3. Social, emotional, and personality development* (5th ed., pp. 701–778). New York: Wiley.

Eisenberg, N., Lennon, R., & Pasternack, J. F. (1986). Altruistic values and moral judgment. In N. Eisenberg (Ed.), *Altruistic emotion, cognition, and behavior.* Mahwah, NJ: Erlbaum.

Eisenberg, N., Martin, C. L., & Fabes, R. A. (1996). Gender development and gender effects. In D. C. Berliner & R. C. Calfee (Eds.), *Handbook of educational psychology.* New York: Macmillan.

Eisenberg, N., Zhou, Q., & Koller, S. (2001). Brazilian adolescents' prosocial moral judgment and behavior: Relations to sympathy, perspective taking, gender-role orientation, and demographic characteristics. *Child Development, 72,* 518–534.

Elder, A. D. (2002). Characterizing fifth grade students' epistemological beliefs in science. In B. K. Hofer & P. R. Pintrich (Eds.), *Personal epistemology: The psychology of beliefs about knowledge and knowing* (pp. 347–363). Mahwah, NJ: Erlbaum.

Elia, J. P. (1994). Homophobia in the high school: A problem in need of a resolution. *Journal of Homosexuality, 77*(1), 177–185.

Elkind, D. (1981). *Children and adolescents: Interpretive essays on Jean Piaget* (3rd ed.). New York: Oxford University Press.

Ellenwood, S., & Ryan, K. (1991). Literature and morality: An experimental curriculum. In W. M. Kurtines & J. L. Gewirtz (Eds.), *Moral behavior and development: Vol. 3. Application.* Mahwah, NJ: Erlbaum.

Elliot, A. J. (2005). A conceptual history of the achievement goal construct. In A. J. Elliot & C. S. Dweck (Eds.), *Handbook of competence and motivation* (pp. 52–72). New York: Guilford Press.

Elliot, A. J., & Dweck, C. S. (2005a). Competence and motivation: Competence as the core of achievement motivation. In A. J. Elliot & C. S. Dweck (Eds.), *Handbook of competence and motivation* (pp. 3–12). New York: Guilford Press.

Elliot, A. J., & Dweck, C. S. (Eds.). (2005b). *Handbook of competence and motivation.* New York: Guilford Press.

Elliot, A. J., & McGregor, H. A. (2000, April). Approach and avoidance goals and autonomous-controlled regulation: Empirical and conceptual relations. In A. Assor (Chair), *Self-determination theory and achievement goal theory: Convergences, divergences, and educational implications.* Symposium conducted at the annual meeting of the American Educational Research Association, New Orleans, LA.

Elliot, A. J., Shell, M. M., Henry, K. B., & Maier, M. A. (2005). Achievement goals, performance contingencies, and performance attainment: An experimental test. *Journal of Educational Psychology, 97,* 630–640.

Elliott, D. J. (1995). *Music matters: A new philosophy of music education.* New York: Oxford University Press.

Elliott, S. N., & Busse, R. T. (1991). Social skills assessment and intervention with children and

adolescents. *School Psychology International, 12,* 63–83.

Ellis, E. S., & Friend, P. (1991). Adolescents with learning disabilities. In B. Y. L. Wong (Ed.), *Learning about learning disabilities.* San Diego, CA: Academic Press.

Ellis, W. E., & Zarbatany, L. (2007). Peer group status as a moderator of group influence on children's deviant, aggressive, and prosocial behavior. *Child Development, 78,* 1240–1254.

Ellison, N. B., Steinfield, C., & Lampe, C. (2007). The benefits of *Facebook* "friends": Social capital and college students' use of online social network sites. *Journal of Computer-Mediated Communication, 12,* 1143–1168.

El-Sheikh, M., Kouros, C. D., Erath, S., Cummings, E. M., Keller, P., & Staton, L. (2009). Marital conflict and children's externalizing behavior: Interactions between parasympathetic and sympathetic nervous system activity. *Monographs of the Society for Research in Child Development, 74*(1, Serial No. 292), 1–78.

Emmer, E. T. (1987). Classroom management and discipline. In V. Richardson-Koehler (Ed.), *Educators' handbook: A research perspective.* White Plains, NY: Longman.

Emmer, E. T. (1994, April). *Teacher emotions and classroom management.* Paper presented at the annual meeting of the American Educational Research Association, New Orleans, LA.

Emmer, E. T., & Evertson, C. M. (1981). Synthesis of research on classroom management. *Educational Leadership, 38*(4), 342–347.

Emmer, E. T., & Evertson, C. M. (2009). *Classroom management for middle and high school teachers* (8th ed.). Upper Saddle River, NJ: Pearson Education.

Emmer, E. T., & Gerwels, M. C. (2006). Classroom management in middle and high school classrooms. In C. M. Evertson & C. S. Weinstein (Eds.), *Handbook of classroom management: Research, practice, and contemporary issues* (pp. 407–437). Mahwah, NJ: Erlbaum.

Emmer, E. T., & Stough, L. M. (2001). Classroom management: A critical part of educational psychology, with implications for teacher education. *Educational Psychologist, 36,* 103–112.

Empson, S. B. (1999). Equal sharing and shared meaning: The development of fraction concepts in a first-grade classroom. *Cognition and Instruction, 17,* 283–342.

Engle, R. A. (2006). Framing interactions to foster generative learning: A situative explanation of transfer in a community of learners classroom. *Journal of the Learning Sciences, 15,* 451–498.

Engle, R. A., & Conant, F. R. (2002). Guiding principles for fostering productive disciplinary engagement: Explaining an emergent argument in a community of learners classroom. *Cognition and Instruction, 20,* 399–483.

Englemann, S., & Carnine, D. (1982). *Theory of instruction: Principles and applications.* New York: Irvington.

Entwisle, N. J., & Ramsden, P. (1983). *Understanding student learning.* London: Croom Helm.

Epstein, J. L. (1986). Friendship selection: Developmental and environmental influences. In E. Mueller & C. Cooper (Eds.), *Process and outcome in peer relationships* (pp. 129–160). New York: Academic Press.

Epstein, J. L. (1989). Family structures and student motivation. In R. E. Ames & C. Ames (Eds.), *Research on motivation in education: Vol. 3. Goals and cognitions* (pp. 259–295). New York: Academic Press.

Epstein, J. L. (1996). Perspectives and previews on research and policy for school, family, and community partnerships. In A. Booth & J. F. Dunn (Eds.), *Family-school links: How do they affect educational outcomes?* Mahwah, NJ: Erlbaum.

Epstein, J. S. (1998). Introduction: Generation X, youth culture, and identity. In J. S. Epstein (Ed.), *Youth culture: Identity in a postmodern world.* Malden, MA: Blackwell.

Erath, S. A., El-Sheikh, M., & Cummings, E. M. (2009). Harsh parenting and child externalizing behavior: Skin conductance level reactivity as a moderator. *Child Development, 80,* 578–592.

Ericsson, K. A. (2003). The acquisition of expert performance as problem solving. In J. E. Davidson & R. J. Sternberg (Eds.), *The psychology of problem solving* (pp. 31–83). Cambridge, England: Cambridge University Press.

Eriks-Brophy, A., & Crago, M. B. (1994). Transforming classroom discourse: An Inuit example. *Language and Education, 8*(3), 105–122.

Erikson, E. H. (1963). *Childhood and society* (2nd ed.). New York: Norton.

Erikson, E. H. (1972). *Eight ages of man.* In C. S. Lavatelli & F. Stendler (Eds.), *Readings in child behavior and child development.* San Diego, CA: Harcourt Brace Jovanovich.

Erwin, P. (1993). *Friendship and peer relations in children.* Chichester, England: Wiley.

Esmonde, I. (2009). Ideas and identities: Supporting equity in cooperative mathematics learning. *Review of Educational Research, 79,* 1008–1043.

Espelage, D. L., Holt, M. K., & Henkel, R. R. (2003). Examination of peer-group contextual effects on aggression during early adolescence. *Child Development, 74,* 205–220.

Espelage, D. L., & Swearer, S. M. (Eds.). (2004). *Bullying in American schools: A social-ecological perspective on prevention and intervention.* Mahwah, NJ: Erlbaum.

Evans, E. D., & Craig, D. (1990). Teacher and student perceptions of academic cheating in middle and senior high schools. *Journal of Educational Research, 84*(1), 44–52.

Evans, E. M. (2001). Cognitive and contextual factors in the emergence of diverse belief systems: Creation versus evolution. *Cognitive Psychology, 42,* 217–266.

Evans, E. M. (2008). Conceptual change and evolutionary biology: A developmental analysis. In S. Vosniadou (Ed.), *International handbook on conceptual change* (pp. 263–294). New York: Routledge.

Evans, G. W. (2004). The environment of childhood poverty. *American Psychologist, 59,* 77–92.

Evans, G. W., & Kim, P. (2007). Childhood poverty and health: Cumulative risk exposure and stress dysregulation. *Psychological Science, 18,* 953–957.

Evans, J. J., Floyd, R. G., McGrew, K. S., & Leforge, M. H. (2001). The relations between measures of Cattell-Horn-Carroll (CHC) cognitive abilities and reading achievement during childhood and adolescence. *School Psychology Review, 31,* 246–262.

Evans-Winters, V., & Ivie, C. (2009). Lost in the shuffle: Re-calling a critical pedagogy for urban girls. In S. R. Steinberg (Ed.), *Diversity and multiculturalism: A reader* (pp. 411–421). New York: Peter Lang.

Evertson, C. M., & Emmer, E. T. (1982). Effective management at the beginning of the year in

junior high classes. *Journal of Educational Psychology, 74,* 485–498.

Evertson, C. M., & Emmer, E. T. (2009). *Classroom management for elementary teachers* (8th ed.). Upper Saddle River, NJ: Pearson Education.

Evertson, C. M., & Harris, A. H. (1992). What we know about managing classrooms. *Educational Leadership, 49*(7), 74–78.

Evertson, C. M., & Weinstein, C. S. (Eds.). (2006). *Handbook of classroom management: Research, practice, and contemporary issues.* Mahwah, NJ: Erlbaum.

Eysenck, M. W. (1992). *Anxiety: The cognitive perspective.* Hove, England: Erlbaum.

Eysink, T. H. S., de Jong, T., Berthold, K., Kolloffel, B., Opfermann, M., & Wouters, P. (2009). Learner performance in multimedia learning arrangements: An analysis across instructional approaches. *American Educational Research Journal, 46,* 1107–1149.

Fabos, B., & Young, M. D. (1999). Telecommunication in the classroom: Rhetoric versus reality. *Review of Educational Research, 69,* 217–259.

Fahrmeier, E. D. (1978). The development of concrete operations among the Hausa. *Journal of Cross-Cultural Psychology, 9,* 23–44.

Fairchild, H. H., & Edwards-Evans, S. (1990). African American dialects and schooling: A review. In A. M. Padilla, H. H. Fairchild, & C. M. Valadez (Eds.), *Bilingual education: Issues and strategies.* Newbury Park, CA: Sage.

Fall, R., Webb, N. M., & Chudowsky, N. (2000). Group discussion and large-scale language arts assessment: Effects on students' comprehension. *American Educational Research Journal, 37,* 911–941.

Fantuzzo, J. W., King, J., & Heller, L. R. (1992). Effects of reciprocal peer tutoring on mathematics and school adjustment: A component analysis. *Journal of Educational Psychology, 84,* 331–339.

Farber, B., Mindel, C. H., & Lazerwitz, B. (1988). The Jewish American family. In C. H. Mindel, R. W. Habenstein, & R. Wright (Eds.), *Ethnic families in America: Patterns and variations.* New York: Elsevier.

Farkas, G. (2008). Quantitative studies of oppositional culture: Arguments and evidence. In J. U. Ogbu (Ed.), *Minority status, oppositional culture, and schooling* (pp. 312–347). New York: Routledge.

Farrell, E. (1990). *Hanging in and dropping out: Voices of at-risk high school students.* New York: Teachers College Press.

Farver, J. A. M., & Branstetter, W. H. (1994). Preschoolers' prosocial responses to their peers' distress. *Developmental Psychology, 30,* 334–341.

Farwell, L., & Weiner, B. (1996). Self-perception of fairness in individual and group contexts. *Personality and Social Psychology Bulletin, 22,* 867–881.

Feather, N. T. (1982). *Expectations and actions: Expectancy-value models in psychology.* Mahwah, NJ: Erlbaum.

Feldhusen, J. F., & Treffinger, D. J. (1980). *Creative thinking and problem solving in gifted education.* Dubuque, IA: Kendall/Hunt.

Feldhusen, J. F., Van Winkle, L., & Ehle, D. A. (1996). Is it acceleration or simply appropriate instruction for precocious youth? *Teaching Exceptional Children, 28*(3), 48–51.

Feldman, A. F., & Matjasko, J. L. (2005). The role of school-based extracurricular activities in adolescent development: A comprehensive review

and future directions. *Review of Educational Research, 75,* 159–210.

Feltz, D. L., Chase, M. A., Moritz, S. E., & Sullivan, P. J. (1999). A conceptual model of coaching efficacy: Preliminary investigation and instrument development. *Journal of Educational Psychology, 91,* 765–776.

Fennema, E. (1987). Sex-related differences in education: Myths, realities, and interventions. In V. Richardson-Koehler (Ed.), *Educators' handbook: A research perspective.* White Plains, NY: Longman.

Fenning, P. A., & Bohanon, H. (2006). Schoolwide discipline policies: An analysis of discipline codes of conduct. In C. M. Evertson & C. S. Weinstein (Eds.), *Handbook of classroom management: Research, practice, and contemporary issues* (pp. 1021–1039). Mahwah, NJ: Erlbaum.

Ferguson, E. L., & Hegarty, M. (1995). Learning with real machines or diagrams: Application of knowledge to real-world problems. *Cognition and Instruction, 13,* 129–160.

Ferguson, R. (1998). Can schools narrow the Black-White test score gap? In C. Jencks & M. Phillips (Eds.), *The Black-White test score gap* (pp. 318–374). Washington, DC: Brookings Institute.

Ferrari, M., & Elik, N. (2003). Influences on intentional conceptual change. In G. M. Sinatra & P. R. Pintrich (Eds.), *Intentional conceptual change* (pp. 21–54). Mahwah, NJ: Erlbaum.

Feuerstein, R., Feuerstein, R., & Gross, S. (1997). The Learning Potential Assessment Device. In D. P. Flanagan, J. L. Genshaft, & P. L. Harrison (Eds.), *Contemporary intellectual assessment: Theories, tests, and issues* (pp. 297–313). New York: Guilford Press.

Feuerstein, R., Klein, P. R., & Tannenbaum, A. (Eds.). (1991). *Mediated learning experience: Theoretical, psychosocial, and learning implications.* London: Freund.

Fiedler, E. D., Lange, R. E., & Winebrenner, S. (1993). In search of reality: Unraveling the myths about tracking, ability grouping and the gifted. *Roeper Review, 16*(1), 4–7.

Fiedler, K. (2008). Language: A toolbox for sharing and influencing social reality. *Perspectives on Psychological Science, 3,* 38–47.

Filax, G. (2007). Queer invisibility: The case of Ellen, Michel, and Oscar. In S. Books (Ed.), *Invisible children in the society and its schools* (3rd ed., pp. 213–234). Mahwah, NJ: Erlbaum.

Finders, M., & Lewis, C. (1994). Why some parents don't come to school. *Educational Leadership, 51*(8), 50–54.

Fingerhut, L. A., & Christoffel, K. K. (2002). Firearm-related death and injury among children and adolescents. *The Future of Children, 12*(2), 25–37.

Finkelhor, D., & Ormrod, R. (2000, December). *Juvenile victims of property crimes.* Washington, DC: U.S. Department of Justice, Office of Justice Programs, Office of Juvenile Justice and Delinquency Prevention.

Finn, J. D. (1989). Withdrawing from school. *Review of Educational Research, 59,* 117–142.

Finn, J. D., Pannozzo, G. M., & Achilles, C. M. (2003). The "why's" of class size: Student behavior in small classes. *Review of Educational Research, 73,* 321–368.

Finnigan, K. S., & Gross, B. (2007). Do accountability policy sanctions influence teacher motivation? Lessons from Chicago's low-performing schools. *American Educational Research Journal, 44,* 594–629.

Fischer, K. W., & Daley, S. G. (2007). Connecting cognitive science and neuroscience to education: Potentials and pitfalls in inferring executive processes. In L. Meltzer (Ed.), *Executive function in education: From theory to practice* (pp. 55–72). New York: Guilford Press.

Fischer, K. W., & Immordino-Yang, M. H. (2006). Cognitive development and education: From dynamic general structure to specific learning and teaching. In W. Damon & R. M. Lerner (Series Eds.), D. Kuhn & R. Siegler (Vol. Eds.), *Handbook of child psychology: Vol. 1. Cognition, perception, and language* (6th ed.). New York: Wiley.

Fischer, K. W., Knight, C. C., & Van Parys, M. (1993). Analyzing diversity in developmental pathways: Methods and concepts. In R. Case & W. Edelstein (Eds.), *The new structuralism in cognitive development: Theory and research on individual pathways.* Basel, Switzerland: Karger.

Fisher, W. W., & Mazur, J. E. (1997). Basic and applied research on choice responding. *Journal of Applied Behavior Analysis, 30,* 387–410.

Fiske, A. P., & Fiske, S. T. (2007). Social relationships in our species and cultures. In S. Kitayama & D. Cohen (Eds.), *Handbook of cultural psychology* (pp. 283–306). New York: Guilford Press.

Flanagan, C. A., & Faison, N. (2001). Youth civic development: Implications of research for social policy and programs. *Social Policy Report of the Society for Research in Child Development, 15*(1), 1–14.

Flanagan, C. A., & Tucker, C. J. (1999). Adolescents' explanations for political issues: Concordance with their views of self and society. *Developmental Psychology, 35,* 1198–1209.

Flanagan, D. P., & Ortiz, S. O. (2001). *Essentials of cross-battery assessment.* New York: Wiley.

Flavell, J. H. (1963). *The developmental psychology of Jean Piaget.* New York: Van Nostrand Reinhold.

Flavell, J. H. (1994). Cognitive development: Past, present, and future. In R. D. Parke, P. A. Ornstein, J. J. Rieser, & C. Zahn-Waxler (Eds.), *A century of developmental psychology.* Washington, DC: American Psychological Association.

Flavell, J. H. (2000). Development of children's knowledge about the mental world. *International Journal of Behavioral Development, 24*(1), 15–23.

Flavell, J. H., Friedrichs, A. G., & Hoyt, J. D. (1970). Developmental changes in memorization processes. *Cognitive Psychology, 1,* 324–340.

Flavell, J. H., Green, F. L., & Flavell, E. R. (1995). Young children's knowledge about thinking. *Monographs of the Society for Research in Child Development, 60*(1, Serial No. 243).

Flavell, J. H., & Miller, P. H. (1998). Social cognition. In W. Damon (Series Ed.), D. Kuhn & R. S. Siegler (Vol. Eds.), *Handbook of child psychology: Vol. 2. Cognition, perception, and language* (5th ed.). New York: Wiley.

Flavell, J. H., Miller, P. H., & Miller, S. A. (2002). *Cognitive development* (4th ed.). Upper Saddle River, NJ: Prentice Hall.

Fleege, P. O., Charlesworth, R., & Burts, D. C. (1992). Stress begins in kindergarten: A look at behavior during standardized testing. *Journal of Research in Childhood Education, 7*(1), 20–26.

Fletcher, J. M., Lyon, G. R., Fuchs, L. S., & Barnes, M. A. (2007). *Learning disabilities: From identification to intervention.* New York: Guilford Press.

Fletcher, K. L., & Bray, N. W. (1995). External and verbal strategies in children with and without mild mental retardation. *American Journal on Mental Retardation, 99,* 363–475.

Flieller, A. (1999). Comparison of the development of formal thought in adolescent cohorts aged 10 to 15 years (1967–1996 and 1972–1993). *Developmental Psychology, 35,* 1048–1058.

Flood, W. A., Wilder, D. A., Flood, A. L., & Masuda, A. (2002). Peer-mediated reinforcement plus prompting as treatment for off-task behavior in children with attention deficit hyperactivity disorder. *Journal of Applied Behavior Analysis, 35,* 199–204.

Flum, H., & Kaplan, A. (2006). Exploratory orientation as an educational goal. *Educational Psychologist, 41,* 99–110.

Flynn, J. R. (2003). Movies about intelligence: The limitations of *g. Current Directions in Psychological Science, 12,* 95–99.

Flynn, J. R. (2007). *What is intelligence? Beyond the Flynn effect.* New York: Cambridge University Press.

Fontaine, R. G., Yang, C., Dodge, K. A., Bates, J. E., & Pettit, G. S. (2008). Testing an individual systems model of response evaluation and decision (RED) and antisocial behavior across adolescence. *Child Development, 79,* 462–475.

Foos, P. W., & Fisher, R. P. (1988). Using tests as learning opportunities. *Journal of Educational Psychology, 80,* 179–183.

Ford, D. Y. (1996). *Reversing underachievement among gifted black students.* New York: Teachers College Press.

Ford, M. E., & Nichols, C. W. (1991). Using goal assessments to identify motivational patterns and facilitate behavioral regulation and achievement. In M. Maehr & P. R. Pintrich (Eds.), *Advances in motivation and achievement: Vol. 7. Goals and self-regulatory processes.* Greenwich, CT: JAI Press.

Ford, M. E., & Smith, P. R. (2007). Thriving with social purpose: An integrative approach to the development of optimal human functioning. *Educational Psychologist, 42,* 153–171.

Forget-Dubois, N., Lemelin, J.-P., Bolvin, M., Dionne, G., Séguin, J. R., Vitaro, F., et al. (2007). Predicting early school achievement with the EDI: A longitudinal population-based study. *Early Education and Development. Special Issue: The Early Development Instrument, 18,* 405–426.

Försterling, F., & Morgenstern, M. (2002). Accuracy of self-assessment and task performance: Does it pay to know the truth? *Journal of Educational Psychology, 94,* 576–585.

Fosnot, C. T. (1996). Constructivism: A psychological theory of learning. In C. T. Fosnot (Ed.), *Constructivism: Theory, perspectives, and practice.* New York: Teachers College Press.

Fowler, S. A., & Baer, D. M. (1981). "Do I have to be good all day?" The timing of delayed reinforcement as a factor in generalization. *Journal of Applied Behavior Analysis, 14,* 13–24.

Fox, E. (2009). The role of reader characteristics in processing and learning from informational text. *Review of Educational Research, 79,* 197–261.

Fox, N. A., Henderson, H. A., Rubin, K. H., Calkins, S. D., & Schmidt, L. A. (2001). Continuity and discontinuity of behavioral inhibition and exuberance: Psychophysical and behavioral influences across the first four years of life. *Child Development, 72,* 1–21.

Fox, P. W., & LeCount, J. (1991, April). *When more is less: Faculty misestimation of student learning.*

Paper presented at the annual meeting of the American Educational Research Association, Chicago.

Frankenberger, K. D. (2000). Adolescent egocentrism: A comparison among adolescents and adults. *Journal of Adolescence, 23,* 343–354.

Frazier, B. N., Gelman, S. A., & Wellman, H. M. (2009). Preschoolers' search for explanatory information within adult–child conversation. *Child Development, 80,* 1592–1611.

Frederiksen, J. R., & Collins, A. (1989). A systems approach to educational testing. *Educational Researcher, 18*(9), 27–32.

Frederiksen, N. (1984a). Implications of cognitive theory for instruction in problem-solving. *Review of Educational Research, 54,* 363–407.

Frederiksen, N. (1984b). The real test bias: Influences of testing on teaching and learning. *American Psychologist, 39,* 193–202.

Fredrickson, B. (2009). *Positivity: Groundbreaking research reveals how to embrace the hidden strength of positive emotions, overcome negativity, and thrive.* New York: Crown Publishing.

The Freedom Writers (with Gruwell, E.). (1999). *The Freedom Writers diary: How a teacher and 150 teens used writing to change themselves and the world around them.* New York: Broadway Books.

Freeman, K. E., Gutman, L. M., & Midgley, C. (2002). Can achievement goal theory enhance our understanding of the motivation and performance of African American young adolescents? In C. Midgley (Ed.), *Goals, goal structures, and patterns of adaptive learning* (pp. 175–204). Mahwah, NJ: Erlbaum.

Frenzel, A. C., Goetz, T., Lüdtke, O., Pekrun, R., & Sutton, R. E. (2009). Emotional transmission in the classroom: Exploring the relationship between teacher and student enjoyment. *Journal of Educational Psychology, 101,* 705–716.

Frey, K. S., Hirschstein, M. K., Edstrom, L. V., & Snell, J. L. (2009). Observed reductions in school bullying, nonbullying aggression, and destructive bystander behavior: A longitudinal evaluation. *Journal of Educational Psychology, 101,* 466–481.

Fries, S., Dietz, F., & Schmid, S. (2008). Motivational interference in learning: The impact of leisure alternatives on subsequent self-regulation. *Contemporary Educational Psychology, 33,* 119–133.

Frisbie, D. A., & Waltman, K. K. (1992). Developing a personal grading plan. *Educational Measurement: Issues and Practice, 11*(3), 35–42. Reprinted in K. M. Cauley, F. Linder, & J. H. McMillan (Eds.), 1994, *Educational psychology 94/95.* Guilford, CT: Dushkin.

Frost, J. L., Shin, D., & Jacobs, P. J. (1998). Physical environments and children's play. In O. N. Saracho & B. Spodek (Eds.), *Multiple perspectives on play in early childhood education.* Albany: State University of New York Press.

Fry, A. F., & Hale, S. (1996). Processing speed, working memory, and fluid intelligence. *Psychological Science, 7,* 237–241.

Fuchs, D., Fuchs, L. S., Mathes, P. G., & Simmons, D. C. (1997). Peer-assisted learning strategies: Making classrooms more responsive to diversity. *American Educational Research Journal, 34,* 174–206.

Fuchs, L. S., Compton, D. L., Fuchs, D., Hollenbeck, K. N., Craddock, C. F., & Hamlett, C. L. (2008). Dynamic assessment of algebraic learning in predicting third graders' development of mathematical problem solving. *Journal of Educational Psychology, 100,* 829–850.

Fuchs, L. S., Compton, D. L., Fuchs, D., Paulsen, K., Bryant, J. D., & Hamlett, C. L. (2005). The prevention, identification, and cognitive determinants of math difficulty. *Journal of Educational Psychology, 97,* 493–513.

Fuchs, L. S., Fuchs, D., Craddock, C., Hollenbeck, K. N., Hamlett, C. L., & Schatschneider, C. (2008). Effects of small-group tutoring with and without validated classroom instruction on at-risk, students' math problem solving: Are two tiers of prevention better than one? *Journal of Educational Psychology, 100,* 491–509.

Fuchs, L. S., Fuchs, D., Karns, K., Hamlett, C. L., Dutka, S., & Katzaroff, M. (1996). The relation between student ability and the quality and effectiveness of explanations. *American Educational Research Journal, 33,* 631–664.

Fuchs, L. S., Fuchs, D., Karns, K., Hamlett, C. L., Katzaroff, M., & Dutka, S. (1997). Effects of task-focused goals on low-achieving students with and without learning disabilities. *American Educational Research Journal, 34,* 513–543.

Fueyo, V., & Bushell, D., Jr. (1998). Using number line procedures and peer tutoring to improve the mathematics computation of low-performing first graders. *Journal of Applied Behavior Analysis, 31,* 417–430.

Fujimura, N. (2001). Facilitating children's proportional reasoning: A model of reasoning processes and effects of intervention on strategy change. *Journal of Educational Psychology, 93,* 589–603.

Fuligni, A. J. (1998). The adjustment of children from immigrant families. *Current Directions in Psychological Science, 7,* 99–103.

Fuligni, A. J., & Hardway, C. (2004). Preparing diverse adolescents for the transition to adulthood. *The Future of Children, 14*(2), 99–119.

Fuller, B., Wright, J., Gesicki, K., & Kang, E. (2007). Gauging growth: How to judge No Child Left Behind. *Educational Researcher, 36*(5), 268–278.

Fuller, M. L. (2001). Multicultural concerns and classroom management. In C. A. Grant & M. L. Gomez, *Campus and classroom: Making schooling multicultural* (2nd ed., pp. 109–134). Upper Saddle River, NJ: Merrill/Prentice Hall.

Furman, W., Brown, B. B., & Feiring, C. (Eds.). (1999). *The development of romantic relationships in adolescence.*. Cambridge, England: Cambridge University Press.

Furman, W., & Buhrmester, D. (1992). Age and sex differences in perceptions of networks and personal relationships. *Child Development, 63,* 103–115.

Furman, W., & Collins, W. A. (2009). Adolescent romantic relationships and experiences. In K. H. Rubin, W. M. Bukowski, & B. Laursen (Eds.), *Handbook of peer interactions, relationships, and groups* (pp. 341–360). New York: Guilford Press.

Furrer, C., & Skinner, E. (2003). Sense of relatedness as a factor in children's academic engagement and performance. *Journal of Educational Psychology, 95,* 148–162.

Gabriele, A. J. (2007). The influence of achievement goals on the constructive activity of low achievers during collaborative problem solving. *British Journal of Educational Psychology, 77,* 121–141.

Gabriele, A. J., & Boody, R. M. (2001, April). *The influence of achievement goals on the constructive activity of low achievers during collaborative problem solving.* Paper presented at the annual meeting of the American Educational Research Association, Seattle, WA.

Gage, N. L. (1991). The obviousness of social and educational research results. *Educational Researcher, 20*(1), 10–16.

Gagné, R. M. (1985). *The conditions of learning and theory of instruction* (4th ed.). New York: Holt, Rinehart & Winston.

Gaines, M. L., & Davis, M. (1990, April). *Accuracy of teacher prediction of elementary student achievement.* Paper presented at the annual meeting of the American Educational Research Association, Boston.

Galambos, N. L., Barker, E. T., & Almeida, D. M. (2003). Parents *do* matter: Trajectories of change in externalizing and internalizing problems in early adolescence. *Child Development, 74,* 578–594.

Gallagher, J. J. (1991). Personal patterns of underachievement. *Journal for the Education of the Gifted, 14,* 221–233.

Gallimore, R., & Goldenberg, C. (2001). Analyzing cultural models and settings to connect minority achievement and school improvement research. *Educational Psychologist, 36,* 45–56.

Ganea, P. A., Shutts, K., Spelke, E. S., & DeLoache, J. S. (2007). Thinking of things unseen: Infants' use of language to update mental representations. *Psychological Science, 18,* 734–739.

Garbarino, J., Bradshaw, C. P., & Vorrasi, J. A. (2002). Mitigating the effects of gun violence on children and youth. *The Future of Children, 12*(2), 73–85.

Garbe, G., & Guy, D. (2006, Summer). No homework left behind. *Educational Leadership* (online issue). Retrieved May 23, 2007, from the Association for Supervision and Curriculum Development Web site: www.ascd.org/portal/site/ascd/menuitem.459dee008f99653fb85516f762108a0c

Garcia, E. E. (1992). "Hispanic" children: Theoretical, empirical, and related policy issues. *Educational Psychology Review, 4,* 69–93.

Garcia, E. E. (1994). *Understanding and meeting the challenge of student cultural diversity.* Boston: Houghton Mifflin.

García, E. E. (1995). Educating Mexican American students: Past treatment and recent developments in theory, research, policy, and practice. In J. A. Banks & C. A. M. Banks (Eds.), *Handbook of research on multicultural education.* New York: Macmillan.

Garcia, E. E. (2005, April). *Any test in English is a test of English: Implications for high stakes testing.* Paper presented at the annual meeting of the American Educational Research Association, Montreal.

Gardiner, H. W., & Kosmitzki, C. (2008). *Lives across cultures: Cross-cultural human development* (4th ed.). Boston: Allyn & Bacon.

Gardner, H. (1983). *Frames of mind: The theory of multiple intelligences.* New York: Basic Books.

Gardner, H. (1995). Reflections on multiple intelligences: Myths and messages. *Phi Delta Kappan, 77,* 200–209.

Gardner, H. (1998, April). *Where to draw the line: The perils of new paradigms.* Paper presented at the annual meeting of the American Educational Research Association, San Diego, CA.

Gardner, H. (1999). *Intelligence reframed: Multiple intelligences for the 21st century.* New York: Basic Books.

Gardner, H. (2000a). A case against spiritual intelligence. *International Journal for the Psychology of Religion, 10*(1), 27–34.

Gardner, H. (2000b). *The disciplined mind: Beyond facts and standardized tests, the K–12 education that every child deserves.* New York: Penguin Books.

Gardner, H. (2003, April). *Multiple intelligences after twenty years.* Paper presented at the annual meeting of the American Educational Research Association, Chicago.

Garibaldi, A. M. (1993). Creating prescriptions for success in urban schools: Turning the corner on pathological explanations for academic failure. In T. M. Tomlinson (Ed.), *Motivating students to learn: Overcoming barriers to high achievement.* Berkeley, CA: McCutchan.

Garner, R., Brown, R., Sanders, S., & Menke, D. J. (1992). "Seductive details" and learning from text. In K. A. Renninger, S. Hidi, & A. Krapp (Eds.), *The role of interest in learning and development.* Mahwah, NJ: Erlbaum.

Garnier, H. E., Stein, J. A., & Jacobs, J. K. (1997). The process of dropping out of high school: A 19-year perspective. *American Educational Research Journal, 34,* 395–419.

Garrett, M. T., Bellon-Harn, M. L., Torres-Rivera, E., Garrett, J. T., & Roberts, L. C. (2003). Open hands, open hearts: Working with Native youth in the schools. *Intervention in School and Clinic, 38,* 225–236.

Gaskill, P. J. (2001, April). *Differential effects of reinforcement feedback and attributional feedback on second-graders' self-efficacy.* Paper presented at the annual meeting of the American Educational Research Association, Seattle, WA.

Gaskins, I. W., & Pressley, M. (2007). Teaching metacognitive strategies that address executive function processes within a schoolwide curriculum. In L. Meltzer (Ed.), *Executive function in education: From theory to practice* (pp. 261–286). New York: Guilford Press.

Gaskins, I. W., Satlow, E., & Pressley, M. (2007). Executive control of reading comprehension in the elementary school. In L. Meltzer (Ed.), *Executive function in education: From theory to practice* (pp. 194–215). New York: Guilford Press.

Gathercole, S. E., & Hitch, G. J. (1993). Developmental changes in short-term memory: A revised working memory perspective. In A. F. Collins, S. E. Gathercole, M. A. Conway, & P. E. Morris (Eds.), *Theories of memory.* Hove, England: Erlbaum.

Gaudry, E., & Bradshaw, G. D. (1971). The differential effect of anxiety on performance in progressive and terminal school examinations. In E. Gaudry & C. D. Spielberger (Eds.), *Anxiety and educational achievement.* Sydney, Australia: Wiley.

Gauvain, M. (2001). *The social context of cognitive development.* New York: Guilford Press.

Gavin, L. A., & Fuhrman, W. (1989). Age differences in adolescents' perceptions of their peer groups. *Developmental Psychology, 25,* 827–834.

Gay, G. (2006). Connections between classroom management and culturally responsive teaching. In C. M. Evertson & C. S. Weinstein (Eds.), *Handbook of classroom management: Research, practice, and contemporary issues* (pp. 343–370). Mahwah, NJ: Erlbaum.

Gayford, C. (1992). Patterns of group behavior in open-ended problem solving in science classes of 15-year-old students in England. *International Journal of Science Education, 14,* 41–49.

Gaynor, J., & Millham, J. (1976). Student performance and evaluation under variant teaching and testing methods in a large college course. *Journal of Educational Psychology, 68,* 312–317.

Gazelle, H., & Ladd, G. W. (2003). Anxious solitude and peer exclusion: A diathesis-stress model of internalizing trajectories in childhood. *Child Development, 74,* 257–278.

Geary, D. C. (1998). What is the function of mind and brain? *Educational Psychology Review, 10,* 377–387.

Geary, D. C. (2005). Folk knowledge and academic learning. In B. J. Ellis & D. F. Bjorklund (Eds.), *Origins of the social mind: Evolutionary psychology and child development* (pp. 493–519). New York: Guilford Press.

Gehlbach, H., Brown, S. W., Ioannou, A., Boyer, M. A., Hudson, N., Niv-Solomon, A., et al. (2008). Increasing interest in social studies: Social perspective taking and self-efficacy in stimulating stimulations. *Contemporary Educational Psychology, 33,* 894–914.

Geiger, M. A. (1997). An examination of the relationship between answer changing, testwiseness and examination performance. *Journal of Experimental Education, 66,* 49–60.

Gelman, S. A. (2003). *The essential child: Origins of essentialism in everyday thought.* New York: Oxford University Press.

Gelman, S. A., & Kalish, C. W. (2006). Conceptual development. In W. Damon & R. M. Lerner (Series Eds.), D. Kuhn & R. Siegler (Vol. Eds.), *Handbook of child psychology: Vol. 1. Cognition, perception, and language* (6th ed.). New York: Wiley.

Genova, W. J., & Walberg, H. J. (1984). Enhancing integration in urban high schools. In D. E. Bartz & M. L. Maehr (Eds.), *Advances in motivation and achievement: Vol. 1. The effects of school desegregation on motivation and achievement.* Greenwich, CT: JAI Press.

Gentry, M., Gable, R. K., & Rizza, M. G. (2002). Students' perceptions of classroom activities: Are there grade-level and gender differences? *Journal of Educational Psychology, 94,* 539–544.

Gerard, J. M., & Buehler, C. (2004). Cumulative environmental risk and youth maladjustment: The role of youth attributes. *Child Development, 75,* 1832–1849.

Gershoff, E. T., Aber, J. L., Raver, C. C., & Lennon, M. C. (2007). Income is not enough: Incorporating material hardship into models of income associations with parenting and child development. *Child Development, 78,* 70–95.

Gerst, M. S. (1971). Symbolic coding processes in observational learning. *Journal of Personality and Social Psychology, 19,* 7–17.

Gettinger, M. (1988). Methods of proactive classroom management. *School Psychology Review, 17,* 227–242.

Gettinger, M., & Kohler, K. M. (2006). Process-outcome approaches to classroom management and effective teaching. In C. M. Evertson & C. S. Weinstein (Eds.), *Handbook of classroom management: Research, practice, and contemporary issues* (pp. 73–95). Mahwah, NJ: Erlbaum.

Ghetti, S., & Angelini, L. (2008). The development of recollection and familiarity in childhood and adolescence: Evidence from the dual-process signal detection model. *Child Development, 79,* 339–358.

Giaconia, R. M. (1988). Teacher questioning and wait-time (Doctoral dissertation, Stanford University, 1988). *Dissertation Abstracts International, 49,* 462A.

Gibbs, J. C. (1995). The cognitive developmental perspective. In W. M. Kurtines & J. L. Gewirtz (Eds.), *Moral development: An introduction.* Boston: Allyn & Bacon.

Gick, M. L., & Holyoak, K. J. (1987). The cognitive basis of knowledge transfer. In S. M. Cormier & J. D. Hagman (Eds.), *Transfer of learning: Contemporary research and applications.* San Diego, CA: Academic Press.

Giedd, J. N., Blumenthal, J., Jeffries, N. O., Castellanos, F. X., Liu, H., Zijdenbos, A., et al. (1999). Brain development during childhood and adolescence: A longitudinal MRI study. *Nature Neuroscience, 2,* 861–863.

Gijbels, D., Dochy, F., Van den Bossche, P., & Segers, M. (2005). Effects of problem-based learning: A meta-analysis from the angle of assessment. *Review of Educational Research, 75,* 27–61.

Gillies, R. M., & Ashman, A. D. (1998). Behavior and interactions of children in cooperative groups in lower and middle elementary grades. *Journal of Educational Psychology, 90,* 746–757.

Gilligan, C. F. (1982). *In a different voice.* Cambridge, MA: Harvard University Press.

Gilligan, C. F. (1987). Moral orientation and moral development. In E. F. Kittay & D. T. Meyers (Eds.), *Women and moral theory.* Totowa, NJ: Rowman & Littlefield.

Gilliland, H. (1988). Discovering and emphasizing the positive aspects of the culture. In H. Gilliland & J. Reyhner (Eds.), *Teaching the Native American.* Dubuque, IA: Kendall/Hunt.

Ginsburg, H. P., Cannon, J., Eisenband, J., & Pappas, S. (2006). Mathematical thinking and learning. In K. McCartney & D. Phillips (Eds.), *Blackwell handbook of early childhood development* (pp. 208–229). Malden, MA: Blackwell.

Ginsburg-Block, M. D., Rohrbeck, C. A., & Fantuzzo, J. W. (2006). A meta-analytic review of social, self-concept, and behavioral outcomes of peer-assisted learning. *Journal of Educational Psychology, 98,* 732–749.

Girotto, V., & Light, P. (1993). The pragmatic bases of children's reasoning. In P. Light & G. Butterworth (Eds.), *Context and cognition: Ways of learning and knowing.* Mahwah, NJ: Erlbaum.

Glaser, D. (2000). Child abuse and neglect and the brain: A review. *Journal of Child Psychology and Psychiatry and Allied Disciplines, 41,* 97–116.

Glover, J. A. (1989). The "testing" phenomenon: Not gone but nearly forgotten. *Journal of Educational Psychology, 81,* 392–399.

Glover, J. A., Ronning, R. R., & Reynolds, C. R. (Eds.). (1989). *Handbook of creativity.* New York: Plenum Press.

Gnepp, J. (1989). Children's use of personal information to understand other people's feelings. In C. Saarni & P. L. Harris (Eds.), *Children's understanding of emotion.* Cambridge, England: Cambridge University Press.

Goddard, R. D., Hoy, W. K., & Woolfolk Hoy, A. (2000). Collective teacher efficacy: Its meaning, measure, and impact on student achievement. *American Educational Research Journal, 37,* 479–507.

Goetz, T., Frenzel, A. C., Hall, N. C., & Pekrun, R. (2008). Antecedents of academic emotions: Testing the internal/external frame of reference model for academic enjoyment. *Contemporary Educational Psychology, 33,* 9–33.

Goldenberg, C. (1992). The limits of expectations: A case for case knowledge about teacher expectancy effects. *American Educational Research Journal, 29,* 517–544.

Goldenberg, C. (2001). Making schools work for low-income families in the 21st century. In S. B. Neuman & D. K. Dickinson (Eds.), *Handbook of early literacy research* (pp. 211–231). New York: Guilford Press.

Goldenberg, C., Gallimore, R., Reese, L., & Garnier, H. (2001). Cause or effect? A longitudinal study of immigrant Latino parents' aspirations and expectations, and their children's school performance. *American Educational Research Journal, 38,* 547–582.

Goldstein, L. S., & Lake, V. E. (2000). "Love, love, and more love for children": Exploring preservice teachers' understanding of caring. *Teaching and Teacher Education, 16,* 861–872.

Goldstein, N. E., Arnold, D. H., Rosenberg, J. L., Stowe, R. M., & Ortiz, C. (2001). Contagion of aggression in day care classrooms as a function of peer and teacher responses. *Journal of Educational Psychology, 93,* 708–719.

Goldstein, S., & Brooks, R. B. (Eds.). (2006). *Handbook of resilience in children.* New York: Springer.

Goldston, D. B., Molock, S. D., Whitbeck, L. B., Murakami, J. L., Zayas, L. H., & Nagayama Hall, G. C. (2008). Cultural considerations in adolescent suicide prevention and psychosocial treatment. *American Psychologist, 63,* 14–31.

Gollwitzer, P. M., & Bargh, J. A. (2005). Automaticity in goal pursuit. In A. J. Elliot & C. S. Dweck (Eds.), *Handbook of competence and motivation* (pp. 624–646). New York: Guilford Press.

Good, C., Aronson, J., & Inzlicht, M. (2003). Improving adolescents' standardized test performance: An intervention to reduce the effects of stereotype threat. *Journal of Applied Developmental Psychology, 24,* 645–662.

Good, T. L., & Brophy, J. E. (1994). *Looking in classrooms* (6th ed.). New York: HarperCollins.

Good, T. L., McCaslin, M. M., & Reys, B. J. (1992). Investigating work groups to promote problem solving in mathematics. In J. Brophy (Ed.), *Advances in research on teaching: Vol. 3. Planning and managing learning tasks and activities.* Greenwich, CT: JAI Press.

Good, T. L., & Nichols, S. L. (2001). Expectancy effects in the classroom: A special focus on improving the reading performance of minority students in first-grade classrooms. *Educational Psychologist, 36,* 113–126.

Goodenow, C. (1993). Classroom belonging among early adolescent students: Relationships to motivation and achievement. *Journal of Early Adolescence, 13,* 21–43.

Goodman, C. S., & Tessier-Lavigne, M. (1997). Molecular mechanisms of axon guidance and target recognition. In W. M. Cowan, T. M. Jessell, & S. L. Zipursky (Eds.), *Molecular and cellular approaches to neural development* (pp. 108–137). New York: Oxford University Press.

Goodman, G. S., Ghetti, S., Quas, J. A., Edelstein, R. S., Alexander, K. W., Redlich, A. D., et al. (2003). A prospective study of memory for child sexual abuse: New findings relevant to the repressed-memory controversy. *Psychological Science, 14,* 113–118.

Goodnow, J. J. (2010). Culture. In M. H. Bornstein (Ed.), *Handbook of cultural developmental science* (pp. 3–19). New York: Psychology Press.

Goodwin, M. H. (2006). *The hidden life of girls: Games of stance, status, and exclusion.* Malden, MA: Blackwell.

Gootman, M. E. (1998). Effective in-house suspension. *Educational Leadership, 56*(1), 39–41.

Gopnik, A., & Meltzoff, A. N. (1997). *Words, thoughts, and theories.* Cambridge, MA: MIT Press.

Gottfredson, D. C. (2001). *Schools and delinquency.* Cambridge, England: Cambridge University Press.

Gottfried, A. E. (1990). Academic intrinsic motivation in young elementary school children. *Journal of Educational Psychology, 82,* 525–538.

Gottfried, A. E., Fleming, J. S., & Gottfried, A. W. (1994). Role of parental motivational practices in children's academic intrinsic motivation and achievement. *Journal of Educational Psychology, 86,* 104–113.

Gottman, J. M. (1986). The world of coordinated play: Same- and cross-sex friendship in young children. In J. M. Gottman & J. G. Parker (Eds.), *Conversations of friends: Speculations on affective development* (pp. 139–191). Cambridge, England: Cambridge University Press.

Gottman, J. M., & Mettetal, G. (1986). Speculations about social and affective development: Friendship and acquaintanceship through adolescence. In J. M. Gottman & J. G. Parker (Eds.), *Conversations of friends: Speculations on affective development* (pp. 192–237). Cambridge, England: Cambridge University Press.

Gould, E., Beylin, A., Tanapat, P., Reeves, A., & Shors, T. J. (1999). Learning enhances adult neurogenesis in the hippocampal formation. *Nature Neuroscience, 2,* 260–265.

Grace, D. M., David, B. J., & Ryan, M. K. (2008). Investigating preschoolers' categorical thinking about gender through imitation, attention, and the use of self-categories. *Child Development, 79,* 1928–1941.

Graesser, A. C., McNamara, D. S., & VanLehn, K. (2005). Scaffolding deep comprehension strategies through Point&Query, AutoTutor, and iSTART. *Educational Psychologist, 40,* 225–234.

Graesser, A., & Person, N. K. (1994). Question asking during tutoring. *American Educational Research Journal, 31,* 104–137.

Graham, S. (1989). Motivation in Afro-Americans. In G. L. Berry & J. K. Asamen (Eds.), *Black students: Psychosocial issues and academic achievement.* Newbury Park, CA: Sage.

Graham, S. (1990). Communicating low ability in the classroom: Bad things good teachers sometimes do. In S. Graham & V. S. Folkes (Eds.), *Attribution theory: Applications to achievement, mental health, and interpersonal conflict.* Mahwah, NJ: Erlbaum.

Graham, S. (2006). Peer victimization in school: Exploring the ethnic context. *Current Directions in Psychological Science, 15,* 317–321.

Graham, S., & Golen, S. (1991). Motivational influences on cognition: Task involvement, ego involvement, and depth of information processing. *Journal of Educational Psychology, 83,* 187–194.

Graham, S., & Harris, K. R. (1996). Addressing problems in attention, memory, and executive functioning. In G. R. Lyon & N. A. Krasnegor (Eds.), *Attention, memory, and executive function* (pp. 349–365). Baltimore: Brookes.

Graham, S., Harris, K. R., & Fink, B. (2000). Is handwriting causally related to learning to write? Treatment of handwriting problems in beginning writers. *Journal of Educational Psychology, 92,* 620–633.

Graham, S., & Hudley, C. (2005). Race and ethnicity in the study of motivation and competence. In A. J. Elliot & C. S. Dweck (Eds.), *Handbook of competence and motivation* (pp. 392–413). New York: Guilford Press.

Graham, S., & Weiner, B. (1996). Theories and principles of motivation. In D. C. Berliner & R. C. Calfee (Eds.), *Handbook of educational psychology.* New York: Macmillan.

Grant, C. A., & Gomez, M. L. (2001). *Campus and classroom: Making schooling multicultural* (2nd ed.). Upper Saddle River, NJ: Merrill/Prentice Hall.

Grant, H., & Dweck, C. (2001). Cross-cultural response to failure: Considering outcome attributions with different goals. In F. Salili & C. Chiu (Eds.), *Student motivation: The culture and context of learning* (pp. 203–219). Dordrecht, The Netherlands: Kluwer Academic.

Gray, M. R., & Steinberg, L. (1999). Unpacking authoritative parenting: Reassessing a multidimensional concept. *Journal of Marriage and the Family, 61,* 574–587.

Gray, W. D., & Orasanu, J. M. (1987). Transfer of cognitive skills. In S. M. Cormier & J. D. Hagman (Eds.), *Transfer of learning: Contemporary research and applications.* San Diego, CA: Academic Press.

Green, C. L., Walker, J. M. T., Hoover-Dempsey, K. V., & Sandler, H. M. (2007). Parents' motivation for involvement in children's education: An empirical test of a theoretical model of parental involvement. *Journal of Educational Psychology, 99,* 532–544.

Green, L., Fry, A. F., & Myerson, J. (1994). Discounting of delayed rewards: A life-span comparison. *Psychological Science, 5,* 33–36.

Greenberg, M. T., Weissberg, R. P., O'Brien, M. U., Zins, J. E., Fredericks, L., Resnik, H., et al. (2003). Enhancing school-based prevention and youth development through coordinated social, emotional, and academic learning. *American Psychologist, 58,* 466–474.

Greene, J. A., & Azevedo, R. (2009). A macro-level analysis of SRL processes and their relations to the acquisition of a sophisticated mental model of a complex system. *Contemporary Educational Psychology, 34,* 18–29.

Greenfield, P. M. (1994). Independence and interdependence as developmental scripts: Implications for theory, research, and practice. In P. M. Greenfield & R. R. Cocking (Eds.), *Cross-cultural roots of minority child development.* Mahwah, NJ: Erlbaum.

Greenfield, P. M., Trumbull, E., Keller, H., Rothstein-Fisch, C., Suzuki, L. K., & Quiroz, B. (2006). Cultural conceptions of learning and development. In P. A. Alexander & P. H. Winne (Eds.), *Handbook of educational psychology* (2nd ed., pp. 675–692). Mahwah, NJ: Erlbaum.

Greenhoot, A. F., Tsethlikai, M., & Wagoner, B. J. (2006). The relations between children's past experiences, social knowledge, and memories for social situations. *Journal of Cognition and Development, 7,* 313–340.

Greenhow, C., Robelia, B., & Hughes, J. E. (2009). Web 2.0 and classroom research: What path should we take now? *Educational Researcher, 38,* 246–259.

Greeno, J. G., Collins, A. M., & Resnick, L. B. (1996). Cognition and learning. In D. C. Berliner & R. C. Calfee (Eds.), *Handbook of educational psychology.* New York: Macmillan.

Greenough, W. T., Black, J. E., & Wallace, C. S. (1987). Experience and brain development. *Child Development, 58,* 539–559.

Greenwood, C. R. (1991). Classwide peer tutoring: Longitudinal effects on the reading, language, and mathematics achievement of at-risk students.

Journal of Reading, Writing, and Learning Disabilities International, 7(2), 105–123.

Greenwood, C. R., Carta, J. J., & Hall, R. V. (1988). The use of peer tutoring strategies in classroom management and educational instruction. *School Psychology Review, 17,* 258–275.

Gregg, M., & Leinhardt, G. (1994, April). *Constructing geography.* Paper presented at the annual meeting of the American Educational Research Association, New Orleans, LA.

Gregoire, M. (2003). Is it a challenge or a threat? A dual-process model of teachers' cognition and appraisal processes during conceptual change. *Educational Psychology Review, 15,* 147–179.

Greif, M. L., Kemler Nelson, D. G., Keil, F. C., & Gutierrez, F. (2006). What do children want to know about animals and artifacts? Domain-specific requests for information. *Psychological Science, 17,* 455–459.

Gresalfi, M. S. (2009). Taking up opportunities to learn: Constructing dispositions in mathematics classrooms. *Journal of the Learning Sciences, 18,* 327–369.

Griffin, M. M., & Griffin, B. W. (1994, April). *Some can get there from here: Situated learning, cognitive style, and map skills.* Paper presented at the annual meeting of the American Educational Research Association, New Orleans, LA.

Griffin, S. A., Case, R., & Capodilupo, A. (1995). Teaching for understanding: The importance of the central conceptual structures in the elementary mathematics curriculum. In A. McKeough, J. Lupart, & A. Marini (Eds.), *Teaching for transfer: Fostering generalization in learning.* Mahwah, NJ: Erlbaum.

Grissmer, D. W., Williamson, S., Kirby, S. N., & Berends, M. (1998). Exploring the rapid rise in Black achievement scores in the United States (1970–1990). In U. Neisser (Ed.), *The rising curve: Long-term gains in IQ and related measures* (pp. 251–285). Washington, DC: American Psychological Association.

Grolnick, W. S., & Ryan, R. M. (1987). Autonomy in children's learning: An experimental and individual difference investigation. *Journal of Personality and Social Psychology, 52,* 890–898.

Gronlund, N. E. (2004). *Writing instructional objectives for teaching and assessment* (7th ed.). Upper Saddle River, NJ: Merrill/Prentice Hall.

Gronlund, N. E., & Brookhart, S. M. (2009). *Writing instructional objectives* (8th ed.). Upper Saddle River, NJ: Merrill/Pearson.

Gronlund, N. E., & Waugh, C. K. (2009). *Assessment of student achievement* (9th ed.). Upper Saddle River, NJ: Pearson.

Gross, E. F. (2004). Adolescent Internet use: What we expect, what teens report. *Journal of Applied Developmental Psychology, 25,* 633–649.

Gross, E. F. (2009). Logging on, bouncing back: An experimental investigation of online communication following social exclusion. *Developmental Psychology, 45,* 1787–1793.

Gross, E. F., Juvonen, J., & Gable, S. L. (2002). Internet use and well-being in adolescence. *Journal of Social Issues, 58,* 75–90.

Grover, R. (Ed.). (1996). *Collaboration: Lessons learned series.* Chicago: American Library Association.

Gruman, D. H., Harachi, T. W., Abbott, R. D., Catalano, R. F., & Fleming, C. B. (2008). Longitudinal effects of student mobility on three dimensions of elementary school engagement. *Child Development, 79,* 1833–1852.

Guay, F., Boivin, M., & Hodges, E. V. E. (1999). Social comparison processes and academic achievement: The dependence of the development of self-evaluations on friends' performance. *Journal of Educational Psychology, 91,* 564–568.

Guay, F., Marsh, H. W., & Boivin, M. (2003). Academic self-concept and academic achievement: Developmental perspectives on their causal ordering. *Journal of Educational Psychology, 95,* 124–136.

Guerra, N. G., Huesmann, L. R., & Spindler, A. (2003). Community violence exposure, social cognition, and aggression among urban elementary school children. *Child Development, 74,* 1561–1576.

Gummerum, M., Keller, M., Takezawa, M., & Mata, J. (2008). To give or not to give: Children's and adolescents' sharing and moral negotiations in economic decision situations. *Child Development, 79,* 562–576.

Gunstone, R. F. (1994). The importance of specific science content in the enhancement of metacognition. In P. J. Fensham, R. F. Gunstone, & R. T. White (Eds.), *The content of science: A constructivist approach to its teaching and learning.* London: Falmer Press.

Gunstone, R. F., & White, R. T. (1981). Understanding of gravity. *Science Education, 65,* 291–299.

Guskey, T. R. (1985). *Implementing mastery learning.* Belmont, CA: Wadsworth.

Guskey, T. R. (2010). Formative assessment: The contributions of Benjamin S. Bloom. In H. L. Andrade & G. J. Cizek (Eds.), *Handbook of formative assessment* (pp. 106–124). New York: Routledge.

Guskey, T. R., & Sparks, D. (2002, April). *Linking professional development to improvements in student learning.* Paper presented at the annual meeting of the American Educational Research Association, New Orleans, LA.

Gustafsson, J. (2008). Schooling and intelligence: Effects of track of study on level and profile of cognitive abilities. In P. C. Kyllonen, R. D. Roberts, & L. Stankov (Eds.), *Extending intelligence: Enhancement and new constructs* (pp. 37–59). New York: Erlbaum/Taylor & Francis.

Gustafsson, J., & Undheim, J. O. (1996). Individual differences in cognitive functions. In D. C. Berliner & R. C. Calfee (Eds.), *Handbook of educational psychology.* New York: Macmillan.

Guthrie, J. T., Wigfield, A., Barbosa, P., Perencevich, K. C., Taboada, A., Davis, M. H., et al. (2004). Increasing reading comprehension and engagement through concept-oriented reading instruction. *Journal of Educational Psychology, 96,* 403–423.

Guthrie, P. (2001). "Catching sense" and the meaning of belonging on a South Carolina Sea island. In S. S. Walker (Ed.), *African roots/American cultures: Africa in the creation of the Americas* (pp. 275–283). Lanham, MD: Rowman & Littlefield.

Gutiérrez, K. D., & Rogoff, B. (2003). Cultural ways of learning: Individual traits or repertoires of practice. *Educational Researcher, 32*(5), 19–25.

Gutman, L. M., & McLoyd, V. C. (2000). Parents' management of their children's education within the home, at school, and in the community: An examination of African-American families living in poverty. *Urban Review, 32*(1), 1–24.

Hacker, D. J. (1998). Self-regulated comprehension during normal reading. In D. J. Hacker, J. Dunlosky, & A. C. Graesser (Eds.), *Metacognition in educational theory and practice* (pp. 165–191). Mahwah, NJ: Erlbaum.

Hacker, D. J., Bol, L., Horgan, D. D., & Rakow, E. A. (2000). Test prediction and performance in a classroom context. *Journal of Educational Psychology, 92,* 160–170.

Haden, C. A., Ornstein, P. A., Eckerman, C. O., & Didow, S. M. (2001). Mother-child conversational interactions as events unfold: Linkages to subsequent remembering. *Child Development, 72,* 1016–1031.

Hadjioannou, X. (2007). Bringing the background to the foreground: What do classroom environments that support authentic discussions look like? *American Educational Research Journal, 44,* 370–399.

Hagger, M. S., Chatzisarantis, N. L. D., Barkoukis, V., Wang, C. K. J., & Baranowski, J. (2005). Perceived autonomy support in physical education and leisure-time physical activity: A cross-cultural evaluation of the trans-contextual model. *Journal of Educational Psychology, 97,* 376–390.

Hagtvet, K. A., & Johnsen, T. B. (Eds.). (1992). *Advances in test anxiety research* (Vol. 7). Amsterdam: Swets & Zeitlinger.

Haier, R. J. (2001). PET studies of learning and individual differences. In J. L. McClelland & R. S. Siegler (Eds.), *Mechanisms of cognitive development: Behavioral and neural perspectives* (pp. 123–145). Mahwah, NJ: Erlbaum.

Haier, R. J. (2003). Positron emission tomography studies of intelligence: From psychometrics to neurobiology. In H. Nyborg (Ed.), *The scientific study of general intelligence.* New York: Pergamon.

Hale-Benson, J. E. (1986). *Black children: Their roots, culture, and learning styles.* Baltimore: Johns Hopkins University Press.

Halford, G. S. (1989). Cognitive processing capacity and learning ability: An integration of two areas. *Learning and Individual Differences, 1,* 125–153.

Halford, G. S., & Andrews, G. (2006). Reasoning and problem solving. In W. Damon & R. M. Lerner (Series Eds.), D. Kuhn & R. Siegler (Vol. Eds.), *Handbook of child psychology: Vol. 2. Cognition, perception, and language* (6th ed.). New York: Wiley.

Halgunseth, L. C., Ispa, J. M., & Rudy, D. (2006). Parental control in Latino families: An integrated review of the literature. *Child Development, 77,* 1282–1297.

Hall, N. C., Goetz, T., Haynes, T. L., Stupnisky, R. H., & Chipperfield, J. G. (2006, April). *Self-regulation of primary and secondary control: Optimizing control striving in an academic achievement setting.* Paper presented at the annual meeting of the American Educational Research Association, San Francisco, CA.

Hall, R. V., Axelrod, S., Foundopoulos, M., Shellman, J., Campbell, R. A., & Cranston, S. S. (1971). The effective use of punishment to modify behavior in the classroom. *Educational Technology, 11*(4), 24–26. Reprinted in K. D. O'Leary & S. O'Leary (Eds.), 1972, *Classroom management: The successful use of behavior modification.* New York: Pergamon.

Hallahan, D. P., Kauffman, J. M., & Pullen, P. C. (2009). *Exceptional learners: An introduction to special education* (11th ed.). Boston: Allyn & Bacon.

Haller, E. P., Child, D. A., & Walberg, H. J. (1988). Can comprehension be taught? A quantitative synthesis of "metacognitive" studies. *Educational Researcher, 17*(9), 5–8.

Halpern, D. F. (1997). *Critical thinking across the curriculum: A brief edition of thought and knowledge.* Mahwah, NJ: Erlbaum.

Halpern, D. F. (1998). Teaching critical thinking for transfer across domains. *American Psychologist, 53,* 449–455.

Halpern, D. F. (2008). Is intelligence critical thinking? Why we need a new definition of intelligence. In P. C. Kyllonen, R. D. Roberts, & L. Stankov (Eds.), *Extending intelligence: Enhancement and new constructs* (pp. 349–370). New York: Erlbaum/Taylor & Francis.

Halpern, D. F., & LaMay, M. L. (2000). The smarter sex: A critical review of sex differences in intelligence. *Educational Psychology Review, 12,* 229–246.

Halpin, G., & Halpin, G. (1982). Experimental investigations of the effects of study and testing on student learning, retention, and ratings of instruction. *Journal of Educational Psychology, 74,* 32–38.

Hambrick, D. Z., & Engle, R. W. (2003). The role of working memory in problem solving. In J. E. Davidson & R. J. Sternberg (Eds.), *The psychology of problem solving* (pp. 176–206). Cambridge, England: Cambridge University Press.

Hammerness, K., Darling-Hammond, L., & Bransford, J. (with Berliner, D., Cochran-Smith, M., McDonald, M., & Zeichner, K.) (2005). How teachers learn and develop. In L. Darling-Hammond & J. Bransford (Eds.), *Preparing teachers for a changing world: What teachers should learn and be able to do* (pp. 358–389). San Francisco: Jossey-Bass/Wiley.

Hamovitch, B. (2007). Hoping for the best: "Inclusion" and stigmatization in a middle school. In S. Books (Ed.), *Invisible children in the society and its schools* (3rd ed., pp. 263–281). Mahwah, NJ: Erlbaum.

Hampson, S. E. (2008). Mechanisms by which childhood personality traits influence adult well-being. *Current Directions in Psychological Science, 17,* 264–268.

Hamre, B. K., & Pianta, R. C. (2005). Can instructional and emotional support in the first-grade classroom make a difference for children at risk of school failure? *Child Development, 76,* 949–967.

Hanish, L. D., Kochenderfer-Ladd, B., Fabes, R. A., Martin, C. L., & Denning, D. (2004). Bullying among young children: The influence of peers and teachers. In D. L. Espelage & S. M. Swearer (Eds.), *Bullying in American schools: A social-ecological perspective on prevention and intervention* (pp. 141–159). Mahwah, NJ: Erlbaum.

Hardré, P. L., Crowson, H. M., DeBacker, T. K., & White, D. (2007). Predicting the motivation of rural high school students. *Journal of Experimental Education, 75,* 247–269.

Hardré, P. L., & Reeve, J. (2003). A motivational model of rural students' intentions to persist in, versus drop out of, high school. *Journal of Educational Psychology, 95,* 347–356.

Hardy, I., Jonen, A., Möller, K., & Stern, E. (2006). Effects of instructional support within constructivist learning environments for elementary school students' understanding of "floating and sinking." *Journal of Educational Psychology, 98,* 307–326.

Hareli, S., & Weiner, B. (2002). Social emotions and personality inferences: A scaffold for a new direction in the study of achievement motivation. *Educational Psychologist, 37,* 183–193.

Harlow, H. F., & Zimmerman, R. R. (1959). Affectional responses in the infant monkey. *Science, 130*, 421–432.

Harmon-Jones, E. (2001). The role of affect in cognitive-dissonance processes. In J. P. Forgas (Ed.), *Handbook of affect and social cognition* (pp. 237–255). Mahwah, NJ: Erlbaum.

Harnishfeger, K. K. (1995). The development of cognitive inhibition: Theories, definitions, and research evidence. In F. N. Dempster & C. J. Brainerd (Eds.), *Interference and inhibition in cognition.* San Diego, CA: Academic Press.

Harris, J. R. (1995). Where is the child's environment? A group socialization theory of development. *Psychological Review, 102*, 458–489.

Harris, J. R. (1998). *The nurture assumption: Why children turn out the way they do.* New York: Free Press.

Harris, K. R. (1982). Cognitive-behavior modification: Application with exceptional students. *Focus on Exceptional Children, 15*, 1–16.

Harris, K. R. (1986). Self-monitoring of attentional behavior versus self-monitoring of productivity: Effects of on-task behavior and academic response rate among learning disabled children. *Journal of Applied Behavior Analysis, 19*, 417–423.

Harris, K. R., & Alexander, P. A. (1998). Integrated, constructivist education: Challenge and reality. *Educational Psychology Review, 10*, 115–127.

Harris, K. R., Santangelo, T., & Graham, S. (2010). Metacognition and strategies instruction in writing. In H. S. Waters & W. Schneider (Eds.), *Metacognition, strategy use, and instruction* (pp. 226–256). New York: Guilford Press.

Harris, M. B. (1997). Preface: Images of the invisible minority. In M. B. Harris (Ed.), *School experiences of gay and lesbian youth: The invisible minority* (pp. xiv–xxii). Binghamton, NY: Harrington Park Press.

Harris, M. J., & Rosenthal, R. (1985). Mediation of interpersonal expectancy effects: 31 meta-analyses. *Psychological Bulletin, 97*, 363–386.

Harris, P. L. (2006). Social cognition. In W. Damon & R. M. Lerner (Series Eds.), D. Kuhn & R. Siegler (Vol. Eds.), *Handbook of child psychology: Vol. 2. Cognition, perception, and language* (6th ed.). New York: Wiley.

Harris, P. L., & Leevers, H. (2000). Pretending imagery and self-awareness in autism. In S. Baron-Cohen, H. Tager-Flusberg, & D. Cohen (Eds.), *Understanding other minds: Perspectives from developmental cognitive neuroscience* (2nd ed., pp. 182–202). Oxford, England: Oxford University Press.

Harris, R. J. (1977). Comprehension of pragmatic implications in advertising. *Journal of Applied Psychology, 62*, 603–608.

Hart, D. (1988). The adolescent self-concept in social context. In D. K. Lapsley & F. C. Power (Eds.), *Self, ego, and identity: Integrative approaches* (pp. 71–90). New York: Springer-Verlag.

Hart, D., & Fegley, S. (1995). Prosocial behavior and caring in adolescence: Relations to self-understanding and social judgment. *Child Development, 66*, 1346–1359.

Hart, E. R., & Speece, D. L. (1998). Reciprocal teaching goes to college: Effects for postsecondary students at risk for academic failure. *Journal of Educational Psychology, 90*, 670–681.

Harter, S. (1983). Children's understanding of multiple emotions: A cognitive-developmental approach. In W. F. Overton (Ed.), *The relationship between social and cognitive development.* Mahwah, NJ: Erlbaum.

Harter, S. (1992). The relationship between perceived competence, affect, and motivational orientation within the classroom: Processes and patterns of change. In A. K. Boggiano & T. S. Pittman (Eds.), *Achievement and motivation: A social-developmental perspective.* Cambridge, England: Cambridge University Press.

Harter, S. (1996). Teacher and classmate influences on scholastic motivation, self-esteem, and level of voice in adolescents. In J. Juvonen & K. Wentzel (Eds.), *Social motivation: Understanding children's school adjustment.* New York: Cambridge University Press.

Harter, S. (1999). *The construction of the self: A developmental perspective.* New York: Guilford Press.

Harter, S., & Whitesell, N. R. (1989). Developmental changes in children's understanding of single, multiple, and blended emotion concepts. In C. Saarni & P. Harris (Eds.), *Children's understanding of emotion* (pp. 81–116). Cambridge, England: Cambridge University Press.

Harter, S., Whitesell, N. R., & Kowalski, P. (1992). Individual differences in the effects of educational transitions on young adolescents' perceptions of competence and motivational orientation. *American Educational Research Journal, 29*, 777–807.

Hartley, J., & Trueman, M. (1982). The effects of summaries on the recall of information from prose: Five experimental studies. *Human Learning, 1*, 63–82.

Hartley, K., & Bendixen, L. D. (2001). Educational research in the Internet age: Examining the role of individual characteristics. *Educational Researcher, 30*(9), 22–26.

Hartup, W. W. (1983). Peer relations. In E. M. Hetherington (Ed.), *Handbook of child psychology: Vol. 4. Socialization, personality, and social development* (4th ed., pp. 103–196). New York: Wiley.

Haskell, R. E. (2001). *Transfer of learning: Cognition, instruction, and reasoning.* San Diego, CA: Academic Press.

Hastings, P. D., Utendale, W. T., & Sullivan, C. (2007). The socialization of prosocial development. In J. E. Grusec & P. D. Hastings (Eds.), *Handbook of socialization: Theory and research* (pp. 638–664). New York: Guilford Press.

Hatano, G., & Inagaki, K. (1991). Sharing cognition through collective comprehension activity. In L. B. Resnick, J. M. Levine, & S. D. Teasley (Eds.), *Perspectives on socially shared cognition.* Washington, DC: American Psychological Association.

Hatano, G., & Inagaki, K. (1993). Desituating cognition through the construction of conceptual knowledge. In P. Light & G. Butterworth (Eds.), *Context and cognition: Ways of learning and knowing.* Mahwah, NJ: Erlbaum.

Hatano, G., & Inagaki, K. (2003). When is conceptual change intended? A cognitive-sociocultural view. In G. M. Sinatra & P. R. Pintrich (Eds.), *Intentional conceptual change* (pp. 407–427). Mahwah, NJ: Erlbaum.

Hattie, J. (2008). Processes of integrating, developing, and processing self information. In H. W. Marsh, R. G. Craven, & D. M. McInerney (Eds.), *Self-processes, learning, and enabling human potential* (pp. 51–85). Charlotte, NC: Information Age.

Hattie, J. A. C. (2009). *Visible learning: A synthesis of over 800 meta-analyses relating to achievement.* London: Routledge.

Hattie, J., Biggs, J., & Purdie, N. (1996). Effects of learning skills interventions on student learning: A meta-analysis. *Review of Educational Research, 66*, 99–136.

Hattie, J., & Timperley, H. (2007). The power of feedback. *Review of Educational Research, 77*, 81–112.

Hawkins, F. P. L. (1997). *Journey with children: The autobiography of a teacher.* Niwot: University Press of Colorado.

Hawley, C. A. (2005). Saint or sinner? Teacher perceptions of a child with traumatic brain injury. *Pediatric Rehabilitation, 8*, 117–129.

Hayslip, B., Jr. (1994). Stability of intelligence. In R. J. Sternberg (Ed.), *Encyclopedia of human intelligence* (Vol. 2). New York: Macmillan.

Haywood, H. C., & Lidz, C. S. (2007). *Dynamic assessment in practice: Clinical and educational applications.* Cambridge, England: Cambridge University Press.

Hearold, S. (1986). A synthesis of 1,043 effects of television on social behavior. In G. Comstock (Ed.), *Public communication and behavior* (Vol. 1). New York: Academic Press.

Heath, S. B. (1980). Questioning at home and at school: A comparative study. In G. Spindler (Ed.), *The ethnography of schooling: Educational anthropology in action.* New York: Holt, Rinehart & Winston.

Heath, S. B. (1989). Oral and literate traditions among black Americans living in poverty. *American Psychologist, 44*, 367–373.

Heatherton, T. F., Macrae, C. N., & Kelley, W. M. (2004). What the social brain sciences can tell us about the self. *Current Directions in Psychological Science, 13*, 190–193.

Hecht, S. A., Close, L., & Santisi, M. (2003). Sources of individual differences in fraction skills. *Journal of Experimental Child Psychology, 86*, 277–302.

Heine, S. J. (2007). Culture and motivation: What motivates people to act in the ways that they do? In S. Kitayama & D. Cohen (Eds.), *Handbook of cultural psychology* (pp. 714–733). New York: Guilford Press.

Helton, G. B., & Oakland, T. D. (1977). Teachers' attitudinal responses to differing characteristics of elementary school students. *Journal of Educational Psychology, 69*, 261–266.

Helwig, C. C., & Jasiobedzka, U. (2001). The relation between law and morality: Children's reasoning about socially beneficial and unjust laws. *Child Development, 72*, 1382–1393.

Helwig, C. C., Zelazo, P. D., & Wilson, M. (2001). Children's judgments of psychological harm in normal and noncanonical situations. *Child Development, 72*, 66–81.

Hembree, R. (1987). Effects of noncontent variables on mathematics test performance. *Journal for Research in Mathematics Education, 18*, 197–214.

Hembree, R. (1988). Correlates, causes, effects, and treatment of test anxiety. *Review of Educational Research, 58*, 47–77.

Hemmings, A. B. (2004). *Coming of age in U.S. high schools: Economic, kinship, religious, and political crosscurrents.* Mahwah, NJ: Erlbaum.

Hemphill, L., & Snow, C. (1996). Language and literacy development: Discontinuities and differences. In D. R. Olson & N. Torrance (Eds.), *The handbook of education and human development: New models of learning, teaching, and schooling.* Cambridge, MA: Blackwell.

Hennessey, B. A. (1995). Social, environmental, and developmental issues and creativity. *Educational Psychology Review, 7,* 163–183.

Hennessey, B. A., & Amabile, T. M. (1987). *Creativity and learning.* Washington, DC: National Education Association.

Hennessey, M. G. (2003). Metacognitive aspects of students' reflective discourse: Implications for intentional conceptual change teaching and learning. In G. M. Sinatra & P. R. Pintrich (Eds.), *Intentional conceptual change* (pp. 103–132). Mahwah, NJ: Erlbaum.

Herbert, J., & Stipek, D. (2005). The emergence of gender differences in children's perceptions of their academic competence. *Journal of Applied Developmental Psychology, 26,* 276–295.

Hernandez, D. J., Denton, N. A., & Macartney, S. E. (2008). Children in immigrant families: Looking to America's future. *Social Policy Report, 22*(3) (Society for Research in Child Development).

Heron, W. (1957). The pathology of boredom. *Scientific American, 196*(1), 52–56.

Herrenkohl, L. R., & Guerra, M. R. (1998). Participant structures, scientific discourse, and student engagement in fourth grade. *Cognition and Instruction, 16,* 431–473.

Hess, R. D., & Azuma, M. (1991). Cultural support for learning: Contrasts between Japan and the United States. *Educational Researcher, 29*(9), 2–8.

Hess, R. D., Chih-Mei, C., & McDevitt, T. M. (1987). Cultural variations in family beliefs about children's performance in mathematics: Comparisons among People's Republic of China, Chinese-American, and Caucasian-American families. *Journal of Educational Psychology, 79,* 179–188.

Hess, R. D., & Holloway, S. D. (1984). Family and school as educational institutions. In R. D. Parke, R. N. Emde, H. P. McAdoo, & G. P. Sackett (Eds.), *Review of child development research* (Vol. 7). Chicago: University of Chicago Press.

Heuer, F., & Reisberg, D. (1992). Emotion, arousal, and memory for detail. In S. Christianson (Ed.), *Handbook of emotion and memory.* Hillsdale, NJ: Erlbaum.

Heward, W. L. (2009). *Exceptional children: An introduction to special education* (9th ed.). Upper Saddle River, NJ: Merrill/Pearson Education.

Hewitt, J., Brett, C., Scardamalia, M., Frecker, K., & Webb, J. (1995, April). *Schools for thought: Transforming classrooms into learning communities.* Paper presented at the annual meeting of the American Educational Research Association, San Francisco.

Hewitt, J., & Scardamalia, M. (1996, April). *Design principles for the support of distributed processes.* Paper presented at the annual meeting of the American Educational Research Association, New York.

Hewitt, J., & Scardamalia, M. (1998). Design principles for distributed knowledge building processes. *Educational Psychology Review, 10,* 75–96.

Heyman, G. D. (2008). Children's critical thinking when learning from others. *Current Directions in Psychological Science, 17,* 344–347.

Hickey, D. T. (1997). Motivation and contemporary socio-constructivist instructional perspectives. *Educational Psychologist, 32,* 175–193.

Hidalgo, N. M., Siu, S., Bright, J. A., Swap, S. M., & Epstein, J. L. (1995). Research on families, schools, and communities: A multicultural perspective. In J. A. Banks & C. A. M. Banks (Eds.), *Handbook of research on multicultural education.* New York: Macmillan.

Hidi, S., & Harackiewicz, J. M. (2000). Motivating the academically unmotivated: A critical issue for the 21st century. *Review of Educational Research, 70,* 151–179.

Hidi, S., & McLaren, J. (1990). The effect of topic and theme interestingness on the production of school expositions. In H. Mandl, E. De Corte, N. Bennett, & H. F. Friedrich (Eds.), *Learning and instruction in an international context.* Oxford, England: Pergamon Press.

Hidi, S., & Renninger, K. A. (2006). The four-phase model of interest development. *Educational Psychologist, 41,* 111–127.

Hidi, S., Renninger, K. A., & Krapp, A. (2004). Interest, a motivational variable that combines affecting and cognitive functioning. In D. Y. Dai & R. J. Sternberg (Eds.), *Motivation, emotion, and cognition: Integrative perspectives on intellectual functioning and development* (pp. 89–115). Mahwah, NJ: Erlbaum.

Hiebert, E. H., & Fisher, C. W. (1992). The tasks of school literacy: Trends and issues. In J. Brophy (Ed.), *Advances in research on teaching: Vol. 3. Planning and managing learning tasks and activities.* Greenwich, CT: JAI Press.

Hiebert, E. H., & Raphael, T. E. (1996). Psychological perspectives on literacy and extensions to educational practice. In D. C. Berliner & R. C. Calfee (Eds.), *Handbook of educational psychology.* New York: Macmillan.

Hiebert, E. H., Valencia, S. W., & Afflerbach, P. P. (1994). Definitions and perspectives. In S. W. Valencia, E. H. Hiebert, & P. P. Afflerbach (Eds.), *Authentic reading assessment: Practices and possibilities.* Newark, DE: International Reading Association.

Hiebert, J., Carpenter, T. P., Fennema, E., Fuson, K. C., Wearne, D., Murray, H., et al. (1997). *Making sense: Teaching and learning mathematics with understanding.* Portsmouth, NH: Heinemann.

Hiebert, J., & Wearne, D. (1996). Instruction, understanding, and skill in multidigit addition and subtraction. *Cognition and Instruction, 14,* 251–283.

Higgins, A. (1995). Educating for justice and community: Lawrence Kohlberg's vision of moral education. In W. M. Kurtines & J. L. Gewirtz (Eds.), *Moral development: An introduction.* Boston: Allyn & Bacon.

Hill, C. (1994). Testing and assessment: An applied linguistic perspective. *Educational Assessment, 2*(3), 179–212.

Hill, C., & Larsen, E. (1992). *Testing and assessment in secondary education: A critical review of emerging practices.* Berkeley: University of California, National Center for Research in Vocational Education.

Hill, H. C., Blunk, M. L., Charalambous, C. Y., Lewis, J. M., Phelps, G. C., Sleep, L., et al. (2008). Mathematical knowledge for teaching and the mathematical quality of instruction: An exploratory study. *Cognition and Instruction, 26,* 430–511.

Hill, K. T. (1984). Debilitating motivation and testing: A major educational problem, possible solutions, and policy applications. In R. Ames & C. Ames (Eds.), *Research on motivation in education: Vol. 1. Student motivation.* San Diego, CA: Academic Press.

Hill, K. T., & Sarason, S. B. (1966). The relation of test anxiety and defensiveness to test and school performance over the elementary school years: A further longitudinal study. *Monographs for the Society of Research in Child Development, 31*(2, Serial No. 104).

Hill, K. T., & Wigfield, A. (1984). Test anxiety: A major educational problem and what can be done about it. *Elementary School Journal, 85,* 105–126.

Hill, N. E., Bush, K. R., & Roosa, M. W. (2003). Parenting and family socialization strategies and children's mental health: Low-income Mexican-American and Euro-American mothers and children. *Child Development, 74,* 189–204.

Hill, N. E., Castellino, D. R., Lansford, J. E., Nowlin, P., Dodge, K. A., Bates, J. E., & Pettit, G. S. (2004). Parent academic involvement as related to school behavior, achievement, and aspirations: Demographic variations across adolescence. *Child Development, 75,* 1491–1509.

Hine, P., & Fraser, B. J. (2002, April). *Combining qualitative and quantitative methods in a study of Australian students' transition from elementary to high school.* Paper presented at the annual meeting of the American Educational Research Association, New Orleans, LA.

Hinkley, J. W., McInerney, D. M., & Marsh, H. W. (2001, April). *The multi-faceted structure of school achievement motivation: A case for social goals.* Paper presented at the annual meeting of the American Educational Research Association, Seattle, WA.

Hinnant, J. B., O'Brien, M., & Ghazarian, S. R. (2009). The longitudinal relations of teacher expectations to achievement in the early school years. *Journal of Educational Psychology, 101,* 662–670.

Hitlin, S., Brown, J. S., & Elder, G. H., Jr. (2006). Racial self-categorization in adolescence: Multiracial development and social pathways. *Child Development, 77,* 1298–1308.

Hmelo-Silver, C. E. (2004). Problem-based learning: What and how do students learn? *Educational Psychology Review, 16,* 235–266.

Hmelo-Silver, C. E. (2006). Design principles for scaffolding technology-based inquiry. In A. M. O'Donnell, C. E. Hmelo-Silver, & G. Erkens (Eds.), *Collaborative learning, reasoning, and technology* (pp. 147–170). Mahwah, NJ: Erlbaum.

Hmelo-Silver, C. E., Duncan, R. G., & Chinn, C. A. (2007). Scaffolding and achievement in problem-based and inquiry learning: A response to Kirschner, Sweller, and Clark (2006). *Educational Psychologist, 42,* 99–107.

Ho, A. D. (2008). The problem with "proficiency": Limitations of statistics and policy under No Child Left Behind. *Educational Researcher, 37,* 351–360.

Ho, D. Y. F. (1994). Cognitive socialization in Confucian heritage cultures. In P. M. Greenfield & R. R. Cocking (Eds.), *Cross-cultural roots of minority child development.* Mahwah, NJ: Erlbaum.

Hobson, P. (2004). *The cradle of thought: Exploring the origins of thinking.* Oxford, England: Oxford University Press.

Hofer, B. K., & Pintrich, P. R. (1997). The development of epistemological theories: Beliefs about knowledge and knowing and their relation to learning. *Review of Educational Research, 67,* 88–140.

Hofer, B. K., & Pintrich, P. R. (Eds.). (2002). *Personal epistemology: The psychology of beliefs about knowledge and knowing.* Mahwah, NJ: Erlbaum.

Hofferth, S. L. (1990). Trends in adolescent sexual activity, contraception, and pregnancy in the United States. In J. Bancroft & J. M. Reinisch

(Eds.), *Adolescence and puberty* (pp. 217–233). New York: Oxford University Press.

Hoffman, M. L. (1970). Moral development. In P. H. Mussen (Ed.), *Carmichael's manual of child psychology* (Vol. 2). New York: Wiley.

Hoffman, M. L. (1975). Altruistic behavior and the parent-child relationship. *Journal of Personality and Social Psychology, 31,* 937–943.

Hoffman, M. L. (1991). Empathy, social cognition, and moral action. In W. M. Kurtines & J. L. Gewirtz (Eds.), *Moral behavior and development: Vol. 1. Theory* (pp. 275–301). Mahwah, NJ: Erlbaum.

Hogan, D. M., & Tudge, J. R. H. (1999). Implications of Vygotsky's theory for peer learning. In A. M. O'Donnell & A. King (Eds.), *Cognitive perspectives on peer learning* (pp. 39–65). Mahwah, NJ: Erlbaum.

Hogan, K., Nastasi, B. K., & Pressley, M. (2000). Discourse patterns and collaborative scientific reasoning in peer and teacher-guided discussions. *Cognition and Instruction, 17,* 379–432.

Hogan, T., Rabinowitz, M., & Craven, J. A., III. (2003). Representation in teaching: Inferences from research of expert and novice teachers. *Educational Psychologist, 38,* 235–247.

Hoge, R. D., & Coladarci, T. (1989). Teacher-based judgments of academic achievement: A review of literature. *Review of Educational Research, 59,* 297–313.

Hoge, R. D., & Renzulli, J. S. (1993). Exploring the link between giftedness and self-concept. *Review of Educational Research, 63,* 449–465.

Hoglund, W. L. G. (2007). School functioning in early adolescence: Gender-linked responses to peer victimization. *Journal of Educational Psychology, 99,* 683–699.

Holland, R. W., Hendriks, M., & Aarts, H. (2005). Smells like clean spirit: Nonconscious effects of scent on cognition and behavior. *Psychological Science, 16,* 689–693.

Holley, C. D., & Dansereau, D. F. (1984). *Spatial learning strategies: Techniques, applications, and related issues.* San Diego, CA: Academic Press.

Holliday, B. G. (1985). Towards a model of teacher-child transactional processes affecting black children's academic achievement. In M. B. Spencer, G. K. Brookins, & W. R. Allen (Eds.), *Beginnings: The social and affective development of black children.* Mahwah, NJ: Erlbaum.

Hollins, E. R. (1996). *Culture in school learning: Revealing the deep meaning.* Mahwah, NJ: Erlbaum.

Hollon, R. E., Roth, K. J., & Anderson, C. W. (1991). Science teachers' conceptions of teaching and learning. In J. Brophy (Ed.), *Advances in research on teaching: Vol. 2. Teachers' knowledge of subject matter as it relates to their teaching practice.* Greenwich, CT: JAI Press.

Holt, M. K., & Keyes, M. A. (2004). Teachers' attitudes toward bullying. In D. L. Espelage & S. M. Swearer (Eds.), *Bullying in American schools: A social-ecological perspective on prevention and intervention* (pp. 121–139). Mahwah, NJ: Erlbaum.

Holt-Reynolds, D. (1992). Personal history-based beliefs as relevant prior knowledge in course work. *American Educational Research Journal, 29,* 325–349.

Hom, A., & Battistich, V. (1995, April). *Students' sense of school community as a factor in reducing drug use and delinquency.* Paper presented at the annual meeting of the American Educational Research Association, San Francisco.

Hong, E., O'Neil, H. F., & Feldon, D. (2005). Gender effects on mathematics achievement: Mediating role of state and trait self-regulation. In A. M. Gallagher & J. C. Kaufman (Eds.), *Gender differences in mathematics: An integrative psychological approach* (pp. 264–293). Cambridge, England: Cambridge University Press.

Hong, Y., Chiu, C., & Dweck, C. S. (1995). Implicit theories of intelligence: Reconsidering the role of confidence in achievement motivation. In M. H. Kernis (Ed.), *Efficacy, agency, and self-esteem.* New York: Plenum Press.

Hong, Y., Morris, M. W., Chiu, C., & Benet-Martínez, V. (2000). Multicultural minds: A dynamic constructivist approach to culture and cognition. *American Psychologist, 55,* 709–720.

Hong, Y., Wan, C., No, S., & Chiu, C.-Y. (2007). Multicultural identities. In S. Kitayama & D. Cohen (Eds.), *Handbook of cultural psychology* (pp. 323–345). New York: Guilford Press.

Hoover-Dempsey, K. V., Battiato, A. C., Walker, J. M. T., Reed, R. P., DeJong, J. M., & Jones, K. P. (2001). Parental involvement in homework. *Educational Psychologist, 36,* 195–209.

Horgan, D. (1990, April). *Students' predictions of test grades: Calibration and metacognition.* Paper presented at the annual meeting of the American Educational Research Association, Boston.

Horgan, D. D., Hacker, D., & Huffman, S. (1997, May). *How students predict their exam performance.* Paper presented at the annual meeting of the Southern Society for Philosophy and Psychology, Atlanta, GA.

Horn, J. L. (2008). Spearman, *g,* expertise, and the nature of human cognitive capability. In P. C. Kyllonen, R. D. Roberts, & L. Stankov (Eds.), *Extending intelligence: Enhancement and new constructs* (pp. 185–230). New York: Erlbaum/Taylor & Francis.

Horne, A. M., Orpinas, P., Newman-Carlson, D., & Bartolomucci, C. L. (2004). Elementary school Bully Busters Program: Understanding why children bully and what to do about it. In D. L. Espelage & S. M. Swearer (Eds.), *Bullying in American schools: A social-ecological perspective on prevention and intervention* (pp. 297–325). Mahwah, NJ: Erlbaum.

Hossler, D., & Stage, F. K. (1992). Family and high school experience influences on the postsecondary educational plans of ninth-grade students. *American Educational Research Journal, 29,* 425–451.

Houtz, J. C. (1990). Environments that support creative thinking. In C. Hedley, J. Houtz, & A. Baratta (Eds.), *Cognition, curriculum, and literacy.* Norwood, NJ: Ablex.

Howe, C. K. (1994). Improving the achievement of Hispanic students. *Educational Leadership, 51*(8), 42–44.

Howell, J. C., & Lynch, J. P. (2000, August). Youth gangs in schools. *Juvenile Justice Bulletin* (OJJDP Publication NCJ-183015). Washington, DC: U.S. Department of Justice, Office of Juvenile Justice and Delinquency Prevention.

Hoy, W. K., Tarter, C. J., & Woolfolk Hoy, A. (2006). Academic optimism of schools: A force for student achievement. *American Educational Research Journal, 43,* 425–446.

Hubbs-Tait, L., Nation, J. R., Krebs, N. F., & Bellinger, D. C. (2005). Neurotoxicants, micronutrients, and social environments: Individual and combined effects on children's development. *Psychological Science in the Public Interest, 6,* 57–121.

Hudley, C., & Graham, S. (1993). An attributional intervention to reduce peer-directed aggression among African American boys. *Child Development, 64,* 124–138.

Huey, E. D., Krueger, F., & Grafman, J. (2006). Representations in the human prefrontal cortex. *Current Directions in Psychological Science, 15,* 167–171.

Huff, J. A. (1988). Personalized behavior modification: An in-school suspension program that teaches students how to change. *School Counselor, 35,* 210–214.

Hufton, N., Elliott, J., & Illushin, L. (2002). Achievement motivation across cultures: Some puzzles and their implications for future research. *New Directions for Child and Adolescent Development, 96,* 65–85.

Hughes, J., & Kwok, O. (2007). Influence of student-teacher and parent-teacher relationships on lower achieving readers' engagement and achievement in the primary grades. *Journal of Educational Psychology, 99,* 39–51.

Hughes, J. M., Bigler, R. S., & Levy, S. R. (2007). Consequences of learning about historical racism among European American and African American children. *Child Development, 78,* 1689–1705.

Hughes, J. N., Luo, W., Kwok, O.-M., & Loyd, L. K. (2008). Teacher-student support, effortful engagement, and achievement: A 3-year longitudinal study. *Journal of Educational Psychology, 100,* 1–14.

Huguet, P., & Régner, I. (2007). Stereotype threat among schoolgirls in quasi-ordinary classroom circumstances. *Journal of Educational Psychology, 99,* 545–560.

Hulit, L. M., & Howard, M. R. (2006). *Born to talk* (4th ed.). Boston: Allyn & Bacon.

Hunt, E. (2008). Improving intelligence: What's the difference from education? In P. C. Kyllonen, R. D. Roberts, & L. Stankov (Eds.), *Extending intelligence: Enhancement and new constructs* (pp. 15–35). New York: Erlbaum/Taylor & Francis.

Hunt, P., & Goetz, L. (1997). Research on inclusive educational programs, practices, and outcomes for students with severe disabilities. *Journal of Special Education, 31,* 3–29.

Hunter, J., & Csikszentmihalyi, M. (2003). The positive psychology of interested adolescents. *Journal of Youth and Adolescence, 32,* 27–35.

Huntsinger, C. S., & Jose, P. E. (2006). A longitudinal investigation of personality and social adjustment among Chinese American and European American adolescents. *Child Development, 77,* 1309–1324.

Hursh, D. (2007). Assessing No Child Left Behind and the rise of neoliberal education policies. *American Educational Research Journal, 44,* 493–518.

Husman, J., & Freeman, B. (1999, April). *The effect of perceptions of instrumentality on intrinsic motivation.* Paper presented at the annual meeting of the American Educational Research Association, Montreal, Canada.

Hutt, S. J., Tyler, S., Hutt, C., & Christopherson, H. (1989). *Play, exploration, and learning: A natural history of the pre-school.* London: Routledge.

Huttenlocher, P. R., & Dabholkar, A. S. (1997). Regional differences in synaptogenesis in human cerebral cortex. *Journal of Comparative Neurology, 387,* 167–178.

Hyde, J. S., & Durik, A. M. (2005). Gender, competence, and motivation. In A. J. Elliot & C. S. Dweck (Eds.), *Handbook of competence and motivation* (pp. 375–391). New York: Guilford Press.

Hyde, J. S., Lindberg, S. M., Linn, M. C., Ellis, A. B., & Williams, C. C. (2008). Gender similarities characterize math performance. *Science, 321*(5888), 494–495.

Hyman, I., Kay, B., Tabori, A., Weber, M., Mahon, M., & Cohen, I. (2006). Bullying: Theory, research, and interventions. In C. M. Evertson & C. S. Weinstein (Eds.), *Handbook of classroom management: Research, practice, and contemporary issues* (pp. 855–884). Mahwah, NJ: Erlbaum.

Hyman, I., Mahon, M., Cohen, I., Snook, P., Britton, G., & Lurkis, L. (2004). Student alienation syndrome: The other side of school violence. In J. C. Conoley & A. P. Goldstein (Eds.), *School violence intervention* (2nd ed., pp. 483–506). New York: Guilford Press.

Hymel, S. (1986). Interpretations of peer behavior: Affective bias in childhood and adolescence. *Child Development, 57,* 431–445.

Hymel, S., Comfort, C., Schonert-Reichl, K., & McDougall, P. (1996). Academic failure and school dropout: The influence of peers. In J. Juvonen & K. R. Wentzel (Eds.), *Social motivation: Understanding children's school adjustment* (pp. 313–345). Cambridge, England: Cambridge University Press.

Hynd, C. (1998a). Conceptual change in a high school physics class. In B. Guzzetti & C. Hynd (Eds.), *Perspectives on conceptual change: Multiple ways to understand knowing and learning in a complex world* (pp. 27–36). Mahwah, NJ: Erlbaum.

Hynd, C. (1998b). Observing learning from different perspectives: What does it mean for Barry and his understanding of gravity? In B. Guzzetti & C. Hynd (Eds.), *Perspectives on conceptual change: Multiple ways to understand knowing and learning in a complex world* (pp. 235–244). Mahwah, NJ: Erlbaum.

Hynd, C. (2003). Conceptual change in response to persuasive messages. In G. M. Sinatra & P. R. Pintrich (Eds.), *Intentional conceptual change* (pp. 291–315). Mahwah, NJ: Erlbaum.

Igoa, C. (1995). *The inner world of the immigrant child.* Mahwah, NJ: Erlbaum.

Inagaki, K., & Hatano, G. (2006). Young children's conception of the biological world. *Current Directions in Psychological Science, 15,* 177–181.

Inglehart, M., Brown, D. R., & Vida, M. (1994). Competition, achievement, and gender: A stress theoretical analysis. In P. R. Pintrich, D. R. Brown, & C. E. Weinstein (Eds.), *Student motivation, cognition, and learning: Essays in honor of Wilbert J. McKeachie.* Mahwah, NJ: Erlbaum.

Inglis, A., & Biemiller, A. (1997, March). *Fostering self-direction in mathematics: A cross-age tutoring program that enhances math problem solving.* Paper presented at the annual meeting of the American Educational Research Association, Chicago.

Inhelder, B., & Piaget, J. (1958). *The growth of logical thinking from childhood to adolescence* (A. Parsons & S. Milgram, Trans.). New York: Basic Books.

Irujo, S. (1988). An introduction to intercultural differences and similarities in nonverbal communication. In J. S. Wurzel (Ed.), *Toward multiculturalism: A reader in multicultural education.* Yarmouth, ME: Intercultural Press.

Irvine, J. J., & York, D. E. (1995). Learning styles and culturally diverse students: A literature review. In J. A. Banks & C. A. M. Banks (Eds.), *Handbook of research on multicultural education.* New York: Macmillan.

Irving, M. A., & Hudley, C. (2008). Oppositional identity and academic achievement among African American males. In J. U. Ogbu (Ed.), *Minority status, oppositional culture, and schooling* (pp. 374–394). New York: Routledge.

Iwata, B. A., & Bailey, J. S. (1974). Reward versus cost token systems: An analysis of the effects on students and teacher. *Journal of Applied Behavior Analysis, 7,* 567–576.

Iyengar, S. S., & Lepper, M. R. (1999). Rethinking the value of choice: A cultural perspective on intrinsic motivation. *Journal of Personality and Social Psychology, 76,* 349–366.

Izard, C., Fine, S., Schultz, D., Mostow, A., Ackerman, B., & Youngstrom, E. (2001). Emotion knowledge as a predictor of social behavior and academic competence in children at risk. *Psychological Science, 12,* 18–23.

Jacob, B. A. (2003). Accountability, incentives, and behavior: The impact of high-stakes testing in the Chicago Public Schools. *Education Next, 3*(1). Retrieved March 10, 2004, from www.education next.org/unabridged/20031/jacob.pdf

Jacobs, J. E., Davis-Kean, P., Bleeker, M., Eccles, J. S., & Malanchuk, O. (2005). "I can, but I don't want to": The impact of parents, interests, and activities on gender differences in math. In A. M. Gallagher & J. C. Kaufman (Eds.), *Gender differences in mathematics: An integrative psychological approach* (pp. 246–263). Cambridge, England: Cambridge University Press.

Jacobs, J. E., & Klaczynski, P. A. (2002). The development of judgment and decision making during childhood and adolescence. *Current Directions in Psychological Science, 11,* 145–149.

Jacobs, J. E., Lanza, S., Osgood, D. W., Eccles, J. S., & Wigfield, A. (2002). Changes in children's self-competence and values: Gender and domain differences across grades one through twelve. *Child Development, 73,* 509–527.

Jagacinski, C. M., & Nicholls, J. G. (1984). Conceptions of ability and related affects in task involvement and ego involvement. *Journal of Educational Psychology, 76,* 909–919.

Jagacinski, C. M., & Nicholls, J. G. (1987). Competence and affect in task involvement and ego involvement: The impact of social comparison information. *Journal of Educational Psychology, 79,* 107–114.

Janos, P. M., & Robinson, N. M. (1985). Psychosocial development in intellectually gifted children. In F. D. Horowitz & M. O'Brien (Eds.), *The gifted and talented: Developmental perspectives.* Washington, DC: American Psychological Association.

Jansen, B. A. (2007). *The Big6 in middle school: Teaching information and communication technology skills.* Columbus, OH: Linworth.

Jansen, B. A. (2009). *The Big6 goes primary: Teaching information and communication technology skills in the K–3 curriculum.* Columbus, OH: Linworth.

Jegede, O. J., & Olajide, J. O. (1995). Wait-time, classroom discourse, and the influence of sociocultural factors in science teaching. *Science Education, 79,* 233–249.

Jenlink, C. L. (1994, April). *Music: A lifeline for the self-esteem of at-risk students.* Paper presented at the annual meeting of the American Educational Research Association, New Orleans, LA.

Jimerson, S., Egeland, B., & Teo, A. (1999). A longitudinal study of achievement trajectories: Factors associated with change. *Journal of Educational Psychology, 91,* 116–126.

Johanning, D. I., D'Agostino, J. V., Steele, D. F., & Shumow, L. (1999, April). *Student writing, postwriting group collaboration, and learning in prealgebra.* Paper presented at the annual meeting of the American Educational Research Association, Montreal, Canada.

Johnson, C. I., & Mayer, R. E. (2009). A testing effect with multimedia learning. *Journal of Educational Psychology, 101,* 621–629.

Johnson, D. W., & Johnson, R. T. (1991). *Learning together and alone: Cooperative, competitive, and individualistic learning* (3rd ed.). Upper Saddle River, NJ: Prentice Hall.

Johnson, D. W., & Johnson, R. T. (1996). Conflict resolution and peer mediation programs in elementary and secondary schools: A review of the research. *Review of Educational Research, 66,* 459–506.

Johnson, D. W., & Johnson, R. T. (2006). Conflict resolution, peer mediation, and peacemaking. In C. M. Evertson & C. S. Weinstein (Eds.), *Handbook of classroom management: Research, practice, and contemporary issues* (pp. 803–832). Mahwah, NJ: Erlbaum.

Johnson, D. W., & Johnson, R. T. (2009a). An educational psychology success story: Social interdependence theory and cooperative learning. *Educational Researcher, 38,* 365–379.

Johnson, D. W., & Johnson, R. T. (2009b). Energizing learning: The instructional power of conflict. *Educational Researcher, 38,* 37–51.

Johnson, D. W., Johnson, R., Dudley, B., Ward, M., & Magnuson, D. (1995). The impact of peer mediation training on the management of school and home conflicts. *American Educational Research Journal, 32,* 829–844.

Johnson, H. C., & Friesen, B. (1993). Etiologies of mental and emotional disorders in children. In H. Johnson (Ed.), *Child mental health in the 1990s: Curricula for graduate and undergraduate.* Washington, DC: U.S. Department of Health and Human Services.

Johnson, M. H., & de Haan, M. (2001). Developing cortical specialization for visual-cognitive function: The case of face recognition. In J. L. McClelland & R. S. Siegler (Eds.), *Mechanisms of cognitive development: Behavioral and neural perspectives* (pp. 253–270). Mahwah, NJ: Erlbaum.

Johnson, R. L., Penny, J. A., & Gordon, B. (2009). *Assessing performance: Designing, scoring, and validating performance tasks.* New York: Guilford Press.

Johnson, R. S., Mims-Cox, J. S., & Doyle-Nichols, A. (2006). *Developing portfolios in education: A guide to reflection, inquiry, and assessment.* Thousand Oaks, CA: Sage.

Johnson, W., McGue, M., & Iacono, W. G. (2005). Disruptive behavior and school grades: Genetic and environmental relations in 11-year-olds. *Journal of Educational Psychology, 97,* 391–405.

Johnson-Glenberg, M. C. (2000). Training reading comprehension in adequate decoders/poor comprehenders: Verbal versus visual strategies. *Journal of Educational Psychology, 92,* 772–782.

John-Steiner, V. (1997). *Notebooks of the mind: Explorations of thinking* (rev. ed.). New York: Oxford University Press.

John-Steiner, V., & Mahn, H. (1996). Sociocultural approaches to learning and development: A Vygotskian framework. *Educational Psychologist, 31,* 191–206.

Jonassen, D. H., & Grabowski, B. L. (1993). *Handbook of individual differences: Learning and instruction.* Mahwah, NJ: Erlbaum.

Jonassen, D. H., Hannum, W. H., & Tessmer, M. (1989). *Handbook of task analysis procedures.* New York: Praeger.

Jones, D., & Christensen, C. A. (1999). Relationship between automaticity in handwriting and students' ability to generate written text. *Journal of Educational Psychology, 91,* 44–49.

Jones, E. E., & Berglas, S. (1978). Control of attributions about the self through self-handicapping strategies: The appeal of alcohol and the role of underachievement. *Personality and Social Psychology Bulletin, 4,* 200–206.

Jones, K. M., Drew, H. A., & Weber, N. L. (2000). Noncontingent peer attention as treatment for disruptive classroom behavior. *Journal of Applied Behavior Analysis, 33,* 343–346.

Jones, M. H., Estell, D. B., & Alexander, J. M. (2008). Friends, classmates, and self-regulated learning: Discussions with peers inside and outside the classroom. *Metacognition Learning, 3,* 1–15.

Jones, M. S., Levin, M. E., Levin, J. R., & Beitzel, B. D. (2000). Can vocabulary-learning strategies and pair-learning formats be profitably combined? *Journal of Educational Psychology, 92,* 256–262.

Jones, V. (2006). How do teachers learn to be effective classroom managers. In C. M. Evertson & C. S. Weinstein (Eds.), *Handbook of classroom management: Research, practice, and contemporary issues* (pp. 887–907). Mahwah, NJ: Erlbaum.

Jonkmann, K., Trautwein, U., & Lüdtke, O. (2009). Social dominance in adolescence: The moderating role of the classroom context and behavioral heterogeneity. *Child Development, 80,* 338–355.

Jozefowicz, D. M., Arbreton, A. J., Eccles, J. S., Barber, B. L., & Colarossi, L. (1994, April). *Seventh grade student, parent, and teacher factors associated with later school dropout or movement into alternative educational settings.* Paper presented at the annual meeting of the American Educational Research Association, New Orleans, LA.

Jussim, L., Eccles, J., & Madon, S. (1996). Social perception, social stereotypes, and teacher expectations: Accuracy and the quest for the powerful self-fulfilling prophecy. In L. Berkowitz (Ed.), *Advances in experimental social psychology.* New York: Academic Press.

Juvonen, J. (2000). The social functions of attributional face-saving tactics among early adolescents. *Educational Psychology Review, 12,* 15–32.

Juvonen, J. (2006). Sense of belonging, social bonds, and school functioning. In P. A. Alexander & P. H. Winne (Eds.), *Handbook of educational psychology* (2nd ed., pp. 655–674). Mahwah, NJ: Erlbaum.

Juvonen, J., & Cadigan, R. J. (2002). Social determinants of public behavior of middle school youth: Perceived peer norms and need to be accepted. In F. Pajares & T. Urdan (Eds.), *Adolescence and education, Vol. 2: Academic motivation of adolescents* (pp. 277–297). Greenwich, CT: Information Age.

Juvonen, J., & Hiner, M. (1991, April). *Perceived responsibility and annoyance as mediators of negative peer reactions.* Paper presented at the annual meeting of the American Educational Research Association, Chicago.

Juvonen, J., & Weiner, B. (1993). An attributional analysis of students' interactions: The social consequences of perceived responsibility. *Educational Psychology Review, 5,* 325–345.

Kagan, J. (2010). Emotions and temperament. In M. H. Bornstein (Ed.), *Handbook of cultural developmental science* (pp. 175–194). New York: Psychology Press.

Kagan, J., Snidman, N., Kahn, V., & Towsley, S. (2007). The preservation of two infant temperaments into adolescence. *Monographs of the Society for Research in Child Development, 72*(2, Serial No. 287).

Kağitçibaşi, Ç. (2007). *Family, self, and human development across cultures: Theory and applications* (2nd ed.). Mahwah, NJ: Erlbaum.

Kahl, B., & Woloshyn, V. E. (1994). Using elaborative interrogation to facilitate acquisition of factual information in cooperative learning settings: One good strategy deserves another. *Applied Cognitive Psychology, 8,* 465–478.

Kahne, J. E., & Sporte, S. E. (2008). Developing citizens: The impact of civic learning opportunities on students' commitment to civic participation. *American Educational Research Journal, 45,* 738–766.

Kail, R. V. (1990). *The development of memory in children* (3rd ed.). New York: Freeman.

Kail, R. V. (1998). *Children and their development.* Upper Saddle River, NJ: Prentice Hall.

Kail, R. V. (2007). Longitudinal evidence that increases in processing speed and working memory enhance children's reasoning. *Psychological Science, 18,* 312–313.

Kalyuga, S., & Sweller, J. (2004). Measuring knowledge to optimize cognitive load factors during instruction. *Journal of Educational Psychology, 96,* 558–568.

Kane, M. T. (2008). Terminology, emphasis, and utility in validation. *Educational Researcher, 37,* 76–82.

Kaplan, A. (1998, April). *Task goal orientation and adaptive social interaction among students of diverse cultural backgrounds.* Paper presented at the annual meeting of the American Educational Research Association, San Diego, CA.

Kaplan, A., & Flum, H. (2009). Motivation and identity: The relations of action and development in educational contexts—An introduction to the special issue. *Educational Psychologist, 44,* 73–77.

Kaplan, A., & Midgley, C. (1997). The effect of achievement goals: Does level of perceived academic competence make a difference? *Contemporary Educational Psychology, 22,* 415–435.

Kaplan, A., & Midgley, C. (1999). The relationship between perceptions of the classroom goal structure and early adolescents' affect in school: The mediating role of coping strategies. *Learning and Individual Differences, 11,* 187–212.

Karau, S. J., & Williams, K. D. (1995). Social loafing: Research findings, implications, and future directions. *Current Directions in Psychological Science, 4,* 134–140.

Kardash, C. A. M., & Amlund, J. T. (1991). Self-reported learning strategies and learning from expository text. *Contemporary Educational Psychology, 16,* 117–138.

Kardash, C. A. M., & Howell, K. L. (2000). Æffects of epistemological beliefs and topic-specific beliefs on undergraduates' cognitive and strategic processing of dual-positional text. *Journal of Educational Psychology, 92,* 524–535.

Kardash, C. A. M., & Scholes, R. J. (1996). Effects of preexisting beliefs, epistemological beliefs, and need for cognition on interpretation of controversial issues. *Journal of Educational Psychology, 88,* 260–271.

Karplus, R., Pulos, S., & Stage, E. K. (1983). Proportional reasoning of early adolescents. In R. Lesh & M. Landau (Eds.), *Acquisition of mathematics concepts and processes.* San Diego, CA: Academic Press.

Karpov, Y. V. (2003). Vygotsky's doctrine of scientific concepts: Its role for contemporary education. In A. Kozulin, B. Gindis, V. S. Ageyev, & S. M. Miller (Eds.), *Vygotsky's educational theory in cultural context* (pp. 65–82). Cambridge, England: Cambridge University Press.

Karpov, Y. V., & Haywood, H. C. (1998). Two ways to elaborate Vygotsky's concept of mediation: Implications for instruction. *American Psychologist, 53,* 27–36.

Katayama, A. D., & Robinson, D. H. (2000). Getting students "partially" involved in note-taking using graphic organizers. *Journal of Experimental Education, 68,* 119–133.

Katchadourian, H. (1990). Sexuality. In S. S. Feldman & G. R. Elliott (Eds.), *At the threshold: The developing adolescent* (pp. 330–351). Cambridge, MA: Harvard University Press.

Katz, L. (1993). All about me: Are we developing our children's self-esteem or their narcissism? *American Educator, 17*(2), 18–23.

Keil, F. C. (1986). The acquisition of natural kind and artifact terms. In W. Demopolous & A. Marras (Eds.), *Language learning and concept acquisition.* Norwood, NJ: Ablex.

Keil, F. C. (1987). Conceptual development and category structure. In U. Neisser (Ed.), *Concepts and conceptual development: Ecological and intellectual factors in categorization.* Cambridge, England: Cambridge University Press.

Keil, F. C. (1989). *Concepts, kinds, and cognitive development.* Cambridge, MA: MIT Press.

Keil, F. C. (1994). The birth and nurturance of concepts by domains: The origins of concepts of living things. In L. A. Hirschfeld & S. A. Gelman (Eds.), *Mapping the mind: Domain specificity in cognition and culture.* New York: Cambridge University Press.

Keil, F. C., & Silberstein, C. S. (1996). Schooling and the acquisition of theoretical knowledge. In D. R. Olson & N. Torrance (Eds.), *The handbook of education and human development: New models of learning, teaching, and schooling.* Cambridge, MA: Blackwell.

Kelemen, D. (2004). Are children "intuitive theists"?: Reasoning about purpose and design in nature. *Psychological Science, 15,* 295–301.

Keller, H. R., & Tapasak, R. C. (2004). Classroom-based approaches. In J. C. Conoley & A. P. Goldstein (Eds.), *School violence intervention* (2nd ed., pp. 103–130). New York: Guilford Press.

Kelly, S., & Monczunski, L. (2007). Overcoming the volatility in school-level gain scores: A new approach to identifying value added with cross-sectional data. *Educational Researcher, 36*(5), 279–287.

Kelly, S. W., Burton, A. M., Kato, T., & Akamatsu, S. (2001). Incidental learning of real-world regularities. *Psychological Science, 12,* 86–89.

Kemler Nelson, D. G., Egan, L. C., & Holt, M. B. (2004). When children ask, "What is it?" what do they want to know about artifacts? *Psychological Science, 15,* 384–389.

Kennedy, R. (1992). What is performance assessment? *New Directions for Education Reform, 1*(2), 21–27.

Keogh, B. K. (2003). *Temperament in the classroom.* Baltimore: Brookes.

Keogh, B. K., & MacMillan, D. L. (1996). Exceptionality. In D. C. Berliner & R. C. Calfee (Eds.), *Handbook of educational psychology.* New York: Macmillan.

Kermani, H., & Moallem, M. (1997, March). *Cross-age tutoring: Exploring features and processes of peer-mediated learning.* Paper presented at the annual meeting of the American Educational Research Association, Chicago.

Kerns, L. L., & Lieberman, A. B. (1993). *Helping your depressed child.* Rocklin, CA: Prima.

Khattri, N., & Sweet, D. (1996). Assessment reform: Promises and challenges. In M. B. Kane & R. Mitchell (Eds.), *Implementing performance assessment: Promises, problems, and challenges* (pp. 1–21). Mahwah, NJ: Erlbaum.

Kiefer, S. M., & Ryan, A. M. (2008). Striving for social dominance over peers: The implications for academic adjustment during early adolescence. *Journal of Educational Psychology, 100,* 417–428.

Kiewra, K. A. (1985). Investigating notetaking and review: A depth of processing alternative. *Educational Psychologist, 20,* 23–32.

Kiewra, K. A. (1989). A review of note-taking: The encoding-storage paradigm and beyond. *Educational Psychology Review, 1,* 147–172.

Killeen, P. R. (2001). The four causes of behavior. *Current Directions in Psychological Science, 10,* 136–140.

Killen, M. (2007). Children's social and moral reasoning about exclusion. *Current Directions in Psychological Science, 16,* 32–36.

Killen, M., & Smetana, J. (2008). Moral judgment and moral neuroscience: Intersections, definitions, and issues. *Child Development Perspectives, 2*(1), 1–6.

Kim, D., Solomon, D., & Roberts, W. (1995, April). *Classroom practices that enhance students' sense of community.* Paper presented at the annual meeting of the American Educational Research Association, San Francisco.

Kim, H. S., & Kamil, M. L. (2004). Adolescents, computer technology, and literacy. In T. L. Jetton & J. A. Dole (Eds.), *Adolescent literacy research and practice* (pp. 351–368). New York: Guilford Press.

Kim, H. S., Sherman, D. K., & Taylor, S. E. (2008). Culture and social support. *American Psychologist, 63,* 518–526.

Kim, J., & Cicchetti, D. (2006). Longitudinal trajectories of self-system processes and depressive symptoms among maltreated and nonmaltreated children. *Child Development, 77,* 624–639.

Kim, J. M., & Turiel, E. (1996). Korean and American children's concepts of adult and peer authority. *Social Development, 5,* 310–329.

Kim-Cohen, J., & Gold, A. L. (2009). Measured gene-environment interactions and mechanisms promoting resilient development. *Current Directions in Psychological Science, 18,* 138–142.

Kincheloe, J. L. (2009). No short cuts in urban education: Metropedagogy and diversity. In S. R. Steinberg (Ed.), *Diversity and multiculturalism: A reader* (pp. 379–409). New York: Peter Lang.

Kindermann, T. A. (2007). Effects of naturally existing peer groups on changes in academic engagement in a cohort of sixth graders. *Child Development, 78,* 1186–1203.

Kindermann, T. A., McCollam, T., & Gibson, E. (1996). Peer networks and students' classroom engagement during childhood and adolescence. In J. Juvonen & K. Wentzel (Eds.), *Social motivation: Understanding children's school adjustment.* Cambridge, England: Cambridge University Press.

King, A. (1992). Comparison of self-questioning, summarizing, and notetaking-review as strategies for learning from lectures. *American Educational Research Journal, 29,* 303–323.

King, A. (1994). Guiding knowledge construction in the classroom: Effects of teaching children how to question and how to explain. *American Educational Research Journal, 31,* 338–368.

King, A. (1997). ASK to THINK—TEL WHY®©: A model of transactive peer tutoring for scaffolding higher level complex learning. *Educational Psychologist, 32,* 221–235.

King, A. (1998). Transactive peer tutoring: Distributing cognition and metacognition. *Educational Psychology Review, 10,* 57–74.

King, A. (1999). Discourse patterns for mediating peer learning. In A. M. O'Donnell & A. King (Eds.), *Cognitive perspectives on peer learning* (pp. 87–115). Mahwah, NJ: Erlbaum.

King, A., Staffieri, A., & Adelgais, A. (1998). Mutual peer tutoring: Effects of structuring tutorial interaction to scaffold peer learning. *Journal of Educational Psychology, 90,* 134–152.

King, N. J., & Ollendick, T. H. (1989). Children's anxiety and phobic disorders in school settings: Classification, assessment, and intervention issues. *Review of Educational Research, 59,* 431–470.

King, P. M., & Kitchener, K. S. (2002). The reflective judgment model: Twenty years of research on epistemic cognition. In B. K. Hofer & P. R. Pintrich (Eds.), *Personal epistemology: The psychology of beliefs about knowledge and knowing* (pp. 37–61). Mahwah, NJ: Erlbaum.

Kinney, D. (1993). From "nerds" to "normals": Adolescent identity recovery within a changing social system. *Sociology of Education, 66,* 21–40.

Kirkland, M. C. (1971). The effect of tests on students and schools. *Review of Educational Research, 41,* 303–350.

Kirschenbaum, R. J. (1989). Identification of the gifted and talented American Indian student. In C. J. Maker & S. W. Schiever (Eds.), *Critical issues in gifted education: Vol. 2. Defensible programs for cultural and ethnic minorities.* Austin, TX: Pro-Ed.

Kirschner, P. A., Sweller, J., & Clark, R. E. (2006). Why minimal guidance during instruction does not work: An analysis of the failure of constructivist, discovery, problem-based, experiential, and inquiry-based teaching. *Educational Psychologist, 41,* 75–86.

Kitayama, S., Duffy, S., & Uchida, Y. (2007). Self as cultural mode of being. In S. Kitayama & D. Cohen (Eds.), *Handbook of cultural psychology* (pp. 136–174). New York: Guilford Press.

Klaczynski, P. A. (2001). Analytic and heuristic processing influences on adolescent reasoning and decision-making. *Child Development, 72,* 844–861.

Klassen, R. (2002). Writing in early adolescence: A review of the role of self-efficacy beliefs. *Educational Psychology Review, 14,* 173–203.

Klassen, R. M., & Lynch, S. L. (2007). Self-efficacy from the perspective of adolescents with LD and their specialist teachers. *Journal of Learning Disabilities, 40,* 494–507.

Klassen, S. (2006). Contextual assessment in science education: Background, issues, and policy. *Science Education, 90,* 820–851.

Knapp, M. S., Turnbull, B. J., & Shields, P. M. (1990). New directions for educating the children of poverty. *Educational Leadership, 48*(1), 4–9.

Kochanska, G., Gross, J. N., Lin, M.-H., & Nichols, K. E. (2002). Guilt in young children: Development, determinants, and relations with a broader system of standards. *Child Development, 73,* 461–482.

Kodluboy, D. W. (2004). Gang-oriented interventions. In J. C. Conoley & A. P. Goldstein (Eds.), *School violence intervention* (2nd ed., pp. 194–232). New York: Guilford Press.

Koedinger, K. R., & Corbett, A. (2006). Cognitive tutors: Technology bringing learning sciences to the classroom. In R. K. Sawyer (Ed.), *The Cambridge handbook of the learning sciences* (pp. 61–77). Cambridge, England: Cambridge University Press.

Koegel, L. K., Koegel, R. L., & Dunlap, G. (Eds.). (1996). *Positive behavioral support: Including people with difficult behavior in the community.* Baltimore: Brookes.

Koestner, R., Ryan, R. M., Bernieri, F., & Holt, K. (1984). Setting limits on children's behavior: The differential effects of controlling versus informational styles on intrinsic motivation and creativity. *Journal of Personality, 52,* 233–248.

Kohlberg, L. (1975). The cognitive-developmental approach to moral education. *Phi Delta Kappan, 57,* 670–677.

Kohlberg, L. (1976). Moral stages and moralization: The cognitive-developmental approach. In T. Lickona (Ed.), *Moral development and behavior: Theory, research, and social issues.* New York: Holt, Rinehart & Winston.

Kohlberg, L. (1981). *The philosophy of moral development: Moral stages and the idea of justice.* San Francisco: Harper & Row.

Kohlberg, L. (1984). *The psychology of moral development: The nature and validity of moral stages.* San Francisco: Harper & Row.

Kohlberg, L. (1986). A current statement on some theoretical issues. In S. Modgil & C. Modgil (Eds.), *Lawrence Kohlberg: Consensus and controversy.* Philadelphia: Falmer Press.

Kohlberg, L., & Candee, D. (1984). The relationship of moral judgment to moral action. In W. M. Kurtines & J. L. Gewirtz (Eds.), *Morality, moral behavior, and moral development.* New York: Wiley.

Kolb, B., Gibb, R., & Robinson, T. E. (2003). Brain plasticity and behavior. *Current Directions in Psychological Science, 12,* 1–5.

Köller, O., Zeinz, H., & Trautwein, U. (2008). Class-average achievement, marks, and academic self-concept in German primary schools. In H. W. Marsh, R. G. Craven, & D. M. McInerney (Eds.), *Self-processes, learning, and enabling human potential* (pp. 331–352). Charlotte, NC: Information Age.

Koltko-Rivera, M. E. (2004). The psychology of worldviews. *Review of General Psychology, 8,* 3–58.

Konishi, C., & Hymel, S. (2008, March). *Examining changes in bullying and social-emotional functioning in early adolescence.* Paper presented at the annual meeting of the American Educational Research Association, New York.

Koob, A. (2009). *The root of thought.* Upper Saddle River, NJ: Pearson.

Koretz, D., Stecher, B., Klein, S., & McCaffrey, D. (1994). The Vermont portfolio assessment program: Findings and implications. *Educational Measurement: Issues and Practice, 13*(3), 5–16.

Kosslyn, S. M. (1985). Mental imagery ability. In R. J. Sternberg (Ed.), *Human abilities: An information-processing approach.* New York: Freeman.

Kosslyn, S. M., Margolis, J. A., Barrett, A. M., Goldknopf, E. J., & Daly, P. F. (1990). Age differences in imagery ability. *Child Development, 61,* 995–1010.

Kounin, J. S. (1970). *Discipline and group management in classrooms.* New York: Holt, Rinehart & Winston.

Kovas, Y., Haworth, C. M. A., Dale, P. S., & Plomin, R. (2007). The genetic and environmental origins of learning abilities and disabilities in the early school years. *Monographs of the Society for Research in Child Development, 72* (3, Serial No. 288).

Kovas, Y., Petrill, S. A., & Plomin, R. (2007). The origins of diverse domains of mathematics: Generalist genes but specialist environments. *Journal of Educational Psychology, 99,* 128–139.

Kovas, Y., & Plomin, R. (2007). Learning abilities and disabilities: Generalist genes, specialist environments. *Current Directions in Psychological Science, 16,* 284–288.

Kowalski, R. M., & Limber, S. P. (2007). Electronic bullying among middle school students. *Journal of Adolescent Health, 41,* S22–S30.

Krajcik, J. S., & Blumenfeld, P. C. (2006). Project-based learning. In R. K. Sawyer (Ed.), *The Cambridge handbook of the learning sciences* (pp. 317–333). Cambridge, England: Cambridge University Press.

Kramarski, B., & Mevarech, Z. R. (2003). Enhancing mathematical reasoning in the classroom: The effects of cooperative learning and metacognitive training. *American Educational Research Journal, 40,* 281–310.

Krampen, G. (1987). Differential effects of teacher comments. *Journal of Educational Psychology, 79,* 137–146.

Krätzig, G. P., & Arbuthnott, K. D. (2006). Perceptual learning style and learning proficiency: A test of the hypothesis. *Journal of Educational Psychology, 98,* 238–246.

Krauss, S., Brunner, M., Kunter, M., Baumert, J., Blum, W., Neubrand, M., et al. (2008). Pedagogical content knowledge and content knowledge of secondary mathematics teachers. *Journal of Educational Psychology, 100,* 716–725.

Krebs, D. L. (2008). Morality: An evolutionary account. *Perspectives on Psychological Science, 3,* 149–172.

Krebs, D. L., & Van Hesteren, F. (1994). The development of altruism: Toward an integrative model. *Developmental Review, 14,* 103–158.

Krumboltz, J. D., & Krumboltz, H. B. (1972). *Changing children's behavior.* Upper Saddle River, NJ: Prentice Hall.

Ku, Y.-M., Chan, W.-C., Wu, Y.-C., & Chen, Y.-H. (2008, March). *Improving children's comprehension of science text: Effects of adjunct questions and notetaking.* Paper presented at the annual meeting of the American Educational Research Association, New York.

Kuhl, J., & Kraska, K. (1989). Self-regulation and metamotivation: Computational mechanisms, development, and assessment. In R. Kanfer, P. L. Ackerman, & R. Cudeck (Eds.), *Abilities, motivation, and methodology: The Minnesota Symposium on Learning and Individual Differences* (pp. 343–374). Mahwah, NJ: Erlbaum.

Kuhn, D. (2001a). How do people know? *Psychological Science, 12,* 1–8.

Kuhn, D. (2001b). Why development does (and does not) occur: Evidence from the domain of inductive reasoning. In J. L. McClelland & R. S. Siegler (Eds.), *Mechanisms of cognitive development: Behavioral and neural perspectives* (pp. 221–249). Mahwah, NJ: Erlbaum.

Kuhn, D. (2006). Do cognitive changes accompany developments in the adolescent brain? *Perspectives on Psychological Science, 1,* 59–67.

Kuhn, D. (2007). Is direct instruction an answer to the right question? *Educational Psychologist, 42,* 109–113.

Kuhn, D. (2009). The importance of learning about knowing: Creating a foundation for development of intellectual values. *Child Development Perspectives, 3,* 112–117.

Kuhn, D., Amsel, E., & O'Loughlin, M. (1988). *The development of scientific thinking skills.* San Diego, CA: Academic Press.

Kuhn, D., Daniels, S., & Krishnan, A. (2003, April). *Epistemology and intellectual values as core metacognitive constructs.* Paper presented at the annual meeting of the American Educational Research Association, Chicago.

Kuhn, D., & Dean, D., Jr. (2005). Is developing scientific thinking all about learning to control variables? *Psychological Science, 16,* 866–870.

Kuhn, D., & Franklin, S. (2006). The second decade: What develops (and how)? In W. Damon & R. M. Lerner (Series Eds.), D. Kuhn & R. Siegler (Vol. Eds.), *Handbook of child psychology: Vol. 1. Cognition, perception, and language* (6th ed.). New York: Wiley.

Kuhn, D., Garcia-Mila, M., Zohar, A., & Andersen, C. (1995). Strategies of knowledge acquisition. *Monographs of the Society for Research in Child Development, 60* (Whole No. 245).

Kuhn, D., & Park, S.-H. (2005). Epistemological understanding and the development of intellectual values. *International Journal of Educational Research, 43,* 111–124.

Kuhn, D., & Pease, M. (2008). What needs to develop in the development of inquiry skills? *Cognition and Instruction, 26,* 512–599.

Kuhn, D., & Pease, M. (2010). The dual components of developing strategy use: Production and inhibition. In H. S. Waters & W. Schneider (Eds.), *Metacognition, strategy use, and instruction* (pp. 135–159). New York: Guilford Press.

Kuhn, D., & Weinstock, M. (2002). What is epistemological thinking and why does it matter? In B. K. Hofer & P. R. Pintrich (Eds.), *Personal epistemology: The psychology of beliefs about knowledge and knowing* (pp. 121–144). Mahwah, NJ: Erlbaum.

Kuiper, E., Volman, M., & Terwel, J. (2005). The Web as an information resource in K–12 education: Strategies for supporting students in searching and processing information. *Review of Educational Research, 75,* 285–328.

Kuklinski, M. R., & Weinstein, R. S. (2001). Classroom and developmental differences in a path model of teacher expectancy effects. *Child Development, 72,* 1554–1578.

Kulik, C. C., Kulik, J. A., & Bangert-Drowns, R. L. (1990). Effectiveness of mastery learning programs: A meta-analysis. *Review of Educational Research, 60,* 265–299.

Kulik, J. A., & Kulik, C. C. (1997). Ability grouping. In N. Colangelo & G. Davis (Eds.), *Handbook of gifted education* (2nd ed., pp. 230–242). Boston: Allyn & Bacon.

Kumar, R., Gheen, M. H., & Kaplan, A. (2002). Goal structures in the learning environment and students' disaffection from learning and schooling. In C. Midgley (Ed.), *Goals, goal structures, and patterns of adaptive learning* (pp. 143–173). Mahwah, NJ: Erlbaum.

Kunzinger, E. L., III (1985). A short-term longitudinal study of memorial development during early grade school. *Developmental Psychology, 21,* 642–646.

Kupchik, A., & Bracy, N. L. (2009). The news media on school crime and violence: Constructing dangerousness and fueling fear. *Youth Violence and Juvenile Justice, 7,* 136–155.

Kurtines, W. M., Berman, S. L., Ittel, A., & Williamson, S. (1995). Moral development: A co-constructivist perspective. In W. M. Kurtines & J. L. Gewirtz (Eds.), *Moral development: An introduction.* Boston: Allyn & Bacon.

Kyle, W. C., & Shymansky, J. A. (1989, April). Enhancing learning through conceptual change teaching. *NARST News, 31,* 7–8.

Labouvie-Vief, G., & González, M. M. (2004). Dynamic integration: Affect optimization and differentiation in development. In D. Y. Dai & R. J. Sternberg (Eds.), *Motivation, emotion, and cognition: Integrative perspectives on intellectual functioning and development* (pp. 237–272). Mahwah, NJ: Erlbaum.

Lackaye, T. D., & Margalit, M. (2006). Comparisons of achievement, effort, and self-perceptions among students with learning disabilities and their peers from different achievement groups. *Journal of Learning Disabilities, 39,* 432–446.

Ladd, G. W. (2006). Peer rejection, aggressive or withdrawn behavior, and psychological maladjustment from ages 5 to 12: An examination of four predictive models. *Child Development, 77,* 822–846.

Ladd, G. W., Herald-Brown, S. L., & Reiser, M. (2008). Does chronic classroom peer rejection predict the development of children's classroom participation during the grade school years? *Child Development, 79,* 1001–1015.

Ladd, G. W., & Troop-Gordon, W. (2003). The role of chronic peer difficulties in the development of children's psychological adjustment problems. *Child Development, 74,* 1344–1367.

Ladson-Billings, G. (1994a). *The dreamkeepers: Successful teachers of African American children.* San Francisco: Jossey-Bass.

Ladson-Billings, G. (1994b). What we can learn from multicultural education research. *Educational Leadership, 51*(8), 22–26.

Ladson-Billings, G. (1995a). But that's just good teaching! The case for culturally relevant pedagogy. *Theory into Practice, 34,* 159–165.

Ladson-Billings, G. (1995b). Toward a theory of culturally relevant pedagogy. *American Educational Research Journal, 32,* 465–491.

LaFromboise, T., Coleman, H. L. K., & Gerton, J. (1993). Psychological impact of biculturalism: Evidence and theory. *Psychological Bulletin, 114,* 395–412.

La Guardia, J. G., (2009). Developing who I am: A self-determination theory approach to the establishment of healthy identities. *Educational Psychologist, 44,* 90–104.

Laird,, J., Kienzl, G., DeBell, M., & Chapman, C. (2007). *Dropout rates in the United States: 2005* (Compendium Report, National Center for Education Statistics 2007-059). Washington: NCES.

Lajoie, S. P., & Derry, S. J. (Eds.). (1993). *Computers as cognitive tools.* Mahwah, NJ: Erlbaum.

Lam, S.-F., Yim, P.-S., & Ng, Y.-L. (2008). Is effort praise motivational? The role of beliefs in the effort-ability relationship. *Contemporary Educational Psychology, 33,* 694–710.

Lambert, M. C., Cartledge, G., Heward, W. L., & Lo, Y.-Y. (2006). Effects of response cards on disruptive behavior and academic responding during math lessons by fourth-grade urban students. *Journal of Positive Behavioral Interventions, 8,* 88–99.

Lamon, M., Chan, C., Scardamalia, M., Burtis, P. J., & Brett, C. (1993, April). *Beliefs about learning and constructive processes in reading: Effects of a computer supported intentional learning environment (CSILE).* Paper presented at the annual meeting of the American Educational Research Association, Atlanta, GA.

Lampert, M. (1990). When the problem is not the question and the solution is not the answer: Mathematical knowing and teaching. *American Educational Research Journal, 27,* 29–63.

Lampert, M., Rittenhouse, P., & Crumbaugh, C. (1996). Agreeing to disagree: Developing sociable mathematical discourse. In D. R. Olson & N. Torrance (Eds.), *The handbook of education and human development: New models of learning, teaching, and schooling.* Cambridge, MA: Blackwell.

Landers, D. M. (2007). The arousal-performance relationship revisited. In D. Smith (Ed.), *Essential readings in sport and exercise psychology* (pp. 211–218). Champaign, IL: Human Kinetics.

Landesman, S., & Ramey, C. (1989). Developmental psychology and mental retardation: Integrating scientific principles with treatment practices. *American Psychologist, 44,* 409–415.

Landrum, T. J., & Kauffman, J. M. (2006). Behavioral approaches to classroom management. In C. M. Evertson & C. S. Weinstein (Eds.), *Handbook of classroom management: Research, practice, and contemporary issues* (pp. 47–71). Mahwah, NJ: Erlbaum.

Lane, K., Falk, K., & Wehby, J. (2006). Classroom management in special education classrooms and resource rooms. In C. M. Evertson & C. S. Weinstein (Eds.), *Handbook of classroom management: Research, practice, and contemporary issues* (pp. 439–460). Mahwah, NJ: Erlbaum.

Langdon, S. (2007). Conceptualizations of *respect:* Qualitative and quantitative evidence of four (five) themes. *Journal of Psychology, 141,* 469–484.

Langer, E. J. (1997). *The power of mindful learning.* Reading, MA: Addison-Wesley.

Langer, E. J. (2000). Mindful learning. *Current Directions in Psychological Science, 9,* 220–223.

Langer, J. A. (2000). Excellence in English in middle and high school: How teachers' professional lives support student achievement. *American Educational Research Journal, 37,* 397–439.

Lansford, J. E., Chang, L., Dodge, K. A., Malone, P. S., Oburu, P., Palmérus, K., et al. (2005). Physical discipline and children's adjustment: Cultural normativeness as a moderator. *Child Development, 76,* 1234–1246.

Lansford, J. E., Deater-Decker, K., Dodge, K. A., Bates, J. E., & Pettit, G. S. (2003). Ethnic differences in the link between physical discipline and later adolescent externalizing behaviors. *Journal of Child Psychology and Psychiatry, 44,* 1–13.

La Paro, K. M., & Pianta, R. C. (2000). Predicting children's competence in the early school years: A meta-analytic review. *Review of Educational Research, 70,* 443–484.

Lapsley, D. K. (1993). Toward an integrated theory of adolescent ego development: The "new look"

at adolescent egocentrism. *American Journal of Orthopsychiatry, 63,* 562–571.

Larkin, S. (2008, March). *The development of metacognition within the context of learning to write.* Paper presented at the annual meeting of the American Educational Research Association, New York.

Larrivee, B. (2006). The convergence of reflective practice and effective classroom management. In C. M. Evertson & C. S. Weinstein (Eds.), *Handbook of classroom management: Research, practice, and contemporary issues* (pp. 983–1001). Mahwah, NJ: Erlbaum.

Larson, R. W. (2000). Toward a psychology of positive youth development. *American Psychologist, 55,* 170–183.

Larson, R. W., & Brown, J. R. (2007). Emotional development in adolescence: What can be learned from a high school theater program? *Child Development, 78,* 1083–1099.

Larson, R. W., Clore, G. L., & Wood, G. A. (1999). The emotions of romantic relationships: Do they wreak havoc on adolescents? In W. Furman, B. B. Brown, & C. Feiring (Eds.), *The development of romantic relationships in adolescence* (pp. 19–49). Cambridge, England: Cambridge University Press.

Larson, R. W., Moneta, G., Richards, M. H., & Wilson, S. (2002). Continuity, stability, and change in daily emotional experience across adolescence. *Child Development, 73,* 1151–1165.

Lau, S., & Nie, Y. (2008). Interplay between personal goals and classroom goal structures in predicting student outcomes: A multilevel analysis of person-context interactions. *Journal of Educational Psychology, 100,* 15–29.

Laupa, M., & Turiel, E. (1995). Social domain theory. In W. M. Kurtines & J. L. Gewirtz (Eds.), *Moral development: An introduction.* Boston: Allyn & Bacon.

Laursen, B., Bukowski, W. M., Aunola, K., & Nurmi, J.-E. (2007). Friendship moderates prospective associations between social isolation and adjustment problems in young children. *Child Development, 78,* 1395–1404.

Lave, J., & Wenger, E. (1991). *Situated learning: Legitimate peripheral participation.* Cambridge, England: Cambridge University Press.

Leadbeater, B. J., & Hoglund, W. L. G. (2009). The effects of peer victimization and physical aggression on changes in internalizing from first to third grade. *Child Development, 80,* 843–859.

Leaper, C., & Friedman, C. K. (2007). The socialization of gender. In J. E. Grusec & P. D. Hastings (Eds.), *Handbook of socialization: Theory and research* (pp. 561–587). New York: Guilford Press.

Learning First Alliance. (2001). *Every child learning: Safe and supportive schools.* Washington, DC: Association for Supervision and Curriculum Development.

Lee, C. D., & Slaughter-Defoe, D. T. (1995). Historical and sociocultural influences on African and American education. In J. A. Banks & C. A. M. Banks (Eds.), *Handbook of research on multicultural education.* New York: Macmillan.

Lee, J. (2008). Is test-driven external accountability effective? Synthesizing the evidence from cross-state causal-comparative and correlational studies. *Review of Educational Research, 78,* 608–644.

Lee, J.-S., & Bowen, N. K. (2006). Parent involvement, cultural capital, and the achievement gap among elementary school children. *American Educational Research Journal, 43,* 193–218.

Lee, K., Ng, E. L., & Ng, S. F. (2009). The contributions of working memory and executive function to problem representation and solution generation in algebraic word problems. *Journal of Educational Psychology, 101,* 373–387.

Lee, O. (1999). Science knowledge, world views, and information sources in social and cultural contexts: Making sense after a natural disaster. *American Educational Research Journal, 36,* 187–219.

Lee, V. E., & Burkam, D. T. (2003). Dropping out of high school: The role of school organization and structure. *American Educational Research Journal, 40,* 353–393.

Lee-Pearce, M. L., Plowman, T. S., & Touchstone, D. (1998). Starbase-Atlantis, a school without walls: A comparative study of an innovative science program for at-risk urban elementary students. *Journal of Education for Students Placed at Risk, 3,* 223–235.

LeFevre, J., Bisanz, J., & Mrkonjic, J. (1988). Cognitive arithmetic: Evidence for obligatory activation of arithmetic facts. *Memory and Cognition, 16,* 45–53.

Legault, L., Green-Demers, I., & Pelletier, L. (2006). Why do high school students lack motivation in the classroom? Toward an understanding of academic amotivation and the role of social support. *Journal of Educational Psychology, 98,* 567–582.

Lehmann, M., & Hasselhorn, M. (2007). Variable memory strategy use in children's adaptive intratask learning behavior: Developmental changes and working memory influences in free recall. *Child Development, 78,* 1068–1082.

Leinhardt, G. (1994). History: A time to be mindful. In G. Leinhardt, I. L. Beck, & C. Stainton (Eds.), *Teaching and learning in history.* Mahwah, NJ: Erlbaum.

Leinhardt, G., & Pallay, A. (1982). Restrictive educational settings: Exile or haven? *Review of Educational Research, 52,* 557–578.

Lejuez, C. W., Schaal, D. W., & O'Donnell, J. (1998). Behavioral pharmacology and the treatment of substance abuse. In J. J. Plaud & G. H. Eifert (Eds.), *From behavior theory to behavior therapy* (pp. 116–135). Boston: Allyn & Bacon.

Lennon, R., Ormrod, J. E., Burger, S. F., & Warren, E. (1990, October). *Belief systems of teacher education majors and their possible influences on future classroom performance.* Paper presented at the Northern Rocky Mountain Educational Research Association, Greeley, CO.

Lenroot, R. K., & Giedd, J. N. (2007). The structural development of the human brain as measured longitudinally with magnetic resonance imaging. In D. Coch, K. W. Fischer, & G. Dawson (Eds.), *Human behavior, learning, and the developing brain: Typical development* (pp. 50–73). New York: Guilford Press.

Lens, W. (2001). How to combine intrinsic task motivation with the motivational effects of the instrumentality of present tasks for future goals. In A. Efklides, J., Kuhl, & R. Sorrentino (Eds.), *Trends and prospects in motivation research* (pp. 37–52). Dordrecht, the Netherlands: Kluwer.

Lens, W., Simons, J., & Dewitte, S. (2002). From duty to desire: The role of students' future time perspective and instrumentality perceptions for study motivation and self-regulation. In F. Pajares & T. Urdan (Eds.), *Adolescence and education: Vol. 2. Academic motivation of adolescents.* Greenwich, CT: Information Age.

Lentz, F. E. (1988). Reductive procedures. In J. C. Witt, S. N. Elliott, & F. M. Gresham (Eds.), *Handbook of behavior therapy in education.* New York: Plenum Press.

Lepper, M. R., Corpus, J. H., & Iyengar, S. S. (2005). Intrinsic and extrinsic motivational orientations in the classroom: Age differences and academic correlates. *Journal of Educational Psychology, 97,* 184–196.

Lepper, M. R., & Hodell, M. (1989). Intrinsic motivation in the classroom. In C. Ames & R. Ames (Eds.), *Research on motivation in education: Vol. 3. Goals and cognitions.* San Diego, CA: Academic Press.

Lerman, D. C., & Vorndran, C. M. (2002). On the status of knowledge for using punishment: Implications for treating behavior disorders. *Journal of Applied Behavior Analysis, 35,* 431–464.

Lerner, R. M. (2002). *Adolescence: Development, diversity, context, and application.* Upper Saddle River, NJ: Prentice Hall.

Lesgold, A. M. (2001). The nature and methods of learning by doing. *American Psychologist, 56,* 965–973.

Lester, F. K., Jr., Lambdin, D. V., & Preston, R. V. (1997). A new vision of the nature and purposes of assessment in the mathematics classroom. In G. D. Phye (Ed.), *Handbook of classroom assessment: Learning, achievement, and adjustment.* San Diego, CA: Academic Press.

Leu, D. J., O'Byrne, W. I., Zawilinski, L., McVerry, J. G., & Everett-Cacopardo, H. (2009). Expanding the new literacies conversation. *Educational Researcher, 38,* 264–269.

Levin, J. R., & Mayer, R. E. (1993). Understanding illustrations in text. In B. K. Britton, A. Woodward, & M. Binkley (Eds.), *Learning from textbooks: Theory and practice.* Mahwah, NJ: Erlbaum.

Levine, D. U., & Lezotte, L. W. (1995). Effective schools research. In J. A. Banks & C. A. M. Banks (Eds.), *Handbook of research on multicultural education.* New York: Macmillan.

Levitt, M. J., Guacci-Franco, N., & Levitt, J. L. (1993). Convoys of social support in childhood and early adolescence: Structure and function. *Developmental Psychology, 29,* 811–818.

Levstik, L. S. (1993). Building a sense of history in a first-grade classroom. In J. Brophy (Ed.), *Advances in research on teaching: Vol. 4. Case studies of teaching and learning in social studies.* Greenwich, CT: JAI Press.

Levy, I., Kaplan, A., & Patrick, H. (2000, April). *Early adolescents' achievement goals, intergroup processes, and attitudes towards collaboration.* Paper presented at the annual meeting of the American Educational Research Association, New Orleans, LA.

Lewis, M. (1991). Self-knowledge and social influence. In M. Lewis & S. Feinman (Eds.), *Social influences and socialization in infancy: Vol. 6. Genesis of behavior* (pp. 111–134). New York: Plenum Press.

Lewis, M., & Sullivan, M. W. (2005). The development of self-conscious emotions. In A. J. Elliot & C. S. Dweck (Eds.), *Handbook of competence and motivation* (pp. 185–201). New York: Guilford Press.

Lewis, T. J., Newcomer, L. L., Trussell, R., & Richter, M. (2006). Schoolwide positive behavior support: Building systems to develop and maintain appropriate social behavior. In C. M. Evertson & C. S. Weinstein (Eds.), *Handbook of classroom management: Research, practice, and contemporary issues* (pp. 833–854). Mahwah, NJ: Erlbaum.

Li, J. (2004). High abilities and excellence: A cultural perspective. In L. V. Shavinina & M. Ferrari (Eds.), *Beyond knowledge: Extracognitive aspects of developing high ability* (pp. 187–208). Mahwah, NJ: Erlbaum.

Li, J. (2005). Mind or virtue: Western and Chinese beliefs about learning. *Current Directions in Psychological Science, 14,* 190–194.

Li, J. (2006). Self in learning: Chinese adolescents' goals and sense of agency. *Child Development, 77,* 482–501.

Li, J., & Fischer, K. W. (2004). Thought and affect in American and Chinese learners' beliefs about learning. In D. Y. Dai & R. J. Sternberg (Eds.), *Motivation, emotion, and cognition: Integrative perspectives on intellectual functioning and development* (pp. 385–418). Mahwah, NJ: Erlbaum.

Li, Y., Anderson, R. C., Nguyen-Jahiel, K., Dong, T., Archodidou, A., Kim, I.-H., et al. (2007). Emergent leadership in children's discussion groups. *Cognition and Instruction, 25,* 75–111.

Liben, L. S., & Bigler, R. S. (2002). The developmental course of gender differentiation: Conceptualizing, measuring, and evaluating constructs and pathways. *Monographs of the Society for Research in Child Development, 67*(2, Serial No. 269).

Liben, L. S., & Myers, L. J. (2007). Developmental changes in children's understanding of maps: What, when, and how? In J. M. Plumert & J. P. Spencer (Eds.), *The emerging spatial mind* (pp. 193–218). New York: Oxford University Press.

Lichtman, J. W. (2001). Developmental neurobiology overview: Synapses, circuits, and plasticity. In D. B. Bailey, Jr., J. T. Bruer, F. J. Symons, & J. W. Lichtman (Eds.), *Critical thinking about critical periods* (pp. 27–42). Baltimore: Brookes.

Lickona, T. (1991). Moral development in the elementary school classroom. In W. M. Kurtines & J. L. Gewirtz (Eds.), *Moral behavior and development: Vol. 3. Application.* Mahwah, NJ: Erlbaum.

Liem, A. D., Lau, S., & Nie, Y. (2008). The role of self-efficacy, task value, and achievement goals in predicting learning strategies, task disengagement, peer relationship, and achievement outcome. *Contemporary Educational Psychology, 33,* 486–512.

Liew, J., McTigue, E., Barrois, L., & Hughes, J. N. (2008, March). *I am, therefore I think: Effortful control, academic self-efficacy, and achievement in early grade school.* Paper presented at the annual meeting of the American Educational Research Association, New York.

Light, P., & Butterworth, G. (Eds.). (1993). *Context and cognition: Ways of learning and knowing.* Mahwah, NJ: Erlbaum.

Linn, M. C. (2008). Teaching for conceptual change: Distinguish or extinguish ideas. In S. Vosniadou (Ed.), *International handbook on conceptual change* (pp. 694–722). New York: Routledge.

Linn, M. C., Clement, C., Pulos, S., & Sullivan, P. (1989). Scientific reasoning during adolescence: The influence of instruction in science knowledge and reasoning strategies. *Journal of Research in Science Teaching, 26,* 171–187.

Linn, M. C., Songer, N. B., & Eylon, B. (1996). Shifts and convergences in science learning and instruction. In D. C. Berliner & R. C. Calfee (Eds.), *Handbook of educational psychology.* New York: Macmillan.

Linn, R. L. (1994). Performance assessment: Policy promises and technical measurement standards. *Educational Researcher, 23*(9), 4–14.

Linn, R. L. (2000). Assessments and accountability. *Educational Researcher, 29*(2), 4–16.

Linn, R. L., & Miller, M. D. (2005). *Measurement and assessment in teaching* (9th ed.). Upper Saddle River, NJ: Merrill/Prentice Hall.

Linnenbrink, E. A. (2005). The dilemma of performance-approach goals: The use of multiple goal contexts to promote students' motivation and learning. *Journal of Educational Psychology, 97,* 197–213.

Linnenbrink, E. A., & Pintrich, P. R. (2002). Achievement goal theory and affect: An asymmetrical bidirectional model. *Educational Psychologist, 37,* 69–78.

Linnenbrink, E. A., & Pintrich, P. R. (2003). Achievement goals and intentional conceptual change. In G. M. Sinatra & P. R. Pintrich (Eds.), *Intentional conceptual change* (pp. 347–374). Mahwah, NJ: Erlbaum.

Linnenbrink, E. A., & Pintrich, P. R. (2004). Role of affect in cognitive processing in academic contexts. In D. Y. Dai & R. J. Sternberg (Eds.), *Motivation, emotion, and cognition: Integrative perspectives on intellectual functioning and development* (pp. 57–87). Mahwah, NJ: Erlbaum.

Lippa, R. A. (2002). *Gender, nature, and nurture.* Mahwah, NJ: Erlbaum.

Lipson, M. Y. (1983). The influence of religious affiliation on children's memory for text information. *Reading Research Quarterly, 18,* 448–457.

Liu, L. G. (1990, April). *The use of causal questioning to promote narrative comprehension and memory.* Paper presented at the annual meeting of the American Educational Research Association, Boston.

Locke, E. A., & Latham, G. P. (2002). Building a practically useful theory of goal setting and task motivation: A 35-year odyssey. *American Psychologist, 57,* 705–717.

Locke, E. A., & Latham, G. P. (2006). New directions in goal-setting theory. *Current Directions in Psychological Science, 15,* 265–268.

Lockhart, K. L., Chang, B., & Story, T. (2002). Young children's beliefs about the stability of traits: Protective optimism? *Child Development, 73,* 1408–1430.

Lodewyk, K. R., & Winne, P. H. (2005). Relations among the structure of learning tasks, achievement, and changes in self-efficacy in secondary students. *Journal of Educational Psychology, 97,* 3–12.

Lodico, M. G., Ghatala, E. S., Levin, J. R., Pressley, M., & Bell, J. A. (1983). The effects of strategy monitoring training on children's selection of effective memory strategies. *Journal of Experimental Child Psychology, 35,* 273–277.

Loftus, E. F., & Loftus, G. R. (1980). On the permanence of stored information in the human brain. *American Psychologist, 35,* 409–420.

Lomawaima, K. T. (1995). Educating Native Americans. In J. A. Banks & C. A. M. Banks (Eds.), *Handbook of research on multicultural education.* New York: Macmillan.

Lopez, A. M. (2003). Mixed-race school-age children: A summary of census 2000 data. *Educational Researcher, 32*(6), 25–37.

López, G. R. (2001). Redefining parental involvement: Lessons from high-performing migrant-impacted schools. *American Educational Research Journal, 38,* 253–288.

Loranger, A. L. (1994). The study strategies of successful and unsuccessful high school students. *Journal of Reading Behavior, 26,* 347–360.

Lorch, R. F., Jr., Calderhead, W. J., Dunlap, E. E., Hodell, E. C., Freer, B. D., & Lorch, E. P. (2008, March). *Teaching the control of variables strategy in fourth grade classrooms.* Paper presented at the annual meeting of the American Educational Research Association, New York.

Lorch, R. F., Jr., Lorch, E. P., & Inman, W. E. (1993). Effects of signaling topic structure on text recall. *Journal of Educational Psychology, 85,* 281–290.

Losey, K. M. (1995). Mexican American students and classroom interaction: An overview and critique. *Review of Educational Research, 65,* 283–318.

Losh, S. C. (2003). On the application of social cognition and social location to creating causal explanatory structures. *Educational Research Quarterly, 26*(3), 17–33.

Lotan, R. A. (2006). Managing groupwork in heterogeneous classrooms. In C. M. Evertson & C. S. Weinstein (Eds.), *Handbook of classroom management: Research, practice, and contemporary issues* (pp. 525–539). Mahwah, NJ: Erlbaum.

Lou, Y., Abrami, P. C., & d'Apollonia, S. (2001). Small group and individual learning with technology: A meta-analysis. *Review of Educational Research, 71,* 449–521.

Lou, Y., Abrami, P. C., Spence, J. C., Poulsen, C., Chambers, B., & d'Apollonia, S. (1996). Within-class grouping: A meta-analysis. *Review of Educational Research, 66,* 423–458.

Lovell, K. (1979). Intellectual growth and the school curriculum. In F. B. Murray (Ed.), *The impact of Piagetian theory: On education, philosophy, psychiatry, and psychology.* Baltimore: University Park Press.

Lovett, S. B., & Flavell, J. H. (1990). Understanding and remembering: Children's knowledge about the differential effects of strategy and task variables on comprehension and memorization. *Child Development, 61,* 1842–1858.

Lubart, T. I., & Mouchiroud, C. (2003). Creativity: A source of difficulty in problem solving. In J. E. Davidson & R. J. Sternberg (Eds.), *The psychology of problem solving* (pp. 127–148). Cambridge, England: Cambridge University Press.

Lubinski, D., & Bleske-Rechek, A. (2008). Enhancing development in intellectually talented populations. In P. C. Kyllonen, R. D. Roberts, & L. Stankov (Eds.), *Extending intelligence: Enhancement and new constructs* (pp. 109–132). New York: Erlbaum/Taylor & Francis.

Lucariello, J., Kyratzis, A., & Nelson, K. (1992). Taxonomic knowledge: What kind and when? *Child Development, 63,* 978–998.

Luchins, A. S. (1942). Mechanization in problem solving: The effect of Einstellung. *Psychological Monographs, 54* (Whole No. 248).

Luciana, M., Conklin, H. M., Hooper, C. J., & Yarger, R. S. (2005). The development of nonverbal working memory and executive control processes in adolescents. *Child Development, 76,* 697–712.

Luckasson, R., Borthwick-Duffy, S., Buntinx, W. H. E., Coulter, D. L., Craig, E. M., Reeve, A., et al. (Eds.). (2002). *Mental retardation: Definition, classification, and systems of supports* (10th ed.). Washington, DC: American Association on Mental Retardation.

Luna, B., Garver, K. E., Urban, T. A., Lazar, N. A., & Sweeney, J. A. (2004). Maturation of cognitive processes from late childhood to adulthood. *Child Development, 75,* 1357–1372.

Lundeberg, M. A., & Fox, P. W. (1991). Do laboratory findings on test expectancy generalize to classroom outcomes? *Review of Educational Research, 61,* 94–106.

Lupart, J. L. (1995). Exceptional learners and teaching for transfer. In A. McKeough, J. Lupart, & A. Marini (Eds.), *Teaching for transfer: Fostering generalization in learning.* Mahwah, NJ: Erlbaum.

Ma, X., & Kishor, N. (1997). Attitude toward self, social factors, and achievement in mathematics: A meta-analytic review. *Educational Psychology Review, 9,* 89–120.

Maccoby, E. E. (2002). Gender and group process: A developmental perspective. *Current Directions in Psychological Science, 11,* 54–58.

Maccoby, E. E. (2007). Historical overview of socialization research and theory. In J. E. Grusec & P. D. Hastings (Eds.), *Handbook of socialization: Theory and research* (pp. 13–41). New York: Guilford Press.

Maccoby, E. E., & Martin, J. A. (1983). Socialization in the context of the family: Parent-child interaction. In E. M. Hetherington (Ed.), *Handbook of child psychology: Vol. 4. Socialization, personality, and social development* (4th ed.). New York: Wiley.

MacDonald, S., Uesiliana, K., & Hayne, H. (2000). Cross-cultural and gender differences in childhood amnesia. *Memory, 8,* 365–376.

Mace, F. C., Belfiore, P. J., & Hutchinson, J. M. (2001). Operant theory and research on self-regulation. In B. Zimmerman & D. Schunk (Eds.), *Learning and academic achievement: Theoretical perspectives* (pp. 39–65). Mahwah, NJ: Erlbaum.

Mace, F. C., Hock, M. L., Lalli, J. S., West, B. J., Belfiore, P., Pinter, E., et al. (1988). Behavioral momentum in the treatment of noncompliance. *Journal of Applied Behavior Analysis, 21,* 123–141.

Mac Iver, D. J., Reuman, D. A., & Main, S. R. (1995). Social structuring of the school: Studying what is, illuminating what could be. In J. T. Spence, J. M. Darley, & D. J. Foss (Eds.), *Annual review of psychology* (Vol. 46, pp. 375–400). Palo Alto, CA: Annual Review.

Mac Iver, D. J., Stipek, D. J., & Daniels, D. H. (1991). Explaining within-semester changes in student effort in junior high school and senior high school courses. *Journal of Educational Psychology, 83,* 201–211.

MacLean, D. J., Sasse, D. K., Keating, D. P., Stewart, B. E., & Miller, F. K. (1995, April). *All-girls' mathematics and science instruction in early adolescence: Longitudinal effects.* Paper presented at the annual meeting of the American Educational Research Association, San Francisco.

MacMaster, K., Donovan, L. A., & MacIntyre, P. D. (2002). The effects of being diagnosed with a learning disability on children's self-esteem. *Child Study Journal, 32,* 101–108.

Maehr, M. L. (1984). Meaning and motivation: Toward a theory of personal investment. In R. Ames & C. Ames (Eds.), *Research on motivation in education: Vol. 1. Student motivation.* San Diego, CA: Academic Press.

Maehr, M. L., & Anderman, E. M. (1993). Reinventing schools for early adolescents: Emphasizing task goals. *Elementary School Journal, 93,* 593–610.

Maehr, M. L., & Meyer, H. A. (1997). Understanding motivation and schooling: Where we've been, where we are, and where we need to go. *Educational Psychology Review, 9,* 371–409.

Magill, R. A. (1993). Modeling and verbal feedback influences on skill learning. *International Journal of Sport Psychology, 24,* 358–369.

Magnusson, S. J., Boyle, R. A., & Templin, M. (1994, April). *Conceptual development: Re-examining knowledge construction in science.* Paper presented at the annual meeting of the American Educational Research Association, New Orleans, LA.

Mahoney, J. L., Cairns, B. D., & Farmer, T. W. (2003). Promoting interpersonal competence and educational success through extracurricular activity participation. *Journal of Educational Psychology, 95,* 409–418.

Maikovich, A. K., Jaffee, S. R., Odgers, C. L., & Gallop, R. (2008). Effects of family violence on psychopathology symptoms in children previously exposed to maltreatment. *Child Development, 79,* 1498–1512.

Maker, C. J., & Schiever, S. W. (Eds.). (1989). *Critical issues in gifted education: Vol. 2. Defensible programs for cultural and ethnic minorities.* Austin, TX: Pro-Ed.

Malti, T., Gummerum, M., Keller, M., & Buchman, M. (2009). Children's moral motivation, sympathy, and prosocial behavior. *Child Development, 80,* 442–460.

Mandara, J., Gaylord-Harden, N. K., Richards, M. H., & Ragsdale, B. L. (2009). The effects of changes in racial identity and self-esteem on changes in African American adolescents' mental health. *Child Development, 80,* 1660–1675.

Mandler, J. M. (2007). On the origins of the conceptual system. *American Psychologist, 62,* 741–751.

Mangels, J. (2004, May). *The influence of intelligence beliefs on attention and learning: A neurophysiological approach.* Invited address presented at the annual meeting of the American Psychological Society, Chicago.

Mantzicopoulos, P. Y., & Knutson, D. J. (2000). Head Start children: School mobility and achievement in the early grades. *Journal of Educational Research, 93,* 305–311.

Marachi, R., Friedel, J., & Midgley, C. (2001, April). *"I sometimes annoy my teacher during math": Relations between student perceptions of the teacher and disruptive behavior in the classroom.* Paper presented at the annual meeting of the American Educational Research Association, Seattle, WA.

Marchand, G., & Skinner, E. A. (2007). Motivational dynamics of children's academic help-seeking and concealment. *Journal of Educational Psychology, 99,* 65–82.

Marcia, J. (1991). Identity and self-development. In R. M. Lerner, A. C. Petersen, & J. Brooks-Gunn (Eds.), *Encyclopedia of adolescence* (Vol. 1, pp. 529–533). New York: Garland.

Marcia, J. E. (1980). Identity in adolescence. In J. Adelson (Ed.), *Handbook of adolescent psychology.* New York: Wiley.

Marcia, J. E. (1988). Common processes underlying ego identity, cognitive/moral development, and individuation. In D. K. Lapsley & F. C. Power (Eds.), *Self, ego, and identity: Integrative approaches* (pp. 211–225). New York: Springer-Verlag.

Marcus, G. (2008). *Kluge: The haphazard construction of the human mind.* Boston: Houghton Mifflin.

Marcus, R. F. (1980). Empathy and popularity of preschool children. *Child Study Journal, 10,* 133–145.

Mareschal, D., Johnson, M. H., Sirois, S., Spratling, M. W., Thomas, M. S. C., & Westermann, G. (2007). *Neuroconstructivism: Vol. 1. How the brain constructs cognition.* Oxford, England: Oxford University Press.

Maria, K. (1998). Self-confidence and the process of conceptual change. In B. Guzzetti & C. Hynd (Eds.), *Perspectives on conceptual change: Multiple ways to understand knowing and learning in a complex world* (pp. 7–16). Mahwah, NJ: Erlbaum.

Markman, E. M. (1977). Realizing that you don't understand: A preliminary investigation. *Child Development, 48,* 986–992.

Markman, E. M. (1979). Realizing that you don't understand: Elementary school children's awareness of inconsistencies. *Child Development, 50,* 643–655.

Marks, H. M. (2000). Student engagement in instructional activity: Patterns in the elementary, middle, and high school years. *American Educational Research Journal, 37,* 153–184.

Markus, H. R., & Hamedani, M. G. (2007). Sociocultural psychology: The dynamic interdependence among self systems and social systems. In S. Kitayama & D. Cohen (Eds.), *Handbook of cultural psychology* (pp. 3–39). New York: Guilford Press.

Marley, S. C., Szabo, Z., Levin, J. R., & Glenberg, A. M. (2008, March). *Activity, observed activity, and children's recall of orally presented narrative passages.* Paper presented at the annual meeting of the American Educational Research Association, New York.

Marsh, H. W., & Craven, R. (1997). Academic self-concept: Beyond the dustbowl. In G. D. Phye (Ed.), *Handbook of classroom assessment: Learning, achievement, and adjustment.* San Diego, CA: Academic Press.

Marsh, H. W., & Craven, R. G. (2006). Reciprocal effects of self-concept and performance from a multidimensional perspective: Beyond seductive pleasure and unidimensional perspectives. *Perspectives on Psychological Science, 1,* 133–163.

Marsh, H. W., Ellis, L., & Craven, R. G. (2002). How do pre-school children feel about themselves? Unraveling measurement and multidimensional self-concept structure. *Developmental Psychology, 38,* 376–393.

Marsh, H. W., Gerlach, E., Trautwein, U., Lüdtke, O., & Brettschneider, W.-D. (2007). Longitudinal study of preadolescent sport self-concept and performance reciprocal effects and causal ordering. *Child Development, 78,* 1640–1656.

Marsh, H. W., & O'Mara, A. J. (2008). Self-concept is as multidisciplinary as it is multidimensional: A review of theory, measurement, and practice in self-concept research. In H. W. Marsh, R. G. Craven, & D. M. McInerney (Eds.), *Self-processes, learning, and enabling human potential* (pp. 87–115). Charlotte, NC: Information Age.

Marshall, H. H. (1992). *Redefining student learning: Roots of educational change.* Norwood, NJ: Ablex.

Martin, A. J. (2008). Enhancing student motivation and engagement: The effects of a multidimensional intervention. *Contemporary Educational Psychology, 33,* 239–269.

Martin, A. J., & Dowson, M. (2009). Interpersonal relationships, motivation, engagement, and achievement: Yields for theory, current issues, and educational practice. *Review of Educational Research, 79,* 327–365.

Martin, A. J., Marsh, H. W., & Debus, R. L. (2001). A quadripolar need achievement representation of self-handicapping and defensive pessimism. *American Educational Research Journal, 38,* 583–610.

Martin, A. J., Marsh, H. W., Williamson, A., & Debus, R. L. (2003). Self-handicapping, defensive pessimism, and goal orientation: A qualitative study of university students. *Journal of Educational Psychology, 95,* 617–628.

Martin, S. S., Brady, M. P., & Williams, R. E. (1991). Effects of toys on the social behavior of preschool children in integrated and nonintegrated groups: Investigation of a setting event. *Journal of Early Intervention, 15,* 153–161.

Martin, T. (2009). A theory of physically distributed learning: How external environments and internal states interact in mathematics learning. *Child Development Perspectives, 3,* 140–144.

Martin, V. L., & Pressley, M. (1991). Elaborative-interrogation effects depend on the nature of the question. *Journal of Educational Psychology, 83,* 113–119.

Martinez-Torteya, C., Bogat, G. A., von Eye, A., & Levendosky, A. A. (2009). Resilience among children exposed to domestic violence: The role of risk and protective factors. *Child Development, 80,* 562–577.

Marzano, R. J. (with Marzano, J. S., & Pickering, D. J.). (2003). *Classroom management that works: Research-based strategies for every teacher.* Alexandria, VA: Association for Supervision and Curriculum Development.

Maslow, A. H. (1973). Theory of human motivation. In R. J. Lowry (Ed.), *Dominance, self-esteem, self-actualization: Germinal papers of A. H. Maslow.* Monterey, CA: Brooks/Cole.

Maslow, A. H. (1987). *Motivation and personality* (3rd ed.). New York: Harper & Row.

Mason, L., Gava, M., & Boldrin, A. (2008). On warm conceptual change: The interplay of text, epistemological beliefs, and topic interest. *Journal of Educational Psychology, 100,* 291–309.

Massialas, B. G., & Zevin, J. (1983). *Teaching creatively: Learning through discovery.* Malabar, FL: Krieger.

Masten, A. S. (2001). Ordinary magic: Resilience processes in development. *American Psychologist, 56,* 227–238.

Masten, A. S., & Coatsworth, J. D. (1998). The development of competence in favorable and unfavorable environments. *American Psychologist, 53,* 205–220.

Mastropieri, M. A., & Scruggs, T. E. (2000). *The inclusive classroom: Strategies for effective instruction.* Upper Saddle River, NJ: Merrill/Prentice Hall.

Mathes, P. G., Torgesen, J. K., & Allor, J. H. (2001). The effects of peer-assisted literacy strategies for first-grade readers with and without additional computer-assisted instruction. *American Educational Research Journal, 38,* 371–410.

Matthews, D. J. (2009). Developmental transitions in giftedness and talent: Childhood into adolescence. In F. D. Horowitz, R. F. Subotnik, & D. J. Matthews (Eds.), *The development of giftedness and talent across the life span* (pp. 89–107). Washington, DC: American Psychological Association.

Matthews, G., Zeidner, M., & Roberts, R. D. (2006). Models of personality and affect for education: A review and synthesis. In P. A. Alexander & P. H. Winne (Eds.), *Handbook of educational psychology* (2nd ed., pp. 163–186). Mahwah, NJ: Erlbaum.

Matthews, J. S., Ponitz, C. C., & Morrison, F. J. (2009). *Journal of Educational Psychology, 101,* 689–704.

Matute-Bianchi, M. E. (2008). Situational ethnicity and patterns of school performance among immigrant and nonimmigrant Mexican-descent students. In J. U. Ogbu (Ed.), *Minority status, oppositional culture, and schooling* (pp. 398–432). New York: Routledge.

Maxmell, D., Jarrett, O. S., & Dickerson, C. (1998, April). *Are we forgetting the children's needs? Recess through the children's eyes.* Paper presented at the annual meeting of the American Educational Research Association, San Diego, CA.

Mayer, J. D., Salovey, P., & Caruso, D. R. (2008). Emotional intelligence: New ability or eclectic traits? *American Psychologist, 63,* 503–517.

Mayer, R. E. (1996). Learning strategies for making sense out of expository text: The SOI model for guiding three cognitive processes in knowledge construction. *Educational Psychology Review, 8,* 357–371.

Mayer, R. E. (1998). Does the brain have a place in educational psychology? *Educational Psychology Review, 10,* 389–396.

Mayer, R. E. (2003). The promise of multimedia learning: Using the same instructional design methods across different media. *Learning and Instruction, 13,* 125–139.

Mayer, R. E. (2004). Should there be a three-strikes rule against pure discovery learning? *American Psychologist, 59,* 14–19.

Mayer, R. E. (2008). Applying the science of learning: Evidence-based principles for the design of multimedia instruction. *American Psychologist, 63,* 760–769.

Mayer, R. E. (2010). Fostering scientific reasoning with multimedia instruction. In H. S. Waters & W. Schneider (Eds.), *Metacognition, strategy use, and instruction* (pp. 160–175). New York: Guilford Press.

Mayer, R. E., & Gallini, J. (1990). When is an illustration worth ten thousand words? *Journal of Educational Psychology, 82,* 715–726.

Mayer, R. E., & Massa, L. J. (2003). Three facets of visual and verbal learners: Cognitive ability, cognitive style, and learning preference. *Journal of Educational Psychology, 95,* 833–846.

Mayer, R. E., & Wittrock, M. C. (1996). Problem-solving transfer. In D. C. Berliner & R. C. Calfee (Eds.), *Handbook of educational psychology.* New York: Macmillan.

Mayer, R. E., & Wittrock, M. C. (2006). Problem solving. In P. A. Alexander & P. H. Winne (Eds.), *Handbook of educational psychology* (2nd ed., pp. 287–303). Mahwah, NJ: Erlbaum.

Mayfield, K. H., & Chase, P. N. (2002). The effects of cumulative practice on mathematics problem solving. *Journal of Applied Behavior Analysis, 35,* 105–123.

McAlpine, L. (1992). Language, literacy and education: Case studies of Cree, Inuit and Mohawk communities. *Canadian Children, 17*(1), 17–30.

McAlpine, L., & Taylor, D. M. (1993). Instructional preferences of Cree, Inuit, and Mohawk teachers. *Journal of American Indian Education, 33*(1), 1–20.

McAshan, H. H. (1979). *Competency-based education and behavioral objectives.* Englewood Cliffs, NJ: Educational Technology.

McBrien, J. L. (2005). *Discrimination and academic motivation in adolescent refugee girls.* Unpublished doctoral dissertation, Emory University, Atlanta, GA.

McCall, R. B., & Plemons, B. W. (2001). The concept of critical periods and their implications for early childhood services. In D. B. Bailey, Jr.,

J. T. Bruer, F. J. Symons, & J. W. Lichtman (Eds.), *Critical thinking about critical periods* (pp. 267–287). Baltimore: Brookes.

McCallum, R. S., & Bracken, B. A. (1993). Interpersonal relations between school children and their peers, parents, and teachers. *Educational Psychology Review, 5,* 155–176.

McCaslin, M., & Good, T. L. (1996). The informal curriculum. In D. C. Berliner & R. C. Calfee (Eds.), *Handbook of educational psychology.* New York: Macmillan.

McClowry, S. G. (1998). The science and art of using temperament as the basis for intervention. *School Psychology Review, 27,* 551–563.

McComas, J. J., Thompson, A., & Johnson, L. (2003). The effects of presession attention on problem behavior maintained by different reinforcers. *Journal of Applied Behavior Analysis, 36,* 297–307.

McCombs, B. L. (1988). Motivational skills training: Combining metacognitive, cognitive, and affective learning strategies. In C. E. Weinstein, E. T. Goetz, & P. A. Alexander (Eds.), *Learning and study strategies: Issues in assessment, instruction, and evaluation.* San Diego, CA: Harcourt Brace Jovanovich.

McCombs, B. L. (1996). Alternative perspectives for motivation. In L. Baker, P. Afflerbach, & D. Reinking (Eds.), *Developing engaged readers in school and home communities.* Hillsdale, NJ: Erlbaum.

McCombs, B. L. (Ed.). (2005). *Learner-centered principles: A framework for teaching.* Mahwah, NJ: Erlbaum.

McCourt, F. (2005). *Teacher man: A memoir.* New York: Scribner.

McCrudden, M. T., & Schraw, G. (2007). Relevance and goal-focusing in text processing. *Educational Psychology Review, 19,* 113–139.

McCutchen, D. (1996). A capacity theory of writing: Working memory in composition. *Educational Psychology Review, 8,* 299–325.

McDaniel, L. (1997). *For better, for worse, forever.* New York: Bantam.

McDaniel, M. A., & Einstein, G. O. (1989). Material-appropriate processing: A contextualist approach to reading and studying strategies. *Educational Psychology Review, 1,* 113–145.

McDevitt, M., & Chaffee, S. H. (1998). Second chance political socialization: "Trickle-up" effects of children on parents. In T. J. Johnson, C. E. Hays, & S. P. Hays (Eds.), *Engaging the public: How government and the media can reinvigorate American democracy* (pp. 57–66). Lanham, MD: Rowman & Littlefield.

McDevitt, T. M., & Ormrod, J. E. (2007). *Child development and education* (3rd ed.). Upper Saddle River, NJ: Merrill/Prentice Hall.

McDevitt, T. M., & Ormrod, J. E. (2008). Fostering conceptual change about child development in prospective teachers and other college students. *Child Development Perspectives, 2,* 85–91.

McDevitt, T. M., & Ormrod, J. E. (2010). *Child development and education* (4th ed.). Upper Saddle River, NJ: Merrill/Pearson Education

McElhaney, K. B., Antonishak, J., & Allen, J. P. (2008). "They like me, they like me not": Popularity and adolescents' perceptions of acceptance predicting social functioning over time. *Child Development, 79,* 720–731.

McGee, K. D., Knight, S. L., & Boudah, D. J. (2001, April). *Using reciprocal teaching in secondary inclusive English classroom instruction.* Paper presented at the annual meeting of the American Educational Research Association, Seattle, WA.

McGee, L. M. (1992). An exploration of meaning construction in first graders' grand conversations. In C. K. Kinzer & D. J. Leu (Eds.), *Literacy research, theory, and practice: Views from many perspectives.* Chicago: National Reading Conference.

McGovern, M. L., Davis, A., & Ogbu, J. U. (2008). The Minority Achievement Committee: Students leading students to greater success in school. In J. U. Ogbu (Ed.), *Minority status, oppositional culture, and schooling* (pp. 560–573). New York: Routledge.

McGregor, H. A., & Elliot, A. J. (2002). Achievement goals as predictors of achievement-relevant processes prior to task engagement. *Journal of Educational Psychology, 94,* 381–395.

McGrew, K. S., Flanagan, D. P., Zeith, T. Z., & Vanderwood, M. (1997). Beyond *g*: The impact of *Gf-Gc* specific cognitive abilities research on the future use and interpretation of intelligence tests in the schools. *School Psychology Review, 26,* 189–210.

McInerney, D. M., Marsh, H. W., & Craven, R. (2008). Self-processes, learning, and enabling human potential. In H. W. Marsh, R. G. Craven, & D. M. McInerney (Eds.), *Self-processes, learning, and enabling human potential* (pp. 3–11). Charlotte, NC: Information Age.

McKerchar, P. M., & Thompson, R. H. (2004). A descriptive analysis of potential reinforcement contingencies in the preschool classroom. *Journal of Applied Behavior Analysis, 37,* 431–444.

McKown, C., & Weinstein, R. S. (2003). The development and consequences of stereotype consciousness in middle childhood. *Child Development, 74,* 498–515.

McLane, J. B., & McNamee, G. D. (1990). *Early literacy.* Cambridge, MA: Harvard University Press.

McLeod, D. B., & Adams, V. M. (Eds.). (1989). *Affect and mathematical problem solving: A new perspective.* New York: Springer-Verlag.

McLoyd, V. C. (1998). Socioeconomic disadvantage and child development. *American Psychologist, 53,* 185–204.

McMillan, J. H., & Reed, D. F. (1994). At-risk students and resiliency: Factors contributing to academic success. *Clearing House, 67*(3), 137–140.

McMillan, J. H., Singh, J., & Simonetta, L. G. (1994). The tyranny of self-oriented self-esteem. *Educational Horizons, 72*(3), 141–145.

McNally, R. J., & Geraerts, E. (2009). A new solution to the recovered memory debate. *Perspectives on Psychological Science, 4,* 126–134.

McNamara, E. (1987). Behavioural approaches in the secondary school. In K. Wheldall (Ed.), *The behaviourist in the classroom.* London: Allen & Unwin.

McNeil, N. M., & Alibali, M. W. (2000). Learning mathematics from procedural instruction: Externally imposed goals influence what is learned. *Journal of Educational Psychology, 92,* 734–744.

McNeil, N. M., & Uttal, D. H. (2009). Rethinking the use of concrete materials in learning: Perspectives from development and education. *Child Development Perspectives, 3,* 137–139.

Medin, D. L. (2005, August). *Role of culture and expertise in cognition.* Invited address presented at the annual meeting of the American Psychological Association, Washington, DC.

Meece, J. L. (1994). The role of motivation in self-regulated learning. In D. H. Schunk & B. J. Zimmerman (Eds.), *Self-regulation of learning and performance: Issues and educational applications.* Mahwah, NJ: Erlbaum.

Meece, J. L., & Holt, K. (1993). A pattern analysis of students' achievement goals. *Journal of Educational Psychology, 85,* 582–590.

Meehan, B. T., Hughes, J. N., & Cavell, T. A. (2003). Teacher-student relationships as compensatory resources for aggressive children. *Child Development, 74,* 1145–1157.

Mehan, H. (1979). *Social organization in the classroom.* Cambridge, MA: Harvard University Press.

Meichenbaum, D. (1977). *Cognitive-behavior modification: An integrative approach.* New York: Plenum Press.

Meichenbaum, D., & Goodman, J. (1971). Training impulsive children to talk to themselves: A means of developing self-control. *Journal of Abnormal Psychology, 77,* 115–126.

Mejía-Arauz, R., Rogoff, B., Dexter, A., & Najafi, B. (2007). Cultural variation in children's social organization. *Child Development, 78,* 1001–1014.

Mellers, B. A., & McGraw, A. P. (2001). Anticipated emotions as guides to choice. *Current Directions in Psychological Science, 10,* 210–214.

Meltzer, L. (Ed.). (2007). *Executive function in education: From theory to practice.* New York: Guilford Press.

Meltzer, L., & Krishnan, K. (2007). Executive function difficulties and learning disabilities: Understandings and misunderstandings. In L. Meltzer (Ed.), *Executive function in education: From theory to practice* (pp. 77–105). New York: Guilford Press.

Meltzer, L., Pollica, L. S., & Barzillai, M. (2007). Executive function in the classroom: Embedding strategy instruction into daily teaching practices. In L. Meltzer (Ed.), *Executive function in education: From theory to practice* (pp. 165–193). New York: Guilford Press.

Mendoza-Denton, R., & Mischel, W. (2007). Integrating system approaches to culture and personality: The cultural cognitive-affective processing system. In S. Kitayama & D. Cohen (Eds.), *Handbook of cultural psychology* (pp. 175–195). New York: Guilford Press.

Menéndez, R. (Director). (1988). *Stand and deliver* [Motion picture]. United States: Warner Studios.

Menon, M., Tobin, D. D., Corby, B. C., Menon, M., Hodges, E. V. E., & Perry, D. G. (2007). The developmental costs of high self-esteem for antisocial children. *Child Development, 78,* 1627–1639.

Menyuk, P., & Menyuk, D. (1988). Communicative competence: A historical and cultural perspective. In J. S. Wurzel (Ed.), *Toward multiculturalism: A reader in multicultural education.* Yarmouth, ME: Intercultural Press.

Mergendoller, J. R., Markham, T., Ravitz, J., & Larmer, J. (2006). Pervasive management of project based learning: Teachers as guides and facilitators. In C. M. Evertson & C. S. Weinstein (Eds.), *Handbook of classroom management: Research, practice, and contemporary issues* (pp. 583–615). Mahwah, NJ: Erlbaum.

Merrill, P. F., Hammons, K., Vincent, B. R., Reynolds, P. L., Christensen, L., & Tolman, M. N. (1996). *Computers in education* (3rd ed.). Boston: Allyn & Bacon.

Mertler, C. A. (2009). *Action research: Teachers as researchers in the classroom* (2nd ed.). Thousand Oaks, CA: Sage.

Merzenich, M. M. (2001). Cortical plasticity contributing to child development. In J. L. McClelland & R. S. Siegler (Eds.), *Mechanisms of cognitive development: Behavioral and neural perspectives* (pp. 67–95). Mahwah, NJ: Erlbaum.

Mesquita, B., & Leu, J. (2007). The cultural psychology of emotion. In S. Kitayama & D. Cohen (Eds.), *Handbook of cultural psychology* (pp. 734–759). New York: Guilford Press.

Messer, S. B. (1976). Reflection-impulsivity: A review. *Psychological Bulletin, 83*, 1026–1052.

Messick, S. (1983). Assessment of children. In W. Kessen (Ed.), *Handbook of child psychology* (Vol. 1). New York: Wiley.

Messick, S. (1994a). The interplay of evidence and consequences in the validation of performance assessments. *Educational Researcher, 23*(2), 13–23.

Messick, S. (1994b). The matter of style: Manifestations of personality in cognition, learning, and testing. *Educational Psychologist, 29*, 121–136.

Metz, K. E. (1995). Reassessment of developmental constraints on children's science instruction. *Review of Educational Research, 65*, 93–127.

Metzger, M. J., Flanagin, A. J., & Zwarun, L. (2003). College student Web use, perceptions of information credibility, and verification behavior. *Computers and Education, 41*, 271–290.

Meyer, D. K., & Turner, J. C. (2002). Discovering emotion in classroom motivation research. *Educational Psychologist, 37*, 107–114.

Meyer, D. K., & Turner, J. C. (2006). Re-conceptualizing emotion and motivation to learn in classroom contexts. *Educational Psychology Review, 18*, 377–390.

Meyer, E. J. (2009). Creating schools that value sexual diversity. In S. R. Steinberg (Ed.), *Diversity and multiculturalism: A reader* (pp. 173–192). New York: Peter Lang.

Meyer, K. A. (1999). Functional analysis and treatment of problem behavior exhibited by elementary school children. *Journal of Applied Behavior Analysis, 32*, 229–232.

Meyer, L. H., Weir, K. F., McClure, J., & Walkey, F. (2008, March). *The relationship of motivation orientations to future achievement in secondary school.* Paper presented at the annual meeting of the American Educational Research Association, New York.

Middleton, M. J., & Midgley, C. (1997). Avoiding the demonstration of lack of ability: An underexplored aspect of goal theory. *Journal of Educational Psychology, 89*, 710–718.

Middleton, M. J., & Midgley, C. (2002). Beyond motivation: Middle school students' perceptions of press for understanding in math. *Contemporary Educational Psychology, 27*, 373–391.

Midgley, C. (Ed.). (2002). *Goals, goal structures, and patterns of adaptive learning.* Mahwah, NJ: Erlbaum.

Midgley, C., Kaplan, A., & Middleton, M. (2001). Performance-approach goals: Good for what, for whom, under what circumstances, and at what cost? *Journal of Educational Psychology, 93*, 77–86.

Midgley, C., Kaplan, A., Middleton, M., Maehr, M., Urdan, T., Anderman, L., et al. (1998). The development and validation of scales assessing students' achievement goal orientations. *Contemporary Educational Psychology, 23*, 113–131.

Midgley, C., Middleton, M. J., Gheen, M. H., & Kumar, R. (2002). Stage-environment fit revisited: A goal theory approach to examining school transitions. In C. Midgley (Ed.), *Goals, goal structures, and patterns of adaptive learning* (pp. 109–142). Mahwah, NJ: Erlbaum.

Mikaelsen, B. (1996). *Countdown.* New York: Hyperion Books for Children.

Miles, S. B., & Stipek, D. (2006). Contemporaneous and longitudinal associations between social behavior and literacy achievement in a sample of low-income elementary school children. *Child Development, 77*, 103–117.

Miller, A. (1987). Cognitive styles: An integrated model. *Educational Psychology, 7*, 251–268.

Miller, A. (2006). Contexts and attributions for difficult behavior in English classrooms. In C. M. Evertson & C. S. Weinstein (Eds.), *Handbook of classroom management: Research, practice, and contemporary issues* (pp. 1093–1120). Mahwah, NJ: Erlbaum.

Miller, B. C., & Benson, B. (1999). Romantic and sexual relationship development during adolescence. In W. Furman, B. B. Brown, & C. Feiring (Eds.), *The development of romantic relationships in adolescence* (pp. 99–121). Cambridge, England: Cambridge University Press.

Miller, D. L., & Kelley, M. L. (1994). The use of goal setting and contingency contracting for improving children's homework performance. *Journal of Applied Behavior Analysis, 27*, 73–84.

Miller, G. A. (1956). The magical number seven, plus or minus two: Some limits on our capacity for processing information. *Psychological Review, 63*, 81–97.

Miller, G. A., & Gildea, P. M. (1987). How children learn words. *Scientific American, 257*, 94–99.

Miller, J. G. (1997). A cultural-psychology perspective on intelligence. In R. J. Sternberg & E. L. Grigorenko (Eds.), *Intelligence, heredity, and environment* (pp. 269–302). Cambridge, England: Cambridge University Press.

Miller, J. G. (2007). Cultural psychology of moral development. In S. Kitayama & D. Cohen (Eds.), *Handbook of cultural psychology* (pp. 477–499). New York: Guilford Press.

Miller, L. S. (1995). *An American imperative: Accelerating minority educational advancement.* New Haven, CT: Yale University Press.

Miller, M. D., Linn, R. L., & Gronlund, N. E. (2009). *Measurement and assessment in teaching* (10th ed.). Upper Saddle River, NJ: Merrill/Pearson.

Miller, P. A., Eisenberg, N., Fabes, R. A., & Shell, R. (1996). Relations of moral reasoning and vicarious emotion to young children's prosocial behavior toward peers and adults. *Developmental Psychology, 32*, 210–219.

Miller, R. B., & Brickman, S. J. (2004). A model of future-oriented motivation and self-regulation. *Educational Psychology Review, 16*, 9–33.

Miller, S. D., Heafner, T., Massey, D., & Strahan, D. B. (2003, April). *Students' reactions to teachers' attempts to create the necessary conditions to promote the acquisition of self-regulation skills.* Paper presented at the annual meeting of the American Educational Research Association, Chicago.

Miller, S. D., & Meece, J. L. (1997). Enhancing elementary students' motivation to read and write: A classroom intervention study. *Journal of Educational Research, 90*, 286–300.

Mills, B., Reyna, V. F., & Estrada, S. (2008). Explaining contradictory relations between risk perception and risk taking. *Psychological Science, 19*, 429–433.

Mills, G. E. (2007). *Action research: A guide for the teacher researcher* (3rd ed.). Upper Saddle River, NJ: Merrill/Prentice Hall.

Milner, H. R. (2006). Classroom management in urban classrooms. In C. M. Evertson & C. S. Weinstein (Eds.), *Handbook of classroom man-agement: Research, practice, and contemporary issues* (pp. 491–522). Mahwah, NJ: Erlbaum.

Minami, M., & McCabe, A. (1996). Compressed collections of experiences: Some Asian American traditions. In A. McCabe (Ed.), *Chameleon readers: Some problems cultural differences in narrative structure pose for multicultural literacy programs* (pp. 72–97). New York: McGraw-Hill.

Minsky, M. (2006). *The emotion machine: Commonsense thinking, artificial intelligence, and the future of the human mind.* New York: Simon and Schuster.

Minstrell, J., & Stimpson, V. (1996). A classroom environment for learning: Guiding students' reconstruction of understanding and reasoning. In L. Schauble & R. Glaser (Eds.), *Innovations in learning: New environments for education.* Mahwah, NJ: Erlbaum.

Mintrop, H., & Sunderman, G. L. (2009). Predictable failure of federal sanctions-driven accountability for school improvement—And why we may retain it anyway. *Educational Researcher, 38*, 353–364.

Mintzes, J. J., Wandersee, J. H., & Novak, J. D. (1997). Meaningful learning in science: The human constructivist perspective. In G. D. Phye (Ed.), *Handbook of academic learning: Construction of knowledge.* San Diego, CA: Academic Press.

Mischel, W., & Shoda, Y. (1995). A cognitive-affective system theory of personality: Reconceptualizing situations, dispositions, dynamics, and invariance in personality structure. *Psychological Review, 102*, 246–268.

Mistry, R. S., Vandewater, E. A., Huston, A. C., & McLoyd, V. C. (2002). Economic well-being and children's social adjustment: The role of family process in an ethnically diverse low-income sample. *Child Development, 73*, 935–951.

Mitchell, D. B. (2006). Nonconscious priming after 17 years: Invulnerable implicit memory? *Psychological Science 17*, 925–929.

Mitchell, M. (1993). Situational interest: Its multifaceted structure in the secondary school mathematics classroom. *Journal of Educational Psychology, 85*, 424–436.

Miyake, N. (2008). Conceptual change through collaboration. In S. Vosniadou (Ed.), *International handbook on conceptual change* (pp. 453–478). New York: Routledge.

Mohan, E. (2009). Putting multiethnic students on the radar: A case for greater consideration of our multiethnic students. In S. R. Steinberg (Ed.), *Diversity and multiculturalism: A reader* (pp. 132–141). New York: Peter Lang.

Mohatt, G., & Erickson, F. (1981). Cultural differences in teaching styles in an Odawa school: A sociolinguistic approach. In H. T. Trueba, G. P. Guthrie, & K. H. Au (Eds.), *Culture and the bilingual classroom: Studies in classroom ethnography.* Rowley, MA: Newbury House.

Moje, E. B., & Hinchman, K. (2004). Culturally reponsive practices for youth literacy learning. In T. L. Jetton & J. A. Dole (Eds.), *Adolescent literacy research and practice* (pp. 321–350). New York: Guilford Press.

Moje, E. B., & Shepardson, D. P. (1998). Social interactions and children's changing understanding of electric circuits: Exploring unequal power relations in "peer"-learning groups. In B. Guzzetti & C. Hynd (Eds.), *Perspectives on conceptual change: Multiple ways to understand knowing and learning in a complex world* (pp. 225–234). Mahwah, NJ: Erlbaum.

Moles, O. C. (Ed.). (1990). *Student discipline strategies: Research and practice.* Albany: State University of New York Press.

Monte-Sano, C. (2008). Qualities of historical writing instruction: A comparative case study of two teachers' practices. *American Educational Research Journal, 45,* 1045–1079.

Moon, J. (2008). *Critical thinking: An exploration of theory and practice.* London: Routledge.

Moon, S. M., Feldhusen, J. F., & Dillon, D. R. (1994). Long-term effects of an enrichment program based on the Purdue Three-Stage Model. *Gifted Child Quarterly, 38,* 38–48.

Mooney, C. M. (1957). Age in the development of closure ability in children. *Canadian Journal of Psychology, 11,* 219–226.

Moore, J. W., & Edwards, R. P. (2003). An analysis of aversive stimuli in classroom demand contexts. *Journal of Applied Behavior Analysis, 36,* 339–348.

Moran, S., & Gardner, H. (2006). Extraordinary achievements: A developmental and systems analysis. In W. Damon & R. M. Lerner (Series Eds.), D. Kuhn & R. Siegler (Vol. Eds.), *Handbook of child psychology: Vol. 2. Cognition, perception, and language* (6th ed.). New York: Wiley.

Morelli, G. A., & Rothbaum, F. (2007). Situating the child in context: Attachment relationships and self-regulation in different cultures. In S. Kitayama & D. Cohen (Eds.), *Handbook of cultural psychology* (pp. 500–527). New York: Guilford Press.

Moreno, R. (2006). Learning in high-tech and multimedia environments. *Current Directions in Psychological Science, 15,* 63–67.

Moreno, R., Mayer, R. E., Spires, H. A., & Lester, J. C. (2001). The case for social agency in computer-based teaching: Do students learn more deeply when they interact with animated pedagogical agents? *Cognition and Instruction, 19,* 177–213.

Morgan, M. (1985). Self-monitoring of attained subgoals in private study. *Journal of Educational Psychology, 77,* 623–630.

Morra, S., Gobbo, C., Marini, Z., & Sheese, R. (2008). *Cognitive development: Neo-Piagetian perspectives.* New York: Erlbaum.

Morrison, G. M., Furlong, M. J., D'Incau, B., & Morrison, R. L. (2004). The safe school: Integrating the school reform agenda to prevent disruption and violence at school. In J. C. Conoley & A. P. Goldstein (Eds.), *School violence intervention* (2nd ed., pp. 256–296). New York: Guilford Press.

Morrow, S. L. (1997). Career development of lesbian and gay youth: Effects of sexual orientation, coming out, and homophobia. In M. B. Harris (Ed.), *School experiences of gay and lesbian youth: The invisible minority* (pp. 1–15). Binghamton, NY: Harrington Park Press.

Mostow, A. J., Izard, C. E., Fine, S., & Trantacosta, C. J. (2002). Modeling emotional, cognitive, and behavioral predictors. *Child Development, 73,* 1775–1787.

Mueller, M. M., Edwards, R. P., & Trahant, D. (2003). Translating multiple assessment techniques into an intervention selection model for classrooms. *Journal of Applied Behavior Analysis, 36,* 563–573.

Muis, K. R. (2004). Personal epistemology and mathematics: A critical review and synthesis of research. *Review of Educational Research, 74,* 317–377.

Muis, K. R. (2007). The role of epistemic beliefs in self-regulated learning. *Educational Psychologist, 42,* 173–190.

Muis, K. R., Bendixen, L. D., & Haerle, F. C. (2006). Domain-generality and domain-specificity in personal epistemology research: Philosophical and empirical reflections in the development of a theoretical framework. *Educational Psychology Review, 18,* 3–54.

Munn, P., Johnstone, M., & Chalmers, V. (1990, April). *How do teachers talk about maintaining effective discipline in their classrooms?* Paper presented at the annual meeting of the American Educational Research Association, Boston.

Munro, D. W., & Stephenson, J. (2009). The effects of response cards on student and teacher behavior during vocabulary instruction. *Journal of Applied Behavior Analysis, 42,* 795–800.

Murdock, T. B. (1999). The social context of risk: Status and motivational predictors of alienation in middle school. *Journal of Educational Psychology, 91,* 62–75.

Murdock, T. B. (2000). Incorporating economic context into educational psychology: Methodological and conceptual challenges. *Educational Psychologist, 35,* 113–124.

Murdock, T. B., & Anderman, E. M. (2006). Motivational perspectives on student cheating: Toward an integrated model of academic dishonesty. *Educational Psychologist, 41,* 129–145.

Murdock, T. B., Hale, N. M., & Weber, M. J. (2001). Predictors of cheating among early adolescents: Academic and social motivations. *Contemporary Educational Psychology, 26,* 96–115.

Murdock, T. B., Miller, A., & Kohlhardt, J. (2004). Effects of classroom context variables on high school students' judgments of the acceptability and likelihood of cheating. *Journal of Educational Psychology, 96,* 765–777.

Murphy, P. K. (2007). The eye of the beholder: The interplay of social and cognitive components in change. *Educational Psychologist, 42,* 41–53.

Murphy, P. K., & Alexander, P. A. (2000). A motivated exploration of motivation terminology. *Contemporary Educational Psychology, 25,* 3–53.

Murphy, P. K., & Mason, L. (2006). Changing knowledge and beliefs. In P. A. Alexander & P. H. Winne (Eds.), *Handbook of educational psychology* (2nd ed., pp. 305–324). Mahwah, NJ: Erlbaum.

Murphy, P. K., Wilkinson, I. A. G., Soter, A. O., Hennessey, M. N., & Alexander, J. F. (2009). Examining the effects of classroom discussion on students' comprehension of text: A meta-analysis. *Journal of Educational Psychology, 101,* 740–764.

Myles, B. S., & Simpson, R. L. (2001). Understanding the hidden curriculum: An essential social skill for children and youth with Asperger syndrome. *Intervention in School and Clinic, 36,* 279–286.

Narváez, D., & Rest, J. (1995). The four components of acting morally. In W. M. Kurtines & J. L. Gewirtz (Eds.), *Moral development: An introduction.* Boston: Allyn & Bacon.

Nasir, N. S., McLaughlin, M. W., & Jones, A. (2009). What does it mean to be African American? Constructions of race and academic identity in an urban public high school. *American Educational Research Journal, 46,* 73–114.

National Association of Secondary School Principals. (2004). *Breaking ranks II: Strategies for leading high school reform.* Reston, VA: Author.

National Center for Education Statistics (2007, September). *Crime, violence, discipline, and safety in U.S. public schools: Findings from the School Survey on Crime and Safety, 2005–06.* Washington: U.S. Department of Education.

National Research Council. (2000). *How people learn: Brain, mind, experience, and school* (expanded ed.). Washington, DC: National Academies Press.

NCSS Task Force on Ethnic Studies Curriculum Guidelines. (1992). Curriculum guidelines for multicultural education. *Social Education, 56,* 274–294.

Neel, R. S., Jenkins, Z. N., & Meadows, N. (1990). Social problem-solving behaviors and aggression in young children: A descriptive observational study. *Behavioral Disorders, 16,* 39–51.

Neisser, U. (1967). *Cognitive psychology.* New York: Appleton-Century-Crofts.

Neisser, U. (1998a). Introduction: Rising test scores and what they mean. In U. Neisser (Ed.), *The rising curve: Long-term gains in IQ and related measures* (pp. 3–22). Washington, DC: American Psychological Association.

Neisser, U. (Ed.). (1998b). *The rising curve: Long-term gains in IQ and related measures.* Washington, DC: American Psychological Association.

Neisser, U., Boodoo, G., Bouchard, T. J., Boykin, A. W., Brody, N., Ceci, S. J., et al. (1996). Intelligence: Knowns and unknowns. *American Psychologist, 51,* 77–101.

Nell, V. (2002). Why young men drive dangerously: Implications for injury prevention. *Current Directions in Psychological Science, 11,* 75–79.

Nelson, C. A., III, Thomas, K. M., & de Haan, M. (2006). Neural bases of cognitive development. In W. Damon & R. M. Lerner (Series Eds.), D. Kuhn, & R. Siegler (Vol. Eds.), *Handbook of child psychology. Vol. 2: Cognition, perception, and language* (6th ed., pp. 3–57). New York: Wiley.

Nelson, K. (1993). The psychological and social origins of autobiographical memory. *Psychological Science, 4,* 7–14.

Nelson, K. (1996). *Language in cognitive development: The emergence of the mediated mind.* Cambridge, England: Cambridge University Press.

Nelson, K., & Fivush, R. (2004). The emergence of autobiographical memory: A social cultural developmental theory. *Psychological Review, 111,* 486–511.

Nelson, T. O., & Dunlosky, J. (1991). When people's judgments of learning (JOLs) are extremely accurate at predicting subsequent recall: The "delayed-JOL effect." *Psychological Science, 2,* 267–270.

Nelson-Barber, S., & Estrin, E. T. (1995). Bringing Native American perspectives to mathematics and science teaching. *Theory into Practice, 34,* 174–185.

Nesbit, J. C., & Adesope, O. O. (2006). Learning with concept and knowledge maps: A meta-analysis. *Review of Educational Research, 76,* 413–448.

Nesdale, D., Maass, A., Durkin, K., & Griffiths, J. (2005). Group norms, threat, and children's racial prejudice. *Child Development, 76,* 652–663.

Nettles, S. M., Caughy, M. O., & O'Campo, P. J. (2008). School adjustment in the early grades: Toward an integrated model of neighborhood, parental, and child processes. *Review of Educational Research, 78,* 3–32.

Neubauer, G., Mansel, J., Avrahami, A., & Nathan, M. (1994). Family and peer support of Israeli and German adolescents. In F. Nestemann & K. Hurrelmann (Eds.), *Social networks and* social support in childhood and adolescence. Berlin, Germany: Aldine de Gruyter.

Nevin, J. A., Mandell, C., & Atak, J. R. (1983). The analysis of behavioral momentum. *Journal of the Experimental Analysis of Behavior, 39,* 49–59.

Newby, T. J., Ertmer, P. A., & Stepich, D. A. (1994, April). *Instructional analogies and the learning of concepts.* Paper presented at the annual meeting of the American Educational Research Association, New Orleans, LA.

Newcomb, A. F., Bukowski, W. M., & Pattee, L. (1993). Children's peer relations: A meta-analytic review of popular, rejected, neglected, controversial, and average sociometric status. *Psychological Bulletin, 113,* 99–128.

Newcombe, N., & Huttenlocher, J. (1992). Children's early ability to solve perspective-taking problems. *Developmental Psychology, 28,* 635–643.

Newgent, R. A., Cavell, T. A., Johnson, C. A., & Stegman, C. E. (2008, March). *Impact of a lunch buddy mentoring program on potential victims of peer harassment.* Paper presented at the annual meeting of the American Educational Research Association, New York.

Newkirk, T. (2002). *Misreading masculinity: Boys, literacy, and popular culture.* Portsmouth, NH: Heinemann.

Newman, L. S. (1990). Intentional and unintentional memory in young children: Remembering vs. playing. *Journal of Experimental Child Psychology, 50,* 243–258.

Newman, R. S. (2008). Adaptive and nonadaptive help seeking with peer harassment: An integrative perspective of coping and self-regulation. *Educational Psychologist, 43,* 1–15.

Newman, R. S., & Murray, B. J. (2005). How students and teachers view the seriousness of peer harassment: When is it appropriate to seek help? *Journal of Educational Psychology, 97,* 347–365.

Newman, R. S., & Schwager, M. T. (1995). Students' help seeking during problem solving: Effects of grade, goal, and prior achievement. *American Educational Research Journal, 32,* 352–376.

Newmann, F. M. (1997). Authentic assessment in social studies: Standards and examples. In G. D. Phye (Ed.), *Handbook of classroom assessment: Learning, achievement, and adjustment.* San Diego, CA: Academic Press.

Newstead, S. (2004). The purposes of assessment. *Psychology of Learning and Teaching, 3,* 97–101.

Ni, Y., & Zhou, Y.-D. (2005). Teaching and learning fractions and rational numbers: The origins and implications of whole number bias. *Educational Psychologist, 40,* 27–52.

Nicholls, J. G. (1984). Conceptions of ability and achievement motivation. In R. Ames & C. Ames (Eds.), *Research on motivation in education: Vol. 1. Student motivation.* San Diego, CA: Academic Press.

Nicholls, J. G. (1990). What is ability and why are we mindful of it? A developmental perspective. In R. J. Sternberg & J. Kolligian (Eds.), *Competence considered.* New Haven, CT: Yale University Press.

Nichols, J. D. (1996). The effects of cooperative learning on student achievement and motivation in a high school geometry class. *Contemporary Educational Psychology, 21,* 467–476.

Nichols, J. D., Ludwin, W. G., & Iadicola, P. (1999). A darker shade of gray: A year-end analysis of discipline and suspension data. *Equity and Excellence in Education, 32*(1), 43–55.

Nickerson, R. S. (1989). New directions in educational assessment. *Educational Researcher, 18*(9), 3–7.

Nippold, M. A. (1988). The literate lexicon. In M. A. Nippold (Ed.), *Later language development: Ages nine through nineteen.* Boston: Little, Brown.

Nisbett, R. E. (2009). *Intelligence and how to get it.* New York: Norton.

Nishina, A., & Juvonen, J. (2005). Daily reports of witnessing and experiencing peer harassment in middle school. *Child Development, 76,* 435–450.

Nixon, A. S. (2005, April). *Moral reasoning in the digital age: How students, teachers, and parents judge appropriate computer uses.* Paper presented at the annual meeting of the American Educational Research Association, Montreal.

Noble, K. G., Tottenham, N., & Casey, B. J. (2005). Neuroscience perspectives on disparities in school readiness and cognitive achievement. *The Future of Children, 15*(1), 71–89.

Nokes, J. D., & Dole, J. A. (2004). Helping adolescent readers through explicit strategy instruction. In T. L. Jetton & J. A. Dole (Eds.), *Adolescent literacy research and practice* (pp. 162–182). New York: Guilford Press.

Nolen, S. B. (1996). Why study? How reasons for learning influence strategy selection. *Educational Psychology Review, 8,* 335–355.

Nolen, S. B. (2007). Young children's motivation to read and write: Development in social contexts. *Cognition and Instruction, 25,* 219–270.

Norenzayan, A., Choi, I., & Peng, K. (2007). Perception and cognition. In S. Kitayama & D. Cohen (Eds.), *Handbook of cultural psychology* (pp. 569–594). New York: Guilford Press.

Noss, R., & Hoyles, C. (2006). Exploring mathematics through construction and collaboration. In R. K. Sawyer (Ed.), *The Cambridge handbook of the learning sciences* (pp. 389–405). Cambridge, England: Cambridge University Press.

Novak, J. D. (1998). *Learning, creating, and using knowledge: Concept maps as facilitative tools in schools and corporations.* Mahwah, NJ: Erlbaum.

Novak, J. D., & Gowin, D. B. (1984). *Learning how to learn.* Cambridge, England: Cambridge University Press.

Nucci, L. (2006). Classroom management for moral and social development. In C. M. Evertson & C. S. Weinstein (Eds.), *Handbook of classroom management: Research, practice, and contemporary issues* (pp. 711–731). Mahwah, NJ: Erlbaum.

Nucci, L. (2009). *Nice is not enough: Facilitating moral development.* Upper Saddle River, NJ: Merrill/Pearson.

Nucci, L. P. (2001). *Education in the moral domain.* Cambridge, England: Cambridge University Press.

Nucci, L. P., & Nucci, M. S. (1982). Children's social interactions in the context of moral and conventional transgressions. *Child Development, 53,* 403–412.

Nucci, L. P., & Weber, E. K. (1995). Social interactions in the home and the development of young children's conceptions of the personal. *Child Development, 66,* 1438–1452.

Nuemi, J.-W. (2008). Self and socialization: How do young people navigate through adolescence? In H. W. Marsh, R. G. Craven, & D. M. McInerney (Eds.), *Self-processes, learning, and enabling human potential* (pp. 305–327). Charlotte, NC: Information Age.

Nussbaum, E. M. (2008). Collaborative discourse, argumentation, and learning: Preface and literature review. *Contemporary Educational Psychology, 33,* 345–359.

Nussbaum, J. (1985). The earth as a cosmic body. In R. Driver (Ed.), *Children's ideas of science.* Philadelphia: Open University Press.

Oakes, J., & Guiton, G. (1995). Matchmaking: The dynamics of high school tracking decisions. *American Educational Research Journal, 32,* 3–33.

Oberheim, N. A., Takano, T., Han, X., He, W., Lin, J. H. C., Wang, F., et al. (2009). Uniquely hominid features of adult human astrocytes. *Journal of Neuroscience, 29,* 3276–3287.

Ochs, E. (1982). Talking to children in western Samoa. *Language and Society, 11,* 77–104.

Ochsner, K. N., & Lieberman, M. D. (2001). The emergence of social cognitive neuroscience. *American Psychologist, 56,* 717–734.

O'Connor, E., & McCartney, K. (2007). Examining teacher-child relationships and achievement as part of an ecological model of development. *American Educational Research Journal, 44,* 340–369.

O'Donnell, A. M. (1999). Structuring dyadic interaction through scripted cooperation. In A. M. O'Donnell & A. King (Eds.), *Cognitive perspectives on peer learning* (pp. 179–196). Mahwah, NJ: Erlbaum.

O'Donnell, A. M. (2006). The role of peers and group learning. In P. A. Alexander & P. H. Winne (Eds.), *Handbook of educational psychology* (2nd ed., pp. 781–802). Mahwah, NJ: Erlbaum.

O'Donnell, A. M., Hmelo-Silver, C. E., & Erkens, G. (Eds.). (2006). *Collaborative learning, reasoning, and technology.* Mahwah, NJ: Erlbaum.

O'Donnell, A. M., & O'Kelly, J. (1994). Learning from peers: Beyond the rhetoric of positive results. *Educational Psychology Review, 6,* 321–349.

O'Donnell, D. A., Schwab-Stone, M. E., & Muyeed, A. Z. (2002). Multidimensional resilience in urban children exposed to community violence. *Child Development, 73,* 1265–1282.

Ogbu, J. U. (1992). Understanding cultural diversity and learning. *Educational Researcher, 21*(8), 5–14, 24.

Ogbu, J. U. (1994). From cultural differences to differences in cultural frame of reference. In P. M. Greenfield & R. R. Cocking (Eds.), *Cross-cultural roots of minority child development.* Mahwah, NJ: Erlbaum.

Ogbu, J. U. (1999). Beyond language: Ebonics, proper English, and identity in a Black-American speech community. *American Educational Research Journal, 36,* 147–184.

Ogbu, J. U. (2003). *Black American students in an affluent suburb: A study of academic disengagement.* Mahwah, NJ: Erlbaum.

Ogbu, J. U. (2008a). Collective identity and the burden of "acting White" in Black history, community, and education. In J. U. Ogbu (Ed.), *Minority status, oppositional culture, and schooling* (pp. 29–63). New York: Routledge.

Ogbu, J. U. (2008b). Multiple sources of peer pressures among African American students. In J. U. Ogbu (Ed.), *Minority status, oppositional culture, and schooling* (pp. 89–111). New York: Routledge.

Öhman, A., & Mineka, S. (2003). The malicious serpent: Snakes as a prototypical stimulus for an evolved module of fear. *Current Directions in Psychological Science, 12,* 5–9.

Okagaki, L. (2001). Triarchic model of minority children's school achievement. *Educational Psychologist, 36,* 9–20.

Okagaki, L. (2006). Ethnicity and learning. In P. A. Alexander & P. H. Winne (Eds.), *Handbook of educational psychology* (2nd ed., pp. 615–634). Mahwah, NJ: Erlbaum.

O'Leary, K. D., Kaufman, K. F., Kass, R. E., & Drabman, R. S. (1970). The effects of loud and soft reprimands on the behavior of disruptive students. *Exceptional Children, 37,* 145–155.

Olneck, M. R. (1995). Immigrants and education. In J. A. Banks & C. A. M. Banks (Eds.), *Handbook of research on multicultural education.* New York: Macmillan.

O'Mara, A. J., Marsh, H. W., Craven, R. G., & Debus, R. L. (2006). Do self-concept interventions make a difference? A synergistic blend of construct validation and meta-analysis. *Educational Psychologist, 41,* 181–206.

Onosko, J. J., & Newmann, F. M. (1994). Creating more thoughtful learning environments. In J. N. Mangieri & C. C. Block (Eds.), *Advanced educational psychology: Enhancing mindfulness.* Fort Worth, TX: Harcourt Brace Jovanovich.

Oppenheimer, L. (1986). Development of recursive thinking: Procedural variations. *International Journal of Behavioral Development, 9,* 401–411.

Orenstein, P. (1994). *Schoolgirls: Young women, self-esteem, and the confidence gap.* New York: Doubleday.

Ormrod, J. E. (2008). *Human learning* (5th ed.). Upper Saddle River, NJ: Merrill/Prentice Hall.

Ormrod, J. E., & McGuire, D. J. (2007). *Case studies: Applying educational psychology* (2nd ed.). Upper Saddle River, NJ: Merrill/Prentice Hall.

Ornstein, P. A., Grammer, J. K., & Coffman, J. L. (2010). Teachers' "mnemonic style" and the development of skilled memory. In H. S. Waters & W. Schneider (Eds.), *Metacognition, strategy use, and instruction* (pp. 23–53). New York: Guilford Press.

Ornstein, R. (1997). *The right mind: Making sense of the hemispheres.* San Diego, CA: Harcourt Brace.

Osborne, J. W., & Simmons, C. M. (2002, April). *Girls, math, stereotype threat, and anxiety: Physiological evidence.* Paper presented at the annual meeting of the American Educational Research Association, New Orleans, LA.

Osher, D., Dwyer, K., & Jimerson, S. R. (2006). Safe, supportive, and effective schools: Promoting school success to reduce school violence. In S. R. Jimerson & M. Furlong (Eds.), *Handbook of school violence and school safety: From research to practice* (pp. 51–71). Mahwah, NJ: Erlbaum.

Oskamp, S. (Ed.). (2000). *Reducing prejudice and discrimination.* Mahwah, NJ: Erlbaum.

Osterman, K. F. (2000). Students' need for belonging in the school community. *Review of Educational Research, 70,* 323–367.

Otis, N., Grouzet, F. M. E., & Pelletier, L. G. (2005). Latent motivational change in an academic setting: A 3-year longitudinal study. *Journal of Educational Psychology, 97,* 170–183.

O'Toole, M. E. (2000). *The school shooter: A threat assessment perspective.* Quantico, VA: Federal Bureau of Investigation. Retrieved February 26, 2004, from www.fbi.gov/publications/school/school2.pdf

Owens, R. E., Jr. (1995). *Language disorders: A functional approach to assessment and intervention* (2nd ed.). Boston: Allyn & Bacon.

Owens, R. E., Jr. (1996). *Language development* (4th ed.). Boston: Allyn & Bacon.

Paciello, M., Fida, R., Tramontano, C., Lupinetti, C., & Caprara, G. V. (2008). Stability and change of moral disengagement and its impact on aggression and violence in late adolescence. *Child Development, 79,* 1288–1309.

Padilla, A. M. (1994). Bicultural development: A theoretical and empirical examination. In R. G. Malgady & O. Rodriguez (Eds.), *Theoretical and conceptual issues in Hispanic mental health* (pp. 20–51). Malabar, FL: Krieger.

Padilla, A. M. (2006). Second language learning: Issues in research and teaching. In P. A. Alexander & P. H. Winne (Eds.), *Handbook of educational psychology* (2nd ed., pp. 571–591). Mahwah, NJ: Erlbaum.

Paget, K. F., Kritt, D., & Bergemann, L. (1984). Understanding strategic interactions in television commercials: A developmental study. *Journal of Applied Developmental Psychology, 5,* 145–161.

Page-Voth, V., & Graham, S. (1999). Effects of goal setting and strategy use on the writing performance and self-efficacy of students with writing and learning problems. *Journal of Educational Psychology, 91,* 230–240.

Pahl, K., & Way, N. (2006). Longitudinal trajectories of ethnic identity among urban Black and Latino adolescents. *Child Development, 77,* 1403–1415.

Pajares, F. (2005). Gender differences in mathematics self-efficacy beliefs. In A. M. Gallagher & J. C. Kaufman (Eds.), *Gender differences in mathematics: An integrative psychological approach* (pp. 294–315). Cambridge, England: Cambridge University Press.

Pajares, F., & Valiante, G. (1999). *Writing self-efficacy of middle school students: Relation to motivation constructs, achievement, gender, and gender orientation.* Paper presented at the annual meeting of the American Educational Research Association, Montreal, Canada.

Paley, V. G. (1984). *Boys and girls: Superheroes in the doll corner.* Chicago: University of Chicago Press.

Palincsar, A. S., & Brown, A. L. (1984). Reciprocal teaching of comprehension-fostering and comprehension-monitoring activities. *Cognition and Instruction, 1,* 117–175.

Palincsar, A. S., & Brown, A. L. (1989). Classroom dialogues to promote self-regulated comprehension. In J. Brophy (Ed.), *Advances in research on teaching* (Vol. 1). Greenwich, CT: JAI Press.

Palincsar, A. S., & Herrenkohl, L. R. (1999). Designing collaborative contexts: Lessons from three research programs. In A. M. O'Donnell & A. King (Eds.), *Cognitive perspectives on peer learning* (pp. 151–177). Mahwah, NJ: Erlbaum.

Palmer, D. J., & Goetz, E. T. (1988). Selection and use of study strategies: The role of the studier's beliefs about self and strategies. In C. E. Weinstein, E. T. Goetz, & P. A. Alexander (Eds.), *Learning and study strategies: Issues in assessment, instruction, and evaluation.* San Diego, CA: Academic Press.

Palmer, E. L. (1965). Accelerating the child's cognitive attainments through the inducement of cognitive conflict: An interpretation of the Piagetian position. *Journal of Research in Science Teaching, 3,* 324.

Pang, V. O. (1995). Asian Pacific American students: A diverse and complex population. In J. A. Banks & C. A. M. Banks (Eds.), *Handbook of research on multicultural education.* New York: Macmillan.

Parada, R. H., Craven, R. G., & Marsh, H. W. (2008). The Beyond Bullying Secondary Program: An innovative program empowering teachers to counteract bullying in schools. In H. W. Marsh, R. G. Craven, & D. M. McInerney (Eds.), *Self-processes, learning, and enabling human potential* (pp. 373–395). Charlotte, NC: Information Age.

Paris, S. G., & Ayres, L. R. (1994). *Becoming reflective students and teachers with portfolios and authentic assessment.* Washington, DC: American Psychological Association.

Paris, S. G., & Byrnes, J. P. (1989). The constructivist approach to self-regulation and learning in the classroom. In B. J. Zimmerman & D. H. Schunk (Eds.), *Self-regulated learning and academic achievement: Theory, research, and practice.* New York: Springer-Verlag.

Paris, S. G., & Cunningham, A. E. (1996). Children becoming students. In D. C. Berliner & R. C. Calfee (Eds.), *Handbook of educational psychology.* New York: Macmillan.

Paris, S. G., Lawton, T. A., Turner, J. C., & Roth, J. L. (1991). A developmental perspective on standardized achievement testing. *Educational Researcher, 20*(5), 12–20, 40.

Paris, S. G., Morrison, F. J., & Miller, K. F. (2006). Academic pathways from preschool through elementary school. In P. A. Alexander & P. H. Winne (Eds.), *Handbook of educational psychology* (2nd ed., pp. 61–85). Mahwah, NJ: Erlbaum.

Paris, S. G., & Paris, A. H. (2001). Classroom applications of research on self-regulated learning. *Educational Psychologist, 36,* 89–101.

Paris, S. G., & Turner, J. C. (1994). Situated motivation. In P. R. Pintrich, D. R. Brown, & C. E. Weinstein (Eds.), *Student motivation, cognition, and learning: Essays in honor of Wilbert J. McKeachie.* Mahwah, NJ: Erlbaum.

Parke, R. D. (1974). Rules, roles, and resistance to deviation: Explorations in punishment, discipline, and self-control. In A. Pick (Ed.), *Minnesota Symposia on Child Psychology* (Vol. 8). Minneapolis: University of Minnesota Press.

Parker, W. D. (1997). An empirical typology of perfectionism in academically talented children. *American Educational Research Journal, 34,* 545–562.

Parkhurst, J. T., & Hopmeyer, A. (1998). Sociometric popularity and peer-perceived popularity: Two distinct dimensions of peer status. *Journal of Early Adolescence, 18,* 125–144.

Parks, C. P. (1995). Gang behavior in the schools: Reality or myth? *Educational Psychology Review, 7,* 41–68.

Pashler, H., McDaniel, M., Rohrer, D., & Bjork, R. (2009). Learning styles: Concepts and evidence. *Psychological Science in the Public Interest, 9,* 105–119.

Pashler, H., Rohrer, D., Cepeda, N. J., & Carpenter, S. K. (2007). Enhancing learning and retarding forgetting: Choices and consequences. *Psychonomic Bulletin & Review, 14,* 187–193.

Patall, E. A., Cooper, H., & Wynn, S. (2008, March). *The importance of providing choices in the classroom.* Paper presented at the annual meeting of the American Educational Research Association, New York.

Patrick, H., Anderman, L. H., & Ryan, A. M. (2002). Social motivation and the classroom social environment. In C. Midgley (Ed.), *Goals, goal structures, and patterns of adaptive learning* (pp. 85–108). Mahwah, NJ: Erlbaum.

Patrick, H., Mantzicopoulos, Y., & Samarapunga-van, A. (2009). Motivation for learning science in kindergarten: Is there a gender gap and does integrated inquiry and literacy instruction make a difference? *Journal of Research in Science Teaching, 46*, 166–191.

Patrick, H., & Pintrich, P. R. (2001). Conceptual change in teachers' intuitive conceptions of learning, motivation, and instruction: The role of motivational and epistemological beliefs. In B. Torff & R. J. Sternberg (Eds.), *Understanding and teaching the intuitive mind: Student and teacher learning* (pp. 117–143). Mahwah, NJ: Erlbaum.

Patrick, H., Ryan, A. M., Anderman, L. H., Middleton, M. J., Linnenbrink, L., Hruda, L. Z. et al. (1997). *Observing Patterns of Adaptive Learning (OPAL): A scheme for classroom observations.* Ann Arbor, MI: The University of Michigan.

Patrick, H., Ryan, A. M., & Kaplan, A. M. (2007). Early adolescents' perceptions of the classroom social environment, motivational beliefs, and engagement. *Journal of Educational Psychology, 99*, 83–98.

Patterson, C. J. (1995). Sexual orientation and human development: An overview. *Developmental Psychology, 31*, 3–11.

Patton, J. R., Blackbourn, J. M., & Fad, K. S. (1996). *Exceptional individuals in focus* (6th ed.). Upper Saddle River, NJ: Merrill/Prentice Hall.

Paulson, F. L., Paulson, P. R., & Meyer, C. A. (1991). What makes a portfolio a portfolio? *Educational Leadership, 49*(5), 60–63.

Paus, T., Zijdenbos, A., Worsley, K., Collins, D. L., Blumenthal, J., Giedd, J. N., et al. (1999). Structural maturation of neural pathways in children and adolescents: In vivo study. *Science, 283*, 1908–1911.

Paxton, R. J. (1999). A deafening silence: History textbooks and the students who read them. *Review of Educational Research, 69*, 315–339.

Pea, R. D. (1987). Socializing the knowledge transfer problem. *International Journal of Educational Research, 11*, 639–663.

Pea, R. D. (1993). Practices of distributed intelligence and designs for education. In G. Salomon (Ed.), *Distributed cognitions: Psychological and educational considerations.* Cambridge, England: Cambridge University Press.

Pea, R. D., & Maldonado, H. (2006). WILD for learning: Interacting through new computing devices anytime, anywhere. In R. K. Sawyer (Ed.), *The Cambridge handbook of the learning sciences* (pp. 427–441). Cambridge, England: Cambridge University Press.

Pedersen, S., Vitaro, F., Barker, E. D., & Borge, A. I. H. (2007). The timing of middle-childhood peer rejection and friendship: Linking early behavior to early-adolescent adjustment. *Child Development, 78*, 1037–1051.

Pekrun, R. (2006). The control-value theory of achievement emotions: Assumptions, corollaries, and implications for educational research and practice. *Educational Psychology Review, 18*, 315–341.

Pekrun, R., Elliot, A., & Maier, M. A. (2006). Achievement goals and discrete achievement emotions: A theoretical model and prospective test. *Journal of Educational Psychology, 98*, 583–597.

Pekrun, R., Goetz, T., Titz, W., & Perry, R. P. (2002). Academic emotions in students' self-regulated learning and achievement: A program of qualitative and quantitative research. *Educational Psychologist, 37*, 91–105.

Pellegrini, A. D. (1998). Play and the assessment of young children. In O. N. Saracho & B. Spodek (Eds.), *Multiple perspectives on play in early childhood education.* Albany: State University of New York Press.

Pellegrini, A. D. (2002). Bullying, victimization, and sexual harassment during the transition to middle school. *Educational Psychologist, 37*, 151–163.

Pellegrini, A. D. (2009). Research and policy on children's play. *Child Development Perspectives, 3*, 131–136.

Pellegrini, A. D., & Archer, J. (2005). Sex differences in competitive and aggressive behavior. In B. J. Ellis & D. F. Bjorklund (Eds.), *Origins of the social mind: Evolutionary psychology and child development* (pp. 219–244). New York: Guilford Press.

Pellegrini, A. D., & Bjorklund, D. F. (1997). The role of recess in children's cognitive performance. *Educational Psychologist, 32*, 35–40.

Pellegrini, A. D., & Bohn, C. M. (2005). The role of recess in children's cognitive performance and school adjustment. *Educational Researcher, 34*(1), 13–19.

Pellegrini, A. D., Huberty, P. D., & Jones, I. (1995). The effects of recess timing on children's playground and classroom behaviors. *American Educational Research Journal, 32*, 845–864.

Pellegrini, A. D., Kato, K., Blatchford, P., & Baines, E. (2002). A short-term longitudinal study of children's playground games across the first year of school: Implications for social competence and adjustment to school. *American Educational Research Journal, 39*, 991–1015.

Pellegrini, A. D., & Long, J. D. (2004). Part of the solution and part of the problem: The role of peers in bullying, dominance, and victimization during the transition from primary school through secondary school. In D. L. Espelage & S. M. Swearer (Eds.), *Bullying in American schools: A social-ecological perspective on prevention and intervention* (pp. 107–117). Mahwah, NJ: Erlbaum.

Pelphrey, K. A., & Carter, E. J. (2007). Brain mechanisms underlying social perception deficits in autism. In D. Coch, G. Dawson, & K. W. Fischer (Eds.), *Human behavior, learning, and the developing brain: Atypical development* (pp. 56–86). New York: Guilford Press.

Peng, K., & Nisbett, R. E. (1999). Culture, dialecticism, and reasoning about contradiction. *American Psychologist, 54*, 741–754.

Pepler, D., Jiang, D., Craig, W., & Connolly, J. (2008). Developmental trajectories of bullying and associated factors. *Child Development, 79*, 325–338.

Pérez, B. (1998). *Sociocultural contexts of language and literacy.* Mahwah, NJ: Erlbaum.

Perfetti, C. A. (1983). Reading, vocabulary, and writing: Implications for computer-based instruction. In A. C. Wilkinson (Ed.), *Classroom computers and cognitive science.* New York: Academic Press.

Perkins, D. N. (1990). The nature and nurture of creativity. In B. F. Jones & L. Idol (Eds.), *Dimensions of thinking and cognitive instruction.* Mahwah, NJ: Erlbaum.

Perkins, D. N. (1992). *Smart schools: From training memories to educating minds.* New York: Free Press/Macmillan.

Perkins, D. N. (1995). *Outsmarting IQ: The emerging science of learnable intelligence.* New York: Free Press.

Perkins, D., & Ritchhart, R. (2004). When is good thinking? In D. Y. Dai & R. J. Sternberg (Eds.), *Motivation, emotion, and cognition: Integrative perspectives on intellectual functioning and development* (pp. 351–384). Mahwah, NJ: Erlbaum.

Perkins, D. N., & Salomon, G. (1989). Are cognitive skills context-bound? *Educational Researcher, 18*(1), 16–25.

Perkins, D. N., Tishman, S., Ritchhart, R., Donis, K., & Andrade, A. (2000). Intelligence in the wild: A dispositional view of intellectual traits. *Educational Psychology Review, 12*, 269–293.

Perkins, S. A., & Turiel, E. (2007). To lie or not to lie: To whom and under what circumstances. *Child Development, 78*, 609–621.

Perner, J., & Wimmer, H. (1985). "John *thinks* that Mary *thinks* that . . ." Attribution of second-order beliefs by 5- to 10-year-old children. *Journal of Experimental Child Psychology, 39*, 437–471.

Perry, D. G., & Perry, L. C. (1983). Social learning, causal attribution, and moral internalization. In J. Bisanz, G. L. Bisanz, & R. Kail (Eds.), *Learning in children: Progress in cognitive development research.* New York: Springer-Verlag.

Perry, N. E. (1998). Young children's self-regulated learning and contexts that support it. *Journal of Educational Psychology, 90*, 715–729.

Perry, N. E., Turner, J. C., & Meyer, D. K. (2006). Classrooms as contexts for motivating learning. In P. A. Alexander & P. H. Winne (Eds.), *Handbook of educational psychology* (2nd ed., pp. 327–348). Mahwah, NJ: Erlbaum.

Perry, N. E., VandeKamp, K. O., Mercer, L. K., & Nordby, C. J. (2002). Investigating teacher-student interactions that foster self-regulated learning. *Educational Psychologist, 37*, 5–15.

Perry, N. E., & Winne, P. H. (2004). Motivational messages from home and school: How do they influence young children's engagement in learning? In D. M. McNerney & S. Van Etten (Eds.), *Big theories revisited* (pp. 199–222). Greenwich, CT: Information Age.

Peterson, C. (1990). Explanatory style in the classroom and on the playing field. In S. Graham & V. S. Folkes (Eds.), *Attribution theory: Applications to achievement, mental health, and interpersonal conflict.* Mahwah, NJ: Erlbaum.

Peterson, C. (2006). *A primer in positive psychology.* New York: Oxford University Press.

Peterson, C., Maier, S., & Seligman, M. (1993). *Learned helplessness: A theory for the age of personal control.* New York: Oxford University Press.

Peterson, L. R., & Peterson, M. J. (1959). Short-term retention of individual items. *Journal of Experimental Psychology, 58*, 193–198.

Petterson, S. M., & Albers, A. B. (2001). Effects of poverty and maternal depression on early child development. *Child Development, 72*, 1794–1813.

Pettito, A. L. (1985). Division of labor: Procedural learning in teacher-led small groups. *Cognition and Instruction, 2*, 233–270.

Peverly, S. T., Brobst, K. E., Graham, M., & Shaw, R. (2003). College adults are not good at self-regulation: A study on the relationship of self-regulation, note taking, and test taking. *Journal of Educational Psychology, 95*, 335–346.

Pfeifer, J. H., Brown, C. S., & Juvonen, J. (2007). Teaching tolerance in schools: Lessons learned since *Brown v. Board of Education* about the development and reduction of children's prejudice. *Social Policy Report, 21*(2), 3–13, 16–17, 20–23. Ann Arbor, MI: Society for Research in Child Development.

Pfeifer, M., Goldsmith, H. H., Davidson, R. J., & Rickman, M. (2002). Continuity and change in inhibited and uninhibited children. *Child Development, 73,* 1474–1485.

Pfiffner, L. J., Barkley, R. A., & DuPaul, G. J. (2006). Treatment of ADHD in school settings. In R. A. Barkley, *Attention-deficit hyperactivity disorder: A handbook for diagnosis and treatment* (3rd ed., pp. 547–589). New York: Guilford Press.

Pfiffner, L. J., & O'Leary, S. G. (1993). School-based psychological treatments. In J. L. Matson (Ed.), *Handbook of hyperactivity in children* (pp. 234–255). Boston: Allyn & Bacon.

Phalet, K., Andriessen, I., & Lens, W. (2004). How future goals enhance motivation and learning in multicultural classrooms. *Educational Psychology Review, 16,* 59–89.

Phelan, P., Davidson, A. L., & Cao, H. T. (1991). Students' multiple worlds: Negotiating the boundaries of family, peer, and school cultures. *Anthropology and Education Quarterly, 22,* 224–250.

Phelan, P., Yu, H. C., & Davidson, A. L. (1994). Navigating the psychosocial pressures of adolescence: The voices and experiences of high school youth. *American Educational Research Journal, 31,* 415–447.

Phelps, E. A., & Sharot, T. (2008). How (and why) emotion enhances the subjective sense of recollection. *Current Directions in Psychological Science, 17,* 147–152.

Phelps, L., McGrew, K. S., Knopik, S. N., & Ford, L. (2005). The general (g), broad, and narrow CHC stratum characteristics of the WJ III and WISC-III tests: A confirmatory cross-battery investigation. *School Psychology Quarterly, 20,* 66–88.

Phillips, B. N., Pitcher, G. D., Worsham, M. E., & Miller, S. C. (1980). Test anxiety and the school environment. In I. G. Sarason (Ed.), *Test anxiety: Theory, research, and applications.* Mahwah, NJ: Erlbaum.

Phillips, D., & Zimmerman, M. (1990). The developmental course of perceived competence and incompetence among competent children. In R. Sternberg & J. Kolligian (Eds.), *Competence considered* (pp. 41–66). New Haven, CT: Yale University Press.

Phillips, G., McNaughton, S., & MacDonald, S. (2004). Managing the mismatch: Enhancing early literacy progress for children with diverse language and cultural identities in mainstream urban schools in New Zealand. *Journal of Educational Psychology, 96,* 309–323.

Phinney, J. (1993). A three-stage model of ethnic identity development in adolescence. In M. E. Bernal & G. P. Knight (Eds.), *Ethnic identity: Formation and transmission among Hispanics and other minorities* (pp. 61–79). Albany: State University of New York Press.

Phinney, J. S. (1989). Stages of ethnic identity development in minority group adolescents. *Journal of Early Adolescence, 9,* 34–39.

Piaget, J. (1928). *Judgment and reasoning in the child* (M. Warden, Trans.). New York: Harcourt, Brace.

Piaget, J. (1952a). *The child's conception of number* (C. Gattegno & F. M. Hodgson, Trans.). London: Routledge & Kegan Paul.

Piaget, J. (1952b). *The origins of intelligence in children* (M. Cook, Trans.). New York: Norton.

Piaget, J. (1959). *The language and thought of the child* (3rd ed.; M. Gabain, Trans.). London: Routledge & Kegan Paul.

Piaget, J. (1960). *The moral judgment of the child* (M. Gabain, Trans.). Glencoe, IL: Free Press. (First published in 1932).

Piaget, J. (1970). Piaget's theory. In P. H. Mussen (Ed.), *Carmichael's manual of psychology.* New York: Wiley.

Piaget, J. (1980). *Adaptation and intelligence: Organic selection and phenocopy* (S. Eames, Trans.). Chicago: University of Chicago Press.

Pianta, R. C. (1999). *Enhancing relationships between children and teachers.* Washington, DC: American Psychological Association.

Pianta, R. C. (2006). Classroom management and relationships between children and teachers: Implications for research and practice. In C. M. Evertson & C. S. Weinstein (Eds.), *Handbook of classroom management: Research, practice, and contemporary issues* (pp. 685–709). Mahwah, NJ: Erlbaum.

Pianta, R. C., Belsky, J., Houts, R., & Morrison, F. (2007). Opportunities to learn in America's elementary classrooms. *Science, 315*(5820), 1795–1796.

Pianta, R. C., Belsky, J., Vandergrift, N., Houts, R., & Morrison, F. J. (2008). Classroom effects on children's achievement trajectories in elementary school. *American Educational Research Journal, 45,* 365–397.

Pianta, R. C., & Hamre, B. K. (2009). Conceptualization, measurement, and improvement of classroom processes: Standardized observation can leverage capacity. *Educational Researcher, 38,* 109–119.

Pickens, J. (2006, Winter). "Poop study" engages primary students. *Volunteer Monitor* (National Newsletter of Volunteer Watershed Monitoring), *18*(1), 13, 21.

Piehler, T. F., & Dishion, T. J. (2007). Interpersonal dynamics within adolescent friendships: Dyadic mutuality, deviant talk, and patterns of antisocial behavior. *Child Development, 78,* 1611–1624.

Piirto, J. (1999). *Talented children and adults: Their development and education* (2nd ed.). Upper Saddle River, NJ: Merrill/Prentice Hall.

Pillow, B. H. (2002). Children's and adults' evaluation of the certainty of deductive inferences, inductive inferences, and guesses. *Child Development, 73,* 779–792.

Pine, K. J., & Messer, D. J. (2000). The effect of explaining another's actions on children's implicit theories of balance. *Cognition and Instruction, 18,* 35–51.

Pintrich, P. R. (2003). Motivation and classroom learning. In W. M. Reynolds, G. E. Miller (Vol. Eds.), & I. B. Weiner (Editor-in-Chief), *Handbook of psychology: Vol. 7. Educational psychology* (pp. 103–122). New York: Wiley.

Pintrich, P. R., & De Groot, E. V. (1990). Motivational and self-regulated learning components of classroom academic performance. *Journal of Educational Psychology, 82,* 33–40.

Pintrich, P. R., Marx, R. W., & Boyle, R. A. (1993). Beyond cold conceptual change: The role of motivational beliefs and classroom contextual factors in the process of conceptual change. *Review of Educational Research, 63,* 167–199.

Pintrich, P. R., & Schrauben, B. (1992). Students' motivational beliefs and their cognitive engagement in academic tasks. In D. Schunk & J. Meece (Eds.), *Students' perceptions in the classroom: Causes and consequences.* Mahwah, NJ: Erlbaum.

Pintrich, P. R., & Schunk, D. H. (2002). *Motivation in education: Theory, research, and applications* (2nd ed.). Upper Saddle River, NJ: Merrill/Prentice Hall.

Plomin, R., & Spinath, F. M. (2004). Intelligence: Genetics, genes, and genomics. *Journal of Personality and Social Psychology, 86,* 112–129.

Plucker, J. A., Beghetto, R. A., & Dow, G. T. (2004). Why isn't creativity more important to educational psychologists? Potentials, pitfalls, and future directions in creativity research. *Educational Psychologist, 39,* 83–96.

Plumert, J. M. (1994). Flexibility in children's use of spatial and categorical organizational strategies in recall. *Developmental Psychology, 30,* 738–747.

Pollack, W. S. (2006). Sustaining and reframing vulnerability and connection: Creating genuine resilience in boys and young males. In. S. Goldstein & R. B. Brooks (Eds.), *Handbook of resilience in children* (pp. 65–77). New York: Springer.

Polman, J. L. (2004). Dialogic activity structures for project-based learning environments. *Cognition and Instruction, 22,* 431–466.

Pomerantz, E. M., & Saxon, J. L. (2001). Conceptions of ability as stable and self-evaluative processes: A longitudinal examination. *Child Development, 72,* 152–173.

Pomeroy, E. (1999). The teacher-student relationship in secondary school: Insights from excluded students. *British Journal of Sociology of Education, 20,* 465–482.

Poole, D. (1994). Routine testing practices and the linguistic construction of knowledge. *Cognition and Instruction, 12,* 125–150.

Popham, W. J. (1990). *Modern educational measurement: A practitioner's perspective* (2nd ed.). Upper Saddle River, NJ: Prentice Hall.

Popham, W. J. (1995). *Classroom assessment: What teachers need to know.* Boston: Allyn & Bacon.

Porat, D. A. (2004). *It's not written here, but this is what happened:* Students' cultural comprehension of textbook narratives on the Israeli-Arab conflict. *American Educational Research Journal, 41,* 963–996.

Porter, A. C. (1989). A curriculum out of balance: The case of elementary school mathematics. *Educational Researcher, 18*(5), 9–15.

Porter, A. C., & Polikoff, M. S. (2007). NCLB: State interpretations, early effects, and suggestions for reauthorization. *Social Policy Report, 21*(4) (Society for Research in Child Development).

Portes, P. R. (1996). Ethnicity and culture in educational psychology. In D. C. Berliner & R. C. Calfee (Eds.), *Handbook of educational psychology.* New York: Macmillan.

Posner, M. I., & Rothbart, M. K. (2007). *Educating the human brain.* Washington, DC: American Psychological Association.

Poulin, F., & Boivin, M. (1999). Proactive and reactive aggression and boys' friendship quality in mainstream classrooms. *Journal of Emotional and Behavioral Disorders, 7,* 168–177.

Powell, S., & Nelson, B. (1997). Effects of choosing academic assignments on a student with attention deficit hyperactivity disorder. *Journal of Applied Behavior Analysis, 30,* 181–183.

Power, F. C., Higgins, A., & Kohlberg, L. (1989). *Lawrence Kohlberg's approach to moral education.* New York: Columbia University Press.

Powers, L. E., Sowers, J. A., & Stevens, T. (1995). An exploratory, randomized study of the impact of mentoring on the self-efficacy and community-based knowledge of adolescents with severe physical challenges. *Journal of Rehabilitation, 61*(1), 33–41.

Prawat, R. S. (1989). Promoting access to knowledge, strategy, and disposition in students: A research synthesis. *Review of Educational Research, 59,* 1–41.

Prawat, R. S. (1993). The value of ideas: Problems versus possibilities in learning. *Educational Researcher, 22*(6), 5–16.

Preckel, F., Holling, H., & Vock, M. (2006). Academic underachievement: Relationship with cognitive motivation, achievement motivation, and conscientiousness. *Psychology in the Schools, 43,* 401–411.

Premack, D. (1959). Toward empirical behavior laws: I. Positive reinforcement. *Psychological Review, 66,* 219–233.

Premack, D. (1963). Rate differential reinforcement in monkey manipulation. *Journal of Experimental Analysis of Behavior, 6,* 81–89.

Presseisen, B. Z., & Beyer, F. S. (1994, April). *Facing history and ourselves: An instructional tool for constructivist theory.* Paper presented at the annual meeting of the American Educational Research Association, New Orleans, LA.

Pressley, M. (1982). Elaboration and memory development. *Child Development, 53,* 296–309.

Pressley, M., Borkowski, J. G., & Schneider, W. (1987). Cognitive strategies: Good strategy users coordinate metacognition and knowledge. In R. Vasta (Ed.), *Annals of child development* (Vol. 4). Greenwich, CT: JAI Press.

Pressley, M., El-Dinary, P. B., Marks, M. B., Brown, R., & Stein, S. (1992). Good strategy instruction is motivating and interesting. In K. A. Renninger, S. Hidi, & A. Krapp (Eds.), *The role of interest in learning and development.* Mahwah, NJ: Erlbaum.

Pressley, M., Harris, K. R., & Marks, M. B. (1992). But good strategy instructors are constructivists! *Educational Psychology Review, 4,* 3–31.

Pressley, M., & Hilden, K. (2006). Cognitive strategies: Production deficiencies and successful strategy instruction everywhere. In W. Damon & R. M. Lerner (Series Eds.), D. Kuhn & R. Siegler (Vol. Eds.), *Handbook of child psychology: Vol. 2. Cognition, perception, and language* (6th ed.). New York: Wiley.

Pressley, M., Levin, J. R., & Delaney, H. D. (1982). The mnemonic keyword method. *Review of Educational Research, 52,* 61–91.

Pribram, K. H. (1997). The work in working memory: Implications for development. In N. A. Krasnegor, G. R. Lyon, & P. S. Goldman-Rakic (Eds.), *Development of the prefrontal cortex: Evolution, neurobiology, and behavior* (pp. 359–378). Baltimore: Brookes.

Price-Williams, D. R., Gordon, W., & Ramirez, M. (1969). Skill and conservation. *Developmental Psychology, 1,* 769.

Pritchard, R. (1990). The effects of cultural schemata on reading processing strategies. *Reading Research Quarterly, 25,* 273–295.

Proctor, B. E., Floyd, R. G., & Shaver, R. B. (2005). Cattell-Horn-Carroll broad cognitive ability profiles of low math achievers. *Psychology in the Schools, 42*(1), 1–12.

Proctor, R. W., & Dutta, A. (1995). *Skill acquisition and human performance.* Thousand Oaks, CA: Sage.

Pruitt, R. P. (1989). Fostering creativity: The innovative classroom environment. *Educational Horizons, 68*(1), 51–54.

Pugh, K. J., & Bergin, D. A. (2006). Motivational influences on transfer. *Educational Psychologist, 41,* 147–160.

Pugh, K. J., Bergin, D. A., & Rocks, J. (2003, April). *Motivation and transfer: A critical review.* Paper presented at the annual meeting of the American Educational Research Association, Chicago.

Pulos, S., & Linn, M. C. (1981). Generality of the controlling variables scheme in early adolescence. *Journal of Early Adolescence, 1,* 26–37.

Purcell-Gates, V. (1995). *Other people's words: The cycle of low literacy.* Cambridge, MA: Harvard University Press.

Purdie, N., & Hattie, J. (1996). Cultural differences in the use of strategies for self-regulated learning. *American Educational Research Journal, 33,* 845–871.

Purdie, N., Hattie, J., & Douglas, G. (1996). Student conceptions of learning and their use of self-regulated learning strategies: A cross-cultural comparison. *Journal of Educational Psychology, 88,* 87–100.

Putnam, R. T. (1992). Thinking and authority in elementary-school mathematics tasks. In J. Brophy (Ed.), *Advances in research on teaching: Vol. 3. Planning and managing learning tasks and activities.* Greenwich, CT: JAI Press.

Putwain, D. W. (2007). Test anxiety in UK schoolchildren: Prevalence and demographic patterns. *British Journal of Educational Psychology, 77,* 579–593.

Qian, G., & Pan, J. (2002). A comparison of epistemological beliefs and learning from science text between American and Chinese high school students. In B. K. Hofer & P. R. Pintrich (Eds.), *Personal epistemology: The psychology of beliefs about knowledge and knowing* (pp. 365–385). Mahwah, NJ: Erlbaum.

Qin, L., Pomerantz, E. M., & Wang, Q. (2009). Are gains in decision-making autonomy during early adolescence beneficial for emotional functioning? The case of the United States and China. *Child Development, 80,* 1705–1721.

Qin, Z., Johnson, D. W., & Johnson, R. T. (1995). Cooperative versus competitive efforts and problem solving. *Review of Educational Research, 65,* 129–143.

Quellmalz, E., & Hoskyn, J. (1997). Classroom assessment of reading strategies. In G. D. Phye (Ed.), *Handbook of classroom assessment: Learning, achievement, and adjustment.* San Diego, CA: Academic Press.

Quinn, P. C. (2002). Category representation in young infants. *Current Directions in Psychological Science, 11,* 66–70.

Quinn, P. C. (2007). On the infant's prelinguistic conception of spatial relations: Three developmental trends and their implications for spatial language learning. In J. M. Plumert & J. P. Spencer (Eds.), *The emerging spatial mind* (pp. 117–141). New York: Oxford University Press.

Quintana, C., Zhang, M., & Krajcik, J. (2005). A framework for supporting metacognitive aspects of online inquiry through software-based scaffolding. *Educational Psychologist, 40,* 235–244.

Quintana, S. M., Aboud, F. E., Chao, R. K., Contreras-Grau, J., Cross, W. E., Jr., Hudley, C., et al. (2006). Race, ethnicity, and culture in child development: Contemporary research and future directions. *Child Development, 77,* 1129–1141.

Raber, S. M. (1990, April). *A school system's look at its dropouts: Why they left school and what has happened to them.* Paper presented at the annual meeting of the American Educational Research Association, Boston.

Rabinowitz, M., & Glaser, R. (1985). Cognitive structure and process in highly competent performance. In F. D. Horowitz & M. O'Brien (Eds.), *The gifted and the talented: Developmental perspectives.* Washington, DC: American Psychological Association.

Radziszewska, B., & Rogoff, B. (1988). Influence of adult and peer collaborators on children's planning skills. *Developmental Psychology, 24,* 840–848.

Raine, A., Reynolds, C., & Venables, P. H. (2002). Stimulation seeking and intelligence: A prospective longitudinal study. *Journal of Personality and Social Psychology, 82,* 663–674.

Raine, A., & Scerbo, A. (1991). Biological theories of violence. In J. S. Milner (Ed.), *Neuropsychology of aggression* (pp. 1–25). Boston: Kluwer.

Ramey, C. T., & Ramey, S. L. (1998). Early intervention and early experience. *American Psychologist, 53,* 109–120.

Ramsey, P. G. (1987). *Teaching and learning in a diverse world: Multicultural education for young children.* New York: Teachers College Press.

Ramsey, P. G. (1995). Growing up with the contradictions of race and class. *Young Children, 50,* 18–22.

Rappaport, N., Osher, D., Garrison, E. G., Anderson-Ketchmark, C., & Dwyer, K. (2003). Enhancing collaboration within and across disciplines to advance mental health in schools. In M. D. Weist, S. W. Evans, & N. A. Lever (Eds.), *Handbook of school mental health: Advancing practice and research* (pp. 107–118). New York: Kluwer Academic Press.

Rapport, M. D., Murphy, H. A., & Bailey, J. S. (1982). Ritalin vs. response cost in the control of hyperactive children: A within-subject comparison. *Journal of Applied Behavior Analysis, 15,* 205–216.

Rasch, B., & Born, J. (2008). Reactivation and consolidation of memory during sleep. *Current Directions in Psychological Science, 17,* 188–192.

Ratelle, C. F., Guay, F., Vallerand, R. J., Larose, S., & Senécal, C. (2007). Autonomous, controlled, and amotivated types of academic motivation: A person-oriented analysis. *Journal of Educational Psychology, 99,* 734–746.

Raudenbush, S. W. (1984). Magnitude of teacher expectancy effects on pupil IQ as a function of credibility induction: A synthesis of findings from 18 experiments. *Journal of Educational Psychology, 76,* 85–97.

Raudenbush, S. W. (2009). The *Brown* legacy and the O'Connor challenge: Transforming schools in the images of children's potential. *Educational Researcher, 38,* 169–180.

Rawson, K. A., & Kintsch, W. (2005). Rereading effects depend on time of test. *Journal of Educational Psychology, 97,* 70–80.

Rawsthorne, L. J., & Elliot, A. J. (1999). Achievement goals and intrinsic motivation: A meta-analytic review. *Personality and Social Psychology Review, 3,* 326–344.

Redfield, D. L., & Rousseau, E. W. (1981). A meta-analysis of experimental research on teacher questioning behavior. *Review of Educational Research, 51,* 237–245.

Reed, J. H., Schallert, D. L., Beth, A. D., & Woodruff, A. L. (2004). Motivated reader, engaged writer: The role of motivation in the literate acts of adolescents. In T. L. Jetton & J. A. Dole (Eds.), *Adolescent literacy research and practice* (pp. 251–282). New York: Guilford Press.

Reeve, J. (2006). Extrinsic rewards and inner motivation. In C. M. Evertson & C. S. Weinstein (Eds.), *Handbook of classroom management:*

Research, practice, and contemporary issues (pp. 645–664.). Mahwah, NJ: Erlbaum.

Reeve, J. (2009). Why teachers adopt a controlling motivating style toward students and how they can become more autonomy supportive. *Educational Psychologist, 44,* 159–175.

Reeve, J., Bolt, E., & Cai, Y. (1999). Autonomy-supportive teachers: How they teach and motivate students. *Journal of Educational Psychology, 91,* 537–548.

Reeve, J., Deci, E. L., & Ryan, R. M. (2004). Self-determination theory: A dialectical framework for understanding sociocultural influences on student motivation. In D. M. McInerney & S. Van Etten (Eds.), *Big theories revisited* (pp. 31–60). Greenwich, CT: Information Age.

Régner, I., Escribe, C., & Dupeyrat, C. (2007). Evidence of social comparison in mastery goals in natural academic settings. *Journal of Educational Psychology, 99,* 575–583.

Reid, R., Trout, A. L., & Schartz, M. (2005). Self-regulation interventions for children with attention deficit/hyperactivity disorder. *Exceptional Children, 71,* 361–377.

Reimer, J., Paolitto, D. P., & Hersh, R. H. (1983). *Promoting moral growth: From Piaget to Kohlberg* (2nd ed.). White Plains, NY: Longman.

Reiner, M., Slotta, J. D., Chi, M. T. H., & Resnick, L. B. (2000). Naive physics reasoning: A commitment to substance-based conceptions. *Cognition and Instruction, 18,* 1–34.

Reinking, D., & Leu, D. J. (Chairs). (2008, March). *Understanding Internet reading comprehension and its development among adolescents at risk of dropping out of school.* Poster session presented at the annual meeting of the American Educational Research Association, New York.

Reisberg, D. (1997). *Cognition: Exploring the science of the mind.* New York: Norton.

Reisberg, D., & Heuer, F. (1992). Remembering the details of emotional events. In E. Winograd & U. Neisser (Eds.), *Affect and accuracy in recall: Studies of "flashbulb" memories.* Cambridge, England: Cambridge University Press.

Reiter, S. N. (1994). Teaching dialogically: Its relationship to critical thinking in college students. In P. R. Pintrich, D. R. Brown, & C. E. Weinstein (Eds.), *Student motivation, cognition, and learning: Essays in honor of Wilbert J. McKeachie.* Mahwah, NJ: Erlbaum.

Renninger, K. A. (2009). Interest and identity development in instruction: An inductive model. *Educational Psychologist, 44,* 105–118.

Renninger, K. A., Hidi, S., & Krapp, A. (Eds.). (1992). *The role of interest in learning and development.* Mahwah, NJ: Erlbaum.

Renzulli, J. S. (2002). Emerging conceptions of giftedness: Building a bridge to the new century. *Exceptionality, 10*(2), 67–75.

Resnick, D. P., & Resnick, L. B. (1996). Performance assessment and the multiple functions of educational measurement. In M. B. Kane & R. Mitchell (Eds.), *Implementing performance assessment: Promises, problems, and challenges* (pp. 23–38). Mahwah, NJ: Erlbaum.

Resnick, L. B. (1989). Developing mathematical knowledge. *American Psychologist, 44,* 162–169.

Resnick, M. D., Bearman, P. S., Blum, R. W., Bauman, K. E., Harris, K. M., Jones, J., et al. (1997). Protecting adolescents from harm: Findings from the National Longitudinal Study on Adolescent Health. *Journal of the American Medical Association, 278,* 823–832.

Rest, J., Narvaez, D., Bebeau, M., & Thoma, S. (1999). A neo-Kohlbergian approach: The DIT and schema theory. *Educational Psychology Review, 11,* 291–324.

Reusser, K. (1990, April). *Understanding word arithmetic problems: Linguistic and situational factors.* Paper presented at the annual meeting of the American Educational Research Association, Boston.

Reyna, C. (2000). Lazy, dumb, or industrious: When stereotypes convey attribution information in the classroom. *Educational Psychology Review, 12,* 85–110.

Reyna, C., & Weiner, B. (2001). Justice and utility in the classroom: An attributional analysis of the goals of teachers' punishment and intervention strategies. *Journal of Educational Psychology, 93,* 309–319.

Reyna, V. F., & Farley, F. (2006). Risk and rationality in adolescent decision making: Implications for theory, practice, and public policy. *Psychological Science in the Public Interest, 7*(1), 1–44.

Reynolds, A. J., & Oberman, G. L. (1987, April). *An analysis of a PSAT preparation program for urban gifted students.* Paper presented at the annual meeting of the American Educational Research Association, Washington, DC.

Reynolds, R. E., & Shirey, L. L. (1988). The role of attention in studying and learning. In C. E. Weinstein, E. T. Goetz, & P. A. Alexander (Eds.), *Learning and study strategies: Issues in assessment, instruction, and evaluation.* San Diego, CA: Academic Press.

Reynolds, R. E., Taylor, M. A., Steffensen, M. S., Shirey, L. L., & Anderson, R. C. (1982). Cultural schemata and reading comprehension. *Reading Research Quarterly, 17,* 353–366.

Rhodes, B. (2008). Challenges and opportunities for intelligence augmentation. In P. C. Kyllonen, R. D. Roberts, & L. Stankov (Eds.), *Extending intelligence: Enhancement and new constructs* (pp. 395–405). New York: Erlbaum/Taylor & Francis.

Rhodes, M., & Gelman, S. A. (2008). Categories influence predictions about individual consistency. *Child Development, 79,* 1270–1287.

Rhodewalt, F., & Vohs, K. D. (2005). Defensive strategies, motivation, and the self: A self-regulatory process view. In A. J. Elliot & C. S. Dweck (Eds.), *Handbook of competence and motivation* (pp. 548–565). New York: Guilford Press.

Ricciuti, H. N. (1993). Nutrition and mental development. *Current Directions in Psychological Science, 2,* 43–46.

Richards, J. M. (2004). The cognitive consequences of concealing feelings. *Current Directions in Psychological Science, 13,* 131–134.

Riding, R. J., & Cheema, I. (1991). Cognitive styles—An overview and integration. *Educational Psychology, 11,* 193–215.

Riggs, J. M. (1992). Self-handicapping and achievement. In A. K. Boggiano & T. S. Pittman (Eds.), *Achievement and motivation: A social-developmental perspective.* Cambridge, England: Cambridge University Press.

Rimm, D. C., & Masters, J. C. (1974). *Behavior therapy: Techniques and empirical findings.* San Diego, CA: Academic Press.

Ripple, R. E. (1989). Ordinary creativity. *Contemporary Educational Psychology, 14,* 189–202.

Rittle-Johnson, B. (2006). Promoting transfer: Effects of self-explanation and direct instruction. *Child Development, 77,* 1–15.

Rittle-Johnson, B., Siegler, R. S., & Alibali, M. W. (2001). Developing conceptual understanding and procedural skill in mathematics: An iterative process. *Journal of Educational Psychology, 93,* 346–362.

Ritts, V., Patterson, M. L., & Tubbs, M. E. (1992). Expectations, impressions, and judgments of physically attractive students: A review. *Review of Educational Research, 62,* 413–426.

Rivers, I., Poteat, V. P., Noret, N., & Ashurst, N. (2009). Observing bullying at school: The mental health implications of witness status. *School Psychology Quarterly, 24*(4), 211–223.

Robbins, P., & Aydede, M. (Eds.). (2009). *The Cambridge handbook of situated cognition.* Cambridge, England: Cambridge University Press.

Roberts, G. C., Treasure, D. C., & Kavussanu, M. (1997). Motivation in physical activity contexts: An achievement goal perspective. *Advances in Motivation and Achievement, 10,* 413–447.

Roberts, T., & Kraft, R. (1987). Reading comprehension performance and laterality: Evidence for concurrent validity of dichotic, haptic, and EEG laterality measures. *Neuropsychologia, 25,* 817–828.

Roberts, T. A. (2005). Articulation accuracy and vocabulary size contributions to phonemic awareness and word reading in English language learners. *Journal of Educational Psychology, 97,* 601–616.

Robins, R. W., & Trzesniewski, K. H. (2005). Self-esteem development across the lifespan. *Current Directions in Psychological Science, 14,* 158–162.

Robinson, C. W., & Sloutsky, V. M. (2004). Auditory dominance and its change in the course of development. *Child Development, 75,* 1387–1401.

Robinson, D. H., & Kiewra, K. A. (1995). Visual argument: Graphic organizers are superior to outlines in improving learning from text. *Journal of Educational Psychology, 87,* 455–467.

Robinson, D. R., Schofield, J. W., & Steers-Wentzell, K. L. (2005). Peer and cross-age tutoring in math: Outcomes and their design implications. *Educational Psychology Review, 17,* 327–362.

Robinson, S. L., & Griesemer, S. M. R. (2006). Helping individual students with problem behavior. In C. M. Evertson & C. S. Weinstein (Eds.), *Handbook of classroom management: Research, practice, and contemporary issues* (pp. 787–802). Mahwah, NJ: Erlbaum.

Roblyer, M. D. (2003). *Integrating educational technology into teaching* (3rd ed.). Upper Saddle River, NJ: Merrill/Prentice Hall.

Roderick, M., & Camburn, E. (1999). Risk and recovery from course failure in the early years of high school. *American Educational Research Journal, 36,* 303–343.

Roediger, H. L., III, & Karpicke, J. D. (2006). The power of testing memory: Basic research and implications for educational practice. *Perspectives on Psychological Science, 1,* 181–210.

Roediger, H. L., III, & Marsh, E. J. (2005). The positive and negative consequences of multiple-choice testing. *Journal of Experimental Psychology: Learning, Memory, and Cognition, 31,* 1155–1159.

Roediger, H. L., III, & McDermott, K. B. (2000). Tricks of memory. *Current Directions in Psychological Science, 9,* 123–127.

Roeser, R. W., Marachi, R., & Gehlbach, H. (2002). A goal theory perspective on teachers' professional identities and the contexts of teaching. In C. Midgley (Ed.), *Goals, goal structures, and patterns of adaptive learning* (pp. 205–241). Mahwah, NJ: Erlbaum.

Rogers, C. R. (1983). *Freedom to learn for the 80's.* Upper Saddle River, NJ: Merrill/Prentice Hall.

Rogers, T. B., Kuiper, N. A., & Kirker, W. S. (1977). Self-reference and the encoding of personal information. *Journal of Personality and Social Psychology, 35,* 677–688.

Rogoff, B. (1990). *Apprenticeship in thinking: Cognitive development in social context.* New York: Oxford University Press.

Rogoff, B. (1991). Social interaction as apprenticeship in thinking: Guidance and participation in spatial planning. In L. B. Resnick, J. M. Levine, & S. D. Teasley (Eds.), *Perspectives on socially shared cognition.* Washington, DC: American Psychological Association.

Rogoff, B. (1994, April). *Developing understanding of the idea of communities of learners.* Paper presented at the annual meeting of the American Educational Research Association, New Orleans, LA.

Rogoff, B. (2003). *The cultural nature of human development.* Oxford, England: Oxford University Press.

Rogoff, B. (2007, March). Cultural perspectives help us see developmental processes. In M. Gauvain & R. L. Munroe (Chairs), *Contributions of socio-historical theory and cross-cultural research to the study of child development.* Symposium conducted at the biennial meeting of the Society for Research in Child Development, Boston.

Rogoff, B., Matusov, E., & White, C. (1996). Models of teaching and learning: Participation in a community of learners. In D. R. Olson & N. Torrance (Eds.), *The handbook of education and human development: New models of learning, teaching, and schooling.* Cambridge, MA: Blackwell.

Rogoff, B., Moore, L., Najafi, B., Dexter, A., Correa-Chávez, M., & Solís, J. (2007). Children's development of cultural repertoires through participation in everyday routines and practices. In J. E. Grusec & P. D. Hastings (Eds.), *Handbook of socialization: Theory and research* (pp. 490–515). New York: Guilford Press.

Rohrbeck, C. A., Ginsburg-Block, M. D., Fantuzzo, J. W., & Miller, T. R. (2003). Peer-assisted learning interventions with elementary school students: A meta-analytic review. *Journal of Educational Psychology, 95,* 240–257.

Rohrer, D., & Pashler, H. (2007). Increasing retention without increasing study time. *Current Directions in Psychological Science, 16,* 183–186.

Root, M. P. P. (1999). The biracial baby boom: Understanding ecological constructions of racial identity in the 21st century. In R. H. Sheets & E. R. Hollins (Eds.), *Racial and ethnic identity in school practices: Aspects of human development* (pp. 67–89). Mahwah, NJ: Erlbaum.

Rortvedt, A. K., & Miltenberger, R. G. (1994). Analysis of a high-probability instructional sequence and time-out in the treatment of child noncompliance. *Journal of Applied Behavior Analysis, 27,* 327–330.

Roscoe, R. D., & Chi, M. T. H. (2007). Understanding tutor learning: Knowledge-building and knowledge-telling in peer tutors' explanations and questions. *Review of Educational Research, 77,* 534–574.

Rose, A. J. (2002). Co-rumination in the friendship of girls and boys. *Child Development, 73,* 1830–1843.

Rose, A. J., & Smith, R. L. (2009). Sex differences in peer relationships. In K. H. Rubin, W. M. Bukowski, & B. Laursen (Eds.), *Handbook of peer interactions, relationships, and groups* (pp. 379–393). New York: Guilford Press.

Rosenshine, B., & Meister, C. (1992). The use of scaffolds for teaching higher-level cognitive strategies. *Educational Leadership, 49*(7), 26–33.

Rosenshine, B., & Meister, C. (1994). Reciprocal teaching: A review of the research. *Review of Educational Research, 64,* 479–530.

Rosenshine, B., Meister, C., & Chapman, S. (1996). Teaching students to generate questions: A review of the intervention studies. *Review of Educational Research, 66,* 181–221.

Rosenshine, B., & Stevens, R. (1986). Teaching functions. In M. C. Wittrock (Ed.), *Handbook of research on teaching* (3rd ed.). New York: Macmillan.

Rosenthal, R. (1994). Interpersonal expectancy effects: A 30-year perspective. *Current Directions in Psychological Science, 3,* 176–179.

Rosenthal, R., & Jacobson, L. (1968). *Pygmalion in the classroom: Teacher expectation and pupils' intellectual development.* New York: Holt, Rinehart & Winston.

Rosenthal, T. L., Alford, G. S., & Rasp, L. M. (1972). Concept attainment, generalization, and retention through observation and verbal coding. *Journal of Experimental Child Psychology, 13,* 183–194.

Ross, J. A. (1988). Controlling variables: A meta-analysis of training studies. *Review of Educational Research, 58,* 405–437.

Ross, S. W, & Horner, R. H. (2009). Bully prevention in positive behavior support. *Journal of Applied Behavior Analysis, 42,* 747–759.

Rosser, R. (1994). *Cognitive development: Psychological and biological perspectives.* Boston: Allyn & Bacon.

Rotenberg, K. J., & Mayer, E. V. (1990). Delay of gratification in Native and White children: A cross-cultural comparison. *International Journal of Behavioral Development, 13,* 23–30.

Roth, K. J., & Anderson, C. (1988). Promoting conceptual change learning from science textbooks. In P. Ramsden (Ed.), *Improving learning: New perspectives.* London: Kogan Page.

Roth, W., & Bowen, G. M. (1995). Knowing and interacting: A study of culture, practices, and resources in a grade 8 open-inquiry science classroom guided by a cognitive apprenticeship metaphor. *Cognition and Instruction, 13,* 73–128.

Rothbart, M. K. (2007). Temperament, development, and personality. *Current Directions in Psychological Science, 16,* 207–212.

Rothbaum, F., & Trommsdorff, G. (2007). Do roots and wings complement or oppose one another? The socialization of relatedness and autonomy in cultural context. In J. E. Grusec & P. D. Hastings (Eds.), *Handbook of socialization: Theory and research* (pp. 461–489). New York: Guilford Press.

Rothbaum, F., Weisz, J. R., & Snyder, S. S. (1982). Changing the world and changing the self: A two-process model of perceived control. *Journal of Personality and Social Psychology, 42,* 5–37.

Rovee-Collier, C. (1999). The development of infant memory. *Current Directions in Psychological Science, 8,* 80–85.

Rowe, D. C., Almeida, D. M., & Jacobson, K. C. (1999). School context and genetic influences on aggression in adolescence. *Psychological Science, 10,* 277–280.

Rowe, M. B. (1974). Wait-time and rewards as instructional variables, their influence on language, logic, and fate control: Part one— Wait time. *Journal of Research in Science Teaching, 11,* 81–94.

Rowe, M. B. (1987). Wait-time: Slowing down may be a way of speeding up. *American Educator, 11,* 38–43, 47.

Rozalski, M. E., & Yell, M. L. (2004). Law and school safety. In J. C. Conoley & A. P. Goldstein (Eds.), *School violence intervention* (2nd ed., pp. 507–523). New York: Guilford Press.

Rubin, K. H. (1982). Nonsocial play in preschoolers: Necessarily evil? *Child Development, 53,* 651–657.

Rubin, K. H., Cheah, C., & Menzer, M. M. (2010). Peers. In M. H. Bornstein (Ed.), *Handbook of cultural developmental science* (pp. 223–237). New York: Psychology Press.

Ruble, D. N., Martin, C. L., & Berebaum, S. A. (2006). Gender development. In W. Damon & R. M. Lerner (Series Eds.) & N. Eisenberg (Vol. Ed.), *Handbook of child psychology: Vol. 3. Social, emotional, and personality development* (6th ed., pp. 858–932). Hoboken, NJ: Wiley.

Rudman, M. K. (1993). Multicultural children's literature: The search for universals. In M. K. Rudman (Ed.), *Children's literature: Resource for the classroom* (2nd ed.). Norwood, MA: Christopher-Gordon.

Rudolph, K. D., Caldwell, M. S., & Conley, C. S. (2005). Need for approval and children's well-being. *Child Development, 76,* 309–323.

Rudolph, K. D., Lambert, S. F., Clark, A. G., & Kurlakowsky, K. D. (2001). Negotiating the transition to middle school: The role of self-regulatory processes. *Child Development, 72,* 929–946.

Rueda, R., & Moll, L. C. (1994). A sociocultural perspective on motivation. In H. F. O'Neil, Jr., & M. Drillings (Eds.), *Motivation: Theory and research.* Mahwah, NJ: Erlbaum.

Ruef, M. B., Higgins, C., Glaeser, B., & Patnode, M. (1998). Positive behavioral support: Strategies for teachers. *Intervention in School and Clinic, 34*(1), 21–32.

Rueger, D. B., & Liberman, R. P. (1984). Behavioral family therapy for delinquent substance-abusing adolescents. *Journal of Drug Abuse, 14,* 403–418.

Ruffman, T., Slade, L., & Crowe, E. (2002). The relation between children's and mothers' mental state language and theory-of-mind understanding. *Child Development, 73,* 734–751.

Rumberger, R. W. (1995). Dropping out of middle school: A multilevel analysis of students and schools. *American Educational Research Journal, 32,* 583–625.

Rumelhart, D. E., & Ortony, A. (1977). The representation of knowledge in memory. In R. C. Anderson, R. J. Spiro, & W. E. Montague (Eds.), *Schooling and the acquisition of knowledge.* Mahwah, NJ: Erlbaum.

Runco, M. A. (2004). Creativity as an extracognitive phenomenon. In L. V. Shavinina & M. Ferrari (Eds.), *Beyond knowledge: Extracognitive aspects of developing high ability* (pp. 17–25). Mahwah, NJ: Erlbaum.

Runco, M. A., & Chand, I. (1995). Cognition and creativity. *Educational Psychology Review, 7,* 243–267.

Rushton, J. P. (1980). *Altruism, socialization, and society.* Upper Saddle River, NJ: Prentice Hall.

Ryan, A. M. (2000). Peer groups as a context for the socialization of adolescents' motivation, engagement, and achievement in school. *Educational Psychologist, 35,* 101–111.

Ryan, A. M. (2001). The peer group as a context for the development of young adolescent motivation and achievement. *Child Development, 72,* 1135–1150.

Ryan, A. M., Hicks, L., & Midgley, C. (1997). Social goals, academic goals, and avoiding help seeking in the classroom. *Journal of Early Adolescence, 17,* 152–171.

Ryan, A. M., & Patrick, H. (2001). The classroom social environment and changes in adolescents' motivation and engagement during middle school. *American Educational Research Journal, 38,* 437–460.

Ryan, A. M., Pintrich, P. R., & Midgley, C. (2001). Avoiding seeking help in the classroom: Who and why? *Educational Psychology Review, 13,* 93–114.

Ryan, K. E., & Ryan, A. M. (2005). Psychological processes underlying stereotype threat and standardized math test performance. *Educational Psychologist, 40,* 53–63.

Ryan, K. E., Ryan, A. M., Arbuthnot, K., & Samuels, M. (2007). Students' motivation for standardized math exams: Insights from students. *Educational Researcher, 36*(1), 5–13.

Ryan, R. M. (2005, April). *Legislating competence: High stakes testing, school reform, and motivation from a self-determination theory viewpoint.* Paper presented at the annual meeting of the American Educational Research Association, Montreal.

Ryan, R. M., Connell, J. P., & Grolnick, W. S. (1992). When achievement is *not* intrinsically motivated: A theory of internalization and self-regulation in school. In A. K. Boggiano & T. S. Pittman (Eds.), *Achievement and motivation: A social-developmental perspective.* Cambridge, England: Cambridge University Press.

Ryan, R. M., & Deci, E. L. (2000). Self-determination theory and the facilitation of intrinsic motivation, social development, and well-being. *American Psychologist, 55,* 68–78.

Ryan, R. M., & Kuczkowski, R. (1994). The imaginary audience, self-consciousness, and public individuation in adolescence. *Journal of Personality, 62,* 219–237.

Ryan, R. M., & Lynch, J. H. (1989). Emotional autonomy versus detachment: Revisiting the vicissitudes of adolescence and young adulthood. *Child Development, 60,* 340–356.

Ryan, R. M., Mims, V., & Koestner, R. (1983). Relation of reward contingency and interpersonal context to intrinsic motivation: A review and test using cognitive evaluation theory. *Journal of Personality and Social Psychology, 45,* 736–750.

Saarni, C., Campos, J. J., Camras, L. A., & Witherington, D. (2006). Emotional development: Action, communication, and understanding. In W. Damon & R. M. Lerner (Eds. in Chief) & N. Eisenberg (Vol. Ed.), *Handbook of child psychology, Vol. 3. Social, emotional, and personality development* (6th ed., pp. 226–299). Hoboken, NJ: Wiley.

Sabers, D. S., Cushing, K. S., & Berliner, D. C. (1991). Differences among teachers in a task characterized by simultaneity, multidimensionality, and immediacy. *American Educational Research Journal, 28,* 63–88.

Sadker, M. P., & Sadker, D. (1994). *Failing at fairness: How our schools cheat girls.* New York: Touchstone.

Sadoski, M., Goetz, E. T., & Fritz, J. B. (1993). Impact of concreteness on comprehensibility, interest, and memory for text: Implications for dual coding theory and text design. *Journal of Educational Psychology, 85,* 291–304.

Sadoski, M., & Paivio, A. (2001). *Imagery and text: A dual coding theory of reading and writing.* Mahwah, NJ: Erlbaum.

Salend, S. J., & Taylor, L. (1993). Working with families: A cross-cultural perspective. *Remedial and Special Education, 14*(5), 25–32, 39.

Säljö, R., & Wyndhamn, J. (1992). Solving everyday problems in the formal setting: An empirical study of the school as context for thought. In S. Chaiklin & J. Lave (Eds.), *Understanding practice.* New York: Cambridge University Press.

Salmivalli, C., & Peets, K. (2009). Bullies, victims, and bully–victim relationships in middle childhood and early adolescence. In K. H. Rubin, W. M. Bukowski, & B. Laursen (Eds.), *Handbook of peer interactions, relationships, and groups* (pp. 322–340). New York: Guilford Press.

Salomon, G. (1993). No distribution without individuals' cognition: A dynamic interactional view. In G. Salomon (Ed.), *Distributed cognitions: Psychological and educational considerations* (pp. 111–138). Cambridge, England: Cambridge University Press.

Sanchez, F., & Anderson, M. L. (1990). Gang mediation: A process that works. *Principal, 69*(4), 54–56.

Sanders, C. E. (1997). Assessment during the preschool years. In G. D. Phye (Ed.), *Handbook of classroom assessment: Learning, achievement, and adjustment.* San Diego, CA: Academic Press.

Sanders, M. G. (1996). Action teams in action: Interviews and observations in three schools in the Baltimore School—Family—Community Partnership Program. *Journal of Education for Students Placed at Risk, 1,* 249–262.

Sapolsky, R. M. (1999). Glucocorticoids, stress, and their adverse neurological effects: Relevance to aging. *Experimental Gerontology, 34,* 721–732.

Sapon-Shevin, M., Dobbelaere, A., Corrigan, C., Goodman, K., & Mastin, M. (1998). Everyone here can play. *Educational Leadership, 56*(1), 42–45.

Sarama, J., & Clements, D. H. (2009). "Concrete" computer manipulatives in mathematics education. *Child Development Perspectives, 3,* 145–150.

Sarason, I. G. (Ed.). (1980). *Test anxiety: Theory, research, and applications.* Mahwah, NJ: Erlbaum.

Sarason, S. B. (1972). What research says about test anxiety in elementary school children. In A. R. Binter & S. H. Frey (Eds.), *The psychology of the elementary school child.* Chicago: Rand McNally.

Sasso, G. M., & Rude, H. A. (1987). Unprogrammed effects of training high-status peers to interact with severely handicapped children. *Journal of Applied Behavior Analysis, 20,* 35–44.

Sattler, J. M. (2001). *Assessment of children: Cognitive applications* (4th ed.). San Diego, CA: Author.

Saudino, K. J., & Plomin, R. (2007). Why are hyperactivity and academic achievement related? *Child Development, 78,* 972–986.

Savin-Williams, R. C. (2008). Then and now: Recruitment, definition, diversity, and positive attributes of same-sex populations. *Developmental Psychology, 44,* 135–138.

Sawyer, R. J., Graham, S., & Harris, K. R. (1992). Direct teaching, strategy instruction, and strategy instruction with explicit self-regulation: Effects on the composition skills and self-efficacy of students with learning disabilities. *Journal of Educational Psychology, 84,* 340–352.

Sawyer, R. K. (2003). Emergence in creativity and development. In R. K. Sawyer, V. John-Steiner, S. Moran, R. J. Sternberg, D. H. Feldman, J. Nakamura, & M. Csikszentmihalyi, *Creativity and development* (pp. 12–60). Oxford, England: Oxford University Press.

Sax, G. (1989). *Principles of educational and psychological measurement and evaluation* (3rd ed.). Belmont, CA: Wadsworth.

Scardamalia, M., & Bereiter, C. (2006). Knowledge building: Theory, pedagogy, and technology. In R. K. Sawyer (Ed.), *The Cambridge handbook of the learning sciences* (pp. 97–115). Cambridge, England: Cambridge University Press.

Scarr, S. (1992). Developmental theories for the 1990s: Development and individual differences. *Child Development, 63,* 1–19.

Scarr, S. (1993). Biological and cultural diversity: The legacy of Darwin for development. *Child Development, 64,* 1333–1353.

Scarr, S., & McCartney, K. (1983). How people make their own environments: A theory of genotype environment effects. *Child Development, 54,* 424–435.

Scarr, S., & Weinberg, R. A. (1976). IQ test performance of black children adopted by white families. *American Psychologist, 31,* 726–739.

Scevak, J. J., Moore, P. J., & Kirby, J. R. (1993). Training students to use maps to increase text recall. *Contemporary Educational Psychology, 18,* 401–413.

Schacter, D. L. (1999). The seven sins of memory: Insights from psychology and neuroscience. *American Psychologist, 54,* 182–203.

Schank, R. C. (1979). Interestingness: Controlling inferences. *Artificial Intelligence, 12,* 273–297.

Schank, R. C., & Abelson, R. P. (1995). Knowledge and memory: The real story. In R. S. Wyer, Jr. (Ed.), *Advances in social cognition: Vol. 8. Knowledge and memory: The real story.* Mahwah, NJ: Erlbaum.

Schauble, L. (1990). Belief revision in children: The role of prior knowledge and strategies for generating evidence. *Journal of Experimental Child Psychology, 49,* 31–57.

Scheier, M. F., & Carver, C. S. (1992). Effects of optimism on psychological and physical well-being: Theoretical overview and empirical update. *Cognitive Therapy and Research, 16,* 201–228.

Schiefele, U. (1991). Interest, learning, and motivation. *Educational Psychologist, 26,* 299–323.

Schiefele, U. (1992). Topic interest and levels of text comprehension. In K. A. Renninger, S. Hidi, & A. Krapp (Eds.), *The role of interest in learning and development.* Mahwah, NJ: Erlbaum.

Schiefele, U. (1998). Individual interest and learning: What we know and what we don't know. In L. Hoffman, A. Krapp, K. Renninger, & J. Baumert (Eds.), *Interest and learning: Proceedings of the Seeon Conference on Interest and Gender* (pp. 91–104). Kiel, Germany: IPN.

Schimmoeller, M. A. (1998, April). *Influence of private speech on the writing behaviors of young children: Four case studies.* Paper presented at the annual meeting of the American Educational Research Association, San Diego, CA.

Schlaefli, A., Rest, J. R., & Thoma, S. J. (1985). Does moral education improve moral judgment? A meta-analysis of intervention studies using the defining issues test. *Review of Educational Research, 55,* 319–352.

Schliemann, A. D., & Carraher, D. W. (1993). Proportional reasoning in and out of school. In P. Light & G. Butterworth (Eds.), *Context and* cognition: Ways of learning and knowing. Mahwah, NJ: Erlbaum.

Schmidt, A. C., Hanley, G. P., & Layer, S. A. (2009). A further analysis of the value of choice: Controlling for illusory discriminative stimuli and evaluating the effects of less preferred items. *Journal of Applied Behavior Analysis, 42*, 711–716.

Schmidt, R. A., & Bjork, R. A. (1992). New conceptualizations of practice: Common principles in three paradigms suggest new concepts for training. *Psychological Science, 3*, 207–217.

Schneider, W. (1993). Domain-specific knowledge and memory performance in children. *Educational Psychology Review, 5*, 257–273.

Schneider, W. (2010). Metacognition and memory development in childhood and adolescence. In H. S. Waters & W. Schneider (Eds.), *Metacognition, strategy use, and instruction* (pp. 54–81). New York: Guilford Press.

Schneider, W., & Pressley, M. (1989). *Memory development between 2 and 20*. New York: Springer-Verlag.

Schoenfeld, A. H., & Hermann, D. J. (1982). Problem perception and knowledge structure in expert and novice mathematical problem solvers. *Journal of Experimental Psychology: Learning, Memory, and Cognition, 8*, 484–494.

Schofield, J. W. (1995). Improving intergroup relations among students. In J. A. Banks & C. A. M. Banks (Eds.), *Handbook of research on multicultural education*. New York: Macmillan.

Schofield, J. W. (2006). Internet use in schools: Promise and problems. In R. K. Sawyer (Ed.), *The Cambridge handbook of the learning sciences* (pp. 521–534). Cambridge, England: Cambridge University Press.

Schommer, M. (1990). Effects of beliefs about the nature of knowledge on comprehension. *Journal of Educational Psychology, 82*, 498–504.

Schommer, M. (1994a). An emerging conceptualization of epistemological beliefs and their role in learning. In R. Garner & P. A. Alexander (Eds.), *Beliefs about text and instruction with text*. Mahwah, NJ: Erlbaum.

Schommer, M. (1994b). Synthesizing epistemological belief research: Tentative understandings and provocative confusions. *Educational Psychology Review, 6*, 293–319.

Schommer, M. (1997). The development of epistemological beliefs among secondary students: A longitudinal study. *Journal of Educational Psychology, 89*, 37–40.

Schommer-Aikins, M. (2002). An evolving theoretical framework for an epistemological belief system. In B. K. Hofer & P. R. Pintrich (Eds.), *Personal epistemology: The psychology of beliefs about knowledge and knowing*. Mahwah, NJ: Erlbaum.

Schoon, I. (2006). *Risk and resilience: Adaptations in changing times*. Cambridge, England: Cambridge University Press.

Schraw, G. (2006). Knowledge: Structures and processes. In P. A. Alexander & P. H. Winne (Eds.), *Handbook of educational psychology* (2nd ed., pp. 245–263). Mahwah, NJ: Erlbaum.

Schraw, G., & Lehman, S. (2001). Situational interest: A review of the literature and directions for future research. *Educational Psychology Review, 13*, 23–52.

Schraw, G., & Moshman, D. (1995). Metacognitive theories. *Educational Psychology Review, 7*, 351–371.

Schraw, G., Potenza, M. T., & Nebelsick-Gullet, L. (1993). Constraints on the calibration of performance. *Contemporary Educational Psychology, 18*, 455–463.

Schroth, M. L. (1992). The effects of delay of feedback on a delayed concept formation transfer task. *Contemporary Educational Psychology, 17*, 78–82.

Schult, C. A. (2002). Children's understanding of the distinction between intentions and desires. *Child Development, 73*, 1727–1747.

Schultheiss, O. C., & Brunstein, J. C. (2005). An implicit motive perspective on competence. In A. J. Elliot & C. S. Dweck (Eds.), *Handbook of competence and motivation* (pp. 31–51). New York: Guilford Press.

Schultz, K., Buck, P., & Niesz, T. (2000). Democratizing conversations: Racialized talk in a post-desegregated middle school. *American Educational Research Journal, 37*, 33–65.

Schunk, D. H. (1981). Modeling and attributional effects on children's achievement: A self-efficacy analysis. *Journal of Educational Psychology, 73*, 93–105.

Schunk, D. H. (1983). Developing children's self-efficacy and skills: The roles of social comparative information and goal setting. *Contemporary Educational Psychology, 8*, 76–86.

Schunk, D. H. (1987). Peer models and children's behavioral change. *Review of Educational Research, 57*, 149–174.

Schunk, D. H. (1990, April). *Socialization and the development of self-regulated learning: The role of attributions*. Paper presented at the annual meeting of the American Educational Research Association, Boston.

Schunk, D. H. (1998). Teaching elementary students to self-regulate practice of mathematical skills with modeling. In D. H. Schunk & B. J. Zimmerman (Eds.), *Self-regulated learning: From teaching to self-reflective practice* (pp. 137–159). New York: Guilford Press.

Schunk, D. H., & Hanson, A. R. (1985). Peer models: Influence on children's self-efficacy and achievement. *Journal of Educational Psychology, 77*, 313–322.

Schunk, D. H., & Pajares, F. (2004). Self-efficacy in education revisited: Empirical and applied evidence. In D. M. McInerney & S. Van Etten (Eds.), *Big theories revisited* (pp. 115–138). Greenwich, CT: Information Age.

Schunk, D. H., & Pajares, F. (2005). Competence perceptions and academic functioning. In A. J. Elliot & C. S. Dweck (Eds.), *Handbook of competence and motivation* (pp. 85–104). New York: Guilford Press.

Schunk, D. H., & Swartz, C. W. (1993). Goals and progress feedback: Effects on self-efficacy and writing achievement. *Contemporary Educational Psychology, 18*, 337–354.

Schunk, D. H., & Zimmerman, B. J. (Eds.). (1998). *Self-regulated learning: From teaching to self-reflective practice*. New York: Guilford Press.

Schunk, D. H., & Zimmerman, B. J. (2006). Competence and control beliefs: Distinguishing the means and ends. In P. A. Alexander & P. H. Winne (Eds.), *Handbook of educational psychology* (2nd ed., pp. 349–367). Mahwah, NJ: Erlbaum.

Schutz, P. A. (1994). Goals as the transactive point between motivation and cognition. In P. R. Pintrich, D. R. Brown, & C. E. Weinstein (Eds.), *Student motivation, cognition, and learning: Essays in honor of Wilbert J. McKeachie*. Mahwah, NJ: Erlbaum.

Schwartz, D., Dodge, K. A., Coie, J. D., Hubbard, J. A., Cillesen, A. H., Lemerise, E. A., et al. (1998). Social-cognitive and behavioral correlates of aggression and victimization in boys' play groups. *Journal of Abnormal Child Psychology, 26*, 431–440.

Schwartz, D., Gorman, A. H., Nakamoto, J., & Toblin, R. L. (2005). Victimization in the peer group and children's academic functioning. *Journal of Educational Psychology, 97*, 425–435.

Schwartz, D. L., & Martin, T. (2004). Inventing to prepare for future learning: The hidden efficiency of encouraging original student production in statistics instruction. *Cognition and Instruction, 22*, 129–184.

Schwarz, B. B., Neuman, Y., & Biezuner, S. (2000). Two wrongs may make a right . . . if they argue together! *Cognition and Instruction, 18*, 461–494.

Scott, J., & Bushell, D. (1974). The length of teacher contacts and students' off-task behavior. *Journal of Applied Behavior Analysis, 7*, 39–44.

Scruggs, T. E., & Lifson, S. A. (1985). Current conceptions of test-wiseness: Myths and realities. *School Psychology Review, 14*, 339–350.

Scruggs, T. E., & Mastropieri, M. A. (1989). Mnemonic instruction of learning disabled students: A field-based evaluation. *Learning Disabilities Quarterly, 12*, 119–125.

Scruggs, T. E., & Mastropieri, M. A. (1994). Successful mainstreaming in elementary science classes: A qualitative study of three reputational cases. *American Educational Research Journal, 31*, 785–811.

Seaton, E. K., Scottham, K. M., & Sellers, R. M. (2006). The status model of racial identity development in African American adolescents: Evidence of structure, trajectories, and well-being. *Child Development, 77*, 1416–1426.

Seaton, M., Craven, R. G., & Marsh, H. W. (2008). East meets west: An examination of the big-fish-little-pond effect in Western and non-Western countries. In H. W. Marsh, R. G. Craven, & D. M. McInerney (Eds.), *Self-processes, learning, and enabling human potential* (pp. 353–371). Charlotte, NC: Information Age.

Sedikides, C., & Gregg, A. P. (2008). Self-enhancement: Food for thought. *Perspectives on Psychological Science, 3*, 102–116.

Segalowitz, S. J. (2007). The role of neuroscience in historical and contemporary theories of human development. In D. Coch, K. W. Fischer, & G. Dawson (Eds.), *Human behavior, learning, and the developing brain: Typical development* (pp. 3–29). New York: Guilford Press.

Seiffge-Krenke, I., Aunola, K., & Nurmi, J.-E. (2009). Changes in stress perception and coping during adolescence: The role of situational and personal factors. *Child Development, 80*, 259–279.

Seligman, M. E. P. (1991). *Learned optimism*. New York: Knopf.

Selman, R. L. (1980). *The growth of interpersonal understanding*. San Diego, CA: Academic Press.

Semb, G. B., & Ellis, J. A. (1994). Knowledge taught in school: What is remembered? *Review of Educational Research, 64*, 253–286.

Serbin, L., & Karp, J. (2003). Intergenerational studies of parenting and the transfer of risk from parent to child. *Current Directions in Psychological Science, 12*, 138–142.

Serpell, R., Baker, L., & Sonnenschein, S. (2005). *Becoming literate in the city: The Baltimore Early*

Childhood Project. Cambridge, England: Cambridge University Press.

Sfard, A. (1998). On two metaphors for learning and the dangers of choosing just one. *Educational Researcher, 27*(2), 4–13.

Shanahan, T. (2004). Overcoming the dominance of communication: Writing to think and to learn. In T. L. Jetton & J. A. Dole (Eds.), *Adolescent literacy research and practice* (pp. 59–74). New York: Guilford Press.

Shapiro, A. M. (2004). How including prior knowledge as a subject variable may change outcomes of learning research. *American Educational Research Journal, 41*, 159–189.

Shariff, S. (2008). *Cyber-bullying: Issues and solutions for the school, the classroom and the home.* London: Routledge.

Shavelson, R. J., & Baxter, G. P. (1992). What we've learned about assessing hands-on science. *Educational Leadership, 49*(8), 20–25.

Shaw, P., Eckstrand, K., Sharp, W., Blumenthal, J., Lerch, J. P., Greenstein, D., et al. (2007). Attention-deficit/hyperactivity disorder is characterized by a delay in cortical maturation. *Proceedings of the National Academy of Sciences, 104*, 19,649–19,654.

Shaw, P., Greenstein, D., Lerch, J., Clasen, L., Lenroot, R., Gogtay, N., et al. (2006). Intellectual ability and cortical development in children and adolescents. *Nature, 440*, 676–679.

Shaywitz, S. E., Mody, M., & Shaywitz, B. A. (2006). Neural mechanisms in dyslexia. *Current Directions in Psychological Science, 15*, 278–281.

Sheets, R. H., & Hollins, E. R. (Eds.). (1999). *Racial and ethnic identity in school practices: Aspects of human development.* Mahwah, NJ: Erlbaum.

Shepard, L. A. (2000). The role of assessment in a learning culture. *Educational Researcher, 29*(7), 4–14.

Shepard, L., Hammerness, K., Darling-Hammond, L., & Rust, F. (with Snowden, J. B., Gordon, E., Gutierrez, C., & Pacheco, A.). (2005). Assessment. In L. Darling-Hammond & J. Bransford (Eds.), *Preparing teachers for a changing world: What teachers should learn and be able to do* (pp. 275–326). San Francisco: Jossey-Bass/Wiley.

Sherman, D. K., & Cohen, G. L. (2002). Accepting threatening information: Self-affirmation and the reduction of defensive biases. *Current Directions in Psychological Science, 11*, 119–123.

Sherman, J., & Bisanz, J. (2009). Equivalence in symbolic and nonsymbolic contexts: Benefits of solving problems with manipulatives. *Journal of Educational Psychology, 101*, 88–100.

Shernoff, D., Csikszentmihalyi, M., Schneider, B., & Shernoff, E. (2003). Student engagement in high school classrooms from the perspective of flow theory. *School Psychology Quarterly, 18*, 158–176.

Shernoff, D. J., & Hoogstra, L. A. (2001). Continuing motivation beyond the high school classroom. In M. Michaelson & J. Nakamura (Eds.), *Supportive frameworks for youth engagement* (pp. 73–87). San Francisco: Jossey-Bass.

Shernoff, D. J., Knauth, S., & Makris, E. (2000). The quality of classroom experiences. In M. Csikszentmihalyi & B. Schneider, *Becoming adult: How teenagers prepare for the world of work.* New York: Basic Books.

Shim, S. S., & Ryan, A. M. (2006, April). *The nature and the consequences of changes in achievement goals during early adolescence.* Paper presented at the annual meeting of the American Educational Research Association, San Francisco, CA.

Shim, S. S., Ryan, A. M., & Anderson, C. J. (2008). Achievement goals and achievement during early adolescence: Examining time-varying predictor and outcome variables in growth-curve analysis. *Journal of Educational Psychology, 100*, 655–671.

Shipman, S., & Shipman, V. C. (1985). Cognitive styles: Some conceptual, methodological, and applied issues. In E. W. Gordon (Ed.), *Review of research in education* (Vol. 12). Washington, DC: American Educational Research Association.

Shores, M., & Shannon, D. (2007). The effects of self-regulation, motivation, anxiety, and attributions on mathematics achievement for fifth and sixth grade students. *School Science and Mathematics, 107*(6), 225–236.

Short, E. J., Schatschneider, C. W., & Friebert, S. E. (1993). Relationship between memory and metamemory performance: A comparison of specific and general strategy knowledge. *Journal of Educational Psychology, 85*, 412–423.

Shrum, W., & Cheek, N. H. (1987). Social structure during the school years: Onset of the degrouping process. *American Sociological Review, 52*, 218–223.

Shuell, T. J. (1996). Teaching and learning in a classroom context. In D. C. Berliner & R. C. Calfee (Eds.), *Handbook of educational psychology.* New York: Macmillan.

Shulman, L. S. (1986). Those who understand: Knowledge growth in teaching. *Educational Researcher, 15*(2), 4–14.

Shure, M. B., & Aberson, B. (2006). Enhancing the process of resilience through effective thinking. In. S. Goldstein & R. B. Brooks (Eds.), *Handbook of resilience in children* (pp. 373–394). New York: Springer.

Shute, V. J. (2008). Focus on formative feedback. *Review of Educational Research, 78*, 153–189.

Shweder, R. A., Mahapatra, M., & Miller, J. G. (1987). Culture and moral development. In J. Kagan & S. Lamb (Eds.), *The emergence of morality in young children* (pp. 1–83). Chicago: University of Chicago Press.

Sideridis, G. D. (2005). Goal orientation, academic achievement, and depression: Evidence in favor of a revised goal theory framework. *Journal of Educational Psychology, 97*, 366–375.

Sieber, J. E., Kameya, L. I., & Paulson, F. L. (1970). Effect of memory support on the problem-solving ability of test-anxious children. *Journal of Educational Psychology, 61*, 159–168.

Siegler, R. S. (2009). Improving the numerical understanding of children from low-income families. *Child Development Perspectives, 3*, 118–124.

Siegler, R. S., & Alibali, M. W. (2005). *Children's thinking* (4th ed.). Upper Saddle River, NJ: Prentice Hall.

Siegler, R. S., & Lin, X. (2010). Self-explanations promote children's learning. In H. S. Waters & W. Schneider (Eds.), *Metacognition, strategy use, and instruction* (pp. 85–112.). New York: Guilford Press.

Siegler, R. S., & Svetina, M. (2006). What leads children to adopt new strategies? A microgenetic/cross-sectional study of class inclusion. *Child Development, 77*, 997–1015.

Sigman, M., & Whaley, S. E. (1998). The role of nutrition in the development of intelligence. In U. Neisser (Ed.), *The rising curve: Long-term gains in IQ and related measures* (pp. 155–182).

Washington, DC: American Psychological Association.

Silberman, M. L., & Wheelan, S. A. (1980). *How to discipline without feeling guilty: Assertive relationships with children.* Champaign, IL: Research Press.

Silverberg, R. P. (2003, April). *Developing relational space: Teachers who came to understand themselves and their students as learners.* Paper presented at the annual meeting of the American Educational Research Association, Chicago.

Silveri, M. M., Rohan, M. L., Pimentel, P. J., Gruber, S. A., Rosso, I. M., & Yurgelun-Todd, D. A. (2006). Sex differences in the relationship between white matter microstructure and impulsivity in adolescents. *Magnetic Resonance Imaging, 24*, 833–841.

Silvia, P. J. (2008). Interest—The curious emotion. *Current Directions in Psychological Science, 17*, 57–60.

Simon, H. A. (1974). How big is a chunk? *Science, 183*, 482–488.

Simons, R. L., Whitbeck, L. B., Conger, R. D., & Conger, K. J. (1991). Parenting factors, social skills, and value commitments as precursors to school failure, involvement with deviant peers, and delinquent behavior. *Journal of Youth and Adolescence, 20*, 645–664.

Simonton, D. K. (2000). Creativity: Cognitive, personal, developmental, and social aspects. *American Psychologist, 55*, 151–158.

Simonton, D. K. (2001). Talent development as a multidimensional, multiplicative, and dynamic process. *Current Directions in Psychological Science, 10*, 39–42.

Sinatra, G. M., & Mason, L. (2008). Beyond knowledge: Learner characteristics influencing conceptual change. In S. Vosniadou (Ed.), *International handbook on conceptual change* (pp. 560–582). New York: Routledge.

Sinatra, G. M., & Pintrich, P. R. (Eds.). (2003). *Intentional conceptual change.* Mahwah, NJ: Erlbaum.

Singer, D. G., & Singer, J. L. (1994). *Barney & Friends as education and entertainment: Phase 3. A national study: Can preschoolers learn through exposure to Barney & Friends?* New Haven, CT: Yale University Family Television Research and Consultation Center.

Sins, P. H. M., van Joolingen, W. R., Savelsbergh, E. R., & van Hout-Wolters, B. (2008). Motivation and performance within a collaborative computer-based modeling task: Relations between students' achievement goal orientation, self-efficacy, cognitive processing, and achievement. *Contemporary Educational Psychology, 33*, 58–77.

Sireci, S. G., Scarpati, S. E., & Li, S. (2005). Test accommodations for students with disabilities: An analysis of the interaction hypothesis. *Review of Educational Research, 75*, 457–490.

Sirin, S. R. (2005). Socioeconomic status and academic achievement: A meta-analytic review of research. *Review of Educational Research, 75*, 417–453.

Sirin, S. R., & Ryce, P. (2010). Cultural incongruence between teachers and families: Implications for immigrant students. In E. L. Grigorenko & R. Takanishi (Eds.), *Immigration, diversity, and education* (pp. 151–169). New York: Routledge.

Sizer, T. R. (1992). *Horace's school: Redesigning the American high school.* Boston: Houghton Mifflin.

Sizer, T. R. (2004). *Horace's compromise: The dilemma of the American high school*. Boston: Houghton Mifflin.

Skaalvik, E. (1997). Self-enhancing and self-defeating ego orientation: Relations with task avoidance orientation, achievement, self-perceptions, and anxiety. *Journal of Educational Psychology, 89*, 71–81.

Skaalvik, E. M., & Skaalvik, S. (2008). Teacher self-efficacy: Conceptual analysis and relations with teacher burnout and perceived school context. In H. W. Marsh, R. G. Craven, & D. M. McInerney (Eds.), *Self-processes, learning, and enabling human potential* (pp. 223–247). Charlotte, NC: Information Age.

Skiba, R. J., & Knesting, K. (2001). Zero tolerance, zero evidence: An analysis of school disciplinary practice. In R. J. Skiba & G. G. Noam (Eds.), *New directions for youth development: Theory, practice, research* (pp. 11–43). San Francisco: Jossey-Bass.

Skiba, R. J., & Rausch, M. K. (2006). Zero tolerance, suspension, and expulsion: Questions of equity and effectiveness. In C. M. Evertson & C. S. Weinstein (Eds.), *Handbook of classroom management: Research, practice, and contemporary issues* (pp. 1063–1089). Mahwah, NJ: Erlbaum.

Skinner, B. F. (1953). *Science and human behavior*. New York: Macmillan.

Skinner, B. F. (1954). The science of learning and the art of teaching. *Harvard Educational Review, 24*, 86–97.

Skinner, B. F. (1968). *The technology of teaching*. New York: Appleton-Century-Crofts.

Skinner, E., Furrer, C., Marchand, G., & Kindermann, T. (2008). Engagement and disaffection in the classroom: Part of a larger motivational dynamic? *Journal of Educational Psychology, 100*, 765–781.

Slater, W. H. (2004). Teaching English from a literacy perspective: The goal of high literacy for all students. In T. L. Jetton & J. A. Dole (Eds.), *Adolescent literacy research and practice* (pp. 40–58). New York: Guilford Press.

Slavin, R. E. (1987). Ability grouping and student achievement in elementary schools: A best-evidence synthesis. *Review of Educational Research, 57*, 293–336.

Slavin, R. E. (1989). Students at risk of school failure: The problem and its dimensions. In R. E. Slavin, N. L. Karweit, & N. A. Madden (Eds.), *Effective programs for students at risk*. Boston: Allyn & Bacon.

Slavin, R. E., Hurley, E. A., & Chamberlain, A. (2003). Cooperative learning and achievement: Theory and research. In W. Reynolds & G. Miller (Eds.), *Handbook of psychology: Vol. 7. Educational psychology* (pp. 177–198). New York: Wiley.

Slavin, R. E., Karweit, N. L., & Madden, N. A. (Eds.). (1989). *Effective programs for students at risk*. Boston: Allyn & Bacon.

Slavin, R. E., & Lake, C. (2008). Effective programs in elementary mathematics: A best-evidence synthesis. *Review of Educational Research, 78*, 427–515.

Slavin, R. E., Lake, C., Chambers, B., Cheung, A., & Davis, S. (2009). Effective reading programs for the elementary grades: A best-evidence synthesis. *Review of Educational Research, 79*, 1391–1466.

Sleeter, C. E., & Grant, C. A. (1999). *Making choices for multicultural education: Five approaches to race, class, and gender* (3rd ed.). Upper Saddle River, NJ: Merrill/Prentice Hall.

Slonim, M. B. (1991). *Children, culture, ethnicity: Evaluating and understanding the impact*. New York: Garland.

Slusher, M. P., & Anderson, C. A. (1996). Using causal persuasive arguments to change beliefs and teach new information: The mediating role of explanation availability and evaluation bias in the acceptance of knowledge. *Journal of Educational Psychology, 88*, 110–122.

Small, M. Y., Lovett, S. B., & Scher, M. S. (1993). Pictures facilitate children's recall of unillustrated expository prose. *Journal of Educational Psychology, 85*, 520–528.

Smetana, J. G. (1981). Preschool children's conceptions of moral and social rules. *Child Development, 52*, 1333–1336.

Smetana, J. G. (2005). Adolescent-parent conflict: Resistance and subversion as developmental process. In L. Nucci (Ed.), *Conflict, contradiction, and contrarian elements in moral development and education* (pp. 69–91). Mahwah, NJ: Erlbaum.

Smetana, J. G. (2006). Social cognitive domain theory: Consistencies and variations in children's moral and social judgments. In M. Killen & J. Smetana (Eds.), *Handbook of moral development* (pp. 119–154). Mahwah, NJ: Erlbaum.

Smetana, J. G., & Braeges, J. L. (1990). The development of toddlers' moral and conventional judgments. *Merrill-Palmer Quarterly, 36*, 329–346.

Smith, C. L. (2007). Bootstrapping processes in the development of students' commonsense matter theories: Using analogical mappings, thought experiments, and learning to measure to promote conceptual restructuring. *Cognition and Instruction, 25*, 337–398.

Smith, C. L., Maclin, D., Grosslight, L., & Davis, H. (1997). Teaching for understanding: A study of students' preinstruction theories of matter and a comparison of the effectiveness of two approaches to teaching about matter and density. *Cognition and Instruction, 15*, 317–393.

Smith, C. L., Maclin, D., Houghton, C., & Hennessey, M. G. (2000). Sixth-grade students' epistemologies of science: The impact of school science experiences on epistemological development. *Cognition and Instruction, 18*, 349–422.

Smith, D. C., & Neale, D. C. (1991). The construction of subject-matter knowledge in primary science teaching. In J. Brophy (Ed.), *Advances in research on teaching: Vol. 2. Teachers' knowledge of subject matter as it relates to their teaching practice*. Greenwich, CT: JAI Press.

Smith, E. E. (2000). Neural bases of human working memory. *Current Directions in Psychological Science, 9*, 45–49.

Smith, E. R., & Semin, G. R. (2007). Situated social cognition. *Current Directions in Psychological Science, 16*, 132–135.

Smith, H. L. (1998). Literacy and instruction in African American communities: Shall we overcome? In B. Pérez (Ed.), *Sociocultural contexts of language and literacy*. Mahwah, NJ: Erlbaum.

Smith, J. L. (2004). Understanding the process of stereotype threat: A review of mediational variables and new performance goal directions. *Educational Psychology Review, 16*, 177–206.

Smitherman, G. (1994). "The blacker the berry the sweeter the juice": African American student writers. In A. H. Dyson & C. Genishi (Eds.), *The need for story: Cultural diversity in classroom and community*. Urbana, IL: National Council of Teachers of English.

Smokowski, P., Buchanan, R. L., & Bacalleo, M, L. (2009). Acculturation and adjustment in Latino adolescents: How cultural risk factors and assets influence multiple domains of adolescent mental health. *Journal of Primary Prevention, 30*, 371–393.

Snarey, J. (1995). In a communitarian voice: The sociological expansion of Kohlbergian theory, research, and practice. In W. M. Kurtines & J. L. Gewirtz (Eds.), *Moral development: An introduction*. Boston: Allyn & Bacon.

Sneider, C., & Pulos, S. (1983). Children's cosmographies: Understanding the earth's shape and gravity. *Science Education, 67*, 205–221.

Snir, J., Smith, C. L., & Raz, G. (2003). Linking phenomena with competing underlying models: A software tool for introducing students to the particulate model of matter. *Science Education, 87*, 794–830.

Snow, R. E., Corno, L., & Jackson, D., III (1996). Individual differences in affective and conative functions. In D. C. Berliner & R. C. Calfee (Eds.), *Handbook of educational psychology*. New York: Macmillan.

Snyder, C, R. (1994). *The psychology of hope: You can get there from here*. New York: Free Press.

Snyder, C. R. (2002). Hope theory: Rainbows in the mind. *Psychological Inquiry, 13*, 249–275.

Snyder, J., Schrepferman, L., McEachern, A., Barner, S., Johnson, K., & Provines, J. (2008). Peer deviancy training and peer coercion: Dual processes associated with early-onset conduct problems. *Child Development, 79*, 252–268.

Solano-Flores, G. (2008). Who is given tests in what language by whom, when, and where? The need for probabilistic views of language in the testing of English language learners. *Educational Researcher, 37*, 189–199.

Solomon, R. C. (1984). Getting angry: The Jamesian theory of emotion in anthropology. In R. Shweder & R. A. Levine (Eds.), *Culture theory: Essays on mind, self, and emotion* (pp. 238–256). Cambridge, England: Cambridge University Press.

Solórzano, R. W. (2008). High stakes testing: Issues, implications, and remedies for English language learners. *Educational Researcher, 78*, 260–329.

Soodak, L. C., & McCarthy, M. R. (2006). Classroom management in inclusive settings. In C. M. Evertson & C. S. Weinstein (Eds.), *Handbook of classroom management: Research, practice, and contemporary issues* (pp. 461–489). Mahwah, NJ: Erlbaum.

Sosniak, L. A., & Stodolsky, S. S. (1994). Making connections: Social studies education in an urban fourth-grade classroom. In J. Brophy (Ed.), *Advances in research on teaching: Vol. 4. Case studies of teaching and learning in social studies*. Greenwich, CT: JAI Press.

Southerland, S. A., & Sinatra, G. M. (2003). Learning about biological evolution: A special case of intentional conceptual change. In G. M. Sinatra & P. R. Pintrich (Eds.), *Intentional conceptual change* (pp. 317–345). Mahwah, NJ: Erlbaum.

Sowell, E. R., & Jernigan, T. L. (1998). Further MRI evidence of late brain maturation: Limbic volume increases and changing asymmetries during childhood and adolescence. *Developmental Neuropsychology, 14*, 599–617.

Sowell, E. R., Thompson, P. M., Holmes, C. J., Jernigan, T. L., & Toga, A. W. (1999). *In vivo* evidence for post-adolescent brain maturation in frontal and striatal regions. *Nature Neuroscience, 2*, 859–861.

Spandel, V. (1997). Reflections on portfolios. In G. D. Phye (Ed.), *Handbook of academic learning: Construction of knowledge.* San Diego, CA: Academic Press.

Spaulding, C. L. (1992). *Motivation in the classroom.* New York: McGraw-Hill.

Spear, L. P. (2000). Neurobehavioral changes in adolescence. *Current Directions in Psychological Science, 9,* 11–114.

Spear, L. P. (2007). Brain development and adolescent behavior. In D. Coch, K. W. Fischer, & G. Dawson (Eds.), *Human behavior, learning, and the developing brain: Typical development* (pp. 362–396). New York: Guilford Press.

Spearman, C. (1904). General intelligence, objectively determined and measured. *American Journal of Psychology, 15,* 201–293.

Spearman, C. (1927). *The abilities of man: Their nature and measurement.* New York: Macmillan.

Spears, A. K. (2007). Improvisation, semantic license, and augmentation. In H. S. Alim & J. Baugh (Eds.), *Talkin Black talk: Language, education, and social change* (pp. 100–111). New York: Teachers College Press.

Spencer, J. P., Blumberg, M. S., McMurray, B., Robinson, S. R., Samuelson, L. K., & Tomblin, J. B. (2009). Short arms and talking eggs: Why we should no longer abide the nativist–empiricist debate. *Child Development Perspectives, 3,* 79–87.

Spera, C. (2005). A review of the relationship among parenting practices, parenting styles, and adolescent school achievement. *Educational Psychology Review, 17,* 125–146.

Sperling, G. (1960). The information available in brief visual presentations. *Psychological Monographs, 74* (Whole No. 498).

Spörer, N., & Brunstein, J. C. (2009). Fostering the reading comprehension of secondary school students through peer-assisted learning: Effects on strategy knowledge, strategy use, and task performance. *Contemporary Educational Psychology, 34,* 289–297.

Squire, L. R., & Alvarez, P. (1998). Retrograde amnesia and memory consolidation: A neurobiological perspective. In L. R. Squire & S. M. Kosslyn (Eds.), *Findings and current opinion in cognitive neuroscience* (pp. 75–84). Cambridge, MA: MIT Press.

Sroufe, L. A., Cooper, R. G., DeHart, G., & Bronfenbrenner, U. (1992). *Child development: Its nature and course* (2nd ed.). New York: McGraw-Hill

Stacey, K. (1992). Mathematical problem solving in groups: Are two heads better than one? *Journal of Mathematical Behavior, 11,* 261–275.

Stack, C. B., & Burton, L. M. (1993). Kinscripts. *Journal of Comparative Family Studies, 24,* 157–170.

Stahl, G., Koschmann, T., & Suthers, D. D. (2006). Computer-supported collaborative learning. In R. K. Sawyer (Ed.), *The Cambridge handbook of the learning sciences* (pp. 409–425). Cambridge, England: Cambridge University Press.

Stahl, S. A., & Shanahan, C. (2004). Learning to think like a historian: Disciplinary knowledge through critical analysis of multiple documents. In T. L. Jetton & J. A. Dole (Eds.), *Adolescent literacy research and practice* (pp. 94–115). New York: Guilford Press.

Stainback, S., & Stainback, W. (1992). Schools as inclusive communities. In W. Stainback & S. Stainback (Eds.), *Controversial issues confronting special education: Divergent perspectives.* Boston: Allyn & Bacon.

Standage, M., Duda, J. L., & Ntoumanis, N. (2003). A model of contextual motivation in physical education: Using constructs from self-determination and achievement goal theories to predict physical activity intentions. *Journal of Educational Psychology, 95,* 97–110.

Stang, J., & Story, M. (2005). Adolescent growth and development. In J. Stang & M. Story (Eds.), *Guidelines for Adolescent Nutrition Services* (pp. 1–8). Retrieved from http://www.epi.umn.edu/let/pubs/img/adol_ch1.pdf

Stanley, J. C. (1980). On educating the gifted. *Educational Researcher, 9*(3), 8–12.

Stanovich, K. E. (1999). *Who is rational? Studies of individual differences in reasoning.* Mahwah, NJ: Erlbaum.

Stanovich, K. E. (2000). *Progress in understanding reading: Scientific foundations and new frontiers.* New York: Guilford Press.

Staples, M. (2007). Supporting whole-class collaborative inquiry in a secondary mathematics classroom. *Cognition and Instruction, 25,* 161–217.

Staub, E. (1995). The roots of prosocial and antisocial behavior in persons and groups: Environmental influence, personality, culture, and socialization. In W. M. Kurtines & J. L. Gewirtz (Eds.), *Moral development: An introduction.* Boston: Allyn & Bacon.

Steele, C. M. (1997). A threat in the air: How stereotypes shape intellectual identity and performance. *American Psychologist, 52,* 613–629.

Stein, B. S. (1989). Memory and creativity. In J. A. Glover, R. R. Ronning, & C. R. Reynolds (Eds.), *Handbook of creativity.* New York: Plenum Press.

Steinberg, L. (1996). *Beyond the classroom: Why school reform has failed and what parents need to do.* New York: Touchstone.

Steinberg, L. (2005). Cognitive and affective development in adolescence. *Trends in Cognitive Sciences, 9*(2), 69–74.

Steinberg, L. (2007). Risk taking in adolescence. *Current Directions in Psychological Science, 16,* 55–59.

Steinberg, L. (2009). Should the science of adolescent brain development inform public policy? *American Psychologist, 64,* 739–750.

Steinberg, L., Cauffman, E., Woolard, J., Graham, S., & Banich, M. (2009). Are adolescents less mature than adults? *American Psychologist, 64,* 583–594.

Steinberg, L., Graham, S., O'Brien, L., Woolard, J., Cauffman, E., & Banich, M. (2009). Age differences in future orientation and delay discounting. *Child Development, 80,* 28–44.

Steiner, H. H., & Carr, M. (2003). Cognitive development in gifted children: Toward a more precise understanding of emerging differences in intelligence. *Educational Psychology Review, 15,* 215–246.

Stepans, J. (1991). Developmental patterns in students' understanding of physics concepts. In S. M. Glynn, R. H. Yeany, & B. K. Britton (Eds.), *The psychology of learning science.* Mahwah, NJ: Erlbaum.

Sternberg, R. J. (1997). The concept of intelligence and its role in lifelong learning and success. *American Psychologist, 52,* 1030–1037.

Sternberg, R. J. (1998). Applying the triarchic theory of human intelligence in the classroom. In R. J. Sternberg & W. M. Williams (Eds.), *Intelligence, instruction, and assessment: Theory into practice.* Mahwah, NJ: Erlbaum.

Sternberg, R. J. (2003). *Wisdom, intelligence, and creativity synthesized.* Cambridge, England: Cambridge University Press.

Sternberg, R. J. (2004). Culture and intelligence. *American Psychologist, 59,* 325–338.

Sternberg, R. J. (2005). Intelligence, competence, and expertise. In A. J. Elliot & C. S. Dweck (Eds.), *Handbook of competence and motivation* (pp. 15–30). New York: Guilford Press.

Sternberg, R. J. (2007). Intelligence and culture. In S. Kitayama & D. Cohen (Eds.), *Handbook of cultural psychology* (pp. 547–568). New York: Guilford Press.

Sternberg, R. J., & Detterman, D. K. (Eds.). (1986). *What is intelligence? Contemporary views on its nature and definition.* Norwood, NJ: Ablex.

Sternberg, R. J., Forsythe, G. B., Hedlund, J., Horvath, J. A., Wagner, R. K., Williams, W. M., et al. (2000). *Practical intelligence in everyday life.* Cambridge, England: Cambridge University Press.

Sternberg, R. J., & Frensch, P. A. (1993). Mechanisms of transfer. In D. K. Detterman & R. J. Sternberg (Eds.), *Transfer on trial: Intelligence, cognition, and instruction.* Norwood, NJ: Ablex.

Sternberg, R. J., Grigorenko, E. L., & Zhang, L.-F. (2008). Styles of learning and thinking matter in instruction and assessment. *Perspectives on Psychological Science, 3,* 486–506.

Sternberg, R. J., & Horvath, J. A. (1995). A prototype view of expert teaching. *Educational Researcher, 24*(6), 9–17.

Sternberg, R. J., & Wagner, R. K. (Eds.). (1994). *Mind in context: Interactionist perspectives on human intelligence.* Cambridge, England: Cambridge University Press.

Stevens, R. J., & Slavin, R. E. (1995). The cooperative elementary school: Effects of students' achievement, attitudes, and social relations. *American Educational Research Journal, 32,* 321–351.

Stevenson, H. W., Chen, C., & Uttal, D. H. (1990). Beliefs and achievement: A study of black, white, and Hispanic children. *Child Development, 61,* 508–523.

Stewart, L., & Pascual-Leone, J. (1992). Mental capacity constraints and the development of moral reasoning. *Journal of Experimental Child Psychology, 54,* 251–287.

Stice, E. (2003). Puberty and body image. In C. Hayward (Ed.), *Gender differences at puberty* (pp. 61–76). Cambridge, England: Cambridge University Press.

Stice, E., & Barrera, M., Jr. (1995). A longitudinal examination of the reciprocal relations between perceived parenting and adolescents' substance use and externalizing behaviors. *Developmental Psychology, 31,* 322–334.

Stiggins, R. (2008). *An introduction to student-involved assessment FOR learning* (5th ed.). Upper Saddle River, NJ: Merrill/Pearson.

Stipek, D. (2002). At what age should children enter kindergarten? A question for policy makers and parents. *Social Policy Report of the Society for Research in Child Development, 16*(2), 3–16.

Stipek, D., & Miles, S. (2008). Effects of aggression on achievement: Does conflict with the teacher make it worse? *Child Development, 79,* 1721–1735.

Stipek, D. J. (1993). *Motivation to learn: From theory to practice* (2nd ed.). Boston: Allyn & Bacon.

Stipek, D. J. (1996). Motivation and instruction. In D. C. Berliner & R. C. Calfee (Eds.), *Handbook of educational psychology.* New York: Macmillan.

Stodolsky, S. S., Salk, S., & Glaessner, B. (1991). Student views about learning math and social studies. *American Educational Research Journal, 28,* 89–116.

Stone, J. R., III, Alfeld, C., & Pearson, D. (2008). Rigor *and* relevance: Enhancing high school students' math skills through career and technical education. *American Educational Research Journal, 45,* 767–795.

Stone, N. J. (2000). Exploring the relationship between calibration and self-regulated learning. *Educational Psychology Review, 12,* 437–475.

Striepling-Goldstein, S. H. (2004). The low-aggression classroom: A teacher's view. In J. C. Conoley & A. P. Goldstein (Eds.), *School violence intervention* (2nd ed., pp. 23–53). New York: Guilford Press.

Stright, A. D., Gallagher, K. C., & Kelley, K. (2008). Infant temperament moderates relations between maternal parenting in early childhood and children's adjustment in first grade. *Child Development, 79,* 186–200.

Stright, A. D., Neitzel, C., Sears, K. G., & Hoke-Sinex, L. (2001). Instruction begins in the home: Relations between parental instruction and children's self-regulation in the classroom. *Journal of Educational Psychology, 93,* 456–466.

Strike, K. A., & Posner, G. J. (1992). A revisionist theory of conceptual change. In R. A. Duschl & R. J. Hamilton (Eds.), *Philosophy of science, cognitive psychology, and educational theory and practice.* New York: State University of New York Press.

Stringer, E. (2008). *Action research in education* (2nd ed.). Upper Saddle River, NJ: Merrill/Pearson Education.

Stringfield, S. C., & Yakimowski-Srebnick, M. E. (2005). Promise, progress, problems, and paradoxes of three phases of accountability: A longitudinal case study of the Baltimore City Public Schools. *American Educational Research Journal, 42,* 43–75.

Sue, D. W. (1990). Culture-specific strategies in counseling: A conceptual framework. *Professional Psychology: Research and Practice, 21,* 424–433.

Sue, S., & Chin, R. (1983). The mental health of Chinese-American children: Stressors and resources. In G. J. Powell (Ed.), *The psychosocial development of minority children.* New York: Brunner/Mazel.

Suh, S., Suh, J., & Houston, I. (2007). Predictors of categorical at-risk high school dropouts. *Journal of Counseling & Development, 85,* 196–203.

Suina, J. H., & Smolkin, L. B. (1994). From natal culture to school culture to dominant society culture: Supporting transitions for Pueblo Indian students. In P. M. Greenfield & R. R. Cocking (Eds.), *Cross-cultural roots of minority child development.* Mahwah, NJ: Erlbaum.

Sullivan, J. R., & Conoley, J. C. (2004). Academic and instructional interventions with aggressive students. In J. C. Conoley & A. P. Goldstein (Eds.), *School violence intervention* (2nd ed., pp. 235–255). New York: Guilford Press.

Sullivan, J. S. (1989). Planning, implementing, and maintaining an effective in-school suspension program. *Clearing House, 62,* 409–410.

Sullivan-DeCarlo, C., DeFalco, K., & Roberts, V. (1998). Helping students avoid risky behavior. *Educational Leadership, 56*(1), 80–82.

Sund, R. B. (1976). *Piaget for educators.* Upper Saddle River, NJ: Merrill/Prentice Hall.

Sutherland, K. S., & Morgan, P. L. (2003). Implications of transactional processes in classrooms for students with emotional/behavioral disorders. *Preventing School Failure, 48*(6), 32–45.

Sutton, R. E., & Wheatley, K. F. (2003). Teachers' emotions and teaching: A review of the literature and directions for future research. *Educational Psychology Review, 15,* 327–358.

Swan, K., Mitrani, M., Guerrero, F., Cheung, M., & Schoener, J. (1990, April). *Perceived locus of control and computer-based instruction.* Paper presented at the annual meeting of the American Educational Research Association, Boston.

Swann, W. B., Jr., Chang-Schneider, C., & McClarty, K. L. (2007). Do people's self-views matter? Self-concept and self-esteem in everyday life. *American Psychologist, 62,* 84–94.

Swanson, D. B., Norman, G. R., & Linn, R. L. (1995). Performance-based assessment: Lessons from the health professions. *Educational Researcher, 24*(5), 5–11, 35.

Swanson, H. L. (2006). Cross-sectional and incremental changes in working memory and mathematical problem solving. *Journal of Educational Psychology, 98,* 265–281.

Swanson, H. L. (2008). Working memory and intelligence in children: What develops? *Journal of Educational Psychology, 100,* 581–602.

Swanson, H. L., & Lussier, C. M. (2001). A selective synthesis of the experimental literature on dynamic assessment. *Review of Educational Research, 71,* 321–363.

Swanson, H. L., O'Connor, J. E., & Cooney, J. B. (1990). An information processing analysis of expert and novice teachers' problem solving. *American Educational Research Journal, 27,* 533–556.

Swearer, S. M., Grills, A. E., Haye, K. M., & Cary, P. T. (2004). Internalizing problems in students involved in bullying and victimization: Implications for intervention. In D. L. Espelage & S. M. Swearer (Eds.), *Bullying in American schools: A social-ecological perspective on prevention and intervention* (pp. 63–83). Mahwah, NJ: Erlbaum.

Sweller, J. (1994). Cognitive load theory, learning difficulty, and instructional design. *Learning and Instruction, 4,* 295–312.

Syvertsen, A. K., Flanagan, C. A., & Stout, M. D. (2009). Code of silence: Students' perceptions of school climate and willingness to intervene in a peer's dangerous plan. *Journal of Educational Psychology, 101,* 219–232.

Tager-Flusberg, H. (2007). Evaluating the theory-of-mind hypothesis of autism. *Current Directions in Psychological Science, 16,* 311–315.

Tamburrini, J. (1982). Some educational implications of Piaget's theory. In S. Modgil & C. Modgil (Eds.), *Jean Piaget: Consensus and controversy.* New York: Praeger.

Tamis-Lemonda, C. S., & McFadden, K. E. (2010). The United States of America. In M. H. Bornstein (Ed.), *Handbook of cultural developmental science* (pp. 299–322). New York: Psychology Press.

Tanner, J. M., & Inhelder, B. (Eds.). (1960). *Discussions of child development: A consideration of the biological, psychological, and cultural approaches to the understanding of human development and behavior: Vol. 4. The proceedings of the fourth meeting of the World Health Organization Study Group on the Psychobiological Development of the Child, Geneva, 1956.* New York: International Universities Press.

Tarver, S. G. (1992). Direct Instruction. In W. Stainback & S. Stainback (Eds.), *Controversial issues confronting special education.* Boston: Allyn & Bacon.

Tate, W. F. (1995). Returning to the root: A culturally relevant approach to mathematics pedagogy. *Theory into Practice, 34,* 166–173.

Tatum, B. D. (1997). *"Why are all the black kids sitting together in the cafeteria?" and other conversations about race.* New York: Basic Books.

Terry, A. W. (2003). Effects of service learning on young, gifted adolescents and their community. *Gifted Child Quarterly, 47,* 295–308.

Terry, A. W. (2008). Student voices, global echoes: Service-learning and the gifted. *Roeper Review, 30,* 45–51.

Terwilliger, J. S. (1989). Classroom standard setting and grading practices. *Educational Measurement: Issues and Practice, 8*(2), 15–19.

Tessler, M., & Nelson, K. (1994). Making memories: The influence of joint encoding on later recall by young children. *Consciousness and Cognition, 3,* 307–326.

Tharp, R. G. (1989). Psychocultural variables and constants: Effects on teaching and learning in schools. *American Psychologist, 44,* 349–359.

Théberge, C. L. (1994, April). *Small-group vs. whole-class discussion: Gaining the floor in science lessons.* Paper presented at the annual meeting of the American Educational Research Association, New Orleans, LA.

Themann, K. S., & Goldstein, H. (2001). Social stories, written text cues, and video feedback: Effects on social communication of children with autism. *Journal of Applied Behavior Analysis, 34,* 425–446.

Théoret, H., Halligan, E., Kobayashi, M., Fregni, F., Tager-Flusberg, H., & Pascual-Leone, A. (2005). Impaired motor facilitation during action observation in individuals with autism spectrum disorder. *Current Biology, 15,* 84–85.

Thomaes, S., Bushman, B. J., Stegge, H., & Olthof, T. (2008). Trumping shame by blasts of noise: Narcissism, self-esteem, shame, and aggression in young adolescents. *Child Development, 79,* 1792–1801.

Thomaes, S., Reijntjes, A., Orobio de Castro, B., & Bushman, B. J. (2009). Reality bites—Or does it? Realistic self-views buffer negative mood following social threat. *Psychological Science, 20,* 1079–1083.

Thomas, A., & Chess, S. (1977). *Temperament and development.* New York: Brunner/Mazel.

Thomas, J. W. (1993). Expectations and effort: Course demands, students' study practices, and academic achievement. In T. M. Tomlinson (Ed.), *Motivating students to learn: Overcoming barriers to high achievement.* Berkeley, CA: McCutchan.

Thomas, M. S. C., & Johnson, M. H. (2008). New advances in understanding sensitive periods in brain development. *Current Directions in Psychological Science, 17,* 1–5.

Thomas, R. M. (2005). *High-stakes testing: Coping with collateral damage.* Mahwah, NJ: Erlbaum.

Thomas, S., & Oldfather, P. (1997). Intrinsic motivations, literacy, and assessment practices: "That's my grade. That's me." *Educational Psychologist, 32,* 107–123.

Thompson, M., & Grace, C. O. (with Cohen, L. J.). (2001). *Best friends, worst enemies: Understanding the social lives of children.* New York: Ballantine.

Thompson, R. A. (1998). Early sociopersonality development. In W. Damon (Series Ed.) & N. Eisenberg (Vol. Ed.), *Handbook of child psychology: Vol. 3: Social, emotional, and personality development* (5th ed.). New York: Wiley.

Thompson, R. A., & Nelson, C. A. (2001). Developmental science and the media: Early brain development. *American Psychologist, 56,* 5–15.

Thompson, R. A., & Wyatt, J. M. (1999). Current research on child maltreatment: Implications for educators. *Educational Psychology Review, 11,* 173–201.

Thorkildsen, T. A. (1995). Conceptions of social justice. In W. M. Kurtines & J. L. Gewirtz (Eds.), *Moral development: An introduction.* Boston: Allyn & Bacon.

Thorndike-Christ, T. (2008, March). *Profiles in failure: The etiology of maladaptive beliefs about mathematics.* Paper presented at the annual meeting of the American Educational Research Association, New York.

Thurstone, L. L. (1938). *Primary mental abilities.* Chicago: University of Chicago Press.

Timm, P., & Borman, K. (1997). The soup pot don't stretch that far no more: Intergenerational patterns of school leaving in an urban Appalachian neighborhood. In M. Sellter & L. Weis (Eds.), *Beyond black and white: New faces and voices in U.S. schools.* Albany: State University of New York Press.

Tirosh, D., & Graeber, A. O. (1990). Evoking cognitive conflict to explore preservice teachers' thinking about division. *Journal for Research in Mathematics Education, 21,* 98–108.

Tisak, M. (1993). Preschool children's judgments of moral and personal events involving physical harm and property damage. *Merrill-Palmer Quarterly, 39,* 375–390.

Tobias, S. (1994). Interest, prior knowledge, and learning. *Review of Educational Research, 64,* 37–54.

Tobin, K. (1987). The role of wait time in higher cognitive level learning. *Review of Educational Research, 57,* 69–95.

Tomback, R. M., Williams, A. Y., & Wentzel, K. R. (2005, April). *Young adolescents' concerns about the transition to high school.* Poster presented at the annual meeting of the American Educational Research Association, Montreal.

Tomlinson, C. A., & McTighe, J. (2006). *Integrating differentiated instruction and understanding by design.* Alexandria, VA: Association for Supervision and Curriculum Development.

Torney-Purta, J. (1994). Dimensions of adolescents' reasoning about political and historical issues: Ontological switches, developmental processes, and situated learning. In M. Carretero & J. F. Voss (Eds.), *Cognitive and instructional processes in history and the social sciences* (pp. 103–122). Mahwah, NJ: Erlbaum.

Torrance, E. P. (1970). *Encouraging creativity in the classroom.* Dubuque, IA: Wm. C. Brown.

Torrance, E. P. (1989). A reaction to "Gifted black students: Curriculum and teaching strategies." In C. J. Maker & S. W. Schiever (Eds.), *Critical issues in gifted education: Vol. 2. Defensible programs for cultural and ethnic minorities.* Austin, TX: Pro-Ed.

Torrance, E. P. (1995). Insights about creativity: Questioned, rejected, ridiculed, ignored. *Educational Psychology Review, 7,* 313–322.

Torres-Guzmán, M. E. (1998). Language, culture, and literacy in Puerto Rican communities. In B. Pérez (Ed.), *Sociocultural contexts of language and literacy.* Mahwah, NJ: Erlbaum.

Tourniaire, F., & Pulos, S. (1985). Proportional reasoning: A review of the literature. *Educational Studies in Mathematics, 16,* 181–204.

Trautwein, U., Gerlach, E., & Lüdtke, O. (2008). Athletic classmates, physical self-concept, and free-time physical activity: A longitudinal study of frame of reference effects. *Journal of Educational Psychology, 100,* 988–1001.

Trautwein, U., & Lüdtke, O. (2007). Students' self-reported effort and time on homework in six school subjects: Between-student differences and within-student variation. *Journal of Educational Psychology, 99,* 432–444.

Trautwein, U., Lüdtke, O., Schnyder, I., & Niggli, A. (2006). Predicting homework effort: Support for a domain-specific, multilevel homework model. *Journal of Educational Psychology, 98,* 438–456.

Trautwein, U., Niggli, A., Schnyder, I., & Lüdtke, O. (2009). Between-teacher differences in homework assignments and the development of students' homework effort, homework emotions, and achievement. *Journal of Educational Psychology, 101,* 176–189.

Trawick-Smith, J. (2003). *Early childhood development: A multicultural perspective* (3rd ed.). Upper Saddle River, NJ: Merrill/Prentice Hall.

Treffert, D. A., & Wallace, G. L. (2002). Islands of genius. *Scientific American, 286*(6), 76–85.

Triandis, H. C. (1995). *Individualism and collectivism.* Boulder, CO: Westview Press.

Troop-Gordon, W., & Ladd, G. W. (2005). Trajectories of peer victimization and perceptions of the self and schoolmates: Precursors to internalizing and externalizing problems. *Child Development, 76,* 1072–1091.

Tsai, J. L. (2007). Ideal affect: Cultural causes and behavioral consequences. *Perspectives on Psychological Science, 2,* 242–259.

Tsai, J. L., & Chentsova-Dutton, Y. (2003). Variation among European Americans in emotional facial expression. *Journal of Cross Cultural Psychology, 34,* 650–657.

Tsai, Y.-M., Kunter, M., Lüdtke, O., Trautwein, U., & Ryan, R. M. (2008). What makes lessons interesting? The role of situational and individual factors in three school subjects. *Journal of Educational Psychology, 100,* 460–472.

Tschannen-Moran, M., Woolfolk Hoy, A., & Hoy, W. K. (1998). Teacher efficacy: Its meaning and measure. *Review of Educational Research, 68,* 202–248.

Tsethlikai, M., & Greenhoot, A. F. (2006). The influence of another's perspective on children's recall of previously misconstrued events. *Developmental Psychology, 42,* 732–745.

Tsethlikai, M., Guthrie-Fulbright, Y., & Loera, S. (2007, March). *Social perspective coordination ability and children's recall of mutual conflict.* Paper presented at the biennial meeting of the Society for Research in Child Development, Boston.

Tucker, V. G., & Anderman, L. H. (1999, April). *Cycles of learning: Demonstrating the interplay between motivation, self-regulation, and cognition.* Paper presented at the annual meeting of the American Educational Research Association, Montreal, Canada.

Tulving, E., & Thomson, D. M. (1973). Encoding specificity and retrieval processes in episodic memory. *Psychological Review, 80,* 352–373.

Tunstall, P., & Gipps, C. (1996). Teacher feedback to young children in formative assessment: A typology. *British Educational Research Journal, 22,* 389–404.

Turiel, E. (1983). *The development of social knowledge: Morality and convention.* Cambridge, England: Cambridge University Press.

Turiel, E. (1998). The development of morality. In W. Damon (Series Ed.) & N. Eisenberg (Vol. Ed.), *Handbook of child psychology: Vol. 3. Social, emotional, and personality development* (5th ed., pp. 863–932). New York: Wiley.

Turiel, E. (2002). *The culture of morality: Social development, context, and conflict.* Cambridge, England: Cambridge University Press.

Turiel, E. (2006). The development of morality. In W. Damon & R. M. Lerner (Eds. in Chief) & N. Eisenberg (Vol. Ed.), *Handbook of child psychology, Vol. 3. Social, emotional, and personality development* (6th ed., pp. 789-857). Hoboken, NJ: Wiley.

Turiel, E., Smetana, J. G., & Killen, M. (1991). Social contexts in social cognitive development. In W. M. Kurtines & J. L. Gewirtz (Eds.), *Moral behavior and development: Vol. 2. Research.* Mahwah, NJ: Erlbaum.

Turkanis, C. G. (2001). Creating curriculum with children. In B. Rogoff, C. G. Turkanis, & L. Bartlett (Eds.), *Learning together: Children and adults in a school community* (pp. 91–102). New York: Oxford University Press.

Turnbull, A. P., Pereira, L., & Blue-Banning, M. (2000). Teachers as friendship facilitators. *Teaching Exceptional Children, 32*(5), 66–70.

Turnbull, A. P., Turnbull, R., & Wehmeyer, M. L. (2007). *Exceptional lives: Special education in today's schools* (5th ed.). Upper Saddle River, NJ: Merrill/Prentice Hall.

Turner, J. C. (1995). The influence of classroom contexts on young children's motivation for literacy. *Reading Research Quarterly, 30,* 410–441.

Turner, J. C., Meyer, D. K., Cox, K. E., Logan, C., DiCintio, M., & Thomas, C. T. (1998). Creating contexts for involvement in mathematics. *Journal of Educational Psychology, 90,* 730–745.

Turner, J. C., & Patrick, H. (2008). How does motivation develop and why does it change? Reframing motivation research. *Educational Psychologist, 43,* 119–131.

Turner, J. C., Thorpe, P. K., & Meyer, D. K. (1998). Students' reports of motivation and negative affect: A theoretical and empirical analysis. *Journal of Educational Psychology, 90,* 758–771.

Turner, J. E., Husman, J., & Schallert, D. L. (2002). The importance of students' goals in their emotional experience of academic failure: Investigating the precursors and consequences of shame. *Educational Psychologist, 37,* 79–89.

Tyler, K. M., Uqdah, A. L., Dillihunt, M. L., Beatty-Hazelbaker, R., Connor, T., Gadson, N., et al. (2008). Cultural discontinuity: Toward a quantitative investigation of a major hypothesis in education. *Educational Researcher, 37,* 280–297.

Tzuriel, D. (2000). Dynamic assessment of young children: Educational and intervention perspectives. *Educational Psychology Review, 12,* 385–435.

Ulichny, P. (1996). Cultures in conflict. *Anthropology and Education Quarterly, 27,* 331–364.

Underwood, J., & Webb, L. D. (2006). *School law for teachers: Concepts and applications.* Upper Saddle River, NJ: Merrill/Prentice Hall.

Urdan, T. C. (1997). Achievement goal theory: Past results, future directions. In M. L. Maehr & P. R. Pintrich (Eds.), *Advances in motivation and achievement* (Vol. 10, pp. 99–141). Greenwich, CT: JAI Press.

Urdan, T. C., & Maehr, M. L. (1995). Beyond a two-goal theory of motivation and achievement: A case for social goals. *Review of Educational Research, 65,* 213–243.

Urdan, T., & Mestas, M. (2006). The goals behind performance goals. *Journal of Educational Psychology, 98,* 354–365.

Urdan, T., & Midgley, C. (2001). Academic self-handicapping: What we know, what more there is to learn. *Educational Psychology Review, 13,* 115–138.

Urdan, T. C., Midgley, C., & Anderman, E. M. (1998). The role of classroom goal structure in students' use of self-handicapping strategies. *American Educational Research Journal, 35,* 101–122.

Urdan, T., Ryan, A. M., Anderman, E. M., & Gheen, M. H. (2002). Goals, goal structures, and avoidance behaviors. In C. Midgley (Ed.), *Goals, goal structures, and patterns of adaptive learning* (pp. 55–83). Mahwah, NJ: Erlbaum.

Urdan, T., & Turner, J. C. (2005). Competence motivation in the classroom. In A. J. Elliot & C. S. Dweck (Eds.), *Handbook of competence and motivation* (pp. 297–317). New York: Guilford Press.

Usher, E. L. (2009). Sources of middle school students' self-efficacy in mathematics: A qualitative investigation. *American Educational Research Journal, 46,* 275–314.

Usher, E. L., & Pajares, F. (2008). Sources of self-efficacy in school: Critical review of the literature and future directions. *Review of Educational Research, 78,* 751–796.

Usher, E. L., & Pajares, F. (2009). Sources of self-efficacy in mathematics: A validation study. *Contemporary Educational Psychology, 34,* 89–101.

U.S. Secret Service National Threat Assessment Center, in collaboration with the U.S. Department of Education. (2000, October). *Safe school initiative: An interim report on the prevention of targeted violence in schools.* Washington, DC: Author.

Valencia, S. W., Hiebert, E. H., & Afflerbach, P. P. (1994). Realizing the possibilities of authentic assessment: Current trends and future issues. In S. W. Valencia, E. H. Hiebert, & P. P. Afflerbach (Eds.), *Authentic reading assessment: Practices and possibilities.* Newark, DE: International Reading Association.

Valentine, J. C., Cooper, H., Bettencourt, B. A., & DuBois, D. L. (2002). Out-of-school activities and academic achievement: The mediating role of self-beliefs. *Educational Psychologist, 37,* 245–256.

Valentine, J. C., DuBois, D. L., & Cooper, H. (2004). The relation between self-beliefs and academic achievement: A meta-analytic review. *Educational Psychologist, 39,* 111–133.

Valiente, C., Lemery-Calfant, K., Swanson, J., & Reiser, M. (2008). Prediction of children's academic competence from their effortful control, relationships, and classroom participation. *Journal of Educational Psychology, 100,* 67–77.

Valkenburg, P. M., & Peter, J. (2007). Preadolescents' and adolescents' online communication and their closeness to friends. *Developmental Psychology, 43,* 267–277.

Valkenburg, P. M., & Peter, J. (2009). Social consequences of the Internet for adolescents: A decade of research. *Current Directions in Psychological Science, 18,* 1–5.

Vallerand, R. J., Fortier, M. S., & Guay, F. (1997). Self-determination and persistence in a real-life setting: Toward a motivational model of high school dropout. *Journal of Personality and Social Psychology, 72,* 1161–1176.

Valli, L., & Buese, D. (2007). The changing roles of teachers in an era of high-stakes accountability. *American Educational Research Journal, 44,* 519–558.

Van Camp, C. M., Lerman, D. C., Kelley, M. E., Roane, H. S., Contrucci, S. A., & Vorndran, C. M. (2000). Further analysis of idiosyncratic antecedent influences during the assessment and treatment of problem behavior. *Journal of Applied Behavior Analysis, 33,* 207–221.

Van Dooren, W., De Bock, D., Hessels, A., Janssens, D., & Verschaffel, L. (2005). Not everything is proportional: Effects of age and problem type on propensities for overgeneralization. *Cognition and Instruction, 23,* 57–86.

van Drie, J., van Boxtel, C., & van der Linden, J. (2006). Historical reasoning in a computer-supported collaborative learning environment. In A. M. O'Donnell, C. E. Hmelo-Silver, & G. Erkens (Eds.), *Collaborative learning, reasoning, and technology* (pp. 265–296). Mahwah, NJ: Erlbaum.

Van Houten, R., Nau, P., MacKenzie-Keating, S., Sameoto, D., & Colavecchia, B. (1982). An analysis of some variables influencing the effectiveness of reprimands. *Journal of Applied Behavior Analysis, 15,* 65–83.

van IJzendoorn, M. H., Juffer, F., & Klein Poelhuis, C. W. (2005). Adoption and cognitive development: A meta-analytic comparison of adopted and nonadopted children's IQ and school performance. *Psychological Bulletin, 131,* 301–316.

van Laar, C. (2000). The paradox of low academic achievement but high self-esteem in African American students: An attributional account. *Educational Psychology Review, 12,* 33–61.

Van Leijenhorst, L., Crone, E. A., & Van der Molen, M. W. (2007). Developmental trends for object and spatial working memory: A psychophysiological analysis. *Child Development, 78,* 987–1000.

Van Meter, P. (2001). Drawing construction as a strategy for learning from text. *Journal of Educational Psychology, 93,* 129–140.

Van Meter, P., & Garner, J. (2005). The promise and practice of learner-generated drawing: Literature review and synthesis. *Educational Psychology Review, 17,* 285–325.

VanSledright, B., & Brophy, J. (1992). Storytelling, imagination, and fanciful elaboration in children's historical reconstructions. *American Educational Research Journal, 29,* 837–859.

VanSledright, B., & Limón, M. (2006). Learning and teaching social studies: A review of cognitive research in history and geography. In P. A. Alexander & P. H. Winne (Eds.), *Handbook of educational psychology* (2nd ed., pp. 545–570). Mahwah, NJ: Erlbaum.

Vansteenkiste, M., Lens, W., & Deci, E. L. (2006). Intrinsic versus extrinsic goal contents in self-determination theory: Another look at the quality of academic motivation. *Educational Psychologist, 41,* 19–31.

Vansteenkiste, M., Zhou, M., Lens, W., & Soenens, B. (2005). Experiences of autonomy and control among Chinese learners: Vitalizing or immobilizing? *Journal of Educational Psychology, 97,* 468–483.

Varma, S., McCandliss, B. D., & Schwartz, D. L. (2008). Scientific and pragmatic challenges for bridging education and neuroscience. *Educational Researcher, 37*(3), 140–152.

Vasquez, J. A. (1988). Contexts of learning for minority students. *Educational Forum, 6,* 243–253.

Vaughn, B. J., & Horner, R. H. (1997). Identifying instructional tasks that occasion problem behaviors and assessing the effects of student versus teacher choice among these tasks. *Journal of Applied Behavior Analysis, 30,* 299–312.

Vaughn, S. (1991). Social skills enhancement in students with learning disabilities. In B. Y. L. Wong (Ed.), *Learning about learning disabilities.* San Diego, CA: Academic Press.

Venn, J. J. (2000). *Assessing students with special needs* (2nd ed.). Upper Saddle River, NJ: Merrill/Prentice Hall.

Verdi, M. P., & Kulhavy, R. W. (2002). Learning with maps and texts: An overview. *Educational Psychology Review, 14,* 27–46.

Verdi, M. P., Kulhavy, R. W., Stock, W. A., Rittschof, K. A., & Johnson, J. T. (1996). Text learning using scientific diagrams: Implications for classroom use. *Contemporary Educational Psychology, 21,* 487–499.

Verkhratsky, A., & Butt, A. (2007). *Glial neurobiology.* Chichester, England: Wiley.

Vernon, P. A. (1993). Intelligence and neural efficiency. In D. K. Detterman (Ed.), *Current topics in human intelligence* (Vol. 3). Norwood, NJ: Ablex.

Véronneau, M.-H., Vitaro, F., Pederson, S., & Tremblay, R. E. (2008). Do peers contribute to the likelihood of secondary school graduation among disadvantaged boys? *Journal of Educational Psychology, 100,* 429–442.

Vintere, P., Hemmes, N. S., Brown, B. L., & Poulson, C. L. (2004). Gross-motor skill acquisition by preschool dance students under self-instruction procedures. *Journal of Applied Behavior Analysis, 37,* 305–322.

Vitaro, F., Brendgen, M., Larose, S., & Tremblay, R. E. (2005). Kindergarten disruptive behaviors, protective factors, and educational achievement by early adulthood. *Journal of Educational Psychology, 97,* 617–629.

Vitaro, F., Gendreau, P. L., Tremblay, R. E., & Oligny, P. (1998). Reactive and proactive aggression differentially predict later conduct problems. *Journal of Child Psychology and Psychiatry and Allied Disciplines, 39,* 377–385.

Volet, S. (1999). Learning across cultures: Appropriateness of knowledge transfer. *International Journal of Educational Research, 31,* 625–643.

Vollmer, T. R., & Hackenberg, T. D. (2001). Reinforcement contingencies and social reinforcement: Some reciprocal relations between basic and applied research. *Journal of Applied Behavior Analysis, 34,* 241–253.

Vosniadou, S. (1991). Conceptual development in astronomy. In S. M. Glynn, R. H. Yeany, & B. K. Britton (Eds.), *The psychology of learning science.* Hillsdale, NJ: Erlbaum.

Vosniadou, S. (1994). Universal and culture-specific properties of children's mental models of the earth. In L. A. Hirschfeld & S. A. Gelman (Eds.), *Mapping the mind: Domain specificity in cognition and culture.* Cambridge, England: Cambridge University Press.

Vosniadou, S. (Ed.) (2008). *International handbook on conceptual change.* New York: Routledge.

Vosniadou, S., & Brewer, W. F. (1987). Theories of knowledge restructuring in development. *Review of Educational Research, 57,* 51–67.

Vosniadou, S., Vamvakoussi, X., & Skopeliti, I. (2008). The framework theory approach to the problem of conceptual change. In S. Vosniadou (Ed.), *International handbook on conceptual change* (pp. 3–34). New York: Routledge.

Voss, J. F., Greene, T. R., Post, T. A., & Penner, B. D. (1983). Problem-solving skill in the social sciences. In G. H. Bower (Ed.), *The psychology of learning and motivation* (Vol. 17). San Diego, CA: Academic Press.

Voss, J. F., & Schauble, L. (1992). Is interest educationally interesting? An interest-related model of learning. In K. A. Renninger, S. Hidi, &

A. Krapp (Eds.), *The role of interest in learning and development.* Mahwah, NJ: Erlbaum.

Vucko, S., & Hadwin, A. (April, 2004). *Going beyond I like it in a portfolio context: Scaffolding the development of six grade-two students' reflections.* Paper presented at the American Educational Research Association, San Diego, CA.

Vye, N. J., Schwartz, D. L., Bransford, J. D., Barron, B. J., Zech, L., & The Cognition and Technology Group at Vanderbilt. (1998). SMART environments that support monitoring, reflection, and revision. In D. J. Hacker, J. Dunlosky, & A. C. Graesser (Eds.), *Metacognition in educational theory and practice* (pp. 305–346). Mahwah, NJ: Erlbaum.

Vygotsky, L. S. (1962). *Thought and language* (E. Haufmann & G. Vakar, Eds. and Trans.). Cambridge, MA: MIT Press.

Vygotsky, L. S. (1978). *Mind in society: The development of higher psychological processes.* Cambridge, MA: Harvard University Press.

Vygotsky, L. S. (1987). *The collected works of L. S. Vygotsky* (Vol. 3; R. W. Rieber & A. S. Carton, Eds.). New York: Plenum Press.

Vygotsky, L. S. (1997). *Educational psychology* (R. Silverman, Trans.). Boca Raton, FL: St. Lucie Press.

Wade, S. E. (1992). How interest affects learning from text. In K. A. Renninger, S. Hidi, & A. Krapp (Eds.), *The role of interest in learning and development.* Mahwah, NJ: Erlbaum.

Wade-Stein, D., & Kintsch, E. (2004). Summary Street: Interactive computer support for writing. *Cognition and Instruction, 22,* 333–362.

Wainryb, C., Brehl, B. A., & Matwin, S. (2005). Being hurt and hurting others: Children's narrative accounts and moral judgments of their own interpersonal conflicts. *Monographs of the Society for Research in Child Development, 70* (3; Serial No. 281).

Walker, E. F. (2002). Adolescent neurodevelopment and psychopathology. *Current Directions in Psychological Science, 11,* 24–28.

Walker, E. N. (2006). Urban high school students' academic communities and their effects on mathematics success. *American Educational Research Journal, 43,* 43–73.

Walker, H. M., Horner, R. H., Sugai, G., Bullis, M., Sprague, J. R., Bricker, D., et al. (1996). Integrated approaches to preventing antisocial behavior patterns among school-age children and youth. *Journal of Emotional and Behavioral Disorders, 4,* 194–209.

Walker, J. M. T., & Hoover-Dempsey, K. V. (2006). Why research on parental involvement is important to classroom management. In C. M. Evertson & C. S. Weinstein (Eds.), *Handbook of classroom management: Research, practice, and contemporary issues* (pp. 665–684). Mahwah, NJ: Erlbaum.

Walls, T. A., & Little, T. D. (2005). Relations among personal agency, motivation, and school adjustment in early adolescence. *Journal of Educational Psychology, 97,* 23–31.

Walshaw, M., & Anthony, G. (2008). The teacher's role in classroom discourse: A review of recent research into mathematics classrooms. *Review of Educational Research, 78,* 516–551.

Walters, G. C., & Grusec, J. E. (1977). *Punishment.* San Francisco: Freeman.

Walton, G. M., & Spencer, S. J. (2009). Latent ability: Grades and test scores systematically underestimate intellectual ability of negatively stereotyped students. *Psychological Science, 20,* 1132–1139.

Wang, J., & Lin, E. (2005). Comparative studies on U.S. and Chinese mathematics learning and the implications for standards-based mathematics teaching reform. *Educational Researcher, 34*(5), 3–13.

Wang, Q. (2006). Culture and the development of self-knowledge. *Current Directions in Psychological Science, 15,* 182–187.

Wang, Q., & Ross, M. (2007). Culture and memory. In S. Kitayama & D. Cohen (Eds.), *Handbook of cultural psychology* (pp. 645–667). New York: Guilford Press.

Warren, J. S., Bohanon-Edmonson, H. M., Turnbull, A. P., Sailor, W., Wickham, D., Griggs, P., et al. (2006). School-wide positive behavior support: Addressing behavior problems that impeded student learning. *Educational Psychology Review, 18,* 187–198.

Wasley, P. A., Hampel, R. L., & Clark, R. W. (1997). *Kids and school reform.* San Francisco: Jossey-Bass.

Waterhouse, L. (2006). Multiple intelligences, the Mozart effect, and emotional intelligence: A critical review. *Educational Psychologist, 41,* 207–225.

Watkins, D. E., & Wentzel, K. R. (2008). Training boys with ADHD to work collaboratively: Social and learning outcomes. *Contemporary Educational Psychology, 33,* 625–646.

Watson, M. (2008). Developmental discipline and moral education. In L. Nucci & D. Narvaez (Eds.), *Handbook of moral and character education* (pp. 175–203). New York: Routledge.

Watson, M., & Battistich, V. (2006). Building and sustaining caring communities. In C. M. Evertson & C. S. Weinstein (Eds.), *Handbook of classroom management: Research, practice, and contemporary issues* (pp. 253–279). Mahwah, NJ: Erlbaum.

Watson, M. W., Andreas, J. B., Fischer, K. W., & Smith, K. (2005). Patterns of risk factors leading to victimization and aggression in children and adolescents. In K. A. Kendall-Tackett & S. M. Giacomoni (Eds.), *Child victimization: Maltreatment, bullying and dating violence, prevention and intervention.* Kingston, NJ: Civic Research Institute.

Watt, H. M. G. (2004). Development of adolescents' self-perceptions, values, and task perceptions according to gender and domain in 7th-through 11th-grade Australian students. *Child Development, 75,* 1556–1574.

Way, N. (1998). *Everyday courage: The lives and stories of urban teenagers.* New York: New York University Press.

Weatherford, J. (1988). *Indian givers: How the Indians of the Americas transformed the world.* New York: Crown.

Weaver, C. A., III, & Kelemen, W. L. (1997). Judgments of learning at delays: Shifts in response patterns or increased metamemory accuracy? *Psychological Science, 8,* 318–321.

Webb, J. T., Meckstroth, E. A., & Tolan, S. S. (1982). *Guiding the gifted child: A practical source for parents and teachers.* Dayton: Ohio Psychology Press.

Webb, N. M. (1989). Peer interaction and learning in small groups. *International Journal of Educational Research, 13,* 21–39.

Webb, N. M., & Farivar, S. (1994). Promoting helping behavior in cooperative small groups in middle school mathematics. *American Educational Research Journal, 31,* 369–395.

Webb, N. M., & Farivar, S. (1999). Developing productive group interaction in middle school mathematics. In A. M. O'Donnell & A. King (Eds.), *Cognitive perspectives on peer learning* (pp. 117–149). Mahwah, NJ: Erlbaum.

Webb, N. M., Franke, M. L., Ing, M., Chan, A., De, T., Freund, D., et al. (2008). The role of teacher instructional practices in student collaboration. *Contemporary Educational Psychology, 33,* 360–381.

Webb, N. M., & Mastergeorge, A. M. (2003). The development of students' helping behavior and learning in peer-directed small groups. *Cognition and Instruction, 21,* 361–428.

Webb, N. M., & Palincsar, A. S. (1996). Group processes in the classroom. In D. C. Berliner & R. C. Calfee (Eds.), *Handbook of educational psychology.* New York: Macmillan.

Webber, J., Scheuermann, B., McCall, C., & Coleman, M. (1993). Research on self-monitoring as a behavior management technique in special education classrooms: A descriptive review. *Remedial and Special Education, 14*(2), 38–56.

Weichold, K., Silbereisen, R. K., & Schmitt-Rodermund, E. (2003). Short-term and long-term consequences of early versus late physical maturation in adolescents. In C. Hayward (Ed.), *Gender differences at puberty* (pp. 241–276). Cambridge, England: Cambridge University Press.

Weiner, B. (1984). Principles for a theory of student motivation and their application within an attributional framework. In R. Ames & C. Ames (Eds.), *Research on motivation in education: Vol. 1. Student motivation.* San Diego, CA: Academic Press.

Weiner, B. (1986). *An attributional theory of motivation and emotion.* New York: Springer-Verlag.

Weiner, B. (2000). Intrapersonal and interpersonal theories of motivation from an attributional perspective. *Educational Psychology Review, 12,* 1–14.

Weiner, B. (2004). Attribution theory revisited: Transforming cultural plurality into theoretical unity. In D. M. McInerney & S. Van Etten (Eds.), *Big theories revisited* (pp. 13–29). Greenwich, CT: Information Age.

Weiner, B. (2005). Motivation from an attribution perspective and the social psychology of perceived competence. In A. J. Elliot & C. S. Dweck (Eds.), *Handbook of competence and motivation* (pp. 73–84). New York: Guilford Press.

Weinert, F. E., & Helmke, A. (1995). Learning from wise Mother Nature or Big Brother Instructor: The wrong choice as seen from an educational perspective. *Educational Psychologist, 30,* 135–142.

Weinstein, R. S. (2002). *Reaching higher: The power of expectations in schooling.* Cambridge, MA: Harvard University Press.

Weinstein, R. S., Madison, S. M., & Kuklinski, M. R. (1995). Raising expectations in schooling: Obstacles and opportunities for change. *American Educational Research Journal, 32,* 121–159.

Weiss, L. H., & Schwarz, J. C. (1996). The relationship between parenting types and older adolescents' personality, academic achievement, adjustment, and substance use. *Child Development, 67,* 2101–2114.

Weissberg, R. P. (1985). Designing effective social problem-solving programs for the classroom. In B. H. Schneider, K. H. Rubin, & J. E. Ledingham (Eds.), *Children's peer relations: Issues in assessment and intervention.* New York: Springer-Verlag.

Welch, G. J. (1985). Contingency contracting with a delinquent and his family. *Journal of Behavior Therapy and Experimental Psychiatry, 16,* 253–259.

Wellman, H. M. (1985). The child's theory of mind: The development of conceptions of cognition. In S. R. Yussen (Ed.), *The growth of reflection in children.* San Diego, CA: Academic Press.

Wellman, H. M. (1990). *The child's theory of mind.* Cambridge, MA: MIT Press.

Wellman, H. M., Cross, D., & Watson, J. (2001). Meta-analysis of theory-of-mind development: The truth about false belief. *Child Development, 72,* 655–684.

Wellman, H. M., & Gelman, S. A. (1998). Acquisition of knowledge. In W. Damon (Series Ed.), D. Kuhn & R. S. Siegler (Vol. Eds.), *Handbook of child psychology: Vol. 2. Cognition, perception, and language* (5th ed.). New York: Wiley.

Wellman, H. M., Phillips, A. T., & Rodriguez, T. (2000). Young children's understanding of perception, desire, and emotion. *Child Development, 71,* 895–912.

Wentzel, K. R. (1999). Social-motivational processes and interpersonal relationships: Implications for understanding motivation at school. *Journal of Educational Psychology, 91,* 76–97.

Wentzel, K. R. (2009). Peers and academic functioning at school. In K. H. Rubin, W. M. Bukowski, & B. Laursen (Eds.), *Handbook of peer interactions, relationships, and groups* (pp. 531–547). New York: Guilford Press.

Wentzel, K. R., & Asher, S. R. (1995). The academic lives of neglected, rejected, popular, and controversial children. *Child Development, 66,* 754–763.

Wentzel, K. R., Barry, C. M., & Caldwell, K. A. (2004). Friendships in middle school: Influences on motivation and school adjustment. *Journal of Educational Psychology, 96,* 195–203.

Wentzel, K. R., Donlan, A. E., Morrison, D. A., Russell, S. L., & Baker, S. A. (2009, April). *Adolescent non-compliance: A social ecological perspective.* Paper presented at the annual meeting of the American Educational Research Association, San Diego, CA.

Wentzel, K. R., Filisetti, L., & Looney, L. (2007). Adolescent prosocial behavior: The role of self-processes and contextual cues. *Child Development, 78,* 895–910.

Wentzel, K. R., & Looney, L. (2007). Socialization in school settings. In J. E. Grusec & P. D. Hastings (Eds.), *Handbook of socialization: Theory and research* (pp. 382–403). New York: Guilford Press.

Wentzel, K. R., & Wigfield, A. (1998). Academic and social motivational influences on students' academic performance. *Educational Psychology Review, 10,* 155–175.

Werner, E. E. (1995). Resilience in development. *Current Directions in Psychological Science, 4,* 81–85.

Werner, E. E., & Smith, R. S. (2001). *Journeys from childhood to midlife: Risk, resilience, and recovery.* Ithaca, NY: Cornell University Press.

West, R. F., Toplak, M. E., & Stanovich, K. E. (2008). Heuristics and biases as measures of critical thinking: Associations with cognitive ability and thinking dispositions. *Journal of Educational Psychology, 100,* 930–941.

Whitaker Sena, J. D., Lowe, P. A., & Lee, S. W. (2007). Significant predictors of test anxiety among students with and without learning disabilities. *Journal of Learning Disabilities, 40,* 360–376.

White, A. G., & Bailey, J. S. (1990). Reducing disruptive behaviors of elementary physical education students with sit and watch. *Journal of Applied Behavior Analysis, 23,* 353–359.

White, B. Y., & Frederiksen, J. R. (1998). Inquiry, modeling, and metacognition: Making science accessible to all students. *Cognition and Instruction, 16,* 3–118.

White, B. Y., & Frederiksen, J. (2005). A theoretical framework and approach for fostering metacognitive development. *Educational Psychologist, 40,* 211–223.

White, J. J., & Rumsey, S. (1994). Teaching for understanding in a third-grade geography lesson. In J. Brophy (Ed.), *Advances in research on teaching: Vol. 4. Case studies of teaching and learning in social studies.* Greenwich, CT: JAI Press.

White, R. (1959). Motivation reconsidered: The concept of competence. *Psychological Review, 66,* 297–333.

White, R., & Cunningham, A. M. (1991). *Ryan White: My own story.* New York: Signet.

Whitesell, N. R., Mitchell, C. M., Kaufman, C. E., Spicer, P., & the Voices of Indian Teens Project Team. (2006). Developmental trajectories of personal and collective self-concept among American Indian adolescents. *Child Development, 77,* 1487–1503.

Whitley, B. E., Jr., & Frieze, I. H. (1985). Children's causal attributions for success and failure in achievement settings: A meta-analysis. *Journal of Educational Psychology, 77,* 608–616.

Wigfield, A. (1994). Expectancy-value theory of achievement motivation: A developmental perspective. *Educational Psychology Review, 6,* 49–78.

Wigfield, A., Byrnes, J. P., & Eccles, J. S. (2006). Development during early and middle adolescence. In P. A. Alexander & P. H. Winne (Eds.), *Handbook of educational psychology* (2nd ed., pp. 87–113). Mahwah, NJ: Erlbaum.

Wigfield, A., & Eccles, J. (1992). The development of achievement task values: A theoretical analysis. *Developmental Review, 12,* 265–310.

Wigfield, A., & Eccles, J. (2000). Expectancy-value theory of achievement motivation. *Contemporary Educational Psychology, 25,* 68–81.

Wigfield, A., & Eccles, J. (2002). The development of competence beliefs, expectancies for success, and achievement values from childhood to adolescence. In A. Wigfield & J. Eccles (Eds.), *Development of achievement motivation* (pp. 91–120). San Diego, CA: Academic Press.

Wigfield, A., Eccles, J., Mac Iver, D., Reuman, D., & Midgley, C. (1991). Transitions at early adolescence: Changes in children's domain-specific self-perceptions and general self-esteem across the transition to junior high school. *Developmental Psychology, 27,* 552–565.

Wigfield, A., Eccles, J. S., & Pintrich, P. R. (1996). Development between the ages of 11 and 25. In D. C. Berliner & R. C. Calfee (Eds.), *Handbook of educational psychology.* New York: Macmillan.

Wigfield, A., & Meece, J. L. (1988). Math anxiety in elementary and secondary school students. *Journal of Educational Psychology, 80,* 210–216.

Wigfield, A., & Wagner, A. L. (2005). Competence, motivation, and identity development during adolescence. In A. J. Elliot & C. S. Dweck (Eds.), *Handbook of competence and motivation* (pp. 222–239). New York: Guilford Press.

Wiggins, G., & McTighe, J. (1998). *Understanding by design.* Alexandria, VA: Association for Supervision and Curriculum Development.

Wilder, A. A., & Williams, J. P. (2001). Students with severe learning disabilities can learn higher order comprehension skills. *Journal of Educational Psychology, 93,* 268–278.

Wiles, J., & Bondi, J. (2001). *The new American middle school: Educating preadolescents in an era of change.* Upper Saddle River, NJ: Merrill/Prentice Hall.

Wiley, J., & Bailey, J. (2006). Effects of collaboration and argumentation on learning from Web pages. In A. M. O'Donnell, C. E. Hmelo-Silver, & G. Erkens (Eds.), *Collaborative learning, reasoning, and technology* (pp. 297–321). Mahwah, NJ: Erlbaum.

Wiley, J., Goldman, S. R., Graesser, A. C., Sanchez, C. A., Ash, I. K., & Hemmerich, J. A. (2009). Source evaluation, comprehension, and learning in Internet science inquiry tasks. *American Educational Research Journal, 46,* 1060–1106.

Willard, N. E. (2007). *Cyberbullying and cyberthreats: Responding to the challenge of online social aggression, threats, and distress.* Champaign, IL: Research Press.

Williams, J. P., Stafford, K. B., Lauer, K. D., Hall, K. M., & Pollini, S. (2009). Embedding reading comprehension training in content-area instruction. *Journal of Educational Psychology, 101,* 1–20.

Williams, K. M. (2001a). "Frontin' it": Schooling, violence, and relationships in the 'hood. In J. N. Burstyn, G. Bender, R. Casella, H. W. Gordon, D. P. Guerra, K. V. Luschen, et al., *Preventing violence in schools: A challenge to American democracy* (pp. 95–108). Mahwah, NJ: Erlbaum.

Williams, K. M. (2001b). What derails peer mediation? In J. N. Burstyn, G. Bender, R. Casella, H. W. Gordon, D. P. Guerra, K. V. Luschen, et al., *Preventing violence in schools: A challenge to American democracy* (pp. 199–208). Mahwah, NJ: Erlbaum.

Willingham, D. T. (2004). *Cognition: The thinking animal* (2nd ed.). Upper Saddle River, NJ: Prentice Hall.

Wilson, B. L., & Corbett, H. D. (2001). *Listening to urban kids: School reform and the teachers they want.* Albany: State University of New York Press.

Wilson, C. C., Piazza, C. C., & Nagle, R. (1990). Investigation of the effect of consistent and inconsistent behavioral examples upon children's donation behaviors. *Journal of Genetic Psychology, 151,* 361–376.

Wilson, P. T., & Anderson, R. C. (1986). What they don't know will hurt them: The role of prior knowledge in comprehension. In J. Orasanu (Ed.), *Reading comprehension: From research to practice.* Mahwah, NJ: Erlbaum.

Wimmer, H., & Perner, J. (1983). Beliefs about beliefs: Representation and constraining function of wrong beliefs in young children's understanding of deception. *Cognition, 13,* 103–128.

Windschitl, M. (2002). Framing constructivism in practice as the negotiation of dilemmas: An analysis of the conceptual, pedagogical, cultural, and political challenges facing teachers. *Review of Educational Research, 72,* 131–175.

Wine, J. D. (1980). Cognitive-attentional theory of test anxiety. In I. G. Sarason (Ed.), *Test anxiety: Theory, research, and applications.* Mahwah, NJ: Erlbaum.

Winn, W. (1991). Learning from maps and diagrams. *Educational Psychology Review, 3,* 211–247.

Winn, W. (2002). Current trends in educational technology research: The study of learning environments. *Educational Psychology Review, 14,* 331–351.

Winne, P. H. (1995a). Inherent details in self-regulated learning. *Educational Psychologist, 30,* 173–187.

Winne, P. H. (1995b). Self-regulation is ubiquitous but its forms vary with knowledge. *Educational Psychologist, 30,* 223–228.

Winne, P. H., & Hadwin, A. F. (1998). Studying as self-regulated learning. In D. J. Hacker, J. Dunlosky, & A. C. Graesser (Eds.), *Metacognition in educational theory and practice* (pp. 277–304). Mahwah, NJ: Erlbaum.

Winner, E. (1988). *The point of words.* Cambridge, MA: Harvard University Press.

Winner, E. (2000a). Giftedness: Current theory and research. *Current Directions in Psychological Science, 9,* 153–156.

Winner, E. (2000b). The origins and ends of giftedness. *American Psychologist, 55,* 159–169.

Winsler, A., & Naglieri, J. (2003). Overt and covert verbal problem-solving strategies: Developmental trends in use, awareness, and relations with task performance in children aged 5 to 17. *Child Development, 74,* 659–678.

Wise, B. W., & Olson, R. K. (1998). Studies of computer-aided remediation for reading disabilities. In C. Hulme & R. M. Joshi (Eds.), *Reading and spelling: Development and disorders.* Mahwah, NJ: Erlbaum.

Wiser, M., & Smith, C. L. (2008). Learning and teaching about matter in grades K–8: When should the atomic–molecular theory be introduced? In S. Vosniadou (Ed.), *International handbook on conceptual change* (pp. 205–231). New York: Routledge.

Wisner Fries, A. B., & Pollak, S. D. (2007). Emotion processing and the developing brain. In D. Coch, K. W. Fischer, & G. Dawson (Eds.), *Human behavior, learning, and the developing brain: Typical development* (pp. 329–361). New York: Guilford Press.

Witkow, M. R., & Fuligni, A. J. (2007). Achievement goals and daily school experiences among adolescents with Asian, Latino, and European American backgrounds. *Journal of Educational Psychology, 99,* 584–596.

Wittrock, M. C. (1994). Generative science teaching. In P. J. Fensham, R. F. Gunstone, & R. T. White (Eds.), *The content of science: A constructivist approach to its teaching and learning.* London: Falmer Press.

Wittwer, J., & Renkl, A. (2008). Why instructional explanations often do not work: A framework for understanding the effectiveness of instructional explanations. *Educational Psychologist, 43,* 49–64.

Wixson, K. K. (1984). Level of importance of postquestions and children's learning from text. *American Educational Research Journal, 21,* 419–433.

Wixted, J. T. (2005). A theory about why we forget what we once knew. *Current Directions in Psychological Science, 14,* 6–9.

Wlodkowski, R. J. (1978). *Motivation and teaching: A practical guide.* Washington, DC: National Education Association.

Wlodkowski, R. J., & Ginsberg, M. B. (1995). *Diversity and motivation: Culturally responsive teaching.* San Francisco: Jossey-Bass.

Wodtke, K. H., Harper, F., & Schommer, M. (1989). How standardized is school testing? An exploratory observational study of standardized group testing in kindergarten. *Educational Evaluation and Policy Analysis, 11,* 223–235.

Wolak, J., Finkelhor, D., Mitchell, K. J., & Ybarra, M. L. (2008). Online "predators" and their victims: Myths, realities, and implications for prevention and treatment. *American Psychologist, 63,* 111–128.

Woloshyn, V. E., Pressley, M., & Schneider, W. (1992). Elaborative-interrogation and prior-knowledge effects on learning of facts. *Journal of Educational Psychology, 84,* 115–124.

Wolters, C. A. (2003). Regulation of motivation: Evaluating an underemphasized aspect of self-regulated learning. *Educational Psychologist, 38,* 189–205.

Wolters, C. A., & Rosenthal, H. (2000). The relation between students' motivational beliefs and their use of motivational regulation strategies. *International Journal of Educational Research, 33,* 801–820.

Wong, B. Y. L. (1985). Self-questioning instructional research: A review. *Review of Educational Research, 55,* 227–268.

Wood, D., Bruner, J. S., & Ross, G. (1976). The role of tutoring in problem-solving. *Journal of Child Psychology and Psychiatry, 17,* 89–100.

Wood, D., Larson, R. W., & Brown, J. R. (2009). How adolescents come to see themselves as more responsible through participation in youth programs. *Child Development, 80,* 285–309.

Wood, D., Wood, H., Ainsworth, S., & O'Malley, C. (1995). On becoming a tutor: Toward an ontogenetic model. *Cognition and Instruction, 13,* 565–581.

Wood, E., Willoughby, T., McDermott, C., Motz, M., Kaspar, V., & Ducharme, M. J. (1999). Developmental differences in study behavior. *Journal of Educational Psychology, 91,* 527–536.

Woolfe, T., Want, S. C., & Siegal, M. (2002). Signposts to development: Theory of mind in deaf children. *Child Development, 73,* 768–778.

Woolfolk, A. E., & Brooks, D. M. (1985). The influence of teachers' nonverbal behaviors on students' perceptions and performances. *Elementary School Journal, 85,* 513–528.

Woolfolk Hoy, A., Davis, H., & Pape, S. J. (2006). Teacher knowledge and beliefs. In P. A. Alexander & P. H. Winne (Eds.), *Handbook of educational psychology* (2nd ed., pp. 715–737). Mahwah, NJ: Erlbaum.

Wright, E. J. (2007, March). *The negative self-focus trap: Emerging self-focused emotion regulation and increased depression risk.* Paper presented at the biennial meeting of the Society for Research in Child Development, Boston.

Wright, L. S. (1982). The use of logical consequences in counseling children. *School Counselor, 30,* 37–49.

Wright, M. O., & Masten, A. S. (2006). Resilience processes in development: Fostering positive adaptation in the context of adversity. In S. Goldstein & R. B. Brooks (Eds.), *Handbook of resilience in children* (pp. 17–37). New York: Springer.

Wright, W. E. (2006). A catch-22 for language learners. *Educational Leadership, 64*(3), 22–27.

Wynne, E. A. (1990). Improving pupil discipline and character. In O. C. Moles (Ed.), *Student discipline strategies: Research and practice.* Albany: State University of New York Press.

Xu, J. (2008). Models of secondary school students' interest in homework: A multilevel analysis. *American Educational Research Journal, 45,* 1180–1205.

Xu, Y., Farver, J., Chang, L, Yu, L., & Zhang, Z. (2006). Culture, family context, and children's coping strategies in peer interactions. In X. Chen, D. French, & B. H. Schneider (Eds.), *Peer relationships in cultural context* (pp. 264–280). New York: Cambridge University Press.

Yates, M., & Youniss, J. (1996). A developmental perspective on community service in adolescence. *Social Development, 5,* 85–111.

Yau, J., & Smetana, J. G. (2003). Conceptions of moral, social-conventional, and personal events among Chinese preschoolers in Hong Kong. *Child Development, 74,* 647–658.

Ybarra, M. L., & Mitchell, K. J. (2007). Prevalence and frequency of Internet harassment instigation: Implications for adolescent health. *Journal of Adolescent Health, 41,* 189–195.

Yell, M. L., Robinson, T. R., & Drasgow, E. (2001). Cognitive behavior modification. In T. J. Zirpoli & K. J. Melloy, *Behavior management: Applications for teachers* (3rd ed., pp. 200–246). Upper Saddle River, NJ: Merrill/Prentice Hall.

Yeung, R. S., & Leadbeater, B. J. (2007, March). *Peer victimization and emotional and behavioral problems in adolescence: The moderating effect of adult emotional support.* Paper presented at the biennial meeting of the Society for Research in Child Development, Boston.

Yip, T., & Fuligni, A. J. (2002). Daily variation in ethnic identity, ethnic behaviors, and psychological well-being among American adolescents of Chinese descent. *Child Development, 73,* 1557–1572.

Youniss, J., & Yates, M. (1999). Youth service and moral-civic identity: A case for everyday morality. *Educational Psychology Review, 11,* 361–376.

Yuker, H. E. (Ed.). (1988). *Attitudes toward persons with disabilities.* New York: Springer.

Zahn-Waxler, C., Friedman, R. J., Cole, P., Mizuta, I., & Hiruma, N. (1996). Japanese and United States preschool children's responses to conflict and distress. *Child Development, 67,* 2462–2477.

Zahn-Waxler, C., Radke-Yarrow, M., Wagner, E., & Chapman, M. (1992). Development of concern for others. *Developmental Psychology, 28,* 126–136.

Zahorik, J. A. (1994, April). *Making things interesting.* Paper presented at the annual meeting of the American Educational Research Association, New Orleans, LA.

Zajonc, R. B. (1980). Feeling and thinking: Preferences need no inferences. *American Psychologist, 35,* 151–175.

Zambo, D. (2003, April). *Thinking about reading: Talking to children with learning disabilities.* Paper presented at the annual meeting of the American Educational Research Association, Chicago.

Zambo, D., & Brem, S. K. (2004). Emotion and cognition in students who struggle to read: New insights and ideas. *Reading Psychology, 25,* 1–16.

Zeelenberg, R., Wagenmakers, E.-J., & Rotteveel, M. (2006). The impact of emotion on perception: Bias or enhanced processing? *Psychological Science, 17,* 287–291.

Zeidner, M. (1998). *Test anxiety: The state of the art.* New York: Plenum Press.

Zeidner, M., & Matthews, G. (2005). Evaluation anxiety: Current theory and research. In A. J. Elliot & C. S. Dweck (Eds.), *Handbook of competence and motivation* (pp. 141–163). New York: Guilford Press.

Zeidner, M., Roberts, R. D., & Matthews, G. (2002). Can emotional intelligence be schooled? A critical review. *Educational Psychologist, 37,* 215–231.

Zelazo, P. D., Müller, U., Frye, D., & Marcovitch, S. (2003). The development of executive function in early childhood. *Monographs of the Society for Research in Child Development, 68*(3), Serial No. 274.

Zeldin, A. L., & Pajares, F. (2000). Against the odds: Self-efficacy beliefs of women in mathematical, scientific, and technological careers. *American Educational Research Journal, 37*, 215–246.

Zelli, A., Dodge, K. A., Lochman, J. E., & Laird, R. D. (1999). The distinction between beliefs legitimizing aggression and deviant processing of social cues: Testing measurement validity and the hypothesis that biased processing mediates the effects of beliefs on aggression. *Journal of Personality and Social Psychology, 77*, 150–166.

Zhang, J., Scardamalia, M., Reeve, R., & Messina, R. (2009). Designs for collective cognitive responsibility in knowledge-building communities. *Journal of the Learning Sciences, 18*(1), 7–44.

Zhang, L.-F., & Sternberg, R. J. (2006). *The nature of intellectual styles*. Mahwah, NJ: Erlbaum.

Zhou, Q., Wang, Y., Deng, X., Eisenberg, N., Wolchik, S. A., & Tein, J.-Y. (2008). Relations of parenting and temperament to Chinese children's experience of negative life events, coping efficacy, and externalizing problems. *Child Development, 79*, 493–513.

Ziegert, D. I., Kistner, J. A., Castro, R., & Robertson, B. (2001). Longitudinal study of young children's responses to challenging achievement situations. *Child Development, 72*, 609–624.

Zigler, E. F., & Finn-Stevenson, M. (1992). Applied developmental psychology. In M. H. Bornstein & M. E. Lamb (Eds.), *Developmental psychology: An advanced textbook*. Mahwah, NJ: Erlbaum.

Zimmer-Gembeck, M. J., & Helfand, M. (2008). Ten years of longitudinal research on U.S. adolescent sexual behavior: Developmental correlates of sexual intercourse and the importance of age, gender and ethnic background. *Developmental Review, 28*, 153–224.

Zimmerman, B. J. (1998). Developing self-fulfilling cycles of academic regulation: An analysis of exemplary instructional models. In D. H. Schunk & B. J. Zimmerman (Eds.), *Self-regulated learning: From teaching to self-reflective practice* (pp. 1–19). New York: Guilford Press.

Zimmerman, B. J. (2004). Sociocultural influence and students' development of academic self-regulation: A social-cognitive perspective. In D. M. McInerney & S. Van Etten (Eds.), *Big theories revisited* (pp. 139–164). Greenwich, CT: Information Age.

Zimmerman, B. J. (2008). In search of self-regulated learning: A personal quest. In H. W. Marsh, R. G. Craven, & D. M. McInerney (Eds.), *Self-processes, learning, and enabling human potential* (pp. 171–191). Charlotte, NC: Information Age.

Zimmerman, B. J., Bandura, A., & Martinez-Pons, M. (1992). Self-motivation for academic attainment: The role of self-efficacy beliefs and personal goal setting. *American Educational Research Journal, 29*, 663–676.

Zimmerman, B. J., & Campillo, M. (2003). Motivating self-regulated problem solvers. In J. E. Davidson & R. J. Sternberg (Eds.), *The psychology of problem solving* (pp. 233–262). Cambridge, England: Cambridge University Press.

Zimmerman, B. J., & Didenedetto, M. K. (2008). Mastery learning and assessment: Implications for students and teachers in an era of high-stakes testing. *Psychology in the Schools, 45*, 206–216.

Zimmerman, B. J., & Kitsantas, A. (1999). Acquiring writing revision skill: Shifting from process to outcome self-regulatory goals. *Journal of Educational Psychology, 91*, 241–250.

Zimmerman, B. J., & Kitsantas, A. (2005). The hidden dimension of personal competence: Self-regulated learning and practice. In A. J. Elliot & C. S. Dweck (Eds.), *Handbook of competence and motivation* (pp. 509–526). New York: Guilford Press.

Zimmerman, B. J., & Risemberg, R. (1997). Self-regulatory dimensions of academic learning and motivation. In G. D. Phye (Ed.), *Handbook of academic learning: Construction of knowledge*. San Diego, CA: Academic Press.

Zimmerman, B. J., & Schunk, D. H. (2004). Self-regulating intellectual processes and outcomes; A social cognitive perspective. In D. Y. Dai & R. J. Sternberg (Eds.), *Motivation, emotion, and cognition: Integrative perspectives on intellectual functioning and development* (pp. 323–349). Mahwah, NJ: Erlbaum.

Zohar, A., & Aharon-Kraversky, S. (2005). Exploring the effects of cognitive conflict and direct teaching for students of different academic levels. *Journal of Research in Science Teaching, 42*, 829–855.

Zook, K. B. (1991). Effects of analogical processes on learning and misrepresentation. *Educational Psychology Review, 3*, 41–72.

Aarts, H., 39
Abbott, R. D., 79
Abelson, R. P., 90
Aber, J. L., 80, 259
Aberson, B., 273
Ablard, K. E., 200
Abrami, P. C., 130, 303
Abuhamdeh, S., 191
Achilles, C. M., 305
Ackerman, B. P., 209
Ackerman, P. L., 160
Adalbjarnardottir S., 271
Adams, V. M., 210
Adelgais, A., 308
Adesope, O. O., 101
Afflerbach, P., 101, 129, 306, 307
Afflerbach, P. P., 377, 383
Aharon-Kraversky, S., 152, 154, 310
Ahn, J., 259
Aikens, N. L., 79
Ainge, D., 341
Ainley, M., 193, 217
Ainsworth, S., 308
Airasian, P. W., 296, 374
Ajzen, I., 205
Akamatsu, S., 20
Alapack, R., 251
Albanese, A. L., 125, 268, 299
Albano, J., 147
Alberg, S. R., 84
Albers, A. B., 336
Alberto, P. A., 344, 350
Alderman, M. K., 225, 268
Alexander, E. S., 225
Alexander, J. F., 90, 301
Alexander, J. L., 148
Alexander, J. M., 110, 112, 147, 155, 195, 208, 248
Alexander, K. L., 266, 267
Alexander, P. A., 10, 20, 36, 43, 50, 104, 105, 155, 194, 195, 200, 224, 225, 316
Alfassi, M., 175
Alfeld, C., 126
Alford, G. S., 86
Alibali, M. W., 35, 130, 154, 201
Alim, H. S., 93, 217, 315
Allday, R. A., 323
Alleman, J., 46, 88, 123, 130, 217, 221, 272, 288, 292, 297, 298, 329, 402
Allen, J., 168, 229
Allen, J. P., 252
Allen, K. D., 126
Allen, L., 259
Allington, R. L., 297
Allison, K. W., 95
Allor, J. H., 308
Alloway, T. P., 27
Almeida, D. M., 248, 255
Altermatt, E. R., 376
Altmann, E. M., 41
Altschul, I., 259
Alvarez, P., 24

Amabile, T. M., 115, 129, 130, 189, 228
Ambrose, D., 168
American Educational Research Association, 369
American Psychiatric Association, 270
American Psychological Association (APA), 3, 6, 369
American Psychological Association Zero Tolerance Task Force, 345
Ames, C., 200, 224, 225, 228
Ames, R., 200, 205
Amlund, J. T., 101, 123
Amrein, A. L., 402
Amsel, E., 51
Amsterlaw, J., 120
Ancess, J., 362
Anderman, E. M., 187, 197, 200, 201, 202, 209, 210, 225, 228, 229, 325, 364, 387, 390
Anderman, L. H., 61, 183, 195, 196, 202, 204, 205, 228, 229, 324, 390
Andersen, C., 104, 152
Anderson, C., 37
Anderson, C. A., 64
Anderson, C. J., 199
Anderson, C. W., 45, 55
Anderson, J. R., 27, 32, 34, 41, 50, 67, 112, 128
Anderson, L. H., 87
Anderson, L. M., 46
Anderson, L. W., 21, 267, 268
Anderson, M. L., 357
Anderson, R. C., 23, 43, 77, 294, 302
Anderson-Ketchmark, C., 355
Andrade, A., 121, 162
Andrade, H. L., 364, 393
Andre, T., 104, 125, 193, 217
Andreas, J. B., 255, 356
Andrews, G., 148, 149, 154
Andriessen, I., 76, 211, 301
Andrzejewski, C. E., 229
Angelini, L., 33
Angold, A., 270
Annahatak, B., 315
Ansley, T., 399
Anthony, G., 90, 301
Antonishak, J., 252
Apperly, I. A., 151
Applebee, A. N., 164
Arbeau, K. A., 170, 274
Arbreton, A. J., 266
Arbuthnot, K., 206
Arbuthnott, K. D., 163
Archer, J., 200, 254
Archer, S. L., 242
Ardoin, S. P., 329
Arlin, M., 316
Arnett, J., 216, 242, 250
Arnold, D. H., 64
Arnold, M. L., 263
Aronson, J., 219

Arroyo, I., 130
Arsenio, W. F., 254, 263
Arter, J. A., 396, 397
Ash, D., 67
Ashcraft, M. H., 214, 216
Asher, S. R., 201, 251, 252, 255
Ashiabi, G. S., 79
Ashley, E., 33
Ashman, A. D., 305
Ashurst, N., 256
Assor, A., 198, 219, 243
Astington, J. W., 104, 105, 253
Astor, R. A., 354
Astuti, R., 75
Atak, J. R., 329
Atance, C. M., 60
Atkinson, R. C., 25
Atkinson, R. K., 47, 123
Atran, S., 75, 94
Attie, I., 246
Au, K. H., 75
Au, W., 401, 402
Aulls, M. W., 297
Aunola, K., 237, 247
Ausubel, D. P., 32, 33, 102, 313
Avni-Babad, D., 328
Avrahami, A., 246
Awh, E., 28
Ayede, M., 66
Ayres, L. R., 111, 125, 126, 366, 389
Azevedo, R., 36, 108, 109, 111, 296, 306
Azuma, M., 211

Babad, E., 226, 328
Bacalleo, M. L., 259
Baddeley, A. D., 27, 28, 106
Baek, S., 364
Baer, D. M., 61
Bagley, C., 163
Baglieri, S., 275, 325
Bailey, J., 68
Bailey, J. S., 344
Baines, E., 248
Bakeman, R., 219
Baker, J., 328
Baker, L., 45, 100, 101, 102, 104, 335
Baker, S. A., 270
Bakermans-Kranenburg, M. J., 140
Balch, W., 39
Balfanz, R., 401
Balch, W., 39
Banaji, M. R., 249
Bandura, A., 196, 256
Bangert-Drowns, R. L., 84, 300, 391, 402
Banich, M., 242
Banks, C. A. M., 75, 93, 225, 251, 259, 315
Banks, J. A., 45, 75, 93, 95, 225, 251, 259, 315
Banta, T. W., 396, 397, 398
Bao, X., 211
Barab, S. A., 164

Baranowski, J., 221
Barbaranelli, C., 256
Barbarin, O., 79, 95
Barber, B. K., 239
Barber, B. L., 266
Barchfeld, P., 152
Barchfield, P., 152, 154
Bargh, J. A., 190
Barker, E. D., 251
Barker, E. T., 248
Barkley, R. A., 53, 213, 344
Barkoukis, V., 221
Barnes, C. D., 255
Barnes, M. A., 53, 78, 316
Barnett, J. E., 102, 104, 122
Barnett, M., 127
Barnett, S. M., 113, 156
Barnett, W. S., 170
Baron, A. S., 249
Baron, J. B., 366
Baron, M. A., 381
Barrera, M., Jr., 239
Barrett, A. M., 36
Barrois, L., 110
Barry, C. M., 247
Bartholomew, D. J., 167
Bartholow, B. D., 64
Bartlett, F. C., 44
Bartolomucci, C. L., 275
Barton, B., 28
Barton, K. C., 171
Barzillai, M., 104, 385
Basso, K., 315
Bassok, M., 112
Bates, J. E., 238, 239, 255, 269, 349
Batsche, C., 64
Batshaw, M. L., 169
Batson, C. D., 257, 263
Battin-Pearson, S., 266
Battistich, V., 192, 326, 333, 334
Bauer, P. J., 24
Baugh, J., 315
Baum, K., 353
Baumeister, A. A., 169
Baumeister, R. F., 243, 255
Baumrind, D., 239
Baxter, G. P., 364, 381
Bay-Hinitz, A. K., 58
Beal, C. R., 130
Beaudin, B. Q., 334
Bebeau, M., 139, 261
Bebko, J. M., 143
Beck, S. R., 151
Becker, B. E., 80, 96, 324
Bédard, J., 46, 155
Beghetto, R. A., 114
Behl-Chadha, G., 142
Behre, W. J., 354
Behrmann, M., 34
Beilock, S. L., 34, 50, 214
Beirne-Smith, M., 169
Beitzel, B. D., 48

Belfiore, P. J., 123, 125, 126, 240, 268, 299, 329, 343
Bell, J. A., 104
Bell, P., 301
Bellinger, D. C., 79
Bellon-Harn, M. L., 75
Belsky, J., 140, 223, 239, 324, 402
Bem, S. L., 244
Bembenutty, H., 107, 195
Bender, G., 354
Bendixen, L. D., 104, 105, 306
Benenson, J. F., 248
Benes, F. M., 141, 216
Benet-Martínez, V., 76
Benner, A. D., 216, 232
Benson, B., 250
Benton, D., 79, 162
Benware, C., 307
Ben-Yehudah, G., 147
Ben-Zeev, T., 219
Bereiter, C., 90, 91, 113, 125, 310, 311
Berenbaum, S. A., 244
Berends, M., 80
Berg, W. K., 83
Bergamo, M., 255
Bergemann, L., 253
Berger, S. R., 279, 309
Bergin, D. A., 113, 200, 259
Berglas, S., 197
Berk, L. E., 143, 274
Berkowitz, L., 213
Berkowitz, R. E., 304
Berliner, D., 362
Berliner, D. C., 10, 11, 79, 323, 402
Berlyne, D. E., 187
Berman, S. L., 262
Bernat, D. H., 259
Berndt, T. J., 247, 248
Bernieri, F., 188, 327
Berthold, K., 101
Berzonsky, M. D., 242
Best, D. L., 248
Beth, A. D., 195
Bettencourt, B. A., 195, 243
Beyer, B. K., 119
Beyer, F. S., 90
Beylin, A., 24
Bialystok, E., 140
Biddlecomb, B., 69
Bielaczyc, K., 90
Biemiller, A., 5, 175, 307, 308, 309
Bierman, K. L., 273, 276
Biezuner, S., 69, 301
Bigbee, M. A., 254, 255
Biggs, J., 122
Bigler, R. S., 93, 94, 244, 249
Bimbela, A., 332
Bisanz, J., 48, 171
Bivens, J. A., 143
Bjork, R., 163
Bjork, R. A., 113
Bjorklund, D. F., 33, 36, 42, 141, 148
Black, J. B., 30
Black, J. E., 24, 140
Blackbourn, J. M., 170
Black-Gutman, D., 277
Blackwell, L. S., 205, 206
Blair, C., 110
Blasi, A., 261, 263
Blatchford, P., 248
Bleeker, M., 197, 208, 385
Bleske-Rechek, A., 167, 168
Block, J. H., 248
Bloom, B. S., 289, 300
Bloom, L., 25
Blue-Banning, M., 334
Blugental, D. B., 332

Blumenfeld, P. C., 128, 190, 201, 208, 223, 224, 296, 303, 305
Boaler, J., 192
Boden, J. M., 255
Boekaerts, M., 201
Bogat, G. A., 269
Boggiano, A. K., 188
Bohanon, H., 345
Bohn, C. M., 53, 247, 274, 345
Boivin, M., 243, 252, 254
Bol, L., 102
Boldrin, A., 105, 193
Boling, C. J., 266
Bolt, E., 221
Bondi, J., 216, 270
Bong, M., 195, 201, 208, 217, 225, 240
Boody, R. M., 200
Boom, J., 260
Borge, A. I. H., 251
Borko, H., 11, 327
Borkowski, J. G., 205
Borman, K., 75, 211
Born, J., 24
Bornholt, L. J., 246
Bornstein, M. H., 93, 159, 239, 336, 349
Bortfeld, H., 140
Bosacki, S. L., 248, 252
Boschee, F., 381
Bouchard, T. J., Jr., 162
Boudah, D. J., 175
Boutte, G. S., 95
Bowen, G. M., 176
Bowen, N. K., 79, 336
Bower, G. H., 30, 31, 32, 33, 212, 213
Bower, J. E., 230
Bowman, K., 39
Bowman, L. G., 83
Boxerman, J. Z., 173
Boyer, E., 64
Boyes, M., 253
Boyle, R. A., 190, 380
Braaksma, M. A. H., 64
Bracken, B. A., 161, 247, 403
Bracy, N. L., 353
Bradley, R. H., 268
Bradshaw, C. P., 350, 354
Bradshaw, G. D., 387
Brady, M. P., 58
Braeges, J. L., 262
Brainerd, C. J., 21, 40, 143
Branch, C., 94
Bransford, J., 5, 10, 11, 112, 128, 285, 362, 379, 402
Bransford, J. D., 113, 126
Branstetter, W. H., 262
Braun, L. J., 87
Bray, N. W., 170
Brayboy, B. M. J., 11, 47, 75, 92, 93, 94, 191, 225, 267, 315, 332, 336, 385
Brem, S. K., 62
Brendgan, M., 243
Brendgen, M., 255, 337, 345
Brenner, M. E., 128
Bressler, J., 102
Bressler, S. L., 24
Brett, C., 104, 310
Brett1, C., 310
Brettschneider, W.-D., 243
Brewer, F. W., 37
Brewer, M. B., 244, 259
Brewer, W. F., 37, 51
Brickman, S. J., 107, 109
Brigham, F. J., 53
Bright, J. A., 336, 349
Brobst, K. E., 101
Broden, M., 343

Brody, G. H., 95, 187, 243, 266
Brody, N., 159, 161
Broekkamp, H., 43
Bronfenbrenner, U., 77, 150
Bronson, M. B., 108, 110, 354
Brooke, R. R., 85
Brookhart, S. M., 285, 288, 393, 395
Brooks, D. M., 323, 333
Brooks, L. W., 112, 113
Brooks, R. B., 269
Brooks-Gunn, J., 79, 80, 162, 246, 250, 267, 268, 336
Brophy, J., 17, 192, 208, 224, 288, 297, 298, 402
Brophy, J. E., 12, 46, 88, 93, 114, 123, 130, 201, 217, 221, 223, 224, 225, 226, 227, 230, 266, 272, 288, 292, 294, 296, 297, 322, 326, 329, 340, 387
Brouwer, A. L., 10
Brown, A. L., 90, 91, 101, 102, 123, 148, 172, 175, 310, 389
Brown, A. S., 366
Brown, B. B., 189, 202, 244, 246, 247, 248, 249, 250, 277
Brown, B. L., 64, 125
Brown, C. S., 95, 249, 277
Brown, D. R., 228
Brown, E. D., 209
Brown, J. R., 216, 268
Brown, J. S., 66, 123, 176, 259
Brown, M. C., 172, 173
Brown, R., 95, 123, 193
Brown, R. D., 141
Brown, R. P., 255
Brown, W. H., 58
Bruer, J. T., 24, 25, 140, 141
Brugman, D., 260
Bruner, J. S., 173, 175
Brunstein, J. C., 164, 202, 308
Bruschi, C. J., 219
Bryan, J. H., 45
Buchanan, R. L., 259
Buchman, M., 257
Buck, P., 93, 95, 277
Buehl, M. M., 104, 105
Buehler, C., 80
Buese, D., 401, 402
Buhrmester, D., 246
Buhs, E. S., 251, 255
Bukowski, W. M., 243, 247, 251, 255, 269, 273, 345
Bulgren, J. A., 48, 294
Bullock, M., 152
Bureau of Justice Statistics, 353
Burger, H. G., 75
Burger, S. F., A-2
Burhans, K. K., 207
Burk-Braxton, C., 214
Burke, L., 143
Burkham, D. T., 267, 322
Burstyn, J. N., 354
Burtis, J., 125
Burtis, P. J., 310
Burton, A. M., 20
Burton, L. M., 75
Burts, D. C., 403
Bush, K. R., 79
Bushell, D., 341
Bushell, D., Jr., 308
Bushman, B. J., 243
Busse, R. T., 273, 350
Butler, D. L., 84, 104, 105, 108, 109, 126
Butler, R., 108, 196, 220, 224, 226, 241, 245
Butt, A., 23, 24

Butterfield, E. C., 169
Butterworth, G., 66
Buunk, A. P., 196, 208, 243, 326
Bybee, D., 259
Byrne, B. M., 240
Byrnes, J. P., 24, 25, 79, 141, 152, 162, 191, 204, 208, 244

Cacioppo, J. T., 163, 187, 191
Cadigan, R. J., 248
Cai, Y., 221
Cairns, B. D., 274, 278
Calderhead, J., 291, 292
Caldwell, C. H., 259
Caldwell, K. A., 247
Caldwell, M. S., 188, 243
Calkins, S. D., 239
Camburn, E., 1, 7, 8, 216, 232
Cameron, J., 192, 222
Cameron, L., 95
Campbell, A., 249
Campbell, C. G., 241
Campbell, J. D., 243
Campillo, M., 118
Campione, J. C., 90, 91, 101, 310, 389
Campos, J. J., 240
Camras, L. A., 219, 240
Candee, D., 263
Candler-Lotven, A., 168
Cannon, J., 171
Cao, H. T., 223
Capodilupo, A., 96
Caprara, G. V., 255, 256, 276
Carbrera, N. J., 336
Card, N. A., 248, 254
Carey, S., 37, 75, 151, 154
Carhill, A., 403
Carlo, G., 253
Carlson, R., 47
Carnagey, N. L., 64
Carney, R. N., 294
Carnine, D., 294
Carpenter, S. K., 366
Carr, A. A., 336
Carr, M., 45, 69, 115, 118, 122, 168
Carr, T. H., 34, 50
Carraher, D. W., 154
Carrasco, R. L., 135, 227
Carroll, D. J., 151
Carroll, J. B., 160
Carta, J. J., 307
Carter, E. J., 78, 270
Carter, K., 275, 323, 327, 330, 332, 340
Carter, K. R., 168
Carter, R., 386
Cartledge, G., 296
Caruso, D. R., 252
Carver, C. S., 206, 210
Carver, S. M., 403
Cary, P. T., 276
Casanova, U., 315
Case, R., 96, 144
Casella, R., 272, 354
Casey, B. J., 79
Caspi, A., 240
Cassady, J. C., 214, 386
Cassel, W. S., 33
Castagno, A. E., 11, 47, 75, 92, 94, 315, 332, 336, 385
Casteneda, A., 377, 379, 381, 389, 396, 398
Castro, R., 207
Catalano, R. F., 79
Cattell, R. B., 159
Cauce, A. M., 246
Cauffman, E., 242
Caughy, M. O., 79

Cauley, K. M., 274, 323
Cavell, T. A., 223, 276, 354
Cazden, C. B., 336
Ceci, S. J., 113, 156, 162
Celio, C. I., 279, 309
Cepeda, N. J., 34, 366
Certo, J. L., 274, 302, 323, 324, 328
Chabrán, M., 214, 216
Chaffee, S. H., 313
Chafin, C., 274, 323
Chalmers, D. J., 25
Chalmers, V., 329
Chamberlain, A., 46, 303
Chambers, B., 171
Chambless, C. B., 324
Chambliss, M. J., 51
Champagne, F. A., 140, 270
Chan, C., 125, 310
Chan, J. M., 270
Chan, W.-C., 42, 104, 124, 294
Chand, I., 115, 118
Chandler, M., 104, 253
Chandler, P., 47
Chang, B., 196, 207, 241
Chang, L., 248, 259, 276
Chang-Schneider, C., 217
Chapman, C., 266
Chapman, D. A., 169
Chapman, J. W., 241
Chapman, M., 262
Chapman, S., 131
Charity, A. H., 315
Charlesworth, R., 403
Chase, M. A., 60, 84
Chase, P. N., 128
Chatzisarantis, N. L. D., 221
Chavous, T. M., 259
Cheah, C., 247, 259
Cheek, N. H., 249
Cheema, I., 163
Chen, C., 79
Chen, E., 255
Chen, J., 195
Chen, W.-B., 334
Chen, X., 75, 239, 248, 259
Chen, Y., 219
Chen, Y.-H., 42, 104, 124, 294
Chen, Z., 28
Cheng, L. R., 387
Cheng, P. W., 34
Chentsova-Dutton, Y., 219
Chess, S., 238, 264
Chester, M. D., 334
Cheung, A., 171
Cheung, M., 296
Chi, M. T. H., 31, 46, 102, 115, 148, 155, 307
Chih-Mei, C., 211
Child, D. A., 102
Chin, R., 211
China, C. A., 128
Chinn, C. A., 51, 69, 131, 217
Chipperfield, J. G., 230
Chisholm, J. S., 92
Chitooran, M. M., 162
Chiu, C., 76, 204
Chiu, C.-Y., 211, 259
Chiu, M. M., 301
Cho, B.-Y., 101, 129, 306, 307
Choi, I., 157, 219
Christensen, C. A., 40
Christenson, S. L., 266, 267, 268, 348
Christoffel, K. K., 332
Christopherson, H., 172
Christou, C., 106
Chudowsky, N., 366
Chun, E., 309

Chung, J., 259
Church, M. A., 225
Cicchetti, D., 269
Cillessen, A. H. N., 251, 255, 273
Cizek, G. G., 364, 393
Cizek, G. J., 61, 208, 332, 387, 388, 393
Clark, A. G., 216, 232
Clark, A.-M., 164, 301, 302
Clark, B., 168
Clark, C. C., 249
Clark, J. M., 34, 290
Clark, M. C., 33
Clark, R. E., 31, 172, 291, 294, 296
Clark, R. M., 269
Clark, R. W., 127, 295
Clarke, S., 270
Clement, C., 130, 154
Clements, D. H., 171
Cleveland, M. J., 187, 243
Clifford, M. M., 204, 220, 221, 391
Clore, G. L., 250
Close, L., 50
Clotfelter, C. T., 10
Coatsworth, J. D., 269
Cobb, P., 301
Coch, D., 53
Cochran, K. F., 11
Cochran-Smith, M., 11
Coffman, J. L., 33, 36
Cognition and Technology Group at Vanderbilt, 127, 310
Cohen, A. B., 70
Cohen, E. G., 301, 305, 309
Cohen, G. L., 188, 231, 277
Cohen, P. R., 130
Cohen, R. L., 50
Coie, J. D., 255, 273
Coladarci, T., 393
Colarossi, L., 266
Colavecchia, B., 344
Colby, A., 260
Cole, A. S., 76
Cole, D. A., 237, 241, 246
Cole, M., 70, 71, 144, 157
Cole, N. S., 288
Cole, P., 219
Cole, P. M., 219, 259
Cole, S. W., 140
Coleman, H. L. K., 76
Coleman, M., 126
Collins, A., 66, 90, 123, 175, 176, 378, 379, 402
Collins, A. M., 66
Collins, W. A., 216, 239, 248, 249, 250, 270
Colvin, G., 341
Combs, A. W., 214
Comfort, C., 223, 266
Compton, D. L., 381
Conant, F. R., 91
Conger, K. J., 249
Conger, R. D., 249
Conklin, H. M., 106, 162
Conley, C. S., 188, 243
Connell, J. P., 189, 198, 219, 243
Connolly, F. W., 296
Connolly, J., 250, 255
Connor, C. M., 316
Connor, D. J., 275, 325
Conoley, J. C., 307, 309
Conway, M. A., 34
Conyers, C., 63, 344
Cook, P. J., 211, 259
Cooks, H. C., 259
Cooney, C., 87
Cooney, G. H., 246
Cooney, J. B., 338

Cooper, H., 195, 221, 243, 297, 298, 299, 313, 345
Cooper, R. G., 150
Copland, R. J., 170, 274
Corbett, A., 296
Corbett, H. D., 123, 208
Corkill, A. J., 294
Cormier, S. M., 113
Cornell, D. G., 168
Corno, L., 108, 109, 161, 210, 221, 291, 298, 316, 345
Cornoldi, C., 159
Corpus, J. H., 191, 200, 208
Correa-Chávez, M., 315
Corrigan, C., 325
Cosden, M., 125, 268, 299
Costa, A. L., 67
Costello, E. J., 270
Cote, L. R., 93, 336
Covington, M. V., 168, 188, 191, 192, 197, 199, 201, 204, 208, 214, 220, 228, 248, 366
Cowan, N., 26, 27, 28, 36
Cox, B. D., 113
Coyle, T. R., 36
Craft, M., 315
Craft, M. A., 84
Crago, M. B., 75, 157, 315
Craig, D., 387, 391
Craig, D. V., 11
Craig, W., 255
Craik, F. I. M., 32, 33
Craven, J., 143
Craven, J. A., III, 11, 333
Craven, R., 217, 240
Craven, R. G., 240, 241, 243, 245, 275
Creasey, G. L., 274
Crehan, K. D., 382
Crick, N. R., 251, 254, 255, 276
Crocker, J., 217, 241
CroCkett, L., 249
Cromley, J. G., 36
Crone, D. A., 351
Crone, E. A., 147
Croninger, R. G., 46
Crook, C., 305
Crooks, T. J., 53, 391
Cross, D., 253
Cross, W. E., Jr., 76, 259
Crosson-Tower, C., 269
Crouter, A. C., 208, 244
Crowder, R. G., 26
Crowe, E., 271
Crowson, H. M., 200, 322
Crumbaugh, C., 90, 301
Csikszentmihalyi, M., 118, 190, 191, 220, 329
Cummings, E. M., 268, 269
Cummings1, J. S., 268
Cummins, J., 403
Cunningham, A. E., 207, 241
Cunningham, A. M., 278
Cunningham, C. E., 276
Cunningham, L. J., 276
Curry, L., 163
Curtis, K. A., 227
Cushing, K. S., 323
Cushing, L. S., 307, 309

Dabholkar, A. S., 141
D'Agostino, J. V., 122
Dahlin, B., 123
Dai, D. Y., 163
d'Ailly, H., 188, 211
Dale, P. S., 162
Daley, S. G., 106
Daley, T. C., 162

Dalrymple, N. J., 270
Daly, P. F., 36
Damasio, A. R., 209
D'Amato, R. C., 162
Damon, W., 110, 255, 257, 261, 263
Daniels, D. H., 197, 395
Daniels, S., 123, 164
Danner, F., 225, 365, 387
Danner, F. W., 154
Dansereau, D. F., 101, 112, 113, 294
D'Apollonia, S., 303
Darch, C. B., 325
Darley, J. M., 375
Darling-Hammond, L., 5, 10, 11, 285, 362, 364, 377, 379, 396, 397, 398
Darwin, C. J., 26
Dauber, S. L., 266
David, B. J., 64
Davidson, A. L., 76, 201, 214, 251
Davidson, F. H., 263
Davidson, J. E., 118
Davidson, R. J., 238
Davies, P. G., 219
Davies, P. T., 268, 270
Davila, J., 250
Davis, A., 268
Davis, C., 335, 336, 348
Davis, G. A., 168, 326, 327, 329, 339, 340, 345
Davis, H., 5, 6, 37, 150, 348
Davis, H. A., 201, 231, 324, 325
Davis, L. E., 205
Davis, M., 393
Davis, O. S. P., 82, 140
Davis, S., 171
Davis-Kean, P., 197, 208, 385
Davis-Kean, P. E., 196, 241, 245
Davison, A. L., 223
Dawson, G., 53
Day, J., 101
Day, J. D., 148
Day, M. C., 154
Dean, D., Jr., 154
Deary, I. J., 159
Deater-Decker, K., 349
Deaux, K., 248
DeBacker, T. K., 200, 322
DeBell, M., 266
De Bock, D., 152
DeBose, C. E., 315
Debus, R. L., 188, 197, 240, 245
deCharms, R., 188
Deci, E. L., 187, 188, 189, 190, 191, 192, 198, 214, 220, 221, 222, 224, 228, 307, 327
De Clercq, A., 130
De Corte, E., 113, 155, 380
Dee-Lucas, D., 101, 102
DeFalco, K., 327
De Groot, E. V., 102, 122
de Haan, M., 24, 141
DeHart, G., 150
de Jong, T., 172, 173, 310
de Koning, E., 201
DeLain, M. T., 77
Delandshere, G., 389
Delaney, H. D., 48
De La Paz, S., 102
deLeeuw, N., 102
Delgado-Gaitan, C., 123, 315
De Lisi, R., 51
DeLisle, J. R., 168
DeLoache, J. S., 36, 143
Demetriou, A., 106
Dempster, F. N., 24, 34, 364, 366
Denning, D., 254
Denton, N. A., 79, 336

DeRidder, L. M., 242
Derry, S., 362
Derry, S. J., 37, 129, 130, 175
Desberg, P., 291
Deshler, D. D., 48, 294
Desimone, L. M., 10
Desoete, A., 130
Detterman, D. K., 156
Deutsch, M., 271, 305, 312
DeVault, G., 351, 352
DeVoe, J. F., 353, 354
DeVries, R., 261
Dewhurst, S. A., 34
Dewitte, S., 198
Dexter, A., 75
Deyhle, D., 75, 92, 211, 349
Diamond, A., 170
Diamond, M., 141
Diamond, S. C., 341
Dickens, W. T., 162
Dickerson, C., 345
Didenedetto, M. K., 300
Didow, S. M., 68
Dien, T., 211, 219, 349
Diener, E., 219
Dietz, F., 110, 299
Dijkstra, P., 196, 208, 218, 231, 243, 326
Dilllon, D. R., 168
Dilworth, J. E., 79
DiMartino, J., 377, 379, 381, 389, 396, 398
D'Incau, B., 354
Dirks, J., 167
diSessa, A. A., 165, 380
Dishion, T. J., 247
Di Vesta, F. J., 42, 101, 112
Dobbelaere, A., 325
Dochy, F., 128
Dodge, K. A., 201, 251, 254, 255, 270, 276, 349
Dole, J. A., 101, 102, 122
Doll, B., 247, 275
Dominowski, R. L., 118, 122
Donaldson, M., 154
Donaldson, S. K., 253
Donis, K., 121, 162
Donlan, A. E., 270
Donohew, L., 187
Donovan, L. A., 264
Dorris, M., 169
Dotterer, A. M., 208
Douch, R., 95
Douglas, G., 105
Dovidio, J. F., 95, 277
Dow, G. T., 114
Dowson, M., 189, 201, 202, 223, 247, 274
Doyle, A., 189, 259
Doyle, W., 37, 201, 247, 275, 312, 322, 323, 327, 328, 329, 330, 332, 333, 337, 338, 339, 340, 341, 344, 384
Doyle-Nichols, A., 396
Drabman, R. S., 344
Drasgow, E., 273
Dreikurs, R., 344
Drew, H. A., 351
Dryfoos, J. G., 355
DuBois, D. L., 195, 214, 216, 243
Dubow, E. F., 277
Duckworth, A. L., 109, 162
Duda, J. L., 221
Dudley, B., 271
Dueck, A., 31, 32
Duffy, G. G., 101
Duffy, S., 70, 349

Duguid, P., 66, 176
Duke, N. K., 313
Dumaret, A., 162
Duncan, G. J., 79, 162, 399
Duncan, R. G., 128
Duncker, K., 117
Dunham, Y., 249
Dunlap, G., 221, 351
Dunlosky, J., 102, 104
Dunning, D., 109, 110, 126
DuPaul, G., 343
DuPaul, G. J., 307, 344
Dupeyrat, C., 199
Duran, B. J., 75
Durik, A. M., 197, 246
Durkin, K., 94, 246, 249
Durlak, J. A., 279, 309
Dutta, A., 34, 40, 50, 155
Duyme, M., 162
Dweck, C., 123, 211
Dweck, C. S., 168, 188, 196, 200, 201, 204, 205, 206, 207, 218, 219, 221, 225, 227, 240, 243, 245
Dwyer, K., 354, 355, 356
Dymond, S. K., 309

Eacott, M. J., 67
Early, S., 290
Eaton, J. F., 55
Eccles, J., 195, 196, 197, 226, 244, 246, 266
Eccles, J. S., 80, 110, 189, 191, 196, 197, 198, 201, 205, 207, 208, 216, 219, 224, 231, 242, 244, 268, 279, 385
Eccles (Parsons), J. S., 206
Eckerman, C. O., 68
Eckert, P., 249, 250
Edens, K. M., 47
Edmonds, M. S., 294
Edstrom, L. V., 273
Edwards, R. P., 58, 330, 351
Edwards-Evans, S., 315
Eeds, M., 301
Egan, L. C., 142
Egbert, J., 307
Egeland, B., 79
Ehle, D. A., 167
Eicher, S. A., 189, 249
Eid, M., 219
Eilam, B., 53, 125, 268, 299
Einstein, G. O., 41, 101, 294
Eisenband, J., 171
Eisenberg, M. B., 304, 305
Eisenberg, N., 239, 248, 253, 257, 261, 262, 263
Eisenberg, T. E., 296
Elder, A. D., 104, 364, 381
Elder, G. H., Jr., 259
El-Dinary, P. B., 123, 130
Elia, J. P., 251
Elik, N., 224
Elkind, D., 154, 216, 242, 244, 245, 247
Ellenwood, S., 278
Elliot, A. J., 188, 199, 200, 201, 224, 225
Elliot, J., 27, 211
Elliott, D. J., 176
Elliott, E. S., 196, 200, 201, 205, 221
Elliott, S. N., 273, 350
Ellis, A. B., 246
Ellis, E. S., 53
Ellis, J. A., 34
Ellis, L., 241
Ellis, W. E., 247, 251
Ellison, N. B., 274

El-Sheikh, M., 268, 269, 270
Emmer, E. T., 119, 120, 312, 322, 323, 325, 327, 329, 330, 332, 337, 338, 340, 341, 348
Empson, S. B., 152, 154
Engle, R. A., 90, 91, 131
Engle, R. W., 115
Englehart, M. D., 289
Englemann, S., 294
Entwisle, D. R., 266
Entwisle, N. J., 200
Epel, E., 230
Epstein, J. L., 228, 229, 249, 334, 335, 336, 349
Epstein, J. S., 249
Erath, S. A., 269
Erickson, F., 47, 315
Ericsson, K. A., 155
Eriks-Brophy, A., 75
Erikson, E. H., 242
Erkens, G., 131
Ertmer, P. A., 294
Ervin, R. A., 307
Erwin, P., 247
Escribe, C., 199
Esmonde, I., 305
Espelage, D. L., 247, 254, 276, 325, 334, 354
Espinosa, M. P., 162
Estell, D. B., 110, 248
Estrada, S., 242
Estrin, E. T., 93
Evans, E. D., 387, 391
Evans, E. M., 75, 94
Evans, G. W., 80, 268
Evans, J. J., 160
Evans, M. A., 255
Evans, W. H., 266
Evans-Winters, V., 87
Everett-Cacopardo, H., 306
Evertson, C. M., 270, 312, 322, 323, 327, 329, 330, 348
Eylon, B., 303
Eysenck, M. W., 214
Eysink, T. H. S., 172

Fabes, R. A., 239, 248, 254, 257, 262, 263
Fabos, B., 310
Fad, K. S., 170
Fahrmeier, E. D., 157
Fairchild, H. H., 315
Faison, N., 262
Fake, S., 351
Falk, B., 362
Falk, K., 221, 341
Fall, R., 366
Fantuzzo, J. W., 303, 308
Farber, B., 315
Farivar, S., 274, 305, 330
Farkas, G., 45, 79
Farley, F., 187, 242, 243
Farmer, W., 274, 278
Farrell, E., 267
Farver, J., 259
Farver, J. A. M., 262
Farwell, L., 375
Fauth, R. C., 79, 268
Feather, N. T., 205
Fegley, S., 262, 263
Feinstein, J. A., 163, 187
Feiring, C., 250
Feldhusen, J. F., 128, 129, 167, 168
Feldman, A. F., 268, 274, 278
Feldon, D., 386
Feldon, D. F., 290

Feltovich, P., 115
Feltz, D. L., 60, 84
Fennema, E., 313
Fenning, P. A., 345
Ferguson, E. L., 294
Ferguson, R., 313
Fernandez, C., 159
Ferrari, M., 224
Ferretti, R. P., 169
Feuerstein, R., 67, 381
Fhagen-Smith, P., 76, 259
Fida, R., 255
Fiedler, E. D., 168
Fiedler, K., 143
Fier, J., 246
Fiez, J. A., 147
Filax, G., 250, 251, 254
Filisetti, L., 201
Finders, M., 336
Fine, S., 251
Fingerhut, L. A., 332
Fink, B., 34
Finkelhor, D., 274, 354
Finn, J. D., 267, 268, 305
Finnigan, K. S., 401
Fischer, K. W., 53, 106, 123, 146, 148, 157, 211, 255, 315, 356, 387
Fisher, C. W., 127
Fisher, R. P., 366
Fisher, W. W., 83
Fiske, A. P., 211
Fiske, S. T., 211
Fivush, R., 143
Flanagan, C. A., 253, 262, 354
Flanagan, D. P., 159, 160
Flanagin, A. J., 120, 129
Flavell, E. R., 253
Flavell, J. H., 35, 104, 139, 147, 148, 154, 253
Fleege, P. O., 403
Fleming, C. B., 79
Fleming, J. S., 168
Fletcher, J. M., 53, 78, 316
Fletcher, K. L., 170
Flieller, A., 151
Flood, A. L., 59
Flood, W. A., 59
Floyd, R. G., 160
Flum, H., 121, 164, 217, 242
Flynn, J. R., 82, 162
Fogel, V., 64
Fontaine, R. G., 255
Foos, P. W., 366
Ford, D. Y., 197
Ford, L., 160
Ford, M. E., 189, 190, 201, 202
Forgas, J. P., 213
Forget-Dubois, N., 399
Försterling, F., 218
Fortier, M. S., 191
Fosnot, C. T., 69, 336
Fowler, S. A., 61
Fox, E., 43
Fox, J. J., 58
Fox, N. A., 24, 239
Fox, P. W., 296, 365
Frankenberger, K. D., 243
Franklin, S., 120, 141, 151, 154, 163
Fraser, B. J., 61, 216, 231, 232
Frazier, B. N., 142
Frecker, K., 104, 310
Frederiksen, J. R., 172, 173, 312, 378, 379, 402
Frederiksen, N., 116, 130, 173, 364, 365, 366
Fredrickson, B., 210, 213

Freedom Writers, 45, 275, 278
Freeman, B., 225
Freeman, K. E., 211
Frensch, P. A., 113, 131
Frenzel, A. C., 210, 217
Frey, K. S., 275, 276
Freygang, T., 147
Friebert, S. E., 104
Friedel, J., 226
Friedman, C. K., 244, 246, 248, 385
Friedman, R. J., 219
Friedrichs, A. G., 104
Friend, P., 53
Fries, S., 110, 299
Friesen, B., 270
Frieze, I. H., 204
Frisbie, D. A., 393, 395
Fritz, J. B., 34
Frost, J. L., 58
Fry, A. F., 61, 147
Frye, D., 106
Fuchs, D., 268, 307
Fuchs, L. S., 53, 78, 200, 268, 300, 307, 308, 316, 381
Fueyo, V., 308
Fuhrman, W., 249
Fujimura, N., 154
Fuligni, A. J., 75, 199, 211, 259
Fuller, B., 401
Fuller, M. L., 344
Furlong, M. J., 354
Furman, W., 246, 248, 249, 250, 270
Furrer, C., 190, 223
Furst, E. J., 289

Gable, R. K., 216
Gable, S. L., 225, 274
Gabriele, A. J., 200, 224
Gaertner, S. L., 95, 277
Gage, N. L., 5, 6
Gagné, R. M., 294
Gaines, M. L., 393
Galambos, N. L., 248
Gallagher, J. J., 167
Gallagher, K. C., 239
Gallimore, R., 75, 349
Gallini, J., 294
Gallop, R., 268
Gamoran, A., 164
Ganea, P. A., 143
Garbarino, J., 354
Garbe, G., 299
García, E. E., 76
Garcia, E. E., 75, 91, 225, 268, 313, 385
Garcia, J., 231, 277
Garcia-Mila, M., 104, 152
Gardiner, H. W., 259
Gardner, H., 25, 156, 157, 160, 167, 177
Garibaldi, A. M., 268
Garner, J., 47
Garner, R., 193
Garnier, H., 75
Garnier, H. E., 266
Garrett, M. T., 75
Garrison, E. G., 355
Garver, K. E., 147
Gaskill, P. J., 234
Gaskins, I. W., 36, 107, 109, 123, 124
Gathercole, S. E., 27, 36
Gaudry, E., 387
Gauvain, M., 68
Gava, M., 105, 193
Gavin, L. A., 249
Gay, G., 315, 338
Gayford, C., 303

Gaylord-Harden, N. K., 259
Gaynor, J., 391
Gazelle, H., 252
Geary, D. C., 31, 140, 223
Gehlbach, H., 227, 272, 310, 311
Geiger, M. A., 402
Gelman, S. A., 30, 31, 142, 246, 253
Gendreau, P. L., 254
Genova, W. J., 274, 278
Gentry, M., 216, 231
Geraerts, E., 213
Gerard, J. M., 80
Gerlach, E., 243
Gerrard, M., 187, 243
Gershoff, E. T., 80
Gerst, M. S., 86
Gerton, J., 76
Gerwels, M. C., 327, 329, 330, 332, 337, 341
Gesicki, K., 401
Gettinger, M., 312, 323, 326, 327, 329, 333, 338
Ghatala, E. S., 104
Ghazarian, S. R., 226
Gheen, M. H., 76, 197, 199, 216, 325
Ghetti, S., 33
Giaconia, R. M., 47
Gibb, R., 141
Gibbons, F. X., 187, 243
Gibbs, J., 260
Gibbs, J. C., 262
Gibson, E., 248
Gick, M. L., 113
Giedd, J. N., 141
Gijbels, D., 128
Gildea, P. M., 139
Gillies, R. M., 305
Gilligan, C. F., 260
Gilliland, H., 94, 315
Ginsberg, M. B., 225
Ginsburg, H. P., 171
Ginsburg-Block, M. D., 303, 305, 307
Gipps, C., 84
Girotto, V., 154
Glaeser, B., 346, 351
Glaessner, B., 210
Glaser, D., 270
Glaser, R., 115, 148, 155, 168, 364, 381
Glenberg, A. M., 33, 172, 173
Glover, J. A., 118, 391
Gnepp, J., 253
Gobbo, C., 148, 154, 157
Goddard, R. D., 334
Goeke-Morey, M. C., 268
Goetz, E. T., 21, 34, 173, 205
Goetz, L., 78
Goetz, T., 209, 210, 217, 230
Golbeck, S. L., 51
Gold, A. L., 269
Goldberg, A., 250
Goldenberg, C., 45, 75, 96, 225, 349
Goldknopf, E. J., 36
Goldsmith, H. H., 238
Goldstein, H., 273
Goldstein, L. S., 5, 6
Goldstein, N. E., 64
Goldstein, S., 269
Goldston, D. B., 259, 270
Golen, S., 220, 228
Gollwitzer, P. M., 190
Gomez, M. L., 315, 387
Gonzales, N., 246
González, M. M., 187, 230
Good, C., 200, 205, 219
Good, T. L., 46, 111, 126, 201, 226, 303, 340, 348

Goodenow, C., 223
Goodman, C. S., 23
Goodman, G. S., 213
Goodman, J., 108, 110
Goodman, K., 325
Goodnow, J. J., 70, 246, 259
Goodwin, M. H., 249, 254, 275
Gootman, M. E., 344
Gopnik, A., 253
Gordon, B., 382
Gordon, W., 157
Gorman, A. H., 255
Gottfredson, D. C., 326
Gottfried, A. E., 168, 191
Gottfried, A. W., 168
Gottman, J. M., 250, 274
Gould, E., 24
Gowin, D. B., 101, 102
Grabowski, B. L., 163
Grace, C. O., 237, 238
Grace, D. M., 64
Graeber, A. O., 112
Graesser, A., 307
Graesser, A. C., 296
Grafman, J., 24
Graham, M., 101
Graham, S., 34, 60, 61, 64, 109, 125, 200, 207, 211, 216, 220, 225, 226, 228, 232, 242, 251, 275, 276
Grammer, J. K., 33, 36
Grant, C. A., 278, 315, 387
Grant, H., 123, 211
Gray, M. R., 239
Gray, S. G., 42, 101
Gray, W. D., 41, 113
Green, C. L., 336
Green, F. L., 253
Green, L., 60, 61
Greenberg, M. T., 355
Green-Demers, I., 192
Greene, J. A., 108
Greene, T. R., 115, 155
Greenfield, P. M., 157, 259, 349
Greenhoot, A. F., 253, 254
Greenhow, C., 245, 274
Greeno, J. G., 66, 112
Greenough, W. T., 24, 140, 141
Greenwood, C. R., 307, 308, 309
Greenwood, D., 277
Greer, B., 155, 380
Gregg, A. P., 188, 197, 211
Gregg, M., 127
Gregoire, M., 5, 6
Gregory, A., 334
Greif, M. L., 31
Gresalfi, M. S., 164
Griesemer, S. M. R., 58, 330
Griesinger, T., 197, 387
Griff, M. M., 128
Griffin, B. w., 128
Griffin, D. M., 315
Griffin, S. A., 96
Griffiths, J., 94, 249
Grigrenko, E. L., 128
Grills, A. E., 276
Grissmer, D. W., 80
Grolnick, W. S., 198, 365
Gronlund, N. E., 285, 288, 375, 379, 383, 385
Gross, B., 401
Gross, E. F., 274
Gross, J. N., 110, 257
Gross, P. H., 375
Gross, S., 381
Grosslight, L., 37, 150

Grotpeter, J. K., 254, 255
Grouzet, F. M. E., 191, 208
Grover, R., 306
Gruman, D. H., 79
Grusec, J. E., 63
Guacci-Franco, N., 237
Guay, F., 191, 224, 243, 252
Guerra, M. R., 301
Guerra, N. G., 64
Guerrero, F., 296
Guiton, G., 226
Gummerum, M., 257, 262
Gunstone, R. F., 51, 105
Guskey, T. R., 10, 300
Gustafsson, J., 159, 162
Guthrie, J. T., 192
Guthrie, P., 259
Guthrie-Fulbright, Y., 253
Gutierrez, F., 31
Gutiérrez, K. D., 71, 95, 315
Gutman, L. M., 211, 334
Guy, D., 299

Hackenberg, T. D., 59
Hacker, D. J., 102, 104
Haden, C. A., 68
Hadjioannou, X., 301, 302
Hadwin, A., 396
Hadwin, A. F., 107
Haerle, F. C., 104, 105
Hagger, M. S., 221
Hagopian, L. P., 83
Hagtvet, K. A., 386
Haier, R. J., 24, 159
Hale, N. M., 332
Hale, S., 147
Hale-Benson, J. E., 75, 239, 315
Halford, G. S., 147, 148, 149, 154
Halgunseth, L. C., 239, 259
Hall, K. M., 104
Hall, N. C., 210, 230
Hall, R. V., 63, 307, 343
Hallahan, D. P., 169
Haller, E. P., 102
Hallett, D., 104
Halpern, D. F., 82, 113, 118, 119, 120, 121, 129, 130, 163, 178
Halpin, G., 364
Hambrick, D. Z., 115
Hamedani, M. G., 68, 72, 246
Hamm, J. V., 244
Hammerness, K., 11, 362, 364
Hamovitch, B., 325
Hampel, R. L., 127, 295
Hampson, S. E., 163, 240, 255
Hamre, B. K., 313, 322, 324, 332
Hanish, L. D., 254
Hanley, G. P., 189
Hannum, W. H., 290
Hanson, A. R., 64, 218
Harachi, T. W., 79
Harackiewicz, J. M., 191, 192, 193, 194, 199, 201, 222
Hardesty, J. L., 214
Hardré, P. L., 191, 200, 221, 267, 322
Hardway, C., 211
Hardy, I., 172, 173
Hareli, S., 205, 209
Harlow, H. F., 59
Harmon-Jones, E., 212
Harnish, J. D., 255
Harnishfeger, K. K., 108
Harper, F., 403
Harris, A. H., 329
Harris, J. R., 239, 248, 249

Harris, K. R., 34, 64, 109, 123, 125, 126, 130, 273, 316, 343
Harris, M. B., 251
Harris, M. J., 243
Harris, P. L., 163, 252, 253
Harris, R. J., 119
Hart, D., 241, 255, 262, 263
Hart, E. R., 175
Harter, S., 109, 188, 189, 191, 198, 201, 209, 214, 217, 220, 224, 240, 241, 243, 244, 245, 246, 253, 257, 263, 264, 386
Hartley, J., 294
Hartley, K., 306
Hartup, W. W., 244
Haskell, R. E., 113, 131
Hasselhorn, M., 36
Hastings, P. D., 262, 263, 279
Hatano, G., 31, 46, 69, 71, 104, 301, 303, 312
Hattie, J., 50, 60, 84, 105, 122, 123, 124, 130, 188, 197, 204, 228, 230, 266
Hattie, J. A. C., 10, 12, 79, 101, 227, 246, 300, 364, 366, 375
Hawkins, F. P. L., 220
Hawley, C. A., 227
Haworth, C. M. A., 82, 140, 162
Haye, K. M., 276
Hayenga, A. O., 191, 200
Hayne, H., 123
Haynes, T. L., 230
Hayslip, B., Jr., 167
Haywood, H. C., 144, 168, 381, 403
He, Y., 248
Heafner, T., 110
Hearold, S., 64, 277
Heath, C., 109
Heath, S. B., 167, 315
Heatherton, T. F., 33
Hecht, S. A., 50
Heck, D. J., 244
Hegarty, M., 294
Heine, S. J., 211, 219
Helfand, M., 250, 251
Heller, L. R., 308
Helmke, A., 293, 294, 295, 312
Helton, G. B., 72
Helwig, C. C., 256, 261, 262
Hembree, R., 214, 386, 402
Hemmes, N. S., 64, 125
Hemmings, A. B., 248, 268
Hemphill, L., 68
Henderson, H. A., 239
Hendriks, M., 39
Henkel, R. R., 247, 354
Hennessey, B. A., 115, 129, 130, 189, 222, 228
Hennessey, M. G., 125, 180
Hennessey, M. N., 90, 301
Henry, K. B., 224
Herald, S. L., 251
Herald-Brown, S. L., 332
Herbert, J., 246
Herman, M., 244
Hermann, D. J., 115
Hernandez, D. J., 79, 336
Heron, W., 187
Herrenkohl, L. R., 68, 131, 172, 301
Hersh, R. H., 260
Hess, R. D., 72, 211
Hessels, A., 152
Hetherington, E. M., 239
Heuer, F., 212, 213
Heward, W. L., 84, 169, 170, 296
Hewitt, J., 68, 91, 104, 310

Heyman, G. D., 119
Hickey, D. T., 172
Hicks, L., 202
Hickson, F., 277
Hidalgo, N. M., 336, 349
Hidi, S., 190, 191, 192, 193, 194, 195, 199, 201, 208, 209, 217, 222
Hiebert, E. H., 69, 90, 127, 301, 377, 383
Hiebert, J., 68, 69, 90, 301, 305
Higgins, A., 261, 268
Higgins, C., 346, 351
Hilden, K., 35, 36, 122, 124
Hildreth, B., 168
Hill, C., 298, 379
Hill, H. C., 11
Hill, K. T., 216, 387
Hill, N. E., 79, 80, 335
Hill, W. H., 289
Hinchman, K., 92, 93
Hine, P., 61, 216, 231, 232
Hiner, M., 277
Hinkley, J. W., 201, 202
Hinnant, J. B., 226
Hiraga, Y., 246
Hirschstein, M. K., 275
Hiruma, N., 219
Hitch, G. J., 36
Hitlin, S., 259
Hmelo-Silver, C. E., 128, 131, 175, 176
Ho, A. D., 401
Ho, D. Y. F., 123
Hobson, P., 270
Hockensmith, M. L., 366
Hodell, M., 217, 222
Hodges, E. V. E., 252
Hofer, B. K., 100, 105
Hoff, K., 343
Hofferth, S. L., 250
Hoffman, M. L., 257, 262, 263, 266
Hogan, D. M., 304
Hogan, K., 69, 301, 312
Hogan, T., 11, 333
Hoge, R. D., 168, 393
Hoglund, W. L. G., 255, 270
Hoke-Sinex, L., 111
Holland, R. W., 39
Holley, C. D., 101
Holliday, B. G., 211
Holling, H., 213
Hollins, E. R., 71, 93, 259
Hollon, R. E., 45
Holloway, S. D., 72
Holmes, C. J., 141
Holt, K., 188, 199, 327
Holt, M. B., 142
Holt, M. K., 247, 255, 354
Holt-Reynolds, D., 5, 6
Holyoak, K. J., 113
Hom, A., 326
Hong, E., 386
Hong, Y., 76, 204, 259
Hong, Y.-Y., 211
Hoogstra, L. A., 200
Hook, C. L., 307
Hooper, C. J., 106, 162
Hoover-Dempsey, K. V., 239, 265, 299, 322, 324, 335, 336
Hopmeyer, A., 251
Hopson, J., 141
Horgan, D., 203
Horgan, D. D., 102, 104
Horger, R. H., 351
Horn, J. L., 155, 160, 177
Horne, A. M., 275

Horner, R. H., 221, 275, 334, 354
Hornyak, R. S., 123, 126, 240, 268, 299
Horvath, J. A., 291
Hoskyn, J., 380
Hossler, D., 75
Houghton, C., 125
Houston, I., 266
Houts, R., 223, 324, 402
Houtz, J. C., 128
Howard, M. R., 315
Howe, C. K., 336
Howell, J. C., 356
Howell, K. L., 105
Hoy, W. K., 12, 333, 334
Hoyles, C., 310
Hoyt, J. D., 104
Hruda, L. Z., 61, 229, 324
Hsiao, C., 259
Hubbs-Tait, L., 79
Huberty, P. D., 345
Hudley, C., 251, 276, 325
Huesmann, L. R., 64, 277
Huey, E. D., 24
Huff, J. A., 344
Huffman, S., 104
Hufton, N., 211
Hughes, J., 334
Hughes, J. E., 245, 274
Hughes, J. N., 110, 223, 324, 332, 354
Huguet, P., 219
Hulit, L. M., 315
Hunt, E., 162
Hunt, P., 78
Hunter, J., 329
Huntley, S. B., 168
Huntsinger, C. S., 259
Hurley, E. A., 46, 303
Hursh, D., 401
Husman, J., 209, 225
Huston, A. C., 336
Hutchinson, J. M., 125, 343
Hutt, C., 172
Hutt, S. J., 172
Huttenlocher, J., 154
Huttenlocher, P. R., 141
Hyde, J. S., 246
Hyman, I., 254, 255, 270, 275, 325, 345, 354, 355
Hymel, S., 223, 254, 266, 277
Hynd, C., 37, 38, 51, 91, 154, 192, 222

Iacono, W. G., 330
Iadicola, P., 345
Ialongo, N. S., 350
Ibarra, R. A., 76
Igoa, C., 76, 219, 313
Illushin, L., 211
Immordino-Yang, M. H., 146, 148
Inagaki, K., 31, 46, 69, 104, 301, 303, 312
Inglehart, M., 228
Inglis, A., 5, 175, 307, 308, 309
Inhelder, B., 136, 148, 154
Inman, W. E., 294
Inzlicht, M., 219
Irujo, S., 75, 315
Irvine, J. J., 163, 164
Irving, M. A., 325
Ispa, J. M., 239, 259
Ittel, A., 262
Ittenbach, R. F., 169
Ivie, C., 87
Iyengar, S. S., 191, 208, 211
Izard, C., 252
Izard, C. E., 209, 251

Jackson, D., III, 210
Jacob, B. A., 402
Jacobs, J. E., 197, 198, 208, 224, 242, 385
Jacobs, J. K., 266
Jacobs, J. W., 36
Jacobs, P. J., 58
Jacobson, K. C., 255
Jacobson, L., 226
Jaffee, S. R., 268
Jagacinski, C. M., 200
Janos, P. M., 168
Jansen, B. A., 304
Janssens, D., 152
Jarrett, O. S., 345
Jarvis, P. A., 274
Jarvis, W. B. G., 163, 187
Jasiobedzka, U., 256, 262
Jegede, O. J., 47
Jenkins, Z. N., 255
Jenlink, C. L., 264, 268
Jernigan, T. L., 141
Jetton, T. L., 43
Jiang, D., 255
Jigjidsuren, D., 95
Jimerson, S., 79, 354
Johanning, D. I., 122
Johnsen, T. B., 386
Johnson, C. A., 276
Johnson, C. I., 36
Johnson, D. W., 228, 271, 301, 303, 304, 305, 312
Johnson, H. C., 270
Johnson, J. T., 47
Johnson, K. E., 112, 147, 155, 195, 208
Johnson, L., 59, 351
Johnson, M. H., 24, 140, 141
Johnson, R., 271
Johnson, R. E., 386
Johnson, R. L., 382
Johnson, R. S., 396, 397, 398, 403
Johnson, R. T., 228, 271, 301, 303, 304, 305, 312
Johnson, W., 330
Johnson-Glenberg, M. C., 34, 175
John-Steiner, V., 67, 176
Johnston, L., 244
Johnstone, M., 329
Jonassen, D. H., 163, 290, 291
Jonen, A., 172, 173
Jones, A., 259
Jones, D., 40
Jones, E. E., 197
Jones, I., 345
Jones, K. M., 351
Jones, L. L., 11
Jones, M. H., 110, 248
Jones, M. S., 48, 130
Jones, V., 322
Jonkmann, K., 248
Jose, P. E., 259
Jovanovic, J., 376
Jozefowicz, D. M., 266
Judy, J. E., 50, 155
Juffer, F., 162
Jussim, L., 226
Juvonen, J., 95, 189, 223, 237, 248, 256, 274, 276, 277, 324, 325, 326

Kagan, J., 139, 219, 238, 259
Kağitçibaşi, Ç., 70, 75, 78, 123, 157, 188, 189, 211, 259, 315, 349
Kahl, B., 131
Kahn, V., 139, 238
Kahne, J. E., 279
Kail, R. V., 147, 161, 169

Kalish, C. W., 31
Kalyuga, S., 316
Kame'enui, E. J., 325
Kameya, L. I., 387
Kamil, M. L., 296
Kane, M. T., 404
Kang, E., 401
Kaplan, A., 76, 121, 164, 198, 199, 200, 201, 217, 242, 303, 325
Kaplan, A. M., 322
Karabenick, S. A., 107, 195
Karau, S. J., 305
Kardash, C. A. M., 101, 105, 120, 123, 124, 129, 163
Karlin, M. B., 31, 32
Karp, J., 268
Karpicke, J. D., 366, 391
Karplus, R., 154
Karpov, Y. V., 144, 172
Karweit, N. L., 268
Kass, R. E., 344
Katayama, A. D., 101
Katchadourian, H., 250, 251
Kato, K., 248
Kato, T., 20
Katz, L., 217
Kauffman, J. M., 63, 169, 343, 344, 345, 346
Kauffman, K. F., 344
Kaufman, C. E., 245, 259
Kavussanu, M., 201
Keating, D. P., 313
Keefe, K., 247, 248
Keil, F. C., 30, 31, 51
Kelemen, D., 75
Kelemen, W. L., 102
Kellam, S. G., 350
Keller, H. R., 341
Keller, M., 257, 262
Kelley, K., 155, 195, 208, 239
Kelley, M. L., 85
Kelley, W. M., 33
Kelly, S., 401
Kelly, S. W., 20
Kemler Nelson, D. G., 31, 142
Kempler, T. M., 190
Kennedy, C. H., 307, 309
Kennedy, R., 381
Keogh, B. K., 139, 167, 169, 239, 264, 325, 330
Kermani, H., 307, 308
Kerns, L. L., 216, 270
Keyes, M. A., 255
Khattri, N., 379
Kiefer, S. M., 255
Kienzl, G., 266
Kiewra, K. A., 42, 101, 123
Killeen, P. R., 48
Killen, M., 95, 261
Kim, D., 192, 243, 325, 326
Kim, H. S., 219, 296
Kim, J., 269
Kim, J. M., 256
Kim, P., 80, 268
Kim-Cohen, J., 269
Kincheloe, J. L., 87, 91
Kindermann, T., 190
Kindermann, T. A., 248, 249
King, A., 69, 102, 122, 124, 131, 303, 308, 309
King, J., 308
King, N. J., 214
King, P. M., 104, 120, 124, 125, 163
Kinney, D., 249
Kintsch, E., 102
Kintsch, W., 101, 102

Kirby, J. R., 294
Kirby, S. N., 80
Kirker, W. S., 33
Kirkland, M. C., 214, 402
Kirkwood, H., 27
Kirschenbaum, R. J., 76, 177
Kirschner, P. A., 31, 172, 173, 294
Kishor, N., 243
Kistner, J. A., 207
Kitayama, S., 70, 349
Kitchener, K. S., 104, 120, 124, 125, 163
Kitsantas, A., 64, 108, 109, 219
Klaczynski, P. A., 148, 242
Klassen, R., 195, 196
Klassen, S., 382
Klebanov, P. K., 162
Klein, P. R., 67
Klein, S., 396
Klein Poelhuis, C. W., 162
Knapp, M. S., 268
Knauth, S., 220
Knight, C. C., 148
Knight, K. M., 217, 241
Knight, S. L., 175
Knighton, B., 46, 88, 123, 130, 217, 272, 288, 292, 329
Knopik, S. N., 160
Knutson, D. J., 79
Kobak, R., 209
Kochanska, G., 110, 257
Kochenderfer-Ladd, B., 254
Kodluboy, D. W., 249, 356, 357
Koedinger, K. R., 296
Koegel, L. K., 351
Koegel, R. L., 351
Koestner, R., 188, 189, 222, 327
Kogan, J. S., 83
Kohlberg, L., 257, 258, 259, 260, 261, 262, 263
Kohler, K. M., 312, 323, 326, 327, 329, 333, 338
Kohlhardt, J., 324, 387
Kolb, B., 141
Kollat, S. H., 241
Köller, O., 246
Koller, S., 257
Koltko-Rivera, M. E., 75
Konishi, C., 254
Koob, A., 23, 24, 104, 141
Koretz, D., 396, 397
Korthagen, F., 10
Koschmann, T., 90, 310
Kosmitzki, C., 259
Kosslyn, S. M., 34, 36
Kounin, J. S., 333
Kovas, Y., 162
Kowalski, P., 386
Kowalski, R. M., 255
Kraft, R., 24
Krajcik, J., 111, 305
Krajcik, J. S., 128, 190
Kramarski, B., 122
Krampen, G., 228, 366
Krapp, A., 193, 195
Kraska, K., 216
Krathwohl, D. R., 289
Krätzig, G. P., 163
Krauss, S., 11
Krebs, D. L., 261, 262
Krebs, N. F., 79
Krishnan, A., 123, 164
Krishnan, K., 122
Kritt, D., 253
Krueger, F., 24

Krueger, J. I., 243
Krug, C., 351
Krumboltz, H. B., 61, 86
Krumboltz, J. D., 61, 86
Ku, Y.-M., 42, 104, 124, 294
Kuczkowski, R., 244
Kuhl, J., 216
Kuhn, D., 51, 68, 104, 105, 120, 121, 123, 129, 141, 151, 152, 154, 162, 163, 164, 172, 178, 211, 285, 301, 310
Kuiper, E., 306
Kuiper, N. A., 33
Kuk, L. S., 242
Kuklinski, M. R., 226, 227
Kulhavy, R. W., 47, 294
Kulik, C. C., 84, 168, 300, 391, 402
Kulik, J. A., 84, 168, 300, 391, 402
Kulikowich, J. M., 36, 195
Kumar, R., 76, 192, 199, 216, 325, 347
Kunter, M., 195
Kunzinger, E. L., III, 36
Kupchik, A., 353
Kurlakowsky, K. D., 216, 232
Kurtines, W. M., 262
Kuyper, H., 196, 208, 243, 326
Kwok, O.-M., 223, 324, 332, 334
Kyle, W. C., 37

Labouvie-Vief, G., 187, 230
Lackaye, T. D., 196
Ladd, G. W., 251, 252, 255, 332
Ladd, H. F., 10
Ladson-Billings, G., 91, 94, 95, 268
LaFromboise, T., 76
La Guardia, J. G., 198, 224, 401
Laird, J., 266
Laird, R. D., 255
Lajoie, S. P., 175
Lake, C., 171, 296, 303
Lake, V. E., 5, 6
Lam, S., 211
Lam, S.-F., 218
LaMay, M. L., 82
Lamb, Shelly, 107
Lambdin, D. V., 377
Lambert, M. C., 296
Lambert, S. F., 216, 232
Lamon, M., 310, 311
Lampe, C., 274
Lampert, M., 90, 301
Landers, D. M., 214
Landesman, S., 169
Landrum, T. J., 63, 343, 344, 345, 346
Lane, K., 221, 341
Langdon, S., 334
Lange, R. E., 168
Langer, D. A., 255
Langer, E. J., 48, 117, 128, 189, 221
Langer, J. A., 12, 164, 227
Lansford, J. E., 239, 349
Lanza, S., 198
La Paro, K. M., 399
Lapsley, D. K., 216, 242
Larkin, J. H., 101, 102
Larkin, S., 131
Larmer, J., 128
Larose, S., 224, 337
Larrivee, B., 11
Larsen, E., 379
Larson, G., 113
Larson, R. W., 190, 191, 192, 216, 221, 222, 250, 268
Latham, G. P., 107, 190, 200, 225
Lau, S., 200
Lauer, K. D., 104

Laupa, M., 256, 262
Laursen, B., 247, 252
Lave, J., 66, 176
Lawton, S. C., 148
Lawton, T. A., 403
Laychak, A. E., 247
Layer, S. A., 189
Lazar, N. A., 147
Lazerwitz, B., 315
Leadbeater, B. J., 270, 276
Leaper, C., 244, 246, 248, 385
Learning First Aliance, 354
LeCompte, M., 75, 92, 211, 349
LeCount, J., 296
Lee, C. D., 76
Lee, D. L., 329
Lee, J., 401
Lee, J.-S., 79, 336
Lee, K., 115
Lee, O., 75, 95
Lee, S. W., 386
Lee, V. E., 267, 322
Lee-Pearce, M. L., 268, 313
Leevers, H., 163
LeFevre, J., 48
LeForgee, M. H., 160
Legault, L., 192
Leggett, E. L., 206
Legters, N., 401
Lehman, S., 193, 194
Lehmann, M., 36
Leibham, M. E., 155, 195, 208
Leinhardt, G., 127, 301, 316
Lejuez, C. W., 59
Lemerise, E. A., 254, 263
Lemery-Calfant, K., 110
Lennon, M. C., 80
Lennon, R., 257, A-2
Lenroot, R. K., 141
Lens, W., 76, 190, 198, 211
Lentz, F. E., 344
Lenz, B. K., 294
LePage, P., 10
Lepper, M. R., 191, 192, 208, 211, 217, 222
Lerman, D. C., 345, 346
Lerner, R. M., 151
Lesgold, A. M., 33, 45
Lester, F. K., Jr., 377, 381
Lester, J. C., 296
Leu, D. J., 175, 306, 307
Leu, J., 219
Levendosky, A. A., 269
Levin, J. R., 33, 48, 104, 130, 294
Levin, M. E., 48
Levine, D. U., 333
Levitt, J. L., 237
Levitt, M. J., 237, 247
Levstik, L. S., 171, 217
Levy, I., 200, 303
Levy, S. R., 93
Lewis, C., 336
Lewis, J. T., 354
Lewis, M., 209, 246, 257, 262
Lewis, T. J., 333
Lezotte, L. W., 333
Li, J., 123, 157, 211, 315, 387
Li, S., 369
Li, Y., 274
Liben, L. S., 68, 94, 165, 244
Liberman, R. P., 85
Lichtman, J. W., 23
Lickona, T., 325
Lidz, C. S., 168, 381, 403
Lieberman, A. B., 216, 270
Lieberman, M., 260

Lieberman, M. D., 209
Liem, A. D., 200
Liew, J., 110
Lifson, S. A., 402
Light, P., 66, 154
Limber, S. P., 255
Limón, M., 104, 125, 301
Lin, E., 218
Lin, E. K., 332
Lin, M.-H., 110, 257
Lin, X., 102, 122, 139, 154
Lindberg, S. M., 246
Linn, M. C., 45, 69, 113, 114, 126, 130, 154, 155, 173, 246, 301, 303
Linn, R. L., 288, 375, 379, 382, 385, 402
Linnenbrink, E., 193, 213
Linnenbrink, E. A., 61, 200, 201, 223, 228, 229, 324
Linver, M. R., 79, 268
Lipko, A. R., 102, 104
Lippa, R. A., 246, 248, 250
Lipschultz, R. E., 200
Lipson, M. Y., 43
Little, T. D., 198, 224, 254
Liu, G., 246
Liu, H., 248
Liu, L. G., 297
Lo, Y.-Y., 296
Lochman, J. E., 255
Locke, E. A., 107, 190, 200, 225
Lockhart, K. L., 196, 207, 219, 241, 243, 245
Lockheed, M. E., 309
Lodewyk, K. R., 175, 219
Lodico, M. G., 104
Loera, S., 253
Loftus, E. F., 41
Loftus, G. R., 41
Lohman, D. F., 160
Lohman, M. R., 309
Lomawaima, K. T., 75
Long, J. D., 231, 254, 255
Looney, L., 72, 201, 247
Lopez, A. M., 71
López, G. R., 335, 336, 337
Loranger, A. L., 104
Lorch, E. P., 294
Lorch, R. F., Jr., 152, 154, 172, 173, 294
Losey, K. M., 315
Losh, S. C., 75, 123, 157
Losoff, M., 249
Lotan, R. A., 301, 305
Lou, Y., 303, 305, 310
Lovell, K., 151, 154
Lovett, S. B., 104, 294
Lowe, P. A., 386
Loyd, L. K., 223, 324, 332
Lubart, T. I., 115, 117, 131
Lubinski, D., 167, 168
Lucariello, J., 36
Luchins, A. S., 117
Luciana, M., 106, 162
Luckasson, R., 169
Lüdtke, O., 163, 195, 217, 243, 248, 298, 299
Ludwig, J., 211, 259
Ludwin, W. G., 345
Luna, B., 147
Lundeberg, M. A., 365
Luo, W., 223, 324, 332
Lupart, J. L., 168
Lupinetti, C., 255
Lussier, C. M., 381
Luthar, S. S., 80, 96, 324
Lynch, J. H., 247

Lynch, J. P., 356
Lynch, S. L., 196
Lyon, G. R., 53, 78, 316
Lyon, J. E., 332
Lytle, S., 11

Ma, X., 243
Maass, A., 94, 249
Macartney, S. E., 79, 336
Maccoby, E. E., 239, 248, 266
MacDonald, S., 96, 123
Mace, F. C., 125, 329, 343
Macias, S., 125, 268, 299
MacIntyre, P. D., 264
Mac Iver, D., 189, 198
Mac Iver, D. J., 58, 197, 295, 330, 364, 390, 395
MacKenzie-Keating, S., 344
MacLean, D. J., 313
Maclin, D., 37, 125, 150
MacMaster, K., 264
MacMillan, D. L., 167, 169
Macrae, C. N., 33
Madden, N. A., 268
Madison, S. M., 227
Madon, S., 226
Maehr, M. L., 190, 200, 201, 223, 225, 228, 229, 231, 247, 364
Magill, R. A., 64
Magnuson, D., 271
Magnuson, K. A., 79
Magnusson, S. J., 380
Mahapatra, M., 259
Mahn, H., 67
Mahoney, J. L., 274, 278
Maier, M. A., 200, 224
Maier, S., 207
Maikovich, A. K., 268
Main, S. R., 58, 295, 330, 364
Maker, C. J., 168, 177
Makris, E., 220
Malanchuk, O., 197, 208, 385
Maldonado, H., 173
Mallick, K., 163
Malti, T., 257, 263
Mandara, J., 259
Mandell, C., 329
Mandler, J. M., 29
Mangels, J. A., 200, 205
Mansel, J., 246
Mantzicopoulos, P. Y., 79
Mantzicopoulos, Y., 217
Marachi, R., 226, 227
Marchand, G., 109, 110, 190, 324
Marcia, J. E., 242, 245
Marcovitch, S., 106
Marcus, G., 120, 212
Marcus, R. F., 255
Mareschal, D., 23, 140
Margalit, M., 196
Margolis, J. A., 36
Margonis, F., 75
Maria, K., 37
Marini, Z., 148, 154, 157
Markell, M., 249
Markham, T., 128
Marks, H. M., 127
Marks, M. B., 123, 130
Marks, P. E. L., 251
Markus, H. R., 68, 72, 246
Marley, S. C., 33, 36
Marsh, E. J., 366
Marsh, H. W., 188, 197, 201, 217, 240, 241, 243, 245, 275
Marshall, H. H., 46
Martens, B. K., 329

Martin, A. J., 188, 189, 197, 218, 228, 247, 274
Martin, C. L., 244, 248, 254
Martin, J. A., 266
Martin, J. M., 246
Martin, S. S., 58
Martin, T., 164, 171, 173
Martin, V. L., 131
Martinez-Pons, M., 196
Martinez-Torteya, C., 269, 270
Marx, R. W., 190, 305
Marzano, R. J., 324
Mashoodh, R., 140, 270
Maslow, A. H., 187
Mason, C., 246
Mason, C. A., 169
Mason, L., 37, 102, 105, 163, 188, 193, 200, 212, 301
Massa, L. J., 163
Massey, D., 110
Massialas, B. G., 131
Masten, A. S., 80, 269, 324
Mastergeorge, A. M., 304
Masters, J. C., 61
Mastin, M., 325
Mastropieri, M. A., 48, 78, 395
Masuda, A., 59
Mata, J., 262
Matjasko, J. L., 268, 274, 278
Matthews, D. J., 167
Matthews, G., 163, 214, 240, 252
Matthews, J. S., 110
Matthews, K. A., 255
Matusov, E., 90
Matute-Bianchi, M. E., 70
Maxmell, D., 345
Mayer, E. V., 61
Mayer, J. D., 252
Mayer, R. E., 25, 33, 47, 48, 113, 116, 163, 172, 293, 294, 296, 366
Mayeux, L., 251
Mayfield, K. H., 128
Mazur, J. E., 83
McAlpine, L., 313, 315
McAshan, H. H., 285
McBrien, J. L., 76, 251
McCabe, A., 157, 315
McCaffrey, D., 396
McCall, C., 126
McCall, R. B., 267
McCallum, R. S., 161, 247
McCandliss, B. D., 24
McCarthy, M. R., 78
McCartney, K., 82, 140, 324, 332
McCaslin, M., 46, 111, 126, 201, 303
McClarty, K. L., 217
McClintic-Gilberg, M. S., 191, 200
McClowry, S. G., 344
McClure, J., 191, 364
McCollam, T., 248
McComas, J. J., 59, 62, 351
McCombs, B. L., 3, 198, 200, 224
McCormick, C. B., 95
McCourt, F., 57, 217, 259
McCrudden, M. T., 104, 124
McCutchen, D., 48
McDaniel, L., 87
McDaniel, M., 163
McDaniel, M. A., 41, 101, 294
McDermott, K. B., 40
McDevitt, M., 313
McDevitt, T. M., 5, 6, 138, 211, 245
McDonald, K. A., 251
McDougall, P., 223, 266
McElhaney, K. B., 252
McFadden, K. E., 71, 79, 211, 259, 349

McGee, K. D., 175
McGee, L. M., 301
McGoey, K. E., 307
McGovern, M. L., 268
McGrath, E. P., 332
McGraw, A. P., 209
McGregor, H. A., 199, 200, 201, 224
McGrew, K. S., 159, 160
McGue, M., 330
McGuire, D. J., 169
McHale, S. M., 208, 244
McInerney, D. M., 189, 201, 202, 223, 240, 247
McKerchar, P. M., 351
McKown, C., 219
McLane, J. B., 138
McLaren, J., 194
McLaughlin, M. W., 259
McLeod, D. B., 210
McLoyd, V. C., 79, 80, 96, 162, 168, 211, 225, 239, 334, 336
McMillan, J. H., 217, 269
McNally, R. J., 213
McNamara, D. S., 296
McNamara, E., 350
McNamee, G. D., 138
McNaughton, S., 96
McNeil, N. M., 151, 172, 173, 201
McTighe, J., 285, 288, 316
McTigue, E., 110
McVerry, J. G., 306
Meadows, N., 255
Meckstroth, E. A., 167
Medin, D. L., 75, 94
Meece, J. L., 199, 200, 214, 220, 221, 225, 297
Meehan, B. T., 223, 354
Mehan, H., 315, 331, 332
Meichenbaum, D., 108, 110, 175, 273, 307
Meister, C., 131, 175
Mejía-Arauz, R., 75
Mejía Arauz, R., 315
Mellers, B. A., 209
Meltzer, L., 53, 100, 104, 109, 110, 111, 118, 122, 125, 130, 131, 385, 389
Meltzoff, A. N., 253
Mendoza-Denton, R., 239, 240
Menéndez, R., 268
Menke, D. J., 193
Menon, M., 243, 255
Menyuk, D., 315
Menyuk, P., 315
Menzer, M. M., 247, 259
Mercado, M., 95
Mercer, L. K., 126
Mergendoller, J. R., 128
Merrill, P. F., 175, 296
Mertler, C. A., 11
Merzenich, M. M., 24, 141
Mesquita, B., 219
Messer, S. B., 178
Messick, S., 162, 163, 382, 403
Messina, R., 90
Mestas, M., 202
Mettetal, G., 250
Metz, K. E., 151, 154
Metzger, M. J., 120, 129
Mevarech, Z. R., 122
Meyer, C. A., 396, 398
Meyer, D. K., 121, 128, 200, 209, 214, 216, 220, 225, 323, 394
Meyer, E. J., 250, 254, 275
Meyer, F., 247
Meyer, H. A., 190, 354
Meyer, K. A., 62, 84

Meyer, L. H., 191, 201, 364
Meyer, R. D., 112
Middleton, M. J., 46, 200, 201, 216, 225
Midgley, C., 46, 108, 188, 189, 197, 198, 199, 200, 201, 202, 211, 216, 225, 226, 231, 232
Mikaelsen, B., 87
Miles, S., 325
Miles, S. B., 354
Miller, A., 163, 324, 330, 348, 387
Miller, B. C., 250
Miller, C. L., 276
Miller, D. L., 85
Miller, F. K., 313
Miller, G. A., 28, 139
Miller, J. G., 157, 259, 260
Miller, K. F., 267
Miller, L. S., 75, 79
Miller, M. D., 288, 375, 385, 393, 403
Miller, P. A., 263
Miller, P. H., 35, 104, 147, 253
Miller, R. B., 107, 109
Miller, S. A., 35, 104, 147, 253
Miller, S. C., 386
Miller, S. D., 110, 220, 225
Miller, T. R., 303
Millham, J., 391
Mills, B., 242
Mills, G. E., 11
Milner, H. R., 223
Miltenberger, R. G., 64, 344
Mimms-Cox, J. S., 396
Mims, V., 222
Minami, M., 157, 315
Mindel, C. H., 315
Mineka, S., 209
Minsky, M., 118, 209
Minstrell, J., 38, 173, 297, 301
Mintrop, H., 401, 402
Mintzes, J. J., 101
Mischel, W., 239, 240
Mistry, R. S., 336
Mitchell, C. M., 245, 259
Mitchell, D. B., 34
Mitchell, K. J., 255, 274
Mitchell, M., 194
Mitrani, M., 296
Mitts, B., 343
Miyake, N., 311
Mizuta, I., 219
Moallem, M., 307, 308
Mody, M., 53
Mohajeri-Nelson, N., 251
Mohan, E., 71
Mohatt, G., 47, 315
Mohler, L., 39
Moje, E. B., 92, 93, 303
Molden, D. C., 206, 225
Moles, O. C., 345, 346
Moll, L. C., 192
Moller, A. C., 187, 188, 192, 198, 222, 224, 228
Möller, K., 172, 173
Monczunski, L., 401
Moneta, G., 216
Monte-Sano, C., 129, 172
Moon, J., 119, 120, 121, 123, 128, 129
Moon, S. M., 168
Mooney, C. M., 22
Moore, C. F., 79
Moore, J. W., 58, 330
Moore, P. J., 294
Moore, S., 64, 204
Moran, S., 167
Morelli, G. A., 123, 211, 219
Moreno, R., 47, 173, 293, 294, 296
Morey, C. C., 27

Morgan, M., 84, 125, 391
Morgan, P. L., 325
Morgenstern, M., 218
Morra, S., 148, 149, 150, 154, 157
Morris, D., 195
Morris, M. W., 76
Morris, P. A., 77
Morrison, D. A., 270
Morrison, F., 223, 324, 402
Morrison, F. J., 110, 267
Morrison, G., 125, 268, 299
Morrison, G. M., 354
Morrison, R. L., 354
Morrow, S. L., 250
Mortiz, S. E., 60, 84
Moshman, D., 109, 124
Moskowitz, J. T., 230
Mostow, A. J., 251
Motzoi, C., 247
Mouchiroud, C., 115, 117, 131
Mrkonjic, J., 48
Müeller, K. J., 188, 191, 199
Mueller, M. M., 351
Ni, Y., 112
Muis, K. R., 100, 104, 105, 107, 124, 131
Müller, U., 106
Munn, P., 329, 340
Munro, D. W., 296
Munro, S., 170
Murdock, T. B., 79, 226, 324, 332, 387
Murphy, B., 253
Murphy, H. A., 344
Murphy, P. K., 37, 90, 102, 163, 200, 225, 301
Murray, B. J., 254, 255, 276
Murray-Close, D., 251
Muyeed, A. Z., 269, 324
Myers, L. J., 68, 165
Myerson, J., 61
Myles, B. S., 270, 331

Nagle, R., 277
Naglieri, J., 143
Najafi, B., 75
Nakamoto, J., 255
Nakamura, J., 190, 191, 220
Narvaez, D., 139, 261
Narváez, D., 257, 263
Nasir, N. S., 259
Nastasi, B. K., 69, 301
Nathan, M., 246
Nation, J. R., 79
National Association of Secondary School Principals (NASSP), 386
National Center for Education Statistics, 354
National Council on Measurement in Education, 369
National Research Council, 3, 11
Nau, P., 344
NCSS Task Force on Ethnic Studies Curriculum Guidelines, 71, 93
Neale, D. C., 11
Nebelsick-Gullet, L., 126
Neel, R. S., 255
Neisser, U., 21, 156, 159, 160, 162, 167, 168, 177
Neitzel, C., 111
Nell, V., 242, 243, 245
Nelson, B., 221
Nelson, C. A., 24, 79, 141
Nelson, K., 68, 143
Nelson, R., 341
Nelson, T. O., 102
Nelson-Barber, S., 93
Nesbit, J. C., 101
Nesdale, D., 94, 249

Nettles, S. M., 79
Neubauer, G., 246
Neuman, Y., 69, 301
Neumann, C., 162
Nevin, J. A., 329
Newby, T. J., 294
Newcomb, A. F., 251
Newcombe, N., 154
Newcomer, L. L., 333
Newgent, R. A., 276
Newkirk, T., 330
Newman, L. S., 36
Newman, R. S., 108, 200, 254, 255, 276
Newman, S. E., 123, 176
Newman-Carlson, D., 275
Newmann, F. M., 129, 379, 381
Newstead, S., 53
Ng, E. L., 115
Ng, S. F., 115
Ng, Y.-L., 218
Ni, Y., 112
Nicholls, J. G., 200, 205, 206, 228
Nichols, C. W., 202
Nichols, J. D., 303, 345
Nichols, K. E., 110, 257
Nichols, S. L., 226, 348
Nickerson, R. S., 379
Nie, Y., 200
Niesz, T., 93, 95, 277
Niggli, A., 163, 298, 299
Ningiuruvik, L., 315
Nippold, M. A., 139
Nisbett, R. E., 156, 159, 162, 168, 177, 211, 219, 401
Nishina, A., 256
Nixon, A. S., 306, 388
No, S., 259
Noar, S., 187
Noble, K. G., 79
Nokes, J. D., 102, 122
Nolen, S. B., 107, 195, 200, 208
Noonan, M., 353
Nordby, C. J., 126
Norenzayan, A., 157, 163, 164, 219
Noret, N., 256
Norman, G. R., 379
Norris, K., 219
North Carolina Department of Public Instruction, 287, 372
Noss, R., 310
Notaro, P. C., 259
Novak, J. D., 33, 101, 102, 313
Ntoumanis, N., 221
Nucci, L., 256, 261, 262, 266, 325, 327, 344
Nucci, L. P., 256, 259, 260, 262, 263, 266, 278, 345, 346
Nucci, M. S., 256
Nuemi, J.-W., 245, 246
Nurmi, J.-E., 237, 247
Nussbaum, E. M., 69, 129, 131, 301
Nussbaum, J., 37
Nystrand, M., 164

Oakes, J., 226
Oakland, T. D., 72
Oberheim, N. A., 23, 24
Oberman, G. L., 402
O'Brien, M., 226
O'Byrne, W. I., 306
O'Campo, P. J., 79
Ochs, E., 315
Ochsner, K. N., 209
O'Connor, E., 324, 332
O'Connor, J. E., 338
Odgers, C. L., 268

O'Donnell, A. M., 131, 301, 303, 305, 307
O'Donnell, D. A., 269, 324
O'Donnell, J., 59
Ogbu, J. U., 76, 167, 232, 259, 268, 277, 315
Öhman, A., 209
Okagaki, L., 75, 349
Okamoto, Y., 144
O'Kelly, J., 303, 305
Olajide, J. O., 47
Oldfather, P., 202
O'Leary, K. D., 344
O'Leary, S. G., 344
Oligny, P., 254
Olivárez, A., 168
Ollendick, T. H., 214
Olneck, M. R., 277
O'Loughlin, M., 51
Olsen, J. A., 239
Olson, R. K., 296
Olthof, T., 243
O'Malley, C., 308
O'Mara, A. J., 240, 243, 245
O'Neal, K. K., 79
O'Neil, H. F., 386
Onosko, J. J., 129
Oppenheimer, L., 253
Orasanu, J. M., 113
O'Reilly, M. F., 270
Orenstein, P., 245
Ormrod, J. E., 5, 6, 138, 168, 169, 245, 350, A-2
Ormrod, J. S., 225, 289
Ormrod, R. K., 37, 354
Ornstein, P. A., 33, 36, 68
Ornstein, R., 24
Orobio de Castro, B., 243
Orpinas, P., 275
Ortiz, C., 64
Ortiz, S. O., 160
Ortony, A., 29
Osana, H. P., 130
Osborne, J. W., 219
Osgood, D. W., 198, 244
Osher, D., 354, 355, 356
Oskamp, S., 95, 277
Osterman, K. F., 325, 326
Osterman, L. L., 255
Otis, N., 191, 198, 208, 224, 232
O'Toole, M. E., 356
Owens, R. E., Jr., 139, 151, 154, 244, 315
Oyserman, D., 259

Pachan, M. K., 279, 309
Paciello, M., 255
Padilla, A. M., 76, 403
Páez, M., 403
Paget, K. F., 253
Page-Voth, V., 225
Pahl, K., 259
Paikoff, R. L., 250
Paivio, A., 34, 47
Pajares, F., 64, 84, 195, 196, 218, 219, 225, 240, 243, 246
Pakurar, K., 323
Paley, V. G., 189, 208
Palincsar, A. S., 68, 69, 123, 131, 172, 174, 175, 303, 305, 309, 313
Pallay, A., 316
Palmer, D. J., 173, 205
Pan, J., 123, 211
Pang, V. O., 95, 219, 349
Pannozzo, G. M., 305
Paolitto, D. P., 260
Pape, S. J., 5, 6, 348

Pappas, S., 171
Paquette, J. A., 252
Parada, R. H., 275
Paris, A. H., 110, 111, 124, 126, 130, 377, 379
Paris, S. G., 110, 111, 124, 125, 126, 130, 192, 204, 207, 241, 267, 365, 366, 377, 379, 389, 403
Park, K., 247
Park, S.-H., 104, 105, 123, 211
Parke, R. D., 346
Parker, J. G., 241
Parker, W. D., 168
Parkhurst, J. T., 201, 251
Parks, C. P., 249
Pascual-Leone, J., 260
Pashler, H., 34, 163, 366
Pasternack, J. F., 257
Pastorelli, C., 256, 276
Patall, E. A., 221, 298, 299
Patnode, M., 346, 351
Patrick, H., 5, 6, 61, 189, 192, 195, 200, 201, 208, 217, 223, 229, 303, 322, 324, 325
Pattee, L., 251
Patterson, C. J., 250, 251
Patterson, M. L., 375
Patton, J. R., 169, 170
Paulson, F. L., 387, 396, 398
Paulson, P. R., 396, 398
Paus, T., 141
Paxton, R. J., 45, 105, 130
Pea, R. D., 131, 164, 173
Pearson, D., 126
Pearson, P. D., 77, 101
Pease, M., 129, 152, 154, 172, 301, 310
Pedersen, S., 251
Pederson, S., 248
Peeke, L. A., 246
Peets, K., 275, 276
Pekrun, R., 200, 205, 209, 210, 213, 217, 228, 230
Pellegrini, A. D., 42, 53, 170, 231, 247, 248, 250, 254, 255, 274, 332, 345, 354, 399
Pelletier, J., 104, 105, 253
Pelletier, L., 192
Pelletier, L. G., 191, 208
Pellicer, L. O., 267, 268
Pelphrey, K. A., 78, 270
Peng, K., 157, 219
Penner, B. D., 115, 155
Penny, J. A., 382
Pepler, D., 255
Pereira, L., 334
Pérez, B., 277, 336
Perfetti, C. A., 48
Perkins, D. N., 100, 104, 112, 113, 120, 121, 128, 130, 131, 162, 163, 164, 167, 177, 178
Perkins, S. A., 261
Perner, J., 253
Perry, D. G., 220, 346
Perry, L. C., 346
Perry, M., 376
Perry, N. E., 111, 125, 126, 391
Perry, R. P., 209
Person, N. K., 307
Peter, J., 255, 274
Peter, K., 353
Petersen, A., 246
Peterson, A. C., 249
Peterson, C., 189, 196, 206, 207, 230
Peterson, L. R., 27
Peterson, M. J., 27
Peterson, R. F., 58

Petrie, S., 189, 249
Petrill, S. A., 162
Petrosky, A. R., 389
Petterson, S. M., 336
Pettit, G. S., 238, 239, 255, 269, 349
Pettito, A. L., 146
Petty, R. E., 163, 187
Peverly, S. T., 101, 112
Pfeifer, J. H., 95, 277
Pfeifer, L. J., 344
Pfeifer, M., 238
Pfiffner, L. J., 344
Phalet, K., 76, 211
Phelan, P., 76, 201, 214, 223, 251
Phelps, E. A., 213
Phelps, L., 168
Phillips, A. T., 253
Phillips, B. N., 386
Phillips, D., 243
Phillips, G., 96
Phinney, J., 259
Phinney, J. S., 244
Piaget, J., 136, 142, 145, 150, 154, 261
Pianta, R. C., 223, 267, 313, 322, 324, 325, 332, 399, 402
Piazza, C. C., 83, 277
Pickens, J., 309
Piehler, T. F., 247
Piirto, J., 168
Pillow, B. H., 120
Pintrich, P. R., 5, 6, 37, 69, 84, 100, 102, 105, 108, 122, 190, 193, 200, 201, 205, 213, 218, 220, 242
Pitcher, G. D., 386
Pittman, T. S., 188
Platsidou, M., 106
Plemons, B. W., 267
Plomin, R., 82, 140, 162, 264
Plowman, T. S., 268, 313
Plucker, J. A., 114, 164
Pluess, M., 239
Plumert, J. M., 36
Polikoff, M. S., 401, 402
Pollack, W. S., 246
Pollak, S. D., 213, 230
Pollica, L. S., 104, 385
Pollini, S., 104
Pelletier, J., 104, 105, 253
Polman, L. L., 128
Pomerantz, E. M., 211
Pomeroy, E., 324
Pomery, E. A., 187, 243
Ponitz, C. C., 110
Poole, D., 379
Popham, W. J., 288, 378, 383, 387, 397, 398, 402
Porat, D. A., 38
Porter, A. C., 114, 401, 402
Portes, P. R., 267, 313
Posner, G. J., 51
Posner, M. I., 24, 42, 141
Post, T. A., 115, 155
Poteat, V. P., 256
Potenza, M. T., 126
Potter, E. F., 47
Poulin, F., 254
Poulson, C. L., 64, 125
Powell, S., 221
Power, F. C., 261
Powers, C. J., 273
Powers, L. E., 87
Prawat, R. S., 46, 102, 122, 130
Preckel, F., 213
Premack, D., 60
Presseisen, B. Z., 90
Pressley, M., 35, 36, 48, 69, 104, 107, 122, 123, 124, 130, 131, 205, 227, 301

Preston, R. V., 377
Pribram, K. H., 141
Price-Williams, D. R., 157
Pritchard, R., 43
Prochnow, J. E., 241
Proctor, B. E., 160
Proctor, R. W., 34, 40, 50, 155
Pruitt, R. P., 129
Pugh, K. J., 113, 200
Pullen, P. C., 169
Pulos, S., 37, 130, 152, 154, 155
Purcell-Gates, V., 315
Purdie, N., 105, 122, 123
Putnam, R. T., 11, 327
Putwain, D. W., 386

Qian, G., 123, 211
Qin, L., 211
Qin, Z., 303
Quellmalz, E., 380
Quilitch, H. R., 58
Quinn, P. C., 29, 142
Quintana, C., 111
Quintana, S. M., 93

Raber, S. M., 267
Rabinowitz, M., 11, 148, 155, 168, 333
Radke-Yarrow, M., 262
Radziszewska, B., 68
Ragsdale, B. L., 259
Raine, A., 163, 187, 255
Rakow, E. A., 102
Ramey, C., 169
Ramey, C. T., 267, 268
Ramey, S. L., 267, 268
Ramirez, M., 157
Ramos, J. F., 248
Ramsden, P., 200
Ramsey, P. G., 93, 95, 277
Raphael, T. E., 69, 90, 301
Raphaelson, Y. E., 255
Rappaport, N., 355
Rapport, M. D., 344
Rasch, B., 24
Rasp, L. M., 86
Ratelle, C. F., 224
Raudenbush, S. W., 11, 12, 144, 226
Rausch, M. K., 345
Raver, C. C., 80
Ravitz, J., 128
Rawson, K. A., 101, 102
Rawsthorne, L. J., 200, 201
Raz, G., 296
Reder, L. M., 50, 67, 112, 128
Redfield, D. L., 297
Reed, D. F., 269
Reed, J. H., 195, 221
Rees, E., 155
Reese, L., 75
Reeve, J., 187, 188, 189, 191, 192, 198, 221, 222, 224, 225, 267
Reeve, R., 90
Reeves, A., 24
Régner, I., 199, 201, 219
Reid, R., 125, 126
Reijntjes, A., 243
Reimer, J., 260, 261, 278
Reiner, M., 31
Reinking, D., 175
Reisberg, D., 25, 27, 41, 212, 213
Reiser, M., 110, 332
Reiter, S. N., 129
Renkl, A., 101, 102, 293
Renninger, K. A., 190, 192, 193, 194, 195, 208, 209, 217
Renshaw, P. D., 251
Renzaglia, A., 309

Renzulli, J. S., 168
Resnick, D. P., 379
Resnick, L. B., 31, 40, 66, 116, 379
Resnick, M. D., 326
Rest, J., 139, 257, 261, 263
Reuman, D., 189, 198
Reuman, D. A., 58, 295, 330, 364
Reusser, K., 116
Reyna, C., 226
Reyna, V. F., 21, 40, 187, 242, 243
Reynolds, A. J., 402
Reynolds, C., 163, 187
Reynolds, C. R., 118
Reynolds, R. E., 21, 43, 77, 102, 124, 294
Reys, B. J., 303
Rhodes, B., 164, 178
Rhodes, M., 246
Rhodewalt, F., 188, 197, 203, 204
Ricciuti, H. N., 162
Richards, A. C., 214
Richards, F., 214
Richards, J. M., 230
Richards, M. H., 216, 259
Richter, M., 333
Rickman, M., 238
Riding, R. J., 163
Riggs, J. M., 197
Rijlaarsdam, G., 43, 64
Rimm, D. C., 61
Rimm, S. B., 168
Ripple, R. E., 114
Risemberg, R., 111
Ritchhart, R., 104, 120, 121, 131, 162, 163, 178
Rittenhouse, P., 90, 301
Rittle-Johnson, B., 130, 294, 295
Ritts, V., 375
Rittschof, K. A., 47
Rivers, I., 256
Rizza, M. G., 216
Robbins, P., 66
Robelia, B., 245, 274
Roberts, G. C., 201
Roberts, L. C., 75
Roberts, R. D., 163, 214, 240, 252
Roberts, T., 24
Roberts, T. A., 315
Roberts, V., 327
Roberts, W., 325
Robertson, B., 207
Robins, R. W., 241, 245
Robinson, C. W., 163
Robinson, D. H., 101, 123
Robinson, D. R., 307, 308
Robinson, E. J., 151
Robinson, J. C., 298
Robinson, N. M., 168
Robinson, S. L., 58, 330
Robinson, T. E., 141
Robinson, T. R., 273
Roblyer, M. D., 296
Rocks, J., 113
Roderick, M., 1, 7, 8, 216, 232
Rodriguez, T., 253
Roediger, H. L., III, 40, 366, 391
Roehler, L. R., 101
Roeser, R. W., 227
Roeyers, H., 130
Rogers, C. R., 326
Rogers, T. B., 33
Rogoff, B., 11, 68, 70, 71, 75, 90, 91, 92, 93, 94, 95, 123, 151, 168, 175, 176, 211, 259, 315, 349, 376
Rohrbeck, C. A., 303
Rohrer, D., 34, 163, 366
Rohrkemper, M. M., 221

Ronning, R. R., 118
Roosa, M. W., 79
Root, M. P. P., 71
Rortvedt, A. K., 344
Roscoe, R. D., 46, 307
Rose, A. J., 216, 247, 248, 251, 254, 255
Rosenberg, J. L., 64
Rosenshine, B., 131, 175, 294, 295, 313, 316
Rosenthal, H., 110
Rosenthal, R., 226, 243, 328
Rosenthal, T. L., 86
Ross, G., 175
Ross, J. A., 221
Ross, M., 123, 143
Ross, N. O., 75, 94
Ross, S. W., 275, 334, 354
Rosser, R., 154
Rotenberg, K. J., 61
Roth, J. L., 403
Roth, K. J., 37, 45, 176
Rothbart, M. K., 24, 42, 139, 141, 163, 238, 264
Rothbaum, F., 123, 211, 219, 230, 239
Rotteveel, M., 212
Rouder, J. N., 28
Rousseau, E. W., 297
Rovee-Collier, C., 190
Rowe, D. C., 255
Rowe, M. B., 47
Rozalski, M. E., 357
Rubin, K. H., 239, 247, 251, 259, 274
Ruble, D. N., 244
Rude, H. A., 64
Rudman, M. K., 336
Rudolph, K. D., 188, 189, 190, 216, 219, 232, 243
Rudy, D., 239, 259
Rueda, R., 192
Ruef, M. B., 346, 351
Rueger, D. B., 85
Ruffman, T., 271
Rumberger, R. W., 266, 267, 354
Rumelhart, D. E., 29
Rumsey, S., 46
Runco, M. A., 114, 115, 118
Rushton, J. P., 64, 261, 262, 266, 277
Russell, S. L., 270
Rust, F., 364
Ruthren, A. J., 85
Rutland, A., 95
Ryan, A. M., 108, 189, 195, 197, 199, 200, 202, 206, 211, 219, 223, 247, 248, 255, 322, 324, 325
Ryan, K., 278
Ryan, K. E., 206, 219
Ryan, M. K., 64
Ryan, R. M., 187, 188, 189, 191, 195, 198, 214, 220, 221, 222, 224, 228, 244, 247, 327, 365, 402
Ryce, P., 76, 95

Saarni, C., 240
Sabers, D. S., 323, 338
Sadker, D., 376
Sadker, M. P., 376
Sadoski, M., 34, 47
Salend, S. J., 336, 348, 349
Säljö, R., 66
Salk, S., 210
Salmivalli, C., 275, 276
Salomon, G., 68, 113, 164, 178
Salovey, P., 252
Samarapungavan, A., 217
Sameoto, D., 344
Samuels, M., 206

Sanchez, F., 357
Sanders, C. E., 399
Sanders, M. G., 61, 268, 336
Sanders, S., 193
Sandler, 336
Sandler, H. M., 241
Santangelo, T., 64, 109
Santisi, M., 50
Sapolsky, R. M., 24
Sapon-Shevin, M., 325
Sarama, J., 171
Sarason, I. G., 214
Sarason, S. B., 214, 216
Sarlo, N., 143
Sasse, D. K., 313
Sasso, G. M., 64
Satlow, E., 107
Sattler, J. M., 159, 161
Saudino, K. J., 264
Saults, J. S., 27
Saunders, J., 205
Savelsbergh, E. R., 190
Savin-Williams, R. C., 250
Sawalani, G. M., 254
Sawyer, R. J., 64
Sawyer, R. K., 114
Sax, G., 387, 391, 402
Scarborough, H. S., 315
Scardamalia, M., 68, 90, 91, 104, 310, 311
Scarpati, S. E., 369
Scarr, S., 82, 140, 162, 239
Scerbo, A., 255
Scevak, J. J., 294
Schaal, D. W., 59
Schacter, D. L., 40, 41, 212
Schallert, D. L., 20, 21, 195, 209
Schank, R. C., 90, 194
Schaps, E., 192, 333
Schartz, M., 125, 126
Schatschneider, C. W., 104
Schauble, L., 154, 190, 191
Scheier, M. F., 206, 210
Scher, M. S., 294
Schermerhorn, A. C., 268
Scheuermann, B., 126
Schiefele, U., 80, 110, 191, 196, 200, 209, 225
Schiever, S. W., 168, 177
Schilling, H. E. H., 366
Schimmoeller, M. A., 143
Schlaefli, A., 261
Schliemann, A. D., 154
Schmid, S., 110, 299
Schmidt, A. C., 189
Schmidt, L. A., 239
Schmidt, R. A., 113
Schmitt-Rodermund, E., 246
Schneider, B., 329
Schneider, W., 33, 36, 102, 108, 110, 131, 205
Schnyder, I., 163, 298, 299
Schoener, J., 296
Schoenfeld, A. H., 115
Schofield, J. W., 277, 278, 306, 307
Scholes, R. J., 120, 124, 129, 163
Schommer, M., 102, 104, 105, 122, 124, 403
Schommer-Aikins, M., 105, 120
Schonert-Reichl, K., 223, 266
School District 6 (Greely/Evans CO), 401
Schoon, I., 269
Schrauben, B., 193
Schraw, G., 29, 104, 109, 124, 126, 193, 194
Schroth, M. L., 126

Schult, C. A., 253
Schultheiss, O. C., 202
Schultz, K., 93, 95, 277, 278
Schulze, S. K., 36, 195
Schumaker, J. B., 48, 294
Schunk, D. H., 64, 84, 105, 107, 109, 195, 196, 204, 205, 206, 208, 218, 219, 220, 225, 240, 243
Schutz, P. A., 201, 324
Schwab-Stone, M. E., 269, 324
Schwager, M. T., 200
Schwartz, D., 255
Schwartz, D. L., 24, 113, 126, 173
Schwarz, B. B., 69, 301
Schwarz, J. C., 239
Scott, B., 112, 147
Scott, J., 341
Scott, K. G., 169
Scottham, K. M., 242, 245
Scruggs, T. E., 48, 53, 78, 395, 402
Searle, K. A., 93, 94, 191, 225, 267
Sears, K. G., 111
Seaton, E. K., 242, 245, 259
Seaton, M., 243
Sedikides, C., 188, 197, 211
Segalowitz, S. J., 21
Segers, M., 128
Seiffge-Krenke, I., 237
Seligman, M., 207
Seligman, M. E. P., 109, 162, 206, 207
Sellers, R. M., 242, 245, 259
Selman, R. L., 253, 271
Semb, G. B., 34
Semin, G. R., 254
Senécal, C., 224
Serbin, L., 268
Seroczynski, A. D., 246
Serpell, R., 45, 335
Sfard, A., 178, 316
Shaffer, D. R., 266
Shanahan, C., 129
Shanahan, T., 102
Shannon, D., 195
Shannon, J. D., 336
Shany, M., 175, 307
Shapiro, A. M., 36, 90
Shapiro, B. K., 169
Shariff, S., 255, 275
Sharot, T., 213
Shaughnessy, M. F., 161
Shavelson, R. J., 381
Shaver, R. B., 160
Shaw, P., 53, 162
Shaw, R., 101
Shaywitz, B. A., 53
Shaywitz, S. E., 53
Sheese, R., 148, 154, 157
Sheets, R. H., 259
Shell, M. M., 224
Shell, R., 263
Shepard, L., 364, 365, 379, 383, 385, 391, 393, 394, 402
Shepard, L. A., 365, 381, 389
Shepardson, D. P., 303
Sheridan, S. M., 348
Sherman, D. K., 188, 219
Sherman, J., 171
Shernoff, D., 329
Shernoff, D. J., 200, 220, 221
Shernoff, E., 329
Shields, P. M., 268
Shiffrin, R. M., 25
Shim, S. S., 199, 211
Shin, D., 58
Shipman, S., 163, 213
Shipman, V. C., 163, 213
Shirey, L. L., 43, 77, 102, 124, 294

Shoda, Y., 239
Shores, M., 195
Shors, T. J., 24
Short, E. J., 104
Shrestha, S., 219
Shrum, W., 249
Shuell, T. J., 300
Shulman, L. S., 11
Shumow, L., 122
Shure, M. B., 273
Shute, V. J., 50, 60, 61, 84, 208, 220, 230, 366, 391
Shutts, K., 143
Shweder, R. A., 259
Shymansky, J. A., 37
Sideridis, G. D., 200
Sieber, J. E., 387
Siegal, M., 271
Siegler, R. S., 35, 45, 96, 102, 122, 130, 139, 149, 154, 171
Siemers, E., 247
Sigman, M., 79, 140
Sigman, M. D., 162
Silbereisen, R. K., 246
Silberman, M. L., 340
Silberstein, C. S., 51
Silverberg, R. P., 325
Silveri, M. M., 141
Silverman, W. K., 386
Silvia, P. J., 193
Simmons, C. M., 219
Simmons, D. C., 307
Simon, H. A., 28, 50, 67, 112, 128
Simonetta, L. G., 217
Simons, J., 198
Simons, R. L., 249
Simonton, D. K., 115, 162
Simpson, R. L., 270, 331
Sinatra, G. M., 37, 69, 94, 102, 105, 121, 163, 188, 200, 212, 301
Singer, D. G., 277
Singer, J. L., 277
Singh, J., 217
Sins, P. H. M., 190, 199, 200
Sireci, S. G., 369
Sirin, S. R., 76, 79, 95
Siu, S., 336, 349
Sizer, T. R., 46
Skaalvik, E., 200
Skaalvik, E. M., 12, 195, 217, 227, 240
Skaalvik, S., 12, 227
Skiba, R. J., 80, 345
Skinner, B. F., 59
Skinner, C. H., 329
Skinner, E., 190, 193, 213, 223
Skinner, E. A., 109, 110, 324
Skopeliti, I., 37
Slade, L., 271
Slater, W. H., 175
Slaughter-Defoe, D. T., 76
Slavin, R. E., 46, 78, 171, 266, 268, 296, 303, 305, 313
Sleeter, C. E., 278
Slonim, M. B., 75
Slotta, J. D., 31
Sloutsky, V. M., 163
Small, M. Y., 294
Smart, L., 255
Smetana, J., 261
Smetana, J. G., 256, 261, 262
Smiley, S. S., 148
Smith, C., 209
Smith, C. L., 37, 90, 125, 150, 154, 296, 301, 302
Smith, D. C., 11
Smith, E. E., 27
Smith, E. L., 55

Smith, E. R., 254
Smith, H. L., 92, 177, 315
Smith, J. L., 219
Smith, K., 255, 356
Smith, P., 159
Smith, P. R., 189, 190, 201
Smith, R. L., 247, 248, 254
Smith, R. S., 269, 324
Smitherman, G., 315
Smokowski, P., 259
Smolkin, L. B., 75, 211, 385
Snarey, J., 259, 260
Sneider, C., 37
Snell, J. L., 275
Snidman, N., 139, 238
Snir, J., 296
Snow, C., 68
Snow, R. E., 210, 213, 216
Snyder, C. R., 196
Snyder, J., 247
Snyder, S. S., 230
Snyder, T. D., 353
Sodian, B., 152
Soenens, B., 211
Sokol, B. W., 104
Solano-Flores, G., 385
Solomon, D., 192, 325, 333
Solomon, G. E. A., 75
Solomon, R. C., 219
Solórzano, R. W., 401, 403
Soloway, E., 305
Song, S., 247
Songer, N. B., 303
Sonnenschein, S., 45, 335
Soodak, L. C., 78
Sosniak, L. A., 90
Soter, A. O., 90, 301
Southerland, S. A., 94, 121,
    163, 200
Sowell, E. R., 141
Sowers, J. A., 87
Spandel, V., 396, 397, 398
Spanoudis, G., 106
Sparks, D., 10
Spaulding, C. L., 217, 221,
    326, 387
Spear, L. P., 141, 216, 245, 265
Spearman, C., 159, 160
Spears, A. K., 315
Speece, D. L., 175
Spelke, E. S., 143
Spencer, J. P., 140
Spencer, S. J., 168, 219
Spera, C., 211, 349
Sperling, G., 26
Spicer, P., 245, 259
Spinath, F. M., 140
Spindler, A., 64
Spires, H. A., 296
Spörer, N., 164, 308
Sporte, S. E., 279
Squire, L. R., 24
Sroufe, L. A., 150, 154
Stabb, S. D., 276
Stacey, K., 303
Stack, C. B., 75
Staffieri, A., 308
Stafford, K. B., 104
Stage, E. K., 154
Stage, F. K., 75
Stahl, G., 90, 310
Stahl, S. A., 129
Stainback, S., 78
Stainback, W., 78
Standage, M., 221
Stang, J., 139

Stanley, J. C., 130, 168
Stanovich, K. E., 40, 121,
    162, 163
Staples, M., 301
Staub, E., 266
Stecher, B., 396
Steele, C. M., 219
Steele, D. F., 122
Steers-Wentzell, K. L., 307
Steffensen, M. S., 43, 77
Stegge, H., 243
Stegman, C. E., 276
Stein, B. S., 131
Stein, J. A., 266
Stein, S., 123
Steinberg, L., 60, 61, 141, 211, 239,
    242, 243, 249, 259, 265
Steiner, H. H., 168
Steinfield, C., 274
Stephenson, J., 296
Stepich, D. A., 294
Stern, E., 172, 173
Sternberg, R. J., 113, 118, 128, 129,
    131, 156, 157, 160, 162, 163, 164,
    168, 177, 291
Stevens, R., 294, 295, 313, 316, 354
Stevens, R. J., 303, 305
Stevens, T., 87
Stevenson, H. W., 79
Steward, B. E., 313
Stewart, L., 260
Stice, E., 239, 241, 246
Stiggins, R., 374, 375, 378, 381, 382,
    383, 389, 394, 398
Stimpson, V., 38, 173, 297, 301
Stipek, D., 246, 325, 354, 399, 403
Stipek, D. J., 197, 198, 200, 214, 217,
    221, 222, 228, 230, 387, 395
Stock, W. A., 47
Stodolsky, S. S., 90, 210, 214
Stolz, H. E., 239
Stone, J. R., 126, 127
Stone, N. J., 102, 104
Story, M., 139
Story, T., 196, 207, 241
Stough, L. M., 338
Stout, M. D., 354
Stowe, R. M., 64
Strahan, D. B., 110
Strand, S., 159
Strauss, L., 76, 259
Striepling-Goldstein, S. H., 335
Stright, A. D., 111, 239
Strike, K. A., 51
Stringer, E., 11
Stringfield, S. C., 401
Stucky, B. D., 254
Stupnisky, R. H., 230
Suárez-Orozco, C., 403
Sue, D. W., 75
Sue, S., 211
Suh, J., 266
Suh, S., 266, 267, 268
Suina, J. H., 75, 211, 385
Sullivan, C., 262, 263
Sullivan, J. R., 307, 309
Sullivan, J. S., 344
Sullivan, M. W., 209, 257, 262
Sullivan, P., 130, 154
Sullivan, P. J., 60, 84
Sullivan-DeCarlo, C., 327
Suls, J. M., 109
Sund, R. B., 154
Sunderman, G. L., 401, 402
Sutherland, K. S., 325
Suthers, D. D., 90, 310

Sutton, R. E., 217, 325
Svetina, M., 149, 154
Swan, K., 296
Swann, W. B., 217
Swanson, D. B., 379, 382
Swanson, H. L., 115, 159, 338, 381
Swanson, J., 110
Swap, S. M., 336, 349
Swartz, C. W., 64
Swearer, S. M., 254, 276, 325, 334
Sweeney, J. A., 147
Sweet, D., 379
Sweller, J., 31, 47, 48, 115, 116, 172,
    294, 316
Swenson, L. P., 214
Syvertsen, A. K., 354
Szabo, Z., 33

Tager-Flusberg, H., 24, 270
Takezawa, M., 262
Tallent-Runnels, M. K., 168
Tamang, B. L., 219
Tamburrini, J., 151, 154
Tamis-Lemonda, C. S., 71, 79, 211,
    259, 349
Tan, P. Z., 219, 259
Tanapat, P., 24
Tannenbaum, A., 67
Tanner, J. M., 148
Tapasak, R. C., 341
Tarter, C. J., 333
Tarver, S. G., 294, 295
Tate, 268
Tatum, B. D., 93, 95, 245, 259, 277,
    278, 315
Taylor, D. M., 313
Taylor, J. H., 291
Taylor, L., 336, 348, 349
Taylor, M. A., 43, 77
Taylor, S. E., 219
Templin, M., 380
Teo, A., 79
Terry, A. W., 168
Terwel, J., 306
Terwilliger, J. S., 394
Tessier-Lavigne, M., 23
Tessler, M., 68
Tessmer, M., 290
Tevendale, H. D., 214
Tharp, R. G., 47, 315
Théberge, C. L., 301, 313
Themann, K. S., 273
Théoret, H., 270
Thoermer, C., 152
Thoma, S., 139, 261
Thomaes, S., 243
Thomas, A., 238, 264
Thomas, J., 170
Thomas, J. W., 102, 104
Thomas, K. M., 24, 141
Thomas, M. A., 326, 327, 329, 339,
    340, 345
Thomas, M. S. C., 24, 140
Thomas, R. M., 400, 401, 402
Thomas, S., 202
Thompson, A., 59, 351
Thompson, E. R., 263
Thompson, M., 237, 238
Thompson, P. M., 141
Thompson, R. A., 79, 239,
    268, 269
Thompson, R. H., 351
Thomson, D. M., 39
Thorkildsen, T. A., 261
Thorndike-Christ, T., 228
Thorpe, P. K., 200, 214

Thurlow, M. L., 266, 267, 268
Thurstone, L. L., 160
Timm, P., 75, 211
Timperley, H., 50, 60, 84, 230
Tinker, E., 25
Tirosh, D., 112
Tisak, M., 256
Tishman, S., 121, 162
Titz, W., 209
Tobias, S., 191, 193, 194
Tobin, K., 47
Toblin, R. L., 255
Todd, C. M., 36
Toga, A. W., 141
Tolan, S. S., 167
Tomback, R. M., 232
Tomkiewecz, S., 162
Tomlinson, C. A., 285, 316
Toplak, M. E., 121, 163
Torgesen, J. K., 308
Torney-Purta, J., 31
Torrance, E. P., 45, 114, 177
Torres-Guzmán, M. E., 75
Torres-Rivera, E., 75
Tottenham, N., 79
Touchstone, D., 268, 313
Tourniaire, F., 152
Townsend, M. A. R., 148
Towsley, S., 139, 238
Trahant, D., 351
Tramontano, C., 255
Trantacosta, C. J., 251
Trautwein, L., 163, 298, 299
Trautwein, U., 195, 243, 246, 248, 299
Trawick-Smith, J., 75, 315
Treasure, D. C., 201
Treffert, D. A., 163
Treffinger, D. J., 128, 129
Tremblay, R. E., 248, 254, 337, 345
Triandis, H. C., 259
Trommsdorff, G., 239
Troop-Gordon, W., 243, 255
Trout, A. L., 125, 126
Troutman, A. C., 344, 350
Trudeau, G. B., 188
Trueman, M., 294
Trussell, R., 333
Trzesniewski, K. H., 205, 206,
    241, 245
Tsai, J. L., 209, 219
Tsai, Y.-M., 195
Tschannen-Moran, M., 12
Tsethlikai, M., 253, 254
Tubbs, M. E., 375
Tucker, C. J., 253
Tucker, V. G., 183, 196, 204, 205
Tudge, J. R. H., 304
Tulving, E., 39
Tunmer, W. E., 241
Tunstall, P., 84
Turiel, E., 256, 257, 259, 261,
    262, 263, 266
Turkanis, C. G., 91
Turnbull, A. P., 169, 170, 269, 334
Turnbull, B. J., 268
Turnbull, R., 169, 170, 269
Turner, J. C., 121, 128, 192, 200, 209,
    214, 216, 220, 221, 225, 323, 365,
    394, 403
Turner, J. E., 209
Turner, T. J., 30
Turvey, M. T., 26
Tyler, K. M., 75, 93, 94, 123, 219, 228,
    313, 315
Tyler, S., 172
Tzuriel, D., 381

Uchida, Y., 70, 349
Uesiliana, K., 123
Ulichny, P., 93
Underwood, J., 392
Undheim, J. O., 159
Urban, T. A., 147
Urdan, T., 188, 197, 200, 202, 220, 225
Urdan, T. C., 200, 201, 223, 231, 247
U.S. Department of Education, 400
Usher, E. L., 108, 195, 196, 387
U.S. Secret Service National Threat Assessment Center, 356
Utendale, W. T., 262, 263
Uttal, D. H., 79, 151

Valencia, S. W., 377, 383, 389
Valiante, G., 246
Valiente, C., 110
Valkenburg, P. M., 255, 274
Vallerand, R. J., 191, 224
Valli, L., 46, 401, 402
Vamvakoussi, X., 37
van Boxtel, C., 301
Van Camp, C. M., 62, 351
Van Court, N., 253
VandeKamp, K. O., 126
van den Bergh, H., 43, 64
Van den Bossche, P., 128
van der Heijden, P. G. M., 260
van der Linden, J., 301
Van der Molen, M. W., 147
van der Werf, G., 196, 208, 243, 326
Vanderwood, M., 159
van der Zee, Y. G., 196, 208, 243, 326
Vandewater, E. A., 336
Van Dooren, W., 152, 154
van Drie, J., 301, 304, 305
Van Hesteren, F., 262
Van Houten, R., 344
van Hout-Wolters, B., 43, 190
van Ijzendoorn, M. H., 140, 162
van Joolingen, 172, 173, 190, 310
van Laar, C., 211
VanLehn, K., 296
Van Leijenhorst, L., 147
van Merriënboer, J. J., 290
Van Meter, P., 47
Van Parys, M., 148
vanSledright, B., 17, 104, 125, 272, 301
Vansteenkiste, M., 190, 198, 211, 224
Van Winkel, L., 167
Vargas, A. U., 329
Varma, S., 24
Vasquez, J. A., 76
Vaughn, B. J., 221
Vaughn, S., 273
Vedder, P., 201
Venables, P. H., 163, 187
Venn, J. J., 395
Verdi, M. P., 47, 294
Verkhratsky, A., 23, 24
Vernon, P. A., 159
Véronneau, M.-H., 248
Verschaffel, L., 152, 155, 380
Vida, M., 197, 228
Vigdor, J., 10
Vintere, P., 64, 86, 125
Vitaro, F., 243, 248, 251, 254, 337, 345
Vock, M., 213
Vogel, E. D., 28
Vohs, K. D., 188, 197, 203, 204, 243
Voices of Indian Teens Project, 245, 259
Volet, S., 113, 315

Vollmer, T. R., 59
Volman, M., 306
von Eye, A., 269
Vorndran, C. M., 345, 346
Vorrasi, J. A., 354
Vosniadou, S., 37, 51, 125
Voss, J. F., 115, 155, 190, 191
Vucko, S., 396
Vul, E., 34
Vye, N. J., 109, 111, 310, 366
Vygotsky, L., 68, 111, 136, 144, 146, 170

Wade, S. E., 101, 194, 294
Wade-Stein, D., 102
Wagenmakers, E.-J., 212
Wagner, A. L., 208
Wagner, E., 262
Wagner, R. K., 164
Wagoner, B. J., 254
Wainryb, 262
Walberg, H. J., 102, 274, 278
Walker, E. F., 141
Walker, E. N., 268
Walker, H. M., 354, 355
Walker, J. M. T., 239, 265, 322, 324, 335, 336
Walker, K. C., 403
Walkey, F., 191, 364
Wallace, C. S., 24, 140
Wallace, G. L., 163
Walls, T. A., 198, 224
Walshaw, M., 90, 301
Walters, G. C., 63
Waltman, K. K., 393, 395
Walton, G. M., 168, 219
Wan, C., 259
Wandersee, J. H., 101
Wang, C. K. J., 221
Wang, J., 218
Wang, L., 75, 239, 259
Wang, Q., 123, 143, 211, 259
Wang, X., 163
Wanner, G., 345
Want, S. C., 271
Ward, M., 271
Warger, C., 356
Warren, E., A-2
Warren, J. S., 333, 351, 354
Wasley, P. A., 127, 295
Waterhouse, L., 5, 161, 252
Watkins, D., 123
Watkins, D. E., 273
Watkins, M. J., 32
Watson, J., 253
Watson, M., 192, 327, 333, 334
Watson, M. W., 255, 356
Watt, H. M. G., 198, 208
Waugh, C. K., 379, 383
Way, N., 259
Wearne, D., 301
Weatherford, J., 94
Weaver, C. A., III, 102
Webb, J., 104, 310
Webb, J. T., 167
Webb, L. D., 392
Webb, N. M., 46, 69, 274, 301, 303, 304, 305, 309, 313, 330, 366
Webber, J., 126
Weber, E. K., 262
Weber, L. M., 401
Weber, M. J., 332
Weber, N. L., 351
Weber, R., 297
Weffer, R. E., 75
Wehby, J., 221, 341

Wehmeyer, M. L., 169, 170, 269
Weichold, K., 246
Weinberg, R. A., 162
Weiner, B., 188, 200, 203, 204, 205, 209, 211, 225, 226, 276, 375
Weinert, F. E., 293, 294, 295, 312
Weinstein, C. S., 270, 322
Weinstein, R. S., 219, 226, 227
Weinstock, M., 104, 129
Weir, K. F., 191, 364
Weiss, L. H., 239
Weissburg, R. P., 273
Weisz, J. R., 230
Welch, G. J., 85
Wellborn, J. G., 189
Wellman, H. M., 30, 31, 104, 142, 253
Wells, D., 301
Wenger, E., 66, 176
Wentzel, K. R., 72, 199, 201, 223, 225, 231, 232, 247, 251, 270, 273
Werner, E. E., 269, 324
West, J., 336
West, R. F., 121, 163
West, T. C., 401
Westerfield, G., 197, 387
Westerman, M. A., 253
Whaley, S. E., 79, 140, 162
Wheatley, K. F., 325
Wheelan, S. A., 340
Whitaker Sena, J. D., 386
Whitbeck, L. B., 249
White, A. G., 344
White, B. Y., 172, 173, 312
White, C., 90
White, D., 200, 322
White, J. J., 46
White, R., 188, 278
White, R. T., 51
Whitehurst, G. J., 140
Whiteman, S. D., 244
Whitesell, N. R., 245, 253, 259, 386
Whitley, B. E., Jr., 204
Whitten, J. D., 162
Wigfield, A., 80, 110, 189, 190, 191, 195, 196, 197, 198, 199, 201, 208, 214, 223, 231, 232, 242, 244, 246, 249, 387
Wiggins, G., 288
Wilder, A. A., 53
Wilder, D. A., 59
Wiles, J., 216, 270
Wiley, J., 68, 129
Wilkinson, I. A. G., 90, 301
Willard, N. E., 275
Williams, A. Y., 232
Williams, C. C., 246
Williams, J. P., 53, 104
Williams, K. D., 305
Williams, K. M., 214, 246, 248, 272, 276, 354
Williams, R. E., 58
Williams, S., 386
Williams, T., 205
Williamson, A., 197
Williamson, S., 80, 262
Willingham, D. T., 25, 29
Wilson, B. L., 123, 208
Wilson, C. C., 277
Wilson, M., 256
Wilson, P. T., 294
Wilson, S., 253
Wimmer, H., 253
Windschitl, M., 11, 104, 125, 193, 217
Wine, J. D., 386
Winebrenner, S., 168

Winn, W., 47, 294, 296, 310
Winne, P. H., 84, 104, 105, 107, 108, 109, 125, 126, 175, 219, 391
Winner, E., 151, 167, 168
Winsler, A., 143
Winzenz, D., 33
Wise, B. W., 296
Wiser, M., 150, 154
Wisner Fries, A. B., 213, 230
Witherington, D., 240
Witkow, M. R., 199
Wittrock, M. C., 48, 105, 113, 116
Wittwer, J., 102, 293
Wixson, K. K., 296
Wixted, J. T., 24, 34
Wlodkowski, R. J., 217, 225
Wodtke, K. H., 403
Woitach, M. J., 268, 270
Wolak, J., 274
Wolfe, L. A., 329
Woloshyn, V. E., 131
Wolters, C. A., 108, 110, 209, 210
Wong, B. Y. L., 175, 268, 308
Wood, D., 175, 268, 308
Wood, E., 131
Wood, G. A., 250
Wood, H., 308
Woodruff, A. L., 195
Woolard, J., 242
Woolfe, T., 271
Woolfolk, A. E., 323, 333
Woolfolk Hoy, A., 5, 6, 12, 333, 334, 348
Worsham, M. E., 386
Worthman, C., 270
Wright, E. J., 241
Wright, J., 401
Wright, L. S., 344
Wright, M. O., 80
Wright, W. E., 401, 403
Wu, Y.-C., 42, 104, 124, 294
Wyatt, J. M., 268, 269
Wyndhamn, J., 66
Wynne, E. A., 340
Wynne, S., 221, 299

Xu, J., 299
Xu, Y., 259

Yakimowski-Srebnick, M. E., 401
Yang, A., 335, 336, 348
Yang, C., 255
Yarger, R. S., 106, 162
Yates, K. A., 290
Yates, M., 208, 262, 263, 279
Yau, J., 262
Ybarra, M. L., 255, 274
Yell, M. L., 273, 357
Yeung, R. S., 276
Yim, P.-S., 218
Yip, T., 259
York, D. E., 163, 164
Young, M. D., 310
Youniss, J., 208, 262, 263, 279
Yu, H. C., 76, 201, 214, 251
Yu, L., 259
Yuker, H. E., 277
Yuki, M., 244, 259

Zahn-Waxler, C., 219, 262
Zahorik, J. A., 194, 217
Zajonc, R. B., 209
Zambo, D., 62, 264
Zan, B., 261
Zarbatany, L., 247, 251
Zawilinski, L., 306
Zeelenberg, R., 212

Zeidner, M., 163, 214, 230, 240, 252
Zeinz, H., 246
Zeith, T. Z., 159
Zelazo, P. D., 106, 256
Zeldin, A. L., 196
Zelli, A., 255, 276
Zhang, J., 90, 131

Zhang, L.-F., 128, 162
Zhang, M., 111
Zhang, Z., 259
Zhou, M., 211
Zhou, Q., 239, 257, 261, 263
Zhou, Y.-D., 112
Ziegert, D. I., 207

Zimbardo, P. G., 256
Zimmer-Gembeck, M. J., 250, 251
Zimmerman, B. J., 64, 105, 107, 108,
    109, 111, 118, 125, 196, 205, 208,
    219, 298, 300
Zimmerman, M., 243
Zimmerman, M. A., 259

Zimmerman, R. R., 59
Zimmerman, R. S., 187
Zmuda, J. H., 350
Zohar, A., 104, 152, 154, 310
Zook, K. B., 294
Zottoli, Brian, 211
Zwarun, L., 120, 129

Abstract concepts
  concrete examples of, 12–13, 154, 171–172
  moral development and, 257–261
  Piaget's stages and, 150–151
Academic achievement
  case study, 1
  competition and, 74, 76, 228
  cooperative learning and, 303
  cultural factors and, 74
  dispositions and, 163
  goals and, 199, 201
  intelligence tests and, 159, 166, 167
  interest and, 193
  peer relationships and, 247–248
  reciprocal causation and, 81, 82
  self-perceptions and, 243
  self-regulation and, 107, 109
  socioeconomic status and, 79–80
  summaries of, 392–397
  teacher-student relationships and, 2, 12, 324
  transition to middle and secondary school and, 2, 232
  values and, 198, 211
Academic disciplines
  applications of, 126–128
  cognitive tools of, 73–74
  complex cognitive processes and, 130, 132
  concrete experiences and, 171
  critical thinking and, 120
  discussions and, 301
  emotions and, 229–230
  epistemic beliefs and, 124
  misconceptions concerning, 104–105
  motivation and, 191–192, 217
  perspective taking and, 272–273
  transfer and, 112–113
  wisdom of previous generations and, 171
Acclimation, 155
Accommodation, defined, 142
Accountability
  defined, 400
  high-stakes testing and, 400–401, 402
Achievement goals, 199, 201–202
Acquired immune deficiency syndrome (AIDS), 251
Action research, defined, 11
Activity reinforcers, 60
Adaptation
  intellectual disabilities and, 169
  intelligence and, 156, 157
Adolescents
  abstract concepts and, 150, 151, 171–172
  anxiety and, 216
  assessment and, 371–372
  brain development, 242
  classroom management and, 332

community service and, 279
  epistemic beliefs of, 105
  homework assignments and, 298
  identity and, 242
  learned helplessness and, 207
  learning strategies and, 36
  logical reasoning and, 154
  metacognition and, 103–104
  moral reasoning and, 262
  motivation and, 208
  multicultural education and, 93
  peer relationships and, 247, 248–251
  personal fable and, 242–243
  recursive thinking and, 253
  reinforcers and, 60, 61
  relatedness and, 189
  risk taking and, 242–243, 264–265
  romantic relationships, 250–251
  self-perceptions and, 241–242
  self-regulation and, 50, 109, 110, 111, 126
  sense of self and, 241, 245
  social groups and, 248–249
  standardized achievement tests and, 403
  synaptic pruning and, 141
  values and, 263
Advance organizer, 294
Affect. See also Emotions
  anxiety and, 213–214, 230–231
  defined, 184
  effects of, 209–216
  instructional strategies and, 228–232
  learning and, 209–213
  moral development and, 261, 263
  motivation and, 209
African American English, 314
African Americans
  "acting white" and, 63
  authoritarian parenting and, 239
  cooperation and, 74
  eye contact and, 74
  intelligence and, 157, 177
  learned helplessness and, 211
  mastery goals and, 211
  personal space and, 74
  playing the dozens, 77, 339
  questions and, 314, 315
  self-determination and, 210
  sense of self and, 258
After-school detentions, 345
Age-equivalent scores, 407
Aggression
  bullies and, 247, 250, 254–255, 256, 274–726
  classroom management and, 353–357
  interventions for, 355–356
  modeling and, 64
  perspective taking and, 255, 276

social cognition and, 254–256
  students at risk and, 355
  three-level approach, 354, 357
  victims of, 254, 255, 256, 275–276
Aggressive behavior, defined, 254
Agreeableness, 240
Alcohol consumption during pregnancy, 162, 169
Alcohol use, 197, 242, 247
Algorithms
  defined, 117
  instructional strategies and, 316
  problem solving and, 117–118
Altruism, 263
Ames, Carol, 186
Analogies, 118
Analytical intelligence, 160
Analytic versus holistic processing, 163
Anderson, John, 19
Animal Hospital (computer simulation), 310
Antecedent stimuli
  defined, 58
  productive behaviors and, 83
Anxiety
  affect and, 213–214, 230–231
  cultural factors, 219
  debilitating anxiety, 213–214
  defined, 213
  developmental trends in, 215–216
  effects of, 5, 213–214
  facilitating anxiety, 213–214, 387
  formal assessment and, 386
  transition to middle and secondary school and, 231–232
APA style, 6
Applied behavior analysis (ABA), 350
Apprenticeships, defined, 176
Argument analysis, 120
Arousal, need for, 187, 217
Articulation, 176
Asian Americans
  authoritarian parenting and, 239
  cooperation and, 74, 339
  critical thinking and, 123
  family relationships, 74, 210
  intelligence and, 157
  mastery goals and, 211
  personality and, 258
  personal space and, 74
  relatedness and, 210–211
  self-determination and, 210
  self-regulation and, 122–123
  values and, 211
Asperger syndrome, 270
Assessment. See also Formal assessment; Informal assessment; Test anxiety
  case study, 361–362
  clinical method and, 165
  cognitive processes and, 50–51, 53, 365

complex cognitive processes and, 131–132
  defined, 362
  determining what students have learned, 364
  diagnosing learning and performance problems, 364
  effects on students' learning, 5
  evaluating quality of instruction, 364
  feedback and, 366
  instructional goals and, 362, 363–364, 371–372
  intrinsic motivation and, 366
  as learning experience, 365–366
  meaningful learning and, 51, 53
  motivation and, 364–365
  practicality of, 366, 373, 374
  promoting learning and, 364, 404
  purposes of, 363–366
  qualities of good assessment, 366–370, 372–373
  reliability of, 366, 367–368, 374
  rote learning and, 53, 121
  standardization of, 366, 369, 374
  standardized tests and, 369, 397–404
  teacher-directed instruction and, 295
  teachers' decisions and, 3
  validity of, 366, 369–370, 372–373, 374
Assimilation, defined, 142
Associations
  long-term memory retrieval and, 38
  mental associations, 18
Astrocytes
  brain development and, 140, 141
  changes in, 24
  defined, 23
Atkinson, Richard, 19
Attention
  affect and, 212–213
  brain development and, 141
  classroom environment and, 323
  classroom strategies and, 42
  defined, 26
  memory and, 26–27, 41
  modeling and, 86
  reciprocal causation and, 81, 82
  sensory register and, 26, 26n24
  social information processing and, 254
  study strategies and, 101
Attention-deficit hyperactivity disorder (ADHD)
  assessment and, 369
  cognitive processes and, 53
  defined, 53
Attributions
  cultural factors and, 211
  defined, 203

Attributions (continued)
    effects on future performance, 204–205
    effort and persistence and, 205–206
    motivation and, 202–207, 209, 225–228
    of teachers, 225–228, 330
Attribution theory, description of, 186
Authentic activities
    critical thinking and, 129
    defined, 127
    formal assessment and, 377–378
    instructional strategies and, 127–128
    learner-directed instruction and, 309–310
    variety of contexts and, 88
Authentic assessment, 377–378
Authoritarian parenting, defined, 239
Authoritative parenting
    classroom management and, 265–266, 322
    defined, 239
    mainstream Western culture and, 239
Autism spectrum disorders, 270
Automaticity
    defined, 34
    practice and, 34, 40, 48
    working memory and, 116, 117
Autonomy
    cultural factors and, 92, 210
    self-determination and, 189

Backup reinforcers, 83
Backward design, defined, 285
Baddeley, Alan, 19
Baillargeon, Renee, 137
Bandura, Albert, 18, 186
Behavioral analysis, 290
Behaviorism
    contexts and, 58
    learning and, 18
    motivation and, 185
Behaviors. See also Misbehavior; On-task behavior; Prosocial behaviors
    acceptable and effective, 65
    affect and, 213
    classroom strategies, 3, 4
    cueing, 83
    culture compatible with, 71–72
    development and, 140
    effects of stimuli on, 58–67
    elicited by stimuli, 58
    encouraging productive behaviors, 83–88
    expectations about outcomes of, 65–66
    incompatible behaviors, 85–86
    influenced by peer relationships, 247–248
    intelligence and, 156
    learners' modifying environmental conditions through, 80–82
    motivation and, 190
    multiple intelligences and, 161
    negative reinforcement and, 60, 62
    person variables, environment and, 80–82, 140
    positive reinforcement and, 59–60
    punishment and, 62–63
    reinforcing productive behaviors, 83–84
    self-perceptions and, 243
    self-regulation and, 105
    social cognition and, 254
    temperament and, 139
Behavior therapy, 350
Belongingness
    classroom environment and, 325–326
    defined, 325
Best-work portfolio, 396
Bias
    confirmation bias, 38, 51, 172, 212
    cultural bias, 383, 384–385
    hostile attributional bias, 255, 341
Big6 approach, 304–305
Binet, Alfred, 158
Bisexuals, 250–251, 254
Black English vernacular, 314
Bloom's taxonomy, 289
Bodily-kinesthetic intelligence, 161
Body language, 248, 339, 340
Brain
    development and, 140–141, 242
    learning and, 23–25
    research on, 24–25
Brainstorming, 118
Bransford, John, 19
Bronfenbrenner, Urie, 138
Bruner, Jerome, 19, 137
Buddhism, 157, 218
Bullies
    classroom environment and, 326
    defined, 254
    forms of, 254–255, 274–275
    peer relationships and, 247, 256
    sexual intimacy and, 250
    teachers' intervention and, 275–276

Capacity
    of attention, 27
    of long-term memory, 28
    of sensory register, 26
    of working memory, 27–28, 40, 41, 42–43, 115–116, 147
Case, Robbie, 136, 137
Cattell, Raymond, 159–160
Cattell–Horn–Carroll theory of cognitive abilities, 160
Causation, correlation and, 8, 9, 119–120
Cause-and-effect relationships, 8, 9
Central executive
    defined, 106
    as memory component, 106, 159
Challenges
    defined, 214
    development and, 146
    performance-avoidance goals and, 199
    practice and, 48
    scaffolding and, 175, 192, 221
    self-efficacy and, 220–221, 264
    self-perceptions and, 243
Cheating
    cultural factors and, 339
    formal assessment and, 387–388
    self-handicapping and, 197
Checklists, 384–385
Childhelp USA, 269
Chomsky, Noam, 137
Class inclusion, 146, 150, 165
Classroom climate, defined, 322
Classroom culture, 131
Classroom environment
    authoritative environment, 265–266, 322

classroom arrangement and, 323
    classroom management and, 322
    community of learners and, 325–326
    developmental differences and, 330–331
    families and, 335–336
    goal-oriented atmosphere, 326
    parent communication and, 334–337
    plans for transitions, 329–330
    productive engagement and, 328–329
    respect for students and, 323–324
    rule enforcement, 328
    rules and procedures, 326–328
    sense of community and, 333–337
    teachers' decisions and, 3
    teacher-student relationships and, 323–325
    withitness and, 333
Classroom management
    aggression and, 353–357
    assessment and, 363
    case study, 321
    classroom environment and, 322
    defined, 322
    developmental trends in, 331–332
    instructional strategies and, 337–338
    reducing unproductive behaviors, 337–353
    self-regulation strategies and, 342–343
    signals and, 340
    teacher-student relationships and, 265–266, 322
Classroom strategies
    assessment promoting learning and achievement, 367
    attention and, 42
    conceptual change and, 52
    cooperative learning and, 305
    critical thinking and, 130
    discovery learning and, 173
    diverse temperaments and, 265
    elaboration and, 4, 46
    feedback and, 84
    instructional goals and objectives, 288
    interactions among diverse groups, 278
    misbehavior consultations with parents, 348
    multiple-choice items and, 380
    new skill acquisition and, 50
    performance assessments, 381
    portfolios and, 398
    productive expectations and attributions and, 227
    promoting productive styles and dispositions, 177, 178
    punishment and, 346
    questions and, 298
    relatedness and, 223
    research on, 4–6
    self-efficacy and self-worth, 220
    self-regulation and, 125
    students at risk and, 268
    students' characteristics and behaviors and, 3, 4
    students' stereotypes and prejudices and, 95
    students with delays in cognitive development, 170
    students with exceptional abilities and talents and, 168

transition to middle and secondary school, 232
Classroom websites, 127, 289, 335
Clinical method
    defined, 165
    problem solving and, 165, 166
Cliques, defined, 249
Coaching, 176
Cognition. See also Metacognition; Situated learning and cognition; Social cognition
    affect and, 209–213
    brain and, 23–25
    defined, 20
    distributed cognition, 68–69, 175
    hot cognition, 212, 278
    moral behavior and, 261, 263
    need for, 163
Cognitive apprenticeship, defined, 176
Cognitive behavioral therapy, 350
Cognitive development. See also Intelligence
    case study, 135
    of elementary school children, 148–150
    fostering of, 170–178
    language and, 143
    Piaget's stages of, 139, 148, 149, 150–152, 172
    social interaction and, 143–144
    trends in, 147–155
Cognitive-developmental theory
    description of, 137
    formal education and, 144
    stage theory and, 139
Cognitive dissonance
    defined, 212
    moral reasoning and, 261
    motivation and, 218–219, 284
Cognitive processes. See also Complex cognitive processes
    assessment and, 50–51, 53, 365
    Bloom's taxonomy, 289
    case study, 99
    defined, 20
    instructional strategies and, 41–53
    integration of, 148
    intelligence and, 159–160
    learning and, 20
    learning processes and, 35
    memory and, 25–38
    motivation and, 190, 192–209, 224–228
    promoting effectiveness in, 41–53
    proving physical and social support for, 88–91
    teacher-directed instruction and, 293, 294
    working memory and, 27, 147
Cognitive styles
    classroom strategies and, 177, 178
    defined, 162
    intelligence and, 162–164
Cognitive tools
    defined, 68
    as products of culture, 72–75
    sociocultural theory and, 68
    supporting effective cognitive processes and, 88
    Vygotsky and, 68
    wisdom of previous generations and, 171
Collaboration
    supporting effective cognitive processes and, 88–90

of teachers, 11–12, 333–334
technology and, 310–311
Collective self-efficacy, 196, 334
Community agencies, 334
Community of learners
classroom environment and, 325–326
defined, 90
technology and, 90–91
Community service, 279
Competence
expertise and, 155
modeling and, 64
motivation and, 184, 187–188, 191, 197
need for, 188, 240
Competency goals, 285, 288
Competition
academic achievement and, 74, 76, 228
minimizing of, 228
peer relationships and, 248
Complex cognitive processes
creativity and, 114–118
critical thinking and, 119–121
defined, 100
metacognition and, 100–105
problem solving and, 100, 114–118
promoting generally, 129–132
promoting specific processes, 121–129
self-regulation and, 105–111
social interaction and, 144
transfer and, 111–114
Comprehension monitoring
defined, 102
self-monitoring and, 108
study strategies and, 13, 102, 104
Computer-based instruction (CBI), 292, 295–296
Computer networks, community of learners, 90–91
Computer simulations, 128, 309–310
Conceptions of time, 75
Concept maps, 101, 102
Concepts. *See also* Abstract concepts
defined, 29
Conceptual change
classroom strategies and, 52
critical thinking and, 120
interest and, 193
misconceptions and, 51
prior knowledge and, 12
self-worth and, 188
Conceptual understanding
defined, 46
problem solving and, 115
transfer and, 113–114
Concrete examples, of abstract concepts, 12–13, 154, 171–172
Concrete operations stage
defined, 150
description of, 149
school years and, 148
Concrete reinforcers, 60
Conditional knowledge, 28
Confidence intervals, 410
Confirmation bias
cognitive dissonance and, 212
defined, 38
discovery learning and, 172
misconceptions and, 38, 51
Conflict resolution, 247, 272
Confucianism, 157
Conscientiousness, 163, 240
Consequences
of behaviors, 59–60

logical consequences, 344
motivation and, 190
patterns in, 65–66
self-regulation and, 109
Conservation
cultural factors and, 156
defined, 149
Piaget's stages and, 149, 150
problem solving and, 165
Conservation of displaced volume, 165, 166
Conservation of liquid, 149, 150
Conservation of weight, 150, 156
Consolidation, 24n15
Constructing meaning, 21–22
Constructivism, 19
Content domains, 120, 196, 217
Content validity, defined, 370
Contexts
cultural factors as, 70–80
environmental conditions as, 58–67
long-term memory retrieval and, 39–40
personality and, 240
providing supportive contexts for learning, 83–96
social interaction as, 67–69
Contingencies
defined, 84, 85
response-reinforcement contingencies, 84–85
self-imposed contingencies, 109, 190, 222, 343
Contingency contracts, 85
Contingency management, 350
Continuous reinforcement, 84
Control groups, defined, 8
Controllability, 203
Controversial students, defined, 251
Conventional morality
defined, 259
Kohlberg's theory on, 259, 260
Conventional transgressions
cultural factors, 259
defined, 256
Convergent thinking
defined, 114
problem solving and, 114–115
working memory capacity and, 114–115
Cooperation
cultural factors and, 74, 92, 94, 211, 313, 339
individual versus cooperative efforts, 74
peer relationships and, 248
social interaction and, 274
Cooperative learning
classroom strategies and, 305
defined, 303
learner-directed instruction and, 302–304
relatedness and, 223
social goals and, 202
Co-regulated learning, 111, 125
Correlation
causation and, 8, 9, 119–120
defined, 7
predictions and, 8
Correlational studies, 7–8, 9
Cortex
brain development and, 141
defined, 23
learning and, 23–24
Course portfolio, 396
Covert strategies

cognitive processes underlying, 101–102
defined, 101
modeling of, 123
Covington, Martin, 185
Crazy Machines (computer simulation), 309
Creative intelligence, 160
Creativity
affect and, 209–210
algorithms and, 117–118
complex cognitive processes and, 114–118
defined, 114
depth of knowledge and, 115
divergent and convergent thinking and, 114–115
instructional strategies and, 128–129
metacognition and, 118
Crick, Nicki, 137
Criterion-referenced scores, defined, 390
Critical thinking
classroom strategies and, 130
complex cognitive processes and, 119–121
cultural factors and, 123
defined, 119
as disposition, 121, 163
epistemic beliefs and, 120
instructional strategies and, 129
of teachers, 11
Crowds, defined, 249
Crystallized intelligence, 159, 160
Csikszentmihalyi, Mihaly, 186
Cueing
defined, 83
misbehavior and, 340, 353
Cultural bias
in assessment, 383
sources of, 384–385
Cultural factors
affect and, 216, 218–219
apprenticeships and, 176
community of learners and, 91
complex cognitive processes and, 122–123
as context, 70–80
cooperation and, 74, 92, 94, 211, 313, 339
cultural bias, 384–385
emotions and, 216, 218, 239
ethnic differences, 74–75
formal operational reasoning skills and, 156–157
giftedness and, 168
inconsistencies between home and school, 75–77
intelligence and, 157, 177
misbehavior and, 338–339
moral development and, 259
motivation and, 208, 210–211
parental discipline and, 349
personality and, 258
prior knowledge and, 44–45
research on, 11
social development and, 258–259
verbal interactions and, 314–315
wait time and, 47, 315
Cultural lens, 91–93
Culturally responsive teaching, defined, 94
Cultural mismatch
anxiety and, 219
defined, 76
problems associated with, 76–77

questions and, 315
Cultures
behaviors compatible with, 71–72
changes in, 70–71
cognitive tools as products of, 72–75
defined, 70
subcultures, 71, 249
variations within, 72, 93
Culture shock, defined, 76
Curriculum
diversity and, 93–94
standardized achievement tests and, 400, 401–402
stereotypes in, 94
Cyberbullying, 255

Daily log sheets, 126
Debilitating anxiety, 213–214
Decay, defined, 41
Deci, Edward, 185
Declarative knowledge
defined, 28
evolution into procedural knowledge, 34
Delay of gratification, defined, 60
Dependent variables, 8
Descriptive studies
defined, 7
questions answered with, 7, 9
Development. *See also* Cognitive development; Moral development; Personal development; Social development; Zone of proximal development (ZPD)
developmental processes, 140–146
general principles of, 136, 138–140
theoretical perspectives on, 137–138
Developmental delays, 169
Developmental differences
accommodating, 164–169
classroom environment and, 330–331
instructional strategies and, 313, 316
standardized achievement tests, 403
Developmental milestones
defined, 136
rate of development and, 138
Developmental portfolio, 396
Developmental trends
in anxiety, 215–216
in assessment matching standards, 371–372
in classroom management, 331–332
in effective reinforcers, 61
in instructional strategies, 286–287
in learning strategies, 35–36, 147
in logical reasoning, 153–154
in metacognition, 102, 103–104, 105, 147
in moral development, 262
in motivation, 207–208
in self-regulation, 109–111, 147
in sense of self, 245
Dialects, defined, 314
Dialogue
reciprocal teaching and, 173–174
supporting effective cognitive processes and, 88–90
Dialogue journals, 323

Direct instruction
defined, 293
teacher-directed instruction and, 292, 293–295
Discovery learning
classroom strategies and, 173
defined, 172
learner-directed instruction and, 304
Discussions
gender differences and, 301, 313
learner-directed instruction and, 300–302
misconceptions and, 91
of moral issues, 278
parent discussion groups, 269
relatedness and, 223
Disequilibrium
cognitive dissonance and, 218
defined, 145
moral reasoning and, 261
and Piaget, 212, 218, 261
prior knowledge inconsistencies and, 187–188
Dispositions
classroom strategies and, 177, 178
critical thinking as, 121, 163
defined, 121, 162
intelligence and, 162–164
Distance learning, 296
Distributed cognition
defined, 68
enhanced understanding and, 68–69
scaffolding and, 175
Distributed intelligence
characteristics of, 164
defined, 164
optimism concerning, 177
scaffolding and, 175
Divergent thinking
creativity and, 114–115
defined, 114
questions and, 128
time for, 129
working memory capacity and, 115–116
Diversity
accommodating developmental differences, 164–169
classroom strategies and, 278
community of learners and, 91
multicultural education and, 93–94
peer mediation and, 272
peer relationships and, 95
in prior knowledge, 43–45
promoting communication among diverse groups, 276–277
in temperaments, 264
Dodge, Kenneth, 137
Down syndrome, 169
Drug use, 197, 242, 247
Duration
of long-term memory, 28, 41
of working memory, 27–28, 41
Dweck, Carol, 186
Dynamic assessment, 381
Dyscalculia, 53
Dyslexia, 53, 264

Eating disorders, 246
Ebonics, 314
Eccles, Jacquelynne, 186
Ecological systems theory, description of, 138

Educational psychology
defined, 2
general guiding principles of, 3–10
Effort and persistence
attributions and, 205–206
individual versus cooperative efforts, 74
motivation and, 190
reducing, 197
Elaboration
classroom strategies and, 4, 46
as cognitive process, 33n43
defined, 4, 33
distributed cognition and, 69
learning strategies and, 13, 35
as meaningful learning, 33, 34
misconceptions and, 37
social information processing and, 254
Elementary school children
abstract concepts and, 151, 154
anxiety and, 215
assessment and, 371
classroom management and, 331
cognitive development of, 148–150
community service and, 279
epistemic beliefs of, 105
homework assignments and, 298
learning strategies and, 35
logical reasoning and, 153
metacognition and, 103
moral reasoning and, 262
motivation and, 191, 207
multicultural education and, 93
play activities and, 170
reinforcers and, 61
retrieval cues and, 50
self-regulation and, 109, 110, 126
sense of self and, 240–241, 245
social cognition and, 253
synaptic pruning and, 141
synaptogenesis and, 140–141
values and, 198
E-mail messages, 335
Emotional and behavioral disorders, 269–270
Emotional intelligence, 252, 252n121
Emotions. *See also* Affect
academic disciplines and, 229–230
attributions and, 204–205
cultural factors and, 216, 218, 239
prosocial behaviors and, 257, 261, 263
risk taking and, 242–243
self-conscious emotions, 209
self-regulation and, 108, 230
situational interest and, 194
social cognition and, 252–253
Emotion self-regulation
defined, 230
peer relationships and, 247
Empathy
defined, 257
encouragement of, 271–273
prosocial behavior and, 263
Encoding
automaticity and, 117
complex cognitive processes and, 128
defined, 20
problem solving and, 116–117
study strategies and, 101
Entity view of intelligence
defined, 206
teachers and, 225–226
Environmental conditions
case study, 57

as contexts, 58–67
development and, 139–140
family relationships and, 267–269
intelligence and, 162
layers of influences, 77–78
learner's modifying, 80–83, 105, 140
motivation and, 192
niche-picking and, 82–83, 105, 140
personality and, 238–239, 240
person variables, behavior and, 80–82, 140
socioeconomic status and, 79
Epistemic beliefs
collaboration and, 310
critical thinking and, 120
cultural factors in, 122
defined, 105
discussions and, 301
distributed cognition and, 69
instructional strategies and, 124–125
metacognition and, 105
misconceptions and, 51
Equilibration, defined, 145
Equilibrium, defined, 144
Erikson, Erik, 138
Ethnic groups
affect and, 218–219
cooperative learning and, 303
cultural bias, 383
cultural factors, 74–75
defined, 71
intelligence and, 162
modeling and, 87
as more-or-less phenomenon, 93
motivation and, 210–211
self-fulfilling prophecies and, 226
sense of self and, 244
stereotypes of, 94–95
variations within, 72, 93
Ethnic identity, 244, 258
ETS scores, 409
European Americans. *See also* Mainstream Western culture
family relationships, 74
personal space and, 74
values and, 211
Evaluations. *See also* Self-evaluation
criteria for, 388
feedback and, 390–391
formal assessment and, 388–392
intrinsic motivation and, 222
learner-direction instruction and, 301–302
objectivity of, 389
risk taking and, 391
RSVP characteristics and, 388
scores and, 390
self-regulation and, 389
students' right to privacy, 391–392
Evidence-based practices, defined, 6
Existential intelligence, 160
Expectancy, 184, 186
Expectancy-value theory, 186
Expectations
cultural factors and, 75–77
environmental conditions and, 65–66
informal assessment and, 375
motivation and, 205, 225–228
reciprocal causation and, 81
Experiential change, 18
Experimental studies
cause-and-effect relationships and, 8, 9
defined, 8

formulating hypotheses and, 152
questions answered with, 7, 8
Expertise, 154–155
Explicit learning, 20
Exploration, 176
Expository instruction, 292
Externalizing behaviors, 270
Extinction, 84, 85
Extraversion, 240
Extrinsic motivation
defined, 191
extrinsic reinforcers and, 222
intrinsic motivation compared to, 191–192
Extrinsic reinforcers, 60, 222
Eye contact, 74, 94

Facilitating anxiety, 213–214, 387
Fading, 175
Failure avoidance, 188
Family Educational Rights and Privacy Act (FERPA), 392
Family relationships. *See also* Parents
classroom environment and, 335–336
cultural factors, 74, 210, 258, 339
environmental conditions and, 267–269
society and, 77
values and, 248
Feedback
assessment and, 366
classroom strategies and, 84
evaluations and, 390–391
positive feedback, 60, 83
reinforcement and, 83
Fischer, Kurt, 136, 137
Flavell, John, 137
Flow, defined, 191
Fluid intelligence, 159–160
Ford, Martin, 186
Foreclosure, identity, 242
Formal assessment
aligning classroom assessments with state standards, 371–372
anxiety and, 386
authentic tasks for, 377–378
cheating and, 387–388
cultural bias in, 383
defined, 362
defining tasks, 383
designing, 376–388
evaluation criteria, 384–385
instructional goals and, 378–379
length of, 376–377
performance and, 386–387
RSVP characteristics of, 382
Formal operations stage
abstract concepts and, 151
cultural factors and, 156–157
defined, 150
description of, 149
school years and, 148
Formative assessment, 363
Freud, Sigmund, 138
Friendships. *See* Peer relationships
Functional analysis, 351

g, defined, 159
general intelligence, 159–160
Gangs
defined, 249
reducing hostilities, 277, 356–357
Gardner, Howard, 160–161
Gary Gadget (computer simulation), 309
Gauvain, Mary, 19, 137

Gays, 250–251, 254
Gender-appropriate behavior, 65
Gender differences
    cooperative learning and, 303
    cultural bias, 383
    discussions and, 301, 313
    giftedness and, 168
    instructional strategies and, 313
    peer relationships and, 248
    self-esteem and, 246
    self-fulfilling prophecies and, 226
    sense of self and, 244, 246
    wait time and, 47
Gender roles, 76
Gender schemas, 244, 246
General transfer, 112–113
Giftedness, 167–168
Glial cells, 23
GLOBE Program, 311
Goals. *See also* Instructional goals;
        Mastery goals; Performance
        goals
    academic achievement and, 199,
        201
    achievement goals, 199, 201–202
    affect and, 209
    classroom environment and, 326
    motivation and, 190, 191–192, 224
    self-chosen goals, 225
    self-handicapping and, 197
    self-perceptions and, 243
    self-regulation and, 107, 109, 111,
        289
    self-serving, 255
    social goals, 201–202
    social information processing
        and, 254
    variety of, 201–202
Goal theory, description of, 186
Goodness of fit, 264
Grade-equivalent scores, 407
Grades
    criteria for, 393
    descriptions of criteria, 394–395
    number of assessments and, 393
    parents and, 393–394
    qualitative information
        accompanying, 395
Graham, Sandra, 186
Group achievement, 74, 211
Group activities
    complex cognitive processes and,
        130–131
    relatedness and, 223
Group membership, 244
Guided participation, 176
Guilt
    defined, 257
    motivation and, 263

Hatano, Giyoo, 19
Hemispheres of the brain, 24
Heredity
    development and, 139–140
    intellectual disabilities and, 169
    intelligence and, 162
    temperaments and, 139, 238–239
Heuristics, 118
Higher-level questions, defined, 297
High-stakes testing, 400–401
Hippocampus, 24
Hispanics
    authoritarian parenting and, 239
    cooperation and, 74, 313, 339
    eye contact and, 74
    family relationships, 74, 210
    intelligence and, 157

personality and, 258
personal space and, 74
questions and, 314
Holistic versus analytic processing,
    163
Homework assignments, 297–299
Hostile attributional bias
    defined, 255
    misbehavior and, 341
Hot cognition
    defined, 212
    moral dilemmas and, 278
Housing, socioeconomic status, 79
Hull, Clark, 185
Humanism, 185
Hypermedia, defined, 306
Hypotheses, formulating and testing,
    120, 125, 151–152, 172
Hypothetical reasoning, 150–151, 156

Identity
    defined, 242
    ethnic identity, 244, 258
    moral values and, 263
Identity achievement, 242
Identity diffusion, 242
Illusion of knowing
    attributions and, 203
    defined, 104
    students' judgment and, 5
Imaginary audience
    defined, 244
    recursive thinking and, 253
Implicit learning, 20
Impulse control, brain development,
    141, 242
Incentives, defined, 66
Inclusion, defined, 4, 78
Incompatible behaviors, 85–86
Incremental view of intelligence
    defined, 206
    teachers and, 228, 240
Incubating situation, 118
Independent practice, 295
Independent variables, 8
In-depth instruction, 130
Individuals with Disabilities
        Education Act (IDEA), 77–78,
        77n57, 369, 395
Induction
    defined, 266
    misbehavior and, 341
Infants, 142, 143
Inferences
    assessments and, 362
    critical thinking and, 120
Informal assessment
    conducting, 374–376
    defined, 362
    expectations and, 375
    observation and, 374–376
    RSVP characteristics of, 376, 382
Information literacy, 304–305
Information processing analysis, 290
Information processing theory
    cognitive development and, 147
    description of, 137
    formal education and, 144
    learning and, 19
Inner-city schools, 232, 356
Inner speech, 143, 144
Inputs, 26
Inquiry learning
    classroom strategies and, 173
    defined, 172
    learner-directed instruction and,
        304

In-school suspension, 344
Instructional goals
    assessment and, 362, 363–364,
        371–372
    choosing instructional strategies
        and, 317
    defined, 284
    lesson plans and, 292
    mastery learning and, 300
    paper-pencil assessment and,
        378–379
    planning instruction and, 285,
        287–289
    standards and, 287–288
Instructional objectives
    assessment and, 371–372
    defined, 285
    lesson plans and, 292, 295
    standards and, 287–288
Instructional strategies
    affect and, 228–232
    assessment and, 364, 371–372
    case study, 283–284
    choices concerning, 317
    classroom management and,
        337–338
    cognitive development and,
        170–178
    cognitive processes and, 41–53
    combining approaches, 316
    complex cognitive processes and,
        121–132
    cultural factors and, 313
    culturally responsive teaching, 94
    developmental needs and, 164–178
    developmental trends in, 286–287
    general strategies, 312–313, 316
    intrinsic motivation and, 216–223
    moral development and, 277–279
    motivation-enhancing cognitive
        processes and, 224–228
    personal development and,
        264–271
    planning and, 284–292
    reciprocal causation and, 82
    social development and, 271–277
    students with special needs and, 4
    supportive contexts for learning
        and, 83–96
    teacher-directed instruction,
        293–300
    teachers' decisions and, 3
Intellectual disabilities
    defined, 168, 169, 169n117
    identification of, 169
Intelligence
    cognitive processes and, 159–160
    cognitive styles and, 162–164
    components of, 156–157
    cultural factors and, 157, 177
    defined, 156
    domains of, 160–161
    g factor, 159–160
    heredity and environment, 162
    measurement of, 158–159
    optimism concerning, 177–178
    physical, symbolic, and social
        support for, 164
    specific processes and abilities,
        160
Intelligence tests
    defined, 158
    development of, 158–159
    as imperfect measures, 157,
        158–159, 162, 177
    intellectual disabilities and, 169
    interpretation of, 166–167

Interest
    defined, 192
    intrinsic motivation and, 193
    motivation and, 192–195
    personal interests, 194–195, 224
    situational interest, 193–194, 217,
        284
Intermittent reinforcement, 84
Internalization
    defined, 144
    peer tutoring and, 307
    scaffolding and, 175
    sociocultural theory and, 172
Internalized motivation
    defined, 198
    extrinsic motivation and, 192
    values and, 198, 224
Internalizing behaviors, 270
Internet
    advantages and potential dangers
        of, 274, 306
    classroom websites, 127
    critical thinking and, 129
    lesson plans and, 292
    student research and, 306–307, 312
    teacher collaboration and, 11
Interpersonal intelligence, 157, 161
Intrapersonal intelligence, 161
Intrinsic motivation
    assessment and, 366
    challenges and, 220–221
    cognitive factors in, 209
    defined, 191
    evaluations and, 222
    extrinsic motivation compared to,
        191–192
    instructional strategies and,
        216–223
    internalized motivation
        distinguished from, 198
    self-determination and, 191,
        221–222, 289
    self-efficacy and, 196, 217–219
Intrinsic reinforcers, 60, 83
IQ scores
    defined, 158
    environmental conditions and, 162
    interpretation of, 399
    ranges of, 158, 159, 409
    reliability of, 167
    standardized achievement tests
        and, 159
IRE cycle, 315

Keyword methods, defined, 49, 50
Kids Voting USA curriculum, 313
Knowledge base
    cognitive development and,
        147–148
    defined, 36
Knowledge construction
    co-construction with experienced
        individuals, 67–68, 88–89
    co-construction with peers, 68–69,
        89–90
    concepts and, 29
    learning and, 21–22
Kohlberg, Lawrence, 137, 139,
        257–261
Kuhn, Deanna, 137

Language
    body language, 248, 339, 340
    cognitive development and, 143
    cognitive tools of, 74–75
    crystallized intelligence and, 160
    sensitive period for, 140

Latham, Gary, 186
Lave, Jean, 19, 137
Learned helplessness
    attributional style and, 206–207
    cultural factors and, 211
    defined, 206
Learner-directed instruction
    authentic activities and, 309–310
    cooperative learning and, 302–304
    defined, 3, 284
    discussions and, 300–302
    evaluation of ideas and, 301–302
    peer tutoring and, 307–309
    scaffolding and, 300, 311–312
    students' research and, 304–307
    technology and, 310–311
Learning. *See also* Meaningful
        learning; Rote learning
    affect and, 209–213
    assessments promoting, 367, 404
    attention and, 26–27
    brain and, 23–25
    case study, 17
    as constructive process, 18–23
    defined, 18
    intelligence and, 156
    long-term memory retrieval and,
        38–39
    mastery learning, 299–300
    misconceptions concerning, 105
    prior knowledge and, 22–23
    self-regulation and, 105, 122–123
    situated learning and cognition,
        66–67, 113
    supportive contexts for, 83–96
    teaching strategies and, 2
    visual versus verbal learning, 163
Learning disabilities
    cognitive processes and, 53
    defined, 53
    developmental delays and, 169
    negative reinforcement and, 62
Learning strategies
    affect and, 213
    attributions and, 205
    cultural factors in, 122
    defined, 35
    developmental trends in, 35–36,
        147
    elaboration and, 13, 35
    explicitly teaching, 122–124
    general transfer and, 112–113
    long-term memory and, 34–35
    organization and, 20, 123
    prior knowledge and, 4–5, 12, 35
    self-regulation and, 107–108
Learning styles, 163
Lerman, Dorothea, 185
Lesbians, 250–251, 254
Less is more principle, 46, 114, 401
Lesson plans, 291–292, 295
Limited English proficiency, 167,
    384–385, 403–404
Linguistic intelligence, 161
Live models, defined, 64
Locke, Edwin, 186
Locus, internal versus external, 203
Loftus, Elizabeth, 19
Logical consequences, 344
Logical-mathematical intelligence,
    161
Logical reasoning
    critical thinking and, 120
    cultural factors and, 155, 156–157
    developmental trends in, 153–154
    prior knowledge and, 152, 154, 155

Long-term change, 18
Long-term memory
    affect and, 213
    anxiety and, 214
    capacity of, 28
    as component of memory, 25, 26
    defined, 28
    duration of, 28, 41
    integration of, 31
    retrieval from, 28, 38–41
    storage processes of, 28, 31–34,
        41–42
Lower-level questions, defined, 296

Mainstream Western culture
    authoritative parenting and, 239
    cognitive tools and, 72–73, 171
    competition and, 228
    conservation and, 156
    context of, 71, 92
    emotional expression and, 218
    epistemic beliefs and, 12
    ethnic identity and, 258
    formal operations reasoning and,
        156–157
    giftedness and, 167–168
    identity and, 242
    intelligence and, 157, 177
    questions and, 314–315
    self-worth and, 210
    verbal interactions and, 314
Maslow, Abraham, 185
Mastery goals
    criterion-referenced scores and,
        390, 394n57
    defined, 199
    focus on, 201, 211, 224–225
    performance goals compared to,
        200, 224–225
Mastery learning, 299–300
Mastery orientation, 206–207
Maturation, 139, 140
Meaningful learning
    assessment and, 51, 53
    defined, 32
    homework assignments and, 298
    long-term memory retrieval and,
        39
    long-term memory storage
        processes and, 32–34
    metacognition and, 101
    prior knowledge and, 36, 43, 45,
        142
    study strategies and, 123
    transfer and, 113–114
    visual imagery as, 33–34
Mean (M), 409
Mediated learning experiences
    defined, 67
    sociocultural theory and, 68, 144
Memory. *See also* Long-term
        memory; Working memory
    attention and, 26–27, 41
    central executive and, 106, 159
    cognitive processes and, 25–38
    defined, 25
    model of, 26, 31, 41, 106
    promoting effective cognitive
        processes and, 41–45
    study strategies and, 101
Mental associations, 18
Mental sets
    automaticity and, 48
    complex cognitive processes and,
        128
    defined, 117

problem solving and, 117
Metacognition
    complex cognitive processes and,
        100–105
    cooperative learning and, 303
    covert strategies and, 101–102
    defined, 100
    developmental trends in, 102,
        103–104, 105, 147
    discovery learning and, 172
    epistemic beliefs and, 105
    instructional strategies and, 122
    intelligence and, 159
    problem solving and creativity
        and, 118
    social cognition and, 253
    study strategies and, 100–101
Michael, Jack, 185
Middle school children
    abstract concepts and, 150,
        171–172
    anxiety and, 215
    assessment and, 371
    classroom management and, 332
    homework assignments and, 298
    learning strategies and, 36
    logical reasoning and, 153
    metacognition and, 103
    moral reasoning and, 262
    motivation and, 208
    reinforcers and, 61
    romantic relationships and, 250
    self-regulation and, 109, 110, 126
    sense of self and, 245
    synaptic pruning and, 141
Misbehavior
    conferring with parents, 345–348,
        353
    cultural factors and, 338–339
    defined, 337
    environmental conditions and, 58
    ignoring of, 339–340, 353
    induction and, 266
    instructional strategies and,
        337–338
    motivation and, 197
    negative reinforcement and, 62
    punishment and, 343–345, 353
    purposes for students, 351–352
    strategies for dealing with, 353
    students' perspectives on,
        341–342
    systematic intervention
        and, 349–350, 353
    transition times and, 329
Misconceptions
    of bullying, 274–275
    conceptual change and, 51
    discovery learning and, 172
    discussions and, 91
    expertise development and, 155
    identifying, 51
    motivation and, 51, 209
    in prior knowledge, 37–38
Missing recess, 345
Mnemonics
    common techniques, 49
    defined, 48
    study strategies and, 123
Modeling
    apprenticeships and, 176
    cooperative learning and, 303
    critical thinking, 129
    defined, 63
    distributed cognition and, 69
    elaboration and, 174

environmental conditions and,
        63–65
    ethnic groups and, 87
    productive behaviors and, 83, 86
    socialization and, 72
Models
    defined, 63
    environmental conditions and,
        63–65
    of prosocial behavior, 277–278
    self-regulation and, 107
    variety of, 86–87
Moral development
    affect and, 261, 263
    challenges to moral reasoning, 261
    cultural factors and, 259
    developmental trends in, 262
    emotions and, 257
    instructional strategies and,
        277–279
    internal standards and, 256
    moral and conventional
        transgressions and, 256
    moral dilemmas and, 257–261, 278
    sense of self and, 263
Morality, defined, 256
Moral reasoning, Kohlberg's stages of,
    260–261
Moral transgressions
    cultural factors, 259
    defined, 256
Moratorium, identity, 242
Motivation. *See also* Extrinsic
        motivation; Intrinsic motivation
    affect and, 209
    assessment and, 364–365
    attributions and, 202–207, 209,
        225–228
    authentic activities and, 127
    case study, 183
    cognitive processes and, 190,
        192–209
    community of learners and, 91
    cultural factors and, 208, 210–211
    defined, 184
    developmental trends in, 207–208
    dispositions and, 162
    expectations and, 205, 225–228
    interest and, 192–195
    internalized motivation, 192, 198,
        224
    intrinsic versus extrinsic
        motivation, 191–192
    misconceptions and, 51, 209
    modeling and, 86
    moral behavior and, 261, 263
    multicultural education and, 93
    self-efficacy and, 184, 195–197, 209
    self-regulation and, 108
    TARGETS, principles of, 228, 229
    teacher-student relationships and,
        324
    theoretical perspectives on,
        185–186
    values and, 197–198, 224
Motor reproduction, modeling and,
    86
Multicultural education, 93–94
Multiple intelligences, 160–161
Musical intelligence, 161
Muslims, 76
Myelin, 23, 141
Myelination, 141

National Child Abuse Hotline, 269
Native Americans

conceptions of time, 75, 339
cooperation and, 74, 92, 211, 313, 339
critical thinking and, 123
emotions and, 218
eye contact and, 74
family relationships, 74, 92, 210, 258
governing practices of, 94
individual autonomy and, 92
intelligence and, 157, 177
public versus private performance and, 74
questions and, 314, 315
self-determination and, 210
sense of self and, 258
Nativism, 137, 139
Naturalist intelligence, 161
Nature versus nurture, 139–140, 162, 239
NCE scores, A-3–A-4
Need for arousal, 187, 217
Need for cognition, 163, 187
Need for competence, 188, 240
Need for relatedness, 189–190, 201, 202, 210–211, 223, 231–232
Need for self-determination, 188–189
Needs. *See also* Students with special needs
arousal and, 187, 217
intrinsic motivation and, 216–223
physical versus psychological well-being, 184, 187
relatedness and, 189–190, 201, 202, 210–211, 223, 231–232
self-determination and, 188–189
self-worth and, 187–188
Negative correlation, 7–8
Negative reinforcement
defined, 60
effects of, 60, 62, 63
positive reinforcement distinguished from, 63
Negative transfer, 111, 112
Neglected students
defined, 251
social skills and, 251–252, 273
Neighborhood influences, 77
Neurons
brain development and, 140, 141
changes in, 24
defined, 23
specialization of, 23
Neuroticism, 240
Niche-picking
defined, 82
environmental conditions and, 82–83, 105, 140
personality and, 239
No Child Left Behind Act (NCLB), 400–401
Normal distribution (normal curve), 408
Norm groups, 390
Norm-referenced scores
comparisons and, 394n57, 399–400
competition and, 228
defined, 390
Note taking
explicit teaching of, 124
metacognition and, 100–101
Nutrition
brain development and, 139
cognitive development and, 140
intellectual disabilities and, 169
intelligence and, 162
socioeconomic status and, 79

Observations, informal assessment and, 374–376
On-task behavior
classroom environment and, 328–329
classroom management and, 337–338
environmental conditions and, 58
incompatible behaviors and, 85–86
need for arousal and, 187
reciprocal causation and, 81
Open-mindedness, 163
Openness, 240
Operant conditioning, defined, 59
Operations, 148
Optimism, 206
Organization
defined, 33
development and, 142
interrelationships and, 45–46
learning strategies and, 20, 123
of long-term memory, 28–31
as meaningful learning, 33, 34
metacognition and, 101
superimposed meaningful structure, 49, 50
Organized presentation, teacher-directed instruction, 294
Ormrod's Own Psychological Survey (OOPS), 4–5
Outlining, as study strategy, 101
Out-of-school suspension, 345
Overt strategies, defined, 100

Pacific Island groups
cooperation and, 74, 211
emotions and, 218
Pacing, teacher-directed instruction, 294
Pajares, Frank, 186
Paper-pencil assessment
authentic assessment and, 377–378
defined, 370
instructional goals and, 378–379
RSVP characteristics of, 378, 382
Parental involvement, 336–337
Parental neglect and abuse, 269
Parent discussion groups, 269
Parenting styles, 239, 268
Parents. *See also* Family relationships
communication with, 251, 269, 334–337
conferring about misbehavior with, 345–348
cultural factors, 349
cultural mismatch and, 315
grades and, 393–394
self-socialization and, 246
Parent-teacher conferences, 269, 334, 337, 389
Pavlov, Ivan, 18
Pedagogical content knowledge, defined, 11
Peer mediation
defined, 271
perspective taking and, 271–272
Peer pressure
behaviors and, 247–248
defined, 247
Peer relationships
behavior influenced by, 247–248
co-construction of knowledge with, 68–69
community of learners and, 91

complex cognitive processes and, 144
diversity and, 95
gender differences and, 248
motivation and, 190
peer tutoring and, 307
personal development and, 247
romantic relationships, 250–251
school culture and, 76
self-efficacy and, 219
sense of self and, 243–244
social goals and, 201–202
Peer tutoring
defined, 307
effects of, 5
learner-directed instruction and, 307–309
scaffolding and, 175
social goals and, 202
Percentile ranks, 407–408
Performance
attribution's effects on, 204–205
formal assessment and, 386–387
motivation and, 191
public versus private performance, 74
reciprocal causation and, 81
self-regulation and, 107, 109, 126
Performance-approach goals, 199, 201
Performance assessment
classroom strategies, 381
defined, 370
RSVP characteristics of, 382
validity and, 379–382
Performance-avoidance goals, 199, 201
Performance goals
defined, 199
mastery goals compared to, 200, 224–225
transition to middle and secondary school, 201
Personal development
instructional strategies, 264–271
peer relationships and, 247
Personal fable
adolescents and, 242–243
defined, 242
fading of, 247
Personal interests
defined, 194
motivation and, 194–195, 224
Personality
Big Five traits, 240
contexts and, 240
cultural factors and, 258
defined, 238
fostering personal development, 264–271
heredity and environment and, 238–239
sense of self and, 238–246, 264
Personal space, defined, 74
Person variables, environment, behavior and, 80–82, 140
Perspective taking
aggression and, 255, 276
defined, 253
encouragement of, 271–273
prosocial behavior and, 263
Pessimism, 206
Peterson, Christopher, 186
Physical aggression, 254, 274–275
Physical appearance, 214, 219, 244, 247

Physical punishment, 344
Piaget, Jean
accommodation and, 142
assimilation and, 142
class inclusion and, 146
clinical method and, 165, 166
cognitive development and, 136, 137, 170
constructivism and, 19
disequilibrium and, 212, 218, 261
equilibration and, 145
equilibrium and, 144–145
experimentation with physical world, 143
integration of cognitive processes, 148, 380
language and, 143
schemes and, 142
social interaction and, 143–144
stages of cognitive development, 139, 148, 149, 150–152, 172
Pintrich, Paul, 186
Planning
assessments and, 363
brain development and, 141
instructional goals and, 285, 287–289
instructional strategies and, 284–292
lesson plans, 291–292
task analysis and, 290–291
teachers' decisions and, 3
Plasticity, defined, 141
Plateaus, in development, 138
Play activities, cognitive development, 170
Playing the dozens, 77, 339
Popular students
defined, 251
sense of self and, 244
social skills and, 251–252
Portfolios
classroom strategies and, 398
complex skills over time and, 395–396
defined, 395
RSVP characteristics, 397
self-assessment and, 389
Positive behavioral support (PBS), 351–352
Positive correlation, 7
Positive feedback, 60, 83
Positive psychology, 186
Positive reinforcement
defined, 59
effects of, 63
forms of, 60
negative reinforcement distinguished from, 63
Positive transfer, 111, 112
Postconventional morality
defined, 259
Kohlberg's theory on, 259, 260
Power, modeling, 64
Practical intelligence, 160, 169
Practicality
of assessment, 366, 373, 374
defined, 373
Practice
automaticity and, 34, 40, 48
promoting effective cognitive processes and, 48
retrieval and, 40
teacher-directed instruction and, 293–295
variety of contexts and, 88

Preconventional morality
  defined, 258
  Kohlberg's theory on, 258–259, 260
Predictions, correlations and, 8
Predispositions, 239
Prefrontal cortex, 23, 24, 140, 141
Prejudices, 95, 277
Preoperational stage, 148, 149
Preschool children
  cognitive development and, 143
  cognitive tools and, 74–75, 171
  environmental conditions and, 58
  play activities and, 170
  reinforcers and, 60
  self-determination and, 189
  synaptic pruning and, 141
Presentation punishment, 62, 63
Prestige, modeling and, 64
Primary reinforcers, defined, 59
Prior beliefs, learning and, 36–38
Prior knowledge
  crystallized intelligence and, 160
  diversity in, 43–45
  intelligence and, 156, 157
  learning and, 22–23, 36–38
  learning strategies and, 4–5, 12, 35
  long-term memory and, 31
  meaningful learning and, 36, 43,
    45, 142
  misconceptions in, 37–38
  socioeconomic status and, 45, 96
  teacher-directed instruction
    and, 293, 294
Prior knowledge activation, defined,
  43
Proactive aggression, 254, 255
Probabilistic reasoning, 120
Problem-based learning, defined, 128
Problem solving
  affect and, 209–210
  algorithms and, 117–118
  clinical method and, 165
  complex cognitive processes and,
    100, 114–118
  convergent and divergent thinking
    and, 114–115
  cooperative learning and, 303
  defined, 114
  depth of knowledge and, 115
  encoding and, 116–117
  instructional strategies and,
    128–129
  metacognition and, 118
  social problem-solving strategies,
    255, 273, 276
  zone of proximal development
    and, 146
Procedural knowledge
  defined, 28
  practice and, 34
Procrastination, self-handicapping,
  197
Project-based learning
  complex cognitive processes and,
    130–131
  defined, 128
Proportional reasoning, 151, 152,
  165, 172
Prosocial behaviors
  cultural factors and, 259
  defined, 64, 256
  developmental trends in, 262
  emotions and, 257, 261, 263
  instructional strategies and,
    277–279
  models of, 277–278

moral and prosocial development
  and, 256–263
Proximal goals, defined, 225
Psychodynamic theory, description
  of, 138
Psychological punishment, 344–345
Puberty, 138, 141, 151, 165, 231, 237,
  242–243
Punishment
  alternatives to, 85–86
  assigning extra classwork as, 345
  classroom management and, 63
  classroom strategies and, 346
  defined, 62
  misbehavior and, 343–345, 353
  presentation punishment, 62, 63
  removal punishment, 62, 63

Qualitative development, 139
Qualitative research
  defined, 6
  questions answered by, 7
Quantitative development, 139
Quantitative research
  defined, 6
  questions answered by, 7
Questions
  complex cognitive processes and,
    128–129
  critical thinking and, 129
  cultural factors, 314–315
  elaboration and, 174
  peer tutoring and, 308
  teacher-directed instruction and,
    296–297
  wait time and, 47, 297, 315

Random assignment, experimental
  studies and, 8, 9
Rating scales, 385, 386
Raw score, 390
Reactive aggression, defined, 254
Reciprocal causation
  defined, 80
  environment, behavior, and person
    variables, 80–82, 105
Reciprocal teaching
  advance reasoning processes and,
    172–175
  defined, 172
Reconstruction error, defined, 41
Recursive thinking, defined, 253
Reeve, Johnmarshall, 185
Reflection, apprenticeships and, 176
Reflective teaching, defined, 11
Rehearsal
  cultural factors and, 122
  defined, 27
  as rote learning, 32
Reinforcement
  defined, 59
  incompatible behaviors and, 85–86
  of productive behaviors, 83–88
  shaping and, 87–88
Reinforcers
  defined, 59
  developmental trends in, 61
  environmental conditions and, 59
  productive behaviors and, 83–84
Rejected students
  defined, 251
  social skills and, 273
Relatedness
  classroom environment and,
    323–324
  classroom strategies for, 223

computer-based instruction and,
  296
cultural factors, 210–211
needs and, 189–190, 201, 202,
  210–211, 223, 231–232
social goals and, 201–202
transition to middle and secondary
  school, 231–232
Relational aggression, 254,
  274–275
Reliability
  of assessment, 366, 367–368, 374
  defined, 367
  intelligence tests and, 167
Remote desktop, 30
Removal punishment
  defined, 62
  effects of, 63
Research
  action research, 11
  on brain, 24–25
  on classroom strategies, 4–6
  developing as teacher and, 10–12
  learner-directed instruction and,
    304–307, 312
  types of, 6–8
Resilient self-efficacy, defined, 196
Resilient students, defined, 269
Response cost, 344
Responses
  defined, 58
  eliciting desired responses, 83
Retention, 86
Retrieval
  affect and, 212–213
  defined, 25
  from long-term memory, 28,
    38–41
  promoting effective cognitive
    processes and, 48–50
Retrieval cues
  appropriate behavior and, 83
  defined, 39
  promoting effective cognitive
    processes and, 48–50
  transfer and, 40, 113
Retrieval failure, defined, 41
Reviews, teacher-directed
  instruction, 294, 295
Rewards, 5
Risk taking
  adolescents and, 242–243, 264–265
  complex cognitive processes and,
    128–129
  formal assessment and, 391
Rogers, Carl, 185
Rogoff, Barbara, 19, 137
Romantic relationships, 250–251
Rote learning
  assessment and, 53, 121
  defined, 32
  long-term memory retrieval and,
    39
  long-term memory storage
    processes and, 32
  misconceptions and, 51
  study strategies and, 122
RSVP characteristics, 366–370,
  372–373, 374, 376, 382, 388
Rubrics, 384–385, 386, 389
Rules and procedures
  classroom environment, 326–328
  enforcement of, 328
Rural areas, family relationships, 74,
  210
Ryan, Richard, 185

Scaffolding
  apprenticeships and, 176
  challenges and, 175, 192, 221
  co-regulated learning and, 111
  defined, 175
  learner-directed instruction and,
    300, 311–312
  motivation and, 192
  peer tutoring and, 309
  shaping and, 87
  student research and, 306–307
Schemas
  defined, 29, 142, 142n25
  long-term memory and, 29–30
Schemes, defined, 142
Scholastic aptitude tests, 399
School community
  collaboration and, 333–334
  nonviolent school environment
    and, 354–355
School culture, 75–77
School readiness tests, 399
Schunk, Dale, 18, 186
Scientific method, 151–152, 156–157
Scoring
  formal assessments, 385, 388, 389
  rubrics for, 384–385, 386, 389
Scripts, defined, 30
Secondary reinforcers, defined, 59
See For Yourself exercises
  affect, 212
  attributions, 202–203
  cognitive tools, 73
  constructing meaning and, 21–22
  convergent and divergent thinking,
    114–115
  cooperative learning, 302–303
  critical thinking, 119–120
  cultural factors, 92
  cultural mismatch, 77
  diversity in prior knowledge,
    43–44
  equilibration, 145–146
  expectations, 65–66
  explicit learning, 20
  hypotheses, 152
  hypothetical reasoning and,
    150–151
  incompatible behaviors, 85–86
  intelligence tests, 158
  interest, 193
  knowledge base, 147–148
  length of formal assessments,
    376–377
  long-term memory, 29, 31–32
  misbehavior, 338–339
  modeling, 64–65
  moral dilemmas, 257–258
  need for arousal, 187
  Ormrod's Own Psychological
    Survey (OOPS), 4–5
  parents, 346–347
  problem solving, 116–117
  reliable assessment, 367–368
  retrieval, 25, 40–41
  retrieval cues, 39
  scaffolding, 311
  schemas, 30
  self-determination, 188–189
  self-efficacy, 195
  self-regulation, 106–107
  sense of self and, 238
  social cognition, 252–253
  task analysis, 290–291
  teacher-directed instruction and,
    293

theories, 30–31
transfer, 112
validity of assessment, 269–270
visual imagery, 33–34
working memory, 28
Self-assessment
self-perceptions and, 243
self-regulation and, 126, 127
Self-concept, sense of self, 240
Self-conscious emotions,
defined, 209
Self-determination
classroom environment and, 327
cultural factors, 210
intrinsic motivation and, 191,
221–222, 289
needs and, 188–189
relatedness and, 210
students at risk and, 267
Self-determination theory, 185
Self-efficacy
challenges and, 220–221, 264
classroom strategies and, 220
defined, 12, 195
expectations and, 66
intrinsic motivation and, 196,
217–219
motivation and, 184, 195–197, 209
sense of self and, 240
social cognitive theory and, 186
teacher-student relationships and,
324
Self-esteem
gender differences and, 246
sense of self and, 240
Self-evaluation
defined, 109
formal assessment and, 389
problem solving and, 118
self-regulation and, 108–109,
125–126
Self-explanation, 102
Self-fulfilling prophecies, 226
Self-handicapping
defined, 197
self-worth theory and, 185
Self-imposed contingencies
defined, 109
misbehavior and, 343
motivation and, 190
self-determination and, 222
self-regulation and, 109
Self-improvement, 210
Self-instructions
defined, 108
misbehavior and, 343
Self-monitoring
defined, 108
self-regulation and, 125–126, 342
Self-perceptions
behaviors influenced by, 243
development of, 241–242
Self-questioning, 102
Self-regulation
assessment and, 366
classroom strategies and, 125
complex cognitive processes and,
105–111
cultural factors and, 122–123
defined, 105
developmental trends in, 109–111,
147
emotions and, 108, 230
goals and, 107, 109, 111, 289
homework assignments and,
298–299

instructional strategies and,
125–126
learning strategies and, 107–108
misbehavior and, 350, 353
retrieval cues and, 50
self-evaluation and, 108–109,
125–126
self-imposed consequences and,
109
study strategies and, 107–108
teaching strategies for, 342–343
values and, 198
Self-serving goals, 255
Self-socialization, 246
Self-talk, 143, 144
Self-worth
anxiety and, 214
classroom strategies and, 220
cultural factors and, 210
defined, 188
motivation and, 184, 187–188, 197
Self-worth theory, 185
Seligman, Martin, 186
Sensation seekers, 187
Sense of community
bullying and, 275
classroom environment and,
333–337
community of learners and, 91
defined, 325
discussions and, 302
norm-referenced scores
inconsistent with, 390
Sense of school community,
333–334
Sense of self
cultural factors, 258
defined, 238
developmental trends in, 245
gender differences and, 244, 246
moral development and, 263
peer relationships and, 243–244
personality and, 238–246, 264
self-concept and, 240
Sensitive periods, defined, 140
Sensorimotor stage, 149
Sensory register
attention and, 26, 26n24
as component of memory, 26
defined, 26
Separating and controlling variables,
8
Service learning, 309
Sexual harassment, 272, 354
Sexual intimacy, 250–251
Shame
attributions and, 204–205
behaviors and, 213
defined, 257
as self-conscious emotion, 209
self-regulation and, 109
Shaping, reinforcement, 87–88
Shiffrin, Richard, 19
Short-term memory. *See* Working
memory
Siegler, Robert, 137
Signals
classroom management and, 340
teacher-directed instruction and,
294
Simulations, 128, 309–310
Situated learning and cognition
defined, 66
environmental conditions and,
66–67
transfer and, 113

Situated motivation, 192, 216
Situational interest
defined, 193
motivation and, 193–194, 217, 284
Skinner, B. F., 18, 59, 185
Social cognition
aggression and, 254–256
awareness of others and, 252–253
behavior towards others and, 254
defined, 252
instructional strategies and,
271–277
Social cognitive theory
contexts and, 58, 80
description of, 186
learning and, 18
Social construction of meaning, 69, 90
Social constructivism, contexts and,
58
Social cues, 255
Social development
case study, 237
instructional strategies and,
271–277
peer relationships and, 247
social cognition and, 252–256
Social goals, 201–202
Social groups, adolescents, 248–249
Social information processing,
defined, 254
Social intelligence, 169
Social interaction
classroom strategies and, 278
cognitive development and,
143–144
computer-based instruction and,
296
as context, 67–69
cooperation and, 274
Socialization
classroom environment and, 326
defined, 72
peer relationships and, 247–248
personality and, 239
self-socialization, 246
Social processes, learning and, 53
Social reinforcers, 60
Social skills
cultural factors and, 258–259
instructional strategies and,
271–277
neglected students and, 251–252,
273
peer relationships and, 247
popular students and, 251–252
Societies
access to resources, 78–80
defined, 70
institutions influencing learning,
77–78
Sociocultural theory
cognitive tools and, 68
contexts and, 58
description of, 137
formal education and, 144
internalization and, 172
learning and, 19
mediated learning experiences
and, 68
self-talk and, 143, 144
Socioeconomic status (SES)
access to resources and, 78–80, 96
community of learners and, 91
cultural bias, 383
defined, 78
modeling and, 87

parenting styles and, 239
peer mediation and, 272
prior knowledge and, 45, 96
Standard English and, 314
Spatial intelligence, 161
Spearman, Charles, 159
Specific aptitude tests, 399
Specific transfer, defined, 112
Spelke, Elizabeth, 137
Spurts, in development, 138
Stability, attributions, 203, 204, 205
Stage theories
defined, 139
prior acquisitions and, 142–143
Standard deviation (SD), A-3
Standard English, defined, 314
Standardization
of assessment, 366, 369, 374
defined, 369
Standardized achievement tests
administration of, 403
high-stakes testing and, 400–401
judicious use of, 401–404
limited English proficiency and,
403–404
preparation for, 402
teaching to the test, 401, 402
uses of, 399–400
validity of, 401–402, 404
Standardized tests
assessment and, 369, 397–404
commonly used tests, 399
defined, 397
norm-referenced scores and, 390
Standards
defined, 285
examples of North Carolina's
standards, 286–287, 371–372
instructional goals and, 287–288
Standard scores, 158, A-2–A-5
Stanines, A-3
Stereotypes
classroom strategies and, 95
cultural factors and, 94–95
cultural variation and, 74
defined, 94
gender stereotypes, 246
self-imposed segregation and, 277
Stereotype threat
anxiety and, 219
defined, 219
Sternberg, Robert, 160
Stimulation seeking, 163
Stimuli
defined, 58
effects on behavior, 58–67
Storage
defined, 25
long-term memory and, 28, 31–34,
41–42
promoting effective cognitive
processes and, 45–48
Strata of intelligence, 160
Students at risk
aggression and, 355
characteristics of, 266–267
classroom environment and, 322
classroom strategies and, 268
cooperative learning and, 303
defined, 266
socioeconomic status and, 80
Students with disabilities
development and, 143
discussions and, 301
emotional and behavioral
disorders and, 269–270

Students with disabilities (*continued*)
  intelligence tests and, 159
  laws concerning, 77–78
  modeling and, 87
Students with special needs
  defined, 4
  instructional strategies for, 4
  intelligence tests and, 159
Study strategies
  complex cognitive processes and, 100
  comprehension monitoring and, 13, 102, 104
  explicit teaching of, 122–124
  metacognition and, 100–101
  reciprocal causation and, 81, 82
  self-regulation and, 107–108
Subcultures, 71, 249
Subgoals, 118
Subject matter analysis, 290
Suicide, 251, 269, 270–271
Summaries
  of academic achievement, 392–397
  grades and, 393–395
  portfolios and, 395–397, 398
  teacher-directed instruction and, 294
Summarizing, as study strategy, 102
Summative assessment, 363
Superimposed meaningful structure, defined, 49, 50
Symbolic models, defined, 64
Sympathy
  defined, 257
  prosocial behavior and, 263
Synapses
  brain development and, 140, 141
  changes in, 24
  defined, 23
Synaptic pruning, defined, 141
Synaptogenesis, defined, 140

Table of specifications
  assessment and, 373
  defined, 370
  standardized achievement tests and, 402n74
Talking versus remaining silent, 314
"TARGETS" approach, to motivation, 228, 229
Task analysis
  defined, 290
  planning and, 290–291
Tasks
  diversity of, 176
  performance assessment and, 383
  time on task, 190
Teachable moments, 292
Teacher-directed instruction
  cognitive processes and, 293, 294
  computer-based instruction and, 292, 295–296
  defined, 284
  direct instruction and, 292, 293–295

examples and practice opportunities, 293–295
  expository instruction, 292
  homework assignments and, 297–299
  instructional strategies, 293–300
  mastery of basic knowledge and, 299–300
  prior knowledge and, 293
  questions and, 296–297
Teachers
  attributions of, 225–228, 330
  collaboration of, 11–12, 333–334
  critical thinking of, 11
  development of, 10–12
  entity view of intelligence and, 225–226
  incremental view of intelligence and, 228, 240
  intervention for bullying incidents, 275–276
  newsletters of, 269, 335
Teacher-student relationships
  academic achievement and, 2, 12, 324
  authoritative environment and, 265–266, 322
  classroom environment and, 323–325
  punishment and, 345
  relatedness and, 223
  self-efficacy and, 12
  teachers' in-depth knowledge of students and, 3–4
Teaching strategies
  developing as teacher and, 10–11
  students' characteristics and behaviors and, 3, 284
Technology
  classroom websites and, 127, 289
  community of learners and, 90–91
  computer simulations, 128, 309–310
  critical thinking and, 129
  learner-directed instruction and, 310–311
Telephone conversations, parent communication, 335
Temperaments
  accommodating diversity in, 264
  classroom environment and, 330
  classroom strategies and, 265
  defined, 139, 238
  heredity and, 139, 238–239
Test anxiety
  defined, 386
  facilitating anxiety, 387
  standardized achievement tests and, 403
Testwiseness, 402
Theoretical perspectives
  on development, 137–138
  on learning, 18–19
  on motivation, 185–186
Theories
  defined, 10, 30

self-constructed theories, 31, 148
  worldview distinguished from, 75
Theory of mind, defined, 253
Thinking. *See* Cognition
Thorndike, Edward, 18
Threat, defined, 214
Time, conceptions of, 171, 339
Time on task, defined, 190
Time-out, 344
Token economy, 83–84
Transfer
  complex cognitive processes and, 111–114
  defined, 111
  general transfer, 112–113
  homework assignments and, 298
  meaningful learning and, 113–114
  retrieval cues and, 40, 113
  similarity between old and new, 112
  situated learning and, 67
  specific transfer, 112
  variety of contexts and, 88
Transition to middle and secondary school
  academic achievement and, 2, 232
  aggression and, 254
  anxiety and, 231–232
  case study, 1
  classroom strategies and, 232
  performance goals and, 201
Treatment groups, defined, 8
Triarchic model of intelligence, 160

Universals (in development), defined, 136

Validity
  of assessment, 366, 369–370, 372–373, 374
  defined, 370
  paper-pencil assessment and, 378
  performance assessment and, 379–382
  of standardized achievement tests, 401–402
Values
  cultural factors, 211
  defined, 197
  family relationships and, 248
  internalization of, 224
  moral values, 263
  motivation and, 197–198, 224
Variables
  experimental studies and, 8
  separating and controlling, 151–152, 165, 172
Verbal interactions, cultural factors, 314–315
Verbal mediators, defined, 49, 50
Verbal reasoning, 120
Verbal reprimands, 343–344
Verbal versus visual learning, 163
Vicarious punishment, defined, 65
Vicarious reinforcement
  defined, 65
  effects of, 5, 65

Violence
  beliefs about appropriateness of, 255
  classroom management and, 353–357
  early warning signs of violent behavior, 356
  modeling and, 64
  three-level approach, 354, 357
Visual aids, 294
Visual imagery
  abstract concepts and, 171
  defined, 33
  as meaningful learning, 33–34
  promoting effective cognitive processes and, 47
  study strategies and, 101
Visual versus verbal learning, 163
Vygotsky, Lev
  cognitive development and, 136, 143, 170
  internalization and, 172
  play activities and, 170
  scaffolding and, 175
  social interaction and, 143–144, 271–272
  sociocultural theory and, 19, 136, 137
  zone of proximal development, 146

Waiting versus interrupting, 315
Wait time
  cultural factors and, 47, 315
  defined, 47
  promoting effective cognitive processes with, 47, 297
Weiner, Bernard, 186
Wigfield, Allan, 186
Withitness, defined, 333
Working memory
  anxiety and, 214
  capacity of, 27–28, 40, 41, 42–43, 115–116, 147
  as component of memory, 25, 26
  components of, 27n26
  defined, 27
  duration of, 27–28, 41
Working portfolio, 396
Worldview
  culturally responsive teaching and, 94
  defined, 75
  formal operational thought and, 156–157
Written communication, parent communication, 334

Zimmerman, Barry, 18, 186
Zone of proximal development (ZPD)
  apprenticeships and, 176
  classroom environment and, 330
  defined, 146
  diversity of learners and, 167–168
  performance assessment and, 381
  scaffolding and, 175
z-scores, 409